PLUNKETT'S E-COMMERCE & INTERNET BUSINESS ALMANAC 2024

The only comprehensive guide to the e-commerce and Internet industry

Jack W. Plunkett

Published by:
Plunkett Research®, Ltd., Houston, Texas
www.plunkettresearch.com

PLUNKETT'S E-COMMERCE & INTERNET BUSINESS ALMANAC 2024

Editor and Publisher:
Jack W. Plunkett

Executive Editor and Database Manager:
Martha Burgher Plunkett

Senior Editor and Researchers:
Isaac Snider

Editors, Researchers and Assistants:
Bryant Huynh
Annie Paynter
Andre Staubo

Information Technology Manager:
Rebeca Tijiboy

Special Thanks to:
eMarketer
Information Technology & Innovation Foundation
Nielsen Online
Pew Internet & American Life Project
U.S. Census Bureau, Economics and Statistics Administration
U.S. Federal Communications Commission (FCC)

Plunkett Research®, Ltd.
P. O. Drawer 541737, Houston, Texas 77254 USA
www.plunkettresearch.com

Plunkett Research®, Ltd.
P. O. Drawer 541737
Houston, Texas 77254-1737
www.plunkettresearch.com

ISBN13 # 978-1-64788-028-6 (eBook Edition # 978-1-64788-522-9)

Limited Warranty and Terms of Use:

PLUNKETT'S E-COMMERCE & INTERNET BUSINESS ALMANAC 2024

CONTENTS

Continued on next page

INTRODUCTION

PLUNKETT'S E-COMMERCE & INTERNET BUSINESS ALMANAC is designed as a general source for researchers of all types.

The data and areas of interest covered are intentionally broad, ranging from the various types of businesses involved in ecommerce and the internet, to technologies and access providers, to an in-depth look at the major firms (which we call "THE E-COMMERCE 500") within the many sectors that make up the ecommerce and internet industry, including technology, services, retailing, telecommunications and much more.

This reference book is designed to assist with market research, strategic planning, employment searches, contact or prospect list creation and financial research, and as a data resource for executives and students of all types.

PLUNKETT'S E-COMMERCE & INTERNET BUSINESS ALMANAC takes a rounded approach for the general reader. This book presents a complete overview of the ecommerce and internet field (see "How To Use This Book"). For example, the impact of the internet upon retail sales is discussed in exacting detail, along with easy-to-use tables on all facets of the internet in general, from the types of services involved to names and descriptions of the

divisions and affiliates of the major firms within this industry.

THE E-COMMERCE 500 is our unique grouping of the biggest, most successful corporations in all segments of the ecommerce and internet industry. Tens of thousands of pieces of information, gathered from a wide variety of sources, have been researched and are presented in a unique form that can be easily understood. This section includes thorough indexes to THE E-COMMERCE 500, by geography, industry, sales, brand names, subsidiary names and many other topics. (See Chapter 4.)

Especially helpful is the way in which PLUNKETT'S E-COMMERCE & INTERNET BUSINESS ALMANAC enables readers who have no business background to readily compare the financial records and growth plans of ecommerce companies and major industry groups. You'll see the mid-term financial record of each firm, along with the impact of earnings, sales and strategic plans on each company's potential to fuel growth, to serve new markets and to provide investment and employment opportunities.

No other source provides this book's easy-to-understand comparisons of growth, expenditures, technologies, corporations and many other items of great importance to people of all types who may be studying this, one of the fastest growing industries in the world today.

By scanning the data groups and the unique indexes, you can find the best information to fit your personal research needs. The major companies in ecommerce and internet fields are profiled and then ranked using several different groups of specific criteria. Which firms are the biggest employers? Which companies earn the most profits? These things and much more are easy to find.

In addition to individual company profiles, an overview of internet technology and its trends is provided. This book's job is to help you sort through easy-to-understand summaries of today's trends in a quick and effective manner.

Whatever your purpose for researching the ecommerce and internet field, you'll find this book to be a valuable guide. Nonetheless, as is true with all resources, this volume has limitations that the reader should be aware of:

- Financial data and other corporate information can change quickly. A book of this type can be no more current than the data that was available as of the time of editing. Consequently, the financial picture, management and ownership of the firm(s) you are studying may have changed since the date of this book. For example, this almanac includes the most up-to-date sales figures and profits available to the editors as of early 2024. That means that we have typically used corporate financial data as of mid-2023.

- Corporate mergers, acquisitions and downsizing are occurring at a very rapid rate. Such events may have created significant change, subsequent to the publishing of this book, within a company you are studying.

- Some of the companies in THE E-COMMERCE 500 are so large in scope and in variety of business endeavors conducted within a parent organization, that we have been unable to completely list all subsidiaries, affiliations, divisions and activities within a firm's corporate structure.

- This volume is intended to be a general guide to a vast industry. That means that researchers should look to this book for an overview and, when

conducting in-depth research, should contact the specific corporations or industry associations in question for the very latest changes and data. Where possible, we have listed contact names, toll-free telephone numbers and internet site addresses for the companies, government agencies and industry associations involved so that the reader may get further details without unnecessary delay.

- Tables of industry data and statistics used in this book include the latest numbers available at the time of printing, generally through mid-2023. In a few cases, the only complete data available was for earlier years.

- We have used exhaustive efforts to locate and fairly present accurate and complete data. However, when using this book or any other source for business and industry information, the reader should use caution and diligence by conducting further research where it seems appropriate. We wish you success in your endeavors, and we trust that your experience with this book will be both satisfactory and productive.

Jack W. Plunkett
Houston, Texas
March 2024

HOW TO USE THIS BOOK

The two primary sections of this book are devoted first to the ecommerce and internet business as a whole and then to the "Individual Data Listings" for THE E-COMMERCE 500. If time permits, you should begin your research in the front chapters of this book. Also, you will find lengthy indexes in Chapter 4 and in the back of the book.

THE E-COMMERCE & INTERNET BUSINESS

Chapter 1: Major Trends Affecting the E-Commerce & Internet Business.
This chapter presents an encapsulated view of the major trends that are creating rapid changes in the ecommerce and internet business today.

Chapter 2: E-Commerce & Internet Business Statistics.
This chapter presents in-depth statistics ranging from an industry overview to the globalization of markets and much more.

Chapter 3: Important E-Commerce & Internet Business Contacts – Addresses, Telephone Numbers and Internet Sites.
This chapter covers contacts for important government agencies, ecommerce and internet organizations and trade groups. Included are numerous important internet sites.

THE E-COMMERCE 500

Chapter 4: THE E-COMMERCE 500: Who They Are and How They Were Chosen.
The companies compared in this book were carefully selected from the ecommerce and internet business, largely in the United States. A number of the firms are based outside the U.S. as well. For a complete description, see THE E-COMMERCE 500 indexes in this chapter.

Individual Data Listings:

Look at one of the companies in THE E-COMMERCE 500's Individual Data Listings. You'll find the following information fields:

Company Name:

The company profiles are in alphabetical order by company name. If you don't find the company you are seeking, it may be a subsidiary or division of one of the firms covered in this book. Try looking it up in the Index by Subsidiaries, Brand Names and Selected Affiliations in the back of the book.

Industry Code:

Industry Group Code: An NAIC code used to group companies within like segments.

Types of Business:

A listing of the primary types of business specialties conducted by the firm.

Brands/Divisions/Affiliations:

Major brand names, operating divisions or subsidiaries of the firm, as well as major corporate affiliations—such as another firm that owns a significant portion of the company's stock. A complete Index by Subsidiaries, Brand Names and Selected Affiliations is in the back of the book.

Contacts:

The names and titles up to 27 top officers of the company are listed, including human resources contacts.

Growth Plans/ Special Features:

Listed here are observations regarding the firm's strategy, hiring plans, plans for growth and product development, along with general information regarding a company's business and prospects.

Financial Data:

Revenue (2022 or the latest fiscal year available to the editors, plus up to five previous years): This figure represents consolidated worldwide sales from all operations. These numbers may be estimates.

R&D Expense (2022 or the latest fiscal year available to the editors, plus up to five previous years): This figure represents expenses associated with the research and development of a company's goods or services. These numbers may be estimates.

Operating Income (2022 or the latest fiscal year available to the editors, plus up to five previous years): This figure represents the amount of profit realized from annual operations after deducting operating expenses including costs of goods sold, wages and depreciation. These numbers may be estimates.

Operating Margin % (2022 or the latest fiscal year available to the editors, plus up to five previous years): This figure is a ratio derived by dividing operating income by net revenues. It is a measurement of a firm's pricing strategy and operating efficiency. These numbers may be estimates.

SGA Expense (2022 or the latest fiscal year available to the editors, plus up to five previous years): This figure represents the sum of selling, general and administrative expenses of a company, including costs such as warranty, advertising, interest, personnel, utilities, office space rent, etc. These numbers may be estimates.

Net Income (2022 or the latest fiscal year available to the editors, plus up to five previous years): This figure represents consolidated, after-tax net profit from all operations. These numbers may be estimates.

Operating Cash Flow (2022 or the latest fiscal year available to the editors, plus up to five previous years): This figure is a measure of the amount of cash generated by a firm's normal business operations. It is calculated as net income before depreciation and after income taxes, adjusted for working capital. It is a prime indicator of a company's ability to generate enough cash to pay its bills. These numbers may be estimates.

Capital Expenditure (2022 or the latest fiscal year available to the editors, plus up to five previous years): This figure represents funds used for investment in or improvement of physical assets such as offices, equipment or factories and the purchase or creation of new facilities and/or equipment. These numbers may be estimates.

EBITDA (2022 or the latest fiscal year available to the editors, plus up to five previous years): This figure is an acronym for earnings before interest, taxes, depreciation and amortization. It represents a company's financial performance calculated as revenue minus expenses (excluding taxes, depreciation and interest), and is a prime indicator of profitability. These numbers may be estimates.

Return on Assets % (2022 or the latest fiscal year available to the editors, plus up to five previous years): This figure is an indicator of the profitability of a company relative to its total assets. It is calculated by dividing annual net earnings by total assets. These numbers may be estimates.

Return on Equity % (2022 or the latest fiscal year available to the editors, plus up to five previous years): This figure is a measurement of net income as a percentage of shareholders' equity. It is also called the rate of return on the ownership interest. It is a vital indicator of the quality of a company's operations. These numbers may be estimates.

Debt to Equity (2022 or the latest fiscal year available to the editors, plus up to five previous years): A ratio of the company's long-term debt to its shareholders' equity. This is an indicator of the overall financial leverage of the firm. These numbers may be estimates.

Address:

The firm's full headquarters address, the headquarters telephone, plus toll-free and fax numbers where available. Also provided is the internet address.

Stock Ticker, Exchange: When available, the unique stock market symbol used to identify this firm's common stock for trading and tracking purposes is indicated. Where appropriate, this field may contain "private" or "subsidiary" rather than a ticker symbol. If the firm is a publicly-held company headquartered outside of the U.S., its international ticker and exchange are given.

    Total Number of Employees: The approximate total number of employees, worldwide, as of the end of 2022 (or the latest data available to the editors).

    Parent Company: If the firm is a subsidiary, its parent company is listed.

Salaries/Bonuses:

    (The following descriptions generally apply to U.S. employers only.)

    Highest Executive Salary: The highest executive salary paid, typically a 2022 amount (or the latest year available to the editors) and typically paid to the Chief Executive Officer.

    Highest Executive Bonus: The apparent bonus, if any, paid to the above person.

    Second Highest Executive Salary: The next-highest executive salary paid, typically a 2022 amount (or the latest year available to the editors) and typically paid to the President or Chief Operating Officer.

    Second Highest Executive Bonus: The apparent bonus, if any, paid to the above person.

Other Thoughts:

    Estimated Female Officers or Directors: It is difficult to obtain this information on an exact basis, and employers generally do not disclose the data in a public way. However, we have indicated what our best efforts reveal to be the apparent number of women who either are in the posts of corporate officers or sit on the board of directors. There is a wide variance from company to company.

    Hot Spot for Advancement for Women/Minorities: A "Y" in appropriate fields indicates "Yes." These are firms that appear either to have posted a substantial number of women and/or minorities to high posts or that appear to have a good record of going out of their way to recruit, train, promote and retain women or minorities. (See the Index of Hot Spots For Women and Minorities in the back of the book.) This information may change frequently and can be difficult to obtain and verify. Consequently, the reader should use caution and conduct further investigation where appropriate.

Glossary: A short list of ecommerce and internet business terms.

Chapter 1

MAJOR TRENDS AFFECTING THE E-COMMERCE & INTERNET BUSINESS

Major Trends Affecting the E-Commerce & Internet Business

1) Introduction to the E-Commerce & Internet Business
2) Bricks, Clicks and Catalogs Create Synergies While Online Sales Growth Surges
3) Amazon's Online Market Share Dominates/Temu & Shein Compete Aggressively)
4) Package and Food Delivery by Drone
5) Wi-Fi Enables Wireless Traffic Growth, Including the Internet of Things (IoT)
6) Global Internet Market Tops 5.40 Billion Users/Ultrafast Broadband Expands, both Fixed and Wireless
7) Fiber-to-the-Home (FTTH) Gains Traction
8) Cloud Computing and Software as a Service (SaaS) Point the Way to the Future
9) China Is the World's Largest E-Commerce Market and Continues to Boom
10) India Is the New E-Commerce Battle Ground
11) Overview of the Social Media Industry/TikTok Soars to 150 U.S. Million Users, Faces Ownership Legislation
12) Social Media Rakes in Global Online Shopping and Ad Revenues
13) Digital & Search Advertising Has Larger Share of U.S. Advertising Market Than TV
14) Programmatic Ad Buying Dominates the Digital Media Market
15) Online Travel Agencies (OTAs) /Hotels Fight to Keep Control of the Customer
16) Pandora and Spotify Lead in Streaming Music Via Internet Radio but Face Challenge from Apple Music/SiriusXM Tops 33.97 Million Subscribers
17) Overview of the Mobile Apps Industry
18) Quality of Care and Health Care Outcomes Data Are Available Online, Creating a New Level of Transparency
19) Smartphones and Neobanks Replace Bank Branches and Tellers
20) Insurance Direct Selling and E-Commerce Grow
21) The Internet of Things (IoT) and M2M to Boom, Enhanced by Artificial Intelligence (AI)/Open New Avenues for Hacking
22) Designers and Manufacturers Bypass the Middleman with Direct-to-Consumer Online Business Models
23) Fashion Rental Pioneered by Online Apparel Firm Rent the Runway
24) Smaller Satellites (SmallSats and CubeSats) and Low Earth Orbit Revolutionize Telecommunications
25) Sharing Economy Gains Market Share in Travel with Online Sites Like Airbnb, Vrbo and Many Global Competitors
26) Digital Assistants Include Amazon's Echo and Google's Home/Alexa and Similar Software Power Third-Party Developers
27) Amazon Becomes One of the World's Leading Sellers of Apparel and Shoes
28) The Metaverse Has Difficulties Gaining Steam
29) OpenAI (ChatGPT), StabilityAI, Anthropic (Claude) and Others Launch Impressive Tools that Generate Text, Art, Code and Smart ChatBots
30) Virtual Reality/Augmented Reality and 3-D Technologies Create Opportunities for the Tech Industry/Immersion Games to Grow
31) Regulatory Environment Is Challenging for Online Businesses and Social Media

1)   Introduction to the E-Commerce & Internet Business

The global internet audience continues to grow steadily, with the worldwide base of broadband internet users (including fixed and wireless) standing in excess of 5.35 billion as 2024 began according to DataReportal. This vast base of high-speed internet users encourages businesses to innovate in order to offer an ever-evolving array of online services. Thanks to the Coronavirus pandemic, even groceries have moved into the fast lane, as online grocery and household product sales are widely available, while consumers enjoy same-day delivery options.

Top Internet Trends
- AI-powered search
- Generative AI tools
- Booming online gaming
- Growth in regulatory concerns and efforts, including consumer privacy, protection of children's online activities, free speech vs. controlled posting and anti-trust issues
- Social platforms extending into additional services, such as merchandising and ecommerce
- Migration of entertainment to streaming services by subscription, and away from traditional cable, satellite and broadcast radio/tv
- Software as a Service (SaaS)

The standout winner in ecommerce merchandising continues to be Amazon, where sales have soared thanks to aggressive pricing, free shipping for its "Prime" members and an ever-growing variety of merchandise and services. The firm's sales outside of North America are booming as well. Meanwhile, Amazon has a massive on-site advertising business and cloud services business, while facing aggressive competition from non-U.S. ecommerce firms, particularly Shein and Temu.

Analysts at eMarketer reported American ecommerce sales in 2023 of an estimated $1.177 trillion, up significantly from $815.4 billion in 2020. This figure includes all goods and services purchased using the internet but excludes travel and event tickets. On the same basis, global internet ecommerce sales exceeded $5.78 trillion in 2023, according to eMarketer. China had an estimated 2023 total of $2.93 trillion.

Digital advertising in the U.S., during 2022, was a projected $239.89 billion, according to eMarketer, up 13.6% from 2021. Mobile advertising was projected at $168.88 billion for the year.

Growth in broadband subscriptions worldwide continues at a strong pace. The number of American homes and businesses with broadband access capabilities topped 126.8 million by the end of 2023, according to Plunkett Research estimates, thanks in part to modest monthly fees at internet service providers. This number does not include mobile broadband subscriptions, estimated at another 390.3 million devices, including smartphones.

A Brief History of the Online Sector: The ecommerce and internet sector has evolved rapidly, going through several distinct stages since its beginnings in the 1970s:

The Internet Is Born: First, there were the early days, when the internet was seen by many as a realm for techies only, one that would produce few, if any, commercial enterprises. Initially designed in 1973, the internet was a series of communication protocols written by Vinton Cerf as part of a project sponsored by the U.S. Department of Defense's Defense Advanced Research Projects Agency (DARPA). The first demonstration of a three-network internet protocol-based connection occurred in November 1977. Eventually, a well-enabled internet was rolled out in 1983, primarily as a failsafe method of defense communications and as a means for researchers at various universities to communicate.

The Web Is Created: Next, the World Wide Web and the coding language of HTML were conceived in 1989 and implemented between 1990 and 1993 by Tim Berners-Lee, enabling a never-ending hyperlinked cyber world where sharing unlimited data became user-friendly thanks to the magic of linked pages.

The Boom Ensues: Starting in 1993 and 1994, entrepreneurs and financiers realized that hyperlinked, electronically posted data could be commercialized with vast, global potential. Amazon.com was launched in 2004. A dramatic revolution in retailing, publishing and entertainment was visualized, one in which consumers and businesspeople alike would eagerly pay for the convenience of online shopping, trading and viewing of published data. An economic boom ensued, the likes of which hadn't been seen since the beginnings of earlier technological breakthroughs: electricity, the railroad, the telephone, the automobile and the passenger-carrying airliner.

Thousands of hopeful new businesses were launched. Capitalization for these new internet-enabled companies ranged from cash-strapped ventures launched in garages with Visa card credit lines, to companies like WebVan that received vast sums from professionally managed venture capital firms only to fail miserably. Roughly 6,000 new firms of significant size raised a cumulative total of more than $100 billion in venture capital in the boom period (1994-2000). About 450 of these companies sold their stock to the public via IPOs (initial public offerings). Stock markets soared and instant billionaires were made, although many of those stocks later plummeted. Venture funds that cashed out early reaped phenomenal gains, and financiers easily found additional investors for new venture capital pools. Companies with little or no sales and profits, led by the success of Netscape's IPO, found eager buyers for their newly issued stocks. The NASDAQ index of stocks rose to 5,000 by early in the year 2000, and the Chairman of the Federal Reserve warned of "exuberant optimism." Some said this boom couldn't last—others said it was the beginning of a "new economy" that would last forever.

The Bust: In mid-2000, the internet industry entered a bleak and dreary phase after the NASDAQ collapsed in March, bringing the entire sector to its knees. By October 10, 2002, the NASDAQ was down to 1,108 from a high of 5,132 in March 2000. Hundreds of thousands of people lost their jobs. Stock portfolio values plummeted. Thousands of firms closed their doors, filed bankruptcy, downsized or were scooped up at bargain prices by competitors. Sellers of hardware, software, consulting and telecommunications services suffered mightily. Entrepreneurs found it nearly impossible to raise funds to launch or sustain their businesses. The dream of a "new economy" became a nightmare for some—profits still matter; business cycles still happen.

The Reality Phase: By early 2003, this sector's dark clouds were abating, and a "reality phase" was taking shape. Well-conceived, internet-based businesses were proving their value. Consumers had become devoted fans of buying over the internet. Businesses of all types found that the internet creates true operating efficiencies and drives profitability (such as booking travel reservations online rather than through costly human agents). "Efficiency" is the most important factor in the ecommerce and internet sector's newfound success. Consumers find the internet to be a terrific way to efficiently expend their shopping and banking efforts. Consumers of all types use eBay to look for bargains, autotrader.com to look for cars at great prices and iTunes to download music. Corporate procurement managers find the internet to be the most efficient way to purchase needed goods and inventory. Billions of people worldwide find e-mail, instant messaging and VOIP telephony to be the most efficient ways to communicate.

Low Costs Fuel the Steady Global Growth: Today, access to fast internet, both wired and wireless, is available at bargain prices in a vast footprint across the globe. Even in relatively undeveloped nations, both consumers and businesses have grown to rely on the internet for everyday needs. Inexpensive devices and wireless networks continue to proliferate in most of the world. Mobile computing is accelerating at blazing speed thanks to moderately-priced smartphones and service plans, offering fast internet access and very advanced features. Meanwhile, the cost of developing and maintaining web sites has plummeted, opening the door to millions of self-funded entrepreneurs, and making it easier for venture capital firms to fund startups using low amounts of cash. Trends such as open software and cloud computing, along with modular software development tools, have made it easier, faster and cheaper to start sophisticated web sites.

Artificial Intelligence (AI): Artificial intelligence is rapidly and dramatically changing three segments of the internet:
1) Creative applications. Generative AI (such as ChatGPT) is enabling content creators to use online tools to write text, design advertising, generate online games and virtual worlds, write software code, create websites and generate graphics.
2) AI-driven search. Search engines are adding artificial intelligence (AI)-driven features that are dramatically changing the nature and effectiveness of search results.
3) Ecommerce sites. Many sites are utilizing AI to better tailor merchandise offerings and to push both streaming entertainment and shopping suggestions to consumers on a predictive and personalized basis.

Cybersecurity and Regulation: The global regulatory environment for the internet, online advertising, social media and ecommerce is more daunting than ever. Governments are attempting to keep up with complex technological advances (such as AI) and privacy issues while addressing anti-trust and competitive concerns and disastrously failing to protect businesses and consumers to any reasonable degree against online fraud and exploitation. Major regulatory acts have been passed in a few areas, particularly in consumer privacy. This puts internet-based companies in a position of continually attempting to meet evolving government requirements while evading potential fines that can run into the billions of dollars or Euros.

One of the biggest, and most poorly addressed, issues is losses and treats relating to cybersecurity, ranging from hackers and fraudsters to online financial fraud, malware, exploitation of children, ransomware and even potential threats from hidden back doors and network/system entry points that could bring down a region's entire energy, water or transportation infrastructure, or disable military communications and command systems. Unfortunately, AI is empowering fraudsters to generate emails, mimic voices, steal identities and scam both consumers and businesses on a global basis.

2) Bricks, Clicks and Catalogs Create Synergies While Online Sales Growth Surges

Several factors have encouraged consumers to do more of their shopping online, including the difficulty of getting to and parking at retail stores, the fact that consumers feel pressed for time, the widespread adoption of high-speed internet access (both at home and on smartphones), and the fact that the lowest prices can often be found online. The Coronavirus gave an immense growth spurt to ecommerce on a worldwide basis. (Nonetheless, when Coronavirus restrictions were loosened, foot traffic at retail stores rebounded. Many consumers had greatly missed the in-person shopping experience.)

Online shopping sometimes goes hand-in-hand with in-store shopping, or at least in-store browsing. A large number of shoppers browse web sites to gain information, later visiting a physical store to make a purchase. The reverse is also often true—many store owners worry that shoppers look at merchandise in their stores and then go home to look for the best possible prices at online sites. Some shoppers add the items that they are considering to their shopping carts on Amazon.com, but don't click the purchase button. Then they go to retail stores, smartphones in hand, and compare prices and features in the stores to their Amazon lists. If the merchandise looks good in person and Amazon's price is better, then they may decide to purchase via Amazon, especially if they belong to the Amazon Prime service that provides free shipping. Best Buy successfully countered this practice by matching the prices of online competitors and emphasizing customers' ability to see and touch the merchandise in-store, speak to experts in-person

and take merchandise home immediately. In addition, Best Buy emphasizes the availability of its experienced service people to install consumer electronics in the home.

Many of the most successful retail firms of the future will be those that take full advantage of the personal touch of traditional, store-based retailing and combine it with the growing popularity of catalog and internet-based retailing.

Best Online Practices for Retailers:
- Seamless integration of store, catalog and internet-based offerings to consumers, providing choices of 1) place and method of purchase, 2) method of pickup or shipment and 3) place or method of returns, repairs and additional services as needed.
- Communication of a seamless brand identity and level of service throughout catalogs, retail stores and web sites.

For good examples of companies that are evolving toward such "seamless" strategies, study Costco, Walmart, REI, The Gap, Staples and Pottery Barn. At Pottery Barn, customers find enhanced flexibility and customer service thanks to the opportunity to shop via the web, Pottery Barn catalogs or Pottery Barn stores. Pottery Barn stores hand out copies of catalogs—which feature the web address of Potterybarn.com, as well as phone ordering options. The point is to create loyalty-inducing convenience for customers, giving them options for purchasing when, where and how they please.

Staff members at Men's Wearhouse are using smartphones to interact with online customers through messaging and video chat, creating an interactive, multi-channel experience for shoppers. Store personnel can send photos of clothing and accessories, field questions and make suggestions, and are paid commissions for the online orders that they facilitate. Men's Wearhouse (which is owned by Tailored Brands, Inc.) is using an app developed by Hero that connects online shoppers with instore employees. In-store staff can wave their smartphones over merchandise tags to generate web links for their online customers. Hero has been improved so that it offers an enhanced shopping experience. Retailers can use it to offer the customer greater product understanding through live product demos, videos and photos. Customers can utilize links within Hero to complete a purchase, while the store employee remains available online to answer questions. Hero was acquired by Klarna, a provider to stores of consumer payment options, in July 2021 (www.klarna.com/us/business).

Nordstrom is experimenting with very small stores that stock no inventory while allowing customers to try on samples, with purchases to be delivered to their homes. These new stores also feature a high level of personal service.

Walmart offers "Pick Up Today," a program in which Walmart customers order items online and then pick them up at their local stores the same day. Best Buy has similar services, as do Bloomingdale's and Macy's.

These shop online—but pickup in the store strategies were born because retailers were fighting a practice called "showrooming," in which shoppers browse for merchandise in stores but buy on rival retailers' web sites, especially Amazon.com. Amazon not only has a vast selection of items and free shipping for Prime members, its prices are also highly competitive.

One thing in favor of brick-and-mortar stores is their ability to accept payments in cash. There are a large number of consumers who are called "underbanked," that is, who are without bank accounts or credit cards. Walmart offers customers the ability to order items online and then pick them up in stores using cash for payment.

Department stores are making a major shift in operations to support online orders. In yet another effort to compete with Amazon.com's success, Macy's converted many of its stores to include expanded storerooms with cutting-edge technology to track inventory and generate shipping labels. Excess store inventory is shifted to highlighted positions on the company's web site, and merchandise that has sold out at the online distribution center may be found in stores, thereby remaining on the web site for sale and delivery by UPS. Online orders are being filled by stores closest to consumers, increasing efficiency and lowering costs. More and more, brick and mortar stores are being used as local warehouses that deliver goods directly to customers.

Macy's is taking the technology a step further in select stores, where it is displaying merchandise with only one item of each style (instead of cramming the racks with every size available). Shoppers can look at the sample, and then use an app on their smartphones to let staff know what size and style they want to try on. Staff members collect the items from stockrooms and send them to fitting rooms via special hatches. Customers are alerted as to which fitting room is theirs via their phones. The practice allows Macy's to display more styles and avoid a cumbersome tangle of vast numbers of coat hangers.

Some brick-and-mortar retailers are opting to make selected merchandise available for online purchase only. Shoppers can browse samples in the stores and then place orders on their phones or at in-store computer stations.

At the same time, a growing number of formerly online-only businesses have opened brick and mortar stores. Examples include women's clothing site Boston Proper (a subsidiary of Chico's FAS) and online eyeglass retailer Warby Parker. Likewise, Bonobos (a clothing retailer now owned by Walmart) has samples in showroom stores but no inventory on-hand. Bonobos has opened these "Guideshops" in dozens of major cities across the U.S. It remains to be seen if this trend will continue after the Coronavirus pandemic.

Another twist to online shopping is to retrain and enable brick and mortar store personnel to connect with shoppers via text, phone, email, Facetime or online chat to personalize the digital shopping experience. Neiman Marcus Group, for example, has an online quiz to match shoppers with store style consultants. Questions include "What do you feel is missing from your closet?" and "Who are you shopping for?" Beauty company Estee Lauder Cos. is hiring online advisers (called online talent) while cutting in-store positions.

As more and more people embrace online shopping, brick and mortar retailers must evolve to offer more convenience and speed. Shoppers are spending less time in stores as they prefer browsing on web sites and social media such as Facebook, Pinterest and Instagram.

Employees at Retail Stores are Fulfilling Online Orders: A Big Logistical Challenge

Walmart is relying on many of its stores as distribution centers for online orders. Target is also fulfilling many of its online orders through its stores. This requires retraining employees to be stockers, packers, shippers and product specialists. Supermarkets are doing the same thing: employees are being retained to first pick items ordered online off the shelves, and then pack and hold them in large, special areas within the stores for delivery or drive-through pickup. The problem with this strategy is that these buildings were designed to be retail stores, not warehouses.

It is unlikely that this fulfilment of online orders through existing stores could ever be as cost-effective or efficient as fulfillment through warehouses that are specifically designed for this purpose. Growing numbers of Amazon competitors are outsourcing logistical needs. Businesses including Shopify, Wix.com and Squarespace offer payment processing while ShipBob and Quiet Logistics fulfill orders through their warehouses. Robotics manufacturers such as 6 River Systems and GreyOrange Pte. offer equipment similar to Amazon's automated internal package systems.

3) Amazon's Online Market Share Dominates/Temu & Shein Compete Aggressively

The standout winner in ecommerce of late is Amazon, where global sales have soared thanks to aggressive discount pricing and an ever-growing variety of merchandise categories. The gross value of merchandise sold through the company's "Marketplace" partners is roughly equal to Amazon's own sales. (Amazon records only the service fees it charges these Marketplace retailers, not the full price of the merchandise sold.) Amazon has become a market leader in vital merchandise categories including apparel and such consumer goods as health and beauty products. By 2022, Amazon accounted for over 40% of all U.S. ecommerce merchandise sales. (Another big winner is the Shopify platform that operates websites for smaller retailers.)

Amazon's phenomenal growth is a result of excellent corporate strategy plus its competitive pricing and convenience. Shoppers don't have to drive to a store, thereby saving on gasoline as well as time. Amazon has also diversified to an amazing extent, offering everything from jewelry to appliances to groceries to industrial and scientific supplies. Shipping can be expedited through the Amazon Prime program which, for a modest annual fee, offers unlimited free two-day shipping, the option to upgrade to one-day shipping for a few dollars and no minimum order size. Amazon had approximately 167.2 million Prime members in the U.S. alone as of 2023 (and more than 200 million globally), according to eMarketer, and those customers spend, on average, considerably more than non-Prime customers. Amazon Prime Now offers two-hour delivery for groceries and other household items in many major U.S. cities.

Also, Amazon has been placing banks of lockers in retailers such as grocery, convenience and drug stores in urban areas. Amazon packages can be placed in these special lockers, so that customers can later pick up packages themselves, using access codes sent by email, instead of trying to be at home to meet delivery by UPS, FedEx or the U.S. Postal Service. Deutsche Post DHL has offered a free locker service in Germany for years.

In 2017, Amazon acquired specialty supermarket firm Whole Foods Market, Inc. for $13.7 billion. This is an extension of Amazon's rapidly expanding grocery sales strategy. The company also offers AmazonFresh, a grocery delivery service for Prime members in select U.S. cities for an additional monthly membership fee.

Amazon is one of the world's largest online beauty product retailers. Amazon designed digital, online storefronts which are special sections for luxury beauty items and for salon, spa and dermatology products to help customers find new products. Amazon also moved into the pharmacy business, fulfilling drug prescriptions that are ordered online. The company's share of U.S. apparel sales is massive as well, although it has to deal with growing competition in low-cost apparel from foreign ecommerce companies.

Amazon has so much online power that manufacturers are building exclusive product lines for the Amazon brand. The initiative markets products in an "Our Brands" campaign to Amazon customers. (Amazon typically markets these products under house brands like Amazon Basics and Amazon Essentials, but it also utilizes a broad range of other brand names that are not as clearly linked to the firm.) It offers participating manufacturers quick customer feedback, top listings in search results and marketing support. Amazon benefits because it does not have to invest money and effort into developing exclusive products. Companies including GNC, Tuft & Needle and the makers of Equal sweeteners have already created exclusive products for Amazon.

The company is facing aggressive competition from China-based Temu and Shein, which are e-tailers with extremely low prices. While neither site offers fast delivery or superb customer service, their rock-bottom prices are attracting increasing numbers of shoppers in the U.S. Comscore estimates that Temu's monthly unique visits from American customers reached 70.5 million in March 2023, while Shein's monthly unique visitors hit 41 million that same month. Comscore also reported that Amazon's unique monthly visitors for March 2023 fell to 211 million, compared to 217.5 million in September 2022.

4) Package and Food Delivery by Drone

The next big step in the use of drones may be package delivery. Could the future for Amazon and other retailers eventually include deliveries by unmanned aerial drones? Amazon has uses drones with a range of 10 miles and a payload of under five pounds (appropriate for about 90% of Amazon's deliveries). The company began drone deliveries in mid-2022 in Lockeford, California, a rural community about 100 miles northeast of San Francisco. Alphabet, Inc. (parent company of Google) has a subsidiary named Wing that began drone delivery in 2022 in the Dallas/Ft. Worth, Texas area. Wing also supplies drones for Walgreens Boots Alliance, Inc. and Walmart deliveries in the Dallas area. Meanwhile, Walmart launched same-day drone delivery in Arizona, Arkansas, Florida, Texas Utah and Virginia in May 2022. In addition, the U.S. Postal Service and Airbus SE have developed and tested units for deliveries. U.S. drone delivery is dependent upon cost, technologies, safety concerns, consumer acceptance and shifts in FAA rules regarding unmanned flight.

In January 2021, the FAA approved the first fully automated commercial drone flights. The approval does have limits, which include drone operation only in rural areas at altitudes of under 400 feet. In late 2020, the FAA established requirements for remote identification of drones and new safeguards for flights across overpopulated areas and at night.

China's number two ecommerce company JD.com is using drones to deliver packages to remote rural villages. The firm has drones that can fly up to 62 mph carrying packages of up to 66 pounds. JD.com is currently testing heavy-duty drones that can carry up to one ton or more and is investing $150 million with the help of the Shaanxi province government. Zipline (www.flyzipline.com), a startup headed by former Google, SpaceX, Boeing and NASA veterans, delivers medical supplies as well as food, retail, agriculture and animal health products by drone in Rwanda, Ghana, Nigeria, Cote d'Ivoire, Kenya, Japan and the U.S. Drone delivery is also a reality in Reykjavik, Iceland, as well as Texas and North Carolina in the U.S., after food delivery company Aha signed a deal with Flytrex (www.flytrex.com) of Israel. The Aha drone weighs 34 pounds (including the drone and the Flytrex attachment) and has a payload of 5.5 pounds.

Delivery drones require more complex designs than those used to gather video footage or sense changes in temperature or pressure. For example, Alphabet's Wing delivery drones have wings capable of switching to upright mode in order to hover while recipients take deliveries. Another Wing model has fixed wings combined with vertical-axis rotors similar to those used on quadcopters. Wing was cleared by the FAA in April 2019 for its first commercial drone delivery.

UPS' Flight Forward drone subsidiary received Part 135 Standard certification from the FAA in October 2019. The firm now delivers medical supplies via drones to hospital campuses in North Carolina, Utah and elsewhere in an agreement with CVS Corporation. Drones are well suited to medical supply delivery, due to the fact that items such as blood and medical specimens tend to be light and of uniform size and require fast turnaround times. In addition, UPS is planning a drone logistics project with Kaiser Permanente for drone delivery between buildings in the company's 39-hospital network. The FAA further authorized the subsidiary to operate drones beyond visual line of sight for small package delivery in September 2023. UPS is planning to conduct flights in North Carolina, Florida and Ohio from its Remote Operations Center in Kentucky.

5) Wi-Fi Enables Wireless Traffic Growth, Including the Internet of Things (IoT)

While cellular phone companies are investing billions of dollars in technologies to give their subscribers enhanced services such and 4G mobile internet, Wi-Fi is more vital than ever for wireless access. As the number of cellular device subscriptions for smartphones, tablets, laptops and aircards has soared, so has the demand placed upon cellular networks. Wi-Fi acts as a vital relief valve. Wireless device owners increasingly want to access immense files, such as Netflix movies on demand. If the world's rapidly increasing wireless data traffic relied solely on cellular networks, the system would be under severe stress. However, since wireless device owners frequently have access to Wi-Fi as an alternative for a large portion of the day, they can switch to Wi-Fi from cellular as needed, reducing their total cellular subscription costs and dramatically reducing the load placed on cellular networks. The role played by Wi-Fi will remain vitally important, even as ultrafast 5G cellular networks are rolled out. At the same time, Wi-Fi will become even more important to the world's technology users as connected devices proliferate in the rapidly growing Internet of Things (IoT).

Experts at Cisco, with their Cisco Visual Networking Index, estimated that by 2023, the global number of internet-connected mobile devices will reach 3.6 per capita (nearly 28.5 billion devices). Smartphones will represent about 44% of these devices and connections. More than 50% of mobile traffic is offloaded to Wi-Fi rather than remaining on cellular networks.

Wi-Fi routers have very high theoretical data transfer speeds, but actual speeds rely on local internet connections. On the fixed end, each Wi-Fi network is tied into an internet router. This means that the actual download speed enjoyed by the Wi-Fi user is limited to the speed of the internet service connected to the router. If a user has a local internet connection with a 50 meg download speed via a cable modem, then the local Wi-Fi system will also be limited to 50 meg.

Wi-Fi is now advancing through enhanced technologies. Recent enhancements include MU-MIMO (multi-user, multiple-input, multiple-output), which allows a Wi-Fi device to handle data requests from multiple sources at once. Another recent technology known as OFDMA (orthogonal frequency-division multiple access) can split a Wi-Fi channel into many data pipes simultaneously. Kumu Networks, Inc., a startup based in Santa Clara, California (kumunetworks.com), has developed "full duplex" technology that enables Wi-Fi to transmit and receive simultaneously, effectively doubling the speed and capability of the network.

In early 2019, Amazon acquired Eero, a Wi-Fi startup that makes small wireless routers for home use, promising no Wi-Fi dead zones within the home. The acquisition enables Amazon to compete with Google's OnHubs.

Amazon and Apple are using devices such as iPhones, smartwatches, "smart" speakers and personal digital assistants such as Alexa to provide connectivity and power wireless networks. The companies use their wireless networks, such as Amazon's Sidewalk, as well as Apple's AirTag and Find My Network, to allow the devices to transmit tiny bits of data from any available wireless connection, thereby supplementing Wi-Fi networks and reducing wireless communication problems. Data is encrypted for security.

6) Global Internet Market Tops 5.40 Billion Users/Ultrafast Broadband Expands, both Fixed and Wireless

The majority of American cellphones are now smartphones. Big improvements in the devices, such as the latest iPhones and Android-based units, along with enhanced high-speed access via 4G networks,

are fueling this growth. More recently, major wireless carriers are offering advanced 5G services with higher potential speeds. Most major e-commerce, news and entertainment sites have carefully designed their web pages to perform reasonably well on the "third screen," that is, cellphones (with TV being the first screen and desktop or laptop computers being the second screen). Globally, the number of internet users was 5.4 billion as of late 2023, (including wireless) according to Plunkett Research estimates.

Internet access speeds continue to increase dramatically. Google launched its "Google Fiber" ultra-high-speed internet service in Kansas City, Kansas in 2012, and soon expanded into other cities.

AT&T initially launched a similar 1 gigabit service in competition with Google in the Austin area called AT&T FIBER. AT&T firm now offers this 1 GB fast service in major cities across the U.S.

What will widespread use of fast internet access mean to consumers? The opportunities for new or enhanced products and services are endless, and the amount of entertainment, news, commerce and personal services designed to take advantage of broadband will continue to grow rapidly. For example, education support and classes via broadband is rapidly growing into a major industry.

Broadband in the home is essential for everyday activities ranging from children's homework to shopping to managing financial accounts. Online entertainment and information options, already vast, will grow daily. Some online services are becoming indispensable, and always-on is the new accepted standard. The quality of streaming video and audio is becoming clear and reliable, making music and movie downloads extremely fast, and allowing internet telephone users to see their parties on the other end as if they were in the same room. Compression and caching techniques are evolving, and distribution and storage costs are expected to plummet. A very significant portion of today's radio, television and movie entertainment has migrated to the web.

7) Fiber-to-the-Home (FTTH) Gains Traction

The major telephone firms are looking for ways to increase revenues through enhanced services while retaining their customer bases. One such way is through the delivery of ultra-high-speed internet access, combined with enhanced entertainment and telephone options, often by installing true fiber-to-the-home (FTTH) networks.

Under traditional telephone and internet service, homes are served by copper wires, which are limited to relatively slow service. However, old-fashioned copper networks are not up to the demands of today's always-on internet consumers. Fiber-optic cable might be used in trunk lines to connect regions and cities to each other at the switch and network level, but speed drops significantly once the service hits local copper lines.

Things are much more advanced in major markets today. In an AT&T project, fiber is being brought into special hubs in existing neighborhoods. From those hubs, fast services are delivered into the home with advanced technologies on short, final runs of copper wire.

FTTH, in contrast, delivers fiber-optic cable all the way from the network to the local switch directly into the living room—with this system, internet delivery speeds and the types of entertainment and data delivered can be astounding. Google's "Google Fiber" service offers extremely fast download speeds of 1,000 Mbps (one gigabit), roughly 50 to 100 times faster than typical DSL or cable service. Recently, Google offered the service in cities including Atlanta, Georgia; Austin, Texas; Charlotte, North Carolina; Kansas City, Missouri; Kansas City, Kansas; Nashville, Tennessee; and Provo Utah, among others. This puts tremendous competitive pressure on other internet access companies. It also makes consumers wonder why they have been paying high monthly rates for slow service for many years. In response, AT&T has begun providing 1,000 Mbps service in several major cities. The long-term result is going to be much better, faster internet access in major U.S. cities, at a reasonable cost.

Verizon has completed a multi-year FTTH program that makes it a U.S. leader in FTTH. Verizon's FTTH (called Fios) offers exceptional speeds up to 1 gigabit.

The Fiber-to-the-Home Council (www.ftthcouncil.org) tracks FTTH trends. In many cases, FTTH has been provided by local government or by subdivision developers who are determined to provide leading-edge connectivity as a value-added feature to new homes.

FTTH technologies, though expensive, may save the Bells from being trampled by the cable companies. Fiber-optic networks can give consumers extremely fast internet connections. Such ultra-high speeds will also allow consumers to download movies in seconds and make videoconferencing a meaningful reality for businesses. (Additional fiber terms used in the industry include FTTP for Fiber-to-the-premises and FTTO for fiber-to-the-office.)

FTTH has been widely adopted in South Korea, Hong Kong, Japan, the United Arab Emirates and Taiwan, according to the FTTH Councils of Asia-Pacific, Europe and North America.

8) Cloud Computing and Software as a Service (SaaS) Point the Way to the Future

There is a now-unstoppable trend toward downplaying the role of packaged software that is installed on the desktop, relying instead on internet-based applications hosted in the cloud. This accelerated dramatically with the onset of the Coronavirus and working-from-home. The trend is called Software as a Service (SaaS). In fact, Sun Microsystem's famous positioning line of long standing, "The network is the computer," pretty well sums up this movement, a thought that "uses the internet as the computing platform of the future." Microsoft, Google, IBM, Salesforce, Oracle and other leading firms are quickly enhancing their own suites of internet-based applications.

Cloud computing is the use of remote servers, often owned and operated by third-party service providers, to store and access data and software, as opposed to servers owned by the user. Firms that offer cloud services run clusters of computers networked together, often based on open standards. Such cloud networks can consist of thousands of computers. Cloud services enable a client company to immediately increase computing capability without any investment in physical infrastructure. (The word "cloud" is also broadly used to describe any data or application that runs via the internet.) The concept of cloud computing is key to the growing use of SaaS.

The Coronavirus pandemic accelerated movement of data from in-house servers to the cloud significantly. Gartner forecasted that global spending on public cloud services on a broad basis would reach $563.6 billion in 2023. The firm further forecasted growth of 20.4% to reach $678.8 billion in 2024.

Spending on cloud infrastructure is spiraling as well. Gartner reported cloud application infrastructure services (Platform as a Service, or PaaS) spending of $145.3 billion in 2023 and forecast growth of 21.5% in 2024 to reach $176.5 billion.

Amazon.com was one of the earliest companies to offer cloud services, and it remains a leader in this field. Since it must operate immense server capacity anyway, Amazon decided in early 2006 to offer cloud computing services, on its servers, to outside parties.

Amazon Web Services (AWS) have been extremely popular. Using AWS requires no long-term contract or up-front investment. Charges are reasonable and usage-based (a few cents per gigabyte per month, in the U.S.). Remote servers, remote storage and the Amazon SimpleDB database are among the most popular AWS tools. Amazon, Microsoft and Google are investing vast sums to build new data centers for cloud services. Artificial intelligence (AI), including tools like ChatGPT, is a key trend driving cloud services demand.

Software that is sold and operates only via the cloud is a growing trend. Adobe Systems, Inc., for example, a maker of extremely popular design software, is selling its biggest software products as online services only available by subscription to Adobe Creative Cloud.

SPOTLIGHT: Hybrid Cloud

The hybrid cloud is a data strategy where some applications and data are moved to cloud-based systems, while highly sensitive data or certain functions are kept on client-owned, local systems. Microsoft began offering hybrid cloud services in 2017 by allowing customers to run a portion of its Azure cloud on in-house servers (built to Microsoft specifications) which work smoothly with Azure data centers. The firm added Azure Stack, a rugged platform designed to support military data needs. Another option is Azure Arc, which affords customers the ability to store more data on their own servers. In 2020, Amazon joined the hybrid cloud movement by offering AWS (Amazon Web Services) server racks called Outposts for local use combined with software that connects it to the AWS cloud. Outposts customers include Disney animators (who demand almost instantaneous connections between in-house data and cloud data), Verizon Communications (needing faster 5G browsing speeds) and Fox Corp. (for video production needs). 2021 saw Microsoft launching Windows 365 (in July) and Windows 11 (in October). Both are cloud-based and part of Microsoft's efforts to regain global operating system market share (which was 85% in 2011 but only 30% in 2021). Windows 365 can be utilized by Apple users without the need to go through Apple's proprietary App Store.

The result of these efforts has become a wide variety of software that is accessed only via the internet instead of the desktop. Some software can be accessed for free, but many rich software applications are rented to the user by subscription or by fees based on the amount of time used. The growing use of smartphones is accelerating this trend. Also, the sharing of data, whether for business collaboration (such as Microsoft's Office 365 and Salesforce's customer management solution) or simply for fun (such as Facebook), has simplified dramatically thanks to the cloud. Business models and profit streams are being altered as a result.

A major goal of publishing software in the cloud is for the user to be able to eliminate much of the money and staff effort that an organization typically invests in building, managing and updating software in the traditional manner on a computer network. At the same time, the cloud enables software providers to build steady streams of renewable subscription revenues. Salesforce, a customer relationship management (CRM) software leader, has achieved great success by selling only internet-based (SaaS) access to its tools. NetSuite is another major provider of internet-based applications. Its offering for businesses includes CRM, enterprise resource planning (ERP), accounting, ecommerce and much more, all on a subscription basis. Among the advantages of SaaS are no software to purchase and no software to install or maintain.

9) China Is the World's Largest E-Commerce Market and Continues to Boom

China is posting phenomenal growth in ecommerce. For 2023, eMarketer forecasted $2.931 trillion in Chinese ecommerce sales, up from $2.682 trillion in 2022 and $2.528 trillion in 2021. (This figure includes most orders of goods and services ordered online, except for travel and event tickets.) This growth is due to widely available internet access, a growing middle class, the development of Chinese ecommerce businesses such as Alibaba.com and Tencent, sophisticated payment technologies and aggressive development of fast product delivery services. The Coronavirus pandemic also played a significant role in ecommerce escalation.

Alibaba.com, the China-based owner of a wide variety of online platforms and services, had 903 million active users in mid-2023. Its flagship web site is Taobao, which is similar to eBay. It offers an enormous array of merchandise but relies on third parties for fulfillment, delivery and logistics as well as other services. Alibaba site Tmall is a marketplace for luxury brands of clothing, food and electronics. Tmall is perfectly positioned to serve China's growing middle class.

China's Singles' Day, an ecommerce holiday and the world's largest internet shopping event, brought in an estimated $156.4 billion in sales across major e-commerce platforms in 2023, up 2.08% over 2022 according to Syntun. A notable difference between Chinese and U.S. online buyers is that in China, shoppers often buy from digital marketplaces rather than traditional brick and mortar retailers' web sites. These marketplaces, including Alibaba, are megasites similar to eBay or Amazon Marketplace.

Alibaba has competitors, including JD.com and Yihaodian. JD.com offers same-day delivery services in cities across China (Alibaba offers it through its Cainiao logistics arm), while Yihaodian became 100% owned by Walmart as of mid-2015. With Walmart's backing, Yihaodian grew to have hundreds of distribution centers. In 2016, Walmart sold the Yihaodian marketplace to JD.com, but retained its direct sales business. Walmart and JD.com are further partnering, in that Sam's Club membership is available on JD.com and Walmart's physical stores are listed on the Chinese firm's O2O JV Dada delivery platform.

Many western companies are enjoying reasonable levels of success in doing business in China. Although the establishment of a Chinese-licensed business unit and the opening of an account in a Chinese bank are still difficult and time consuming requirements, there are some initiatives that are making the effort easier. Alibaba created Tmall Global, an international marketplace in which foreign companies can sell to Chinese customers without creating Chinese subsidiaries or setting up bank accounts. Ant Financial, an Alibaba spinoff, takes care of transaction processing with the firms' home-country banks, while shipping and handling are overseen by delivery firm Cainiao. Another Tmall Global plus is that it has worked with the Chinese government to create bonded warehouses in several cities that are free from standard import duties in some cases and taxed at a lower rate than wholesale purchases.

The big news in Asia's e-commerce sector is the soaring growth of Temu and Shein, both retailers of massive numbers of items at rock bottom prices. Temu, owned by Pinduoduo, launched service in the U.S. in late 2022 and in select EU countries in 2023. Its monthly gross merchandise volume reached $1 billion in June 2023. Shein, which operates on a similar model, is an online-only fashion retailer selling in more than 150 countries worldwide (however, it does not sell to customers in China). By the end of 2022, Shein had about 74.7 million total global users.

Internet Research Tip: The Internet in China
For the latest information on internet usage and web sites in China, visit the China Internet Network Information Center, www.cnnic.net.cn. The group publishes extremely useful research and survey results, and its web site is available in English as well as the Chinese language.

---

10) India Is the New E-Commerce Battle Ground

Of India's 1.4 billion people, roughly one-half live in rural areas with little if any access to traditional retailers. With the rollout of 4G wireless service in much of the country, those millions of shoppers are front and center for marketing efforts by the world's e-tailers. This market poses unique challenges, since many of these potential customers don't have credit cards or delivery addresses and are new to online shopping. Some don't have smartphones. eMarketer estimated that retail ecommerce revenue in India could rise from the 2022 level of $83.75 billion to reach $102.45 billion in 2023 and $122.94 billion in 2024. There is clearly room for significant additional growth.

Amazon bet heavily on the explosive growth potential in India, where it began operations in 2014. To win over customers, Amazon enabled motorbike delivery centers around the country, with riders who understand confusing streets and arcane addresses and offers customers the ability to pay in cash when items are delivered.

The company redesigned its shopping app in India. It offers tips in Hindi on how to find products (after humans translated descriptions of thousands of items, machine learning is now doing the Hindi translation, with more languages to follow), no email address is required to establish an account (just a phone number) and customers can pay by cash on delivery or using the Amazon Pay digital wallet (no credit cards or bank accounts required).

Amazon is attempting to overcome the fact that many poorly-educated rural consumers do not know how to type, don't understand how to conduct an effective online search, and often are unable to read. Amazon works with small, local stores that it refers to as Easy Stores, with well-trained storeowners available to assist new consumers in online buying. The store owners provide online shopping expertise that many consumers still lack, accept the payments and allow the consumers to pick up the packages at the stores upon arrival.

U.S.-based retail giant Walmart acquired India's Flipkart in 2018. Flipkart is India's largest ecommerce firm. The site offers guaranteed same-day delivery in India's largest cities. In July 2020, Flipkart Wholesale, a digital marketplace for small mom-and-pop businesses, was launched.

While U.S.-based firms Walmart and Amazon were making massive investments in Indian ecommerce in an effort to dominate massive market share, the Indian government stepped in to make their strategies much more difficult. Government leaders noted how China had encouraged the growth of highly innovative local ecommerce firms (including Alibaba and JD.com) by making it difficult for foreign-owned companies to participate in the market. Effective February 1, 2019, foreign-owned firms are prohibited from entering into exclusive agreements for the online sale of other companies' products. The new rules also cracked down on practices whereby ecommerce firms were shifting merchandise distribution to networks of wholesale distributors that they controlled, thereby circumventing rules intended to control growth of foreign companies. (Rules prohibited foreign firms selling multiple brands from holding their own inventory or shipping merchandise directly to consumers.) India hopes to protect the interests of local storeowners in this manner, while fostering the growth of its own domestic online platforms. Despite a recent Competition Commission of India antitrust investigation of both Amazon and Flipkart, both firms continue to dominate the e-commerce market in India. As of early 2024, Flipkart was planning to launch an instant-delivery service in select locations.

Meanwhile, domestic investment and innovation is growing. Giant India-based conglomerate Tata Group offers its own ecommerce platform called Tata CLiQ. Another major Indian firm, Reliance Industries (which spent $35 billion to create India's first all-4G wireless network in 2018), has its own ecommerce platform called Jio. Meesho enables users to sell items to friends on WhatsApp, Facebook and Instagram (Meta Platforms is a Meesho investor). In late 2022, the Indian government launched an e-commerce aggregator that allows users to search across multiple platforms (including Amazon and Meesho) for price comparisons and purchases.

11) Overview of the Social Media Industry/TikTok Soars to 170 Million U.S. Users, Faces Ownership Legislation

Since most social media accounts and activities are free-of-charge, the challenge for social media firms has been to monetize their vast user bases. As of the first quarter of 2024, Facebook had 3.05 billion monthly active users (the majority are on mobile devices), Instagram had 2.4 billion and TikTok had 1.1 billion according to DataReportal and Insider Intelligence.

Meanwhile, LinkedIn has been quite successful in generating revenues. It not only sells advertising, but also sells subscriptions to account upgrades for users who are interested in deeper services. Since LinkedIn, largely aimed at business professionals and job seekers, is a popular way for salespeople to initiate conversations with potential customers, and for corporate recruiters and human resources managers to seek new hires, the site has had significant success in generating recurring revenues. In late 2016, LinkedIn was acquired by Microsoft for about $26.2 billion.

Facebook has rapidly become one of the most successful of all the world's advertising platforms. Both Facebook and LinkedIn have made it extremely easy for small to mid-size businesses to design and initiate their own ads on social media, where these advertisers have the option of carefully targeting their ads to select groups of users by interest, occupation, education, geography or habits. At the same time, these sites have broad appeal to major national advertisers.

TikTok, owned by Chinese company ByteDance, is the international version of the video sharing social network app called Douyin in China. TikTok was released in 2017, and its users are comprised mainly of Generation Z and younger Millennials, in more than 150 countries. The app specializes in short-form entertainment (often about 15 to 30 seconds in length) and utilizes a powerful engine that suggests content tailored to each users' taste and viewing history. It has become so popular that consumers worldwide are highly influenced, in terms of tastes and trends, by what they see on the platform. In the U.S., TikTok had 170 million users as of 2024. It is expanding into online e-commerce sales via the TikTok site, bringing it into direct competition with Amazon.

However, TikTok has drawn the ire and concern of many government legislators. Part of their concern is TikTok's immense popularity with young children and teens, where the firm's largely unregulated short-form video content could be used to manipulate (politically or otherwise), misinform or exploit young people. The other major concern is the platform's ability to intensely monitor the online activities of users in the U.S., EU and elsewhere, and then report massive amounts of useful personal information back to the government of China, the nation where TikTok's owners re headquartered. Some members of the U.S. Congress cite national security concerns, and lawmakers have banned the use of the app on government-owned devices. In the U.S., TikTok is attempting to defuse the controversy by separating out and storing American user data in servers based in America and operated by Oracle's cloud services, but that doesn't necessarily ensure that the data could not be copied and transferred. There is some chance that the eventual result could be a sale of all or part of TikTok to non-Chinese owners.

A service of great interest is Pinterest, a virtual pin board on which users post photos, recipes, notes, lists or anything else pertaining to hobbies, projects and other interests. As of April 2023, Pinterest had 463 million global monthly active users, according to DataReportal. This visual platform heavily influences consumers who are seeking ideas for fashion, interior decor, cooking/food and events such as weddings.

While the social media pioneers were largely U.S.-based, and the audiences of leading sites like Facebook are global, many nations can boast of their own local social media success stories. This is particularly important in China, where the government limits access to many of the outside world's most popular sites such as YouTube and Facebook. Popular Chinese services include 51.com, Weixin/WeChat and Kaixin0001.com. Moreover, Ushi.cn is a Chinese service targeted at the LinkedIn-type of professional user.

The biggest news in social media involves Twitter. It was acquired by Elon Musk and a few partners in October 2022 for $44 billion. Musk renamed the platform as X and plans ongoing changes and innovations, and eventually hopes to evolve the platform into an all-purpose app similar to China's WeChat, with multiple entertainment, shopping and financial services features.

X faces new competition, however. In mid-2023, Facebook launched an X-like short-form text platform named Threads. Users can share posts of up to 500 characters, photos and videos of up to five minutes in length. Thread integrates with Facebook's popular Instagram service, and it immediately garnered a huge user base. There are other competitors as well, including Mastodon. Bluesky and Spill.

The best known social media platforms are in a mature state, with vast user bases. That is, their early phases of rapid growth in numbers are past them. Now, they want to capitalize on profit potential through the sale of advertising, and sometimes through the sale of merchandise and value-added subscription services. Consequently, these platforms are focused on driving both user engagement and advertising revenues via new features.

12) Social Media Rakes in Global Online Shopping and Ad Revenues

With more than 3 billion social media users worldwide, global ad spending on such platforms is soaring. Facebook (www.facebook.com), owned by Meta Platforms, continues to be the dominant site among social media worldwide. As of January 2024, Facebook had 3.05 billion monthly active users. The company is building targeted advertising revenues based on likes and dislikes established in users' profiles, to the extent that it is now one of the largest generators of online advertising revenue. Advertisers want to be where potential customers are, and Facebook reported in early 2021 that its average user spends 33 minutes each day on the site.

In May 2020, Facebook announced the launch of its Shops ecommerce initiative. Shops enables small businesses to set up ecommerce stores on Facebook or Instagram. Other sites such as Shopify can link to those sites. While the virtual storefronts are free, Facebook is generating revenue from in-house payment system users who will pay to increase stores' visibility. Shopping within social media is an important trend, and social media firms hope to make this into a very significant revenue generator by collecting fees on each sale made.

Advertisers have control of where ads appear on Facebook, either in users' newsfeeds or in a column of ads on the right side of the site's pages. In addition, advertisers can use the site's Custom Audience tool to specify potential customer attributes (gender, interests, location, etc.) and the Lookalike Audiences tool to find potential customers who are similar to existing customers.

LinkedIn is designed to help users network for business opportunities, and to help job seekers and recruiters connect. The site was launched in 2003, and by early 2022, it had exceeded 810 million registered users in 24 different languages. LinkedIn has revolutionized the employee recruiting industry single-handed, as each user's home page's functions well as an online resume. Recruiters constantly comb the users' information in order to identify people with certain qualifications, using sophisticated online tools provided by LinkedIn on a monthly subscription basis. In 2016, LinkedIn was acquired by Microsoft for about $26 billion. Microsoft is focusing on adding services and features to its cloud-based businesses and sees LinkedIn as a logical extension of Microsoft's services for business customers.

China's TikTok global music video platform and social network, owned by ByteDance, is one of the top global social networks. TikTok had 1.1 billion monthly active users according to Insider Intelligence as of early 2024.

On the video front, YouTube (www.youtube.com), part of Google, has long been a free-of-charge site for sharing video uploaded by YouTube members. The company earns very significant revenues through the sale of online ads. In addition, it intends to be a major provider of premium online content for paid subscribers. The site has social media elements, since members connect to create video groups that share similar interests. Videos can be uploaded by their creators as available for public viewing, or as private videos with limited access.

In order to add to its videos contributed by amateur users and professionals or corporations who want to build video audiences, YouTube has partnered with major content providers such as CBS, Sony Music Group, the BBC, NBA, Warner Music Group, The Sundance Channel and Universal Music Group. YouTube is truly global in scope. In an effort to encourage international users, YouTube has established local sites in dozens of nations.

X (formerly Twitter) is working to attract advertisers with tools such as Amplify Pre-roll, which allows X to sell ads in conjunction with television and other media companies. Using Amplify, networks post brief video replays of just-aired programming sponsored by advertisers. A&E Networks, BBC America and ESPN were early partners with Amplify. Many TV ads and some programs feature X hashtags to promote discussions.

X and Facebook face stiff competition from other social outlets including Pinterest and Snapchat. Snapchat users share photos and videos taken on their smartphones. Snapchat offers Discover, a service that links content from a broad array of sources such as ESPN, the Food Network, CNN, National Geographic, Yahoo! News and Warner Music Group.

Users swipe their mobile screens from left to right to change images, and up and down to view full video or news articles posted by the content sources, which include advertising.

Pinterest is an extremely social site that enables users to create online bulletin boards ("pinboards") of photos, videos, ideas, dreams and comments. Each image posted is called a "pin."

Some observers expect Google's and Facebook's market share of digital ad spending in the U.S. to be on the decline, due to brands spending ad dollars on alternative sites and formats, such as the wildly popular TikTok. Also, Amazon is earning an ever-growing share of the online advertising market, with its services that allow merchandise sellers to boost and advertise their products directly on Amazon.com.

In China, a social media app called Weixin/WeChat has largely taken the place of Facebook and Twitter (both of which are officially banned in China). Google sites, including YouTube, as well as Instagram, are also banned. The Weixin/WeChat app features games, chat and social media in one package. Weixin is owned by Tencent, a Chinese internet firm known for its online games and the QQ instant messenger service. Tencent markets Weixin outside China, particularly in Southeast Asia, Europe and Latin America under the brand WeChat.

13) Digital & Search Advertising Has Larger Market Share of U.S. Advertising Than TV

After a surge in online advertising during the Coronavirus era, ads had slipped by early 2023, returning to massive but more normal levels. Recent changes in consumer privacy protection rules have also slowed online advertising. Both the online audience and the level of sophistication in online advertising continue to increase dramatically. Advertisers large and small have made the internet a significant part of their advertising strategies. Digital advertising in the U.S. during 2023 was a projected $263.89 billion, compared to $244.78 billion in 2022 according to eMarketer.

Digital marketing technologies, and the vast volume of personal data gathered on consumers and utilized in such advertising, has sparked deep concern about consumer privacy throughout much of the world. An enhanced degree of government regulation has resulted, particularly in the EU. This will be an evolving process in governments worldwide.

Online advertising includes paid search, display ads, video ads and other categories. To take advantage of the growing base of online consumers, as well as the increases in connection and computing speeds, advertisers have developed rich media techniques such as very catchy ads and video content.

The digital advertising market has expanded to include social media such as Facebook and LinkedIn, where advertising has been growing at a fast clip. Advertisers, including national firms, are taking social media very seriously. Consumers are spending a significant amount of time each day on Facebook and similar pages, and these sites offer tremendous tools that enable advertisers to reach specific, niche markets. Sophisticated tracking technology that is now commonplace on the internet allows advertisers to see how online ads are performing in real-time. Meanwhile, Amazon.com has become one of the most successful online advertising platforms, generating billions of dollars yearly in fees for display ads on its shopping sites. Google remains the dominant player in online shopping searches. People who are shopping for a specific product often tend to go straight to Amazon to search, rather than going first to a platform like Google. This has had the interesting effect of making Amazon's own paid placement and display advertising revenues surge, as many companies are willing to pay Amazon to make their items more prominent.

Advertising Via Paid Search Results: Search engines such as Google provide targeted search result placement, also known as "paid search results," in the form of prominent links to a client's site. Ads on Google's search results pages appear near the "natural" search results. What is vital about these ads is that they are generated by the key words a user enters in his or her search. Advertisers pay search engines to have their links appear whenever certain words or collections of words are part of a search. For example, a paid search result for a light fixture company might appear whenever "lighting" or "lamp" is entered as part of a search. Advertisers pay for each user click on their ads. Google and other search engine sites generally sell keyword placements to the highest bidders.

Another popular online method is "pay-per-click" advertising. For example, Google's extremely successful AdSense program enables an advertiser to upload a text- or image-based ad into Google's system. Google's sophisticated technology places the ads on third-party sites that contain content related to the advertisement inserted there. Every time a consumer clicks on the ad, he or she is taken to the

advertiser's own web site, which results in a small pay-per-click fee being charged to the advertiser. This fee is shared between Google and the owner of the third-party site where the click originated.

Yet another method of online advertising is "textual" or "in-text." Advertisers pay for certain words in news or general interest articles to by hyperlinked on third-party sites. When users click the underlined word, a related ad pops up, complete with a link to the advertiser's web site. Online advertising company Vibrant Media, Inc., (www.vibrantmedia.com) for example, offers in-text ad products that can include text, flash media and video.

SPOTLIGHT: Nielsen and Partners Track Mobile Video Viewing

In partnership with Facebook, Google and other sites, Nielsen is tracking video viewers on smartphones, tablets and laptops. Video player manufacturers now include code that send pings to Nielsen servers with information about the device used to watch a video. Nielsen's servers communicate with Facebook about those device addresses, and the social media site matches the addresses with member information. Facebook sends Nielsen data such as age and sex of the associated viewers. Experian, another partner, adds buying patter information related to those viewers. Nielsen sells this information to advertisers, enabling these advertisers to best tailor their ads to reach specific audiences on specific devices.

Behavioral Targeting: A concept sometimes called "behavioral targeting" uses technology to analyze an individual internet user's tastes, habits, interests and concerns. A primary method of such targeting has long been the placement of cookies on users' computers. Cookies track a user's actions, such as web sites visited, and relay data on these actions to marketing analysis databases. (Cookies are also used to enable a web site to recognize a user when he or she returns to a web page.) Over a period of time, a pattern of web site visits will show a user's unique interests, enabling targeting of ads. Data may also be gathered every time a user clicks on an ad.

An enhancement to this idea is technology that tracks all page visits of all internet subscribers within a given geographical area. This site visit history can be analyzed at the individual level, enabling an internet service provider to offer highly targeted ads based on a subscriber's internet use history and apparent interests. Acxiom Corp.

(www.acxiom.com) is a major player in targeted online ads, maintaining a database of households with information taken from a wide variety of sources, including public real estate and motor vehicle records, warranty cards that customers complete and return to manufacturers and travel histories.

Google uses extremely sophisticated technology to gauge the interests of online consumers and to place relevant ads in their view. Google's effort to target ads in this manner vastly improves its ability to deliver relevant ads to consumers and serve advertisers' interests, all while increasing Google's ability to generate revenues.

Privacy: Google and Apple Alter the Rules

Consumers' online activity is generally tracked at the individual user's level by cookies and other means. This is extremely useful to advertisers who want to a) serve up their ads to viewers who are most likely to have an interest in their content, and b) better understand what types of people are viewing their ads. However, it runs counter to growing consumer and regulatory backlash about consumers' lack of privacy and control over their own online activities. During 2020, Google announced that it would remove support for third-party cookies from its popular Chrome internet browser. In the spring of 2021, it announced that it will not create alternative digital identifiers to track individuals as they browse across the internet, nor will it use such identifiers in Google products.

Rather than track individuals' viewing habits, one alternate trend within the digital advertising realm is to create groups or cohorts of non-identifiable users according to their apparent interests. One goal is to give users more control over their identities and to give them more trust in both internet use and in the ads that are presented to them.

In another important development, Apple announced in early 2021 that apps used by the hundreds of millions of iPhones worldwide must ask users for permission to track them individually for advertising purposes. The query occurs at the time that an app is downloaded.

The net effect of these trends has been higher advertising costs for many advertisers, with lower results. Some advertisers are reporting very substantial increases in their ad costs. For example, a tooth whitening products company in the UK called smirk (getsmirk.com), saw its Facebook ad prices soar due to Apple's privacy policy change.

Another company, Get Stix, Inc. which makes and markets pregnancy and fertility tests (getstix.co), is sharply cutting its monthly ad spending on Facebook after costs ballooned. This is an evolving situation in which the leading technology companies are attempting to better protect consumer privacy and online safety in a more proactive manner. Part of their strategy is to attempt to show the government that the industry can self-regulate without additional government control. However, there is broad interest in government in the EU to protect consumers, as well as strong feelings about better protection from members in both parties in the U.S. Congress.

Another practice is "retargeting," which displays ads for items that were viewed on an advertiser's web site but were not yet purchased. For example, a user might browse for dog beds on a pet-related site. When that user moves to an unrelated site, perhaps a news site, an ad showing the very dog beds previously viewed appears on the news page.

To some extent, internet companies make it possible for consumers to opt-out of these practices, when consumers are willing to take the time to manage their user profiles. In addition, web browser options and security settings within Apple, Microsoft and other popular software enable consumers, who are willing to take the time and trouble, to restrict the use of cookies and other tracking technology.

The EU has enacted a "General Data Protection Regulation (GDPR)" that requires websites to alert consumers to the use of cookies. Many other aspects of a site's use of consumer information are also tightly controlled by GDPR, with companies of all types required to take significant steps to protect consumers' privacy and data security.

14) Programmatic Ad Buying Dominates the Digital Media Market

Technology experts have devised automated systems in which advertisers specify the type of ad, types of page locations and price they are willing to pay for an ad. The ads are then placed by a third party (an "exchange") into vacant slots that match the advertiser's criteria. The practice, which is also referred to as programmatic buying, utilizes a set of complicated algorithms running during the milliseconds it takes for a web page to load. Omnicom Group reports that it can bid for up to 10 million online ads every second. The practice already places ads on smartphones, tablets and desktops, but will exponentially grow as televisions and billboards increasingly become connected to the internet.

Sophisticated online ad management systems make it relatively simple for advertisers, agencies and web site owners to track ad space inventories and advertising campaigns. This ability for advertisers and their agencies to tightly control their advertising spending creates new cost-effectiveness and is a powerful boost to overall online ad spending.

15) Online Travel Agencies (OTAs)/Hotels Fight to Keep Control of the Customer

The Coronavirus slashed business for travel booking agencies of all types. It remains to be seen what the long-term effect will be, but it was quickly clear that revenues would plummet along with customer counts. Meanwhile, airlines, hotels and online booking sites will continue to battle for control of customers and their loyalty.

One of the biggest single changes in the travel industry has been the exceptionally rapid rise of online travel agencies, also known as OTAs. Around the globe, vast numbers of business and leisure travelers alike rely on the internet as their primary means of gaining travel information, reserving hotels or booking air tickets.

Expedia, Travelocity, Orbitz, Hotwire and Booking Holdings, Inc. (formerly Priceline Group and owner of Booking.com) are among the largest firms offering online travel booking services in North America. In Europe, major online travel booking firms include EasyGroup (a holding company that owns and operates a number of travel and entertainment brands including easyCar, easyHotel and easyJet), Lastminute.com (a subsidiary of Travelocity Europe Limited) and eBookers. The numbers involved are massive.

Other important players include China's Ctrip.com and eLong, UK-based Opodo and India's MakeMyTrip. Meanwhile, Airbnb began allowing hotels to list on its site in 2018, charging the hotels a lower booking fee (compared to the 12%-25% fee hotels are charged by booking sites such as Expedia and Priceline).

In September 2015, Expedia completed its $1.3 billion acquisition of Orbitz. Expedia already owned several sites, including hotels.com and Travelocity. From a U.S. travel market perspective, there will now be only two significant corporate OTA groups: Expedia and Priceline. Together, these corporate enterprises control about 95% of the American OTA market. The two giants, Priceline and Expedia, each now have massive existing customer bases. They

have enormous marketing budgets that can be used to battle competitors that might emerge. Both have extremely powerful, deeply experienced digital marketing and technology teams that may be able to out-produce and out-compete the strategies of emerging firms. They each own several respected, dominant booking brands. The firms also have reached the point of massive scale whereby they have significant clout with suppliers, and they have the potential to make their loyalty programs even more compelling and competitive due to scale.

Meanwhile, an extremely popular travel reviews and information site, TripAdvisor, has evolved into an online booking site. It is in a good position to compete head-on with Priceline and Expedia. There are even more changes in store with the online travel booking business thanks to recent entries by Google and Amazon.

Consumers like OTAs because they offer a wide choice of hotel brands, prices and locations in one view. Some sites operate as "metasearch" engines, enabling the consumer to link directly to a hotel's site for booking. The largest, however, operate as true online booking agencies.

Hotels typically pay from 12% to as much as 25% commission for these bookings. In addition to the fees, OTAs are causing serious alarm at hotel chains, which fear they are losing control of the loyalty of and relationship with their customers. This is due to several strategies employed by the OTAs, including continual addition of new travel planning features to their web sites and apps, as well as extremely popular loyalty points programs of their own. Hotels.com, for example, offers a free hotel night, with no restrictions, after booking 10 nights total. This is a much simpler, easier-to-use program than those offered by most chains.

Major hotel chains and airlines have invested immense sums in their own, branded internet sites. These travel providers benefit because the use of their own online booking systems eliminates fees to middlemen and wages to human reservation agents. Encouraging travelers to book through the hotel and airline companies' own sites also gives the firms control over marketing and branding and enables them to promote loyalty programs. Consumers benefit because they have seamless access to travel information, frequent flyer accounts and other perks. A major consideration is access to loyalty points. Hotel chains are also offering discounts through their loyalty programs.

Most, if not all, chains have adopted aggressive online tactics and are denying awards points to customers who book their rooms through third-party sites. In addition, chains are offering "best price guarantees." For example, if a guest sees a better price at an OTA but books through the hotel chain, the hotel will give the guest another 25% off. Hotels are also boosting their digital offerings for loyalty program members who book directly with the hotels. These include smartphone apps that enable instant check-in, fast check-out, smartphone-based electronic room keys, digital concierge services and smartphone-based scheduling of hotel services and room service orders.

In most cases, hotels and OTAs have rate parity agreements in their contracts. This means that hotels may not be able to offer lower prices than those provided to the OTAs. However, the hotel chains may offer special prices to select groups of guests, such as loyalty plan members. This means that competitive advantage has to be created in some other manner, like loyalty programs, or special free perks for guests. In this regard, it's vital for hotel chains to take advantage of assets that they control. For example, Hyatt is among chains enabling direct booking guests to look at a floor plan and choose the actual room that they will stay in. Other hotels are including free meals or drinks for certain guests.

Traditional travel agencies have endured vast changes in recent years, including the growing trend among corporate travelers to use online booking services. Some travel agents have successfully repositioned themselves as "consultants," charging hourly fees for their expertise. Others specialize in providing unique knowledge about travel to out-of-the-way places such as Cambodia, French Polynesia or Africa.

The largest national travel agencies run sophisticated web sites of their own. They act as outsourced travel departments for their major corporate clients and arrange discounts for clients who purchase massive amounts of travel. For example, Carlson Wagonlit is a leading global business travel agency. Many large travel agencies that focus on leisure travelers buy hotel and aircraft space at wholesale and then create highly profitable tour packages to popular tourist destinations such as Cancun, Jamaica and Orlando.

16) Pandora and Spotify Lead in Streaming Music Via Internet Radio but Face Challenge from Apple Music/SiriusXM Tops 33.97 Million Subscribers

More and more people are shifting to streaming music services, accessed via online subscriptions or ad-supported plans. This is hurting recorded music sales, as consumers who subscribe to Pandora and similar services see little need to buy their own copies of their favorite songs. However, music publishers offset this revenue loss by licensing music to Pandora, Spotify and similar subscription services. In fact, streaming music over the internet means that more people are accessing more music than ever before.

For all of 2022, RIAA (Recording Industry Association of America) reported that music subscription services, such as those from Apple, Inc., Amazon.com and Spotify Technology SA, saw revenues rise 8% over 2021 to reach $10.2 billion. Streaming music accounted for 84% of all recorded music revenues in the U.S.

Streaming Music: A number of services offer ad-supported free streaming music services including Spotify, Pandora, Amazon Music, Google Play music, and the recently launched Apple Music. Most also offer premium subscription access for a few dollars per month that is ad free.

Pandora's web-based platform allows its 46.6 U.S. million active users (as of early 2023) to build unique virtual radio stations based on their personal music preferences. Pandora allows up to 250 personalized stations to be created per account. The firm's technology is based in part on the Music Genome Project, which analyzes and catalogues thousands of songs from multiple genres to create a comprehensive database that breaks down songs by 450 individual musical attributes. (In February 2019, Pandora was acquired by SiriusXM Holdings, Inc., the satellite radio service provider, for $3.5 billion, creating one of the largest audio entertainment companies in the world.)

Pandora offers free accounts, which are ad-supported but restrict the ability to skip songs, as well as premium subscriptions through Pandora One, which give listeners the ability to skip an unlimited number of songs, has no limit on monthly listening hours, delivers higher quality audio and removes advertisements. The firm branched out into mobile listening by releasing software for internet-enabled smartphones and tablets. It has also established partnerships with consumer electronics manufacturers, including Panasonic, Pioneer, Samsung and Sony, to integrate its software into new devices, as well as automakers like Honda, Ford, Lexus and Mercedes to include its software pre-installed on certain new model vehicles.

Competitor Spotify, Ltd. also offers a wide range of listening options. Spotify is a web-based subscription music service offering streaming music to registered users with roughly 456 global listeners to the free service, plus more than 195 million paying subscribers by early 2023 (North America accounted for 28% of Spotify listeners). The firm's library of 80 million songs is accessed via its proprietary Spotify streaming music player program, which users can download and install on a variety of platforms, offering them access to Spotify's entire music library and the ability to listen to chosen tracks at any time and in any order. Spotify is investing heavily in podcast content with great success.

Spotify users can create personalized playlists and have the option to share these playlists with other Spotify users who can then edit the playlists and make their own updates, enabling a collaborative approach to online, peer-to-peer music sharing. The company offers two main access tiers. Spotify Free allows free access to the online music library and is supported through advertisements, while the fee-based subscription service, Spotify Premium, offer a variety of upgraded features and does not include advertising. Subscribers to Spotify Premium can access Spotify on a variety of mobile platforms, including the iPhone, the iPod Touch, Android-based phones and Windows Mobile-based phones. Spotify also connects users to a range of music sellers, providing links to online music stores where customers can purchase albums and individual songs for download. Additionally, it introduced Spotify Platform, which allows third-party developers to create music-based apps.

Apple Music has been attempting to catch up with pioneers Spotify and Pandora. Paid subscribers are charged a modest fee per month for ad-free service. In addition to on-demand streaming service, Apple Music offers a 24-hour global internet radio station and a portal in which artists connect with listeners. The service had 88 million users as of late 2023. The fact that Amazon Music can be controlled conveniently and easily by voice via the Alexa personal assistant has been an immense boost.

A major competitor is Tencent Music Entertainment Group in China. The firm's apps include QQ Music, Kugou and Kuwo. Parent Tencent Holdings Limited acquired China Music

Corporation in 2016 to strengthen its music offerings, and subsequently changed China Music's name to Tencent Music Entertainment Group.

Satellite Radio: While Spotify and Pandora have gained tremendous audiences in internet radio, they have not benefited financially as much as the world leader in delivering radio via satellite: SiriusXM.

Sirius XM Holdings, Inc., operating as Sirius XM Radio, is a U.S.-based satellite radio provider. (It also owns an interest in a related company Canada, where broadcasts are made in French and English.) It offers hundreds of channels to its more than 33.97 million SiriusXM subscribers (as of September 2023), consisting of dozens of channels of commercial-free music; as well as popular channels of sports, news and talk that may include advertising in some cases, traffic and weather; and Latino channels.

The company's primary source of revenue is subscription fees, with most of its customers subscribing to Sirius on an annual basis. Sirius radios for the car, truck, home, RV, boat, office and store are distributed through automakers and retail locations nationwide as well as online through SiriusXM.com. Sirius also has agreements with every major automaker to offer its radios as factory or dealer-installed options in their vehicles. In addition, satellite radio services are offered to customers of certain rental car companies.

Sirius Internet Radio is an internet-only version of the firm's service that delivers a simulcast of select music and non-music channels. Additional services provided by the firm include Travel Link, a collection of data services that provides users with information on weather, fuel prices, movie listing and sports scores and scheduling; and both real-time weather and traffic services. The fact that voice-activated personal assistants, such as Amazon Echo and Google Home, can take verbal commands to find play music (by artist, genre or specific title), will add to the subscription music trend.

17) Overview of the Mobile Apps Industry

Mobile apps (short for "applications"), including those for magazines, information services such as health site WebMD, games, newspapers, catalogs and ebooks, to name but a few of the tens of thousands of uses, didn't really exist before the introduction of the iconic iPhone smartphone (although online "widgets," which offer similar features, had been around for quite some time). The Apple App Store launched in July 2008 with only about 500 apps available. By 2024, Apple's store had 1.96 million apps that were either for sale or downloadable free-of-charge. Sensor Tower reports that Apple's App Store sales grew to $89.3 billion in 2023, up from $86.8 billion in 2022 and $85.1 billion in 2021.

The vast majority of apps are downloadable free-of-charge, as they are offered to consumers to enable them to more quickly access internet-based stores and services via mobile devices. You might think of this as app-based advertising. For example, airlines such as United Airlines and Singapore Airlines offer free apps that make it easier to make purchases from the airlines. Apps sold for a fee generate only modest revenues per average app, with roughly 500 downloads daily per average app. App fees tend to be in the $3.00 range. Paid apps usually are free of advertisements. However, Apple announced plans to reduce fees from 30% to 15% of app store sales for small developers (those with no more than $1 million in revenue). Sensor Tower estimated that only about 0.2% of the apps in the Apple App Store generated more than $1 million in 2019.

Meanwhile, vast numbers of apps are also available for the Android mobile phone operating system (the world's leading smartphone platform). Android is the mobile operating system developed by Google, and it is the most popular operating system in the mobile world.

On all platforms, the most popular apps include games such as *Candy Crush;* tools such as Google Maps; and entertainment- and media-related apps, such as those for Pandora internet-based radio. At the same time, apps provide tools for business people, travelers, students, hobbyists, wine drinkers, people who like to cook, job seekers, children, sports fans, shoppers, car enthusiasts and myriad other special interest niches.

The number of apps on the market has become so massive that consumers are less likely to be willing to sort through app stores to find useful tools. Instead, to a growing extent, they rely on recommendations from friends, emails from trusted sources and magazine reviews in order to find new apps to download. Many smartphone users have downloaded a large number of apps, but only use a few of them on a regular basis.

Microsoft's Windows 11, the first new version of its operating system since 2015, was released in late 2021. The new system features an apps store that collaborates with Amazon, enabling PC app stores to operate as simply as those used on smartphones. Users are able to choose apps formerly limited to Android operating systems such as TikTok for video sharing and Uber for ride sharing. The long-term intent is to make the PC experience more app-driven, and thus more like using a smartphone.

18) Quality of Care and Health Care Outcomes Data Are Available Online, Creating a New Level of Transparency

From the earliest days of the internet, one of the most popular activities online has been searching for information about illness, disease, pharmaceuticals and their side effects, as well as information related to care and diagnosis, such as options for surgery. Now, online activity about health care has risen to a massive level. With rapidly rising health care costs and concerns about the quality of care received for the dollar spent, many patients, employers and insurance providers are using online databases for information regarding doctors and hospitals—call it comparison shopping for health care. For example, there are growing numbers of web sites that track data on hospitals, such as the U.S. Department of Health and Human Services' web site, Hospital Compare (www.medicare.gov/hospitalcompare/search.html). Hospital Compare uses data from Medicare and Medicaid to track performance at thousands of facilities across the U.S. Also, many insurers make hospital data available to members on their web sites.

These databases typically enable an insurer or patient to compare specific hospitals to the national average on statistics such as mortality rates. For example, the Hospital Compare site compares each hospital in Houston, Texas to the Texas state average and to the national average. Data includes many items concerning patient experiences and satisfaction, surgical outcomes, readmission, hospital-related infections, and time spent waiting for care in emergency rooms. Also, average costs for various types of procedures are now available online on web sites that are attempting to earn profits from such services, although the quality of the data may vary.

Internet Research Tip: Getting Hospital Ratings Online

Patients and concerned family members can now use any of several web sites to check on the quality of hospitals before checking in for treatment. Available data typically includes patient outcomes, fees and whether the latest in technology is available. For patients needing specialized care, this knowledge can be a real windfall. WebMD Health Services, at www.webmdhealthservices.com, (formerly Subimo) gets high marks for its ease of use.

It sells subscriptions to major employers and health plans, whose members can then log in.

Other sites include HealthGrades, www.healthgrades.com, Medicare's Hospital Compare at www.medicare.gov/hospitalcompare/search.html and United Healthcare's www.myUHC.com, designed to be used by the millions of patients who are covered by United's health plans.

The Medicare claims database is a digital record of the bills Medicare pays. It is used by federal investigators to sniff out fraud and for analysis by researchers and consultants for cost and utilization studies. Medicare has begun making some data about payments to individual physicians available. The database covers millions of caregivers and beneficiaries, but it is prohibited by law from disclosing patients' names.

Internet Research Tip:
Top web sites for health care information include:
National Cancer Institute, www.cancer.gov
Centers for Disease Control and Prevention (CDC), www.cdc.gov
FamilyDoctor.org, www.familydoctor.org
Health Finder, www.healthfinder.gov , a service of the U.S. Dept. of Health & Human Services
KidsHealth, kidshealth.org
Mayo Clinic, www.mayoclinic.org
NIH National Institute on Aging, www.nia.nih.gov/health
Medscape, www.medscape.com

Elsewhere, corporations in various segments of the health industry may publish interesting cost and outcomes information. For example, health diagnostics and monitoring devices from Abbott, provide an online database giving the exact CPT procedure code and Medicare reimbursement rate for hundreds of procedures such as cholesterol tests at www.codemap.com/alere. The data is sorted geographically as well as by type of care.

Data on individual doctors is becoming available online, at such web sites as www.findadoc.com. The quality of the data from such sites may vary, and one should use caution. Nonetheless, the information is intriguing. Findadoc, for example, enables the user to look up doctors by location and specialty, and then view their hospital affiliations, languages spoken and patient ratings for such qualities as bedside manner and wait time.

Quantum Health (www.quantum-health.com), a Columbus, Ohio health care coordinator, offers comparative health care data to its corporate clients, plus a laundry list of services that help employees covered by company insurance navigate the often confusing health care system and get the most out of their health benefits. Quantum Health services include informing patients of what questions they should ask their physicians about their conditions, assistance in finding specialists, advice on medical tests that should or should not be taken and education on disease management and prevention. Quantum reports that its employer clients have enjoyed reduced spending on workers' health care, thanks to reductions in waste and unnecessary care, better results from disease management and a 25% reduction in health benefits-related workload. Two of its most impressive statistics are a 22% reduction in readmissions and a 4% reduction in emergency room usage.

The Affordable Care Act of 2010 (ACA) includes a provision that hospitals and doctors that score poorly on patient surveys can be denied Medicare reimbursement fees. Surveys such as those from Press Ganey, Gallup and National Research Corp., on which patients score health care providers on care experiences (based on patient surveys) including waiting times, pain relief and bedside manner, are becoming powerful arbiters in how patients are treated.

Internet Research Tip:
To compare costs for procedures, try the following site:
www.healthcarebluebook.com

For bill negotiation services, see:
www.medicalcostadvocate.com

To determine whether or not a physician is board certified:
www.abms.org

19) Smartphones and Neobanks Replace Bank Branches and Tellers

Banks have learned that combining the convenience of online banking with a chain of branch locations and ATMs allows them to fill the entire range of many customers' needs. This is similar to the trend among major retailers of combining ecommerce and physical storefronts, thereby creating synergies between bricks and clicks. Virtually all banks now have web sites where customers can monitor the status of their accounts, including checking, savings, investments and loans; make money-transfers to pay bills; and apply for services online. Online banking has been an enormous success, and was boosted even further by the Coronavirus pandemic, as people curtailed trips to physical bank offices.

Thousands of U.S. branch locations have closed in recent years. Online banking, in combination with ATMs, goes a long way to fill the gap left by fewer brick and mortar bank locations. The end result is greater operating efficiency for banks. Nonetheless, providing online banking poses operational costs and challenges, including security and hacking issues.

The popularity of mobile and online banking has enabled a highly competitive segment within banking known as "challenger banks" or "neobanks." These are companies that offer traditional bank services, such as deposit accounts and debit cards, but have no physical locations whatsoever. In an effort to build market share, they often offer higher interest rates on deposit accounts, generous loyalty rewards and other perks that exceed those of traditional banks. This is a global trend, and it is being fostered by "open banking" laws and technologies that make it easy for new challenger banks to startup. Among the biggest players in this sector are Ant, in China; Revolut, in the UK; as well as Chime and Brex in the U.S.

E*Trade Financial, a major online stockbroker, entered the online and electronic banking field in a big way. It owns a nationwide system of ATMs under the E*Trade brand and has a rapidly growing base of online bank deposits.

Brick and mortar branches still offer a few services that online banks cannot, such as cashier's checks and safe deposit boxes, and a large percentage of customers want to know they can walk into a branch for assistance when needed. Bank of America has opened a small number of employee-free branches, where customers can use ATMs and converse with remote tellers via video phones.

Security of online and mobile banking remains a daunting challenge, and banks are struggling to attempt to stay ahead of online fraudsters. Bank of America offers SafePass, a 6-digit, one-time passcode sent as a text message to customers' smartphones which can then be used to authorize fund transfers, administer the online payment system and receive higher transfer limits. Major security software providers include RSA, the security division of EMC Corporation (www.rsa.com/en-us), Broadcom, which acquired Symantec in 2019 (www.broadcom.com) and Entrust (www.entrust.com).

Biometrics are becoming more common with regard to smartphone security. Customers by the millions at Wells Fargo, Bank of America and JP Morgan Chase use fingerprints to log into their bank accounts via smartphone. Retinal scans are also in use at Wells Fargo for corporate accounts. In addition, Citigroup uses voice recognition to verify its credit card customers. However, the most advanced technologies being applied to mobile and online account and payments security are now based on artificial intelligence (AI) and machine learning (ML). One of the most useful developments is "behavioral analytics." This is the application of ML to compare a customer's activities in making a current transaction to the customer's behavior patterns in previous transactions. For example, a signal of fraud is if the user misspells words or otherwise enters data very differently than his/her known habits. ML systems can analyze such patterns and flag potential fraud with lightning speed.

20) Insurance Direct Selling and E-Commerce Grow

The roles of insurance intermediaries and agents, along with the overall structure of the insurance market, are changing dramatically as a result of ecommerce influences. Insurance sites on the internet enable consumers to generate a large number of competing insurance quotes within seconds. Because the tasks of providing information and writing transactions have typically been the primary functions of insurance agents, electronic markets that can perform these tasks more efficiently and with fewer costs threaten to displace agents. The future role of the insurance agent may evolve toward value-added customer service and consultation. This is similar to the evolution of the role of travel agents since the booming popularity of booking travel reservations via the internet. The extremely rapid adoption of smartphones on a global basis means that firms that deal with consumer lines such as auto insurance must adopt mobile strategies in order to gain new customers and satisfy the service needs of existing accounts.

Thanks to extremely successful direct sales efforts by firms like GEICO and Progressive, direct sales in the U.S. personal auto insurance market are booming. Direct marketing is also taking over in nations other than the U.S., with a signification portion of all new car insurance policies in the UK, for example, sold through direct marketing. Independent agencies will continue to lose market share as technology and direct sales gain in use.

Independent agents face tough and growing competition from internet-based sales. At the same time, underwriters utilizing captive agency systems have found growth opportunities by increasing ecommerce efforts or acquiring independent agencies and integrating them into their captive systems. The internet is an extremely effective way for underwriter web sites to generate leads for captive agencies.

Moreover, thanks to the growing success of internet sites that enable consumers to shop for the best life insurance prices, direct selling is playing a growing role in the life sector as well. Nonetheless, many insurance consumers prefer to deal with live agents in person or via the telephone. For example, Liberty Mutual, GEICO and State Farm make it extremely fast and convenient for consumers to get homeowner's quotes online.

Thanks in part to the rising popularity of ecommerce, many insurance underwriters are now utilizing both direct sales and sales through agents in their business models. For example, the Progressive Corporation, an underwriter of automobile insurance, makes buying insurance online or over the phone extremely user-friendly. At the same time, it offers its auto insurance policies through about 30,000 independent agents, one of the largest agent networks in the U.S. Log onto www.progressive.com and you can get an instant quote on a policy for an automobile, motorcycle, boat or recreational vehicle, in addition to homeowner's and renter's insurance. Customers can also use the Progressive web site to file a claim or make a payment. Its easy-to-use web site (which includes pages in Spanish) is part of Progressive's overall strategy to utilize a high level of service, advanced technologies and direct sales to offer a competitive combination of coverage, service and pricing. Meanwhile, Progressive also uses the internet to promote business for its independent agents.

Insurers selling over the internet may enjoy a substantial cost advantage over the course of a customer's lifetime, relative to non-internet-based insurers. This is due to reduced sales costs, lower customer service expenses and more advanced information-gathering capacities. Consequently, ecommerce has prompted many insurers to upgrade and integrate their information systems.

The increased value of online connections results in decreased transaction costs. Products such as travel, credit or burial insurance have relatively high fixed costs and low value, but nonetheless have significant transaction costs when sold via traditional methods. Consequently, customers purchasing these products generally pay a high price per dollar of coverage. The internet can automate the sales and underwriting process for such insurance products. This means that prices can be lowered, and more insurance can be sold by reducing transaction costs. Increased access through ecommerce is also influencing some consumers to purchase broader, high-value insurance products, such as liability umbrellas. Meanwhile, the security of insurance customers' data online is an important consideration, since large amounts of highly personal information are at stake.

Banks are becoming increasingly competitive in insurance sales, partly because they are adopting direct marketing methods. Large numbers of bank holding companies have acquired or established insurance agency subsidiaries. While these subsidiaries may operate using traditional agents, many of them use substantial direct marketing as well. For example, if you are a Bank of America customer, you are likely to receive life insurance offers in your monthly bank statements. This generates insurance leads for Bank of America at nominal cost.

Major Insurance-Comparing and Selling Sites on the Internet

Insure.com
www.insure.com provides instant insurance quotes from the most diverse array of insurers offered by any one source. The site works with over 200 insurance companies in all 50 states.

Insurance.com
www.insurance.com is an online insurance agency that offers all types of insurance with emphasis on auto coverage.

CoverHound
Coverhound.com is a San Francisco-based firm that compares options from insurers including Progressive, esurance and Safeco, and links users directly with the selected company for policy purchase.

PolicyGenius
www.policygenius.com sells a variety of insurance products from top insurers such as AIG, MetLife, Prudential and Embrace Pet Insurance.

A growing list of major insurers are investing in online technology, as are venture capitalists with interests in the insurance industry. In October 2019, Prudential Financial, Inc. completed the acquisition of startup Assurance IQ, Inc. for $2.35 billion. Softbank Group Corp. headed a $300 million investment round for Lemonade Insurance Co. which offers online renter's and homeowner's insurance. Clover Health, a startup in San Francisco that offers Medicare Advantage health insurance, raised $500 million. The industry is going to see a growing list of such startups that are focused on making it easier, faster and less expensive for consumer to purchase insurance. That goes for business insurance as well; Berkshire Hathaway, owner of major insurance companies of many types, offers a small business insurance package called THREE, a program that includes workers' compensation, multiple liability coverages (including general liability and cyber insurance), property and auto insurance products into one accessible package. It is marketed directly to business owners via the internet only, not through agents.

21) The Internet of Things (IoT) and M2M to Boom, Enhanced by Artificial Intelligence (AI)/Open New Avenues for Hacking

The phrase "Internet of Things" or "IoT" will become increasingly commonplace. It refers to wireless communications known as M2M or machine-to-machine. M2M can be as simple as a refrigerator that lets a smartphone app know when you are running low on milk (via Wi-Fi) to a vast, exceedingly complex network of wireless devices connecting all of the devices in a massive factory. Analysts at network device giant Cisco expected M2M connections to grow dramatically and rapidly, to 14.7 billion by 2023.

A Wireless Sensor Network (WSN) consists of a grouping of remote sensors that transmit data wirelessly to a receiver that is collecting information into a database. Special controls may alert the network's manager to changes in the environment, traffic or hazardous conditions within the vicinity of the sensors. Long-term collection of data from remote sensors can be used to establish patterns and make predictions, as well as to manage surveillance in real time. Another term that is coming into wide use is M2M2P or machine-to-machine-to-people. The "to-people" part refers to the fact that consumers, workers and professionals will increasingly be actively involved in the gathering of data, its analysis and its usage. For example, M2M2P systems that automatically collect data from patients' bedsides; analyze, chart and store that data; and make the data available to doctors or nurses so that they may take any necessary actions are becoming increasingly powerful. Such systems, part of the growing trend of

electronic health records (EHR), can also include bedside comments spoken into tablet computers by physicians that are transcribed automatically by voice recognition software and then stored into EHR.

Connected Devices are a Notorious Channel for Hackers' Entry into Networks and Data

The Internet of Things (IoT) is a vital component of machine-to-machine (M2M) communications and will become even more important with the rollout of fast, urban 5G wireless networks. IoT sensors, monitors and cameras can gather the types of data that can make cities more efficient (in a wide range of areas, from traffic flow to lighting efficiency); make agricultural technology advance (such as better efficiency in irrigation and fertilization) and enhance operations in manufacturing and distribution facilities of all types. However, connected devices such as these are notorious nodes through which hackers have had stunning and costly success at taking over networks and stealing data. There is a massive need, and an accompanying business opportunity, to make M2M networks as cybersafe as possible.

The long-term trend of miniaturization is playing a vital role in M2M. Intel and other firms are working on convergence of MEMS (microelectromechanical systems—tiny devices or switches that can measure changes such as acceleration or vibration), RFID (wireless radio frequency identification devices) and sometimes tiny computer processors (microprocessors embedded with software). In a small but powerful package, such remote sensors can monitor and transmit the stress level or metal fatigue in a highway bridge or an aircraft wing or monitor manufacturing processes and product quality in a factory. In our age of growing focus on environmental quality, they can be designed to analyze surrounding air for chemicals, pollutants or particles, using lab on a chip technology that already largely exists. Some observers have referred to these wireless sensors as "smart dust," expecting vast quantities of them to be scattered about the Earth as the sensors become smaller and less expensive over the near future. Energy efficiency is going to benefit greatly, particularly in newly built offices and factories. An important use of advanced sensors will be to monitor and control energy efficiency on a room-by-room, or even square meter-by-square meter, basis in large buildings. Turntide Technologies (turntide.com), a California company offers systems comprised of electric motors and small computers that analyze building occupant patterns and then more efficiently manage heating and cooling systems. German firm Envio Systems, now a unit of JLL, has similar technology to adjust lighting, heating and cooling.

In an almost infinite variety of possible, efficiency-enhancing applications, artificial intelligence (AI) software can use data gathered from smart dust to forecast needed changes, and robotics or microswitches can then act upon that data, making adjustments in processes automatically. For example, such a system of sensors and controls could make adjustments to the amount of an ingredient being added to the assembly line in a paint factory or food processing plant; increase fresh air flow to a factory room; or adjust air conditioning output in one room while leaving a nearby hallway as is. The ability to monitor conditions such as these 24/7, and provide instant analysis and reporting to engineers, means that potential problems can be deterred, manufacturing defects can be avoided, and energy efficiency can be enhanced dramatically. Virtually all industry sectors and processes will benefit.

Look for data sensors in homes to proliferate over the mid-term. In the insurance business, live data emanating from sensors in homes could lead to more intelligent policies. Monitoring data via smartphone could be a significant opportunity for companies in the senior care, childcare and pet care sectors.

Internet Research Tip: The Internet of Things Infographic:
Cisco posts a highly informative Internet of Things page at www.cisco.com/web/solutions/trends/iot/overview.html which includes a one-minute IoT video.

Meanwhile, French technology firm SigFox offers a simple, inexpensive wireless network, designed specifically for M2M needs. The network transmits data at a rate of 100 bits per second, which is slower by a factor of 1,000 than most smartphone networks but does so cheaply while it fills simple transmission needs such as those from many wireless sensors (such as Whistle, a clip-on collar sensor that tracks dog activity levels). Base stations use a wireless chip that costs only $1 to $2, and customers pay modest service charges per year per device. As of early-2023, SigFox had deployed its technology in about 70 countries, covering more than 1 billion people within its network range.

Intel and other firms have developed methods that enable such remote sensors to bypass the need for internal batteries. Instead, they can run on "power harvesting circuits" that are able to reap power from nearby television signals, FM radio signals, Wi-Fi networks or RFID readers.

Memory chips used in sensors are much smaller than those in smartphones and laptops, opening a major opportunity for manufacturers such as Adesto Technologies. The firm makes chips that store between 32 kilobits and one megabit of data, making them a good fit for small monitors such as fitness data tracking wristbands. Meanwhile, Wiliot (www.wiliot.com), a supply chain technology firm in Israel, has developed a combination sensor and mini-computer tag for use by retailers desiring to track merchandise in the supply chain. The tags do not require batteries and promise to ultimately cost a few pennies each. Future applications might include location-based beacons in retail stores that alert nearby customers to selected items by cellphone. Smoke detectors with small memory chips could sense battery life, while blood transfusion bags could track their locations, ages and content viability.

Amazon offers a variety of IoT devices, including the Astro robot for home monitoring and Halo Rise for tracking sleep patterns. Both communicate with Amazon's Alexa personal assistant. In the fall of 2022, the Connectivity Standards Alliance launched Matter, an interoperability standard that specifies how smart devices talk to each other. Many platforms have embraced Matter, including Amazon Alexa, Apple Home, Google Home and Samsung SmartThings.

Internet Research Tip: Internet of Things (IoT) Networks:
For more information on wireless network systems and remote sensors, see:
Analog Devices, Inc. (which acquired Linear Technology Corp.), www.analog.com/en/applications/technology/smartmesh-pavilion-home.html%20#
Moog, Inc., www.moog.com
C3ai, c3iot.com/industries

---

22) Designers and Manufacturers Bypass the Middleman with Direct-to-Consumer Online Business Models

Digital marketing, the power of ecommerce and today's simple access to global manufacturers have combined to launch another interesting trend: companies that claim to source their merchandise at the same manufacturers used by well-known brands, and then sell, via their web sites only, high quality items direct to consumers are modest prices. The intent is to bypass middlemen and retail stores, and thus offer very high value. Shopping from home during the Coronavirus pandemic boosted this trend.

New apparel companies are among the leaders in this field. One of the better-known companies with this business model is Everlane, www.everlane.com, which states, "We spend months finding the best factories around the world—the very same ones that produce your favorite designer labels." Online apparel firms with similar business models include JustFab, ShoeDazzle and BirchBox. In fact, the list has gotten very long.

Such companies must offer excellent service, reasonable prices and cost-free returns, in addition to a compelling merchandise line, in order to be competitive. Even when they do so, there is reason to question whether or not they can compete successfully against companies such as Ralph Lauren that have massive supply chains, unbeatable design and marketing teams and immense buying power. If apparel manufacturers that rely on traditional marketing feel threatened by online-only, off-brand upstarts, it would be simple enough for them to launch their own businesses based on this business model, using a different brand name in order to avoid sales channel conflicts.

Meanwhile, brands and logos owned by companies like Ralph Lauren are extremely powerful in the minds of consumers and are exceptionally difficult for smaller firms to compete against. There is also the "wait for name brands to go on sale" mentality that is now standard in consumer behavior. That is, department stores and specialty clothing retailers have essentially trained consumers to expect their favorite apparel brands to be on sale. If you see something new that you like in stores today at full retail price, you know that it will almost undoubtedly be marked down by 25% to 40% soon. At the end of the season, it may be marked down by as much as 70%.

Nonetheless, there are some niche markets where the direct-to-consumer model may make a lot of sense. Eyeglasses are a standout in this regard. Once a consumer's eye exam is completed and a prescription written, glasses can be made virtually anywhere. Traditionally, however, consumers have ordered their eyeglasses (in particular, expensive designer frames) in expensive retail store fronts that operate at high overhead. Consumers can try out various styles of frames in these stores and turn over their prescription to a salesclerk so that glasses can be custom ordered. However, the actual manufacturing

of lenses, and their assembly into frames, will be done elsewhere.

This is where a successful new company called Warby Parker comes in. Its founder saw opportunity in this multi-step supply chain and notoriously high prices. At www.warbyparker.com, customers can select from basic frame styles, upload their prescriptions and order attractive glasses for around $100 to $300, which is a comparative bargain. While Warby Parker has built a considerable following with its online business model, its strategy includes both bricks and clicks, as it is opening a growing number of retail showrooms in major cities in the U.S. Executives of the company reported that when a physical location opens in a new market, online sales in the area typically triple. The firm plans to open as many as 900 U.S. stores. (Of course, there has long been a modestly priced alternative in the eyeglasses market: companies that operate hundreds of storefronts that offer both eye exams and frame selections. After the exam and sale, the eyeglasses are manufactured in a lab owned by the same firm that owns and operates the stores. This vertical integration can offer relatively low prices at high volume but may not appeal to fashion conscious consumers.)

Large numbers of direct-to-consumer businesses are springing up offering everything from custom shirts to bed linens to shoes. Deal Décor sells furniture under this model. Crane and Canopy has gotten good press coverage of its business model, which is very similar to that of Everlane. This firm, at www.craneandcanopy.com, sells sheets, duvet covers and other bed linens that it claims are from the same factories, with the same quality textiles, as those offered by designer labels. Here again, the price is lower than standard retail prices found in stores, at least until such stores put their goods on sale.

The business of shipping goods directly from manufacturers in China to consumers around the world is booming. Chinese retailer LightInTheBox offers hundreds of thousands of items, from wedding dresses to table linens to iPhone chargers to faucets, at competitive prices that are free of middleman markups. Costs are kept down further by LightInTheBox's proximity to its suppliers, so that its inventory is kept low. The company does business in multiple languages, so it employs part-time workers from around the world who connect with customers via phone and email.

23) Fashion Rental Pioneered by Online Apparel Firm Rent the Runway

Rent the Runway, an online site that rents dresses, jewelry and accessories, makes luxury affordable to its subscribers. The site offers tens of thousands of dresses, tops, pants, skirts, as well as accessories and jewelry (many from top designers such as Badgley Mischka, Herve Leger and Vera Wang) which members rent for a few days and return in prepaid and addressed folding garment bags. The company's warehouse operations are housed in a 160,000-square-foot facility. In addition to packing and shipping, the facility has been carefully designed to incorporate dry-cleaning and sterilization of returned apparel, making Rent the Runway the largest dry-cleaning operation, in one building, in the U.S. Members may also purchase clothing and accessories, rather than rent.

Starting in 2017, Rent the Runway varied its offerings from one-time, one–item rentals to monthly subscriptions, including RTR Unlimited which allows the rental of unlimited numbers of pieces on rotation with no return dates. Rent the Runway also opened a small number of brick-and-mortar stores. The company reported that most people wear only 20% of their closets. This indicates that a continual stream of rented attire may have great appeal to certain consumers.

The Coronavirus pandemic hit Rent the Runway hard. Much of its business focused on clothing for the office or for parties, proms, weddings and other social gatherings and special events. By mid-2020, the firm had closed its brick-and-mortar stores permanently, and instituted layoffs. It also expanded its drop-off and pickup locations for online orders, utilizing some of its former stores. Business rebounded by late 2021, and the company conducted a successful IPO in late October of that year.

Top Fashion Rental Companies:
Gwynnie Bee, closet.gwynniebee.com
Rent the Runway, www.renttherunway.com
Taelor, taelor.style

---

24) Smaller Satellites (SmallSats and CubeSats) and Low Earth Orbit Revolutionize Telecommunications

Until recently, satellites orbiting the Earth were large, heavy craft. In recent years, however, a growing fleet of smaller satellites has been launched, ranging from the size of kitchen refrigerators down to golf balls. These relatively tiny SmallSats have an exponentially growing number of uses and, thanks to their miniaturization coupled with rocket technology innovation, are far cheaper to launch and maintain than ever before. A class of the smallest SmallSats are called CubeSats, which, according to NASA, refers to a class of nanosatellites that use a standard size and form factor. The standard CubeSat size uses one standard module or unit ("1U") measuring 10x10x10 centimeters, and is extendable to larger sizes; 1.5, 2, 3, 6 and even 12U. They are particularly easy to launch because they have electronic and physical interfaces that allow 1U modules to stack together in a dispenser that increases payload in a rocket, sometimes called a "secondary payload." CubeSats were originally developed in 1999 by California Polytechnic State University at San Luis Obispo (Cal Poly) and Stanford University to provide a platform for education and space exploration.

Satellites of all sizes are being streamlined to rely more on 3-D printing which saves manufacturing costs and increases orbit efficiency. For example, Boeing Co. is incorporating 3-D printing in the development of its Phoenix satellites.

Internet Research Tip: CubeSats

For more on CubeSats, see NASA's web site which includes comprehensive images, videos and media resources:
www.nasa.gov/mission_pages/cubesats/index.html

Some of the uses for these new baby satellites include gathering weather data to aid farmers, transportation and logistics firms, and disaster relief workers. Environmental impact data can be used by government agencies to monitor deforestation, polar icecap and ocean changes over time. Satellites are also bringing internet service to all parts of the globe, including rural areas that other providers cannot reach.

SmallSats promise vast increases in cost-efficiency, utility and flexibility. Today's state-of-the-art satellites feature computer circuitry that can be reprogrammed from the ground, on an as-needed basis. This is vast improvement over traditional satellites. SmallSats are easier and faster to manufacture as well.

Thanks to advanced technologies and miniaturization, today's tiny satellites are much lighter in weight than former generations. This means that a launch rocket can carry a much higher number of satellites in one payload. This is important, because launch costs are one of the major investments required in completing the tasks required to get satellites into service. Entrepreneur Elon Musk, founder of electric car company Tesla, is revolutionizing satellite launches. His SpaceX firm has shown that rocket bodies can be recovered and reused in a highly efficient manner. His methods are slashing the cost of putting satellites into orbit.

Space launch firm SpaceX has its own system, called Starlink, planning to expand it to as many as 12,000 LOE satellites, and perhaps even more over the long term. As of March 2024, the company had launched 5,504 Starlink satellites and reported 1.3 million subscribers worldwide for its satellite internet service. Officials at NASA have stated concern over the potential of this huge number of satellites to cause space collisions. This firm, associated with Tesla founder Elon Musk, will have significant advantages, since it operates an extremely cost-effective rocket launch service. Starlink's satellites are deployed at three different altitudes. Its satellites weigh only about 200 kilograms each. A grouping of 60 of these units can provide up to 1 terabit per second of bandwidth. In June 2022, the U.S. Federal Communications Commission (FCC) approved the firm's request to service moving vehicles including boats, airplanes and recreational vehicles, as well as commercial trucks and consumer's cars. This will open up a very broad new market.

A firm called OneWeb owns system that may eventually encompass from 648 low-Earth orbit (LOE) satellites. This will drive down costs and improve performance in telecommunications and internet applications. Unfortunately, after raising $1.7 billion and launching only 75 satellites, OneWeb took bankruptcy in the spring of 2020 during the Coronavirus pandemic. It was quickly acquired, in July 2020, by the UK Department for Business, Energy and Industrial Strategy.

LEO satellites are typically in orbit at altitudes of 400 to 1,000 miles and are used for telecommunications and internet access. Because of their low altitude, the time required to send and receive Earth signals is shorter. This can be extremely advantageous in many circumstances. For example, passengers on cruise ships are dependent upon satellite systems for internet access, which traditionally has been much slower than land-based access. LEO satellites are speeding up ship-board internet to the extent that movies, gaming and intense business applications are much more practical.

Cruise ships are perfect customers for fast internet access via low-orbit satellites. Guests are encouraged to Tweet, Skype, Stream movies (using accounts with DIRECTV, Netflix or Hulu), connect with friends or play Xbox Live with gamers worldwide.

Jeff Bezos' Blue Origin is investing $10 billion to launch more than 3,200 low-Earth-orbit satellites between 2020 and 2029. The network, called Project Kuiper, received FCC approval in July 2020 and promises to provide reliable, affordable broadband service to underserved communities around the globe. By late 2023, Project Kuiper plans had launched two prototype satellites, and it has scheduled 83 multi-satellite launches over a five-year period.

SpaceX and T-Mobile US, Inc. are working together to utilize SpaceX satellites to boost T-Mobile wireless connections. By the end of 2023, the companies began testing text messaging services in select U.S. markets, with an ultimate goal of coast-to-coast voice and data service without using cell towers. The intent is to determine the feasibility of working together to provide satellite-based wireless phone services in remote areas, far from cell towers.

25) Sharing Economy Gains Market Share in Travel with Online Sites Like Airbnb, Vrbo and Many Global Competitors

One of the most remarkable growth stories in ecommerce has been the advent of new ways to book non-traditional accommodations for travelers. This "sharing economy" (also known as collaborative consumption) affords consumers the ability to rent or borrow everything from hotel rooms to cars to private homes. As with all hospitality sectors, shared accommodation has been hard hit by the Coronavirus pandemic. Many travelers may feel safer in small independent properties, away from crowds, rather than in large hotels. While the early months of the Coronavirus saw plummeting demand for travel and for accommodations, short-term home rental sites such as Vrbo soon found popularity among travelers who wanted to avoid hotels.

Vrbo, which stands for Vacation Rental by Owner, is a site that allows property owners, especially owners of second homes and resort condos, to advertise their properties online to people seeking vacation accommodations. Vrbo was acquired by startup HomeAway, Inc., a firm that originated when venture capital firm Austin Ventures agreed to back entrepreneur Brian Sharples in this promising business sector. HomeAway also owns Travelmob, a sharing-economy accommodations site focused on Asia. HomeAway was acquired by

Expedia in 2015 for $3.9 billion, and the HomeAway name was dropped in favor of Vrbo.

Internet platforms that focus primarily on hotel room reservations are also adding homes and apartments as alternative places to stay. For example, Booking.com, a major presence in online hotel room booking and a subsidiary of Priceline, is also offering shared-space and vacation property listings on its site.

The biggest disruptor to the hotel industry is San Francisco-based Airbnb, Inc., founded in 2008. Airbnb.com members who are willing to let travelers stay in their homes can post their information, including pricing and accommodation details. The accommodations range from a bedroom in an occupied house or apartment to a luxury apartment or condo reserved entirely for the guest. In turn, travelers may search in a given market for members who are willing to accommodate them. Airbnb offers more than 5.6 million accommodations in 220 countries. Members are encouraged to write reviews describing the positive and/or negative aspects of their stays. These reviews are partially encouraged so that renters and travelers may view profiles and feedback before staying in homes or letting others stay in their homes, thereby reducing the risk of danger or other negative situations. The Airbnb network is also connected to Facebook, allowing members to search the social networking platform for additional information regarding certain hosts and guests. Airbnb charges room owners a 3% host fee and an additional fee of 6% to 12% per guest. The average commission is about 12% of total revenues. The typical guest stays longer, on average, than a guest in a traditional hotel.

Airbnb has expanded to offer local-led activities in cities around the world. Activities are varied and may include bike rides, walking tours or fishing trips, to name a few, and are typically provided by Airbnb hosts.

Airbnb wrote more exacting standards for hosts with regard to cleanliness, communication and cancellations, and offers a mobile app to facilitate communication between hosts and guests. Hosts are encouraged to earn badges for "business travel ready" listings that offer such amenities as Wi-Fi and hairdryers. In growing numbers of cities, hosts are now required to purchase short-term rental licenses and collect and remit municipal taxes.

Literally hundreds of competitors and imitators have sprung up around the world. Some are focused on particular locales, travelers or types of accommodations. For example, OneFineStay.com (which was acquired by AccorHotels) is focused on renting a curated collection of better homes and condos in major cities, including New York, Paris, Los Angeles and London as well as resort destinations in the Caribbean, Hawaii and Central America, among others.

Despite their wide popularity, room- and home-sharing sites face multiple challenges. Fraud has been a problem, with unscrupulous site members collecting fees for rentals of properties that they claim to own but are in fact owned by others. Guest safety is a serious issue. There have been accidents, dog bites, even a guest locked into his room by a host seeking sexual favors. At most sites, there are no room inspections and no way to enforce room standards. Guest room rentals may not be covered under a homeowner's insurance policy. Likewise, such rentals may not be allowed under homeowner's association rules and municipal law. Last, but not least, the market may become saturated, with only a limited number of properties available to add to inventory.

Nonetheless, the traditional hotel industry sees room-sharing as a significant competitive threat that is already taking market share. The long-term result may be hotel chains creating their own branded sharing sites, listing both their own hotel properties and rooms or condos owned by others. Hotels may build hybrid properties as well, with apartment towers for room sharing next door to traditional hotel properties. The hotels could run the apartments to high standards, and could build oversized pools, spas and other common area facilities to be shared with guests from the apartments next door.

Marriott International offers a vacation property-sharing venture called Homes & Villas by Marriott International. The division offers 2,000 luxury properties worldwide with options ranging from one-bedroom homes to a castle in Ireland. Marriott is partnering with LaCure and Lloyd & Townsend Rose to vet and manage unique properties.

SPOTLIGHT: Short Term Apartment Rentals Compete with Hotels

Travelers are finding furnished apartments in cities around the world available for short term rentals. In some cases, large buildings built especially for this apartment-hotel purpose are springing up. Similar to an Airbnb stay, the apartments offer kitchens and washers and dryers for about 20% to 30% lower nightly rates than hotels. Management companies typically lease a few floors in a condo or apartment building, although Sonder Corp. (www.sonder.com) manages all 270 units in the Butler Brothers building in downtown Dallas.

---

26) Digital Assistants Include Amazon's Echo and Google's Home/Alexa and Similar Software Power Third-Party Developers

Apple, Google, Amazon and Microsoft are competing to offer the best voice-activated systems that can do anything from reporting the time and weather, to playing music on request, to performing web searches, to telling jokes, to making purchases from internet sites and operating appliances and thermostats. These platforms utilize the latest in artificial intelligence in order to become more useful over time. Apple's Siri is available on iPhones, iPads, Apple Watches and through an app in some vehicles. Google Now is an app available on a variety of mobile devices as is Microsoft's Cortana app. Amazon's Alexa web app is installed on a gadget called Amazon Echo that sits on a countertop, desk or shelf. Alexa software can be installed on other devices as well. Google offers a similar device called Google Home. All of these apps and platforms are voice-activated and use connections to other apps and systems to find information such as directions, time, date, weather and trivia, or make purchases, which are reported audibly (users can choose their device's voice gender and language). The next step for these handy assistants is the ability to connect with apps relating to climate control, lighting and/or security enabling users to simply say, for example, "Set home temperature to 72 degrees," or "Activate alarm system," and have the action performed, even from remote locations.

Importantly, most systems are open to third-party developers. For example, Amazon has opened "Lex" to developers, which is the artificial intelligence engine behind the Alexa and Echo platforms. Lex is tied into Amazon's AWS cloud computing system. Software and product developers can incorporate Lex, enabling voice-activated or click-activated responsiveness (often in the form of specific task-oriented icons or apps known as "bots"). This gives these developers instant access to extremely powerful cloud computing, artificial intelligence and voice-activation in one easy-to-launch package. Amazon charges a modest fee per thousand uses or data accesses. This ease-of-use has spurred a tidal wave of new product development worldwide, with the potential to revolutionize the manner in which consumers interface with their digital devices and the internet. Smart device and digital assistant manufacturers have banded together to adopt a technology standard called "Matter" to evolve their devices to communicate with various platforms.

Top Voice-Activated Technology Platforms and their Unique Advantages:

Alexa: Owned by Amazon. Connects to Amazon AWS Cloud services, making it easy to embed Alexa software in third-party products.

Siri: Owned by Apple. Siri, already familiar to hundreds of millions of iPhone users worldwide, has evolved into a very sophisticated digital assistant.

Cortana: Owned by Microsoft. Microsoft had deep partnerships and experience with third-party corporate software and technology firms, making this an easy platform for others to embed.

Google Assistant: Owned by Google. Assistant capitalizes on Google's constantly evolving expertise in search and artificial intelligence.

Source: Plunkett Research, Ltd.

---

27) Amazon Becomes One of the World's Leading Sellers of Apparel and Shoes

Amazon.com is attempting to dominate online fashion shopping in the same way it has revolutionized other retail categories including books, electronics and groceries. It first jumped into the fashion pool with the acquisition of Shopbop in 2006, followed by the purchase of online footwear site Zappos in 2009 and discount luxury clothing and accessories site MyHabit in 2011. Starting in 2013, Amazon began taking on high fashion, working out deals with designers such as Michael Kors, Calvin Klein, Catherine Malandrino and Vivienne Westwood. In 2016, Amazon launched seven in-house fashion lines, including Lark & Ro women's clothing, Franklin Tailored men's suits and accessories and Scout + Ro children's clothing.

The company invested heavily in improving selection and photography of the items for better presentation. Amazon's Prime Wardrobe service lets customers subscribe to a service that ships apparel on a regular basis. Members can try on the clothing, keep what they like, and return the rest with no shipping charges.

By 2021, analysts at Cowen forecast that Amazon's share of the U.S. apparel market reached 16%. The giant online retailer was granted a patent in 2017 for on-demand apparel panel cutting and manufacturing, making Amazon part of the robotic "click, buy and make" movement. In addition, the firm has developed a technology system utilizing a camera and scanning software to automatically take customers' measurements and upload them to Amazon accounts. The system is powered by Amazon's Alexa tabletop personal assistant.

Amazon has also invested heavily in tools and content that can help online customers make better choices while they shop. For example, it operates a massive photography studio where models try on apparel and shoes. This studio makes hundreds of thousands of apparel and shoe photos yearly for use on the Amazon websites. They also may make notes about how the items fit. Amazon also posts comments from customers about how items fit. For example, items may be rated as fits as expected, too small, somewhat small, somewhat large or too large. This not only drives customer satisfaction and confidence, it also reduces return shipping costs.

28) The Metaverse Has Difficulties Gaining Steam

The metaverse refers to a life-like scene, representation or virtual world that has been generated by specialized software. The user's experience is enhanced significantly when viewing and participating in virtual reality (VR) environments through special VR viewing equipment (such as a helmet/googles with 3-D viewing screens and earphones, sometimes used with gloves that contain sensors). VR creates an experience that is immersive to the user. Many observers consider the emerging metaverse to be a segment of virtual reality, but some metaverse sites may be accessed without VR headsets. To get a clear idea of the potential of this technology, imagine riding a unicorn, fighting as a gladiator in Rome's Colosseum in the 4th century B.C. or walking your dog on the moon, in a life-like, immersive, 3-D experience, made possible by specialized headsets that you wear. VR headsets are made by firms like Oculus, HTC and Sony, and start at $299.

Large tech companies are investing billions in metaverse technology, and Facebook even changed its corporate parent's name to Meta Platforms, Inc. The company reportedly spent $10 billion in 2021 on its Facebook Reality Labs unit. One project, Horizon Workrooms, is an app that enables Oculus Quest 2 headset wearing users to enter virtual offices as avatars to participate in meetings. Despite huge investments, the metaverse in general is having difficulty gaining broad adoption by consumers or businesses.

Meanwhile, Unity Software, Inc. provides a software platform for creating and operating interactive, real-time 3D content. The platform can be used to create, run and monetize interactive, real-time 2D and 3D content for mobile phones, tablets, PCs, consoles and augmented and virtual reality devices. In addition to gaming and entertainment, the metaverse has industrial and educational applications. For example, Unity Software's products are used in the gaming industry, architecture and construction sector, animation industry and designing sector. Other leaders in the metaverse sector include Microsoft, Epic Games, Roblox Corp., Sony, Samsung, HTC, iTechArt, Alphabet/Google, Oculus (part of Meta Platforms) and Nvidia Corp.

29) OpenAI (ChatGPT), StabilityAI, Anthropic (Claude) and Others Launch Impressive Tools that Generate Text, Art, Code and Smart ChatBots

OpenAI (openai.com) created GPT, or Generative Pre-trained Transformer. It uses language-processing algorithms mined from massive numbers of gigabytes of data gathered by internet crawling, enabling it study digital files (machine learning) in order to answer questions, write essays and summaries, translate languages, create memos or program computer code, among other tasks. (This process is known as "generative AI.")

By 2023, OpenAI had accepted substantial investments from Microsoft. Importantly, it had launched leading-edge AI interfaces, including ChatGPT that are easy to use in the automated creation of text (such as magazine articles), art (such as illustrations for websites), music and even complex computer code. While these AI tools produce very impressive results, they remain a work in progress, with continuing refinement needed.

In addition to ChatGPT, OpenAI's other impressive AI-driven tools include Dall-E, for creation of art images and Codex, which utilizes AI to help programmers create lines of code. (Codex is the basis for Microsoft's popular GitHub Copilot programming aid.) OpenAI launched a business version of ChatGPT called ChatGPT Enterprise in mid-2023, which focuses on protecting proprietary data.

OpenAI and Microsoft have many competitors in the generative AI arena, not the least of which is Google's parent company Alphabet and owner of the DeepMind AI lab. Alphabet developed its own Smart Chat system. It was initially called Bard, but the name was changed to Gemini in early 2024. It is based on the firm's long-standing project known as LaMDA, or Language Model for Dialogue Applications. Other pioneers include Stability AI, AI21 Labs, Character AI, Cohere, Runway, Hugging Face and Anthropic (backed with $7 billion in investment from Amazon, Google and others). Web services leaders like Amazon's AWS and Baidu are also very active in AI-driven tools such as chatbots and automated computer code. China's Baidu launched Ernie Bot in March 2023. China-based Huawei has also invested heavily in AI, including development of a Smart Chat bot. Watch especially for big leaps forward in AI-enhanced search engines as a result of this competition.

The use of AI tools such as these that learn from the works of millions of human producers (machine learning), and then create new text, art, etc., is leading to significant debate as to copyrights, fair use and other aspects of ownership. Getty Images, a company that sells licenses for photos available for commercial use via its websites, sued Stability AI in courts in London, England claiming breach of copyright. In addition, the ability of students to use tools like ChatGPT to create essays and other homework is sparking significant controversy within the education sector. (Several tools exist to aid teachers and editors in determining whether or not text was generated by AI, but such tools are likely to lag by the ever-growing capabilities of AI platforms.)

Meanwhile, SmartBots, including the ability of tools like ChatGPT to write intelligent answers and search results on-the-fly go far beyond writing essays and providing customer service. Microsoft is incorporating Chat AI into its Edge/Bing search tools, and Google launched similar search enhancements of its own. Product suggestions and search results on websites, such as those of retailers like H&M or Saks, may become significantly more effective thanks to incorporation of these AI tools. This will lead to systems that literally act as virtual salespeople, which will boost revenues at retailers and also increase customer satisfaction. The ability of these tools to study massive amounts of

background and reference data (machine learning) could lead to virtual teachers, counselors and business professionals in the not-too-distant future. For example, students could ask for auto-generated textbooks tailored to their specific, personal needs and interests. (Virtual tutors may be the first step.) Business owners could query virtual human resources SmartBots, deeply immersed in legal material—even specific to specific job types, state jurisdictions or management problems. The owners could obtain guidance on how to deal with (or even dismiss) problem employees.

30) Virtual Reality/Augmented Reality and 3-D Technologies Create Opportunities for the Tech Industry/Immersion Games to Grow

Virtual Reality (VR): One of the most closely watched developments in the technology sector, especially in electronic games, is virtual reality, or "VR." In addition to gaming, potential major uses for VR include training/education as well as entertainment in general. Growth will be boosted by the ability to connect VR and augmented reality (AR) devices to IoT.

California-based Oculus VR headsets make virtual reality seem startlingly lifelike. Its Oculus Rift S headset makes stereoscopic 3-D gaming players using PCs feel immersed in the game, using some components that are commonly found in smartphones and tablets. This is sometimes referred to as "immersion" gaming. The Oculus Go headset requires no PC, no wires and no controller, while the Oculus Quest headset works with an app and a game controller.

Facebook acquired Oculus VR for $2 billion in March 2014. Today's Meta Quest headsets (originally developed by Oculus) bring a realistic feeling to virtual meetings and entertainment, in addition to the obvious advantages for games. Meta planned to release its latest headset, Quest 3, in 2023.

Sony's virtual reality headset, the PlayStation VR, was released in October 2016. Another virtual reality headset is HTC Corporation's Vive. Its price tag includes two wireless controllers and two base stations for 360-degree room-scale motion-tracking.

Google has had a major focus on the potential of VR since 2014. It was the lead investor in a $542 million funding round for Magic Leap, Inc., the developer of an eyeglass-based device that can project computer generated images over real settings (a twist on VR called augmented reality). The Magic Leap One device was released in early 2019.

Microsoft's 3D offering, HoloLens, made its debut in 2015. Another device that promises augmented reality, HoloLens imposes holograms over real views. The headset is designed to allow users to play electronic games, build 3D models and conduct immersive videoconferencing. Microsoft offers a HoloLens Commercial Suite for organizations and a Development Edition for individual developers. In late 2019, Microsoft released Hololens 2, a next generation version designed for the enterprise sector with a wider field of view and hand and eye-tracking.

Microsoft's artificial intelligence capabilities (including its collaboration with OpenAI), its cloud computing platform Azure, its business enterprise tools and its video gaming products all have massive potential to work together with the HoloLens product to create highly innovative services and add-on tools. Microsoft's Windows operating system supports VR headsets from a variety of manufacturers including Acer, Dell, HP, Lenovo Group and Samsung. Samsung's HMD Odyssey headset, for example, features OLED displays and includes headphones and a built-in microphone.

VR equipment sales have seen a disappointing adoption rate, particularly among video gamers, as of early 2023. Sony launched PlayStation VR2 in February 2023, despite sales of its earlier version (PlayStation VR) coming in at only about 5 million units between 2016 and 2019 (less than 10% of the number of traditional PlayStation gaming consoles sold during the same period). Meta Platforms' sales of its Quest VR headsets have been similarly lackluster. Part of the problem is the relatively high cost. HTC and Samsung have also been developing VR sets.

Augmented Reality (AR): AR is a technology that superimposes computer-generated, digital images on a real-time view, creating a composite view. For example, health technicians may use smart glasses, with AR installed, to see the location of a patient's veins before drawing blood, or technicians may wear smart glasses to see schematics and instructions relating to nearby equipment that needs fixing. AR equipment currently available includes Microsoft's HoloLens 2 headset (at about $3,500) and Lenovo's ThinkReality A3 smart glasses (at about $1,500).

SPOTLIGHT: AR Boosts Online Retail

Online shoppers are embracing AR as a way of "trying on" clothing, accessories, cosmetics and more, by imposing images of items for sale on their own faces or bodies captured by cameras on their mobile devices. Warby Parker, for example, has long offered an app on which online shoppers see different glasses frames on their digital faces. Cosmetics retailers Ulta Beauty and MAC Cosmetics launched an AR shoppable filter from Snapchat in February 2022. Snapchat parent Snap, Inc. reported that as of mid-2022, 200 million people were utilizing AR on a daily basis. The company commissioned a study from Deloitte Digital that concluded that online shoppers who use AR had a 94% higher conversion rate than those without.

The Coronavirus pandemic accelerated the adoption of AR since social distancing requires people to stay far apart. Business travel virtually shut down for several months and will likely continue to be curtailed even as businesses reopen. AR technology allows team members to interact from a distance. For example, due to a global curtailment of travel, an Intel engineer in Germany was unable to fly to a chip plant in Arizona that needed his expertise. Intel relayed a video to the engineer of real-time work at the plant via AR goggles, and he was able to walk the plant workers through a vital repair. Volkswagen AG's Porsche subsidiary reported that use of AR glasses in U.S. service departments more than tripled during the pandemic when technicians got virtual help from counterparts in different cities and different countries. Other sectors that are embracing the technology include health care and defense.

Apple, Inc. was investing heavily in both VR and AR technology. Its headset, called Vision Pro, is expected to offer an 8K display for each eye and has an anticipated release in early 2024 at a price of about $3,500. The company also offers certain AR features on iPhones which, as early as 2018, were equipped with cameras that enable composite images, and it offers tens of thousands of AR apps in its store. Among the more popular AR features for iPhones are the ability to transform a screen within Snapchat with special effects—such as tropical flowers or a star-filled sky. Arki enables users to visualize projects and designs in 3D. The app from eyeglasses retailer Warby Parker utilizes AR to enable users to virtually see, on their faces onscreen, a pair of glasses that they are considering. VR apps for interactive learning are also available. For example, JigSpace enables an in-depth view of a coral reef, and the ability to visualize a machine such as a jet engine from the inside out. Another retailer, IKEA, has an AR-featured app that enables the user to visualize pieces of specific furniture in their homes.

VR and AR uses are stretching far beyond gaming. Surgeons can practice complicated techniques before cutting into patients (Medivis is a pioneer in this field). Corporate training is another area where VR is coming into play. Wal-Mart, Inc., for example, now utilizes VR training in all 200 of its training centers, which serve 140,000 new hires per year.

31) Regulatory Environment Is Challenging for Online Businesses and Social Media

The online industry continues to slowly move towards better protection of the privacy of consumers—sometimes voluntarily, and sometimes through regulation. The EU has enacted a "General Data Protection Regulation (GDPR)" that requires websites to alert consumers to the use of cookies (bits of code that record a website visitor's actions). Many other aspects of a site's use of consumer information are also tightly controlled by GDPR, with companies of all types required to take significant steps to protect consumers' privacy and data security. One very conspicuous result is the cookies settings screen that users must face when they first visit a website. It may seem a waste of time to many consumers in the habit of clicking "accept cookies" or "accept only necessary cookies" so that they can continue using the site (their alternative is to click into a second screen that enables consumers to have greater control over cookies and tracking when on-site). Meanwhile, website operators can fairly state that they have notified consumers that cookies are used. Nonetheless, the fines for noncompliance can be steep.

In 2021, Google announced that it would stop utilizing technologies that are able to identify unique, individual users as they click from page to page online. Instead, Google is using tools that enable advertisers to target their ads without collecting information on users. Consumers are grouped with other people who have similar habits, placed into cohorts that can then be targeted by ads. That is, the advertiser can target large groups of people, but cannot identify individuals. The net result is that many advertisers are altering both their strategies and their budgets, sometimes to the extent of reducing budgets on sites like Google. Many are concerned that their ads are much less effective. Email advertising has also been somewhat regulated in recent years, with commercial senders now required to offer consumers the opportunity to easily opt out of receiving further emails. Starting in 2024, email blast senders are also required to provide more transparency as to the ownership of the IP addresses from which high-volume emails are originating.

With advertising, privacy and cookie tracking somewhat addressed by these measures, there are other significant regulatory issues afoot. Freedom of speech has long been a massive controversy in the digital space. Should consumers be free to express opinions and post graphics and text to the extent of inciting hatred and violence, posting disinformation or attempting to manipulate readers? Or should potentially harmful communications be prohibited by law? A primary consideration is whether or not (and to what extent) social media like Facebook and X should be allowed (or required) to enhance or restrict certain points of view and types of content. For example, should users be able to freely express (post) whatever they want, or should site operators (whether with human intervention or automatic algorithms) be allowed to remove posts or news? Various social media and news outlets have been accused of blocking or removing posts with certain points of view, for political purposes. Some operators might find it logical to remove posts that appear to be racial, religious or sexual slurs or harassment. Who is to decide what is and is not appropriate? At the same time, it is clear that certain types of posts incite or encourage behavior that is dangerous or antisocial, such as crime or terrorism. The U.S. Supreme Court had two cases (Florida and Texas state-level laws) on its docket as of early 2024, and many such cases are likely to ensue globally over the mid-term.

Chapter 2

ECOMMERCE & INTERNET BUSINESS STATISTICS

Contents:

Ecommerce & Internet Business Statistics and Market Size Overview

Worldwide Ecommerce & Internet Market	Amount	Units	Year	Source
Retail ecommerce Sales, Worldwide [1]	5.78	Tril. US$	2023	eMarketer
Digital Ad Spending as a Percent of All Ad Spending, Worldwide	67.4	%	2023	eMarketer
Percentage of Individuals Using the Internet, Worldwide	65.7	%	2023	DR

U.S. ecommerce & Internet Market	Amount	Units	Year	Source
Total Retail Sales, U.S.[2] (includes Ecommerce)	8.33	Tril. US$	2023	Census
Previous Year Total Retail Sales, U.S.[2] (includes Ecommerce)	8.07	Tril. US$	2022	Census
Retail ecommerce Sales, U.S.[1]	1.177	Tril. US$	2023	eMarketer
Percent of U.S. Adults Who Use the Internet	93	%	2021	PEW
High Speed Internet Subscribers, U.S., Fixed, Home & Business	126.8	Million	2023	PRE
High Speed Internet Subscribers, U.S., Wireless, incl. Smartphone	390.3	Million	2023	PRE
Home Broadband Adoption, U.S.	98	%	2023	ITIF

[1] These revenues include products or services ordered using the internet, regardless of the method of payment or fulfillment, but exclude travel, event tickets, money transfers food services and gambling.

[2] Including food services.

ITU = International Telecommunication Union

DR = DataReportal

PEW = Source: Internet/Broadband Fact Sheet. Pew Research Center, Washington D.C. (2022) www.pewresearch.org/internet/fact-sheet/internet-broadband/

ITIF - Information Technology & Innovation Foundation

Census = U.S. Census Bureau

PRE = Plunkett Research Estimate

Source: Plunkett Research, ® Ltd.

U.S. Computer Software & Related Services Quarterly Revenue: Q4 2022-Q3 2023

(In Millions of US$)

NAICS Code[1]	Kind of business	2023			2022
		1Q	2Q	3Q	4Q
5112	Software publishers	124,481	125,840	132,540	120,707
	Government	10,163	10,925	11,158	11,162
	Business	82,525	83,856	85,252	81,474
	Households consumers & individuals	31,793	30,933	32,154	31,934
5171	Wired telecommunications carriers	78,181	77,569	77,223	79,293
	Government	3,400	3,348	3,278	3,649
	Business	22,873	22,556	22,457	23,217
	Households consumers & individuals	51,908	51,665	51,488	52,427
5172	Wireless telecommunications carriers (except satellite)	75,746	74,397	76,834	79,330
	Government	1,512	1,417	1,600	1,517
	Business	23,452	23,106	24,046	24,761
	Households consumers & individuals	50,782	49,874	51,188	53,052
518	Data processing, hosting & related services	81,527	83,244	85,161	83,472
5415	Computer systems design & related services	168,096	168,366	162,373	164,203
	Government	50,216	49,948	S	49,418
	Business	113,878	S	S	S
	Households consumers & individuals	4,002	3,917	3,993	4,258
5417	Scientific research and development services	68,147	73,876	74,764	74,335
	Government	15,849	16,284	17,707	16,163
	Households consumers & individuals	S	S	S	3,169

Notes: Estimates have not been adjusted for seasonal variation, holiday or trading-day differences, or price changes. Estimates are based on data from the Quarterly Services Survey and have been adjusted using results of the 2007 Service Annual Survey. Detail percents may not add to 100 percent due to rounding.

S = Estimate does not meet publication standards because of high sampling variability (coefficient of variation is greater than 30%) or poor response quality (total quantity response rate is less than 50%). Unpublished estimates derived from this table by subtraction are subject to these same limitations and should not be attributed to the U.S. Census Bureau.

[1] For a full description of the NAICS codes used in this table, see www.census.gov/eos/www/naics/.

Source: U.S. Census Bureau
Plunkett Research, ® Ltd.
www.plunkettresearch.com

U.S. Retail Trade and Ecommerce Sales: 2019-2022

(In Millions of US$; Latest Year Available)

NAICS Code	Kind of Business	2022		2021		2020		2019	
		Retail	Ecomm.	Retail	Ecomm.	Retail	Ecomm.	Retail	Ecomm.
	Total Retail Trade	**7,040,995**	**1,012,636**	**6,519,845**	**951,027**	**5,565,713**	**810,758**	**5,401,470**	**571,088**
441	Motor vehicles & parts dealers	1,521,010	D	1,478,354	D	1,206,588	D	1,235,246	38,709
442	Furniture & home furnishings stores	143,646	4,779	141,087	4,554	113,545	3,806	120,509	2,337
443	Electronics & appliance stores	92,760	2,788	94,097	2,983	74,804	2,341	90,841	1,793
444	Building materials & garden equipment & supplies stores	511,690	3,878	481,171	3,286	421,003	2,297	372,473	2,086
445	Food & beverage stores	957,185	27,445	890,689	26,345	849,573	23,172	774,417	8,525
446	Health & personal care stores	402,880	D	386,734	D	354,683	D	347,004	D
447	Gasoline Stations	736,082	D	572,654	S	429,353	S	513,686	S
448	Clothing & clothing accessories stores	303,413	20,968	292,402	19,454	201,521	15,898	268,025	12,363
451	Sporting goods, hobby, book & music stores	102,993	6,128	102,641	6,362	83,802	5,483	79,367	3,376
452	General merchandise stores	862,133	D	797,486	D	728,695	D	715,524	D
453	Miscellaneous store retailers	171,265	S	160,004	8,503	128,793	6,546	131,848	5,415
454	Nonstore retailers	1,235,938	873,421	1,122,526	818,347	973,353	704,002	752,530	494,030
4541	Electronic shopping & mail order houses	1,117,046	870,459	1,019,866	815,430	884,382	701,437	659,251	492,023

Notes: Estimates are not adjusted for price changes and include data for businesses with or without paid employees..

D = Denotes an estimate withheld to avoid disclosing data of individual companies; data are included in higher-level totals.

S = Estimate does not meet publication standards because of high sampling variability (coefficient of variation is greater than 30%) or poor response quality (total quantity response rate is less than 50%). Unpublished estimates derived from this table by subtraction are subject to these same limitations and should not be attributed to the U.S. Census Bureau.

NA = Not Available

Total & Ecommerce Sales for Electronic Shopping & Mail-Order Houses, by Merchandise Line, U.S.: 2019-2022

(In Millions of US$; Latest Year Available)

Merchandise Lines[1]	2022		2021		2020		2019	
	Total	Ecomm.	Total	Ecomm.	Total	Ecomm.	Total	Ecomm.
Total Electronic Shopping & Mail-Order Houses (NAICS 4541)	**1,117,046**	**870,459**	**1,027,971**	**820,843**	**888,502**	**703,017**	**657,089**	**489,094**
Books & magazines	22,846	21,238	22,524	20,966	20,998	18,772	16,808	14,813
Clothing & clothing accessories (includes footwear)	S	S	133,146	124,365	115,735	108,485	92,995	84,951
Computer hardware	S	S	S	S	S	S	S	S
Computer software	S	S	S	S	19,839	18,575	15,278	14,267
Drugs, health aids & beauty aids	258,144	84,354	214,603	76,883	197,936	75,114	163,823	51,633
Electronics & appliances	92,252	85,507	88,930	82,274	S	S	56,113	50,891
Food, beer & wine	41,505	38,287	40,663	37,856	29,094	26,787	19,067	16,995
Furniture & home furnishings	137,588	131,165	131,773	124,311	115,900	109,898	73,627	68,471
Jewelry	S	S	14,183	12,015	12,512	10,542	9,471	7,618
Audio and video recordings (includes purchased downloads)	20,602	19,410	18,392	17,286	16,400	15,403	11,964	11,091
Office equipment & supplies	S	S	S	S	10,801	9,330	S	S
Sporting Goods	39,083	33,642	40,515	37,040	35,918	32,800	22,679	20,420
Toys, hobby goods & games	30,902	28,682	30,041	28,042	25,959	24,149	17,872	16,335
Other merchandise[2]	153,080	132,182	150,805	132,399	125,581	107,869	83,641	68,241
Nonmerchandise receipts[3]	74,545	68,610	S	S	46,232	42,322	34,454	30,645

Notes: Estimates are not adjusted for price changes.

[1] Estimates include data for businesses with or without paid employees and are grouped according to merchandise categories used in the Annual Retail Trade Survey.

[2] Includes other merchandise such as collectibles, souvenirs, auto parts and accessories, hardware, lawn and garden equipment and supplies, and jewelry.

[3] Includes nonmerchandise receipts such as auction commissions, customer training, customer support, advertising, and shipping and handling.

* Plunkett Research Estimate

NA = Not Available

Source: U.S. Census Bureau
Plunkett Research, ® Ltd.

Internet Publishing & Broadcasting & Web Search Portals: Estimated Revenue U.S.: 2017-2023

(In Millions of US$; Latest Year Available)

NAICS Code 51913	2023	2022	2021	2020	2019	2018	2017
Total Operating Revenue	339,574	317,358	311,136	245,601	218,580	193,119	165,430

Notes: Estimates are based on data from the Service Annual Survey and administrative data. Dollar volume estimates are published in millions of dollars; consequently, results may not be additive.

Source: Plunkett Research Online Estimates, U.S. Census Bureau

Plunkett Research, Ltd.

www.plunkettresearch.com

Internet Access Technologies Compared

(In Millions of Bits per Second - Mbps)

Type of Access	Maximum Data Rate (In Mbps)	Characteristics
Dialup		
Dialup	.0288, .0336, .056	Analog modems that require dialup connection. Slowest method of Internet access.
ISDN	.064, .128	Integrated Services Digital Network. Digital access that requires dialup connection.
Wired Broadband		
ADSL	1.5 - 24 Downstream .5 - 3.5 Upstream	Asymmetrical Digital Subscriber Line. Highest speeds are on ADSL2+ (ULL).
SDSL	2.3	Symmetric Digital Subscriber Line. Downstream and upstream data transfer rates are similar. Ideal for businesses because of synchronous speed and high-speed router capabilities.
VDSL	24 - 100 Downstream 2.3 - 16 Upstream	Very High bit-Rate DSL.
Cable Modem	4 - 2,000 Downstream .384 - 50 Upstream	2 Gigabyte (2 GB) speeds are possible with DOCSIS 3.1 technology.
FTTH	15 to 1,000 Downstream 5 to 1,000 Upstream	Fiber to the x (Home, Node, Premises, etc). Google Fiber is a leading provider. Google is developing future 10 Gigabyte (10 GB) technologies.
T1/DS1	1.544	Ideal for businesses with high bandwidth requirements.
T3/DS3	44.736	Equivalent to 30 T1 circuits.
E1 (Europe)	2.048	European version of T1.
E3 (Europe)	34.368	European version of T3.
OC3	155.52	High-speed access. Uses optical fiber technology.
OC12	622.08	Offers higher speed access than OC3. Uses optical fiber technology.
OC48	2,488.32	Offers one of the fastest data rates. Uses optical fiber technology. Extremely expensive to setup and maintain.
OC768	39,813.12	Network line used by AT&T, Cisco and others.
Wireless Broadband		
802.15.3 (UWB)	100 - 2,000	UWB stands for ultrawideband. It is useful for high-speed, short distance data transfer.
802.11b-g (Wi-Fi)	11 - 54	Typical home and office wireless networks.
802.11n (MIMO), 802.11ac	100 - 2,000	Faster data transmission rates and broader area coverage than other 802.11 technologies.
802.15 (Bluetooth) versions 1.0 - 2.0	1 - 3	Useful for high-speed, short distance data transfer.
802.15 Bluetooth version 3.0	24	Bluetooth 3.0 offers high speed data transfer at short range of up to 10 meters.
802.16e (WiMAX)	15 - 70	Has the potential to be useful for distances of up to 30 miles.
802.16m (WiMAX2)	110-365 Download 70-376 Upload	Also known as WiMAX Advanced, this technology is classified by the ITU as true 4G.
Satellite	5 to 20	Limited upstream speeds. Low-Earth Orbit satellites may offer faster speeds.
CDMA2000 EV-DO	2.4	Popular cellular technology. EV-DO Rev. A is 3.1 Mbps, Rev. B is 14.7 Mbps
HSPA	14.4	Popular 3G cellular
HSPA+	42 - 168	Advanced cellular, Release 8 is 42 Mbps, Release 9 is 84 Mbps and Release 10 is 168 Mbps.
LTE (3G-4G)	36 to 326	"Long Term Evolution" technology for cellular networks.
LTE Advanced (4G, Release 10)	100-1,000 Download up to 500 Upload	An upgraded version of LTE that is classified by the ITU as 4G. Sometimes called an IMT-Advanced technology.
5G	200 - 10,000	Download speeds of as much 10 Gigabytes are theoretically possible.

Note: 1 Mbps = 1,000 Kbps; 1,000 Mbps = 1 Gigabyte (1 GB)

Source: Plunkett Research, ® Ltd.

Number of Business & Residential High Speed Internet Lines, U.S.: 2019-2024

(In Thousands)

Types of Technology	19-Dec	20-Dec	21-Dec	22-Dec*	23-Dec*	24-Dec*
Total Fixed (e.g. cable, satellite, fiber to the premises)	114,291	121,250	125,777	129,550	133,437	137,440
Mobile Wireless (e.g. smartphone, tablet)	352,012	369,638	362,241	376,006	390,294	405,126
Total Lines	466,302	490,888	510,198	535,708	562,493	590,618
Yearly Change	15,240	23,735	25,510	26,785	28,125	29,531

Notes: High-speed lines are connections to end-user locations that deliver services at speeds exceeding 200 kbps in at least one direction. Advanced services lines, which are a subset of high-speed lines, are connections that deliver services at speeds exceeding 200 kbps in both directions. Line counts presented in this report are not adjusted for the number of persons at a single end-user location who have access to, or who use, the Internet-access services that are delivered over the high-speed connection to that location.

* Plunkett Research Estimate.

Copyright © 2024, Plunkett Research, Ltd.

Source: U.S. Federal Communications Bureau (FCC)

www.plunkettresearch.com

Amazon.com, Inc. Annual Sales & Income: 2017-2023

(In Millions of US$)

Region/Product Line	2023	2022	2021	2020	2019	2018	2017
Net Sales	574,785	513,983	469,822	386,064	280,522	232,887	177,866
North America	352,828	315,880	279,833	236,282	170,773	141,366	106,110
International	131,200	118,007	127,787	104,412	74,723	65,866	54,297
Amazon Web Services (AWS)	90,757	80,096	62,202	45,370	35,026	25,655	NA
Net Income	30,425	-2,722	33,364	21,331	11,588	10,073	3,033

NA = Not Available

Source: Amazon.com, Inc.
Plunkett Research, ® Ltd.
www.plunkettresearch.com

Employment in Ecommerce & Internet-related Fields, U.S.: 2002-2023*

(In Thousands of Employed Workers)

Year	Software Publishers	Data Processing, Hosting & Related Services	Web Search Portals, Libraries, Archives, and Other Information Centers
2002	253.3	303.9	71.1
2003	238.9	280.0	68.4
2004	235.9	267.1	69.8
2005	237.9	262.5	70.1
2006	244.0	263.2	71.7
2007	255.3	267.8	74.8
2008	263.6	260.3	77.6
2009	257.7	248.5	77.7
2010	260.9	243.0	79.6
2011	271.4	245.8	87.5
2012	287.1	254.9	95.3
2013	299.6	269.6	103.9
2014	315.5	279.5	114.1
2015	334.4	296.2	124.0
2016	358.8	303.9	133.3
2017	381.2	318.0	144.4
2018	416.3	331.0	154.6
2019	466.0	343.2	166.9
2020	504.4	361.7	173.8
2021	559.2	401.7	179.2
2022	635.8	466.3	189.2
2023*	653.6	495.6	191.6

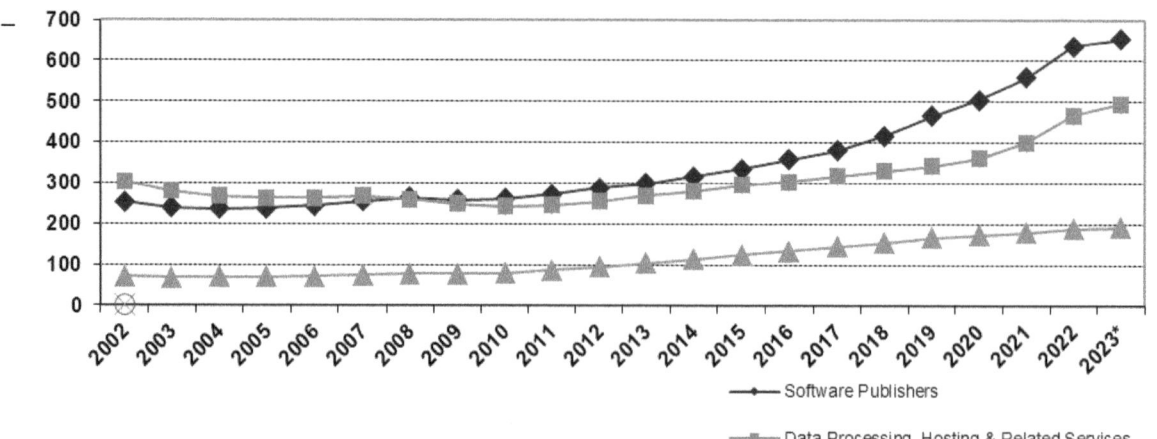

* Preliminary estimate as of October 2023.
Source: U.S. Bureau of Labor Statistics
Plunkett Research, ® Ltd.
www.plunkettresearch.com

Estimated Quarterly U.S. Retail and Ecommerce Sales:
1st Quarter 2012-3rd Quarter 2023

(In Millions of US$; Not Seasonally Adjusted, Holiday & Trading-Day Differences;
Does Not Include Food Services)

Quarter	Retail Sales in US$ Mil.		E-commerce as a % of Total Retail Sales	% Change Over Same Quarter Previous Year	
	Retail	E-commerce*		Retail	E-commerce
2012 Q1	1,015,512	51,722	5.1	7.6	16.9
2012 Q2	1,078,406	52,542	4.9	4.2	15.7
2012 Q3	1,067,088	53,832	5.0	3.9	16.6
2012 Q4	1,141,223	73,827	6.5	4.0	14.6
2013 Q1	1,040,435	58,355	5.6	2.5	12.8
2013 Q2	1,121,958	60,181	5.4	4.0	14.5
2013 Q3	1,117,600	61,344	5.5	4.7	14.0
2013 Q4	1,178,457	83,766	7.1	3.3	13.5
2014 Q1	1,060,492	66,148	6.2	1.9	13.4
2014 Q2	1,177,252	69,715	5.9	4.9	15.8
2014 Q3	1,170,225	71,331	6.1	4.7	16.3
2014 Q4	1,231,471	95,830	7.8	4.5	14.4
2015 Q1	1,084,374	75,918	7.0	2.3	14.8
2015 Q2	1,194,480	79,916	6.7	1.5	14.6
2015 Q3	1,193,142	81,769	6.9	2.0	14.6
2015 Q4	1,253,997	109,362	8.7	1.8	14.1
2016 Q1	1,120,887	86,811	7.7	3.4	14.3
2016 Q2	1,218,921	91,969	7.5	2.0	15.1
2016 Q3	1,217,376	93,830	7.7	2.0	14.8
2016 Q4	1,294,590	124,697	9.6	3.2	14.0
2017 Q1	1,156,810	99,805	8.6	3.2	15.0
2017 Q2	1,266,215	107,094	8.5	3.9	16.4
2017 Q3	1,262,868	108,905	8.6	3.7	16.1
2017 Q4	1,361,001	145,230	10.7	5.1	16.5
2018 Q1	1,219,133	115,602	9.5	5.4	15.8
2018 Q2	1,332,848	122,934	9.2	5.3	14.8
2018 Q3	1,323,360	124,214	9.4	4.8	14.1
2018 Q4	1,407,934	160,894	11.4	3.4	10.8
2019 Q1	1,241,540	129,015	10.4	1.8	11.6
2019 Q2	1,367,413	134,714	10.1	3.3	13.6
2019 Q3	1,365,135	140,538	10.3	3.8	16.8
2019 Q4	1,446,906	178,865	12.4	3.7	15.3
2020 Q1	1,264,772	141,521	11.2	2.7	13.8
2020 Q2	1,320,701	193,624	14.7	-3.4	43.7
2020 Q3	1,460,101	191,573	13.1	7.0	36.3
2020 Q4	1,548,016	235,957	15.2	7.0	31.9
2021 Q1	1,472,314	196,808	13.4	16.4	39.1
2021 Q2	1,691,751	211,437	12.5	28.1	9.2
2021 Q3	1,641,507	227,234	13.8	12.9	9.4
2021 Q4	1,770,273	281,576	15.9	14.6	9.7
2022 Q1	1,621,623	231,320	14.3	10.5	6.7
2022 Q2	1,818,833	252,087	13.9	7.9	7.3
2022 Q3	1,791,015	251,713	14.1	9.1	10.8
2022 Q4	1,857,200	303,120	16.3	3.7	20.2
2023 Q1	1,680,614	252,773	15.0	-9.5	-16.6
2023 Q2	1,831,959	269,287	14.7	9.0	6.5
2023 Q3ᴾ	1,827,617	271,653	14.9	-0.2	0.9

ᴾ Preliminary Estimate.

* E-commerce sales are sales of goods and services over the Internet, an extranet, Electronic Data Interchange (EDI) or other online system. Payment may or may not be made online.

Source: U.S. Census Bureau
Plunkett Research, ® Ltd.
www.plunkettresearch.com

Chapter 3

IMPORTANT E-COMMERCE & INTERNET BUSINESS CONTACTS

Addresses, Telephone Numbers and Internet Sites

Contents:

1) Advertising Resources

AdAsia
160 Robinson Rd., Ste. #13-01 SBF Center

Singapore, 068914 Singapore
Phone: 65-6386-7368
Fax: 65-6386-8036
E-mail Address: info@adasia.com.sg
Web Address: www.adasiaholdings.com
AdAsia is an online magazine for the advertising,
marketing and media community in Singapore and
the Asia-Pacific region. The website includes news
articles, events, jobs and general industry links and
information.

Interactive Advertising Bureau (IAB)
116 E. 27th St., Fl. 6
New York, NY 10016 USA
Phone: 212-380-4700
E-mail Address: iab@kcsa.com
Web Address: www.iab.net
The Interactive Advertising Bureau (IAB) is
dedicated to helping online, email, wireless and
interactive advertisers increase their revenues. The
organization publishes numerous research reports and
articles regarding the Internet advertising industry.

Practical Ecommerce
125 S. Park St., Ste.430
Traverse City, MI 49684 USA
Phone: 231-946-0606
E-mail Address: contact@practicalecommerce.com
Web Address: www.practicalecommerce.com
Practical Ecommerce is an independent publishing
company, unaffiliated with any e-commerce platform
or provider. Its mission is to help online merchants
improve their businesses by providing expert guides,
articles, webinars, and podcasts.

2)   Advertising/Marketing Associations

4A's (American Association of Advertising Agencies)
1065 Ave. of the Americas, Fl. 16
New York, NY 10018 USA
Phone: 212-682-2500
Web Address: www.aaaa.org
The 4A's (American Association of Advertising
Agencies) is the national trade association
representing the advertising agency industry in the
U.S.

Advertising Research Foundation (ARF)
432 Park Ave. S., Fl. 4
New York, NY 10016-8013 USA
Phone: 212-751-5656
Fax: 212-689-1859

E-mail Address: Membership@thearf.org
Web Address: www.thearf.org
The Advertising Research Foundation (ARF), a
nonprofit corporate-membership association, is a
leading professional organization in the fields of
advertising, marketing and media research.

American Advertising Federation, Inc. (AAF)
1101 K St. NW, Ste. 420
Washington, DC 20005 USA
Phone: 202-898-0089
E-mail Address: addyinfo@aaf.org
Web Address: www.aaf.org
The American Advertising Federation, Inc. (AAF)
protects and promotes the well-being of advertising
through a nationally coordinated network of
advertisers, agencies, media companies, local
advertising clubs and college chapters.

American Institute of Graphic Arts (AIGA)
222 Broadway
New York, NY 10038 USA
Phone: 212-807-1990
Web Address: www.aiga.org
The American Institute of Graphic Arts (AIGA)
strives to further excellence in communication
design, both as a strategic tool for business and as a
cultural force.

American Marketing Association (AMA)
130 E. Randolph St., Fl. 22
Chicago, IL 60601 USA
Phone: 312-542-9000
Fax: 312-542-9001
Toll Free: 800-262-1150
Web Address: www.ama.org
The American Marketing Association (AMA) is a
massive association for marketing professionals in
both business and education and serves all levels of
marketing practitioners, educators and students,
across all industries.

Association of National Advertisers
155 E 44th St.
New York, NY 10017 USA
Phone: 212-697-5950
Fax: 212-687-7310
Web Address: www.ana.net
The Association of National Advertisers', which
absorbed the Data & Marketing Association, mission
is to drive growth for marketing professionals, for
brands and businesses, and for the industry.

eMarketing Association (eMA)
40 Blue Ridge Dr.
Charlestown, RI 02813 USA
Fax: 408-884-2461
Toll Free: 800-496-2950
E-mail Address: ema@emarketingassociation.com
Web Address: www.emarketingassociation.com
eMarketing Association (eMA) is the largest
international association of electronic marketing
professionals, with members in over 40 countries
worldwide. The organization provides a forum to
exchange knowledge and ideas and to make
professional contacts.

International Advertising Association (IAA)
511 Ave. of Americas, Ste. 4017
New York, NY 10011 USA
Phone: 646-849-9908
E-mail Address: iaa@iaaglobal.org
Web Address: www.iaaglobal.org
The International Advertising Association (IAA) is a
strategic partnership that champions the common
interests of disciplines across the full spectrum of the
marketing communications industry.

Mobile Marketing Association (MMA)
2020 Maltby Rd., PMB 123
Bothell, WA 98201 USA
Phone: 646-257-4515
E-mail Address: mma@mmaglobal.com
Web Address: www.mmaglobal.com
The Mobile Marketing Association (MMA) is a
global organization with offices in many cities,
including a New York headquarters, a Bothell,
Washington correspondence office, and chapters
throughout Europe, Asia-Pacific, the Middle East and
Latin America. MMA members include agencies,
advertisers, handheld device manufacturers, carriers
and operators, retailers, software providers and
service providers, as well as companies focused on
the potential of marketing via mobile devices.

**NEMOA (National Etailing & Mailing
Organization of America)**
396 Washington St., Ste. 387
Wellesley Hills, MA 02481 USA
Phone: 781-237-7483
E-mail Address: beth@nemoa.org
Web Address: www.nemoa.org
NEMOA offers direct marketing merchants of all
sizes, and the vendors that service them, an
affordable network to share knowledge, learn about

industry trends and connect with peers and experts in
a non-selling environment.

One Club for Creativity (The)
450 W 31st St., Fl. 6
New York, NY 10001 USA
Phone: 212-979-1900
Fax: 212-643-4266
E-mail Address: info@oneclub.org
Web Address: www.oneclub.org
The One Club for Creativity is an international not-
for-profit organization of creative leaders in
advertising, graphic design, interactive media,
broadcast design, typography, packaging,
environmental design, photography, illustration and
related disciplines.

Shop! Association
Phone: 212-981-0845
E-mail Address: info@shopassociation.org
Web Address: www.shopassociation.org
Shop! Association (formerly the Shop Environments
Association which absorbed POPAI) provides
research, education, conferences and networking to
member companies and affiliates globally.

3)   Apps Industry Associations

ACT | The App Association
1401 K St. NW, Ste. 501
Washington, DC 20005 USA
Phone: 202-331-2130
Fax: 202-331-2139
E-mail Address: info@ACTonline.org
Web Address: www.actonline.org
ACT | The App Association gives a voice to small
technology companies. Its mission is to help
members promote an environment that inspires and
rewards innovation while providing resources to help
them raise capital, create jobs, and continue creating
incredible technology.

4)   Artificial Intelligence Associations

OpenAI
3180 18th St.
San Francisco, CA 94110 USA
E-mail Address: info@openai.com
Web Address: www.openai.com
Near the end of 2015, a group of well-known Silicon
Valley investors, including Elon Musk and Peter
Thiel, announced a long-term commitment to raise

funds of as much a $1 billion for a new organization to be known as OpenAI, www.openai.com. OpenAI is a nonprofit research organization focused on long-term, fundamental AI projects. In 2023, the organization created a for-profit partnership to commercialize its ChatGPT tool. Microsoft provided multi-billion funding for and owns an interest in this for-profit unit.

5)   Audience & Circulation Research

Alliance for Audited Media (AAM)
48 W. Seegers Rd.
Arlington Heights, IL 60005-3913 USA
Phone: 224-366-6939
Fax: 224-366-6949
Toll Free: 800-285-2220
Web Address: www.auditedmedia.com
The Alliance for Audited Media (AAM), formerly the Audit Bureau of Circulations, is the leading magazine circulation auditing organization for newspaper and magazine publishers in the U.S. and Canada, as well as advertising agencies and advertisers. It aims to conduct audits that set the industry standard for integrity, objectivity and accuracy.

Media Rating Council (MRC)
420 Lexington Ave., Ste. 343
New York, NY 10170 USA
Phone: 212-972-0300
Fax: 212-972-2786
E-mail Address: staff@mediaratingcouncil.org
Web Address: www.mediaratingcouncil.org
The Media Rating Council (MRC) is a nonprofit regulatory agency that promotes valid, accurate audience measurement services for the media industry.

6)   Broadcasting, Cable, Radio & TV Associations

National Cable and Telecommunications Association (NCTA)
25 Massachusetts Ave. NW, Ste. 100
Washington, DC 20001-1413 USA
Phone: 202-222-2300
Fax: 202-222-2514
E-mail Address: info@ncta.com
Web Address: www.ncta.com
The National Cable and Telecommunications Association (NCTA) is the principal trade association of the cable television industry in the United States. It represents cable operators as well as over 200 cable program networks that produce TV shows.

7)   Canadian Government Agencies- General

Canadian Intellectual Property Office (CIPO)
Place du Portage, 50 Victoria St., Rm. C-229
Gatineau, QC K1A 0C9 Canada
Phone: 819-934-0544
Fax: 819-953-2476
Toll Free: 866-997-1936
Web Address: www.cipo.ic.gc.ca
The Canadian Intellectual Property Office (CIPO) is the agency responsible for the administration and processing of intellectual property in Canada, including patents, trademarks, copyrights, industrial designs and integrated circuit topographies.

8)   Careers-Computers/Technology

ComputerJobs.com, Inc.
675 Alpha Dr., Ste. E
Highland Heights, OH 44143 USA
Toll Free: 800-850-0045
Web Address: www.computerjobs.com
ComputerJobs.com, Inc. is an employment web site that offers users links to computer-related job opportunities organized by skill and market.

Dice.com
6465 S. Greenwood Plaza Blvd., Ste. 400
Centennial, CO 80111 USA
Phone: 515-280-1144
Fax: 515-280-1452
Toll Free: 888-321-3423
E-mail Address: techsupport@dice.com
Web Address: www.dice.com
Dice.com provides free employment services for IT jobs. The site includes advanced job searches by geographic location and category, availability announcements and resume postings, as well as employer profiles, a recruiter's page and career links. It is maintained by Dice Holdings, Inc., a publicly traded company.

Institute for Electrical and Electronics Engineers (IEEE) Job Site
445 Hoes Ln.
Piscataway, NJ 08855-1331 USA
Phone: 732-981-0060
Toll Free: 800-678-4333

E-mail Address: candidatejobsite@ieee.org
Web Address: careers.ieee.org
The Institute for Electrical and Electronics Engineers (IEEE) Job Site provides a host of employment services for technical professionals, employers and recruiters. The site offers job listings by geographic area, a resume bank and links to employment services.

Pencom Systems, Inc.
152 Remsen St.
Brooklyn, NY 11201 USA
Phone: 718-923-1111
Fax: 718-923-6065
E-mail Address: tom@pencom.com
Web Address: www.pencom.com
Pencom Systems, Inc., an open system recruiting company, hosts a career web site geared toward high-technology and scientific professionals, featuring an interactive salary survey, career advisor, job listings and technology resources. Its focus is the financial services industry within the New York City area.

9) Careers-First Time Jobs/New Grads

CollegeGrad.com, Inc.
950 Tower Ln., Fl. 6
Foster City, CA 94404 USA
E-mail Address: info@quinstreet.com
Web Address: www.collegegrad.com
CollegeGrad.com, Inc. offers in-depth resources for college students and recent grads seeking entry-level jobs.

National Association of Colleges and Employers (NACE)
62 Highland Ave.
Bethlehem, PA 18017-9085 USA
Phone: 610-868-1421
E-mail Address: customerservice@naceweb.org
Web Address: www.naceweb.org
The National Association of Colleges and Employers (NACE) is a premier U.S. organization representing college placement offices and corporate recruiters who focus on hiring new grads.

10) Careers-General Job Listings

CareerBuilder, Inc.
200 N La Salle Dr., Ste. 1100
Chicago, IL 60601 USA
Phone: 773-527-3600
Fax: 773-353-2452
Toll Free: 800-891-8880
Web Address: www.careerbuilder.com
CareerBuilder, Inc. focuses on the needs of companies and also provides a database of job openings. The site has over 1 million jobs posted by 300,000 employers and receives an average of 23 million unique visitors monthly. The company also operates online career centers for 140 newspapers and 9,000 online partners. Resumes are sent directly to the company, and applicants can set up a special e-mail account for job-seeking purposes. CareerBuilder is primarily a joint venture between three newspaper giants: The McClatchy Company, Gannett Co., Inc. and Tribune Company.

CareerOneStop
Toll Free: 877-872-5627
E-mail Address: info@careeronestop.org
Web Address: www.careeronestop.org
CareerOneStop is operated by the employment commissions of various state agencies. It contains job listings in both the private and government sectors, as well as a wide variety of useful career resources and workforce information. CareerOneStop is sponsored by the U.S. Department of Labor.

LaborMarketInfo (LMI)
Employment Development Dept.
P.O. Box 826880, MIC 57
Sacramento, CA 94280-0001 USA
Phone: 916-262-2162
Fax: 916-262-2352
Web Address: www.labormarketinfo.edd.ca.gov
LaborMarketInfo (LMI) provides job seekers and employers a wide range of resources, namely the ability to find, access and use labor market information and services. It provides statistics for employment demographics on both a local and regional level, as well as career searching tools for California residents. The web site is sponsored by California's Employment Development Office.

Recruiters Online Network
E-mail Address: rossi.tony@comcast.net
Web Address: www.recruitersonline.com
The Recruiters Online Network provides job postings from thousands of recruiters, Careers Online Magazine, a resume database, as well as other career resources.

USAJOBS
USAJOBS Program Office
1900 E St. NW, Ste. 6500
Washington, DC 20415-0001 USA
Phone: 818-934-6600
Web Address: www.usajobs.gov
USAJOBS, a program of the U.S. Office of Personnel
Management, is the official job site for the U.S.
Federal Government. It provides a comprehensive list
of U.S. government jobs, allowing users to search for
employment by location; agency; type of work; or by
senior executive positions. It also has special
employment sections for individuals with disabilities,
veterans and recent college graduates; an information
center, offering resume and interview tips and other
information; and allows users to create a profile and
post a resume.

11) Careers-Job Reference Tools

Vault.com, Inc.
132 W. 31st St., Fl. 16
New York, NY 10001 USA
Fax: 212-366-6117
Toll Free: 800-535-2074
E-mail Address: customerservice@vault.com
Web Address: www.vault.com
Vault.com, Inc. is a comprehensive career web site
for employers and employees, with job postings and
valuable information on a wide variety of industries.
Its features and content are largely geared toward
MBA degree holders.

12) Computer & Electronics Industry Associations

**Asian-Oceanian Computing Industry
Organization (ASOCIO)**
No. 2, Jalan PJU 8/8A,
c/o PIKOM, Block E1, Empire Damansara E-01-G,
Petaling Jaya, Selangor 47820 Malaysia
Phone: 603-7622-0079
Fax: 603-7622-4879
E-mail Address: secretariat@asocio.org
Web Address: www.asocio.org
The Asian-Oceanian Computing Industry
Organization's (ASOCIO) objective is to promote the
development of the computing industry in the region.

**China Electronics Chamber of Commerce
(CECC)**
No. 15 Bldg., Cuiwei Zhongli

Haidian District
Beijing, 100036 China
Phone: 86-10-6825-6762
Fax: 86-10-6825-6764
E-mail Address: info@cecc.org.cn
Web Address: www.cecc.org.cn
China Electronics Chamber of Commerce (CECC),
which is led by the Ministry of Information Industry,
is the national professional organization for
telecommunications and mobile electronics. The
group circulates industry information and mediates
between its members and the government.

**Communications and Information Network
Association of Japan (CIAJ)**
21-7 Nihonbashi Kabutocho, Chuo-ku
6th Fl., HF Nihonbashi Kabutocho Bldg.
Tokyo, 103-0026 Japan
Phone: 81-3-5962-3455
Web Address: www.ciaj.or.jp/en/
Communications and Information Network
Association of Japan (CIAJ) works to help the
development of the communication and information
network industry in Japan through the promotion of
info-communication technologies.

**Computer & Communications Industry
Association (CCIA)**
25 Massachusetts Ave., Ste. 300C
Washington, DC 20001 USA
Phone: 202-783-0070
Fax: 202-783-0534
Web Address: www.ccianet.org
The Computer & Communications Industry
Association (CCIA) is a non-profit membership
organization for companies and senior executives
representing the computer, Internet, information
technology (IT) and telecommunications industries.

**Computer Technology Industry Association
(CompTIA)**
3500 Lacey Rd., Ste. 100
Downers Grove, IL 60515 USA
Phone: 630-678-8300
Fax: 630-678-8384
Toll Free: 866-835-8020
Web Address: www.comptia.org
The Computer Technology Industry Association
(CompTIA) is the leading association representing
the international technology community. Its goal is to
provide a unified voice, global advocacy and
leadership, and to advance industry growth through

standards, professional competence, education and business solutions.

Electronic Industries Association of India (ELCINA)
422 Okhla Industrial Estate
ELCINA House
New Delhi, Delhi 110020 India
Phone: 91-11-2692-4597
Fax: 91-11-2692-3440
E-mail Address: info@elcina.com
Web Address: www.elcina.com
The Electronic Industries Association of India (ELCINA) is an organization for the promotion of electronic hardware manufacturing through active representation and advice to the Indian government.

Electronics and Computer Software Export Promotion Council (ESC)
ESC House, 155 Okhla Industrial Estate
New Delhi, Delhi 110020 India
Phone: 91-11-47480000
Fax: 91-11-2685-3412
E-mail Address: info@escindia.com
Web Address: www.escindia.in
The Electronics and Computer Software Export Promotion Council (ESC) represents the info-communication technology industry through electronics and IT trade facilitation.

Information Technology Association of Canada (ITAC)
5090 Explorer Dr., Ste. 801
Mississauga, ON L4W 4T9 Canada
Phone: 905-602-8345
Fax: 905-602-8346
E-mail Address: dwhite@itac.ca
Web Address: www.itac.ca
The Information Technology Association of Canada (ITAC) represents the IT, software, computer and telecommunications industries in Canada.

Information Technology Industry Council (ITI)
700 K St. NW, Ste. 600
Washington, DC 20001 USA
Phone: 202-737-8888
Fax: 202-638-4922
E-mail Address: info@itic.org
Web Address: www.itic.org
The Information Technology Industry Council (ITI) is a premier group of the nation's leading high-tech companies and widely recognized as one of the tech industry's most effective lobbying organization in Washington, in various foreign capitals and the World Trade Organization (WTO).

Information Technology Management Association (ITMA)
Robinson Rd.
P.O. Box 3297
Singapore, 905297 Singapore
Phone: 65-8171-4456
Fax: 65-6410-8008
E-mail Address: secretariat@itma.org.sg
Web Address: www.itma.org.sg
Information Technology Management Association (ITMA) represents professionals working in the field of IT management in Singapore.

Korea Association of Information and Telecommunications (KAIT)
NO. 1678-2, 2nd Fl. Dong-Ah Villat 2 Town
Seocho-dong, Seocho-gu
Seoul, 137-070 Korea
Phone: 82-2-580-0582
E-mail Address: webmaster@kait.or.kr
Web Address: www.kait.or.kr/eng
The Korea Association of Information and Telecommunications (KAIT) was created to develop and promote the InfoTech, computer, consumer electronics, wireless, software and telecommunications sectors in Korea.

Manufacturers' Association for Information Technology (MAIT)
4/2, Siri Institutional Area, August Kranti Marg
Fl. 4, PHD House, Ramakrishna Dalmia Wing
New Delhi, Delhi 110-016 India
Phone: 91-11-2685-5487
Fax: 91-11-2685-1321
E-mail Address: contact@mait.com
Web Address: www.mait.com
The Manufacturers' Association for Information Technology (MAIT) is an organization that focuses on the promotion of the hardware, training, design/R&D and the associated services sectors of the Indian IT industry.

Singapore Computer Society
53/53A Neil Rd.
Singapore, 088891 Singapore
Phone: 65-6226-2567
Fax: 65-6226-2569
E-mail Address: scs.secretariat@scs.org.sg
Web Address: www.scs.org.sg

The Singapore Computer Society is a membership society for infocomm professionals in Singapore.

World Information Technology and Services Alliance (WITSA)
8300 Boone Blvd., Ste. 450
Vienna, VA 22182 USA
Phone: 571-265-5964
Fax: 703-893-1269
E-mail Address: admin@witsa.org
Web Address: www.witsa.org
The World Information Technology and Services Alliance (WITSA) is a consortium of over 70 information technology (IT) industry associations from economies around the world. WITSA members represent over 90% of the world IT market. Founded in 1978 and originally known as the World Computing Services Industry Association, WITSA is an advocate in international public policy issues affecting the creation of a robust global information infrastructure.

13) Computer & Electronics Industry Resources

Centre for Development of Advanced Computing (C-DAC)
Pune University Campus
Ganesh Khind
Pune, 411 007 India
Phone: 91-20-2570-4100
Fax: 91-20-2569-4004
Web Address: www.cdac.in
The Centre for Development of Advanced Computing (C-DAC) is a research and development institution created for the design, development and deployment information technology solutions for economic and human advancement. C-DAC is a branch of India's Department of Information Technology (DIT), Ministry of Communications & Information Technology (MCIT).

EETimes
Web Address: www.eetimes.com
The EETimes is an online magazine devoted to electronic engineers in the semiconductor, systems and software design fields.

Information Technology and Innovation Foundation (ITIF)
700 K St. NW, Ste. 600
Washington, DC 20001 USA
Phone: 202-449-1351

E-mail Address: mail@itif.org
Web Address: www.itif.org
Information Technology and Innovation Foundation (ITIF) is a non-partisan research and educational institute (a think tank) with a mission to formulate and promote public policies to advance technological innovation and productivity internationally, in Washington, and in the States. Recognizing the vital role of technology in ensuring American prosperity, ITIF focuses on innovation, productivity, and digital economy issues.

Ministry of Electronics and Information Technology (India)
Electronics Niketan
6 CGO Complex, Lodhi Rd.
New Delhi, 110003 India
Phone: 91-11-2430-1851
E-mail Address: webmaster@deity.gov.in
Web Address: www.meity.gov.in
Ministry of Communications & Information Technology (MIT) of the Government of India, is charged with promoting the information technology and communications industries.

14) Consulting Industry Associations

Institute of Certified E-Commerce Consultants (ICECC)
E-mail Address: info@icecc.com
Web Address: www.icecc.com
The Institute of Certified E-Commerce Consultants (ICECC) is a global association for the accreditation of ecommerce professionals.

TechServe Alliance
1420 King St., Ste. 610
Alexandria, VA 22314 USA
Phone: 703-838-2050
E-mail Address: staff@techservealliance.org
Web Address: www.techservealliance.org
The TechServe Alliance is an association that aims to advance excellence and ethics within the IT & engineering staffing and solutions industry. Its membership offers collaborative networking and knowledge sharing, updated operational and market trends and commitment to fair business practices and ethical codes of conduct.

15) Corporate Information Resources

Business Journals (The)
120 W. Morehead St., Ste. 400
Charlotte, NC 28202 USA
Toll Free: 866-853-3661
E-mail Address: gmurchison@bizjournals.com
Web Address: www.bizjournals.com
Bizjournals.com is the online media division of
American City Business Journals, the publisher of
dozens of leading city business journals nationwide.
It provides access to research into the latest news
regarding companies both small and large. The
organization maintains 42 websites and 64 print
publications and sponsors over 700 annual industry
events.

Business Wire
101 California St., Fl. 20
San Francisco, CA 94111 USA
Phone: 415-986-4422
Fax: 415-788-5335
Toll Free: 800-227-0845
E-mail Address: info@businesswire.com
Web Address: www.businesswire.com
Business Wire offers news releases, industry- and
company-specific news, top headlines, conference
calls, IPOs on the Internet, media services and access
to tradeshownews.com and BW Connect On-line
through its informative and continuously updated
web site.

Edgar Online, Inc.
35 W. Wacker Dr.
Chicago, IL 60601 USA
Phone: 301-287-0300
Fax: 301-287-0390
Toll Free: 800-823-5304
Web Address: www.edgar-online.com
Edgar Online, Inc. is an SEC gateway and search tool
for viewing corporate documents, such as annual
reports on Form 10-K, filed with the U.S. Securities
and Exchange Commission.

PR Newswire Association LLC
200 Vesey St., Fl. 19
New York, NY 10281 USA
Fax: 800-793-9313
Toll Free: 800-776-8090
E-mail Address: mediainquiries@cision.com
Web Address: www.prnewswire.com
PR Newswire Association LLC provides
comprehensive communications services for public

relations and investor relations professionals, ranging
from information distribution and market intelligence
to the creation of online multimedia content and
investor relations web sites. Users can also view
recent corporate press releases from companies
across the globe. The Association is owned by United
Business Media plc.

Silicon Investor
E-mail Address: si.admin@siliconinvestor.com
Web Address: www.siliconinvestor.com
Silicon Investor is focused on providing information
about technology companies. Its web site serves as a
financial discussion forum and offers quotes, profiles
and charts.

16) Ecommerce and Data Interchange Technology Associations

Center for Research in Electronic Commerce
McCombs School of Business
CBA 6.426, 2100 Speedway, Stop B6500
Austin, TX 78712-1170 USA
Phone: 512-471-7962
Fax: 512-471-3034
E-mail Address: abw@uts.cc.utexas.edu
Web Address: cism.mccombs.utexas.edu/
The Center for Research in Electronic Commerce at
the University of Texas is a leading research
institution in generating critical knowledge and
understanding in the fields of information systems
and management, electronic commerce and the
digital economy.

RosettaNet
7877 Washington Village Dr., Ste. 300
Dayton, OH 45459 USA
Phone: 937-435-3870
E-mail Address: info@gs1us.org
Web Address: www.resources.gs1us.org/rosettanet
RosettaNet, a subsidiary of GS1 US, is a nonprofit
organization whose mission is to develop e-business
process standards that serve as a frame of reference
for global trading networks. The organization's
standards provide a common language for companies
within the global supply chain.

17) Ecommerce Education & Training

eLab
Owen Graduate School of Management
Vanderbilt University, 401 21st Ave. S.

Nashville, TN 37203 USA
Phone: 615-322-7217
Fax: 615-343-7177
E-mail Address: elab@owen.vanderbilt.edu
Web Address: elab.vanderbilt.edu
eLab, located at the Sloan Center for Internet
Retailing at Vanderbilt University, was chartered to
perform cutting-edge ecommerce research, often in
cooperation with private enterprise.

18) Economic Data & Research

Centre for European Economic Research (The, ZEW)
L 7, 1
Mannheim, 68161 Germany
Phone: 49-621-1235-01
Fax: 49-621-1235-224
E-mail Address: empfang@zew.de
Web Address: www.zew.de/en
Zentrum fur Europaische Wirtschaftsforschung, The
Centre for European Economic Research (ZEW),
distinguishes itself in the analysis of internationally
comparative data in a European context and in the
creation of databases that serve as a basis for
scientific research. The institute maintains a special
library relevant to economic research and provides
external parties with selected data for the purpose of
scientific research. ZEW also offers public events and
seminars concentrating on banking, business and
other economic-political topics.

Economic and Social Research Council (ESRC)
Polaris House
North Star Ave.
Swindon, SN2 1UJ UK
Phone: 44-01793 413000
E-mail Address: esrcenquiries@esrc.ac.uk
Web Address: www.esrc.ac.uk
The Economic and Social Research Council (ESRC)
funds research and training in social and economic
issues. It is an independent organization, established
by Royal Charter. Current research areas include the
global economy; social diversity; environment and
energy; human behavior; and health and well-being.

Eurostat
5 Rue Alphonse Weicker
Joseph Bech Bldg.
Luxembourg, L-2721 Luxembourg
Phone: 00 800 6789 1011
E-mail Address:
https://ec.europa.eu/eurostat/web/main/home

Web Address: ec.europa.eu/eurostat
Eurostat is the European Union's service that
publishes a wide variety of comprehensive statistics
on European industries, population, trade, agriculture,
technology, environment and other vital business
topics.

Federal Statistical Office of Germany
Gustav-Stresemann-Ring 11
Wiesbaden, D-65189 Germany
Phone: 49-611-75-2405
Fax: 49-611-72-4000
Web Address: www.destatis.de
Federal Statistical Office of Germany publishes a
wide variety of nation and regional economic data of
interest to anyone who is studying Germany, one of
the world's leading economies. Data available
includes population, consumer prices, labor markets,
health care, industries and output.

India Brand Equity Foundation (IBEF)
Fl. 20, Jawahar Vyapar Bhawan
Tolstoy Marg
New Delhi, 110001 India
Phone: 91-11-43845500
Fax: 91-11-23701235
E-mail Address: info.brandindia@ibef.org
Web Address: www.ibef.org
India Brand Equity Foundation (IBEF) is a public-
private partnership between the Ministry of
Commerce and Industry, the Government of India
and the Confederation of Indian Industry. The
foundation's primary objective is to build positive
economic perceptions of India globally. It aims to
effectively present the India business perspective and
leverage business partnerships in a globalizing
marketplace.

National Bureau of Statistics (China)
57, Yuetan Nanjie, Sanlihe
Xicheng District
Beijing, 100826 China
Fax: 86-10-6878-2000
E-mail Address: info@gj.stats.cn
Web Address: www.stats.gov.cn/english
The National Bureau of Statistics (China) provides
statistics and economic data regarding China's
economy and society.

Organization for Economic Co-operation and Development (OECD)
2 rue Andre Pascal, Cedex 16
Paris, 75775 France

Phone: 33-1-45-24-82-00
Fax: 33-1-45-24-85-00
E-mail Address: webmaster@oecd.org
Web Address: www.oecd.org
The Organization for Economic Co-operation and
Development (OECD) publishes detailed economic,
government, population, social and trade statistics on
a country-by-country basis for over 30 nations
representing the world's largest economies. Sectors
covered range from industry, labor, technology and
patents, to health care, environment and
globalization.

**Statistics Bureau, Director-General for Policy
Planning (Japan)**
19-1 Wakamatsu-cho
Shinjuku-ku
Tokyo, 162-8668 Japan
Phone: 81-3-5273-2020
E-mail Address: toukeisoudan@soumu.go.jp
Web Address: www.stat.go.jp/english
The Statistics Bureau, Director-General for Policy
Planning (Japan) and Statistical Research and
Training Institute, a part of the Japanese Ministry of
Internal Affairs and Communications, plays the
central role of producing and disseminating basic
official statistics and coordinating statistical work
under the Statistics Act and other legislation.

Statistics Canada
150 Tunney's Pasture Driveway
Ottawa, ON K1A 0T6 Canada
Phone: 514-283-8300
Fax: 514-283-9350
Toll Free: 800-263-1136
E-mail Address: STATCAN.infostats-
infostats.STATCAN@canada.ca
Web Address: www.statcan.gc.ca
Statistics Canada provides a complete portal to
Canadian economic data and statistics. Its conducts
Canada's official census every five years, as well as
hundreds of surveys covering numerous aspects of
Canadian life.

19) Electronic Health Records/Continuity of Care Records

**American Health Information Management
Association (AHIMA)**
233 N. Michigan Ave., Fl. 21
Chicago, IL 60601-5809 USA
Phone: 312-233-1100
Fax: 312-233-1090

Toll Free: 800-335-5535
E-mail Address: info@ahima.org
Web Address: www.ahima.org
The American Health Information Management
Association (AHIMA) is a professional association
that consists of health information management
professionals who work throughout the health care
industry.

20) Electronic Publishing Associations

**International Digital Enterprise Alliance
(IDEAlliance)**
1800 Diagonal Rd., Ste. 320
Alexandria, VA 22314-2862 USA
Phone: 703-837-1070
Fax: 703-837-1072
Web Address: www.idealliance.org
IDEAlliance (International Digital Enterprise
Alliance) is a non-profit membership organization
supporting the digital media industry. It seeks to
advance core technologies and develop standards and
best practices that enhance the flow of information
across the digital media supply chain, from creation
and production to management and delivery, both in
print and digital formats.

International Digital Publishing Forum (IDPF)
113 Cherry St., Ste. 70-719
Seattle, WA 98104 USA
Phone: 206-451-7250
E-mail Address: membership@idpf.org
Web Address: www.idpf.org
The International Digital Publishing Forum (IDPF) is
a trade and standards organization dedicated to the
development and promotion of electronic publishing,
including electronic newspapers, books and other
types of media. Members include software
developers, authors and publishers of many types.
The organization developed the ePub (electronic
publication) open standard for the publication of
eBooks.

21) Engineering, Research & Scientific Associations

**American Society for Engineering Education
(ASEE)**
1818 North St. NW, Ste. 600
Washington, DC 20036-2479 USA
Phone: 202-331-3500
Fax: 202-265-8504

E-mail Address: board@asee.org
Web Address: www.asee.org
The American Society for Engineering Education
(ASEE) is nonprofit organization dedicated to
promoting and improving engineering and
technology education.

IEEE Communications Society (ComSoc)

3 Park Ave., Fl. 17
New York, NY 10016 USA
Phone: 212-705-8900
Fax: 212-705-8999
Web Address: www.comsoc.org
The IEEE Communications Society (ComSoc) is
composed of industry professionals with a common
interest in advancing communications technologies.

Institute of Electrical and Electronics Engineers (IEEE)

3 Park Ave., Fl. 17
New York, NY 10016-5997 USA
Phone: 212-419-7900
Fax: 212-752-4929
Toll Free: 800-678-4333
E-mail Address: society-info@ieee.org
Web Address: www.ieee.org
The Institute of Electrical and Electronics Engineers
(IEEE) is a nonprofit, technical professional
association of more than 430,000 individual members
in approximately 160 countries. The IEEE sets global
technical standards and acts as an authority in
technical areas ranging from computer engineering,
biomedical technology and telecommunications to
electric power, aerospace and consumer electronics.

Optical Society of America (OSA)

2010 Massachusetts Ave. NW
Washington, DC 20036-1023 USA
Phone: 202-223-8130
Fax: 202-223-1096
E-mail Address: info@osa.org
Web Address: www.osa.org
The Optical Society of America (OSA) is an
interdisciplinary society offering synergy between all
components of the optics industry, from basic
research to commercial applications such as fiber-
optic networks. It has a membership group of over
16,000 individuals from over 100 countries.
Members include scientists, engineers, educators,
technicians and business leaders.

Society of Cable Telecommunications Engineers (SCTE)

140 Philips Rd.
Exton, PA 19341-1318 USA
Phone: 610-363-6888
Fax: 610-884-7237
Toll Free: 800-542-5040
E-mail Address: info@scte.org
Web Address: www.scte.org
The Society of Cable Telecommunications Engineers
(SCTE) is a nonprofit professional association
dedicated to advancing the careers and serving the
industry of telecommunications professionals by
providing technical training, certification and
information resources.

22) Entertainment & Amusement Associations-General

Airline Passenger Experience Association (APEX)

355 Lexington Ave., Fl. 15
New York, NY 10017-6603 USA
Phone: 212-297-2177
Fax: 212-370-9047
E-mail Address: info@apex.aero
Web Address: apex.aero
The Airline Passenger Experience Association
(APEX), formerly the World Airline Entertainment
Association (WAEA), is a worldwide network
representing airlines, airline suppliers and related
companies committed to excellence in inflight
entertainment (IFE), communications and services.

23) Entertainment and Video Statistics in Europe

European Audiovisual Observatory

76 Allee de la Robertsau
Strasbourg, 67000 France
Phone: 33-0-3-9021-6000
Fax: 33-0-3-9021-6019
Web Address: www.obs.coe.int
The European Audiovisual Observatory is part of the
Council of Europe in Strasbourg, France. It is a
public service organization. The Observatory was
created in 1992 in order to collect and distribute
information about the audiovisual industries in
Europe. The group publishes statistics and research
on film, broadcasting (including TV and radio),
video, satellite, cable and DVD markets. The
Observatory provides information on the various
audiovisual markets in Europe and their financing. It

also analyses and reports on the legal issues affecting the different sectors of the audiovisual industry.

24) Financial Technology Associations

Financial Technology Association (FTA)
E-mail Address: info@ftassociation.org
Web Address: www.ftassociation.com
The Financial Technology Association (FTA) represents industry leaders shaping the future of finance. We champion the power of technology-centered financial services and advocate for the modernization of financial regulation to support inclusion and responsible innovation.

25) Financial Technology Associations, FinTech

Electronic Transactions Association
1300 Connecticut Ave., Ste. 475
Washington, DC 20036 USA
Phone: 202-828-2635
Fax: 202-828-2639
Toll Free: 800-695-5509
E-mail Address: info@electran.org
Web Address: www.electran.org
The Electronic Transactions Association is the leading trade association for the payments industry, representing 550 companies worldwide involved in electronic transaction processing products and services. The purpose of ETA is to influence, monitor and shape the payments industry by providing leadership through education, advocacy and the exchange of information. ETA's membership spans the breadth of the payments industry to include independent sales organizations (ISOs), payments networks, financial institutions, transaction processors, mobile payments products and services, payments technologies, and software providers (ISV) and hardware suppliers.

26) Games Industry Associations

Entertainment Software Association (ESA)
601 Massachusetts Ave. NW, Ste. 300
Washington, DC 20001 USA
Phone: 202-223-2400
E-mail Address: esa@theesa.com
Web Address: www.theesa.com
The Entertainment Software Association (ESA) is a U.S. trade association for companies that publish video and computer games for consoles, personal computers and the Internet. The ESA owns the E3 Media & Business Summit, a major invitation-only annual trade show for the video game industry.

Game Manufacturers Association (GAMA)
258 E. Campus View Blvd.
Columbus, OH 43235 USA
Phone: 614-255-4500
Fax: 614-255-4499
E-mail Address: ed@gama.org
Web Address: www.gama.org
The Game Manufacturers Association (GAMA) is an international non-profit trade association serving the hobby games industry. It hosts two annual events, the GAMA Trade Show and Origins Game Fair, and publishes a quarterly information newsletter, GAMATimes.

Hong Kong Digital Entertainment Industry Support Centre
78 Tat Chee Ave.
HKPC Building
Kowloon, Hong Kong Hong Kong
Phone: 852-2788-5678
Fax: 852-2788-5900
E-mail Address: hkpcenq@hkpc.org
Web Address: www.hkpc.org/en/industry-support-services/support-centres/hong-kong-software-industry-information-centre
The Hong Kong Digital Entertainment Industry Support Centre comprises three major sectors in Hong Kong, namely entertainment software, computer animation and digital effects in the production of videos and films. The center supports the development of professionals in the field of animation, design and programming, as well as promotes traditional industries through business development, marketing and branding.

International Game Developers Association (IGDA)
1 Eglinton Ave. E., Ste. 705
Toronto, ON M4P 3A1 Canada
Phone: 856-423-2990
E-mail Address: info@igda.org
Web Address: www.igda.org
The International Game Developers Association (IGDA) represents members involved in the video game production industry. The firm aims to promote professional development within the gaming industry and advocates for issues that affect the game developer community, including anti-censorship issues.

27) Identity Theft Resources

Identity Theft Resource Center (ITRC)
2514 Jamacha Rd., Ste. 502-525
El Cajon, CA 92019-4492 USA
Toll Free: 888-400-5530
E-mail Address: itrc@idtheftcenter.org
Web Address: www.idtheftcenter.org
The Identity Theft Resource Center (ITRC) is a
nonprofit organization established to support victims
of identity theft in resolving their cases, and to
broaden public education and awareness in the
understanding of identity theft, data breaches, cyber
security, scams/fraud and privacy issues.

28) Industry Research/Market Research

ClickZ
119 W 24th St., Fl. 4
New York, NY 10011 USA
Phone: 44-208-0806-489
E-mail Address: info@clickz.com
Web Address: www.clickz.com
ClickZ, is an online publication that offers news,
information and ecommerce statistics.

Forrester Research
60 Acorn Park Dr.
Cambridge, MA 02140 USA
Phone: 617-613-5730
Toll Free: 866-367-7378
E-mail Address: press@forrester.com
Web Address: www.forrester.com
Forrester Research is a publicly traded company that
identifies and analyzes emerging trends in technology
and their impact on business. Among the firm's
specialties are the financial services, retail, health
care, entertainment, automotive and information
technology industries.

Gartner, Inc.
56 Top Gallant Rd.
Stamford, CT 06902 USA
Phone: 203-964-0096
E-mail Address: info@gartner.com
Web Address: www.gartner.com
Gartner, Inc. is a publicly traded IT company that
provides competitive intelligence and strategic
consulting and advisory services to numerous clients
worldwide.

MarketResearch.com
6116 Executive Blvd., Ste. 550
Rockville, MD 20852 USA
Phone: 240-747-3093
Fax: 240-747-3004
Toll Free: 800-298-5699
E-mail Address:
customerservice@marketresearch.com
Web Address: www.marketresearch.com
MarketResearch.com is a leading broker for
professional market research and industry analysis.
Users are able to search the company's database of
research publications including data on global
industries, companies, products and trends.

Plunkett Research, Ltd.
P.O. Drawer 541737
Houston, TX 77254-1737 USA
Phone: 713-932-0000
Fax: 713-932-7080
E-mail Address:
customersupport@plunkettresearch.com
Web Address: www.plunkettresearch.com
Plunkett Research, Ltd. is a leading provider of
market research, industry trends analysis and
business statistics. Since 1985, it has served clients
worldwide, including corporations, universities,
libraries, consultants and government agencies. At
the firm's web site, visitors can view product
information and pricing and access a large amount of
basic market information on industries such as
financial services, InfoTech, ecommerce, health care
and biotech.

29) Internet & Online Business Resources

E-Commerce Guide
950 Tower Ln., 6th Fl.
Foster City, CA 94404 USA
E-mail Address: info@quinstreet.com
Web Address: www.ecommerce-guide.com
E-Commerce Guide, a QuinStreet, Inc. company,
provides news, trends, products and solutions guides.

E-Commerce Times News Network (ECT)
16133 Ventura Blvd., Ste. 700
Encino, CA 91436 USA
Phone: 818-461-9700
Fax: 818-461-9710
Toll Free: 877-238-5500
E-mail Address: contact@ectnews.com
Web Address: www.ecommercetimes.com

The E-Commerce Times News Network (ECT) provides news and information about ecommerce.

InternetNews.com
3343 Perimeter Hill Dr., Ste. 100
Nashville, TN 37211 USA
Phone: 877-822-9526
E-mail Address: info@technologyadvice.com
Web Address: www.internetnews.com
InternetNews.com offers real-time business news specifically designed for Internet technology managers. News categories include hardware, software, mobility, content, networking and search.

30) Internet Industry Associations

Asia & Pacific Internet Association (APIA)
P.O. Box 1908
Milton, 4064 Australia
E-mail Address: apiasec@apia.org
Web Address: www.apia.org
Asia & Pacific Internet Association (APIA) is a nonprofit trade association whose aim is to promote the business interests of the Internet-related service industry in the Asia Pacific region. The site contains a list of organizations, standards, regional Internet registries and related Asia Pacific organizations.

China Internet Network Information Center
4, S. 4th St., Zhongguancun
Fl. 1, Bldg. 1, Software Park
Beijing, 100190 China
Phone: 86-10-58813000
Fax: 86-10-58812666
E-mail Address: service@cnnic.cn
Web Address: www.cnnic.cn
The China Internet Network Information Center compiles Internet information and databases regarding the Internet community and facilitates the development and application of Internet resources and relevant technologies in China.

Cooperative Association for Internet Data Analysis (CAIDA)
9500 Gilman Dr.
Mail Stop 0505
La Jolla, CA 92093-0505 USA
Phone: 858-534-5000
E-mail Address: info@caida.org
Web Address: www.caida.org
The Cooperative Association for Internet Data Analysis (CAIDA), representing organizations from the government, commercial and research sectors, works to promote an atmosphere of greater cohesion in the engineering and maintenance of the Internet. CAIDA is located at the San Diego Supercomputer Center (SDSC) on the campus of the University of California, San Diego (UCSD).

Federation of Internet Service Providers of the Americas (FISPA)
c/o Jim Hollis
8200 Raintree Ln., Ste. 100
Charlotte, NC 28277 USA
Phone: 704-844-2540
Fax: 704-844-2728
Toll Free: 813-574-2556
E-mail Address: executive.director@fipsa.org
Web Address: www.fispa.org
The Federation of Internet Service Providers of the Americas (FISPA) encourages discussion, education and collective buying power for organizations involved in providing Internet access, web hosting, web design and other Internet products and services.

International Academy of Digital Arts and Sciences (IADAS)
22 W. 21st St., Fl. 7
New York, NY 10010 USA
Phone: 212-675-4890
E-mail Address: dmdavies@iadas.net
Web Address: www.iadas.net
The International Academy of Digital Arts and Sciences (IADAS) is dedicated to the progress of new media worldwide. It runs The Webby Awards, honoring web sites for technological and creative achievements, as well as The Lovie Awards, honoring individuals involved in managing, designing, marketing online web sites, advertising, mobile apps and social content for European market.

Internet and Mobile Association of India (IAMAI)
406 Ready Money Terr.
167 Dr. Annie Besant Rd.
Mumbai, 400 018 India
E-mail Address: k.ayesha@iamai.in
Web Address: www.iamai.in
The Internet & Mobile Association of India (IAMAI) is an industry organization representing the interests of India's online and mobile value-added services industry.

Internet Association
Phone: 202-869-8680
E-mail Address: info@internetassociation.org
Web Address: https://internetassociation.org

The Internet Association is a trade association that exclusively represents leading global internet companies on matters of public policy. It offers posts, reports and resources relating to election advertising, patents, net neutrality, trade, privacy, data security, sharing economy and global internet governance.

Internet Law & Policy Forum (ILPF)

2440 Western Ave., Ste. 709
Seattle, WA 98121 USA
Phone: 206-727-0700
Fax: 206-374-2263
E-mail Address: admin@ilpf.org
Web Address: www.ilpf.org
The Internet Law & Policy Forum (ILPF) is dedicated to the global development of the Internet through legal and public policy initiatives. It is an international nonprofit organization whose member companies develop and deploy the Internet in every aspect of business today.

Internet Society (ISOC)

11710 Plaza America Dr., Ste. 400
Reston, VA 20190 USA
Phone: 703-439-2120
Fax: 703-326-9881
E-mail Address: isoc@isoc.org
Web Address: www.isoc.org
The Internet Society (ISOC) is a nonprofit organization that provides leadership in public policy issues that influence the future of the Internet. The organization is the home of groups that maintain infrastructure standards for the Internet, such as the Internet Engineering Task Force (IETF) and the Internet Architecture Board (IAB).

Internet Systems Consortium, Inc. (ISC)

P.O. Box 360
Newmarket, NH 03857 USA
Phone: 650-423-1300
Fax: 650-423-1355
E-mail Address: info@isc.org
Web Address: www.isc.org
The Internet Systems Consortium, Inc. (ISC) is a nonprofit organization with extensive expertise in the development, management, maintenance and implementation of Internet technologies.

Organization for the Advancement of Structured Information Standards (OASIS)

35 Corporate Dr., Ste. 150
Burlington, MA 01803-4238 USA
Phone: 781-425-5073
Fax: 781-425-5072
E-mail Address: info@oasis-open.org
Web Address: www.oasis-open.org
The Organization for the Advancement of Structured Information Standards (OASIS) is a consortium which drives the development and adoption of e-business standards. It produces Web services standards, along with standards for security, e-business, and standardization efforts in the public sector and for application-specific markets. Founded in 1993, OASIS has more than 5,000 participants representing over 600 organizations and individual members in 100 countries.

U.S. Internet Service Provider Association (US ISPA)

700 12th St. NW, Ste. 700E
Washington, DC 20005 USA
Phone: 202-904-2351
E-mail Address: kdean@usispa.org
Web Address: www.usispa.org
U.S. Internet Service Provider Association (US ISPA) is a leading provider of technical, business, policy and regulatory support to ISPs (Internet service providers).

W3C (World Wide Web Consortium)

32 Vassar St., Bldg. 32-G515
Cambridge, MA 02139 USA
Phone: 617-253-2613
Fax: 617-258-5999
E-mail Address: susan@w3.org
Web Address: www.w3.org
The World Wide Web Consortium (W3C) develops technologies and standards to enhance the performance and utility of the World Wide Web. The W3C is hosted by three different organizations: the European Research Consortium for Informatics and Mathematics (ERICM) handles inquiries about the W3C in the EMEA region; Keio University handles W3C's Japanese and Korean correspondence; and the Computer Science & Artificial Intelligence Lab (CSAIL) at MIT handles all other countries, include Australia and the U.S.

31) Internet Industry Resources

American Registry for Internet Numbers (ARIN)

P.O. Box 232290
Centreville, VA 20120 USA
Phone: 703-227-9840
Fax: 703-263-0417
E-mail Address: info@arin.net

Web Address: www.arin.net
The American Registry for Internet Numbers (ARIN) is a nonprofit organization that administers and registers Internet protocol (IP) numbers. The organization also develops policies and offers educational outreach services.

Berkman Center for Internet & Society
23 Everett St., Fl. 2
Cambridge, MA 02138 USA
Phone: 617-495-7547
Fax: 617-495-7641
E-mail Address: cyber@law.harvard.edu
Web Address: cyber.law.harvard.edu
The Berkman Center for Internet & Society, housed at Harvard University's law school, focuses on the exploration of the development and inner workings of laws pertaining to the Internet. The center offers Internet courses, conferences, advising and advocacy.

CommerceNet
5050 El Camino Real, Ste. 215
Los Altos, CA 94022 USA
Phone: 650-289-4040
Fax: 650-289-4041
E-mail Address: info@commerce.net
Web Address: www.commerce.net
CommerceNet, an entrepreneurial research institute, is also an industry consortium for companies using, promoting and building electronic commerce solutions on the Internet.

Computer Emergency Response Team (CERT)
4500 5th Ave.
Pittsburgh, PA 15213-2612 USA
Phone: 412-268-7090
Fax: 412-268-6989
E-mail Address: cert@cert.org
Web Address: www.cert.org
The Computer Emergency Response Team (CERT) is part of the Software Engineering Institute (SEI), a federally funded research and development center at Carnegie Mellon University in Pittsburgh, Pennsylvania. CERT develops and promotes systems management practices to resist Internet security incidents.

Congressional Internet Caucus Advisory Committee (CICA)
1440 G St. NW
Washington, DC 20005 USA
Phone: 202-638-4370
E-mail Address: tlordan@netcaucus.org

Web Address: www.netcaucus.org
The Congressional Internet Caucus Advisory Committee (ICAC) works to educate the public, as well as a bipartisan group from the U.S. House and Senate about Internet-related policy issues.

InformationWeek
5 Howick Pl.
London, SW1P 1WG UK
Phone: 415-947-6000
Web Address: www.informationweek.com
InformationWeek is an online community comprising of a diverse range of IT professionals who offer insights and share their experiences with technologies, products and technology trends. It mainly consists of nine technology and vertical communities: strategic CIO, software, cloud, big data, mobile, government, security, healthcare and infrastructure.

Internet Assigned Numbers Authority (IANA)
12025 Waterfront Dr., Ste. 300
Los Angeles, CA 90094 USA
Phone: 424-254-5300
Fax: 424-254-5033
E-mail Address: iana@iana.org
Web Address: www.iana.org
The Internet Assigned Numbers Authority (IANA) serves as the central coordinator for the assignment of parameter values for Internet protocols. IANA is operated by the Internet Corporation for Assigned Names and Numbers (ICANN).

Internet Education Foundation
1440 G St. NW
Washington, DC 20005 USA
Phone: 202-638-4370
Fax: 202-637-0968
E-mail Address: tlordan@neted.org
Web Address: www.neted.org
The Internet Education Foundation is a nonprofit organization dedicated to educating the public and policymakers about the potential of the global Internet to promote democracy, communications and commerce.

InterNIC
Web Address: www.internic.net
InterNIC provides public information regarding Internet domain name registration services.

National Informatics Centre (NIC)
Lodhi Rd.

A-Block, CGO Complex
New Delhi, Delhi 110 003 India
Phone: 91-11-24305000
E-mail Address: wim@nic.in
Web Address: www.nic.in
The National Informatics Centre (NIC), under the
Department of Information Technology of the
Government of India, provides support to India's
governmental agencies through the applications of
information technology and technological activities.

Web3 Foundation
Zug, 6300 Switzerland
Web Address: web3.foundation
Web3 Foundation funds research and development
teams building the technology stack of the
decentralized web. It was established in Zug,
Switzerland by Ethereum co-founder Gavin Wood.
Polkadot is the Foundation's flagship project.

32) Internet Usage Statistics

ClickZ Network
119 W 24th St., Fl. 4
New York, NY 10011 USA
Phone: 646-736-1844
E-mail Address: kamaljeet.kalsi@contentive.com
Web Address: www.clickz.com
The ClickZ Network, part of Contentive Media
Group, is a resource for interactive marketing news,
information, commentary, advice and opinions. The
web site seeks to provide valuable tools for
marketers.

comScore, Inc.
11950 Democracy Dr., Ste. 600
Reston, VA 20190 USA
Phone: 703-438-2000
Fax: 703-438-2051
Toll Free: 866-276-6972
Web Address: www.comscore.com
comScore, Inc. provides excellent data on consumer
behavior and audiences, particularly in terms of how
consumers access and use online sites and digital data
and entertainment. They are global leaders in Internet
usage data.

eMarketer
11 Times Square
New York, NY 10036 USA
Toll Free: 800-405-0844
Web Address: www.emarketer.com

eMarketer is a comprehensive, objective and easy-to-
use resource for statistics and trends in online
marketing and emerging media. The firm offers news
articles, market projections and analytical
commentaries.

Nielsen
85 Broad St.
New York, NY 10004 USA
Toll Free: 800-864-1224
Web Address: www.nielsen.com
Nielsen offers detailed, real-time Internet, retail and
media audiences research and analysis.

Pew Internet & American Life Project
1615 L St. NW, Ste. 800
Washington, DC 20036 USA
Phone: 202-419-4300
Fax: 202-857-8562
E-mail Address: info@pewinternet.org
Web Address: www.pewinternet.org
The Pew Internet & American Life Project, an
initiative of the Pew Research Center, produces
reports that explore the impact of the Internet on
families, communities, work and home, daily life,
education, health care and civic and political life.

33) Logistics & Supply Chain Associations

Reverse Logistics Association (RLT)
2300 Lakeview Pkwy., Ste. 700
Alpharetta, GA 30009 USA
Phone: 801-331-8949
Toll Free: 866-801-6332
E-mail Address: info@RLA.org
Web Address: www.reverselogisticstrends.com
The Reverse Logistics Association (RLT) provides
news and information for third party service
providers involved in the management and movement
of goods that are returned for replacement, repair,
refurbishment or recycling.

34) MBA Resources

MBA Depot
Web Address: www.mbadepot.com
MBA Depot is an online community and information
portal for MBAs, potential MBA program applicants
and business professionals.

35) Outsourcing Industry Resources

CIO Outsourcing Center
492 Old Connecticut Path
P.O. Box 9208
Framingham, MA 01701-9208 USA
Phone: 508-872-0080
E-mail Address: rhein@cio.com
Web Address: www.cio.com/topic/3195/Outsourcing
CIO Outsourcing Center, a feature on CIO.com, provides data for chief information officers about technology outsourcing. CIO.com and the Outsourcing Center are products of CXO Media Inc., which is itself a division of International Data Group.

36) Payments Industry Associations

Payments Association, The
20 St Thomas St.
London, SE1 9RS UK
Phone: 44 20 7378 9890
Web Address: www.thepaymentsassociation.org
The Payments Association operates as an independent representative for the payments industry and its interests, and drive collaboration within the payments sector in order to bring about meaningful change and innovation.

37) Printers & Publishers Associations

MPA-The Association of Magazine Media
1211 Connecticut Ave. NW, Ste. 610
Washington, DC 20036 USA
Phone: 202-296-7277
E-mail Address: mpa@magazine.org
Web Address: www.magazine.org
MPA-The Association of Magazine Media (formerly the Magazine Publishers of America, Inc.) is the industry association for consumer magazines in all formats, including printed, mobile and online.

38) Privacy & Consumer Matters

Electronic Frontier Foundation (EFF)
815 Eddy St.
San Francisco, CA 94109 USA
Phone: 415-436-9333
Fax: 415-436-9993
E-mail Address: info@eff.org
Web Address: www.eff.org
The Electronic Frontier Foundation (EFF) is a nonprofit, non-partisan organization that strives to protect user privacy and free speech online, fight illegal surveillance, support freedom-enhancing technologies and advocate for users and innovators. It advances its mission through impact litigation, policy analysis, grassroots activism and technology development.

Electronic Privacy Information Center (EPIC)
1519 New Hampshire Ave. NW
Washington, DC 20036 USA
Phone: 202-483-1140
Fax: 202-483-1248
E-mail Address: info@epic.org
Web Address: www.epic.org
The Electronic Privacy Information Center (EPIC) is a public interest research center, established to focus public attention on emerging civil liberties issues and to protect privacy, the First Amendment and constitutional values.

Federal Trade Commission-Privacy and Security
600 Pennsylvania Ave. NW
Washington, DC 20580 USA
Phone: 202-326-2222
Web Address: business.ftc.gov/privacy-and-security
Federal Trade Commission-Privacy and Security is responsible for many aspects of business-to-consumer and business-to-business trade and regulation.

Get Safe Online
Cygnet House
Exchange Rd.
Lincoln, LN6 3JZ UK
Phone: 44-7507-309212
E-mail Address: info@getsafeonline.org
Web Address: www.getsafeonline.org
Get Safe Online is a joint initiative between the U.K. government, law enforcement, leading businesses and the public sector. Its aim is to provide computer users and small businesses with free, independent, user-friendly advice that will allow them to use the internet confidently, safely and securely. It provides videos and online advice about such subjects as identify theft, computer security and safe purchasing practices for products, services and travel.

National Fraud Information Center (NFIC)
1701 K St. NW, Ste. 1200
c/o National Consumers League
Washington, DC 20006 USA
Phone: 202-835-3323
Fax: 202-835-0747

Toll Free: 800-876-7060
E-mail Address: info@nclnet.org
Web Address: www.fraud.org
The National Fraud Information Center (NFIC) covers all types of fraud and provides information about reporting fraud, as well as posting fraud alerts.

Privacy International

62 Britton St.
London, EC1M 5UY UK
Phone: 44-20-3422-4321
E-mail Address: info@privacy.org
Web Address: www.privacyinternational.org
Privacy International is a government and business watchdog, alerting individuals to wiretapping and national security activities, medical privacy infringement, police information systems and the use of ID cards, video surveillance and data matching.

Privacy Times

P.O. Box 302
Cabin John, MD 20818 USA
Phone: 301-229-7002
Fax: 301-229-8011
E-mail Address: evan@privacytimes.com
Web Address: www.privacytimes.com
Privacy Times is a publication targeting attorneys and professionals wishing to follow legislation and developments in the information privacy arena, including the Freedom of Information Act, direct marketing, Caller ID and credit reports.

TRUSTe

111 Sutter St., Ste. 600
San Francisco, CA 94104 USA
Phone: 415-520-3490
Fax: 415-520-3420
Toll Free: 888-878-7830
E-mail Address: trustarc-info@trustarc.com
Web Address: trustarc.com/consumer-info/privacy-certification-standards/
TRUSTe formed an alliance with all major portal sites to launch the Privacy Partnership campaign, a consumer education program designed to raise awareness of Internet privacy issues. The organization works to meet the needs of business web sites while protecting user privacy.

39) Research & Development, Laboratories

Electronics and Telecommunications Research Institute (ETRI)

218 Gajeongno
Yuseong-gu
Daejeon, 34129 Korea
Phone: 82-42-860-6114
E-mail Address: k21human@etri.re.kr
Web Address: www.etri.re.kr
Established in 1976, the Electronics and Telecommunications Research Institute (ETRI) is a nonprofit government-funded research organization that promotes technological excellence. The research institute has successfully developed information technologies such as TDX-Exchange, High Density Semiconductor Microchips, Mini-Super Computer (TiCOM), and Digital Mobile Telecommunication System (CDMA). ETRI's focus is on information technologies, robotics, telecommunications, digital broadcasting and future technology strategies.

Institute for Telecommunication Sciences (ITS)

325 Broadway
Boulder, CO 80305-3337 USA
Phone: 303-497-3571
E-mail Address: info@its.bldrdoc.gov
Web Address: www.its.bldrdoc.gov
The Institute for Telecommunication Sciences (ITS) is the research and engineering branch of the National Telecommunications and Information Administration (NTIA), a division of the U.S. Department of Commerce (DOC). Its research activities are focused on advanced telecommunications and information infrastructure development.

40) Science & Technology Resources

Technology Review

1 Main St., Fl. 13
Cambridge, MA 02142 USA
Phone: 617-475-8000
Fax: 617-475-8000
Web Address: www.technologyreview.com
Technology Review, an MIT enterprise, publishes tech industry news, covers innovation and writes in-depth articles about research, development and cutting-edge technologies.

41) Software Industry Associations

Apache Software Foundation
401 Edgewater Pl., Ste. 600
Wakefield, MA 01880 USA
Fax: 919-573-9199
E-mail Address: apache@apache.org
Web Address: www.apache.org
Apache Software Foundation is one of the largest
open software successes. Apache is used by about
two-thirds of all web sites worldwide. Its software
manages the interaction between a web site and the
viewer's browser.

Business Software Alliance (BSA)
20 F St. NW, Ste. 800
Washington, DC 20001 USA
Phone: 202-872-5500
Fax: 202-872-5501
E-mail Address: info@bsa.org
Web Address: www.bsa.org
The Business Software Alliance (BSA) is a leading
global software industry association. BSA educates
consumers regarding software management,
copyright protection, cyber security, trade,
ecommerce and other Internet-related issues.

Colorado Technology Association
1245 Champa St., Ste. 200
Denver, CO 80204 USA
Phone: 303-592-4070
E-mail Address: info@coloradotechnology.org
Web Address: www.coloradotechnology.org/
The Colorado Technology Association, formerly the
Colorado Software & Internet Association, promotes
the technology industry in Colorado through
networking and organization.

European Software Institute (ESI)
Parque Tecnologico de Bizkaia
Edificio 202
Zamudio, Bizkaia E-48170 Spain
Phone: 34-946-430-850
Fax: 34-901-706-009
Web Address: www.esi.es
The European Software Institute (ESI) is a nonprofit
foundation launched as an initiative of the European
Commission, with the support of leading European
companies working in the information technology
field.

Information Systems Security Association (ISSA)
1964 Gallows Rd., Ste. 210

Vienna, VA 22182 USA
Phone: 703-982-8205
Fax: 703-495-2973
Toll Free: 866-349-5818
E-mail Address: mdelacruz@issa.org
Web Address: www.issa.org
The Information Systems Security Association
(ISSA) is an international nonprofit organization of
information security professionals. It offers
educational forums, publishes resources and
networking opportunities to its members.

Korea Software Industry Association (KOSA)
IT Venture Tower W., 12F
135 Jung-daero, Songpa-gu
Seoul, 05717 South Korea
Phone: 82-2-2188-6900
Fax: 82-2-2188-6901
E-mail Address: choicy@sw.or.kr
Web Address: www.sw.or.kr
The Korea Software Industry Association (KOSA) is
Korea's nonprofit trade organization representing
more than 1,200 member companies in the software
industry.

Linux Foundation (The)
1 Letterman Dr.
Building D, Ste. D4700
San Francisco, CA 94129 USA
Phone: 415-723-9709
E-mail Address: info@linuxfoundation.org
Web Address: www.linuxfoundation.org
The Linux Foundation, founded in 2007 by the
merger of Open Source Development Labs (OSDL)
and the Free Standards Group, is a nonprofit
organization that standardizes, protects and promotes
the work of Linux creator Linus Torvalds. It provides
necessary services and resources to make and keep
open source software competitive with closed
platforms. The foundation is supported by a global
consortium of global open source IT industry leaders,
with facilities in the U.S. and Japan.

New Mexico Technology Council (NMTC)
200 Broadway Blvd. NE
Albuquerque, NM 87102 USA
Phone: 505-847-6840
E-mail Address: info@nmtechcouncil.org
Web Address: www.nmtechcouncil.org
The New Mexico Technology Council (NMTC)
represents the interests of the software industry in
New Mexico. Its members include businesses, tech

professionals and organizations who work to promote technology industry in New Mexico.

Singapore Infocomm Technology Federation (SiTF)
79 Ayer Rajah Crescent, Ste. 02-03/04/05
Singapore, 139955 Singapore
Phone: 65-6325-9700
Fax: 65-6325-4993
E-mail Address: info@sitf.org.sg
Web Address: sitf.org.sg
Singapore Infocomm Technology Federation (SiTF) is an infocom industry association that has four chapters: Cloud Computing Chapter, Digital Media Wireless Chapter, Security and Governance Chapter and Singapore Enterprise Chapter.

Software & Information Industry Association (SIIA)
1090 Vermont Ave. NW, Fl. 6
Washington, DC 20005-4095 USA
Phone: 202-289-7442
Fax: 202-289-7097
Web Address: www.siia.net
The Software & Information Industry Association (SIIA) is a principal trade association for the software and digital content industry.

Software Association of Oregon (SAO)
123 NE Third Ave., Ste. 210
Portland, OR 97232 USA
Phone: 503-228-5401
Web Address: www.techoregon.org
The Technology Association of Oregon, formerly Software Association of Oregon (SAO) promotes the growth of technology industry by offering opportunities, such as networking, professional and business development programs, advocacy, industry promotions and talent development.

Washington Technology Industry Association
1721 8th Ave. N
Seattle, WA 98109 USA
Phone: 206-448-3033
E-mail Address: info@washingtontechnology.org
Web Address: www.washingtontechnology.org
The Washington Technology Industry Association promotes and helps coordinate the software industry in the state of Washington.

42) Software Industry Resources

Software Engineering Institute (SEI)-Carnegie Mellon
4500 5th Ave.
Pittsburgh, PA 15213-2612 USA
Phone: 412-268-5800
Fax: 412-268-5758
Toll Free: 888-201-4479
E-mail Address: info@sei.cmu.edu
Web Address: www.sei.cmu.edu
The Software Engineering Institute (SEI) is a federally funded research and development center at Carnegie Mellon University, sponsored by the U.S. Department of Defense through the Office of the Under Secretary of Defense for Acquisition, Technology, and Logistics [OUSD (AT&L)]. The SEI's core purpose is to help users make measured improvements in their software engineering capabilities.

43) Stocks & Financial Markets Data

SiliconValley.com
4 N. Second St., Ste. 700
San Jose, CA 95113 USA
Phone: 408-920-5000
Fax: 408-228-8060
E-mail Address: svfeedback@mercurynews.com
Web Address: www.siliconvalley.com
SiliconValley.com, run by San Jose Mercury News and owned by MediaNews Group, offers a summary of current financial news and information regarding the field of technology.

44) Technology Law Associations

International Technology Law Association (ITechLaw)
7918 Jones Branch Dr., Ste. 300
McLean, VA 22102 USA
Phone: 703-506-2895
Fax: 703-506-3266
E-mail Address: memberservices@itechlaw.org
Web Address: www.itechlaw.org
The International Technology Law Association (ITechLaw) offers information concerning Internet and converging technology law. It represents lawyers in the field of technology law.

45) Technology Transfer Associations

Licensing Executives Society (USA and Canada), Inc.
11130 Sunrise Valley Dr., Ste. 350
Reston, VA 20191 USA
Phone: 703-234-4058
Fax: 703-435-4390
E-mail Address: info@les.org
Web Address: www.lesusacanada.org
Licensing Executives Society (USA and Canada), Inc., established in 1965, is a professional association composed of about 3,000 members who work in fields related to the development, use, transfer, manufacture and marketing of intellectual property. Members include executives, lawyers, licensing consultants, engineers, academic researchers, scientists and government officials. The society is part of the larger Licensing Executives Society International, Inc. (same headquarters address), with a worldwide membership.

46) Telecommunications Industry Associations

Asia-Pacific Telecommunity (APT)
Chaengwattana Rd.
12/49 Soi 5
Bangkok, 10210 Thailand
Phone: 66-2-573-0044
Fax: 66-2-573-7479
E-mail Address: aptmail@apt.int
Web Address: www.aptsec.org
The Asia-Pacific Telecommunity (APT) is an organization of governments, telecom service providers, manufacturers of communication equipment, research & development organizations and other stakeholders active in the field of communication and information technology. APT serves as the focal organization for communication and information technology in the Asia-Pacific region.

DigitalEurope
Rue de la Science 14
Brussels, 1040 Belgium
Phone: 32-2-609-5310
Fax: 32-2-609-5339
E-mail Address: info@digitaleurope.org
Web Address: www.digitaleurope.org
DigitalEurope is dedicated to improving the business environment for the European information and communications technology and consumer electronics sector. Its members include 57 leading corporations and 37 national trade associations from across Europe.

European Telecommunications Standards Institute (ETSI)
ETSI Secretariat
650, route des Lucioles
Sophia-Antipolis Cedex, 06921 France
Phone: 33-4-92-94-42-00
Fax: 33-4-93-65-47-16
E-mail Address: info@etsi.org
Web Address: www.etsi.org
The European Telecommunications Standards Institute (ETSI) is a non-profit organization whose mission is to produce telecommunications standards to be implemented throughout Europe.

INCOMPAS
1100 G St. NW, Ste. 800
Washington, DC 20005 USA
Phone: 202-296-6650
E-mail Address: gnorris@comptel.org
Web Address: www.incompas.org
CompTel is a trade organization representing voice, data and video communications service providers and their supplier partners. Members are supported through education, networking, policy advocacy and trade shows.

International Federation for Information Processing (IFIP)
Hofstrasse 3
Laxenburg, A-2361 Austria
Phone: 43-2236-73616
Fax: 43-2236-73616-9
E-mail Address: ifip@ifip.org
Web Address: www.ifip.org
The International Federation for Information Processing (IFIP) is a multinational, apolitical organization in information & communications technologies and sciences recognized by the United Nations and other world bodies. It represents information technology societies from 56 countries or regions, with over 500,000 members in total.

International Telecommunications Union (ITU)
Place des Nations
Geneva 20, 1211 Switzerland
Phone: 41-22-730-5111
Fax: 41-22-733-7256
E-mail Address: itumail@itu.int

Web Address: www.itu.int
The International Telecommunications Union (ITU) is an international organization for the standardization of the radio and telecommunications industry. It is an agency of the United Nations (UN).

MEF

12130 Millennium Dr., Ste. 2-167
Los Angeles, CA 90094 USA
Phone: 310-642-2800
Web Address: www.mef.net
MEF is a global industry association of network, cloud, and technology providers working together to accelerate enterprise digital transformation through a better-together ecosystem.

Pacific Telecommunications Council (PTC)

914 Coolidge St.
Honolulu, HI 96826-3085 USA
Phone: 808-941-3789
Fax: 833-944-0749
E-mail Address: info@ptc.org
Web Address: www.ptc.org
The Pacific Telecommunications Council (PTC), through its member network, promotes the development and use of telecommunications and information and communications technologies to enhance the lives of people living in the Pacific hemisphere.

Telecommunications Industry Association (TIA)

1310 N. Courthouse Rd., Ste. 890
Arlington, VA 22201 USA
Phone: 703-907-7700
Fax: 703-907-7727
E-mail Address: smontgomery@tiaonline.org
Web Address: www.tiaonline.org
The Telecommunications Industry Association (TIA) is a leading trade association in the information, communications and entertainment technology industry. TIA focuses on market development, trade promotion, trade shows, domestic and international advocacy, standards development and enabling e-business.

TeleManagement Forum (TM Forum)

240 Headquarters Plz.
E. Twr., 10th Fl.
Morristown, NJ 07960-6628 USA
Phone: 973-944-5100
E-mail Address: info@tmforum.org
Web Address: www.tmforum.org

The TeleManagement Forum (TM Forum) is a nonprofit global organization that provides leadership, strategic guidance and practical solutions to improve the management and operation of information and communications services.

Voice On the Net (VON) Coalition, Inc.

1200 Seventh St. NW
Pillsbury Winthrop Shaw Pittman LLP
Washington, DC 20036-3006 USA
Phone: 202-663-8215
E-mail Address: glenn.richards@pillsburylaw.com
Web Address: www.von.org
Voice On the Net (VON) Coalition, Inc. is an advocational organization for the IP telephony industry. The VON Coalition supports the premise that the IP industry should remain free of governmental regulations. It also serves to educate consumers and the media on internet communications technologies.

47) Telecommunications Resources

Department of Telecommunication (Gov. of India)

20 Ashoka Rd.
Sanchar Bhawan
New Delhi, 110001 India
Phone: 91-11-2373-9191
Fax: 91-11-2372-3330
E-mail Address: secy-dot@nic.in
Web Address: www.dot.gov.in
The Government of India's Department of Telecommunication web site provides information, directories, guidelines, news and information related to the telecom, Internet, Wi-Fi and wireless communication industries. It is a branch of India's Ministry of Communications & Information Technology.

International Communications Project (The)

Unit 2, Marine Action
Birdhill Industrial Estate
Birdhill, Co Tipperary Ireland
Phone: 353-86-108-3932
Fax: 353-61-749-801
E-mail Address: robert.alcock@intercomms.net
Web Address: www.intercomms.net
The International Communications Project (InterComms) is an authoritative policy, strategy and reference publication for the international telecommunications industry.

48) Trade Associations-General

BUSINESSEUROPE
168 Ave. de Cortenbergh 168
Brussels, 1000 Belgium
Phone: 32-2-237-65-11
Fax: 32-2-231-14-45
E-mail Address: main@businesseurope.eu
Web Address: www.businesseurope.eu
BUSINESSEUROPE is a major European trade federation that operates in a manner similar to a chamber of commerce. Its members are the central national business federations of the 34 countries throughout Europe from which they come. Companies cannot become direct members of BUSINESSEUROPE, though there is a support group which offers the opportunity for firms to encourage BUSINESSEUROPE objectives in various ways.

United States Council for International Business (USCIB)
1212 Ave. of the Americas
New York, NY 10036 USA
Phone: 212-354-4480
Fax: 212-575-0327
E-mail Address: news@uscib.org
Web Address: www.uscib.org
The United States Council for International Business (USCIB) promotes an open system of world trade and investment through its global network. Standard USCIB members include corporations, law firms, consulting firms and industry associations. Limited membership options are available for chambers of commerce and sole legal practitioners.

VR/AR Association (VRARA)
Palo Alto, CA 94303 USA
Phone: 314-640-1404
E-mail Address: info@thevrara.com
Web Address: www.thevrara.com
The VR/AR Association (VRARA) is an international organization designed to foster collaboration between solution providers and end-users that accelerates growth, fosters research and education, helps develop industry best practices, connects member organizations and promotes the services of member companies.

49) Trade Associations-Global

World Trade Organization (WTO)
Centre William Rappard
Rue de Lausanne 154
Geneva 21, CH-1211 Switzerland
Phone: 41-22-739-51-11
Fax: 41-22-731-42-06
E-mail Address: enquiries@wto.og
Web Address: www.wto.org
The World Trade Organization (WTO) is a global organization dealing with the rules of trade between nations. To become a member, nations must agree to abide by certain guidelines. Membership increases a nation's ability to import and export efficiently.

50) U.S. Government Agencies

Bureau of Economic Analysis (BEA)
4600 Silver Hill Rd.
Washington, DC 20233 USA
Phone: 301-278-9004
E-mail Address: customerservice@bea.gov
Web Address: www.bea.gov
The Bureau of Economic Analysis (BEA), is an agency of the U.S. Department of Commerce, is the nation's economic accountant, preparing estimates that illuminate key national, international and regional aspects of the U.S. economy.

Bureau of Labor Statistics (BLS)
2 Massachusetts Ave. NE
Washington, DC 20212-0001 USA
Phone: 202-691-5200
Fax: 202-691-7890
Toll Free: 800-877-8339
E-mail Address: blsdata_staff@bls.gov
Web Address: stats.bls.gov
The Bureau of Labor Statistics (BLS) is the principal fact-finding agency for the Federal Government in the field of labor economics and statistics. It is an independent national statistical agency that collects, processes, analyzes and disseminates statistical data to the American public, U.S. Congress, other federal agencies, state and local governments, business and labor. The BLS also serves as a statistical resource to the Department of Labor.

Cybersecurity & Infrastructure Security Agency (CISA)
245 Murray Ln.
Washington, D.C. 20528-0380 USA
Phone: 888-282-0870
E-mail Address: central@cisa.gov
Web Address: www.cisa.gov
The Cybersecurity & Infrastructure Security Agency (CISA) is the U.S. government agency focused on

defending against cyber attacks and the development of new cybersecurity tools. The CISA also responds to attacks against the U.S. Government.

FCC-VoIP Division
445 12th St. SW
Washington, DC 20554 USA
Fax: 866-418-0232
Toll Free: 888-225-5322
E-mail Address: FOIA@fcc.gov
Web Address: www.fcc.gov/voip
The FCC-VoIP Division is dedicated to the promotion and regulation of the VoIP (Voice over Internet Protocol) industry. It operates as part of the Federal Communications Commission (FCC). VoIP allows users to call from their computer (or adapters) over the Internet to regular telephone numbers.

Federal Communications Commission (FCC)
445 12th St. SW
Washington, DC 20554 USA
Fax: 866-418-0232
Toll Free: 888-225-5322
E-mail Address: PRA@fcc.gov
Web Address: www.fcc.gov
The Federal Communications Commission (FCC) is an independent U.S. government agency established by the Communications Act of 1934 responsible for regulating interstate and international communications by radio, television, wire, satellite and cable.

Federal Communications Commission (FCC)-Wireless Telecommunications Bureau
445 12th St. SW
Washington, DC 20554 USA
Phone: 202-418-0600
Fax: 202-418-0787
Toll Free: 888-225-5322
E-mail Address: PRA@fcc.gov
Web Address: www.fcc.gov/wireless-telecommunications#block-menu-block-4
The Federal Communications Commission (FCC)-Wireless Telecommunications Bureau handles nearly all FCC domestic wireless telecommunications programs and policies, including cellular and smarftphones, pagers and two-way radios. The bureau also regulates the use of radio spectrum for businesses, aircraft/ship operators and individuals.

National Telecommunications and Information Administration (NTIA)
1401 Constitution Ave. NW
Herbert C. Hoover Bldg.
Washington, DC 20230 USA
Phone: 202-482-2000
Web Address: www.ntia.doc.gov
The National Telecommunications and Information Administration (NTIA), an agency of the U.S. Department of Commerce, is the Executive Branch's principal voice on domestic and international telecommunications and information technology issues.

U.S. Census Bureau
4600 Silver Hill Rd.
Washington, DC 20233-8800 USA
Phone: 301-763-4636
Toll Free: 800-923-8282
E-mail Address: pio@census.gov
Web Address: www.census.gov
The U.S. Census Bureau is the official collector of data about the people and economy of the U.S. Founded in 1790, it provides official social, demographic and economic information. In addition to the Population & Housing Census, which it conducts every 10 years, the U.S. Census Bureau conducts numerous other surveys annually.

U.S. Department of Commerce (DOC)
1401 Constitution Ave. NW
Washington, DC 20230 USA
Phone: 202-482-2000
E-mail Address: publicaffairs@doc.gov
Web Address: www.commerce.gov
The U.S. Department of Commerce (DOC) regulates trade and provides valuable economic analysis of the economy.

U.S. Department of Labor (DOL)
200 Constitution Ave. NW
Washington, DC 20210 USA
Phone: 202-693-4676
Toll Free: 866-487-2365
E-mail Address: m-DOLPublicAffairs@dol.gov
Web Address: www.dol.gov
The U.S. Department of Labor (DOL) is the government agency responsible for labor regulations. The Department of Labor's goal is to foster, promote, and develop the welfare of the wage earners, job seekers, and retirees of the United States; improve working conditions; advance opportunities for profitable employment; and assure work-related benefits and rights.

U.S. Patent and Trademark Office (PTO)
600 Dulany St.
Madison Bldg.
Alexandria, VA 22314 USA
Phone: 571-272-1000
Toll Free: 800-786-9199
E-mail Address: usptoinfo@uspto.gov
Web Address: www.uspto.gov
The U.S. Patent and Trademark Office (PTO)
administers patent and trademark laws for the U.S.
and enables registration of patents and trademarks.

U.S. Securities and Exchange Commission (SEC)
100 F St. NE
Washington, DC 20549 USA
Phone: 202-942-8088
Fax: 202-772-9295
Toll Free: 800-732-0330
E-mail Address: help@sec.gov
Web Address: www.sec.gov
The U.S. Securities and Exchange Commission
(SEC) is a nonpartisan, quasi-judicial regulatory
agency responsible for administering federal
securities laws. These laws are designed to protect
investors in securities markets and ensure that they
have access to disclosure of all material information
concerning publicly traded securities. Visitors to the
web site can access the EDGAR database of
corporate financial and business information.

51) Wireless & Cellular Industry Associations

Broadband Wireless Association (BWA)
Phone: 44-7765-250610
E-mail Address: Stephen@thebwa.eu
Web Address: www.thebwa.eu
The Broadband Wireless Association (BWA)
provides representation, news and information for the
European broadband wireless industry.

Industrial Internet Consortium
9C Medway Rd., PMB 274
Milford, MA 01757 USA
Phone: 781-444-0404
E-mail Address: info@iiconsortium.org
Web Address: www.iiconsortium.org
The Industrial Internet Consortium was founded in
2014 to further development, adoption and widespread use of interconnected machines, intelligent
analytics and people at work. Through an
independently-run consortium of technology
innovators, industrial companies, academia and

government, the goal of the IIC is to accelerate the
development and availability of intelligent industrial
automation for the public good.

Open Mobile Alliance (OMA)
2907 Shelter Island, Ste. 105-273
San Diego, CA 92106 USA
Phone: 858-623-0742
Fax: 858-623-0743
E-mail Address: snewberry@omaorg.org
Web Address: www.openmobilealliance.org
The Open Mobile Alliance (OMA) facilitates global
user adoption of mobile data services by specifying
market driven mobile service enablers that ensure
service interoperability across devices, geographies,
service providers, operators and networks, while
allowing businesses to compete through innovation
and differentiation.

Wi-Fi Alliance
10900-B Stonelake Blvd., Ste. 126
Austin, TX 78759 USA
Phone: 512-498-9434
Fax: 512-498-9435
Web Address: www.wi-fi.org
The Wi-Fi Alliance is a non-profit group that
promotes wireless interoperability via Wi-Fi (802.11
standards). It also provides consumers with current
information about Wi-Fi systems. The alliance
currently includes over 350 member organizations.

WiMAX Forum
9009 SE Adams St., Ste. 2259
Clackamas, OR 97015 USA
Phone: 858-605-0978
Fax: 858-461-6041
Web Address: www.wimaxforum.org
The WiMAX Forum supports the implementation and
standardization of long-range wireless Internet
connections. It is a non-profit organization dedicated
to the promotion and certification of interoperability
and compatibility of broadband wireless products.

Wireless Communications Alliance (WCA)
1510 Page Mill Rd.
Palo Alto, CA 94304-1125 USA
E-mail Address: promote@wca.org
Web Address: www.wca.org
The Wireless Communications Alliance (WCA) is a
non-profit business association for companies and
organizations working with wireless technologies. It
promotes networking, education and the exchange of
information amongst its members.

**Wireless Communications Association
International (WCAI)**
1333 H St. NW, Ste. 700 W
Washington, DC 20005-4754 USA
Phone: 202-452-7823
Web Address: www.wcainternational.com/
The Wireless Communications Association
International (WCAI) is a nonprofit trade association
representing the wireless broadband industry.

Chapter 4

THE E-COMMERCE 500: WHO THEY ARE AND HOW THEY WERE CHOSEN

Includes Indexes by Company Name, Industry & Location

The companies chosen to be listed in PLUNKETT'S E-COMMERCE & INTERNET BUSINESS ALMANAC comprise a unique list. THE E-COMMERCE 500 were chosen specifically for their dominance in the many facets of the ecommerce and internet business in which they operate. Complete information about each firm can be found in the "Individual Profiles," beginning at the end of this chapter. These profiles are in alphabetical order by company name.

THE E-COMMERCE 500 companies are from all parts of the United States, Canada, Europe, Asia/Pacific and beyond. THE E-COMMERCE 500 includes companies that are deeply involved in the technologies, services and trends that keep the entire industry forging ahead.

Simply stated, THE E-COMMERCE 500 contains the largest, most successful, fastest growing firms in ecommerce and related industries in the world. To be included in our list, the firms had to meet the following criteria:

1) Generally, these are corporations based in the U.S., however, the headquarters of many firms are located in other nations.

2) Prominence, or a significant presence, in ecommerce, ecommerce-based services, equipment and supporting fields. (See the following Industry Codes section for a complete list of types of businesses that are covered).

3) The companies in THE E-COMMERCE 500 do not have to be exclusively in the ecommerce field.

4) Financial data and vital statistics must have been available to the editors of this book, either directly from the company being written about or from outside sources deemed reliable and accurate by the editors. A small number of companies that we would like to have included are not listed because of a lack of sufficient, objective data.

INDEX OF COMPANIES WITHIN INDUSTRY GROUPS

The industry codes shown below are based on the 2012 NAIC code system (NAIC is used by many analysts as a replacement for older SIC codes because NAIC is more specific to today's industry sectors, see www.census.gov/NAICS). Companies are given a primary NAIC code, reflecting the main line of business of each firm.

Industry Group/Company	Industry Code	2022 Sales	2022 Profits
Advertising and Marketing - Online			
AKQA Inc	541810E	800,000,000	
Carta Communications Inc	541810E	880,000,000	
CDK Global LLC	541810E	1,725,000,000	
Critical Mass Inc	541810E		
Groupon Inc	541810E	599,084,992	-237,608,992
InMobi Pte Ltd	541810E	62,000,000	
LivingSocial LLC	541810E		
Macquarium Inc	541810E		
MoreVisibility.com Inc	541810E		
Onstream Media Corporation	541810E	19,400,000	
Performics Inc	541810E		
Quotient Technology Inc	541810E	288,766,016	-76,511,000
Rakuten Marketing LLC	541810E		
Taboola Inc	541810E	1,401,149,952	-11,975,000
VerticalResponse Inc	541810E		
Vibrant Media Inc	541810E		
Xaxis LLC	541810E	1,910,000,000	
Advertising, Public Relations and Marketing Services			
Digitas	541800	735,000,000	
MKTG Sports + Entertainment	541800	171,000,000	
Student Advantage LLC	541800		
Automobile (Car) and Light Truck Dealers (Used)			
Carvana Co	441120	13,603,999,744	-1,587,000,064
Book Stores			
LifeWay Christian Resources	451211	1,838,720	
Cable TV Programming, Cable Networks and Subscription Video			
Hulu LLC	515210	10,700,000,000	
Netflix Inc	515210	31,615,549,440	4,491,923,968
Walt Disney Company (The)	515210	82,721,996,800	3,144,999,936
Cloud, Data Processing, Business Process Outsourcing (BPO) and Internet Content Storage			
Automatic Data Processing Inc (ADP)	518210	16,046,499,840	2,948,900,096
Cyxtera Technologies Inc	518210	746,000,000	-355,100,000
GoDaddy Inc	518210	4,091,300,096	352,200,000
Health Catalyst Inc	518210	276,236,000	-137,403,008
Neustar Inc	518210	621,000,000	
Newfold Digital Inc	518210	901,243,200	
Register.com Inc	518210		
Switch Inc	518210	615,700,000	
Tucows Inc	518210	321,142,016	-27,571,000

Industry Group/Company	Industry Code	2022 Sales	2022 Profits
Computer and Data Systems Design, Consulting and Integration Services			
Accenture plc	541512	61,594,304,512	6,877,169,152
Atos SE	541512	12,110,888,960	-1,080,700,160
Infosys Limited	541512	16,311,000,064	2,963,000,064
Perficient Inc	541512	905,062,016	104,392,000
Publicis Sapient	541512	2,085,000,000	
Sopra Steria Group SA	541512	5,445,479,988	265,805,010
Tata Consultancy Services Limited (TCS)	541512	25,700,000,000	2,379,843,586
Wipro Limited	541512	9,583,245,312	1,480,510,976
Computer Manufacturing, Including PCs, Laptops, Mainframes and Tablets			
Dell Technologies Inc	334111	101,196,996,608	5,562,999,808
Computer Networking & Related Equipment Manufacturing (may incl. Wireless)			
Arista Networks Inc	334210A	4,381,309,952	1,352,445,952
Cisco Systems Inc	334210A	51,556,999,168	11,811,999,744
Juniper Networks Inc	334210A	5,301,199,872	471,000,000
Computer Programming and Custom Software Development and Consulting			
Lionbridge Technologies LLC	541511	575,000,000	
Squarespace Inc	541511	866,972,032	-252,220,992
Computer Software: Accounting, Banking & Financial			
Avalara Inc	511210Q	700,000,000	
Bill.com Holdings Inc	511210Q	641,958,976	-326,360,992
BlackLine Inc	511210Q	522,937,984	-29,391,000
Bottomline Technologies Inc	511210Q	480,000,000	
Conga (Appextremes LLC)	511210Q	416,000,000	
Coupa Software Incorporated	511210Q	725,289,024	-379,039,008
DocuSign Inc	511210Q	2,107,213,056	-69,976,000
Expensify Inc	511210Q	169,495,008	-27,009,000
Gusto	511210Q		
Intuit Inc	511210Q	12,725,999,616	2,066,000,000
Namely Inc	511210Q	41,600,000	
Sage Intacct Inc	511210Q	195,771,000	
SAP Ariba	511210Q	1,670,000,000	
Computer Software: Business Management & Enterprise Resource Planning (ERP)			
Alteryx Inc	511210H	855,000,000	-319,000,000
Anaplan Inc	511210H	592,200,000	-200,700,000
Apptio Inc	511210H	350,000,000	
Asana Inc	511210H	378,436,992	-288,342,016
BMC Software Inc	511210H	2,120,000,000	
Greenhouse Software Inc	511210H		
iCIMS Inc	511210H		
Intralinks Inc	511210H	359,868,600	
Microsoft Corporation	511210H	198,269,992,960	72,737,996,800
Oracle Corporation	511210H	42,439,999,488	6,717,000,192
Oracle NetSuite	511210H	1,144,000,000	
RealPage Inc	511210H	1,500,000,000	

Industry Group/Company	Industry Code	2022 Sales	2022 Profits
SAP SE	511210H	32,966,692,864	2,439,050,496
ServiceMax Inc	511210H	82,000,000	
Sisense Inc	511210H		
Smartsheet Inc	511210H	550,832,000	-171,096,992
SMS Assist LLC	511210H		
Symphony Technology Group	511210H	3,120,000,000	
TIBCO Software Inc	511210H	1,369,470,374	
Workday Inc	511210H	5,138,798,080	29,373,000
Yardi Systems Inc	511210H		
Zoho Corporation Pvt Ltd	511210H	925,216,000	
Computer Software: Content & Document Management			
Box Inc	511210L	874,332,032	-41,459,000
EasyAsk Technologies Inc	511210L		
Open Text Corporation	511210L	3,493,843,968	397,089,984
Computer Software: Data Base & File Management			
Domo Inc	511210J	257,960,992	-102,111,000
Embarcadero Inc	511210J	150,000,000	
MongoDB Inc	511210J	873,782,016	-306,865,984
Qualtrics International Inc	511210J	1,458,627,968	-1,061,478,016
Segment.io Inc	511210J		
Sumo Logic Inc	511210J	242,124,992	-123,365,000
Teradata Corporation	511210J	1,795,000,064	33,000,000
Computer Software: E-Commerce, Web Analytics & Applications Management			
Acquia Inc	511210M	232,814,400	
AppDirect Inc	511210M		
AppDynamics LLC	511210M	233,099,767	
BigCommerce Holdings Inc	511210M	279,075,008	-139,919,008
BroadVision Group	511210M	5,050,000	
Digital River Inc	511210M	255,783,528	
Computer Software: E-Commerce, Web Analytics & Applications Management			
Dynatrace Inc	511210m	929,444,992	52,451,000
Computer Software: E-Commerce, Web Analytics & Applications Management			
Fast AF Inc	511210M		
Fastly Inc	511210M	432,724,992	-190,774,000
iCrossing Inc	511210M		
Computer Software: E-Commerce, Web Analytics & Applications Management			
Infor	511210m	3,629,227,000	
Computer Software: E-Commerce, Web Analytics & Applications Management			
Kibo Software Inc	511210M		
Mixpanel Inc	511210M	114,400,000	
Sea Limited	511210M	12,449,704,960	-1,651,421,056
Ushahidi Inc	511210M		
Computer Software: Electronic Games, Apps & Entertainment			
Badoo Trading Limited	511210G	209,200,000	

Industry Group/Company	Industry Code	2022 Sales	2022 Profits
DeNA Co Ltd	511210G	883,729,728	206,177,488
Electronic Arts Inc (EA)	511210G	6,991,000,064	789,000,000
Happn (SAS HAPPN)	511210G		
Linden Research Inc (Linden Lab)	511210G		
Optimizely Inc	511210G		
PoF (Plentyoffish Media ULC)	511210G		
Tantan (Tantan Cultural Development Beijing Co Ltd)	511210G		
Tinder Inc	511210G	1,790,000,000	
Zynga Inc	511210G	2,159,200,000	
Computer Software: Healthcare (Medical) & Biotechnology			
Flatiron Health Inc	511210D		
MedeAnalytics Inc	511210D		
PointClickCare	511210D	196,365,000	
Computer Software: Multimedia, Advertising, Graphics & Publishing			
Adobe Inc	511210F	17,606,000,640	4,755,999,744
Campaign Monitor Pty Ltd	511210F		
Canva Pty Ltd	511210F	193,378,000	
Extreme Reach Inc	511210F		
Hootsuite Inc	511210F		
Khoros LLC	511210F	313,040,000	
MediaPlatform Inc	511210F		
Piksel Inc	511210F	70,000,000	
RealNetworks LLC	511210F	47,865,400	
SendGrid Inc	511210F	215,000,000	
Sprinklr Inc	511210F	492,393,984	-111,470,000
Computer Software: Network Management, System Testing, & Storage			
F5 Inc	511210B	2,695,845,120	322,160,000
NetScout Systems Inc	511210B	855,574,976	35,874,000
Nutanix Inc	511210B	1,580,796,032	-798,945,984
Radware Ltd	511210B	293,425,984	-166,000
ServiceNow Inc	511210B	7,245,000,192	325,000,000
Veeam Software	511210B		
Computer Software: Operating Systems, Languages & Development Tools, Artificial Intelligence (AI)			
Datadog Inc	511210I	1,675,100,032	-50,160,000
MuleSoft LLC	511210I	480,300,000	
Progress Software Corporation	511210I	602,012,992	95,069,000
Red Hat Inc	511210I	3,483,000,000	
Computer Software: Product Lifecycle, Engineering, Design & CAD			
InVisionApp Inc	511210N		
Procore Technologies Inc	511210N	720,203,008	-286,931,008
Computer Software: Sales & Customer Relationship Management			
Corcentric Inc	511210K	31,200,000	
Gainsight Inc	511210K		
InsideSales	511210K		
Lightspeed Commerce Inc	511210K	548,371,968	-288,432,992

Industry Group/Company	Industry Code	2022 Sales	2022 Profits
LivePerson Inc	511210K	514,800,000	-225,747,008
LiveRamp Holdings Inc	511210K	528,656,992	-33,833,000
Medallia Inc	511210K	435,304,000	
Salesforce Inc	511210K	26,492,000,256	1,444,000,000
Shopify Inc	511210K	5,600,000,000	-3,460,000,000
SugarCRM Inc	511210K	348,795,720	
Talkdesk Inc	511210K		
US Interactive Inc	511210K		
WalkMe Inc	511210K		
Computer Software: Security & Anti-Virus			
Axway Inc	511210E	335,224,952	-42,743,367
Check Point Software Technologies Ltd	511210E	2,329,900,032	796,899,968
Cloudflare Inc	511210E	975,241,024	-193,380,992
Cylance Inc	511210E	196,560,000	
Duo Security Inc	511210E		
Entrust Corporation	511210E	915,200,000	
Forescout Technologies Inc	511210E	382,500,000	
Gen Digital Inc	511210E	2,796,000,000	836,000,000
Geocomply Solutions Inc	511210E		
Illumio	511210E		
Lookout Inc	511210E		
McAfee Corp	511210E	2,000,000,000	
Netskope Inc	511210E		
OneSpan Inc	511210E	219,006,000	-14,434,000
Trend Micro Inc	511210E	1,511,250,176	201,524,784
Veracode Inc	511210E		
VeriSign Inc	511210E	1,424,899,968	673,800,000
WatchGuard Technologies Inc	511210E		
Zscaler Inc	511210E	1,090,946,048	-390,278,016
Computer Software: Supply Chain & Logistics, (may incl. Artificial Intelligence, AI)			
Blue Yonder Group Inc	511210A	1,352,000,000	
JAGGAER	511210A	208,208,000	
Manhattan Associates Inc	511210A	767,084,032	128,959,000
Steel Connect Inc	511210A	203,272,000	-10,968,000
Computer Software: Telecom, Communications & VOIP, Internet of Things (IoT)			
Fuze Inc	511210C		
Intercom Inc	511210C	150,000,000	
PagerDuty Inc	511210C	281,396,000	-107,455,000
Skype Technologies Sarl	511210C		
Slack Technologies LLC	511210C	681,864,453	
Twilio Inc	511210C	3,826,320,896	-1,256,145,024
WhatsApp LLC	511210C		
Zoom Video Communications Inc	511210C	4,099,864,064	1,375,639,040
Consulting Services, Marketing			
comScore Inc	541613	376,423,008	-66,561,000
Consumer Loans and Consumer Lending			
Klarna Bank AB	522291	1,743,162,600	-954,152,160

Industry Group/Company	Industry Code	2022 Sales	2022 Profits
Credit Card Processing, Online Payment Processing, EFT, ACH and Clearinghouses			
Adyen NV	522320	9,542,209,536	602,435,904
Authorize.net	522320		
CyberSource Corporation	522320	453,881,610	
Elavon Inc	522320	2,100,000,000	
Fiserv Inc	522320	17,737,000,960	2,529,999,872
Global Payments Inc	522320	8,975,514,624	111,493,000
PayPal Holdings Inc	522320	27,517,999,104	2,419,000,064
Paysafe Limited	522320	1,496,136,960	-1,862,654,976
Stripe Inc	522320	25,000,000,000	
Total System Services LLC (TSYS)	522320	4,264,000,000	
VeriFone Inc	522320	1,800,000,000	
Zuora Inc	522320	346,737,984	-99,425,000
Ecommerce, Catalog, Home Shopping Networks, Mail Order and Other Non-Store Retailers			
1-800 Contacts Inc	454110	509,600,000	
1-800-Flowers.Com Inc	454110	2,207,885,056	29,610,000
3 Suisses	454110	2,860,000,000	
a.k.a. Brands Holding Corp	454110	611,737,984	-176,696,992
AbeBooks Inc	454110		
AG Interactive Inc	454110	70,589,610	
Alibris Inc	454110	211,120,000	
Amazon.com Inc	454110	513,982,988,288	-2,721,999,872
Americanas SA	454110	4,880,258,000	-2,441,469,000
AptDeco Inc	454110		
ASOS plc	454110	4,970,767,360	-38,892,328
Audible Inc	454110		
BackCountry.com LLC	454110		
Beyond Inc	454110	1,929,334,016	-35,236,000
Blue Nile Inc	454110	555,580,000	
Bonobos Inc	454110	200,000,000	
Boohoo.com PLC	454110	2,503,756,544	-5,050,952
Build.com Inc	454110	2,072,900,000	
Chewy Inc (Chewy.com)	454110	8,890,773,504	-73,817,000
Coupang Inc	454110	20,582,615,040	-92,042,000
Deem Inc	454110		
Dingdong (Cayman) Ltd	454110	3,410,913,024	-114,682,656
eBay Inc	454110	9,795,000,320	-1,268,999,936
eMusic.com Inc	454110		
Etsy Inc	454110	2,566,110,976	-694,288,000
Eventbrite Inc	454110	260,927,008	-55,384,000
Everlane	454110	121,000,000	
Fanatics Inc	454110	6,300,000,000	
Fandango Inc	454110		
Farfetch Limited	454110	2,316,679,936	359,287,008
Flipkart Internet Private Limited	454110	6,765,262,496	-444,495,830
Fredericks of Hollywood	454110	86,500,000	
Free People	454110		

Industry Group/Company	Industry Code	2022 Sales	2022 Profits
FreshDirect LLC	454110	1,144,000,000	
Freshly Inc	454110		
Grove Collaborative Holdings Inc	454110	321,527,008	-87,715,000
Gwynnie Bee (CaaStle Inc)	454110		
Heyday (HYDY Inc)	454110	20,904,000	
Houzz Inc	454110	476,985,600	
JD.com Inc	454110	147,334,365,184	1,461,745,536
Kidpik Corp	454110	16,477,984	-7,615,261
Le Tote Inc	454110		
Lillian Vernon Corporation	454110		
Meesho (Fashnear Technologies Private Limited)	454110		
MercadoLibre Inc	454110	10,536,999,936	482,000,000
MovieTickets.com Inc	454110		
Newegg Commerce Inc	454110	1,720,273,024	-57,429,000
Ocado Group PLC	454110	3,174,270,464	-575,177,088
Ozon Holdings PLC	454110	3,784,800,000	-794,700,000
PDD Holdings Inc	454110	18,385,545,216	4,441,292,800
Polished.com Inc	454110	534,473,984	-125,965,000
Poshmark Inc	454110	339,050,000	
Princess Polly Group Pty Ltd	454110	40,000,000	
PSI Capital Inc	454110		
Qurate Retail Inc	454110	12,106,000,384	-2,593,999,872
Rakuten (Ebates Inc)	454110		
Rakuten Inc	454110	13,018,638,336	-2,518,023,424
Reformation (LYMI Inc)	454110	94,100,000	
Rent the Runway Inc	454110	203,300,000	-211,800,000
Revolve Group Inc	454110	1,101,415,936	58,697,000
SHEIN	454110	23,800,000,000	800,000,000
Shopping.com Ltd	454110		
Snapdeal	454110	131,683,000	
Solo Brands Inc	454110	517,627,008	-4,945,000
Stamps.com Inc	454110	819,831,000	
Stitch Fix Inc	454110	2,072,812,032	-207,120,992
Suning.com Co Ltd	454110	10,305,143,000	-2,341,945,000
Teespring Inc (dba SPRING)	454110	165,000,000	
Temu	454110		
TheRealReal Inc	454110	603,492,992	-196,444,992
VANCL	454110		
Veepee	454110	3,842,964,000	
Vipshop Holdings Limited	454110	14,526,270,464	887,019,776
VitaCost.com Inc	454110	487,000,000	
Wayfair LLC	454110	12,218,000,384	-1,331,000,064
Wish.com (ContextLogic Inc)	454110	571,000,000	-384,000,000
YOOX Net-A-Porter Group SpA (YNAP)	454110	1,580,000,000	
Zalando SE	454110	11,047,062,528	17,940,476
Zappos.com LLC	454110	4,950,000,000	
Zozo Inc	454110	1,122,314,112	232,918,704
Financial Data Publishing - Print & Online			
Bloomberg LP	511120A	13,150,000,000	

Industry Group/Company	Industry Code	2022 Sales	2022 Profits
FactSet Research Systems Inc	511120A	1,843,891,968	396,916,992
Thomson Reuters Corporation	511120A	6,626,999,808	1,338,000,000
Flower, Nursery Stock and Florists' Supplies Wholesale Distribution			
FTD LLC	424930	1,100,000,000	
Greeting Card Publishers			
American Greetings Corporation LLC	511191	2,328,144,000	
Hallmark Cards Inc	511191	3,952,000,000	
Insurance Agencies, Risk Management Consultants and Insurance Brokers			
eHealth Inc	524210	405,356,000	-88,722,000
Life Quotes Inc	524210		
Internet Search Engines, Online Publishing, Sharing, Streaming Entertainment, Social Media			
Alibaba Group Holding Limited	519130	120,130,969,600	8,766,107,648
Alphabet Inc (Google)	519130	282,836,008,960	59,972,001,792
Ancestry.com Inc	519130	1,275,000,000	
Angi Inc	519130	1,891,523,968	-128,450,000
Autohome Inc	519130	977,430,080	273,871,104
Automattic Inc	519130		
AutoWeb Inc	519130	74,448,400	
Avantax Inc	519130	666,496,000	420,247,000
Baidu Inc	519130	17,416,316,928	1,064,483,008
Bankrate LLC	519130	557,178,804	
Brightcove Inc	519130	211,008,000	-9,015,000
BuzzFeed Inc	519130	436,673,984	-200,956,992
Cars.com Inc	519130	653,875,968	17,206,000
CoStar Group Inc	519130	2,182,398,976	369,452,992
Cox Automotive Inc	519130	7,000,000,000	
Crackle Plus LLC	519130		
Craigslist Inc	519130	694,000,000	
D&B Hoovers	519130		
Data.ai	519130		
Digg Inc	519130		
Dotdash Meredith	519130	1,934,699,000	-188,091,000
Dropbox Inc	519130	2,324,900,096	553,200,000
eHarmony Inc	519130	422,580,000	
Endeavor Streaming	519130	114,400,000	
Evernote Corporation	519130	26,000,000	
Everyday Health Inc	519130	280,134,400	
GitHub Inc	519130	1,000,000,000	
Gree Inc	519130	505,827,712	68,352,176
IAC/InterActiveCorp	519130	5,235,279,872	-1,170,169,984
Indiegogo Inc	519130		
Instagram	519130	33,300,000,000	
Intuit MailChimp (The Rocket Science Group LLC)	519130	1,000,000,000	
Jumia Technologies AG	519130	221,882,000	-238,232,000
Kakao Corporation	519130	5,637,420,000	1,073,200,000
Kickstarter PBC	519130		

Industry Group/Company	Industry Code	2022 Sales	2022 Profits
Leaf Group Ltd	519130	220,000,000	
LinkedIn Corporation	519130	14,000,000,000	
LiveWorld Inc	519130	9,000,000	
LookSmart Group Inc	519130	1,719,000	-63,000
Major League Baseball Advanced Media LP (MLBAM)	519130	105,000,000	
MapQuest.com Inc	519130		
Marchex Inc	519130	52,170,000	-8,245,000
MarketWatch Inc	519130		
Match Group Inc	519130	3,188,843,008	361,945,984
Meituan Dianping	519130	30,974,773,248	-941,559,808
Meta Platforms Inc (Facebook)	519130	116,608,999,424	23,200,000,000
MH Sub I LLC (dba Internet Brands)	519130	167,440,000	
mixi Inc	519130	824,048,192	69,297,568
Moatable Inc	519130	45,808,000	-75,244,000
MOGU Inc	519130	47,523,484	-90,098,720
Move Inc	519130	687,000,000	
MyHeritage Ltd	519130	187,200,000	
Myspace LLC	519130		
Naver Corporation	519130	6,191,589,888	572,649,408
NaviSite LLC	519130		
NetEase Inc	519130	13,588,854,784	2,864,007,168
OfferUp Inc	519130		
OpenTable Inc	519130	420,000,000	
Paramount Streaming	519130		
Perplexity AI	519130		
Photobucket Inc	519130		
Ping An Healthcare and Technology Company Limited	519130	867,446,016	-85,559,848
Pinterest Inc	519130	2,802,574,080	-96,047,000
ProQuest LLC	519130	634,400,000	
REA Group Ltd	519130	958,243,840	258,324,400
Rocket Internet SE	519130	131,040,000	
Ruhnn Holding Limited	519130	197,943,000	
Salon.com LLC	519130		
Seek Limited	519130	749,530,112	113,319,024
Shutterfly LLC	519130	3,536,000,000	
SINA Corporation	519130	2,833,817,132	
Snap Inc (Snapchat)	519130	4,601,846,784	-1,429,652,992
Sogou Inc	519130	967,200,000	
Sohu.com Limited	519130	733,872,000	-17,343,000
SurveyMonkey Inc	519130	480,916,992	-89,891,000
Tencent Holdings Limited	519130	78,093,819,904	26,508,992,512
TheStreet Inc	519130	76,500,000	
Thumbtack Inc	519130	205,000,000	
TikTok (ByteDance Ltd)	519130	80,000,000,000	40,000,000,000
TrueCar Inc	519130	161,524,000	-118,685,000
Vimeo Inc	519130	433,028,000	-79,591,000
VK Company Limited	519130	1,335,342,660	-42,940,752
WebMD Health Corp	519130	922,504,156	
Whitepages Inc	519130		

Industry Group/Company	Industry Code	2022 Sales	2022 Profits
Wikimedia Foundation	519130	154,686,521	8,173,996
X Corp (Twitter)	519130	3,000,000,000	
Yahoo Inc	519130	1,491,110,720	
Yandex NV	519130	5,763,992,576	436,029,152
Yelp Inc	519130	1,193,506,048	36,347,000
Youku Tudou Inc	519130	1,280,000,000	
YouTube LLC	519130	29,200,000,000	
Zillow Group Inc	519130	1,958,000,000	-101,000,000
ZipRecruiter Inc	519130	904,649,024	61,494,000
Local Messengers and Food Delivery, Gig Economy			
Deliveroo plc	492210	2,381,133,000	-354,632,000
Delivery Hero SE	492210	9,156,182,000	-3,191,795,000
Grubhub Inc	492210	2,050,000,000	
Instacart (Maplebear Inc)	492210	2,551,000,064	428,000,000
Market Research, Business Intelligence and Opinion Polling			
Forrester Research Inc	541910	537,787,008	21,806,000
Gartner Inc	541910	5,475,846,144	807,798,976
Mortgage Brokers and Loan Brokers			
Eloan	522310		
Newspaper Publishing			
Dow Jones & Company Inc	511110	1,845,000,000	
New York Times Company (The)	511110	2,308,321,024	173,904,992
News Corporation	511110	10,385,000,448	623,000,000
Optical Goods Stores			
Warby Parker Inc	446130	598,112,000	-110,393,000
Outsourced Computer Facilities Management and Operations Services			
International Business Machines Corporation (IBM)	541513	60,529,999,872	1,640,000,000
Personal Care Products; Consumer; Cosmetics; Makeup; Fragrances; Perfumes; Hair Care Manufacturing			
Honest Company Inc (The)	325620	313,651,008	-49,019,000
Professional Training, Management Development and Corporate Employee Training			
HealthStream Inc	611430	266,826,000	12,091,000
Radio Networks, Incl Commercial Networks Supporting Radio Broadcasting			
Pandora Media LLC	515111	1,576,000,000	
Spotify Technology SA	515111	12,523,092,992	-459,190,784
Tencent Music Entertainment Group	515111	3,990,790,144	517,807,104
Recruiting & Job Services Online			
CareerBuilder LLC	561311A	820,000,000	
HeadHunter Group PLC	561311A	235,101,232	47,472,340
Ladders (The)	561311A		
Monster Worldwide Inc	561311A	688,000,000	
Reservations, Car Rentals, Car Sharing, Ticket Offices, Time Share and Vacation Club Rentals			
Amadeus IT Group SA	561599	4,788,653,391	709,133,607
DiDi Global Inc	561599	19,826,743,296	-3,349,244,928
Lyft Inc	561599	4,095,134,976	-1,584,510,976

Industry Group/Company	Industry Code	2022 Sales	2022 Profits
Uber Technologies Inc	561599	31,876,999,168	-9,141,000,192
viagogo Entertainment Inc	561599		
Satellite Telecommunication Services (Including Satellite Telephone Companies)			
OneWeb Ltd	517410	9,600,000	-389,800,000
Planet Labs PBC	517410	131,209,000	-137,124,000
Securities Brokerage, Discount Brokers and Online Stock Brokers			
Boursorama	523120	302,020,000	
Charles Schwab Corporation (The)	523120	20,761,999,360	7,183,000,064
E-Trade from Morgan Stanley	523120	2,710,300,441	
TradeStation Group Inc	523120	142,000,000	
Telecommunications, Telephone & Network Equip Manufacturing, Routers, Switches, Handsets			
ADTRAN Inc	334210	1,025,536,000	-2,037,000
Avaya Holdings Corp	334210	3,000,000,000	
Ciena Corporation	334210	3,632,660,992	152,902,000
Harmonic Inc	334210	624,956,992	28,182,000
Huawei Technologies Co Ltd	334210		
Tellabs Inc	334210	1,660,000,000	
Westell Technologies Inc	334210	37,990,000	3,870,000
Television Broadcasting			
TEGNA Inc	515120	3,279,245,056	629,908,992
Travel Agencies and Room or Accommodation Sharing Services			
Airbnb Inc	561510	8,399,000,064	1,892,999,936
Booking Holdings Inc	561510	17,089,999,872	3,057,999,872
Expedia Group Inc	561510	11,667,000,320	352,000,000
Hotels.com LP	561510		
Hotwire Inc	561510		
KAYAK	561510	501,552,607	
lastminute.com NV (lm group)	561510	314,226,356	-16,160,731
MakeMyTrip Limited	561510	303,921,984	-45,405,000
Orbitz LLC	561510	932,000,000	
Sabre Corporation	561510	2,537,015,040	-435,448,000
Travelport Worldwide Limited	561510	1,950,033,370	
Travelscape LLC (Travelocity.com)	561510		
Travelzoo Inc	561510	70,599,000	6,634,000
Trip.com Group Limited	561510	2,821,957,376	197,575,040
TripAdvisor Inc	561510	1,492,000,000	20,000,000
trivago NV	561510	571,323,008	-135,854,256
Tujia Online Information Technology (Beijing) Co Ltd	561510		
Wired Telephone and Telecommunications Carriers and Services (Phone Companies)			
Akamai Technologies Inc	517311	3,616,654,080	523,672,000
Altice USA Inc	517311	9,647,659,008	194,563,008
Amazon Web Services Inc (AWS)	517311	80,096,000,000	22,841,000,000
AT&T Inc	517311	120,741,003,264	-8,524,000,256
Boingo Wireless Inc	517311	256,771,840	
Charter Communications Inc	517311	54,022,000,640	5,055,000,064

Industry Group/Company	Industry Code	2022 Sales	2022 Profits
Cincinnati Bell Inc (altafiber)	517311	1,796,000,000	-130,900,000
Cisco Webex	517311		
Cogent Communications Group Inc	517311	599,603,968	5,146,000
Comcast Corporation	517311	121,427,001,344	5,369,999,872
Consensus Cloud Solutions Inc	517311	362,422,016	72,714,000
CoreSite an American Tower Company	517311	743,400,000	
Cox Communications Inc	517311	13,800,000,000	
DigitalOcean Inc	517311	576,321,984	-27,804,000
DirecTV LLC (DIRECTV)	517311	31,400,000,000	
EarthLink LLC	517311	1,280,229,350	
Equinix Inc	517311	7,263,105,024	704,345,024
Frontier Communications Corporation	517311	5,786,999,808	441,000,000
INNOVATE Corp	517311	1,637,299,968	-35,900,000
Internap Corporation	517311	307,931,520	
Internet Initiative Japan Inc	517311	1,528,402,432	105,830,400
Liberty Global plc	517311	7,195,700,224	1,473,200,000
Lumen Technologies Inc	517311	17,478,000,640	-1,548,000,000
Net2Phone Inc	517311	58,654,451	
Rackspace Technology Inc	517311	3,122,299,904	-804,800,000
Rogers Communications Inc	517311	11,229,922,304	1,225,400,832
Shaw Communications Inc	517311	3,984,174,592	558,720,512
SoftBank Group Corp	517311	42,012,979,200	-11,534,033,920
Telecomunicaciones de Puerto Rico Inc	517311	1,001,669,760	
Telephone and Data Systems Inc (TDS)	517311	5,413,000,192	62,000,000
United Internet AG	517311	6,314,267,000	391,982,000
United Online Inc	517311	204,584,640	
Vonage Holdings Corp	517311	1,435,320,000	
Windstream Holdings Inc	517311	5,200,000,000	
Wireless (Cellphone, Cellular) Telecommunications Carriers (Except Satellite)			
America Movil SAB de CV	517312	49,544,241,152	4,468,032,000
China Mobile Limited	517312	135,323,328,938	18,315,289,846
Jio (Reliance Jio Infocomm Ltd)	517312	11,093,896,524	
KDDI Corporation	517312	36,780,707,840	4,541,185,536
Mobile TeleSystems PJSC	517312	7,293,372,000	444,896,000
NTT DOCOMO Inc	517312	49,695,675,640	8,972,124,044
SK Telecom Co Ltd	517312	13,034,582,016	687,244,800
Telenor ASA	517312	9,351,427,072	4,244,402,944
T-Mobile US Inc	517312	79,571,001,344	2,590,000,128
Veon Ltd	517312	3,755,000,064	-162,000,000
Verio Inc	517312		
Verizon Communications Inc	517312	136,834,998,272	21,255,999,488
Vodafone Group plc	517312	48,674,222,080	2,229,744,896
Wireless Communications & Radio, TV Broadcasting Equipment Manufacturing, incl Cellphones (Handsets)			
Apple Inc	334220	394,328,014,848	99,802,996,736

ALPHABETICAL INDEX

Dell Technologies Inc
DeNA Co Ltd
DiDi Global Inc
Digg Inc
Digital River Inc
DigitalOcean Inc
Digitas
Dingdong (Cayman) Ltd
DirecTV LLC (DIRECTV)
DocuSign Inc
Domo Inc
Dotdash Meredith
Dow Jones & Company Inc
Dropbox Inc
Duo Security Inc
Dynatrace Inc
EarthLink LLC
EasyAsk Technologies Inc
eBay Inc
eHarmony Inc
eHealth Inc
Elavon Inc
Electronic Arts Inc (EA)
Eloan
Embarcadero Inc
eMusic.com Inc
Endeavor Streaming
Entrust Corporation
Equinix Inc
E-Trade from Morgan Stanley
Etsy Inc
Eventbrite Inc
Everlane
Evernote Corporation
Everyday Health Inc
Expedia Group Inc
Expensify Inc
Extreme Reach Inc
F5 Inc
FactSet Research Systems Inc
Fanatics Inc
Fandango Inc
Farfetch Limited
Fast AF Inc
Fastly Inc
Fiserv Inc
Flatiron Health Inc
Flipkart Internet Private Limited
Forescout Technologies Inc
Forrester Research Inc
Fredericks of Hollywood
Free People
FreshDirect LLC
Freshly Inc
Frontier Communications Corporation
FTD LLC
Fuze Inc
Gainsight Inc

Gartner Inc
Gen Digital Inc
Geocomply Solutions Inc
GitHub Inc
Global Payments Inc
GoDaddy Inc
Gree Inc
Greenhouse Software Inc
Groupon Inc
Grove Collaborative Holdings Inc
Grubhub Inc
Gusto
Gwynnie Bee (CaaStle Inc)
Hallmark Cards Inc
Happn (SAS HAPPN)
Harmonic Inc
HeadHunter Group PLC
Health Catalyst Inc
HealthStream Inc
Heyday (HYDY Inc)
Honest Company Inc (The)
Hootsuite Inc
Hotels.com LP
Hotwire Inc
Houzz Inc
Huawei Technologies Co Ltd
Hulu LLC
IAC/InterActiveCorp
iCIMS Inc
iCrossing Inc
Illumio
Indiegogo Inc
Infor
Infosys Limited
InMobi Pte Ltd
INNOVATE Corp
InsideSales
Instacart (Maplebear Inc)
Instagram
Intercom Inc
Internap Corporation
International Business Machines Corporation (IBM)
Internet Initiative Japan Inc
Intralinks Inc
Intuit Inc
Intuit MailChimp (The Rocket Science Group LLC)
InVisionApp Inc
JAGGAER
JD.com Inc
Jio (Reliance Jio Infocomm Ltd)
Jumia Technologies AG
Juniper Networks Inc
Kakao Corporation
KAYAK
KDDI Corporation
Khoros LLC
Kibo Software Inc
Kickstarter PBC

Kidpik Corp
Klarna Bank AB
Ladders (The)
lastminute.com NV (lm group)
Le Tote Inc
Leaf Group Ltd
Liberty Global plc
Life Quotes Inc
LifeWay Christian Resources
Lightspeed Commerce Inc
Lillian Vernon Corporation
Linden Research Inc (Linden Lab)
LinkedIn Corporation
Lionbridge Technologies LLC
LivePerson Inc
LiveRamp Holdings Inc
LiveWorld Inc
LivingSocial LLC
Lookout Inc
LookSmart Group Inc
Lumen Technologies Inc
Lyft Inc
Macquarium Inc
Major League Baseball Advanced Media LP (MLBAM)
MakeMyTrip Limited
Manhattan Associates Inc
MapQuest.com Inc
Marchex Inc
MarketWatch Inc
Match Group Inc
McAfee Corp
Medallia Inc
MedeAnalytics Inc
MediaPlatform Inc
Meesho (Fashnear Technologies Private Limited)
Meituan Dianping
MercadoLibre Inc
Meta Platforms Inc (Facebook)
MH Sub I LLC (dba Internet Brands)
Microsoft Corporation
mixi Inc
Mixpanel Inc
MKTG Sports + Entertainment
Moatable Inc
Mobile TeleSystems PJSC
MOGU Inc
MongoDB Inc
Monster Worldwide Inc
MoreVisibility.com Inc
Move Inc
MovieTickets.com Inc
MuleSoft LLC
MyHeritage Ltd
Myspace LLC
Namely Inc
Naver Corporation
NaviSite LLC
Net2Phone Inc

NetEase Inc
Netflix Inc
NetScout Systems Inc
Netskope Inc
Neustar Inc
New York Times Company (The)
Newegg Commerce Inc
Newfold Digital Inc
News Corporation
NTT DOCOMO Inc
Nutanix Inc
Ocado Group PLC
OfferUp Inc
OneSpan Inc
OneWeb Ltd
Onstream Media Corporation
Open Text Corporation
OpenTable Inc
Optimizely Inc
Oracle Corporation
Oracle NetSuite
Orbitz LLC
Ozon Holdings PLC
PagerDuty Inc
Pandora Media LLC
Paramount Streaming
PayPal Holdings Inc
Paysafe Limited
PDD Holdings Inc
Perficient Inc
Performics Inc
Perplexity AI
Photobucket Inc
Piksel Inc
Ping An Healthcare and Technology Company Limited
Pinterest Inc
Planet Labs PBC
PoF (Plentyoffish Media ULC)
PointClickCare
Polished.com Inc
Poshmark Inc
Princess Polly Group Pty Ltd
Procore Technologies Inc
Progress Software Corporation
ProQuest LLC
PSI Capital Inc
Publicis Sapient
Qualtrics International Inc
Quotient Technology Inc
Qurate Retail Inc
Rackspace Technology Inc
Radware Ltd
Rakuten (Ebates Inc)
Rakuten Inc
Rakuten Marketing LLC
REA Group Ltd
RealNetworks LLC
RealPage Inc

Red Hat Inc
Reformation (LYMI Inc)
Register.com Inc
Rent the Runway Inc
Revolve Group Inc
Rocket Internet SE
Rogers Communications Inc
Ruhnn Holding Limited
Sabre Corporation
Sage Intacct Inc
Salesforce Inc
Salon.com LLC
SAP Ariba
SAP SE
Sea Limited
Seek Limited
Segment.io Inc
SendGrid Inc
ServiceMax Inc
ServiceNow Inc
Shaw Communications Inc
SHEIN
Shopify Inc
Shopping.com Ltd
Shutterfly LLC
SINA Corporation
Sisense Inc
SK Telecom Co Ltd
Skype Technologies Sarl
Slack Technologies LLC
Smartsheet Inc
SMS Assist LLC
Snap Inc (Snapchat)
Snapdeal
SoftBank Group Corp
Sogou Inc
Sohu.com Limited
Solo Brands Inc
Sopra Steria Group SA
Spotify Technology SA
Sprinklr Inc
Squarespace Inc
Stamps.com Inc
Steel Connect Inc
Stitch Fix Inc
Stripe Inc
Student Advantage LLC
SugarCRM Inc
Sumo Logic Inc
Suning.com Co Ltd
SurveyMonkey Inc
Switch Inc
Symphony Technology Group
Taboola Inc
Talkdesk Inc
Tantan (Tantan Cultural Development Beijing Co Ltd)
Tata Consultancy Services Limited (TCS)
Teespring Inc (dba SPRING)

TEGNA Inc
Telecomunicaciones de Puerto Rico Inc
Telenor ASA
Telephone and Data Systems Inc (TDS)
Tellabs Inc
Temu
Tencent Holdings Limited
Tencent Music Entertainment Group
Teradata Corporation
TheRealReal Inc
TheStreet Inc
Thomson Reuters Corporation
Thumbtack Inc
TIBCO Software Inc
TikTok (ByteDance Ltd)
Tinder Inc
T-Mobile US Inc
Total System Services LLC (TSYS)
TradeStation Group Inc
Travelport Worldwide Limited
Travelscape LLC (Travelocity.com)
Travelzoo Inc
Trend Micro Inc
Trip.com Group Limited
TripAdvisor Inc
trivago NV
TrueCar Inc
Tucows Inc
Tujia Online Information Technology (Beijing) Co Ltd
Twilio Inc
Uber Technologies Inc
United Internet AG
United Online Inc
US Interactive Inc
Ushahidi Inc
VANCL
Veeam Software
Veepee
Veon Ltd
Veracode Inc
VeriFone Inc
Verio Inc
VeriSign Inc
Verizon Communications Inc
VerticalResponse Inc
viagogo Entertainment Inc
Vibrant Media Inc
Vimeo Inc
Vipshop Holdings Limited
VitaCost.com Inc
VK Company Limited
Vodafone Group plc
Vonage Holdings Corp
WalkMe Inc
Walt Disney Company (The)
Warby Parker Inc
WatchGuard Technologies Inc
Wayfair LLC

WebMD Health Corp
Westell Technologies Inc
WhatsApp LLC
Whitepages Inc
Wikimedia Foundation
Windstream Holdings Inc
Wipro Limited
Wish.com (ContextLogic Inc)
Workday Inc
X Corp (Twitter)
Xaxis LLC
Yahoo Inc
Yandex NV
Yardi Systems Inc
Yelp Inc
YOOX Net-A-Porter Group SpA (YNAP)
Youku Tudou Inc
YouTube LLC
Zalando SE
Zappos.com LLC
Zillow Group Inc
ZipRecruiter Inc
Zoho Corporation Pvt Ltd
Zoom Video Communications Inc
Zozo Inc
Zscaler Inc
Zuora Inc
Zynga Inc

INDEX OF HEADQUARTERS LOCATION BY U.S. STATE

To help you locate the firms geographically, the city and state of the headquarters of each company are in the following index.

ALABAMA
ADTRAN Inc; Huntsville

ARIZONA
Axway Inc; Phoenix
Blue Yonder Group Inc; Scottsdale
Carvana Co; Tempe
Gen Digital Inc; Tempe
GoDaddy Inc; Tempe
Moatable Inc; Phoenix

ARKANSAS
Windstream Holdings Inc; Little Rock

CALIFORNIA
a.k.a. Brands Holding Corp; San Francisco
Adobe Inc; San Jose
Airbnb Inc; San Francisco
AKQA Inc; San Francisco
Alibris Inc; Berkeley
Alphabet Inc (Google); Mountain View
Alteryx Inc; Irvine
Anaplan Inc; San Francisco
AppDirect Inc; San Francisco
AppDynamics LLC; San Francisco
Apple Inc; Cupertino
Arista Networks Inc; Santa Clara
Asana Inc; San Francisco
Automattic Inc; San Francisco
Avaya Holdings Corp; Santa Clara
Bill.com Holdings Inc; San Jose
BlackLine Inc; Woodland Hills
Boingo Wireless Inc; Los Angeles
Box Inc; Redwood City
BroadVision Group; Redwood City
Build.com Inc; Chico
Cisco Systems Inc; San Jose
Cisco Webex; San Jose
Cloudflare Inc; San Francisco
Consensus Cloud Solutions Inc; Los Angeles
Coupa Software Incorporated; San Mateo
Crackle Plus LLC; Culver City
Craigslist Inc; San Francisco
CyberSource Corporation; Foster City
Cylance Inc; Irvine
Data.ai; San Francisco
Deem Inc; Oakland
DirecTV LLC (DIRECTV); El Segundo
DocuSign Inc; San Francisco

Dropbox Inc; San Francisco
eBay Inc; San Jose
eHarmony Inc; Los Angeles
eHealth Inc; Santa Clara
Electronic Arts Inc (EA); Redwood City
Equinix Inc; Redwood City
Eventbrite Inc; San Francisco
Everlane; San Francisco
Evernote Corporation; Redwood City
Expensify Inc; San Francisco
Fandango Inc; Beverly Hills
Fast AF Inc; San Francisco
Fastly Inc; San Francisco
Forescout Technologies Inc; San Jose
Gainsight Inc; San Francisco
GitHub Inc; San Francisco
Grove Collaborative Holdings Inc; San Francisco
Gusto; San Francisco
Harmonic Inc; San Jose
Heyday (HYDY Inc); San Francisco
Honest Company Inc (The); Santa Monica
Hotwire Inc; San Francisco
Houzz Inc; Palo Alto
Hulu LLC; Santa Monica
Illumio; Sunnyvale
Indiegogo Inc; San Francisco
Instacart (Maplebear Inc); San Francisco
Instagram; Menlo Park
Intercom Inc; San Francisco
Intuit Inc; Mountain View
Juniper Networks Inc; Sunnyvale
Le Tote Inc; San Francisco
Leaf Group Ltd; Santa Monica
Linden Research Inc (Linden Lab); San Francisco
LinkedIn Corporation; Sunnyvale
LiveRamp Holdings Inc; San Francisco
LiveWorld Inc; Campbell
Lookout Inc; San Francisco
LookSmart Group Inc; San Francisco
Lyft Inc; San Francisco
MarketWatch Inc; San Francisco
McAfee Corp; San Jose
Medallia Inc; Pleasanton
MediaPlatform Inc; North Hollywood
Meta Platforms Inc (Facebook); Menlo Park
MH Sub I LLC (dba Internet Brands); El Segundo
Mixpanel Inc; San Francisco
Move Inc; Santa Clara
MuleSoft LLC; San Francisco
Myspace LLC; Beverly Hills
Netflix Inc; Los Gatos
Netskope Inc; Santa Clara
Newegg Commerce Inc; City of Industry
Nutanix Inc; San Jose
OpenTable Inc; San Francisco
PagerDuty Inc; San Francisco
Pandora Media LLC; Oakland
Paramount Streaming; San Francisco

PayPal Holdings Inc; San Jose
Perplexity AI; San Francisco
Pinterest Inc; San Francisco
Planet Labs PBC; San Francisco
Poshmark Inc; Redwood City
Procore Technologies Inc; Carpinteria
PSI Capital Inc; Santa Monica
Quotient Technology Inc; Mountain View
Rakuten (Ebates Inc); San Mateo
Rakuten Marketing LLC; San Mateo
Reformation (LYMI Inc); Vernon
Revolve Group Inc; Cerritos
Sage Intacct Inc; San Jose
Salesforce Inc; San Francisco
Salon.com LLC; San Francisco
SAP Ariba; Palo Alto
Segment.io Inc; San Francisco
ServiceMax Inc; Pleasanton
ServiceNow Inc; Santa Clara
Shopping.com Ltd; San Jose
Shutterfly LLC; San Jose
Slack Technologies LLC; San Francisco
Snap Inc (Snapchat); Santa Monica
Stamps.com Inc; El Segundo
Stitch Fix Inc; San Francisco
Stripe Inc; San Francisco
SugarCRM Inc; Cupertino
Sumo Logic Inc; Redwood City
SurveyMonkey Inc; San Mateo
Symphony Technology Group; Menlo Park
Talkdesk Inc; San Francisco
Teespring Inc (dba SPRING); San Francisco
Teradata Corporation; San Diego
TheRealReal Inc; San Francisco
Thumbtack Inc; San Francisco
TIBCO Software Inc; Palo Alto
Tinder Inc; Los Angeles
TrueCar Inc; Santa Monica
Twilio Inc; San Francisco
Uber Technologies Inc; San Francisco
United Online Inc; Woodland Hills
US Interactive Inc; Santa Clara
WalkMe Inc; San Francisco
Walt Disney Company (The); Burbank
WhatsApp LLC; Menlo Park
Wikimedia Foundation; San Francisco
Wish.com (ContextLogic Inc); San Francisco
Workday Inc; Pleasanton
X Corp (Twitter); San Francisco
Yardi Systems Inc; Santa Barbara
Yelp Inc; San Francisco
YouTube LLC; San Bruno
ZipRecruiter Inc; Santa Monica
Zoom Video Communications Inc; San Jose
Zscaler Inc; San Jose
Zuora Inc; Redwood City
Zynga Inc; San Mateo

COLORADO
Angi Inc; Denver
Conga (Appextremes LLC); Broomfield
CoreSite an American Tower Company; Denver
Lillian Vernon Corporation; Colorado Springs
MapQuest.com Inc; Denver
Photobucket Inc; Denver
Qurate Retail Inc; Englewood
SendGrid Inc; Denver

CONNECTICUT
Booking Holdings Inc; Norwalk
Charter Communications Inc; Stamford
FactSet Research Systems Inc; Norwalk
Frontier Communications Corporation; Norwalk
Gartner Inc; Stamford
KAYAK; Stamford

DELAWARE
viagogo Entertainment Inc; Dover

DISTRICT OF COLUMBIA
Cogent Communications Group Inc; Washington
LivingSocial LLC; Washington

FLORIDA
AutoWeb Inc; Tampa
Chewy Inc (Chewy.com); Dania Beach
Cyxtera Technologies Inc; Coral Gables
Fanatics Inc; Jacksonville
MoreVisibility.com Inc; Boca Raton
MovieTickets.com Inc; Boca Raton
Newfold Digital Inc; Jacksonville
Onstream Media Corporation; Fort Lauderdale
Register.com Inc; Jacksonville
TradeStation Group Inc; Plantation
Ushahidi Inc; Orlando
VeriFone Inc; Coral Springs
Verio Inc; Jacksonville
VerticalResponse Inc; St. Petersburg
VitaCost.com Inc; Boca Raton

GEORGIA
Cox Automotive Inc; Atlanta
Cox Communications Inc; Atlanta
EarthLink LLC; Atlanta
Elavon Inc; Atlanta
Global Payments Inc; Atlanta
Internap Corporation; Atlanta
Intuit MailChimp (The Rocket Science Group LLC); Atlanta
Macquarium Inc; Atlanta
Manhattan Associates Inc; Atlanta
Total System Services LLC (TSYS); Columbus

ILLINOIS
CareerBuilder LLC; Chicago

Cars.com Inc; Chicago
CDK Global LLC; Hoffman Estates
FTD LLC; Downers Grove
Groupon Inc; Chicago
Grubhub Inc; Chicago
Life Quotes Inc; Darien
OneSpan Inc; Chicago
Orbitz LLC; Chicago
Performics Inc; Chicago
SMS Assist LLC; Chicago
Telephone and Data Systems Inc (TDS); Chicago
Westell Technologies Inc; Aurora

LOUISIANA
Lumen Technologies Inc; Monroe

MARYLAND
Ciena Corporation; Hanover

MASSACHUSETTS
Acquia Inc; Boston
Akamai Technologies Inc; Cambridge
Brightcove Inc; Cambridge
Digitas; Boston
Dynatrace Inc; Waltham
EasyAsk Technologies Inc; Bedford
Extreme Reach Inc; Dedham
Forrester Research Inc; Cambridge
Fuze Inc; Boston
Lionbridge Technologies LLC; Waltham
NaviSite LLC; Andover
NetScout Systems Inc; Westford
Progress Software Corporation; Bedford
Publicis Sapient; Boston
Temu; Boston
TripAdvisor Inc; Needham
Veracode Inc; Burlington
Wayfair LLC; Boston

MICHIGAN
Duo Security Inc; Ann Arbor
ProQuest LLC; Ann Arbor

MINNESOTA
Digital River Inc; Minnetonka
Entrust Corporation; Shakopee

MISSOURI
Hallmark Cards Inc; Kansas City
Perficient Inc; Saint Louis
Polished.com Inc; St. Louis

NEVADA
Switch Inc; Las Vegas
Zappos.com LLC; Las Vegas

NEW HAMPSHIRE
Bottomline Technologies Inc; Portsmouth

NEW JERSEY
Audible Inc; Newark
Automatic Data Processing Inc (ADP); Roseland
Corcentric Inc; Cherry Hill
D&B Hoovers; Short Hills
iCIMS Inc; Holmdel
Net2Phone Inc; Newark
Vonage Holdings Corp; Holmdel

NEW YORK
1-800-Flowers.Com Inc; Carle Place
Altice USA Inc; Long Island City
AptDeco Inc; New York
Bankrate LLC; New York
Bloomberg LP; New York
Bonobos Inc; New York
BuzzFeed Inc; New York
Datadog Inc; New York
Digg Inc; Brooklyn
DigitalOcean Inc; New York
Dotdash Meredith; New York
Dow Jones & Company Inc; New York
Eloan; New York
eMusic.com Inc; New York
Endeavor Streaming; Plainview
Etsy Inc; Brooklyn
Everyday Health Inc; New York
Flatiron Health Inc; New York
Fredericks of Hollywood; New York
FreshDirect LLC; Bronx
Freshly Inc; New York
Greenhouse Software Inc; New York
Gwynnie Bee (CaaStle Inc); New York
IAC/InterActiveCorp; New York
iCrossing Inc; New York
Infor; New York
INNOVATE Corp; New York
International Business Machines Corporation (IBM); Armonk
Intralinks Inc; New York
InVisionApp Inc; New York
Kickstarter PBC; Brooklyn
Kidpik Corp; New York
Ladders (The); New York
LivePerson Inc; New York
Major League Baseball Advanced Media LP (MLBAM); New York
MKTG Sports + Entertainment; New York
MongoDB Inc; New York
Monster Worldwide Inc; New York
Namely Inc; New York
New York Times Company (The); New York
News Corporation; New York
Optimizely Inc; New York
Rent the Runway Inc; New York

Sisense Inc; New York
Sprinklr Inc; New York
Squarespace Inc; New York
Student Advantage LLC; Ithaca
Taboola Inc; New York
TheStreet Inc; New York
Travelzoo Inc; New York
Verizon Communications Inc; New York
Vibrant Media Inc; New York
Vimeo Inc; New York
Warby Parker Inc; New York
WebMD Health Corp; New York
Xaxis LLC; New York
Yahoo Inc; New York

NORTH CAROLINA
JAGGAER; Morrisville
Red Hat Inc; Raleigh

OHIO
AG Interactive Inc; Cleveland
American Greetings Corporation LLC; Cleveland
Cincinnati Bell Inc (altafiber); Cincinnati

PENNSYLVANIA
Comcast Corporation; Philadelphia
Free People; Philadelphia

TENNESSEE
HealthStream Inc; Nashville
LifeWay Christian Resources; Nashville
Steel Connect Inc; Smyrna

TEXAS
AT&T Inc; Dallas
Avantax Inc; Dallas
BigCommerce Holdings Inc; Austin
BMC Software Inc; Houston
Charles Schwab Corporation (The); Westlake
Dell Technologies Inc; Round Rock
Embarcadero Inc; Austin
Hotels.com LP; Dallas
InsideSales; Austin
Khoros LLC; Austin
Kibo Software Inc; Dallas
Match Group Inc; Dallas
MedeAnalytics Inc; Richardson
Oracle Corporation; Austin
Oracle NetSuite; Austin
Rackspace Technology Inc; San Antonio
RealPage Inc; Richardson
Sabre Corporation; Southlake
Solo Brands Inc; Southlake
Tellabs Inc; Carrollton
Travelscape LLC (Travelocity.com); Dallas

UTAH

1-800 Contacts Inc; Draper
Ancestry.com Inc; Lehi
Authorize.net; American Fork
BackCountry.com LLC; Park City
Beyond Inc; Midvale
Domo Inc; American Fork
Health Catalyst Inc; South Jordan
Qualtrics International Inc; Provo

VIRGINIA

comScore Inc; Reston
E-Trade from Morgan Stanley; Arlington
Neustar Inc; Reston
TEGNA Inc; Tysons
VeriSign Inc; Reston

WASHINGTON

Amazon Web Services Inc (AWS); Seattle
Amazon.com Inc; Seattle
Apptio Inc; Bellevue
Avalara Inc; Seattle
Blue Nile Inc; Bellevue
CoStar Group Inc; Northwest
Expedia Group Inc; Seattle
F5 Inc; Seattle
Marchex Inc; Seattle
Microsoft Corporation; Redmond
OfferUp Inc; Bellevue
RealNetworks LLC; Seattle
Smartsheet Inc; Bellevue
T-Mobile US Inc; Bellevue
WatchGuard Technologies Inc; Seattle
Whitepages Inc; Seattle
Zillow Group Inc; Seattle

WISCONSIN

Fiserv Inc; Brookfield

INDEX OF NON-U.S. HEADQUARTERS LOCATION BY COUNTRY

ARGENTINA

MercadoLibre Inc; Buenos Aires

AUSTRALIA

Campaign Monitor Pty Ltd; Sydney
Canva Pty Ltd; Surry Hills
Princess Polly Group Pty Ltd; Gold Coast MC
REA Group Ltd; Richmond
Seek Limited; Melbourne

BRAZIL

Americanas SA; Rio de Janeiro

CANADA

AbeBooks Inc; Victoria
Critical Mass Inc; Calgary
Geocomply Solutions Inc; Vancouver
Hootsuite Inc; Vancouver
Lightspeed Commerce Inc; Montreal
Open Text Corporation; Waterloo
PoF (Plentyoffish Media ULC); Vancouver
PointClickCare; Mississauga
Rogers Communications Inc; Toronto
Shaw Communications Inc; Calgary
Shopify Inc; Ottawa
Thomson Reuters Corporation; Toronto
Tucows Inc; Toronto

CHINA

Autohome Inc; Beijing
Baidu Inc; Beijing
DiDi Global Inc; Beijing
Dingdong (Cayman) Ltd; Shanghai
Huawei Technologies Co Ltd; Shenzhen
JD.com Inc; Beijing
Meituan Dianping; Beijing
MOGU Inc; Hangzhou
NetEase Inc; Beijing
Ping An Healthcare and Technology Company Limited; Shanghai
Ruhnn Holding Limited; Hangzhou
SHEIN; Guangzhou
SINA Corporation; Shanghai
Sogou Inc; Beijing
Sohu.com Limited; Beijing
Suning.com Co Ltd; Nanjing
Tantan (Tantan Cultural Development Beijing Co Ltd); Beijing
Tencent Holdings Limited; Shenzhen
Tencent Music Entertainment Group; Shenzhen
TikTok (ByteDance Ltd); Beijing
Trip.com Group Limited; Shanghai

Tujia Online Information Technology (Beijing) Co Ltd;
Beijing
VANCL; Beijing
Vipshop Holdings Limited; Guangzhou
Youku Tudou Inc; Beijing

CYPRUS
Ozon Holdings PLC; Nicosia

FRANCE
3 Suisses; Paris
Atos SE; Bezons
Boursorama; Boulogne-Billancourt
Happn (SAS HAPPN); Paris
Sopra Steria Group SA; Paris
Veepee; Saint-Denis

GERMANY
Delivery Hero SE; Berlin
Jumia Technologies AG; Berlin
Rocket Internet SE; Berlin
SAP SE; Walldorf
trivago NV; Dusseldorf
United Internet AG; Montabaur
Zalando SE; Berlin

HONG KONG
Alibaba Group Holding Limited; Hong Kong
China Mobile Limited; Hong Kong

INDIA
Flipkart Internet Private Limited; Bengaluru, Karnataka
Infosys Limited; Bengaluru
Jio (Reliance Jio Infocomm Ltd); Ambawadi
MakeMyTrip Limited; Gurgaon
Meesho (Fashnear Technologies Private Limited);
Bengaluru
Snapdeal; Gurugram, Haryana
Tata Consultancy Services Limited (TCS); Mumbai
Wipro Limited; Bengaluru
Zoho Corporation Pvt Ltd; Vallancherry Village

IRELAND
Accenture plc; Dublin
PDD Holdings Inc; Dublin

ISRAEL
Check Point Software Technologies Ltd; Tel Aviv
MyHeritage Ltd; Or Yehuda
Radware Ltd; Tel Aviv

ITALY
Piksel Inc; Milan
YOOX Net-A-Porter Group SpA (YNAP); Milan

JAPAN
Carta Communications Inc; Tokyo
DeNA Co Ltd; Tokyo
Gree Inc; Tokyo
Internet Initiative Japan Inc; Tokyo
KDDI Corporation; Tokyo
mixi Inc; Tokyo
NTT DOCOMO Inc; Tokyo
Rakuten Inc; Tokyo
SoftBank Group Corp; Tokyo
Trend Micro Inc; Tokyo
Zozo Inc; Chiba

KOREA
Coupang Inc; Seoul
Kakao Corporation; Jeju-si Jeju-do
Naver Corporation; Bundang-gu
SK Telecom Co Ltd; Seoul

LUXEMBOURG
Skype Technologies Sarl; Luxembourg
Spotify Technology SA; Luxembourg City

MEXICO
America Movil SAB de CV; Mexico City

NORWAY
Telenor ASA; Fornebu

PUERTO RICO
Telecomunicaciones de Puerto Rico Inc; Guaynabo

RUSSIA
HeadHunter Group PLC; Moscow
Mobile TeleSystems PJSC; Moscow
VK Company Limited; Moscow

SINGAPORE
InMobi Pte Ltd; Singapore
Sea Limited; Singapore

SPAIN
Amadeus IT Group SA; Madrid

SWEDEN
Klarna Bank AB; Stockholm

SWITZERLAND
Veeam Software; Baar

THE NETHERLANDS
Adyen NV; Amsterdam
lastminute.com NV (lm group); Amsterdam
Veon Ltd; Amsterdam
Yandex NV; Shiphol

UNITED KINGDOM

ASOS plc; London
Badoo Trading Limited; London
Boohoo.com PLC; Manchester
Deliveroo plc; London
Farfetch Limited; London
Liberty Global plc; London
Ocado Group PLC; Hatfield
OneWeb Ltd; London
Paysafe Limited; London
Travelport Worldwide Limited; Berkshire
Vodafone Group plc; Newbury

Individual Profiles
On Each Of
THE E-COMMERCE 500

1-800 Contacts Inc

www.1800contacts.com

NAIC Code: 454110

TYPES OF BUSINESS:

Direct Selling-Contact Lenses & Supplies
Contact Lens Manufacturing
Optical Retail Referral
Online Sales
Contact Lens Accessories
Eyeglasses
Online Eye Exams
Ecommerce

BRANDS/DIVISIONS/AFFILIATES:

KKR & Co LP
ExpressExam
Liingo Eyewear
Boomerang

CONTACTS: *Note: Officers with more than one job title may be intentionally listed here more than once.*

John Graham, CEO
John F. Nichols, VP-Trade Rel.

GROWTH PLANS/SPECIAL FEATURES:

1-800 Contacts, Inc. is a provider of prescription contact lenses by mail, as well as other related services. The firm sells popular brands of contact lenses, including Acuvue, Air Optix, Biofinity, clarity, DAILIES, Bausch+Lomb and CooperVision and more. 1-800 Contacts' central distribution facility has an inventory of more than 15 million contacts. 1-800 Contacts offers customer service 24 hours a day, seven days a week, filling orders by phone at 1-800-CONTACTS and through the internet at 1800Contacts.com as well as via mobile app. Orders can also be placed by mail or fax. Order services include email or short message system (SMS) shipping confirmation, online order tracking and online/mobile correspondence. The firm also sells related contact lens accessories such as lens and eyecare solutions and lens cases. Additional services include ExpressExam, a free online prescription renewal process by taking an eye exam through the firm's website (but is not a comprehensive eye exam); Liingo Eyewear, offering affordable eyeglasses and sunglasses, and consumers can try five frames within five days' time at home for free; and Boomerang, offering re-lensing services. 1-800 Contacts is owned by KKR & Co. Inc.

1-800 Contacts offers its employees comprehensive health insurance, life and disability insurance, and a 401(k).

FINANCIAL DATA: *Note: Data for latest year may not have been available at press time.*

In U.S. $	2022	2021	2020	2019	2018	2017
Revenue	509,600,000	490,000,000	484,312,500	472,500,000	450,000,000	431,000,000
R&D Expense						
Operating Income						
Operating Margin %						
SGA Expense						
Net Income						
Operating Cash Flow						
Capital Expenditure						
EBITDA						
Return on Assets %						
Return on Equity %						
Debt to Equity						

CONTACT INFORMATION:

Phone: 801-924-9900   Fax: 801-924-9923
Toll-Free: 800-266-8228
Address: 261 W. Data Dr., Draper, UT 84020 United States

STOCK TICKER/OTHER:

Stock Ticker: Private   Exchange:
Employees: 1,300   Fiscal Year Ends: 12/31
Parent Company: KKR & Co LP

SALARIES/BONUSES:

Top Exec. Salary: $ Bonus: $
Second Exec. Salary: $ Bonus: $

OTHER THOUGHTS:

Estimated Female Officers or Directors:
Hot Spot for Advancement for Women/Minorities:

1-800-Flowers.Com Inc

www.1800flowers.com

NAIC Code: 454110

TYPES OF BUSINESS:

Direct Selling-Flowers
Online & Catalog Sales
Wine Distribution
Gardening Accessories
Gourmet Foods
Gifts
Retail Stores

BRANDS/DIVISIONS/AFFILIATES:

BloomNet
Fruit Bouquet
Cheryl's & Co
Popcorn Factory (The)
Harry & David
Cushman's
Moose Munch
Napco

CONTACTS: *Note: Officers with more than one job title may be intentionally listed here more than once.*

Christopher McCann, CEO
William Shea, CFO
James Mccann, Chairman of the Board
Arnold Leap, Chief Information Officer
Michael Manley, General Counsel
Steven Lightman, President, Divisional
Thomas Hartnett, President, Divisional
Dinesh Popat, President, Subsidiary

GROWTH PLANS/SPECIAL FEATURES:

1-800-Flowers.com Inc is a provider of gifts designed to help customers express, connect and celebrate. The company's e-commerce business platform features all brands, including 1-800-Flowers.com, 1-800-Baskets.com, Cheryl's Cookies, Harry and David, PersonalizationMall.com, Shari's Berries, FruitBouquets.com, Moose Munch, The Popcorn Factory, Wolferman's Bakery, Stock Yards, and Simply Chocolate. Through the Celebrations Passport loyalty program, which provides members with free standard shipping and no service charge across its portfolio of brands, the firm strives to deepen relationships with customers. The company also operates BloomNet, an international floral and gift industry service provider; Napco, a resource for floral gifts and seasonal decor; and DesignPac Gifts, LLC.

1-800-Flowers.com offers its employees a 401(k) plan, a profit-sharing plan and health coverage.

FINANCIAL DATA: *Note: Data for latest year may not have been available at press time.*

In U.S. $	2022	2021	2020	2019	2018	2017
Revenue	2,207,885,000	2,122,245,000	1,489,637,000	1,248,623,000	1,151,921,000	
R&D Expense	56,561,000	54,428,000	48,698,000	43,758,000	39,258,000	
Operating Income	42,101,000	149,087,000	80,364,000	45,108,000	41,048,000	
Operating Margin %	.02%	.07%	.05%	.04%	.04%	
SGA Expense	673,998,000	650,404,000	460,621,000	407,290,000	376,250,000	
Net Income	29,610,000	118,652,000	58,998,000	34,766,000	40,791,000	
Operating Cash Flow	5,189,000	173,290,000	139,417,000	78,100,000	58,341,000	
Capital Expenditure	66,408,000	55,219,000	34,703,000	32,560,000	33,306,000	
EBITDA	85,847,000	197,485,000	112,793,000	75,717,000	74,122,000	
Return on Assets %	.03%	.13%	.09%	.06%	.07%	
Return on Equity %	.06%	.26%	.16%	.11%	.14%	
Debt to Equity	.52%	.47%	0.374	0.268	.29%	

CONTACT INFORMATION:

Phone: 516 237-6000   Fax:
Toll-Free:
Address: One Old Country Rd., Carle Place, NY 11514 United States

STOCK TICKER/OTHER:

Stock Ticker: FLWS   Exchange: NAS
Employees: 4,200   Fiscal Year Ends: 06/30
Parent Company:

SALARIES/BONUSES:

Top Exec. Salary: $975,000   Bonus: $
Second Exec. Salary: Bonus: $
$775,000

OTHER THOUGHTS:

Estimated Female Officers or Directors: 1
Hot Spot for Advancement for Women/Minorities:

Sales, profits and employees may be estimates. Financial information, benefits and other data can change quickly and may vary from those stated here.

3 Suisses

www.3suisses.fr

NAIC Code: 454110

TYPES OF BUSINESS:

Fashion Apparel
Online Retail
Ecommerce
Fashion Apparel
Athleticwear
Handbags
Footwear
Accessories

BRANDS/DIVISIONS/AFFILIATES:

Shopinvest Group (The)

GROWTH PLANS/SPECIAL FEATURES:

3 Suisses is a designer and online retailer of high fashion apparel for men, women and children based in France. Apparel includes dresses, swimwear, blouses, shirts, sweaters, coats, pants, skirts, jackets, athleticwear, sleepwear and outerwear. Related items include shoes, jewelry, bags, scarves, belts, hats, gloves and sunglasses. Additionally, the company offers household and leisure products. Customers can place orders by phone, online or through its catalog. The firm is a subsidiary of The Shopinvest Group.

CONTACTS: *Note: Officers with more than one job title may be intentionally listed here more than once.*

Karine Schrenzel, CEO-Shopinvest
Diego du Monceau, Chmn.-3 Suisses Int'l Group
Denis Terrien, CEO-3 Suisses Int'l Group

FINANCIAL DATA: *Note: Data for latest year may not have been available at press time.*

In U.S. $	2022	2021	2020	2019	2018	2017
Revenue	2,860,000,000	2,750,000,000	3,009,825,000	3,087,000,000	2,940,000,000	2,800,000,000
R&D Expense						
Operating Income						
Operating Margin %						
SGA Expense						
Net Income						
Operating Cash Flow						
Capital Expenditure						
EBITDA						
Return on Assets %						
Return on Equity %						
Debt to Equity						

CONTACT INFORMATION:

Phone: 33-892-69-15-00   Fax:
Toll-Free:
Address: 49 Avenue Kleber, Paris, 75116 France

STOCK TICKER/OTHER:

Stock Ticker: Subsidiary   Exchange:
Employees: 2,500   Fiscal Year Ends: 12/31
Parent Company: Shopinvest Group (The)

SALARIES/BONUSES:

Top Exec. Salary: $ Bonus: $
Second Exec. Salary: $ Bonus: $

OTHER THOUGHTS:

Estimated Female Officers or Directors: 1
Hot Spot for Advancement for Women/Minorities:

a.k.a. Brands Holding Corp

www.aka-brands.com

NAIC Code: 454110

TYPES OF BUSINESS:
Online Sales, B2C Ecommerce, Sharing Economy Platforms

GROWTH PLANS/SPECIAL FEATURES:
a.k.a. Brands Holding Corp is an online fashion retailer focused on acquiring and accelerating the growth of next-generation, digitally native fashion brands targeting Gen Z and Millennial customers.

BRANDS/DIVISIONS/AFFILIATES:

CONTACTS: *Note: Officers with more than one job title may be intentionally listed here more than once.*
Ciaron Long, Interim CEO
Michael Trembley, CIO

FINANCIAL DATA: *Note: Data for latest year may not have been available at press time.*

In U.S. $	2022	2021	2020	2019	2018	2017
Revenue	611,738,000	562,191,000	215,916,000	102,440,000		
R&D Expense						
Operating Income	1,747,000	16,383,000	22,140,000	2,593,000		
Operating Margin %	.00%	.03%	.10%			
SGA Expense	335,500,000	291,281,000	104,261,000	53,272,000		
Net Income	-176,697,000	-5,968,000	14,334,000	1,394,000		
Operating Cash Flow	-319,000	23,968,000	21,712,000	511,000		
Capital Expenditure	19,993,000	8,575,000	1,779,000	1,403,000		
EBITDA	-153,223,000	20,956,000	28,746,000	8,953,000		
Return on Assets %	-.30%	-.01%	.09%			
Return on Equity %	-.51%	-.02%	.12%			
Debt to Equity	.70%	.28%	0.025			

CONTACT INFORMATION:
Phone: 415 295-6085   Fax:
Toll-Free:
Address: 100 Montgomery Street, San Francisco, CA 94104 United States

STOCK TICKER/OTHER:
Stock Ticker: AKA
Employees: 1,000
Parent Company:

Exchange: NYS
Fiscal Year Ends: 12/31

SALARIES/BONUSES:
Top Exec. Salary: $601,511   Bonus: $233,184
Second Exec. Salary: $416,155   Bonus: $105,000

OTHER THOUGHTS:
Estimated Female Officers or Directors:
Hot Spot for Advancement for Women/Minorities:

AbeBooks Inc

NAIC Code: 454110

www.abebooks.com

TYPES OF BUSINESS:

Online Book Sales
Book Inventory & Order Management
Ecommerce
Online Bookstore
Online Rare Books
Online Art and Collectibles
Websites
Book Search Engine

BRANDS/DIVISIONS/AFFILIATES:

Amazon.com Inc
Abebooks.com
Abebooks.co.uk
AbeBooks.de
AbeBooks.fr
IberLibros.com
ZVAB.com
BookFinder.com

CONTACTS: *Note: Officers with more than one job title may be intentionally listed here more than once.*

Hannes Blum, Pres.
Richard Davies, Public Relations Manager
Richard Davies, Mgr.-Public Rel. & Publicity

GROWTH PLANS/SPECIAL FEATURES:

AbeBooks, Inc., a subsidiary of Amazon.com, Inc., is one of the world's largest online marketers of new, used, out-of-print and rare books. Its website features millions of books offered through independent book dealers, who pay a monthly membership fee to sell their books through the firm's portal. The fee is based on how many books they sell. Aside from its English language websites (Abebooks.com, Abebooks.ca, AbeBooks Aus/NZ and Abebooks.co.uk), the company maintains AbeBooks.de for German language shoppers, AbeBooks.fr for French shoppers, AbeBooks.it for Italian shoppers and IberLibro.com for Spanish language books. Affiliated companies include ZVAB.com, a global marketplace for rare German books, offering millions of used, antiquarian and out-of-print books; and BookFinder.com, a price comparison shopping service dedicated to books. AbeBooks also offers art and collectibles sold by professional sellers around the world, including photographs, comics, sheet music, manuscripts, rare maps and more.

FINANCIAL DATA: *Note: Data for latest year may not have been available at press time.*

In U.S. $	2022	2021	2020	2019	2018	2017
Revenue						
R&D Expense						
Operating Income						
Operating Margin %						
SGA Expense						
Net Income						
Operating Cash Flow						
Capital Expenditure						
EBITDA						
Return on Assets %						
Return on Equity %						
Debt to Equity						

CONTACT INFORMATION:

Phone: 250-412-3258   Fax: 250-475-6014
Toll-Free:
Address: 655 Tyee Rd., Ste. 500, Victoria, BC V9A 6X5 Canada

STOCK TICKER/OTHER:

Stock Ticker: Subsidiary   Exchange:
Employees: 135   Fiscal Year Ends: 12/31
Parent Company: Amazon.com Inc

SALARIES/BONUSES:

Top Exec. Salary: $ Bonus: $
Second Exec. Salary: $ Bonus: $

OTHER THOUGHTS:

Estimated Female Officers or Directors:
Hot Spot for Advancement for Women/Minorities:

Accenture plc

www.accenture.com

NAIC Code: 541512

TYPES OF BUSINESS:

IT Consulting
Technology
Artificial Intelligence
Data
Analytics
Supply Chain Management
Cloud
Automation

BRANDS/DIVISIONS/AFFILIATES:

Zestgroup

GROWTH PLANS/SPECIAL FEATURES:

Accenture is a leading global IT-services firm that provides consulting, strategy, and technology and operational services. These services run the gamut from aiding enterprises with digital transformation to procurement services to software system integration. The company provides its IT offerings to a variety of sectors, including communications, media and technology, financial services, health and public services, consumer products, and resources. Accenture employs just under 500,000 people throughout 200 cities in 51 countries.

CONTACTS: Note: Officers with more than one job title may be intentionally listed here more than once.

Julie Sweet, CEO
Jo Deblaere, COO
KC McClure, CFO
Jill Kramer, CMO
Ellyn J. Shook, Chief Human Resources Officer
Paul R. Daugherty, CTO
Martin I. Cole, Group CEO-Tech.
Sander vant Noordende, Group CEO-Prod.
Richard Lumb, Group CEO-Financial Services
Stephen J Rohleder, Group CEO-Health & Public Service
Michael J Salvino, Group CEO-Business Process Outsourcing
Julie Spellman Sweet, General Counsel
David C. Thomlinson, Chief Oper. & Geographic Strategy Officer
Shawn Collinson, Chief Strategy Officer
Michael R. Sutcliff, Group CEO-Accenture Digital
Robert E. Sell, Group CEO-Comm., Media & Tech.
Mark A. Knickrehm, Group CEO-Accenture Strategy
Gianfranco Casati, Group CEO-Growth Markets
Adrian Lajtha, Chief Leadership Officer
Jean-Marc Ollagnier, Group CEO-Resources
Julie Sweet, Chmn.

FINANCIAL DATA: Note: Data for latest year may not have been available at press time.

In U.S. $	2022	2021	2020	2019	2018	2017
Revenue	61,594,300,000	50,533,390,000	44,327,040,000	43,215,010,000	40,992,530,000	
R&D Expense						
Operating Income	9,367,181,000	7,621,529,000	6,513,644,000	6,305,074,000	5,898,779,000	
Operating Margin %	.15%	.15%	.15%	.15%	.14%	
SGA Expense	10,334,360,000	8,742,599,000	7,462,514,000	7,009,614,000	6,594,585,000	
Net Income	6,877,169,000	5,906,809,000	5,107,839,000	4,779,112,000	4,059,907,000	
Operating Cash Flow	9,541,129,000	8,975,148,000	8,215,152,000	6,626,953,000	6,026,691,000	
Capital Expenditure	717,998,000	580,132,000	599,132,000	599,009,000	619,187,000	
EBITDA	10,554,220,000	9,711,850,000	8,580,526,000	7,167,520,000	6,754,408,000	
Return on Assets %	.15%	.15%	.15%	.18%	.17%	
Return on Equity %	.33%	.32%	.33%	.39%	.42%	
Debt to Equity	.12%	.14%	0.16	0.001	.00%	

CONTACT INFORMATION:

Phone: 353 1-646-2000   Fax:
Toll-Free:
Address: 1 Grand Canal Sq., Dublin, 2 Ireland

STOCK TICKER/OTHER:

Stock Ticker: ACN   Exchange: NYS
Employees: 733,000   Fiscal Year Ends: 08/31
Parent Company:

SALARIES/BONUSES:

Top Exec. Salary: $1,537,500   Bonus: $
Second Exec. Salary: Bonus: $
$1,100,000

OTHER THOUGHTS:

Estimated Female Officers or Directors: 6
Hot Spot for Advancement for Women/Minorities: Y

Sales, profits and employees may be estimates. Financial information, benefits and other data can change quickly and may vary from those stated here.

Acquia Inc

NAIC Code: 511210M

www.acquia.com

TYPES OF BUSINESS:

Computer Software, E-Commerce & Web Analytics
Digital Experience Software
Opensource Software Platform
Web and App Development Solutions
Cloud Integrated Development
Digital Asset Management
Customer Data Technology
Brand Expansion Solutions

BRANDS/DIVISIONS/AFFILIATES:

Vista Equity Partners Management LLC
Widen Enterprises Inc
Acquia Cloud
Site Studio
Edge CDN
Site Factory
Cloud IDE
Acquia DAM

CONTACTS: *Note: Officers with more than one job title may be intentionally listed here more than once.*

Stephen Reny, CEO
Chris Andersen, CFO
Jennifer Griffin Smith, CMO
Heather Hartford, Chief People Officer
Dries Buytaert, CTO
Chris Doggett, Chief Revenue Officer

GROWTH PLANS/SPECIAL FEATURES:

Acquia, Inc. is an opensource digital experience firm that helps brands innovate and create customer connections through its software and services. Acquia gives enterprise companies the ability to build, operate and optimize websites, apps and other digital experiences. Its products are built around the Drupal opensource web content management system and include Acquia Cloud, Site Studio, Edge CDN (content delivery network), Site Factory, Cloud IDE (integrated development environment), Acquia DAM (digital asset management), personalization, customer data platform, campaign studio and campaign factory. Widen Enterprises, Inc. is an Acquia technology company that designs, develops and provides DAM and product information management software, as well as digital asset management services. Widen helps brands simplify their digital expansion. Headquartered in Boston, Massachusetts, Acquia has domestic locations in Oregon and California, as well as international locations in Canada, the U.K., Germany, France, India, Japan, Singapore and Australia. Vista Equity Partners Management, LLC owns a majority stake in Acquia. In January 2024, the firm completed its acquisition of the Monsido platform, a website accessibility and optimization solution, from CivicPlus.

Acquia offers employee benefits, but vary per location.

FINANCIAL DATA: *Note: Data for latest year may not have been available at press time.*

In U.S. $	2022	2021	2020	2019	2018	2017
Revenue	232,814,400	223,860,000	215,250,000	210,000,000	200,000,000	175,000,000
R&D Expense						
Operating Income						
Operating Margin %						
SGA Expense						
Net Income						
Operating Cash Flow						
Capital Expenditure						
EBITDA						
Return on Assets %						
Return on Equity %						
Debt to Equity						

CONTACT INFORMATION:

Phone: 336 525-6131   Fax:
Toll-Free: 888-922-7842
Address: 53 State St., Fl. 10, Boston, MA 02109 United States

STOCK TICKER/OTHER:

Stock Ticker: Private   Exchange:
Employees: 900   Fiscal Year Ends: 12/31
Parent Company: Vista Equity Partners Management LLC

SALARIES/BONUSES:

Top Exec. Salary: $ Bonus: $
Second Exec. Salary: $ Bonus: $

OTHER THOUGHTS:

Estimated Female Officers or Directors:
Hot Spot for Advancement for Women/Minorities:

Adobe Inc

www.adobe.com

NAIC Code: 511210F

TYPES OF BUSINESS:

Computer Software, Multimedia, Graphics & Publishing
Document Management Software
Photo Editing & Management Software
Graphic Design Software
Digital Media Solutions
Marketing Solutions
Workflow Solutions
Cloud Solutions

BRANDS/DIVISIONS/AFFILIATES:

Adobe Experience Cloud
Adobe LiveCycle
Adobe Connect
Frame.io

GROWTH PLANS/SPECIAL FEATURES:

Adobe provides content creation, document management, and digital marketing and advertising software and services to creative professionals and marketers for creating, managing, delivering, measuring, optimizing and engaging with compelling content multiple operating systems, devices and media. The company operates with three segments: digital media content creation, digital experience for marketing solutions, and publishing for legacy products (less than 5% of revenue).

Adobe offers its employees comprehensive benefits.

CONTACTS: Note: Officers with more than one job title may be intentionally listed here more than once.

Shantanu Narayen, CEO
John Murphy, CFO
Mark Garfield, Chief Accounting Officer
Ann Lewnes, Chief Marketing Officer
Abhay Parasnis, Chief Technology Officer
John Warnock, Co-Founder
Scott Belsky, Executive VP, Divisional
Gloria Chen, Executive VP, Divisional
Dana Rao, Executive VP
Anil Chakravarthy, Executive VP

FINANCIAL DATA: Note: Data for latest year may not have been available at press time.

In U.S. $	2022	2021	2020	2019	2018	2017
Revenue	17,606,000,000	15,785,000,000	12,868,000,000	11,171,000,000	9,030,000,000	
R&D Expense	2,987,000,000	2,540,000,000	2,188,000,000	1,930,000,000	1,538,000,000	
Operating Income	6,098,000,000	5,802,000,000	4,237,000,000	3,268,000,000	2,840,000,000	
Operating Margin %	.35%	.37%	.33%	.29%	.31%	
SGA Expense	6,187,000,000	5,406,000,000	4,559,000,000	4,125,000,000	3,366,000,000	
Net Income	4,756,000,000	4,822,000,000	5,260,000,000	2,951,000,000	2,591,000,000	
Operating Cash Flow	7,838,000,000	7,230,000,000	5,727,000,000	4,422,000,000	4,029,000,000	
Capital Expenditure	442,000,000	348,000,000	419,000,000	395,000,000	267,000,000	
EBITDA	6,976,000,000	6,606,000,000	5,049,000,000	4,119,000,000	3,229,000,000	
Return on Assets %	.17%	.19%	.23%	.15%	.16%	
Return on Equity %	.33%	.34%	.44%	.30%	.29%	
Debt to Equity	.29%	.31%	0.348	0.094	.44%	

CONTACT INFORMATION:

Phone: 408 536-6000   Fax: 408 536-6799
Toll-Free: 800-833-6687
Address: 345 Park Ave., San Jose, CA 95110-2704 United States

STOCK TICKER/OTHER:

Stock Ticker: ADBE   Exchange: NAS
Employees: 29,945   Fiscal Year Ends: 11/30
Parent Company:

SALARIES/BONUSES:

Top Exec. Salary: $850,000   Bonus: $3,100,000
Second Exec. Salary: $750,000   Bonus: $1,666,667

OTHER THOUGHTS:

Estimated Female Officers or Directors: 5
Hot Spot for Advancement for Women/Minorities: Y

Sales, profits and employees may be estimates. Financial information, benefits and other data can change quickly and may vary from those stated here.

ADTRAN Inc

NAIC Code: 334210

www.adtran.com

TYPES OF BUSINESS:

Carrier Networks
Network Platforms
Communications Platforms
Broadband Access
Internet of Things
Cloud
Gateways
Fiber Optics

BRANDS/DIVISIONS/AFFILIATES:

GROWTH PLANS/SPECIAL FEATURES:

Adtran Inc is a provider of networking and communications platforms, software, and services focused on the broadband access market. It operates under two reportable segments: Network Solutions, which includes hardware and software products, and Services & Support, which includes a portfolio of network implementation services, support services, and cloud-hosted SaaS applications that complement the product portfolio and can be utilized to support other platforms as well. These two segments span across their three revenue categories: Access & Aggregation, Subscriber Solutions, and Optical Networking Solutions.

ADTRAN offers its employees comprehensive health benefits, life and disability insurance, flexible spending accounts and a variety of employee assistance programs and incentives.

CONTACTS: Note: Officers with more than one job title may be intentionally listed here more than once.

Thomas Stanton, CEO
Michael Foliano, CFO
Raymond Harris, Chief Information Officer
Daniel Whalen, Other Executive Officer
James Wilson, Other Executive Officer
Ronald Centis, Senior VP, Divisional
Marc Kimpe, Senior VP, Divisional

FINANCIAL DATA: Note: Data for latest year may not have been available at press time.

In U.S. $	2022	2021	2020	2019	2018	2017
Revenue	1,025,536,000	563,004,000	506,510,000	530,061,000	529,277,000	666,900,000
R&D Expense	173,757,000	108,663,000	113,287,000	126,200,000	124,547,000	130,666,000
Operating Income	-55,394,000	-14,700,000	-9,708,000	-37,321,000	-45,422,000	37,386,000
Operating Margin %	- .05%	- .03%	- .02%	- .07%	- .09%	.06%
SGA Expense	208,889,000	124,414,000	113,972,000	130,288,000	124,440,000	135,583,000
Net Income	-2,037,000	-8,635,000	2,378,000	-52,982,000	-19,342,000	23,840,000
Operating Cash Flow	-44,228,000	3,008,000	-16,518,000	-2,472,000	55,454,000	-42,379,000
Capital Expenditure	17,072,000	5,669,000	6,413,000	9,494,000	8,110,000	14,720,000
EBITDA	27,000	9,813,000	10,386,000	-6,495,000	-16,947,000	60,935,000
Return on Assets %	.00%	- .02%	.00%	- .09%	- .03%	.04%
Return on Equity %	.00%	- .02%	.01%	- .13%	- .04%	.05%
Debt to Equity	.02%	.01%			.06%	0.051

CONTACT INFORMATION:

Phone: 256 963-8000   Fax: 256 963-8004
Toll-Free: 800-923-8726
Address: 901 Explorer Blvd., Huntsville, AL 35806-2807 United States

STOCK TICKER/OTHER:

Stock Ticker: ADTN   Exchange: NAS
Employees: 3,307   Fiscal Year Ends: 12/31
Parent Company:

SALARIES/BONUSES:

Top Exec. Salary: $400,123   Bonus: $500,000
Second Exec. Salary: Bonus: $
$865,676

OTHER THOUGHTS:

Estimated Female Officers or Directors:
Hot Spot for Advancement for Women/Minorities:

Adyen NV

www.adyen.com

NAIC Code: 522320

TYPES OF BUSINESS:
Payment Processing-Intermediary
Online Electronic Payment Processing Platform

BRANDS/DIVISIONS/AFFILIATES:

GROWTH PLANS/SPECIAL FEATURES:
Adyen is a payment company that provides merchants with a single platform to accept e-commerce, mobile, and point-of-sale payments in multiple countries using various payment schemes and methodologies. Adyen started out providing only gateway and payment processing services to merchants but soon expanded into merchant acquiring services as well. Adyen obtained a banking license to improve settlement of merchant accounts.

CONTACTS:
Note: Officers with more than one job title may be intentionally listed here more than once.

Pieter Willem van der Does, CEO
Kamran Zaki, COO
Ingo Uytdehaage, CFO
Roelant Prins, CCO

FINANCIAL DATA:
Note: Data for latest year may not have been available at press time.

In U.S. $	2022	2021	2020	2019	2018	2017
Revenue	9,645,521,000	6,471,739,000	3,930,687,000	2,867,847,000	1,784,270,000	1,092,876,000
R&D Expense						
Operating Income	717,539,900	641,980,700	403,421,800	317,804,400	186,819,900	100,813,900
Operating Margin %	.07%	.10%	.10%	.11%	.10%	.09%
SGA Expense	60,049,650	39,274,610	42,759,060	34,840,240	23,013,820	15,925,090
Net Income	608,958,300	507,034,700	281,756,300	252,897,200	141,565,200	76,972,140
Operating Cash Flow	2,181,733,000	1,964,752,000	1,097,417,000	571,518,800	414,513,200	216,550,100
Capital Expenditure	106,971,100	58,663,640	23,631,260	21,544,690	14,907,170	11,905,220
EBITDA	858,716,500	678,590,200	389,845,600	347,405,000	188,862,300	106,795,100
Return on Assets %	.08%	.09%	.08%	.10%	.09%	.06%
Return on Equity %	.27%	.31%	.25%	.32%	.27%	.20%
Debt to Equity	.07%	.07%	0.097		0.059	

CONTACT INFORMATION:
Phone: 31-20-240-1660   Fax:
Toll-Free:
Address: Simon Carmiggeltstraat 6-50, Amsterdam, 1011 DJ Netherlands

STOCK TICKER/OTHER:
Stock Ticker: ADYEY   Exchange: PINX
Employees: 3,332   Fiscal Year Ends: 12/31
Parent Company:

SALARIES/BONUSES:
Top Exec. Salary: $ Bonus: $
Second Exec. Salary: $ Bonus: $

OTHER THOUGHTS:
Estimated Female Officers or Directors:
Hot Spot for Advancement for Women/Minorities:

AG Interactive Inc

www.americangreetings.com

NAIC Code: 454110

TYPES OF BUSINESS:
Online Greeting Cards
Wallpapers & Screensavers
Online Invitations
Avatars
Emoticons, Winks & Expressions
Instant Messaging Desktop Backgrounds
Mobile Wallpapers
Reminders

BRANDS/DIVISIONS/AFFILIATES:
American Greetings Corporation LLC
AmericanGreetings.com
BlueMoutain.com
justWink
SmashUps

CONTACTS: *Note: Officers with more than one job title may be intentionally listed here more than once.*
Joe Arcuri, CEO
Kathy McConaughy, Chief Creative Officer
Ned Newhouse, Sr. VP-Advertising

GROWTH PLANS/SPECIAL FEATURES:
AG Interactive, Inc. produces and distributes online greetings, photo/video sharing and customized printing services and other personalized digital content through a network of websites including AmericanGreetings.com and BlueMountain.com, as well as the justWink and SmashUps mobile apps. Customers may purchase single items or an annual subscription that allows unlimited use of the company's e-card and photo customizing services. Besides subscription fees, AG generates sales from advertising. Users can choose among several different products and services, including typical online messages, personalized cards designed to be printed on printers and customized gifts with their digital photos rendered on coffee mugs, t-shirts and other items. In addition to e-cards and gifts, AG's products include video-sharing e-cards, online avatars, active backgrounds for instant messaging desktops, screensavers and wallpapers, mobile wallpapers, an online reminders service and online invitations. Its services are produced in more than 20 languages for distribution in nearly 80 countries worldwide. AG is a subsidiary of American Greetings Corporation, LLC.

FINANCIAL DATA: *Note: Data for latest year may not have been available at press time.*

In U.S. $	2022	2021	2020	2019	2018	2017
Revenue	70,589,610	67,874,625	66,543,750	68,250,000	65,000,000	60,000,000
R&D Expense						
Operating Income						
Operating Margin %						
SGA Expense						
Net Income						
Operating Cash Flow						
Capital Expenditure						
EBITDA						
Return on Assets %						
Return on Equity %						
Debt to Equity						

CONTACT INFORMATION:
Phone: 216 252-7300   Fax:
Toll-Free: 800-711-4474
Address: One American Rd., Cleveland, OH 44145 United States

STOCK TICKER/OTHER:
Stock Ticker: Subsidiary   Exchange:
Employees: 650   Fiscal Year Ends: 02/28
Parent Company: American Greetings Corporation LLC

SALARIES/BONUSES:
Top Exec. Salary: $ Bonus: $
Second Exec. Salary: $ Bonus: $

OTHER THOUGHTS:
Estimated Female Officers or Directors: 3
Hot Spot for Advancement for Women/Minorities: Y

Airbnb Inc

NAIC Code: 561510

www.airbnb.com

TYPES OF BUSINESS:

Travel Agencies
Online Homestay Reservations
Room Rental Reservations
Tour Booking Online
Restaurant Reservations
Luxury Accommodations Booking
Insurance Protection

BRANDS/DIVISIONS/AFFILIATES:

Airbnb.com
Airbnb for Business
Airbnb Experiences
Beyond by Airbnb
Airbnb Plus
Airbnb Citizen
AirCover

CONTACTS: *Note: Officers with more than one job title may be intentionally listed here more than once.*

Brian Chesky, CEO
David Stephenson, CFO
Joseph Gebbia, Chairman, Divisional
David Bernstein, Chief Accounting Officer
Nathan Blecharczyk, Chief Strategy Officer
Aristotle Balogh, Chief Technology Officer
Catherine Powell, Other Corporate Officer

GROWTH PLANS/SPECIAL FEATURES:

Started in 2008, Airbnb is the world's largest online alternative accommodation travel agency, also offering booking services for boutique hotels and experiences. Airbnb's platform offered over 7 million active accommodation listings as of Sept. 30, 2023. Listings from the company's over 4 million hosts are spread over almost every country in the world. In the fourth quarter of 2022, 47% of revenue was from the North American region. Transaction fees for online bookings account for all its revenue.

About 41% of employees are women.

FINANCIAL DATA: *Note: Data for latest year may not have been available at press time.*

In U.S. $	2022	2021	2020	2019	2018	2017
Revenue	8,399,000,000	5,992,000,000	3,378,199,000	4,805,239,000	3,651,985,000	
R&D Expense	1,502,000,000	1,425,000,000	2,752,872,000	976,695,000	579,193,000	
Operating Income	1,891,000,000	542,000,000	-3,438,792,000	-501,543,000	18,744,000	
Operating Margin %	.23%	.09%	-1.02%	-.10%	.01%	
SGA Expense	2,466,000,000	2,022,000,000	2,310,176,000	2,318,700,000	1,580,814,000	
Net Income	1,893,000,000	-352,000,000	-4,584,716,000	-674,339,000	-16,860,000	
Operating Cash Flow	3,430,000,000	2,313,000,000	-629,732,000	222,727,000	595,557,000	
Capital Expenditure			37,371,000	125,452,000	90,624,000	
EBITDA	2,094,000,000	276,000,000	-4,384,374,000	-287,573,000	155,577,000	
Return on Assets %	.13%	-.03%	-.49%	-.09%	.00%	
Return on Equity %	.37%	-.09%	-4.38%			
Debt to Equity	.41%	.49%	0.774			

CONTACT INFORMATION:

Phone: 415-510-4027   Fax:
Toll-Free:
Address: 888 Brannan St., San Francisco, CA 94103 United States

STOCK TICKER/OTHER:

Stock Ticker: ABNB   Exchange: NAS
Employees: 6,811   Fiscal Year Ends: 12/31
Parent Company:

SALARIES/BONUSES:

Top Exec. Salary: $600,000   Bonus: $
Second Exec. Salary: Bonus: $
$600,000

OTHER THOUGHTS:

Estimated Female Officers or Directors:
Hot Spot for Advancement for Women/Minorities: Y

Akamai Technologies Inc

www.akamai.com

NAIC Code: 517311

TYPES OF BUSINESS:

Online Information Service-Streaming Content
Content Delivery Protection
Business Content Applications
Internet Protection
Security Solutions
Edge Computing
Cloud Optimization

BRANDS/DIVISIONS/AFFILIATES:

Guardicore Ltd

GROWTH PLANS/SPECIAL FEATURES:

Akamai operates a content delivery network, or CDN, which entails locating servers at the edges of networks so its customers, which store content on Akamai servers, can reach their own customers faster, more securely, and with better quality. Akamai has over 325,000 servers distributed over 4,100 points of presence in more than 1,000 cities worldwide. The firm also offers security and cloud computing for its customers, and those businesses have grown to be bigger than the legacy CDN.

Akamai offers its employees health and dental care, time off, fitness/wellness options and more.

CONTACTS: Note: Officers with more than one job title may be intentionally listed here more than once.

F. Leighton, CEO
Edward McGowan, CFO
Daniel Hesse, Chairman of the Board
Laura Howell, Chief Accounting Officer
Mani Sundaram, Chief Information Officer
Kim Salem-Jackson, Chief Marketing Officer
Robert Blumofe, Chief Technology Officer
Adam Karon, COO
Paul Joseph, Executive VP, Divisional
Aaron Ahola, Executive VP
Anthony Williams, Executive VP
Rick Mcconnell, General Manager, Divisional

FINANCIAL DATA: Note: Data for latest year may not have been available at press time.

In U.S. $	2022	2021	2020	2019	2018	2017
Revenue	3,616,654,000	3,461,223,000	3,198,149,000	2,893,617,000	2,714,474,000	2,489,035,000
R&D Expense	391,434,000	335,372,000	269,315,000	261,365,000	246,165,000	222,434,000
Operating Income	708,874,000	807,202,000	701,674,000	577,991,000	416,052,000	392,546,000
Operating Margin %	.20%	.23%	.22%	.20%	.15%	.16%
SGA Expense	986,277,000	918,977,000	966,696,000	947,545,000	982,775,000	887,977,000
Net Income	523,672,000	651,642,000	557,054,000	478,035,000	298,373,000	222,766,000
Operating Cash Flow	1,274,676,000	1,404,563,000	1,215,000,000	1,058,304,000	1,008,327,000	800,983,000
Capital Expenditure	458,302,000	545,230,000	731,872,000	562,077,000	405,741,000	414,778,000
EBITDA	1,261,853,000	1,351,185,000	1,163,591,000	1,022,519,000	820,811,000	705,344,000
Return on Assets %	.06%	.08%	.08%	.08%	.06%	.05%
Return on Equity %	.12%	.15%	.14%	.14%	.09%	.07%
Debt to Equity	.68%	.59%	0.617	0.692	.27%	0.197

CONTACT INFORMATION:

Phone: 617 444-3000   Fax:
Toll-Free: 877-425-2624
Address: 145 Broadway, Cambridge, MA 02142 United States

STOCK TICKER/OTHER:

Stock Ticker: AKAM   Exchange: NAS
Employees: 9,800   Fiscal Year Ends: 12/31
Parent Company:

SALARIES/BONUSES:

Top Exec. Salary: $550,000   Bonus: $
Second Exec. Salary: Bonus: $
$515,000

OTHER THOUGHTS:

Estimated Female Officers or Directors: 4
Hot Spot for Advancement for Women/Minorities: Y

AKQA Inc

www.akqa.com

NAIC Code: 541810E

TYPES OF BUSINESS:

Online Marketing
Email Marketing
Website Design
Website Hosting
Digital Creation Services
Online Interactive Advertising Services
Digital Innovation and Design
Software and Analytics

BRANDS/DIVISIONS/AFFILIATES:

WPP plc
AKQA Bloom
Aleph
Made Thought
MAP Project Office
Grey
ArcTouch
Universal

CONTACTS: Note: Officers with more than one job title may be intentionally listed here more than once.

Tesa Aragones, Pres.
Stuart Sproule, Managing Dir.

GROWTH PLANS/SPECIAL FEATURES:

AKQA, Inc. is an agency specializing in creating digital services and products. The company creates websites, conducts email marketing campaigns and produces online interactive advertising. Additionally, the firm offers website hosting services. AKQA's digital innovation and service is recognized worldwide for its design and delivery of iconic digital products. Its social media team provides a sustained, integrated, managed and measurable ecosystem that is guided by its clients' commercial requirements and new opportunities, across multiple channels and platforms. AKQA's data science team delivers solutions to complex and challenging client requirements, offering advanced algorithm, analytic, software and technological expertise. The company's engineering approach delivers digital ecosystems that improve performance and is motivated by engineering frictionless solutions. Companies and brands within AKQA's global network include AKQA Bloom, Aleph, ArcTouch, Grey, Made Thought, MAP Project Office and Universal. Clients have included Rolls-Royce, Nike, Google, Tidal x Usher, Starbucks, Jordan and Verizon. AKQA has offices worldwide, has won more than 80 Agency of the Year awards and operates as a subsidiary of WPP plc.

FINANCIAL DATA: Note: Data for latest year may not have been available at press time.

In U.S. $	2022	2021	2020	2019	2018	2017
Revenue	800,000,000	780,000,000	766,080,000	798,000,000	760,000,000	731,000,000
R&D Expense						
Operating Income						
Operating Margin %						
SGA Expense						
Net Income						
Operating Cash Flow						
Capital Expenditure						
EBITDA						
Return on Assets %						
Return on Equity %						
Debt to Equity						

CONTACT INFORMATION:

Phone: 415-645-9400   Fax: 415-645-9420
Toll-Free:
Address: 360 Third St., Fl. 5, San Francisco, CA 94107 United States

STOCK TICKER/OTHER:

Stock Ticker: Subsidiary   Exchange:
Employees: 2,200   Fiscal Year Ends: 12/31
Parent Company: WPP plc

SALARIES/BONUSES:

Top Exec. Salary: $ Bonus: $
Second Exec. Salary: $ Bonus: $

OTHER THOUGHTS:

Estimated Female Officers or Directors:
Hot Spot for Advancement for Women/Minorities:

Alibaba Group Holding Limited www.alibabagroup.com/en/global/home
NAIC Code: 519130

TYPES OF BUSINESS:
Internet Publishing and Broadcasting and Web Search Portals
Internet Platforms
Ecommerce
Online Payment Solutions
Cloud Computing
Business-to-Consumer Solutions

BRANDS/DIVISIONS/AFFILIATES:
Taobao Marketplace (Taobao.com)
Tmall.com
Freshippo
AliExpress
Lazada
Ele.me
Youku
DingTalk

CONTACTS: Note: Officers with more than one job title may be intentionally listed here more than once.
Daniel Zhang, CEO
J. Michael Evans, Pres.
Maggie Wu, CFO
Chris Tung, CMO
Judy Tong, Chief People Officer
Li Cheng, CTO
Polo Shao, Group Sec.
Zeng Ming, Chief Strategy Officer
Joe Tsai, Vice-Chmn.
Lucy Peng, CEO-Small & Micro Financial Svcs. Group
Leo Jiang, Sr. VP
Zhang Yu, VP
Daniel Zhang, Chmn.

GROWTH PLANS/SPECIAL FEATURES:
Alibaba is the world's largest online and mobile commerce company as measured by gross merchandise volume. It operates China's online marketplaces, including Taobao (consumer-to-consumer) and Tmall (business-to-consumer). The China commerce retail division is the most valuable cash-flow-generating business at Alibaba. Additional revenue sources include China commerce wholesale, international commerce retail/wholesale, local consumer services, cloud computing, digital media and entertainment platforms, Cainiao logistics services, and innovation initiatives/other.

FINANCIAL DATA: Note: Data for latest year may not have been available at press time.

In U.S. $	2022	2021	2020	2019	2018	2017
Revenue	117,309,400,000	98,638,450,000	70,093,230,000	51,821,940,000	34,415,480,000	
R&D Expense	7,627,305,000	7,870,845,000	5,924,173,000	5,147,898,000	3,129,031,000	
Operating Income	13,033,590,000	12,332,130,000	12,652,260,000	7,849,942,000	9,676,013,000	
Operating Margin %	.11%	.13%	.18%	.15%	.28%	
SGA Expense	20,864,010,000	18,804,300,000	10,845,860,000	8,892,999,000	5,987,431,000	
Net Income	8,560,211,000	20,706,830,000	20,549,370,000	12,085,700,000	8,813,789,000	
Operating Cash Flow	19,631,600,000	31,874,200,000	24,836,280,000	20,761,420,000	17,300,150,000	
Capital Expenditure	7,332,884,000	5,938,613,000	6,241,284,000	6,826,689,000	4,102,916,000	
EBITDA	17,633,080,000	29,973,320,000	29,463,000,000	19,044,680,000	17,325,460,000	
Return on Assets %	.04%	.10%	.13%	.10%	.10%	
Return on Equity %	.07%	.18%	.24%	.20%	.20%	
Debt to Equity	.17%	.17%	0.184	0.227	.33%	

CONTACT INFORMATION:
Phone: 852 2215-5100   Fax:
Toll-Free:
Address: Fl. 26, Tower One, 1 Matheson St., Causeway Bay, Hong Kong, Hong Kong 999077 Hong Kong

STOCK TICKER/OTHER:
Stock Ticker: BABA   Exchange: NYS
Employees: 235,216   Fiscal Year Ends: 03/31
Parent Company:

SALARIES/BONUSES:
Top Exec. Salary: $ Bonus: $
Second Exec. Salary: $ Bonus: $

OTHER THOUGHTS:
Estimated Female Officers or Directors: 4
Hot Spot for Advancement for Women/Minorities: Y

Alibris Inc

NAIC Code: 454110

www.alibris.com

TYPES OF BUSINESS:

Online Bookseller-Rare & Used
Business-to-Business Services
Rare Manuscripts & Prints
Online Retailer-DVDs & CDs
Ecommerce
Online Bookstore
Online Music Store

BRANDS/DIVISIONS/AFFILIATES:

Alibris for Libraries
Alibris UK

CONTACTS: *Note: Officers with more than one job title may be intentionally listed here more than once.*

Anindo Dey, CEO
Erich Heston, CFO

GROWTH PLANS/SPECIAL FEATURES:

Alibris, Inc. provides an online marketplace for independent sellers of new, used and hard-to-find books, music, video games and movies. The firm provides bookstores, online booksellers, libraries and consumers in the U.S. and the U.K. with out-of-print, used, foreign-language and rare and collectible materials. The Alibris website contains a database of millions of books and textbooks, manuscripts, movies, music and eBooks from thousands of sellers worldwide. If a product is not currently being sold in the marketplace, customers can submit a Book Fetch request, and the company will email them when the product is available. Students also have the option to rent textbooks for up to 90% off the purchase price. In addition, the company offers the Alibris for Libraries Service, which offers libraries one-stop search and acquisition solutions as well as acceptance of purchase orders, free search services, want list matching and consolidated shipping services. The firm has partnerships with a number of major retail companies, including Amazon.com, Barnes & Noble, Chapters/Indigo (Canada) and Waterstone's (UK). The program allows anyone to sell their new and used books, used textbooks, DVDs and CDs and video games, as well as rare and out-of-print books across Alibris's network of sales channels. Alibris operates in Europe through Alibris U.K.

FINANCIAL DATA: *Note: Data for latest year may not have been available at press time.*

In U.S. $	2022	2021	2020	2019	2018	2017
Revenue	211,120,000	203,000,000	123,480,000	154,350,000	147,000,000	140,000,000
R&D Expense						
Operating Income						
Operating Margin %						
SGA Expense						
Net Income						
Operating Cash Flow						
Capital Expenditure						
EBITDA						
Return on Assets %						
Return on Equity %						
Debt to Equity						

CONTACT INFORMATION:

Phone: 510-594-4500   Fax:
Toll-Free:
Address: 2560 9th St., Ste. 215, Berkeley, CA 94710-2565 United States

STOCK TICKER/OTHER:

Stock Ticker: Private   Exchange:
Employees: 120   Fiscal Year Ends: 12/31
Parent Company:

SALARIES/BONUSES:

Top Exec. Salary: $ Bonus: $
Second Exec. Salary: $ Bonus: $

OTHER THOUGHTS:

Estimated Female Officers or Directors:
Hot Spot for Advancement for Women/Minorities: Y

Alphabet Inc (Google)

NAIC Code: 519130

TYPES OF BUSINESS:

Search Engine-Internet
Paid Search Listing Advertising Services
Online Software and Productivity Tools
Online Video and Photo Services
Travel Booking
Web Analytical Tools
Venture Capital
Online Ad Exchanges

BRANDS/DIVISIONS/AFFILIATES:

Google LLC
Android
YouTube
GooglePlay
Gmail
Google Ad Manager
AdSense
AdMob

CONTACTS: *Note: Officers with more than one job title may be intentionally listed here more than once.*

Sundar Pichai, CEO
Ruth Porat, CFO
John Hennessy, Chairman of the Board
Amie OToole, Chief Accounting Officer
Sergey Brin, Co-Founder
Larry Page, Co-Founder
Kent Walker, Other Executive Officer
Philipp Schindler, Other Executive Officer
Prabhakar Raghavan, Senior VP, Subsidiary

GROWTH PLANS/SPECIAL FEATURES:

Alphabet is a holding company. Internet media giant Google is a wholly owned subsidiary. Google generates 99% of Alphabet revenue, of which more than 85% is from online ads. Google's other revenue is from sales of apps and content on Google Play and YouTube, as well as cloud service fees and other licensing revenue. Sales of hardware such as Chromebooks, the Pixel smartphone, and smart home products, which include Nest and Google Home, also contribute to other revenue. Alphabet's moonshot investments are in its other bets segment, where it bets on technology to enhance health (Verily), provide faster internet access (Google Fiber), enable self-driving cars (Waymo), and more.

FINANCIAL DATA: *Note: Data for latest year may not have been available at press time.*

In U.S. $	2022	2021	2020	2019	2018	2017
Revenue	282,836,000,000	257,637,000,000	182,527,000,000	161,857,000,000	136,819,000,000	
R&D Expense	39,500,000,000	31,562,000,000	27,573,000,000	26,018,000,000	21,419,000,000	
Operating Income	74,842,000,000	78,714,000,000	41,224,000,000	35,928,000,000	32,595,000,000	
Operating Margin %	.26%	.31%	.23%	.22%	.24%	
SGA Expense	42,291,000,000	36,422,000,000	28,998,000,000	28,015,000,000	23,256,000,000	
Net Income	59,972,000,000	76,033,000,000	40,269,000,000	34,343,000,000	30,736,000,000	
Operating Cash Flow	91,495,000,000	91,652,000,000	65,124,000,000	54,520,000,000	47,971,000,000	
Capital Expenditure	31,485,000,000	24,640,000,000	22,281,000,000	23,548,000,000	25,139,000,000	
EBITDA	85,160,000,000	103,521,000,000	61,914,000,000	51,506,000,000	44,062,000,000	
Return on Assets %	.17%	.22%	.14%	.14%	.14%	
Return on Equity %	.24%	.32%	.19%	.18%	.19%	
Debt to Equity	.11%	.10%	0.113	0.073	.02%	

CONTACT INFORMATION:

Phone: 650 253-0000   Fax: 650 253-0001
Toll-Free:
Address: 1600 Amphitheatre Pkwy., Mountain View, CA 94043 United States

STOCK TICKER/OTHER:

Stock Ticker: GOOGL   Exchange: NAS
Employees: 18,502   Fiscal Year Ends: 12/31
Parent Company:

SALARIES/BONUSES:

Top Exec. Salary: $2,000,000   Bonus: $
Second Exec. Salary: $1,000,000   Bonus: $

OTHER THOUGHTS:

Estimated Female Officers or Directors: 3
Hot Spot for Advancement for Women/Minorities: Y

Alteryx Inc

www.alteryx.com

NAIC Code: 511210H

TYPES OF BUSINESS:
Computer Software, Business Management & ERP
Advanced Analytics Software
Machine Learning
Artificial Intelligence
Cloud

BRANDS/DIVISIONS/AFFILIATES:
Alteryx Designer
Alteryx Server
Alteryx Connect
Alteryx Promote
Alteryx Analytics Gallery
Alteryx Community
Alteryx Intelligence Suite

CONTACTS: Note: Officers with more than one job title may be intentionally listed here more than once.
Mark Anderson, CEO
Kevin Rubin, CFO
Dean Stoecker, Chairman of the Board
Christopher Lal, Chief Legal Officer
Sharmila Mulligan, Chief Marketing Officer
Olivia Adams, Co-Founder
Scott Davidson, COO
Dean Darwin, Other Corporate Officer
Suresh Vittal, Other Executive Officer

GROWTH PLANS/SPECIAL FEATURES:
Alteryx Inc is a software company that provides self-service data analytics software. Alteryx delivers easy end-to-end automation of data engineering, analytics, reporting, machine learning, and data science processes, enabling enterprises everywhere to democratize data analytics across their organizations for a broad range of use cases. The company generates its revenue from the sale of a subscription-based software platform.

FINANCIAL DATA: Note: Data for latest year may not have been available at press time.

In U.S. $	2022	2021	2020	2019	2018	2017
Revenue	855,000,000	536,000,000	495,308,000	417,910,000	253,570,000	
R&D Expense	221,000,000	132,000,000	101,117,000	69,100,000	43,449,000	
Operating Income	-258,000,000	-136,000,000	-3,907,000	37,981,000	29,770,000	
Operating Margin %	-.30%	-.25%	-.01%	.09%	.12%	
SGA Expense	774,000,000	484,000,000	354,259,000	271,678,000	157,551,000	
Net Income	-319,000,000	-180,000,000	-24,374,000	27,143,000	28,020,000	
Operating Cash Flow	-105,000,000	63,000,000	74,782,000	34,192,000	26,089,000	
Capital Expenditure	36,000,000	33,000,000	26,358,000	11,453,000	6,728,000	
EBITDA	-268,000,000	-122,000,000	22,575,000	36,200,000	38,030,000	
Return on Assets %	-.20%	-.12%	-.02%	.03%	.06%	
Return on Equity %	-1.11%	-.41%	-.05%	.07%	.12%	
Debt to Equity	4.92%	1.90%	1.492	1.552	.58%	

CONTACT INFORMATION:
Phone: 888-836-4274   Fax: 714-516-2410
Toll-Free:
Address: 3345 Michelson Dr., Ste. 400, Irvine, CA 92612 United States

STOCK TICKER/OTHER:
Stock Ticker: AYX   Exchange: NYS
Employees: 2,900   Fiscal Year Ends: 12/31
Parent Company:

SALARIES/BONUSES:
Top Exec. Salary: $650,000   Bonus: $
Second Exec. Salary: Bonus: $
$541,667

OTHER THOUGHTS:
Estimated Female Officers or Directors:
Hot Spot for Advancement for Women/Minorities:

Altice USA Inc

NAIC Code: 517311

www.alticeusa.com

TYPES OF BUSINESS:

Cable Television Service
Professional Sports Teams
Television Programming
Communications Services
Movie Theatres
Voice Over Internet Protocol
High-Speed Internet

BRANDS/DIVISIONS/AFFILIATES:

Optimum
Suddenlink
Altice Mobile
News 12 Networks
Cheddar
i24NEWS
a4
New York Interconnect

GROWTH PLANS/SPECIAL FEATURES:

Altice Europe acquired privately held U.S. cable company Suddenlink in 2015 and Cablevision in 2016. Suddenlink's networks provide television, internet access, and phone services to roughly 3.5 million U.S. homes and businesses located primarily in smaller markets, with major clusters in Texas, West Virginia, Idaho, Arizona, and Louisiana. Cablevision provides comparable services to about 5.5 million homes and business in the New York City metro area. Both regions operate under the Optimum brand name. Altice Europe spun off Altice USA, which includes both the Suddenlink and Cablevision operations, to shareholders in 2018. Altice USA also owns News 12 Networks, which broadcasts local news in New York and i24News, a news operation focused on the Middle East.

CONTACTS: Note: Officers with more than one job title may be intentionally listed here more than once.

Dexter Goei, CEO
Michael Grau, CFO
Patrick Drahi, Chairman of the Board
Layth Taki, Chief Accounting Officer
Colleen Schmidt, Executive VP, Divisional
Michael Olsen, Executive VP

FINANCIAL DATA: Note: Data for latest year may not have been available at press time.

In U.S. $	2022	2021	2020	2019	2018	2017
Revenue	9,647,659,000	10,090,850,000	9,894,642,000	9,760,859,000	9,566,608,000	
R&D Expense						
Operating Income	1,932,879,000	2,541,803,000	2,206,362,000	1,896,789,000	1,720,927,000	
Operating Margin %	.20%	.25%	.22%	.19%	.18%	
SGA Expense						
Net Income	194,563,000	990,311,000	436,183,000	138,936,000	18,833,000	
Operating Cash Flow	2,366,901,000	2,854,078,000	2,980,164,000	2,554,169,000	2,508,317,000	
Capital Expenditure	1,914,282,000	1,231,715,000	1,073,955,000	1,355,350,000	1,153,589,000	
EBITDA	3,622,038,000	4,359,650,000	4,019,127,000	3,986,832,000	3,920,560,000	
Return on Assets %	.01%	.03%	.01%	.00%	.00%	
Return on Equity %			.77%	.05%	.00%	
Debt to Equity				10.801	6.17%	

CONTACT INFORMATION:

Phone: 516 803-2300   Fax: 516 803-2273
Toll-Free:
Address: 1 Court Square West, Long Island City, NY 11101 United States

STOCK TICKER/OTHER:

Stock Ticker: ATUS
Employees: 11,000
Parent Company: Next Alt Sarl

Exchange: NYS
Fiscal Year Ends: 12/31

SALARIES/BONUSES:

Top Exec. Salary: $680,769   Bonus: $
Second Exec. Salary: $400,000   Bonus: $

OTHER THOUGHTS:

Estimated Female Officers or Directors: 4
Hot Spot for Advancement for Women/Minorities: Y

Amadeus IT Group SA

www.amadeus.com

NAIC Code: 561599

TYPES OF BUSINESS:
Reservation Services
Online Travel Services
Corporate Travel Software-Hosted

GROWTH PLANS/SPECIAL FEATURES:
Among the top three operators, Amadeus' 40%-plus market share in air global distribution system bookings is the largest in the industry. The GDS segment represented 56% of total pre-pandemic sales in 2019. The company has a growing IT solutions division (44% of 2019 revenue) that addresses the airline, airport, rail, hotel, and business intelligence markets. Transaction fees, which are tied to volume and not price, account for the bulk of sales and profits.

BRANDS/DIVISIONS/AFFILIATES:
Amadeus Altea Suite
Altea Reservation
Altea Inventory
Altea Departure Control
Altea eCommerce
Amadeus.net
CheckMyTrip.com
Amadeus IT Holding SA

CONTACTS: Note: Officers with more than one job title may be intentionally listed here more than once.
Luis Maroto, CEO
Till Streichert, CFO
Herve Couturier, Exec. VP-R&D
Christophe Bousquet, CTO
Denis Lacroix, VP-Product Dev. & Sales
Tomas Lopez Fernebrand, General Counsel
Eberhard Haag, Exec. VP-Global Oper.
Alex Luzarraga, VP-Corp. Strategy
Denis Lacroix, VP-e-commerce Platforms
Francisco Perez-Lozao Ruter, Sr. VP-New Bus.
Julia Sattel, VP-Airline IT
Claude Giafferri, VP
Petra Euler, Managing Dir.- Amadeus Germany
Jose Antonio Tazon Garcia, Chmn.
David Brett, Pres., Amadeus Asia Pacific
Holger Taubmann, Sr. VP-Dist.

FINANCIAL DATA: Note: Data for latest year may not have been available at press time.

In U.S. $	2022	2021	2020	2019	2018	2017
Revenue	4,842,292,000	2,882,124,000	2,346,718,000	6,012,630,000	5,327,828,000	5,005,613,000
R&D Expense						
Operating Income	1,039,184,000	-89,594,120	-832,038,000	1,592,616,000	1,503,454,000	1,422,712,000
Operating Margin %		- .03%	- .35%	.26%	.28%	.28%
SGA Expense						
Net Income	717,508,600	-153,713,300	-675,086,300	1,201,533,000	1,082,038,000	1,082,362,000
Operating Cash Flow	1,555,268,000	686,852,400	35,621,760	1,945,164,000	1,863,774,000	1,680,699,000
Capital Expenditure	611,722,800	496,761,600	541,342,800	794,581,100	775,259,000	660,729,700
EBITDA	1,765,112,000	621,653,700	31,411,920	2,399,395,000	2,169,473,000	2,003,886,000
Return on Assets %		- .01%	- .06%	.11%	.11%	.13%
Return on Equity %		- .04%	- .17%	.32%	.35%	.37%
Debt to Equity		1.16%	1.16	0.616	.91%	0.668

CONTACT INFORMATION:
Phone: 34 915820100   Fax: 34 915820188
Toll-Free:
Address: Salvador de Madariaga, 1, Madrid, 28027 Spain

STOCK TICKER/OTHER:
Stock Ticker: AMADY   Exchange: PINX
Employees: 17,070   Fiscal Year Ends: 12/31
Parent Company:

SALARIES/BONUSES:
Top Exec. Salary: $ Bonus: $
Second Exec. Salary: $ Bonus: $

OTHER THOUGHTS:
Estimated Female Officers or Directors: 4
Hot Spot for Advancement for Women/Minorities: Y

Amazon Web Services Inc (AWS)

www.aws.amazon.com

NAIC Code: 517311

TYPES OF BUSINESS:

Cloud Computing Services
Cloud Software
Cloud Computing Services
Database Storage
Cloud Applications
Internet Solutions
Virtual Servers
Machine Learning

BRANDS/DIVISIONS/AFFILIATES:

Amazon.com Inc
Amazon EC2
Amazon Simple Storage Service
Amazon Aurora
Amazon DynamoDB
Amazon RDS
Amazon VPC
Amazon Lightsail

CONTACTS: *Note: Officers with more than one job title may be intentionally listed here more than once.*

Adam Selipsky, CEO

GROWTH PLANS/SPECIAL FEATURES:

Amazon Web Services, Inc. (AWS) is a business unit within Amazon.com, Inc. that offers a suite of cloud-computing services. Cloud computing is the on-demand delivery of computer power, database storage, applications and other IT resources through a cloud services platform via the internet. AWS' platform offers more than 200 fully featured services, which operate from strategically located data centers worldwide, including North America, South America, Europe, and Asia Pacific. AWS' services help clients build applications with increased flexibility, scalability and reliability. Solutions by industry include advertising/marketing, aerospace/satellite, automotive, consumer packaged goods, education, energy, financial services, game technology, government, health care, life sciences, industrial, manufacturing, media/entertainment, nonprofit, power/utilities, retail, semiconductor, sports, sustainability, telecommunications, and travel/hospitality. Featured services by AWS include Amazon EC2 virtual servers in the cloud, Amazon Simple Storage Service for storage in the cloud, Amazon Aurora for a high-performance managed relational database, Amazon DynamoDB for a managed NoSQL database, Amazon RDS for a managed relational database service for MySQL and other servers, AWS Lambda for a run code, Amazon VPC for isolated cloud resources, Amazon LightSail for launching and managing virtual private servers, and Amazon SageMaker for building and deploying machine learning and Internet of Things (IoT) models at scale. AWS offers price options without long-term contracts, as well as free short-term offers.

FINANCIAL DATA: *Note: Data for latest year may not have been available at press time.*

In U.S. $	2022	2021	2020	2019	2018	2017
Revenue	80,096,000,000	62,200,000,000	45,370,000,000	35,026,000,000	25,655,000,000	17,459,000,000
R&D Expense						
Operating Income						
Operating Margin %						
SGA Expense						
Net Income	22,841,000,000	18,532,000,000	13,531,000,000	9,201,000,000	7,296,000,000	4,331,000,000
Operating Cash Flow						
Capital Expenditure						
EBITDA						
Return on Assets %						
Return on Equity %						
Debt to Equity						

CONTACT INFORMATION:

Phone: 206 266-1000   Fax:
Toll-Free:
Address: 410 Terry Ave. N., Seattle, WA 98109 United States

STOCK TICKER/OTHER:

Stock Ticker: Subsidiary   Exchange:
Employees: Fiscal Year Ends: 12/31
Parent Company: Amazon.com Inc

SALARIES/BONUSES:

Top Exec. Salary: $ Bonus: $
Second Exec. Salary: $ Bonus: $

OTHER THOUGHTS:

Estimated Female Officers or Directors:
Hot Spot for Advancement for Women/Minorities:

Amazon.com Inc

www.amazon.com

NAIC Code: 454110

TYPES OF BUSINESS:

Online Retailing and Related Services
Robotics and Automation
Cloud Computing Services
Logistics Services
Retail Supermarkets & Grocery Delivery
Department Stores
Convenience Stores
E-Commerce Support & Hosting

BRANDS/DIVISIONS/AFFILIATES:

Amazon Web Services (AWS)
Amazon Marketplace
Amazon Prime
Echo
Whole Foods Market
Amazon Go
Amazon Fresh
Kindle Direct Publishing

CONTACTS: Note: Officers with more than one job title may be intentionally listed here more than once.

David Clark, CEO, Divisional
Andrew Jassy, CEO
Brian Olsavsky, CFO
Jeffrey Bezos, Chairman of the Board
Shelley Reynolds, Chief Accounting Officer
David Zapolsky, General Counsel
Jeffrey Blackburn, On Leave

GROWTH PLANS/SPECIAL FEATURES:

Amazon is a leading online retailer and one of the highest-grossing e-commerce aggregators, with $386 billion in net sales and approximately $578 billion in estimated physical/digital online gross merchandise volume in 2021. Retail-related revenue represents approximately 80% of the total, followed by Amazon Web Services' cloud computing, storage, database, and other offerings (10%-15%), advertising services (5%), and other. International segments constitute 25%-30% of Amazon's non-AWS sales, led by Germany, the United Kingdom, and Japan.

Qualified employees receive generous medical and drugs coverage, dental and vision benefits. A 401(k) savings plan, stock incentives, disability insurance, flexible spending accounts, legal services, family care benefits and a 10% Amazon merchandise disco

FINANCIAL DATA: Note: Data for latest year may not have been available at press time.

In U.S. $	2022	2021	2020	2019	2018	2017
Revenue	513,983,000,000	469,822,000,000	386,064,000,000	280,522,000,000	232,887,000,000	
R&D Expense						
Operating Income	12,248,000,000	24,879,000,000	22,899,000,000	14,541,000,000	12,421,000,000	
Operating Margin %	.02%	.05%	.06%	.05%	.05%	
SGA Expense	54,129,000,000	41,374,000,000	28,676,000,000	24,081,000,000	18,150,000,000	
Net Income	-2,722,000,000	33,364,000,000	21,331,000,000	11,588,000,000	10,073,000,000	
Operating Cash Flow	46,752,000,000	46,327,000,000	66,064,000,000	38,514,000,000	30,723,000,000	
Capital Expenditure	63,645,000,000	61,053,000,000	40,140,000,000	16,861,000,000	13,427,000,000	
EBITDA	38,352,000,000	74,393,000,000	51,076,000,000	37,365,000,000	28,019,000,000	
Return on Assets %	-.01%	.09%	.08%	.06%	.07%	
Return on Equity %	-.02%	.29%	.27%	.22%	.28%	
Debt to Equity	.96%	.84%	0.903	1.018	.76%	

CONTACT INFORMATION:

Phone: 206 266-1000   Fax:
Toll-Free:
Address: 410 Terry Ave. N., Seattle, WA 98109 United States

STOCK TICKER/OTHER:

Stock Ticker: AMZN   Exchange: NAS
Employees: 1,525,000   Fiscal Year Ends: 12/31
Parent Company:

SALARIES/BONUSES:

Top Exec. Salary: $317,500   Bonus: $
Second Exec. Salary: Bonus: $
$317,500

OTHER THOUGHTS:

Estimated Female Officers or Directors: 3
Hot Spot for Advancement for Women/Minorities: Y

America Movil SAB de CV

www.americamovil.com

NAIC Code: 517312

TYPES OF BUSINESS:

Wireless Telecommunications Carriers (except Satellite)
Wireless Internet
Local & Long Distance
Satellite & Cable TV

BRANDS/DIVISIONS/AFFILIATES:

Telcel
Telmex
Claro
TracFone
A1
Straight Talk
KPN

GROWTH PLANS/SPECIAL FEATURES:

America Movil is the largest telecom carrier in Latin America, serving about 285 million wireless customers across the region. It also provides fixed-line phone, internet access, and television services in most of the countries it serves. Mexico is the firm's largest market, providing about 35% of service revenue. Movil dominates the Mexican wireless market with more than 60% customer share and also serves about half of fixed-line internet access customers in the country. Brazil, its second most important market, provides about 20% of service revenue. Movil sold its low-margin wireless resale business in the U.S. to Verizon in 2021 and now owns a 1.4% stake in the U.S. telecom giant. The firm also holds a 58% stake in Telekom Austria and a 15% stake in Dutch carrier KPN.

CONTACTS:
Note: Officers with more than one job title may be intentionally listed here more than once.

Daniel Hajj Aboumrad, CEO
Carlos Garcia Moreno Elizondo, CFO
Patric Slim Domit, Vice Chmn.
Alejandro Cantu Jimenez, General Counsel
Salvador Cortes Gomez, COO-Mexico
Fernando Ocampo Carapia, CFO-Mexico
Juan Antonio Aguilar, CEO-Central America
Enrique Luna Roshard, CFO-Central America
Juan Carlos Archila Cabal, CEO-Colombia
Fernando Gonzalez Apango, CFO-Colombia
Carlos Slim Domit, Chmn.

FINANCIAL DATA:
Note: Data for latest year may not have been available at press time.

In U.S. $	2022	2021	2020	2019	2018	2017
Revenue	49,167,290,000	48,363,040,000	47,472,940,000	49,573,790,000	60,444,970,000	59,480,010,000
R&D Expense						
Operating Income	9,948,180,000	9,755,209,000	8,663,955,000	8,372,008,000	8,125,088,000	5,830,393,000
Operating Margin %		.19%	.17%	.17%	.13%	.10%
SGA Expense	10,447,900,000	10,105,900,000	10,724,590,000	11,382,570,000	13,227,260,000	14,009,860,000
Net Income	4,434,038,000	11,202,970,000	2,727,782,000	3,943,326,000	3,060,430,000	1,707,370,000
Operating Cash Flow	13,116,320,000	15,031,460,000	16,349,920,000	13,639,810,000	14,457,930,000	12,678,820,000
Capital Expenditure	9,190,337,000	8,907,259,000	7,344,098,000	8,837,703,000	8,839,134,000	7,960,121,000
EBITDA	20,098,600,000	18,044,880,000	14,927,220,000	18,366,970,000	17,290,440,000	14,841,810,000
Return on Assets %		.12%	.03%	.05%	.04%	.02%
Return on Equity %		.60%	.22%	.36%	.27%	.15%
Debt to Equity		1.26%	2.254	3.315	2.77%	3.328

CONTACT INFORMATION:

Phone: 52 55-2581-4449   Fax: 52-55-2581-4422
Toll-Free:
Address: Lago Zurich 245, Colonia Granada, Ampliacion, Mexico City, DF 11529 Mexico

STOCK TICKER/OTHER:

Stock Ticker: AMX   Exchange: NYS
Employees: 176,014   Fiscal Year Ends: 12/31
Parent Company:

SALARIES/BONUSES:

Top Exec. Salary: $ Bonus: $
Second Exec. Salary: $ Bonus: $

OTHER THOUGHTS:

Estimated Female Officers or Directors: 2
Hot Spot for Advancement for Women/Minorities:

Sales, profits and employees may be estimates. Financial information, benefits and other data can change quickly and may vary from those stated here.

American Greetings Corporation LLC   www.americangreetings.com

NAIC Code: 511191

TYPES OF BUSINESS:

Greeting Cards
Gift Wrap
Party Supplies
Stationery
Digital Media Marketing
Online Greetings Cards
Greeting Card Design and Manufacture
eCards

BRANDS/DIVISIONS/AFFILIATES:

Clayton Dubilier & Rice LLC
AG Interactive Inc
american greetings
Papyrus
Recycled Paper Greetings
SmashUps
Paper Rebel
CreataCard

CONTACTS: Note: Officers with more than one job title may be intentionally listed here more than once.

Joe Acuri, CEO
Lorna Street, CFO
Aaron Siegel, CMO
Chris Haffke, Chief Human Resources Officer
Joel Lee, CIO
Thomas H. Johnston, Sr. VP-Creative & Merch.
Christopher W. Haffke, General Counsel
Robert D. Tyler, Corp. Controller
Erwin Weiss, Sr. VP
Jeffrey Weiss, Co-CEO
Gregory Steinberg, Treas.

GROWTH PLANS/SPECIAL FEATURES:

American Greetings Corporation, LLC designs, manufactures and sells every day/seasonal greeting cards, as well as other social expression products. The company markets its products through AG Interactive, Inc. (AGI), a subsidiary focused on digital media marketing. American Greetings' major greeting card brands are American greetings, Papyrus, Recycled Paper Greetings, and SmashUps. Additional brands include Paper Rebel, justWink, plus mark, Today and Always, Blue Mountain, Carlton cards, CreataCard, DesignWare, Jacquie Lawson, and Kathy Davis. AmericanGreetings.com offers consumers paper cards, eCards, printables, party supplies and gift wrap, along with useful content that educates and inspires visitors to connect more meaningfully. American Greetings Corporation has been in business since 1906. The firm is based in Cleveland, Ohio, and its products can be found in retail outlets worldwide. American Greetings is 60%-owned by private equity company Clayton, Dubilier & Rice LLC, with the Weiss family retaining a 40% share.

American Greetings offers its employees health benefits, life and disability insurance, a 401(k) retirement plan and other plans and programs.

FINANCIAL DATA: Note: Data for latest year may not have been available at press time.

In U.S. $	2022	2021	2020	2019	2018	2017
Revenue	2,328,144,000	2,238,600,000	2,152,500,000	2,100,000,000	2,000,000,000	1,900,000,000
R&D Expense						
Operating Income						
Operating Margin %						
SGA Expense						
Net Income						
Operating Cash Flow						
Capital Expenditure						
EBITDA						
Return on Assets %						
Return on Equity %						
Debt to Equity						

CONTACT INFORMATION:

Phone: 216 252-7300   Fax: 216 255-6777
Toll-Free:
Address: One American Blvd., Cleveland, OH 44145-8151 United States

STOCK TICKER/OTHER:

Stock Ticker: Joint Venture   Exchange:
Employees: 27,000   Fiscal Year Ends: 02/28
Parent Company: Clayton Dubilier & Rice LLC

SALARIES/BONUSES:

Top Exec. Salary: $ Bonus: $
Second Exec. Salary: $ Bonus: $

OTHER THOUGHTS:

Estimated Female Officers or Directors:
Hot Spot for Advancement for Women/Minorities: Y

Americanas SA

NAIC Code: 454110

/ri.americanas.com

TYPES OF BUSINESS:
Online Retailing
Ecommerce Retailing
Digital Brands
Delivery Services
Payment Solutions
Digital Marketing Solutions
Digital Ordering
Business-to-Business Ecommerce Integration

BRANDS/DIVISIONS/AFFILIATES:
Americanas.com
Submarino
Shoptime
Sou Barato
Loas Americanas
Local Americanas
Ame Go
+AQUI

CONTACTS: *Note: Officers with more than one job title may be intentionally listed here more than once.*
Leonardo Coelho, Co-CEO
Camille Loyo Faria, Co-CEO
Cruz Marcio Meirelles, Chief Commercial Officer
Fabio da Silva Abrate, Investor Rel. Officer
Timotheo Jose Barros, Co-COO
Carlos Eduardo Rosalba Padilha, Co-COO
Carlos Henreique de Lucca Strong Gatto, Co-COO
Jean Pierre Lessa, Co-COO
Santos Ferriera, Co-COO

GROWTH PLANS/SPECIAL FEATURES:
Americanas SA is a leading ecommerce retailer in Latin America. Based in Brazil, the firm operates through a portfolio of online/digital brands. Americanas.com offers millions of products available, including electronics, CDs, DVDs, computers/IT, home appliances, books, games, toys, stationery, fragrances and wines. Items can be purchased through the website, by telephone, at kiosks within brick-and-mortar stores and at Lojas Americanas stores. Submarino sells books, games, technology and entertainment products such as CDs, DVDs and software. Shoptime is Brazil's first home shopping channel and operates through internet, telesales and catalogues. Shoptime specializes in the demonstration of products on its 24/7 on-air programming channels, with its own brands including Casa & Conforto (bed, bath, kitchen), Fun Kitchen (small appliances), La Cuisine (housewares) and Life Zone (sports and leisure). Americanas Empresas facilitates business-to-business ecommerce sales and purchase system integration. Lojas Americanas has retail stores that stock an assortment of products of up to 60,000 items. Americanas Express are neighborhood stores with an assortment of up to 15,000 items. Ame is the financial platform of Americanas S.A. and its purpose is to democratize access to financial and non-financial products, services, simplifying the way people relate to money. Other brands include Puket, MinD, Imaginarium, Lovebrands, Hortifruti Natural da Terra and Skoob.

FINANCIAL DATA: *Note: Data for latest year may not have been available at press time.*

In U.S. $	2022	2021	2020	2019	2018	2017
Revenue	4,880,258,000	5,282,032,000	2,421,650,000	2,069,110,000	1,582,747,392	1,736,986,624
R&D Expense						
Operating Income						
Operating Margin %						
SGA Expense						
Net Income	-2,441,469,000	140,375,000	-39,181,400	-96,951,600	-96,945,232	-100,365,888
Operating Cash Flow						
Capital Expenditure						
EBITDA						
Return on Assets %						
Return on Equity %						
Debt to Equity						

CONTACT INFORMATION:
Phone: 55 22066000   Fax: 55 22066898
Toll-Free:
Address: Rua Sacadura Cabral, 102-Part, Rio de Janeiro, RJ 20081902 Brazil

STOCK TICKER/OTHER:
Stock Ticker: AMER3   Exchange: Sao Paulo
Employees: 10,781   Fiscal Year Ends: 12/31
Parent Company:

SALARIES/BONUSES:
Top Exec. Salary: $ Bonus: $
Second Exec. Salary: $ Bonus: $

OTHER THOUGHTS:
Estimated Female Officers or Directors:
Hot Spot for Advancement for Women/Minorities:

Anaplan Inc

www.anaplan.com

NAIC Code: 511210H

TYPES OF BUSINESS:
Computer Software, Business Management & ERP
Enterprise Software
Enterprise Planning Solutions
Enterprise Business Performance Solutions
Predictive Insights
Enterprise Performance Technologies
Platform Training
Community Support

BRANDS/DIVISIONS/AFFILIATES:
Thoma Bravo LP
Polaris Calculation Engine
Hyperblock

GROWTH PLANS/SPECIAL FEATURES:
Anaplan, Inc. is a cloud-native, enterprise software-as-a-service (SaaS) company that helps enterprises see, plan and drive business performance. The firm's Polaris Calculation Engine and Hyperblock technology present what-if scenarios through the Anaplan platform for forecasting future outcomes swiftly and for making strategic business decisions. Performance can be contextualized in real time. Solutions by function span finance, sales, supply chain, human resources, workforce and marketing. The Anaplan platform encompasses connected planning, user experience, intelligence, planning and modeling, extensibility, enterprise scale, security, predictive insights and pricing. Services by Anaplan include platform training and hypercare. Based in the U.S., Anaplan has offices worldwide, including Europe and Asia Pacific. Anaplan is a subsidiary of Thoma Bravo LP.

CONTACTS:
Note: Officers with more than one job title may be intentionally listed here more than once.

Charlie Gottdiener, CEO
Hemant Kapadia, CFO
Jim Freeze, CMO
Carey Pellock, Chief People Officer
Adam Their, CTO
Ana Pinczuk, Other Executive Officer

FINANCIAL DATA:
Note: Data for latest year may not have been available at press time.

In U.S. $	2022	2021	2020	2019	2018	2017
Revenue	592,200,000	447,755,008	348,022,016	240,642,000	168,347,008	120,499,000
R&D Expense						
Operating Income						
Operating Margin %						
SGA Expense						
Net Income	-200,700,000	-153,967,008	-149,216,992	-131,016,000	-47,554,000	-40,194,000
Operating Cash Flow						
Capital Expenditure						
EBITDA						
Return on Assets %						
Return on Equity %						
Debt to Equity						

CONTACT INFORMATION:
Phone: 415-742-8199   Fax: 415-202-6481
Toll-Free:
Address: 50 Hawthorne St., San Francisco, CA 94105 United States

STOCK TICKER/OTHER:
Stock Ticker: Private   Exchange:
Employees: 2,200   Fiscal Year Ends: 01/31
Parent Company: Thoma Bravo LP

SALARIES/BONUSES:
Top Exec. Salary: $ Bonus: $
Second Exec. Salary: $ Bonus: $

OTHER THOUGHTS:
Estimated Female Officers or Directors:
Hot Spot for Advancement for Women/Minorities:

Ancestry.com Inc

www.ancestry.com

NAIC Code: 519130

TYPES OF BUSINESS:

Internet-Based Genealogy Database
Family History Records
Digital Historical Records
DNA Tests
Genetic Origin Search Engine
Genealogy Solutions and Services
Military Records
Digital Newspaper Archive

BRANDS/DIVISIONS/AFFILIATES:

Blackstone Group Inc (The)
GIC Private Limited
AncestryDNA
AncestryProGenealogists
Ancestry Academy
Ancestry Institution
Fold3
RootsWeb

CONTACTS: *Note: Officers with more than one job title may be intentionally listed here more than once.*

Deborah Liu, CEO
Howard Hochhauser, COO
Tim Sullivan, Pres.
Brian Donnelly, Chief Commercial Officer
Shane Koller, Sr. VP-People
Sriram Thiagarajan, CTO
Eric Shoup, Exec. VP-Prod.
William Stern, General Counsel
Ken Chahine, Sr. VP
Julie Miller, Chief Communications Officer
Olivier Van Calster, Sr. VP-Int'l

GROWTH PLANS/SPECIAL FEATURES:

Ancestry.com, Inc. creates, updates and maintains an online family history resource that provides access to 60 billion digitized historical records on a subscription basis. Family trees are created from the ancestral profiles, with records dating back to the thirteenth century. AncestryDNA offers a fee-based, mail-in saliva sample DNA test designed to help customers learn more about their genetic origins; AncestryProGenealogists comprises a team of expert researchers and genealogists to help conduct research, trace family trees and help clients connect with their past; Ancestry Academy offers video instruction from family history and genealogy experts; Ancestry Institution is a family history resource of more than 10,000 archives, ancestry libraries, schools and other institutions; Fold3 offers global military records, including stories, photos and personal documents, of men and women who have served; RootsWeb is a free online community for sharing family history information at RootsWeb.Ancestry.com; Newspapers.com comprises an historical digital archive of newspapers dating to the 1700s; We Remember is a place to collect and preserve memories; Find A Grave is a free resource for finding grave sites of famous people, friends and family; Archives.com, is a site for anyone who wants to begin discovering heritage roots; and Forces War Records is a British military genealogy-specialist website that helps people discover and contextualize their family's military history. Ancestry's corporate headquarters are in Utah, USA, and international headquarters are in Dublin, Ireland. The Blackstone Group, Inc. holds the majority stake in Ancestry.com, while GIC Private Limited holds a significant minority interest.

FINANCIAL DATA: *Note: Data for latest year may not have been available at press time.*

In U.S. $	2022	2021	2020	2019	2018	2017
Revenue	1,275,000,000	1,250,000,000	1,074,937,500	1,102,500,000	1,050,000,000	1,000,000,000
R&D Expense						
Operating Income						
Operating Margin %						
SGA Expense						
Net Income						
Operating Cash Flow						
Capital Expenditure						
EBITDA						
Return on Assets %						
Return on Equity %						
Debt to Equity						

CONTACT INFORMATION:

Phone: 801 705-7000   Fax: 901 705-7001
Toll-Free: 800-262-3787
Address: 1300 W. Traverse Pkwy., Lehi, UT 84043 United States

STOCK TICKER/OTHER:

Stock Ticker: Private   Exchange:
Employees: 1,400   Fiscal Year Ends: 12/31
Parent Company: Blackstone Group Inc (The)

SALARIES/BONUSES:

Top Exec. Salary: $ Bonus: $
Second Exec. Salary: $ Bonus: $

OTHER THOUGHTS:

Estimated Female Officers or Directors:
Hot Spot for Advancement for Women/Minorities:

Angi Inc

NAIC Code: 519130

www.angihomeservices.com

TYPES OF BUSINESS:
Online Business Reviews
Consumer Information and Help
Handyman Marketplace
Home Services

GROWTH PLANS/SPECIAL FEATURES:
Angi Inc connects quality home service professionals across different categories, from repairing and remodeling to cleaning and landscaping, with consumers. The Company has four operating segments: (i) Ads and Leads; (ii) Services; (iii) Roofing; and (iv) International (Europe and Canada). Majority of the revenue is earned from United States.

BRANDS/DIVISIONS/AFFILIATES:
Angies List
HomeAdvisor
Fixd Repair
CraftJack
HomeStars
Instapro
MyBuilder
Travaux

CONTACTS: *Note: Officers with more than one job title may be intentionally listed here more than once.*
Jeffrey Kip, CEO, Subsidiary
Oisin Hanrahan, CEO
Jeff Pedersen, CFO
Joseph Levin, Chairman of the Board
Christopher Bohnert, Chief Accounting Officer
Shannon Shaw, Chief Legal Officer
Allison Lowrie, Chief Marketing Officer
Kulesh Shanmugasundaram, Chief Technology Officer
Angela Hicks Bowman, Co-Founder

FINANCIAL DATA: *Note: Data for latest year may not have been available at press time.*

In U.S. $	2022	2021	2020	2019	2018	2017
Revenue	1,891,524,000	1,685,438,000	1,467,925,000	1,326,205,000	1,132,241,000	736,386,000
R&D Expense	73,821,000	70,933,000	68,803,000	64,200,000	61,143,000	47,907,000
Operating Income	-100,300,000	-76,513,000	-6,368,000	38,645,000	63,906,000	-147,871,000
Operating Margin %	-.05%	-.05%	.00%	.03%	.06%	-.20%
SGA Expense	1,387,232,000	1,289,462,000	1,136,686,000	1,081,470,000	864,931,000	764,473,000
Net Income	-128,450,000	-71,378,000	-6,283,000	34,829,000	77,318,000	-103,118,000
Operating Cash Flow	27,069,000	6,209,000	188,419,000	214,161,000	223,700,000	41,823,000
Capital Expenditure	116,352,000	70,215,000	52,488,000	68,804,000	46,976,000	26,837,000
EBITDA	-32,416,000	-3,346,000	90,373,000	140,536,000	168,169,000	-108,093,000
Return on Assets %	-.07%	-.03%	.00%	.02%	.05%	-.12%
Return on Equity %	-.12%	-.06%	.00%	.03%	.07%	-.18%
Debt to Equity	.47%	.44%	0.56	0.176	.19%	0.262

CONTACT INFORMATION:
Phone: 303-963-7200   Fax:
Toll-Free:
Address: 3601 Walnut St., Denver, CO 80205 United States

STOCK TICKER/OTHER:
Stock Ticker: ANGI   Exchange: NAS
Employees: 4,600   Fiscal Year Ends: 12/31
Parent Company:

SALARIES/BONUSES:
Top Exec. Salary: $444,231   Bonus: $1,250,000
Second Exec. Salary: $575,000   Bonus: $350,000

OTHER THOUGHTS:
Estimated Female Officers or Directors: 2
Hot Spot for Advancement for Women/Minorities:

Sales, profits and employees may be estimates. Financial information, benefits and other data can change quickly and may vary from those stated here.

AppDirect Inc

www.appdirect.com

NAIC Code: 511210M

TYPES OF BUSINESS:

Cloud Applications Management Tools
Subscription Commerce Platform
Ecommerce
Digital Monetization Solutions
Digital Engagement Solutions
Business-to-Business Marketplace Solutions
Subscription Billing Solutions
App Store Launching Services

BRANDS/DIVISIONS/AFFILIATES:

VEEUE

CONTACTS: *Note: Officers with more than one job title may be intentionally listed here more than once.*

Nicolas Desmarais, CEO
Renee Bergeron, COO
Emanuel Bertolin, Chief Revenue Officer
Andy Sen, CTO
Deb Tenenbaum, Chief People Officer
Pierre-Luc Bisaillon, CIO
Nicolas Desmarais, Chmn.

GROWTH PLANS/SPECIAL FEATURES:

AppDirect, Inc. provides a subscription commerce platform for selling, distributing and managing digital products and services. This platform enables organizations of all sizes the capability of getting to market quickly. AppDirect's capabilities include business-to-business (B2B) marketplace, partner relationship management, subscription billing, cloud distribution, device application management, digital engagement capabilities, procurement marketplace, workforce identity and data management, spend management, support solutions and advisory services. The company's solutions are many and include software-as-a-service (SaaS), infrastructure-as-a-service, third-party digital services, managed services, customer support services, app store launching, scaling a partner ecosystem, managing a reseller program, selling services for connected devices, automating subscription billing, offering self-service procurement and selling through third-party marketplaces. Headquartered in California, USA, AppDirect has additional offices in the U.S., Canada, Germany, India, Australia, the U.K. and Argentina. In August 2023, the firm announced it had acquired ADCom Solutions' Network Operations Center and VEEUE platform. The VEEUE platform provides network and cloud monitoring with powerful analytics to deliver advanced monitoring, incident management, and business intelligence with actionable insights into the work and compute environment.

FINANCIAL DATA: *Note: Data for latest year may not have been available at press time.*

In U.S. $	2022	2021	2020	2019	2018	2017
Revenue						
R&D Expense						
Operating Income						
Operating Margin %						
SGA Expense						
Net Income						
Operating Cash Flow						
Capital Expenditure						
EBITDA						
Return on Assets %						
Return on Equity %						
Debt to Equity						

CONTACT INFORMATION:

Phone: 415-852-3919   Fax: 415-874-3001
Toll-Free: 833-427-7762
Address: 650 California St., Fl. 25, San Francisco, CA 94108 United States

STOCK TICKER/OTHER:

Stock Ticker: Private   Exchange:
Employees: 650   Fiscal Year Ends:
Parent Company:

SALARIES/BONUSES:

Top Exec. Salary: $ Bonus: $
Second Exec. Salary: $ Bonus: $

OTHER THOUGHTS:

Estimated Female Officers or Directors:
Hot Spot for Advancement for Women/Minorities:

Sales, profits and employees may be estimates. Financial information, benefits and other data can change quickly and may vary from those stated here.

AppDynamics LLC

www.appdynamics.com

NAIC Code: 511210M

TYPES OF BUSINESS:

Application Performance Management Software
Application Performance Monitoring Solutions
Data Insight
User Experience Technology
Cloud Monitoring and Migration
Microservices
On-Premise and Cloud Management
Software-as-a-Service

BRANDS/DIVISIONS/AFFILIATES:

Cisco Systems Inc
Cisco AppDynamics

CONTACTS: Note: Officers with more than one job title may be intentionally listed here more than once.

Ronak Desai, General Mngr.
Bhaskar Sunkara, VP-Prod. Mgmt.
Ed Rowe, Sr. VP-Eng.
Joe Sexton, Pres., Worldwide Field Oper.
Stuart Horne, VP-Bus. Dev.
Hatim Shafique, VP-Customer Success & Oper.

GROWTH PLANS/SPECIAL FEATURES:

AppDynamics, LLC, doing business as Cisco AppDynamics, is a leading provider of observability and application performance monitoring technology. The company helps customers observe matters inside and beyond their IT environments and can therefore turn the data insights toward delivering enhanced user experiences. Solutions offered by AppDynamics include cloud monitoring, cloud migration, AWS monitoring, Microsoft Azure, microservices, SAP monitoring and continuous delivery. The company's products address areas such as correlating performance metrics with business outcomes, providing continual strategic user experiences, ensuring quality software delivery with application performance monitoring, managing on-premises and cloud-native environments, isolating performance issues across third-party networks and software-a-s-a-service (SaaS), and automating and continuously adapting application security. Based in San Francisco, California, the company has offices spanning North America, Europe, Asia and Oceania. AppDynamics is a subsidiary of Cisco Systems, Inc., an American multinational technology conglomerate based in California.

FINANCIAL DATA: Note: Data for latest year may not have been available at press time.

In U.S. $	2022	2021	2020	2019	2018	2017
Revenue	233,099,767	209,999,790	201,922,875	203,962,500	194,250,000	185,000,000
R&D Expense						
Operating Income						
Operating Margin %						
SGA Expense						
Net Income						
Operating Cash Flow						
Capital Expenditure						
EBITDA						
Return on Assets %						
Return on Equity %						
Debt to Equity						

CONTACT INFORMATION:

Phone: 628-263-8000   Fax:
Toll-Free:
Address: 500 Terry A. Francois Blvd., Fl. 3, San Francisco, CA 94158 United States

STOCK TICKER/OTHER:

Stock Ticker: Subsidiary
Employees: 1,200
Parent Company: Cisco Systems Inc

Exchange:
Fiscal Year Ends: 07/31

SALARIES/BONUSES:

Top Exec. Salary: $ Bonus: $
Second Exec. Salary: $ Bonus: $

OTHER THOUGHTS:

Estimated Female Officers or Directors:
Hot Spot for Advancement for Women/Minorities:

Apple Inc

NAIC Code: 334220

TYPES OF BUSINESS:

Electronics Design and Manufacturing
Software
Computers and Tablets
Retail Stores
Smartphones
Online Music Store
Apps Store
Home Entertainment Software & Systems

BRANDS/DIVISIONS/AFFILIATES:

iPhone
iPad
Apple Watch
Apple TV
iOS
watchOS
HomePod
AirPods

GROWTH PLANS/SPECIAL FEATURES:

Apple is among the largest companies in the world, with a broad portfolio of hardware and software products targeted at consumers and businesses. Apple's iPhone makes up a majority of the firm sales, and Apple's other products like Mac, iPad, and Watch are designed around the iPhone as the focal point of an expansive software ecosystem. Apple has progressively worked to add new applications, like streaming video, subscription bundles, and augmented reality. The firm designs its own software and semiconductors while working with subcontractors like Foxconn and TSMC to build its products and chips. Slightly less than half of Apple's sales come directly through its flagship stores, with a majority of sales coming indirectly through partnerships and distribution.

Apple offers employees comprehensive health benefits, retirement plans and various employee assistance programs.

CONTACTS:
Note: Officers with more than one job title may be intentionally listed here more than once.

Timothy Cook, CEO
Luca Maestri, CFO
Arthur Levinson, Chairman of the Board
Chris Kondo, Chief Accounting Officer
Jeffery Williams, COO
Katherine Adams, General Counsel
Deirdre OBrien, Senior VP, Divisional

FINANCIAL DATA:
Note: Data for latest year may not have been available at press time.

In U.S. $	2022	2021	2020	2019	2018	2017
Revenue	394,328,000,000	365,817,000,000	274,515,000,000	260,174,000,000	265,595,000,000	
R&D Expense	26,251,000,000	21,914,000,000	18,752,000,000	16,217,000,000	14,236,000,000	
Operating Income	119,437,000,000	108,949,000,000	66,288,000,000	63,930,000,000	70,898,000,000	
Operating Margin %	.30%	.30%	.24%	.25%	.27%	
SGA Expense	25,094,000,000	21,973,000,000	19,916,000,000	18,245,000,000	16,705,000,000	
Net Income	99,803,000,000	94,680,000,000	57,411,000,000	55,256,000,000	59,531,000,000	
Operating Cash Flow	122,151,000,000	104,038,000,000	80,674,000,000	69,391,000,000	77,434,000,000	
Capital Expenditure	10,708,000,000	11,085,000,000	7,309,000,000	10,495,000,000	13,313,000,000	
EBITDA	133,138,000,000	123,136,000,000	81,020,000,000	81,860,000,000	87,046,000,000	
Return on Assets %	.28%	.28%	.17%	.16%	.16%	
Return on Equity %	1.75%	1.47%	.74%	.56%	.49%	
Debt to Equity	1.95%	1.73%	1.51	1.015	.87%	

CONTACT INFORMATION:

Phone: 408 996-1010   Fax: 408 974-2483
Toll-Free: 800-692-7753
Address: One Apple Park Way, Cupertino, CA 95014 United States

STOCK TICKER/OTHER:

Stock Ticker: AAPL   Exchange: NAS
Employees: 161,000   Fiscal Year Ends: 09/30
Parent Company:

SALARIES/BONUSES:

Top Exec. Salary: $3,000,000   Bonus: $
Second Exec. Salary: Bonus: $
$1,000,000

OTHER THOUGHTS:

Estimated Female Officers or Directors:
Hot Spot for Advancement for Women/Minorities:

Apptio Inc

www.apptio.com

NAIC Code: 511210H

TYPES OF BUSINESS:

Computer Software, Business Management & ERP
Business Management Software
Advanced Data and Analytics
Technology Business Management
Digital Transformation Services
Machine Learning
IT Finance Solutions
Cloud and Agile Solutions

BRANDS/DIVISIONS/AFFILIATES:

Vista Equity Partners
ApptioOne
Cloudability
Targetprocess

CONTACTS: *Note: Officers with more than one job title may be intentionally listed here more than once.*

Ajay Patel, Gen. Mgr.
Larry Blasko, Pres.-Field Oper.
Kurt Shintaffer, CFO
Allison Breeding, CMO
Missy Waggoner, Chief People Officer
Jeremy Ung, CTO
John Morrow, Executive VP, Divisional
Lawrence Blasko, Other Executive Officer
Eugene Khvostov, Chief Product Officer

GROWTH PLANS/SPECIAL FEATURES:

Apptio, Inc., privately-owned by Vista Equity Partners, is a Software-as-a-Service (SaaS) solutions provider that builds advanced data and analytics applications for technology business management (TBM) purposes. The company helps information technology (IT) leaders make informed decisions as they plan, analyze and optimize technology investments in pursuit of digital transformation. Apptio's software utilizes machine learning to translate technology costs and it spans across on-premises systems, vendors, projects, agile and cloud systems to provide end-to-end visibility. Solutions are grouped into four categories: IT Finance, Cloud, Agile and Public Sector IT. IT Finance solutions include application rationalization, IT benchmarking, IT cost optimization, IT cost reduction, IT metrics and KPIs, IT planning, IT financial management and TBM. Cloud solutions include cost management, migration, SaaS license management, finance operations and cloud center of excellence. Agile solutions span initiatives, frameworks and roles, and include agile portfolio management, ideas management, lean portfolio management, remote PI planning, remote retrospectives, requests management, risk management, value stream management, Full SAFe, Kanban, OKRs, Scrum, agile PMO, product management and product owner. Last, Public Sector IT solutions include government, higher education, U.S. Department of Defense and Public Sector Summits. Companies of all sizes and geographies use Apptio, Fortune 100s. Product brands include ApptioOne, Cloudability and Targetprocess. Headquartered in the U.S., Apptio has global offices in The Netherlands, Denmark, France, Germany, Poland, Sweden, Australia, India, Japan and the U.K.

FINANCIAL DATA: *Note: Data for latest year may not have been available at press time.*

In U.S. $	2022	2021	2020	2019	2018	2017
Revenue	350,000,000	325,000,000	270,000,000	207,842,206	197,944,958	188,519,008
R&D Expense						
Operating Income						
Operating Margin %						
SGA Expense						
Net Income						
Operating Cash Flow						
Capital Expenditure						
EBITDA						
Return on Assets %						
Return on Equity %						
Debt to Equity						

CONTACT INFORMATION:

Phone: 425 453-5861   Fax:
Toll-Free: 866-470-0320
Address: 11100 NE 8th St., Ste. 600, Bellevue, WA 98004 United States

STOCK TICKER/OTHER:

Stock Ticker: Private   Exchange:
Employees: 1,300   Fiscal Year Ends:
Parent Company: Vista Equity Partners

SALARIES/BONUSES:

Top Exec. Salary: $ Bonus: $
Second Exec. Salary: $ Bonus: $

OTHER THOUGHTS:

Estimated Female Officers or Directors:
Hot Spot for Advancement for Women/Minorities:

AptDeco Inc

NAIC Code: 454110

www.aptdeco.com

TYPES OF BUSINESS:

Electronic Shopping
Furniture Ecommerce Platform
Used Furniture Marketplace
Retail Furniture Marketplace
Designer Trade Program
Seller and Buyer Furniture Transactions
Payments and Delivery Solutions
Ecommerce Technology

BRANDS/DIVISIONS/AFFILIATES:

CONTACTS: *Note: Officers with more than one job title may be intentionally listed here more than once.*

Reham Fagiri, CEO

GROWTH PLANS/SPECIAL FEATURES:

AptDeco, Inc. operates an online marketplace for selling and purchasing furniture. Sellers can list their own used furniture for sale. The AptDeco platform takes care of the payments, scheduling, pickup and delivery, insurance and other services in order to maintain security between verified buyers and sellers from start to finish. Furniture can be listed, purchased and delivered anywhere in the contiguous U.S. How AptDeco works: sellers list the furniture being sold and include photos and details; shoppers browse furniture according to brand, category, color or other options; shoppers request to purchase; AptDeco authorizes payment, which is only charged if the seller confirms the sale within 24 hours of the buyer's request; once confirmed, pickup and delivery is scheduled through the AptDeco system, as well as assembly and logistics services; purchases are confirmed within 24 hours after delivery; and payment is processed and seller's earnings are deposited into an uploaded account within 2-5 business days. Payments are handled through Stripe. Unconfirmed buyer requests cancels the transaction and no payments are processed. AptDeco offers a money back guarantee. The platform has a designer trade program, and a business program for furniture retailers.

AptDeco offers its employees comprehensive medical benefits, learning and development programs, paid parental leave and other benefits, programs and perks.

FINANCIAL DATA: *Note: Data for latest year may not have been available at press time.*

In U.S. $	2022	2021	2020	2019	2018	2017
Revenue						
R&D Expense						
Operating Income						
Operating Margin %						
SGA Expense						
Net Income						
Operating Cash Flow						
Capital Expenditure						
EBITDA						
Return on Assets %						
Return on Equity %						
Debt to Equity						

CONTACT INFORMATION:

Phone: 347-367-2744   Fax:
Toll-Free:
Address: 330 W. 38th St., New York, NY 10018 United States

STOCK TICKER/OTHER:

Stock Ticker: Private   Exchange:
Employees: Fiscal Year Ends:
Parent Company:

SALARIES/BONUSES:

Top Exec. Salary: $ Bonus: $
Second Exec. Salary: $ Bonus: $

OTHER THOUGHTS:

Estimated Female Officers or Directors:
Hot Spot for Advancement for Women/Minorities:

Arista Networks Inc

www.aristanetworks.com

NAIC Code: 334210A

TYPES OF BUSINESS:
Cloud Computing Routers
Cloud Networking Solutions

BRANDS/DIVISIONS/AFFILIATES:
EOS+
Cognitive Cloud Networking
CloudVision
Big Switch Networks Inc
Awake Security Inc

GROWTH PLANS/SPECIAL FEATURES:
Arista Networks Inc is a networking equipment provider that primarily sells Ethernet switches and software to data centers. Its marquee product is its extensible operating system, or EOS, that runs a single image across every single one of its devices. The firm operates as one reportable segment. It has steadily gained market share since its founding in 2004, with a focus on high-speed applications. Arista counts Microsoft and Meta Platforms as its largest customers and derives roughly three quarters of its sales from North America.

CONTACTS:
Note: Officers with more than one job title may be intentionally listed here more than once.

Jayshree Ullal, CEO
Ita Brennan, CFO
Andy Bechtolsheim, Chairman of the Board
Kenneth Duda, Chief Technology Officer
Anshul Sadana, COO
Marc Taxay, General Counsel
John McCool, Other Executive Officer

FINANCIAL DATA:
Note: Data for latest year may not have been available at press time.

In U.S. $	2022	2021	2020	2019	2018	2017
Revenue	4,381,310,000	2,948,037,000	2,317,512,000	2,410,706,000	2,151,369,000	
R&D Expense	728,394,000	586,752,000	486,594,000	462,759,000	442,468,000	
Operating Income	1,527,106,000	924,739,000	699,684,000	805,774,000	678,347,000	
Operating Margin %	.35%	.31%	.30%	.33%	.32%	
SGA Expense	420,196,000	369,288,000	295,608,000	275,805,000	252,562,000	
Net Income	1,352,446,000	840,854,000	634,557,000	859,867,000	328,115,000	
Operating Cash Flow	492,813,000	1,015,856,000	735,114,000	963,034,000	503,119,000	
Capital Expenditure	44,644,000	64,736,000	15,384,000	15,751,000	23,830,000	
EBITDA	1,589,806,000	975,073,000	734,842,000	838,623,000	319,173,000	
Return on Assets %	.22%	.16%	.14%	.24%	.12%	
Return on Equity %	.31%	.23%	.20%	.34%	.17%	
Debt to Equity	.01%	.01%	0.022	0.029	.02%	

CONTACT INFORMATION:
Phone: 408-547-5500   Fax: 408-538-8920
Toll-Free: 866-547-5502
Address: 5453 Great America Pkwy., Santa Clara, CA 95054 United States

STOCK TICKER/OTHER:
Stock Ticker: ANET
Employees: 3,612
Parent Company:

Exchange: NYS
Fiscal Year Ends: 12/31

SALARIES/BONUSES:
Top Exec. Salary: $308,077   Bonus: $
Second Exec. Salary: $308,077   Bonus: $

OTHER THOUGHTS:
Estimated Female Officers or Directors: 1
Hot Spot for Advancement for Women/Minorities:

Asana Inc

NAIC Code: 511210H

TYPES OF BUSINESS:

Computer Software, Business Management & ERP
Software
Task Management

BRANDS/DIVISIONS/AFFILIATES:

GROWTH PLANS/SPECIAL FEATURES:

Asana is a provider of collaborative work management software delivered via a cloud-based SaaS model. The firm's solution offers scalable, dynamic tools to improve the efficiency of project and process management across countless use cases, including marketing programs, managing IT approvals, and performance management. Asana's offering supports workflow management across teams, provides real time visibility into projects, and reporting and automation capabilities. The firm generates revenue via software subscriptions on a per seat basis.

CONTACTS: Note: Officers with more than one job title may be intentionally listed here more than once.

Dustin Moskovitz, CEO
Tim Wan, CFO
Justin Rosenstein, Co-Founder
Anne Raimondi, COO
Eleanor Lacey, General Counsel

FINANCIAL DATA: Note: Data for latest year may not have been available at press time.

In U.S. $	2022	2021	2020	2019	2018	2017
Revenue	378,437,000	227,004,000	142,606,000	76,770,000		
R&D Expense	203,124,000	121,139,000	89,675,000	42,585,000		
Operating Income	-265,184,000	-175,567,000	-119,631,000	-52,013,000		
Operating Margin %	- .70%	- .77%	- .84%			
SGA Expense	401,600,000	252,691,000	152,681,000	72,366,000		
Net Income	-288,342,000	-211,710,000	-118,589,000	-50,928,000		
Operating Cash Flow	-83,785,000	-92,870,000	-40,136,000	-30,180,000		
Capital Expenditure	42,719,000	58,306,000	7,262,000	3,407,000		
EBITDA	-258,256,000	-170,513,000	-116,033,000	-46,669,000		
Return on Assets %	- .40%	- .37%	- .44%			
Return on Equity %	-3.02%					
Debt to Equity	1.19%					

CONTACT INFORMATION:

Phone: 415-525-3888   Fax:
Toll-Free:
Address: 1550 Bryant St., Ste. 200, San Francisco, CA 94103 United States

STOCK TICKER/OTHER:

Stock Ticker: ASAN
Employees: 1,782
Parent Company:

Exchange: NYS
Fiscal Year Ends: 01/31

SALARIES/BONUSES:

Top Exec. Salary: $745,833   Bonus: $
Second Exec. Salary: $706,667   Bonus: $

OTHER THOUGHTS:

Estimated Female Officers or Directors:
Hot Spot for Advancement for Women/Minorities:

Sales, profits and employees may be estimates. Financial information, benefits and other data can change quickly and may vary from those stated here.

ASOS plc

NAIC Code: 454110

www.asosplc.com

TYPES OF BUSINESS:

Online Apparel Sales
eCommerce
Online Fashion Marketplace

GROWTH PLANS/SPECIAL FEATURES:

Asos is a global e-commerce player focusing on fashion and cosmetics and targeting the youth segment (20-somethings) globally. Of its revenue, 45% comes from its U.K. home market, 30% from other European Union countries, 13% from the United States, 12% from the rest of the world. The company ships to 240 countries from its three warehouses located in the U.K., continental Europe, and the United States. It offers over 85 000 products on its website from third-party brands and its own labels (Asos Design, Collusion).

BRANDS/DIVISIONS/AFFILIATES:

ASOS White
ASOS Black
ASOS Maternity
ASOS Swim
ASOS Curve
ASOS Tall
Green Room (The)
Collusion

CONTACTS: *Note: Officers with more than one job title may be intentionally listed here more than once.*

Nick Beighton, CEO
Mat Dunn, CFO
Nick Beighton, Corp. Sec.
Adam Crozier, Chmn.
Jon Kamaluddin, Dir.-Intl

FINANCIAL DATA: *Note: Data for latest year may not have been available at press time.*

In U.S. $	2022	2021	2020	2019	2018	2017
Revenue	4,969,073,000	4,936,253,000	4,119,540,000	3,450,517,000	3,051,376,000	
R&D Expense						
Operating Income	42,161,070	239,964,600	190,734,700	44,306,990	128,629,100	
Operating Margin %	.00%	.05%	.05%	.01%	.04%	
SGA Expense	2,138,349,000	2,002,398,000	1,762,560,000	1,639,990,000	1,432,971,000	
Net Income	-38,879,070	162,080,300	143,019,400	31,052,760	104,014,100	
Operating Cash Flow	-151,981,800	271,522,300	509,088,600	113,229,000	118,530,700	
Capital Expenditure	230,876,000	198,308,500	147,185,000	279,727,300	268,871,500	
EBITDA	177,859,100	411,259,700	339,560,700	134,309,500	197,929,800	
Return on Assets %	- .01%	.05%	.07%	.02%	.09%	
Return on Equity %	- .03%	.14%	.18%	.06%	.23%	
Debt to Equity	.82%	.74%	0.359			

CONTACT INFORMATION:

Phone: 44 2077561000   Fax: 44 2077561001
Toll-Free:
Address: Hampstead Road, London, NW1 7FB United Kingdom

STOCK TICKER/OTHER:

Stock Ticker: ASOMY   Exchange: PINX
Employees: 3,042   Fiscal Year Ends: 08/31
Parent Company:

SALARIES/BONUSES:

Top Exec. Salary: $890,877   Bonus: $
Second Exec. Salary: Bonus: $
$110,452

OTHER THOUGHTS:

Estimated Female Officers or Directors: 3
Hot Spot for Advancement for Women/Minorities: Y

AT&T Inc

www.att.com

NAIC Code: 517311

TYPES OF BUSINESS:

Local Telephone Service
Telecommunications
Media Services
Technology
Video Services
Broadband
Television and Film Production
Entertainment Services

BRANDS/DIVISIONS/AFFILIATES:

WanerMedia
HBO Max
Home Box Office
Warner Bros
Xandr
Otter Media Holdings
Vrio

GROWTH PLANS/SPECIAL FEATURES:

The wireless business contributes about two thirds of AT&T's revenue following the spinoff of Warner Media. The firm is the third-largest U.S. wireless carrier, connecting 71 million postpaid and 17 million prepaid phone customers. Fixed-line enterprise services, which account for about 17% of revenue, include internet access, private networking, security, voice, and wholesale network capacity. Residential fixed-line services, about 11% of revenue, primarily consist of broadband internet access. AT&T also has a sizable presence in Mexico, serving 22 million customers, but this business only accounts for 3% of revenue. The firm still holds a 70% equity stake in satellite television provider DirecTV but does not consolidate this business in its financial statements.

CONTACTS:
Note: Officers with more than one job title may be intentionally listed here more than once.

Jason Kilar, CEO, Subsidiary
Jeffery McElfresh, CEO, Subsidiary
Lori Lee, CEO, Subsidiary
John Stankey, CEO
Pascal Desroches, CFO
William Kennard, Chairman of the Board
David Huntley, Chief Compliance Officer
David McAtee, General Counsel
Angela Santone, Senior Executive VP, Divisional
Edward Gillespie, Senior Executive VP, Subsidiary

FINANCIAL DATA: *Note: Data for latest year may not have been available at press time.*

In U.S. $	2022	2021	2020	2019	2018	2017
Revenue	120,741,000,000	134,038,000,000	171,760,000,000	181,193,000,000	170,756,000,000	160,546,000,000
R&D Expense						
Operating Income	22,911,000,000	26,110,000,000	25,285,000,000	29,413,000,000	26,142,000,000	22,884,000,000
Operating Margin %	.19%	.19%	.15%	.16%	.15%	.14%
SGA Expense	28,961,000,000	29,669,000,000	38,039,000,000	39,422,000,000	36,765,000,000	35,465,000,000
Net Income	-8,524,000,000	20,081,000,000	-5,176,000,000	13,903,000,000	19,370,000,000	29,450,000,000
Operating Cash Flow	32,023,000,000	41,958,000,000	43,130,000,000	48,668,000,000	43,602,000,000	38,010,000,000
Capital Expenditure	19,626,000,000	15,545,000,000	15,675,000,000	19,635,000,000	21,251,000,000	20,647,000,000
EBITDA	21,035,000,000	53,739,000,000	33,585,000,000	55,107,000,000	61,260,000,000	45,826,000,000
Return on Assets %	-.02%	.04%	-.01%	.03%	.04%	.07%
Return on Equity %	-.07%	.12%	-.03%	.08%	.12%	.22%
Debt to Equity	1.51%	1.02%	1.088	0.94	.90%	0.894

CONTACT INFORMATION:

Phone: 210 821-4105   Fax:
Toll-Free:
Address: 208 S. Akard St., Dallas, TX 75202 United States

STOCK TICKER/OTHER:

Stock Ticker: T   Exchange: NYS
Employees: 160,700   Fiscal Year Ends: 12/31
Parent Company:

SALARIES/BONUSES:

Top Exec. Salary: $2,400,000   Bonus: $
Second Exec. Salary: Bonus: $
$1,300,000

OTHER THOUGHTS:

Estimated Female Officers or Directors: 4
Hot Spot for Advancement for Women/Minorities: Y

Atos SE

NAIC Code: 541512

TYPES OF BUSINESS:

IT Consulting
Business Process Outsourcing
Payment Solutions
e-Commerce Consulting
Supply Chain Management
Customer Relationship Management
Product Lifecycle Management
Web Design

BRANDS/DIVISIONS/AFFILIATES:

Atos
Atos Syntel
Unify
Worldgrid

GROWTH PLANS/SPECIAL FEATURES:

Atos SE is an information technology company offering clients a full-stack range of digital solutions and products alongside consultancy services, digital security and decarbonization offerings. Its operating segments include North America, Northern Europe, Central Europe, Southern Europe and Growing Markets. Its purpose is to help design the future of the information space. The company enables its customers and employees, and members of society to live, work and develop sustainably, in a safe and secure information space.

CONTACTS: Note: Officers with more than one job title may be intentionally listed here more than once.

Pierre Barnabe, Co-CEO
Adrian Gregory, Co-CEO
Robert Goegele, Head-Mfg., Retail & Svcs.
Philippe Mareine, Gen. Sec.
Charles Dehelly, Sr. Exec. VP-Global Oper.
Marc Meyer, Head-Talent & Comm.
Michel-Alain Proch, Head-Finance
Francis Meston, Head-System Integration
Eric Grall, Head-Managed Svcs.
Ingo Juraske, Head-Public Sector, Health Care & Transport
Jeremy Hore, Head-Siemens Account
Gilles Grapinet, Sr. Exec. VP-Global Functions

FINANCIAL DATA: Note: Data for latest year may not have been available at press time.

In U.S. $	2022	2021	2020	2019	2018	2017
Revenue	12,242,010,000	11,700,130,000	12,069,300,000	12,508,640,000	11,493,960,000	12,949,050,000
R&D Expense						
Operating Income	-166,234,900	-878,670,100	950,993,000	930,483,500	879,749,500	1,158,247,000
Operating Margin %		-.08%	.08%	.07%	.08%	.09%
SGA Expense	463,082,900	459,844,500	524,611,400	528,929,200	508,419,600	338,946,400
Net Income	-1,092,401,000	-3,197,323,000	593,696,000	3,669,041,000	680,051,800	648,747,800
Operating Cash Flow	460,924,000	409,110,500	1,315,846,000	1,468,048,000	860,319,500	1,335,276,000
Capital Expenditure	270,941,300	293,609,700	345,423,100	349,740,900	400,474,900	567,789,200
EBITDA	-66,925,730	-2,155,656,000	1,612,694,000	1,478,843,000	1,120,466,000	1,504,749,000
Return on Assets %		-.17%	.03%	.17%	.04%	.04%
Return on Equity %		-.52%	.08%	.52%	.12%	.13%
Debt to Equity		.82%	0.531	0.506	.72%	0.266

CONTACT INFORMATION:

Phone: 33 173260000   Fax:
Toll-Free:
Address: River Ouest 80, Quai Voltaire, Bezons, 95877 France

STOCK TICKER/OTHER:

Stock Ticker: AEXAY   Exchange: PINX
Employees: 111,000   Fiscal Year Ends: 12/31
Parent Company:

SALARIES/BONUSES:

Top Exec. Salary: $ Bonus: $
Second Exec. Salary: $ Bonus: $

OTHER THOUGHTS:

Estimated Female Officers or Directors: 5
Hot Spot for Advancement for Women/Minorities: Y

Audible Inc

NAIC Code: 454110

www.audible.com

TYPES OF BUSINESS:

Audio Books-Online Sales
Audio Programming Software
Time-Shifted Radio Programming
Digital Audio Players
Educational Audio Materials
Audio Content

BRANDS/DIVISIONS/AFFILIATES:

Amazon.com Inc
Audible Plus
Audible.com

CONTACTS: *Note: Officers with more than one job title may be intentionally listed here more than once.*

Bob Carrigan, CEO
Cynthia Chu, CFO
Anne Erni, Chief People Officer
Guy A. Story, Jr., Chief Scientist
Tim Martin, CTO
Beth Anderson, Exec. VP
Foy C. Sperring, Jr., Exec. VP-Customer Experience
Don Katz, Chmn.

GROWTH PLANS/SPECIAL FEATURES:

Audible, Inc., a subsidiary of Amazon.com, Inc., provides internet-delivered premium spoken audio content for playback on personal computers and mobile devices. The company offers a variety of software systems and audio programming software designed to download, store and play content from its online store, Audible.com. Audible sells a wide array of audio content, including educational materials, humor, periodicals, fiction, nonfiction and time-shifted radio programming comprised of different programs and thousands of content providers. For an annual membership fee, the company's plans provide up to one free audiobook per month, two Audible originals, discounts on additional purchases, exposure to periodic sales and member-only free content offerings. Audible Plus is a subscription service within Audible that offers unlimited access to a wide variety of love stories. The firm also has partnerships with leading audiobook, magazine and newspaper publishers as well as broadcasters, business information providers and educational and cultural institutions. For example, Audible.com features daily selected audio content from The Wall Street Journal and The New York Times, both available on a subscription basis. In addition, the site offers a large collection of audiobook bestsellers and classics by authors such as Stephen King, James Patterson, William Shakespeare and Jane Austen as well as speeches, lectures and on-demand radio programs. Many titles are available for purchase on Audible's global websites.

Audible offers its employees health benefits, 401(k) and stock plans, and other employee benefits and programs.

FINANCIAL DATA: *Note: Data for latest year may not have been available at press time.*

In U.S. $	2022	2021	2020	2019	2018	2017
Revenue						
R&D Expense						
Operating Income						
Operating Margin %						
SGA Expense						
Net Income						
Operating Cash Flow						
Capital Expenditure						
EBITDA						
Return on Assets %						
Return on Equity %						
Debt to Equity						

CONTACT INFORMATION:

Phone: 973-820-0400   Fax:
Toll-Free: 888-283-5051
Address: 1 Washington Park, Fl. 16, Newark, NJ 07102 United States

STOCK TICKER/OTHER:

Stock Ticker: Subsidiary   Exchange:
Employees: 400   Fiscal Year Ends: 12/31
Parent Company: Amazon.com Inc

SALARIES/BONUSES:

Top Exec. Salary: $ Bonus: $
Second Exec. Salary: $ Bonus: $

OTHER THOUGHTS:

Estimated Female Officers or Directors: 2
Hot Spot for Advancement for Women/Minorities: Y

Authorize.net

www.authorize.net

NAIC Code: 522320

TYPES OF BUSINESS:

Software-Payment Processing & Antifraud
Payment Transaction Products & Services
Ecommerce Payment Solutions
Online and Mobile App Payments
Business Payment Devices
Billing and Invoicing Solutions
Virtual Payment Terminal Solutions
Fraud Protection

BRANDS/DIVISIONS/AFFILIATES:

Visa Inc
CyberSource Corporation

CONTACTS: Note: Officers with more than one job title may be intentionally listed here more than once.

Ryan McInerney, CEO-Visa Inc
Roy D. Banks, Pres.
Eugene J. DiDonato, VP
Alfred F. Kelly, Jr., Chmn.-Visa Inc

GROWTH PLANS/SPECIAL FEATURES:

Authorize.net is a payment processing services company, serving more than 445,000 merchants. Authorize.net's payment solutions include: ecommerce, offering customers a variety of payment options online; point of sale, for connecting a compatible card reader to the business' computer for accepting payments; mobile payments, for accepting payments from customers using mobile devices; billing, offering easy-to-use tools for managing ongoing billing needs; eCheck, for accepting electronic check payments from customers; and phone payments, for submitting manual orders swiftly and securely with Authorize's virtual terminal solution. Features offered by Authorize.com include advanced fraud protection, customer information management, recurring/installment payment submission and acceptance, account updater, digital invoicing and a buy now or donate button on the business' website. The firm operates as a subsidiary of CyberSource Corporation, itself a subsidiary of Visa, Inc.

FINANCIAL DATA: Note: Data for latest year may not have been available at press time.

In U.S. $	2022	2021	2020	2019	2018	2017
Revenue						
R&D Expense						
Operating Income						
Operating Margin %						
SGA Expense						
Net Income						
Operating Cash Flow						
Capital Expenditure						
EBITDA						
Return on Assets %						
Return on Equity %						
Debt to Equity						

CONTACT INFORMATION:

Phone: 801-492-6450   Fax: 801-492-6489
Toll-Free: 888-323-4289
Address: 808 E. Utah Valley Dr., American Fork, UT 84003 United States

SALARIES/BONUSES:

Top Exec. Salary: $ Bonus: $
Second Exec. Salary: $ Bonus: $

STOCK TICKER/OTHER:

Stock Ticker: Subsidiary   Exchange:
Employees: 200   Fiscal Year Ends: 12/31
Parent Company: Visa Inc

OTHER THOUGHTS:

Estimated Female Officers or Directors:
Hot Spot for Advancement for Women/Minorities:

Autohome Inc

NAIC Code: 519130

TYPES OF BUSINESS:

Automobile Information for Consumers
Online Portal
Automobile Marketplace
Used Cars

BRANDS/DIVISIONS/AFFILIATES:

Autohome Mall
autohome.com.cn
che168.com
TTP Car Inc

GROWTH PLANS/SPECIAL FEATURES:

Founded in 2008 as a media content platform, Autohome is the leading online automobile platform in China, ranking first among automotive service platforms in terms of mobile daily active users, according to QuestMobile. Through its two websites, autohome.com.cn and che168.com, Autohome delivers comprehensive, independent and interactive content and tools to automobile consumers as well as a full suite of services to automakers and dealers. According to iResearch, the company was the largest online automotive advertising and lead generation service provider with 30% market share, in terms of media services and lead generation revenue, in China's online auto platform media advertising market in 2019.

CONTACTS: *Note: Officers with more than one job title may be intentionally listed here more than once.*

Quan Long, CEO

FINANCIAL DATA: *Note: Data for latest year may not have been available at press time.*

In U.S. $	2022	2021	2020	2019	2018	2017
Revenue	954,472,400	995,201,200	1,190,687,000	1,157,985,000	994,671,400	853,997,000
R&D Expense	194,872,600	192,251,900	187,602,500	177,540,100	156,114,200	120,845,000
Operating Income	171,553,800	244,999,500	432,902,900	444,972,000	394,522,000	282,158,700
Operating Margin %		.25%	.36%	.38%	.40%	.33%
SGA Expense	463,227,700	454,310,900	498,954,800	469,108,700	378,179,300	265,332,300
Net Income	267,438,500	352,089,200	450,454,200	440,045,300	394,809,400	275,253,900
Operating Cash Flow	352,737,900	484,596,000	457,326,200	397,333,400	427,871,400	338,797,100
Capital Expenditure	16,163,860	30,199,530	36,368,070	28,068,730	15,663,030	14,785,960
EBITDA	229,862,900	304,291,300	471,294,300	478,117,400	408,533,900	294,375,300
Return on Assets %		.08%	.16%	.18%	.20%	.18%
Return on Equity %		.11%	.21%	.25%	.30%	.28%
Debt to Equity		.00%	0.005	0.002		

CONTACT INFORMATION:

Phone: 86 10-5985-7001   Fax:
Toll-Free:
Address: 18/Fl, Tower B, 3 Dan Ling St., Haidian Distr., Beijing, Beijing 100080 China

STOCK TICKER/OTHER:

Stock Ticker: ATHM   Exchange: NYS
Employees: 5,355   Fiscal Year Ends: 12/31
Parent Company:

SALARIES/BONUSES:

Top Exec. Salary: $ Bonus: $
Second Exec. Salary: $ Bonus: $

OTHER THOUGHTS:

Estimated Female Officers or Directors:
Hot Spot for Advancement for Women/Minorities:

Automatic Data Processing Inc (ADP)

www.adp.com

NAIC Code: 518210

TYPES OF BUSINESS:

Data Processing Services
Business Outsourcing Solutions
Information Services
Payroll Processing

BRANDS/DIVISIONS/AFFILIATES:

RUN Powered by ADP
ADP Vantage HCM
ADP SmartCompliance
ADP Workforce Now
ADP GlobalView HCM
ADP TotalSource

GROWTH PLANS/SPECIAL FEATURES:

ADP is a provider of payroll and human capital management solutions servicing the full scope of businesses from micro to global enterprises. ADP was established in 1949 and serves over 1 million clients primarily in the United States. ADP's employer services segment offers payroll, human capital management solutions, human resources outsourcing, insurance and retirement services. The smaller but faster-growing professional employer organization segment provides HR outsourcing solutions to small and midsize businesses through a co-employment model.

CONTACTS: Note: Officers with more than one job title may be intentionally listed here more than once.

Carlos Rodriguez, CEO
Laura Brown, Pres., Geographical
Kathleen Winters, CFO
John Jones, Chairman of the Board
Brock Albinson, Chief Accounting Officer
Michael Bonarti, Chief Administrative Officer
Christopher D'Ambrosio, Chief Strategy Officer
Sreeni Kutam, Other Executive Officer
Alexander Quevedo, President, Divisional
Joseph DeSilva, President, Divisional
Brian Michaud, President, Divisional
Deborah Dyson, President, Divisional
Maria Black, President, Divisional
Don McGuire, President, Divisional
John Ayala, President, Geographical
Michael Eberhard, Treasurer
David Kwon, Vice President
Stuart Sackman, Vice President, Divisional

FINANCIAL DATA: Note: Data for latest year may not have been available at press time.

In U.S. $	2022	2021	2020	2019	2018	2017
Revenue	16,046,500,000	14,583,000,000	14,044,600,000	13,548,300,000	12,807,700,000	
R&D Expense						
Operating Income	3,351,400,000	2,902,200,000	2,596,500,000	2,462,500,000	2,090,900,000	
Operating Margin %	.21%	.20%	.18%	.18%	.16%	
SGA Expense	3,233,200,000	3,040,500,000	3,003,000,000	3,064,200,000	2,959,400,000	
Net Income	2,948,900,000	2,598,500,000	2,466,500,000	2,292,800,000	1,884,900,000	
Operating Cash Flow	3,099,500,000	3,093,300,000	3,026,200,000	2,688,300,000	2,515,200,000	
Capital Expenditure	553,400,000	505,900,000	616,400,000	566,500,000	470,800,000	
EBITDA	4,401,100,000	3,931,600,000	3,769,700,000	3,544,500,000	2,762,900,000	
Return on Assets %	.05%	.06%	.06%	.06%	.05%	
Return on Equity %	.66%	.45%	.44%	.45%	.43%	
Debt to Equity	1.04%	.59%	0.234	0.371	.42%	

CONTACT INFORMATION:

Phone: 973 974-5000   Fax: 973 974-5390
Toll-Free: 800-225-5237
Address: 1 ADP Blvd., Roseland, NJ 07068 United States

STOCK TICKER/OTHER:

Stock Ticker: ADP   Exchange: NAS
Employees: 60,000   Fiscal Year Ends: 06/30
Parent Company:

SALARIES/BONUSES:

Top Exec. Salary: $966,000   Bonus: $
Second Exec. Salary: $908,100   Bonus: $

OTHER THOUGHTS:

Estimated Female Officers or Directors: 1
Hot Spot for Advancement for Women/Minorities: Y

Sales, profits and employees may be estimates. Financial information, benefits and other data can change quickly and may vary from those stated here.

Automattic Inc

automattic.com

NAIC Code: 519130

TYPES OF BUSINESS:

Internet Publishing and Broadcasting and Web Search Portals
Website Operations
Mobile App Operations
Writing Platforms
Ecommerce Platforms
Spam Filter Solutions
Stream Solutions
Podcast Solution

BRANDS/DIVISIONS/AFFILIATES:

WordPress.com
WooCommerce
Simplenote
Longreads
VaultPress
Akismet
Day One
Pocket Casts

CONTACTS: *Note: Officers with more than one job title may be intentionally listed here more than once.*

Matt Mullenweg, CEO

GROWTH PLANS/SPECIAL FEATURES:

Automattic, Inc. builds and operates websites worldwide. The company's sites include, but are not limited to, WordPress.com, for blogging or as a website; WooCommerce, an ecommerce site; Jetpack, a plugin for sites and includes stats, backups, speed and power; Simplenote, which synchronizes notes across devices; Longreads, for storytelling; WPScan, providing enterprise protection concerning vulnerabilities affecting WordPress installation, plugins and themes; VaultPress, providing automatic backups and scanning for website security purposes; Akismet, which filters spam; Gravatar, which syncs a picture across all of a user's profiles; Crowdsignal, which collects readers' opinions; Cloudup, for streaming videos, photos, music, links and documents; Tumblr, a microblogging and social networking website; Day One, a place for journaling and adding photos, videos, drawings or audio recordings in relation to the journal written; and Pocket Casts, a podcast platform that provides enhanced listening, search and discovery tools. Automattic also serves nonprofit and opensource projects in the U.S. and internationally. The company is headquartered in San Francisco, California, USA, but has employees across 93 countries, speaking more than 119 different languages.

Automatic offers employee benefits, which vary by location.

FINANCIAL DATA: *Note: Data for latest year may not have been available at press time.*

In U.S. $	2022	2021	2020	2019	2018	2017
Revenue						
R&D Expense						
Operating Income						
Operating Margin %						
SGA Expense						
Net Income						
Operating Cash Flow						
Capital Expenditure						
EBITDA						
Return on Assets %						
Return on Equity %						
Debt to Equity						

CONTACT INFORMATION:

Phone: 877-273-3049   Fax: 415-840-0710
Toll-Free:
Address: 60 29th St., #343, San Francisco, CA 94110 United States

STOCK TICKER/OTHER:

Stock Ticker: Private   Exchange:
Employees: 1,275   Fiscal Year Ends:
Parent Company:

SALARIES/BONUSES:

Top Exec. Salary: $ Bonus: $
Second Exec. Salary: $ Bonus: $

OTHER THOUGHTS:

Estimated Female Officers or Directors:
Hot Spot for Advancement for Women/Minorities:

Sales, profits and employees may be estimates. Financial information, benefits and other data can change quickly and may vary from those stated here.

AutoWeb Inc

www.autoweb.com

NAIC Code: 519130

TYPES OF BUSINESS:

Automotive Media & Marketing Services
Online Car Sales Support
Digital Marketing

BRANDS/DIVISIONS/AFFILIATES:

Payment Pro
Autobytel
WebLeads+
MyGarage
iControl
TextShield
CarZeus

GROWTH PLANS/SPECIAL FEATURES:

AutoWeb Inc is a digital marketing company for the automotive industry. The company helps automotive retail dealers and automotive manufacturers to market and sell new and used vehicles to consumers through the company's programs for online lead and traffic referrals, dealer marketing products and services, online advertising and mobile products. Through its owned and operated flagship entities, namely car.com, usedcars.com, and Autobytel, AutoWeb equips consumers with the knowledge to make the best car-buying decisions possible. The firm has offices in the U.S., Canada, Ukraine, Armenia and Guatemala.

CONTACTS: Note: Officers with more than one job title may be intentionally listed here more than once.

Jared Rowe, CEO
Carlton Hamer, CFO
Cheray Duran, Chief Accounting Officer
Glenn Fuller, Chief Legal Officer
Daniel Ingle, COO
Sara Partin, Other Executive Officer
Michael Fuchs, Chmn.

FINANCIAL DATA: Note: Data for latest year may not have been available at press time.

In U.S. $	2022	2021	2020	2019	2018	2017
Revenue	74,448,400	71,585,000	76,570,000	113,981,000	125,589,000	142,124,992
R&D Expense						
Operating Income						
Operating Margin %						
SGA Expense						
Net Income		-5,659,000	-6,820,000	-15,229,000	-38,816,000	-64,964,000
Operating Cash Flow						
Capital Expenditure						
EBITDA						
Return on Assets %						
Return on Equity %						
Debt to Equity						

CONTACT INFORMATION:

Phone: 949-225-4500   Fax:
Toll-Free:
Address: 400 N. Ashley Dr., Ste. 300, Tampa, FL 33602 United States

STOCK TICKER/OTHER:

Stock Ticker: Private   Exchange:
Employees: 150   Fiscal Year Ends: 12/31
Parent Company: One Planet Group LLC

SALARIES/BONUSES:

Top Exec. Salary: $ Bonus: $
Second Exec. Salary: $ Bonus: $

OTHER THOUGHTS:

Estimated Female Officers or Directors: 1
Hot Spot for Advancement for Women/Minorities:

Avalara Inc

NAIC Code: 511210Q

TYPES OF BUSINESS:

Computer Software: Accounting, Banking & Financial
Tax Compliance Software
Cloud

BRANDS/DIVISIONS/AFFILIATES:

Vista Equity Partners Management LLC

GROWTH PLANS/SPECIAL FEATURES:

Avalara, Inc., privately-owned by Vista Equity Partners Management LLC, provides compliance solutions. For its over 30,000 business and government customers in over 90 countries, the firm provides software solutions that help them comply with tax requirements for transactions worldwide. Avalara offers a broad and growing suite of compliance solutions for transaction taxes, such as sales and use tax, VAT, fuel excise tax, beverage alcohol, cross-border taxes, lodging tax, and communications tax. These solutions enable customers to automate the process of determining taxability, identifying applicable tax rates, determining and collecting taxes, preparing and filing returns, remitting taxes, maintaining tax records, and managing compliance documents. The firm generates revenue in the form of subscriptions and professional services.

CONTACTS: *Note: Officers with more than one job title may be intentionally listed here more than once.*

Scott McFarlane, CEO
Ross Tennenbaum, CFO
Ross Tennenbaum, CFO
Jay Lee, CMO
Ee Lyn Khoo, Chief People Officer
Danny Fields, Chief Technology Officer

FINANCIAL DATA: *Note: Data for latest year may not have been available at press time.*

In U.S. $	2022	2021	2020	2019	2018	2017
Revenue	700,000,000	698,977,024	500,568,992	382,420,992	272,097,984	213,159,008
R&D Expense						
Operating Income						
Operating Margin %						
SGA Expense						
Net Income		-135,618,000	-55,320,000	-51,951,000	-75,550,000	-64,126,000
Operating Cash Flow						
Capital Expenditure						
EBITDA						
Return on Assets %						
Return on Equity %						
Debt to Equity						

CONTACT INFORMATION:

Phone: 206 826-4900   Fax: 206 780-5011
Toll-Free: 877-780-4848
Address: 255 S. King St., Ste. 1800, Seattle, WA 98104 United States

STOCK TICKER/OTHER:

Stock Ticker: Private   Exchange:
Employees: 4,400   Fiscal Year Ends: 12/31
Parent Company: Vista Equity Partners Management LLC

SALARIES/BONUSES:

Top Exec. Salary: $ Bonus: $
Second Exec. Salary: $ Bonus: $

OTHER THOUGHTS:

Estimated Female Officers or Directors:
Hot Spot for Advancement for Women/Minorities:

Avantax Inc

www.avantax.com

NAIC Code: 519130

TYPES OF BUSINESS:

Internet Search Engines
Federal Tax Preparation Software
Technology
Wealth Management
Digital Tax

BRANDS/DIVISIONS/AFFILIATES:

Cetera Holdings
Cetera Financial Group Inc
Avantax Wealth Management
Avantax Planning Partners

CONTACTS: Note: Officers with more than one job title may be intentionally listed here more than once.

Todd Mackay, Pres., Avantax Wealth Management
Marc Mehlman, CFO
Andrew Duggan, VP-Finance
Blynn Austin, VP-Mktg. & Comm.
Curtis Campbell, President, Divisional
Todd Mackay, President, Subsidiary

GROWTH PLANS/SPECIAL FEATURES:

Avantax, Inc. is a provider of tax-intelligent wealth management solutions for financial professionals, tax professionals and CPA firms, supporting its goal of minimizing clients' tax burdens through comprehensive tax-intelligent financial planning. Avantax has two distinct models within its business: the independent Financial Professional model and the employee-based model. Avantax refers to its independent Financial Professional model as Avantax Wealth Management. Avantax Wealth Management works with a nationwide network of Financial Professionals operating as independent contractors and offers its services through its U.S. independent broker-dealer, registered investment advisor (RIA), and insurance agency subsidiaries. The firm's employee-based model, Avantax Planning Partners, offers services through its RIA and insurance agency by partnering with CPA firms to provide their consumer and small-business clients with holistic financial planning and advisory services. Collectively, Avantax manages $92 billion in total client assets across all 50 states in the U.S. In November 2023, Avantax was acquired by wealth hub and financial services provider Cetera Financial Group, Inc., part of Cetera Holdings.

FINANCIAL DATA: Note: Data for latest year may not have been available at press time.

In U.S. $	2022	2021	2020	2019	2018	2017
Revenue	666,496,000	658,213,000	546,189,000	507,979,000	373,174,000	348,620,000
R&D Expense						
Operating Income						
Operating Margin %						
SGA Expense						
Net Income	420,247,000	7,757,000	-342,755,008	48,148,000	51,569,000	29,376,000
Operating Cash Flow						
Capital Expenditure						
EBITDA						
Return on Assets %						
Return on Equity %						
Debt to Equity						

CONTACT INFORMATION:

Phone: 972-870-6000   Fax:
Toll-Free:
Address: 3200 Olympus Blvd., Ste. 100, Dallas, TX 75019 United States

STOCK TICKER/OTHER:

Stock Ticker: Subsidiary   Exchange:
Employees: 727   Fiscal Year Ends: 12/31
Parent Company: Cetera Holdings

SALARIES/BONUSES:

Top Exec. Salary: $ Bonus: $
Second Exec. Salary: $ Bonus: $

OTHER THOUGHTS:

Estimated Female Officers or Directors: 3
Hot Spot for Advancement for Women/Minorities: Y

Avaya Holdings Corp

www.avaya.com

NAIC Code: 334210

TYPES OF BUSINESS:

Telecommunications Systems
Telecommunications Software
Consulting Services
Networking Systems & Software
Network Maintenance, Management & Security Services
Systems Planning & Integration
Unified Communications Systems

BRANDS/DIVISIONS/AFFILIATES:

Avaya Inc

GROWTH PLANS/SPECIAL FEATURES:

Avaya Holdings Corp provides digital communications products, solutions, and services for businesses. The company has two operating segments namely Products and Solutions and Services. Products and Solutions offer Unified Communications and Contact Center platforms, applications and devices. It helps to offer an open, extensible development platform so that customers and third parties can easily create custom applications and automated workflows for their unique needs. Whereas Services consists of three business areas: Global Support Services, Enterprise Cloud and Managed Services and Professional Services. The company generates maximum revenue from the Services segment. Geographically, it derives a majority of its revenue from the U.S. In August 2023, Avaya was awarded a cooperative purchasing contract in the Unified Communications and Contact Center categories at Sourcewell. This comes only months after Avaya entered bankruptcy protection as it restructured its operations and finances.

CONTACTS:
Note: Officers with more than one job title may be intentionally listed here more than once.

Alan Masarek, CEO
Amy O'Keefe, CFO
Josh Mueller, CMO
Stephen Spears, Executive VP

FINANCIAL DATA:
Note: Data for latest year may not have been available at press time.

In U.S. $	2022	2021	2020	2019	2018	2017
Revenue	3,000,000,000	2,972,999,936	2,872,999,936	2,887,000,064	2,887,000,064	3,272,000,000
R&D Expense						
Operating Income						
Operating Margin %						
SGA Expense						
Net Income		-13,000,000	-680,000,000	-671,000,000	-671,000,000	-182,000,000
Operating Cash Flow						
Capital Expenditure						
EBITDA						
Return on Assets %						
Return on Equity %						
Debt to Equity						

CONTACT INFORMATION:

Phone: 908 953-6000   Fax:
Toll-Free: 866-462-8292
Address: 4655 Great American Pkwy., Santa Clara, CA 95054 United States

STOCK TICKER/OTHER:

Stock Ticker: Private   Exchange:
Employees: 8,266   Fiscal Year Ends: 09/30
Parent Company:

SALARIES/BONUSES:

Top Exec. Salary: $ Bonus: $
Second Exec. Salary: $ Bonus: $

OTHER THOUGHTS:

Estimated Female Officers or Directors: 1
Hot Spot for Advancement for Women/Minorities:

Axway Inc

www.axway.com

NAIC Code: 511210E

TYPES OF BUSINESS:

Computer Software, Network Security, Managed Access, Digital ID,
Cybersecurity & Anti-Virus
Email, Firewall & Anti-Spam Software
Secure File Transfer Software
Professional Services
Security Software
Business Processing Management
Tracking Software
Data Integration and Transformation

BRANDS/DIVISIONS/AFFILIATES:

Axway AMPLIFY

CONTACTS:
Note: Officers with more than one job title may be intentionally listed here more than once.

Patrick Donovan, CEO
Mark Fairbrother, Exec. VP-R&D
Cecile Allmacher, CFO
Paul French, CMO
Dominique Fougerat, Exec. VP-People & Culture
Vince Padua, CTO
Rohit Khanna, Sr. VP-Consulting & Professional Svcs.
Pierre Pasquier, Chmn.

GROWTH PLANS/SPECIAL FEATURES:

Axway, Inc. is a leading provider of multi-enterprise solutions, serving more than 11,000 enterprises in 100 countries. Its Axway AMPLIFY platform unifies a business' employees, suppliers, partners and developers in order to create a powerful customer experience network that meets consumer demands. The platform's capabilities include analytics, application program interface (API) lifecycle management, app development, community management and integration. For IT and architects, Axway's product offers big data integration, cloud integration, identity federation, identity validation, mobility and Internet of Things (IoT). For developers, it offers cross-platform application, development, API development and DevOps. Businesses and industries served by the firm include automotive, banking/financial services, healthcare, life sciences, manufacturing, consumer packaged goods, retail, U.S. federal government and many more. Axway offers various types of support, including downloads, documentation, contact support, how-to videos, webinars, training courses, resource library, cloud consulting, API management consulting and managed file transfer consulting. Corporately headquartered in Arizona, USA, the firm has global headquarters in France, Singapore and Brazil, and offices throughout North America, Asia-Pacific, Europe and Latin America.

FINANCIAL DATA:
Note: Data for latest year may not have been available at press time.

In U.S. $	2022	2021	2020	2019	2018	2017
Revenue	335,224,952	293,923,350	365,076,000	395,928,698	377,074,950	359,119,000
R&D Expense						
Operating Income						
Operating Margin %						
SGA Expense						
Net Income	-42,743,367	20,832,462	10,413,100	11,565,164	12,581,700	5,270,600
Operating Cash Flow						
Capital Expenditure						
EBITDA						
Return on Assets %						
Return on Equity %						
Debt to Equity						

CONTACT INFORMATION:

Phone: 480 627-1800   Fax: 480-627-1801
Toll-Free: 877-564-7700
Address: 6811 E. Mayo Blvd., Ste. 400, Phoenix, AZ 85054 United States

STOCK TICKER/OTHER:

Stock Ticker: AXW
Employees: 1,885
Parent Company: Sopra Steria Group SA

Exchange: Paris
Fiscal Year Ends: 12/31

SALARIES/BONUSES:

Top Exec. Salary: $ Bonus: $
Second Exec. Salary: $ Bonus: $

OTHER THOUGHTS:

Estimated Female Officers or Directors:
Hot Spot for Advancement for Women/Minorities:

BackCountry.com LLC

www.backcountrycorp.com

NAIC Code: 454110

TYPES OF BUSINESS:

Sporting Goods-Online Retail
Outdoor Sports Equipment
Athletic Apparel
Ski Equipment
Ecommerce Retailer

BRANDS/DIVISIONS/AFFILIATES:

TSG Consumer Partners LLC
competitivecyclist.com
motorsport.com
steapandcheap.com

CONTACTS: *Note: Officers with more than one job title may be intentionally listed here more than once.*

Melanie Cox, CEO
Steve Lyman, Chief Supply Chain & Vendor Oper. Officer
Judd Tirnauer, CFO
Colby Black, Chief Product Officer
Ben Gross, Chief People Officer
Scott Huddleston, Chief Digital Officer
Jonathan Nielson, Exec. VP-Prod.
Brendan Quirk, Exec. VP-Customer Experience

GROWTH PLANS/SPECIAL FEATURES:

BackCountry.com LLC, owned by private equity firm TSG Consumer Partners, LLC, is an online retailer of outdoor gear. The company was founded by Jim Holland, a two-time Olympian and six-time national champion Nordic ski jumper; and John Bresee, former editor of Powder Magazine. BackCountry offers a wide selection of goods for outdoor activities, including men's, women's and children's clothing, shoes, skis and skiing accessories, snowboards and snowboard accessories, hiking and camping gear, trail running products, snowshoeing products, technical climbing gear, kayaks and kayak accessories and outdoor travel products (backpacks, car racks, etc.). The company's selection of goods encompasses over 1,000 brands, including The North Face, Oakley, Patagonia, Marmot, Oakley, Rossignol, K2 and more. BackCountry has been expanding since its inception and has fostered spin-off ecommerce storefronts, each focused on a specific niche of the outdoor sporting market. These internet stores include: competitivecyclist.com, a source for pro-caliber cycling gear and clothing; motosport.com for motorcycle enthusiasts; and steapandcheap.com, a showroom of limited-time, limited quantity deals. The company processes orders and ships from a 200,000-square-foot distribution center in Utah, and a 320,000-square-foot distribution center in Virginia. The firm also maintains offices in Portland, Oregon, the motosport.com headquarters; and Costa Rica, BackCountry's first international office.

BackCountry offers its employees comprehensive health benefits, life and disability insurance, 401(k) and a variety of employee assistance programs and company perks.

FINANCIAL DATA: *Note: Data for latest year may not have been available at press time.*

In U.S. $	2022	2021	2020	2019	2018	2017
Revenue						
R&D Expense						
Operating Income						
Operating Margin %						
SGA Expense						
Net Income						
Operating Cash Flow						
Capital Expenditure						
EBITDA						
Return on Assets %						
Return on Equity %						
Debt to Equity						

CONTACT INFORMATION:

Phone: 801 746-7580   Fax: 801-973-4552
Toll-Free: 800-409-4502
Address: 1678 W. Redstone Center Dr., Ste. 210, Park City, UT 84098 United States

STOCK TICKER/OTHER:

Stock Ticker: Private   Exchange:
Employees: 1,200   Fiscal Year Ends: 12/31
Parent Company: TSG Consumer Partners LLC

SALARIES/BONUSES:

Top Exec. Salary: $ Bonus: $
Second Exec. Salary: $ Bonus: $

OTHER THOUGHTS:

Estimated Female Officers or Directors: 1
Hot Spot for Advancement for Women/Minorities:

Badoo Trading Limited

badoo.com

NAIC Code: 511210G

TYPES OF BUSINESS:

Computer Software, Electronic Games, Apps & Entertainment
Dating App
Online Dating Platform

GROWTH PLANS/SPECIAL FEATURES:

Badoo Trading Limited operates Badoo, a free online dating platform that combines photos with instant messaging. The site comprises millions of members across the world. Badoo enables people to build connections by expressing who they are and what they want in a relationship. Safety is the firm's number one priority and has a safety center containing all the information and support a person needs to date with confidence. Badoo is privately-owned by Bumble, Inc.

Parent Bumble offers its employees benefits, which vary by location.

BRANDS/DIVISIONS/AFFILIATES:

Bumble Inc

CONTACTS: Note: Officers with more than one job title may be intentionally listed here more than once.

Whitney Wolfe Herd, CEO-Corporate

FINANCIAL DATA: Note: Data for latest year may not have been available at press time.

In U.S. $	2022	2021	2020	2019	2018	2017
Revenue	209,200,000	232,744,000	630,827,000	502,444,000	342,486,000	194,418,000
R&D Expense						
Operating Income						
Operating Margin %						
SGA Expense						
Net Income			-55,175,200	-60,028,200	-4,265,190	-7,946,340
Operating Cash Flow						
Capital Expenditure						
EBITDA						
Return on Assets %						
Return on Equity %						
Debt to Equity						

CONTACT INFORMATION:

Phone: 44 20 7440 7000   Fax:
Toll-Free:
Address: The Broadgate Twr., Fl. 3, 20 Primrose St., London, EC2A 2RS United Kingdom

STOCK TICKER/OTHER:

Stock Ticker: Private   Exchange:
Employees: Fiscal Year Ends: 12/31
Parent Company: Bumble Inc

SALARIES/BONUSES:

Top Exec. Salary: $ Bonus: $
Second Exec. Salary: $ Bonus: $

OTHER THOUGHTS:

Estimated Female Officers or Directors:
Hot Spot for Advancement for Women/Minorities:

Baidu Inc

NAIC Code: 519130

TYPES OF BUSINESS:

Online Search Portals
Online Advertising Services
Social Networking
Entertainment
News
Online Payment Services

BRANDS/DIVISIONS/AFFILIATES:

Baidu App
Baidu Search
Haokan
Baidu Post Bar
Baidu Knows
Baidu Maps
Baidu Input Method Editor
iQIYI

CONTACTS: Note: Officers with more than one job title may be intentionally listed here more than once.

Robin Li, CEO
Dou Shen, Exec. VP
Rong Luo, CFO
Shanshan Cui, Sr. VP
Victor Zhixiang Liang, Sr. VP
Haifeng Wang, CTO
Jing Wang, VP-Eng.
Victor Liang, VP-Legal Affairs
Hailong Xiang, VP-Commercial Oper.
Guang Zhu, VP-Public Rel.
Robin Li, Chmn.

GROWTH PLANS/SPECIAL FEATURES:

Baidu is the largest internet search engine in China with 84% share of the search engine market in September 2021 per web analytics firm, Statcounter. The firm generated 72% of core revenue from online marketing services from its search engine in 2022. Outside its search engine, Baidu is a technology-driven company and its other major growth initiatives are artificial intelligence cloud, video streaming services, voice recognition technology, and autonomous driving.

FINANCIAL DATA: Note: Data for latest year may not have been available at press time.

In U.S. $	2022	2021	2020	2019	2018	2017
Revenue	17,007,250,000	17,119,730,000	14,724,350,000	14,770,970,000	14,064,690,000	11,662,560,000
R&D Expense	3,206,177,000	3,429,365,000	2,683,343,000	2,522,862,000	2,168,897,000	1,777,802,000
Operating Income	2,188,011,000	1,446,389,000	1,971,974,000	867,311,100	2,135,618,000	2,157,758,000
Operating Margin %		.08%	.13%	.06%	.15%	.19%
SGA Expense	2,820,996,000	3,399,799,000	2,483,945,000	2,737,936,000	2,644,563,000	1,805,305,000
Net Income	1,039,481,000	1,406,235,000	3,090,251,000	282,869,700	3,791,719,000	2,516,674,000
Operating Cash Flow	3,598,784,000	2,767,089,000	3,327,878,000	3,913,420,000	4,946,025,000	4,514,363,000
Capital Expenditure	1,140,692,000	1,535,912,000	734,058,400	2,628,474,000	3,062,748,000	1,910,642,000
EBITDA	4,553,005,000	5,054,800,000	6,725,477,000	3,404,612,000	6,579,023,000	4,875,892,000
Return on Assets %		.03%	.07%	.01%	.10%	.08%
Return on Equity %		.05%	.13%	.01%	.20%	.18%
Debt to Equity		.35%	0.356	0.383	.34%	0.31

CONTACT INFORMATION:

Phone: 86 10-5992-8888   Fax: 86 1059920000
Toll-Free:
Address: No. 10 Shangdi, 10th St., Beijing, Beijing 100085 China

STOCK TICKER/OTHER:

Stock Ticker: BIDU   Exchange: NAS
Employees: 41,300   Fiscal Year Ends: 12/31
Parent Company:

SALARIES/BONUSES:

Top Exec. Salary: $ Bonus: $
Second Exec. Salary: $ Bonus: $

OTHER THOUGHTS:

Estimated Female Officers or Directors: 1
Hot Spot for Advancement for Women/Minorities:

Bankrate LLC

www.bankrate.com

NAIC Code: 519130

TYPES OF BUSINESS:

Portal-Financial Services
Financial Information
Banking Information
Online Finance Calculation Tools
Financial Comparison Information
Online Financial Strategies
Online Publisher
Online Information Aggregation

BRANDS/DIVISIONS/AFFILIATES:

Red Ventures Holdco LP
Bankrate.com
Bankrate.com/uk/

GROWTH PLANS/SPECIAL FEATURES:

Bankrate, LLC offers an online consumer banking and personal finance platform for guiding savers and spenders. The company publishes, aggregates and distributes finance-related information, offering free tools and resources to help individuals reach their goals. Bankrate is compensated in exchange for featured placement of sponsored ad products and services, or by the clicks on the advertisements themselves. Flagship website, Bankrate.com, aggregates information about financial products and fees, including mortgages, banking, credit cards, loans, investing, home equity, insurance and retirement. The information enables people to compare financial product rates and fees as well as financial strategies. Bankrate.com regularly aggregates data from thousands of financial institutions in all 50 U.S. states, as well as in the U.K. via Bankrate.com/uk/. Bankrate is privately-owned by Red Ventures Holdco, LP, a leading digital consumer choice platform.

CONTACTS: *Note: Officers with more than one job title may be intentionally listed here more than once.*

Kenneth Esterow, CEO
Christopher Speltz, CEO, Subsidiary
Peter Morse, Director
James Gilmartin, General Counsel

FINANCIAL DATA: *Note: Data for latest year may not have been available at press time.*

In U.S. $	2022	2021	2020	2019	2018	2017
Revenue	557,178,804	535,748,850	515,143,125	490,612,500	467,250,000	445,000,000
R&D Expense						
Operating Income						
Operating Margin %						
SGA Expense						
Net Income						
Operating Cash Flow						
Capital Expenditure						
EBITDA						
Return on Assets %						
Return on Equity %						
Debt to Equity						

CONTACT INFORMATION:

Phone: 917-368-8600   Fax:
Toll-Free: 855-733-0700
Address: 1675 Broadway, New York, NY 10019 United States

STOCK TICKER/OTHER:

Stock Ticker: Private   Exchange:
Employees: 600   Fiscal Year Ends: 12/31
Parent Company: Red Ventures Holdco LP

SALARIES/BONUSES:

Top Exec. Salary: $ Bonus: $
Second Exec. Salary: $ Bonus: $

OTHER THOUGHTS:

Estimated Female Officers or Directors:
Hot Spot for Advancement for Women/Minorities:

Beyond Inc

NAIC Code: 454110

TYPES OF BUSINESS:

Online Retail, General
Online Retail
Ecommerce
Blockchain Technology
Order Fulfillment

GROWTH PLANS/SPECIAL FEATURES:

Beyond, Inc., based in Midvale, Utah, is an ecommerce company that focuses on the home furnishing and décor markets. The company owns Overstock, Bed Bath & Beyond, Baby & Beyond and other related brands and associated intellectual property. Its suite of online shopping brands features millions of products for various life stages that millions of customers visit each month. In 2023, Beyond (formerly Overstock.com, Inc.) acquired the Bed Bath & Beyond brand and associated intellectual property. Following the acquisition, the firm rebranded its ecommerce platform to Bed Bath & Beyond.

BRANDS/DIVISIONS/AFFILIATES:

Overstock.com
Bed Bath & Beyond
Baby & Beyond

CONTACTS: *Note: Officers with more than one job title may be intentionally listed here more than once.*

Jonathan Johnson, CEO
Adrianne Lee, CFO
Allison Abraham, Chairman of the Board
Carter Lee, Chief Administrative Officer
E. Nickle, Chief Legal Officer
Joel Weight, Chief Technology Officer
Ronald Hilton, COO
Meghan Tuohig, Other Executive Officer
Krista Mathews, Other Executive Officer
Mark Baker, Other Executive Officer
David Nielsen, President, Divisional

FINANCIAL DATA: *Note: Data for latest year may not have been available at press time.*

In U.S. $	2022	2021	2020	2019	2018	2017
Revenue						
R&D Expense						
Operating Income						
Operating Margin %						
SGA Expense						
Net Income						
Operating Cash Flow						
Capital Expenditure						
EBITDA						
Return on Assets %						
Return on Equity %						
Debt to Equity						

CONTACT INFORMATION:

Phone: 801 947-3100   Fax: 801 944-4629
Toll-Free: 800-989-0135
Address: 799 West Coliseum Way, Midvale, UT 84047 United States

STOCK TICKER/OTHER:

Stock Ticker: BYON   Exchange: NYS
Employees: 1,050   Fiscal Year Ends: 12/31
Parent Company:

SALARIES/BONUSES:

Top Exec. Salary: $871,154   Bonus: $
Second Exec. Salary: Bonus: $
$573,077

OTHER THOUGHTS:

Estimated Female Officers or Directors: 2
Hot Spot for Advancement for Women/Minorities: Y

BigCommerce Holdings Inc

www.bigcommerce.com

NAIC Code: 511210M

TYPES OF BUSINESS:

Computer Software: E-Commerce & Web Analytics
Ecommerce Platform
Business Website
Business Commerce
Online
Application Programming Interface
Marketplace

BRANDS/DIVISIONS/AFFILIATES:

BigCommerce Pty Ltd

GROWTH PLANS/SPECIAL FEATURES:

BigCommerce Holdings Inc is engaged in offering Software-as-a-service (SaaS) e-commerce platform. The company's SaaS platform engages in the creation of online stores by delivering a combination of ease-of-use, enterprise functionality, and flexibility. It powers both the customers' branded ecommerce stores and their cross-channel connections to popular online marketplaces, social networks, and offline point-of-sale systems. The group operates in a single segment covering geographical areas of Americas-U.S.; Americas-other; EMEA; and APAC, of which a majority of revenue is generated from Americas-U.S.

CONTACTS: Note: Officers with more than one job title may be intentionally listed here more than once.

Brent Bellm, CEO
Robert Alvarez, CFO
Thomas Aylor, Chief Accounting Officer
Jeff Mengoli, Chief Legal Officer
Lisa Pearson, Chief Marketing Officer
Brian Dhatt, Chief Technology Officer
Marc Ostryniec, Other Executive Officer
Paul Vaillancourt, Other Executive Officer
Jimmy Duvall, Other Executive Officer
Russell Klein, Other Executive Officer

FINANCIAL DATA: Note: Data for latest year may not have been available at press time.

In U.S. $	2022	2021	2020	2019	2018	2017
Revenue	279,075,000	219,855,000	152,368,000	112,103,000	91,867,000	
R&D Expense	88,253,000	64,547,000	48,332,000	43,123,000	42,485,000	
Operating Income	-98,019,000	-52,644,000	-38,697,000	-40,987,000	-37,980,000	
Operating Margin %	-.35%	-.24%	-.25%	-.37%		
SGA Expense	210,783,000	156,189,000	108,607,000	82,944,000	65,425,000	
Net Income	-139,919,000	-76,677,000	-37,560,000	-42,590,000	-38,878,000	
Operating Cash Flow	-89,357,000	-40,300,000	-26,529,000	-39,969,000	-30,591,000	
Capital Expenditure	5,196,000	3,304,000	1,964,000	5,579,000	3,326,000	
EBITDA	-127,140,000	-70,306,000	-31,348,000	-38,381,000	-35,535,000	
Return on Assets %	-.27%	-.18%	-.23%	-.87%		
Return on Equity %	-1.52%	-.43%				
Debt to Equity	7.61%	2.50%	0.058			

CONTACT INFORMATION:

Phone: 512-758-7588   Fax:
Toll-Free: 888-699-8911
Address: 11305 Four Points Dr., Bldg. 2, 3/Fl, Austin, TX 78726 United States

STOCK TICKER/OTHER:

Stock Ticker: BIGC
Employees: 1,500
Parent Company:

Exchange: NAS
Fiscal Year Ends: 12/31

SALARIES/BONUSES:

Top Exec. Salary: $469,231   Bonus: $206,860
Second Exec. Salary: $390,385   Bonus: $111,857

OTHER THOUGHTS:

Estimated Female Officers or Directors:
Hot Spot for Advancement for Women/Minorities:

Sales, profits and employees may be estimates. Financial information, benefits and other data can change quickly and may vary from those stated here.

Bill.com Holdings Inc

NAIC Code: 511210Q

www.bill.com

TYPES OF BUSINESS:

Computer Software: Accounting, Banking & Financial
Cloud-based Business Software
Cash Management
Accounts Payable Automation
Supplier and Customer Collaboration
Storage Solutions
Transaction Dashboard
Document Processing Solution

BRANDS/DIVISIONS/AFFILIATES:

Invoice2go

GROWTH PLANS/SPECIAL FEATURES:

BILL Holdings Inc is a provider of software-as-a-service, cloud-based payments and spend and expense management products, which allow users to automate accounts payable and accounts receivable transactions, enable businesses to easily connect with their suppliers or customers to do business, eliminate expense reports, manage cash flows and improve back office efficiency. Initial Public Offering and Follow-on Offering.

CONTACTS: Note: Officers with more than one job title may be intentionally listed here more than once.

Blake Murray, CEO, Subsidiary
Rene Lacerte, CEO
John Rettig, CFO
Raj Aji, Chief Compliance Officer
Mark Lenhard, COO
Thomas Clayton, Other Executive Officer
Bora Chung, Other Executive Officer

FINANCIAL DATA: Note: Data for latest year may not have been available at press time.

In U.S. $	2022	2021	2020	2019	2018	2017
Revenue	641,959,000	238,265,000	157,600,000	108,351,000	64,865,000	
R&D Expense	219,818,000	89,503,000	52,996,000	28,924,000	17,986,000	
Operating Income	-316,818,000	-113,967,000	-34,198,000	-9,803,000	-7,817,000	
Operating Margin %	- .49%	- .48%	- .22%	- .09%		
SGA Expense	548,325,000	196,051,000	98,520,000	59,312,000	35,324,000	
Net Income	-326,361,000	-98,720,000	-31,091,000	-7,314,000	-7,195,000	
Operating Cash Flow	-18,093,000	4,623,000	-4,430,000	-3,949,000	-8,356,000	
Capital Expenditure	15,636,000	21,206,000	12,076,000	4,299,000	2,046,000	
EBITDA	-233,756,000	-100,170,000	-26,552,000	-3,491,000	-4,444,000	
Return on Assets %	- .04%	- .02%	- .02%	- .01%		
Return on Equity %	- .10%	- .06%	- .10%			
Debt to Equity	.44%	.43%				

CONTACT INFORMATION:

Phone: 650-621-7700   Fax:
Toll-Free:
Address: 6220 America Center Dr., Ste. 100, San Jose, CA 95022 United States

STOCK TICKER/OTHER:

Stock Ticker: BILL
Employees: 2,521
Parent Company:

Exchange: NYS
Fiscal Year Ends: 06/30

SALARIES/BONUSES:

Top Exec. Salary: $550,000   Bonus: $
Second Exec. Salary: $351,479   Bonus: $145,224

OTHER THOUGHTS:

Estimated Female Officers or Directors:
Hot Spot for Advancement for Women/Minorities:

BlackLine Inc

www.blackline.com

NAIC Code: 511210Q

TYPES OF BUSINESS:

Computer Software: Accounting, Banking & Financial
Cloud Software
Finance and Accounting

BRANDS/DIVISIONS/AFFILIATES:

Rimilia Holdings Ltd

GROWTH PLANS/SPECIAL FEATURES:

BlackLine Inc is engaged in providing financial accounting close solutions delivered as Software as a Service (SaaS). The Company's solutions enable its customers to address various aspects of their financial close process including account reconciliations, variance analysis of account balances, journal entry capabilities, and certain types of data matching capabilities. The majority of the revenue of the company is earned in the United States.

BlackLine offers its employees health benefits and company perks.

CONTACTS:
Note: Officers with more than one job title may be intentionally listed here more than once.

Marc Huffman, CEO
Mark Partin, CFO
Therese Tucker, Chairman of the Board
Patrick Villanova, Chief Accounting Officer
Karole Morgan-Prager, Chief Administrative Officer
Peter Hirsch, Chief Technology Officer
Mark Woodhams, Other Executive Officer

FINANCIAL DATA:
Note: Data for latest year may not have been available at press time.

In U.S. $	2022	2021	2020	2019	2018	2017
Revenue	522,938,000	425,706,000	351,737,000	288,976,000	227,788,000	175,603,000
R&D Expense	108,893,000	77,322,000	56,464,000	43,006,000	30,754,000	23,874,000
Operating Income	-52,357,000	-38,614,000	-19,891,000	-27,899,000	-29,836,000	-30,409,000
Operating Margin %	-.10%	-.09%	-.06%	-.10%	-.13%	-.17%
SGA Expense	337,017,000	289,127,000	246,192,000	214,894,000	175,996,000	140,753,000
Net Income	-29,391,000	-115,161,000	-46,911,000	-32,535,000	-28,714,000	-33,408,000
Operating Cash Flow	56,013,000	80,093,000	54,735,000	29,724,000	16,140,000	6,424,000
Capital Expenditure	30,182,000	23,265,000	19,424,000	9,692,000	11,959,000	8,626,000
EBITDA	1,255,000	-10,786,000	5,503,000	-497,000	-5,364,000	-12,859,000
Return on Assets %	-.02%	-.08%	-.04%	-.04%	-.06%	-.08%
Return on Equity %	-.13%	-.31%	-.11%	-.09%	-.09%	-.11%
Debt to Equity	12.46%	3.47%	0.982	0.991		

CONTACT INFORMATION:

Phone: 818-223-9008 Fax:
Toll-Free:
Address: 21300 Victory Blvd., 12/Fl, Woodland Hills, CA 91367 United States

STOCK TICKER/OTHER:

Stock Ticker: BL Exchange: NAS
Employees: 1,814 Fiscal Year Ends: 12/31
Parent Company:

SALARIES/BONUSES:

Top Exec. Salary: $475,000 Bonus: $
Second Exec. Salary: $387,500 Bonus: $

OTHER THOUGHTS:

Estimated Female Officers or Directors:
Hot Spot for Advancement for Women/Minorities:

Sales, profits and employees may be estimates. Financial information, benefits and other data can change quickly and may vary from those stated here.

Bloomberg LP

NAIC Code: 511120A

TYPES OF BUSINESS:

Financial Data and News Publishing
Financial Software
Financial Data
Financial Media Platform
Financial Software Tools
Data Analytics and Services
Equity Trading Platform
Technology Platform Development

BRANDS/DIVISIONS/AFFILIATES:

CONTACTS: *Note: Officers with more than one job title may be intentionally listed here more than once.*

Vladimir Kliatchko, CEO
Jean-Paul Zammitt, Pres.
Jason Schechter, Chief Communications Officer
Matthew Winkler, Editor-in-Chief, Bloomberg News
Thomas Secunda, Vice Chmn.
Mark Carney, Chmn.

GROWTH PLANS/SPECIAL FEATURES:

Bloomberg LP is a financial, software, data and media company, serving customers worldwide. The firm provides financial software tools such as an analytics and equity trading platform, data services, and news to financial companies and organizations. Bloomberg utilizes technology to connect customers so they can make informed decisions. The company's engineers and data scientists build and advance new solutions, rolling out software that integrates seamlessly into client workflows. Its data department turns data points into insights and answers, and produces the algorithms, research and analysis that fuel all of Bloomberg's products. The product department brainstorms, builds and implements tools for clients to navigate markets across the entire range of products and solutions offered by Bloomberg. The technology department engages in continual research and innovation, quantitative finance, machine learning, software development and open technologies for Bloomberg's financial products and services. Bloomberg's global office locations include the U.S., U.K., Australia, China, Hong Kong, India, Japan and Singapore.

Bloomberg offers its employees benefits, which vary by location, and may include comprehensive health plans and a retirement savings plan.

FINANCIAL DATA: *Note: Data for latest year may not have been available at press time.*

In U.S. $	2022	2021	2020	2019	2018	2017
Revenue	13,150,000,000	12,350,000,000	11,500,000,000	10,500,000,000	10,000,000,000	9,658,000,000
R&D Expense						
Operating Income						
Operating Margin %						
SGA Expense						
Net Income						
Operating Cash Flow						
Capital Expenditure						
EBITDA						
Return on Assets %						
Return on Equity %						
Debt to Equity						

CONTACT INFORMATION:

Phone: 212-318-2000   Fax: 917-369-5000
Toll-Free:
Address: 731 Lexington Ave., New York, NY 10022 United States

STOCK TICKER/OTHER:

Stock Ticker: Private   Exchange:
Employees: 21,000   Fiscal Year Ends: 12/31
Parent Company:

SALARIES/BONUSES:

Top Exec. Salary: $ Bonus: $
Second Exec. Salary: $ Bonus: $

OTHER THOUGHTS:

Estimated Female Officers or Directors: 8
Hot Spot for Advancement for Women/Minorities: Y

Blue Nile Inc

www.bluenile.com

NAIC Code: 454110

TYPES OF BUSINESS:

Jewelry, Online Retail
Jewelry Design
Diamonds
Handcrafted Jewelry
Ecommerce Retailing
Engagement Rings
Fine Jewelry
Showrooms

BRANDS/DIVISIONS/AFFILIATES:

Signet Jewelers Ltd

CONTACTS: Note: Officers with more than one job title may be intentionally listed here more than once.

Sean Kell, CEO
Dominique Bourgault, CFO
Lauren Neiswender, General Counsel
Jon Sainsbury, Other Executive Officer

GROWTH PLANS/SPECIAL FEATURES:

Blue Nile, Inc. is an American jewelry company founded in 1999. The firm specializes in the diamond and engagement ring business as an ecommerce retailer, making it possible to shop for high-quality products at a great value. Once purchases are made, the order is either sent to a showroom or shipped directly to the customer, free of charge. Blue Nile showrooms are located throughout the U.S. so that clients can look, touch and try on the purchased jewelry and/or engagement rings with a representative present. Blue Nile offers hand-crafted engagement rings and fine jewelry, and constantly innovates ways to design and deliver its pieces for all occasions. Hand-crafted engagement rings are quadruple checked to ensure the quality of the diamonds and jewelry before being shipped. Blue Nile purchases only ethically sourced diamonds through suppliers who adhere to and enforce Kimberley Process standards. The company offers more than 150,000 loose diamonds (D-K color grade) with FI-SI2 clarity. Blue Nile provides diamond buying tips and education guides, with experts available 24/7 to answer questions. Blue Nile provides Diamond Certification, 30-day returns, and lifetime guarantees for its products. Diamond shapes include round, princess, cushion, oval, emerald, pear, Asscher, heart, radiant and marquise. Blue Nile is a subsidiary of Signet Jewelers Ltd. Blue Nile is headquartered in Washington and has showrooms in shopping malls across the U.S.

Blue Nile offers its employees comprehensive benefits

FINANCIAL DATA: Note: Data for latest year may not have been available at press time.

In U.S. $	2022	2021	2020	2019	2018	2017
Revenue	555,580,000	539,398,125	523,687,500	551,250,000	525,000,000	500,000,000
R&D Expense						
Operating Income						
Operating Margin %						
SGA Expense						
Net Income						
Operating Cash Flow						
Capital Expenditure						
EBITDA						
Return on Assets %						
Return on Equity %						
Debt to Equity						

CONTACT INFORMATION:

Phone: 206 336-6700   Fax: 206 336-6750
Toll-Free: 800-242-2728
Address: 3380 146th Pl. SE, Bellevue, WA 98007 United States

STOCK TICKER/OTHER:

Stock Ticker: Subsidiary   Exchange:
Employees: 350   Fiscal Year Ends: 01/31
Parent Company: Signet Jewelers Ltd

SALARIES/BONUSES:

Top Exec. Salary: $ Bonus: $
Second Exec. Salary: $ Bonus: $

OTHER THOUGHTS:

Estimated Female Officers or Directors: 4
Hot Spot for Advancement for Women/Minorities: Y

Blue Yonder Group Inc

NAIC Code: 511210A

TYPES OF BUSINESS:

Computer Software: Supply Chain & Logistics
Digital Supply Chain
Commerce
Logistics
Business Planning
Artificial Intelligence
Machine Learning
Internet of Things

BRANDS/DIVISIONS/AFFILIATES:

Panasonic Corporation
Luminate

CONTACTS: *Note: Officers with more than one job title may be intentionally listed here more than once.*

Duncan Angove, CEO
Edward Auriemma, COO
Mark Henry, CFO
Patricia Harris, CMO
Salil Joshi, CTO
David King, Exec. VP-Prod. Dev.
David Kennedy, Chief Legal Officer
David Gai, Exec. VP-Svcs.
Yasu Higuchi, Chmn.

GROWTH PLANS/SPECIAL FEATURES:

Blue Yonder Group, Inc. offers a digital supply chain platform that delivers dynamic commerce experiences from beginning to end. The Luminate platform helps clients predict potential disruptions, find growth opportunities and optimize inventory replenishment. It provides synchronized business planning, execution, delivery and labor solutions by leveraging artificial intelligence (AI) and machine learning (ML) capabilities, as well as workflow-driven user experiences across the entire workplace. Other technologies include cloud transformation, data management, microservices, Internet of Things (IoT), infrastructure orchestration and more. Solutions by Luminate include planning for the delivery of goods to market, inventory optimization, financial management, warehouse integration, transportation/logistics and labor/operations planning and fulfillment (including micro-fulfillment) information. Blue Yonder serves more than 3,000 companies worldwide and is comprised of over 400 granted patents and patents pending. Services by Blue Yonder include cloud transformation, discovery services, education, enablement and expansion. Blue Yonder has offices in more than 28 locations worldwide, including major cities in the U.S., Asia Pacific, Canada, Latin America, Europe, Australia and the Middle East. Blue Yonder is a wholly owned subsidiary of Panasonic Corporation.

FINANCIAL DATA: *Note: Data for latest year may not have been available at press time.*

In U.S. $	2022	2021	2020	2019	2018	2017
Revenue	1,352,000,000	1,300,000,000	1,240,312,500	1,181,250,000	1,125,000,000	935,000,000
R&D Expense						
Operating Income						
Operating Margin %						
SGA Expense						
Net Income						
Operating Cash Flow						
Capital Expenditure						
EBITDA						
Return on Assets %						
Return on Equity %						
Debt to Equity						

CONTACT INFORMATION:

Phone: 480 308-3000   Fax: 480 308-3001
Toll-Free: 800-438-5301
Address: 15059 N. Scottsdale Rd., Ste. 400, Scottsdale, AZ 85254-2666
United States

STOCK TICKER/OTHER:

Stock Ticker: Subsidiary   Exchange:
Employees: 5,500   Fiscal Year Ends: 12/31
Parent Company: Panasonic Corporation

SALARIES/BONUSES:

Top Exec. Salary: $ Bonus: $
Second Exec. Salary: $ Bonus: $

OTHER THOUGHTS:

Estimated Female Officers or Directors: 2
Hot Spot for Advancement for Women/Minorities:

BMC Software Inc

www.bmc.com

NAIC Code: 511210H

TYPES OF BUSINESS:

Computer Software, Mainframe Related
Systems Management Software
eBusiness Software
Consulting & Training Services
Workload Automation
Multi-Cloud Management Solutions
Security and Compliance Solutions
Artificial Intelligence

BRANDS/DIVISIONS/AFFILIATES:

KKR & Co Inc

CONTACTS: Note: Officers with more than one job title may be intentionally listed here more than once.

Ayman Sayed, CEO
Michelle Carbone, Sr. VP-Oper.
Marc Rothman, CFO
Martyn Etherington, CMO
Eric Olmo, Sr. VP-People & Spaces
Ali Siddiqui, Chief Product Officer
Hollie Castro, Sr. VP-Admin.
Patrick K. Tagtow, General Counsel
Steve Goddard, Sr. VP-Bus. Oper.
Ken Berryman, Sr. VP-Strategy & Corp. Dev.
Ann Duhon, Mgr.-Comm.
Derrick Vializ, VP-Investor Rel.
T. Cory Bleuer, Chief Acct. Officer
Patrick K. Tagtow, Chief Compliance Officer
Paul Avenant, Sr. VP-Solutions
Bill Green, Chmn.

GROWTH PLANS/SPECIAL FEATURES:

BMC Software, Inc. is a software vendor company that provides system management, service management and automation solutions primarily for large companies. BMC's software products span mainframe systems, IT service management, cloud management, IT operations, digital, chatbot, software-as-a-service (SaaS)-based solutions, workflow orchestration workload automation and IT automation. BMC's solutions are grouped into seven categories: multi-cloud management, security and compliance, artificial intelligence and machine learning, automation and DevOps, observation and AIOps, industry/technology and service management. Multi-cloud management solutions include multi-cloud cost control, asset visibility, cloud performance management, automation across clouds, cloud security, cloud migration and services management across clouds. Security and compliance solutions include building a SecOps strategy, ensuring GDPR compliance, remediating vulnerabilities and managing policies and compliance. AI & machine learning solutions include cognitive service management, AI application to IT, big data insights, and acceleration via self-managing mainframe. Automation and DevOps solutions include automating workloads, file transfers, application deployment and data centers. , Observation and AIOps leverages the power of Generative AI and Observability to identify and prevent IT issues before they arise. Industry/technology solutions are offers Amazon Web Services (AWB) to manage your cloud and offers guidance in sectors such as Communications, finances, healthcare, manufacturing, public and retail. Last, service management solutions offer transformation, modernization, IT asset visibility and digital workplace enhancement. BMC Software operates as a subsidiary of KKR & Co., Inc.

FINANCIAL DATA: Note: Data for latest year may not have been available at press time.

In U.S. $	2022	2021	2020	2019	2018	2017
Revenue	2,120,000,000	2,080,000,000	2,000,000,000	2,200,000,000	2,000,000,000	2,500,000,000
R&D Expense						
Operating Income						
Operating Margin %						
SGA Expense						
Net Income						
Operating Cash Flow						
Capital Expenditure						
EBITDA						
Return on Assets %						
Return on Equity %						
Debt to Equity						

CONTACT INFORMATION:

Phone: 713 918-8800   Fax: 713 918-8000
Toll-Free: 800-793-4262
Address: 2103 Citywest Blvd., Houston, TX 77042 United States

STOCK TICKER/OTHER:

Stock Ticker: Subsidiary   Exchange:
Employees: 6,000   Fiscal Year Ends: 03/31
Parent Company: KKR & Co LP

SALARIES/BONUSES:

Top Exec. Salary: $ Bonus: $
Second Exec. Salary: $ Bonus: $

OTHER THOUGHTS:

Estimated Female Officers or Directors: 2
Hot Spot for Advancement for Women/Minorities: Y

Boingo Wireless Inc

NAIC Code: 517311

TYPES OF BUSINESS:

Wi-Fi Internet Access
Next-Generation Wireless Connectivity
Neutral Host Networks
5G
Distributed Antenna Systems
Small Cell Deployment
Citizen Broadband Radio Service (CBRS)
Digital Services and Solutions

BRANDS/DIVISIONS/AFFILIATES:

DigitalBridge Group Inc

CONTACTS: *Note: Officers with more than one job title may be intentionally listed here more than once.*

Mike Finley, CEO
Peter Hovenier, CFO
Dawn Callahan, CMO
Derek Peterson, CTO
Michael Zeto, Chief Commercial Officer

GROWTH PLANS/SPECIAL FEATURES:

Boingo Wireless, Inc. provides next-generation wireless connectivity through neutral host networks. The firm's solutions connect people and things 24/7 with cellular, Wi-Fi 6 and shared-spectrum technologies. Boingo powers 5G connectivity using a combination of licensed, unlicensed and shared spectrum. Other wireless solutions include citizens broadband radio service (CBRS) for macro networks, distributed antenna system (DAS) deployment, small cell deployment, private networks and more. Products and services include network monetization, customizable digital services, passpoint and roaming solutions, unlimited free Wi-Fi at more than 1 million hotspots worldwide, managed wireless services, a single Wi-Fi network for venues, Edge and cloud computing, Internet of Things (IoT), digital transformation, and advertising solutions. Industries served by Boingo Wireless include airports, transportation, sports, entertainment, military, government, commercial real estate, healthcare, manufacturing and logistics. Boingo operates as a subsidiary of DigitalBridge Group, Inc. Headquartered in Los Angeles, Boingo Wireless also has regional offices in New York. NY; Frisco. TX; Chicago, IL; and Las Vegas, NV.

Boingo Wireless offers its employees health benefits, life and AD&D insurance, a 401(k) savings plan, flexible spending accounts, training and development programs, tuition reimbursement and company programs and perks.

FINANCIAL DATA: *Note: Data for latest year may not have been available at press time.*

In U.S. $	2022	2021	2020	2019	2018	2017
Revenue	256,771,840	246,896,000	237,400,000	263,790,000	250,820,992	204,368,992
R&D Expense						
Operating Income						
Operating Margin %						
SGA Expense						
Net Income			-17,100,000	-10,296,000	-1,220,000	-19,366,000
Operating Cash Flow						
Capital Expenditure						
EBITDA						
Return on Assets %						
Return on Equity %						
Debt to Equity						

CONTACT INFORMATION:

Phone: 310 586-5180   Fax: 310 586-4060
Toll-Free: 800-880-4117
Address: 10960 Wilshire Blvd., Fl. 23, Los Angeles, CA 90024 United States

STOCK TICKER/OTHER:

Stock Ticker: Subsidiary
Employees: 420
Parent Company: DigitalBridge Group Inc

Exchange:
Fiscal Year Ends: 12/31

SALARIES/BONUSES:

Top Exec. Salary: $ Bonus: $
Second Exec. Salary: $ Bonus: $

OTHER THOUGHTS:

Estimated Female Officers or Directors: 1
Hot Spot for Advancement for Women/Minorities:

Bonobos Inc

bonobos.com

NAIC Code: 454110

TYPES OF BUSINESS:

Men's Apparel Online
Ecommerce Men's Apparel
Online Clothing
Apparel Design
Custom Apparel

BRANDS/DIVISIONS/AFFILIATES:

Express Inc
WHP Global

CONTACTS: *Note: Officers with more than one job title may be intentionally listed here more than once.*

John Hutchison, Brand Pres.

GROWTH PLANS/SPECIAL FEATURES:

Bonobos, Inc. is an ecommerce apparel company that designs and sells men's clothing. The firm's signature line of curved waste banded pants is designed to conform to the natural shape of a man's waist, with a unique cut and medium rise. Bonobos set out to build the best online shopping experience, and claims to be the largest clothing brand ever built on the web in the U.S. What sets the company apart from other online retail sites is that shipping is entirely free, whether receiving a package or returning it. Returns and exchanges are simple. Apparel options include bottoms, tops, tailored clothing, outerwear, golf attire, accessories (ties, belts, scarves and cashmere hats) and shoes. Bonobos' guide shop locations enable customers to schedule fittings ahead of time. The guide shop process includes a guide that walks the customer through the Bonobos catalog, helps them find the perfect fit from all available options and places orders, which are shipped directly to the customer's home or office. Bonobos has more than 60 locations throughout the U.S. The firm offers both digital and physical gift cards. In May 2023, fashion apparel retailer Express, Inc. and global brand management firm WHP Global acquired Bonobos from Walmart, Inc. WHP Global acquired the Bonobos brand for $50 million, while Express acquired the operating assets and assumed related liabilities of the Bonobos business for $25 million.

FINANCIAL DATA: *Note: Data for latest year may not have been available at press time.*

In U.S. $	2022	2021	2020	2019	2018	2017
Revenue	200,000,000	107,111,550	82,393,500	139,650,000	147,000,000	140,000,000
R&D Expense						
Operating Income						
Operating Margin %						
SGA Expense						
Net Income						
Operating Cash Flow						
Capital Expenditure						
EBITDA						
Return on Assets %						
Return on Equity %						
Debt to Equity						

CONTACT INFORMATION:

Phone: 877-294-7737   Fax:
Toll-Free:
Address: 45 W. 25th St., Fl. 5, New York, NY 10010 United States

STOCK TICKER/OTHER:

Stock Ticker: Subsidiary   Exchange:
Employees: 550   Fiscal Year Ends: 01/31
Parent Company: Express Inc

SALARIES/BONUSES:

Top Exec. Salary: $ Bonus: $
Second Exec. Salary: $ Bonus: $

OTHER THOUGHTS:

Estimated Female Officers or Directors:
Hot Spot for Advancement for Women/Minorities:

Boohoo.com PLC

www.boohoo.com

NAIC Code: 454110

TYPES OF BUSINESS:

Electronic Shopping

GROWTH PLANS/SPECIAL FEATURES:

Boohoo Group PLC is an online fashion retailer catering to young people in the UK and internationally. The company markets and retails its own-brand clothing and accessories through its website www.boohoo.com. Its brand includes boohoo, PrettyLittleThing, Nasty Gal, and Others. The company's geographical segment includes United Kingdom; Rest of Europe; USA and Rest of world. It derives a majority of its revenue from the United Kingdom. Its product offering includes clothing, footwear, and related fashion accessories.

BRANDS/DIVISIONS/AFFILIATES:

boohoo
boohooMAN
PrettyLittleThing
Nasty Gal
MissPap
Karen Millen
Coast
Debenhams Retail Limited

CONTACTS: Note: Officers with more than one job title may be intentionally listed here more than once.

Mahmud Kamani, Co-CEO
John Lyttle, Co-CEO
Carol Kane, Exec. Dir.

FINANCIAL DATA: Note: Data for latest year may not have been available at press time.

In U.S. $	2022	2021	2020	2019	2018	2017
Revenue	2,502,903,000	2,203,105,000	1,558,823,000	1,081,697,000	731,885,800	
R&D Expense						
Operating Income	11,739,460	155,390,000	114,491,300	82,186,310	53,680,880	
Operating Margin %	.00%	.07%	.07%	.08%	.07%	
SGA Expense	1,286,291,000	1,030,800,000	720,146,300	504,212,300	327,417,300	
Net Income	-5,049,230	114,491,300	80,408,980	55,016,400	39,954,550	
Operating Cash Flow	13,001,770	205,503,600	146,049,000	128,202,500	87,116,880	
Capital Expenditure	330,093,400	154,885,100	57,561,220	59,160,560	58,550,870	
EBITDA	79,777,830	195,405,200	148,068,700	93,311,020	68,716,230	
Return on Assets %	.00%	.13%	.13%	.11%	.12%	
Return on Equity %	- .01%	.23%	.22%	.19%	.21%	
Debt to Equity	.09%	.02%	0.042	0.018	.04%	

CONTACT INFORMATION:

Phone: 44 1612332050   Fax:
Toll-Free:
Address: 49/51 Dale St., Manchester, M1 2HF United Kingdom

STOCK TICKER/OTHER:

Stock Ticker: BHOOY
Employees: 6,190
Parent Company:

Exchange: PINX
Fiscal Year Ends: 02/28

SALARIES/BONUSES:

Top Exec. Salary: $821,594   Bonus: $821,593
Second Exec. Salary: $601,169   Bonus: $601,169

OTHER THOUGHTS:

Estimated Female Officers or Directors:
Hot Spot for Advancement for Women/Minorities:

Booking Holdings Inc

www.bookingholdings.com

NAIC Code: 561510

TYPES OF BUSINESS:

Online Retail-Travel Services
Auction-Based Travel Sales
Online Financial Services
Commission-Based Travel Bookings (Travel Agency Model)

BRANDS/DIVISIONS/AFFILIATES:

Booking.com
KAYAK
Priceline
Agoda
Rentalcars.com
OpenTable
Trip Builder

GROWTH PLANS/SPECIAL FEATURES:

Booking is the world's largest online travel agency by sales, offering booking and payment services for hotel and alternative accommodation rooms, airline tickets, rental cars, restaurant reservations, cruises, experiences, and other vacation packages. The company operates a number of branded travel booking sites, including Booking.com, Agoda, OpenTable, and Rentalcars.com, and has expanded into travel media with the acquisitions of Kayak and Momondo. Transaction fees for online bookings account for the bulk of revenue and profits.

CONTACTS: Note: Officers with more than one job title may be intentionally listed here more than once.

Glenn Fogel, CEO
David Goulden, CFO
Robert Mylod, Chairman of the Board
Sue DEmic, Chief Accounting Officer
Peter Millones, Executive VP

FINANCIAL DATA: Note: Data for latest year may not have been available at press time.

In U.S. $	2022	2021	2020	2019	2018	2017
Revenue	17,090,000,000	10,958,000,000	6,796,000,000	15,066,000,000	14,527,000,000	12,681,000,000
R&D Expense						
Operating Income	4,903,000,000	2,509,000,000	580,000,000	5,345,000,000	5,341,000,000	4,538,000,000
Operating Margin %	.29%	.23%	.09%	.35%	.37%	.36%
SGA Expense	11,210,000,000	7,616,000,000	5,459,000,000	8,967,000,000	8,527,000,000	7,349,000,000
Net Income	3,058,000,000	1,165,000,000	59,000,000	4,865,000,000	3,998,000,000	2,341,000,000
Operating Cash Flow	6,554,000,000	2,820,000,000	85,000,000	4,865,000,000	5,338,000,000	4,662,000,000
Capital Expenditure	368,000,000	304,000,000	286,000,000	368,000,000	442,000,000	288,000,000
EBITDA	4,921,000,000	2,398,000,000	1,565,000,000	6,865,000,000	5,530,000,000	5,016,000,000
Return on Assets %	.12%	.05%	.00%	.22%	.17%	.10%
Return on Equity %	.68%	.21%	.01%	.66%	.40%	.22%
Debt to Equity	4.51%	1.50%	2.329	1.366	.98%	0.782

CONTACT INFORMATION:

Phone: 203-2998000   Fax:
Toll-Free:
Address: 800 Connecticut Ave., Norwalk, CT 06854 United States

STOCK TICKER/OTHER:

Stock Ticker: BKNG   Exchange: NAS
Employees: 21,600   Fiscal Year Ends: 12/31
Parent Company:

SALARIES/BONUSES:

Top Exec. Salary: $750,000   Bonus: $
Second Exec. Salary: Bonus: $
$625,000

OTHER THOUGHTS:

Estimated Female Officers or Directors: 1
Hot Spot for Advancement for Women/Minorities: Y

Bottomline Technologies Inc

www.bottomline.com

NAIC Code: 511210Q

TYPES OF BUSINESS:

Software-Electronic Banking
Financial Technology
Business Payments Solutions
Business Financial Process Solutions
Electronic Payment Solutions
Digital Banking Solutions
Global Payments and Cash Management
Accounts Payable Automation

BRANDS/DIVISIONS/AFFILIATES:

Thoma Bravo LP
Paymode-X
Nexus Systems

CONTACTS: *Note: Officers with more than one job title may be intentionally listed here more than once.*

Craig Saks, CEO
Adam Bowden, CFO
Eric Morgan, Controller
Andrew Mintzer, Executive VP, Divisional
David Sweet, Executive VP, Divisional
Danielle Sheer, General Counsel
John Kelly, General Manager, Divisional
Tom Dolan, General Manager, Divisional
Paul Fannon, Managing Director, Divisional
Norman Deluca, Managing Director, Divisional
Brian McLaughlin, Other Executive Officer
Kimberly Hannemann, Other Executive Officer
Angela White, Vice President, Divisional

GROWTH PLANS/SPECIAL FEATURES:

Bottomline Technologies, Inc. provides financial technology regarding business payments and processes, serving companies and financial institutions worldwide. Solutions offered include, but are not limited to: Paymode-X, for making and receiving electronic payments; digital banking, a digital banking and payments platform that enables customer engagement for acquiring and retaining customers; financial messaging and bank connectivity, for communicating, reconciling and managing financial transactions across the global financial supply chain; legal spend management, offering data insight and bill review solutions for enhanced efficiency, decision making and vendor relationships; accounts payable automation, for streamlining invoice receipts, automating workflows, accelerating approvals and making electronic payments through a single source; fraud and financial crime management, offering protection from internal fraud and external financial crime, and for meeting compliance and regulations; and global payments and cash management, enabling banking and payments consolidation departmentally through a streamlined, comprehensive solutions. Bottomline has headquarter locations in New Hampshire, USA; Sydney, Australia; Singapore; and Reading, England. Bottomline is owned by Thoma Bravo, LP, a private-equity, software investment firm.

FINANCIAL DATA: *Note: Data for latest year may not have been available at press time.*

In U.S. $	2022	2021	2020	2019	2018	2017
Revenue	480,000,000	471,403,008	442,220,992	421,961,984	394,096,000	349,412,000
R&D Expense						
Operating Income						
Operating Margin %						
SGA Expense						
Net Income		-16,288,000	-9,229,000	9,432,000	9,328,000	-33,137,000
Operating Cash Flow						
Capital Expenditure						
EBITDA						
Return on Assets %						
Return on Equity %						
Debt to Equity						

CONTACT INFORMATION:

Phone: 603 436-0700   Fax: 603 436-0300
Toll-Free: 800-243-2528
Address: 325 Corporate Dr., Portsmouth, NH 03801 United States

STOCK TICKER/OTHER:

Stock Ticker: Private   Exchange:
Employees: 2,000   Fiscal Year Ends: 06/30
Parent Company: Thoma Bravo LP

SALARIES/BONUSES:

Top Exec. Salary: $ Bonus: $
Second Exec. Salary: $ Bonus: $

OTHER THOUGHTS:

Estimated Female Officers or Directors:
Hot Spot for Advancement for Women/Minorities:

Boursorama

groupe.boursorama.fr

NAIC Code: 523120

TYPES OF BUSINESS:

Online Brokerage Services
Online Banking Services
Online Brokerage Services
Insurance
Wealth Management
Financial Information Services
Digital and Alternative Banking Services

BRANDS/DIVISIONS/AFFILIATES:

Societe Generale Group
Boursorama Banque

CONTACTS: Note: Officers with more than one job title may be intentionally listed here more than once.

Benoit Grisoni, Gen. Mgr.
Nicole Viviand, Dir-Oper.
Jean-Philippe Lavenir, Dir.-Finance
Xavier Prin, Dir.-Mktg.
Lucie Petyst de Morcourt, Dir.-Human Resources
David Godat, Dir.-Information Systems
Diane-Charlotte Kermorgant, Head-Press Rel.
Diane-Charlotte Kermorgant, Head-Investor Rel.
Ralf Oetting, Managing Dir.-Onvista AG Germany
Xavier Prin, Portal Dir.
Benoit Grisoni, Managing Dir.-Boursorama Banque
Patrick Sommelet, Deputy CEO
Philippe Aymerich, Chmn.
Alberto Navarro, Managing Dir.-Selftrade Bank, Spain

GROWTH PLANS/SPECIAL FEATURES:

Boursorama, a subsidiary of the Societe Generale Group, is a leading European online financial and insurance services provider which operates through Boursorama Banque. The company has three main areas of activity: online banking, online brokerage and financial information on the internet. The online banking division has more than 5.4 million customers, providing several services areas free of charge. Boursorama Banque offers account banking, mortgage lending and other money-related services all online. The online brokerage division provides access to major exchanges with rates tailored to the investor's profile. Its products include equities, options, futures, warrants, turbos, certificates, bonds and trackers. The internet portal division comprises the boursorama.com website, which offers a wide array of financial information and averages more than 54.7 million monthly visits every year. The website disseminates market and economic news and offers general information, as well as video content and discussion forums. In addition, Boursorama's customers can use Google Assistant (including connected Google Home speakers) on all compatible devices for managing their bank accounts autonomously and securely. Boursorama's mobile platform is compatible with Samsung Pay, Apple Pay and Google Pay.

FINANCIAL DATA: Note: Data for latest year may not have been available at press time.

In U.S. $	2022	2021	2020	2019	2018	2017
Revenue	302,020,000	287,469,000	276,412,500	283,500,000	270,000,000	255,000,000
R&D Expense						
Operating Income						
Operating Margin %						
SGA Expense						
Net Income						
Operating Cash Flow						
Capital Expenditure						
EBITDA						
Return on Assets %						
Return on Equity %						
Debt to Equity						

CONTACT INFORMATION:

Phone: 33-1-46-09-50-00   Fax:
Toll-Free:
Address: 18 Quai du Point du Jour, Boulogne-Billancourt, 92659 France

STOCK TICKER/OTHER:

Stock Ticker: Subsidiary   Exchange:
Employees: 825   Fiscal Year Ends: 12/31
Parent Company: Societe Generale Group

SALARIES/BONUSES:

Top Exec. Salary: $ Bonus: $
Second Exec. Salary: $ Bonus: $

OTHER THOUGHTS:

Estimated Female Officers or Directors: 5
Hot Spot for Advancement for Women/Minorities: Y

Box Inc

www.box.com

NAIC Code: 511210L

TYPES OF BUSINESS:

Application Software
Cloud
Storage
Security
Data Management

GROWTH PLANS/SPECIAL FEATURES:

Box is a cloud-based content services platform that provides cloud-based storage and workflow collaboration services for enterprise customers. The firm was founded in 2005 as a file-sync and sharing provider. More recently, however, the company has focused on bolstering its product portfolio by adding tools such as governance and e-signature to enhance workflow management and collaboration.

Box offers its employees medical, dental and vision coverage, and a variety of company perks.

BRANDS/DIVISIONS/AFFILIATES:

Box Solution (The)

CONTACTS: *Note: Officers with more than one job title may be intentionally listed here more than once.*

Aaron Levie, CEO
Dylan Smith, CFO
Bethany Mayer, Chairman of the Board
Eliahu Berkovitch, Chief Accounting Officer
Stephanie Carullo, COO

FINANCIAL DATA: *Note: Data for latest year may not have been available at press time.*

In U.S. $	2022	2021	2020	2019	2018	2017
Revenue	874,332,000	770,770,000	696,264,000	608,386,000	506,142,000	
R&D Expense	218,523,000	201,262,000	199,750,000	163,750,000	136,791,000	
Operating Income	-27,626,000	-37,642,000	-139,472,000	-134,237,000	-154,021,000	
Operating Margin %	-.03%	-.05%	-.20%	-.22%	-.30%	
SGA Expense	433,951,000	382,412,000	420,409,000	405,279,000	388,124,000	
Net Income	-41,459,000	-43,433,000	-144,348,000	-134,612,000	-154,960,000	
Operating Cash Flow	234,818,000	196,834,000	44,713,000	55,321,000	35,391,000	
Capital Expenditure	10,487,000	16,490,000	13,401,000	17,567,000	11,822,000	
EBITDA	50,608,000	37,836,000	-80,048,000	-86,578,000	-113,120,000	
Return on Assets %	-.04%	-.04%	-.18%	-.22%	-.30%	
Return on Equity %		-.50%	-5.37%	-5.81%	-3.46%	
Debt to Equity		3.64%	14.741	2.694	4.47%	

CONTACT INFORMATION:

Phone: 877-729-4269　　　　　Fax:
Toll-Free: 877-729-4269
Address: 900 Jefferson Ave., Redwood City, CA 94063 United States

STOCK TICKER/OTHER:

Stock Ticker: BOX　　　　　　　　Exchange: NYS
Employees: 2,487　　　　　　　　Fiscal Year Ends: 01/31
Parent Company:

SALARIES/BONUSES:

Top Exec. Salary: $411,250　　　　Bonus: $
Second Exec. Salary: $392,500　　　Bonus: $

OTHER THOUGHTS:

Estimated Female Officers or Directors: 2
Hot Spot for Advancement for Women/Minorities:

Brightcove Inc

www.brightcove.com

NAIC Code: 519130

TYPES OF BUSINESS:

Internet TV Broadcasting
Internet Television Broadcasting
Media Services
Content Creation and Distribution
Live Streaming Solutions
Over-the-Top Video
Cloud-Based Technology
Video Encoding

BRANDS/DIVISIONS/AFFILIATES:

Brightcove Video Cloud
Brightcove Live
Brightcove Beacon
Brightcove Player
Zencoder
Brightcove SSAI
Brightcove Video Marketing Suite
Brightcove Enterprise Video Suite

GROWTH PLANS/SPECIAL FEATURES:

Brightcove Inc is a provider of cloud-based services for the video ecosystem. The firm targets its solutions at media companies, broadcasters, publishers, and corporations. Brightcove Video Cloud is the firm's flagship product, enabling customers to publish and distribute video to Internet-connected devices. Video Cloud generates a significant portion of the firm's revenue through a subscription-based software-as-a-service model. Other products include Zencoder, a cloud-based video encoding service. It generates a large majority of its revenue in North America and Asia.

Brightcove offers its employees health benefits, 401(k) and savings plans, tuition reimbursement programs and other benefits.

CONTACTS:
Note: Officers with more than one job title may be intentionally listed here more than once.

Hugh Ray, CEO
Robert Noreck, CFO
Deborah Besemer, Chairman of the Board
David Plotkin, Chief Legal Officer

FINANCIAL DATA:
Note: Data for latest year may not have been available at press time.

In U.S. $	2022	2021	2020	2019	2018	2017
Revenue	211,008,000	211,093,000	197,353,000	184,455,000	164,833,000	155,913,000
R&D Expense	33,524,000	31,718,000	33,978,000	32,535,000	31,716,000	31,850,000
Operating Income	-7,285,000	7,874,000	445,000	-9,616,000	-12,385,000	-19,696,000
Operating Margin %	- .03%	.04%	.00%	- .05%	- .08%	- .13%
SGA Expense	106,547,000	100,438,000	86,833,000	86,067,000	78,878,000	79,141,000
Net Income	-9,015,000	5,397,000	-5,813,000	-21,903,000	-14,028,000	-19,519,000
Operating Cash Flow	25,421,000	19,563,000	21,312,000	2,708,000	2,550,000	-6,441,000
Capital Expenditure	24,552,000	8,842,000	8,724,000	7,279,000	4,531,000	4,112,000
EBITDA	1,629,000	14,521,000	3,705,000	-12,914,000	-5,589,000	-12,439,000
Return on Assets %	- .04%	.03%	- .03%	- .14%	- .11%	- .15%
Return on Equity %	- .09%	.06%	- .08%	- .30%	- .20%	- .27%
Debt to Equity	.20%	.24%	0.069	0.158		

CONTACT INFORMATION:

Phone: 617-500-4947   Fax: 617-261-4830
Toll-Free: 888-882-1880
Address: 290 Congress St., Cambridge, MA 02210 United States

STOCK TICKER/OTHER:

Stock Ticker: BCOV   Exchange: NAS
Employees: 725   Fiscal Year Ends: 12/31
Parent Company:

SALARIES/BONUSES:

Top Exec. Salary: $400,000   Bonus: $
Second Exec. Salary: $385,000   Bonus: $

OTHER THOUGHTS:

Estimated Female Officers or Directors: 1
Hot Spot for Advancement for Women/Minorities: Y

Sales, profits and employees may be estimates. Financial information, benefits and other data can change quickly and may vary from those stated here.

BroadVision Group

broadvision.com

NAIC Code: 511210M

TYPES OF BUSINESS:

Software-Web Site Tools
eBusiness Solutions
Software Collaboration Solutions
Software Communication Solutions
App Development

BRANDS/DIVISIONS/AFFILIATES:

ESW Capital

GROWTH PLANS/SPECIAL FEATURES:

BroadVision Group is a US-based private asset management firm focusing on funding, incubating, and operating cutting-edge business ventures globally across artificial intelligence, cleantech, cloudtech, fintech, healthtech, medtech, biotech, and other innovative technology domains. The firm creates and nurtures unique solutions through digital transformation, delivering compelling growth and profitability for businesses as well as generating robust returns for its investors. Since its inception, BroadVision has made direct investments in more than 50 startup ventures, plus many more indirectly as a limited partner via several special purpose vehicles and venture/private equity funds. Headquartered in the U.S., the firm has offices worldwide. BroadVision is owned by private equity firm ESW Capital.

CONTACTS: *Note: Officers with more than one job title may be intentionally listed here more than once.*

A.R.. Weiler, Managing Dir.-Americas
Andrea Rubei, Managing Dir.-EMEA
Toshi Sakayori, Managing Dir.-Japan
Yin-Ping Hsu, Managing Dir.-Asia Pacific
Pehong Chen, Chmn.

FINANCIAL DATA: *Note: Data for latest year may not have been available at press time.*

In U.S. $	2022	2021	2020	2019	2018	2017
Revenue	5,050,000	4,600,000	4,510,000	4,400,000	5,051,000	6,357,000
R&D Expense						
Operating Income						
Operating Margin %						
SGA Expense						
Net Income						
Operating Cash Flow						
Capital Expenditure						
EBITDA						
Return on Assets %						
Return on Equity %						
Debt to Equity						

CONTACT INFORMATION:

Phone: 650 331-1000   Fax: 650 364-3425
Toll-Free: 866-246-4887
Address: 460 Seaport Ct., Ste. 102, Redwood City, CA 94063 United States

STOCK TICKER/OTHER:

Stock Ticker: Private
Employees: 145
Parent Company: ESW Capital

Exchange:
Fiscal Year Ends: 12/31

SALARIES/BONUSES:

Top Exec. Salary: $ Bonus: $
Second Exec. Salary: $ Bonus: $

OTHER THOUGHTS:

Estimated Female Officers or Directors:
Hot Spot for Advancement for Women/Minorities:

Sales, profits and employees may be estimates. Financial information, benefits and other data can change quickly and may vary from those stated here.

Build.com Inc

NAIC Code: 454110

TYPES OF BUSINESS:

Electronic Shopping
Online Hardware Store
Ecommerce
Online Home Improvement Products
Home Appliances
Flooring
Kitchen and Bath
HVAC

BRANDS/DIVISIONS/AFFILIATES:

Ferguson plc

CONTACTS: Note: Officers with more than one job title may be intentionally listed here more than once.

Nicole Creech, Pres.

GROWTH PLANS/SPECIAL FEATURES:

Build.com, Inc. is an ecommerce home improvement retailer offering over 1 million home improvement products. The firm's website offers products in a variety of categories, including bathroom, which features faucets, sinks, bathtubs, bathroom hardware and accessories; kitchen, which includes kitchen appliances, garbage disposals, kitchen sinks and faucet and cabinet hardware; lighting, which includes chandeliers, pendant lighting, ceiling lights and outdoor lighting; fans, including indoor and outdoor ceiling fans, air circulators and related accessories; hardware, including door knobs, deadbolts, door levers and door entry sets; decors, including area rugs, decorative mirrors, clocks, home accents and decorative pillows; appliances, including dishwashers, refrigeration, range hoods and laundry; heating & air, including stoves and fireplaces, chimney pipes, thermostats and tankless water heaters; outdoor, which includes patio furniture, barbecue grills, firepits and outdoor kitchens; and flooring, which includes wood, laminate, cork and bamboo flooring and tile. In addition, the company offers smart home products, such as hubs and controllers, security solutions, smart locks and smart lighting among others. Build.com partners with vendors to offer end-to-end solutions to its customers. Through its website, customers can explore do-it-yourself (DIY) project ideas, seek help and lookup contact information for professional contractors. Build.com operates as a subsidiary of Ferguson plc.

FINANCIAL DATA: Note: Data for latest year may not have been available at press time.

In U.S. $	2022	2021	2020	2019	2018	2017
Revenue	2,072,900,000	2,147,800,000	1,508,560,000	1,468,640,000	847,980,000	807,600,000
R&D Expense						
Operating Income						
Operating Margin %						
SGA Expense						
Net Income						
Operating Cash Flow						
Capital Expenditure						
EBITDA						
Return on Assets %						
Return on Equity %						
Debt to Equity						

CONTACT INFORMATION:

Phone: 530 566-1893   Fax:
Toll-Free: 800-375-3403
Address: 402 Otterson Dr., Ste. 100, Chico, CA 95928 United States

STOCK TICKER/OTHER:

Stock Ticker: Subsidiary   Exchange:
Employees: 700   Fiscal Year Ends: 07/31
Parent Company: Ferguson plc

SALARIES/BONUSES:

Top Exec. Salary: $ Bonus: $
Second Exec. Salary: $ Bonus: $

OTHER THOUGHTS:

Estimated Female Officers or Directors:
Hot Spot for Advancement for Women/Minorities:

BuzzFeed Inc

www.buzzfeed.com

NAIC Code: 519130

TYPES OF BUSINESS:

Internet Publishing and Broadcasting and Web Search Portals
Digital Media
News
Entertainment

GROWTH PLANS/SPECIAL FEATURES:

BuzzFeed Inc is a tech-powered, diversified media company that reaches hundreds of millions globally through its cross-platform news and entertainment network. The company produces articles, lists, quizzes, videos, and original series; lifestyle content through brands including Tasty, the world's largest social food network; original reporting and investigative journalism through BuzzFeed News and HuffPost; an industry-leading affiliate business, strategic partnerships, licensing and product development through BuzzFeed Commerce; and original productions across broadcast, cable, SVOD, film and digital platforms for BuzzFeed Studios.

BRANDS/DIVISIONS/AFFILIATES:

BuzzFeed Originals
BuzzFeed Media Brands
BuzzFeed Studios
BuzzFeed Marketing
BuzzFeed News
Nifty
Goodful
Tasty

CONTACTS: Note: Officers with more than one job title may be intentionally listed here more than once.

Jonah Peretti, CEO
Felicia DellaFortuna, CFO
Carole Robinson, Chief Communications Officer
Katie Sitter, Chief People Officer
Peter Wang, CTO
Mark Schoofs, Editor-in-Chief

FINANCIAL DATA: Note: Data for latest year may not have been available at press time.

In U.S. $	2022	2021	2020	2019	2018	2017
Revenue	436,674,000	397,564,000	321,324,000	317,923,000	307,251,000	
R&D Expense	30,597,000	24,928,000	17,669,000	21,129,000	26,516,000	
Operating Income	-79,807,000	-25,154,000	12,138,000	-40,268,000	-80,078,000	
Operating Margin %	- .18%	- .06%	.04%	- .13%		
SGA Expense	188,996,000	167,533,000	133,741,000	167,262,000	169,355,000	
Net Income	-200,957,000	24,712,000	10,336,000	-37,192,000	-77,535,000	
Operating Cash Flow	-7,857,000	797,000	27,553,000	-20,243,000	-72,743,000	
Capital Expenditure	17,785,000	16,022,000	14,538,000	8,589,000	17,865,000	
EBITDA	-143,072,000	25,217,000	30,506,000	-20,818,000	-58,251,000	
Return on Assets %	- .34%			- .15%		
Return on Equity %	- .72%					
Debt to Equity	1.11%	.38%				

CONTACT INFORMATION:

Phone: 212-431-7464   Fax: 212-431-7461
Toll-Free:
Address: 111 E. 18th Street, 13/Fl, New York, NY 10003 United States

STOCK TICKER/OTHER:

Stock Ticker: BZFD   Exchange: NAS
Employees: 1,368   Fiscal Year Ends: 12/31
Parent Company:

SALARIES/BONUSES:

Top Exec. Salary: $400,000   Bonus: $970,000
Second Exec. Salary: Bonus: $517,175
$187,250

OTHER THOUGHTS:

Estimated Female Officers or Directors:
Hot Spot for Advancement for Women/Minorities:

Sales, profits and employees may be estimates. Financial information, benefits and other data can change quickly and may vary from those stated here.

Campaign Monitor Pty Ltd

www.campaignmonitor.com

NAIC Code: 511210F

TYPES OF BUSINESS:

Computer Software, Multimedia, Graphics & Publishing
Email Marketing Solutions
Software
Automation Solutions
Online Surveys
Online Marketing Technology
Analytics Technology

BRANDS/DIVISIONS/AFFILIATES:

CM Group

CONTACTS: *Note: Officers with more than one job title may be intentionally listed here more than once.*

Wellford Dillard, CEO
Micki Howl, COO
Lisa Mayer, CFO
Wendy Werve, CMO
Sharon Strauss, Chief People Officer

GROWTH PLANS/SPECIAL FEATURES:

Campaign Monitor, part of the CM Group of brands, provides email marketing, automation and online surveys to help small- and medium-sized businesses grow. The company's technology solves complex problems having to do with online marketing delivery. Its products and feature tools provide everything needed to run marketing campaigns, including an email template builder, segmentation, personalization, marketing automation, transactional email, analytics, integrations, signup forms, short message system (SMS) and more. With Campaign Monitor's application programming interface (API), customers can connect its core business apps to meet email marketing and automation needs. Price ranges depend on the amount of people the campaign will be sent to and begin at $11 per month for 2,500 emails and up to $149 per month for unlimited emails. Customers served include agencies, retailers, non-profits and those within the entertainment, media, publishing, travel and hospitality industries. Headquartered in Tennessee, the firm has additional locations in California and Indiana, and internationally in London and Sydney.

FINANCIAL DATA: *Note: Data for latest year may not have been available at press time.*

In U.S. $	2022	2021	2020	2019	2018	2017
Revenue						
R&D Expense						
Operating Income						
Operating Margin %						
SGA Expense						
Net Income						
Operating Cash Flow						
Capital Expenditure						
EBITDA						
Return on Assets %						
Return on Equity %						
Debt to Equity						

CONTACT INFORMATION:

Phone: 61 2-9521-5312   Fax:
Toll-Free: 888-533-8098
Address: Fl. 38, 201 Elizabeth St., Sydney, NSW 2000 Australia

STOCK TICKER/OTHER:

Stock Ticker: Private   Exchange:
Employees: 250   Fiscal Year Ends:
Parent Company: CM Group

SALARIES/BONUSES:

Top Exec. Salary: $ Bonus: $
Second Exec. Salary: $ Bonus: $

OTHER THOUGHTS:

Estimated Female Officers or Directors: 2
Hot Spot for Advancement for Women/Minorities: Y

Canva Pty Ltd

www.canva.com

NAIC Code: 511210F

TYPES OF BUSINESS:

Computer Software: Multimedia, Advertising, Graphics & Publishing
Software Development
Online Templates
Photo Editing Solutions
Printing Solutions
Infographic Solutions

BRANDS/DIVISIONS/AFFILIATES:

CONTACTS: *Note: Officers with more than one job title may be intentionally listed here more than once.*

Melanie Perkins, CEO

GROWTH PLANS/SPECIAL FEATURES:

Canva Pty Ltd. designs, develops and sells application software. Canva's website offers a wide variety of design types, templates, photos and icons, with features including graphs, photo editing and printing. Design types include logos, posters, business cards, flyers, resumes and infographics. Templates span flyers, resume, brochures, invitations, business cards and presentations. Photos include free photos, backgrounds, nature, animals, food, people, among many others. And icons can be created for social media, web, files, folders, business, weather, computer and other purposes. Price plans include: Free (individuals and small groups working on quick projects), offering free templates, design types and free photos and graphics; Pro (individuals and small teams who need more customization and productivity), offering everything in free plus creating a brand's visual identity with logos, colors, fonts and more, 250,000+ free templates, 100+ million free photos, videos, audios and graphics; and Canvas for Teams (for larger teams needing advanced brand and collaboration control), offering everything in Pro and establishing brand and logos, control of what team members access Canvas, built-in workflows to get approval on designs, advanced template locking, unlimited storage, single sign-on and 24/7 support. Canva offers resources about font, photo editing, color, making logos and more. Headquartered in Australia, Canva has office located in the Philippines and China.

FINANCIAL DATA: *Note: Data for latest year may not have been available at press time.*

In U.S. $	2022	2021	2020	2019	2018	2017
Revenue	193,378,000	185,940,248	178,788,700	174,428,000	148,807,550	99,615,100
R&D Expense						
Operating Income						
Operating Margin %						
SGA Expense						
Net Income						
Operating Cash Flow						
Capital Expenditure						
EBITDA						
Return on Assets %						
Return on Equity %						
Debt to Equity						

CONTACT INFORMATION:

Phone: 61 2 8006 6883   Fax:
Toll-Free:
Address: 110 Kippax St., Surry Hills, NSW 2010 Australia

STOCK TICKER/OTHER:

Stock Ticker: Private   Exchange:
Employees: 2,000   Fiscal Year Ends: 06/30
Parent Company:

SALARIES/BONUSES:

Top Exec. Salary: $ Bonus: $
Second Exec. Salary: $ Bonus: $

OTHER THOUGHTS:

Estimated Female Officers or Directors:
Hot Spot for Advancement for Women/Minorities:

CareerBuilder LLC

www.careerbuilder.com

NAIC Code: 561311A

TYPES OF BUSINESS:

Portal-Career Support
Career Services
Online Recruiting
Resume Writing
Artificial Intelligence

BRANDS/DIVISIONS/AFFILIATES:

Apollo Global Management LLC
CareerBuilder.com
Broadbean

CONTACTS: *Note: Officers with more than one job title may be intentionally listed here more than once.*

Jeff Furman, CEO
Leigh-Margaret Stull, COO
Brett Rasmussen, Pres., North America
Ahern Dull, Exec. VP-Finance
Kristin Kelley, CMO
Brian Burbank, VP-Human Resources
Hope Gurion, Chief Prod. Officer
Alex Green, General Counsel
Hunter Arnold, Pres., Asia Pacific
Tony Roy, Pres., EMEA

GROWTH PLANS/SPECIAL FEATURES:

CareerBuilder, LLC is a global, end-to-end human capital solutions company in business since 1995. The firm provides targeted interactive recruiting through its flagship CareerBuilder.com website, as well as through dozens of affiliated career sites. The company's products and services include a talent discovery platform, a talent network, sourcing solutions, screening solutions, hiring events, social referrals, applicant tracking, hiring solutions, international solutions and more. CareerBuilder also offers supply and demand data to inform and provide insights of an organization's overall strategy. The company serves hundreds of thousands of employers; serves specialized markets across the globe; and powers more than 1,000 partner's career sites, including newspapers and leading portals. CareerBuilder's mission is to empower employment. The firm's platform utilizes advanced artificial intelligence (AI) technology built on a foundation of billions of data points and client and user feedback, enabling companies to find and hire jobseekers swiftly. CareerBuilder owns recruitment software company Broadbean; and operates in the U.S., Canada, Europe and Asia. CareerBuilder itself is majority-owned by Apollo Global Management, LCC. Headquartered in Illinois, USA, CareerBuilder has a European headquarter in London, U.K., and technology hubs in Georgia, USA and Shanghai, China.

FINANCIAL DATA: *Note: Data for latest year may not have been available at press time.*

In U.S. $	2022	2021	2020	2019	2018	2017
Revenue	820,000,000	812,000,000	787,929,188	808,132,500	769,650,000	733,000,000
R&D Expense						
Operating Income						
Operating Margin %						
SGA Expense						
Net Income						
Operating Cash Flow						
Capital Expenditure						
EBITDA						
Return on Assets %						
Return on Equity %						
Debt to Equity						

CONTACT INFORMATION:

Phone: 773-527-3600   Fax: 773-399-6313
Toll-Free: 800-638-4212
Address: 200 N. LaSalle St., Ste. 1100, Chicago, IL 60601 United States

STOCK TICKER/OTHER:

Stock Ticker: Joint Venture   Exchange:
Employees: 3,200   Fiscal Year Ends: 12/31
Parent Company: Apollo Global Management LLC

SALARIES/BONUSES:

Top Exec. Salary: $ Bonus: $
Second Exec. Salary: $ Bonus: $

OTHER THOUGHTS:

Estimated Female Officers or Directors: 2
Hot Spot for Advancement for Women/Minorities: Y

Cars.com Inc

NAIC Code: 519130

www.cars.com

TYPES OF BUSINESS:

Internet Publishing and Broadcasting and Web Search Portals
Cars for Sale
Ecommerce
Website

GROWTH PLANS/SPECIAL FEATURES:

Cars.com Inc is an online destination for buying and selling new and used vehicles. The company brands include Dealer Inspire, DealerRater, FUEL, Accu-Trade, PickupTrucks.com, CreditIQ, and NewCars.com., websites directed towards different consumer segments.

BRANDS/DIVISIONS/AFFILIATES:

Cars.com
Dealer Inspire
DealerRater
Auto.com
PickupTrucks.com
NewCars.com

CONTACTS: *Note: Officers with more than one job title may be intentionally listed here more than once.*

Thomas Vetter, CEO
Sonia Jain, CFO
Scott Forbes, Chairman of the Board
James Rogers, Chief Legal Officer
Douglas Miller, Other Executive Officer
Jeanette Tomy, Treasurer

FINANCIAL DATA: *Note: Data for latest year may not have been available at press time.*

In U.S. $	2022	2021	2020	2019	2018	2017
Revenue	653,876,000	623,683,000	547,503,000	606,682,000	662,127,000	626,262,000
R&D Expense						
Operating Income	66,036,000	48,338,000	29,528,000	36,193,000	99,412,000	143,204,000
Operating Margin %	.10%	.08%	.05%	.06%	.15%	.23%
SGA Expense	378,487,000	359,213,000	303,163,000	354,063,000	368,472,000	328,878,000
Net Income	17,206,000	10,791,000	-817,120,000	-445,324,000	38,809,000	224,443,000
Operating Cash Flow	128,511,000	138,003,000	138,616,000	101,484,000	163,548,000	185,929,000
Capital Expenditure	19,714,000	19,192,000	16,712,000	21,257,000	14,233,000	32,774,000
EBITDA	152,290,000	150,144,000	-785,277,000	-327,628,000	188,456,000	231,843,000
Return on Assets %	.02%	.01%	-.53%	-.19%	.02%	.09%
Return on Equity %	.04%	.03%	-1.10%	-.32%	.02%	.11%
Debt to Equity	1.19%	1.15%	1.694	0.536	.41%	0.332

CONTACT INFORMATION:

Phone: 312-601-5000   Fax:
Toll-Free: 888-780-1286
Address: 300 S. Riverside Plaza, Ste. 1000, Chicago, IL 60606 United States

STOCK TICKER/OTHER:

Stock Ticker: CARS   Exchange: NYS
Employees: 1,700   Fiscal Year Ends: 12/31
Parent Company:

SALARIES/BONUSES:

Top Exec. Salary: $737,500   Bonus: $
Second Exec. Salary: $298,876   Bonus: $389,099

OTHER THOUGHTS:

Estimated Female Officers or Directors:
Hot Spot for Advancement for Women/Minorities:

Carta Communications Inc

www.cci.co.jp/en

NAIC Code: 541810E

TYPES OF BUSINESS:

Internet Advertising
Marketing Support
Travel Agencies
Software Development
Insert Advertising
RSS Feed Advertising

BRANDS/DIVISIONS/AFFILIATES:

Dentsu Inc
Carta Holdings Inc

GROWTH PLANS/SPECIAL FEATURES:

Carta Communications, Inc. (CCI), based in Japan, is an internet advertising company focused on buying, marketing and selling internet advertising space as well as providing advertising delivery technology and support services. The company serves advertising agencies. As an advertising media representative, the firm acts as a marketing company, linking internet media and advertising agencies with advertisers and purchasing and selling advertising space. Its specialties include smart device marketing, solution services, social media marketing and ad platforms. Other services include advertising effectiveness analysis, creative production services and cross-media and technology. Headquartered in Tokyo, CCI has branch offices in Osaka, Nagoya and Fukuoka, Japan. The firm is a subsidiary of Carta Holdings, Inc., itself a subsidiary of Dentsu Inc.

CONTACTS: Note: Officers with more than one job title may be intentionally listed here more than once.

Taku Meguro, CEO
Shinsuke Usami, Chmn.

FINANCIAL DATA: Note: Data for latest year may not have been available at press time.

In U.S. $	2022	2021	2020	2019	2018	2017
Revenue	880,000,000	842,914,800	810,495,000	871,500,000	830,000,000	815,000,000
R&D Expense						
Operating Income						
Operating Margin %						
SGA Expense						
Net Income						
Operating Cash Flow						
Capital Expenditure						
EBITDA						
Return on Assets %						
Return on Equity %						
Debt to Equity						

CONTACT INFORMATION:

Phone: 81-3-4560-4196   Fax:
Toll-Free:
Address: Toranomon Hills Station Twr., Fl. 36, 2-6-1, Toranomon, Minato-ku, Tokyo, 105-5536 Japan

STOCK TICKER/OTHER:

Stock Ticker: Subsidiary   Exchange:
Employees: 730   Fiscal Year Ends: 03/31
Parent Company: Dentsu Inc

SALARIES/BONUSES:

Top Exec. Salary: $ Bonus: $
Second Exec. Salary: $ Bonus: $

OTHER THOUGHTS:

Estimated Female Officers or Directors: 2
Hot Spot for Advancement for Women/Minorities:

Sales, profits and employees may be estimates. Financial information, benefits and other data can change quickly and may vary from those stated here.

Carvana Co
NAIC Code: 441120

www.carvana.com

TYPES OF BUSINESS:
Used Car Dealers
Ecommerce Used Cars
Transportation Management System
Vehicle Inspection

BRANDS/DIVISIONS/AFFILIATES:

GROWTH PLANS/SPECIAL FEATURES:
Carvana Co is an e-commerce platform for buying and selling used cars. The company derives revenue from used vehicle sales, wholesale vehicle sales and other sales and revenues. The other sales and revenues include sales of loans originated and sold in securitization transactions or to financing partners, commissions received on VSCs and sales of GAP waiver coverage. The foundation of the business is retail vehicle unit sales. This drives the majority of the revenue and allows the company to capture additional revenue streams associated with financing, VSCs, auto insurance and GAP waiver coverage, as well as trade-in vehicles.

Carvana offers employees health benefits.

CONTACTS: *Note: Officers with more than one job title may be intentionally listed here more than once.*
Ernie Garcia, CEO
Mark Jenkins, CFO
Stephen Palmer, Chief Accounting Officer
Benjamin Huston, Co-Founder
Ryan Keeton, Co-Founder
Daniel Gill, Other Executive Officer
Tom Taira, President, Divisional
Paul Breaux, Vice President

FINANCIAL DATA: *Note: Data for latest year may not have been available at press time.*

In U.S. $	2022	2021	2020	2019	2018	2017
Revenue	13,604,000,000	12,814,000,000	5,587,000,000	3,940,000,000	1,955,467,000	858,870,000
R&D Expense						
Operating Income	-1,490,000,000	-104,000,000	-332,000,000	-280,000,000	-228,549,000	-155,309,000
Operating Margin %	-.11%	-.01%	-.06%	-.07%	-.12%	-.18%
SGA Expense	2,736,000,000	2,033,000,000	1,126,000,000	787,000,000	425,258,000	223,400,000
Net Income	-1,587,000,000	-135,000,000	-171,000,000	-115,000,000	-55,476,000	-18,313,000
Operating Cash Flow	-1,324,000,000	-2,594,000,000	-608,000,000	-757,000,000	-414,340,000	-199,924,000
Capital Expenditure	512,000,000	557,000,000	360,000,000	231,000,000	143,668,000	78,490,000
EBITDA	-2,146,000,000	-5,000,000	-257,000,000	-243,000,000	-206,188,000	-145,089,000
Return on Assets %	-.20%	-.03%	-.07%	-.08%	-.07%	-.04%
Return on Equity %		-.39%	-.70%	-1.29%	-1.13%	
Debt to Equity		11.66%	4.549	10.184	5.34%	1.694

CONTACT INFORMATION:
Phone: 480-719-8809   Fax:
Toll-Free:
Address: 1930 W. Rio Salado Pkwy, Tempe, AZ 85821 United States

STOCK TICKER/OTHER:
Stock Ticker: CVNA   Exchange: NYS
Employees: 16,600   Fiscal Year Ends: 12/31
Parent Company:

SALARIES/BONUSES:
Top Exec. Salary: $1,011,375   Bonus: $
Second Exec. Salary: $322,771   Bonus: $

OTHER THOUGHTS:
Estimated Female Officers or Directors:
Hot Spot for Advancement for Women/Minorities:

CDK Global LLC

www.cdkglobal.com

NAIC Code: 541810E

TYPES OF BUSINESS:

Advertising-Automotive Dealerships & Manufacturers
Automotive Retail Information Technology
Training & Consulting Services
Technology Integration Solutions
Vehicle Sales and Financing
Vehicle Insurance Solutions
Parts and Repair Software Solutions

BRANDS/DIVISIONS/AFFILIATES:

Brookfield Business Partners LP
CDK Global University

GROWTH PLANS/SPECIAL FEATURES:

CDK Global, LLC provides integrated information technology solutions to the automotive retail and adjacent industries in North America. The company's software-as-a-service (SaaS) solutions connect people with technology by automating and integrating all parts of the dealership and buying process, including the acquisition, sale, financing, insuring, parts supply, repair, and maintenance of vehicles. CDK works with more than 15,000 retail client locations, including most original equipment manufacturers (OEMs) across the auto, truck, agriculture, recreation, marine and powersports industries. CDK Global University offers product education, process and skill education and leadership development to dealerships. CDK is privately-owned by the investment firm Brookfield Business Partners LP.

CONTACTS:
Note: Officers with more than one job title may be intentionally listed here more than once.

Brian P. MacDonald, CEO
Eric Guerin, CFO
Joseph Tautges, COO
Lee Brunz, Executive VP
Amy Byrne, Executive VP

FINANCIAL DATA:
Note: Data for latest year may not have been available at press time.

In U.S. $	2022	2021	2020	2019	2018	2017
Revenue	1,725,000,000	1,673,200,000	1,960,099,968	1,914,800,000	2,273,200,128	2,220,199,936
R&D Expense						
Operating Income						
Operating Margin %						
SGA Expense						
Net Income		1,034,300,032	207,500,000	124,000,000	380,800,000	295,600,000
Operating Cash Flow						
Capital Expenditure						
EBITDA						
Return on Assets %						
Return on Equity %						
Debt to Equity						

CONTACT INFORMATION:

Phone: 847-397-1700   Fax: 206-269-6350
Toll-Free: 800-909-8244
Address: 1950 Hassell Rd., Hoffman Estates, IL 60169 United States

STOCK TICKER/OTHER:

Stock Ticker: Subsidiary   Exchange:
Employees: 6,500   Fiscal Year Ends: 06/30
Parent Company: Brookfield Business Partners LP

SALARIES/BONUSES:

Top Exec. Salary: $ Bonus: $
Second Exec. Salary: $ Bonus: $

OTHER THOUGHTS:

Estimated Female Officers or Directors: 1
Hot Spot for Advancement for Women/Minorities:

Charles Schwab Corporation (The)

www.schwab.com

NAIC Code: 523120

TYPES OF BUSINESS:

Stock Brokerage-Retail, Online & Discount
Investment Services
Physical Branch Investment Offices
Mutual Funds
Wealth Management
Financial Information
Retail Banking
Online Trading Platform

BRANDS/DIVISIONS/AFFILIATES:

Charles Schwab & Co Inc
Charles Schwab Bank
Charles Schwab Investment Management Inc
TD Ameritrade Holding Corporation
TD Ameritrade Inc
TD Ameritrade Clearing Inc

GROWTH PLANS/SPECIAL FEATURES:

Charles Schwab operates in brokerage, wealth management, banking, and asset-management businesses. The company runs a large network of brick-and-mortar brokerage branch offices, a well-established online investing website, and has mobile trading capabilities. It also operates a bank and a proprietary asset management business and offers services to independent investment advisors. The company is among the largest firms in the investment business, with over $7 trillion of client assets at the end of December 2022. Nearly all of its revenue is from the United States.

CSC offers employees health benefits; 401(k) and savings plans; education reimbursement; and on-the-job training and support.

CONTACTS:
Note: Officers with more than one job title may be intentionally listed here more than once.

Walter Bettinger, CEO
Jonathan Craig, Sr. Exec. VP
Peter Crawford, CFO
Charles Schwab, Chairman of the Board
Nigel Murtagh, Chief Risk Officer
Joseph Martinetto, COO
Bernard Clark, Executive VP, Divisional
Peter Morgan, Executive VP
Richard Wurster, President

FINANCIAL DATA:
Note: Data for latest year may not have been available at press time.

In U.S. $	2022	2021	2020	2019	2018	2017
Revenue	20,762,000,000	18,520,000,000	11,691,000,000	10,721,000,000	10,132,000,000	8,618,000,000
R&D Expense						
Operating Income						
Operating Margin %						
SGA Expense	6,355,000,000	5,935,000,000	4,280,000,000	4,002,000,000	3,801,000,000	3,415,000,000
Net Income	7,183,000,000	5,855,000,000	3,299,000,000	3,704,000,000	3,507,000,000	2,354,000,000
Operating Cash Flow	2,057,000,000	2,118,000,000	6,852,000,000	9,325,000,000	12,456,000,000	-839,000,000
Capital Expenditure	971,000,000	916,000,000	631,000,000	708,000,000	570,000,000	400,000,000
EBITDA						
Return on Assets %	.01%	.01%	.01%	.01%	.01%	.01%
Return on Equity %	.18%	.11%	.09%	.19%	.20%	.15%
Debt to Equity	.77%	.41%	0.282	0.392	.38%	0.302

CONTACT INFORMATION:

Phone: 817 859-5000   Fax:
Toll-Free: 800-648-5300
Address: TX-114 Circle T Ranch, Westlake, TX 76262 United States

STOCK TICKER/OTHER:

Stock Ticker: SCHW   Exchange: NYS
Employees: 35,300   Fiscal Year Ends: 12/31
Parent Company:

SALARIES/BONUSES:

Top Exec. Salary: $1,484,615   Bonus: $
Second Exec. Salary: $879,231   Bonus: $

OTHER THOUGHTS:

Estimated Female Officers or Directors: 6
Hot Spot for Advancement for Women/Minorities: Y

Charter Communications Inc

corporate.charter.com

NAIC Code: 517311

TYPES OF BUSINESS:

Cable TV Service
Internet Access
Advanced Broadband Cable Services
Telephony Services
Voice Over Internet Protocol

BRANDS/DIVISIONS/AFFILIATES:

Spectrum
Spectrum TV
Spectrum Internet Gig
Spectrum Voice
Spectrum Mobile
Spectrum Enterprise Solutions
Spectrum Community Solutions
Spectrum Reach

CONTACTS: *Note: Officers with more than one job title may be intentionally listed here more than once.*

Thomas Rutledge, CEO
Catherine Bohigian, Exec. VP, Divisional
Jessica Fischer, CFO
Kevin Howard, Chief Accounting Officer
Jonathan Hargis, Chief Marketing Officer
Stephanie Mitchko-Beale, Chief Technology Officer
Richard DiGeronimo, Chief Technology Officer
Christopher Winfrey, COO
Tom Montemagno, Executive VP, Divisional
Charles Fisher, Executive VP, Divisional
Cliff Hagan, Executive VP, Divisional
Thomas Adams, Executive VP, Divisional
James Nuzzo, Executive VP, Divisional
Adam Ray, Executive VP, Divisional
Magesh Srinivasan, Executive VP, Divisional

GROWTH PLANS/SPECIAL FEATURES:

Charter is the product of the 2016 merger of three cable companies, each with a decades-long history in the business: Legacy Charter, Time Warner Cable, and Bright House Networks. The firm now holds networks capable of providing television, internet access, and phone services to roughly 56 million U.S. homes and businesses, around 40% of the country. Across this footprint, Charter serves 30 million residential and 2 million commercial customer accounts under the Spectrum brand, making it the second-largest U.S. cable company behind Comcast. The firm also owns, in whole or in part, sports and news networks, including Spectrum SportsNet (long-term local rights to Los Angeles Lakers games), SportsNet LA (Los Angeles Dodgers), SportsNet New York (New York Mets), and Spectrum News NY1.

Charter Communications offers its employees comprehensive benefits and retirement options.

FINANCIAL DATA: *Note: Data for latest year may not have been available at press time.*

In U.S. $	2022	2021	2020	2019	2018	2017
Revenue	54,022,000,000	51,682,000,000	48,097,000,000	45,764,000,000	43,634,000,000	
R&D Expense						
Operating Income	12,497,000,000	11,160,000,000	8,397,000,000	6,545,000,000	5,648,000,000	
Operating Margin %	.23%	.21%	.18%	.14%	.13%	
SGA Expense	3,331,000,000	2,951,000,000	3,097,000,000	3,113,000,000	2,850,000,000	
Net Income	5,055,000,000	4,654,000,000	3,222,000,000	1,668,000,000	1,230,000,000	
Operating Cash Flow	14,925,000,000	16,239,000,000	14,562,000,000	11,748,000,000	11,767,000,000	
Capital Expenditure	8,823,000,000	7,555,000,000	7,956,000,000	7,140,000,000	9,595,000,000	
EBITDA	20,921,000,000	19,770,000,000	17,854,000,000	16,154,000,000	15,544,000,000	
Return on Assets %	.04%	.03%	.02%	.01%	.01%	
Return on Equity %	.44%	.25%	.12%	.05%	.03%	
Debt to Equity	10.54%	6.30%	3.434	2.403	1.92%	

CONTACT INFORMATION:

Phone: 203 905-7801   Fax:
Toll-Free:
Address: 400 Atlantic St., Stamford, CT 06901 United States

STOCK TICKER/OTHER:

Stock Ticker: CHTR   Exchange: NAS
Employees: 101,100   Fiscal Year Ends: 12/31
Parent Company:

SALARIES/BONUSES:

Top Exec. Salary: $2,447,115   Bonus: $
Second Exec. Salary: $1,359,038   Bonus: $

OTHER THOUGHTS:

Estimated Female Officers or Directors: 1
Hot Spot for Advancement for Women/Minorities:

Check Point Software Technologies Ltd
www.checkpoint.com

NAIC Code: 511210E

TYPES OF BUSINESS:
Computer Software: Network Security, Managed Access, Digital ID, Cybersecurity & Anti-Virus
Security Software Development
Network Security
Cloud Security
User Access Security
Software Management Solutions

BRANDS/DIVISIONS/AFFILIATES:
Quantum
CloudGuard
Harmony
Infinity-Vision
Avanan

CONTACTS: Note: Officers with more than one job title may be intentionally listed here more than once.
Gil Shwed, CEO
Tal Payne, CFO
Peter Alexander, CMO
Yiftah Yoffe, Chief Human Resources Officer
Dorit Dor, Chief Product Officer
Jerry Ungerman, Chmn.

GROWTH PLANS/SPECIAL FEATURES:
Check Point Software Technologies is a pure-play cybersecurity vendor. The company offers solutions for network, endpoint, cloud, and mobile security in addition to security management. Check Point, a software specialist, sells to enterprises, businesses, and consumers. Around 50% of revenue is generated in Europe, the Middle East, and Africa, 40% from the Americas, and 10% from the Asia-Pacific region. The firm, based in Tel Aviv, Israel, was founded in 1993 and has about 5,000 employees.

FINANCIAL DATA: Note: Data for latest year may not have been available at press time.

In U.S. $	2022	2021	2020	2019	2018	2017
Revenue	2,329,900,000	2,166,800,000	2,064,900,000	1,994,800,000	1,916,500,000	1,854,700,000
R&D Expense	349,900,000	292,700,000	252,800,000	239,200,000	211,500,000	192,400,000
Operating Income	884,300,000	907,500,000	904,200,000	881,800,000	913,800,000	923,900,000
Operating Margin %		.42%	.44%	.44%	.48%	.50%
SGA Expense	791,300,000	708,500,000	681,400,000	658,400,000	589,800,000	525,400,000
Net Income	796,900,000	815,600,000	846,600,000	825,700,000	821,300,000	802,900,000
Operating Cash Flow	1,098,500,000	1,203,900,000	1,161,000,000	1,104,300,000	1,143,600,000	1,109,600,000
Capital Expenditure	22,100,000	15,900,000	19,300,000	25,900,000	17,200,000	28,800,000
EBITDA	920,500,000	938,200,000	931,300,000	905,800,000	934,600,000	940,600,000
Return on Assets %		.14%	.15%	.14%	.15%	.15%
Return on Equity %		.24%	.24%	.22%	.22%	.23%
Debt to Equity						

CONTACT INFORMATION:
Phone: 972 37534555   Fax: 972 35759256
Toll-Free: 800-429-4391
Address: 5 Shlomo Kaplan St., Tel Aviv, 6789159 Israel

STOCK TICKER/OTHER:
Stock Ticker: CHKP   Exchange: NAS
Employees: 6,026   Fiscal Year Ends: 12/31
Parent Company:

SALARIES/BONUSES:
Top Exec. Salary: $400,200   Bonus: $276,700
Second Exec. Salary: $352,200   Bonus: $254,600

OTHER THOUGHTS:
Estimated Female Officers or Directors: 3
Hot Spot for Advancement for Women/Minorities: Y

Chewy Inc (Chewy.com)

www.chewy.com

NAIC Code: 454110

TYPES OF BUSINESS:

Online Pet Supplies Sales
Pharmacy for Pets

BRANDS/DIVISIONS/AFFILIATES:

PetSmart Inc
Chewy.com
Chewy.com Rescue and Shelter Network

GROWTH PLANS/SPECIAL FEATURES:

Chewy is the largest e-commerce pet care retailer in the U.S., generating $10.1 billion in 2022 sales across pet food, treats, hard goods, and pharmacy categories. The firm was founded in 2011, acquired by PetSmart in 2017, and tapped public markets as a standalone company in 2019 after spending a couple of years developing under the aegis of the pet superstore chain. The firm generates sales from pet food, treats, over-the-counter medications, medical prescription fulfillment, and hard goods, like crates, leashes, and bowls.

CONTACTS: Note: Officers with more than one job title may be intentionally listed here more than once.

Sumit Singh, CEO
Mario Marte, CFO
Raymond Svider, Chairman of the Board
Stacy Bowman, Chief Accounting Officer
Satish Mehta, Chief Technology Officer
Susan Helfrick, General Counsel

FINANCIAL DATA: Note: Data for latest year may not have been available at press time.

In U.S. $	2022	2021	2020	2019	2018	2017
Revenue	8,890,774,000	7,146,264,000	4,846,743,000	3,532,837,000	2,104,287,000	
R&D Expense						
Operating Income	-72,178,000	-90,464,000	-252,726,000	-267,766,000	-337,851,000	
Operating Margin %	-.01%	-.01%	-.05%	-.08%	-.16%	
SGA Expense	2,445,760,000	1,911,271,000	1,396,786,000	982,571,000	705,401,000	
Net Income	-73,817,000	-92,486,000	-252,370,000	-267,890,000	-338,057,000	
Operating Cash Flow	191,739,000	132,755,000	46,581,000	-13,415,000	-79,747,000	
Capital Expenditure	183,186,000	130,743,000	48,636,000	44,160,000	40,282,000	
EBITDA	-17,169,000	-54,800,000	-222,081,000	-244,556,000	-325,315,000	
Return on Assets %	-.04%	-.07%	-.34%	-.51%	-1.39%	
Return on Equity %	-11.60%					
Debt to Equity	27.83%					

CONTACT INFORMATION:

Phone: 954-793-4144   Fax:
Toll-Free: 800-672-4399
Address: 1855 Griffin Rd., Dania Beach, FL 33004 United States

STOCK TICKER/OTHER:

Stock Ticker: CHWY
Employees: 19,400
Parent Company: PetSmart Inc

Exchange: NYS
Fiscal Year Ends: 01/31

SALARIES/BONUSES:

Top Exec. Salary: $1,200,000   Bonus: $
Second Exec. Salary: $595,000   Bonus: $

OTHER THOUGHTS:

Estimated Female Officers or Directors:
Hot Spot for Advancement for Women/Minorities:

China Mobile Limited

www.chinamobileltd.com

NAIC Code: 517312

TYPES OF BUSINESS:

Mobile Phone Service
Communication and Information Services
Telecommunication Services
Voice and Data Services
Broadband Services
International Data Communications
Cloud Computing
Internet of Things

BRANDS/DIVISIONS/AFFILIATES:

China Mobile Communications Group Co Ltd

GROWTH PLANS/SPECIAL FEATURES:

China Mobile Limited (CML) is a leading provider of communications and information services in all 31 provinces, autonomous regions and municipalities of mainland China and in Hong Kong. CML is also a leading telecommunications and information operator, with a network that offers voice, data, broadband, dedicated lines, international data communications (IDC), cloud computing, Internet of Things (IoT) and other services to consumers and businesses. As of January 2024, CML had 985 million mobile customers and 2,866 million wireline broadband customers. The firm is majority-owned by China Mobile Communications Group Co. Ltd. (approximately 69.79%), with the remainder held by public investors.

CONTACTS: *Note: Officers with more than one job title may be intentionally listed here more than once.*

Xin Dong, CEO
Ronghua Li, CFO
Huang Wnelin, VP
Sha Yuejia, VP
Liu Aili, VP
Jie Yang, Chmn.

FINANCIAL DATA: *Note: Data for latest year may not have been available at press time.*

In U.S. $	2022	2021	2020	2019	2018	2017
Revenue	135,323,328,938	133,089,135,426	117,674,000,000	110,869,217,280	109,516,939,264	104,327,135,232
R&D Expense						
Operating Income						
Operating Margin %						
SGA Expense						
Net Income	18,315,289,846	18,248,062,482	16,567,600,000	15,850,562,560	17,506,353,152	16,100,168,704
Operating Cash Flow						
Capital Expenditure						
EBITDA						
Return on Assets %						
Return on Equity %						
Debt to Equity						

CONTACT INFORMATION:

Phone: 852 3121-8888   Fax: 85 225119092
Toll-Free:
Address: 99 Queen's Rd. Central, The Center, Fl. 60, Hong Kong, Hong Kong 999077 Hong Kong

STOCK TICKER/OTHER:

Stock Ticker: 941   Exchange: Hong Kong
Employees: 450,698   Fiscal Year Ends: 12/31
Parent Company: China Mobile Communications Group Co Ltd

SALARIES/BONUSES:

Top Exec. Salary: $ Bonus: $
Second Exec. Salary: $ Bonus: $

OTHER THOUGHTS:

Estimated Female Officers or Directors: 1
Hot Spot for Advancement for Women/Minorities: Y

Ciena Corporation

www.ciena.com

NAIC Code: 334210

TYPES OF BUSINESS:
Communications Networking Equipment
Software & Support Services
Consulting Services
Switching Platforms
Packet Interworking Products
Access Products
Network & Service Management Tools

BRANDS/DIVISIONS/AFFILIATES:
Blue Planet Automation
Adaptive Network

GROWTH PLANS/SPECIAL FEATURES:
Ciena Corp is a network and technology company. It provides network hardware, software, and services that support the transport, switching, aggregation, service delivery, and management of video, data, and voice traffic on communications networks. It serves various industries such as communication services providers, web-scale providers, cable operators, government, and large enterprises world-wide. The business activities function through Networking Platforms; Platform Software and Services; Blue Planet Automation Software, and Global Services segments. Geographically, its presence is seen in the markets of the United States, Canada, the Caribbean, Latin America, Europe, the Middle East, Africa, the Asia Pacific, Japan, and India. The maximum revenue is generated from Americas.

CONTACTS:
Note: Officers with more than one job title may be intentionally listed here more than once.

Gary Smith, CEO
James Moylan, CFO
Patrick Nettles, Chairman of the Board
Andrew Petrik, Chief Accounting Officer
Mary Yang, Chief Strategy Officer
Stephen Alexander, Chief Technology Officer
David Rothenstein, General Counsel
Scott McFeely, Senior VP, Divisional
Jason Phipps, Senior VP, Divisional
Rick Hamilton, Senior VP, Divisional

FINANCIAL DATA:
Note: Data for latest year may not have been available at press time.

In U.S. $	2022	2021	2020	2019	2018	2017
Revenue	3,632,661,000	3,620,684,000	3,532,157,000	3,572,131,000	3,094,286,000	
R&D Expense	624,656,000	536,666,000	529,888,000	548,139,000	491,564,000	
Operating Income	257,230,000	527,493,000	513,647,000	374,674,000	253,196,000	
Operating Margin %	.07%	.15%	.15%	.10%	.08%	
SGA Expense	645,947,000	634,088,000	585,973,000	597,445,000	554,193,000	
Net Income	152,902,000	500,196,000	361,291,000	253,434,000	-344,690,000	
Operating Cash Flow	-167,756,000	541,646,000	493,654,000	413,140,000	229,261,000	
Capital Expenditure	90,818,000	79,550,000	82,667,000	62,579,000	67,616,000	
EBITDA	369,758,000	625,854,000	619,809,000	473,354,000	314,050,000	
Return on Assets %	.03%	.11%	.09%	.07%	- .09%	
Return on Equity %	.05%	.18%	.15%	.12%	- .17%	
Debt to Equity	.43%	.26%	0.319	0.343	.39%	

CONTACT INFORMATION:
Phone: 410 694-5700   Fax: 410 694-5750
Toll-Free: 800-921-1144
Address: 7035 Ridge Rd., Hanover, MD 21076 United States

STOCK TICKER/OTHER:
Stock Ticker: CIEN
Employees: 8,483
Parent Company:

Exchange: NYS
Fiscal Year Ends: 10/31

SALARIES/BONUSES:
Top Exec. Salary: $1,000,000   Bonus: $
Second Exec. Salary: $591,369   Bonus: $

OTHER THOUGHTS:
Estimated Female Officers or Directors: 2
Hot Spot for Advancement for Women/Minorities:

Cincinnati Bell Inc (altafiber)

www.cincinnatibell.com

NAIC Code: 517311

TYPES OF BUSINESS:

Local Telephone Service
Integrated Communications Services
IT Network Solutions
Fiber-Optic Networks
Internet Services
Video and Voice Services
Data Solutions
IT Hardware

BRANDS/DIVISIONS/AFFILIATES:

Macquarie Group Limited
Macquarie Infrastructure and Real Assets
altafiber
Hawaiian Telecom
CBTS
OnX

CONTACTS: *Note: Officers with more than one job title may be intentionally listed here more than once.*

Leigh R. Fox, CEO
Suzanne Maratta, Controller
Joshua T. Duckworth, CFO
Kevin Murray, CIO
Leigh Fox, Director
Christi Cornette, Other Executive Officer
Shannon Mullen, Vice President, Divisional
Joshua Duckworth, Vice President, Divisional
Christopher Wilson, Vice President

GROWTH PLANS/SPECIAL FEATURES:

Cincinnati Bell, Inc., doing business as altafiber, provides integrated communications and information technology (IT) solutions to residential and business customers. The Company operates its businesses through the following segments: Network and IT Services and Hardware. The Network segment serves customers in the Greater Cincinnati region through the altafiber brand and services customers in Hawaii through our Hawaiian Telcom brand. This segment provides high-speed data, video and voice solutions to consumers and businesses over an expanding fiber network and a legacy copper network. The IT Services and Hardware segment services customers in the U.S. and Europe through the CBTS brand and in Canada through the OnX brand. This segment provides a full range of managed IT solutions, telephony and IT equipment sales, and professional IT staffing services. These services and products are provided through subsidiaries in various geographic areas throughout the U.S., Canada, Europe and India. By offering a full range of infrastructure solutions in addition to cloud, communications and consulting services, the segment provides end-to-end IT solutions designed to reduce cost and mitigate risk while optimizing performance for its customers. Cincinnati Bell operates under Macquarie Infrastructure and Real Assets, a subsidiary of Macquarie Group Limited. In June 2023, the firm and Bridgewired executed an agreement under which the firm will acquire the broadband infrastructure assets of Bridgewired, LLC. In February 2024, Cincinnati Bell announced that TowerBrook Capital Partners had agreed to acquire CBTS.

FINANCIAL DATA: *Note: Data for latest year may not have been available at press time.*

In U.S. $	2022	2021	2020	2019	2018	2017
Revenue	1,796,000,000	1,693,100,000	1,559,800,064	1,536,700,032	1,378,200,064	1,288,499,968
R&D Expense						
Operating Income						
Operating Margin %						
SGA Expense						
Net Income	-130,900,000	-108,500,000	-55,600,000	-66,600,000	-69,800,000	35,100,000
Operating Cash Flow						
Capital Expenditure						
EBITDA						
Return on Assets %						
Return on Equity %						
Debt to Equity						

CONTACT INFORMATION:

Phone: 513 397-9900   Fax:
Toll-Free: 877-649-6332
Address: 221 E. Fourth St., Cincinnati, OH 45202 United States

STOCK TICKER/OTHER:

Stock Ticker: Subsidiary   Exchange:
Employees: 5,800   Fiscal Year Ends: 12/31
Parent Company: Macquarie Group Limited

SALARIES/BONUSES:

Top Exec. Salary: $ Bonus: $
Second Exec. Salary: $ Bonus: $

OTHER THOUGHTS:

Estimated Female Officers or Directors:
Hot Spot for Advancement for Women/Minorities: Y

Cisco Systems Inc

www.cisco.com

NAIC Code: 334210A

TYPES OF BUSINESS:

Computer Networking Equipment
Routers & Switches
Real-Time Conferencing Technology
Server Virtualization Software
Data Storage Products
Security Products
Teleconference Systems and Technology
Unified Communications Systems

BRANDS/DIVISIONS/AFFILIATES:

AppDynamics Inc
Acacia Communications Inc

GROWTH PLANS/SPECIAL FEATURES:

Cisco Systems is the largest provider of networking equipment in the world and one of the largest software companies in the world. Its largest businesses are selling networking hardware and software (where it has leading market shares) and cybersecurity software like firewalls. It also has collaboration products, like its Webex suite, and observability tools. It primarily outsources its manufacturing to third parties and has a large sales and marketing staff, 25,000 strong across 90 countries. Overall, Cisco employees 80,000 employees and sells its products globally.

CONTACTS: Note: Officers with more than one job title may be intentionally listed here more than once.

Charles Robbins, CEO
R. Herren, CFO
Prat Bhatt, Chief Accounting Officer
Deborah Stahlkopf, Chief Legal Officer
Maria Martinez, COO
Geraldine Elliott, Executive VP

FINANCIAL DATA: Note: Data for latest year may not have been available at press time.

In U.S. $	2022	2021	2020	2019	2018	2017
Revenue	51,557,000,000	49,818,000,000	49,301,000,000	51,904,000,000	49,330,000,000	
R&D Expense	6,774,000,000	6,549,000,000	6,347,000,000	6,577,000,000	6,332,000,000	
Operating Income	13,975,000,000	13,719,000,000	14,101,000,000	14,541,000,000	12,667,000,000	
Operating Margin %	.27%	.28%	.29%	.28%	.26%	
SGA Expense	11,186,000,000	11,411,000,000	11,094,000,000	11,398,000,000	11,386,000,000	
Net Income	11,812,000,000	10,591,000,000	11,214,000,000	11,621,000,000	110,000,000	
Operating Cash Flow	13,226,000,000	15,454,000,000	15,426,000,000	15,831,000,000	13,666,000,000	
Capital Expenditure	477,000,000	692,000,000	770,000,000	909,000,000	834,000,000	
EBITDA	16,794,000,000	15,558,000,000	16,363,000,000	17,327,000,000	16,174,000,000	
Return on Assets %	.12%	.11%	.12%	.11%	.00%	
Return on Equity %	.29%	.27%	.31%	.30%	.00%	
Debt to Equity	.21%	.22%	0.305	0.431	.47%	

CONTACT INFORMATION:

Phone: 408 526-4000   Fax: 408 526-4100
Toll-Free: 800-553-6387
Address: 170 W. Tasman Dr., San Jose, CA 95134-1706 United States

STOCK TICKER/OTHER:

Stock Ticker: CSCO   Exchange: NAS
Employees: 84,900   Fiscal Year Ends: 07/31
Parent Company:

SALARIES/BONUSES:

Top Exec. Salary: $1,390,000   Bonus: $
Second Exec. Salary: Bonus: $
$869,231

OTHER THOUGHTS:

Estimated Female Officers or Directors: 10
Hot Spot for Advancement for Women/Minorities: Y

Sales, profits and employees may be estimates. Financial information, benefits and other data can change quickly and may vary from those stated here.

Cisco Webex

NAIC Code: 517311

www.webex.com

TYPES OF BUSINESS:

Videoconferencing Services
Workplace Collaboration Cloud Solutions
Workplace Meetings Solutions
Training and Conferencing Applications
Workplace Mobile App
Hybrid Work Solutions
Customer Experience Solutions
Collaboration and Meetings Devices

BRANDS/DIVISIONS/AFFILIATES:

Cisco Systems Inc
Webex App
Webex Suite

CONTACTS: *Note: Officers with more than one job title may be intentionally listed here more than once.*

Chuck Robbins, CEO

GROWTH PLANS/SPECIAL FEATURES:

Cisco Webex, a subsidiary of Cisco Systems, Inc., provides cloud-based collaboration, meeting, training and conferencing applications for teams of all sizes. Webex's services scale to business needs to reach and deliver anywhere in the world. For example, staff meetings, presentations and trainings can be accessed anywhere, any time, on any device, including mobile. Products by Webex are grouped into four categories: the Webex App, an all-in-one app for calling, meeting, messaging and getting work done; the Webex Suite, a suite for hybrid work, including calling, meetings, messaging, polling, events and webinars; customer experience solutions, for connecting the customer journey and creating experiences across contact center, artificial intelligence (AI), workforce optimization and communications-platform-as-a-service (CPaaS); and a platform, offering enterprise-grade security, administration and management solutions across a company-wide control hub, with AI collaboration capabilities. Devices offered by Webex include headsets, cameras, desktops, video and multi-screen video conferencing devices for rooms, presentation displays and digital whiteboards, business phones and related accessories. App integrations are offered by Webex. The firm's products and solutions primarily serve the education, healthcare, government, finance, sports, entertainment, frontline, non-profit and startup industries.

FINANCIAL DATA: *Note: Data for latest year may not have been available at press time.*

In U.S. $	2022	2021	2020	2019	2018	2017
Revenue						
R&D Expense						
Operating Income						
Operating Margin %						
SGA Expense						
Net Income						
Operating Cash Flow						
Capital Expenditure						
EBITDA						
Return on Assets %						
Return on Equity %						
Debt to Equity						

CONTACT INFORMATION:

Phone: 408 435-7048   Fax:
Toll-Free: 877-509-3239
Address: 855 E. Tasman Dr., San Jose, CA 95035 United States

STOCK TICKER/OTHER:

Stock Ticker: Subsidiary   Exchange:
Employees: 230   Fiscal Year Ends: 12/31
Parent Company: Cisco Systems Inc

SALARIES/BONUSES:

Top Exec. Salary: $ Bonus: $
Second Exec. Salary: $ Bonus: $

OTHER THOUGHTS:

Estimated Female Officers or Directors:
Hot Spot for Advancement for Women/Minorities:

Cloudflare Inc

www.cloudflare.com

NAIC Code: 511210E

TYPES OF BUSINESS:

Computer Software, Network Security, Managed Access, Digital ID, Cybersecurity & Anti-Virus
Web Content Delivery
Cloud Platform
Business Network Services
Software

BRANDS/DIVISIONS/AFFILIATES:

GROWTH PLANS/SPECIAL FEATURES:

Cloudflare is a software company based in San Francisco, California, that offers security and web performance offerings by utilizing a distributed, serverless content delivery network, or CDN. The firm's edge computing platform, Workers, leverages this network by providing clients the ability to deploy, and execute code without maintaining servers.

Cloudflare offers health benefits and other employee assistance programs.

CONTACTS: Note: Officers with more than one job title may be intentionally listed here more than once.

Matthew Prince, CEO
Thomas Seifert, CFO
Paul Underwood, Chief Accounting Officer
Michelle Zatlyn, Co-Founder
Douglas Kramer, General Counsel

FINANCIAL DATA: Note: Data for latest year may not have been available at press time.

In U.S. $	2022	2021	2020	2019	2018	2017
Revenue	975,241,000	656,426,000	431,059,000	287,022,000	192,674,000	134,915,000
R&D Expense	298,303,000	189,408,000	127,144,000	90,669,000	54,463,000	33,650,000
Operating Income	-201,203,000	-127,684,000	-106,768,000	-107,946,000	-84,899,000	-9,730,000
Operating Margin %	- .21%	- .19%	- .25%	- .38%	- .44%	- .07%
SGA Expense	645,531,000	447,568,000	309,628,000	240,876,000	179,573,000	82,207,000
Net Income	-193,381,000	-260,309,000	-119,370,000	-105,828,000	-87,164,000	-10,748,000
Operating Cash Flow	123,595,000	64,648,000	-17,129,000	-38,917,000	-43,281,000	3,167,000
Capital Expenditure	163,364,000	107,738,000	74,962,000	57,279,000	34,839,000	22,975,000
EBITDA	-83,414,000	-132,135,000	-50,622,000	-74,122,000	-66,190,000	3,321,000
Return on Assets %	- .08%	- .14%	- .11%	- .19%	- .38%	- .07%
Return on Equity %	- .27%	- .32%	- .15%	- .35%		
Debt to Equity	2.47%	1.54%	0.503	0.014		

CONTACT INFORMATION:

Phone: 888 993-5273   Fax:
Toll-Free:
Address: 101 Townsend St., San Francisco, CA 94107 United States

STOCK TICKER/OTHER:

Stock Ticker: NET
Employees: 3,217
Parent Company:

Exchange: NYS
Fiscal Year Ends: 12/31

SALARIES/BONUSES:

Top Exec. Salary: $650,000   Bonus: $
Second Exec. Salary: $550,000   Bonus: $

OTHER THOUGHTS:

Estimated Female Officers or Directors: 1
Hot Spot for Advancement for Women/Minorities:

Cogent Communications Group Inc

www.cogentco.com

NAIC Code: 517311

TYPES OF BUSINESS:
Facilities-Based Internet Service Provider
VoIP Service

BRANDS/DIVISIONS/AFFILIATES:

GROWTH PLANS/SPECIAL FEATURES:
Cogent carries over one fifth of the world's internet traffic over its network and is a broadband provider for businesses. Cogent's corporate customers are in high-rise office buildings; the firm provides them with two types of connections: dedicated internet access, which connects them to the internet, and virtual private networking, which offers an internal network for employees in different locations. Cogent's corporate customers are exclusively in North America and account for over half of the firm's revenue. Cogent's netcentric customers include internet service providers and content providers, to which Cogent provides internet transit. They hand traffic to Cogent in data centers and rely on Cogent to deliver it. About half of netcentric revenue is from outside the U.S.

CONTACTS:
Note: Officers with more than one job title may be intentionally listed here more than once.

David Schaeffer, CEO
Sean Wallace, CFO
John Chang, Chief Legal Officer
R. Kummer, Chief Technology Officer
James Bubeck, Other Executive Officer
Thaddeus Weed, Senior VP, Divisional
Bryant Banks, Vice President, Divisional
Henry Kilmer, Vice President, Divisional

FINANCIAL DATA:
Note: Data for latest year may not have been available at press time.

In U.S. $	2022	2021	2020	2019	2018	2017
Revenue	599,604,000	589,797,000	568,103,000	546,159,000	520,193,000	485,175,000
R&D Expense						
Operating Income	116,207,000	111,840,000	106,993,000	99,198,000	85,576,000	72,056,000
Operating Margin %	.19%	.19%	.19%	.18%	.16%	.15%
SGA Expense	163,021,000	162,380,000	158,476,000	146,913,000	133,858,000	127,915,000
Net Income	5,146,000	48,185,000	6,216,000	37,520,000	28,667,000	5,876,000
Operating Cash Flow	173,707,000	170,257,000	140,320,000	148,809,000	133,921,000	111,702,000
Capital Expenditure	78,971,000	69,916,000	55,952,000	46,958,000	49,937,000	45,801,000
EBITDA	186,182,000	218,719,000	156,275,000	190,374,000	173,671,000	155,511,000
Return on Assets %	.01%	.05%	.01%	.04%	.04%	.01%
Return on Equity %						
Debt to Equity						

CONTACT INFORMATION:
Phone: 202 295-4200   Fax:
Toll-Free: 877-875-4432
Address: 2450 N St. NW, Washington, DC 20037 United States

STOCK TICKER/OTHER:
Stock Ticker: CCOI   Exchange: NAS
Employees: 1,076   Fiscal Year Ends: 12/31
Parent Company:

SALARIES/BONUSES:
Top Exec. Salary: $335,551   Bonus: $
Second Exec. Salary: Bonus: $
$266,678

OTHER THOUGHTS:
Estimated Female Officers or Directors:
Hot Spot for Advancement for Women/Minorities:

Comcast Corporation

corporate.comcast.com

NAIC Code: 517311

TYPES OF BUSINESS:

Cable Television
VoIP Service
Cable Network Programming
High-Speed Internet Service
Video-on-Demand
Advertising Services
Streaming TV Programming
Wireless Services

BRANDS/DIVISIONS/AFFILIATES:

Sky Limited
XFINITY
NBCUniversal
Sky News
Sky Sports
Philadelphia Flyers
Universal Studios
Peacock

GROWTH PLANS/SPECIAL FEATURES:

Comcast is made up of three parts. The core cable business owns networks capable of providing television, internet access, and phone services to 62 million U.S. homes and businesses, or nearly half of the country. About 55% of the homes in this territory subscribe to at least one Comcast service. Comcast acquired NBCUniversal from General Electric in 2011. NBCU owns several cable networks, including CNBC, MSNBC, and USA, the NBC broadcast network, the Peacock streaming platform, several local NBC affiliates, Universal Studios, and several theme parks. Sky, acquired in 2018, is the dominant television provider in the U.K. and has invested heavily in proprietary content to build this position. Sky is also the largest pay-television provider in Italy and has a presence in Germany and Austria.

CONTACTS: Note: Officers with more than one job title may be intentionally listed here more than once.

Jeffrey Shell, CEO, Subsidiary
David Watson, CEO, Subsidiary
Brian Roberts, CEO
Michael Cavanagh, CFO
Daniel Murdock, Chief Accounting Officer
Adam Miller, Chief Administrative Officer
Thomas Reid, Chief Legal Officer
Sheldon Bonovitz, Director Emeritus

FINANCIAL DATA: Note: Data for latest year may not have been available at press time.

In U.S. $	2022	2021	2020	2019	2018	2017
Revenue	121,427,000,000	116,385,000,000	103,564,000,000	108,942,000,000	94,507,000,000	
R&D Expense						
Operating Income	22,624,000,000	20,817,000,000	17,493,000,000	21,125,000,000	19,009,000,000	
Operating Margin %	.19%	.18%	.17%	.19%	.20%	
SGA Expense	46,769,000,000	43,314,000,000	39,850,000,000	40,424,000,000	35,130,000,000	
Net Income	5,370,000,000	14,159,000,000	10,534,000,000	13,057,000,000	11,731,000,000	
Operating Cash Flow	26,413,000,000	29,146,000,000	24,737,000,000	25,697,000,000	24,297,000,000	
Capital Expenditure	13,767,000,000	12,057,000,000	11,634,000,000	12,428,000,000	11,709,000,000	
EBITDA	27,001,000,000	37,178,000,000	31,753,000,000	34,516,000,000	29,801,000,000	
Return on Assets %	.02%	.05%	.04%	.05%	.05%	
Return on Equity %	.06%	.15%	.12%	.17%	.17%	
Debt to Equity	1.15%	.96%	1.114	1.182	1.50%	

CONTACT INFORMATION:

Phone: 215 286-1700   Fax:
Toll-Free: 800-266-2278
Address: One Comcast Center, Philadelphia, PA 19103 United States

STOCK TICKER/OTHER:

Stock Ticker: CMCSA   Exchange: NAS
Employees: 186,000   Fiscal Year Ends: 12/31
Parent Company:

SALARIES/BONUSES:

Top Exec. Salary: $2,500,000   Bonus: $
Second Exec. Salary: Bonus: $
$2,500,000

OTHER THOUGHTS:

Estimated Female Officers or Directors: 16
Hot Spot for Advancement for Women/Minorities: Y

comScore Inc

www.comscore.com

NAIC Code: 541613

TYPES OF BUSINESS:

Marketing Consulting Services
Analytics
Advertising Measurement
Content Measurement
Consumer Audience Measurement
Consulting

BRANDS/DIVISIONS/AFFILIATES:

GROWTH PLANS/SPECIAL FEATURES:

comScore Inc is a United States-based company that provides digital media analytics services to customers in the media, advertising, and marketing industries. Its products are categorized into audience measurement products and services, advertising products and services, and enterprise solutions. The audience measurement products and services help clients measure the size and features of online users. The advertising products and services provide customers with solutions to optimize and assess digital advertising performance. The enterprise solutions help customers optimize businesses through digital media analytics. The company generates almost all its revenue from the United States, Europe, and Canada.

CONTACTS: Note: Officers with more than one job title may be intentionally listed here more than once.

William Livek, CEO
Brent Rosenthal, Chairman of the Board
Christopher Wilson, Other Executive Officer

FINANCIAL DATA: Note: Data for latest year may not have been available at press time.

In U.S. $	2022	2021	2020	2019	2018	2017
Revenue	376,423,000	367,013,000	356,036,000	388,645,000	419,482,000	403,549,000
R&D Expense	36,987,000	39,123,000	38,706,000	61,802,000	76,979,000	89,023,000
Operating Income	-22,607,000	-28,865,000	-16,604,000	-61,997,000	-120,883,000	-201,477,000
Operating Margin %	-.06%	-.08%	-.05%	-.16%	-.29%	-.50%
SGA Expense	124,136,000	122,568,000	118,909,000	156,651,000	226,591,000	284,427,000
Net Income	-66,561,000	-50,037,000	-47,918,000	-338,996,000	-159,268,000	-281,393,000
Operating Cash Flow	34,937,000	9,856,000	717,000	-4,636,000	-72,575,000	-56,405,000
Capital Expenditure	17,822,000	15,550,000	15,555,000	14,236,000	13,814,000	10,182,000
EBITDA	-17,634,000	1,642,000	31,724,000	-263,210,000	-88,974,000	-225,287,000
Return on Assets %	-.13%	-.09%	-.07%	-.40%	-.16%	-.26%
Return on Equity %	-.45%	-.28%	-.20%	-.84%	-.26%	-.36%
Debt to Equity	.32%	.23%	1.00	0.923	.32%	0.003

CONTACT INFORMATION:

Phone: 703 438-2000   Fax: 703 438-2051
Toll-Free:
Address: 11950 Democracy Dr., Ste. 600, Reston, VA 20190 United States

STOCK TICKER/OTHER:

Stock Ticker: SCOR   Exchange: NAS
Employees: 1,556   Fiscal Year Ends: 12/31
Parent Company:

SALARIES/BONUSES:

Top Exec. Salary: $572,808   Bonus: $300,000
Second Exec. Salary: Bonus: $100,000
$312,517

OTHER THOUGHTS:

Estimated Female Officers or Directors: 1
Hot Spot for Advancement for Women/Minorities:

Conga (Appextremes LLC)

conga.com

NAIC Code: 511210Q

TYPES OF BUSINESS:

Computer Software: Accounting, Banking & Financial
Cloud Software
Digital Document Transformation Solutions
Cash Quotes
Contract Software Solutions
Artificial Intelligence
Machine Learning
Revenue and Risk Protection Solutions

BRANDS/DIVISIONS/AFFILIATES:

Thoma Bravo LP

CONTACTS: Note: Officers with more than one job title may be intentionally listed here more than once.

Noel Goggin, CEO
Chris Bishop, Chief Customer Officer
Simon Edwards, CFO
Randy Littleson, CMO
Dayna Perry, Chief People Officer
Koti Reddy, CTO
Grant Peterson, Chief Product Officer

GROWTH PLANS/SPECIAL FEATURES:

Conga provides cloud-based quote-to-cash software and digital document transformation solutions. The firm's products help businesses simplify and automate their approach to quotes, contracts and documents for commerce success. Conga's products document generation, contract lifecycle management, configure, price, quote, eSignature and salesforce optimization. Businesses can streamline documents, manage contracts and automate order/billing revenue. Conga serves a wide range of industries, including energy, healthcare, higher education, life sciences, manufacturing, media, nonprofit, financial services, public sector, retail and technology. Business departments within these industries primarily include business operations, finance, legal, procurement and sales. Conga has more than 12,000 customers worldwide. Headquartered in California, USA, the company has additional offices in the U.S., as well as international locations in India, Ireland, the U.K. and Australia. Conga is privately-owned by Thoma Bravo LP.

FINANCIAL DATA: Note: Data for latest year may not have been available at press time.

In U.S. $	2022	2021	2020	2019	2018	2017
Revenue	416,000,000	400,000,000	194,512,500	199,500,000	190,000,000	185,000,000
R&D Expense						
Operating Income						
Operating Margin %						
SGA Expense						
Net Income						
Operating Cash Flow						
Capital Expenditure						
EBITDA						
Return on Assets %						
Return on Equity %						
Debt to Equity						

CONTACT INFORMATION:

Phone: 303-465-1616   Fax:
Toll-Free:
Address: 390 Interlocken Crescent, Ste. 500, Broomfield, CO 80021 United States

STOCK TICKER/OTHER:

Stock Ticker: Private   Exchange:
Employees: 1,400   Fiscal Year Ends:
Parent Company: Thoma Bravo LP

SALARIES/BONUSES:

Top Exec. Salary: $ Bonus: $
Second Exec. Salary: $ Bonus: $

OTHER THOUGHTS:

Estimated Female Officers or Directors:
Hot Spot for Advancement for Women/Minorities:

Consensus Cloud Solutions Inc

NAIC Code: 517311

www.j2global.com

TYPES OF BUSINESS:

Unified Messaging & Communication Services
Internet-Based Faxing
Internet Conferencing
Cloud-Based Communications Services
Customer Relationship Management Solutions

GROWTH PLANS/SPECIAL FEATURES:

Consensus Cloud Solutions Inc is a provider of secure information delivery services with a scalable Software-as-a-Service SaaS platform. It is engaged in fax cloud. Geographically, it derives a maximum revenue from the United States.

BRANDS/DIVISIONS/AFFILIATES:

MyFax
eVoice
LiveDrive
IPVanish
Campaigner
IGN
Mashable
Everyday Health

CONTACTS: *Note: Officers with more than one job title may be intentionally listed here more than once.*

R. Turicchi, CEO
Steve Emberland, Chief Accounting Officer
Jeffrey Sullivan, Chief Technology Officer
John Nebergall, COO

FINANCIAL DATA: *Note: Data for latest year may not have been available at press time.*

In U.S. $	2022	2021	2020	2019	2018	2017
Revenue	362,422,000	352,664,000	331,168,000	322,559,000	597,975,000	
R&D Expense	10,018,000	7,652,000	7,146,000	9,745,000	27,656,000	
Operating Income	151,918,000	175,136,000	196,675,000	189,827,000	230,120,000	
Operating Margin %		.50%	.59%	.59%		
SGA Expense	138,535,000	111,876,000	73,968,000	72,997,000	218,045,000	
Net Income	72,714,000	109,001,000	152,913,000	212,967,000	152,058,000	
Operating Cash Flow	83,149,000	233,675,000	238,789,000	226,702,000	235,805,000	
Capital Expenditure	31,045,000	34,509,000	35,573,000	22,943,000	14,191,000	
EBITDA	165,638,000	227,167,000	307,998,000	270,173,000	289,982,000	
Return on Assets %		.11%	.10%	.14%		
Return on Equity %		.28%	.19%	.46%		
Debt to Equity			0.023	1.491		

CONTACT INFORMATION:

Phone: 323 860-9200   Fax: 323 860-9201
Toll-Free:
Address: 700 S. Flower St., Fl. 15, Los Angeles, CA 90017 United States

STOCK TICKER/OTHER:

Stock Ticker: CCSI
Employees: 581
Parent Company:

Exchange: NAS
Fiscal Year Ends: 12/31

SALARIES/BONUSES:

Top Exec. Salary: $750,000   Bonus: $
Second Exec. Salary: $450,000   Bonus: $

OTHER THOUGHTS:

Estimated Female Officers or Directors: 2
Hot Spot for Advancement for Women/Minorities:

Corcentric Inc

www.corcentric.com

NAIC Code: 511210K

TYPES OF BUSINESS:

Contract Lifecycle Management Software
Payment and Procurement Software
Payment Advisory Services
Payment Solutions
Source-to-Pay
ePayments
Order-to-Cash
Fleet and Group Purchasing Organization Solutions

BRANDS/DIVISIONS/AFFILIATES:

CONTACTS: Note: Officers with more than one job title may be intentionally listed here more than once.

Matt Clark, Pres.
Chuck Bernicker, CFO
Nancy D. Pearson, CMO
Buffi Gibbons, Chief Human Resources Officer
Manish Jaiswal, CTO
Alan Howe, Director
Douglas W. Clark, Chmn.

GROWTH PLANS/SPECIAL FEATURES:

Corcentric, Inc. offers software, advisory services and payment solutions that transform how companies purchase, pay and receive payment. The company's source-to-pay platform covers sourcing, procurement and financial processes and is trusted by thousands of companies, small and large. Corcentric's integrated platform features source-to-contract, supplier management, contract lifecycle management, procure-to-pay, invoice management, financial management, analytics and core framework capabilities. Its business-to-business (B2B) ePayments solutions help boost cash flow, supplier relations and fraud control. Other source-to-pay platform solutions include accounts payable automation in regards to electronic purchase orders, workflow approval and three-way matching; strategic advisory services in regards to sourcing services, procurement, finance and digital transformation; and managed services, including procurement and help desk. Order-to-cash solutions by Corcentric include managed accounts receivable, supply chain finance, centralized billing for national account programs, electronic invoice presentment, electronic and online payments, managed postal solutions and accounts receivable automation. Fleet solutions are offered for construction and agriculture fleets, as well as for material handling equipment, and includes fleet procurement, fleet financing, fleet analytics, fleet suppliers and fleet remarketing solutions. Group purchasing organization (GPO) solutions by Corcentric help optimize and streamline indirect spend management, and therefore provides procure-to-pay savings as a result. Corcentric's fleet procurement solutions offer discounts on truck parts, from tires to parts to lubricants.

FINANCIAL DATA: Note: Data for latest year may not have been available at press time.

In U.S. $	2022	2021	2020	2019	2018	2017
Revenue	31,200,000	30,000,000	28,786,826	29,524,950	28,119,000	27,463,000
R&D Expense						
Operating Income						
Operating Margin %						
SGA Expense						
Net Income						
Operating Cash Flow						
Capital Expenditure						
EBITDA						
Return on Assets %						
Return on Equity %						
Debt to Equity						

CONTACT INFORMATION:

Phone: 856 773-0600   Fax:
Toll-Free: 800-608-0809
Address: 200 Lake Dr. E., Ste. 200, Cherry Hill, NJ 08002 United States

STOCK TICKER/OTHER:

Stock Ticker: Private   Exchange:
Employees: 150   Fiscal Year Ends:
Parent Company:

SALARIES/BONUSES:

Top Exec. Salary: $ Bonus: $
Second Exec. Salary: $ Bonus: $

OTHER THOUGHTS:

Estimated Female Officers or Directors: 2
Hot Spot for Advancement for Women/Minorities:

CoreSite an American Tower Company

NAIC Code: 517311

www.coresite.com

TYPES OF BUSINESS:

Data Center Operation
Hybrid IT Solutions
Business IT Solutions
Interconnected Data Centers
Native Digital Supply Chain
Direct Cloud Onramps
Digital Transformation Solutions
Cloud Networking

BRANDS/DIVISIONS/AFFILIATES:

American Tower Corporation

CONTACTS: *Note: Officers with more than one job title may be intentionally listed here more than once.*

Juan Font, CEO
Robert Stuckey, Chairman of the Board
Adam Post, Sr. VP-Finance & Corp. Dev.
Maile Kaiser, Sr. VP-Sales & Mktg.
Leslie McIntosh, Sr. VP-Human Resources
Aleks Krusko, Sr. VP-IT & Digitalization
Derek McCandless, General Counsel
Steven Smith, Other Executive Officer
Paul Szurek, President
Brian Warren, Senior VP, Divisional
Juan Font, Senior VP, Divisional
Maile Kaiser, Senior VP, Divisional
Anthony Hatzenbuehler, Senior VP, Divisional
Aleksandra Krusko, Senior VP, Divisional

GROWTH PLANS/SPECIAL FEATURES:

CoreSite, an American Tower Company, provides hybrid information technology (IT) solutions for enterprises, cloud, network and IT service providers so they can monetize and secure their digital businesses. The firm's interconnected data center campuses offer a native digital supply chain that features direct cloud onramps, enabling customers to build customized hybrid IT infrastructure and apply digital transformation. CoreSite's solutions are grouped into four categories: cloud networking, offering open cloud exchange, interconnect gateway, AWS direct connect, Azure ExpressRoute connect, Google Cloud interconnect, Oracle FastConnect and cloud infrastructure services; interconnection, offering peering exchanges, cross connects, inter-site connectivity and blended IP; colocation, offering cabinet colocation, cage colocation, private data center suites, move-in assistance and remote solutions; Industries solutions include artificial intelligence providers, cloud and it service providers, digital media providers, education, financial services, healthcare providers, network providers, public sector, retail it solutions and software as a service (SaaS) providers. CoreSite operates as a subsidiary of American Tower Corporation, a global real estate investment trust and owner, operator and developer of multi-tenant communications real estate.

CoreSite offers its employees comprehensive health benefits, 401(k), short- and long-term disability insurance, life insurance and a variety of employee plans, programs and perks.

FINANCIAL DATA: *Note: Data for latest year may not have been available at press time.*

In U.S. $	2022	2021	2020	2019	2018	2017
Revenue	743,400,000	667,506,400	606,824,000	572,726,976	544,392,000	481,820,992
R&D Expense						
Operating Income						
Operating Margin %						
SGA Expense						
Net Income			79,309,000	75,840,000	77,922,000	74,855,000
Operating Cash Flow						
Capital Expenditure						
EBITDA						
Return on Assets %						
Return on Equity %						
Debt to Equity						

CONTACT INFORMATION:

Phone: 866-777-2673   Fax:
Toll-Free:
Address: 1001 17th St., Ste. 500, Denver, CO 80202 United States

STOCK TICKER/OTHER:

Stock Ticker: Subsidiary   Exchange:
Employees: 480   Fiscal Year Ends: 12/31
Parent Company: American Tower Corporation

SALARIES/BONUSES:

Top Exec. Salary: $ Bonus: $
Second Exec. Salary: $ Bonus: $

OTHER THOUGHTS:

Estimated Female Officers or Directors: 2
Hot Spot for Advancement for Women/Minorities: Y

CoStar Group Inc

NAIC Code: 519130

www.costar.com

TYPES OF BUSINESS:

Online Commercial Real Estate Information
Real Estate Platform
Online Marketplace
Commercial
Residential

GROWTH PLANS/SPECIAL FEATURES:

CoStar Group is a leading provider of commercial real estate data and marketplace listing platforms. Its data offering contains in-depth analytical information on over 5 million commercial real estate properties related to various subsectors including office, retail, hotels, multifamily, healthcare, industrial, self-storage, and data centers. It operates many flagship brands such as CoStar Suite, LoopNet, Apartments.com, BizBuySell, and LandsofAmerica, with more than 80% of its revenue classified as subscription-based. The company also recently expanded its presence in Canada, the United Kingdom, Spain, and France.

BRANDS/DIVISIONS/AFFILIATES:

CoStar
STR
Ten-X
LoopNet
Realla
Apartments.com
Homesnap
Houses.com

CONTACTS:
Note: Officers with more than one job title may be intentionally listed here more than once.

Andrew Florance, CEO
Scott Wheeler, CFO
Michael Klein, Chairman of the Board
Frank Simuro, Chief Technology Officer
Jaye Campbell, General Counsel
Matthew Green, Managing Director, Geographical
Michael Desmarais, Other Executive Officer
Frederick Saint, President, Subsidiary
Lisa Ruggles, Senior VP, Divisional
Jack Spivey, Senior VP, Divisional

FINANCIAL DATA:
Note: Data for latest year may not have been available at press time.

In U.S. $	2022	2021	2020	2019	2018	2017
Revenue	2,182,399,000	1,944,135,000	1,659,019,000	1,399,719,000	1,191,832,000	965,230,000
R&D Expense	220,923,000	201,022,000	162,916,000	125,602,000	100,937,000	88,850,000
Operating Income	450,949,000	432,337,000	289,202,000	363,547,000	273,564,000	173,816,000
Operating Margin %	.21%	.22%	.17%	.26%	.23%	.18%
SGA Expense	1,022,959,000	878,718,000	835,476,000	587,336,000	516,517,000	464,490,000
Net Income	369,453,000	292,564,000	227,128,000	314,963,000	238,334,000	122,695,000
Operating Cash Flow	478,620,000	469,731,000	486,106,000	457,780,000	335,458,000	234,703,000
Capital Expenditure	58,574,000	65,220,000	48,347,000	46,197,000	29,632,000	24,499,000
EBITDA	588,834,000	571,895,000	406,146,000	444,712,000	351,307,000	237,715,000
Return on Assets %	.05%	.04%	.04%	.09%	.08%	.05%
Return on Equity %	.06%	.05%	.05%	.10%	.08%	.06%
Debt to Equity	.16%	.19%	0.207	0.039	.00%	

CONTACT INFORMATION:

Phone: 202-346-6500   Fax: 202 346-6370
Toll-Free: 800-204-5960
Address: 1331 L Street NW, Northwest, WA 20005 United States

STOCK TICKER/OTHER:

Stock Ticker: CSGP   Exchange: NAS
Employees: 5,653   Fiscal Year Ends: 12/31
Parent Company:

SALARIES/BONUSES:

Top Exec. Salary: $971,962   Bonus: $
Second Exec. Salary: $535,892   Bonus: $

OTHER THOUGHTS:

Estimated Female Officers or Directors:
Hot Spot for Advancement for Women/Minorities: Y

Coupa Software Incorporated

coupa.com

NAIC Code: 511210Q

TYPES OF BUSINESS:

Computer Software: Accounting, Banking & Financial
Cloud Software
Business Spend Management

BRANDS/DIVISIONS/AFFILIATES:

Thoma Bravo LP

GROWTH PLANS/SPECIAL FEATURES:

Coupa Software is a cloud-based provider of business spending management (BSM) solutions. Its BSM platform provides visibility into all spending, allowing companies to gain control over their spending, optimize their supplier network and supply chains, and manage liquidity. The platform's transactional core consists of procurement, invoicing, expense management, and payment solutions, while supporting modules ranging from strategic sourcing solutions to supply chain design and planning solutions round out the comprehensive spending management ecosystem. In February 2023, Coupa was acquired by the private equity, software investment firm Thoma Bravo LP.

Coupa Software offers its employees health benefits, 401(k), an employee stock purchase plan, paid time off and more.

CONTACTS: *Note: Officers with more than one job title may be intentionally listed here more than once.*

Leagh Turner, CEO
Stephen Knipe, COO
Kevin Burns, CFO
Kevin Iaquinto, CMO
Susan Tohyama, Chief Human Resources Officer
Amy Sweeney, CIO
Robert Glenn, Executive VP, Divisional
Mark Riggs, Other Executive Officer
Todd Ford, President, Divisional

FINANCIAL DATA: *Note: Data for latest year may not have been available at press time.*

In U.S. $	2022	2021	2020	2019	2018	2017
Revenue	725,289,024	541,643,008	389,719,008	260,366,000	186,780,000	133,775,000
R&D Expense						
Operating Income						
Operating Margin %						
SGA Expense						
Net Income	-379,039,008	-180,116,992	-90,832,000	-55,524,000	-43,805,000	-37,607,000
Operating Cash Flow						
Capital Expenditure						
EBITDA						
Return on Assets %						
Return on Equity %						
Debt to Equity						

CONTACT INFORMATION:

Phone: 650-931-3200   Fax:
Toll-Free:
Address: 1855 S. Grant St., San Mateo, CA 94402 United States

STOCK TICKER/OTHER:

Stock Ticker: Private   Exchange:
Employees: 3,000   Fiscal Year Ends: 01/31
Parent Company: Thoma Bravo LP

SALARIES/BONUSES:

Top Exec. Salary: $ Bonus: $
Second Exec. Salary: $ Bonus: $

OTHER THOUGHTS:

Estimated Female Officers or Directors:
Hot Spot for Advancement for Women/Minorities:

Coupang Inc

www.coupang.com

NAIC Code: 454110

TYPES OF BUSINESS:

Electronic Shopping
Ecommerce
Merchandise
Travel Booking

BRANDS/DIVISIONS/AFFILIATES:

GROWTH PLANS/SPECIAL FEATURES:

Coupang Inc is an e-commerce company. The company sells apparel, electronics, footwear, food products, furniture, nutritional supplements, and other products. Its segments include Product Commerce and Developing Offerings. The company generates maximum revenue from the Product Commerce segment. Product Commerce includes core retail (owned inventory) and marketplace offerings (third-party merchants) and Rocket Fresh, fresh grocery offering, as well as advertising products associated with these offerings.

CONTACTS: *Note: Officers with more than one job title may be intentionally listed here more than once.*

Bom Suk Kim, CEO

FINANCIAL DATA: *Note: Data for latest year may not have been available at press time.*

In U.S. $	2022	2021	2020	2019	2018	2017
Revenue	20,582,620,000	18,406,370,000	11,967,340,000	6,273,263,000	4,053,589,000	
R&D Expense						
Operating Income	-112,019,000	-1,493,962,000	-515,994,000	-641,923,000	-1,052,406,000	
Operating Margin %	-.01%	-.08%	-.04%	-.10%		
SGA Expense	4,821,892,000	4,445,090,000	2,502,231,000	1,675,145,000	1,241,790,000	
Net Income	-92,042,000	-1,542,590,000	-463,157,000	-696,885,000	-1,097,532,000	
Operating Cash Flow	565,439,000	-410,578,000	301,554,000	-311,843,000	-694,465,000	
Capital Expenditure	824,262,000	673,663,000	484,630,000	217,823,000	93,401,000	
EBITDA	165,029,000	-1,294,750,000	-227,584,000	-529,311,000	-970,688,000	
Return on Assets %	-.01%	-.23%	-.13%	-.24%		
Return on Equity %	-.04%					
Debt to Equity	.73%	.68%				

CONTACT INFORMATION:

Phone: 82 2-1577-7011   Fax: 82 2-3441-7011
Toll-Free:
Address: 570, Tower 730, Songpa-daero, Songpa-gu, Seoul, 05510 South Korea

STOCK TICKER/OTHER:

Stock Ticker: CPNG   Exchange: NYS
Employees: 63,000   Fiscal Year Ends: 12/31
Parent Company:

SALARIES/BONUSES:

Top Exec. Salary: $774,024   Bonus: $637,012
Second Exec. Salary: $1,100,000   Bonus: $

OTHER THOUGHTS:

Estimated Female Officers or Directors:
Hot Spot for Advancement for Women/Minorities:

Cox Automotive Inc

www.coxautoinc.com

NAIC Code: 519130

TYPES OF BUSINESS:

Internet Search Portals
Automotive Resources
Innovative Online Communication
Technologies
Vehicle Inventory Resources
Vehicle Service Resources
Fleet Service Resources

BRANDS/DIVISIONS/AFFILIATES:

Cox Enterprises Inc
Autotrader
Cox Automotive Mobility
Dealer.com
Fyusion
Kelley Blue Book
NextGear Capital
Xtime

CONTACTS: *Note: Officers with more than one job title may be intentionally listed here more than once.*

Stephen M. Rowley, Pres.
Mark F. Bowser, CFO
Ken Kraft, CMO
Michele Parks, Chief People Officer
Tim McKinley, Chief Sales Officer

GROWTH PLANS/SPECIAL FEATURES:

Cox Automotive, Inc. provides automotive resources and tools for consumers, dealers and manufacturers. The firm's six business units are inventory, for identifying, acquiring and financing inventory; marketing, for planning, pricing and marketing vehicles in showrooms and online; sales, for making in-store sales go more smoothly; service, for scheduling service appointments; operations, for the management of dealerships; and mobility, offering fleet services and solutions for fleet operations, including EV battery solutions and more. Brands include Autotrader, Cox Automotive Mobility, Dealertrack, Dealer.com, Dealer-Auction.com, Dealertrack, Dickinson Fleet Services, F&I Express, Fyusion, Jingzhengu, Kelley Blue Book, Mahindra First Choice, Manheim, Modix, Molicar, Movex, NextGear Capital, Ready Logistics, vAuto, VinSolutions and Xtime. Cox Automotive has more than 40,000 auto dealer clients across five continents. Cox Automotive operates as a subsidiary of Cox Enterprises, Inc.

FINANCIAL DATA: *Note: Data for latest year may not have been available at press time.*

In U.S. $	2022	2021	2020	2019	2018	2017
Revenue	7,000,000,000	7,280,000,000	7,000,000,000	8,169,525,000	7,780,500,000	7,410,000,000
R&D Expense						
Operating Income						
Operating Margin %						
SGA Expense						
Net Income						
Operating Cash Flow						
Capital Expenditure						
EBITDA						
Return on Assets %						
Return on Equity %						
Debt to Equity						

CONTACT INFORMATION:

Phone: 404 568-8000   Fax:
Toll-Free: 855-449-0010
Address: 3003 Summit Blvd., Ste. 200, Atlanta, GA 30319 United States

STOCK TICKER/OTHER:

Stock Ticker: Subsidiary   Exchange:
Employees: 27,000   Fiscal Year Ends: 12/31
Parent Company: Cox Enterprises Inc

SALARIES/BONUSES:

Top Exec. Salary: $ Bonus: $
Second Exec. Salary: $ Bonus: $

OTHER THOUGHTS:

Estimated Female Officers or Directors:
Hot Spot for Advancement for Women/Minorities:

Cox Communications Inc

www.cox.com/aboutus/home.html

NAIC Code: 517311

TYPES OF BUSINESS:

Cable TV Service and Internet Access
Broadband
Internet
TV
Streaming
Smart Home
Security
Telephone Service

BRANDS/DIVISIONS/AFFILIATES:

Cox Enterprises Inc

GROWTH PLANS/SPECIAL FEATURES:

Cox Communications, Inc., a subsidiary of Cox Enterprises, Inc., is a broadband communications and entertainment company, serving millions of customers throughout the U.S. Cox Communications' products and services include internet, TV, streaming, smart home, security, home phone and bundled deals. The company serves both residential and business customers, with business solutions also including security systems, networking, collaboration and cloud services. Cox Business solutions primarily serve the education, healthcare, government, hospitality and wireless carrier industries.

Cox offers its employees comprehensive health care, a 401(k), continuing education and professional development funds and other benefits.

CONTACTS:
Note: Officers with more than one job title may be intentionally listed here more than once.

Mark Greatrex, Pres.
Colleen Langner, COO
Perley McBride, CFO
Kia Painter, Chief People Officer
Len Barlik, CTO
Len Barlik, Exec. VP-Prod. Mgmt. & Dev.
Asheesh Saksena, Chief Strategy Officer
Joseph J. Rooney, Sr. VP-Social Media, Advertising & Brand Mktg.
William (Bill) J. Fitzsimmons, Chief Acct. Officer
Philip G. Meeks, Sr. VP-Cox Bus.
Jennifer W. Hightower, Sr. VP-Law & Policy
David Pugliese, Sr. VP-Product Mktg.
Mark A. Kaish, Sr. VP-Tech. Oper.
George Richter, VP-Supply Chain Mgmt.

FINANCIAL DATA:
Note: Data for latest year may not have been available at press time.

In U.S. $	2022	2021	2020	2019	2018	2017
Revenue	13,800,000,000	13,104,000,000	12,600,000,000	12,300,000,000	12,000,000,000	11,550,000,000
R&D Expense						
Operating Income						
Operating Margin %						
SGA Expense						
Net Income						
Operating Cash Flow						
Capital Expenditure						
EBITDA						
Return on Assets %						
Return on Equity %						
Debt to Equity						

CONTACT INFORMATION:

Phone: 404-843-5000   Fax: 404-843-5939
Toll-Free: 888-566-7751
Address: 6205-B Peachtree Dunwoody Rd. NE, Atlanta, GA 30328 United States

STOCK TICKER/OTHER:

Stock Ticker: Subsidiary   Exchange:
Employees: 18,000   Fiscal Year Ends: 12/31
Parent Company: Cox Enterprises Inc

SALARIES/BONUSES:

Top Exec. Salary: $ Bonus: $
Second Exec. Salary: $ Bonus: $

OTHER THOUGHTS:

Estimated Female Officers or Directors: 3
Hot Spot for Advancement for Women/Minorities: Y

Crackle Plus LLC

www.crackle.com

NAIC Code: 519130

TYPES OF BUSINESS:

Internet Streaming Movies & Television Shows
Over-the-Top Media Platform
Television and Movie Programming

BRANDS/DIVISIONS/AFFILIATES:

Chicken Soup for the Soul LLC

GROWTH PLANS/SPECIAL FEATURES:

Crackle Plus, LLC offers a U.S.-based over-the-top (OTT) media platform called Crackle that offers a free to use streaming service. The company generates its revenue from advertising while watching TV shows and movies. Crackle's library consists of original content as well as programming acquired from other companies, spanning genres such as action, comedy, crime, drama, horror and sci-fi. Crackle, Inc. is a subsidiary of Chicken Soup for the Soul LLC (CSS). The service is available in the U.S. for free and can be accessed through connected devices including smart TVs, mobile devices, set-top boxes, video game consoles and online at Crackle.com. Crackle is ad-supported, enabling the company to offer all content free of charge. Some movies and shows on Crackle are only available for a limited time due to agreements with programming providers.

CONTACTS: Note: Officers with more than one job title may be intentionally listed here more than once.

Eric Berger, Sr. VP-Digital Networks
William J. Rouhana, Jr., Chmn.-CSS

FINANCIAL DATA: Note: Data for latest year may not have been available at press time.

In U.S. $	2022	2021	2020	2019	2018	2017
Revenue						
R&D Expense						
Operating Income						
Operating Margin %						
SGA Expense						
Net Income						
Operating Cash Flow						
Capital Expenditure						
EBITDA						
Return on Assets %						
Return on Equity %						
Debt to Equity						

CONTACT INFORMATION:

Phone: 310-244-4000   Fax:
Toll-Free: 800-952-5210
Address: 9336 Washington Blvd., Culver City, CA 90232 United States

STOCK TICKER/OTHER:

Stock Ticker: Subsidiary   Exchange:
Employees: 100   Fiscal Year Ends: 12/31
Parent Company: Chicken Soup For The Soul LLC

SALARIES/BONUSES:

Top Exec. Salary: $ Bonus: $
Second Exec. Salary: $ Bonus: $

OTHER THOUGHTS:

Estimated Female Officers or Directors:
Hot Spot for Advancement for Women/Minorities:

Craigslist Inc

www.craigslist.org

NAIC Code: 519130

TYPES OF BUSINESS:
Online Classified Ads Platform
Online Classified Ads
Online Community Forums
Job Postings
Items for Sale
Services for Hire
Technology
Ecommerce

BRANDS/DIVISIONS/AFFILIATES:
Craigslist.org
Craigslist Charitable Fund

CONTACTS: Note: Officers with more than one job title may be intentionally listed here more than once.
Jim Buckmaster, CEO
Craig Newmark, Chmn.

GROWTH PLANS/SPECIAL FEATURES:

Craigslist, Inc. operates Craigslist.org, an online community offering local classifieds and forums in more than 70 countries. The platform enables users to post listings for everything from classified and personal ads to jobs, housing, goods, services, local activities and advice. In addition to English, sites are available in 15 languages such as Catalan, Danish, Dutch, Filipino, French, German, Italian, Norwegian, Portuguese, Spanish, Swedish, Turkish and more. Craigslist users create millions of classified ads for jobs, housing, goods, services, romance and local activities each month. People use Craigslist to post their views across different discussion forums on many different subjects. Although Craigslist is a commercial enterprise, it retains its original .org URL to emphasize its mission as a community service and to reflect its non-corporate culture. The company relies almost entirely on word-of-mouth advertising and has resisted the efforts of advertisers to purchase space on its sites, meaning that users may navigate without seeing banner ads or other advertisements. Through its Craigslist Charitable Fund, the company creates grants for 501(c)3 nonprofit organizations. Craigslist has released many opensource projects that are available for download.

Craigslist offers its employees health and retirement benefits, as well as a variety of employee assistance programs.

FINANCIAL DATA: Note: Data for latest year may not have been available at press time.

In U.S. $	2022	2021	2020	2019	2018	2017
Revenue	694,000,000	660,000,000	517,000,000	651,420,000	1,034,000,000	850,000,000
R&D Expense						
Operating Income						
Operating Margin %						
SGA Expense						
Net Income						
Operating Cash Flow						
Capital Expenditure						
EBITDA						
Return on Assets %						
Return on Equity %						
Debt to Equity						

CONTACT INFORMATION:
Phone: 415-566-6394   Fax: 415-504-6394
Toll-Free:
Address: 1381 9th Ave., San Francisco, CA 94122 United States

STOCK TICKER/OTHER:
Stock Ticker: Private   Exchange:
Employees: 50   Fiscal Year Ends:
Parent Company:

SALARIES/BONUSES:
Top Exec. Salary: $ Bonus: $
Second Exec. Salary: $ Bonus: $

OTHER THOUGHTS:
Estimated Female Officers or Directors: 4
Hot Spot for Advancement for Women/Minorities: Y

Critical Mass Inc

www.criticalmass.com

NAIC Code: 541810E

TYPES OF BUSINESS:

Online Advertising & Marketing
Digital Marketing Services
Brand Development Services
Ecommerce Services
Marketing Design and Implementation Services
Marketing Campaign Management
Automated and Real-time Analytics
Customer Engagement Solutions

BRANDS/DIVISIONS/AFFILIATES:

Omnicom Group Inc
DAS Group of Companies

CONTACTS: *Note: Officers with more than one job title may be intentionally listed here more than once.*

Michael Larson, CEO-DAS
Scott Ross, Exec. Tech. Dir.
Jaime Escobar, Dir.-Oper.
Diane Heun, VP-Bus. Dev.
Katy Zack, Dir.-Comm.
Darren Delichte, Sr. VP
Matt Di Paolo, Sr. VP
Amanda Levy, Sr. VP
Shaina Boone, Sr. VP-Mktg. Science
Jaime Escobar, Gen. Mgr.-Latin America

GROWTH PLANS/SPECIAL FEATURES:

Critical Mass, Inc. is a digital marketing company. The firm offers web design services as well as solutions in regard to new products, driving sales, reducing customer support costs, building customer loyalty and increasing the use of online and digital channels. Services by Critical Mass include creating marketing strategies through its insight and planning unit; eMarketing, including email campaign management; experience design, which helps clients develop brands and brand presence; technology support, including ecommerce and application development, as well as automated and real-time analytics and on-demand content; and social media, which connects people in order to engage and activate them. The firm's associated web design services include the production of computer graphics and animation. Through its services, the company aids clients in improving marketing efforts in online environments, reengineering websites, standardizing brand presence, moving customers to online channels and personalizing a customer's electronic experience. Besides its Calgary headquarters, the company has primary offices in Chicago, Cupertino, London, Los Angeles, Nashville, New York, San Jose, Sao Paulo, Tokyo and Toronto. Critical Mass operates as a subsidiary of DAS Group of Companies, a division of Omnicom Group, Inc.

FINANCIAL DATA: *Note: Data for latest year may not have been available at press time.*

In U.S. $	2022	2021	2020	2019	2018	2017
Revenue						
R&D Expense						
Operating Income						
Operating Margin %						
SGA Expense						
Net Income						
Operating Cash Flow						
Capital Expenditure						
EBITDA						
Return on Assets %						
Return on Equity %						
Debt to Equity						

CONTACT INFORMATION:

Phone: 403-262-3006   Fax: 403-262-7185
Toll-Free:
Address: 1011 9th Ave. SE, Ste. 300, Calgary, AB T2G 0H7 Canada

STOCK TICKER/OTHER:

Stock Ticker: Subsidiary   Exchange:
Employees: 1,130   Fiscal Year Ends: 12/31
Parent Company: Omnicom Group Inc

SALARIES/BONUSES:

Top Exec. Salary: $ Bonus: $
Second Exec. Salary: $ Bonus: $

OTHER THOUGHTS:

Estimated Female Officers or Directors: 6
Hot Spot for Advancement for Women/Minorities: Y

CyberSource Corporation

www.cybersource.com

NAIC Code: 522320

TYPES OF BUSINESS:

E-Commerce Processing Services & Systems
Risk Management Solutions
Credit Card Processing
Tax Calculation
Fraud Screening
Compliance Services
Consulting Services
Digital Payment Solutions

BRANDS/DIVISIONS/AFFILIATES:

Visa Inc

CONTACTS: Note: Officers with more than one job title may be intentionally listed here more than once.

Ryan McInerney, CEO-Visa Inc
Michael Walsh, Pres.
Neil Buckley, VP-Prod. Dev.
David J. Kim, General Counsel
John McDonnell, VP-Bus. Dev.
Carolyn Brackett, VP-Channels & Alliances
David A. Glaser, VP-Professional Svcs.
Trish Martin, VP-Customer Support
John Bodine, VP-Sales & Mktg.

GROWTH PLANS/SPECIAL FEATURES:

CyberSource Corporation, a subsidiary of Visa, Inc., provides secure electronic payment and risk management services to organizations that sell products and services over the internet and through mobile apps. The company's payment systems allow ecommerce merchants to accept a range of payment options, including credit cards, electronic checks and global payment options. CyberSource's payment management platform helps companies optimize business results by actively managing every aspect of its payment operations, from payment acceptance and processing to order screening, fraud management and enterprise payment security. Payment processing solutions include cross-channel payments, gateway and processing connections, payment cards, online and mobile digital payments, direct debit and bank transfers, reconciliation reports, payer authentication, global tax calculation, recurring billing and account updater. Fraud management solutions include managed risk services, payer authentication, account takeover protection, loyalty fraud management, fraud alert, delivery address verification and export compliance. Payment security solutions include secure acceptance via web and mobile channels, as well as payment tokenization. CyberSource's solutions serve merchants of all sizes, operating in the most varied geographies and industry verticals. Its partner program is available to technology providers, system integrators, financial institutions and payment solution providers. Businesses worldwide use CyberSource solutions. Based in the U.S., CyberSource has international office locations.

FINANCIAL DATA: Note: Data for latest year may not have been available at press time.

In U.S. $	2022	2021	2020	2019	2018	2017
Revenue	453,881,610	453,881,610	436,424,625	415,642,500	395,850,000	377,000,000
R&D Expense						
Operating Income						
Operating Margin %						
SGA Expense						
Net Income						
Operating Cash Flow						
Capital Expenditure						
EBITDA						
Return on Assets %						
Return on Equity %						
Debt to Equity						

CONTACT INFORMATION:

Phone: 650-432-7350   Fax: 650-625-9145
Toll-Free: 800-530-9095
Address: 900 Metro Center Blvd., Foster City, CA 94404 United States

STOCK TICKER/OTHER:

Stock Ticker: Subsidiary   Exchange:
Employees: 700   Fiscal Year Ends: 12/31
Parent Company: Visa Inc

SALARIES/BONUSES:

Top Exec. Salary: $ Bonus: $
Second Exec. Salary: $ Bonus: $

OTHER THOUGHTS:

Estimated Female Officers or Directors: 2
Hot Spot for Advancement for Women/Minorities: Y

Sales, profits and employees may be estimates. Financial information, benefits and other data can change quickly and may vary from those stated here.

Cylance Inc
NAIC Code: 511210E

www.blackberry.com/us/en/cylance

TYPES OF BUSINESS:
Computer Software: Network Security, Managed Access, Digital ID, Cybersecurity & Anti-Virus
Security Technology
Cyber Security Solutions
Artificial Intelligence
Machine Learning
Offline Protection
User Behavior Analytics
Access Solutions

BRANDS/DIVISIONS/AFFILIATES:
BlackBerry Limited
Cylance AI
CylanceENDPOINT
CylanceEDGE
CylanceGUARD
CylanceINTELLIGENCE

CONTACTS: Note: Officers with more than one job title may be intentionally listed here more than once.
Richard Lynch, Chmn.-BlackBerry Limited

GROWTH PLANS/SPECIAL FEATURES:
Cylance, Inc., a subsidiary of BlackBerry Limited, offers technology that provides customers endpoint security that proactively detects cyber threats and prevents cyberattacks. The company's cybersecurity products are artificial intelligence (AI)- and machine learning (ML)-driven, and work to protect organizations with a unified endpoint security solution, offering enhanced visibility, endpoint detection and response to smart antivirus. Cylance products prevent breaches and provide added controls to ward off cyber threats without human intervention. They work to protect devices when offline. Its endpoint user and entry behavior analytics solution use predictive AI to adapt security policy in real-time, based on user location, device and other factors. The Cylance gateway is a Zero Trust network access solution that protects systems and data while simultaneously providing access to software-as-a-service (SaaS) and on-premises apps for hybrid workforces. Product lines include Cylance AI, CylanceENDPOINT, CylanceEDGE, CylanceGUARD and CylanceINTELLIGENCE. Industries served by Cylance include financial services, professional services, government, healthcare, consumer industries, transportation, education, utilities and manufacturing.

Parent BlackBerry offers Cylance employees comprehensive health benefits, retirement savings programs, an education reimbursement program and other company plans, programs and perks.

FINANCIAL DATA: Note: Data for latest year may not have been available at press time.

In U.S. $	2022	2021	2020	2019	2018	2017
Revenue	196,560,000	189,000,000	151,000,000	184,000,000	105,000,000	100,000,000
R&D Expense						
Operating Income						
Operating Margin %						
SGA Expense						
Net Income						
Operating Cash Flow						
Capital Expenditure						
EBITDA						
Return on Assets %						
Return on Equity %						
Debt to Equity						

CONTACT INFORMATION:
Phone: 519 888-7465   Fax:
Toll-Free: 888-997-6795
Address: 400 Spectrum Center Dr., Ste. 900, Irvine, CA 92618 United States

STOCK TICKER/OTHER:
Stock Ticker: Subsidiary   Exchange:
Employees: 760   Fiscal Year Ends: 02/28
Parent Company: BlackBerry Limited

SALARIES/BONUSES:
Top Exec. Salary: $ Bonus: $
Second Exec. Salary: $ Bonus: $

OTHER THOUGHTS:
Estimated Female Officers or Directors:
Hot Spot for Advancement for Women/Minorities:

Cyxtera Technologies Inc

www.cyxtera.com

NAIC Code: 518210

TYPES OF BUSINESS:

Hosting & Collocation Services
Data Centers
Networking
Digital Computing
Artificial Intelligence
Machine Learning

BRANDS/DIVISIONS/AFFILIATES:

Medina Capital
BC Partners LLP

GROWTH PLANS/SPECIAL FEATURES:

Cyxtera Technologies Inc is engaged in data center colocation and interconnection services. The company operates a footprint of more than 60 data centers around the world, providing services to more than 2,300 leading enterprises and U.S. federal government agencies. Cyxtera brings proven operational excellence, global scale, flexibility and customer-focused innovation together to provide a comprehensive portfolio of data center and interconnection services.

CONTACTS: Note: Officers with more than one job title may be intentionally listed here more than once.

Nelson Fonseca, CEO
Carlos Sagasta, CFO
Manuel Medina, Chairman of the Board
Victor Semah, Chief Compliance Officer
Randy Rowland, COO
Leo Taddeo, Other Executive Officer

FINANCIAL DATA: Note: Data for latest year may not have been available at press time.

In U.S. $	2022	2021	2020	2019	2018	2017
Revenue	746,000,000	703,699,968	690,499,968	679,000,000	685,755,000	653,100,000
R&D Expense						
Operating Income						
Operating Margin %						
SGA Expense						
Net Income	-355,100,000	-257,900,000	-122,800,000	-295,000,000		
Operating Cash Flow						
Capital Expenditure						
EBITDA						
Return on Assets %						
Return on Equity %						
Debt to Equity						

CONTACT INFORMATION:

Phone: 305 537-9500   Fax:
Toll-Free: 855-699-8372
Address: BAC Colonnade Office Twr., 2333 Ponce De Leon Blvd, Coral Gables, FL 33134 United States

STOCK TICKER/OTHER:

Stock Ticker: Subsidiary
Employees: 755
Parent Company: Evoque Data Center Solutions
Exchange:
Fiscal Year Ends: 12/31

SALARIES/BONUSES:

Top Exec. Salary: $ Bonus: $
Second Exec. Salary: $ Bonus: $

OTHER THOUGHTS:

Estimated Female Officers or Directors: 1
Hot Spot for Advancement for Women/Minorities:

Sales, profits and employees may be estimates. Financial information, benefits and other data can change quickly and may vary from those stated here.

D&B Hoovers
www.dnb.com/products/marketing-sales/dnb-hoovers.html
NAIC Code: 519130

TYPES OF BUSINESS:
Online Corporate Intelligence
Reference Books
Ecommerce
Advertising Services
Sales & Marketing Lists

BRANDS/DIVISIONS/AFFILIATES:
Dun & Bradstreet Inc

GROWTH PLANS/SPECIAL FEATURES:
D&B Hoovers, a division of Dun & Bradstreet, Inc., offers a sales intelligence solution that enables sales and marketing professionals to generate business growth. D&B Hoovers leverages a global commercial database business records and analytics to deliver its sales intelligence solution. The platform provides real-time trigger alerts, predictive indicators, industry analysis, extensive market research reports and more. It encompasses sales prospecting capabilities for building highly targeted campaign lists and creating leads and monitors the market 24/7 to ensure the list of prospects is always current. Users can send marketing and sales leads directly to their customer relations marketing and marketing automation platforms (CRM/MAP). D&B Hoovers seamlessly integrates directly with the systems that its customers use, such as Salesforce, Microsoft, etc. Sales pitches can be personalized and developments can be monitored.

CONTACTS: *Note: Officers with more than one job title may be intentionally listed here more than once.*
Hyune Hand, Pres.
William P. Foley II, Chmn.-Corp.

FINANCIAL DATA: *Note: Data for latest year may not have been available at press time.*

In U.S. $	2022	2021	2020	2019	2018	2017
Revenue						
R&D Expense						
Operating Income						
Operating Margin %						
SGA Expense						
Net Income						
Operating Cash Flow						
Capital Expenditure						
EBITDA						
Return on Assets %						
Return on Equity %						
Debt to Equity						

CONTACT INFORMATION:
Phone: 512-374-4500   Fax: 512-374-4501
Toll-Free: 866-473-3932
Address: 103 John F Kennedy Parkway, Short Hills, NJ 07078 United States

STOCK TICKER/OTHER:
Stock Ticker: Subsidiary   Exchange:
Employees: 200   Fiscal Year Ends: 12/31
Parent Company: Dun & Bradstreet Inc

SALARIES/BONUSES:
Top Exec. Salary: $ Bonus: $
Second Exec. Salary: $ Bonus: $

OTHER THOUGHTS:
Estimated Female Officers or Directors:
Hot Spot for Advancement for Women/Minorities: Y

Data.ai

NAIC Code: 519130

TYPES OF BUSINESS:

Internet Publishing and Broadcasting and Web Search Portals
Artificial Intelligent Data Platform
Consumer and Market Data Software
Analytics Technology
Data Aggregation Solutions
App Marketing Solutions
Business Insights

BRANDS/DIVISIONS/AFFILIATES:

Unified Data AI
App Annie Limited

CONTACTS: Note: Officers with more than one job title may be intentionally listed here more than once.

Ted Krantz, CEO
Alfred Chak, CFO

GROWTH PLANS/SPECIAL FEATURES:

Data.ai (formerly App Annie Limited) offers an artificial intelligence (AI)-powered platform so businesses can leverage consumer and market data to generate insights and outcomes. Data.ai's mobile and digital strategy is presented through its Unified Data AI platform, which combines data estimates for insights, adjustment-making and on-point execution. Data is aggregated from over 1 million apps, consumer panels, networks and more, with the connections offering a view of market data and a company's own analytics to maximize return on investment (ROI). Data.ai's products support seven languages. Its solutions span industries including gaming, banking, FinTech, retail, ecommerce, advertising, media and entertainment and more. Headquartered in San Francisco, California, Data.ai has additional office locations in 15 countries.

Data.ai is a remote-first company and offers professional growth and training.

FINANCIAL DATA: Note: Data for latest year may not have been available at press time.

In U.S. $	2022	2021	2020	2019	2018	2017
Revenue						
R&D Expense						
Operating Income						
Operating Margin %						
SGA Expense						
Net Income						
Operating Cash Flow						
Capital Expenditure						
EBITDA						
Return on Assets %						
Return on Equity %						
Debt to Equity						

CONTACT INFORMATION:

Phone: 415-638-6840   Fax:
Toll-Free:
Address: 44 Montgomery St., Fl. 3, San Francisco, CA 94104 United States

STOCK TICKER/OTHER:

Stock Ticker: Private   Exchange:
Employees: 450   Fiscal Year Ends:
Parent Company:

SALARIES/BONUSES:

Top Exec. Salary: $ Bonus: $
Second Exec. Salary: $ Bonus: $

OTHER THOUGHTS:

Estimated Female Officers or Directors:
Hot Spot for Advancement for Women/Minorities:

Datadog Inc

NAIC Code: 511210I

www.datadoghq.com

TYPES OF BUSINESS:

Computer Software, Operating Systems, Languages & Development Tools
Software

BRANDS/DIVISIONS/AFFILIATES:

Madumbo
Undefined Labs

GROWTH PLANS/SPECIAL FEATURES:

Datadog is a cloud-native company that focuses on analyzing
machine data. The firm's product portfolio, delivered via
software as a service, allows a client to monitor and analyze its
entire IT infrastructure. Datadog's platform can ingest and
analyze large amounts of machine-generated data in real time,
allowing clients to utilize it for a variety of applications
throughout their businesses.

The company offers its employees medical insurance, open
paid time off, commuter benefits, a 401(k), catered lunches and
other perks.

CONTACTS: *Note: Officers with more than one job title may be intentionally listed here more than once.*

Olivier Pomel, CEO
David Obstler, CFO
Alexis Le-Quoc, Chief Technology Officer
Laszlo Kopits, General Counsel
Armelle Madre, Other Executive Officer
Amit Agarwal, Other Executive Officer
Dan Fougere, Other Executive Officer

FINANCIAL DATA: *Note: Data for latest year may not have been available at press time.*

In U.S. $	2022	2021	2020	2019	2018	2017
Revenue	1,675,100,000	1,028,784,000	603,466,000	362,780,000	198,077,000	100,761,000
R&D Expense	752,351,000	419,769,000	210,626,000	111,425,000	55,176,000	24,734,000
Operating Income	-58,695,000	-19,156,000	-13,773,000	-20,140,000	-11,033,000	-2,956,000
Operating Margin %	- .04%	- .02%	- .02%	- .06%	- .06%	
SGA Expense	634,701,000	393,926,000	276,416,000	182,546,000	107,405,000	55,569,000
Net Income	-50,160,000	-20,745,000	-24,547,000	-16,710,000	-10,762,000	-2,570,000
Operating Cash Flow	418,407,000	286,545,000	109,091,000	24,234,000	10,829,000	13,832,000
Capital Expenditure	64,889,000	36,025,000	25,883,000	23,443,000	15,838,000	7,803,000
EBITDA	13,094,000	25,568,000	23,662,000	-3,574,000	-4,214,000	-252,000
Return on Assets %	- .02%	- .01%	- .02%	- .03%	- .07%	
Return on Equity %	- .04%	- .02%	- .03%	- .05%		
Debt to Equity	.58%	.76%	0.655	0.062		

CONTACT INFORMATION:

Phone: Fax:
Toll-Free: 866-329-4466
Address: 620 8th Ave., Fl. 45, New York, NY 10018 United States

STOCK TICKER/OTHER:

Stock Ticker: DDOG   Exchange: NAS
Employees: 4,800   Fiscal Year Ends: 12/31
Parent Company:

SALARIES/BONUSES:

Top Exec. Salary: $395,833   Bonus: $
Second Exec. Salary: Bonus: $
$395,833

OTHER THOUGHTS:

Estimated Female Officers or Directors:
Hot Spot for Advancement for Women/Minorities:

Deem Inc

www.deem.com

NAIC Code: 454110

TYPES OF BUSINESS:

Online Business Services and Travel Marketplace
Corporate Travel Management Software
Technology
Cloud Based Travel Solutions
Mobile Travel Solutions
Travel Booking Solutions
Ground Transportation Management

BRANDS/DIVISIONS/AFFILIATES:

Enterprise Holdings
Deem
Deem Go

GROWTH PLANS/SPECIAL FEATURES:

Deem, Inc., wholly owned by Enterprise Holdings, is a technology company that offers corporate travel management software. The firm's Deem is a mobile cloud-based travel solution that allows for over 300 employees to shop for, book, customize and manage their travel. Deem Go is a self-onboarding travel management platform for companies with one to 300 employees. As of February 2024, Deem has 8.6 million annual searches and has booked 1.8 million yearly trips. Deem is headquartered in California, with global offices in India and Ireland.

Deem offers its employees medical insurance, career development, flexible time off and company perks.

CONTACTS: Note: Officers with more than one job title may be intentionally listed here more than once.

Kyle Moore, General Manager
Jazeb Malik, Manager Finance
My Phung, Director Product Marketing
Van Williams, VP-Technology
Gabriel Sandoval, Chief Legal Officer
Andrew McGraw, Sr. VP-Bus. Travel
Wade Jones, Gen. Mgr.-Deem Offers

FINANCIAL DATA: Note: Data for latest year may not have been available at press time.

In U.S. $	2022	2021	2020	2019	2018	2017
Revenue						
R&D Expense						
Operating Income						
Operating Margin %						
SGA Expense						
Net Income						
Operating Cash Flow						
Capital Expenditure						
EBITDA						
Return on Assets %						
Return on Equity %						
Debt to Equity						

CONTACT INFORMATION:

Phone: 415-590-8300   Fax: 415-590-8301
Toll-Free:
Address: 1330 Broadway, Fl. 7, Oakland, CA 94612 United States

STOCK TICKER/OTHER:

Stock Ticker: Private   Exchange:
Employees: 250   Fiscal Year Ends:
Parent Company: Enterprise Holdings

SALARIES/BONUSES:

Top Exec. Salary: $ Bonus: $
Second Exec. Salary: $ Bonus: $

OTHER THOUGHTS:

Estimated Female Officers or Directors: 2
Hot Spot for Advancement for Women/Minorities: Y

Sales, profits and employees may be estimates. Financial information, benefits and other data can change quickly and may vary from those stated here.

Deliveroo plc

NAIC Code: 492210

TYPES OF BUSINESS:

On Demand Food Delivery
Food Delivery Service
Online Ordering
Grocery Delivery
Bike Rider Delivery Service
Retail Kiosk Grocery Store
Bespoke Kitchens

BRANDS/DIVISIONS/AFFILIATES:

Deliveroo
Editions
Deliveroo HOP

CONTACTS: Note: Officers with more than one job title may be intentionally listed here more than once.

Will Shu, CEO

GROWTH PLANS/SPECIAL FEATURES:

Deliveroo plc offers an on-demand food delivery service called Deliveroo, operating in 10 markets worldwide. The delivery platform connects local consumers, restaurants and grocers, as well as bike riders who deliver the food ordered. More than 160,000 restaurants and grocers are partners of Deliveroo. The firm's Editions kitchen concept enables partners to prepare food for customers at delivery-only kitchens created by Deliveroo. Deliveroo's delivery-only kitchens concept called Editions is an innovation we pioneered that helps restaurants expand to new areas at lower cost and with lower risk. A percentage fee covers upkeep costs, marketing support and a growth manager for building the preparer's own brand. Deliveroo has built technology to simultaneously complete hundreds of thousands of orders across the globe. Delivery riders have full flexibility in when and where they work, as well as what orders to accept. Free accident insurance is provided to riders, and additional benefits are offered depending on location. Deliveroo HOP, a new brick-and-mortar grocery store concept enables customers to shop in-store by ordering through digital kiosks, or to order online and have the groceries delivered via riders.

FINANCIAL DATA: Note: Data for latest year may not have been available at press time.

In U.S. $	2022	2021	2020	2019	2018	2017
Revenue	2,381,133,000	2,340,411,000	1,616,772,976	1,012,292,880	604,269,000	373,899,000
R&D Expense						
Operating Income						
Operating Margin %						
SGA Expense						
Net Income	-354,632,000	-369,631,000	-302,907,332	-417,219,960	-294,428,000	-247,601,000
Operating Cash Flow						
Capital Expenditure						
EBITDA						
Return on Assets %						
Return on Equity %						
Debt to Equity						

CONTACT INFORMATION:

Phone: 44 20 3699 9977   Fax:
Toll-Free:
Address: 1 Cousin Ln., The River Bldg., Level 1, London, EC4R 3TE United Kingdom

STOCK TICKER/OTHER:

Stock Ticker: ROO
Employees: 4,046
Parent Company:

Exchange: London
Fiscal Year Ends: 12/31

SALARIES/BONUSES:

Top Exec. Salary: $ Bonus: $
Second Exec. Salary: $ Bonus: $

OTHER THOUGHTS:

Estimated Female Officers or Directors:
Hot Spot for Advancement for Women/Minorities:

Delivery Hero SE

www.deliveryhero.com

NAIC Code: 492210

TYPES OF BUSINESS:

Online Restaurant Meals Delivery Services
Online Food Order & Delivery
Ecommerce
Household Goods

GROWTH PLANS/SPECIAL FEATURES:

Delivery Hero is an online food delivery provider and active delivery service headquartered in Germany. It operates in over 70 countries across five continents. Commission rate per order, the company's largest source of revenue, varies across the countries in its four geographic segments--the Americas, Asia, Europe, and the Middle East and North Africa--as well as the type of restaurant and the provided service.

BRANDS/DIVISIONS/AFFILIATES:

DX Ventures
Instashop
Glovo
Woowa Brothers Corp

CONTACTS: *Note: Officers with more than one job title may be intentionally listed here more than once.*

Niklas Ostberg, CEO
Emmanuel Thomassin, CFO

FINANCIAL DATA: *Note: Data for latest year may not have been available at press time.*

In U.S. $	2022	2021	2020	2019	2018	2017
Revenue	9,258,743,000	6,320,812,000	2,668,178,000	1,335,816,000	717,940,400	489,745,200
R&D Expense						
Operating Income	-913,644,200	-1,180,160,000	-691,925,700	-523,100,200	-143,134,700	-185,233,200
Operating Margin %		-.19%	-.26%	-.39%	-.20%	-.38%
SGA Expense	1,351,036,000	1,143,674,000	609,132,200	491,472,400	284,866,100	257,016,400
Net Income	-3,227,547,000	-1,213,623,000	-1,521,049,000	249,784,100	-41,234,880	-372,517,200
Operating Cash Flow	-743,523,300	-973,013,800	-572,107,100	-393,782,400	-177,677,000	-227,331,600
Capital Expenditure	272,884,300	346,610,500	224,956,800	102,655,400	53,216,750	24,935,230
EBITDA	-2,302,785,000	-544,365,200	-1,260,471,000	-590,241,800	-213,946,400	-268,350,600
Return on Assets %		-.12%	-.33%	.10%	-.02%	-.19%
Return on Equity %		-.33%	-.93%	.13%	-.02%	-.26%
Debt to Equity		.81%	2.658	0.048	.00%	

CONTACT INFORMATION:

Phone: 49-30-54-4459100   Fax:
Toll-Free:
Address: Oranienburger Strasse 70, Berlin, 10117 Germany

STOCK TICKER/OTHER:

Stock Ticker: DELHY
Employees: 51,118
Parent Company:

Exchange: PINX
Fiscal Year Ends: 12/31

SALARIES/BONUSES:

Top Exec. Salary: $ Bonus: $
Second Exec. Salary: $ Bonus: $

OTHER THOUGHTS:

Estimated Female Officers or Directors:
Hot Spot for Advancement for Women/Minorities:

Dell Technologies Inc

www.delltechnologies.com/en-us/index.htm

NAIC Code: 334111

TYPES OF BUSINESS:

Computer Manufacturing
Information Technology
IT Device Development
IT Device Production
Hardware
Software
Storage Solutions
Networking Products

BRANDS/DIVISIONS/AFFILIATES:

Client Solutions Group
Infrastructure Solutions Group
Dell EMC
Virtustream

GROWTH PLANS/SPECIAL FEATURES:

Dell Technologies is a broad information technology vendor, primarily supplying hardware to enterprises. It is focused on premium personal computers and enterprise on-premises data center hardware. It holds top-three shares in its core markets of personal computers, peripheral displays, mainstream servers, and external storage. Dell is vertically-integrated but has a robust ecosystem of component and assembly partners, and also relies heavily on channel partners to fulfill its sales.

CONTACTS: *Note: Officers with more than one job title may be intentionally listed here more than once.*

Michael Dell, CEO
Thomas Sweet, CFO
Brunilda Rios, Chief Accounting Officer
Allison Dew, Chief Marketing Officer
Jeffrey Clarke, COO
Richard Rothberg, General Counsel
Jennifer Saavedra, Other Executive Officer
Howard Elias, Other Executive Officer
William Scannell, President, Divisional

FINANCIAL DATA: *Note: Data for latest year may not have been available at press time.*

In U.S. $	2022	2021	2020	2019	2018	2017
Revenue	101,197,000,000	86,670,000,000	84,815,000,000	90,621,000,000	79,040,000,000	
R&D Expense	2,577,000,000	2,455,000,000	2,454,000,000	4,604,000,000	4,384,000,000	
Operating Income	4,659,000,000	3,685,000,000	2,366,000,000	-191,000,000	-2,416,000,000	
Operating Margin %	.05%	.04%	.03%	.00%	-.03%	
SGA Expense	14,655,000,000	14,000,000,000	15,819,000,000	20,640,000,000	18,569,000,000	
Net Income	5,563,000,000	3,250,000,000	4,616,000,000	-2,310,000,000	-2,849,000,000	
Operating Cash Flow	10,307,000,000	11,407,000,000	9,291,000,000	6,991,000,000	6,843,000,000	
Capital Expenditure	2,796,000,000	2,082,000,000	2,576,000,000	1,497,000,000	1,581,000,000	
EBITDA	12,016,000,000	9,788,000,000	8,426,000,000	7,873,000,000	6,271,000,000	
Return on Assets %	.05%	.03%	.04%	-.02%	-.02%	
Return on Equity %	8.79%	3.24%		-.61%	-.22%	
Debt to Equity		11.14%			3.64%	

CONTACT INFORMATION:

Phone: 512 338-4400   Fax: 512 283-6161
Toll-Free: 800-289-3355
Address: One Dell Way, Round Rock, TX 78682 United States

STOCK TICKER/OTHER:

Stock Ticker: DELL   Exchange: NYS
Employees: 133,000   Fiscal Year Ends: 01/31
Parent Company:

SALARIES/BONUSES:

Top Exec. Salary: $1,013,195   Bonus: $
Second Exec. Salary: $986,538   Bonus: $

OTHER THOUGHTS:

Estimated Female Officers or Directors: 1
Hot Spot for Advancement for Women/Minorities: Y

DeNA Co Ltd

www.dena.jp

NAIC Code: 511210G

TYPES OF BUSINESS:

Computer Software, Electronic Games, Apps & Entertainment
Social Networking
Online Payment Service
Online Travel Service
Online Auctions
Apps

BRANDS/DIVISIONS/AFFILIATES:

AI Business
Mobage
Anyca
MYCODE
SHOWROOM
Everystar
Yokohama DeNA Baystars
Strategic Investment Office

CONTACTS: Note: Officers with more than one job title may be intentionally listed here more than once.

Isao Moriyasu, CEO
Tomoko Namba, Chmn.

GROWTH PLANS/SPECIAL FEATURES:

DeNA Co Ltd is primarily a social media service provider in Japan. It generates the major portion of its revenue by providing social media and Internet marketing related services through its Social Media segment. The E-commerce segment offers E-Commerce related services, including the operation of auction shopping and cellular phone websites under the names DeNA shopping and Mobaoku respectively. The Others segment is engaged in travel agency and insurance agency services, and professional baseball related business. The Company has its primary market in North America.

FINANCIAL DATA: Note: Data for latest year may not have been available at press time.

In U.S. $	2022	2021	2020	2019	2018	2017
Revenue	893,034,800	934,681,300	828,337,100	846,959,600	951,188,400	
R&D Expense						
Operating Income	78,215,940	153,504,400	-311,690,100	92,198,190	187,685,500	
Operating Margin %	.09%	.16%	-.38%	.11%	.20%	
SGA Expense	390,465,600	396,265,900	414,656,400	388,493,500	434,773,400	
Net Income	208,348,400	174,897,500	-335,505,600	86,725,400	156,820,900	
Operating Cash Flow	125,389,800	204,492,900	88,342,670	156,807,200	257,071,300	
Capital Expenditure	43,898,380	63,278,350	97,316,140	136,990,500	125,539,900	
EBITDA	248,903,000	259,985,100	-191,923,200	202,125,000	290,829,300	
Return on Assets %	.09%	.09%	-.18%	.04%	.07%	
Return on Equity %	.13%	.13%	-.23%	.05%	.09%	
Debt to Equity	.03%	.11%	0.039			

CONTACT INFORMATION:

Phone: 81 353041701   Fax:
Toll-Free:
Address: 2-21-1 Shibuya, Shibuya-ku, Tokyo, 150-8510 Japan

STOCK TICKER/OTHER:

Stock Ticker: DNACF   Exchange: PINX
Employees: 3,334   Fiscal Year Ends: 03/31
Parent Company:

SALARIES/BONUSES:

Top Exec. Salary: $ Bonus: $
Second Exec. Salary: $ Bonus: $

OTHER THOUGHTS:

Estimated Female Officers or Directors: 1
Hot Spot for Advancement for Women/Minorities:

DiDi Global Inc

NAIC Code: 561599

www.didiglobal.com

TYPES OF BUSINESS:

Ride Sharing and Car Sharing Platform
Mobility Technology
Mobile Apps
Ride Hailing
Taxi Hailing
Shared Mobility
Automotive Solutions
Artificial Intelligence

BRANDS/DIVISIONS/AFFILIATES:

DiDi
DiDi Finance
DiDi Consumer Loans
DiDi Driver Insurance

GROWTH PLANS/SPECIAL FEATURES:

DiDi Global Inc is a mobility technology platform. It is building four key components of its platform that work together to improve the consumer experience: shared mobility, auto solutions, electric mobility, and autonomous driving. It is a go-to brand in China for shared mobility, providing consumers with a range of safe, affordable, and convenient mobility services, including ride-hailing, taxi-hailing, chauffeur, hitch, and other forms of shared mobility. The company operates in three segments: China Mobility, which mainly includes ride-hailing services to riders, and also acts as an agent by connecting end-users to service providers who provide taxi hailing, chauffeur, hitch, and other services; International; and Other Initiatives.

CONTACTS: Note: Officers with more than one job title may be intentionally listed here more than once.

Will Wei Cheng, CEO
Jean Qing Liu, Pres.

FINANCIAL DATA: Note: Data for latest year may not have been available at press time.

In U.S. $	2022	2021	2020	2019	2018	2017
Revenue	19,361,060,000	23,903,980,000	19,490,940,000	21,285,510,000	18,604,220,000	
R&D Expense	1,311,283,000	1,294,661,000	868,659,100	735,353,900	601,968,100	
Operating Income	-2,451,142,000	-6,277,922,000	-1,896,058,000	-1,101,965,000	-1,711,042,000	
Operating Margin %		-.26%	-.10%	-.05%		
SGA Expense	3,680,081,000	6,281,238,000	2,569,819,000	1,885,259,000	1,628,970,000	
Net Income	-3,270,578,000	-6,785,525,000	-1,445,908,000	-1,337,815,000	-2,059,679,000	
Operating Cash Flow	-1,313,867,000	-1,844,616,000	156,440,800	198,662,000	-1,269,056,000	
Capital Expenditure	351,185,800	910,379,800	797,466,500	309,752,300	754,093,700	
EBITDA	-2,535,535,000	-5,891,910,000	-757,065,400	-824,962,400	-1,741,466,000	
Return on Assets %		-.33%	-.07%	-.07%		
Return on Equity %		-2.79%				
Debt to Equity		.02%				

CONTACT INFORMATION:

Phone: 86 40 0766 6998   Fax:
Toll-Free:
Address: No. 1 Blk B, No. 8 Dongbeiwang W. Rd., Haidian Dist., Beijing, Beijing 100000 China

STOCK TICKER/OTHER:

Stock Ticker: DIDIY   Exchange: PINX
Employees: 20,870   Fiscal Year Ends: 12/31
Parent Company:

SALARIES/BONUSES:

Top Exec. Salary: $ Bonus: $
Second Exec. Salary: $ Bonus: $

OTHER THOUGHTS:

Estimated Female Officers or Directors:
Hot Spot for Advancement for Women/Minorities:

Digg Inc

www.digg.com

NAIC Code: 519130

TYPES OF BUSINESS:

Online Media Aggregator
Digital News and Story Sharing
Advertising Services
Video Sharing
Opinion Sharing
Social Platform
Online and Mobile App
Content Ratings and Comments

BRANDS/DIVISIONS/AFFILIATES:

BuySellAds.com Inc
Digg Editions

GROWTH PLANS/SPECIAL FEATURES:

Digg, Inc. operates a community platform that allows users to share stories and videos found elsewhere on digital channels (websites and mobile apps). Digg content is generated by individuals submitting links and small descriptor blurbs for pieces of media they find interesting. Other users can vote up or down on the submissions to rate their popularity. Featured content spans across video, data viz, movies and tv, real estate, internet culture, news, one main character, memes, relationships, gaming and more. Each submission includes an area for community comments and viewpoints. Items can be re-shared through certain social media networks, such as Facebook and Twitter. Digg's daily newsletter can be delivered to user inboxes via Digg Editions, featuring recent stories and uploads. Digg is owned by BuySellAds.com, Inc.

CONTACTS: Note: Officers with more than one job title may be intentionally listed here more than once.

Todd Garland, CEO-BuySellAds
Kevin Barnett, Dir.-Front End Dev.
John Borthwick, CEO-betaworks

FINANCIAL DATA: Note: Data for latest year may not have been available at press time.

In U.S. $	2022	2021	2020	2019	2018	2017
Revenue						
R&D Expense						
Operating Income						
Operating Margin %						
SGA Expense						
Net Income						
Operating Cash Flow						
Capital Expenditure						
EBITDA						
Return on Assets %						
Return on Equity %						
Debt to Equity						

CONTACT INFORMATION:

Phone: 415-355-3000   Fax:
Toll-Free:
Address: 109 S. 5th St., Brooklyn, NY 11249 United States

STOCK TICKER/OTHER:

Stock Ticker: Subsidiary   Exchange:
Employees: 25   Fiscal Year Ends:
Parent Company: BuySellAds.com Inc

SALARIES/BONUSES:

Top Exec. Salary: $ Bonus: $
Second Exec. Salary: $ Bonus: $

OTHER THOUGHTS:

Estimated Female Officers or Directors: 2
Hot Spot for Advancement for Women/Minorities:

Sales, profits and employees may be estimates. Financial information, benefits and other data can change quickly and may vary from those stated here.

Digital River Inc

www.digitalriver.com

NAIC Code: 511210M

TYPES OF BUSINESS:

E-Commerce Software
Global Commerce Solutions
Commerce Payment Solutions
Commerce Tax Solutions
Online Fraud Solutions
Commerce Compliance Solutions
Commerce Logistics Solutions
Brand Marketing Solutions

BRANDS/DIVISIONS/AFFILIATES:

Siris Capital Group LLC

GROWTH PLANS/SPECIAL FEATURES:

Digital River, Inc. offers global commerce solutions for established and growing brands. Solutions offered by the firm span areas such as payments, tax, online fraud, compliance and logistics. Digital River's solutions and products help sell products by simplifying cross-border duties, taxes and logistics; by localizing ecommerce checkout and minimizing involuntary return; by delivering consumer-like experiences and business-to-business payment options; and by growing brand recognition and international sales through an online direct-to-consumer channel. Commerce partners that enable commerce technology integrations include Adobe Exchange Partners, BigCommerce, commercetools, Salesforce, VTEX and WooCommerce. Digital River is based in the U.S. and Brazil, and has teams across the Americas, Europe/Middle East/Africa and Asia-Pacific. The firm is owned by private equity firm Siris Capital Group, LLC.

CONTACTS: Note: Officers with more than one job title may be intentionally listed here more than once.

Vic Pacor, CEO
Ryan Douglas, COO
Keith Bush, CFO
Ted Rogers, CMO
Kumar Dasani, CIO
Kevin Crudden, General Counsel

FINANCIAL DATA: Note: Data for latest year may not have been available at press time.

In U.S. $	2022	2021	2020	2019	2018	2017
Revenue	255,783,528	245,945,700	236,486,250	242,550,000	231,000,000	325,993,125
R&D Expense						
Operating Income						
Operating Margin %						
SGA Expense						
Net Income						
Operating Cash Flow						
Capital Expenditure						
EBITDA						
Return on Assets %						
Return on Equity %						
Debt to Equity						

CONTACT INFORMATION:

Phone: 952 253-1234   Fax: 952 646-5604
Toll-Free:
Address: 10380 Bren Rd. W., Minnetonka, MN 55343 United States

STOCK TICKER/OTHER:

Stock Ticker: Private   Exchange:
Employees: 1,700   Fiscal Year Ends: 12/31
Parent Company: Siris Capital Group LLC

SALARIES/BONUSES:

Top Exec. Salary: $ Bonus: $
Second Exec. Salary: $ Bonus: $

OTHER THOUGHTS:

Estimated Female Officers or Directors: 3
Hot Spot for Advancement for Women/Minorities: Y

DigitalOcean Inc

NAIC Code: 517311

www.digitalocean.com

TYPES OF BUSINESS:

Web Hosting Services
Cloud Hosting
Developer Tools

GROWTH PLANS/SPECIAL FEATURES:

DigitalOcean Holdings Inc is a cloud computing platform offering on-demand infrastructure and platform tools for developers, start-ups and small and medium-sized businesses. The customers use the platform for a wide range of cases, such as web and mobile applications, website hosting, e-commerce, media and gaming, personal web projects, and managed services, among many others. The group has a business presence in North America, Europe, Asia and Other countries.

DigitalOcean offers its employees comprehensive health benefits, commuter benefits, 401(k) and education support.

BRANDS/DIVISIONS/AFFILIATES:

Droplet

CONTACTS: Note: Officers with more than one job title may be intentionally listed here more than once.

Yancey Spruill, CEO
William Sorenson, CFO
Carly Brantz, Chief Marketing Officer
Barry Cooks, Chief Technology Officer
Jeffrey Guy, COO
Alan Shapiro, General Counsel
Matthew Norman, Other Executive Officer

FINANCIAL DATA: Note: Data for latest year may not have been available at press time.

In U.S. $	2022	2021	2020	2019	2018	2017
Revenue	576,322,000	428,561,000	318,380,000	254,823,000	203,136,000	
R&D Expense	143,885,000	115,684,000	74,970,000	59,973,000	44,934,000	
Operating Income	-25,697,000	-11,186,000	-15,791,000	-29,905,000	-27,294,000	
Operating Margin %	-.05%	-.03%	-.05%	-.12%		
SGA Expense	246,207,000	153,468,000	113,669,000	102,496,000	88,454,000	
Net Income	-27,804,000	-19,503,000	-43,568,000	-40,390,000	-35,999,000	
Operating Cash Flow	195,152,000	133,109,000	58,458,000	39,902,000	37,954,000	
Capital Expenditure	120,217,000	109,099,000	115,806,000	84,499,000	61,254,000	
EBITDA	86,743,000	73,915,000	46,527,000	32,840,000	23,949,000	
Return on Assets %	-.01%	-.02%	-.12%	-.13%		
Return on Equity %	-.08%	-.08%				
Debt to Equity	30.90%	2.53%				

CONTACT INFORMATION:

Phone: 347 903-7918   Fax:
Toll-Free:
Address: 101 Ave. of Americas, 10/Fl, New York, NY 10013 United States

STOCK TICKER/OTHER:

Stock Ticker: DOCN
Employees: 1,024
Parent Company:

Exchange: NYS
Fiscal Year Ends: 12/31

SALARIES/BONUSES:

Top Exec. Salary: $514,000   Bonus: $
Second Exec. Salary: $441,667   Bonus: $

OTHER THOUGHTS:

Estimated Female Officers or Directors:
Hot Spot for Advancement for Women/Minorities:

Digitas
NAIC Code: 541800

TYPES OF BUSINESS:
Database Marketing Services
Strategic Consulting Services
Customer Relationship Management
Online Advertising & Marketing Services
Ecommerce Platforms, Web Design & Development

BRANDS/DIVISIONS/AFFILIATES:
Publicis Groupe SA

CONTACTS: *Note: Officers with more than one job title may be intentionally listed here more than once.*
Jill Kelly, Exec. VP-Corp. Comm.
Tony Weisman, CEO-North America
Lincoln Bjorkman, Chief Creative Officer-North America
Vincent Digonnet, Pres., Asia Pacific
Sav Evangelous, Exec. Creative Dir.-Int'l
Arthur Sadou, Chmn.-Publicis Groupe SA
Stephan Beringer, Pres.

GROWTH PLANS/SPECIAL FEATURES:
Digitas is a leading marketing and technology agency. The firm specializes in creating marketing engines that drive customer acquisition, cross-selling, loyalty and customer care operations across digital and direct media. Its marketing channels include direct mail, websites, online advertising, email, print advertising, mobile applications, television commercials, events and promotions. Digitas offers a cloud-based marketing suite of processes and tools designed to help clients engage audiences on a global scale, across multiple platforms in real time. The company designs and builds web portals from scratch, provides affiliate marketing, designs brand content, engages and measures user experience, creates mobile applications, embeds its social media expertise into its technology and products, manages/hosts websites, provides analytics services, provides search engine optimization, sets up pay-per-click marketing strategies, provides user research solutions and more. Headquartered in Massachusetts, the firm has additional U.S. offices as well as many international offices located across Latin America, Europe, Asia Pacific, the Middle East and Africa. Digitas operates as a subsidiary of Publicis Groupe SA.

Digitas offers employees health, dental and vision insurance; vacation days; flex days; paid holidays; and a 401(k) plan.

FINANCIAL DATA: *Note: Data for latest year may not have been available at press time.*

In U.S. $	2022	2021	2020	2019	2018	2017
Revenue	735,000,000	717,471,300	689,876,250	673,050,000	641,000,000	622,000,000
R&D Expense						
Operating Income						
Operating Margin %						
SGA Expense						
Net Income						
Operating Cash Flow						
Capital Expenditure						
EBITDA						
Return on Assets %						
Return on Equity %						
Debt to Equity						

CONTACT INFORMATION:
Phone: 617-867-1000   Fax:
Toll-Free:
Address: 40 Water St., Boston, MA 02109 United States

STOCK TICKER/OTHER:
Stock Ticker: Subsidiary   Exchange:
Employees: 3,500   Fiscal Year Ends: 12/31
Parent Company: Publicis Groupe SA

SALARIES/BONUSES:
Top Exec. Salary: $ Bonus: $
Second Exec. Salary: $ Bonus: $

OTHER THOUGHTS:
Estimated Female Officers or Directors: 6
Hot Spot for Advancement for Women/Minorities: Y

Dingdong (Cayman) Ltd

www.100.me

NAIC Code: 454110

TYPES OF BUSINESS:

Online Sales, B2C Ecommerce, Sharing Economy Platforms

GROWTH PLANS/SPECIAL FEATURES:

Dingdong (Cayman) Ltd is the fastest growing on-demand e-commerce company in China. It directly provides users and households with fresh produce, meat and seafood, and other daily necessities through a convenient shopping experience supported by an extensive self-operated frontline fulfillment grid. It recognizes revenues from product sales of fresh groceries and other daily necessities through Dingdong Fresh APP and mini-programs and membership services.

BRANDS/DIVISIONS/AFFILIATES:

Dingdong Fresh APP

CONTACTS: *Note: Officers with more than one job title may be intentionally listed here more than once.*

Changlin Liang, CEO

FINANCIAL DATA: *Note: Data for latest year may not have been available at press time.*

In U.S. $	2022	2021	2020	2019	2018	2017
Revenue	3,330,798,000	2,766,970,000	1,558,848,000	533,576,100		
R&D Expense	137,959,100	124,452,600	44,238,360	12,533,860		
Operating Income	-104,895,400	-872,789,900	-434,478,800	-239,460,800		
Operating Margin %		-.32%	-.28%			
SGA Expense	148,898,800	302,180,400	141,193,600	318,366,200		
Net Income	-111,989,000	-884,096,100	-436,875,300	-257,619,500		
Operating Cash Flow	12,014,190	-779,237,600	-282,690,500	-132,602,900		
Capital Expenditure	17,448,950	62,103,160	34,169,340	17,163,600		
EBITDA	-63,562,480	-841,795,500	-415,682,500	-244,849,200		
Return on Assets %		-.94%	-.99%			
Return on Equity %						
Debt to Equity		1.71%				

CONTACT INFORMATION:

Phone: 86 21-6858-5011   Fax:
Toll-Free:
Address: 500 Shengxia Road, Shanghai, Shanghai 200125 China

STOCK TICKER/OTHER:

Stock Ticker: DDL   Exchange: NYS
Employees: 3,363   Fiscal Year Ends: 12/31
Parent Company:

SALARIES/BONUSES:

Top Exec. Salary: $ Bonus: $
Second Exec. Salary: $ Bonus: $

OTHER THOUGHTS:

Estimated Female Officers or Directors:
Hot Spot for Advancement for Women/Minorities:

DirecTV LLC (DIRECTV)

www.directv.com

NAIC Code: 517311

TYPES OF BUSINESS:

Satellite Broadcasting
Satellite TV
Streaming Services
Bundled Services
Media Entertainment
Multi-language Programming

BRANDS/DIVISIONS/AFFILIATES:

AT&T Inc
TPG Capital

CONTACTS: *Note: Officers with more than one job title may be intentionally listed here more than once.*

Bill Morrow, CEO
Ray Carpenter, CFO
Vince Torres, CMO
Scott S. Smith, Chief Human Resources Officer
Debbie Taylor, CIO

GROWTH PLANS/SPECIAL FEATURES:

DirecTV, LLC is a leading provider of DIRECTV branded satellite TV and streaming TV services via televisions, online or mobile app. DirecTV offers four satellite TV packages, including Entertainment (with 75+ channels), Choice (105+ channels), Ultimate (140+ channels) and Premier (340+ channels), which differ in price depending on what the package offers. On the streaming side, the firm offers four packages as well: Entertainment (75+ channels), Choice (105+ channels), Ultimate (150+ channels) and Premier (150+ channels). Packages can be bundled with AT&T offerings, which are subject to location availability. Channels include ESPN, CBS, NBC, ABC, FOX, TNT, CNN, Comedy Central, FX, National Geographic, tbs, Discovery, Disney Channel, amc, USA and TLC. The firm also offers international packages for multi-language programming. Premium sports entertainment is provided. AT&T owns a 70% stake in the company, and TPG Capital owns the remaining 30%.

DirecTV employees receive medical, dental and vision coverage; flexible spending accounts; wellness plans; employee assistance programs; and a 401(k) savings plan with a matching contribution opportunity.

FINANCIAL DATA: *Note: Data for latest year may not have been available at press time.*

In U.S. $	2022	2021	2020	2019	2018	2017
Revenue	31,400,000,000	29,039,677,664	27,922,766,985	31,025,296,650	30,416,957,500	32,017,850,000
R&D Expense						
Operating Income						
Operating Margin %						
SGA Expense						
Net Income						
Operating Cash Flow						
Capital Expenditure						
EBITDA						
Return on Assets %						
Return on Equity %						
Debt to Equity						

CONTACT INFORMATION:

Phone: 310 964-5000   Fax:
Toll-Free:
Address: 2260 E. Imperial Hwy., El Segundo, CA 90245 United States

STOCK TICKER/OTHER:

Stock Ticker: Subsidiary   Exchange:
Employees: 30,000   Fiscal Year Ends: 12/31
Parent Company: AT&T Inc

SALARIES/BONUSES:

Top Exec. Salary: $ Bonus: $
Second Exec. Salary: $ Bonus: $

OTHER THOUGHTS:

Estimated Female Officers or Directors: 3
Hot Spot for Advancement for Women/Minorities: Y

Sales, profits and employees may be estimates. Financial information, benefits and other data can change quickly and may vary from those stated here.

DocuSign Inc

www.docusign.com

NAIC Code: 511210Q

TYPES OF BUSINESS:

Online Signature Management Software
Cloud
Electronic Signature

GROWTH PLANS/SPECIAL FEATURES:

DocuSign offers the Agreement Cloud, a broad cloud-based software suite that enables users to automate the agreement process and provide legally binding e-signatures from nearly any device. The company was founded in 2003 and completed its IPO in May 2018.

BRANDS/DIVISIONS/AFFILIATES:

DocuSign Agreement Cloud
DocuSign eSignature
Seal Software Group Limited
Liveoak Technololgies Inc

CONTACTS: Note: Officers with more than one job title may be intentionally listed here more than once.

Daniel Springer, CEO
Cynthia Gaylor, CFO
Mary Agnes Wilderotter, Chairman of the Board
Scott Olrich, COO
Tram Phi, General Counsel
Loren Alhadeff, Other Executive Officer
Michael Sheridan, President, Divisional

FINANCIAL DATA: Note: Data for latest year may not have been available at press time.

In U.S. $	2022	2021	2020	2019	2018	2017
Revenue	2,107,213,000	1,453,047,000	973,971,000	700,969,000	518,504,000	
R&D Expense	393,362,000	271,522,000	185,552,000	185,968,000	92,428,000	
Operating Income	-61,884,000	-173,855,000	-193,509,000	-426,323,000	-51,653,000	
Operating Margin %	-.03%	-.12%	-.20%	-.61%	-.10%	
SGA Expense	1,309,284,000	991,322,000	738,694,000	748,903,000	359,456,000	
Net Income	-69,976,000	-243,267,000	-208,359,000	-426,458,000	-52,276,000	
Operating Cash Flow	506,467,000	296,954,000	115,696,000	76,086,000	54,979,000	
Capital Expenditure	61,396,000	82,395,000	72,046,000	30,413,000	18,929,000	
EBITDA	21,442,000	-127,603,000	-126,098,000	-380,315,000	-16,768,000	
Return on Assets %	-.03%	-.12%	-.12%	-.38%	-.10%	
Return on Equity %	-.23%	-.56%	-.36%	-3.09%		
Debt to Equity	3.07%	2.65%	1.149	0.714		

CONTACT INFORMATION:

Phone: 866-219-4318   Fax:
Toll-Free:
Address: 221 Main St., Ste. 1550, San Francisco, CA 94105 United States

STOCK TICKER/OTHER:

Stock Ticker: DOCU   Exchange: NAS
Employees: 7,336   Fiscal Year Ends: 01/31
Parent Company:

SALARIES/BONUSES:

Top Exec. Salary: $267,308   Bonus: $325,000
Second Exec. Salary: $228,669   Bonus: $336,415

OTHER THOUGHTS:

Estimated Female Officers or Directors:
Hot Spot for Advancement for Women/Minorities:

Sales, profits and employees may be estimates. Financial information, benefits and other data can change quickly and may vary from those stated here.

Domo Inc

NAIC Code: 511210J

www.domo.com

TYPES OF BUSINESS:

Computer Software, Data Base & File Management
Software
Business Intelligence
Internet of Things
Cloud
Applications

BRANDS/DIVISIONS/AFFILIATES:

GROWTH PLANS/SPECIAL FEATURES:

Domo Inc provides a cloud-based platform that digitally connects all the data, systems and people in an organization, giving them access to real-time data and insights and allowing them to manage their business from their smartphones. The company offers a platform to its customers as a subscription-based service. Users receive notifications on any device and immediately act on the invitation, after which the system can write back to the original system of record. The company derives revenue from subscriptions to its cloud-based platform and professional services.

CONTACTS: Note: Officers with more than one job title may be intentionally listed here more than once.

Joshua James, CEO
Bruce Felt, CFO
Catherine Wong, Executive VP, Divisional

FINANCIAL DATA: Note: Data for latest year may not have been available at press time.

In U.S. $	2022	2021	2020	2019	2018	2017
Revenue	257,961,000	210,180,000	173,395,000	142,464,000	108,524,000	
R&D Expense	81,027,000	66,474,000	69,224,000	75,740,000	78,261,000	
Operating Income	-88,470,000	-73,085,000	-115,267,000	-144,087,000	-175,781,000	
Operating Margin %	-.34%	-.35%	-.66%	-1.01%	-1.62%	
SGA Expense	198,258,000	160,043,000	163,508,000	161,257,000	161,125,000	
Net Income	-102,111,000	-84,634,000	-125,656,000	-154,309,000	-176,562,000	
Operating Cash Flow	379,000	-15,872,000	-80,219,000	-131,367,000	-148,657,000	
Capital Expenditure	6,517,000	5,811,000	6,531,000	7,976,000	7,596,000	
EBITDA	-83,107,000	-68,320,000	-108,350,000	-135,300,000	-167,650,000	
Return on Assets %	-.44%	-.39%	-.49%	-.69%	-1.20%	
Return on Equity %						
Debt to Equity				2.184		

CONTACT INFORMATION:

Phone: 801-899-1000   Fax:
Toll-Free: 800-899-1000
Address: 772 E. Utah Valley Dr., American Fork, UT 84003 United States

STOCK TICKER/OTHER:

Stock Ticker: DOMO
Employees: 967
Parent Company:

Exchange: NAS
Fiscal Year Ends: 01/31

SALARIES/BONUSES:

Top Exec. Salary: $515,385   Bonus: $
Second Exec. Salary: $449,255   Bonus: $

OTHER THOUGHTS:

Estimated Female Officers or Directors:
Hot Spot for Advancement for Women/Minorities:

Dotdash Meredith

www.dotdash.com

NAIC Code: 519130

TYPES OF BUSINESS:

Online Information
Digital Publisher
Print Publisher
Magazines
Advertising Studio
Content Development
Content Marketing Programs

BRANDS/DIVISIONS/AFFILIATES:

IAC/InterActiveCorp
Foundry 360
verywell
Investopedia
allrecipes
Better Home & Gardens
Travel + Leisure
Meredith Premium Publishing

CONTACTS: *Note: Officers with more than one job title may be intentionally listed here more than once.*

Neil Vogel, CEO
Alex Ellerson, COO
Tim Quinn, CFO
Tory Brangham, Chief Commerce Officer
Ellen Shultz, Chief Human Resources Officer
Nabil Ahmad, CTO
Tricia Han, Sr. VP-Product
Brad Simon, General Counsel
Chris Coluzzi, Sr. VP-Oper.
Igor Lebovic, Sr. VP-Growth
Alex Ellerson, Sr. VP-Content
Brian Colbert, Chief Revenue Officer
Jack Griffin, Chmn.

GROWTH PLANS/SPECIAL FEATURES:

Dotdash Meredith is a digital and print publisher based in the U.S. Nearly 200 million readers trust the company's information and content to help them make decisions, take action and find inspiration. Dotdash Meredith comprises over 40 brands across subject areas including health, finance, food and beverage, home, beauty and style, travel, technical, sustainability, entertainment and publishing. Dotdash Meredith's advertising studio develop content for Dotdash Meredith brands, all of which is data-driven to capture, retain and inspire audiences. The firm's Foundry 360 division creates content marketing programs for the brands' owned and operated channels. Dotdash Meredith brands include, but are not limited to, verywell, Investopedia, allrecipes, Better Homes & Gardens, Brides, Travel + Leisure, Lifewire, People, and Meredith Premium Publishing. Headquartered in New York, Dotdash Meredith has additional offices in Alabama and Iowa. The company is an operating business of IAC/InterActiveCorp.

FINANCIAL DATA: *Note: Data for latest year may not have been available at press time.*

In U.S. $	2022	2021	2020	2019	2018	2017
Revenue	1,934,699,000	456,273,000	213,753,000	167,594,000	130,991,000	90,890,000
R&D Expense						
Operating Income						
Operating Margin %						
SGA Expense						
Net Income	-188,091,000	7,176,000	50,241,000	29,021,000	18,778,000	
Operating Cash Flow						
Capital Expenditure						
EBITDA						
Return on Assets %						
Return on Equity %						
Debt to Equity						

CONTACT INFORMATION:

Phone: 212-204-4000   Fax:
Toll-Free:
Address: 225 Liberty St., Fl. 4, New York, NY 10281 United States

STOCK TICKER/OTHER:

Stock Ticker: Subsidiary   Exchange:
Employees: Fiscal Year Ends: 12/31
Parent Company: IAC/InterActiveCorp

SALARIES/BONUSES:

Top Exec. Salary: $ Bonus: $
Second Exec. Salary: $ Bonus: $

OTHER THOUGHTS:

Estimated Female Officers or Directors: 1
Hot Spot for Advancement for Women/Minorities: Y

Sales, profits and employees may be estimates. Financial information, benefits and other data can change quickly and may vary from those stated here.

Dow Jones & Company Inc

NAIC Code: 511110

TYPES OF BUSINESS:

Newspaper Publishing-Financial News
Business Publishing
Community Newspapers
Electronic & Online Publishing
Financial Indices
Financial Information Services
Ecommerce

BRANDS/DIVISIONS/AFFILIATES:

Dow Jones Curation Services
Dow Jones Risk & Compliance
Dow Jones Newswires
WSJ Pro
Wall Street Journal (The)
Barrons
MarketWatch
News Corporation

CONTACTS: *Note: Officers with more than one job title may be intentionally listed here more than once.*

Almar Latour, CEO
Edwin A. Finn, Jr., Pres.
Elizabeth O'Melia, CFO
Sherry Weiss, CMO
Dianne Desevo, Chief People Officer
Artem Fishman, CTO
Stephen Orban, Head-Tech.
Dean Del Vecchio, Chief Admin. Officer
Mark H. Jackson, General Counsel
Joseph Vincent, Head-Oper.
Ingrid Verschuren, Head-Data Strategy
Michael Rolnick, Head-Digital
Paula Keve, Chief Comm. Officer
Christina Komporlis, Head-Print Circulation
Daniel Hayter, Head-Institutional Sales
Georgene Huang, Head-Institutional Products
Daniel Hayter, Head-Institutional Sales, Americas
Kelly E. Leach, Managing Dir.-EMEA

GROWTH PLANS/SPECIAL FEATURES:

Dow Jones & Company, Inc., a subsidiary of News Corporation, is a global provider of business and financial news information. With millions of readers worldwide, the firm distributes information through newspapers, newswires, magazines, television, radio stations and the internet. Its products include: Dow Jones Curation Services, a curation offering providing relevant world news content grouped by subject matter according to personal business needs; Dow Jones Factiva, a global news database featuring nearly 33,000 sources; Dow Jones Risk & Compliance, a provider of third-party risk management and regulatory compliance solutions; and Dow Jones Newswires, delivering comprehensive global business insights, rolling market commentary and expert analysis. Other products include: WSJ Pro, a global, industry-specific membership offering reporting, insight and data; Dow Jones Private Equity & Venture Capital, a suite of news and data on companies backed by venture capital and private equity in every region, industry and stage of development; and The Wall Street Journal, which includes coverage of U.S. and world news, politics, arts, culture, lifestyle, sports, health and more. Barron's is a source of market ideas and insights to help self-directed investors grow their portfolios; MarketWatch provides financial news and market data; Financial News provides news, analysis and commentary on wholesale financial and European securities industries across the sectors of investment banking, asset management, private equity, trading and technology and Fintech; Buy Side, an ecommerce shopping platform for helping readers to make smart decisions about how to spend their time; Dow Jones Developer Platform, an open intelligence platform for industry data, news and analytics for enterprise customers; and Dow Jones Reprints provides transaction-based services for the licensing of Dow Jones' branded content.

FINANCIAL DATA: *Note: Data for latest year may not have been available at press time.*

In U.S. $	2022	2021	2020	2019	2018	2017
Revenue	1,845,000,000	1,702,000,000	1,590,000,000	1,549,000,000	1,511,000,000	1,479,000,000
R&D Expense						
Operating Income						
Operating Margin %						
SGA Expense						
Net Income						
Operating Cash Flow						
Capital Expenditure						
EBITDA						
Return on Assets %						
Return on Equity %						
Debt to Equity						

CONTACT INFORMATION:

Phone: 212-416-2000   Fax: 212-416-4348
Toll-Free: 800-223-2274
Address: 1211 Avenue of the Americas, New York, NY 10036 United States

STOCK TICKER/OTHER:

Stock Ticker: Subsidiary   Exchange:
Employees: 7,100   Fiscal Year Ends: 06/30
Parent Company: News Corporation

SALARIES/BONUSES:

Top Exec. Salary: $ Bonus: $
Second Exec. Salary: $ Bonus: $

OTHER THOUGHTS:

Estimated Female Officers or Directors: 10
Hot Spot for Advancement for Women/Minorities: Y

Dropbox Inc

www.dropbox.com

NAIC Code: 519130

TYPES OF BUSINESS:

Online Data Storage and Sharing
Online Storage and Sharing Database
Digital Platform
Smart Workspace

GROWTH PLANS/SPECIAL FEATURES:

Dropbox is a leading provider of cloud-storage and content collaboration tools with an emphasis on individuals and SMB. The company was founded in 2007 and was a pioneer in cloud storage and cross-platform file syncing. Utilizing inorganic and organic means, the firm has been working on diversifying its product mix and pivoting away from the cloud-storage space.

BRANDS/DIVISIONS/AFFILIATES:

CONTACTS: *Note: Officers with more than one job title may be intentionally listed here more than once.*

Andrew Houston, CEO
Timothy Regan, CFO
Bart Volkmer, Chief Legal Officer
Olivia Nottebohm, COO
Timothy Young, President

FINANCIAL DATA: *Note: Data for latest year may not have been available at press time.*

In U.S. $	2022	2021	2020	2019	2018	2017
Revenue	2,324,900,000	2,157,900,000	1,913,900,000	1,661,300,000	1,391,700,000	
R&D Expense	891,900,000	755,900,000	727,500,000	662,100,000	768,200,000	
Operating Income	356,500,000	305,700,000	121,200,000	-80,500,000	-494,000,000	
Operating Margin %	.15%	.14%	.06%	-.05%	-.35%	
SGA Expense	632,300,000	652,100,000	650,600,000	668,700,000	722,800,000	
Net Income	553,200,000	335,800,000	-256,300,000	-52,700,000	-484,900,000	
Operating Cash Flow	797,300,000	729,800,000	570,800,000	528,500,000	425,400,000	
Capital Expenditure	34,900,000	28,900,000	80,300,000	137,800,000	66,000,000	
EBITDA	513,600,000	457,100,000	280,500,000	93,000,000	-327,200,000	
Return on Assets %	.18%	.12%	-.10%	-.02%	-.36%	
Return on Equity %		16.83%	-.45%	-.07%	-5.90%	
Debt to Equity			2.79	1.052	.13%	

CONTACT INFORMATION:

Phone: 415-857-6800   Fax:
Toll-Free:
Address: 1800 Owens St., San Francisco, CA 94158 United States

STOCK TICKER/OTHER:

Stock Ticker: DBX
Employees: 3,118
Parent Company:

Exchange: NAS
Fiscal Year Ends: 12/31

SALARIES/BONUSES:

Top Exec. Salary: $625,000   Bonus: $
Second Exec. Salary: $600,000   Bonus: $

OTHER THOUGHTS:

Estimated Female Officers or Directors: 1
Hot Spot for Advancement for Women/Minorities:

Sales, profits and employees may be estimates. Financial information, benefits and other data can change quickly and may vary from those stated here.

Duo Security Inc

NAIC Code: 511210E

duo.com

TYPES OF BUSINESS:

Computer Software: Network Security, Managed Access, Digital ID,
Cybersecurity & Anti-Virus
Cloud-based Access Software
Security Solutions
Multi-factor Authentication
Device Trust Solutions
Adaptive Access Solutions
Remote Access Solutions
Biometrics

BRANDS/DIVISIONS/AFFILIATES:

Cisco Systems Inc

CONTACTS: *Note: Officers with more than one job title may be intentionally listed here more than once.*

Dug Song, Gen. Mngr.

GROWTH PLANS/SPECIAL FEATURES:

Duo Security, Inc. provides cloud-based access security for companies of all sizes. The firm protects organizations against data breaches by ensuring that only legitimate users and appropriate devices have access to sensitive data and applications anytime, anywhere. Duo Security's platform offers five capabilities: Multi-Factor Authentication (MFA); Device Trust; Adaptive Access Policies; Remote Access; and Single Sign-On (SSO). MFA ensures that users are who they say they are at every access attempt and regularly reaffirms their trustworthiness. Device Trust identifies risky devices, enforces contextual access policies and reports on device health. Adaptive Access Policies assign granular and contextual access policies, limiting data exposure to as few users and devices as possible. Remote Access provides appropriate permissions for every user at any time and from anywhere. SSO reduces the risk of credential theft by enabling users to securely access their applications with a single username and password. Duo Security has 1 billion authentications each month and more than 40,000 paying customers in 100 countries. The firm is a subsidiary of Cisco Systems, Inc. Based in Michigan, Duo Security has additional U.S. locations in California and Texas, as well as in London, U.K.

FINANCIAL DATA: *Note: Data for latest year may not have been available at press time.*

In U.S. $	2022	2021	2020	2019	2018	2017
Revenue						
R&D Expense						
Operating Income						
Operating Margin %						
SGA Expense						
Net Income						
Operating Cash Flow						
Capital Expenditure						
EBITDA						
Return on Assets %						
Return on Equity %						
Debt to Equity						

CONTACT INFORMATION:

Phone: 866-760-4247   Fax:
Toll-Free:
Address: 123 N. Ashley St., Ann Arbor, MI 48104 United States

STOCK TICKER/OTHER:

Stock Ticker: Subsidiary   Exchange:
Employees: 740   Fiscal Year Ends:
Parent Company: Cisco Systems Inc

SALARIES/BONUSES:

Top Exec. Salary: $ Bonus: $
Second Exec. Salary: $ Bonus: $

OTHER THOUGHTS:

Estimated Female Officers or Directors:
Hot Spot for Advancement for Women/Minorities:

Dynatrace Inc

www.dynatrace.com

NAIC Code: 511210m

TYPES OF BUSINESS:

Application Performance Management Tools
Software
Multi-cloud Environments
Artificial Intelligence
Automation

GROWTH PLANS/SPECIAL FEATURES:

Dynatrace is a cloud-native company that focuses on analyzing machine data. Its product portfolio, delivered as software as a service, allows a client to monitor and analyze its entire IT infrastructure. Dynatrace's platform can ingest and analyze large amounts of machine-generated data in real time, allowing clients to use it for a variety of applications throughout their businesses.

BRANDS/DIVISIONS/AFFILIATES:

CONTACTS: *Note: Officers with more than one job title may be intentionally listed here more than once.*

John Van Siclen, CEO
Kevin Burns, CFO
Jill Ward, Chairman of the Board
Bernd Greifeneder, Chief Technology Officer
Stephen Pace, Senior VP, Divisional

FINANCIAL DATA: *Note: Data for latest year may not have been available at press time.*

In U.S. $	2022	2021	2020	2019	2018	2017
Revenue	929,445,000	703,509,000	545,803,000	430,966,000	398,047,000	
R&D Expense	156,342,000	111,415,000	119,281,000	76,759,000	58,320,000	
Operating Income	81,332,000	91,936,000	-170,847,000	-70,944,000	-16,769,000	
Operating Margin %	.09%	.13%	- .31%	- .16%	- .04%	
SGA Expense	488,738,000	337,706,000	428,158,000	270,664,000	209,464,000	
Net Income	52,451,000	75,714,000	-413,817,000	-116,194,000	9,222,000	
Operating Cash Flow	250,917,000	220,436,000	-142,455,000	147,141,000	118,838,000	
Capital Expenditure	17,695,000	13,879,000	20,613,000	9,250,000	15,229,000	
EBITDA	138,727,000	153,022,000	-106,815,000	10,045,000	65,683,000	
Return on Assets %	.02%	.04%	- .21%	- .06%	.00%	
Return on Equity %	.04%	.07%	-1.44%			
Debt to Equity	.25%	.39%	0.528			

CONTACT INFORMATION:

Phone: 781-530-1000 Fax:
Toll-Free: 888-833-3652
Address: 1601 Trapelo Rd., Ste. 116, Waltham, MA 02451 United States

STOCK TICKER/OTHER:

Stock Ticker: DT
Employees: 4,180
Parent Company:

Exchange: NYS
Fiscal Year Ends: 03/31

SALARIES/BONUSES:

Top Exec. Salary: $630,000   Bonus: $
Second Exec. Salary: $450,000   Bonus: $

OTHER THOUGHTS:

Estimated Female Officers or Directors:
Hot Spot for Advancement for Women/Minorities:

EarthLink LLC

NAIC Code: 517311

TYPES OF BUSINESS:

Internet Service Provider (ISP)
High-Speed Internet
Fiber and Wireless Internet
Satellite Internet
Digital Marketing Solutions
Website Development
Security and Privacy Solutions
Television Streaming Services

BRANDS/DIVISIONS/AFFILIATES:

Trive Capital

GROWTH PLANS/SPECIAL FEATURES:

EarthLink LLC is a leading next-generation internet service provider. With access available across the U.S., the firm offers fast and reliable connectivity, customer support and customizable features. High-speed internet access offerings include fiber internet, wireless home internet and satellite internet. Internet services are provided for businesses, residences and rural areas. EarthLink also provides: digital marketing solutions, such as website development, custom branding and find my business services; security and privacy solutions, such as cybersecurity, parental control, remote information technology (IT) support and data backup services; and EarthLink television streaming services. EarthLink is owned by private equity firm Trive Capital.

EarthLink offers its employees health plan options, 401(k), life and disability insurance, and a variety of assistance plans and company perks.

CONTACTS:
Note: Officers with more than one job title may be intentionally listed here more than once.

Glenn Goad, CEO
Michael Toplisek, Pres.
Julie Shimer, Chairman of the Board
Michael Morrison, CFO
Christopher Roy, Chief Strategy Officer
Scott Klinger, Chief People Officer
Bobby Nix, VP
Bradley Ferguson, Executive VP, Divisional
Louis Alterman, Executive VP
Samuel Desimone, Executive VP
John Dobbins, Executive VP
Gerard Brossard, Executive VP
Rick Froehlich, Executive VP
Valerie Benjamin, Senior VP, Divisional
R. Thurston, Vice President
Brian McLaughlin, CTO

FINANCIAL DATA:
Note: Data for latest year may not have been available at press time.

In U.S. $	2022	2021	2020	2019	2018	2017
Revenue	1,280,229,350	1,230,989,760	1,183,644,000	1,212,750,000	1,155,000,000	1,100,000,000
R&D Expense						
Operating Income						
Operating Margin %						
SGA Expense						
Net Income						
Operating Cash Flow						
Capital Expenditure						
EBITDA						
Return on Assets %						
Return on Equity %						
Debt to Equity						

CONTACT INFORMATION:

Phone: 404 815-0770   Fax:
Toll-Free: 888-327-8454
Address: 980 Hammond Dr. NE, Ste. 400, Atlanta, GA 30328 United States

STOCK TICKER/OTHER:

Stock Ticker: Private   Exchange:
Employees: 2,100   Fiscal Year Ends: 12/31
Parent Company: Trive Capital

SALARIES/BONUSES:

Top Exec. Salary: $ Bonus: $
Second Exec. Salary: $ Bonus: $

OTHER THOUGHTS:

Estimated Female Officers or Directors:
Hot Spot for Advancement for Women/Minorities:

EasyAsk Technologies Inc

www.easyask.com

NAIC Code: 511210L

TYPES OF BUSINESS:

Software-Search & Information Retrieval
Ecommerce Software
Natural Language Technology
Artificial Intelligence
Analytics
Customer Relations Management
Business-to-Business
Merchandise and Shopping Intelligence

BRANDS/DIVISIONS/AFFILIATES:

CONTACTS: *Note: Officers with more than one job title may be intentionally listed here more than once.*

Craig Bassin, CEO
Richard Wood, VP-Dev.
Evan Bobotas, VP-Sales & Bus. Dev.
Nick Halsey, Dir.-Mktg. Strategy
John Morrell, VP-Prod. Mktg.

GROWTH PLANS/SPECIAL FEATURES:

EasyAsk Technologies, Inc. is a natural language search and information retrieval solutions company that provides single-point access to content for ecommerce and business optimization. EasyAsk's natural language technology applies advanced linguistic understanding to break down content and produce better answers to search engine queries. The technology also interprets the intent of the question so customers can use their own vocabulary and still get useful results without being dependent on typical search engine text-matching. EasyAsk utilizes an artificial intelligence (AI)-based natural language query (NLQ) for business intelligence, analytics and customer relations management. This feature enables users to type a question in English and get an immediate answer, with no data hierarchies, no coding, no report building, etc. EasyAsk also provides merchandising tools designed specifically for merchandisers, such as for business-to-business (B2B) and Business-to-commerce (B2C) tasks, voice-driven searches on smartphones and other devices; or for rolling out merchandising across multiple local language sites on a global scale; or for providing customers with new merchandise categories, and for providing feedback and insights about shoppers. Headquartered in Massachusetts, the firm has a global office in the U.K.

FINANCIAL DATA: *Note: Data for latest year may not have been available at press time.*

In U.S. $	2022	2021	2020	2019	2018	2017
Revenue						
R&D Expense						
Operating Income						
Operating Margin %						
SGA Expense						
Net Income						
Operating Cash Flow						
Capital Expenditure						
EBITDA						
Return on Assets %						
Return on Equity %						
Debt to Equity						

CONTACT INFORMATION:

Phone: 781-402-5635   Fax: 781-280-7380
Toll-Free: 800-425-8200
Address: 19 Crosby Dr., Ste. 150, Bedford, MA 01730 United States

STOCK TICKER/OTHER:

Stock Ticker: Private
Employees: 20
Parent Company:

Exchange:
Fiscal Year Ends: 12/31

SALARIES/BONUSES:

Top Exec. Salary: $ Bonus: $
Second Exec. Salary: $ Bonus: $

OTHER THOUGHTS:

Estimated Female Officers or Directors:
Hot Spot for Advancement for Women/Minorities:

eBay Inc

NAIC Code: 454110

www.ebay.com

TYPES OF BUSINESS:

Online Retail-Auctions
Online Payment Processing
Memorabilia & Collectibles
Ecommerce Services

BRANDS/DIVISIONS/AFFILIATES:

Marketplace
www.ebay.com

GROWTH PLANS/SPECIAL FEATURES:

EBay operates one of the largest e-commerce marketplaces in the world, with $74 billion in 2022 gross merchandise volume, or GMV, rendering the firm a top 10 global e-commerce company. eBay generates revenue from listing fees, advertising, revenue-sharing arrangements with service providers, and managed payments, with its platform connecting more than 132 million buyers and roughly 20 million sellers across almost 190 global markets at the end of 2022. eBay generates just north of 50% of its GMV in international markets, with a large presence in the U.K., Germany, and Australia.

Employees of eBay are offered health and wellness benefits, financial benefits and employee assistance programs.

CONTACTS: Note: Officers with more than one job title may be intentionally listed here more than once.

Jamie Iannone, CEO
Steve Priest, CFO
Paul Pressler, Chairman of the Board
Brian Doerger, Chief Accounting Officer
Marie Huber, Chief Legal Officer
Pierre Omidyar, Director Emeritus
Kristin Yetto, Other Executive Officer
Cornelius Boone, Other Executive Officer
Peter Thompson, Other Executive Officer
Julie Loeger, Other Executive Officer

FINANCIAL DATA: Note: Data for latest year may not have been available at press time.

In U.S. $	2022	2021	2020	2019	2018	2017
Revenue	9,795,000,000	10,420,000,000	8,894,000,000	7,429,000,000	8,650,000,000	9,927,000,000
R&D Expense	1,330,000,000	1,325,000,000	1,028,000,000	930,000,000	1,051,000,000	1,224,000,000
Operating Income	2,350,000,000	2,923,000,000	2,636,000,000	1,770,000,000	1,752,000,000	2,264,000,000
Operating Margin %	.24%	.28%	.30%	.24%	.20%	.23%
SGA Expense	3,099,000,000	3,091,000,000	3,076,000,000	2,854,000,000	3,555,000,000	3,908,000,000
Net Income	-1,269,000,000	13,608,000,000	5,667,000,000	1,786,000,000	2,530,000,000	-1,017,000,000
Operating Cash Flow	2,254,000,000	2,657,000,000	2,419,000,000	3,114,000,000	2,658,000,000	3,146,000,000
Capital Expenditure	449,000,000	444,000,000	463,000,000	508,000,000	623,000,000	666,000,000
EBITDA	-924,000,000	1,169,000,000	4,232,000,000	2,563,000,000	3,226,000,000	3,243,000,000
Return on Assets %	-.05%	.59%	.30%	.09%	.10%	-.04%
Return on Equity %	-.17%	2.04%	1.76%	.39%	.35%	-.11%
Debt to Equity	1.58%	.81%	2.259	2.508	1.22%	1.147

CONTACT INFORMATION:

Phone: 408 376-7400   Fax: 408 558-7401
Toll-Free: 800-322-9266
Address: 2025 Hamilton Ave., San Jose, CA 95125 United States

STOCK TICKER/OTHER:

Stock Ticker: EBAY   Exchange: NAS
Employees: 11,600   Fiscal Year Ends: 12/31
Parent Company:

SALARIES/BONUSES:

Top Exec. Salary: $788,462   Bonus: $1,750,000
Second Exec. Salary: $668,077   Bonus: $830,000

OTHER THOUGHTS:

Estimated Female Officers or Directors: 1
Hot Spot for Advancement for Women/Minorities: Y

eHarmony Inc

www.eharmony.com

NAIC Code: 519130

TYPES OF BUSINESS:
Online Dating Services
Digital Dating Platform
Algorithm Matching Technology
Online Advisory Resources
Compatibility Software and Technology

BRANDS/DIVISIONS/AFFILIATES:
eHarmony.com

GROWTH PLANS/SPECIAL FEATURES:
eHarmony, Inc. operates eHarmony.com, a subscription-based online dating portal. The firm uses a patented compatibility algorithm matching system that focuses on multiple dimensions of compatibility. Potential users answer a comprehensive questionnaire to create an introductory profile before qualifying as members. These questions also form the basis of the user's profile, which is used in the algorithm to determine a compatibility score with other subscribers. Popular demographic categories include Asian dating, Black dating, Christian dating, Senior dating, Free dating, Latin dating, International dating and more. eHarmony.com offers resource links that offer dating and relationship advice, dating tips, date ideas and information concerning first dates. Outside the U.S., service is available internationally in Canada, Australia and the U.K. eHarmony's membership pool comprises singles living in all 50 U.S. states, and more than 125 countries worldwide.

CONTACTS:
Note: Officers with more than one job title may be intentionally listed here more than once.

Gareth Mandel, COO
Stefan Schulze, CFO
Carlos Robles, CCO
Ron Sarian, VP
David Chen, VP-Corp. Dev.
Jaime Rupert, Dir.-Corp. Comm.
David Chen, VP-Finance
Steve Carter, VP-Matching
Grant Langston, VP-Customer Experience
Dan Erickson, Dir.-Special Projects

FINANCIAL DATA:
Note: Data for latest year may not have been available at press time.

In U.S. $	2022	2021	2020	2019	2018	2017
Revenue	422,580,000	406,326,375	386,977,500	396,900,000	378,000,000	360,000,000
R&D Expense						
Operating Income						
Operating Margin %						
SGA Expense						
Net Income						
Operating Cash Flow						
Capital Expenditure						
EBITDA						
Return on Assets %						
Return on Equity %						
Debt to Equity						

CONTACT INFORMATION:
Phone: 424-258-1199   Fax:
Toll-Free:
Address: 10900 Wilshire Blvd, Fl. 17, Los Angeles, CA 90024 United States

STOCK TICKER/OTHER:
Stock Ticker: Private   Exchange:
Employees: 250   Fiscal Year Ends:
Parent Company:

SALARIES/BONUSES:
Top Exec. Salary: $ Bonus: $
Second Exec. Salary: $ Bonus: $

OTHER THOUGHTS:
Estimated Female Officers or Directors:
Hot Spot for Advancement for Women/Minorities:

eHealth Inc

www.ehealthinsurance.com

NAIC Code: 524210

TYPES OF BUSINESS:

Health Insurance Brokerage-Online
Health Insurance
Student Health Insurance
Short-term Health Insurance
Health Savings Accounts
Dental Insurance
Term Life Insurance
Dental Discount Cards

BRANDS/DIVISIONS/AFFILIATES:

eHealthInsurance Services Inc
eHealth.com
eHealthInsurance.com
eHealthMedicare.com
Medicare.com
GoMedigap.com
PlanPrescriber.com

GROWTH PLANS/SPECIAL FEATURES:

eHealth Inc offers a private health insurance exchange where individuals and small businesses can compare health insurance products from leading insurers. Users can purchase the insurance online. The exchange includes Medicare options, and seniors can enroll in those plans online or via phone. The company primarily generates revenue through commissions it receives from health insurance carriers. EHealth has relationships with the health insurance carriers in the United States and offers thousands of plans online. All of the company's revenue is from the United States.

CONTACTS: Note: Officers with more than one job title may be intentionally listed here more than once.

Scott Flanders, CEO
Christine Janofsky, CFO
Dale Wolf, Chairman of the Board
John Pierantoni, Chief Accounting Officer
Timothy Hannan, Other Executive Officer
Phillip Morelock, Other Executive Officer

FINANCIAL DATA: Note: Data for latest year may not have been available at press time.

In U.S. $	2022	2021	2020	2019	2018	2017
Revenue	405,356,000	538,199,000	582,774,000	506,201,000	251,395,000	190,706,000
R&D Expense						
Operating Income	-83,097,000	-74,423,000	53,323,000	105,488,000	16,792,000	-8,831,000
Operating Margin %	-.20%	-.14%	.09%	.21%	.07%	-.05%
SGA Expense	266,898,000	346,999,000	285,792,000	214,399,000	128,767,000	105,843,000
Net Income	-88,722,000	-104,375,000	45,450,000	66,887,000	241,000	25,426,000
Operating Cash Flow	-26,869,000	-162,622,000	-107,860,000	-71,492,000	-3,230,000	-15,541,000
Capital Expenditure	15,506,000	20,857,000	23,756,000	16,872,000	10,828,000	5,078,000
EBITDA	-61,989,000	-55,556,000	66,266,000	114,479,000	23,563,000	-3,490,000
Return on Assets %	-.11%	-.11%	.05%	.11%	.00%	.11%
Return on Equity %	-.17%	-.15%	.07%	.16%	.00%	.14%
Debt to Equity	.15%	.05%	0.049	0.065	.02%	

CONTACT INFORMATION:

Phone: 650 584-2700   Fax: 650 961-2153
Toll-Free: 800-977-8860
Address: 2625 Augustine Dr., 2/Fl, Santa Clara, CA 95054 United States

STOCK TICKER/OTHER:

Stock Ticker: EHTH   Exchange: NAS
Employees: 1,515   Fiscal Year Ends: 12/31
Parent Company:

SALARIES/BONUSES:

Top Exec. Salary: $665,630   Bonus: $
Second Exec. Salary: Bonus: $337,877
$196,154

OTHER THOUGHTS:

Estimated Female Officers or Directors: 1
Hot Spot for Advancement for Women/Minorities:

Elavon Inc

NAIC Code: 522320

TYPES OF BUSINESS:

Payment Processing Terminal Products
Payment Processing Software
Seamless Payment Processing Solutions
Contactless Payment Solutions
Ecommerce Payment Solutions
In-Person Payments
Digital Payments Solutions
Payment Gateway Solutions

BRANDS/DIVISIONS/AFFILIATES:

US Bancorp

CONTACTS: *Note: Officers with more than one job title may be intentionally listed here more than once.*

Jamie Walker, CEO
Manny Cofresi Jr., Exec. VP
Simon Haslam, Pres.
Brad W. Hoffelt, CFO
Pari Sawant, Chief Product Officer
Kim Osborn, Chief of Staff
Rachel Hansen, CIO
Marianne Johnson, Head-Prod. & Innovation
Mindy Doster, General Counsel
Brian Mahony, Chief Strategy Officer
Guy Harris, Pres., North America
Carlos Navarro, Pres., Latin America

GROWTH PLANS/SPECIAL FEATURES:

Elavon, Inc. provides end-to-end payment processing solutions to businesses in 36 countries and in more than 131 currencies. Elavon's payment processing solutions enable a swift and secure checkout experience, whether customers shop online, in-person or via mobile app. Solutions include in-person payments transformation, contactless payments, ecommerce payments, payment gateways for flexible payment authorization options, chargeback management, security and payment card industry data security standard (PCI DSS) compliance, value-added services for optimizing business operations, enhanced reporting and reconciliation management, and software/gateway connectivity. Elavon's platform enables seamless integration and protects sensitive data. The company's locally based, multilingual support team is available 24/7/365. Businesses of all sizes can use Elavon, with primary industries served including retail, restaurants, services, travel and hospitality. Partners of Elavon span payment facilitators, referral partners, independent sales organizations, agent partners, financial institutions and affinity partners. Elavon operates as a subsidiary of U.S. Bancorp.

FINANCIAL DATA: *Note: Data for latest year may not have been available at press time.*

In U.S. $	2022	2021	2020	2019	2018	2017
Revenue	2,100,000,000	2,000,000,000	1,808,100,000	1,764,000,000	1,680,000,000	1,600,000,000
R&D Expense						
Operating Income						
Operating Margin %						
SGA Expense						
Net Income						
Operating Cash Flow						
Capital Expenditure						
EBITDA						
Return on Assets %						
Return on Equity %						
Debt to Equity						

CONTACT INFORMATION:

Phone: 678-731-5000   Fax:
Toll-Free:
Address: Two Concourse Pkwy., Ste. 800, Atlanta, GA 30328 United States

STOCK TICKER/OTHER:

Stock Ticker: Subsidiary   Exchange:
Employees: 1,400   Fiscal Year Ends: 12/31
Parent Company: US Bancorp

SALARIES/BONUSES:

Top Exec. Salary: $ Bonus: $
Second Exec. Salary: $ Bonus: $

OTHER THOUGHTS:

Estimated Female Officers or Directors: 5
Hot Spot for Advancement for Women/Minorities: Y

Electronic Arts Inc (EA)

www.ea.com

NAIC Code: 511210G

TYPES OF BUSINESS:

Computer Software, Electronic Games, Apps & Entertainment
Online Interactive Games
E-Commerce Sales
Mobile Games
Apps

BRANDS/DIVISIONS/AFFILIATES:

Battlefield
Sims (The)
Apex Legends
Need for Speed
Plants vs Zombies

GROWTH PLANS/SPECIAL FEATURES:

EA is one of the world's largest third-party video game publishers and has transitioned from a console-based video game publisher to the one of the largest publishers on consoles, PC, and mobile. The firm owns number of large franchises, including Madden, EA Sports FC (formerly FIFA), Battlefield, Apex Legends, Mass Effect, Dragon's Age, and Need for Speed.

EA offers its employees health care coverage, retirement and financial plans, and company perks.

CONTACTS: Note: Officers with more than one job title may be intentionally listed here more than once.

Andrew Wilson, CEO
Blake Jorgensen, CFO
Eric Kelly, Chief Accounting Officer
Jacob Schatz, Chief Legal Officer
Kenneth Moss, Chief Technology Officer
Christopher Bruzzo, Other Executive Officer
Laura Miele, Other Executive Officer
Vijayanthimala Singh, Other Executive Officer
Kenneth Barker, Senior VP, Divisional

FINANCIAL DATA: Note: Data for latest year may not have been available at press time.

In U.S. $	2022	2021	2020	2019	2018	2017
Revenue	6,991,000,000	5,629,000,000	5,537,000,000	4,950,000,000	5,150,000,000	
R&D Expense	2,186,000,000	1,778,000,000	1,559,000,000	1,433,000,000	1,320,000,000	
Operating Income	1,129,000,000	1,046,000,000	1,450,000,000	1,010,000,000	1,434,000,000	
Operating Margin %	.16%	.19%	.26%	.20%	.28%	
SGA Expense	1,634,000,000	1,281,000,000	1,137,000,000	1,162,000,000	1,110,000,000	
Net Income	789,000,000	837,000,000	3,039,000,000	1,019,000,000	1,043,000,000	
Operating Cash Flow	1,899,000,000	1,934,000,000	1,797,000,000	1,547,000,000	1,692,000,000	
Capital Expenditure	188,000,000	124,000,000	140,000,000	119,000,000	107,000,000	
EBITDA	1,625,000,000	1,243,000,000	1,702,000,000	1,267,000,000	1,627,000,000	
Return on Assets %	.06%	.07%	.30%	.12%	.13%	
Return on Equity %	.10%	.11%	.48%	.21%	.24%	
Debt to Equity	.25%	.24%	0.053	0.186	.22%	

CONTACT INFORMATION:

Phone: 650 628-1500   Fax: 650 628-1414
Toll-Free:
Address: 209 Redwood Shores Pkwy., Redwood City, CA 94065 United States

STOCK TICKER/OTHER:

Stock Ticker: EA   Exchange: NAS
Employees: 12,730   Fiscal Year Ends: 03/31
Parent Company:

SALARIES/BONUSES:

Top Exec. Salary: $1,300,000   Bonus: $
Second Exec. Salary: $800,000   Bonus: $

OTHER THOUGHTS:

Estimated Female Officers or Directors: 2
Hot Spot for Advancement for Women/Minorities:

Sales, profits and employees may be estimates. Financial information, benefits and other data can change quickly and may vary from those stated here.

Eloan

www.eloan.com

NAIC Code: 522310

TYPES OF BUSINESS:

Online Mortgage Broker
Lending Referral Services
Loan Search Technology
Online Lending Services
Online Financial Tools

BRANDS/DIVISIONS/AFFILIATES:

Popular Inc
Banco Popular de Puerto Rico

GROWTH PLANS/SPECIAL FEATURES:

Eloan is a division of Banco Popular de Puerto Rico and offers online lending referral services on behalf of lending institutions. The company used to operate as an online direct lender until transforming its business to a referral program. Whether consumers need a personal loan for consolidating debts or needing a loan to purchase a home, Eloan provides financial research experience based on the customer's needs. Eloan also offers online financial tools to simplify their research process. The company's financial technology transforms data into solutions, assisting consumers during their decision-making process. Banco Popular de Puerto Rico is a subsidiary of Popular, Inc.

CONTACTS:
Note: Officers with more than one job title may be intentionally listed here more than once.

Manuel Chinea, COO
Mark Lefanowicz, Pres.

FINANCIAL DATA:
Note: Data for latest year may not have been available at press time.

In U.S. $	2022	2021	2020	2019	2018	2017
Revenue						
R&D Expense						
Operating Income						
Operating Margin %						
SGA Expense						
Net Income						
Operating Cash Flow						
Capital Expenditure						
EBITDA						
Return on Assets %						
Return on Equity %						
Debt to Equity						

CONTACT INFORMATION:

Phone: 847-994-5800   Fax:
Toll-Free:
Address: 85 Broad St., Fl. 10, New York, NY 10004 United States

SALARIES/BONUSES:

Top Exec. Salary: $ Bonus: $
Second Exec. Salary: $ Bonus: $

STOCK TICKER/OTHER:

Stock Ticker: Subsidiary   Exchange:
Employees: 930   Fiscal Year Ends: 12/31
Parent Company: Popular Inc

OTHER THOUGHTS:

Estimated Female Officers or Directors:
Hot Spot for Advancement for Women/Minorities:

Embarcadero Inc

www.embarcadero.com

NAIC Code: 511210J

TYPES OF BUSINESS:

Software, Application & Database Management
Software Development Tools
Application Development Tools
Embedded Structural Query Language
Mobile Enterprise Application Platform
Creating and Testing Code
App Deployment Tools

BRANDS/DIVISIONS/AFFILIATES:

Idera Inc
RESTful MEAP
RAD Studio
Delphi
C++ Builder
INterBase

CONTACTS: *Note: Officers with more than one job title may be intentionally listed here more than once.*

Randy Jacops, CEO
Chris Smith, COO
Trey Chambers, CFO
Michael Swindell, Sr. VP-Prod. Mgmt.
Tony de la Lama, Sr. VP-Eng.
Michael Swindell, Sr. VP-Strategy
David Intersimone, VP-Developer Rel.
Steve Young, Chmn.
Nigel Brown, Gen. Mgr.-Int'l

GROWTH PLANS/SPECIAL FEATURES:

Embarcadero, Inc. designs and produces tools for software developers, data architects and database management professionals for designing, building, optimizing and running applications and database systems across multiple platforms. The company's products are grouped into three categories: development tools, embedded structural query language (SQL) database and RESTful MEAP. Development tools include: RAD Studio, an integrated development environment (IDE) for coding, debugging, testing and designing for cross-platform mobile and desktop deployment; Delphi, for Object Pascal developers worldwide to create apps across devices; and C++ Builder, for creating and testing code in order to deploy apps. The embedded SQL database category offers InterBase, an ultrafast, scalable, embedded SQL database equipped with commercial-grade data security, disaster recovery and change synchronization. The RESTful MEAP (mobile enterprise application platform) is a turnkey application server that provides an out-of-the-box backend platform on which to build and deploy Delphi and C++ Builder application services. Free development tools offered by Embarcadero include C++ compiler, community education platforms, REST debugger, InterBase developer edition, FMX stencils, PyScripter and more. Embarcadero is a subsidiary of Idera, Inc., the parent company of global business-to-business software productivity brands.

FINANCIAL DATA: *Note: Data for latest year may not have been available at press time.*

In U.S. $	2022	2021	2020	2019	2018	2017
Revenue	150,000,000	180,000,000	174,636,000	176,400,000	168,000,000	160,000,000
R&D Expense						
Operating Income						
Operating Margin %						
SGA Expense						
Net Income						
Operating Cash Flow						
Capital Expenditure						
EBITDA						
Return on Assets %						
Return on Equity %						
Debt to Equity						

CONTACT INFORMATION:

Phone: 512-226-8080   Fax: 415-434-1721
Toll-Free:
Address: 10801 North Mopac Expressway, Bldg. 1, Ste. 100, Austin, TX 78759 United States

STOCK TICKER/OTHER:

Stock Ticker: Private   Exchange:
Employees: 220   Fiscal Year Ends: 12/31
Parent Company: Idera Inc

SALARIES/BONUSES:

Top Exec. Salary: $ Bonus: $
Second Exec. Salary: $ Bonus: $

OTHER THOUGHTS:

Estimated Female Officers or Directors: 1
Hot Spot for Advancement for Women/Minorities:

eMusic.com Inc

NAIC Code: 454110

www.emusic.com

TYPES OF BUSINESS:

Online Music-Retail
MP3 Subscription Services
Audiobook Subscription Services
Music Discovery Platform
Ecommerce

BRANDS/DIVISIONS/AFFILIATES:

TriPlay Communications Ltd
eStories

CONTACTS: *Note: Officers with more than one job title may be intentionally listed here more than once.*

Tamir Koch, CEO-TriPlay
Molly Neuman, VP-Label Relations
Daniel C. Stein, Pres., JDS Capital Management, Inc.
Madeline Milne, Managing Dir.-Europe

GROWTH PLANS/SPECIAL FEATURES:

eMusic.com, Inc. is a discovery-and-download ecommerce marketplace for people who like music. Discovery is the heart of eMusic, and believes the best discoveries are inspired by unique and personal interest. eMusic enables listeners to explore its dynamic assortment of features designed to tap into those music interests and tastes, leading them to music they will enjoy. After exploring the eMusic catalog, listeners can purchase discoveries a la carte at any time or become an eMusic member and save 25-50%. Every penny of membership goes directly toward downloading music. Member plans charge a monthly fee, and can be changed, supplemented or canceled at any time. Music purchases are automatically uploaded to a personal eMusic cloud account. Listeners can upload and store an unlimited number of tracks for free; use the smart playlist feature to rediscover music or build a mix for any occasion; and/or sync and play the entire collection wherever they go via iPhone and Android apps. The eMusic website features new albums and bands via staff interviews, and within the site's Editors' Picks. Users can dig further into a musician's catalog through eMusic's search engine and locate like-kind music types with its browse function. Personalized recommendations will be provided as well. In addition, the company has an eStories website, delivering audiobook service that comprises more than 120,000 audiobook titles. These titles include best-sellers spanning every genre, and new releases are added every week. Personalized search and discovery tools make it easy to find interesting stories. After an initial trial period, members pay a monthly fee, with the basic plan including one audiobook each month. Audiobooks can be listened to via iPhone and Android apps, and stories will automatically sync across up to 10 devices. eMusic is owned by Israeli-based TriPlay Communications Ltd.

FINANCIAL DATA: *Note: Data for latest year may not have been available at press time.*

In U.S. $	2022	2021	2020	2019	2018	2017
Revenue						
R&D Expense						
Operating Income						
Operating Margin %						
SGA Expense						
Net Income						
Operating Cash Flow						
Capital Expenditure						
EBITDA						
Return on Assets %						
Return on Equity %						
Debt to Equity						

CONTACT INFORMATION:

Phone: 212-201-9240   Fax: 212-201-9204
Toll-Free:
Address: 215 Lexington Ave., New York, NY 10016 United States

STOCK TICKER/OTHER:

Stock Ticker: Private   Exchange:
Employees: 180   Fiscal Year Ends: 12/31
Parent Company: TriPlay Communications Ltd

SALARIES/BONUSES:

Top Exec. Salary: $ Bonus: $
Second Exec. Salary: $ Bonus: $

OTHER THOUGHTS:

Estimated Female Officers or Directors:
Hot Spot for Advancement for Women/Minorities:

Sales, profits and employees may be estimates. Financial information, benefits and other data can change quickly and may vary from those stated here.

Endeavor Streaming

www.endeavorstreaming.com

NAIC Code: 519130

TYPES OF BUSINESS:

Internet Protocol Television
Television, web, sports media, mobile solutions and services.
Global Streaming Services
Live Content Services
On-Demand Digital Services and Solutions
Digital Business Solutions
Real-time Analytics Solutions
Audio Codecs and Plugins

BRANDS/DIVISIONS/AFFILIATES:

Endeavor Operating Company LLC
MainConcept GmbH

CONTACTS: *Note: Officers with more than one job title may be intentionally listed here more than once.*

Fred Santarpia, Pres.
Charles Wang, Chmn.
Fern Pucheu, CMO
Greg Willis, Sr. VP-Global Sales
Goncalo Luiz, CTO
Roy Reichbach, Director
J. Wagner, Executive VP, Divisional
Ronald Nunn, Executive VP, Divisional
Horngwei Her, Executive VP, Divisional
Alexander Arato, General Counsel
Nancy Li, Vice Chairman of the Board
Peter Bellamy, Chief Commercial Officer

GROWTH PLANS/SPECIAL FEATURES:

Endeavor Streaming is a global streaming provider specializing in the broadcasting, distribution and monetization of live and on-demand digital content services. The firm's streaming solutions are end-to-end seamless, from content aggregation and management through monetization and end-user experience. Clients can manage their video library from a centralized console, including users, content metadata, user experience, user interface, products, packages, promotional campaigns and more. Clients can provide their viewers with premium streaming experiences up to 4K HDR on smart and connected devices. A number of business models are offered through Endeavor's streaming platforms, including subscription, advertising, transactional, authentication and hybrid combinations. Clients can create custom packages for their customers. Real-time analytics in regards to audience consumption and behavior habits across live and on-demand video are part of what Endeavor's solutions have to offer. Subsidiary MainConcept GmbH provides video and audio codecs, plugins and applications to the production, streaming and broadcast industries. Endeavor Streaming is a subsidiary of Endeavor Operating Company LLC, based in California.

FINANCIAL DATA: *Note: Data for latest year may not have been available at press time.*

In U.S. $	2022	2021	2020	2019	2018	2017
Revenue	114,400,000	110,000,000	108,000,073	105,365,925	100,348,500	95,570,000
R&D Expense						
Operating Income						
Operating Margin %						
SGA Expense						
Net Income						
Operating Cash Flow						
Capital Expenditure						
EBITDA						
Return on Assets %						
Return on Equity %						
Debt to Equity						

CONTACT INFORMATION:

Phone: 516 622-830   Fax:
Toll-Free:
Address: 1600 Old Country Rd., Plainview, NY 11803 United States

STOCK TICKER/OTHER:

Stock Ticker: Subsidiary   Exchange:
Employees: 650   Fiscal Year Ends: 12/31
Parent Company: Endeavor Operating Company LLC

SALARIES/BONUSES:

Top Exec. Salary: $ Bonus: $
Second Exec. Salary: $ Bonus: $

OTHER THOUGHTS:

Estimated Female Officers or Directors: 2
Hot Spot for Advancement for Women/Minorities: Y

Entrust Corporation

www.entrust.com

NAIC Code: 511210E

TYPES OF BUSINESS:

Computer Software, Network Security, Managed Access, Digital ID,
Cybersecurity & Anti-Virus
Digital Identification & Certificates
Digital Security Solutions
Security Application Developer
Digital Signature Solutions
Financial Issuance Solutions
Multi-Cloud Security Solutions

BRANDS/DIVISIONS/AFFILIATES:

Evidos

CONTACTS: *Note: Officers with more than one job title may be intentionally listed here more than once.*

Todd Wilkinson, CEO
Anudeep Parhar, COO
Kurt Ishaug, CFO
Karen Kaukol, CMO
Beth Klehr, Chief Human Resources Officer
Anudeep Parhar, CIO
Robert (Bob) VanKirk, Sr. VP-American Sales
Mike Baxter, Sr. VP-Product Dev.
Mark Reeves, Sr. VP-Int'l Sales

GROWTH PLANS/SPECIAL FEATURES:

Entrust Corporation is a global provider of security applications that protect and secure digital identities and information. The firm designs, produces and sells security, policy and access management software products and related services. Solutions span identity verification, ID issuance, user identity, machine identity, electronic signature, financial issuance, digital card, secure transactions, digital onboarding, post quantum cryptography, database security and multi-cloud security. Entrust products are grouped into several categories, including issuance, cloud security posture management, key management and encryption, hardware security modules, digital certificates, identity and access management (IAM), electronic and digital signing, public key infrastructure (PKI). Entrust offers support and services concerning product downloads, technical support, marketing development funds, digital security guides and white papers, User guides and technotes, custom cryptographic solutions, product deployment services, packaged services, training and more. Based in Minnesota, Entrust has offices in the U.S., Asia Pacific, Canada, Europe, Latin America, the Caribbean and the Middle East.

FINANCIAL DATA: *Note: Data for latest year may not have been available at press time.*

In U.S. $	2022	2021	2020	2019	2018	2017
Revenue	915,200,000	880,000,000	840,000,000	800,000,000	700,000,000	600,000,000
R&D Expense						
Operating Income						
Operating Margin %						
SGA Expense						
Net Income						
Operating Cash Flow						
Capital Expenditure						
EBITDA						
Return on Assets %						
Return on Equity %						
Debt to Equity						

CONTACT INFORMATION:

Phone: 952 933-1223   Fax:
Toll-Free: 800-621-6972
Address: 1187 Park Pl., Shakopee, MN 55379 United States

STOCK TICKER/OTHER:

Stock Ticker: Private   Exchange:
Employees: 2,500   Fiscal Year Ends: 12/31
Parent Company:

SALARIES/BONUSES:

Top Exec. Salary: $ Bonus: $
Second Exec. Salary: $ Bonus: $

OTHER THOUGHTS:

Estimated Female Officers or Directors:
Hot Spot for Advancement for Women/Minorities:

Equinix Inc
NAIC Code: 517311

TYPES OF BUSINESS:
Data Networks
Internet Exchange Services

BRANDS/DIVISIONS/AFFILIATES:
International Business Exchange (IBX)
xScale
Equinix Internet Exchange
Equinix Fabric
Equinix SmartKey
Bare Metal

GROWTH PLANS/SPECIAL FEATURES:
Equinix operates 260 data centers in 71 markets worldwide. It generates 44% of total revenue in the Americas, 35% in Europe, the Middle East, and Africa, and 21% in Asia-Pacific. The firm has more than 10,000 customers, including 2,100 network providers, that are dispersed over five verticals: cloud and IT services, content providers, network and mobile services, financial services, and enterprise. About 70% of Equinix's revenue comes from renting space to tenants and related services, and more than 15% comes from interconnection. Equinix operates as a real estate investment trust.

Equinix offers its employees health and financial benefit options, depending on location.

CONTACTS:
Note: Officers with more than one job title may be intentionally listed here more than once.

Charles Meyers, CEO
Keith Taylor, CFO
Peter Van Camp, Chairman of the Board
Simon Miller, Chief Accounting Officer
Brandi Morandi, Chief Legal Officer
Karl Strohmeyer, Other Executive Officer
Michael Campbell, Other Executive Officer

FINANCIAL DATA:
Note: Data for latest year may not have been available at press time.

In U.S. $	2022	2021	2020	2019	2018	2017
Revenue	7,263,105,000	6,635,537,000	5,998,545,000	5,562,140,000	5,071,654,000	
R&D Expense						
Operating Income	1,226,343,000	1,120,086,000	1,114,868,000	1,165,892,000	1,005,783,000	
Operating Margin %	.17%	.17%	.19%	.21%	.20%	
SGA Expense	2,285,261,000	2,043,029,000	1,809,337,000	1,586,064,000	1,460,396,000	
Net Income	704,345,000	500,191,000	369,777,000	507,450,000	365,359,000	
Operating Cash Flow	2,963,182,000	2,547,206,000	2,309,826,000	1,992,728,000	1,815,426,000	
Capital Expenditure	2,278,004,000	2,751,512,000	2,282,504,000	2,079,521,000	2,096,174,000	
EBITDA	2,921,914,000	2,601,324,000	2,346,060,000	2,457,118,000	2,182,021,000	
Return on Assets %	.02%	.02%	.01%	.02%	.02%	
Return on Equity %	.06%	.05%	.04%	.06%	.05%	
Debt to Equity	1.41%	1.35%	1.26	1.396	1.51%	

CONTACT INFORMATION:
Phone: 650 598-6000   Fax: 650 513-7900
Toll-Free: 800-322-9280
Address: 1 Lagoon Dr., Redwood City, CA 94065 United States

STOCK TICKER/OTHER:
Stock Ticker: EQIX   Exchange: NAS
Employees: 12,097   Fiscal Year Ends: 12/31
Parent Company:

SALARIES/BONUSES:
Top Exec. Salary: $1,050,000   Bonus: $
Second Exec. Salary: Bonus: $
$680,000

OTHER THOUGHTS:
Estimated Female Officers or Directors: 3
Hot Spot for Advancement for Women/Minorities: Y

E-Trade from Morgan Stanley

www.etrade.com

NAIC Code: 523120

TYPES OF BUSINESS:

Stock Brokerage/Investment Management-Online
Financial Services
Banking Services
Stock Services
Online Banking
Online Trading
Retirement Financial Solutions

BRANDS/DIVISIONS/AFFILIATES:

Morgan Stanley
ETRADE Securities LLC
ETRADE Capital Management LLC
ETRADE Futures LLC
ETRADE Fomamcoa; Corporate Services Inc
Morgan Stanley Private Bank NA

CONTACTS: *Note: Officers with more than one job title may be intentionally listed here more than once.*

Ted Pick, CEO-Morgan Stanley
Chad Turner, CFO
Michael Curcio, Executive VP, Divisional
James P Gorman, Chmn.-Morgan Stanley

GROWTH PLANS/SPECIAL FEATURES:

E*TRADE from Morgan Stanley is a global financial services company that offers banking and stock plans to retail customers. The firm provides access digital resources for its online services, as well as market insights, webinars and answers to a variety of questions. Types of accounts include brokerage, retirement, core portfolios, managed portfolios, small business and bank. Investment choices span stocks, options, mutual funds, exchange traded funds (ETFs), futures, bonds and certificates of deposit (CDs), pre-built portfolios and initial public offerings (IPOs). The trading division encompasses platforms, margin trading and execution. E*TRADE offers information for those new to trading. Trading prices range from free to $1.50, depending on the stock, option, contract and/or bond. Prices for other services are listed on the company's website and mobile app. Securities products and services are offered by E*TRADE Securities LLC; investment advisory services by E*TRADE Capital Management LLC; commodity futures and options on futures products and services by E*TRADE Futures LLC; stock plan administration solutions and services by E*TRADE Financial Corporate Services Inc.; and banking products and services are provided by Morgan Stanley Private Bank, N.A. E*TRADE from Morgan Stanley is a wholly-owned subsidiary of Morgan Stanley, and each of the companies under E*TRADE are separate but affiliated subsidiaries of Morgan Stanley.

FINANCIAL DATA: *Note: Data for latest year may not have been available at press time.*

In U.S. $	2022	2021	2020	2019	2018	2017
Revenue	2,710,300,441	3,151,512,140	3,030,300,134	2,886,000,128	2,872,999,936	2,366,000,128
R&D Expense						
Operating Income						
Operating Margin %						
SGA Expense						
Net Income				955,000,000	1,052,000,000	614,000,000
Operating Cash Flow						
Capital Expenditure						
EBITDA						
Return on Assets %						
Return on Equity %						
Debt to Equity						

CONTACT INFORMATION:

Phone: 646 521-4300   Fax:
Toll-Free: 800-387-2331
Address: 671 N. Glebe Rd., Arlington, VA 22203 United States

STOCK TICKER/OTHER:

Stock Ticker: Subsidiary   Exchange:
Employees: 4,000   Fiscal Year Ends: 12/31
Parent Company: Morgan Stanley

SALARIES/BONUSES:

Top Exec. Salary: $ Bonus: $
Second Exec. Salary: $ Bonus: $

OTHER THOUGHTS:

Estimated Female Officers or Directors: 3
Hot Spot for Advancement for Women/Minorities: Y

Etsy Inc

www.etsy.com

NAIC Code: 454110

TYPES OF BUSINESS:

Online Craft Marketplace
Handmade Arts & Crafts
Crafting Supplies
Vintage Clothing & Goods

GROWTH PLANS/SPECIAL FEATURES:

Etsy operates a top-10 e-commerce marketplace operator in the U.S. and the U.K., with sizable operations in Germany, France, Australia, and Canada. The firm dominates an interesting niche, connecting buyers and sellers through its online market to exchange vintage and craft goods. With $13.3 billion in 2022 consolidated gross merchandise volume, the firm has cemented itself as one of the largest players in a quickly growing space, generating revenue from listing fees, commissions on sold items, advertising services, payment processing, and shipping labels. As of the end of 2022, the firm connected more than 95 million buyers and 7.5 million sellers on its marketplace properties: Etsy, Reverb (musical equipment), and Depop (clothing resale).

BRANDS/DIVISIONS/AFFILIATES:

Etsy.com

CONTACTS: *Note: Officers with more than one job title may be intentionally listed here more than once.*

Josh Silverman, CEO
Rachel Glaser, CFO
Frederick Wilson, Chairman of the Board
Merilee Buckley, Chief Accounting Officer
Jill Simeone, Chief Legal Officer
Ryan Scott, Chief Marketing Officer
Michael Fisher, Chief Technology Officer
Raina Moskowitz, COO, Divisional
Kruti Goyal, Other Executive Officer

FINANCIAL DATA: *Note: Data for latest year may not have been available at press time.*

In U.S. $	2022	2021	2020	2019	2018	2017
Revenue	2,566,111,000	2,329,114,000	1,725,625,000	818,379,000	603,693,000	441,231,000
R&D Expense	412,398,000	271,535,000	180,080,000	121,878,000	97,249,000	74,616,000
Operating Income	386,462,000	465,732,000	424,009,000	88,761,000	74,786,000	15,058,000
Operating Margin %	.15%	.20%	.25%	.11%	.12%	.03%
SGA Expense	1,022,659,000	937,335,000	656,791,000	336,704,000	240,896,000	200,571,000
Net Income	-694,288,000	493,507,000	349,246,000	95,894,000	77,491,000	81,800,000
Operating Cash Flow	683,612,000	651,551,000	678,956,000	206,920,000	198,925,000	69,101,000
Capital Expenditure	30,743,000	28,170,000	7,110,000	15,278,000	20,556,000	13,156,000
EBITDA	-551,108,000	555,806,000	465,923,000	152,997,000	103,998,000	70,592,000
Return on Assets %	-.21%	.16%	.18%	.08%	.10%	.14%
Return on Equity %	-17.07%	.72%	.61%	.24%	.19%	.22%
Debt to Equity		3.80%	1.491	2.063	.84%	0.162

CONTACT INFORMATION:

Phone: 718-880-3660   Fax:
Toll-Free:
Address: 117 Adams St., Brooklyn, NY 11201 United States

STOCK TICKER/OTHER:

Stock Ticker: ETSY   Exchange: NAS
Employees: 2,790   Fiscal Year Ends: 12/31
Parent Company:

SALARIES/BONUSES:

Top Exec. Salary: $622,500   Bonus: $
Second Exec. Salary: $468,750   Bonus: $

OTHER THOUGHTS:

Estimated Female Officers or Directors:
Hot Spot for Advancement for Women/Minorities: Y

Eventbrite Inc

www.eventbrite.com

NAIC Code: 454110

TYPES OF BUSINESS:

Online Event Ticket Sales
Credit Card Charge Processing
Event Promotion
Ticketing
RSVP

GROWTH PLANS/SPECIAL FEATURES:

Eventbrite Inc is a United States based self-service ticketing and experience technology platform that serves event creators. It is engaged in creating a platform to enable creators to solve many challenges associated with creating live experiences. The Company's platform integrates components needed to seamlessly plan, promote and produce live events. Its platform helps to plan, promote and produce live events, thereby allowing creators to reduce friction and costs, increase reach and drive ticket sales. Geographically, it generates maximum revenue from the United States.

BRANDS/DIVISIONS/AFFILIATES:

Eventbrite.com

CONTACTS: Note: Officers with more than one job title may be intentionally listed here more than once.

Julia Hartz, CEO
Charles Baker, CFO
Kevin Hartz, Chairman of the Board
Xiaojing Fan, Chief Accounting Officer
Vivek Sagi, Chief Technology Officer

FINANCIAL DATA: Note: Data for latest year may not have been available at press time.

In U.S. $	2022	2021	2020	2019	2018	2017
Revenue	260,927,000	187,134,000	106,006,000	326,801,000	291,611,000	201,597,000
R&D Expense	86,346,000	66,303,000	54,551,000	64,196,000	46,071,000	30,608,000
Operating Income	-46,742,000	-67,778,000	-198,280,000	-69,951,000	-38,675,000	-33,407,000
Operating Margin %	-.18%	-.36%	-1.87%	-.21%	-.13%	-.17%
SGA Expense	130,577,000	118,315,000	187,405,000	203,415,000	163,562,000	122,729,000
Net Income	-55,384,000	-139,080,000	-224,718,000	-68,760,000	-64,078,000	-38,547,000
Operating Cash Flow	8,610,000	85,834,000	-157,957,000	29,955,000	7,162,000	29,821,000
Capital Expenditure	4,451,000	2,533,000	6,282,000	13,598,000	12,650,000	8,678,000
EBITDA	-29,129,000	-102,669,000	-177,602,000	-41,642,000	-17,025,000	-12,680,000
Return on Assets %	-.06%	-.16%	-.28%	-.08%	-.09%	-.09%
Return on Equity %	-.33%	-.57%	-.61%	-.16%	-.49%	
Debt to Equity	2.15%	2.13%	0.691	0.038	.23%	

CONTACT INFORMATION:

Phone: 415-692-7779   Fax: 415-520-3420
Toll-Free: 888-810-2063
Address: 155 5th St., 7/F, San Francisco, CA 94103 United States

STOCK TICKER/OTHER:

Stock Ticker: EB   Exchange: NYS
Employees: 881   Fiscal Year Ends: 12/31
Parent Company:

SALARIES/BONUSES:

Top Exec. Salary: $475,000   Bonus: $
Second Exec. Salary: $430,000   Bonus: $

OTHER THOUGHTS:

Estimated Female Officers or Directors: 3
Hot Spot for Advancement for Women/Minorities: Y

Everlane

NAIC Code: 454110

TYPES OF BUSINESS:

Online Apparel Sales
Apparel Ecommerce Platform
Retail
Apparel Factories
Apparel and Footwear
Bags, Purses and Backpacks
Scarves, Hats and Gloves
Mobile App

BRANDS/DIVISIONS/AFFILIATES:

Tread
Gum Sole Collection
Core Collection

CONTACTS: *Note: Officers with more than one job title may be intentionally listed here more than once.*

Andrea O'Donnell, CEO
Michael Preysman, Chmn.

GROWTH PLANS/SPECIAL FEATURES:

Everlane is primarily an ecommerce shopping retailer. The company discloses the origin of all products, as well as the cost breakdown of each garment, such as labor, materials, transportation and taxes/fees. The site also provides price comparison with traditional retailers' merchandise. Everlane products include men's and women's apparel and accessories. Apparel consists of sweaters, outerwear, tops, t-shirts, sweatshirts, pants, denim, shorts, skirts, dresses and undergarments; and accessories consist of backpacks/bags, ties, leather goods, scarves, hats, gloves and shoes. In addition, Everlane produces and distributes the Tread line of men's and women's environmentally friendly, low-impact sneakers. Tread collections include the Gum Sole Collection and the Core Collection. The firm's mobile app enables shoppers to browse and buy its luxury items directly from their smartphones. The app features the current weather in order to offer suggestions of what to wear. Everlane's factories are based in the South America, India, Europe, Africa and Asia. Everlane's 11 brick-and-mortar stores are located throughout the U.S. in cities such as Austin, Washington DC, Los Angeles, New York City, Brooklyn, Boston, Palo Alto, San Francisco, King of Prussia, Seattle and Georgetown.

FINANCIAL DATA: *Note: Data for latest year may not have been available at press time.*

In U.S. $	2022	2021	2020	2019	2018	2017
Revenue	121,000,000	112,467,128	86,513,175	146,632,500	139,650,000	133,000,000
R&D Expense						
Operating Income						
Operating Margin %						
SGA Expense						
Net Income						
Operating Cash Flow						
Capital Expenditure						
EBITDA						
Return on Assets %						
Return on Equity %						
Debt to Equity						

CONTACT INFORMATION:

Phone: 415-209-5195   Fax:
Toll-Free:
Address: 461 Valencia St., San Francisco, CA 94103 United States

STOCK TICKER/OTHER:

Stock Ticker: Private   Exchange:
Employees: 200   Fiscal Year Ends:
Parent Company:

SALARIES/BONUSES:

Top Exec. Salary: $ Bonus: $
Second Exec. Salary: $ Bonus: $

OTHER THOUGHTS:

Estimated Female Officers or Directors:
Hot Spot for Advancement for Women/Minorities:

Evernote Corporation

www.evernote.com

NAIC Code: 519130

TYPES OF BUSINESS:

Online Scheduling and Organizing Tool
Handwriting Recognition Software
Online Notes
Note Software
Online Schedule Reminders
Voice Filing
Note Sharing
Search Tools

BRANDS/DIVISIONS/AFFILIATES:

Evernote
Evernote Teams

CONTACTS: *Note: Officers with more than one job title may be intentionally listed here more than once.*

Ian Small, CEO
Alex Pashintsev, VP-R&D
Philip Constantinou, VP-Prod.
Alice Harmon, VP-Admin.
Alex Pachikov, VP-Bus. Dev.
Leonora Teng, VP-Finance
Linda Kozlowski, Head-Int'l Mktg.
Seth Hitchings, VP-Evernote Platform
Luis Samra, Gen. Mgr.-Latin America
Troy Malone, Gen. Mgr.-Asia Pacific
Hitoshi Hokamura, Chmn.-Evernote Japan

GROWTH PLANS/SPECIAL FEATURES:

Evernote Corporation is a software company focused on developing tools for users to create, archive and access data in the form of notes, images, reminders and voice files. On the Evernote platform, users can compile clippings from web pages, handwritten notes, photos, computer documents and voice memos into notebooks where the information can be quickly accessed later. The program also enables notebook sharing, allowing users to collaborate on various projects regardless of distance. The firm's free subscription allows users to upload 60 megabytes (MB) per month and sync capabilities across two devices. For $10.83 per month, Evernote offers 10 gigabytes (GB) per month across an unlimited number of devices; and $14.17 per month, for 20GB per month for professionals who work either on premises or at home. Evernote Teams is $20.83 per user per month and useful for collaborating and sharing information. The Evernote program is compatible with Windows and Mac desktop operating systems as well as iOS, Android and Windows mobile operating systems. Evernote Web Clipper allows users to click and save part or all of web pages for later reference. Templates are available online, as well as system integrations. The company's search handwriting platform can identify 28 typewritten and 11 handwritten languages, enabling users to locate hand-written notes that they have uploaded to Evernote via scan or photo. The handwriting search tool locates notes when searching a key word. Based in San Diego, California, the firm has an additional office in Zurich, Switzerland.

Evernote offers its employees comprehensive health benefits, life and disability insurance, employee development opportunities and more.

FINANCIAL DATA: *Note: Data for latest year may not have been available at press time.*

In U.S. $	2022	2021	2020	2019	2018	2017
Revenue	26,000,000	25,000,000	223,689,375	229,425,000	241,500,000	230,000,000
R&D Expense						
Operating Income						
Operating Margin %						
SGA Expense						
Net Income						
Operating Cash Flow						
Capital Expenditure						
EBITDA						
Return on Assets %						
Return on Equity %						
Debt to Equity						

CONTACT INFORMATION:

Phone: 408-746-9900   Fax:
Toll-Free:
Address: 305 Walnut St., Redwood City, CA 94063 United States

STOCK TICKER/OTHER:

Stock Ticker: Private   Exchange:
Employees: 300   Fiscal Year Ends:
Parent Company:

SALARIES/BONUSES:

Top Exec. Salary: $ Bonus: $
Second Exec. Salary: $ Bonus: $

OTHER THOUGHTS:

Estimated Female Officers or Directors: 4
Hot Spot for Advancement for Women/Minorities: Y

Everyday Health Inc

www.everydayhealth.com

NAIC Code: 519130

TYPES OF BUSINESS:

Online Health Information Services
Health Care Digital Platform
Communications Services
Marketing Services
Data Analytics
Health Care Information
Wellness Management
Healthcare News and Tools for Professionals

BRANDS/DIVISIONS/AFFILIATES:

j2 Global Inc
Ziff Davis Inc

CONTACTS: *Note: Officers with more than one job title may be intentionally listed here more than once.*

Dan Stone, CEO
Brian Cooper, CFO
Scott Wolf, Executive VP
Jed Savage, Executive VP
Alan Shapiro, General Counsel

GROWTH PLANS/SPECIAL FEATURES:

Everyday Health, Inc. operates a digital marketing and communications platform for health care marketers primarily in the U.S. The platform combines digital content from leading health brands with data and analytics technology to present updated, informed content for users. The content can be accessed by Everyday Health's consumers and professionals anytime, anywhere, across multiple channels, including the web, mobile devices, video and social media. The multi-brand, multi-channel content experience helps with decision making, and allows companies to engage with consumers and healthcare professionals. Its portfolio of properties consists of websites, mobile applications and social media destinations. Consumers use Everyday Health's tools to manage health and wellness needs such as weight loss, exercise, healthy pregnancy, nutrition and medical conditions. The company also provides health care professionals with news, tools and information needed to keep in touch with current industry, legislative and regulatory developments in major medical specialties. More than 890,000 practicing U.S. physicians can be reached, ranging across numerous specialty areas. Everyday Health's website offers links and access to free newsletters, a symptom checker, drug finder, calorie counter, meal planner and recipes. Everyday Health operates as a subsidiary of Ziff Davis, Inc., itself a subsidiary of j2 Global, Inc. Headquartered in New York, USA, Everyday Health has additional offices across the U.S., as well as international offices in the U.K. and India.

FINANCIAL DATA: *Note: Data for latest year may not have been available at press time.*

In U.S. $	2022	2021	2020	2019	2018	2017
Revenue	280,134,400	269,360,000	259,000,000	280,000,000	279,300,000	266,000,000
R&D Expense						
Operating Income						
Operating Margin %						
SGA Expense						
Net Income						
Operating Cash Flow						
Capital Expenditure						
EBITDA						
Return on Assets %						
Return on Equity %						
Debt to Equity						

CONTACT INFORMATION:

Phone: 646-728-9500   Fax: 646-728-9501
Toll-Free:
Address: 114 Fifth Ave., Fl. 15, New York, NY 10011 United States

STOCK TICKER/OTHER:

Stock Ticker: Subsidiary   Exchange:
Employees: 560   Fiscal Year Ends:
Parent Company: j2 Global Inc

SALARIES/BONUSES:

Top Exec. Salary: $ Bonus: $
Second Exec. Salary: $ Bonus: $

OTHER THOUGHTS:

Estimated Female Officers or Directors: 4
Hot Spot for Advancement for Women/Minorities: Y

Expedia Group Inc

www.expedia.com

NAIC Code: 561510

TYPES OF BUSINESS:
Online Travel Services
Online Reservations
Corporate Travel Services
Vacation Packages
Retail Travel Services Kiosks
Destination Activities & Tours
Online Travel Information
Inventory-Based Hotel Room Offerings

BRANDS/DIVISIONS/AFFILIATES:
Brand Expedia
Hotels.com
Expedia Partner Solutions
Vrbo
Egencia
Travelocity
CarRentals.com
VacationRentals.com

GROWTH PLANS/SPECIAL FEATURES:
Expedia is the world's second-largest online travel agency by bookings, offering services for lodging (80% of total 2023 sales), air tickets (3%), rental cars, cruises, in-destination, and other (11%), and advertising revenue (6%). Expedia operates a number of branded travel booking sites, but its three core onlint travel agency brands are Expedia, Hotels.com, and Vrbo. It also has a metasearch brand, Trivago. Transaction fees for online bookings account for the bulk of sales and profits.

Expedia Group offers employees medical, life, AD&D, disability, dental and vision insurance; 401(k); and various employee assistance programs.

CONTACTS: Note: Officers with more than one job title may be intentionally listed here more than once.
Peter Kern, CEO
Eric Hart, CFO
Barry Diller, Chairman of the Board
Lance Soliday, Chief Accounting Officer
Robert Dzielak, Chief Legal Officer

FINANCIAL DATA: Note: Data for latest year may not have been available at press time.

In U.S. $	2022	2021	2020	2019	2018	2017
Revenue	11,667,000,000	8,598,000,000	5,199,000,000	12,067,000,000	11,223,000,000	
R&D Expense	1,181,000,000	1,074,000,000	1,068,000,000	1,263,000,000	1,122,000,000	
Operating Income	1,189,000,000	262,000,000	-1,527,000,000	961,000,000	783,000,000	
Operating Margin %	.10%	.03%	-.29%	.08%	.07%	
SGA Expense	1,420,000,000	1,427,000,000	3,116,000,000	6,867,000,000	6,495,000,000	
Net Income	352,000,000	12,000,000	-2,612,000,000	565,000,000	406,000,000	
Operating Cash Flow	3,440,000,000	3,748,000,000	-3,834,000,000	2,767,000,000	1,975,000,000	
Capital Expenditure	662,000,000	673,000,000	797,000,000	1,160,000,000	878,000,000	
EBITDA	1,607,000,000	1,127,000,000	-1,898,000,000	1,858,000,000	1,676,000,000	
Return on Assets %	.02%	-.01%	-.13%	.03%	.02%	
Return on Equity %	.16%	-.15%	-.98%	.14%	.09%	
Debt to Equity	2.87%	3.93%	5.781	1.19	.91%	

CONTACT INFORMATION:
Phone: 425 679-7200   Fax: 425 564-7240
Toll-Free: 800-397-3342
Address: 1111 Expedia Group Way. W., Seattle, WA 98119 United States

STOCK TICKER/OTHER:
Stock Ticker: EXPE   Exchange: NAS
Employees: 16,500   Fiscal Year Ends: 12/31
Parent Company:

SALARIES/BONUSES:
Top Exec. Salary: $999,999   Bonus: $
Second Exec. Salary: $950,001   Bonus: $

OTHER THOUGHTS:
Estimated Female Officers or Directors: 1
Hot Spot for Advancement for Women/Minorities:

Expensify Inc

NAIC Code: 511210Q

use.expensify.com

TYPES OF BUSINESS:

Computer Software: Accounting, Banking & Financial
Software
Expense Reporting
Receipt Scan

BRANDS/DIVISIONS/AFFILIATES:

SmartScan

GROWTH PLANS/SPECIAL FEATURES:

Expensify Inc is a cloud-based expense management software
platform that helps the smallest to the largest businesses
simplify the way they manage money. Over 12 million people
use Expensify's free features, which include corporate cards,
expense tracking, next-day reimbursement, invoicing, bill pay,
and travel booking in one app.

Expensify offers its employees comprehensive health benefits,
401(k) and company perks.

CONTACTS: *Note: Officers with more than one job title may be intentionally listed here more than once.*

David Barrett, CEO
Ryan Schaffer, CFO
Anuradha Muralidharan, COO

FINANCIAL DATA: *Note: Data for latest year may not have been available at press time.*

In U.S. $	2022	2021	2020	2019	2018	2017
Revenue	169,495,000	142,835,000	88,072,000	80,460,000		
R&D Expense	13,692,000	10,988,000	6,728,000	4,110,000		
Operating Income	-15,232,000	-10,252,000	5,670,000	1,247,000		
Operating Margin %	- .09%	- .07%	.06%			
SGA Expense	108,366,000	88,406,000	43,260,000	43,118,000		
Net Income	-27,009,000	-13,558,000	-1,710,000	1,241,000		
Operating Cash Flow	32,876,000	5,486,000	7,585,000	12,430,000		
Capital Expenditure	2,204,000	7,614,000	4,297,000	4,908,000		
EBITDA	-9,844,000	-5,055,000	8,918,000	4,092,000		
Return on Assets %	- .14%	- .10%	- .02%			
Return on Equity %	- .31%	- .59%				
Debt to Equity	.53%	.69%				

CONTACT INFORMATION:

Phone: 570-123-4567   Fax:
Toll-Free: 800-745-9064
Address: 548 Market St., Ste. 61434, San Francisco, CA 94104 United
States

STOCK TICKER/OTHER:

Stock Ticker: EXFY
Employees: 138
Parent Company:

Exchange: NAS
Fiscal Year Ends: 12/31

SALARIES/BONUSES:

Top Exec. Salary: $1,606,327   Bonus: $
Second Exec. Salary: Bonus: $
$864,750

OTHER THOUGHTS:

Estimated Female Officers or Directors:
Hot Spot for Advancement for Women/Minorities:

Extreme Reach Inc

extremereach.com

NAIC Code: 511210F

TYPES OF BUSINESS:

Computer Software, Multimedia, Graphics & Publishing
Digital Advertising Software
Ad Technology
Advertising Management Solutions
Omnichannel Ad Campaigns
Ad Pitching Solutions
Data Analytics and Insights
Video Workflow Technology Integrations

BRANDS/DIVISIONS/AFFILIATES:

Gamut Capital Management LP

CONTACTS: Note: Officers with more than one job title may be intentionally listed here more than once.

Louisa Wong, CEO
Chandler Bigelow, CFO
Meredith Brace, CMO
Jennifer Wambold, Chief Human Resources Officer
Dan Brackett, CTO

GROWTH PLANS/SPECIAL FEATURES:

Extreme Reach, Inc. provides digital solutions for advertising workflow. The company's technology manages, deploys and tracks TV and video ads across every screen. At the same time, the platform and Extreme Reach teams manage the talent and rights that go along with the ads, wherever they play. The firm's technology platform moves its creative capabilities across media channels, which simplifies the activation and optimization of omnichannel campaigns for brands and agencies via control, visibility and analytic insights. This creative-to-media strategy helps to define and answer supply chain challenges across the marketplace landscape. Its technology solution integrates all forms of linear TV and non-linear video workflow seamlessly with talent payments and rights management. As a result, brands and agencies can optimize campaigns as consumer consumption shifts across TV, CTV, OTT, addressable TV, mobile, desktop and video-on-demand. Extreme Reach is present in 140 countries and capable of communicating with customers across 45 languages, serving thousands of clients worldwide. Headquartered in Massachusetts, USA, the company has office locations throughout the U.S. as well as in Canada, South America, Southwest Asisa/India, Middle East/Africa, Europe, and Australia/New Zealand.

FINANCIAL DATA: Note: Data for latest year may not have been available at press time.

In U.S. $	2022	2021	2020	2019	2018	2017
Revenue						
R&D Expense						
Operating Income						
Operating Margin %						
SGA Expense						
Net Income						
Operating Cash Flow						
Capital Expenditure						
EBITDA						
Return on Assets %						
Return on Equity %						
Debt to Equity						

CONTACT INFORMATION:

Phone: 781-577-2016   Fax: 877-484-8836
Toll-Free: 877-769-9382
Address: 3 Allied Dr., Ste. 130, Dedham, MA 02026 United States

STOCK TICKER/OTHER:

Stock Ticker: Private   Exchange:
Employees: 1,100   Fiscal Year Ends:
Parent Company: Gamut Capital Management LP

SALARIES/BONUSES:

Top Exec. Salary: $ Bonus: $
Second Exec. Salary: $ Bonus: $

OTHER THOUGHTS:

Estimated Female Officers or Directors:
Hot Spot for Advancement for Women/Minorities:

F5 Inc

www.f5.com

NAIC Code: 511210B

TYPES OF BUSINESS:

Computer Software: Network Management (IT), System Testing & Storage
Multi-Cloud
Security
Managed Services
Software
Hardware

BRANDS/DIVISIONS/AFFILIATES:

Volterra

GROWTH PLANS/SPECIAL FEATURES:

F5 is a market leader in the application delivery controller market. The company sells products for security, application performance, and automation. Its three customer verticals are enterprises, service providers, and government entities. Revenue is evenly split between its services business and products business with revenue trending toward products due to software adoption. The Seattle-based firm was incorporated in 1996, has about 6,500 employees, and generates about 55% its revenue within the Americas, 25% in EMEA, and 20% in APAC/Japan.

F5 Networks offers its employees comprehensive health benefits and a variety of assistance programs.

CONTACTS: *Note: Officers with more than one job title may be intentionally listed here more than once.*

Francis Pelzer, CFO
Mika Yamamoto, Chief Marketing Officer
Tom Fountain, Chief Strategy Officer
Geng Lin, Chief Technology Officer
Alan Higginson, Director
Francois Locoh-Donou, Director
Chad Whalen, Executive VP, Divisional
Scot Rogers, Executive VP
Kara Sprague, Executive VP
Haiyan Song, Executive VP
Ana White, Executive VP

FINANCIAL DATA: *Note: Data for latest year may not have been available at press time.*

In U.S. $	2022	2021	2020	2019	2018	2017
Revenue	2,695,845,000	2,603,416,000	2,350,822,000	2,242,447,000	2,161,407,000	
R&D Expense	543,368,000	512,627,000	441,324,000	408,058,000	366,084,000	
Operating Income	411,701,000	394,025,000	400,067,000	518,463,000	609,325,000	
Operating Margin %	.15%	.15%	.17%	.23%	.28%	
SGA Expense	1,201,149,000	1,203,618,000	1,101,544,000	959,349,000	824,517,000	
Net Income	322,160,000	331,241,000	307,441,000	427,734,000	453,689,000	
Operating Cash Flow	442,631,000	645,196,000	660,898,000	747,841,000	761,068,000	
Capital Expenditure	33,624,000	30,651,000	59,940,000	103,542,000	53,465,000	
EBITDA	527,310,000	509,449,000	495,924,000	586,970,000	668,816,000	
Return on Assets %	.06%	.07%	.08%	.14%	.18%	
Return on Equity %	.13%	.14%	.15%	.28%	.36%	
Debt to Equity	.11%	.27%	0.317			

CONTACT INFORMATION:

Phone: 206 272-5555   Fax: 206 272-5556
Toll-Free: 888-882-4447
Address: 801 5th Ave., Seattle, WA 98104 United States

STOCK TICKER/OTHER:

Stock Ticker: FFIV   Exchange: NAS
Employees: 6,524   Fiscal Year Ends: 09/30
Parent Company:

SALARIES/BONUSES:

Top Exec. Salary: $962,000   Bonus: $
Second Exec. Salary: Bonus: $
$582,000

OTHER THOUGHTS:

Estimated Female Officers or Directors: 3
Hot Spot for Advancement for Women/Minorities: Y

FactSet Research Systems Inc

www.factset.com

NAIC Code: 511120A

TYPES OF BUSINESS:

Online Financial & Economic Data
Financial Software
Consulting Services

GROWTH PLANS/SPECIAL FEATURES:

FactSet provides financial data and portfolio analytics to the Global investment community. The company aggregates data from third-party data suppliers, news sources, exchanges, brokerages, and contributors into its workstations. In addition, it provides essential portfolio analytics that companies use to monitor portfolios and address reporting requirements. Buy-side clients account for 82% of FactSet's annual subscription value. In 2015, the company acquired Portware, a provider of trade execution software. In 2017, it acquired BISAM, a risk management and performance measurement provider. In 2022, it completed its purchase of CUSIP Global Services.

BRANDS/DIVISIONS/AFFILIATES:

CONTACTS:
Note: Officers with more than one job title may be intentionally listed here more than once.

F. Snow, CEO
Linda Huber, CFO
Robin Abrams, Chairman of the Board
Gregory Moskoff, Chief Accounting Officer
Rachel Stern, Chief Legal Officer
Gene Fernandez, Chief Technology Officer
Goran Skoko, Executive VP
Robert Robie, Executive VP
Jonathan Reeve, Executive VP
Kristina Karnovsky, Executive VP
Daniel Viens, Executive VP
Helen Shan, Other Executive Officer

FINANCIAL DATA:
Note: Data for latest year may not have been available at press time.

In U.S. $	2022	2021	2020	2019	2018	2017
Revenue	1,843,892,000	1,591,445,000	1,494,111,000	1,435,351,000	1,350,145,000	
R&D Expense						
Operating Income	539,754,000	474,041,000	456,160,000	438,035,000	366,204,000	
Operating Margin %	.29%	.30%	.31%	.31%	.27%	
SGA Expense	433,032,000	331,004,000	342,505,000	333,870,000	324,645,000	
Net Income	396,917,000	399,590,000	372,938,000	352,790,000	267,085,000	
Operating Cash Flow	538,277,000	555,226,000	505,840,000	427,136,000	385,668,000	
Capital Expenditure	51,156,000	61,325,000	77,642,000	59,370,000	33,520,000	
EBITDA	609,006,000	583,139,000	537,762,000	499,052,000	425,409,000	
Return on Assets %	.13%	.19%	.20%	.24%	.19%	
Return on Equity %	.34%	.42%	.48%	.59%	.49%	
Debt to Equity	1.65%	.82%	0.944	0.854	1.09%	

CONTACT INFORMATION:

Phone: 203 810-1000   Fax: 203 810-1001
Toll-Free:
Address: 45 Glover Ave., Norwalk, CT 06850 United States

STOCK TICKER/OTHER:

Stock Ticker: FDS   Exchange: NYS
Employees: 12,237   Fiscal Year Ends: 08/31
Parent Company:

SALARIES/BONUSES:

Top Exec. Salary: $746,154   Bonus: $
Second Exec. Salary: Bonus: $
$573,077

OTHER THOUGHTS:

Estimated Female Officers or Directors: 3
Hot Spot for Advancement for Women/Minorities: Y

Fanatics Inc

www.fanaticsinc.com

NAIC Code: 454110

TYPES OF BUSINESS:

Electronic Shopping of Licensed Sports Merchandise
Ecommerce
Vertical Commerce
Licensed Sports Merchandise
Digital Sports Platform
Sports Product Design and Manufacturing
Ecommerce Supply Chain and Logistics
Betting and Gaming Databases

BRANDS/DIVISIONS/AFFILIATES:

Fanatics Commerce
Fanatics Collectibles
Fanatics Betting & Gaming

CONTACTS: *Note: Officers with more than one job title may be intentionally listed here more than once.*

Michael Rubin, CEO
Tucker Kain, Chief Strategy Officer
Jamie Davis, Pres.
Glenn H. Schiffman, CFO
Meier Raivich, Exec. VP-Global Communications
Orlando Ashford, Chief People Officer
Kelly Guo, Chief Information Security Officer
Jack Boyle, Pres., Merch.
Mitch Trager, Chief Strategy Officer
Meier Raivich, VP-Branding
Gary Gertzog, Exec. VP-Bus. Affairs

GROWTH PLANS/SPECIAL FEATURES:

Fanatics, Inc. is an online retailer of licensed sports merchandise. The firm's global digital sports platform also features NFTs/digital collectibles, sports betting and iGaming, trading cards and more. Fanatics has relationships with over 900 properties and includes many prominent brands. Subsidiary Fanatics Commerce comprises an innovative vertical commerce business strategy that allows the company to swiftly design, manufacture and distribute high-quality fan gear, jerseys, lifestyle and streetwear products, as well as headwear and hardgoods. This division offers a broad assortment of first and third-party fan merchandise and memorabilia, whether manufactured in-house, sourced from fan apparel brands or available via drop-ship. Fanatics Collectibles implements a vertical commerce model, an innovative technology platform and an agile supply chain to offer a mobile-first consumer brand. Its operations encompass technology, on-demand manufacturing and logistics. Fanatics Betting & Gaming combines global databases of sports fans, creative marketing, social strategies, technology and brand recognition. Fanatics, Inc. is headquartered in Florida, with international headquarter locations in the U.K. and Japan.

FINANCIAL DATA: *Note: Data for latest year may not have been available at press time.*

In U.S. $	2022	2021	2020	2019	2018	2017
Revenue	6,300,000,000	4,000,000,000	2,887,500,000	2,500,000,000	2,475,375,000	2,415,000,000
R&D Expense						
Operating Income						
Operating Margin %						
SGA Expense						
Net Income						
Operating Cash Flow						
Capital Expenditure						
EBITDA						
Return on Assets %						
Return on Equity %						
Debt to Equity						

CONTACT INFORMATION:

Phone: 904-421-1897   Fax:
Toll-Free: 877-833-7397
Address: 8100 Nations Way, Jacksonville, FL 32256 United States

STOCK TICKER/OTHER:

Stock Ticker: Private   Exchange:
Employees: 18,200   Fiscal Year Ends: 12/31
Parent Company:

SALARIES/BONUSES:

Top Exec. Salary: $ Bonus: $
Second Exec. Salary: $ Bonus: $

OTHER THOUGHTS:

Estimated Female Officers or Directors:
Hot Spot for Advancement for Women/Minorities:

Fandango Inc

www.fandango.com

NAIC Code: 454110

TYPES OF BUSINESS:

Online Movie Ticket Sales
Digital Movie Ticket Sales
Movie and Television Programming Information
Movie and TV Show Trailer Content
Original Video and Home Entertainment Services
Entertainment Reviews
On-Demand Streaming Services
Advertising and Business Development Solutions

BRANDS/DIVISIONS/AFFILIATES:

Comcast Corporation
Warner Bros Discovery
Fandango
MovieTickets.com
Flixter
Rotten Tomatoes
Rotten Tomatoes Movieclips
Vudu

CONTACTS: Note: Officers with more than one job title may be intentionally listed here more than once.

Will McIntosh, Pres.
Justin Tupper, Sr. VP-Content & Strategy
Jason Cuthbertson, CFO
Jody Vogelaar, CMO
Simeon Hardy, VP-Human Resources
Jessica Yi, Chief Prod. Officer
Dana Henry Benson, Exec. Dir.-Comm.

GROWTH PLANS/SPECIAL FEATURES:

Fandango, Inc. offers a digital network for accessing information on movies and television programming, serving more than 50 million unique visitors every month. The firm's platform offers movie and TV information, movie ticketing, trailers and original video, as well as home entertainment. The company's portfolio features online ticketers Fandango, MovieTickets.com and Flixster; entertainment review site Rotten Tomatoes; and Rotten Tomatoes Movieclips, a movie trailer and content channel on YouTube. Fandango's on-demand streaming services, Vudu, offers over 200,000 new release and catalog movies, as well as next-day TV shoes to more than 200 million connected, over-the-top (OTT) and mobile devices. Advertising and business development opportunities are provided by Fandango, with a link for related online proposal forms obtainable on the fandango.com website. Affiliate program information can also be obtained on the site. Gift cards are available. Fandango is majority-owned (75%) by Comcast Corporation and 25-%-owned by Warner Bros. Discovery.

Fandango offers its employees health benefits and related options, a 401(k) and company perks.

FINANCIAL DATA: Note: Data for latest year may not have been available at press time.

In U.S. $	2022	2021	2020	2019	2018	2017
Revenue						
R&D Expense						
Operating Income						
Operating Margin %						
SGA Expense						
Net Income						
Operating Cash Flow						
Capital Expenditure						
EBITDA						
Return on Assets %						
Return on Equity %						
Debt to Equity						

CONTACT INFORMATION:

Phone: 310-451-7690   Fax: 310-451-7861
Toll-Free: 855-646-2580
Address: 407 N. Maple Dr., Ste. 300, Beverly Hills, CA 90210 United States

STOCK TICKER/OTHER:

Stock Ticker: Subsidiary
Employees: 425
Parent Company: Comcast Corporation

Exchange:
Fiscal Year Ends: 01/31

SALARIES/BONUSES:

Top Exec. Salary: $ Bonus: $
Second Exec. Salary: $ Bonus: $

OTHER THOUGHTS:

Estimated Female Officers or Directors: 2
Hot Spot for Advancement for Women/Minorities: Y

Farfetch Limited

www.farfetch.com

NAIC Code: 454110

TYPES OF BUSINESS:

Electronic Shopping
Ecommerce
Fashion
Designers

GROWTH PLANS/SPECIAL FEATURES:

Farfetch is an online platform connecting sellers and buyers of personal luxury goods. It was founded in 2008. The company partners with over 1,000 luxury goods sellers to offer their inventory on the platform. When making the retailers' stock available to almost a million active customers, the company charges a cut of around 30% (third-party take rate). The company operates digital marketplace platform Farfetch, Browns stores and acquired branded company New Guard Group.

BRANDS/DIVISIONS/AFFILIATES:

Farfetch.com
Farfetch Second Life

CONTACTS: Note: Officers with more than one job title may be intentionally listed here more than once.

Jose Neves, CEO
Luis Teixeira, COO
Elliot Jordan, CFO
Giorgio Belloli, CCO
Sian Keane, Chief People Officer
Cipriano Sousa, CTO
Jose Neves, Chmn.

FINANCIAL DATA: Note: Data for latest year may not have been available at press time.

In U.S. $	2022	2021	2020	2019	2018	2017
Revenue	2,316,680,000	2,256,608,000	1,673,922,000	1,021,037,000	602,384,000	385,966,000
R&D Expense						
Operating Income	-710,428,000	-464,457,000	-580,555,000	-429,575,000	-173,316,000	-91,194,000
Operating Margin %						
SGA Expense	1,400,828,000	1,229,770,000	1,134,260,000	775,830,000	448,229,000	284,980,000
Net Income	359,287,000	1,466,487,000	-3,333,171,000	-405,109,000	-155,575,000	-112,275,000
Operating Cash Flow	-536,598,000	-282,154,000	116,315,000	-126,642,000	-116,205,000	-59,320,000
Capital Expenditure	170,870,000	196,561,000	120,944,000	112,497,000	72,115,000	31,613,000
EBITDA	754,546,000	1,802,117,000	-3,061,480,000	-270,492,000	-129,343,000	-80,650,000
Return on Assets %						
Return on Equity %						
Debt to Equity						

CONTACT INFORMATION:

Phone: 44-20-7549-5400   Fax:
Toll-Free:
Address: 211 Old St., The Bower, 4/Fl, London, EC1V 9NR United Kingdom

STOCK TICKER/OTHER:

Stock Ticker: FTCHF   Exchange: PINX
Employees: 6,728   Fiscal Year Ends: 12/31
Parent Company:

SALARIES/BONUSES:

Top Exec. Salary: $ Bonus: $
Second Exec. Salary: $ Bonus: $

OTHER THOUGHTS:

Estimated Female Officers or Directors:
Hot Spot for Advancement for Women/Minorities:

Fast AF Inc

www.fast.co

NAIC Code: 511210M

TYPES OF BUSINESS:

Computer Software: E-Commerce, Web Analytics & Applications
Management
Ecommerce Payment Solutions
Online and Mobile App Shopping
Fraud Detection Technology
Security Technology
Micro Fulfillment Centers

BRANDS/DIVISIONS/AFFILIATES:

Fast Login
Fast Checkout
Darkstore

GROWTH PLANS/SPECIAL FEATURES:

Fast AF, Inc. offers an online and mobile platform, Fast, for managing transactions from a single dashboard. The firm's login and checkout features enable a one-click sign-in and ecommerce purchase experience, making it easy for consumers to buy products and for merchants to sell them. No passwords required. Fast products work on any browser, device or platform. After users sign up for Fast, they can start purchasing items from ecommerce sites that have installed Fast's checkout platform. The company has invested in fraud detection, payment processing and security technology, which enables the selling/purchase process to occur swiftly and securely. Fast offers a zero-fraud guarantee and uses micro fulfillment centers, enabling the company's two-hour delivery service.

CONTACTS: *Note: Officers with more than one job title may be intentionally listed here more than once.*

Lee Hnetinka, CEO

FINANCIAL DATA: *Note: Data for latest year may not have been available at press time.*

In U.S. $	2022	2021	2020	2019	2018	2017
Revenue						
R&D Expense						
Operating Income						
Operating Margin %						
SGA Expense						
Net Income						
Operating Cash Flow						
Capital Expenditure						
EBITDA						
Return on Assets %						
Return on Equity %						
Debt to Equity						

CONTACT INFORMATION:

Phone: 415 548-4827   Fax:
Toll-Free:
Address: 349 9th St., San Francisco, CA 94103 United States

STOCK TICKER/OTHER:

Stock Ticker: Private   Exchange:
Employees: Fiscal Year Ends:
Parent Company:

SALARIES/BONUSES:

Top Exec. Salary: $ Bonus: $
Second Exec. Salary: $ Bonus: $

OTHER THOUGHTS:

Estimated Female Officers or Directors:
Hot Spot for Advancement for Women/Minorities:

Fastly Inc

NAIC Code: 511210M

www.fastly.com

TYPES OF BUSINESS:

Computer Software, E-Commerce & Web Analytics
Software Development
Content Delivery Network
Edge
Cloud

BRANDS/DIVISIONS/AFFILIATES:

Signal Sciences

GROWTH PLANS/SPECIAL FEATURES:

Fastly operates a content delivery network, which is necessary for entities to provide faster and more reliable online content. Fastly's strategy differs from traditional CDNs, which focus on locating servers in as many locations as possible to store copies of files that consumers most use. Fastly is in far fewer sites than traditional CDNs, but it houses servers in the most network-dense data centers. Instead of simply storing static content, it allows its customers to program on its platform, enabling edge computing and better service of the more dynamic content that was traditionally not well served by CDNs. Fastly gears its service to the largest, most sophisticated enterprises rather than small companies and generated nearly three fourths of its revenue in the United States in 2022.

CONTACTS: *Note: Officers with more than one job title may be intentionally listed here more than once.*

Joshua Bixby, CEO
Ronald Kisling, CFO
Artur Bergman, Chairman of the Board
Paul Luongo, General Counsel
Brett Shirk, Other Executive Officer

FINANCIAL DATA: *Note: Data for latest year may not have been available at press time.*

In U.S. $	2022	2021	2020	2019	2018	2017
Revenue	432,725,000	354,330,000	290,874,000	200,462,000	144,563,000	104,900,000
R&D Expense	155,308,000	126,859,000	74,814,000	46,492,000	34,618,000	28,989,000
Operating Income	-246,199,000	-219,021,000	-107,212,000	-46,548,000	-29,138,000	-31,030,000
Operating Margin %	-.57%	-.62%	-.37%	-.23%	-.20%	
SGA Expense	300,672,000	279,490,000	203,265,000	112,196,000	73,584,000	58,269,000
Net Income	-190,774,000	-222,697,000	-95,932,000	-51,550,000	-30,935,000	-32,450,000
Operating Cash Flow	-69,632,000	-38,482,000	-19,916,000	-31,303,000	-16,985,000	-25,861,000
Capital Expenditure	80,318,000	50,387,000	37,511,000	20,100,000	19,657,000	13,248,000
EBITDA	-120,478,000	-167,346,000	-80,806,000	-29,269,000	-15,540,000	-21,484,000
Return on Assets %	-.09%	-.13%	-.12%	-.21%	-.22%	
Return on Equity %	-.19%	-.21%	-.15%	-.82%		
Debt to Equity	.82%	1.00%	0.056	0.098		

CONTACT INFORMATION:

Phone: 844 432-7859   Fax:
Toll-Free:
Address: 475 Brannan St., Ste. 300, San Francisco, CA 94107 United States

STOCK TICKER/OTHER:

Stock Ticker: FSLY
Employees: 1,112
Parent Company:

Exchange: NYS
Fiscal Year Ends: 12/31

SALARIES/BONUSES:

Top Exec. Salary: $200,000   Bonus: $1,000,000
Second Exec. Salary: $600,000   Bonus: $

OTHER THOUGHTS:

Estimated Female Officers or Directors:
Hot Spot for Advancement for Women/Minorities:

Fiserv Inc

www.fiserv.com

NAIC Code: 522320

TYPES OF BUSINESS:
Financial Services
Investment Services
Online Banking
Electronic Billing & Payment
Software Applications & Investment Management Solutions

GROWTH PLANS/SPECIAL FEATURES:
Fiserv is a leading provider of core processing and complementary services, such as electronic funds transfer, payment processing, and loan processing, for U.S. banks and credit unions, with a focus on small and midsize banks. Through the merger with First Data in 2019, Fiserv also provides payment processing services for merchants. About 10% of the company's revenue is generated internationally.

BRANDS/DIVISIONS/AFFILIATES:
First Data
STAR

CONTACTS: Note: Officers with more than one job title may be intentionally listed here more than once.
Frank Bisignano, CEO
Robert Hau, CFO
Denis OLeary, Chairman of the Board
Kenneth Best, Chief Accounting Officer
Lynn McCreary, Chief Legal Officer
Guy Chiarello, COO
Christopher Foskett, Executive VP, Divisional
Devin McGranahan, Other Corporate Officer
Suzan Kereere, Other Executive Officer
Byron Vielehr, Other Executive Officer

FINANCIAL DATA: Note: Data for latest year may not have been available at press time.

In U.S. $	2022	2021	2020	2019	2018	2017
Revenue	17,737,000,000	16,226,000,000	14,852,000,000			
R&D Expense						
Operating Income	3,686,000,000	2,288,000,000	1,388,000,000			
Operating Margin %						
SGA Expense	6,059,000,000	5,810,000,000	5,652,000,000			
Net Income	2,530,000,000	1,334,000,000	958,000,000			
Operating Cash Flow	4,618,000,000	4,034,000,000	4,147,000,000			
Capital Expenditure	1,479,000,000	1,160,000,000	900,000,000			
EBITDA	6,828,000,000	5,558,000,000	5,097,000,000			
Return on Assets %						
Return on Equity %						
Debt to Equity						

CONTACT INFORMATION:
Phone: 262 879-5000   Fax: 262 879-5275
Toll-Free: 800-872-7882
Address: 255 Fiserv Dr., Brookfield, WI 53045 United States

STOCK TICKER/OTHER:
Stock Ticker: FI   Exchange: NYS
Employees: 41,000   Fiscal Year Ends: 12/31
Parent Company:

SALARIES/BONUSES:
Top Exec. Salary: $1,320,000   Bonus: $
Second Exec. Salary: Bonus: $
$1,000,000

OTHER THOUGHTS:
Estimated Female Officers or Directors: 1
Hot Spot for Advancement for Women/Minorities:

Sales, profits and employees may be estimates. Financial information, benefits and other data can change quickly and may vary from those stated here.

Flatiron Health Inc

www.flatiron.com

NAIC Code: 511210D

TYPES OF BUSINESS:

Computer Software, Healthcare & Biotechnology
Healthcare Technology
Data Gathering
Data Storage
Research and Development
Healthcare Software Solutions
Connected Data Platform

BRANDS/DIVISIONS/AFFILIATES:

Roche Holding AG

CONTACTS: *Note: Officers with more than one job title may be intentionally listed here more than once.*

Carolyn Starrett, CEO
Bruce Gottlieb, COO
Ara Tucker, Chief People Officer
Jamie Lopez, CMO

GROWTH PLANS/SPECIAL FEATURES:

Flatiron Health, Inc. is a healthcare technology company engaged in building data pipelines and structured databases for oncology, as well as healthcare markets. The company's goal is to make a difference in the fight against cancer, and therefore focuses on researching and developing software solutions that seamlessly connect cancer centers, clinics, medical centers and hospitals, gathering and storing disconnected, unstructured clinical data into a connected, structured platform. With this data strategy, Flatiron and the healthcare industry can improve treatment, accelerate research and better serve customers and cancer patients. Flatiron Health partners with hundreds of cancer centers, global developers of oncology therapeutics and researchers and regulators throughout the world. The firm's employees consist of software engineers, data scientists, biostatisticians, epidemiologists, health professionals and other experts. Flatiron partners with the U.S. Food and Drug Administration, the National Comprehensive Cancer Network and others. Insights from its database have helped expand treatment alternatives for people with gastric, esophageal and breast cancer. The firm is a subsidiary of Roche Holding AG, a world-leading healthcare and biotechnology company. Headquartered in New York, Flatiron has an additional office in San Francisco, California.

FINANCIAL DATA: *Note: Data for latest year may not have been available at press time.*

In U.S. $	2022	2021	2020	2019	2018	2017
Revenue						
R&D Expense						
Operating Income						
Operating Margin %						
SGA Expense						
Net Income						
Operating Cash Flow						
Capital Expenditure						
EBITDA						
Return on Assets %						
Return on Equity %						
Debt to Equity						

CONTACT INFORMATION:

Phone: 888-662-6367   Fax:
Toll-Free:
Address: 233 Spring St., New York, NY 10013 United States

STOCK TICKER/OTHER:

Stock Ticker: Subsidiary   Exchange:
Employees: 950   Fiscal Year Ends:
Parent Company: Roche Holding AG

SALARIES/BONUSES:

Top Exec. Salary: $ Bonus: $
Second Exec. Salary: $ Bonus: $

OTHER THOUGHTS:

Estimated Female Officers or Directors:
Hot Spot for Advancement for Women/Minorities:

Sales, profits and employees may be estimates. Financial information, benefits and other data can change quickly and may vary from those stated here.

Flipkart Internet Private Limited

www.flipkart.com

NAIC Code: 454110

TYPES OF BUSINESS:

Electronic Retailing
Online Apparel Sales
Ecommerce
Payment Solutions
Delivery Solutions

BRANDS/DIVISIONS/AFFILIATES:

Walmart Inc
Flipkart First

CONTACTS: *Note: Officers with more than one job title may be intentionally listed here more than once.*

Kalyan Krishnamurthy, CEO
Amod Malviya, Sr. VP

GROWTH PLANS/SPECIAL FEATURES:

Flipkart Internet Private Limited is an ecommerce firm based in India. The firm began as an online book dealer in 2007, but soon expanded its product base to include a myriad of other products such as electronic goods, movies, clothing, footwear, watches, beauty and personal care, jewelry, home appliances and stationary products. The company boasts a marketplace of over 150 million products across more than 80 categories. Its 500 million registered users clock millions of daily visits. In addition to regular payment options, such as credit cards and internet banking, Flipkart also offers cash on delivery (CoD). CoD allows a customer to order a product online and then pay for it in cash when the item is delivered. Flipkart offers an in-day guarantee and a same-day guarantee in select cities. The firm also provides a paid annual subscription service, Flipkart Plus. Member benefits include additional super coins (points towards rewards), incentives to use super coins, a welcome reward of 500 super coins and early access to sales events. Members may also choose to upgrade their membership for additional rewards

FINANCIAL DATA: *Note: Data for latest year may not have been available at press time.*

In U.S. $	2022	2021	2020	2019	2018	2017
Revenue	6,765,262,496	5,909,255,601	4,974,700,000	4,445,900,000	4,636,970,000	3,336,940,000
R&D Expense						
Operating Income						
Operating Margin %						
SGA Expense						
Net Income	-444,495,830	-333,236,385	-452,768,000	-553,815,000	-7,209,720,000	-318,164,000
Operating Cash Flow						
Capital Expenditure						
EBITDA						
Return on Assets %						
Return on Equity %						
Debt to Equity						

CONTACT INFORMATION:

Phone: 91-80-4274-9527   Fax: 91-80-0793-1547
Toll-Free: 800-208-9898
Address: Outer Ring Rd., Devarabeesanahalli Village, Bengaluru, Karnataka, 560103 India

STOCK TICKER/OTHER:

Stock Ticker: Subsidiary   Exchange:
Employees: 33,000   Fiscal Year Ends: 03/31
Parent Company: Walmart Inc

SALARIES/BONUSES:

Top Exec. Salary: $ Bonus: $
Second Exec. Salary: $ Bonus: $

OTHER THOUGHTS:

Estimated Female Officers or Directors:
Hot Spot for Advancement for Women/Minorities:

Forescout Technologies Inc

www.forescout.com

NAIC Code: 511210E

TYPES OF BUSINESS:

Computer Software, Network Security, Managed Access, Digital ID, Cybersecurity & Anti-Virus
Network Security Solutions
Cybersecurity Solutions
IT and Internet of Things Security Solutions
Cyber Risk Insights
Automated Cybersecurity Monitoring
Security Software Development
Security Technology

BRANDS/DIVISIONS/AFFILIATES:

Advent International Corporation
eyeSight
eyeInspect
eyeSegment
eyeControl
eyeExtend
XDR
Crosspoint Capital

CONTACTS: *Note: Officers with more than one job title may be intentionally listed here more than once.*

Barry Mainz, CEO
Ellen Sundra, Chief Customer Officer
Yehezkel Yeshurun, Chairman of the Board
Rob Gillespie, CFO
Kevin O'Leary, Chief Product Officer
Duncan Macmurdy, Chief People Officer
Sloane Stricker, CIO
Michael DeCesare, Director
David Dewalt, Director
Pedro Abreu, Other Executive Officer
George McTaggart, CMO

GROWTH PLANS/SPECIAL FEATURES:

Forescout Technologies, Inc. develops network security solutions that enable enterprises and government organizations to monitor and mitigate security exposures and cyberattacks. The firm's products and solutions deliver automated cybersecurity across digital platforms and asset types, including information technology (IT), Internet of Things (IoT), operational technology (OT) and Internet of Medial Things (IoMT). Through these technologies, Forescout also manages cyber risk via data-powered insights. The Forescout Continuum platform offers complete coverage security coverage and visibility through three steps: discover, knowing how many assets are connected to the network; assess, continually assessing compliance and risk without requiring agents across all cyber assets, and integrated with third-party cybersecurity products to enhance native assessment capabilities; and govern, for scaling and governing the entire digital terrain by shrinking the attack surface and minimizing the impact of breaches via pinpoint controls that proactively remediate and segmentize. Platform product lines include eyeSight, eyeInspect, eyeSegment, eyeControl, eyeExtend, XDR and risk/exposure management. Industries served include financial services, government, healthcare, energy and utilities, oil and gas, manufacturing and education. Based in California, the firm has global locations throughout the Americas, Europe, the Middle East, and Asia-Pacific.

FINANCIAL DATA: *Note: Data for latest year may not have been available at press time.*

In U.S. $	2022	2021	2020	2019	2018	2017
Revenue	382,500,000	367,786,684	353,641,042	336,800,992	297,651,008	220,871,008
R&D Expense						
Operating Income						
Operating Margin %						
SGA Expense						
Net Income				-118,535,000	-74,836,000	-91,205,000
Operating Cash Flow						
Capital Expenditure						
EBITDA						
Return on Assets %						
Return on Equity %						
Debt to Equity						

CONTACT INFORMATION:

Phone: 408-213-3191   Fax: 408-371-2284
Toll-Free: 866-377-8771
Address: 300 Santana Row, Ste. 400, San Jose, CA 95128 United States

SALARIES/BONUSES:

Top Exec. Salary: $ Bonus: $
Second Exec. Salary: $ Bonus: $

STOCK TICKER/OTHER:

Stock Ticker: Private   Exchange:
Employees: 1,217   Fiscal Year Ends: 12/31
Parent Company:

OTHER THOUGHTS:

Estimated Female Officers or Directors:
Hot Spot for Advancement for Women/Minorities:

Forrester Research Inc

www.forrester.com

NAIC Code: 541910

TYPES OF BUSINESS:

Market Research
Consulting & Advisory
Workshops & Events

BRANDS/DIVISIONS/AFFILIATES:

Research
Forrester Wave (The)
Age of the Customer Research
Forrester Connect
Leadership Boards
ForecastView
FeedbackNow

GROWTH PLANS/SPECIAL FEATURES:

Forrester Research Inc is a United States-based company that provides independent research, data, and advisory services. It operates through the following segments: The Research segment develops and delivers research, connect, and analytics products; The consulting segment includes the revenues and the related costs of the company's consulting organization, and the Events segment is engaged in developing and hosting in-person and virtual events.

Forrester employees receive medical and dental insurance, retirement savings and employee perks, which may be differentiated by location.

CONTACTS: Note: Officers with more than one job title may be intentionally listed here more than once.

George Colony, CEO
Michael Doyle, CFO
Scott Chouinard, Chief Accounting Officer
Mike Kasparian, Chief Information Officer
Ryan Darrah, Chief Legal Officer
Shirley Macbeth, Chief Marketing Officer
Kelley Hippler, Other Executive Officer
Carrie Fanlo, Other Executive Officer
Sherri Kottmann, Other Executive Officer
Steven Peltzman, Other Executive Officer

FINANCIAL DATA: Note: Data for latest year may not have been available at press time.

In U.S. $	2022	2021	2020	2019	2018	2017
Revenue	537,787,000	494,315,000	448,984,000	461,697,000	357,575,000	337,673,000
R&D Expense						
Operating Income	41,989,000	38,976,000	21,954,000	7,873,000	26,212,000	27,549,000
Operating Margin %	.08%	.08%	.05%	.02%	.07%	.08%
SGA Expense	249,595,000	229,005,000	216,569,000	225,907,000	175,744,000	165,823,000
Net Income	21,806,000	24,844,000	9,990,000	-9,570,000	15,380,000	15,140,000
Operating Cash Flow	39,425,000	107,067,000	47,754,000	48,406,000	38,418,000	37,493,000
Capital Expenditure	5,663,000	10,745,000	8,905,000	11,890,000	5,049,000	7,861,000
EBITDA	70,126,000	73,347,000	61,232,000	42,238,000	32,642,000	34,800,000
Return on Assets %	.03%	.04%	.02%	-.02%	.04%	.04%
Return on Equity %	.10%	.13%	.06%	-.06%	.11%	.10%
Debt to Equity	.45%	.69%	0.892	1.191		

CONTACT INFORMATION:

Phone: 617 613-5730   Fax:
Toll-Free:
Address: 60 Acorn Park Dr., Cambridge, MA 02140 United States

STOCK TICKER/OTHER:

Stock Ticker: FORR   Exchange: NAS
Employees: 2,033   Fiscal Year Ends: 12/31
Parent Company:

SALARIES/BONUSES:

Top Exec. Salary: $597,896   Bonus: $
Second Exec. Salary: Bonus: $
$428,750

OTHER THOUGHTS:

Estimated Female Officers or Directors: 3
Hot Spot for Advancement for Women/Minorities: Y

Fredericks of Hollywood

Fredericks.com

NAIC Code: 454110

TYPES OF BUSINESS:

Lingerie & Sleepwear
Loungewear and Intimate Apparel
Apparel Manufacturing and Marketing
Ecommerce

GROWTH PLANS/SPECIAL FEATURES:

Frederick's of Hollywood, a subsidiary of Authentic Brands Group, LLC, operates and sells the Fredrick's of Hollywood brand of merchandise through its global ecommerce platform, Fredericks.com. The firm manufactures, markets and sells an extensive line of ladies' intimate apparel. Product categories include lingerie, bras, panties, plus size, ultra-sexy, sleepwear, shapewear, corsets and more. Some of the company's brands and trademarks include Hollywood Exxtreme, Hollywood Heartthrob and Pleasure State. Services offered by Frederick's of Hollywood include order status, a frequently-asked questions page, returns information, gift cards and more.

BRANDS/DIVISIONS/AFFILIATES:

Authentic Brands Group LLC
Fredericks.com
Hollywood Exxtreme
Hollywood Heartthrob
Pleasure State

CONTACTS: *Note: Officers with more than one job title may be intentionally listed here more than once.*

Candice Cuoco, Creative Director
Jamie Salter, Chmn.- Authentic Brands

FINANCIAL DATA: *Note: Data for latest year may not have been available at press time.*

In U.S. $	2022	2021	2020	2019	2018	2017
Revenue	86,500,000	60,394,621	58,071,751	59,560,770	61,087,969	64,303,125
R&D Expense						
Operating Income						
Operating Margin %						
SGA Expense						
Net Income						
Operating Cash Flow						
Capital Expenditure						
EBITDA						
Return on Assets %						
Return on Equity %						
Debt to Equity						

CONTACT INFORMATION:

Phone: 212-760-2410   Fax:
Toll-Free:
Address: 1411 Broadway Fl. 4, New York, NY 10018 United States

STOCK TICKER/OTHER:

Stock Ticker: Private   Exchange:
Employees: 902   Fiscal Year Ends: 06/30
Parent Company: Authentic Brands Group LLC

SALARIES/BONUSES:

Top Exec. Salary: $ Bonus: $
Second Exec. Salary: $ Bonus: $

OTHER THOUGHTS:

Estimated Female Officers or Directors:
Hot Spot for Advancement for Women/Minorities: Y

Free People

NAIC Code: 454110

TYPES OF BUSINESS:

Women's Clothing Online Stores
Women's Apparel
Retail Stores
Ecommerce
Beauty Products
Wellness Products
Product Design and Manufacture

BRANDS/DIVISIONS/AFFILIATES:

Urban Outfitters Inc

GROWTH PLANS/SPECIAL FEATURES:

Free People is a specialty clothing brand featuring trends and vintage collections for women. The eclectic look consists of quality apparel, shoes and accessories that invoke attributes of femininity, spirit and creativity with its design. Free People also offers intimate apparel, swimwear and beauty/wellness products. Free People designs and sews its apparel, which is distributed globally via direct channels such as Free People digital sites and mobile applications, as well as specialty boutiques, top department stores, and the brand's own freestanding retail locations in the U.S. and in London, U.K. Free People operates as a subsidiary of Urban Outfitters, Inc.

Parent Urban Outfitters offers Free People employees health and financial planning benefits, as well as employee assistance programs and company perks.

CONTACTS: *Note: Officers with more than one job title may be intentionally listed here more than once.*

Sheila Harrington, Global CEO

FINANCIAL DATA: *Note: Data for latest year may not have been available at press time.*

In U.S. $	2022	2021	2020	2019	2018	2017
Revenue						
R&D Expense						
Operating Income						
Operating Margin %						
SGA Expense						
Net Income						
Operating Cash Flow						
Capital Expenditure						
EBITDA						
Return on Assets %						
Return on Equity %						
Debt to Equity						

CONTACT INFORMATION:

Phone: 215-454-5000   Fax: 800-436-2618
Toll-Free: 800 309-1500
Address: 5000 S. Broad St., B25, Philadelphia, PA 19112-1495 United States

STOCK TICKER/OTHER:

Stock Ticker: Subsidiary   Exchange:
Employees: 4,633   Fiscal Year Ends:
Parent Company: Urban Outfitters Inc

SALARIES/BONUSES:

Top Exec. Salary: $ Bonus: $
Second Exec. Salary: $ Bonus: $

OTHER THOUGHTS:

Estimated Female Officers or Directors:
Hot Spot for Advancement for Women/Minorities:

FreshDirect LLC

www.freshdirect.com

NAIC Code: 454110

TYPES OF BUSINESS:

Online Grocery Sales
Home Grocery Delivery
Catering
Online Ordering
Business Grocery Delivery
Processing Facility

BRANDS/DIVISIONS/AFFILIATES:

CONTACTS: *Note: Officers with more than one job title may be intentionally listed here more than once.*

David McInerney, CEO
Tina Bourbeau, Exec. Chef
Amaury Garcia, Mgr.-Sortation

GROWTH PLANS/SPECIAL FEATURES:

FreshDirect, LLC is an online retail grocery business serving customers in New York City metropolitan area, with seasonal service to eastern Long Island and the New Jersey shore. FreshDirect offers fresh food and grocery items, including fruits and vegetables, meat, seafood, deli items, cheese, dairy, coffee, tea, bakery goods, pasta and frozen food as well as kosher and gluten free foods, local and organic produce, health and beauty items and wine. It also provides catering services and a full line of ready-to-heat meals prepared by its on-staff chefs. FreshDirect owns and operates a processing facility, which enables the firm to process and ship fresh meats, produce and dairy products quickly and efficiently. The company is also able to offer lower prices, on average lower than traditional retail grocers, due to the lack of intermediary distribution channels. There is a minimum order amount for home deliveries, and each order is charged a delivery fee depending on location. For offices, there is a minimum order amount of 50$ and a delivery fee. Customers can also pick up their orders at the facility. FreshDirect offers gift cards. Getir a Turkish deliver company owns FreshDirect.

FreshDirect offers its employees health coverage, learning and development opportunities and company perks.

FINANCIAL DATA: *Note: Data for latest year may not have been available at press time.*

In U.S. $	2022	2021	2020	2019	2018	2017
Revenue	1,144,000,000	1,100,000,000	1,100,000,000	678,037,500	645,750,000	615,000,000
R&D Expense						
Operating Income						
Operating Margin %						
SGA Expense						
Net Income						
Operating Cash Flow						
Capital Expenditure						
EBITDA						
Return on Assets %						
Return on Equity %						
Debt to Equity						

CONTACT INFORMATION:

Phone: 718-928-1000   Fax: 718-433-0648
Toll-Free: 866-283-7374
Address: 2 Saint Anns Ave., Bronx, NY 10454 United States

STOCK TICKER/OTHER:

Stock Ticker: Subsidiary   Exchange:
Employees: 3,400   Fiscal Year Ends: 12/31
Parent Company: Getir

SALARIES/BONUSES:

Top Exec. Salary: $ Bonus: $
Second Exec. Salary: $ Bonus: $

OTHER THOUGHTS:

Estimated Female Officers or Directors: 1
Hot Spot for Advancement for Women/Minorities:

Freshly Inc

www.freshly.com

NAIC Code: 454110

TYPES OF BUSINESS:

Meal Delivery Service
Prepared Meals
Delivered Meals
Fresh Food
Online Ordering
Mobile App Ordering
Business and Partnership Meals

BRANDS/DIVISIONS/AFFILIATES:

Nestle SA
FreshlyFit
FreshlyWell

CONTACTS: Note: Officers with more than one job title may be intentionally listed here more than once.

Craig Hurlbert, CO-CEO
Travis Joyner, CO-CEO

GROWTH PLANS/SPECIAL FEATURES:

Freshly, Inc. offers an online platform from which customers can order healthy meals prepared by local chefs and delivered to their home or business. The firm's plans range from six to 18 per week. The more meals ordered, the less they are per meal. Plans can be paused, canceled or changed at any time. Menus are updated weekly, and Freshly offers dozens of lunch and dinner options to choose from. Meals are delivered ready-to-eat and are never frozen, and come with nutritional information, a full ingredient list and heating instructions. They are packaged in a refrigerated recycled-materials box and shipped with ice packs to be kept cold. Shipments are delivered directly to the premises and left at the door if unanswered. Freshly accommodates a variety of dietary preferences, and its entire menu is free of gluten and peanuts. FreshlyFit specifically caters to active lifestyles, offering low-carb, high-protein meals. FreshlyWell provides tailored, freshly prepared meals for making life easier, including on-site grab-and-go options or flexible meal delivery solutions. FreshlyWell offers its custom solutions to employers, healthcare systems, colleges and universities, health plans, senior living and other similar partnerships. Examples of meals include Homestyle Chicken with Butternut Mac and Cheese, Penne Bolognese, Sausage Baked Penne with Sauteed Zucchini and Spinach, Chicken Tikka Masala, Slow-cooked Beef Chili, Turkey Shepherd's Pie and Southwest Veggie Bowl. Meals are made with all-natural ingredients, are high in protein and nutrient-dense vegetables. eGifts are available. Freshly is a subsidiary of Nestle SA.

FINANCIAL DATA: Note: Data for latest year may not have been available at press time.

In U.S. $	2022	2021	2020	2019	2018	2017
Revenue						
R&D Expense						
Operating Income						
Operating Margin %						
SGA Expense						
Net Income						
Operating Cash Flow						
Capital Expenditure						
EBITDA						
Return on Assets %						
Return on Equity %						
Debt to Equity						

CONTACT INFORMATION:

Phone: 212 702-8791   Fax:
Toll-Free: 844 373-7459
Address: 115 E. 23rd St., New York, NY 10010-4508 United States

STOCK TICKER/OTHER:

Stock Ticker: Subsidiary   Exchange:
Employees: 1,100   Fiscal Year Ends:
Parent Company: Nestle SA

SALARIES/BONUSES:

Top Exec. Salary: $ Bonus: $
Second Exec. Salary: $ Bonus: $

OTHER THOUGHTS:

Estimated Female Officers or Directors:
Hot Spot for Advancement for Women/Minorities:

Sales, profits and employees may be estimates. Financial information, benefits and other data can change quickly and may vary from those stated here.

Frontier Communications Corporation

www.frontier.com

NAIC Code: 517311

TYPES OF BUSINESS:

Telecommunications
Internet Services
Long-Distance Phone Services
Directory Service
Access Services
Wireless Internet Services

GROWTH PLANS/SPECIAL FEATURES:

Frontier Communications Parent Inc offers a variety of services to residential and business customers over its fiber-optic and copper networks, including video, high-speed internet, advanced voice, and Frontier Secure digital protection solutions. It offers communications solutions to small, medium, and enterprise businesses.

BRANDS/DIVISIONS/AFFILIATES:

FiOS
Vantage

CONTACTS: Note: Officers with more than one job title may be intentionally listed here more than once.

Bernard Han, CEO
Scott Beasley, CFO
Donald Daniels, Chief Accounting Officer
Mark Nielsen, Chief Legal Officer

FINANCIAL DATA: Note: Data for latest year may not have been available at press time.

In U.S. $	2022	2021	2020	2019	2018	2017
Revenue	5,787,000,000		7,155,000,000	8,107,000,000		
R&D Expense						
Operating Income	691,000,000		1,208,000,000	1,466,000,000		
Operating Margin %	.12%		.17%			
SGA Expense	1,745,000,000		1,648,000,000	1,804,000,000		
Net Income	441,000,000		-402,000,000	-5,911,000,000		
Operating Cash Flow	1,401,000,000		1,989,000,000	1,508,000,000		
Capital Expenditure	2,738,000,000		1,181,000,000	1,226,000,000		
EBITDA	2,273,000,000		1,874,000,000	-3,207,000,000		
Return on Assets %	.03%		- .02%			
Return on Equity %	.09%					
Debt to Equity	1.77%					

CONTACT INFORMATION:

Phone: 203 614-5600   Fax: 203 614-4602
Toll-Free:
Address: 401 Merritt 7, Norwalk, CT 06851 United States

STOCK TICKER/OTHER:

Stock Ticker: FYBR   Exchange: NAS
Employees: 14,700   Fiscal Year Ends: 12/31
Parent Company:

SALARIES/BONUSES:

Top Exec. Salary: $650,000   Bonus: $1,500,000
Second Exec. Salary: Bonus: $
$1,300,000

OTHER THOUGHTS:

Estimated Female Officers or Directors: 7
Hot Spot for Advancement for Women/Minorities: Y

FTD LLC

www.ftd.com

NAIC Code: 424930

TYPES OF BUSINESS:

Flower, Nursery Stock and Florists' Supplies Wholesale Distribution
Flowers and Plants
Retail
Ecommerce
Online Ordering
Payment Solutions
Ecommerce and Payments Technology
Marketing Solutions

BRANDS/DIVISIONS/AFFILIATES:

Nexus Capital Management LP
FTD.com
ProFlowers.com

GROWTH PLANS/SPECIAL FEATURES:

FTD LLC is a floral and gifting company, in business since 1910. FTD stands for Florists' Transworld Delivery. FTD merchandise is displayed in floral shops in more than 150 countries, as well as online and mobile app. FTD partners with local florists to hand-craft floral arrangements available for same-day or scheduled delivery on FTD.com and ProFlowers.com. The sites also offer live potted plants, including flowering plants and indoor plants. In addition to delivering flowers and plants, the company supports locally owned retail florists by providing technology, marketing and digital services to members within its network. FTD is privately-owned by Nexus Capital Management LP.

FTD offers its employees health care benefits and onsite company perks.

CONTACTS: *Note: Officers with more than one job title may be intentionally listed here more than once.*

Charlie Cole, CEO
Tom Moeller, Pres.
Steven Barnhart, CFO
Tom Moeller, Executive VP, Subsidiary
Rhys Hughes, President, Divisional

FINANCIAL DATA: *Note: Data for latest year may not have been available at press time.*

In U.S. $	2022	2021	2020	2019	2018	2017
Revenue	1,100,000,000	1,000,000,000	939,443,476	963,531,770	1,014,243,968	1,084,028,032
R&D Expense						
Operating Income						
Operating Margin %						
SGA Expense						
Net Income						
Operating Cash Flow						
Capital Expenditure						
EBITDA						
Return on Assets %						
Return on Equity %						
Debt to Equity						

CONTACT INFORMATION:

Phone: 630-719-7800   Fax:
Toll-Free:
Address: 3113 Woodcreek Dr., Downers Grove, IL 60515 United States

STOCK TICKER/OTHER:

Stock Ticker: Private   Exchange:
Employees: 1,000   Fiscal Year Ends: 12/31
Parent Company: Nexus Capital Management LP

SALARIES/BONUSES:

Top Exec. Salary: $ Bonus: $
Second Exec. Salary: $ Bonus: $

OTHER THOUGHTS:

Estimated Female Officers or Directors:
Hot Spot for Advancement for Women/Minorities:

Fuze Inc

NAIC Code: 511210C

www.8x8.com/fuze

TYPES OF BUSINESS:

Computer Software: Telecom, Communications & VOIP
Enterprise Communications Platform
Video and Voice Calling
Contact Center
Communication APIs
Cloud Architecture
Meetings and Chat Messaging
Notifications and Message Saving, Archiving

BRANDS/DIVISIONS/AFFILIATES:

8x8 Inc
Fuze Desktop

CONTACTS: *Note: Officers with more than one job title may be intentionally listed here more than once.*

Samuel Wilson, CEO-8x8 Inc

GROWTH PLANS/SPECIAL FEATURES:

Fuze, Inc. provides a communications platform for the global enterprise, both in the U.S. and internationally. As a subsidiary of 8x8, Inc., Fuze's platform is enhanced by 8x8's contact center and communication application programming interfaces (APIs). Fuze designs and sells its user platform, which handles voice, video and messaging into a single interface through a cloud architecture that is reliable, scalable and secure. Fuze Desktop provides the full unified communications experience directly from the web screen. Its mobile app enables users to stay connected with colleagues from anywhere, any time. The Fuze platform displays user presence to other people, such as being available and updates automatically when joining or leaving calls and meetings. The presence feature can be manually set and enables custom messages to be created. All communications are retained within the platform and can be accessed when needed. Other access features include settings for calls, audio/video, notifications, meetings, connected accounts and app behaviors. Chat messaging is offered, with the ability to share content, including details about saved calls and meetings. Group messaging is also available, and others can be alerted by using mentions such as @Lily. Fuze integrates with Office365 and Chrome, enabling users to make calls and schedule meetings without leaving the browser.

FINANCIAL DATA: *Note: Data for latest year may not have been available at press time.*

In U.S. $	2022	2021	2020	2019	2018	2017
Revenue						
R&D Expense						
Operating Income						
Operating Margin %						
SGA Expense						
Net Income						
Operating Cash Flow						
Capital Expenditure						
EBITDA						
Return on Assets %						
Return on Equity %						
Debt to Equity						

CONTACT INFORMATION:

Phone: 617-453-2052   Fax: 617-453-0170
Toll-Free: 800-890-1553
Address: 2 Copley Place, Fl. 7, Boston, MA 02116 United States

STOCK TICKER/OTHER:

Stock Ticker: Subsidiary   Exchange:
Employees: 700   Fiscal Year Ends:
Parent Company: 8x8 Inc

SALARIES/BONUSES:

Top Exec. Salary: $ Bonus: $
Second Exec. Salary: $ Bonus: $

OTHER THOUGHTS:

Estimated Female Officers or Directors:
Hot Spot for Advancement for Women/Minorities:

Gainsight Inc

www.gainsight.com

NAIC Code: 511210K

TYPES OF BUSINESS:

Computer Software, Sales & Customer Relationship Management
Enterprise Software
Customer Lifecycle Management
Information Technology
Data Insight
Analytics
Product Adoption Solutions
Business Community Platform

BRANDS/DIVISIONS/AFFILIATES:

Vista Equity Partners Management LLC
Gainsight Platform
Gainsight CS
Gainsight PX
inSided

CONTACTS: Note: Officers with more than one job title may be intentionally listed here more than once.

Nick Mehta, CEO
Denise Stokowski, SVP- Product Management
Alka Tandan, CFO
Scott Salkin, CMO
Robin Merritt, Chief People and Operations Officer
Kellie Capote, Chief Customer Officer

GROWTH PLANS/SPECIAL FEATURES:

Gainsight, Inc. provides enterprise software solutions that leverage customer data to identify at-risk customers and build and enhance beneficial ones. The Gainsight Platform enables businesses to easily integrate key customer technologies into their technology stack; implement integrations to systems across categories such as customer relations management (CRM), support, business intelligence and analytics; and push data and power activities via Gainsight's application programming interfaces (APIs). Products, deployments and services sold to customers can be managed within the platform, which provides insights about those customers. Data can be edited and optimized through an administrative interface; and intuitive signals across complex datasets can be uncovered to perform statistics, aggregations, mergers, formulas, calculations and more for the purpose of deriving customer data. Products by Gainsight include: Gainsight CS (customer service), for retaining and growing customers at scale; Gainsight PX (product experience), a software solution for utilizing advanced analytics to increase user engagement, reveal best opportunities for growth, identify friction points, mitigate adoption risk and navigate integrations with CS and CRM; and inSided, offering a community platform for customers to connect, share best practices, provide feedback and build relationships with products. Gainsight is headquartered in California, USA, with additional offices in the U.S., India, Japan, Israel and the U.K. The firm is privately-owned by Vista Equity Partners Management LLC.

FINANCIAL DATA: Note: Data for latest year may not have been available at press time.

In U.S. $	2022	2021	2020	2019	2018	2017
Revenue						
R&D Expense						
Operating Income						
Operating Margin %						
SGA Expense						
Net Income						
Operating Cash Flow						
Capital Expenditure						
EBITDA						
Return on Assets %						
Return on Equity %						
Debt to Equity						

CONTACT INFORMATION:

Phone: 650 622-4947   Fax:
Toll-Free: 888-623-8562
Address: 350 Bay St., Ste. 100, San Francisco, CA 94133 United States

STOCK TICKER/OTHER:

Stock Ticker: Private   Exchange:
Employees: 700   Fiscal Year Ends:
Parent Company: Vista Equity Partners Management LLC

SALARIES/BONUSES:

Top Exec. Salary: $ Bonus: $
Second Exec. Salary: $ Bonus: $

OTHER THOUGHTS:

Estimated Female Officers or Directors: 2
Hot Spot for Advancement for Women/Minorities: Y

Sales, profits and employees may be estimates. Financial information, benefits and other data can change quickly and may vary from those stated here.

Gartner Inc

www.gartner.com

NAIC Code: 541910

TYPES OF BUSINESS:

Research-Computer Hardware & Software
Industry Research
IT Symposia & Conferences
Measurement & Advisory Services

GROWTH PLANS/SPECIAL FEATURES:

Based in Stamford, Conn., Gartner provides independent research and analysis on information technology and other related technology industries. Its research is delivered to clients' desktops in the form of reports, briefings, and updates. Typical clients are chief information officers and other business executives who help plan companies' IT budgets. Gartner also provides consulting services and hosted nearly 80 IT conferences across the globe in 2007.

BRANDS/DIVISIONS/AFFILIATES:

Symposium/Xpo

CONTACTS: *Note: Officers with more than one job title may be intentionally listed here more than once.*

Eugene Hall, CEO
Craig Safian, CFO
James Smith, Chairman of the Board
Michael Diliberto, Chief Information Officer
Kenneth Allard, Chief Marketing Officer
Yvonne Genovese, Executive VP, Divisional
Joe Beck, Executive VP, Divisional
Alwyn Dawkins, Executive VP, Divisional
Scott Hensel, Executive VP, Divisional
Michael Harris, Executive VP, Divisional
Claire Herkes, Executive VP, Divisional
Jules Kaufman, Executive VP
Robin Kranich, Executive VP
Akhil Jain, Senior VP, Divisional

FINANCIAL DATA: *Note: Data for latest year may not have been available at press time.*

In U.S. $	2022	2021	2020	2019	2018	2017
Revenue	5,475,846,000	4,733,962,000	4,099,403,000	4,245,321,000	3,975,454,000	
R&D Expense						
Operating Income	1,109,185,000	921,806,000	496,432,000	379,550,000	366,912,000	
Operating Margin %	.20%	.19%	.12%	.09%	.09%	
SGA Expense	2,480,944,000	2,155,658,000	2,038,963,000	2,103,424,000	1,884,141,000	
Net Income	807,799,000	793,560,000	266,745,000	233,290,000	122,456,000	
Operating Cash Flow	1,101,422,000	1,312,470,000	903,278,000	565,436,000	471,158,000	
Capital Expenditure	108,050,000	59,834,000	83,888,000	149,016,000	126,873,000	
EBITDA	1,345,344,000	1,300,788,000	660,753,000	590,349,000	563,496,000	
Return on Assets %	.11%	.11%	.04%	.03%	.02%	
Return on Equity %	2.70%	1.09%	.26%	.26%	.13%	
Debt to Equity	13.39%	8.50%	2.511	3.065	2.68%	

CONTACT INFORMATION:

Phone: 203 316-1111   Fax:
Toll-Free:
Address: 56 Top Gallant Rd., Stamford, CT 06902-7700 United States

STOCK TICKER/OTHER:

Stock Ticker: IT   Exchange: NYS
Employees: 19,500   Fiscal Year Ends: 12/31
Parent Company:

SALARIES/BONUSES:

Top Exec. Salary: $935,443   Bonus: $
Second Exec. Salary: Bonus: $
$644,175

OTHER THOUGHTS:

Estimated Female Officers or Directors: 3
Hot Spot for Advancement for Women/Minorities: Y

Sales, profits and employees may be estimates. Financial information, benefits and other data can change quickly and may vary from those stated here.

Gen Digital Inc

www.gendigital.com

NAIC Code: 511210E

TYPES OF BUSINESS:

Computer Software: Network Security, Managed Access, Digital ID,
Cybersecurity & Anti-Virus
Cybersecurity
Identity Security

GROWTH PLANS/SPECIAL FEATURES:

Gen is a cybersecurity pure-play that offers security, identity
protection, and privacy solutions to individual consumers. The
firm's cyber safety offerings, via brands such as Norton, Avast,
and LifeLock, have long maintained their positions as some of
the most recognizable consumer-focused security and identity-
protection products.

BRANDS/DIVISIONS/AFFILIATES:

NortonLifeLock
Norton 360
Avast

CONTACTS: Note: Officers with more than one job title may be intentionally listed here more than once.

Vincent Pilette, CEO
Natalie Derse, CFO
Frank Dangeard, Chairman of the Board
Bryan Ko, Chief Legal Officer

FINANCIAL DATA: Note: Data for latest year may not have been available at press time.

In U.S. $	2022	2021	2020	2019	2018	2017
Revenue	2,796,000,000	2,551,000,000	2,490,000,000	2,456,000,000	2,559,000,000	
R&D Expense	253,000,000	267,000,000	328,000,000	420,000,000	455,000,000	
Operating Income	1,036,000,000	1,057,000,000	621,000,000	379,000,000	226,000,000	
Operating Margin %	.37%	.41%	.25%	.15%	.09%	
SGA Expense	1,014,000,000	791,000,000	1,069,000,000	1,122,000,000	1,328,000,000	
Net Income	836,000,000	554,000,000	3,887,000,000	31,000,000	1,138,000,000	
Operating Cash Flow	974,000,000	706,000,000	-861,000,000	1,495,000,000	950,000,000	
Capital Expenditure	6,000,000	6,000,000	89,000,000	207,000,000	142,000,000	
EBITDA	1,308,000,000	1,166,000,000	1,376,000,000	716,000,000	1,140,000,000	
Return on Assets %	.13%	.08%	.33%	.00%	.07%	
Return on Equity %			1.35%	.01%	.27%	
Debt to Equity			353.80	0.69	1.00%	

CONTACT INFORMATION:

Phone: 650 527-2900   Fax:
Toll-Free:
Address: 60 E. Rio Salado Pkwy, Ste. 1000, Tempe, AZ 85281 United
States

STOCK TICKER/OTHER:

Stock Ticker: GEN   Exchange: NAS
Employees: 3,700   Fiscal Year Ends: 03/31
Parent Company:

SALARIES/BONUSES:

Top Exec. Salary: $940,385   Bonus: $
Second Exec. Salary: Bonus: $
$540,385

OTHER THOUGHTS:

Estimated Female Officers or Directors: 3
Hot Spot for Advancement for Women/Minorities: Y

Geocomply Solutions Inc

www.geocomply.com

NAIC Code: 511210E

TYPES OF BUSINESS:

Computer Software: Security & Anti-Virus
KYC
AML
Geofencing

BRANDS/DIVISIONS/AFFILIATES:

GeoComply Core
PinPoint
IDComply
Geoguard
OneComply
GeoComply Chargeback Integrator (CGI)

GROWTH PLANS/SPECIAL FEATURES:

Geocomply Solutions, founded in 2011, is a leading technology company specializing in geolocation and fraud prevention services. The firm services the online gaming, entertainment, banking and cybersecurity industries. Geocomply's products use cutting-edge location detection and verification technologies to provide accurate and secure geolocation data. Products include GeoCore, an anti-fraud and geolocation compliance solution; IDComply, an all-in-one KYC & AML solution; PinPoint, a custom, on-property geofencing solution; GeoGuard, an award-winning VPN and proxy detection tool; GeoComply Chargeback Integrator (GCI), a product designed to fight and win chargeback disputes; OneComply, a tool to streamline, manage, and automate licensing in one secure place. Geocomply has offices in the U.S., U.K., Poland, Canada and Vietnam.

CONTACTS: *Note: Officers with more than one job title may be intentionally listed here more than once.*

Anna Sainsbury, CEO

FINANCIAL DATA: *Note: Data for latest year may not have been available at press time.*

In U.S. $	2022	2021	2020	2019	2018	2017
Revenue						
R&D Expense						
Operating Income						
Operating Margin %						
SGA Expense						
Net Income						
Operating Cash Flow						
Capital Expenditure						
EBITDA						
Return on Assets %						
Return on Equity %						
Debt to Equity						

CONTACT INFORMATION:

Phone: Fax:
Toll-Free: 888-822-9339
Address: 545 Robson St., Ste. 5, Vancouver, BC V6B 1A6 Canada

STOCK TICKER/OTHER:

Stock Ticker: Private   Exchange:
Employees: Fiscal Year Ends:
Parent Company:

SALARIES/BONUSES:

Top Exec. Salary: $ Bonus: $
Second Exec. Salary: $ Bonus: $

OTHER THOUGHTS:

Estimated Female Officers or Directors:
Hot Spot for Advancement for Women/Minorities:

GitHub Inc

github.com

NAIC Code: 519130

TYPES OF BUSINESS:

Internet Publishing and Broadcasting and Web Search Portals
Version Control Repository
Internet Hosting
Platform Development
Artificial Intelligence
Software Development
Workflow Automation
Collaboration

BRANDS/DIVISIONS/AFFILIATES:

Microsoft Corporation

CONTACTS: *Note: Officers with more than one job title may be intentionally listed here more than once.*

Thomas Dohmke, CEO
Kyle Daigle, COO
Dan Whittle, CFO
Inbal Shani, Chief Product Officer
Dawn Beatty, Chief Human Resources Officer
Mike Hanley, Chief Security Officer

GROWTH PLANS/SPECIAL FEATURES:

GitHub, Inc. provides a web-based version control repository (Git) and internet hosting service. The company offers all the distributed version control and source code management functionality of Git, as well as its own features. The GitHub platform allows developers and individuals to build software for open source and private projects. GitHub supports a community of over 100 million who learn, share and work together in order to build software. Once a user's code is on GitHub, they can invite others to join in with a link or an @mention. Or users can collaborate with other developers in public or invite them to join the GitHub community's unlimited private repositories. Small businesses and startups can securely develop company software on GitHub and can work together as a team in creating it. Developers will be able to champion new ideas, work together on code and track bugs on a single integrated platform. Product categories by GitHub include actions, such as automating workflows; packages, hosting and managing packages; security, finding and fixing vulnerabilities; code spaces, offering instant development environments; co-pilot, for writing enhanced code with artificial intelligence (AI); code review, managing code changes; issues, planning and tracking work; and discussions, collaborating outside of code. Price plans for GitHub range from free to enterprise, and offer monthly or annual rates. GitHub has hosted more than 420 million repositories on the platform. GitHub is a subsidiary of Microsoft Corporation.

FINANCIAL DATA: *Note: Data for latest year may not have been available at press time.*

In U.S. $	2022	2021	2020	2019	2018	2017
Revenue	1,000,000,000					
R&D Expense						
Operating Income						
Operating Margin %						
SGA Expense						
Net Income						
Operating Cash Flow						
Capital Expenditure						
EBITDA						
Return on Assets %						
Return on Equity %						
Debt to Equity						

CONTACT INFORMATION:

Phone: 415-735-4488   Fax: 415-520-5597
Toll-Free:
Address: 88 Colin P Kelly Junior St., San Francisco, CA 94107 United States

STOCK TICKER/OTHER:

Stock Ticker: Subsidiary   Exchange:
Employees: 5,595   Fiscal Year Ends:
Parent Company: Microsoft Corporation

SALARIES/BONUSES:

Top Exec. Salary: $ Bonus: $
Second Exec. Salary: $ Bonus: $

OTHER THOUGHTS:

Estimated Female Officers or Directors:
Hot Spot for Advancement for Women/Minorities:

Global Payments Inc

www.globalpaymentsinc.com

NAIC Code: 522320

TYPES OF BUSINESS:

Electronic Payment Processing
Credit & Debit Card Processing
Funds Transfer Services
Check Guarantee Services
Merchant Services
Payment Technology

BRANDS/DIVISIONS/AFFILIATES:

GROWTH PLANS/SPECIAL FEATURES:

Global Payments is a leading provider of payment processing and software solutions and focuses on serving small and midsize merchants. The company operates in 30 countries and generates about one fourth of its revenue from outside North America, primarily in Europe and Asia. In 2019, Global Payments merged with Total System Services in an all-stock deal that gave Total System Services shareholders 48% of the combined company's shares. The merger added issuer processing operations.

CONTACTS: Note: Officers with more than one job title may be intentionally listed here more than once.

Jeffrey Sloan, CEO
Paul Todd, CFO
M. Woods, Chairman of the Board
David Sheffield, Chief Accounting Officer
Guido Sacchi, Chief Information Officer
Cameron Bready, COO
David Green, General Counsel

FINANCIAL DATA: Note: Data for latest year may not have been available at press time.

In U.S. $	2022	2021	2020	2019	2018	2017
Revenue	8,975,515,000	8,523,762,000	7,423,558,000	4,911,892,000	3,366,366,000	
R&D Expense						
Operating Income	1,672,320,000	1,358,876,000	893,953,000	791,417,000	737,055,000	
Operating Margin %	.19%	.16%	.12%	.16%	.22%	
SGA Expense	3,524,578,000	3,391,161,000	2,878,878,000	2,046,672,000	1,534,297,000	
Net Income	111,493,000	965,460,000	584,520,000	430,613,000	452,053,000	
Operating Cash Flow	2,244,040,000	2,780,825,000	2,314,150,000	1,391,278,000	1,106,082,000	
Capital Expenditure	615,652,000	493,216,000	436,236,000	307,868,000	213,290,000	
EBITDA	2,336,210,000	3,069,580,000	2,551,944,000	1,701,165,000	1,280,587,000	
Return on Assets %	.00%	.02%	.01%	.01%	.03%	
Return on Equity %	.00%	.04%	.02%	.03%	.12%	
Debt to Equity	.55%	.45%	0.31	0.326	1.26%	

CONTACT INFORMATION:

Phone: 770 829-8000   Fax:
Toll-Free: 800-560-2960
Address: 3550 Lenox Rd., Atlanta, GA 30326 United States

STOCK TICKER/OTHER:

Stock Ticker: GPN
Employees: 25,000
Parent Company:

Exchange: NYS
Fiscal Year Ends: 05/31

SALARIES/BONUSES:

Top Exec. Salary: $1,200,000   Bonus: $
Second Exec. Salary: $725,000   Bonus: $

OTHER THOUGHTS:

Estimated Female Officers or Directors: 2
Hot Spot for Advancement for Women/Minorities: Y

GoDaddy Inc

www.goDaddy.com

NAIC Code: 518210

TYPES OF BUSINESS:

Domain Name Registration
Domain Name Reselling
Research & Development, Internet Services

BRANDS/DIVISIONS/AFFILIATES:

Poynt

GROWTH PLANS/SPECIAL FEATURES:

GoDaddy is a provider of domain registration and aftermarket services, website hosting, security, design, and business productivity tools, commerce solutions, and domain registry services. The company primarily targets micro- to small businesses, website design professionals, registrar peers, and domain investors. Since acquiring payment processing platform Poynt in 2021, the company has expanded into omnicommerce solutions, including offering an online payment gateway and offline point-of-sale devices.

GoDaddy offers its employees 100% paid medical and dental premiums, employee appreciation outings, a 401(k) plan, life and disability insurance, maternity and paternity leave, adoption assistance, subsidized lunches and employee discounts.

CONTACTS: Note: Officers with more than one job title may be intentionally listed here more than once.

Amanpal Bhutani, CEO
Ray Winborne, CFO
Charles Robel, Chairman of the Board
Nick Daddario, Chief Accounting Officer
Nima Kelly, Chief Legal Officer

FINANCIAL DATA: Note: Data for latest year may not have been available at press time.

In U.S. $	2022	2021	2020	2019	2018	2017
Revenue	4,091,300,000	3,815,700,000	3,316,700,000	2,988,100,000	2,660,100,000	2,231,900,000
R&D Expense	794,000,000	706,300,000	560,400,000	492,600,000	434,000,000	355,800,000
Operating Income	514,500,000	381,800,000	-358,900,000	211,300,000	164,500,000	190,100,000
Operating Margin %	.13%	.10%	-.11%	.07%	.06%	.09%
SGA Expense	797,800,000	849,700,000	762,300,000	707,700,000	625,400,000	535,600,000
Net Income	352,200,000	242,300,000	-495,100,000	137,000,000	77,100,000	136,400,000
Operating Cash Flow	979,700,000	829,300,000	764,600,000	723,400,000	559,800,000	475,600,000
Capital Expenditure	60,100,000	253,200,000	81,500,000	92,300,000	97,000,000	135,200,000
EBITDA	697,400,000	579,200,000	-201,400,000	428,200,000	405,500,000	395,600,000
Return on Assets %	.05%	.03%	-.08%	.02%	.01%	.03%
Return on Equity %		7.04%	-1.30%	.18%	.12%	.26%
Debt to Equity		48.97%		3.329	3.02%	4.955

CONTACT INFORMATION:

Phone: 480 505-8800   Fax: 480-505-8844
Toll-Free:
Address: 2155 E. GoDaddy Way, Tempe, AZ 85284 United States

STOCK TICKER/OTHER:

Stock Ticker: GDDY   Exchange: NYS
Employees: 6,910   Fiscal Year Ends: 12/31
Parent Company:

SALARIES/BONUSES:

Top Exec. Salary: $1,000,000   Bonus: $
Second Exec. Salary: Bonus: $
$525,000

OTHER THOUGHTS:

Estimated Female Officers or Directors: 3
Hot Spot for Advancement for Women/Minorities: Y

Sales, profits and employees may be estimates. Financial information, benefits and other data can change quickly and may vary from those stated here.

Gree Inc

gree.jp

NAIC Code: 519130

TYPES OF BUSINESS:

Social Networking Platform
Mobile Applications
Online Games
Information Technology
Investment
Online Advertising
Social Entertainment

BRANDS/DIVISIONS/AFFILIATES:

funplex inc
ExPlay Inc
GREE VR Studio
XTELE
MINE
STRIVE
GREE Ads Rewards
QUANT

CONTACTS: *Note: Officers with more than one job title may be intentionally listed here more than once.*

Yoshikazu Tanaka, CEO
Taisei Yoshida, Sr. VP-Prod.
Masaki Fujimoto, Sr. VP-Eng.
Naoki Aoyagi, Sr. VP-Global Oper.
Kotaru Yamagishi, Exec. VP
Yuta Maeda, VP
Shozo Mizuno, VP
Naoki Aoyagi, CEO-GREE Intl

GROWTH PLANS/SPECIAL FEATURES:

Gree is a Japanese internet media company headquartered in Tokyo. Its business is divided into games, media, advertising, and investment. The games division provides games internationally via the App Store and Google Play from the company's studios in Japan and North America. The media segment is engaged in a variety of IT businesses, including services and media. The advertising segment targets mainly the smartphone advertising market. The company has investments in Internet technology services companies in Japan, North America, and Southeast Asia.

FINANCIAL DATA: *Note: Data for latest year may not have been available at press time.*

In U.S. $	2022	2021	2020	2019	2018	2017
Revenue	511,153,700	431,341,000	427,621,900	484,062,700	531,755,200	
R&D Expense						
Operating Income	78,461,620	74,121,590	21,577,280	37,374,700	64,288,300	
Operating Margin %	.15%	.17%	.05%	.08%	.12%	
SGA Expense						
Net Income	69,071,880	92,348,320	18,486,040	23,781,410	32,127,090	
Operating Cash Flow	90,198,780	46,716,660	13,866,240	49,528,120	62,282,060	
Capital Expenditure	9,212,313	341,197	2,047,181	8,325,202	3,637,158	
EBITDA	104,174,200	97,206,960	46,041,090	44,000,740	56,004,040	
Return on Assets %	.08%	.10%	.02%	.03%	.04%	
Return on Equity %	.10%	.12%	.02%	.03%	.04%	
Debt to Equity	.09%	.07%				

CONTACT INFORMATION:

Phone: 81 357709500   Fax:
Toll-Free:
Address: 6-10-1 Roppongi, Minato-ku, Tokyo, 106-6112 Japan

STOCK TICKER/OTHER:

Stock Ticker: GREZF   Exchange: PINX
Employees: 2,568   Fiscal Year Ends: 06/30
Parent Company:

SALARIES/BONUSES:

Top Exec. Salary: $ Bonus: $
Second Exec. Salary: $ Bonus: $

OTHER THOUGHTS:

Estimated Female Officers or Directors:
Hot Spot for Advancement for Women/Minorities:

Greenhouse Software Inc

www.greenhouse.io

NAIC Code: 511210H

TYPES OF BUSINESS:

Computer Software, Business Management & ERP
Recruitment Software
Software-as-a-Service Platform
Hiring and Job Recruitment Management

BRANDS/DIVISIONS/AFFILIATES:

TPG Inc
Rise Fund (The)

GROWTH PLANS/SPECIAL FEATURES:

Greenhouse Software, Inc. provides recruiting software-as-a-service (SaaS). The firm's SaaS platform enables companies to plan and outline hiring processes, get new jobs approved, accept applications online, provide various job recruitment search options, post jobs to boards and social networks, learn how to boost referrals, manage candidates and prospects, schedule interviews, create interview kits, score candidates, manage the recruitment pipeline and decide who to hire, as well as make and manage offers. Greenhouse also offers solutions for managing hiring teams, configuring notifications, controlling user permissions, streamline communications and create/share reports via application program interfaces (APIs). Greenhouse provides resources including eBooks, webinars, events and case studies. Investors of Greenhouse Software include TPG Inc. and The Rise Fund. The company is headquartered in New York.

CONTACTS: Note: Officers with more than one job title may be intentionally listed here more than once.

Daniel Chait, CEO
Jon Stross, Pres.
Sean Murray, Chief Revenue Officer
Carin van Vuuren, CMO
Donald Knight, Chief People Officer
Andrew Lister, Head of Technology

FINANCIAL DATA: Note: Data for latest year may not have been available at press time.

In U.S. $	2022	2021	2020	2019	2018	2017
Revenue						
R&D Expense						
Operating Income						
Operating Margin %						
SGA Expense						
Net Income						
Operating Cash Flow						
Capital Expenditure						
EBITDA						
Return on Assets %						
Return on Equity %						
Debt to Equity						

CONTACT INFORMATION:

Phone: 917-780-4130   Fax:
Toll-Free: 800-790-9789
Address: 18 West 18th St., Fl. 11, New York, NY 10011 United States

STOCK TICKER/OTHER:

Stock Ticker: Private   Exchange:
Employees: 200   Fiscal Year Ends:
Parent Company: TPG Inc

SALARIES/BONUSES:

Top Exec. Salary: $ Bonus: $
Second Exec. Salary: $ Bonus: $

OTHER THOUGHTS:

Estimated Female Officers or Directors:
Hot Spot for Advancement for Women/Minorities:

Groupon Inc

www.groupon.com

NAIC Code: 541810E

TYPES OF BUSINESS:

Online Marketing Services
Ecommerce
Local Goods
Local Services
Website
Mobile App
Travel

GROWTH PLANS/SPECIAL FEATURES:

Groupon acts as the middleman between consumers and merchants, offering a variety of products and services at discounts via its online store. It offers consumers daily deals from local merchants. It generates revenue from the take rate on the vouchers' purchase and/or usage. More than 60% of Groupon's revenue comes from North America.

BRANDS/DIVISIONS/AFFILIATES:

CONTACTS: *Note: Officers with more than one job title may be intentionally listed here more than once.*

Aaron Cooper, CEO
Melissa Thomas, CFO
Eric Lefkofsky, Chairman of the Board
Kerrie Dvorak, Chief Accounting Officer
Dane Drobny, Chief Administrative Officer
Damien Schmitz, Senior VP, Divisional

FINANCIAL DATA: *Note: Data for latest year may not have been available at press time.*

In U.S. $	2022	2021	2020	2019	2018	2017
Revenue	599,085,000	967,108,000	1,416,868,000	2,218,915,000	2,636,746,000	2,843,877,000
R&D Expense						
Operating Income	-107,782,000	37,240,000	-80,425,000	39,829,000	53,903,000	31,114,000
Operating Margin %	-.18%	.04%	-.06%	.02%	.02%	.01%
SGA Expense	630,606,000	699,876,000	757,719,000	1,146,300,000	1,266,698,000	1,302,747,000
Net Income	-237,609,000	118,668,000	-287,931,000	-22,377,000	-11,079,000	14,040,000
Operating Cash Flow	-135,987,000	-123,958,000	-63,598,000	71,283,000	190,855,000	128,127,000
Capital Expenditure	38,845,000	52,761,000	52,951,000	71,066,000	87,957,000	60,217,000
EBITDA	-114,927,000	178,050,000	-173,352,000	115,827,000	138,768,000	194,652,000
Return on Assets %	-.24%	.09%	-.19%	-.01%	-.01%	.01%
Return on Equity %	-2.18%	.75%	-1.15%	-.06%	-.04%	.05%
Debt to Equity	27.64%	1.34%	2.976	0.84	.56%	0.83

CONTACT INFORMATION:

Phone: 312 676-5773   Fax:
Toll-Free: 877-788-7858
Address: 600 W. Chicago Ave., Ste. 400, Chicago, IL 60654 United States

STOCK TICKER/OTHER:

Stock Ticker: GRPN
Employees: 2,904
Parent Company:

Exchange: NAS
Fiscal Year Ends: 03/31

SALARIES/BONUSES:

Top Exec. Salary: $42,192   Bonus: $1,000,000
Second Exec. Salary: $590,000   Bonus: $

OTHER THOUGHTS:

Estimated Female Officers or Directors: 1
Hot Spot for Advancement for Women/Minorities:

Grove Collaborative Holdings Inc

www.grove.co

NAIC Code: 454110

TYPES OF BUSINESS:
Electronic Shopping
Natural Home & Personal Care Products
Product Innovation and Development
Ecommerce
Online and Mobile App Marketplaces
Online Payment Solution
Wholesale Retailing
Sustainable Packaging Design

BRANDS/DIVISIONS/AFFILIATES:

GROWTH PLANS/SPECIAL FEATURES:

Grove Collaborative Holdings Inc is engaged in providing consumer products. It offers Cleaning accessories, Home and Pantry, Personal care products, Pets supplements and Other products.

CONTACTS: *Note: Officers with more than one job title may be intentionally listed here more than once.*
Sergio Cervantes, CFO

FINANCIAL DATA: *Note: Data for latest year may not have been available at press time.*

In U.S. $	2022	2021	2020	2019	2018	2017
Revenue	321,527,000	383,685,000	364,271,000	233,116,000		
R&D Expense	22,503,000	23,408,000	18,655,000	13,604,000		
Operating Income	-140,983,000	-128,855,000	-66,493,000	-163,169,000		
Operating Margin %	- .44%	- .34%	- .18%			
SGA Expense	273,132,000	293,951,000	223,842,000	233,000,000		
Net Income	-87,715,000	-135,896,000	-72,260,000	-161,470,000		
Operating Cash Flow	-96,261,000	-127,089,000	-83,656,000	-124,805,000		
Capital Expenditure	4,222,000	5,768,000	4,820,000	11,617,000		
EBITDA	-72,260,000	-125,650,000	-62,497,000	-157,045,000		
Return on Assets %	- .49%	- .60%	- .27%			
Return on Equity %						
Debt to Equity	2.89%					

CONTACT INFORMATION:
Phone: 844 476-8375   Fax:
Toll-Free: 800-231-8527
Address: 1301 Sansome St., San Francisco, CA 94111 United States

STOCK TICKER/OTHER:
Stock Ticker: GROV   Exchange: NYS
Employees: 550   Fiscal Year Ends: 12/31
Parent Company:

SALARIES/BONUSES:
Top Exec. Salary: $363,637   Bonus: $150,000
Second Exec. Salary: $450,000   Bonus: $

OTHER THOUGHTS:
Estimated Female Officers or Directors:
Hot Spot for Advancement for Women/Minorities:

Grubhub Inc

www.grubhub.com

NAIC Code: 492210

TYPES OF BUSINESS:

Online Restaurant Pick-Up and Delivery
Online Food Ordering Services
Food Delivery Services
Catering Delivery Services
Ecommerce Payment Solutions
Corporate Credit Cards

BRANDS/DIVISIONS/AFFILIATES:

Just Eat Takeaway.com NV
Grubhub+
Grubhub Pay Card

GROWTH PLANS/SPECIAL FEATURES:

Grubhub, Inc. is an online and mobile food ordering company that connects diners with local takeout restaurants. Its online and mobile ordering platforms allows millions of active diners to order directly from more than 365,000 takeout restaurants in over 4,000 U.S. cities. Every order is supported by the company's 24/7 customer service teams. Grubhub also provides catering delivery services, in which users can schedule an order from a local restaurant and have it delivered. Grubhub offers gift cards. Grubhub+ is a membership program that costs about $10 per month and offers unlimited delivery fees on eligible orders, as well as exclusive rewards and other perks. GrubHub operates as a subsidiary of Just Eat Takeaway.com N.V., an Amsterdam-based food delivery service. Grubhubs corporate pay card is coming soon (as of February 2024) to help drive orders to local restaurants and increase order flexibility for in-office and at-home employees.

CONTACTS: *Note: Officers with more than one job title may be intentionally listed here more than once.*

Howard Migdal, CEO
Adam Patnaude, CFO
Maggie Drucker, Chief Legal Officer
Greg Russell, CTO
Margo Drucker, General Counsel
Samuel Hall, Other Executive Officer

FINANCIAL DATA: *Note: Data for latest year may not have been available at press time.*

In U.S. $	2022	2021	2020	2019	2018	2017
Revenue	2,050,000,000	1,910,981,049	1,819,981,952	1,312,151,040	1,007,257,024	683,067,008
R&D Expense						
Operating Income						
Operating Margin %						
SGA Expense						
Net Income			-155,860,992	-18,566,000	78,481,000	98,983,000
Operating Cash Flow						
Capital Expenditure						
EBITDA						
Return on Assets %						
Return on Equity %						
Debt to Equity						

CONTACT INFORMATION:

Phone: 877-585-7878   Fax:
Toll-Free:
Address: 111 W. Washington St., Ste. 2100, Chicago, IL 60602 United States

STOCK TICKER/OTHER:

Stock Ticker: Subsidiary   Exchange:
Employees: 2,450   Fiscal Year Ends: 12/31
Parent Company: Just Eat Takeaway.com NV

SALARIES/BONUSES:

Top Exec. Salary: $ Bonus: $
Second Exec. Salary: $ Bonus: $

OTHER THOUGHTS:

Estimated Female Officers or Directors: 2
Hot Spot for Advancement for Women/Minorities: Y

Gusto

NAIC Code: 511210Q

TYPES OF BUSINESS:

Computer Software: Accounting, Banking & Financial
Cloud Software and Storage
Automated Payroll Solutions
Employee Benefits Solutions
Human Resources Solutions
Attendance Tracking
Hiring Documents
Technology

BRANDS/DIVISIONS/AFFILIATES:

Ardius

GROWTH PLANS/SPECIAL FEATURES:

Gusto provides a cloud-based payroll, benefits and human resource solution for businesses throughout the U.S. The firm serves more than 300,000 small business customers nationwide, with offices in San Francisco, Denver and New York City. The Gusto platform is a single system of record comprised of automated payroll, which includes tax filings, employee paystubs, W-2s and more; benefits administration tailored to each firm's needs; streamlined HR solutions, including emergency contacts, new hire documents and employee anniversaries; and 401(k) integration. Tools offered by Gusto include small business financial relief, employer tax calculator, burn rate calculator, salary comparison, time attendance and time-off, new hire checklist and small business information. Pricing starts at $40 per month.

Gusto offers its employees health and wellness benefits and a variety of assistance plans and company perks.

CONTACTS: Note: Officers with more than one job title may be intentionally listed here more than once.

Joshua Reeves, CEO

FINANCIAL DATA: Note: Data for latest year may not have been available at press time.

In U.S. $	2022	2021	2020	2019	2018	2017
Revenue						
R&D Expense						
Operating Income						
Operating Margin %						
SGA Expense						
Net Income						
Operating Cash Flow						
Capital Expenditure						
EBITDA						
Return on Assets %						
Return on Equity %						
Debt to Equity						

CONTACT INFORMATION:

Phone: 415 864-4273   Fax:
Toll-Free: 800-936-0383
Address: 525 20th St., San Francisco, CA 94107 United States

STOCK TICKER/OTHER:

Stock Ticker: Private   Exchange:
Employees: 300   Fiscal Year Ends:
Parent Company:

SALARIES/BONUSES:

Top Exec. Salary: $ Bonus: $
Second Exec. Salary: $ Bonus: $

OTHER THOUGHTS:

Estimated Female Officers or Directors:
Hot Spot for Advancement for Women/Minorities:

Gwynnie Bee (CaaStle Inc)

closet.gwynniebee.com

NAIC Code: 454110

TYPES OF BUSINESS:

Online Rental of Luxury Apparel and Accessories
Apparel Sharing
Clothing Rental
Online Ordering
Mobile App Ordering
Payment Solution
Analytics
Algorithms

BRANDS/DIVISIONS/AFFILIATES:

Gwynnie Bee
Pepperjam

CONTACTS: *Note: Officers with more than one job title may be intentionally listed here more than once.*

Christine Hunsicker, CEO

GROWTH PLANS/SPECIAL FEATURES:

CaaStle, Inc. offers an online/mobile service that provides unlimited fashion styles for women for rent or for sale. The online/mobile service is called Gwynnie Bee. CaaStle's customer-as-a-service (hence, CaaS-tle) platform builds and manages all aspects of the subscription model, including the website, databases, algorithms and analytics. Gwynnie Bee's apparel categories include shirts, blouses, dresses, denim, pants, cardigans, sweaters, jackets, outerwear, skirts and more. Prices for each item are displayed on the app or website, and other features include size advisory and fit guide. Suggestions for weekend and work wear are offered on the site, as well as styles to consider. The company's distribution centers comprise state-of-the-art inventory and garment care systems that manage the cleaning, shipping and receiving processes for its customers. Subscribers choose apparel as often as they'd like, anytime, anywhere, complimented with free shipping and unlimited returns. Subscribers can explore top brands and curated collections and wear them as often as they'd like. Those who wish to purchase an item can do so for less than retail price. CaaStle's affiliate program is built on rewarding subscribers for being an advocate to its attire-sharing marketplace via Pepperjam. Affiliates get paid for: displaying related ads, banners and links; reviewing the service and collections; and advertising CaaStle/Gwynnie Bee promotions.

FINANCIAL DATA: *Note: Data for latest year may not have been available at press time.*

In U.S. $	2022	2021	2020	2019	2018	2017
Revenue						
R&D Expense						
Operating Income						
Operating Margin %						
SGA Expense						
Net Income						
Operating Cash Flow						
Capital Expenditure						
EBITDA						
Return on Assets %						
Return on Equity %						
Debt to Equity						

CONTACT INFORMATION:

Phone: 718 752-1470   Fax:
Toll-Free: 855 499-6643
Address: 5 Penn Plaza, Fl. 4, New York, NY 10001 United States

STOCK TICKER/OTHER:

Stock Ticker: Private   Exchange:
Employees: Fiscal Year Ends:
Parent Company:

SALARIES/BONUSES:

Top Exec. Salary: $ Bonus: $
Second Exec. Salary: $ Bonus: $

OTHER THOUGHTS:

Estimated Female Officers or Directors:
Hot Spot for Advancement for Women/Minorities:

Hallmark Cards Inc

www.hallmark.com

NAIC Code: 511191

TYPES OF BUSINESS:

Greeting Cards Publishing
Cable Television Broadcasting
Crayons & Art Products
Movie Production & Distribution
Streaming Services
Retail and Department Stores
Real Estate Development
Hotels and Entertainment

BRANDS/DIVISIONS/AFFILIATES:

Hallmark
Hallmark Media
Crayola
Crown Center Redevelopment Corporation
Hallmark Channel
Hallmark Movies & Mysteries
Hallmark Publishing
Halls Kansas City

CONTACTS: *Note: Officers with more than one job title may be intentionally listed here more than once.*

Mike Perry, CEO
David E. Hall, Vice Chmn.
David E. Hall, Pres., North America Div.
Donald J. Hall, Jr., Chmn.

GROWTH PLANS/SPECIAL FEATURES:

Hallmark Cards, Inc. operates a diverse group of businesses that offer greeting cards, entertainment and more. The company's businesses are divided into four segments: Hallmark, Hallmark Media, Crayola, and Crown Center Redevelopment Corporation. Hallmark offers a wide range of greeting cards, gift wrap and related products in more than 100 countries and 100,000 retailer stores worldwide. This includes a network of company-owned and independently-owned Hallmark Gold Crown stores in the U.S., Canada, England, Ireland and Scotland. Products are also sold on hallmark.com. Related companies within Hallmark include DaySpring Cards (including Mary & Martha) and Hallmark Business Connections. Hallmark Media (formerly Crown Media) operates three cable networks, namely Hallmark Channel, Hallmark Movies & Mysteries, and Hallmark Drama. This division's Hallmark Publishing offers eBooks in relation to the Hallmark channels; Hallmark Movies Now is a subscription-based streaming service; and Hallmark Hall of Fame is a movie franchise. Crayola sells art materials and toys, operates Crayola retail stores and operates Crayola Experience interactive attractions. Crayola's popular product lines include coloring and drawing, toys and activities and mess-free coloring. Last, Crown Center is a real estate development business that manages the 85-acre hotel, office, entertainment and residential complex that surrounds Hallmark's world headquarters in Kansas City, Missouri. Crown Center also features: Halls Kansas City, a specialty department store offering apparel for men and women, including high-end designer brands, cosmetics, crystal and decorative home accessories; Sheraton Kansas City Hotel at Crown Center and The Westin Kansas City at Crown Center, which offers hotel and meetings accommodations as well as a variety of shopping, dining and entertainment options in the heart of Kansas City.

Hallmark offers its employees comprehensive benefits, retirement options and employee assistance programs.

FINANCIAL DATA: *Note: Data for latest year may not have been available at press time.*

In U.S. $	2022	2021	2020	2019	2018	2017
Revenue	3,952,000,000	3,800,000,000	3,500,000,000	4,200,000,000	4,000,000,000	3,912,000,000
R&D Expense						
Operating Income						
Operating Margin %						
SGA Expense						
Net Income						
Operating Cash Flow						
Capital Expenditure						
EBITDA						
Return on Assets %						
Return on Equity %						
Debt to Equity						

CONTACT INFORMATION:

Phone: 816-274-5111   Fax:
Toll-Free: 800-425-5627
Address: 2501 McGee Trafficway, Kansas City, MO 64108 United States

STOCK TICKER/OTHER:

Stock Ticker: Private   Exchange:
Employees: 27,000   Fiscal Year Ends: 12/31
Parent Company:

SALARIES/BONUSES:

Top Exec. Salary: $ Bonus: $
Second Exec. Salary: $ Bonus: $

OTHER THOUGHTS:

Estimated Female Officers or Directors:
Hot Spot for Advancement for Women/Minorities:

Happn (SAS HAPPN)

NAIC Code: 511210G

TYPES OF BUSINESS:

Computer Software, Electronic Games, Apps & Entertainment
Online and Mobile Dating App
Location-Based Technology
Voice Feature

BRANDS/DIVISIONS/AFFILIATES:

GROWTH PLANS/SPECIAL FEATURES:

SAS HAPPN operates Happn, a location-based social search mobile app and online site that connects users to people they've happened to cross paths with. Happn keeps track of where its users are, in real-time. When another user passes by the same spot, their profile will show up on the app feed. Since there is already something in common between the two, the users can look up the other and decide to either like or dislike them in the app. When two users like each other, the mode for communication between them becomes available on the app. Happn has more than 100 million users, with new users added each month. Nearly 5 million messages are sent and received between Happn users every day. Happn is available worldwide, including the Americas, Europe, Asia and Oceania.

CONTACTS: Note: Officers with more than one job title may be intentionally listed here more than once.

Karima ben Abdelmalek, CEO

FINANCIAL DATA: Note: Data for latest year may not have been available at press time.

In U.S. $	2022	2021	2020	2019	2018	2017
Revenue						
R&D Expense						
Operating Income						
Operating Margin %						
SGA Expense						
Net Income						
Operating Cash Flow						
Capital Expenditure						
EBITDA						
Return on Assets %						
Return on Equity %						
Debt to Equity						

CONTACT INFORMATION:

Phone: 5653 5211723   Fax:
Toll-Free:
Address: 8 Rue de Sentier, Paris, 75002 France

STOCK TICKER/OTHER:

Stock Ticker: Private   Exchange:
Employees: Fiscal Year Ends:
Parent Company:

SALARIES/BONUSES:

Top Exec. Salary: $ Bonus: $
Second Exec. Salary: $ Bonus: $

OTHER THOUGHTS:

Estimated Female Officers or Directors:
Hot Spot for Advancement for Women/Minorities:

Harmonic Inc

www.harmonicinc.com

NAIC Code: 334210

TYPES OF BUSINESS:

Networking Equipment
Video Stream Processing
Cable Edge & Access
Software

BRANDS/DIVISIONS/AFFILIATES:

GROWTH PLANS/SPECIAL FEATURES:

Harmonic Inc designs and manufactures video infrastructure products and system solutions to deliver video and broadband services to consumer devices. The firm operates in two segments: Video, which sells video processing, production, and playout solutions to cable operators and satellite and telecommunications providers; and Broadband which sells broadband access solutions and related services. Majority of the revenue generated from the company is from United States.

CONTACTS: Note: Officers with more than one job title may be intentionally listed here more than once.

Patrick Harshman, CEO
Sanjay Kalra, CFO
Patrick Gallagher, Chairman of the Board
Nimrod Ben-Natan, General Manager, Divisional
Ian Graham, Senior VP, Divisional
Neven Haltmayer, Senior VP, Divisional

FINANCIAL DATA: Note: Data for latest year may not have been available at press time.

In U.S. $	2022	2021	2020	2019	2018	2017
Revenue	624,957,000	507,149,000	378,831,000	402,874,000	403,558,000	
R&D Expense	120,307,000	102,231,000	82,494,000	84,614,000	89,163,000	
Operating Income	48,860,000	18,919,000	-10,127,000	16,224,000	-2,093,000	
Operating Margin %	.08%	.04%	-.03%	.04%	-.01%	
SGA Expense	146,717,000	138,085,000	119,611,000	119,035,000	118,952,000	
Net Income	28,182,000	13,254,000	-29,271,000	-5,924,000	-21,035,000	
Operating Cash Flow	5,476,000	41,017,000	39,163,000	31,295,000	12,284,000	
Capital Expenditure	9,250,000	12,975,000	32,205,000	10,328,000	7,044,000	
EBITDA	61,785,000	32,549,000	999,000	24,661,000	15,791,000	
Return on Assets %	.04%	.02%	-.05%	-.01%	-.04%	
Return on Equity %	.09%	.05%	-.11%	-.02%	-.09%	
Debt to Equity	.11%	.48%	0.641	0.49	.56%	

CONTACT INFORMATION:

Phone: 408 542-2500 Fax:
Toll-Free: 800-788-1330
Address: 2590 Orchard Pkwy., San Jose, CA 95131 United States

STOCK TICKER/OTHER:

Stock Ticker: HLIT Exchange: NAS
Employees: 1,340 Fiscal Year Ends: 12/31
Parent Company:

SALARIES/BONUSES:

Top Exec. Salary: $545,592 Bonus: $
Second Exec. Salary: $402,463 Bonus: $

OTHER THOUGHTS:

Estimated Female Officers or Directors: 1
Hot Spot for Advancement for Women/Minorities:

HeadHunter Group PLC   www.hh.ru

NAIC Code: 561311A

TYPES OF BUSINESS:
Online Job Recruitment
Job Recruitment
Online Recruitment
Job Postings
Job Searches
Websites
Online Platform

BRANDS/DIVISIONS/AFFILIATES:

GROWTH PLANS/SPECIAL FEATURES:
HeadHunter Group PLC is an online recruitment platform in Russia and the Commonwealth of Independent States region and focuses on connecting job seekers with employers. The company offers employers and recruiters paid access to its resume database and job postings platform. It also provides job seekers and employers with a value-added services portfolio centered around their recruitment needs. The company engages with job seekers and employers via its own desktop sites, mobile sites and mobile applications.

CONTACTS: Note: Officers with more than one job title may be intentionally listed here more than once.
Mikhail Zhukov, CEO

FINANCIAL DATA: Note: Data for latest year may not have been available at press time.

In U.S. $	2022	2021	2020	2019	2018	2017
Revenue	235,101,232	218,695,232	133,927,984	106,673,160	82,184,832	64,304,212
R&D Expense						
Operating Income						
Operating Margin %						
SGA Expense						
Net Income	47,472,340	73,829,720	28,282,016	19,831,788	12,752,784	5,453,456
Operating Cash Flow						
Capital Expenditure						
EBITDA						
Return on Assets %						
Return on Equity %						
Debt to Equity						

CONTACT INFORMATION:
Phone: 7 495-974-64-27   Fax:
Toll-Free:
Address: 9/10 Godovikova St., Moscow, 129085 Russia

STOCK TICKER/OTHER:
Stock Ticker: HHRU   Exchange: Moscow
Employees: 1,515   Fiscal Year Ends: 12/31
Parent Company:

SALARIES/BONUSES:
Top Exec. Salary: $ Bonus: $
Second Exec. Salary: $ Bonus: $

OTHER THOUGHTS:
Estimated Female Officers or Directors:
Hot Spot for Advancement for Women/Minorities:

Health Catalyst Inc

NAIC Code: 518210

www.healthcatalyst.com

TYPES OF BUSINESS:

Data Processing, Hosting, and Related Services
Healthcare Data Technology
Healthcare Analytics Technology
Software
Cloud

BRANDS/DIVISIONS/AFFILIATES:

GROWTH PLANS/SPECIAL FEATURES:

Health Catalyst Inc is engaged in providing data and analytics technology and services to healthcare organizations. It has two operating segments. The Technology segment, which is the key revenue driver, includes data platform, analytics applications and support services. This generates revenues primarily from contracts that are cloud-based subscription arrangements, time-based license arrangements, and maintenance and support fees; and Professional Services segment is generally the combination of analytics, implementation, strategic advisory, outsource, and improvement services to deliver expertise to its customers to more fully configure and utilize the benefits of the technology offerings.

CONTACTS: Note: Officers with more than one job title may be intentionally listed here more than once.

Daniel Burton, CEO
Bryan Hunt, CFO
John Kane, Chairman of the Board
Jason Alger, Chief Accounting Officer
Bryan Hinton, Chief Technology Officer
Paul Horstmeier, COO
Daniel Orenstein, General Counsel
Linda Llewelyn, Other Executive Officer
James Nelli, President

FINANCIAL DATA: Note: Data for latest year may not have been available at press time.

In U.S. $	2022	2021	2020	2019	2018	2017
Revenue	276,236,000	241,926,000	188,845,000	154,941,000	112,574,000	73,081,000
R&D Expense	75,680,000	62,733,000	53,517,000	46,252,000	38,592,000	28,470,000
Operating Income	-140,005,000	-143,650,000	-96,125,000	-54,865,000	-60,095,000	-45,540,000
Operating Margin %	-.51%	-.59%	-.51%	-.35%	-.53%	
SGA Expense	149,215,000	160,961,000	114,651,000	78,997,000	66,813,000	40,617,000
Net Income	-137,403,000	-153,210,000	-115,017,000	-60,096,000	-61,984,000	-47,035,000
Operating Cash Flow	-35,270,000	-23,123,000	-26,148,000	-32,184,000	-40,296,000	-36,829,000
Capital Expenditure	17,414,000	18,467,000	10,465,000	4,334,000	2,503,000	3,344,000
EBITDA	-86,147,000	-105,267,000	-85,914,000	-47,323,000	-52,683,000	-39,648,000
Return on Assets %	-.17%	-.22%	-.26%	-1.17%	-1.03%	
Return on Equity %	-.29%	-.38%	-.48%			
Debt to Equity	.58%	.39%	0.698	0.248		

CONTACT INFORMATION:

Phone: 801-708-6800   Fax:
Toll-Free:
Address: 10897 S. River Front Pkwy. #300, South Jordan, UT 84095 United States

STOCK TICKER/OTHER:

Stock Ticker: HCAT   Exchange: NAS
Employees: 1,200   Fiscal Year Ends: 12/31
Parent Company:

SALARIES/BONUSES:

Top Exec. Salary: $316,667   Bonus: $
Second Exec. Salary: Bonus: $
$300,000

OTHER THOUGHTS:

Estimated Female Officers or Directors:
Hot Spot for Advancement for Women/Minorities:

HealthStream Inc

www.healthstream.com

NAIC Code: 611430

TYPES OF BUSINESS:

Educational & Training Content
Internet-based Educational Programs
Workforce Management
Credentialing
Online Training
Online Learning

BRANDS/DIVISIONS/AFFILIATES:

hStream
VerityStream
EchoCredentialing
MSOW
EchoOneApp
CredentialMyDoc
EchoAccess
ComplyALIGN

CONTACTS: *Note: Officers with more than one job title may be intentionally listed here more than once.*

Robert Frist, CEO
Scott Roberts, CFO
Jeffrey Cunningham, Chief Technology Officer
J. Pearson, COO
Michael Collier, General Counsel
Trisha Coady, General Manager, Divisional
Michael Sousa, President, Subsidiary
Michael McQuigg, Senior VP, Divisional
Scott Fenstermacher, Senior VP, Divisional
Kevin OHara, Senior VP, Divisional

GROWTH PLANS/SPECIAL FEATURES:

HealthStream Inc provides workforce and provider solutions for healthcare organizations. Its reportable segments include Workforce Solutions and Provider Solutions. Workforce development solutions consist of SaaS, subscription-based products that are used by healthcare organizations. Its Provider Solutions products offer healthcare organizations software applications for administering and tracking provider credentialing, privileging, call center and enrollment activities. The company generates a majority of its revenue from the Workforce solutions segment.

FINANCIAL DATA: *Note: Data for latest year may not have been available at press time.*

In U.S. $	2022	2021	2020	2019	2018	2017
Revenue	266,826,000	256,712,000	244,826,000	254,112,000	231,616,000	214,899,000
R&D Expense	44,277,000	41,659,000	32,305,000	29,109,000	25,735,000	24,148,000
Operating Income	12,449,000	8,055,000	15,818,000	14,720,000	15,491,000	9,407,000
Operating Margin %	.05%	.03%	.06%	.06%	.07%	.04%
SGA Expense	81,012,000	79,152,000	77,182,000	78,524,000	70,145,000	70,089,000
Net Income	12,091,000	5,845,000	14,091,000	15,770,000	32,217,000	10,004,000
Operating Cash Flow	51,188,000	42,385,000	35,874,000	65,657,000	43,246,000	46,712,000
Capital Expenditure	25,102,000	25,346,000	18,803,000	36,510,000	18,450,000	15,112,000
EBITDA	50,394,000	44,868,000	46,007,000	42,589,000	39,722,000	33,454,000
Return on Assets %	.02%	.01%	.03%	.03%	.08%	.02%
Return on Equity %	.04%	.02%	.04%	.05%	.10%	.03%
Debt to Equity	.07%	.08%	0.085	0.091		

CONTACT INFORMATION:

Phone: 615 301-3100   Fax: 615 301-3200
Toll-Free: 800-521-0574
Address: 500 11th Ave. N., Ste. 1000, Nashville, TN 37203 United States

STOCK TICKER/OTHER:

Stock Ticker: HSTM   Exchange: NAS
Employees: 1,154   Fiscal Year Ends: 12/31
Parent Company:

SALARIES/BONUSES:

Top Exec. Salary: $375,000   Bonus: $
Second Exec. Salary: Bonus: $
$368,333

OTHER THOUGHTS:

Estimated Female Officers or Directors:
Hot Spot for Advancement for Women/Minorities:

Heyday (HYDY Inc)   www.heyday.co

NAIC Code: 454110

TYPES OF BUSINESS:

Electronic Shopping
Entrepreneur Partnerships
Brand Building
Ecommerce Strategies
Next-Generation Consumer Product Design
Product Development
Technology Innovation
Mergers and Acquisitions, Operations

BRANDS/DIVISIONS/AFFILIATES:

GROWTH PLANS/SPECIAL FEATURES:

Heyday partners with entrepreneurs in their journey to build and brand next-generation consumer products for the ecommerce marketplace. Heyday's platform provides the capital, tools, insights and expertise for all stages of a brand's lifecycle, from incubation to acquisition. The platform is built via technology, data and operations tailored specifically for the ecommerce marketplace. As a partner, Heyday's three-stage strategy consists of incubating the brand, growing the brand and selling the brand. Heyday specializes in mergers and acquisitions, operations, technology and brand building. Heyday investors include RAINE, PremjiInvest, General Catalyst, Khosla Ventures and Arbor Ventures, having raised over $800 million since its 2013 inception.

CONTACTS: Note: Officers with more than one job title may be intentionally listed here more than once.

Andy Taylor, CEO

FINANCIAL DATA: Note: Data for latest year may not have been available at press time.

In U.S. $	2022	2021	2020	2019	2018	2017
Revenue	20,904,000	20,100,000	200,000,000			
R&D Expense						
Operating Income						
Operating Margin %						
SGA Expense						
Net Income						
Operating Cash Flow						
Capital Expenditure						
EBITDA						
Return on Assets %						
Return on Equity %						
Debt to Equity						

CONTACT INFORMATION:

Phone: 415 284-4515   Fax:
Toll-Free:
Address: 180 Spear St., San Francisco, CA 94105 United States

STOCK TICKER/OTHER:

Stock Ticker: Private   Exchange:
Employees: 240   Fiscal Year Ends:
Parent Company:

SALARIES/BONUSES:

Top Exec. Salary: $ Bonus: $
Second Exec. Salary: $ Bonus: $

OTHER THOUGHTS:

Estimated Female Officers or Directors:
Hot Spot for Advancement for Women/Minorities:

Honest Company Inc (The)

www.honest.com

NAIC Code: 325620

TYPES OF BUSINESS:

Consumer and Personal Care Goods
Sanitary Paper Product Manufacturing
Infant Formula Manufacturing
Baby Powder and Baby Oil Manufacturing
Ecommerce
Retail
Subscription

BRANDS/DIVISIONS/AFFILIATES:

NO List

GROWTH PLANS/SPECIAL FEATURES:

The Honest Co Inc is a digitally-native consumer products company to make purpose-driven consumer products designed for all people. It is an omnichannel brand, ensuring its products are available wherever its consumers shop through company's Retail and Digital channels. It has three product categories namely; Diapers and Wipes, Skin and Personal Care, and Household and Wellness, out of which the majority of its revenue is generated from the sale of diapers and wipes. The company operates only in the United States.

CONTACTS: *Note: Officers with more than one job title may be intentionally listed here more than once.*

Nikolaos Vlahos, CEO
Kelly Kennedy, CFO
Jessica Alba, Chairman of the Board
Sharareh Parvaneh, Chief Information Officer
Glenn Klages, Executive VP, Divisional
Brendan Sheehey, General Counsel
Rick Rexing, Other Executive Officer
Jasmin Manner, Other Executive Officer
Donald Frey, Other Executive Officer
Janis Hoyt, Other Executive Officer

FINANCIAL DATA: *Note: Data for latest year may not have been available at press time.*

In U.S. $	2022	2021	2020	2019	2018	2017
Revenue	313,651,000	318,639,000	300,522,000	235,587,000		
R&D Expense	6,996,000	7,679,000	5,705,000	5,137,000		
Operating Income	-49,780,000	-36,826,000	-13,540,000	-31,457,000		
Operating Margin %	-.16%	-.12%	-.05%			
SGA Expense	135,099,000	138,319,000	115,731,000	102,174,000		
Net Income	-49,019,000	-38,679,000	-14,466,000	-31,083,000		
Operating Cash Flow	-76,275,000	-38,154,000	-12,066,000	-19,992,000		
Capital Expenditure	1,617,000	220,000	200,000	661,000		
EBITDA	-47,027,000	-32,702,000	-8,686,000	-23,785,000		
Return on Assets %	-.19%	-.12%	-.06%			
Return on Equity %	-.30%					
Debt to Equity	.20%	.21%				

CONTACT INFORMATION:

Phone: 310 917-9199   Fax:
Toll-Free: 888-862-8818
Address: 2700 Pennsylvania Ave., Ste. 1200, Santa Monica, CA 90404
United States

STOCK TICKER/OTHER:

Stock Ticker: HNST   Exchange: NAS
Employees: 198   Fiscal Year Ends: 12/31
Parent Company:

SALARIES/BONUSES:

Top Exec. Salary: $846,154   Bonus: $
Second Exec. Salary: Bonus: $
$688,077

OTHER THOUGHTS:

Estimated Female Officers or Directors:
Hot Spot for Advancement for Women/Minorities: Y

Hootsuite Inc

hootsuite.com

NAIC Code: 511210F

TYPES OF BUSINESS:

Computer Software, Multimedia, Graphics & Publishing
Social Media Management Solutions
Software
Marketing Solutions
Artificial Intelligence
Customer Service and Engagement Solutions
Platform Management Solutions
Social Selling

BRANDS/DIVISIONS/AFFILIATES:

CONTACTS: Note: Officers with more than one job title may be intentionally listed here more than once.

Irina Novoselsky, CEO
Dave Wynne, CFO
Elina Vilk, CMO
Tara Ataya, Chief People Officer
Antonis Papatsaras, CTO
Julie Herendeen, Chmn.

GROWTH PLANS/SPECIAL FEATURES:

Hootsuite, Inc. provides social media management solutions for organizations worldwide. The firm's products enable companies to form relationships on social media via artificial intelligence (AI)-based technology across engagement, publishing, analytics, insights, campaigns, employee advocacy, platform management and more. Hootsuite extensions and tools enable app creation, which subsequently offers content recommendations to app users. Hootsuite solutions include social marketing, social selling, customer service and employee advocacy. Hootsuite has several price plans: professional ($99/month), offering 10 social profiles/1 user and online tools; team ($249/month), offering 20 social profiles/3 users and expanded tools; business (Pricing varies), offering 50 social profiles/5 users, unlimited scheduling and advanced tools; and enterprise (custom pricing), which offers a variety of enhanced customizable features and personalized training. Primary industries served by the company include financial services, healthcare, higher education, agencies and government. Hootsuite has more than 200 thousand users worldwide. The firm is headquartered in Canada, with offices across North America, the U.K., Europe and Australia.

FINANCIAL DATA: Note: Data for latest year may not have been available at press time.

In U.S. $	2022	2021	2020	2019	2018	2017
Revenue						
R&D Expense						
Operating Income						
Operating Margin %						
SGA Expense						
Net Income						
Operating Cash Flow						
Capital Expenditure						
EBITDA						
Return on Assets %						
Return on Equity %						
Debt to Equity						

CONTACT INFORMATION:

Phone: 604-681-4668   Fax: 604-681-4668
Toll-Free:
Address: 111 E. 5th Ave., Vancouver, BC V5T 4L1 Canada

STOCK TICKER/OTHER:

Stock Ticker: Private   Exchange:
Employees: 1,000   Fiscal Year Ends:
Parent Company:

SALARIES/BONUSES:

Top Exec. Salary: $ Bonus: $
Second Exec. Salary: $ Bonus: $

OTHER THOUGHTS:

Estimated Female Officers or Directors: 2
Hot Spot for Advancement for Women/Minorities: Y

Hotels.com LP

NAIC Code: 561510

TYPES OF BUSINESS:

Online Hotel Reservations System
Online Travel Information
Lodging Options
Search Engine
Technology

BRANDS/DIVISIONS/AFFILIATES:

Expedia Group Inc
Hotels.com Rewards

CONTACTS: *Note: Officers with more than one job title may be intentionally listed here more than once.*

Adam Jay, Pres.
Taylor Cole, Dir.-Public Rel.
Dara Khoosrowshahi, CEO-Expedia, Inc.

GROWTH PLANS/SPECIAL FEATURES:

Hotels.com, LP, a subsidiary of Expedia Group, Inc., is a specialized provider of discount lodging reservation services for destinations around the world. Hotels.com's room supply relationships include a wide range of independent hotel operators, lodging properties, bed & breakfasts as well as hotels associated with several national chains such as Hilton, Sheraton, Radisson and Best Western. Through its website, mobile app and telephone call centers, customers have access to hundreds of thousands of properties worldwide, with accommodations ranging from standard hotels to condos and all-inclusive resorts. The firm's booking engine allows users to quickly compare price, quality, amenities, location and availability of hotel rooms in seconds. The site also provides extensive virtual tours of rooms being offered along with user reviews, as well as package deals such as hotel/flight/things to do, deals for groups, space for meetings and more. Hotels.com offers various perks to its customers, including Hotels.com Rewards programs that provides customers with a one-night-free stay after every ten bookings at a partner hotel.

FINANCIAL DATA: *Note: Data for latest year may not have been available at press time.*

In U.S. $	2022	2021	2020	2019	2018	2017
Revenue						
R&D Expense						
Operating Income						
Operating Margin %						
SGA Expense						
Net Income						
Operating Cash Flow						
Capital Expenditure						
EBITDA						
Return on Assets %						
Return on Equity %						
Debt to Equity						

CONTACT INFORMATION:

Phone: 214-361-7311   Fax: 214-361-7299
Toll-Free: 800-246-8357
Address: 5400 LBJ Freeway, Ste. 500, Dallas, TX 75240 United States

STOCK TICKER/OTHER:

Stock Ticker: Subsidiary   Exchange:
Employees: 1,000   Fiscal Year Ends: 12/31
Parent Company: Expedia Group Inc

SALARIES/BONUSES:

Top Exec. Salary: $ Bonus: $
Second Exec. Salary: $ Bonus: $

OTHER THOUGHTS:

Estimated Female Officers or Directors: 2
Hot Spot for Advancement for Women/Minorities:

Hotwire Inc

www.hotwire.com

NAIC Code: 561510

TYPES OF BUSINESS:

Online Reservation Systems
Online Hotel Booking
Car Rental Reservations
Discount Airfare
Cruise Reservations
Vacation Packages

BRANDS/DIVISIONS/AFFILIATES:

Expedia Group Inc

CONTACTS: Note: Officers with more than one job title may be intentionally listed here more than once.

Heather Kernahan, CEO
Pierre-Etienne Chartier, VP-Oper.

GROWTH PLANS/SPECIAL FEATURES:

Hotwire, Inc., wholly owned by Expedia Group, Inc., offers discount prices on airfare, hotel accommodations, rental cars, cruises and vacation packages through its website and mobile app. The company offers discounts to customers by helping travel suppliers book unsold airline seats, hotel rooms and rental cars. The site also features the opaque purchase service, allowing customers to book travel arrangements based on hotel price, star rating and neighborhood preferences, without knowing the name of the hotel until after purchase. Hotwire offers airline tickets from domestic and international airlines. It partners with several U.S. carriers as well as international airlines. Additionally, the firm partners with a variety of hotels chains, car rental companies and technology suppliers to offer a wide range of options, services and solutions for consumers. Travel planning tools available through Hotwire's site include trip planning, offering ideal travel times to destination cities by aggregating historic airfare and hotel pricing data as well as compiling historic weather information; and trip watching, allowing users to flag certain travel options and receive price status alerts.

FINANCIAL DATA: Note: Data for latest year may not have been available at press time.

In U.S. $	2022	2021	2020	2019	2018	2017
Revenue						
R&D Expense						
Operating Income						
Operating Margin %						
SGA Expense						
Net Income						
Operating Cash Flow						
Capital Expenditure						
EBITDA						
Return on Assets %						
Return on Equity %						
Debt to Equity						

CONTACT INFORMATION:

Phone: 415-343-8400   Fax: 415-343-8401
Toll-Free: 866-468-9473
Address: 114 Sansome St., #400, San Francisco, CA 94104 United States

STOCK TICKER/OTHER:

Stock Ticker: Subsidiary   Exchange:
Employees: 350   Fiscal Year Ends: 12/31
Parent Company: Expedia Group Inc

SALARIES/BONUSES:

Top Exec. Salary: $ Bonus: $
Second Exec. Salary: $ Bonus: $

OTHER THOUGHTS:

Estimated Female Officers or Directors:
Hot Spot for Advancement for Women/Minorities: Y

Sales, profits and employees may be estimates. Financial information, benefits and other data can change quickly and may vary from those stated here.

Houzz Inc

NAIC Code: 454110

TYPES OF BUSINESS:

Home Furnishings Online
Home Remodeling
Home Design
Hire Professionals Online
Online and Mobile Platform
Construction Professionals
Ecommerce
Social Community

BRANDS/DIVISIONS/AFFILIATES:

Houzz.com
houzz

CONTACTS: Note: Officers with more than one job title may be intentionally listed here more than once.

Adi Tatarko, CEO

GROWTH PLANS/SPECIAL FEATURES:

Houzz, Inc. offers an online and mobile platform (houzz) for home remodeling and design, providing everything needed to improve the home from start to finish. The Houzz.com website showcases portfolios created by construction and design professionals for users to browse, and they can save the ones they like. The houzz platform comprises a community of more than 65 million homeowners, design enthusiasts and improvement professionals throughout the U.S., and around the world. Design segments span kitchen and dining, bath, bedroom, living room, lighting, furniture, decor, home improvement, outdoor and more. Designers and professionals post their photos, overviews and ideas. Homeowners write reviews, ask questions and share current home improvement activities. Users can connect with a construction professional through houzz. Businesses and professionals can sell on the platform, enabling consumers to purchase directly through the website or mobile app. The company offers houzz credit cards as well as gift cards. Headquartered in California, USA, the firm has offices in Arkansas and Germany.

FINANCIAL DATA: Note: Data for latest year may not have been available at press time.

In U.S. $	2022	2021	2020	2019	2018	2017
Revenue	476,985,600	458,640,000	441,000,000	420,000,000	400,000,000	350,000,000
R&D Expense						
Operating Income						
Operating Margin %						
SGA Expense						
Net Income						
Operating Cash Flow						
Capital Expenditure						
EBITDA						
Return on Assets %						
Return on Equity %						
Debt to Equity						

CONTACT INFORMATION:

Phone: 650-326-3000   Fax: 650-433-4249
Toll-Free:
Address: 285 Hamilton Ave., Fl. 4, Palo Alto, CA 94301 United States

STOCK TICKER/OTHER:

Stock Ticker: Private   Exchange:
Employees: 1,500   Fiscal Year Ends: 12/31
Parent Company:

SALARIES/BONUSES:

Top Exec. Salary: $ Bonus: $
Second Exec. Salary: $ Bonus: $

OTHER THOUGHTS:

Estimated Female Officers or Directors:
Hot Spot for Advancement for Women/Minorities:

Huawei Technologies Co Ltd

www.huawei.com

NAIC Code: 334210

TYPES OF BUSINESS:

Telecommunications Equipment Manufacturing
Network Equipment
Software
Wireless Technology
Smartphones
5G Wireless Technology
Watches

BRANDS/DIVISIONS/AFFILIATES:

Union of Huawei Investment & Holding Co
Huaewi

CONTACTS:
Note: Officers with more than one job title may be intentionally listed here more than once.

Ren Zhengfi, CEO
Ren Zhengfei, Pres.
Meng Wanzhou, CFO
Ding Yun (Ryan Ding), Chief Prod. & Solutions Officer
Yu Chengdong (Richard Yu), Chief Strategy Officer
Chen Lifang, Corp. Sr. VP-Public Affairs & Comm. Dept.
Guo Ping, Chmn.-Finance Committee
Zhang Ping'an (Alex Zhang), CEO-Huawei Symantec
Hu Houkun (Ken Hu), Chmn.-Huawei USA
Liang Hua, Chmn.
Wan Biao, Pres., Russia

GROWTH PLANS/SPECIAL FEATURES:

Huawei Technologies Co., Ltd., founded in 1987, is a leading global information and communications technology (ICT) solutions provider. Huawei is one of the world's leading manufacturers of smartphones. The company's ICT portfolio of end-to-end solutions in telecom, enterprise networks, and consumers are used in more than 170 countries and regions, serving more than one-third of the world's population. Huawei's consumer products include the Huawei brand of mobile smart phones, the laptops, tablets, watches, ear buds, speakers, Wi-Fi connection devices and more. The company's business products include switches, routers, WLAN (wireless local area network), servers, storage, cloud computing, network energy services and more. Its carrier products include cloud data centers, wireless network, fixed network, cloud core network, carrier software, IT infrastructure and network energy global services. Huawei Technologies' NB-IoT city-aware network, a one network/one platform/N-tier applications model. NB-IoT stands for NarrowBand Internet of Things, and is a low-power, wide-area network radio technology standard that enables a wide range of devices and services to be connected using cellular telecommunications bands. Huawei's smart city solutions senses, processes and delivers informed decisions for improving the environment for citizens, with recent information and communications technology (ICT) offering real-time situation reporting and analysis, empowered by a combination of cloud computing, IoT technologies, big data analytics and artificial intelligence (AI). The company has global joint innovation centers and research and development centers. Huawei Technologies operates as a subsidiary of the Union of Huawei Investment & Holding Co., Ltd.

FINANCIAL DATA:
Note: Data for latest year may not have been available at press time.

In U.S. $	2022	2021	2020	2019	2018	2017
Revenue						
R&D Expense						
Operating Income						
Operating Margin %						
SGA Expense						
Net Income						
Operating Cash Flow						
Capital Expenditure						
EBITDA						
Return on Assets %						
Return on Equity %						
Debt to Equity						

CONTACT INFORMATION:

Phone: 86 755-28780808   Fax: 86-755-28789251
Toll-Free:
Address: Section H, Bantian, Longgang Distr., Shenzhen, Guangdong 518129 China

STOCK TICKER/OTHER:

Stock Ticker: Subsidiary   Exchange:
Employees: 195,000   Fiscal Year Ends: 12/31
Parent Company: Union of Huawei Investment & Holding Co Ltd

SALARIES/BONUSES:

Top Exec. Salary: $ Bonus: $
Second Exec. Salary: $ Bonus: $

OTHER THOUGHTS:

Estimated Female Officers or Directors: 3
Hot Spot for Advancement for Women/Minorities: Y

Hulu LLC

NAIC Code: 515210

TYPES OF BUSINESS:

Streaming Entertainment Online, Including Movies and TV Shows
Entertainment Streaming Services
Life and On-Demand Entertainment
Television Shows and Films
News and Sports Entertainment
Subscription Viewing Services
Ecommerce

BRANDS/DIVISIONS/AFFILIATES:

Walt Disney Company (The)
Comcast Corporation
Hulu Originals
Hulu + Live TV
Shop Hulu

CONTACTS: *Note: Officers with more than one job title may be intentionally listed here more than once.*

Joe Earley, Pres.
Chadwick Ho, General Counsel
Jean-Paul Colaco, Sr. VP-Advertising

GROWTH PLANS/SPECIAL FEATURES:

Hulu, LLC provides a subscription streaming service that offers instant access to live and on-demand entertainment, both in and outside the home. Hulu has more than 48.5 million subscribers in the U.S. (as of January 2024), who have access to over 70,000 TV episodes and movies and 95+ live channels. As part of Disney's media and entertainment distribution division, Hulu provides access to shows from every major U.S. broadcast network, libraries of hit TV series and films (including licensed content) and Hulu Originals, both with and without commercials. Hulu + Live TV offers a combination of access to live news, entertainment and sports TV channels from 20th Television, The Walt Disney Company, ABC, NBCUniversal, CBS Corporation, The CW, Turner Networks, A+E Networks and Discovery Networks, as well as Disney+ and ESPN+ as part of its base plan. Hulu also offers an online shopping destination, Shop Hulu, which features exclusive limited editions of apparel and lifestyle products as well as products inspired by Hulu Originals, popular titles in Hulu's on-demand library and Hulu branded merchandise. The Walt Disney Company owns two-thirds of Hulu, and Comcast Corporation owns the remaining 33%.

FINANCIAL DATA: *Note: Data for latest year may not have been available at press time.*

In U.S. $	2022	2021	2020	2019	2018	2017
Revenue	10,700,000,000	9,600,000,000	7,200,000,000	3,164,175,000	3,013,500,000	2,870,000,000
R&D Expense						
Operating Income						
Operating Margin %						
SGA Expense						
Net Income						
Operating Cash Flow						
Capital Expenditure						
EBITDA						
Return on Assets %						
Return on Equity %						
Debt to Equity						

CONTACT INFORMATION:

Phone: 310-571-4700   Fax: 310-571-4701
Toll-Free:
Address: 2500 Broadway, Fl. 2, Santa Monica, CA 90404 United States

STOCK TICKER/OTHER:

Stock Ticker: Joint Venture   Exchange:
Employees: 3,000   Fiscal Year Ends: 09/30
Parent Company: Walt Disney Company (The)

SALARIES/BONUSES:

Top Exec. Salary: $ Bonus: $
Second Exec. Salary: $ Bonus: $

OTHER THOUGHTS:

Estimated Female Officers or Directors: 2
Hot Spot for Advancement for Women/Minorities: Y

IAC/InterActiveCorp

www.iac.com

NAIC Code: 519130

TYPES OF BUSINESS:

E-Commerce, Online Advertising & Search Engines
Online Personals & Dating Services
Online Entertainment & Shopping Directories
Service Provider Listings Online

GROWTH PLANS/SPECIAL FEATURES:

IAC is an internet media company with segments that include Angi (33% of total revenue), Dotdash Meredith (39%), search (14%), and emerging and other (14%). The firm spun off the narrow-moat dating app provider Match Group in second-quarter 2020 and the no-moat video software provider Vimeo in second-quarter 2021.

BRANDS/DIVISIONS/AFFILIATES:

ANGI Homeservices Inc
Angie's List
HomeAdvisor
Vivian
Dotdash Meredith
Ask Media Group
Care.com
Daily Beast

CONTACTS: *Note: Officers with more than one job title may be intentionally listed here more than once.*

Joseph Levin, CEO
Glenn Schiffman, CFO
Barry Diller, Chairman of the Board
Michael Schwerdtman, Chief Accounting Officer
Mark Stein, Chief Strategy Officer
Victor Kaufman, Director
Kendall Handler, General Counsel

FINANCIAL DATA: *Note: Data for latest year may not have been available at press time.*

In U.S. $	2022	2021	2020	2019	2018	2017
Revenue	5,235,280,000	3,699,627,000	2,764,536,000	2,509,980,000	2,533,048,000	3,307,239,000
R&D Expense	332,873,000	230,810,000	185,335,000	132,640,000	177,298,000	250,879,000
Operating Income	-568,440,000	-154,925,000	-272,517,000	9,052,000	35,835,000	188,466,000
Operating Margin %	-.07%	-.04%	-.10%	.00%	.01%	
SGA Expense	3,109,446,000	2,177,606,000	1,910,691,000	1,690,942,000	1,669,289,000	2,100,478,000
Net Income	-1,170,170,000	597,547,000	269,726,000	22,895,000	246,772,000	304,924,000
Operating Cash Flow	-82,791,000	136,953,000	154,581,000	251,800,000	369,435,000	416,699,000
Capital Expenditure	139,753,000	90,210,000	60,726,000	95,097,000	54,680,000	75,523,000
EBITDA	-977,367,000	913,924,000	455,988,000	175,907,000	468,104,000	288,661,000
Return on Assets %	-.10%	.05%	.04%	.00%	.04%	
Return on Equity %	-.18%	.08%	.06%	.01%	.09%	
Debt to Equity	.34%	.29%	0.108	0.091	.79%	

CONTACT INFORMATION:

Phone: 212 314-7300 Fax: 212 314-7399
Toll-Free:
Address: 555 W. 18th St., New York, NY 10011 United States

STOCK TICKER/OTHER:

Stock Ticker: IAC Exchange: NAS
Employees: 11,000 Fiscal Year Ends: 12/31
Parent Company:

SALARIES/BONUSES:

Top Exec. Salary: $1,000,000 Bonus: $3,000,000
Second Exec. Salary: $549,231 Bonus: $2,000,000

OTHER THOUGHTS:

Estimated Female Officers or Directors: 6
Hot Spot for Advancement for Women/Minorities: Y

iCIMS Inc

www.icims.com

NAIC Code: 511210H

TYPES OF BUSINESS:

Computer Software, Business Management & ERP
Talent Acquisition Software Solutions
Recruitment Management
Software Development
Artificial Intelligence
Machine Learning
Talent Data and Analytics
Skills and Digital Reference Technology

BRANDS/DIVISIONS/AFFILIATES:

Talent Cloud
SkillSurvey

CONTACTS: *Note: Officers with more than one job title may be intentionally listed here more than once.*

Jason Edelboim, CEO
Diane Fanelli, COO
Nathan Anastasoff, CFO
Ari Osur, CMO
Laura Coccaro, Chief People Officer
Al Smith, CTO
Fernando Correa Arango, Chief Strategy Officer

GROWTH PLANS/SPECIAL FEATURES:

iCIMS, Inc. provides software-as-a-service (SaaS) talent acquisition solutions for businesses in the U.S. and internationally. iCIMS stands for internet collaborative information management system. Recruit software of iCIMS allows business users to easily find and screen people through its applicant tracking and management system, called Talent Cloud, a single platform. Talent Cloud encompasses technologies such as artificial intelligence (AI), machine learning, a vide studio, analytics, innovation, integrations, trust and security. Products of the platform span career sites, candidate relationship management, digital assistant, employee onboarding, marketing automation, opportunity marketplace, SkillSurvey, text engagement, video studio, analytics/advanced analytics, talent cloud applied intelligence (AI), insights and insights advisor. Headquartered in New Jersey, the firm has additional offices in Colorado and New York, and international offices in Ireland, Scotland, the U.K., India, Italy and France.

iCIMS offers its employees health benefits and retirement plans.

FINANCIAL DATA: *Note: Data for latest year may not have been available at press time.*

In U.S. $	2022	2021	2020	2019	2018	2017
Revenue						
R&D Expense						
Operating Income						
Operating Margin %						
SGA Expense						
Net Income						
Operating Cash Flow						
Capital Expenditure						
EBITDA						
Return on Assets %						
Return on Equity %						
Debt to Equity						

CONTACT INFORMATION:

Phone: 732 847-1941   Fax:
Toll-Free: 800-889-4422
Address: 101 Crawfords Corner Rd., Ste. 3-100, Holmdel, NJ 07733
United States

STOCK TICKER/OTHER:

Stock Ticker: Private
Employees: 800
Parent Company:

Exchange:
Fiscal Year Ends:

SALARIES/BONUSES:

Top Exec. Salary: $ Bonus: $
Second Exec. Salary: $ Bonus: $

OTHER THOUGHTS:

Estimated Female Officers or Directors:
Hot Spot for Advancement for Women/Minorities:

iCrossing Inc

www.iCrossing.com

NAIC Code: 511210M

TYPES OF BUSINESS:

Search Engine Marketing
Web Analytics Software
Marketing Solutions
Data and Consumer Insights
Data Management
Customer Experience
Digital Transformation Solutions
Search Engine Optimization

BRANDS/DIVISIONS/AFFILIATES:

Hearst Communications Inc

CONTACTS: *Note: Officers with more than one job title may be intentionally listed here more than once.*

Steven R. Swartz, Pres.
Rod Lenniger, Chief Admin. Officer
Adam Lavelle, Chief Strategy Officer
Patrick Bertermann, CEO-iCrossing Munich
Patrick Stern, Chief Creative Officer
Marlin Jackson, Exec. VP-Global Dev.
Amanda McElroy, Sr. VP-Bus. Dev.
William Randolph Hearst III, Chmn.-Hearst
Paul Doleman, CEO-iCrossing U.K.

GROWTH PLANS/SPECIAL FEATURES:

iCrossing, Inc., a subsidiary of Hearst Communications Inc., builds marketing solutions for businesses. The firm has a business-to-business (B2B) and business-to-consumer (C2B) strategy, with a focus on consumer touchpoints for brands to follow and analyze. iCrossing helps businesses measure, organize and analyze consumer and user data to guide strategy and deliver enhanced results. Data and consumer insight capabilities include attribution, business intelligence, 360 customer profiles, data management, data strategy, analytics audits, consultancy, training, measurement, reporting and web analytics. Customer and user experience capabilities include creative strategy and design, digital creative production, experience mapping, digital and enablement strategy, employee experience and enablement design, channel architecture, copywriting, web design, brand strategy, content marketing and social media assets. Digital transformation and technology capabilities include commerce, headless implementation, cross-platform integration, engineering, product management, quality assurance, managed services, intelligent automation, virtual/augmented reality, and data platforms. Search engine optimization (SEO) and performance media capabilities span media strategy, SEO, eRetail/Amazon, paid search, programmatic, paid social, audience planning and media analytics. Headquartered in Chicago, Mexico City and New York, iCrossing has offices throughout the U.S., Europe, Latin America and Asia.

FINANCIAL DATA: *Note: Data for latest year may not have been available at press time.*

In U.S. $	2022	2021	2020	2019	2018	2017
Revenue						
R&D Expense						
Operating Income						
Operating Margin %						
SGA Expense						
Net Income						
Operating Cash Flow						
Capital Expenditure						
EBITDA						
Return on Assets %						
Return on Equity %						
Debt to Equity						

CONTACT INFORMATION:

Phone: 212 649-3900 Fax: 646-280-1091
Toll-Free:
Address: 320 W. 57th St., New York, NY 10019 United States

STOCK TICKER/OTHER:

Stock Ticker: Subsidiary Exchange:
Employees: 1,000 Fiscal Year Ends: 12/31
Parent Company: Hearst Communications Inc

SALARIES/BONUSES:

Top Exec. Salary: $ Bonus: $
Second Exec. Salary: $ Bonus: $

OTHER THOUGHTS:

Estimated Female Officers or Directors: 7
Hot Spot for Advancement for Women/Minorities: Y

Illumio

www.illumio.com

NAIC Code: 511210E

TYPES OF BUSINESS:

Computer Software: Network Security, Managed Access, Digital ID, Cybersecurity & Anti-Virus
Zero Trust Segmentation Products
Cyber Attack Solutions
Workload Security
Cloud Security
Endpoint Security

BRANDS/DIVISIONS/AFFILIATES:

Illumio Core
Illumio CloudSecure
Illumio Edge

GROWTH PLANS/SPECIAL FEATURES:

Illumio provides Zero Trust segmentation products and solutions against cyber attacks. The company's offerings protect critical applications and digital assets by identifying risks, isolating attacks and securing data across cloud-native apps, hybrid and multi-clouds, data centers and endpoints. Illumio's products span workload security, cloud security and endpoint security through its Illumio Core, Illumio CloudSecure Illumio Endpoint and Illumio for Microsoft Azure Firewall product lines. Solutions include Cloud Security, Compliance, Cyber Resilience, Ransomware Risk Reduction and Zero Trust. Industries served by Illumio include Banking and Financial Services, Energy and Utilities, Government, Healthcare and Small/Midsize Businesses.

CONTACTS: Note: Officers with more than one job title may be intentionally listed here more than once.

Andrew Rubin, CEO
Anup Singh, CFO
Gautam Mehandru, CMO
Ben Verghese, CTO

FINANCIAL DATA: Note: Data for latest year may not have been available at press time.

In U.S. $	2022	2021	2020	2019	2018	2017
Revenue						
R&D Expense						
Operating Income						
Operating Margin %						
SGA Expense						
Net Income						
Operating Cash Flow						
Capital Expenditure						
EBITDA						
Return on Assets %						
Return on Equity %						
Debt to Equity						

CONTACT INFORMATION:

Phone: 669-800-5000   Fax:
Toll-Free:
Address: 920 De Guigne Dr., Sunnyvale, CA 94085 United States

STOCK TICKER/OTHER:

Stock Ticker: Private   Exchange:
Employees: 160   Fiscal Year Ends:
Parent Company:

SALARIES/BONUSES:

Top Exec. Salary: $ Bonus: $
Second Exec. Salary: $ Bonus: $

OTHER THOUGHTS:

Estimated Female Officers or Directors:
Hot Spot for Advancement for Women/Minorities:

Indiegogo Inc

www.indiegogo.com

NAIC Code: 519130

TYPES OF BUSINESS:

Crowdfunding
Crowdfunding Campaign Technology
Crowdfunding Online Platform
Ecommerce
Innovative Products
Product Investment
Product Payments and Fulfillment Services
Retail, Licensing and Distribution Services

BRANDS/DIVISIONS/AFFILIATES:

InDemand
Crowdfunding Field Guide

CONTACTS: *Note: Officers with more than one job title may be intentionally listed here more than once.*

Becky Center, CEO

GROWTH PLANS/SPECIAL FEATURES:

Indiegogo, Inc. offers live crowdfunding campaigns as well as an innovative product shopping and ecommerce marketplace. As for funding, thousands of crowdfunding and InDemand campaigns are launched and discovered on the Indiegogo site every week. Backers are people who contribute to campaigns, whether a project is in its early stages of development or ready to be shipped as a product. Equity crowdfunding is available for those who want to invest in innovative startups and growing companies, from software to hardware, film, restaurant and more. Just as with crowdfunding, the products come straight from entrepreneurs and their teams all over the world. Marketplace orders have guaranteed shipping, and if a seller does not stick to their shipping schedule, Indiegogo will refund the purchase. Entrepreneurs download Indiegogo's Crowdfunding Field Guide to get started, then funds are raised with a crowdfunding campaign. After the campaign, money continues to be raised with InDemand, with no fundraising target and no deadline limits. Early sales are generated in the Indiegogo marketplace, from which products are sold directly to the audience. Investments can also be raised, including via securities, revenue sharing and cryptocurrency or token sales. Services offered by Indiegogo include creative; fulfillment; marketing and communications; prototyping and production; and retail, licensing and distribution. Pre-launches are free, crowdfunding has a 5% platform fee as well as third-party credit card fees, and InDemand has a 5% platform fee as well as third-party credit card fees.

FINANCIAL DATA: *Note: Data for latest year may not have been available at press time.*

In U.S. $	2022	2021	2020	2019	2018	2017
Revenue						
R&D Expense						
Operating Income						
Operating Margin %						
SGA Expense						
Net Income						
Operating Cash Flow						
Capital Expenditure						
EBITDA						
Return on Assets %						
Return on Equity %						
Debt to Equity						

CONTACT INFORMATION:

Phone: 866-641-4646   Fax:
Toll-Free:
Address: 965 Mission St., Fl. 6, San Francisco, CA 94103 United States

STOCK TICKER/OTHER:

Stock Ticker: Private   Exchange:
Employees: 85   Fiscal Year Ends:
Parent Company:

SALARIES/BONUSES:

Top Exec. Salary: $ Bonus: $
Second Exec. Salary: $ Bonus: $

OTHER THOUGHTS:

Estimated Female Officers or Directors:
Hot Spot for Advancement for Women/Minorities:

Sales, profits and employees may be estimates. Financial information, benefits and other data can change quickly and may vary from those stated here.

Infor

www.infor.com

NAIC Code: 511210m

TYPES OF BUSINESS:

Cloud Applications Management and Analytics
Cloud-based Software
Enterprise Resource Management
Artificial Intelligence and Machine Learning
Human Capital Management
Financial and Supply Chain Management
Workforce Management
Cloud Technology

BRANDS/DIVISIONS/AFFILIATES:

Koch Industries Inc

CONTACTS: *Note: Officers with more than one job title may be intentionally listed here more than once.*

Kevin Samuelson, CEO
Soma Somasundaram, CTO

GROWTH PLANS/SPECIAL FEATURES:

Infor is a cloud-based business applications software provider. The company builds and designs its software for specific industry needs across verticals such as distribution, manufacturing and service. Over 60,000 organizations in more than 175 countries rely on Infor to help overcome market disruptions and achieve business-wide digital transformation. Infor's industry solutions include enterprise resource planning (ERP), financials, human capital management (HCM), supply chain management, product lifecycle management and workforce management, human resources and talent management, community development and regulations, clinical interoperability and many more. Infor's platform capabilities include machine learning, artificial intelligence (AI), analytics and reporting, an application programming interface (API) gateway, an app designer, cloud technology, governance, risk and compliance, marketplace and enterprise automation. Infor Marketplace provides complete visibility into all the innovations available for industry-specific customer needs. Services offered by the firm include consulting, managed services, education services and related support services. Infor operates as a subsidiary of Koch Industries, Inc.

FINANCIAL DATA: *Note: Data for latest year may not have been available at press time.*

In U.S. $	2022	2021	2020	2019	2018	2017
Revenue	3,629,227,000	3,489,641,610	3,355,424,625	3,273,585,000	3,117,700,000	2,855,800,000
R&D Expense						
Operating Income						
Operating Margin %						
SGA Expense						
Net Income						
Operating Cash Flow						
Capital Expenditure						
EBITDA						
Return on Assets %						
Return on Equity %						
Debt to Equity						

CONTACT INFORMATION:

Phone: 646-336-1700   Fax:
Toll-Free: 866-244-5479
Address: 641 Avenue of the Americas, New York, NY 10011 United States

STOCK TICKER/OTHER:

Stock Ticker: Subsidiary   Exchange:
Employees: 17,000   Fiscal Year Ends: 04/30
Parent Company: Koch Industries Inc

SALARIES/BONUSES:

Top Exec. Salary: $ Bonus: $
Second Exec. Salary: $ Bonus: $

OTHER THOUGHTS:

Estimated Female Officers or Directors:
Hot Spot for Advancement for Women/Minorities:

Infosys Limited

www.infosys.com

NAIC Code: 541512

TYPES OF BUSINESS:
IT Consulting
Software Development & Services
Business Process Outsourcing

GROWTH PLANS/SPECIAL FEATURES:
Infosys is a leading global IT services provider, with nearly 250,000 employees. Based in Bangalore, the Indian IT services firm leverages its offshore outsourcing model to derive 60% of its revenue from North America. The company offers traditional IT services offerings: consulting, managed services and cloud infrastructure services, and business process outsourcing as a service (BPaaS).

BRANDS/DIVISIONS/AFFILIATES:
Finacle
Global Delivery Model
EdgeVerve Systems Limited
Infosys BPM
Infosys Consulting
Infosys Public Services

CONTACTS: *Note: Officers with more than one job title may be intentionally listed here more than once.*
Salil Parekh, CEO
Mohit Joshi, Co-Pres.
Nilnajan Roy, CFO
Inderpreet Sawhney, Chief Compliance Officer
Krishnamurthy Shankar, Exec. VP-Human Resources
Subrahmanyan Goparaju, Sr. VP-Infosys Labs
Ravi Kumar S., Co-Pres.
Sanjay Purohit, Sr. VP-Prod., Platforms & Solutions
Sanjay Jalona, Sr. VP-Mfg. & Eng. Svcs.
Nithyanandan Radhakrishnan, Sr. VP
K. Murali Krishna, Sr. VP-Computers & Comm.
N.R. Narayana Murthy, Co-Chmn.
V. Balakrishnan, Head-Infosys BPO, Fin. & India Bus. Unit
Srinath Batni, Head-Delivery Excellence
Nandita Gurjar, Sr. VP-Education & Research
Nandan Nilekani, Chmn.
Dheeshjith V.G., Sr. VP-Asia Pacific, Middle East & Africa
Chandrashekar Kakal, Sr. VP-Global Delivery

FINANCIAL DATA: *Note: Data for latest year may not have been available at press time.*

In U.S. $	2022	2021	2020	2019	2018	2017
Revenue	16,311,000,000	13,561,000,000	12,780,000,000	11,799,000,000	10,939,000,000	
R&D Expense						
Operating Income	3,779,000,000	3,325,000,000	2,724,000,000	2,696,000,000	2,659,000,000	
Operating Margin %	.23%	.25%	.21%	.23%	.24%	
SGA Expense	1,391,000,000	1,408,000,000	1,504,000,000	1,416,000,000	1,279,000,000	
Net Income	2,963,000,000	2,613,000,000	2,331,000,000	2,199,000,000	2,486,000,000	
Operating Cash Flow	3,345,000,000	3,258,000,000	2,611,000,000	2,262,000,000	2,257,000,000	
Capital Expenditure	290,000,000	285,000,000	465,000,000	349,000,000	310,000,000	
EBITDA	4,529,000,000	4,063,000,000	3,526,000,000	3,290,000,000	3,432,000,000	
Return on Assets %	.20%	.19%	.19%	.18%	.20%	
Return on Equity %	.29%	.27%	.26%	.23%	.24%	
Debt to Equity	.06%	.06%	0.061			

CONTACT INFORMATION:
Phone: 91 8028520261   Fax: 91 8028520362
Toll-Free:
Address: Hosur Rd., Electronics City, Bengaluru, Karnataka 560 100 India

STOCK TICKER/OTHER:
Stock Ticker: INFY   Exchange: NYS
Employees: 368,125   Fiscal Year Ends: 03/31
Parent Company:

SALARIES/BONUSES:
Top Exec. Salary: $827,890   Bonus: $2,306,531
Second Exec. Salary: $761,219   Bonus: $630,062

OTHER THOUGHTS:
Estimated Female Officers or Directors: 2
Hot Spot for Advancement for Women/Minorities: Y

Sales, profits and employees may be estimates. Financial information, benefits and other data can change quickly and may vary from those stated here.

InMobi Pte Ltd

www.inmobi.com

NAIC Code: 541810E

TYPES OF BUSINESS:

Online Marketing Services
Cloud-Based Advertising Services
Marketing Technology Platforms
Customer Feedback Solutions
Customer Engagement Solutions
Mobile App Marketing
In-App Monetizing Solutions
Ad Revenue Optimization

BRANDS/DIVISIONS/AFFILIATES:

Pulse
Audiences
Exchange
DSP
InMobi University
Appsumer

CONTACTS: *Note: Officers with more than one job title may be intentionally listed here more than once.*

Naveen Tewari, CEO
Marc Steifman, CFO
Sahil Mathur, Chief Human Resources Officer
Mohit Saxena, CTO

GROWTH PLANS/SPECIAL FEATURES:

InMobi Pte., Ltd. provides cloud-based mobile advertising services. The firm connects brands and consumers by leveraging its technology platforms and providing access to its mobile intelligence capabilities. InMobi's cloud-based marketing strategy creates a way for brands to understand, identify, engage and acquire connected consumers. Solutions for Advertisement include: Pulse, which combines direct feedback and unaided mobile data sources to connect with consumers and to act immediately; Audiences, for harnessing the power of unique, always-on segments to engage and activate the best prospective customers; Exchange, for reaching premium in-app audiences programmatically, so as to maximize return-on-investment (ROI) for mobile marketing campaigns; and DSP, an in-app, demand-side platform (DSP) for advertising, guaranteeing ROI and complete transparency. For publishers, InMobi offers a comprehensive in-app monetization platform for maximizing inventory yield; a mediation platform for maximizing ad revenue with a unified auction across multiple demand sources; and an in-app audience bidding solution. For the retail industry, InMobi offers a retail media solution for monetizing media and secured data. Its telecommunications solutions offer technology for products and company growth. InMobi University is an education platform for marketers and publishers. InMobi is headquartered in India, with offices strategically located worldwide.

FINANCIAL DATA: *Note: Data for latest year may not have been available at press time.*

In U.S. $	2022	2021	2020	2019	2018	2017
Revenue	62,000,000	59,715,136	57,418,400	55,224,800	49,499,600	44,219,300
R&D Expense						
Operating Income						
Operating Margin %						
SGA Expense						
Net Income			-10,234,300	-7,761,740	-5,000,000	1,828,860
Operating Cash Flow						
Capital Expenditure						
EBITDA						
Return on Assets %						
Return on Equity %						
Debt to Equity						

CONTACT INFORMATION:

Phone: 65 6820 2953   Fax:
Toll-Free:
Address: 11-03, 80 Robinson Rd., Singapore, 068898 Singapore

STOCK TICKER/OTHER:

Stock Ticker: Private   Exchange:
Employees: 800   Fiscal Year Ends: 03/31
Parent Company:

SALARIES/BONUSES:

Top Exec. Salary: $ Bonus: $
Second Exec. Salary: $ Bonus: $

OTHER THOUGHTS:

Estimated Female Officers or Directors:
Hot Spot for Advancement for Women/Minorities:

INNOVATE Corp

innovatecorp.com

NAIC Code: 517311

TYPES OF BUSINESS:

International & Long-Distance Telephone Service
Industrial Construction Services
Structural Steel
Water Pipes
Digital Engineering
Healthcare Product Development
Medical Technologies
Over-the-Air Broadcasting Stations

BRANDS/DIVISIONS/AFFILIATES:

DBM Global Inc
GrayWolf
Panseed Life Sciences LLC
HC2 Broadcasting Holdings Inc
Azteca America
INNOVATE Corp

GROWTH PLANS/SPECIAL FEATURES:

Innovate Corp is a diversified holding company that has a portfolio of subsidiaries in a variety of operating segments which are; The infrastructure segment is comprised of DBM Global Inc, a fully integrated industrial construction, structural steel, and facility maintenance provider that provides fabrication and erection of structural steel and heavy steel plate services, The Life Sciences segment is comprised of Pansend Life Sciences which seeks to develop products to treat early osteoarthritis of the knee and aesthetic and medical technologies for the skin, and Spectrum segment is comprised of HC2 Broadcasting Holdings Inc which operates over-the-air broadcasting stations across the United States.

CONTACTS:
Note: Officers with more than one job title may be intentionally listed here more than once.

Philip Falcone, CEO
Michael Sena, CFO
Suzi Herbst, Chief Administrative Officer
Joseph Ferraro, Other Executive Officer

FINANCIAL DATA:
Note: Data for latest year may not have been available at press time.

In U.S. $	2022	2021	2020	2019	2018	2017
Revenue	1,637,300,000	1,205,200,000	716,900,000	1,077,000,000	1,976,700,000	1,634,100,000
R&D Expense						
Operating Income	13,400,000	-10,600,000	-28,300,000	75,300,000	-54,800,000	-1,100,000
Operating Margin %	.01%	-.01%	-.04%	.07%	-.03%	.00%
SGA Expense	180,100,000	168,300,000	145,500,000	177,300,000	218,400,000	182,800,000
Net Income	-35,900,000	-227,500,000	-92,000,000	-31,500,000	162,000,000	-46,900,000
Operating Cash Flow	-9,500,000	27,000,000	41,100,000	110,700,000	341,400,000	6,600,000
Capital Expenditure	20,700,000	24,100,000	17,800,000	24,700,000	39,700,000	31,900,000
EBITDA	53,100,000	16,000,000	54,900,000	42,500,000	296,700,000	51,900,000
Return on Assets %	-.04%	-.06%	-.01%	.00%	.03%	-.02%
Return on Equity %		-.97%	-.21%	-.14%	1.72%	-.85%
Debt to Equity			0.285	1.887	8.06%	8.115

CONTACT INFORMATION:

Phone: 212 235-2690   Fax:
Toll-Free:
Address: 295 Madison Ave. Fl. 12, New York, NY 10017 United States

STOCK TICKER/OTHER:

Stock Ticker: VATE   Exchange: NYS
Employees: 3,761   Fiscal Year Ends: 12/31
Parent Company:

SALARIES/BONUSES:

Top Exec. Salary: $550,000   Bonus: $
Second Exec. Salary: Bonus: $
$506,000

OTHER THOUGHTS:

Estimated Female Officers or Directors:
Hot Spot for Advancement for Women/Minorities:

InsideSales

NAIC Code: 511210K

TYPES OF BUSINESS:

Computer Software, Sales & Customer Relationship Management
Enterprise Revenue Solutions
Cloud
Data
Insights
Marketing
Sales
Account Management

BRANDS/DIVISIONS/AFFILIATES:

Aurea Software Inc
InsideSales
Revenue Acceleration Cloud

GROWTH PLANS/SPECIAL FEATURES:

InsideSales has developed a Revenue Acceleration Cloud that provides enterprise revenue teams with the data, insights and solutions necessary to drive results. Solutions offered include marketing, sales development, account executives, account management, sales operations and sales leaders, as well as use-case solutions such as lead follow-up, opportunity engagement, outbound engagement and customer relationship. Products offered include playbooks, cadence, automation, prioritization, reporting, scoring, scoreboards and buyer intelligence, as well as integrations with Salesforce, Microsoft and SAP. InsideSales operates as a wholly owned subsidiary of Aurea Software, Inc.

CONTACTS: Note: Officers with more than one job title may be intentionally listed here more than once.

Kathy Slowinski, CEO-Aurea

FINANCIAL DATA: Note: Data for latest year may not have been available at press time.

In U.S. $	2022	2021	2020	2019	2018	2017
Revenue						
R&D Expense						
Operating Income						
Operating Margin %						
SGA Expense						
Net Income						
Operating Cash Flow						
Capital Expenditure						
EBITDA						
Return on Assets %						
Return on Equity %						
Debt to Equity						

CONTACT INFORMATION:

Phone: 512 201-8287   Fax:
Toll-Free:
Address: 2028 E. Ben White Blvd., Ste. 240-2650, Austin, TX 78741
United States

STOCK TICKER/OTHER:

Stock Ticker: Subsidiary   Exchange:
Employees: 500   Fiscal Year Ends:
Parent Company: Aurea Software Inc

SALARIES/BONUSES:

Top Exec. Salary: $ Bonus: $
Second Exec. Salary: $ Bonus: $

OTHER THOUGHTS:

Estimated Female Officers or Directors:
Hot Spot for Advancement for Women/Minorities:

Instacart (Maplebear Inc)

www.instacart.com

NAIC Code: 492210

TYPES OF BUSINESS:

Grocery Delivery Services
Online Food Order
Food Delivery
Curbside Service
Food Delivery Membership Service
API Technology Solutions
Nano-Fulfillment Centers
Data and Insights

BRANDS/DIVISIONS/AFFILIATES:

Maplebear Inc
Instacart+
Instacart Connect
Instacart Platform

GROWTH PLANS/SPECIAL FEATURES:

Maplebear, which does business as Instacart, is an online grocery pickup and delivery service provider currently in the United States and Canada. Instacart partners with local and national grocers who provide their selection of food and other goods to customers through Instacart's mobile app or website. After a customer places an order, an independent personal shopper employed by Instacart will pick the order and either prepare it for pickup or deliver it to the customer's chosen location. Instacart's revenue model consists of transaction revenue in the form of retailer and customer fees, as well as advertising revenue from brand advertising on Instacart platforms.

CONTACTS: Note: Officers with more than one job title may be intentionally listed here more than once.

Fidji Simo, CEO

FINANCIAL DATA: Note: Data for latest year may not have been available at press time.

In U.S. $	2022	2021	2020	2019	2018	2017
Revenue	2,551,000,000	1,834,000,000	1,477,000,000			
R&D Expense	518,000,000	368,000,000	194,000,000			
Operating Income	62,000,000	-86,000,000	-75,000,000			
Operating Margin %						
SGA Expense	999,000,000	682,000,000	436,000,000			
Net Income	428,000,000	-73,000,000	-70,000,000			
Operating Cash Flow	277,000,000	-204,000,000	-91,000,000			
Capital Expenditure	26,000,000	22,000,000	7,000,000			
EBITDA	109,000,000	-59,000,000	-55,000,000			
Return on Assets %						
Return on Equity %						
Debt to Equity						

CONTACT INFORMATION:

Phone: 415 932-6695   Fax:
Toll-Free: 888 246-7822
Address: 50 Beale, Ste. 600, San Francisco, CA 94107 United States

STOCK TICKER/OTHER:

Stock Ticker: CART   Exchange: NAS
Employees: 3,486   Fiscal Year Ends: 12/31
Parent Company:

SALARIES/BONUSES:

Top Exec. Salary: $500,000   Bonus: $1,000,000
Second Exec. Salary: $500,000   Bonus: $360,000

OTHER THOUGHTS:

Estimated Female Officers or Directors:
Hot Spot for Advancement for Women/Minorities: Y

Sales, profits and employees may be estimates. Financial information, benefits and other data can change quickly and may vary from those stated here.

Instagram

instagram.com

NAIC Code: 519130

TYPES OF BUSINESS:

Social Media
Online Advertising
Social App
Brand Building
Online Community Platform
Content Sharing
Pictures and Videos
In-App Features

BRANDS/DIVISIONS/AFFILIATES:

Meta Platforms Inc
Instagram Stories
Reels
IGTV

CONTACTS: *Note: Officers with more than one job title may be intentionally listed here more than once.*

Adam Mosseri, CEO

GROWTH PLANS/SPECIAL FEATURES:

Instagram, founded in 2010, is an online community of more than two billion members who capture and share pictures and videos every month. The social networking service enables users to share content either publicly or privately on its platform, as well as through a variety of other social networking platforms such as Facebook, Twitter, Tumblr and Flickr. Users can also apply digital filters to their images. The maximum duration for Instagram in feed videos is 60 minutes. Instagram Stories is a feature of the app dedicated to posting temporary moments of the day. These moments automatically disappear after a 24-hour period. The Reels feature enables users to create, watch and share short videos (up to 90 seconds). Other features include saving posts, customizable stickers used in Instagram stories and direct messages, four or more people can go live together, closed captioning and more. Instagram's shopping link enables users to explore new products and shop online. IGTV is a standalone vertical video application primarily made for smartphones. It allows users to upload vertical videos up to 10 minutes in length or up to 60 minutes if you are verified or popular. It is available within the Instagram app and website. For creators and businesses, Instagram offers tools for engaging with audiences and building brands. The tools offer education content, insights, profile controls and more. Instagram is owned by Meta Platforms, Inc.

FINANCIAL DATA: *Note: Data for latest year may not have been available at press time.*

In U.S. $	2022	2021	2020	2019	2018	2017
Revenue	33,300,000,000	23,331,000,000	19,442,500,000	17,675,000,000	8,500,000,000	3,500,000,000
R&D Expense						
Operating Income						
Operating Margin %						
SGA Expense						
Net Income						
Operating Cash Flow						
Capital Expenditure						
EBITDA						
Return on Assets %						
Return on Equity %						
Debt to Equity						

CONTACT INFORMATION:

Phone: 650-543-4800   Fax:
Toll-Free:
Address: 1 Hacker Way, Bldg. 14, Fl. 1, Menlo Park, CA 94025 United States

STOCK TICKER/OTHER:

Stock Ticker: Subsidiary   Exchange:
Employees: Fiscal Year Ends:
Parent Company: Meta Platforms Inc

SALARIES/BONUSES:

Top Exec. Salary: $ Bonus: $
Second Exec. Salary: $ Bonus: $

OTHER THOUGHTS:

Estimated Female Officers or Directors:
Hot Spot for Advancement for Women/Minorities:

Intercom Inc

www.intercom.com

NAIC Code: 511210C

TYPES OF BUSINESS:

Computer Software: Telecom, Communications & VOIP
Message Software
Marketing Communication Solutions
Customer Relations
Chat Bots
Marketing Software
Ecommerce

BRANDS/DIVISIONS/AFFILIATES:

CONTACTS: Note: Officers with more than one job title may be intentionally listed here more than once.

Eogham McCabe, CEO
Des Traynor, Chief Strategy Officer
Dan Griggs, CFO
Paul Adams, Chief Product Officer
Darragh Curran, CTO
Eoghan McCabe, Chmn.

GROWTH PLANS/SPECIAL FEATURES:

Intercom, Inc. provides a messaging platform for sales, marketing and customer service teams. The platform enables business teams to talk to customers via company apps, websites, social media and email. Intercom's products feature a business manager, customizable bots, automated answers, product tours, targeted messages, team inbox, help center articles, account-based marketing, apps, integrations, customer data, live chat and iOS/Android apps and related integrations. More than 25,000 businesses use Intercom to connect with people worldwide. Industries served by Intercom primarily include financial services, ecommerce, education and healthcare. Intercom is headquartered in San Francisco, California, with a domestic office in Chicago, Illinois, as well as international offices in Australia, Ireland and the U.K. Investors of the firm include Bessemer Venture Partners, ICONIQ, Index Ventures, Social Capital, Kleiner Perkins and others.

Intercom offers its employees comprehensive health benefits, continuing education options and more.

FINANCIAL DATA: Note: Data for latest year may not have been available at press time.

In U.S. $	2022	2021	2020	2019	2018	2017
Revenue	150,000,000	100,700,000	95,000,000	89,900,000	61,500,000	
R&D Expense						
Operating Income						
Operating Margin %						
SGA Expense						
Net Income						
Operating Cash Flow						
Capital Expenditure						
EBITDA						
Return on Assets %						
Return on Equity %						
Debt to Equity						

CONTACT INFORMATION:

Phone: 877-595-5175   Fax:
Toll-Free:
Address: 55 2nd St., Fl. 4, San Francisco, CA 94105 United States

STOCK TICKER/OTHER:

Stock Ticker: Private   Exchange:
Employees: 600   Fiscal Year Ends: 01/31
Parent Company:

SALARIES/BONUSES:

Top Exec. Salary: $ Bonus: $
Second Exec. Salary: $ Bonus: $

OTHER THOUGHTS:

Estimated Female Officers or Directors:
Hot Spot for Advancement for Women/Minorities:

Sales, profits and employees may be estimates. Financial information, benefits and other data can change quickly and may vary from those stated here.

Internap Corporation

www.inap.com

NAIC Code: 517311

TYPES OF BUSINESS:

Internet Access Provider
Hybrid Infrastructure Solutions
Multi-platform Cloud Solutions
Data Centers
Intelligent Managed Services
Network Solutions

BRANDS/DIVISIONS/AFFILIATES:

Internap Holding LLC
INAP

GROWTH PLANS/SPECIAL FEATURES:

Internap Corporation, branded as INAP, is a global provider of performance-driven, secure hybrid infrastructure solutions. INAP's suite of multi-platform cloud, modern data center, optimized network and intelligent managed services solutions help businesses flexibly move workloads, and thus reducing risk and maximizing value. Cloud solutions include bare metal and multi-cloud, as well as cloud backup for data protection. Network solutions include performance internet protocol (IP) and connectivity solutions. Managed services include intelligent monitoring, managed security, managed storage and managed backups. INAP's data centers are located throughout North America, as well as in Amsterdam, London, Singapore, Sydney and Tokyo/Osaka. Internap Corporation operates as a subsidiary of Internap Holding, LLC.

Internap offers its employees comprehensive health benefits, 401(k), paid time off and more.

CONTACTS: Note: Officers with more than one job title may be intentionally listed here more than once.

John Scanlon, CEO
Jason Kiser, Sr. VP-Oper.
Kevin Bostick, CFO
Ali Marashi, CTO
Richard Diegnan, Executive VP
Richard Ramlall, Other Executive Officer
Joseph DuFresne, Vice President, Divisional

FINANCIAL DATA: Note: Data for latest year may not have been available at press time.

In U.S. $	2022	2021	2020	2019	2018	2017
Revenue	307,931,520	296,088,000	284,700,000	292,000,000	317,372,992	280,718,016
R&D Expense						
Operating Income						
Operating Margin %						
SGA Expense						
Net Income				-138,000,000	-62,500,000	-45,343,000
Operating Cash Flow						
Capital Expenditure						
EBITDA						
Return on Assets %						
Return on Equity %						
Debt to Equity						

CONTACT INFORMATION:

Phone: 404 302-9700   Fax: 404 475-0520
Toll-Free: 877-843-7627
Address: 250 Williams St., Ste. E-100, Atlanta, GA 30303 United States

STOCK TICKER/OTHER:

Stock Ticker: Private   Exchange:
Employees: 530   Fiscal Year Ends: 12/31
Parent Company: Internap Holding LLC

SALARIES/BONUSES:

Top Exec. Salary: $ Bonus: $
Second Exec. Salary: $ Bonus: $

OTHER THOUGHTS:

Estimated Female Officers or Directors: 2
Hot Spot for Advancement for Women/Minorities: Y

International Business Machines Corporation (IBM)

www.ibm.com
NAIC Code: 541513

TYPES OF BUSINESS:

Computer Facilities and Business Process Outsourcing
Computer Facilities Management
Business Process Outsourcing
Software & Hardware
Cloud-Based Computer Services
IT Consulting & Outsourcing
Financial Services
Data Analytics and Health Care Analytics

BRANDS/DIVISIONS/AFFILIATES:

Aspera
Cognos
IBM
Red Hat OpenShift
Watson
Kyndryl Holdings Inc

GROWTH PLANS/SPECIAL FEATURES:

IBM looks to be a part of every aspect of an enterprise's IT needs. The company primarily sells software, IT services, consulting, and hardware. IBM operates in 175 countries and employs approximately 350,000 people. The company has a robust roster of 80,000 business partners to service 5,200 clients, which includes 95% of all Fortune 500. While IBM is a B2B company, IBM's outward impact is substantial. For example, IBM manages 90% of all credit card transactions globally and is responsible for 50% of all wireless connections in the world.

IBM offers employees medical, vision, dental and disability insurance; a flexible spending account; and 401(k) and stock purchase options.

CONTACTS: *Note: Officers with more than one job title may be intentionally listed here more than once.*

Arvind Krishna, CEO
James Kavanaugh, CFO, Divisional
Robert Del Bene, Chief Accounting Officer
Nickle Lamoreaux, Other Executive Officer
Michelle Browdy, Senior VP, Divisional
Gary Cohn, Vice Chairman

FINANCIAL DATA: *Note: Data for latest year may not have been available at press time.*

In U.S. $	2022	2021	2020	2019	2018	2017
Revenue	60,530,000,000	57,351,000,000	55,179,000,000	57,714,000,000	79,591,000,000	79,139,000,000
R&D Expense	6,567,000,000	6,488,000,000	6,262,000,000	5,910,000,000	5,379,000,000	5,590,000,000
Operating Income	8,154,000,000	6,832,000,000	4,662,000,000	7,538,000,000	13,217,000,000	13,139,000,000
Operating Margin %	.13%	.12%	.08%	.13%	.17%	.17%
SGA Expense	17,483,000,000	17,699,000,000	20,561,000,000	18,724,000,000	19,366,000,000	19,680,000,000
Net Income	1,640,000,000	5,742,000,000	5,590,000,000	9,431,000,000	8,728,001,000	5,753,000,000
Operating Cash Flow	10,435,000,000	12,796,000,000	18,197,000,000	14,770,000,000	15,247,000,000	16,724,000,000
Capital Expenditure	1,972,000,000	2,768,000,000	3,230,000,000	2,907,000,000	3,964,000,000	3,773,000,000
EBITDA	7,174,000,000	12,409,000,000	10,555,000,000	14,609,000,000	16,545,000,000	16,556,000,000
Return on Assets %	.01%	.04%	.04%	.07%	.07%	.05%
Return on Equity %	.08%	.29%	.27%	.50%	.51%	.32%
Debt to Equity	2.20%	2.51%	2.764	2.782	2.12%	2.264

CONTACT INFORMATION:

Phone: 914 499-1900   Fax: 800-314-1092
Toll-Free: 800-426-4968
Address: 1 New Orchard Rd., Armonk, NY 10504 United States

STOCK TICKER/OTHER:

Stock Ticker: IBM   Exchange: NYS
Employees: 311,300   Fiscal Year Ends: 12/31
Parent Company:

SALARIES/BONUSES:

Top Exec. Salary: $1,500,000   Bonus: $
Second Exec. Salary: Bonus: $
$1,170,000

OTHER THOUGHTS:

Estimated Female Officers or Directors: 6
Hot Spot for Advancement for Women/Minorities: Y

Sales, profits and employees may be estimates. Financial information, benefits and other data can change quickly and may vary from those stated here.

Internet Initiative Japan Inc

NAIC Code: 517311

www.iij.ad.jp

TYPES OF BUSINESS:

Internet Service Provider
Internet Access
Wide Area Network
Systems Integration
Outsourcing Services

GROWTH PLANS/SPECIAL FEATURES:

Internet Initiative Japan Inc. is a provider of a variety of services including Internet access, outsourcing, and systems integration. Its Internet access services span dial-up, mobile, and broadband technologies. Its wide area network services allow secure data sharing over Internet virtual private networks, independently developed routers, and closed wide area networks. Its outsourcing services include cloud, content delivery, data center, and security services. The firm generates nearly all its revenue in Japan.

BRANDS/DIVISIONS/AFFILIATES:

Trust Networks Inc
PTC Systems Pte Ltd

CONTACTS: *Note: Officers with more than one job title may be intentionally listed here more than once.*

Koichi Suzuki, CEO
Eijiro Katsu, Pres.
Kazuhiro Tokita, Sr. Exec. Officer
Masayoshi Tobita, Exec. Managing Officer
Junichi Shimagami, Exec. Managing Officer
Kiyoshi Ishida, Exec. Managing Officer

FINANCIAL DATA: *Note: Data for latest year may not have been available at press time.*

In U.S. $	2022	2021	2020	2019	2018	2017
Revenue	1,544,495,000	1,453,511,000	1,395,314,000	1,313,131,000	1,202,605,000	
R&D Expense						
Operating Income	160,683,200	97,225,540	56,128,040	41,100,470	46,195,430	
Operating Margin %	.10%	.07%	.04%	.03%	.04%	
SGA Expense	190,858,700	173,946,700	164,291,400	154,576,000	146,533,800	
Net Income	106,944,700	66,271,050	27,341,960	24,024,120	30,181,740	
Operating Cash Flow	297,339,300	276,670,800	227,876,800	171,638,000	100,065,000	
Capital Expenditure	78,591,260	75,113,350	80,788,000	85,167,840	117,462,300	
EBITDA	362,774,100	290,631,000	247,637,100	149,466,800	141,419,400	
Return on Assets %	.07%	.05%	.02%	.02%	.03%	
Return on Equity %	.16%	.11%	.05%	.05%	.06%	
Debt to Equity	.05%	.08%	0.154	0.184	.21%	

CONTACT INFORMATION:

Phone: 81 352056500   Fax: 81 352596311
Toll-Free:
Address: Iidabashi Grand Bloom, 2-10-2 Fujimi, Tokyo, 102-0071 Japan

STOCK TICKER/OTHER:

Stock Ticker: IIJIY   Exchange: PINX
Employees: 4,451   Fiscal Year Ends: 03/31
Parent Company:

SALARIES/BONUSES:

Top Exec. Salary: $ Bonus: $
Second Exec. Salary: $ Bonus: $

OTHER THOUGHTS:

Estimated Female Officers or Directors:
Hot Spot for Advancement for Women/Minorities:

Intralinks Inc

www.intralinks.com

NAIC Code: 511210H

TYPES OF BUSINESS:

Software-as-a-Service Technologies
Cloud Financial Technology
Secure Data Solutions
Global Banking Technology
Deal-Making Solutions
Capital Markets Solutions
Virtual Data Platform

BRANDS/DIVISIONS/AFFILIATES:

SS&C Technologies Holdings Inc
SS&C Intralinks

CONTACTS: Note: Officers with more than one job title may be intentionally listed here more than once.

Ken Bisconti, Co-CEO
Bob Petrocchi, Co-CEO
Christopher Lafond, CFO
Michal Kimeldorfer, Executive VP, Divisional
Aditya Joshi, Executive VP, Divisional
Leif OLeary, Executive VP, Divisional
Scott Semel, Executive VP

GROWTH PLANS/SPECIAL FEATURES:

Intralinks, Inc., operating as SS&C Intralinks, provides cloud-based financial technology for global banking, deal-making and capital market industries. The firm pioneered the virtual data room, and its technologies enable and secure the flow of information. Intralinks facilitates strategic initiatives such as mergers and acquisitions, capital raising and investor reporting. Its solutions enhance these activities by streamlining operations, reducing risk, improving client experiences and increasing visibility. Intralinks serves nearly all of the Fortune 1000 and has executed trillions worth of financial transactions on its platform. Products of the company are grouped into four categories: mergers and acquisitions, offering a virtual data room, marketing deals, buy-side due diligence, deal management and post-merger integration; alternative investments, offering fund reporting, fundraising, portfolio reporting and accounting solutions; banking and securities, offering capital market, corporate lending and debt sale solutions, as well as retail and private banking, regulatory risk and compliance and LIBOR transition services and solutions; and platform, offering application programming interfaces (APIs) and platform accelerators, as well as audit, certification, security, governance and mobile solutions. Intralinks operates as a subsidiary of SS&C Technologies Holdings, Inc., and has 25 offices in 19 countries worldwide.

FINANCIAL DATA: Note: Data for latest year may not have been available at press time.

In U.S. $	2022	2021	2020	2019	2018	2017
Revenue	359,868,600	346,027,500	332,718,750	341,250,000	325,000,000	303,000,000
R&D Expense						
Operating Income						
Operating Margin %						
SGA Expense						
Net Income						
Operating Cash Flow						
Capital Expenditure						
EBITDA						
Return on Assets %						
Return on Equity %						
Debt to Equity						

CONTACT INFORMATION:

Phone: 212 543-7700   Fax: 212 543-7978
Toll-Free: 866-468-7254
Address: 622 3rd Ave., Fl 10, New York, NY 10017 United States

STOCK TICKER/OTHER:

Stock Ticker: Subsidiary   Exchange:
Employees: 810   Fiscal Year Ends: 12/31
Parent Company: SS&C Technologies Holdings Inc

SALARIES/BONUSES:

Top Exec. Salary: $ Bonus: $
Second Exec. Salary: $ Bonus: $

OTHER THOUGHTS:

Estimated Female Officers or Directors: 1
Hot Spot for Advancement for Women/Minorities:

Intuit Inc

NAIC Code: 511210Q

www.intuit.com

TYPES OF BUSINESS:

Computer Software-Financial Management
Business Accounting Software
Consumer Finance Software
Tax Preparation Software
Online Financial Services

GROWTH PLANS/SPECIAL FEATURES:

Intuit is a provider of small-business accounting software (QuickBooks), personal tax solutions (TurboTax), and professional tax offerings (Lacerte). Founded in the mid-1980s, Intuit controls the majority of U.S. market share for small-business accounting and DIY tax-filing software.

BRANDS/DIVISIONS/AFFILIATES:

Credit Karma
ProConnect
QuickBooks
TurboTax
Mint
Lacerte
ProFile
Rocket Science Group LLC (The)

CONTACTS: Note: Officers with more than one job title may be intentionally listed here more than once.

Sasan Goodarzi, CEO
Michelle Clatterbuck, CFO
Brad Smith, Chairman of the Board
Mark Flournoy, Chief Accounting Officer
Marianna Tessel, Chief Technology Officer
Lauren Hotz, Controller
Kerry McLean, Executive VP
J. Chriss, Executive VP
Gregory Johnson, Executive VP
Laura Fennell, Executive VP
Scott Cook, Founder

FINANCIAL DATA: Note: Data for latest year may not have been available at press time.

In U.S. $	2022	2021	2020	2019	2018	2017
Revenue	12,726,000,000	9,633,000,000	7,679,000,000	6,784,000,000	6,025,000,000	
R&D Expense	2,347,000,000	1,678,000,000	1,392,000,000	1,233,000,000	1,186,000,000	
Operating Income	2,571,000,000	2,500,000,000	2,176,000,000	1,854,000,000	1,560,000,000	
Operating Margin %	.20%	.26%	.28%	.27%	.26%	
SGA Expense	4,986,000,000	3,626,000,000	2,727,000,000	2,524,000,000	2,295,000,000	
Net Income	2,066,000,000	2,062,000,000	1,826,000,000	1,557,000,000	1,329,000,000	
Operating Cash Flow	3,889,000,000	3,250,000,000	2,414,000,000	2,324,000,000	2,112,000,000	
Capital Expenditure	229,000,000	125,000,000	137,000,000	155,000,000	124,000,000	
EBITDA	3,369,000,000	2,948,000,000	2,425,000,000	2,118,000,000	1,832,000,000	
Return on Assets %	.10%	.16%	.21%	.27%	.29%	
Return on Equity %	.16%	.28%	.41%	.47%	.64%	
Debt to Equity	.42%	.24%	0.441	0.103	.14%	

CONTACT INFORMATION:

Phone: 650 944-6000   Fax: 650 944-3060
Toll-Free: 800-446-8848
Address: 2700 Coast Ave., Mountain View, CA 94043 United States

STOCK TICKER/OTHER:

Stock Ticker: INTU
Employees: 18,200
Parent Company:

Exchange: NAS
Fiscal Year Ends: 07/31

SALARIES/BONUSES:

Top Exec. Salary: $1,100,000   Bonus: $
Second Exec. Salary: Bonus: $
$770,000

OTHER THOUGHTS:

Estimated Female Officers or Directors: 5
Hot Spot for Advancement for Women/Minorities: Y

Intuit MailChimp (The Rocket Science Group LLC) mailchimp.com

NAIC Code: 519130

TYPES OF BUSINESS:

E-mail Platform
Digital Marketing Tools
Marketing Campaigns
Marketing Strategies
Email Marketing
Website Ads
Printed Postcards
Social Media Marketing

BRANDS/DIVISIONS/AFFILIATES:

Intuit Inc
Intuit MailChimp

CONTACTS: Note: Officers with more than one job title may be intentionally listed here more than once.

Sasan K. Goodarzi, CEO-Corp.

GROWTH PLANS/SPECIAL FEATURES:

The Rocket Science Group, LLC offers Intuit MailChimp, an all-in-one marketing platform for small businesses. Products by Intuit MailChimp help market businesses through strategies such as establishing a web domain name, creating business web and ecommerce sites, sending emails and printed postcards, and through establishing landing pages, digital advertisements and social media engagement. Platform products are categorized into audience management, creative tools, marketing automation, insights and analytics, with features ranging from customer relations management, behavioral targeting and predicted demographics to content studio, campaign templates, marketing integrations, surveys and performance tracking and reports. Intuit MailChimp serves a range of industries, including ecommerce, retail, startups, agencies, freelancers and developers. Marketing price plans range from free to premium (starting at $350/month sending 150,000 emails/month); website and commerce price plans range from free to Essentials (starting at $13/month); and transactional email price plans are either based on an estimated amount of sends per month or by blocks of emails sent each month. The Rocket Science Group is a subsidiary of Intuit, Inc.

FINANCIAL DATA: Note: Data for latest year may not have been available at press time.

In U.S. $	2022	2021	2020	2019	2018	2017
Revenue	1,000,000,000	967,435,000	917,000,000	700,000,000	600,000,000	588,000,000
R&D Expense						
Operating Income						
Operating Margin %						
SGA Expense						
Net Income						
Operating Cash Flow						
Capital Expenditure						
EBITDA						
Return on Assets %						
Return on Equity %						
Debt to Equity						

CONTACT INFORMATION:

Phone: 678-999-0141 Fax:
Toll-Free:
Address: 675 Ponce de Leon Ave. N.E., Ste. 5000, Atlanta, GA 30308 United States

STOCK TICKER/OTHER:

Stock Ticker: Subsidiary Exchange:
Employees: 1,147 Fiscal Year Ends: 07/31
Parent Company: Intuit Inc

SALARIES/BONUSES:

Top Exec. Salary: $ Bonus: $
Second Exec. Salary: $ Bonus: $

OTHER THOUGHTS:

Estimated Female Officers or Directors:
Hot Spot for Advancement for Women/Minorities:

InVisionApp Inc
NAIC Code: 511210N

TYPES OF BUSINESS:
Computer Software, Product Lifecycle, Engineering, Design & CAD
Workplace Online Collaboration
Workplace Mobile Collaboration
Software Solutions
Design Tools
Task Management Solutions
Prototyping Solutions

BRANDS/DIVISIONS/AFFILIATES:

GROWTH PLANS/SPECIAL FEATURES:
InVisionApp, Inc. offers a web and mobile collaboration platform for businesses. InVision gives companies of all sizes the ability to design, review and user-test products without writing code. InVision's intuitive tools for prototyping, task management and version control unify the entire design process within a singular place, digitally. Features offered by the platform include design prototyping, design sharing and presentation, design feedback and commenting, real-time design meetings and whiteboarding, design organization and collaboration, project management for designers, inspection and user-testing and research. Collaboration and product templates are available (from planning to launch), as well as security solutions and support services. InVision is used for prototyping websites, web apps, mobile apps, wearables and more. Over 7 million people utilize InVision across the globe.

InVisionApp offers its employees a monthly allowance for wellness reimbursement and a variety of assistance plans and programs. The company is a 100% remote-first organization.

CONTACTS:
Note: Officers with more than one job title may be intentionally listed here more than once.

Michael Shenkman, CEO

FINANCIAL DATA:
Note: Data for latest year may not have been available at press time.

In U.S. $	2022	2021	2020	2019	2018	2017
Revenue						
R&D Expense						
Operating Income						
Operating Margin %						
SGA Expense						
Net Income						
Operating Cash Flow						
Capital Expenditure						
EBITDA						
Return on Assets %						
Return on Equity %						
Debt to Equity						

CONTACT INFORMATION:
Phone: 212-209-3061   Fax: 212-371-5500
Toll-Free: 877-932-7111
Address: 41 Madison Ave., New York, NY 10010 United States

STOCK TICKER/OTHER:
Stock Ticker: Private   Exchange:
Employees: 220   Fiscal Year Ends:
Parent Company:

SALARIES/BONUSES:
Top Exec. Salary: $ Bonus: $
Second Exec. Salary: $ Bonus: $

OTHER THOUGHTS:
Estimated Female Officers or Directors:
Hot Spot for Advancement for Women/Minorities:

JAGGAER

NAIC Code: 511210A

www.jaggaer.com

TYPES OF BUSINESS:

Computer Software, Supply Chain & Logistics
Autonomous Commerce Solutions
Business-to-Business Commerce
Intelligent Procurement Solutions
Artificial Intelligence
Machine Learning
Source-to-Contact Solutions
Supply Chain Management Solutions

BRANDS/DIVISIONS/AFFILIATES:

Cinven
JAGGAER ONE

CONTACTS: Note: Officers with more than one job title may be intentionally listed here more than once.

Andy Hovancik, CEO
Jeff Laborde, CFO
Eva Skidmore, CMO
Martin Kersch, CTO
Grant Collingsworth, General Counsel
Teresa Jamison, Senior VP, Divisional
Douglas Keister, Senior VP, Divisional

GROWTH PLANS/SPECIAL FEATURES:

JAGGAER provides autonomous commerce solutions, offering a self-governing business-to-business (B2B) commerce experience between buyers, suppliers, things (IoT) and partners. The company's intelligent procurement solutions leverage artificial intelligence (AI) and machine learning to provide enterprise buyers and suppliers match recommendations that align buyer needs with supplier capabilities. They autonomously execute many repetitive, behind the scenes tasks required to facilitate enterprise commerce. JAGGAER's solutions are grouped into four categories: JAGGAER ONE Source to Contract offers spend analytics, category management, supplier management, savings management, sourcing, advanced sourcing optimizer, advanced rates, contracts ai and contract management; JAGGAER ONE Supply Chain Management includes supply chain collaboration and quality management; JAGGAER ONE Procure to Pay offers eProcurement, invoicing, digital capture, digital mailroom, global eInvoice compliance, payment solutions, inventory management and research material management; Lastly, JAGGAER ONE Platform includes autonomous commerce, analytics, supplier network, supplier identity management, adopt, assist and advise. JAGGAER serves industries including education, energy, utilities, financial services, healthcare, life sciences, pharmaceuticals, retail, manufacturing, aerospace and defense, consumer packaged goods, public sector, transportation and logistics. JAGGAER holds more than 37 patents and connects customers to a network of 10 million suppliers worldwide. JAGGAER's global offices span North America, Latin America, Europe, Australia, Asia and the Middle East. U.K.-based private equity firm Cinven owns a majority holding in JAGGAER.

JAGGAER offers its employees comprehensive health benefits and career growth programs.

FINANCIAL DATA: Note: Data for latest year may not have been available at press time.

In U.S. $	2022	2021	2020	2019	2018	2017
Revenue	208,208,000	200,200,000	131,142,375	134,505,000	128,100,000	122,000,000
R&D Expense						
Operating Income						
Operating Margin %						
SGA Expense						
Net Income						
Operating Cash Flow						
Capital Expenditure						
EBITDA						
Return on Assets %						
Return on Equity %						
Debt to Equity						

CONTACT INFORMATION:

Phone: 919 659-2100   Fax: 919 659-2199
Toll-Free: 888-638-7322
Address: 3020 Carrington Mill Blvd., Ste. 100, Morrisville, NC 27560 United States

STOCK TICKER/OTHER:

Stock Ticker: Private   Exchange:
Employees: 1,000   Fiscal Year Ends: 12/31
Parent Company: Cinven

SALARIES/BONUSES:

Top Exec. Salary: $ Bonus: $
Second Exec. Salary: $ Bonus: $

OTHER THOUGHTS:

Estimated Female Officers or Directors: 3
Hot Spot for Advancement for Women/Minorities: Y

Sales, profits and employees may be estimates. Financial information, benefits and other data can change quickly and may vary from those stated here.

JD.com Inc

NAIC Code: 454110

ir.jd.com

TYPES OF BUSINESS:

Online Retailer
Ecommerce Platform
Retail
Warehouses
Logistics Services and Solutions
Technology
Artificial Intelligence

BRANDS/DIVISIONS/AFFILIATES:

GROWTH PLANS/SPECIAL FEATURES:

JD.com is a leading e-commerce platform with its 2022 China GMV being similar to Pinduoduo (GMV not reported), on our estimate, but still lower than Alibaba. it offers a wide selection of authentic products with speedy and reliable delivery. The company has built its own nationwide fulfilment infrastructure and last-mile delivery network, staffed by its own employees, which supports both its online direct sales, its online marketplace and omnichannel businesses.

CONTACTS: Note: Officers with more than one job title may be intentionally listed here more than once.

Richard Qiangdong Liu, CEO
Lei Xu, Pres.
Sandy Ran Xu, CFO
Chengfeng He, Chief Compliance Officer
Pang Zhang, Chief Human Resources Officer
Peng Cao, Dir.-Technology
Richard Qiangdong Liu, Chmn.

FINANCIAL DATA: Note: Data for latest year may not have been available at press time.

In U.S. $	2022	2021	2020	2019	2018	2017
Revenue	143,873,800,000	130,858,800,000	102,559,400,000	79,331,120,000	63,534,940,000	49,826,280,000
R&D Expense	2,323,052,000	2,245,905,000	2,220,740,000	2,010,341,000	1,670,042,000	914,805,400
Operating Income	2,903,918,000	805,291,600	1,820,569,000	1,008,265,000	-272,577,400	1,096,137
Operating Margin %		.01%	.02%	.01%	.00%	.00%
SGA Expense	6,714,201,000	6,917,724,000	4,615,712,000	8,896,161,000	7,756,716,000	6,187,932,000
Net Income	1,427,412,000	-489,555,600	6,793,960,000	1,675,491,000	-342,638,500	17,707,060
Operating Cash Flow	7,951,016,000	5,817,049,000	5,850,465,000	3,407,775,000	2,871,522,000	3,693,220,000
Capital Expenditure	3,150,896,000	3,063,574,000	1,712,895,000	1,237,503,000	2,938,639,000	1,561,610,000
EBITDA	3,191,600,000	669,013,600	7,977,557,000	2,784,142,000	555,686,100	725,727,500
Return on Assets %		-.01%	.14%	.05%	-.01%	.00%
Return on Equity %		-.02%	.37%	.17%	-.04%	.00%
Debt to Equity		.11%	0.121	0.19	.17%	0.21

CONTACT INFORMATION:

Phone: 86 10 8262 5500   Fax: 86-10 8261-5208
Toll-Free:
Address: Fl. 20, Bldg. A, No. 18 Kechuang 11 St., Daxing Dist., Beijing, Beijing 101111 China

STOCK TICKER/OTHER:

Stock Ticker: JD   Exchange: NAS
Employees: 450,679   Fiscal Year Ends: 12/31
Parent Company:

SALARIES/BONUSES:

Top Exec. Salary: $ Bonus: $
Second Exec. Salary: $ Bonus: $

OTHER THOUGHTS:

Estimated Female Officers or Directors:
Hot Spot for Advancement for Women/Minorities:

Jio (Reliance Jio Infocomm Ltd)

www.jio.com

NAIC Code: 517312

TYPES OF BUSINESS:

Wireless Telecommunications Carriers (except Satellite)
LTE Network
Mobile Network Operations
Fiber-to-the-Home
Internet Services
Communication Technologies
Payment Solutions
Mobile Apps

BRANDS/DIVISIONS/AFFILIATES:

Reliance Industries Limited
Jio
JioFi
JioFiber

CONTACTS: *Note: Officers with more than one job title may be intentionally listed here more than once.*

Mukesh D. Ambani, Managing Dir.

GROWTH PLANS/SPECIAL FEATURES:

Reliance Jio Infocomm Ltd. (popularly known as Jio), a subsidiary of Reliance Industries Limited, is an Indian mobile network operator and fiber-to-the-home (FTTH) provider serving the Indian market. Jio operates a national long-term evolution (LTE) network with coverage across all telecommunication circles. The firm has built a world-class, all-IP data network with next-generation LTE technology, which utilizes voice over LTE (VoLTE) to provide voice service on its network. The company's future-ready network can be easily upgraded to support even more data as technologies advance, including 5G. Its data routers and phones are marketed under the JioFi and Jio brand names. Jio apps enable users to manage their Jio accounts and related devices, connect to Wi-Fi, chat, watch entertainment, listen to music, read online magazines and news, browse the web, secure data, file into the cloud, make payments, make calls, make online purchases, and connect with doctors and health test results. Devices can be purchased in-store (in the Mumbai area), as well as online at www.jio.com or via mobile app. Jio can offer free calls and very cheap internet access by relying on advertising and content revenues. JioFiber offers FTTH broadband throughout a home or business, separate Wi-Fi identifications for guests, Norton's mobile security for a select number of devices, high-definition (HD) voice calls throughout India, TV video calling and conferencing, integrated TV, home networking, security and surveillance solutions, a multi-player platform and more. AirFiber is the firms latest offering and allows for over 550 digital channels, 15 or more over the top media subscriptions, Unlimited Wifi and devices at no extra cost.

FINANCIAL DATA: *Note: Data for latest year may not have been available at press time.*

In U.S. $	2022	2021	2020	2019	2018	2017
Revenue	11,093,896,524	9,599,828,802	8,504,180,000	6,889,980,000	3,645,450,000	17,797,100
R&D Expense						
Operating Income						
Operating Margin %						
SGA Expense						
Net Income		1,637,569,936	734,478,000	426,095,000	111,143,000	-5,235,450
Operating Cash Flow						
Capital Expenditure						
EBITDA						
Return on Assets %						
Return on Equity %						
Debt to Equity						

CONTACT INFORMATION:

Phone: 91 79-3503-1200   Fax:
Toll-Free:
Address: 101, Saffron, Nr. Cntr. Point Panchwati 5 Rast, Ambawadi, Ahmedabad 380006 India

STOCK TICKER/OTHER:

Stock Ticker: Subsidiary   Exchange:
Employees: Fiscal Year Ends: 03/31
Parent Company: Reliance Industries Limited

SALARIES/BONUSES:

Top Exec. Salary: $ Bonus: $
Second Exec. Salary: $ Bonus: $

OTHER THOUGHTS:

Estimated Female Officers or Directors:
Hot Spot for Advancement for Women/Minorities:

Jumia Technologies AG

NAIC Code: 519130

group.jumia.com

TYPES OF BUSINESS:
Internet Publishing and Broadcasting and Web Search Portals
Ecommerce
Logistics
Online Payments
Delivery

BRANDS/DIVISIONS/AFFILIATES:
Jumia
JumiaPay

GROWTH PLANS/SPECIAL FEATURES:
Jumia Technologies AG is the pan-African e-commerce platform. The company's platform consists of a marketplace, which connects sellers with consumers. Its logistics service enables the shipment and delivery of packages from sellers to consumers, and the company's payment service facilitates transactions among participants active on its platform in selected markets. Jumia generates revenue from Sales of goods, Commissions, Fulfillment, Value-added services, and Marketing & Advertising. Its geographical segments are West Africa, North Africa, East & South Africa, Europe, and United Arab Emirates. The firm generates majority of its revenue from the West Africa segment.

CONTACTS:
Note: Officers with more than one job title may be intentionally listed here more than once.

Sacha Poignonnec, CEO

FINANCIAL DATA:
Note: Data for latest year may not have been available at press time.

In U.S. $	2022	2021	2020	2019	2018	2017
Revenue	221,882,000	177,934,000	159,366,000	179,540,000	147,629,800	111,637,100
R&D Expense	55,252,000	39,197,000	31,781,000	30,528,000	25,660,030	24,697,080
Operating Income	-215,918,000	-238,539,000	-164,032,000	-245,264,000	-185,677,200	-179,593,100
Operating Margin %		-1.33%	-1.02%	-1.37%	-1.26%	
SGA Expense	194,668,000	220,739,000	157,569,000	279,464,000	196,495,100	170,621,700
Net Income	-238,232,000	-226,865,000	-183,682,000	-253,755,000	-194,544,700	-193,846,700
Operating Cash Flow	-240,178,000	-171,179,000	-112,389,000	-204,387,000	-159,016,200	-140,336,400
Capital Expenditure	11,147,000	7,185,000	2,874,000	6,456,000	4,043,697	2,702,930
EBITDA	-217,926,000	-215,201,000	-169,867,000	-243,214,000	-191,173,600	-182,598,300
Return on Assets %		-.45%	-.48%	-1.02%	-1.57%	
Return on Equity %		-.66%	-.76%	-1.93%	-6.38%	
Debt to Equity		.02%	0.035	0.033		

CONTACT INFORMATION:
Phone: 49 30398203451   Fax:
Toll-Free:
Address: Charlottenstrasse 4, Berlin, 10969 Germany

STOCK TICKER/OTHER:
Stock Ticker: JMIA   Exchange: NYS
Employees: 4,318   Fiscal Year Ends: 12/31
Parent Company:

SALARIES/BONUSES:
Top Exec. Salary: $355,000   Bonus: $
Second Exec. Salary: Bonus: $
$339,000

OTHER THOUGHTS:
Estimated Female Officers or Directors:
Hot Spot for Advancement for Women/Minorities:

Juniper Networks Inc

www.juniper.net

NAIC Code: 334210A

TYPES OF BUSINESS:

Networking Equipment
Network Product Development
Network Security Solutions
Artificial Intelligence
Machine Learning
Automated WAN Solutions
Cloud-Based Data Center Solutions

BRANDS/DIVISIONS/AFFILIATES:

Mist
EX
128 Technology
SRX
MX
PTX
ACX
Apstra

GROWTH PLANS/SPECIAL FEATURES:

Juniper Networks Inc is engaged in designing, developing, and selling products and services for high-performance networks to enable customers to build scalable, reliable, secure, and cost-effective networks for their businesses while achieving agility and improved operating efficiency through automation. The company's high-performance network and service offerings include routing, switching, Wi-Fi, network security, artificial intelligence (AI) or AI-enabled enterprise networking operations (AIOps), and software-defined networking (SDN) technologies. In addition to the company's products, the company offers its customers a variety of services, including maintenance and support, professional services, Software-as-a-Service ("SaaS"), and education and training programs.

Juniper Networks offers medical, dental, prescription and vision insurance; paid time off; and stock/savings plans.

CONTACTS: Note: Officers with more than one job title may be intentionally listed here more than once.

Rami Rahim, CEO
Kenneth Miller, CFO
Scott Kriens, Chairman of the Board
Thomas Austin, Chief Accounting Officer
Manoj Leelanivas, COO
Anand Athreya, Executive VP
Brian Martin, Senior VP

FINANCIAL DATA: Note: Data for latest year may not have been available at press time.

In U.S. $	2022	2021	2020	2019	2018	2017
Revenue	5,301,200,000	4,735,400,000	4,445,100,000	4,445,400,000	4,647,500,000	
R&D Expense	1,036,100,000	1,007,200,000	958,400,000	955,700,000	1,003,200,000	
Operating Income	539,300,000	430,400,000	421,100,000	477,500,000	579,500,000	
Operating Margin %	.10%	.09%	.09%	.11%	.12%	
SGA Expense	1,382,900,000	1,302,500,000	1,194,200,000	1,183,600,000	1,158,500,000	
Net Income	471,000,000	252,700,000	257,800,000	345,000,000	566,900,000	
Operating Cash Flow	97,600,000	689,700,000	612,000,000	528,900,000	861,100,000	
Capital Expenditure	105,100,000	100,000,000	100,400,000	109,600,000	147,400,000	
EBITDA	812,600,000	598,300,000	554,600,000	713,400,000	846,400,000	
Return on Assets %	.05%	.03%	.03%	.04%	.06%	
Return on Equity %	.11%	.06%	.06%	.07%	.12%	
Debt to Equity	.38%	.42%	0.411	0.40	.37%	

CONTACT INFORMATION:

Phone: 408 745-2000   Fax: 408 745-2100
Toll-Free: 888-586-4737
Address: 1133 Innovation Way, Sunnyvale, CA 94089 United States

STOCK TICKER/OTHER:

Stock Ticker: JNPR   Exchange: NYS
Employees: 10,901   Fiscal Year Ends: 12/31
Parent Company:

SALARIES/BONUSES:

Top Exec. Salary: $1,000,000   Bonus: $
Second Exec. Salary: $132,292   Bonus: $650,000

OTHER THOUGHTS:

Estimated Female Officers or Directors: 3
Hot Spot for Advancement for Women/Minorities: Y

Kakao Corporation

www.kakaocorp.com

NAIC Code: 519130

TYPES OF BUSINESS:
Internet Portal Service
Mobile Platforms
Online Platforms
Communications
Artificial Intelligence
Development Software
Payment Solutions
Blockchain Technology

BRANDS/DIVISIONS/AFFILIATES:

GROWTH PLANS/SPECIAL FEATURES:

Kakao Corporation is a Korea-based global mobile platform company, with services that connect people via technology. The firm's offerings are divided into two segments: technology and service. The technology segment consists of artificial intelligence (AI) services, opensource services, people and technology connection software, development software, machine learning services, teaching software, blockchain technology, mobility solutions and more. The service segment consists of online/mobile calendars, communication platforms, ecommerce platforms, business platforms, social platforms, lifestyle platforms, AI-based business-to-business (B2B) connections, daily routine platforms, banking platforms, emoticon platform, payment solutions, story reading sharing, self-care platforms, television and content viewing, food ordering platform, and writing platform, among many others.

CONTACTS: Note: Officers with more than one job title may be intentionally listed here more than once.

Hong Eun Taek, CEO
Jaehyuk Lee, Head-Strategy
Hyunyoung Kim, Head-Global Mgmt.
Yun Seok, Chmn.

FINANCIAL DATA: Note: Data for latest year may not have been available at press time.

In U.S. $	2022	2021	2020	2019	2018	2017
Revenue	5,637,420,000	4,933,370,000	3,818,970,780	2,668,300,000	2,163,380,000	1,846,900,000
R&D Expense						
Operating Income						
Operating Margin %						
SGA Expense						
Net Income	1,073,200,000	1,170,570,000	153,498,000	-293,466,000	14,262,900	119,449,000
Operating Cash Flow						
Capital Expenditure						
EBITDA						
Return on Assets %						
Return on Equity %						
Debt to Equity						

CONTACT INFORMATION:
Phone: 82-064-795-1500   Fax: 82-2-60035401
Toll-Free:
Address: 242, Cheomdan-ro, Jeju-si Jeju-do, 63309 South Korea

STOCK TICKER/OTHER:
Stock Ticker: 35720
Employees: 2,450
Parent Company:

Exchange: Seoul
Fiscal Year Ends: 12/31

SALARIES/BONUSES:
Top Exec. Salary: $ Bonus: $
Second Exec. Salary: $ Bonus: $

OTHER THOUGHTS:
Estimated Female Officers or Directors: 1
Hot Spot for Advancement for Women/Minorities:

Sales, profits and employees may be estimates. Financial information, benefits and other data can change quickly and may vary from those stated here.

KAYAK

NAIC Code: 561510

www.kayak.com

TYPES OF BUSINESS:

Online Travel Services
Online and Mobile Travel Planning Platform
Digital Travel Booking Services
Travel Rate Comparison Services
Travel Search Engine
Trip Status and Alerts
Trip Management Solutions
Software and Technology

BRANDS/DIVISIONS/AFFILIATES:

Booking Holdings Inc
KAYAK.com
KAYAK Trips
Explore
SWOODOO
checkfelix
momondo
Cheapflights

GROWTH PLANS/SPECIAL FEATURES:

KAYAK operates travel planning search and aggregation sites that allow users to compile and compare data gathered from hundreds of travel sites. The company offers users comparison rates for hotels, airfare, rental cars, trains, buses and vacation packages. KAYAK.com's tools and features include KAYAK Trips and Explore, along with its mobile application. KAYAK Trips allows users to create, manage and share trips, and includes the capability of receiving flight status alerts in real-time. Explore is an internet feature that displays prices to various places around the world, on a map, derived from the user's existing location. Prices vary depending on when flights are chosen and purchased by the consumer. KAYAK also operates a portfolio of international seven brands. The firm is owned by Booking Holdings, Inc. KAYAK for business offers memberships for company to help them on their travels. Headquartered in the U.S., KAYAK has more than 26 international office locations.

CONTACTS:
Note: Officers with more than one job title may be intentionally listed here more than once.

Steve Hafner, CEO
Paul M. English, Pres.
Paul D. Schwenk, Sr. VP-Eng.
Keith D. Melnick, Chief Comm. Officer

FINANCIAL DATA:
Note: Data for latest year may not have been available at press time.

In U.S. $	2022	2021	2020	2019	2018	2017
Revenue	501,552,607	335,711,250	268,569,000	479,587,500	456,750,000	435,000,000
R&D Expense						
Operating Income						
Operating Margin %						
SGA Expense						
Net Income						
Operating Cash Flow						
Capital Expenditure						
EBITDA						
Return on Assets %						
Return on Equity %						
Debt to Equity						

CONTACT INFORMATION:

Phone: 203 899-3100   Fax: 203-899-3125
Toll-Free:
Address: 7 Market St., Stamford, CT 06902 United States

STOCK TICKER/OTHER:

Stock Ticker: Subsidiary   Exchange:
Employees: 1,000   Fiscal Year Ends: 12/31
Parent Company: Booking Holdings Inc

SALARIES/BONUSES:

Top Exec. Salary: $ Bonus: $
Second Exec. Salary: $ Bonus: $

OTHER THOUGHTS:

Estimated Female Officers or Directors: 1
Hot Spot for Advancement for Women/Minorities: Y

KDDI Corporation

www.kddi.com

NAIC Code: 517312

TYPES OF BUSINESS:

Wireless Telecommunications Carriers (except Satellite)
Telecommunications
Communication Technology
Internet of Things
Business Services
Internet Service

BRANDS/DIVISIONS/AFFILIATES:

GROWTH PLANS/SPECIAL FEATURES:

KDDI is Japan's second-largest wireless operator (31% market share), the largest pay-TV operator (53% market share) and the second-largest provider of fiber-to-the-home broadband (12% market share). It has grown through acquisition and is focusing on increasing the number of customers who subscribe to more than one telecommunication service. It is also looking to grow its Life Design business which includes commerce, energy, and finance and had over 45 million Internet of Things connections by the end of December 2023.

CONTACTS: *Note: Officers with more than one job title may be intentionally listed here more than once.*

Makoto Takahashi, CEO
Makoto Takahashi, Sr. VP
Kanichiro Aritomi, Vice Chmn.
Hirofumi Morozumi, Exec. VP
Hideo Yuasa, Associate Sr. VP

FINANCIAL DATA: *Note: Data for latest year may not have been available at press time.*

In U.S. $	2022	2021	2020	2019	2018	2017
Revenue	37,167,980,000	36,252,830,000	35,738,460,000	34,668,000,000	34,406,130,000	
R&D Expense						
Operating Income	7,197,887,000	7,045,789,000	6,973,933,000	6,885,003,000	6,538,695,000	
Operating Margin %	.19%	.19%	.20%	.20%	.19%	
SGA Expense	9,707,314,000	9,309,444,000	8,867,731,000	8,260,169,000	8,674,689,000	
Net Income	4,589,001,000	4,445,767,000	4,365,729,000	4,214,934,000	3,906,894,000	
Operating Cash Flow	10,021,960,000	11,478,990,000	9,030,496,000	7,025,972,000	7,242,959,000	
Capital Expenditure	4,610,025,000	4,262,476,000	4,226,090,000	4,108,951,000	3,827,395,000	
EBITDA	12,285,430,000	12,106,430,000	11,750,840,000	10,800,170,000	10,331,080,000	
Return on Assets %	.06%	.06%	.08%	.09%	.09%	
Return on Equity %	.14%	.14%	.15%	.16%	.16%	
Debt to Equity	.24%	.30%	0.323	0.249	.19%	

CONTACT INFORMATION:

Phone: 81 333470077 Fax:
Toll-Free:
Address: Garden Air Tower, 3-10-10, Iidabashi, Chiyoda-ku, Tokyo, 102-8460 Japan

STOCK TICKER/OTHER:

Stock Ticker: KDDIY   Exchange: PINX
Employees: 78,337   Fiscal Year Ends: 03/31
Parent Company:

SALARIES/BONUSES:

Top Exec. Salary: $ Bonus: $
Second Exec. Salary: $ Bonus: $

OTHER THOUGHTS:

Estimated Female Officers or Directors:
Hot Spot for Advancement for Women/Minorities:

Khoros LLC

khoros.com

NAIC Code: 511210F

TYPES OF BUSINESS:

Computer Software, Multimedia, Graphics & Publishing
Customer Engagement Software
Software Platform Development
Product and Brand Marketing
Contact Center Automation Solutions
Digital Messaging Solutions
Social Marketing Solutions
Social Media Content Solutions

BRANDS/DIVISIONS/AFFILIATES:

Vista Equity Partners Management LLC
Khoros Platform

CONTACTS: Note: Officers with more than one job title may be intentionally listed here more than once.

Chris Tranquill, CEO
Jeff Yentis, CFO
Lindsey Sanchez, CMO
Dustin Williams, CTO

GROWTH PLANS/SPECIAL FEATURES:

Khoros, LLC provides a software platform to help companies connect, engage and understand their customers. The Khoros Platform seamlessly integrates across digital channels and offers solutions across customer engagement, contact center automation and insights, community engagement and social media management. Products by the firm span areas including brand communities, messaging (SMS, apps, etc.) website chat, chatbots, social media, review sites, social marketing, social listening and finding/curating/sharing social media content. Solutions include call AI/automation, Khoros communities, Khoros service and Khoros social media management. Services include strategic services, professional services and product coaching. Resources offered on Khoros' website include podcasts, guides and tips, ebooks, webinars, channel integrations, developer information, a blog and customer stories. Based in Texas, the firm has additional U.S. office in Oregon, as well as internationally in the U.K., Germany, France, India, Netherlands and Australia. Khoros is backed by Vista Equity Partners Management, LLC.

Khoros offers its employees comprehensive benefits, 401(k), life and disability insurance, flexible hours and company perks.

FINANCIAL DATA: Note: Data for latest year may not have been available at press time.

In U.S. $	2022	2021	2020	2019	2018	2017
Revenue	313,040,000	301,000,000	255,937,500	262,500,000	250,000,000	
R&D Expense						
Operating Income						
Operating Margin %						
SGA Expense						
Net Income						
Operating Cash Flow						
Capital Expenditure						
EBITDA						
Return on Assets %						
Return on Equity %						
Debt to Equity						

CONTACT INFORMATION:

Phone: 512-201-4090   Fax:
Toll-Free:
Address: 7300 Ranch Rd. 2222, Bldg. 1, Austin, TX 78730-3204 United States

STOCK TICKER/OTHER:

Stock Ticker: Private
Employees: 1,200
Parent Company:

Exchange:
Fiscal Year Ends:

SALARIES/BONUSES:

Top Exec. Salary: $ Bonus: $
Second Exec. Salary: $ Bonus: $

OTHER THOUGHTS:

Estimated Female Officers or Directors:
Hot Spot for Advancement for Women/Minorities:

Sales, profits and employees may be estimates. Financial information, benefits and other data can change quickly and may vary from those stated here.

Kibo Software Inc

kibocommerce.com

NAIC Code: 511210M

TYPES OF BUSINESS:

E-Commerce Software
Cloud-Based Software Solutions
Business-to-Consumer Commerce
Business-to-Business Commerce
Consumer Experiences
Ecommerce
Machine Learning
Professional Development Tools

BRANDS/DIVISIONS/AFFILIATES:

Vista Equity Partners
Kibo Commerce

GROWTH PLANS/SPECIAL FEATURES:

Kibo Software, Inc. operates as Kibo Commerce and provides cloud-based, omnichannel software solutions for retailers and branded manufacturers. The company's products and solutions help customers achieve optimal performance of business-to-consumer (B2C) and business-to-business (B2B) commerce via unified consumer experiences. The firm's products cover unified commerce, headless ecommerce, personalization, order management, point of sale and subscription management. Kibo's unified commerce platform encompasses microservices, machine learning, solutions/tools for developers, and is application programming interface (API)-first. Resources on Kibo's website include reports and analysis, blog posts, documentation, resources by industry, professional services, client support and other types of support. Kibo is privately-owned by Vista Equity Partners.

CONTACTS: *Note: Officers with more than one job title may be intentionally listed here more than once.*

Ram Venkataraman, CEO
Brandon Flora, CFO
Marjorie Edwards, Chief People Officer
Thom Phipps, CTO
Sam Hogin, VP-Prod. Mgmt.
James Miller, Exec. VP-Client Svcs.
George Loyer, VP-Managed Svcs.

FINANCIAL DATA: *Note: Data for latest year may not have been available at press time.*

In U.S. $	2022	2021	2020	2019	2018	2017
Revenue						
R&D Expense						
Operating Income						
Operating Margin %						
SGA Expense						
Net Income						
Operating Cash Flow						
Capital Expenditure						
EBITDA						
Return on Assets %						
Return on Equity %						
Debt to Equity						

CONTACT INFORMATION:

Phone: 877-350-3866   Fax:
Toll-Free:
Address: 717 N. Harwood St., Ste. 1900, Dallas, TX 75201 United States

STOCK TICKER/OTHER:

Stock Ticker: Private   Exchange:
Employees: 110   Fiscal Year Ends: 12/31
Parent Company: Vista Equity Partners

SALARIES/BONUSES:

Top Exec. Salary: $ Bonus: $
Second Exec. Salary: $ Bonus: $

OTHER THOUGHTS:

Estimated Female Officers or Directors: 1
Hot Spot for Advancement for Women/Minorities:

Kickstarter PBC   www.kickstarter.com

NAIC Code: 519130

TYPES OF BUSINESS:

Crowdfunding
Crowd Funding
Online Platform

BRANDS/DIVISIONS/AFFILIATES:

CONTACTS: *Note: Officers with more than one job title may be intentionally listed here more than once.*

Everette Taylor, CEO
Yancey Strickler, Head-Comm.
Charles Adler, Creative Dir.
Perry Chen, Chmn.

GROWTH PLANS/SPECIAL FEATURES:

Kickstarter PBC (public benefit corporation) is a crowd funding platform for creative projects, enabling creators to receive funding directly from the public. This alternative form of funding lets audiences engage with creators and their projects early in the process and gives creators greater freedom than traditional routes of funding. Contributors receive different incentives in accordance with the level of funding they provide for projects. Incentives can include a signed copy of the finished product, acknowledgement on the finished product, an original piece related to the project, VIP access to performances, private screenings and special editions of finished products. Creators, as a part of creating their project's Kickstarter, choose what incentives will be offered. Originally begun as a venue for crowd funded independent film projects, the company has expanded to fund projects in art, comics, dance, design, fashion, food, games, music, photography, publishing, technology and theater. Film and video still represents the largest percentage of funded projects, with games following. The firm has backed 50,000 projects since the site's 2009 inception, over 23 million people have backed a project, $7.8 billion has been pledged and 254,202 projects have been successfully funded (as of February 2024). The site operates on an all-or-nothing basis. Projects must achieve their set funding goal to receive their proceeds. Contributors are charged for their contribution at the end of a successful project's funding cycle, with Kickstarter charging 5% of the total funds raised. Since the funds go directly to the project creators, Kickstarter is not responsible for project and incentive fulfillment.

FINANCIAL DATA: *Note: Data for latest year may not have been available at press time.*

In U.S. $	2022	2021	2020	2019	2018	2017
Revenue						
R&D Expense						
Operating Income						
Operating Margin %						
SGA Expense						
Net Income						
Operating Cash Flow						
Capital Expenditure						
EBITDA						
Return on Assets %						
Return on Equity %						
Debt to Equity						

CONTACT INFORMATION:

Phone: 866-749-7545   Fax:
Toll-Free:
Address: 58 Kent St., Brooklyn, NY 11222 United States

STOCK TICKER/OTHER:

Stock Ticker: Private   Exchange:
Employees: 125   Fiscal Year Ends:
Parent Company:

SALARIES/BONUSES:

Top Exec. Salary: $ Bonus: $
Second Exec. Salary: $ Bonus: $

OTHER THOUGHTS:

Estimated Female Officers or Directors: 12
Hot Spot for Advancement for Women/Minorities: Y

Sales, profits and employees may be estimates. Financial information, benefits and other data can change quickly and may vary from those stated here.

Kidpik Corp

NAIC Code: 454110

TYPES OF BUSINESS:

Online Sales, B2C Ecommerce, Sharing Economy Platforms

GROWTH PLANS/SPECIAL FEATURES:

Kidpik Corp is a subscription-based e-commerce business geared toward kid products for girl's and boy's apparel, footwear, and accessories. The Company serves its customers through the clothing subscription box business, its retail website and 3rd party websites.

BRANDS/DIVISIONS/AFFILIATES:

CONTACTS: *Note: Officers with more than one job title may be intentionally listed here more than once.*

Ezra Dabah, CEO
Moshe Dabah, COO
Adir Katzav, CFO
Ezra Dabah, Chmn.

FINANCIAL DATA: *Note: Data for latest year may not have been available at press time.*

In U.S. $	2022	2021	2020	2019	2018	2017
Revenue	16,477,980	21,834,520	16,936,390	13,518,710		
R&D Expense						
Operating Income	-7,823,409	-5,663,286	-3,665,811	-4,093,997		
Operating Margin %		-.26%	-.22%			
SGA Expense	13,338,540	12,546,720	13,482,640	12,236,260		
Net Income	-7,615,261	-5,947,547	-4,188,360	-4,603,314		
Operating Cash Flow	-6,650,537	-11,015,870	-3,550,328	-4,214,518		
Capital Expenditure	48,903	45,394	11,470	4,193		
EBITDA	-7,508,701	-5,207,327	-3,602,968	-4,047,246		
Return on Assets %		-.38%	-.48%			
Return on Equity %		-.72%	-4.97%			
Debt to Equity			0.197			

CONTACT INFORMATION:

Phone: 212 399-2323   Fax:
Toll-Free:
Address: 200 Park Avenue South, New York, NY 10003 United States

STOCK TICKER/OTHER:

Stock Ticker: PIK
Employees: 25
Parent Company:

Exchange: NAS
Fiscal Year Ends: 12/31

SALARIES/BONUSES:

Top Exec. Salary: $260,000   Bonus: $
Second Exec. Salary: Bonus: $
$215,000

OTHER THOUGHTS:

Estimated Female Officers or Directors:
Hot Spot for Advancement for Women/Minorities:

Klarna Bank AB

klarna.com

NAIC Code: 522291

TYPES OF BUSINESS:

Consumer Lending
Online Payment Solutions
Ecommerce
Digital Technology
ePayment Technology
Ecommerce Marketing Solutions
Merchant Portal Solution
Consumer Payments

BRANDS/DIVISIONS/AFFILIATES:

Klarna Inc
Klarna
PriceRunner

CONTACTS: Note: Officers with more than one job title may be intentionally listed here more than once.

Sebastian Siemiatkowski, CEO
Camilla Giesecke, COO
Niclas Neglen, CFO
David Sandstrom, CMO
David Fock, Chief Product Officer
Yaron Shaer, CTO
Michael Moritz, Chmn.

GROWTH PLANS/SPECIAL FEATURES:

Klarna Bank AB is a Swedish banking company under the supervision of the Swedish Financial Supervisory Authority. The firm operates Klarna, a Swedish ePayment platform that provides online payment services to ecommerce merchants. Klarna has a customer base of approximately 150 million and works with over 500,000 merchants across some 45 countries. The firm offers direct payments, pay after delivery options and installment plans in a smooth, single-click purchase experience that lets consumers pay when and how they want. The purpose at Klarna is to simplify buying by making the process simple and safe for consumers and merchants. Other solutions offered to businesses include marketing, sales channels and a merchant portal. For consumers, Klarna offers a wide range of shopping categories, as well as deals and loyalty rewards. Consumers can compare prices on thousands of products. Subsidiary Klarna, Inc. is based in the U.S., with offices in Ohio and New York.

Klarna Bank offers its employees a health subsidy, pension and retirement contributions, and on-the-job training.

FINANCIAL DATA: Note: Data for latest year may not have been available at press time.

In U.S. $	2022	2021	2020	2019	2018	2017
Revenue	1,743,162,600	1,520,008,579	1,220,800,000	766,759,000	606,525,000	550,718,000
R&D Expense						
Operating Income						
Operating Margin %						
SGA Expense						
Net Income	-954,152,160	-783,792,507	-167,958,000	-96,704,700	11,708,600	42,054,900
Operating Cash Flow						
Capital Expenditure						
EBITDA						
Return on Assets %						
Return on Equity %						
Debt to Equity						

CONTACT INFORMATION:

Phone: 46-8-120-120-10   Fax:
Toll-Free:
Address: Sveavagen 46, Stockholm, 111 34 Sweden

STOCK TICKER/OTHER:

Stock Ticker: Private
Employees: 5,441
Parent Company:

Exchange:
Fiscal Year Ends: 12/31

SALARIES/BONUSES:

Top Exec. Salary: $ Bonus: $
Second Exec. Salary: $ Bonus: $

OTHER THOUGHTS:

Estimated Female Officers or Directors: 1
Hot Spot for Advancement for Women/Minorities:

Ladders (The)

NAIC Code: 561311A

TYPES OF BUSINESS:

Online Job Postings
High-Level Job Search
Online Job Search
Online Resume Templates
Job Application Service
Online Job Posting
Company Information Data
Job Application Status

BRANDS/DIVISIONS/AFFILIATES:

Apply4Me

CONTACTS: *Note: Officers with more than one job title may be intentionally listed here more than once.*

Marc Cenedella, CEO
Shankar Mishra, VP-Data Science & Analytics
Kyri Sarantakos, VP-Eng.
Tarmi Addonizio, VP-Legal Affairs

GROWTH PLANS/SPECIAL FEATURES:

The Ladders helps job-seeking professionals connect with recruiters and employers. The firm is one of the leading companies in the over $100,000 job search category, serving professionals who want to advance in their $100,000-$500,000+ careers. The Ladders community consists of high-end employers and high-end talent. Approximately 22,000 employers use Ladders across industries and company needs. Ladders members are experts in their fields and are focused on achievement goals and strategies. Ladder members have access to high-level job search, which includes in-depth company information including salaries. Resume templates are offered, resume review and related advice. Ladders News offers cutting-edge headlines, statistics and insights. The Ladders' Apply4Me feature asks the member a set of questions online, then fills out application forms for job opportunities that the member chooses. Ladders then applies the applications on the member's behalf and keeps them up to date on the application/job status. Ladders' online Press & Media link offers news, opinion, analysis and advice in regards to the changing workplace and the future of work.

FINANCIAL DATA: *Note: Data for latest year may not have been available at press time.*

In U.S. $	2022	2021	2020	2019	2018	2017
Revenue						
R&D Expense						
Operating Income						
Operating Margin %						
SGA Expense						
Net Income						
Operating Cash Flow						
Capital Expenditure						
EBITDA						
Return on Assets %						
Return on Equity %						
Debt to Equity						

CONTACT INFORMATION:

Phone: 866-800-4640   Fax:
Toll-Free:
Address: 244 Fifth Ave., Ste. D100, New York, NY 10001 United States

STOCK TICKER/OTHER:

Stock Ticker: Private   Exchange:
Employees: 150   Fiscal Year Ends:
Parent Company:

SALARIES/BONUSES:

Top Exec. Salary: $ Bonus: $
Second Exec. Salary: $ Bonus: $

OTHER THOUGHTS:

Estimated Female Officers or Directors:
Hot Spot for Advancement for Women/Minorities:

lastminute.com NV (lm group)

lmgroup.lastminute.com

NAIC Code: 561510

TYPES OF BUSINESS:

Online Travel Agency
Online Reservations & Ticket Sales
Vacation packages
Entertainment packages
Dining discounts/packages

BRANDS/DIVISIONS/AFFILIATES:

Lastminute.com
Volagratis
Rumbo
weg.de
Bravofly
Jetcost
Hotelscan
Crocierissime

CONTACTS: *Note: Officers with more than one job title may be intentionally listed here more than once.*

Luca Concone, Interim CEO
Matthew Crummack, Pres.
Marco Forasassi Torresani, Chmn.

GROWTH PLANS/SPECIAL FEATURES:

Lastminute.com NV is a European travel company that operates a portfolio of online brands for travel purposes. These brands include lastminute.com, Volagratis, Rumbo, weg.de, Bravofly, Jetcost, Hotelscan, Crocierissime, and Forward (fwd), each of which offer search and information capabilities for booking travel itineraries. The websites and apps are present across 58 countries and in multiple languages, and customers can search, compare and/or book places to go to, stay at and attend. Lastminute.com offers all kinds of booking capabilities, including hotels, entertainment, spa treatments and more. Volagratis is an Italy-based search engine that offers a range of flights, holiday packages, hotels, cruises and car rentals. Rumbo enables users to search, compare and book good deals on hotels, flights, packages, escapes and cruises. weg.de is online travel website based in Germany, offering package tours and all-inclusive trips, as well as hotels, flights, rental cars and ski holidays. Bravofly offers flights, hotels, cars, tours and more, with core markets being France and Germany. Jetcost is a metasearch website that enables users to search for and compare flights, hotels and rental cars from a range of suppliers, operating across Europe, Asia and America. Hotelscan is a metasearch website that enables users to search and compare hotels, vacation rentals, bed-and-breakfasts and other lodging accommodations from a wide range of suppliers. Crocierissime is a cruise booking platform that offers destinations across the Mediterranean, Greek Islands and the fjords of northern Europe. Last, Forward is a travel marketer who helps brands design and activate content for driving measurable impact.

FINANCIAL DATA: *Note: Data for latest year may not have been available at press time.*

In U.S. $	2022	2021	2020	2019	2018	2017
Revenue	314,226,356	161,488,167	129,045,000	410,080,384	341,311,872	279,779,904
R&D Expense						
Operating Income						
Operating Margin %						
SGA Expense						
Net Income	-16,160,731	-10,835,936	-76,210,100	29,319,988	11,990,695	-6,972,068
Operating Cash Flow						
Capital Expenditure						
EBITDA						
Return on Assets %						
Return on Equity %						
Debt to Equity						

CONTACT INFORMATION:

Phone: 4143-244-8140   Fax:
Toll-Free: 800-083-4000
Address: Basisweg 10, Amsterdam, 1043 AP Netherlands

STOCK TICKER/OTHER:

Stock Ticker: LMN   Exchange: Zurich
Employees: 1,200   Fiscal Year Ends: 12/31
Parent Company:

SALARIES/BONUSES:

Top Exec. Salary: $ Bonus: $
Second Exec. Salary: $ Bonus: $

OTHER THOUGHTS:

Estimated Female Officers or Directors:
Hot Spot for Advancement for Women/Minorities:

Le Tote Inc

NAIC Code: 454110

letote.com

TYPES OF BUSINESS:

Online Rental of Luxury Apparel and Accessories
Online Clothing Rental
Clothes Sharing
Ecommerce

BRANDS/DIVISIONS/AFFILIATES:

Saadia Group LLC

CONTACTS: *Note: Officers with more than one job title may be intentionally listed here more than once.*

Rakesh Tondon, CEO

GROWTH PLANS/SPECIAL FEATURES:

Le Tote, Inc. operates an ecommerce clothing and accessories rental business. The firm's online platform provides customers access to women's clothing and accessories for a monthly membership fee. Featured brands include Splendid, Vince Camuto, BCBGeneration, French Connection, Rebecca Minkoff, Rachel Roy, Adrianna Papell and KUT from the Kloth, among others. Le Tote utilizes an analytical, data-driven and customer-first approach, serving consumers in 48 U.S. states. How it works: members browse styles and pick items they want to rent; once received by mail, wear them as often as preferred; and then either return items in a provided, pre-paid USPS envelope or keep items and pay up to 50% off retail price. Payment capabilities are offered online or through the app. Fashion styles include casual, athletic leisure, going to an event, business casual, professional or going out. Monthly rental plans start at $59. There is no commitment with Le Tote, memberships can be changed, paused or canceled at any time. Gift cards are available online. Le Tote owns the Lord + Taylor brand. Le Tote operates as a subsidiary of Saadia Group LLC.

FINANCIAL DATA: *Note: Data for latest year may not have been available at press time.*

In U.S. $	2022	2021	2020	2019	2018	2017
Revenue						
R&D Expense						
Operating Income						
Operating Margin %						
SGA Expense						
Net Income						
Operating Cash Flow						
Capital Expenditure						
EBITDA						
Return on Assets %						
Return on Equity %						
Debt to Equity						

CONTACT INFORMATION:

Phone: 415 260-1809   Fax:
Toll-Free: 844 899-8683
Address: 3130 20th St., Ste. 225, San Francisco, CA 94110 United States

STOCK TICKER/OTHER:

Stock Ticker: Subsidiary   Exchange:
Employees: Fiscal Year Ends: 12/31
Parent Company: Saadia Group LLC

SALARIES/BONUSES:

Top Exec. Salary: $ Bonus: $
Second Exec. Salary: $ Bonus: $

OTHER THOUGHTS:

Estimated Female Officers or Directors:
Hot Spot for Advancement for Women/Minorities:

Leaf Group Ltd

NAIC Code: 519130

www.leafgroup.com

TYPES OF BUSINESS:

Internet Portals
Consumer Internet Sites
Online Leisure Activities Information
How-to Internet Sites
Fitness and Wellness Websites
Art and Design Websites
Animal and Pet Publishing Site
Practical Solutions and Information Sites

BRANDS/DIVISIONS/AFFILIATES:

Graham Holdings Company
Well + Good
Livestrong.com
Saatchi Art
society6
cuteness
eHOW
Only In Your State

CONTACTS: Note: Officers with more than one job title may be intentionally listed here more than once.

Sean Moriarty, CEO
James Quandt, Chairman of the Board
Sean Moriarty, Director
Adam Wergeles, Executive VP, Divisional

GROWTH PLANS/SPECIAL FEATURES:

Leaf Group Ltd. is a diversified consumer internet company that builds brands that reach audiences in lifestyle categories. The firm's brands are grouped into three categories: fitness and wellness, art and design, and publishing. Brands within the fitness and wellness category are housed under the subsidiary World of Good and includes Well + Good, specializing in health via fitness, super foods, natural beauty and more; and Livestrong.com, specializing in healthy living by helping people to live stronger, healthier and happier lives. Other fitness and wellness brands include Good Collective, Hunker, House of Good and many more. Brands within the art and design category are housed under subsidiary Saatchi Art, offering an online art gallery that connect people with art and artists; society6, offering an online marketplace that features unique wall art, home decorations and lifestyle goods created by independent artists; hunker, which features property tours and design advice; Headquartered in California, Leaf Group has offices in New York and Colorado, as well as in Australia and the U.K. Leaf Group is a subsidiary of Graham Holdings Company.

FINANCIAL DATA: Note: Data for latest year may not have been available at press time.

In U.S. $	2022	2021	2020	2019	2018	2017
Revenue	220,000,000	220,543,432	212,060,992	154,956,000	155,042,000	128,990,000
R&D Expense						
Operating Income						
Operating Margin %						
SGA Expense						
Net Income			-8,860,000	-26,838,000	-23,190,000	-31,133,000
Operating Cash Flow						
Capital Expenditure						
EBITDA						
Return on Assets %						
Return on Equity %						
Debt to Equity						

CONTACT INFORMATION:

Phone: 310-656-6253   Fax:
Toll-Free:
Address: 1655 26th St., Santa Monica, CA 90404 United States

STOCK TICKER/OTHER:

Stock Ticker: Subsidiary   Exchange:
Employees: 400   Fiscal Year Ends: 12/31
Parent Company: Graham Holdings Company

SALARIES/BONUSES:

Top Exec. Salary: $ Bonus: $
Second Exec. Salary: $ Bonus: $

OTHER THOUGHTS:

Estimated Female Officers or Directors: 2
Hot Spot for Advancement for Women/Minorities: Y

Liberty Global plc

www.libertyglobal.com

NAIC Code: 517311

TYPES OF BUSINESS:

Video, Voice & Broadband Internet Access Services
Telephony Services
VoIP Services
Mobile Telephony Services
Video on Demand Services

GROWTH PLANS/SPECIAL FEATURES:

Liberty Global is a holding company with interests in several telecom companies in the U.K., Netherlands, Belgium, Switzerland, Ireland, and Slovakia. Liberty is the owner of the main cable network in each of these geographies and has pursued a strategy since 2016 to merge or partner with mobile-network-operators to be able to offer converged services. Liberty also owns minority stakes in other media, entertainment, and cloud companies.

BRANDS/DIVISIONS/AFFILIATES:

Virgin Media
Telenet
UPC
Vodafone Ziggo
ITV
All3Media
ITI Neovision
Sunrise Communications AG

CONTACTS: *Note: Officers with more than one job title may be intentionally listed here more than once.*

Michael Fries, CEO
John Malone, Chairman of the Board
Charlie Bracken, CFO
Amy Blair, Sr. VP
Enrique Rodriguez, Exec. VP
Bryan Hall, Executive VP
Diederik Karsten, Executive VP
Leonard Stegman, Managing Director
John C. Malone, Chmn.

FINANCIAL DATA: *Note: Data for latest year may not have been available at press time.*

In U.S. $	2022	2021	2020	2019	2018	2017
Revenue	7,195,700,000	10,311,300,000	11,545,400,000	11,115,800,000	11,957,900,000	
R&D Expense						
Operating Income	231,900,000	1,301,300,000	2,128,300,000	815,300,000	1,087,300,000	
Operating Margin %	.03%	.13%	.18%	.07%	.09%	
SGA Expense	1,623,400,000	2,154,100,000	2,150,000,000	2,044,200,000	2,049,100,000	
Net Income	1,473,200,000	13,426,800,000	-1,628,000,000	11,521,400,000	725,300,000	
Operating Cash Flow	2,837,800,000	3,549,000,000	4,185,800,000	4,585,400,000	5,963,100,000	
Capital Expenditure	1,303,200,000	1,408,000,000	1,292,800,000	1,168,200,000	1,453,000,000	
EBITDA	4,184,900,000	17,236,600,000	1,613,000,000	3,688,600,000	5,498,700,000	
Return on Assets %	.03%	.25%	-.03%	.23%	.01%	
Return on Equity %	.06%	.68%	-.12%	1.26%	.13%	
Debt to Equity	.65%	.59%	1.106	1.786	5.59%	

CONTACT INFORMATION:

Phone: 44 208-483-6300   Fax:
Toll-Free:
Address: Griffin House, 161 Hammersmith Rd., London, W6 8BS United Kingdom

STOCK TICKER/OTHER:

Stock Ticker: LBTYA   Exchange: NAS
Employees: 10,100   Fiscal Year Ends: 12/31
Parent Company:

SALARIES/BONUSES:

Top Exec. Salary: $2,563,000   Bonus: $
Second Exec. Salary: $1,143,569   Bonus: $78,706

OTHER THOUGHTS:

Estimated Female Officers or Directors: 3
Hot Spot for Advancement for Women/Minorities: Y

Life Quotes Inc

NAIC Code: 524210

TYPES OF BUSINESS:

Online Insurance Broker
Online Price Comparison Services
Insurance Quotes
Customer and Insurance Broker Connection
Online Price Quotes
Personalized Insurance Brokering
Policy Placement Services
Online Technology and Lead Generation

BRANDS/DIVISIONS/AFFILIATES:

LifeQuotes.com
Consumerinsuranceguide.com

CONTACTS: Note: Officers with more than one job title may be intentionally listed here more than once.

Robert S. Bland, CEO
Margaret Thornton, Dir.-New Bus.
Robert Goss, Exec. VP

GROWTH PLANS/SPECIAL FEATURES:

Life Quotes, Inc. owns and operates an online consumer insurance information service, accessible at LifeQuotes.com and Consumerinsuranceguide.com, which provides self-directed personal and corporate insurance shoppers instant quotes for various insurance products. The firm's proprietary and comprehensive insurance price comparison and order-entry technologies produce instant quotes from various life insurance companies. Types of insurance include life, auto, health, homeowners, renters, long-term care, Medicare supplement, Medicare Advantage and travel. When shopping for insurance, customers may specify the amount of coverage they are looking for. Life Quotes also provides personalized insurance brokerage and policy placement services. The company generates revenues from the receipt of commissions and fees paid by insurers based on the volume of business produces and also generates revenues from the sale of website traffic and insurance leads to agents and brokers. Life Quotes provides toll-free advice to its website visitors and customers.

FINANCIAL DATA: Note: Data for latest year may not have been available at press time.

In U.S. $	2022	2021	2020	2019	2018	2017
Revenue						
R&D Expense						
Operating Income						
Operating Margin %						
SGA Expense						
Net Income						
Operating Cash Flow						
Capital Expenditure						
EBITDA						
Return on Assets %						
Return on Equity %						
Debt to Equity						

CONTACT INFORMATION:

Phone: 630 515-0170   Fax:
Toll-Free: 800 556-9393
Address: 850 N. Cass Ave., Ste. 102, Darien, IL 60559 United States

STOCK TICKER/OTHER:

Stock Ticker: Private   Exchange:
Employees: 106   Fiscal Year Ends: 12/31
Parent Company:

SALARIES/BONUSES:

Top Exec. Salary: $ Bonus: $
Second Exec. Salary: $ Bonus: $

OTHER THOUGHTS:

Estimated Female Officers or Directors: 2
Hot Spot for Advancement for Women/Minorities:

LifeWay Christian Resources

www.lifeway.com

NAIC Code: 451211

TYPES OF BUSINESS:

Christian Books, Retail
Christian Book Publishing
Conference Centers
Online Sales
Church Supplies

BRANDS/DIVISIONS/AFFILIATES:

LifeWay Christian Stores
LifeWay Ridgecrest Conference Center
B&H Publishing Group
Holman Christian Standard Bible
LifeWay.com
LifeWay Research
Southern Baptist Convention

CONTACTS: *Note: Officers with more than one job title may be intentionally listed here more than once.*

Ben Mandrell, CEO
Joe Walker, SVP-CFO
Coniia Nelson, SVP- Chief Human Resources Officer
Ed Stetzer, VP-Insights Div.
Jamies Adams, SVP-CTO
Brad Waggoner, Exec. VP-Oper.
Jerry Rhyne, VP-Finance & Bus. Svcs.
Tim Vineyard, VP-LifeWay Christian Stores
Eric Geiger, VP-Church Resources Div.
Selma Wilson, VP-B&H Publishing Group

GROWTH PLANS/SPECIAL FEATURES:

LifeWay Christian Resources is a nonprofit organization founded in 1891, and a world-leading provider of Christian products and digital services. The firm sells Bibles; church literature; software; books; music; DVDs and videos; teaching recordings; and church supplies, such as furniture and signs. It operates LifeWay Christian Stores across the U.S., and its products are offered via ecommerce channels. LifeWay products are used in more than 160 countries. The LifeWay.com website includes resources such as links to counseling, Bible study courses and links to multimedia Bible stories for children. In addition, the organization owns and operates LifeWay Ridgecrest Conference Center in North Carolina, offering various types of events such as summer camps for boys and girls on Ridgecrest's 1,300-acre campus. Through B&H Publishing Group, LifeWay produces a bible translation called the Holman Christian Standard Bible. The organization coordinates its activities and initiates retail operations through a 1.3-million-square-foot office space in Nashville, Tennessee. The firm's LifeWay Research division explores new ministry ventures. LifeWay operates as a subsidiary of Southern Baptist Convention.

FINANCIAL DATA: *Note: Data for latest year may not have been available at press time.*

In U.S. $	2022	2021	2020	2019	2018	2017
Revenue	1,838,720	1,768,000	1,700,000	3,307,500	3,150,000	3,000,000
R&D Expense						
Operating Income						
Operating Margin %						
SGA Expense						
Net Income						
Operating Cash Flow						
Capital Expenditure						
EBITDA						
Return on Assets %						
Return on Equity %						
Debt to Equity						

CONTACT INFORMATION:

Phone: 615-251-2000   Fax: 615-251-3899
Toll-Free:
Address: One Lifeway Plz., Nashville, TN 37234 United States

STOCK TICKER/OTHER:

Stock Ticker: Nonprofit   Exchange:
Employees: 4,000   Fiscal Year Ends: 09/30
Parent Company: Southern Baptist Convention

SALARIES/BONUSES:

Top Exec. Salary: $ Bonus: $
Second Exec. Salary: $ Bonus: $

OTHER THOUGHTS:

Estimated Female Officers or Directors: 2
Hot Spot for Advancement for Women/Minorities: Y

Lightspeed Commerce Inc

www.lightspeedhq.com

NAIC Code: 511210K

TYPES OF BUSINESS:

Computer Software, Sales & Customer Relationship Management
Point of Sale Systems
Point of Sale Software
eCommerce
Merchant
Restaurant
Golf Course

BRANDS/DIVISIONS/AFFILIATES:

ShopKeep Inc
Upserve Inc

GROWTH PLANS/SPECIAL FEATURES:

Lightspeed Commerce Inc provides an omni-channel commerce-enabling SaaS platform. Its software platform provides customers with the functionality it needs to engage with consumers, manage their operations, accept payments, and grow their business. The company sells its platform through a direct sales force in the United States, Canada, New Zealand, United Kingdom, Australia and other countries. It derives a majority of its revenue from the United States.

CONTACTS: Note: Officers with more than one job title may be intentionally listed here more than once.

Dax Dasilva, CEO
Brandon Nussey, CFO
Patrick Pichette, Chairman of the Board
Jean Chauvet, Director
Steve Midgley, Executive VP, Divisional
Asha Bakshani, Executive VP, Divisional
Lory Ajamian, Executive VP, Divisional
Daniel Micak, Executive VP
Jean-David Saint-Martin, Other Executive Officer

FINANCIAL DATA: Note: Data for latest year may not have been available at press time.

In U.S. $	2022	2021	2020	2019	2018	2017
Revenue	548,372,000	221,728,000	120,637,000	77,451,000	57,079,000	
R&D Expense	121,150,000	55,303,000	31,812,000	18,283,000	13,295,000	
Operating Income	-266,437,000	-114,052,000	-47,715,000	-21,775,000	-21,267,000	
Operating Margin %	-.49%	-.51%	-.40%	-.28%	-.37%	
SGA Expense	311,912,000	149,935,000	79,874,000	52,833,000	42,453,000	
Net Income	-288,433,000	-124,278,000	-53,531,000	-183,525,000	-96,179,000	
Operating Cash Flow	-87,218,000	-93,064,000	-28,550,000	-7,556,000	-10,023,000	
Capital Expenditure	10,653,000	1,794,000	3,609,000	2,030,000	1,485,000	
EBITDA	-207,939,000	-90,690,000	-34,248,000	-17,238,000	-16,148,000	
Return on Assets %	-.10%	-.10%	-.15%	-1.15%	-1.61%	
Return on Equity %	-.11%	-.11%	-.20%			
Debt to Equity	.02%	.03%	0.126			

CONTACT INFORMATION:

Phone: 514-907-1801   Fax: 514-221-4499
Toll-Free: 855-300-7108
Address: 700 Saint Antoine Street East, Montreal, QC H2Y1A6 Canada

STOCK TICKER/OTHER:

Stock Ticker: LSPD   Exchange: NYS
Employees: 3,000   Fiscal Year Ends: 12/31
Parent Company:

SALARIES/BONUSES:

Top Exec. Salary: $369,450   Bonus: $
Second Exec. Salary: $323,269   Bonus: $

OTHER THOUGHTS:

Estimated Female Officers or Directors:
Hot Spot for Advancement for Women/Minorities:

Sales, profits and employees may be estimates. Financial information, benefits and other data can change quickly and may vary from those stated here.

Lillian Vernon Corporation

www.lillianvernon.com

NAIC Code: 454110

TYPES OF BUSINESS:

Gifts & Housewares, Catalogs
Ecommerce
Gifts and Houseware Products
Children's Products
Garden Products
Personalized Products
Outdoor and Home Decorations
Personalized Gifts and Products

BRANDS/DIVISIONS/AFFILIATES:

Regent LP
Current
colorful images
FineStationery

GROWTH PLANS/SPECIAL FEATURES:

Lillian Vernon Corporation, privately-owned by Regent LP, is a national online ecommerce retailer of gifts, housewares, gardening, season and children's products. The firm's wide range of products span totes and bags, jewelry, apparel and accessories, mugs, bar and grill products, cutting boards, wall decorations, holiday and occasion decorations, coasters and trivets, pillows and blankets, linens, utensils and gadgets, photo gifts, gifts for weddings, gifts for pets, gifts for new babies, memorial gifts, garden and outdoor supplies, calendars, office accessories, stationery, travel essentials, luggage for kids, lunch bags, pencils and pencil cases, school supplies, teacher gifts, puzzles and games, toys and much more. Personalization on applicable gifts is free. Customer service concerning products, order status, shipping, returns and exchanges is offered via telephone or online chat. Exclusive and special offer notifications can be received via email or text message. Sister companies of Lillian Vernon include Current, colorful images, and FineStationery.

CONTACTS:
Note: Officers with more than one job title may be intentionally listed here more than once.

Michael D. Muoio, Pres.
Ralph J. Thomann, Sr. VP-Oper.
Norman Foster, Sr. VP-Quality Assurance
Michael A. Reinstein, Chmn.-Regent

FINANCIAL DATA:
Note: Data for latest year may not have been available at press time.

In U.S. $	2022	2021	2020	2019	2018	2017
Revenue						
R&D Expense						
Operating Income						
Operating Margin %						
SGA Expense						
Net Income						
Operating Cash Flow						
Capital Expenditure						
EBITDA						
Return on Assets %						
Return on Equity %						
Debt to Equity						

CONTACT INFORMATION:

Phone: 719-594-4100   Fax:
Toll-Free:
Address: 1005 E. Woodmen Rd, Colorado Springs, CO 80920-3522
United States

STOCK TICKER/OTHER:

Stock Ticker: Private
Employees: 1,200
Parent Company: Regent LP

Exchange:
Fiscal Year Ends: 02/28

SALARIES/BONUSES:

Top Exec. Salary: $ Bonus: $
Second Exec. Salary: $ Bonus: $

OTHER THOUGHTS:

Estimated Female Officers or Directors: 1
Hot Spot for Advancement for Women/Minorities:

Linden Research Inc (Linden Lab)

lindenlab.com

NAIC Code: 511210G

TYPES OF BUSINESS:

Computer Software, Electronic Games, Apps & Entertainment
Application Developer
Platform Creator
Development Tools
Registered Money Services
eWallet
Innovative Technology

BRANDS/DIVISIONS/AFFILIATES:

Linden Lab
Second Life
Tilia LLC
High Fidelity
JP Morgan Payments

CONTACTS: Note: Officers with more than one job title may be intentionally listed here more than once.

Philip Rosedale, CEO

GROWTH PLANS/SPECIAL FEATURES:

Linden Research, Inc. (dba Linden Lab) develops platforms for creating and sharing virtual experiences. Linden Lab established Second Life, an online collaborative 3D virtual build-and-play environment that millions of users have utilized for gaming and development purposes. Second Life differs from a typical massively multiplayer online role-playing game (MMORPG) in that it provides nearly unlimited interactive and creative freedom as well as providing its users with the opportunity to retain intellectual property (IP) rights over creations. Once an object has been built, its creator has the IP rights to it and can sell it to other users, called Residents. A Second Life account includes access to an avatar personalization tool, as well as building tools using geometric primitives and scripting language, adding functionality to created objects. Linden's Sansar platform was created for virtual reality (VR) concert experiences. Players can see concerts from their favorite artists, buy merchandise, take selfies and dance, while also upgrading their tickets for VIP and exclusive experiences. Subsidiary Tilia LLC is a registered money services business licensed in the U.S. as a money transmitter. Tilia provides secure transactions at a massive scale and enables end-users to have a stored value wallet in compliance with legal obligations. Headquartered in San Francisco, California, Linden has additional offices in Boston, Charlottesville, Davis and Seattle. High Fidelity owns an interest in Linden Research Inc., with the deal including distributed computing patents in regards to Second Life. High Fidelity is a real-time communications company whose mission is to build technology that powers more human experiences in the digital world, including the metaverse.

FINANCIAL DATA: Note: Data for latest year may not have been available at press time.

In U.S. $	2022	2021	2020	2019	2018	2017
Revenue						
R&D Expense						
Operating Income						
Operating Margin %						
SGA Expense						
Net Income						
Operating Cash Flow						
Capital Expenditure						
EBITDA						
Return on Assets %						
Return on Equity %						
Debt to Equity						

CONTACT INFORMATION:

Phone: 415-243-9000   Fax: 415-243-9045
Toll-Free:
Address: 548 Market St., PMB 59201, San Francisco, CA 94104-5401
United States

STOCK TICKER/OTHER:

Stock Ticker: Private   Exchange:
Employees: 200   Fiscal Year Ends:
Parent Company:

SALARIES/BONUSES:

Top Exec. Salary: $ Bonus: $
Second Exec. Salary: $ Bonus: $

OTHER THOUGHTS:

Estimated Female Officers or Directors:
Hot Spot for Advancement for Women/Minorities:

Sales, profits and employees may be estimates. Financial information, benefits and other data can change quickly and may vary from those stated here.

LinkedIn Corporation

www.linkedin.com

NAIC Code: 519130

TYPES OF BUSINESS:

Business-Oriented Social Networking
Advertising Services
Recruiting and Marketing Tools
Online Business Social Network
Social Network Platform
Job Search and Hire
Skill Learning and Talent Development

BRANDS/DIVISIONS/AFFILIATES:

Microsoft Corporation
LinkedIn.com
LinkedIn for Journalists
EduBrite

CONTACTS: *Note: Officers with more than one job title may be intentionally listed here more than once.*

Ryan Roslansky, CEO
Dan Roth, Editor in Chief

GROWTH PLANS/SPECIAL FEATURES:

LinkedIn Corporation operates an online social networking site targeting the business and professional community. On LinkedIn.com users can post profiles, connect with co-workers, post resumes and search for job openings. The website offers a suite of business solutions for hiring, marketing, social selling, learning skills and developing talent. In addition, LinkedIn for Journalists is a program that provides access to training sessions, LinkedIn experts and tools. Its membership base had more than 875 million users worldwide (as of late-2022), and is available in multiple languages including English, French, German, Italian, Portuguese, Spanish, Japanese, Korean, Russian, Arabic and Turkish. The LinkedIn website generates revenue through ad sales, user subscription fees on premium accounts and enterprise hiring software licensing fees. LinkedIn operates as a subsidiary of Microsoft Corporation. During 2022, LinkedIn acquired EduBrite, a platform that specializes in creating, hosting and deploying professional certificates. EduBrite would be integrated into LinkedIn's learning platform to better test and verify the skills people have to help them grow in their careers and enable them to earn credentials from organizations.

FINANCIAL DATA: *Note: Data for latest year may not have been available at press time.*

In U.S. $	2022	2021	2020	2019	2018	2017
Revenue	14,000,000,000	10,500,000,000	7,140,000,000	6,200,000,000	5,050,000,000	2,600,000,000
R&D Expense						
Operating Income						
Operating Margin %						
SGA Expense						
Net Income						
Operating Cash Flow						
Capital Expenditure						
EBITDA						
Return on Assets %						
Return on Equity %						
Debt to Equity						

CONTACT INFORMATION:

Phone: 650 687-3600   Fax:
Toll-Free:
Address: 1000 W. Maude, Sunnyvale, CA 94085 United States

STOCK TICKER/OTHER:

Stock Ticker: Subsidiary   Exchange:
Employees: 19,450   Fiscal Year Ends: 06/30
Parent Company: Microsoft Corporation

SALARIES/BONUSES:

Top Exec. Salary: $ Bonus: $
Second Exec. Salary: $ Bonus: $

OTHER THOUGHTS:

Estimated Female Officers or Directors: 4
Hot Spot for Advancement for Women/Minorities: Y

Lionbridge Technologies LLC

www.lionbridge.com

NAIC Code: 541511

TYPES OF BUSINESS:

Software Development and Testing
Website Language Translation
Interpretation Communication Services
Localization Services
Marketing Solutions
Content Services
Quality Assurance and Testing Services
Artificial Intelligence

BRANDS/DIVISIONS/AFFILIATES:

HIG Capital LLC

CONTACTS: Note: Officers with more than one job title may be intentionally listed here more than once.

John Fennelly, CEO
Rich Tobin, COO
Will Rowlands-Rees, Chief Product Officer
Ann Lazarus-Barnes, Chief People Officer
Marcus Casal, CTO
Rory Cowan, Founder
Margaret Shukur, General Counsel
Richard Tobin, General Manager, Divisional
Paula Shannon, Other Executive Officer
Marc Osofsky, Senior VP, Divisional

GROWTH PLANS/SPECIAL FEATURES:

Lionbridge Technologies, Inc. provides translation, localization and marketing solutions to businesses. The company's language tools help users to decide the best form of language, translation, localization and other features for marketing to their audiences. Lionbridge's localization technology adapts products to a market and internationalizes them for its customers to create and market products on a global scale. The firm's localization tools are powered by artificial intelligence (AI), and its machine translation technology localizes the customers' entire journey, for every market. Lionbridge also offers content services include technical writing, training/eLearning, financial reports, multicultural marketing, and digital experience assessments; translation services encompass video localization, software localization, translation for regulated companies, interpretation, live events, multilingual SEO/digital marketing, content optimization, and website localization; testing services feature functional QA/testing, compatibility testing, interoperability testing, performance testing, accessibility testing, and UX/CX testing; solutions cover translation service models, digital marketing, machine translation, and START onboarding; lionbridge knowledge hubs comprise positive patient outcomes, modern clinical trial solutions, future of localization, innovation to immunity, covid-19 resource center, disruption series, patient engagement, and lionbridge insights. The company's language cloud platform supports end-to-end localization and content lifecycle. Testing services span functional quality assurance and testing, compatibility testing, interoperability testing, performance testing, accessibility testing, and user experience/customer experience testing. Resources and webinars are offered on Lionbridge's website. Industries served include life sciences, banking and finance, retail, ecommerce, games, automotive, consumer packaged goods, technology, industrial manufacturing, legal services, travel and hospitality. Lionbridge Technologies is a subsidiary of H.I.G. Capital LLC.

FINANCIAL DATA: Note: Data for latest year may not have been available at press time.

In U.S. $	2022	2021	2020	2019	2018	2017
Revenue	575,000,000	661,342,500	648,375,000	682,500,000	650,000,000	595,000,000
R&D Expense						
Operating Income						
Operating Margin %						
SGA Expense						
Net Income						
Operating Cash Flow						
Capital Expenditure						
EBITDA						
Return on Assets %						
Return on Equity %						
Debt to Equity						

CONTACT INFORMATION:

Phone: 781-434-6000   Fax: 781 434-6034
Toll-Free: 866-267-0437
Address: 1050 Winter St., Ste. 2300, Waltham, MA 02451 United States

STOCK TICKER/OTHER:

Stock Ticker: Private   Exchange:
Employees: 6,000   Fiscal Year Ends: 12/31
Parent Company: HIG Capital LLC

SALARIES/BONUSES:

Top Exec. Salary: $ Bonus: $
Second Exec. Salary: $ Bonus: $

OTHER THOUGHTS:

Estimated Female Officers or Directors: 5
Hot Spot for Advancement for Women/Minorities: Y

Sales, profits and employees may be estimates. Financial information, benefits and other data can change quickly and may vary from those stated here.

LivePerson Inc

www.liveperson.com

NAIC Code: 511210K

TYPES OF BUSINESS:

E-Commerce Software
Customer Service Software
Sales & Marketing Service Software
Live Chat Applications
Conversational Cloud Engine
Online Business Messaging
Technologies
Artificial Intelligence

BRANDS/DIVISIONS/AFFILIATES:

VoiceBase
Tenfold

GROWTH PLANS/SPECIAL FEATURES:

LivePerson Inc offers cloud-based platform solutions. It enables businesses and consumers to connect through conversational interfaces, such as in-app and mobile messaging, while leveraging bots and Artificial Intelligence (AI) to increase efficiency. The company has two reportable segments namely Business and Consumer. It generates maximum revenue from the Business segment. The Business segment enables brands to leverage the Conversational Cloud's sophisticated intelligence engine to connect with consumers through an integrated suite of mobile and online business messaging technologies. The company has a presence in the United Kingdom, Asia-Pacific, Latin America, and Europe.

CONTACTS: Note: Officers with more than one job title may be intentionally listed here more than once.

Robert Locascio, CEO
John Collins, CFO
Daryl Carlough, Chief Accounting Officer
Norman Osumi, Chief Accounting Officer
Alexander Spinelli, Chief Technology Officer
Andrew Hamel, Executive VP, Divisional
Monica Greenberg, Executive VP, Divisional

FINANCIAL DATA: Note: Data for latest year may not have been available at press time.

In U.S. $	2022	2021	2020	2019	2018	2017
Revenue	514,800,000	469,624,000	366,620,000	291,609,000	249,838,000	218,876,000
R&D Expense	193,688,000	158,390,000	108,414,000	82,145,000	55,707,000	40,034,000
Operating Income	-201,917,000	-89,869,000	-60,031,000	-84,989,000	-19,235,000	-15,232,000
Operating Margin %	- .39%	- .19%	- .16%	- .29%	- .08%	- .07%
SGA Expense	331,749,000	239,570,000	207,823,000	212,873,000	148,134,000	134,029,000
Net Income	-225,747,000	-124,974,000	-107,594,000	-96,071,000	-25,032,000	-18,191,000
Operating Cash Flow	-62,101,000	3,247,000	33,605,000	-59,158,000	4,779,000	10,290,000
Capital Expenditure	51,166,000	48,313,000	43,476,000	48,506,000	21,938,000	17,390,000
EBITDA	-169,272,000	-53,222,000	-64,416,000	-66,521,000	-2,234,000	1,808,000
Return on Assets %	- .20%	- .11%	- .14%	- .24%	- .10%	- .08%
Return on Equity %	-1.08%	- .42%	- .55%	- .60%	- .16%	- .13%
Debt to Equity	10.84%	1.65%	2.237	1.292		

CONTACT INFORMATION:

Phone: 212 609-4200   Fax: 212 609-4201
Toll-Free:
Address: 530 7th Ave., Fl. M1, New York, NY 10018 United States

STOCK TICKER/OTHER:

Stock Ticker: LPSN   Exchange: NAS
Employees: 1,301   Fiscal Year Ends: 12/31
Parent Company:

SALARIES/BONUSES:

Top Exec. Salary: $611,820   Bonus: $
Second Exec. Salary: Bonus: $
$506,250

OTHER THOUGHTS:

Estimated Female Officers or Directors: 2
Hot Spot for Advancement for Women/Minorities:

LiveRamp Holdings Inc

liveramp.com/about-us

NAIC Code: 511210K

TYPES OF BUSINESS:

Consumer Data Management
Consumer Databases
Consulting and Analytics
Risk Mitigation Services
CDI Technology
Consumer Privacy Solutions
Data Marketplace

BRANDS/DIVISIONS/AFFILIATES:

LiveRamp Safe Haven

GROWTH PLANS/SPECIAL FEATURES:

LiveRamp's cloud-based software helps businesses combine their data (first-party data) about customer touch points such as on webpages, mobile apps, in stores, and on other devices with data from other sources to get a better view of a current or potential customer's activity. Such combined data can help businesses and advertisers create better profiles of their customers. The software is also used by publishers to easily combine their data with that of advertisers, helping them to optimize their ad inventory. LiveRamp generates revenue through a one-year subscription model (around 80% of total revenue) for its software. The firm also provides a marketplace for third-party data owners and data buyers, around 20% of total revenue.

CONTACTS: *Note: Officers with more than one job title may be intentionally listed here more than once.*

Gerald Jones, Assistant Secretary
Scott Howe, CEO
Warren Jenson, CFO
Clark Kokich, Chairman of the Board
Anneka Gupta, Co-President

FINANCIAL DATA: *Note: Data for latest year may not have been available at press time.*

In U.S. $	2022	2021	2020	2019	2018	2017
Revenue	528,657,000	443,026,000	380,572,000	285,620,000	220,101,000	
R&D Expense	157,935,000	135,111,000	105,981,000	85,697,000	60,713,000	
Operating Income	-64,059,000	-117,833,000	-175,921,000	-178,213,000	-130,801,000	
Operating Margin %	-.12%	-.27%	-.46%	-.62%	-.59%	
SGA Expense	287,354,000	281,744,000	297,808,000	257,418,000	193,793,000	
Net Income	-33,833,000	-90,268,000	-124,511,000	1,028,547,000	23,480,000	
Operating Cash Flow	78,077,000	-20,560,000	-28,782,000	-460,503,000	111,555,000	
Capital Expenditure	4,499,000	2,182,000	11,711,000	8,642,000	12,641,000	
EBITDA	-39,811,000	-90,092,000	-140,020,000	-144,431,000	-93,154,000	
Return on Assets %	-.03%	-.07%	-.09%	.77%	.02%	
Return on Equity %	-.03%	-.08%	-.10%	.99%	.03%	
Debt to Equity	.05%	.00%	0.011		.30%	

CONTACT INFORMATION:

Phone: 866-352-3267   Fax:
Toll-Free:
Address: 225 Bush St., Fl. 17, San Francisco, CA 94104 United States

STOCK TICKER/OTHER:

Stock Ticker: RAMP   Exchange: NYS
Employees: 1,370   Fiscal Year Ends: 03/31
Parent Company:

SALARIES/BONUSES:

Top Exec. Salary: $690,000   Bonus: $
Second Exec. Salary: Bonus: $
$590,000

OTHER THOUGHTS:

Estimated Female Officers or Directors: 4
Hot Spot for Advancement for Women/Minorities: Y

LiveWorld Inc

www.liveworld.com

NAIC Code: 519130

TYPES OF BUSINESS:

Diversified Internet Portal
Online Communities
Online Business Services
Online Marketing Services
Online Events

BRANDS/DIVISIONS/AFFILIATES:

Conversational Messaging
Enterprise Chatbot Management Platform

GROWTH PLANS/SPECIAL FEATURES:

LiveWorld Inc is a social content marketing company. The Company's principal business is a combination of digital agency services and software that empower companies to deepen customer relationships with emotion-driven behavior change through campaigns with a human touch. The company provides consulting strategy, and creativity along with human agents for moderation, engagement, customer care, and adverse events management, as well as conversation management software, and chatbots for digital campaigns and social media programs.

LiveWorld offers its employees health benefits and a 401(k).

CONTACTS: *Note: Officers with more than one job title may be intentionally listed here more than once.*

Peter Friedman, CEO
David Houston, CFO
Jason Kapler, VP-Mktg.
Jason Liebowitz, VP-Sales
Frank Chevallier, VP-Prod. Mgmt.
Trevor Griffiths, VP-Eng.
Trevor Griffiths, VP-Oper.
Jenna Woodul, Chief Community Officer
Bruce Dembecki, VP-Moderation Svcs.
Virginie Glaenzer, VP-Mktg.
Martin Bishop, VP-Account Mgr.-Wal-Mart
Peter Friedman, Chmn.

FINANCIAL DATA: *Note: Data for latest year may not have been available at press time.*

In U.S. $	2022	2021	2020	2019	2018	2017
Revenue	9,000,000	8,800,000	8,560,000	7,374,000	7,709,000	9,949,000
R&D Expense						
Operating Income						
Operating Margin %						
SGA Expense						
Net Income			366,000	-449,000	-637,000	-1,338,000
Operating Cash Flow						
Capital Expenditure						
EBITDA						
Return on Assets %						
Return on Equity %						
Debt to Equity						

CONTACT INFORMATION:

Phone: 408 871-5200   Fax:
Toll-Free: 800-301-9507
Address: 2105 S. Bascom Ave., Ste. 159, Campbell, CA 95008 United States

STOCK TICKER/OTHER:

Stock Ticker: LVWD   Exchange: PINX
Employees: 185   Fiscal Year Ends: 12/31
Parent Company:

SALARIES/BONUSES:

Top Exec. Salary: $ Bonus: $
Second Exec. Salary: $ Bonus: $

OTHER THOUGHTS:

Estimated Female Officers or Directors: 7
Hot Spot for Advancement for Women/Minorities: Y

LivingSocial LLC

www.livingsocial.com

NAIC Code: 541810E

TYPES OF BUSINESS:

Online Coupons and Discount Offers
Ecommerce
Local Discounts
Coupons and Discount Codes
Business-to-Consumer Solutions
Business-to-Business Solutions
Ecommerce Technology
Payment Technology

BRANDS/DIVISIONS/AFFILIATES:

Groupon Inc

GROWTH PLANS/SPECIAL FEATURES:

LivingSocial, LLC operates an ecommerce platform that offers online coupons and discounts, locally and abroad. Deals offered span a range of interests, such as things to do in select cities; travel and hotel deals and packages; spa and wellness services; high-quality products; events such as sports, music or theater; and home improvement or design products and services. The site also offers promotion codes, digital coupons and information on sales from online brands. LivingSocial's vast network enables businesses to market themselves and grow. LivingSocial offers deals up to 95% off their regular prices, with some consisting of last-chance getaways to particular destinations. LivingSocial operates as a subsidiary of Groupon, Inc.

CONTACTS: Note: Officers with more than one job title may be intentionally listed here more than once.

Dusan Sekypl, CEO-Corp.
Jake Maas, Sr. VP-Merch. Solutions
Ryan Owens, VP-Eng.
Jim Bramson, General Counsel
Jake Maas, Sr. VP-Oper.
Doug Miller, Sr. VP-New Bus. Initiatives
Mitch Spolan, Sr. VP-National Sales
Eric Eichmann, Pres., Int'l

FINANCIAL DATA: Note: Data for latest year may not have been available at press time.

In U.S. $	2022	2021	2020	2019	2018	2017
Revenue						
R&D Expense						
Operating Income						
Operating Margin %						
SGA Expense						
Net Income						
Operating Cash Flow						
Capital Expenditure						
EBITDA						
Return on Assets %						
Return on Equity %						
Debt to Equity						

CONTACT INFORMATION:

Phone: 202-695-7000   Fax:
Toll-Free: 888-808-6676
Address: 1445 New York Ave. NW, Washington, DC 20005 United States

STOCK TICKER/OTHER:

Stock Ticker: Subsidiary   Exchange:
Employees: 188   Fiscal Year Ends:
Parent Company: Groupon Inc

SALARIES/BONUSES:

Top Exec. Salary: $ Bonus: $
Second Exec. Salary: $ Bonus: $

OTHER THOUGHTS:

Estimated Female Officers or Directors: 3
Hot Spot for Advancement for Women/Minorities: Y

Lookout Inc

www.lookout.com

NAIC Code: 511210E

TYPES OF BUSINESS:

Computer Software: Network Security, Managed Access, Digital ID,
Cybersecurity & Anti-Virus
Cybersecurity Solutions
Cybersecurity Technology
Cyber Attack Prediction
Cloud Data Security Solutions

BRANDS/DIVISIONS/AFFILIATES:

Lookout Security Cloud
Lookout for Small Business
Lookout App Defense
Lookout Personal
SaferPass

CONTACTS: *Note: Officers with more than one job title may be intentionally listed here more than once.*

Jim Dolce, CEO
Mark Nasiff, COO
Aaron Cockerill, Chief Strategy Officer
Deb Wolf, CMO
Missy Ballew, Chief Human Resources Officer
Sundaram Lakshmanan, CTO
Jim Dolce, Chmn.

GROWTH PLANS/SPECIAL FEATURES:

Lookout, Inc. is a cybersecurity company that predicts and stops mobile attacks before harm is done to an individual or an enterprise. The company's cloud-based technology is generated by a global network of millions of endpoints and analyzed applications. Within this data, Lookout identifies connections that would otherwise go unseen and stop cybercriminals from attacking mobile devices. The platform comes with easy-to-use cloud modules for security detection, visibility, response and remediation. Products include mobile endpoint security, which is powered by telemetry from hundreds of millions of mobile apps, devices and web items to detect mobile compromise and phishing attacks. Threat Intelligence Services leverage advanced mobile threat intelligence, by reconstructing kill chains to respond to attacks, and proactively hunt for threats. Secure Cloud Access provides visibility into data, devices and users, continuous monitoring of user and entity behavior analytics and advanced data protection controls, enabling users to securely collaborate in a hybrid work environment. Secure Internet Access is a cloud delivered solution, built on the principles of zero trust, offering inline and API security controls to protect users, networks and corporate data from Internet based threats. Secure Private Access verifies the security posture of users and only grants access to apps that users require for work. Partners of the company include Google, Microsoft and VMware, as well as AT&T, NTT Docomo, Orange, Telefonica, Telstra, T-Mobile, Verizon and Vodafone. Based in San Francisco, California, Lookout has additional offices in the U.S., Australia, Canada, India, Japan, Netherlands, Singapore, Slovakia, the UK and the UAE.

FINANCIAL DATA: *Note: Data for latest year may not have been available at press time.*

In U.S. $	2022	2021	2020	2019	2018	2017
Revenue						
R&D Expense						
Operating Income						
Operating Margin %						
SGA Expense						
Net Income						
Operating Cash Flow						
Capital Expenditure						
EBITDA						
Return on Assets %						
Return on Equity %						
Debt to Equity						

CONTACT INFORMATION:

Phone: 415-281-2820   Fax:
Toll-Free:
Address: 275 Battery St., Ste. 200, San Francisco, CA 94111 United States

STOCK TICKER/OTHER:

Stock Ticker: Private   Exchange:
Employees: 347   Fiscal Year Ends:
Parent Company:

SALARIES/BONUSES:

Top Exec. Salary: $ Bonus: $
Second Exec. Salary: $ Bonus: $

OTHER THOUGHTS:

Estimated Female Officers or Directors:
Hot Spot for Advancement for Women/Minorities:

LookSmart Group Inc

www.looksmart.com

NAIC Code: 519130

TYPES OF BUSINESS:

Search Portal-Directory Model
Customer Analysis Software
Advertising Services
Publisher Services
Vertical Search Services
Bookmarking Services

BRANDS/DIVISIONS/AFFILIATES:

LookSmart Network
LookSmart Publisher Solutions

CONTACTS: *Note: Officers with more than one job title may be intentionally listed here more than once.*

Michael Onghai, CEO

GROWTH PLANS/SPECIAL FEATURES:

LookSmart Group, Inc., is a search advertising network and management company with over 6 billion monthly queries, including 50 million monthly unique visitors. The firm is focused on supporting its advertiser base through a syndicated network specializing in pay-per-click text ads. LookSmart optimizes traffic from publishers and other networks to ultimately benefit its advertisers. LookSmart serves small businesses, brands and agencies and affiliate marketing firms. The firm has developed its own tools and processes to help identify and filter invalid traffic. These processes include automated fraud detection controls to help catch instances of unusual activity such as spiders, bots and click fraud; filtering software to help identify and remove non-converting traffic from customer's bills; and filtering software to pre-screen sites for traffic quality and click-through rate consistency. LookSmart's account managers do a thorough analysis of the client's current campaigns and identify the ones with the highest odds for success on the LookSmart Network. Once an advertising plan has been agreed upon, the firm tracks the clicks and obtains/tests data feedback; launches an initial 10-day evaluation period of the product, which is optimized continually to reach KPI (key performance indicator) goals; and then presents the initial campaign evaluation to the client, makes recommendations for ongoing spend and ramps the campaign accordingly. LookSmart Publisher Solutions can be purchased and used a la carte or as a package. Clients receive personalized service, unique analytics and transparent reporting.

FINANCIAL DATA: *Note: Data for latest year may not have been available at press time.*

In U.S. $	2022	2021	2020	2019	2018	2017
Revenue	1,719,000	18,560,000	7,840,527	5,985,135	6,138,600	6,296,000
R&D Expense						
Operating Income						
Operating Margin %						
SGA Expense						
Net Income	-63,000	565,000	222,000			
Operating Cash Flow						
Capital Expenditure						
EBITDA						
Return on Assets %						
Return on Equity %						
Debt to Equity						

CONTACT INFORMATION:

Phone: 415 348-7000   Fax:
Toll-Free:
Address: 50 California St., Fl. 16, San Francisco, CA 94111-4684 United States

STOCK TICKER/OTHER:

Stock Ticker: LKST   Exchange: OTC
Employees: 10   Fiscal Year Ends: 12/31
Parent Company:

SALARIES/BONUSES:

Top Exec. Salary: $ Bonus: $
Second Exec. Salary: $ Bonus: $

OTHER THOUGHTS:

Estimated Female Officers or Directors:
Hot Spot for Advancement for Women/Minorities:

Lumen Technologies Inc

NAIC Code: 517311

TYPES OF BUSINESS:

Local Telephone Service
Enterprise Technology
Industry 4.0
Advanced Architecture
Machine Learning
Artificial Intelligence
Internet of Things

BRANDS/DIVISIONS/AFFILIATES:

Lumen
CenturyLink Inc

GROWTH PLANS/SPECIAL FEATURES:

With 450,000 route miles of fiber, Lumen Technologies is one of the United States' largest telecommunications carriers serving global enterprises. Its merger with Level 3 in 2017 and divestiture of much of its incumbent local exchange carrier, or ILEC, business in 2022 has shifted the company's operations away from its legacy consumer business and toward enterprises (now nearly 80% of revenue). Lumen offers businesses a full menu of communications services, providing colocation and data center services, data transportation, and end-user phone and internet service. On the consumer side, Lumen provides broadband and phone service across 37 states, where it has 4.5 million broadband customers.

Lumen offers its employees health coverage, life and disability insurance, 401(k) and many other benefits.

CONTACTS: *Note: Officers with more than one job title may be intentionally listed here more than once.*

Andrea Genschaw, Assistant Controller
Jeffrey Storey, CEO
Indraneel Dev, CFO
T. Glenn, Chairman of the Board
Eric Mortensen, Chief Accounting Officer
Shaun Andrews, Chief Marketing Officer
W. Hanks, Director
Scott Trezise, Executive VP, Divisional
Stacey Goff, Executive VP

FINANCIAL DATA: *Note: Data for latest year may not have been available at press time.*

In U.S. $	2022	2021	2020	2019	2018	2017
Revenue	17,478,000,000	19,687,000,000	20,712,000,000	21,458,000,000	22,580,000,000	17,656,000,000
R&D Expense						
Operating Income	3,293,000,000	4,285,000,000	3,604,000,000	3,780,000,000	3,296,000,000	2,009,000,000
Operating Margin %	.19%	.22%	.17%	.18%	.15%	.11%
SGA Expense	3,078,000,000	2,895,000,000	3,464,000,000	3,715,000,000	4,165,000,000	3,508,000,000
Net Income	-1,548,000,000	2,033,000,000	-1,232,000,000	-5,269,000,000	-1,733,000,000	1,389,000,000
Operating Cash Flow	4,735,000,000	6,501,000,000	6,524,000,000	6,680,000,000	7,032,000,000	3,878,000,000
Capital Expenditure	3,016,000,000	2,900,000,000	3,729,000,000	3,628,000,000	3,175,000,000	3,106,000,000
EBITDA	3,580,000,000	8,242,000,000	5,596,000,000	2,084,000,000	5,734,000,000	5,957,000,000
Return on Assets %	-.03%	.03%	-.02%	-.08%	-.02%	.02%
Return on Equity %	-.14%	.18%	-.10%	-.32%	-.08%	.08%
Debt to Equity	1.96%	2.32%	2.635	2.405	1.79%	1.587

CONTACT INFORMATION:

Phone: 318 388-9000   Fax: 318 789-8656
Toll-Free:
Address: 100 CenturyLink Dr., Monroe, LA 71203 United States

SALARIES/BONUSES:

Top Exec. Salary: $1,800,011   Bonus: $
Second Exec. Salary: Bonus: $1,000,000
$180,840

STOCK TICKER/OTHER:

Stock Ticker: LUMN   Exchange: NYS
Employees: 29,000   Fiscal Year Ends: 12/31
Parent Company:

OTHER THOUGHTS:

Estimated Female Officers or Directors: 5
Hot Spot for Advancement for Women/Minorities: Y

Lyft Inc

www.lyft.me

NAIC Code: 561599

TYPES OF BUSINESS:

Car Ride Dispatch Service, Mobile App-Based
Bicycle Rental & Sharing Systems
Augmented Reality Technology
Rental Cars
Vehicle Sharing

BRANDS/DIVISIONS/AFFILIATES:

Lyft
Lyft Rental

GROWTH PLANS/SPECIAL FEATURES:

Lyft is the second-largest ride-sharing service provider in the U.S. and Canada, connecting riders and drivers over the Lyft app. Incorporated in 2013, Lyft offers a variety of rides via private vehicles, including traditional private rides, shared rides, and luxury ones. Besides ride-share, Lyft also has entered the bike- and scooter-share market to bring multimodal transportation options to users.

CONTACTS: Note: Officers with more than one job title may be intentionally listed here more than once.

Logan Green, CEO
Brian Roberts, CFO
Prashant Aggarwal, Chairman of the Board
Lisa Blackwood-Kapral, Chief Accounting Officer
John Zimmer, Co-Founder
Eisar Lipkovitz, Executive VP, Divisional
Lindsay Llewellyn, General Counsel
Ashwin Raj, Other Corporate Officer
Kristin Sverchek, President, Divisional

FINANCIAL DATA: Note: Data for latest year may not have been available at press time.

In U.S. $	2022	2021	2020	2019	2018	2017
Revenue	4,095,135,000	3,208,323,000	2,364,681,000	3,615,960,000	2,156,616,000	
R&D Expense	856,777,000	911,946,000	909,126,000	1,505,640,000	300,836,000	
Operating Income	-1,458,916,000	-1,135,217,000	-1,808,382,000	-2,702,480,000	-977,711,000	
Operating Margin %	-.36%	-.35%	-.76%	-.75%	-.45%	
SGA Expense	1,817,692,000	1,327,044,000	1,362,458,000	2,000,215,000	1,251,689,000	
Net Income	-1,584,511,000	-1,062,144,000	-1,752,857,000	-2,602,241,000	-911,335,000	
Operating Cash Flow	-237,285,000	-101,721,000	-1,378,899,000	-105,702,000	-280,673,000	
Capital Expenditure	114,970,000	79,176,000	93,639,000	178,088,000	70,868,000	
EBITDA	-1,404,106,000	-859,937,000	-1,607,360,000	-2,491,456,000	-891,845,000	
Return on Assets %	-.34%	-.22%	-.34%	-.55%	-.27%	
Return on Equity %	-1.83%	-.70%	-.77%			
Debt to Equity	2.52%	.65%	0.543	0.134		

CONTACT INFORMATION:

Phone: 412 620-6133   Fax:
Toll-Free: 844-250-2773
Address: 185 Berry St., Ste. 5000, San Francisco, CA 94107 United States

STOCK TICKER/OTHER:

Stock Ticker: LYFT   Exchange: NAS
Employees: 4,419   Fiscal Year Ends: 12/31
Parent Company:

SALARIES/BONUSES:

Top Exec. Salary: $527,308   Bonus: $1,500,000
Second Exec. Salary: $537,692   Bonus: $

OTHER THOUGHTS:

Estimated Female Officers or Directors: 2
Hot Spot for Advancement for Women/Minorities:

Macquarium Inc

NAIC Code: 541810E

www.macquarium.com

TYPES OF BUSINESS:

Consulting-Web Development
Interactive Marketing
Internet Training Systems
Ecommerce Consulting
Computer Animation
Customer Experience Solutions
Web Development Consulting

BRANDS/DIVISIONS/AFFILIATES:

Synoptek LLC

CONTACTS: *Note: Officers with more than one job title may be intentionally listed here more than once.*

Carlos Pimenta, CEO
Will Payman, VP-Strategy
Carlos Pimenta, Pres.
Connie McClung, CFO
Brett Sharp, VP-Customer Experience
Jay Cann, CTO
Marc Adler, Chmn.

GROWTH PLANS/SPECIAL FEATURES:

Macquarium, Inc. is an interactive agency and web development consulting firm. The company collaborates with clients to create eBusiness services designed to generate revenue, reduce costs and enhance user efficiency. Macquarium employs a design thinking methodology to achieve results for its clients and their customers, including understanding problems through the customer's perspective, designing customer touchpoint experiences that enhance their journey, eliminating journey gaps by orchestrating a unified experience and leveraging qualitative and quantitative research for continual improvement. The firm's services include: establishing a customer experience program for gaining insight and understanding about them; planning and building interactive experiences to increase customer satisfaction; creating relevant, personalized and timely content that serve customers, including loyalty programs; and addressing journey friction points by testing customer experience and optimizing experiences in order to meet and exceed business goals. Industries served by Macquarium include technology, entertainment, utilities, restaurants, quick service restaurants, consumer goods, travel, tourism, healthcare, education, telecommunications, financial services, manufacturing and retail. The firm, which is owned by Synoptek LLC, is based in Atlanta, and has offices in Washington DC, Houston, Chicago, Charlotte and San Francisco.

FINANCIAL DATA: *Note: Data for latest year may not have been available at press time.*

In U.S. $	2022	2021	2020	2019	2018	2017
Revenue						
R&D Expense						
Operating Income						
Operating Margin %						
SGA Expense						
Net Income						
Operating Cash Flow						
Capital Expenditure						
EBITDA						
Return on Assets %						
Return on Equity %						
Debt to Equity						

CONTACT INFORMATION:

Phone: 404-554-4000   Fax: 404-554-4001
Toll-Free:
Address: 1800 Peachtree St., Ste. 250, Atlanta, GA 30309 United States

STOCK TICKER/OTHER:

Stock Ticker: Private   Exchange:
Employees: 60   Fiscal Year Ends:
Parent Company: Synoptek LLC

SALARIES/BONUSES:

Top Exec. Salary: $ Bonus: $
Second Exec. Salary: $ Bonus: $

OTHER THOUGHTS:

Estimated Female Officers or Directors: 2
Hot Spot for Advancement for Women/Minorities: Y

Major League Baseball Advanced Media LP (MLBAM)
www.mlb.com
NAIC Code: 519130

TYPES OF BUSINESS:
Online Delivery of Sporting Events
Streaming Sports Media
Digital Baseball Content
Web Applications
Mobile Applications
Content Strategy
User Experience and Product Design
Proprietary Software

BRANDS/DIVISIONS/AFFILIATES:
MLB.com
MLB Network
MLB Productions
At Bat

CONTACTS: *Note: Officers with more than one job title may be intentionally listed here more than once.*
Lara Pitaro Wisch, Exec. VP
Chris Marinak, COO
Bob Starkey, CFO
Karin Timpone, CMO
Tony Reagins, Chief Baseball Dev. Officer
Pat Courtney, CCO
Rob Manfred, Commissioner

GROWTH PLANS/SPECIAL FEATURES:
Major League Baseball Advanced Media LP (MLBAM) is a full-service solutions provider that delivers digital content through all forms of interactive media. Its capabilities are designed for web, mobile applications and connected devices while integrating live and on-demand multimedia. MLB.com, MLB Network and MLB Productions are all under MLBAM. The company's services include business and content strategy, delivering back-end infrastructure, as well as development and operational management of custom multi-platform applications; UX (user experience) and product design, providing solutions for all forms of digital presence such as websites, mobile web applications, connected devices, marketing campaigns and social media; social media and marketing, a suite of marketing solutions that are fully customizable and able to develop, integrate and manage initiatives; ticketing, which supports digital ticketing strategies such as print-at-home, mobile, season and package plans, secondary market, dynamic pricing and interactive seating; sponsorship and advertising; eCommerce and paid content, a subscription platform that supports digital products such as live and on-demand multimedia, fantasy games, gamecast applications and fan clubs with password-protected login; multimedia and live streaming, which operates and distributes live events and daily streams; mobile web and applications; and statistics and data applications, which deploys proprietary software to chronicle every pitch of every game throughout the season, in-game highlights, box scores and player stats. The firm's At Bat offering is a subscription-based application that provides live scores, statistics, pitch tracking, player cards, notifications and news via online and mobile devices.

FINANCIAL DATA: *Note: Data for latest year may not have been available at press time.*

In U.S. $	2022	2021	2020	2019	2018	2017
Revenue	105,000,000	99,225,000	94,500,000	135,000,000	130,000,000	110,000,000
R&D Expense						
Operating Income						
Operating Margin %						
SGA Expense						
Net Income						
Operating Cash Flow						
Capital Expenditure						
EBITDA						
Return on Assets %						
Return on Equity %						
Debt to Equity						

CONTACT INFORMATION:
Phone: 212-931-7800   Fax:
Toll-Free:
Address: 1271 Avenue of the Americas, New York, NY 10020 United States

STOCK TICKER/OTHER:
Stock Ticker: Subsidiary   Exchange:
Employees: Fiscal Year Ends:
Parent Company: Major League Baseball

SALARIES/BONUSES:
Top Exec. Salary: $ Bonus: $
Second Exec. Salary: $ Bonus: $

OTHER THOUGHTS:
Estimated Female Officers or Directors:
Hot Spot for Advancement for Women/Minorities:

MakeMyTrip Limited

www.makemytrip.com

NAIC Code: 561510

TYPES OF BUSINESS:

Online Travel Services

BRANDS/DIVISIONS/AFFILIATES:

MakeMyTrip (India) Private Limited
Ibibo Group Holdings (Singapore) Pte Ltd
Ibibo Group Private Limited
ITC Bangkok Co Ltd
Luxury Tours & Travel Pte Ltd
Luxury Tours (Malaysia) Sdn Bhd
MakeMyTrip Inc
Bitla Software Private Limited

CONTACTS: *Note: Officers with more than one job title may be intentionally listed here more than once.*

Rajesh Magow, CEO
Mohit Kabra, CFO
Amit Somani, Chief Prod. Officer
Keyur Joshi, Chief Commercial Officer
Mohit Gupta, Chief Bus. Officer-Holidays
Deep Kalra, Chmn.
Amit Saberwal, Chief Bus. Officer-Intl Markets

GROWTH PLANS/SPECIAL FEATURES:

MakeMyTrip Ltd is an online travel company, which provides online booking solutions for day-to-day travel needs. The company's operating segment includes Air ticketing; Hotels and packages; Bus ticketing and Others. It generates maximum revenue from the Hotels and packages segment. The Hotels and packages segments include internet-based platforms, call-centers, and branch offices, which provide holiday packages and hotel reservations. Its Air ticketing segment includes internet-based platforms, provides the facility to book domestic and international air tickets. Geographically, it derives a majority of revenue from India and also has a presence in the United States; South East Asia; Europe, and other countries.

FINANCIAL DATA: *Note: Data for latest year may not have been available at press time.*

In U.S. $	2022	2021	2020	2019	2018	2017
Revenue	303,922,000	163,440,000	511,529,000	486,011,000	675,256,000	
R&D Expense						
Operating Income	-32,885,000	-69,189,000	-157,931,000	-152,993,000	-216,139,000	
Operating Margin %	- .11%	- .42%	- .31%	- .31%	- .32%	
SGA Expense	178,866,000	135,870,000	316,905,000	329,128,000	589,963,000	
Net Income	-45,405,000	-55,639,000	-447,781,000	-167,759,000	-218,412,000	
Operating Cash Flow	5,998,000	64,526,000	-112,733,000	-78,927,000	-125,478,000	
Capital Expenditure	12,911,000	8,770,000	12,761,000	9,703,000	12,095,000	
EBITDA	-2,003,000	-23,637,000	-410,976,000	-141,507,000	-189,889,000	
Return on Assets %	- .03%	- .05%	- .34%	- .10%	- .13%	
Return on Equity %	- .05%	- .06%	- .40%	- .12%	- .15%	
Debt to Equity	.24%	.23%	0.025	0.00	.00%	

CONTACT INFORMATION:

Phone: 91 1244395000   Fax:
Toll-Free: 800-102-8747
Address: 19/Fl, Bldg. 5, DLF Cyber City, Gurgaon, 122002 India

STOCK TICKER/OTHER:

Stock Ticker: MMYT   Exchange: NAS
Employees: 4,090   Fiscal Year Ends: 03/31
Parent Company:

SALARIES/BONUSES:

Top Exec. Salary: $ Bonus: $
Second Exec. Salary: $ Bonus: $

OTHER THOUGHTS:

Estimated Female Officers or Directors:
Hot Spot for Advancement for Women/Minorities:

Manhattan Associates Inc

www.manh.com

NAIC Code: 511210A

TYPES OF BUSINESS:
Computer Software, Supply Chain & Logistics
Consulting & Support
RFID System Integration
Consulting Services

GROWTH PLANS/SPECIAL FEATURES:
Manhattan Associates provides software that helps users manage their supply chains, inventory, and omnichannel operations. Customers are generally retailers, wholesalers, manufacturers, and logistics providers. The company was founded in 1990 and serves more than 1,200 customers around the world.

BRANDS/DIVISIONS/AFFILIATES:

CONTACTS: Note: Officers with more than one job title may be intentionally listed here more than once.
Eddie Capel, CEO
Dennis Story, CFO
John Huntz, Chairman of the Board
Linda Pinne, Chief Accounting Officer
Bruce Richards, Chief Legal Officer
Deepak Raghavan, Co-Founder
Robert Howell, Senior VP, Geographical

FINANCIAL DATA: Note: Data for latest year may not have been available at press time.

In U.S. $	2022	2021	2020	2019	2018	2017
Revenue	767,084,000	663,643,000	586,372,000	617,949,000	559,157,000	
R&D Expense	111,877,000	97,628,000	84,276,000	87,608,000	71,896,000	
Operating Income	152,700,000	134,333,000	114,061,000	115,924,000	133,887,000	
Operating Margin %	.20%	.20%	.19%	.19%	.24%	
SGA Expense	137,607,000	125,941,000	109,202,000	121,463,000	103,880,000	
Net Income	128,959,000	110,472,000	87,240,000	85,762,000	104,690,000	
Operating Cash Flow	179,630,000	185,183,000	140,885,000	146,908,000	137,349,000	
Capital Expenditure	6,587,000	4,016,000	2,730,000	15,193,000	7,306,000	
EBITDA	159,363,000	142,247,000	123,007,000	123,911,000	142,500,000	
Return on Assets %	.23%	.22%	.21%	.25%	.34%	
Return on Equity %	.54%	.47%	.48%	.59%	.65%	
Debt to Equity	.06%	.09%	0.127	0.228		

CONTACT INFORMATION:
Phone: 770 955-7070   Fax: 770 995-0302
Toll-Free:
Address: 2300 Windy Ridge Pkwy., 10/Fl, Atlanta, GA 30339 United States

STOCK TICKER/OTHER:
Stock Ticker: MANH   Exchange: NAS
Employees: 2,500   Fiscal Year Ends: 12/31
Parent Company:

SALARIES/BONUSES:
Top Exec. Salary: $665,000   Bonus: $
Second Exec. Salary: $450,000   Bonus: $3,000

OTHER THOUGHTS:
Estimated Female Officers or Directors:
Hot Spot for Advancement for Women/Minorities:

MapQuest.com Inc

www.mapquest.com

NAIC Code: 519130

TYPES OF BUSINESS:

Online Mapping Services
Driving Directions
Trip and Route Planners
Live Traffic Reports
Advertising Services
Travel Booking Services
Destination Information

BRANDS/DIVISIONS/AFFILIATES:

System1 Inc
MapQuest Mobile
MapQuest Enterprise Solutions
MapQuest Developer Network
MapQuest Route Planner
MapQuest Travel

CONTACTS: *Note: Officers with more than one job title may be intentionally listed here more than once.*

James W. Thomas, VP-Admin.
James W. Thomas, Sec.
William Muenster, Sr. VP-Dev. & Prod.
James W. Thomas, Principal Acct. Officer
Michael Blend, CEO

GROWTH PLANS/SPECIAL FEATURES:

MapQuest.com, Inc., a subsidiary of System1, Inc., operates a website that allows users to access interactive maps and driving directions via online, mobile app and in print. MapQuest's navigation software platform is utilized by millions of users every month. MapQuest offers additional information such as restaurant and lodging locations and city information to help with trip planning as well as computer applications for information kiosks and hotel reservation systems. The company also provides state-of-the-art mapping technology products and services for the information publishing industry as well as for the commercial, internet, telecommunications and real estate markets. The firm generates revenue through paid advertisements, including a service that pinpoints advertisers' store locations on a user's map. MapQuest Mobile enables consumers to plan trips and access directions from their mobile devices. It utilizes the latest wireless and voice recognition technologies to provide travelers with the tools needed to continually access navigation and travel information. MapQuest Enterprise Solutions helps global brands build engaging business mapping applications with MapQuest geospatial web services. MapQuest Developer Network provides free, flexible and customizable APIs and web services to help add and enhance location content on websites. MapQuest's Route Planner optimizes routes for drivers with multiple destinations on their trips. MapQuest Travel provides information on destinations, places to eat and drink, U.S. national parks, family destinations, luxury destinations, destinations on a budget and more. In addition, MapQuest offers a travel booking platform powered by Priceline, spanning hotels, car rentals, flights, vacation packages and activities.

FINANCIAL DATA: *Note: Data for latest year may not have been available at press time.*

In U.S. $	2022	2021	2020	2019	2018	2017
Revenue						
R&D Expense						
Operating Income						
Operating Margin %						
SGA Expense						
Net Income						
Operating Cash Flow						
Capital Expenditure						
EBITDA						
Return on Assets %						
Return on Equity %						
Debt to Equity						

CONTACT INFORMATION:

Phone: 303-486-4000   Fax: 303-486-4001
Toll-Free:
Address: 1555 Blake St., Fl. 3, Denver, CO 80202 United States

STOCK TICKER/OTHER:

Stock Ticker: Subsidiary   Exchange:
Employees: 335   Fiscal Year Ends: 12/31
Parent Company: System1 Inc

SALARIES/BONUSES:

Top Exec. Salary: $ Bonus: $
Second Exec. Salary: $ Bonus: $

OTHER THOUGHTS:

Estimated Female Officers or Directors:
Hot Spot for Advancement for Women/Minorities:

Marchex Inc

www.marchex.com

NAIC Code: 519130

TYPES OF BUSINESS:

Online Marketing
Conversation Analytics
Voice
Text
Marketing
Artificial Intelligence
Machine Learning

BRANDS/DIVISIONS/AFFILIATES:

Marchex Call Analytics

GROWTH PLANS/SPECIAL FEATURES:

Marchex Inc is a conversational analytics and solutions company that helps businesses connect, drive, measure, convert callers into customers, and connect the voice of the customer to their business. It delivers data insights and incorporates artificial intelligence (AI)-powered functionality that drives insights and solutions to help companies find, engage, and support their customers across voice and text-based communication channels. The group enables sales and marketing teams to deliver the buying experiences that today's customers expect. The company generates the majority of its revenues from core analytics and solutions services. Company operates in United States, Canada and other countries.

CONTACTS: Note: Officers with more than one job title may be intentionally listed here more than once.

Leila Kirske, CFO
Russell Horowitz, Chairman of the Board
Michael Arends, Co-CEO
Ryan Polley, COO
John Roswech, Other Executive Officer

FINANCIAL DATA: Note: Data for latest year may not have been available at press time.

In U.S. $	2022	2021	2020	2019	2018	2017
Revenue	52,170,000	53,476,000	51,218,000	54,489,000	85,251,000	90,291,000
R&D Expense	14,355,000	16,112,000	21,001,000	17,879,000	15,423,000	18,094,000
Operating Income	-8,075,000	-11,654,000	-25,454,000	-14,407,000	-3,426,000	-6,361,000
Operating Margin %		-.22%	-.50%	-.26%	-.04%	-.07%
SGA Expense	23,304,000	22,843,000	29,452,000	26,751,000	24,669,000	29,219,000
Net Income	-8,245,000	-4,390,000	-38,446,000	-4,042,000	-2,678,000	-6,087,000
Operating Cash Flow	-2,292,000	-6,342,000	-3,373,000	5,094,000	5,051,000	1,692,000
Capital Expenditure	2,865,000	1,351,000	1,357,000	1,683,000	2,228,000	1,577,000
EBITDA	-4,017,000	1,849,000	-36,657,000	-6,282,000	-828,000	-3,570,000
Return on Assets %		-.06%	-.38%	-.03%	-.02%	-.05%
Return on Equity %		-.08%	-.50%	-.04%	-.03%	-.06%
Debt to Equity		.03%	0.06	0.057		

CONTACT INFORMATION:

Phone: 206 331-3300   Fax: 206 331-3695
Toll-Free: 800-840-1012
Address: 520 Pike St., Ste. 2000, Seattle, WA 98101 United States

STOCK TICKER/OTHER:

Stock Ticker: MCHX   Exchange: NAS
Employees: 193   Fiscal Year Ends: 12/31
Parent Company:

SALARIES/BONUSES:

Top Exec. Salary: $400,000   Bonus: $214,733
Second Exec. Salary: $350,000   Bonus: $172,779

OTHER THOUGHTS:

Estimated Female Officers or Directors: 1
Hot Spot for Advancement for Women/Minorities:

MarketWatch Inc

www.marketwatch.com

NAIC Code: 519130

TYPES OF BUSINESS:

Online Financial Information
Television & Radio Programming

BRANDS/DIVISIONS/AFFILIATES:

News Corporation
Dow Jones & Company Inc
Barrons.com
Financial News London
Moneyish
Mansion Global

CONTACTS: *Note: Officers with more than one job title may be intentionally listed here more than once.*

Almar Latour, CEO- Dow Jones
Raju Narisetti, Managing Editor-WSJ.com

GROWTH PLANS/SPECIAL FEATURES:

MarketWatch, Inc. is a financial media company providing web-based, real-time business news, analysis, and stock market data. MarketWatch is a wholly-owned subsidiary of publishing firm Dow Jones & Company Inc., itself a subsidiary of News Corporation, a U.S. mass media and publishing company. The firm is a member of Dow Jones Media Group, which also includes: Barrons.com, a financial information website; Financial News London, a financial newspaper and news website published in London; Moneyish, offering features, essays, videos and news about money; and Mansion Global, offering digital content about the global real estate market, featuring luxury listings for sale around the world. These free, advertising-supported websites serve the business and financial communities with timely market news and information, provided by bureaus in the U.S., Europe and Asia. In addition to business and financial news, MarketWatch sites offer in-depth commentary on trends and events, personal finance commentary and data, community features and other services designed to provide a one-stop-shop for audiences. Other features include a mutual fund center, a seasonal tax guide, market advisors and research columns. Customers have the ability to create personal user settings including portfolio trackers, news and quotes, custom views, allocation analysis, financials and charting. MarketWatch also delivers relevant financial news to user e-mail accounts, hosts investment discussion communities, offers personalized automatic alerts and provides customers with wireless capabilities. In addition, the firm sells subscription-based content for individual investors that includes unlimited access across devices and platforms, member-exclusive content and fewer ads.

MarketWatch offers employees health care coverage, a retirement savings program and tuition assistance.

FINANCIAL DATA: *Note: Data for latest year may not have been available at press time.*

In U.S. $	2022	2021	2020	2019	2018	2017
Revenue						
R&D Expense						
Operating Income						
Operating Margin %						
SGA Expense						
Net Income						
Operating Cash Flow						
Capital Expenditure						
EBITDA						
Return on Assets %						
Return on Equity %						
Debt to Equity						

CONTACT INFORMATION:

Phone: 415-439-6400   Fax: 415-439-6485
Toll-Free:
Address: 825 Battery St., San Francisco, CA 94111 United States

STOCK TICKER/OTHER:

Stock Ticker: Subsidiary   Exchange:
Employees: 206   Fiscal Year Ends: 12/31
Parent Company: News Corporation

SALARIES/BONUSES:

Top Exec. Salary: $ Bonus: $
Second Exec. Salary: $ Bonus: $

OTHER THOUGHTS:

Estimated Female Officers or Directors:
Hot Spot for Advancement for Women/Minorities: Y

Match Group Inc

www.match.com

NAIC Code: 519130

TYPES OF BUSINESS:

Internet Dating Sites
Dating Platforms
Online

GROWTH PLANS/SPECIAL FEATURES:

Match Group is a provider of online dating products. The firm became public in 2015 and was more than 80% owned by IAC/InterActiveCorp until IAC spun it off in 2020. The company has a vast portfolio of different online dating service providers, including Tinder, Hinge, BLK, Chispa, Match.com, OkCupid, PlentyOfFish, and Meetic. Match Group has more than 45 brands of online dating sites and/or apps, from which it generates user fee revenue (95%) and advertising revenue (5%).

BRANDS/DIVISIONS/AFFILIATES:

Match
OKCupid
PlentyOfFish
Tinder
Meetic
OurTime
Pairs
Hinge

CONTACTS:

Note: Officers with more than one job title may be intentionally listed here more than once.

Sharmistha Dubey, CEO
Gary Swidler, CFO
Thomas Mcinerney, Chairman of the Board
Philip Eigenmann, Chief Accounting Officer
Jared Sine, Chief Legal Officer

FINANCIAL DATA:

Note: Data for latest year may not have been available at press time.

In U.S. $	2022	2021	2020	2019	2018	2017
Revenue	3,188,843,000	2,983,277,000	2,391,269,000	2,051,258,000	1,729,850,000	3,307,239,000
R&D Expense	333,639,000	241,049,000	169,811,000	151,960,000	132,030,000	250,879,000
Operating Income	881,262,000	880,238,000	753,240,000	645,454,000	549,469,000	188,466,000
Operating Margin %	.28%	.30%	.31%	.31%	.32%	.06%
SGA Expense	970,385,000	981,280,000	791,114,000	683,578,000	602,206,000	2,100,478,000
Net Income	361,946,000	277,723,000	162,329,000	453,838,000	626,961,000	304,924,000
Operating Cash Flow	525,688,000	912,499,000	802,182,000	937,938,000	988,127,000	416,699,000
Capital Expenditure	49,125,000	79,971,000	42,376,000	39,035,000	31,397,000	75,523,000
EBITDA	566,632,000	428,043,000	802,847,000	686,510,000	593,124,000	288,661,000
Return on Assets %	.08%	.07%	.03%	.06%	.10%	.06%
Return on Equity %			.21%	.16%	.24%	.14%
Debt to Equity				0.987	.79%	0.815

CONTACT INFORMATION:

Phone: 214-576-9352   Fax:
Toll-Free:
Address: 8750 N. Central Expressway, Ste. 1400, Dallas, TX 75231
United States

STOCK TICKER/OTHER:

Stock Ticker: MTCH
Employees: 2,720
Parent Company:

Exchange: NAS
Fiscal Year Ends: 12/31

SALARIES/BONUSES:

Top Exec. Salary: $675,000   Bonus: $2,000,000
Second Exec. Salary: $553,846   Bonus: $2,000,000

OTHER THOUGHTS:

Estimated Female Officers or Directors:
Hot Spot for Advancement for Women/Minorities:

McAfee Corp

NAIC Code: 511210E

TYPES OF BUSINESS:
Computer Software: Network Security, Managed Access, Digital ID, Cybersecurity & Anti-Virus
Virus Protection Software
Identity Protection Software
Cybersecurity
Malware Protection
Software Design and Development
Software Technology
Virtual Private Network Solution

BRANDS/DIVISIONS/AFFILIATES:
Advent International Corporation
McAfee+
McAfee+ Ultimate
Total Protection

CONTACTS: *Note: Officers with more than one job title may be intentionally listed here more than once.*
Greg Johnson, CEO
Jennifer Biry, CFO
Chatelle Lynch, Chief People Officer
Steve Grobman, CTO
Lynne Doherty McDonald, Executive VP, Divisional
Gagan Singh, Executive VP
Ashish Agarwal, Senior VP, Divisional

GROWTH PLANS/SPECIAL FEATURES:
McAfee Corp. is an online protection company offering products and solutions that protect user privacy and identity across devices and locations. All-in-one protection products include: McAfee+, offering privacy, identity and device protection for individuals and families; McAfee+ Ultimate, offering privacy, identity and device protection as well as $2 million in ID theft coverage; and Total Protection, which protects devices with identity monitoring and virtual private network (VPN), enabling users to securely send/receive data across shared or public networks. Protection products for devices are available for antivirus, VPN and mobile security needs. Security features span personal data cleanup, identity monitoring, credit monitoring, security freeze, identity theft coverage and restoration, password manager, antivirus, web protection, parental controls and more. McAfee offers free tools and downloads on its website, as well as services regarding PC optimizing, technical and virus removal. McAfee serves more than 100 million customers in over 180 countries. The firm is privately-owned by Advent International Corporation.

McAfee offers its employees health and retirement plans, as well as skill and learning development opportunities.

FINANCIAL DATA: *Note: Data for latest year may not have been available at press time.*

In U.S. $	2022	2021	2020	2019	2018	2017
Revenue	2,000,000,000	1,920,000,000	1,558,000,000	1,303,000,000	2,408,999,936	2,076,000,000
R&D Expense						
Operating Income						
Operating Margin %						
SGA Expense						
Net Income		2,688,000,000	-289,000,000	-236,000,000	-512,000,000	-686,000,000
Operating Cash Flow						
Capital Expenditure						
EBITDA						
Return on Assets %						
Return on Equity %						
Debt to Equity						

CONTACT INFORMATION:
Phone: 866 622-3911   Fax:
Toll-Free:
Address: 6220 America Center Dr., San Jose, CA 95002 United States

STOCK TICKER/OTHER:
Stock Ticker: Private   Exchange:
Employees: 6,900   Fiscal Year Ends: 12/31
Parent Company: Advent International Corporation

SALARIES/BONUSES:
Top Exec. Salary: $ Bonus: $
Second Exec. Salary: $ Bonus: $

OTHER THOUGHTS:
Estimated Female Officers or Directors: 3
Hot Spot for Advancement for Women/Minorities: Y

Medallia Inc

www.medallia.com

NAIC Code: 511210K

TYPES OF BUSINESS:

Computer Software, Sales & Customer Relationship Management
Customer Experience Software Development
Enterprise Software Solutions
Customer Experience
Artificial Intelligence
Machine Learning
Behavior Prediction and Analytics

BRANDS/DIVISIONS/AFFILIATES:

Thoma Bravo LP
Medallia Experience Cloud
Medallia Athena
Thunderhead
CXTeam
Mindful

CONTACTS: *Note: Officers with more than one job title may be intentionally listed here more than once.*

Joe Tyrrell, CEO
Dan madden, CFO
Ashwin Ballal, CIO
Stefanie Wittner, Chief People Officer
Robert Baca, CTO

GROWTH PLANS/SPECIAL FEATURES:

Medallia, Inc. develops and provides software that improves customer experience. The firm's cloud-based software-as-a-service (SaaS) platform, the Medallia Experience Cloud, captures feedback from people no matter where they are (mobile, social, web, in-store). This data provides insight to solve issues, drive innovation and implement ideas that are customer centric. Medallia Athena brings artificial intelligence (AI) to the Medallia Experience Cloud, detecting patterns, anticipating needs, predicting behavior and focusing attention on smarter experience decisions. The system delivers intuitive experience management applications for discovering insights and taking action. Medallia's solutions are primarily used by customer experience professionals, human resource professionals, account managers, contact centers, location-based operators and research/insight professionals. Industries served by Medallia include automotive, energy/utilities, financial services, government, healthcare, higher education, insurance, life sciences, manufacturing, nonprofit, restaurants/food service, retail, technology, telecommunications, media, travel and hospitality. Medallia is headquartered in California, USA and has 11 global offices in San Mateo, New York, London, Paris, Sydney, Buenos Aires and Tel Aviv. The firm is privately owned by software investment firm Thoma Bravo LP.

FINANCIAL DATA: *Note: Data for latest year may not have been available at press time.*

In U.S. $	2022	2021	2020	2019	2018	2017
Revenue	435,304,000	418,561,528	402,463,008	313,641,984	261,195,008	137,812,500
R&D Expense						
Operating Income						
Operating Margin %						
SGA Expense						
Net Income			-112,333,000	-82,234,000	-70,361,000	
Operating Cash Flow						
Capital Expenditure						
EBITDA						
Return on Assets %						
Return on Equity %						
Debt to Equity						

CONTACT INFORMATION:

Phone: 650-321-3000   Fax:
Toll-Free:
Address: 6220 Stoneridge Mall Rd., Fl. 2, Pleasanton, CA 94588 United States

STOCK TICKER/OTHER:

Stock Ticker: Private   Exchange:
Employees: 2,040   Fiscal Year Ends: 01/31
Parent Company: Thoma Bravo LP

SALARIES/BONUSES:

Top Exec. Salary: $ Bonus: $
Second Exec. Salary: $ Bonus: $

OTHER THOUGHTS:

Estimated Female Officers or Directors:
Hot Spot for Advancement for Women/Minorities: Y

MedeAnalytics Inc

medeanalytics.com

NAIC Code: 511210D

TYPES OF BUSINESS:

Computer Software, Healthcare & Biotechnology
Cloud Software
Healthcare Data Management
Performance Management Solutions
Healthcare Provider and Payer Solutions
Government Healthcare Program Solutions

BRANDS/DIVISIONS/AFFILIATES:

JLL Partners

CONTACTS: *Note: Officers with more than one job title may be intentionally listed here more than once.*

Steve Grieco, CEO
Saleem Tahir, COO
Reese Feuerman, CFO
Andy De, CMO
Lisa King, Chief People Officer
Sree Ghantasala, CTO
David Bartley, Chief Product Officer

GROWTH PLANS/SPECIAL FEATURES:

MedeAnalytics, Inc. provides cloud-based performance management software to the healthcare industry. The firm's software-as-a-service (SaaS) healthcare analytics solutions normalize vast amounts of complex data across multiple sources to produce clear, human-powered insights. For providers, the company's solutions include enterprise analytics, patient access, business office, revenue integrity, population health, performance management and provider implementation services. For payers, its solutions include health plans, state government, employers, brokers/consultants and payer implementation services. The firm's solutions are utilized by more than 22,000 users worldwide, including 2,000 hospitals, health systems, health plans, state Medicaid programs and more. MedeAnalytics' partners include Optum, R1, Conifer Health Solutions, Deloitte, CTG, Bohemia Hospital, UST Global, Bakertilly, Waystar, Change Healthcare and TransUnion. Based in Texas, USA, the firm has a domestic office in California and international offices in the U.K. and Ukraine. MedeAnalytics is owned by New York-based private equity firm JLL Partners.

FINANCIAL DATA: *Note: Data for latest year may not have been available at press time.*

In U.S. $	2022	2021	2020	2019	2018	2017
Revenue						
R&D Expense						
Operating Income						
Operating Margin %						
SGA Expense						
Net Income						
Operating Cash Flow						
Capital Expenditure						
EBITDA						
Return on Assets %						
Return on Equity %						
Debt to Equity						

CONTACT INFORMATION:

Phone: 469-916-3300   Fax: 469-916-3355
Toll-Free:
Address: 501 W. President George Bush Highway, Ste. 250, Richardson, TX 75080 United States

STOCK TICKER/OTHER:

Stock Ticker: Private   Exchange:
Employees: 370   Fiscal Year Ends:
Parent Company: JLL Partners

SALARIES/BONUSES:

Top Exec. Salary: $ Bonus: $
Second Exec. Salary: $ Bonus: $

OTHER THOUGHTS:

Estimated Female Officers or Directors:
Hot Spot for Advancement for Women/Minorities:

MediaPlatform Inc

www.mediaplatform.com

NAIC Code: 511210F

TYPES OF BUSINESS:

Computer Software, Multimedia, Graphics & Publishing
Webcasting Software
Business Software
Video Streaming Solutions
Executive Broadcasts
Webinars
Video Training Solutions
Video Recruiting and Retention Solutions

BRANDS/DIVISIONS/AFFILIATES:

CONTACTS: *Note: Officers with more than one job title may be intentionally listed here more than once.*

Mike Newman, CEO
Shaun Brown, Gen. Mngr.-Services Oper.
Dena Kendros, VP-Finance & Administration
Darian Germain, VP-Mktg.
John Frederick, Head-Global Sales
Bill Accola, VP-Professional and Customer Services
Dena Kendros, VP-Admin.
Dena Kendros, VP-Finance
Tom Dunlap, Dir.-Client Svcs.

GROWTH PLANS/SPECIAL FEATURES:

MediaPlatform, Inc. provides webcast software. The company's end-to-end enterprise video platform enables businesses to webcast, capture, stream, transcode, host, deliver and govern all live and on-demand video assets within a single source built for enterprise environments. MediaPlatform's video management portal is a place for publishing and managing the recorded assets, and from which viewers can search and find the information needed, while administrators set viewer access and content governance policies. Live video assets can be securely streamed across devices on-demand, and the real-time dashboard lets producers monitor viewers' quality of experience, track audience sentiment and give IT teams actionable information about quality of service. MediaPlatform solutions include server, mining, industrial, gaming, edge and digital signage solutions. Products offered include computer cases, CPU/processors, DAS/NAS/SAN, desktops, dram memory, electronics, fans/PC cooling, flash memory, hard drives, monitors, motherboards, networking, notebooks, optical drives, pc components, power supplies, servers, software, solid state drives, storage/memory, tablets and video adapters

FINANCIAL DATA: *Note: Data for latest year may not have been available at press time.*

In U.S. $	2022	2021	2020	2019	2018	2017
Revenue						
R&D Expense						
Operating Income						
Operating Margin %						
SGA Expense						
Net Income						
Operating Cash Flow						
Capital Expenditure						
EBITDA						
Return on Assets %						
Return on Equity %						
Debt to Equity						

CONTACT INFORMATION:

Phone: 310 909-8410   Fax: 310-295-1110
Toll-Free:
Address: 5200 Lankershim Blvd., Ste. 420, North Hollywood, CA 91601
United States

STOCK TICKER/OTHER:

Stock Ticker: Private   Exchange:
Employees: 35   Fiscal Year Ends: 12/31
Parent Company:

SALARIES/BONUSES:

Top Exec. Salary: $ Bonus: $
Second Exec. Salary: $ Bonus: $

OTHER THOUGHTS:

Estimated Female Officers or Directors: 1
Hot Spot for Advancement for Women/Minorities: Y

Meesho (Fashnear Technologies Private Limited)

www.meesho.com

NAIC Code: 454110

TYPES OF BUSINESS:

Online Sales, B2C Ecommerce, Sharing Economy Platforms
Ecommerce Platform
Apparel Products
Consumer Products
Payments Technology
Delivery Services
Seller and Reseller Capabilities
Online and Mobile App Shopping

BRANDS/DIVISIONS/AFFILIATES:

Meesho Inc

CONTACTS: *Note: Officers with more than one job title may be intentionally listed here more than once.*

Vidit Aatrey, CEO
Dhiresh Bansal, CFO
Ashish Kumar Singh, Chief Human Resources Officer
Sanjeev Barnwal, CTO

GROWTH PLANS/SPECIAL FEATURES:

Fashnear Technologies Private Limited operates Meesho, a Bengaluru-based ecommerce, hyperlocal fashion discovery platform founded in 2015. The Meesho online and mobile platform helps shop owners to sell on leading social media sites, including Meesho, Facebook and WhatsApp. The affordable ecommerce platform is comprised of product categories, which includes apparel (men, women and children), footwear, jewelry, apparel accessories, health and beauty, home and kitchen, and electronics. Ethnic wear and western wear are available. Meesho offers multiple payment options, including debit and credit cards, real-time unified payments interface (UPI) system and cash on delivery (COD). Sellers register on Meesho, upload products on the supplier panel, and Meesho receives orders, charges low shipping costs for deliveries across India, and deposits sellers' payments directly into their accounts. There is a seven-day payment cycle from order to delivery to deposit. Resellers are encouraged to do business with Meesho. Meesho, Inc. is the firm's U.S. subsidiary.

FINANCIAL DATA: *Note: Data for latest year may not have been available at press time.*

In U.S. $	2022	2021	2020	2019	2018	2017
Revenue						
R&D Expense						
Operating Income						
Operating Margin %						
SGA Expense						
Net Income						
Operating Cash Flow						
Capital Expenditure						
EBITDA						
Return on Assets %						
Return on Equity %						
Debt to Equity						

CONTACT INFORMATION:

Phone: 91 81-0523-6065   Fax:
Toll-Free:
Address: C/O Vaishnavi Signature No. 78/9, Outer Ring Rd., Bengaluru, Karnataka 560103 India

STOCK TICKER/OTHER:

Stock Ticker: Private   Exchange:
Employees: Fiscal Year Ends:
Parent Company:

SALARIES/BONUSES:

Top Exec. Salary: $ Bonus: $
Second Exec. Salary: $ Bonus: $

OTHER THOUGHTS:

Estimated Female Officers or Directors:
Hot Spot for Advancement for Women/Minorities:

Meituan Dianping

NAIC Code: 519130

TYPES OF BUSINESS:

Online Reviews
Food Delivery
Attraction Tickets
Hotel Booking
Bike Sharing
Websites
Mobile Apps

BRANDS/DIVISIONS/AFFILIATES:

Dianping.com
Meituan.com

GROWTH PLANS/SPECIAL FEATURES:

Meituan is the largest food delivery service in China, with a 70.7% share of the market in 2020 per the Chinese government. For the quarter-ended Sept. 30, 2021, the firm generated 54.2% of revenue from food delivery services, 17.7% from hotel booking, coupon sales, advertising, and 28.1% from new initiatives. In the long term, its new initiatives business may transform the company into an all-encompassing grocer and logistics business involving community group buying, nonfood delivery, and online grocery, overtaking food delivery as its main business.

CONTACTS: *Note: Officers with more than one job title may be intentionally listed here more than once.*

Wang Xing, CEO
Zhang Tao, CEO-Shanghai Han Tao

FINANCIAL DATA: *Note: Data for latest year may not have been available at press time.*

In U.S. $	2022	2021	2020	2019	2018	2017
Revenue	30,247,250,000	24,632,900,000	15,786,040,000	13,411,700,000	8,969,770,000	4,665,629,000
R&D Expense	2,852,056,000	2,293,155,000	1,497,891,000	1,161,411,000	972,496,800	501,469,200
Operating Income	-889,863,900	-3,024,568,000	-265,485,900	179,680,000	-1,814,002,000	-613,545,400
Operating Margin %		-.12%	-.02%	.01%	-.20%	-.13%
SGA Expense	6,809,351,000	6,778,942,000	3,640,944,000	3,184,590,000	2,945,302,000	1,798,718,000
Net Income	-919,444,700	-3,236,895,000	647,466,700	307,865,700	-15,879,920,000	-2,601,330,000
Operating Cash Flow	1,569,252,000	-551,638,100	1,165,447,000	766,542,400	-1,262,369,000	-42,657,350
Capital Expenditure	788,143,900	1,239,078,000	2,176,107,000	412,785,600	313,530,300	102,577,200
EBITDA	626,793,800	-1,864,404,000	1,372,058,000	1,070,479,000	-15,140,390,000	-2,487,304,000
Return on Assets %		-.12%	.03%	.02%	-1.13%	-.28%
Return on Equity %		-.21%	.05%	.03%	-5.03%	
Debt to Equity		.36%	0.17	0.016	.01%	

CONTACT INFORMATION:

Phone: 86 215-355-9777   Fax:
Toll-Free:
Address: No. 4 Wang Jing East Rd., Beijing, Beijing 100102 China

STOCK TICKER/OTHER:

Stock Ticker: MPNGF   Exchange: PINX
Employees: 91,932   Fiscal Year Ends: 12/31
Parent Company:

SALARIES/BONUSES:

Top Exec. Salary: $ Bonus: $
Second Exec. Salary: $ Bonus: $

OTHER THOUGHTS:

Estimated Female Officers or Directors:
Hot Spot for Advancement for Women/Minorities:

MercadoLibre Inc

NAIC Code: 454110

www.mercadolibre.com

TYPES OF BUSINESS:

Electronic Shopping
Ecommerce Platform
Ecommerce Solutions
Online Marketplace
Shipping
Logistics
Technology
Financial Services

BRANDS/DIVISIONS/AFFILIATES:

Mercado Pago
Mercado Envios
MercadoShops
Mercado Credito
Mercado Fondo

GROWTH PLANS/SPECIAL FEATURES:

MercadoLibre runs the largest e-commerce marketplace in Latin America, connecting a network of more than 148 million active users and 1 million active sellers as of the end of 2022 across an 18-country footprint. The company also operates a host of complementary businesses, with shipping solutions (Mercado Envios), a payment and financing operation (Mercado Pago and Mercado Credito), advertisements (Mercado Clics), classifieds, and a turnkey e-commerce solution (Mercado Shops) rounding out its arsenal. MercadoLibre generates revenue from final value fees, advertising royalties, payment processing, insertion fees, subscription fees, and interest income from consumer and small-business lending.

CONTACTS:
Note: Officers with more than one job title may be intentionally listed here more than once.

Marcos Galperin, CEO
Pedro Arnt, CFO

FINANCIAL DATA:
Note: Data for latest year may not have been available at press time.

In U.S. $	2022	2021	2020	2019	2018	2017
Revenue	10,537,000,000	7,069,000,000	3,974,000,000	2,296,314,000	1,439,653,000	1,216,542,000
R&D Expense	1,099,000,000	590,000,000	353,000,000	223,807,000	146,273,000	127,160,000
Operating Income	1,034,000,000	441,000,000	128,000,000	-153,161,000	-69,482,000	144,871,000
Operating Margin %	.10%	.06%	.03%	-.07%	-.05%	.12%
SGA Expense	1,957,000,000	1,539,000,000	1,095,000,000	1,031,477,000	620,217,000	447,569,000
Net Income	482,000,000	83,000,000	-1,000,000	-171,999,000	-36,585,000	13,780,000
Operating Cash Flow	2,940,000,000	965,000,000	1,182,000,000	451,091,000	230,907,000	269,010,000
Capital Expenditure	455,000,000	609,000,000	247,000,000	136,870,000	97,754,000	74,884,000
EBITDA	1,504,000,000	674,000,000	293,000,000	31,950,000	36,589,000	121,460,000
Return on Assets %	.04%	.01%	.00%	-.05%	-.02%	.01%
Return on Equity %	.29%	.05%	.00%	-.16%	-.11%	.04%
Debt to Equity	1.72%	1.70%	0.669	0.407	1.79%	0.958

CONTACT INFORMATION:

Phone: 54 1146408000   Fax:
Toll-Free:
Address: Arias 3751, 7/Fl, Buenos Aires, C1430CRG Argentina

STOCK TICKER/OTHER:

Stock Ticker: MELI   Exchange: NAS
Employees: 40,548   Fiscal Year Ends: 12/31
Parent Company:

SALARIES/BONUSES:

Top Exec. Salary: $448,824   Bonus: $2,046,528
Second Exec. Salary: Bonus: $615,667
$537,875

OTHER THOUGHTS:

Estimated Female Officers or Directors:
Hot Spot for Advancement for Women/Minorities:

Meta Platforms Inc (Facebook)

investor.fb.com

NAIC Code: 519130

TYPES OF BUSINESS:

Social Networking
Advertising Services
Metaverse Technologies and Platforms
Online Video
3-D Headset Manufacturing
In-App Merchandising and Ecommerce
Virtual Reality (VR) and Augmented Reality (AR)
Instant Messaging

BRANDS/DIVISIONS/AFFILIATES:

Facebook
Instagram
Meta Quest
WhatsApp Messenger
Oculus
Llama
Meta Spark
Meta Horizon

CONTACTS: Note: Officers with more than one job title may be intentionally listed here more than once.

Mark Zuckerberg, CEO
David Wehner, CFO
Susan Taylor, Chief Accounting Officer
Michael Schroepfer, Chief Technology Officer
Sheryl Sandberg, COO
Jennifer Newstead, General Counsel
Christopher Cox, Other Executive Officer
David Fischer, Other Executive Officer

GROWTH PLANS/SPECIAL FEATURES:

Meta is the world's largest online social network, with nearly 4 billion family of apps monthly active users. Users engage with each other in different ways, exchanging messages and sharing news events, photos, and videos. The firm's ecosystem consists mainly of the Facebook app, Instagram, Messenger, WhatsApp, and many features surrounding these products. Users can access Facebook on mobile devices and desktops. Advertising revenue represents more than 90% of the firm's total revenue, with more than 45% coming from the U.S. and Canada and over 20% from Europe.

FINANCIAL DATA: Note: Data for latest year may not have been available at press time.

In U.S. $	2022	2021	2020	2019	2018	2017
Revenue	116,609,000,000	117,929,000,000	85,965,000,000	70,697,000,000	55,838,000,000	
R&D Expense	35,338,000,000	24,655,000,000	18,447,000,000	13,600,000,000	10,273,000,000	
Operating Income	28,944,000,000	46,753,000,000	32,671,000,000	23,986,000,000	24,913,000,000	
Operating Margin %	.25%	.40%	.38%	.34%	.45%	
SGA Expense	27,078,000,000	23,872,000,000	18,155,000,000	20,341,000,000	11,297,000,000	
Net Income	23,200,000,000	39,370,000,000	29,146,000,000	18,485,000,000	22,112,000,000	
Operating Cash Flow	50,475,000,000	57,683,000,000	38,747,000,000	36,314,000,000	29,274,000,000	
Capital Expenditure	31,431,000,000	18,690,000,000	15,163,000,000	15,102,000,000	13,915,000,000	
EBITDA	37,690,000,000	55,274,000,000	39,533,000,000	29,727,000,000	29,228,000,000	
Return on Assets %	.13%	.24%	.20%	.16%	.24%	
Return on Equity %	.19%	.31%	.25%	.20%	.28%	
Debt to Equity	.20%	.10%	0.075	0.094		

CONTACT INFORMATION:

Phone: 650 543-4800   Fax:
Toll-Free:
Address: 1601 Willow Rd., Menlo Park, CA 94025 United States

STOCK TICKER/OTHER:

Stock Ticker: META   Exchange: NAS
Employees: 67,317   Fiscal Year Ends: 12/31
Parent Company:

SALARIES/BONUSES:

Top Exec. Salary: $893,846   Bonus: $940,214
Second Exec. Salary: Bonus: $786,552
$987,046

OTHER THOUGHTS:

Estimated Female Officers or Directors: 2
Hot Spot for Advancement for Women/Minorities: Y

MH Sub I LLC (dba Internet Brands)   www.internetbrands.com

NAIC Code: 519130

TYPES OF BUSINESS:

Auto Sales-Online
Ecommerce Management Solutions
Website Management Solutions
Automotive Online Solutions
Healthcare Online Solutions
Home and Travel Online Solutions
Legal Online Solutions

BRANDS/DIVISIONS/AFFILIATES:

KKR & Co LP
Internet Brands
CarsDirect
Medscape
SatisFacts
Martindale-Avvo
Lawyers.com
PulsePoint

CONTACTS: *Note: Officers with more than one job title may be intentionally listed here more than once.*

Bob Brisco, CEO
Robert N. Brisco, Pres.
B. Lynn Walsh, General Counsel
B. Lynn Walsh, Exec. VP-Corp. Dev.
Gregory T. Perrier, CEO

GROWTH PLANS/SPECIAL FEATURES:

MH Sub I, LLC does business as Internet Brands, and owns and operates ecommerce and community websites. The firm's fully integrated vertical approach combines web solutions for businesses and media websites for consumers, serving more than 100,000 business clients and 250 million monthly website visitors. These sites are grouped into five categories: automotive, health, home/travel, legal and diversified media. The automotive segment operates ecommerce automotive websites that enable consumers to research and buy cars, including CarsDirect, Auto Credit Express, The Car Connection, NewCarTestDrive.com, RacingJunk.com, Honda-tech.com, Corvette Forum, MBWorld, AudiWorld, Club Lexus, F150online, YoTaTech and Internet Brands Automotive Group. The health segment operates websites for health professionals as well as sites that connect people with health professionals, with websites including Medscape, HenryScheinONE, Demandforce, Officite, eDoctors, and WebMD. Home and travel websites help people find homes and places to travel to, and include SatisFacts, doityourself, weddingbee and Fodor's Travel. Legal websites help people solve their legal problems and include Martindale-Avvo, Martindale Hubbell, total attorneys and Lawyers.com. Last, the diversified media segment provides consumers content in a range of categories, including bargain shopping, coupons, bike online communities and small business management. Brands within this division include Ben's Bargains, PromotionalCodes.org.uk, ultimate coupons, High-Def Digest, Bike Forums, DVD talk, HuntingNet.com, Model Mayhem, Professional Pilots Rumour Network, Class A Drivers, and Hospital Jobs Online, among others. MH Sub I operates as a subsidiary of KKR & Co. LP. Based in California, USA, the firm has additional offices in California, New Jersey and Oregan , as well as in Maharashtra, India and London, U.K.

MH Sub offers its employees comprehensive health and retirement benefits.

FINANCIAL DATA: *Note: Data for latest year may not have been available at press time.*

In U.S. $	2022	2021	2020	2019	2018	2017
Revenue	167,440,000	161,000,000	188,114,063	192,937,500	183,750,000	175,000,000
R&D Expense						
Operating Income						
Operating Margin %						
SGA Expense						
Net Income						
Operating Cash Flow						
Capital Expenditure						
EBITDA						
Return on Assets %						
Return on Equity %						
Debt to Equity						

CONTACT INFORMATION:

Phone: 310-280-4000   Fax:
Toll-Free: 800-692-2200
Address: 909 N. Pacific Coast Hwy, Fl. 11, El Segundo, CA 90245 United States

STOCK TICKER/OTHER:

Stock Ticker: Private   Exchange:
Employees: 5,000   Fiscal Year Ends: 12/31
Parent Company: KKR & Co LP

SALARIES/BONUSES:

Top Exec. Salary: $ Bonus: $
Second Exec. Salary: $ Bonus: $

OTHER THOUGHTS:

Estimated Female Officers or Directors:
Hot Spot for Advancement for Women/Minorities:

Microsoft Corporation

www.microsoft.com

NAIC Code: 511210H

TYPES OF BUSINESS:

Computer Software, Operating Systems, Languages & Development Tools
Enterprise Software
Game Consoles
Operating Systems
Software as a Service (SAAS)
Search Engine and Advertising
E-Mail Services
Instant Messaging

BRANDS/DIVISIONS/AFFILIATES:

Office 365
Exchange
SharePoint
Microsoft Teams
Skype for Business
Outlook.com
OneDrive
LinkedIn

CONTACTS: *Note: Officers with more than one job title may be intentionally listed here more than once.*

Satya Nadella, CEO
Amy Hood, CFO
Alice Jolla, Chief Accounting Officer
Bradford Smith, Chief Legal Officer
Christopher Capossela, Chief Marketing Officer
Christopher Young, Executive VP, Divisional
Kathleen Hogan, Executive VP, Divisional
Judson Althoff, Executive VP
Jean-Philippe Courtois, Executive VP

GROWTH PLANS/SPECIAL FEATURES:

Microsoft develops and licenses consumer and enterprise software. It is known for its Windows operating systems and Office productivity suite. The company is organized into three equally sized broad segments: productivity and business processes (legacy Microsoft Office, cloud-based Office 365, Exchange, SharePoint, Skype, LinkedIn, Dynamics), intelligence cloud (infrastructure- and platform-as-a-service offerings Azure, Windows Server OS, SQL Server), and more personal computing (Windows Client, Xbox, Bing search, display advertising, and Surface laptops, tablets, and desktops).

Microsoft offers its employees comprehensive benefits, a 401(k) and employee stock purchase plans; and employee assistance programs.

FINANCIAL DATA: *Note: Data for latest year may not have been available at press time.*

In U.S. $	2022	2021	2020	2019	2018	2017
Revenue	198,270,000,000	168,088,000,000	143,015,000,000	125,843,000,000	110,360,000,000	
R&D Expense	24,512,000,000	20,716,000,000	19,269,000,000	16,876,000,000	14,726,000,000	
Operating Income	83,383,000,000	69,916,000,000	52,959,000,000	42,959,000,000	35,058,000,000	
Operating Margin %	.42%	.42%	.37%	.34%	.32%	
SGA Expense	27,725,000,000	25,224,000,000	24,709,000,000	23,098,000,000	22,223,000,000	
Net Income	72,738,000,000	61,271,000,000	44,281,000,000	39,240,000,000	16,571,000,000	
Operating Cash Flow	89,035,000,000	76,740,000,000	60,675,000,000	52,185,000,000	43,884,000,000	
Capital Expenditure	23,886,000,000	20,622,000,000	15,441,000,000	13,925,000,000	11,632,000,000	
EBITDA	100,239,000,000	85,134,000,000	68,423,000,000	58,056,000,000	49,468,000,000	
Return on Assets %	.21%	.19%	.15%	.14%	.07%	
Return on Equity %	.47%	.47%	.40%	.42%	.19%	
Debt to Equity	.35%	.42%	0.568	0.712	.94%	

CONTACT INFORMATION:

Phone: 425 882-8080   Fax: 425 936-7329
Toll-Free: 800-642-7676
Address: One Microsoft Way, Redmond, WA 98052 United States

STOCK TICKER/OTHER:

Stock Ticker: MSFT   Exchange: NAS
Employees: 221,000   Fiscal Year Ends: 06/30
Parent Company:

SALARIES/BONUSES:

Top Exec. Salary: $2,500,000   Bonus: $
Second Exec. Salary: $1,000,000   Bonus: $

OTHER THOUGHTS:

Estimated Female Officers or Directors: 4
Hot Spot for Advancement for Women/Minorities: Y

mixi Inc

mixi.co.jp

NAIC Code: 519130

TYPES OF BUSINESS:

Social Networking & Advertising Services
Online Networking
Online Entertainment
Media Services
Information Technology
Gaming
Sports Betting
Photo Storage

BRANDS/DIVISIONS/AFFILIATES:

mixi recruitment inc
Chariloto Co Ltd
SFIDANTE Inc
Chiba Jets Funabashi Co Ltd
Net Dreamers Co Ltd
i-mercury Capital Inc
mixi empowerment Inc
mixi America Inc

GROWTH PLANS/SPECIAL FEATURES:

mixi Inc is a Japanese company which provides social networking services. The company conducts its business activities mainly including the operation of websites and provision of native smartphone games on the Internet. It business segments include, Entertainment Business and Media Platform Business. mixi provides games mainly including native smartphone games through Entertainment Business, and operates business-to-consumer and consumer-to-consumer services utilizing the Internet and invests in operating companies of these services through Media Platform Business.

CONTACTS:
Note: Officers with more than one job title may be intentionally listed here more than once.

Koki Kimura, Pres.

FINANCIAL DATA:
Note: Data for latest year may not have been available at press time.

In U.S. $	2022	2021	2020	2019	2018	2017
Revenue	832,724,900	814,225,200	765,447,700	982,865,200	1,290,365,000	
R&D Expense						
Operating Income	121,527,500	156,466,000	117,016,800	280,013,300	493,780,000	
Operating Margin %	.14%	.19%	.15%	.28%	.38%	
SGA Expense						
Net Income	70,027,220	107,081,200	73,425,540	180,977,600	285,158,600	
Operating Cash Flow	18,062,960	236,599,500	121,411,500	123,601,900	341,026,200	
Capital Expenditure	26,572,410	32,741,240	67,788,980	25,692,120	11,327,730	
EBITDA	138,935,300	187,071,400	129,027,000	273,783,100	507,605,200	
Return on Assets %	.05%	.07%	.05%	.14%	.23%	
Return on Equity %	.05%	.08%	.06%	.15%	.26%	
Debt to Equity	.04%	.04%	0.016	0.003		

CONTACT INFORMATION:

Phone: 81-03-5738-5900　　　Fax:
Toll-Free:
Address: Scramble Square, 2-24-12 Shibuya, 36/Fl, Tokyo, 150-6136 Japan

STOCK TICKER/OTHER:

Stock Ticker: MIXIF　　　　　　　Exchange: PINX
Employees: 1,041　　　　　　　　Fiscal Year Ends: 03/31
Parent Company:

SALARIES/BONUSES:

Top Exec. Salary: $　　　　Bonus: $
Second Exec. Salary: $　　　Bonus: $

OTHER THOUGHTS:

Estimated Female Officers or Directors:
Hot Spot for Advancement for Women/Minorities:

Mixpanel Inc

mixpanel.com

NAIC Code: 511210M

TYPES OF BUSINESS:

Computer Software, E-Commerce & Web Analytics
Business Analytics Products
Software and Technology Development
Data Management
Product Usage Analytics
Product Conversion Rate Data
User Retention Measurement

BRANDS/DIVISIONS/AFFILIATES:

CONTACTS: Note: Officers with more than one job title may be intentionally listed here more than once.

Amir Movafaghi, CEO

GROWTH PLANS/SPECIAL FEATURES:

Mixpanel, Inc. is a business analytics service and company. The firm builds advanced analytic products for mobile and web devices that help companies understand product usage, conversion rates and user retention. Mixpanel analyzes and measures billions of user actions monthly. Understanding what users are doing can be attained by installing Mixpanel's software development kit (SDK), which allows businesses to pick and choose which actions to track in their applications. SDK features include the ability to segment data for easy-to-find focus areas, to bookmark and save reports, to visualize the data in various ways and to make annotations to highlight significant events that have or have not yet occurred. Mixpanel has an SDK that can be installed on every major platform, and produces data that measures the actions people take in a company's application, pinpoints where and why customers are being lost, discovers who one's users are and what they do, finds out if people love the app by seeing if they return, embeds email and push notifications, and provides A/B testing to see if presented ideas are liked. Overall, the company's services and solutions include interactive reports, team dashboards and alerts, limitless segmentation, group analytics, scalable infrastructure, data integrations, data management, security/privacy, and integration directory connection tools.

FINANCIAL DATA: Note: Data for latest year may not have been available at press time.

In U.S. $	2022	2021	2020	2019	2018	2017
Revenue	114,400,000	110,000,000	107,493,750	110,250,000	105,000,000	100,000,000
R&D Expense						
Operating Income						
Operating Margin %						
SGA Expense						
Net Income						
Operating Cash Flow						
Capital Expenditure						
EBITDA						
Return on Assets %						
Return on Equity %						
Debt to Equity						

CONTACT INFORMATION:

Phone: 415-688-4001 Fax:
Toll-Free:
Address: One Front St., Fl. 28, San Francisco, CA 94111 United States

STOCK TICKER/OTHER:

Stock Ticker: Private Exchange:
Employees: 300 Fiscal Year Ends:
Parent Company:

SALARIES/BONUSES:

Top Exec. Salary: $ Bonus: $
Second Exec. Salary: $ Bonus: $

OTHER THOUGHTS:

Estimated Female Officers or Directors:
Hot Spot for Advancement for Women/Minorities:

MKTG Sports + Entertainment

mktgse.com

NAIC Code: 541800

TYPES OF BUSINESS:

Marketing Services
Sports and Entertainment Marketing
Marketing Design and Execution
Marketing Management
Marketing Solutions and Testing
Commercial Rights Negotiation and Management
Messaging and Communication Strategies
Qualitative and Quantitative Research

BRANDS/DIVISIONS/AFFILIATES:

Dentsu Group Inc
Dentsu Aegis Network Ltd

CONTACTS: Note: Officers with more than one job title may be intentionally listed here more than once.

Charles W. Horsey, CEO
Charles Horsey, Pres.
Matt Manning, Sr. VP-Corp. Dev.
James R. Haughton, Sr. VP

GROWTH PLANS/SPECIAL FEATURES:

MKTG Sports + Entertainment is a global integrated agency that offers sports and entertainment marketing solutions. The company utilizes consumer insights to create marketing experiences for venues, entities and brands. MKTG connects the sports and entertainment industry and companies worldwide across strategy, measurement, content, hospitality and events in order to deliver its marketing solutions and experiences. Core capabilities of the firm are vast, and include portfolio review and optimization, commercial rights/sales negotiation and management, sponsorship identification/negotiation/implementation, rightsholder/stakeholder management, messaging and communication strategy and implementation, talent procurement and management, property and platform development, market research and measurement, consumer insights, return on investment prediction, qualitative and quantitative research, concept testing, sponsorship and IP valuation, digital communication planning, culture-first creative ideation, social strategy and execution, talent and influencer partnerships, creative design, video product and more. MKTG has offices throughout the U.S., as well as in Canada, Australia, Japan, Singapore and the U.K. MKTG operates as a subsidiary of Dentsu Aegis Network Ltd., itself a part of Dentsu Group, Inc.

FINANCIAL DATA: Note: Data for latest year may not have been available at press time.

In U.S. $	2022	2021	2020	2019	2018	2017
Revenue	171,000,000	163,505,160	157,216,500	169,050,000	161,000,000	155,000,000
R&D Expense						
Operating Income						
Operating Margin %						
SGA Expense						
Net Income						
Operating Cash Flow						
Capital Expenditure						
EBITDA						
Return on Assets %						
Return on Equity %						
Debt to Equity						

CONTACT INFORMATION:

Phone: 212 366-3400   Fax:
Toll-Free:
Address: 489 Fifth Ave., Fl. 23, New York, NY 10017 United States

STOCK TICKER/OTHER:

Stock Ticker: Subsidiary   Exchange:
Employees: 4,750   Fiscal Year Ends: 03/31
Parent Company: Dentsu Aegis Network Ltd

SALARIES/BONUSES:

Top Exec. Salary: $ Bonus: $
Second Exec. Salary: $ Bonus: $

OTHER THOUGHTS:

Estimated Female Officers or Directors:
Hot Spot for Advancement for Women/Minorities: Y

Moatable Inc

www.moatable.com

NAIC Code: 519130

TYPES OF BUSINESS:

Social Networking
Online Games
Social Commerce
E-Commerce
Application Development

GROWTH PLANS/SPECIAL FEATURES:

Moatable Inc provides management expertise, support services, and capital to help its SaaS businesses grow, scale, and reach their full potential. The Chime division includes the Company's all-in-one real estate sales acceleration and client lifecycle management platform. The Trucker Path division includes the Company's driver-centric online transportation management platform.

BRANDS/DIVISIONS/AFFILIATES:

Trucker Path
Ping An Bank
Kaixin Auto Group
Chime
Geographic Farming LLC

CONTACTS: Note: Officers with more than one job title may be intentionally listed here more than once.

Joseph Chen, CEO
James Jian Liu, COO
Yi Yang, Acting CFO
Rita Yi, VP-Human Resources
Jing Huang, VP-Renren.com
Ripley Hu, VP-Mktg.
Kitty Zhou, VP-56.com
Joseph Chen, Chmn.

FINANCIAL DATA: Note: Data for latest year may not have been available at press time.

In U.S. $	2022	2021	2020	2019	2018	2017
Revenue	45,808,000	32,219,000	18,106,000	15,085,000	66,794,000	174,624,000
R&D Expense	16,187,000	10,721,000	11,347,000	22,791,000	21,930,000	17,435,000
Operating Income	-15,251,000	-32,696,000	-27,227,000	-48,119,000	-76,200,000	-77,689,000
Operating Margin %						
SGA Expense	34,412,000	34,128,000	30,535,000	20,869,000	58,567,000	71,564,000
Net Income	-75,244,000	13,663,000	-19,220,000	-51,097,000	72,540,000	-110,427,000
Operating Cash Flow	-3,822,000	-18,108,000	-15,601,000	-33,147,000	-59,985,000	-114,964,000
Capital Expenditure	7,615,000	103,000	221,000	412,000	132,000	135,000
EBITDA	-66,582,000	-44,994,000	-15,665,000	-27,639,000	-56,304,000	-36,406,000
Return on Assets %						
Return on Equity %						
Debt to Equity						

CONTACT INFORMATION:

Phone: Fax:
Toll-Free: 833-258-7482
Address: 45 W Buchanan St., Phoenix, AZ 85003 United States

STOCK TICKER/OTHER:

Stock Ticker: MTBL   Exchange: NYS
Employees: 601   Fiscal Year Ends: 12/31
Parent Company:

SALARIES/BONUSES:

Top Exec. Salary: $491,027   Bonus: $50,000
Second Exec. Salary: Bonus: $46,500
$372,862

OTHER THOUGHTS:

Estimated Female Officers or Directors: 3
Hot Spot for Advancement for Women/Minorities: Y

Mobile TeleSystems PJSC

NAIC Code: 517312

TYPES OF BUSINESS:

Mobile Telephone Service
Mobile Operations
Digital and Media Services
Wireless and Wireline Connectivity Services
Television Services
Digital Banking and Financial Services
Cloud Computing Services
Internet of Things Services

BRANDS/DIVISIONS/AFFILIATES:

Sistema JSGC
Gulfstream Security Systems JSC

GROWTH PLANS/SPECIAL FEATURES:

Mobile TeleSystems PJSC (MTS) is a leading mobile operator based in Russia and provides digital and media services. MTS' wide range of solutions for consumers and businesses span wireless and wireline connectivity, over-the-top (OTT)/linear/satellite television, digital banking, financial services, unified communications, cloud computing and Internet of Things (IoT). The firm serves more than 88 million mobile subscribers through its operations in Russia, Armenia and Belarus, including approximately 80 million subscribers in Russia alone. MTS comprises a nationwide network of 5,400 owned and franchised retail outlets in Russia, and provides broadband, television (via OTT and Pay-tv) and fixed-line telephone connectivity. MTS is a subsidiary of Sistema JSGC. In June 2023, MTS announced that it acquired an additional 41.62% stake in Gulfstream Security Systems JSC and wholly-owns the company. Gulfstream Security Systems is based in Russia, and is a provider of security services and smart home solutions for individuals and businesses.

CONTACTS:
Note: Officers with more than one job title may be intentionally listed here more than once.

Vyacheslav Nikolaev, CEO
Ruslan Ibragimov, VP-Corp. & Legal Matters
Michael Hecker, VP-Strategy & Corp. Dev.
Vadim Savchenko, VP-Sales & Customer Svcs.
Konstantin Markov, Dir.
Ivan Zolochevskiy, CEO
Valery Shorzhin, Dir.-Procurement Mgmt.

FINANCIAL DATA:
Note: Data for latest year may not have been available at press time.

In U.S. $	2022	2021	2020	2019	2018	2017
Revenue	7,293,372,000	7,179,053,568	6,648,728,064	6,395,904,512	6,452,151,808	6,016,063,488
R&D Expense						
Operating Income						
Operating Margin %						
SGA Expense						
Net Income	444,896,000	852,682,496	824,995,456	728,661,824	91,994,544	761,218,880
Operating Cash Flow						
Capital Expenditure						
EBITDA						
Return on Assets %						
Return on Equity %						
Debt to Equity						

CONTACT INFORMATION:

Phone: 7 4952232025 Fax: 7 4959116567
Toll-Free:
Address: 4, Marksistskaya St., Moscow, 109147 Russia

STOCK TICKER/OTHER:

Stock Ticker: MTSS Exchange: Moscow
Employees: 60,000 Fiscal Year Ends: 12/31
Parent Company: Sistema JSGC

SALARIES/BONUSES:

Top Exec. Salary: $ Bonus: $
Second Exec. Salary: $ Bonus: $

OTHER THOUGHTS:

Estimated Female Officers or Directors: 1
Hot Spot for Advancement for Women/Minorities:

MOGU Inc

www.mogu-inc.com

NAIC Code: 519130

TYPES OF BUSINESS:
Internet Publishing and Broadcasting and Web Search Portals
Apparel
Ecommerce

BRANDS/DIVISIONS/AFFILIATES:

GROWTH PLANS/SPECIAL FEATURES:
MOGU Inc is an online fashion and lifestyle destination in China. The company's online platform includes Mogu.com, Mogujie.com, and Meilishuo.com. Its platform allows people to discover and share fashion trends while fully enjoying the shopping experience. The company on its platform provides content related to fashion and lifestyle guides in various multi-media formats which include Live Video Broadcasts, Short-form Videos, Photography, and Online Review Community. The company derives revenues from within China.

CONTACTS: Note: Officers with more than one job title may be intentionally listed here more than once.
Qi Chen, CEO
Xuqiang Yue, COO

FINANCIAL DATA: Note: Data for latest year may not have been available at press time.

In U.S. $	2022	2021	2020	2019	2018	2017
Revenue	46,407,260	66,336,440	114,868,700	147,730,000	133,831,200	
R&D Expense	11,364,430	14,229,290	23,534,010	32,515,020	39,779,700	
Operating Income	-62,144,280	-63,668,360	-94,689,140	-78,316,660	-119,262,800	
Operating Margin %	-1.33%	-.95%	-.82%	-.53%	-.89%	
SGA Expense	31,296,910	45,766,990	101,945,200	125,429,500	116,617,800	
Net Income	-87,982,500	-45,101,140	-305,785,000	-66,870,420	-76,756,970	
Operating Cash Flow	-15,733,030	-10,716,730	-42,875,860	-44,803,690	-43,298,450	
Capital Expenditure	7,582,337	22,793,360	8,644,645	2,720,884	768,575	
EBITDA	-44,389,630	3,892,105	-48,144,500	-49,935,500	-57,876,070	
Return on Assets %	-.43%	-.15%	-.63%	-.27%	-.30%	
Return on Equity %	-.57%	-.19%	-.74%			
Debt to Equity						

CONTACT INFORMATION:
Phone: 86 571-8605-2790   Fax:
Toll-Free:
Address: Fl. 23, Bldg. G, No. 77 Xueyuan Rd., Xihu Dist., Hangzhou, Zhejiang 310012 China

STOCK TICKER/OTHER:
Stock Ticker: MOGU
Employees: 407
Parent Company:

Exchange: NYS
Fiscal Year Ends: 03/31

SALARIES/BONUSES:
Top Exec. Salary: $ Bonus: $
Second Exec. Salary: $ Bonus: $

OTHER THOUGHTS:
Estimated Female Officers or Directors:
Hot Spot for Advancement for Women/Minorities:

MongoDB Inc

NAIC Code: 511210J

www.mongodb.com

TYPES OF BUSINESS:

Computer Software, Data Base & File Management
Database Platform
Applications
Cloud Data
Application Development Solutions
Software
Consulting Services

BRANDS/DIVISIONS/AFFILIATES:

MongoDB

GROWTH PLANS/SPECIAL FEATURES:

Founded in 2007, MongoDB is a document-oriented database with nearly 33,000 paying customers and well past 1.5 million free users. MongoDB provides both licenses as well as subscriptions as a service for its NoSQL database. MongoDB's database is compatible with all major programming languages and is capable of being deployed for a variety of use cases.

CONTACTS: *Note: Officers with more than one job title may be intentionally listed here more than once.*

Dev Ittycheria, CEO
Michael Gordon, CFO
Peter Killalea, Chairman of the Board
Thomas Bull, Chief Accounting Officer
Mark Porter, Chief Technology Officer
Dwight Merriman, Co-Founder
Cedric Pech, Other Executive Officer

FINANCIAL DATA: *Note: Data for latest year may not have been available at press time.*

In U.S. $	2022	2021	2020	2019	2018	2017
Revenue	873,782,000	590,380,000	421,720,000	267,016,000	166,028,000	
R&D Expense	308,820,000	205,161,000	149,033,000	89,854,000	62,202,000	
Operating Income	-289,364,000	-209,304,000	-147,866,000	-97,765,000	-84,881,000	
Operating Margin %	-.33%	-.35%	-.35%	-.37%	-.51%	
SGA Expense	594,834,000	417,447,000	295,197,000	201,359,000	145,848,000	
Net Income	-306,866,000	-266,944,000	-175,522,000	-99,011,000	-83,973,000	
Operating Cash Flow	6,980,000	-42,673,000	-29,540,000	-41,989,000	-44,881,000	
Capital Expenditure	8,072,000	11,773,000	3,564,000	6,848,000	2,135,000	
EBITDA	-267,118,000	-182,054,000	-135,421,000	-86,247,000	-78,975,000	
Return on Assets %	-.16%	-.20%	-.17%	-.17%	-.28%	
Return on Equity %	-.92%	-6.47%	-1.01%	-.39%		
Debt to Equity	1.76%		11.094	0.82		

CONTACT INFORMATION:

Phone: 646-727-4092   Fax:
Toll-Free:
Address: 1633 Broadway, Fl. 38, New York, NY 10019 United States

STOCK TICKER/OTHER:

Stock Ticker: MDB   Exchange: NAS
Employees: 4,619   Fiscal Year Ends: 01/31
Parent Company:

SALARIES/BONUSES:

Top Exec. Salary: $400,000   Bonus: $
Second Exec. Salary: Bonus: $
$325,000

OTHER THOUGHTS:

Estimated Female Officers or Directors: 2
Hot Spot for Advancement for Women/Minorities:

Monster Worldwide Inc

www.monster.com

NAIC Code: 561311A

TYPES OF BUSINESS:
Online Job Recruitment
Employment Advertising
Applicant Recruitment
Online Employment Platform
Resume Services
Career Advisory Services
Job Search Engine

BRANDS/DIVISIONS/AFFILIATES:
Randstad Holding NV
Monster
Monster.com

GROWTH PLANS/SPECIAL FEATURES:

Monster Worldwide, Inc. operates Monster, a global online employment services platform designed to advance careers and connect people with jobs. Monster is available in the U.S. and internationally. It leverages advanced technology using intelligent digital, social and mobile solutions, including the flagship website Monster.com, the Monster mobile app and a wide array of products and services. Employers can post jobs and search resumes. Job seekers can browse for jobs, upload resumes, utilize salary tools, and obtain career and resume advice. Beyond the U.S., Monster offers jobs in Austria, Belgium, Canada, France, Germany, Ireland, Italy, Luxembourg, Netherlands, Spain, Sweden, Switzerland and the U.K. Monster is a subsidiary of the Dutch multinational human resource consulting firm, Randstad Holding NV.

Monster offers its employees comprehensive health benefits, a retirement plan, employee training and development programs, an employee assistance program and more.

CONTACTS: *Note: Officers with more than one job title may be intentionally listed here more than once.*

Scott Gutz, CEO
Timothy Yates, Director
Mark Stoever, President

FINANCIAL DATA: *Note: Data for latest year may not have been available at press time.*

In U.S. $	2022	2021	2020	2019	2018	2017
Revenue	688,000,000	654,885,000	623,700,000	693,000,000	660,000,000	660,000,000
R&D Expense						
Operating Income						
Operating Margin %						
SGA Expense						
Net Income						
Operating Cash Flow						
Capital Expenditure						
EBITDA						
Return on Assets %						
Return on Equity %						
Debt to Equity						

CONTACT INFORMATION:
Phone: 212-351-7000 Fax:
Toll-Free:
Address: 622 Third Ave. Fl. 39, New York, NY 10017 United States

STOCK TICKER/OTHER:
Stock Ticker: Subsidiary Exchange:
Employees: 4,000 Fiscal Year Ends: 12/31
Parent Company: Randstad Holding NV

SALARIES/BONUSES:
Top Exec. Salary: $ Bonus: $
Second Exec. Salary: $ Bonus: $

OTHER THOUGHTS:
Estimated Female Officers or Directors: 3
Hot Spot for Advancement for Women/Minorities: Y

MoreVisibility.com Inc

www.morevisibility.com

NAIC Code: 541810E

TYPES OF BUSINESS:

Search Engine Optimization (SEO)
Marketing Outsourcing Services
Search Engine Optimization
Social Media Marketing Services
Search Engine Marketing
Social Medica Marketing
Web Design Services
Analytics Consulting Services

BRANDS/DIVISIONS/AFFILIATES:

Healthcare Privacy Platform
American College of Healthcare Executives

CONTACTS: *Note: Officers with more than one job title may be intentionally listed here more than once.*

Dennis Pushkin, CEO
Andrew Wetzler, Pres.
Danielle Leitch, COO
Max Braglia, VP-Digital Advertising
Matt Crowley, VP-Digital Svcs.
Danielle Leitch, Exec. VP-Client Strategy
Khrysti Nazzaro, Dir.-Optimized Svcs.
Khrysti Nazzaro, Exec. VP- Client Services

GROWTH PLANS/SPECIAL FEATURES:

MoreVisibility.com, Inc. offers digital marketing strategies that relate to online businesses. Emphasizing search engine optimization (SEO), the company seeks to help customers effectively utilize the complex online environment. MoreVisibility.com also specializes in search engine marketing (SEM), social media marketing, analytics consulting and implementation, full-service website design and custom development services. Each team member of the firm is an expert within his/her field to serve the specific needs of every client; and the team also works collaboratively to offer strategic plans in regards to enhanced brand awareness, traffic, leads and/or sales. Resources are provided on MoreVisibility.com, such as newsletters, white papers, webinars, an online marketing blog and more. In January 2024, MoreVisibility partnered with Freshpaint to offer clients an industry first Healthcare Privacy Platform and the American College of Healthcare Executives (ACHE) to increase online presence and marketing results.

MoreVisibility offers its employees comprehensive health benefits, a 401(k) and a variety of employee assistance programs and company perks.

FINANCIAL DATA: *Note: Data for latest year may not have been available at press time.*

In U.S. $	2022	2021	2020	2019	2018	2017
Revenue						
R&D Expense						
Operating Income						
Operating Margin %						
SGA Expense						
Net Income						
Operating Cash Flow						
Capital Expenditure						
EBITDA						
Return on Assets %						
Return on Equity %						
Debt to Equity						

CONTACT INFORMATION:

Phone: 561-620-9682   Fax: 561-620-9684
Toll-Free: 800-787-0497
Address: 975 S. Federal Hwy., Fl. 2, Boca Raton, FL 33432 United States

STOCK TICKER/OTHER:

Stock Ticker: Private   Exchange:
Employees: 45   Fiscal Year Ends:
Parent Company:

SALARIES/BONUSES:

Top Exec. Salary: $ Bonus: $
Second Exec. Salary: $ Bonus: $

OTHER THOUGHTS:

Estimated Female Officers or Directors: 2
Hot Spot for Advancement for Women/Minorities:

Move Inc

NAIC Code: 519130

TYPES OF BUSINESS:

Online Portal-Real Estate Data
Real Estate Software
Real Estate Publishing
Real Estate Advertising
Home Search
Home Rental Software
Real Estate Professional Tools

BRANDS/DIVISIONS/AFFILIATES:

News Corporation
Realtor.com
Moving.com
Doorsteps
Avail
UpNest
ListHub
www.seniorhousingnet.com

CONTACTS: *Note: Officers with more than one job title may be intentionally listed here more than once.*

Robert Thomson, CEO-Corp.
Raymond Picard, Executive VP, Divisional
James Caulfield, Executive VP
Errol Samuelson, President, Subsidiary

GROWTH PLANS/SPECIAL FEATURES:

Move, Inc. operates a network of brands engaged in real estate and moving services. The company divides its brands into two categories: consumer brands and professional brands. Consumer brands include: realtor.com, a resource about homes, primarily displaying home properties listed for-sale; moving.com, a search service for contacting movers and comparing their quotes before choosing which one to hire; Doorsteps, offering residential properties for rent; Avail, a platform that gives do-it-yourself landlords and tenants online rental tools, support and educational content concerning the rental process; and UpNest, which allows consumers to compare top real estate agents in their area, with online tools for making decisions. Professional brands include: realtor.com for professionals, offering lead generation, brand building and other solutions to help agents, teams and brokers reach home buyers and sellers; and ListHub, a platform that enables brokers to deliver accurate, multiple listing service (MLS)-sourced listings to consumers. Move also offers a site that provides senior living options, including 55+ living, assisted living, Alzheimer's care and other options via www.seniorhousingnet.com. Moreover, Move offers software products, solutions and services to help real estate professionals serve their clients and grow their business. Move is a subsidiary of News Corporation.

FINANCIAL DATA: *Note: Data for latest year may not have been available at press time.*

In U.S. $	2022	2021	2020	2019	2018	2017
Revenue	687,000,000	641,000,000	473,000,000	484,600,000	452,000,000	394,000,000
R&D Expense						
Operating Income						
Operating Margin %						
SGA Expense						
Net Income						
Operating Cash Flow						
Capital Expenditure						
EBITDA						
Return on Assets %						
Return on Equity %						
Debt to Equity						

CONTACT INFORMATION:

Phone: 408 558-7100 Fax:
Toll-Free:
Address: 3315 Scott Blvd., Ste. 250, Santa Clara, CA 95054 United States

STOCK TICKER/OTHER:

Stock Ticker: Subsidiary
Employees: 943
Parent Company: News Corporation

Exchange:
Fiscal Year Ends: 06/30

SALARIES/BONUSES:

Top Exec. Salary: $ Bonus: $
Second Exec. Salary: $ Bonus: $

OTHER THOUGHTS:

Estimated Female Officers or Directors:
Hot Spot for Advancement for Women/Minorities:

MovieTickets.com Inc

www.movietickets.com

NAIC Code: 454110

TYPES OF BUSINESS:

Online Movie Ticket Sales
Online Ticketing
Movies
Mobile App Ticketing
Payment Solutions
Movie Information and Reviews
Technology
Ecommerce

BRANDS/DIVISIONS/AFFILIATES:

Comcast Corporation
Warner Bros Discovery
Fandango Inc

GROWTH PLANS/SPECIAL FEATURES:

MovieTickets.com, Inc. is an online ticketing service based in the U.S. that provides customers with online access to movie tickets at theater chains all over the world. The company's connected sites enable customers to purchase movie tickets online, through mobile devices or by phone; access local show times; view movie trailers; and read reviews. The firm's partner theaters include Regal Cinemas, Regal Entertainment Group, AMC Theaters, Georgia Theater Company, Starlight Cinemas, IMAX and Cinemark Theaters. Fandango gift cards can be used to purchase tickets through MovieTickets.com. MovieTickets.com operates as a subsidiary of Fandango, Inc., itself being majority-owned (75%) by Comcast Corporation and 25%-owned by Warner Bros. Discovery.

CONTACTS:
Note: Officers with more than one job title may be intentionally listed here more than once.

Paul Yanover, CEO-Fandango

FINANCIAL DATA:
Note: Data for latest year may not have been available at press time.

In U.S. $	2022	2021	2020	2019	2018	2017
Revenue						
R&D Expense						
Operating Income						
Operating Margin %						
SGA Expense						
Net Income						
Operating Cash Flow						
Capital Expenditure						
EBITDA						
Return on Assets %						
Return on Equity %						
Debt to Equity						

CONTACT INFORMATION:

Phone: 561-322-3200   Fax: 561-322-3222
Toll-Free:
Address: 2255 Glades Rd., Ste. 100E, Boca Raton, FL 33431 United States

STOCK TICKER/OTHER:

Stock Ticker: Subsidiary   Exchange:
Employees: 10   Fiscal Year Ends: 03/31
Parent Company: Comcast Corporation

SALARIES/BONUSES:

Top Exec. Salary: $ Bonus: $
Second Exec. Salary: $ Bonus: $

OTHER THOUGHTS:

Estimated Female Officers or Directors:
Hot Spot for Advancement for Women/Minorities:

MuleSoft LLC

www.mulesoft.com

NAIC Code: 511210I

TYPES OF BUSINESS:

Computer Software, Operating Systems, Language & Development Tools
Software Development
Software Integration
Application Network Solutions
Software-as-a-Service Architecture
Application Program Interfaces
Platform Deployment Solutions
API Management and Monitoring

BRANDS/DIVISIONS/AFFILIATES:

Salesforce.com Inc
Anypoint Platform

CONTACTS: Note: Officers with more than one job title may be intentionally listed here more than once.

Marc Benioff, CEO- Corp.
Matthew Langdon, CFO

GROWTH PLANS/SPECIAL FEATURES:

MuleSoft, LLC is a software company that designs, develops and markets an integration platform for connecting applications, data sources and devices on-premises and in the cloud. This offering enables corporations to reach customers, employees and partners. The company's Anypoint Platform connects the application network, solving complex connectivity issues across service-oriented architecture, software-as-a-service (SaaS) architecture and application program interfaces (APIs). The runtime engine of Anypoint Platform combines data and application integration across legacy systems, SaaS applications and APIs with hybrid deployment options for maximum flexibility. Anypoint features low-friction development tools that make it easy to design and test APIs, implement data and application integration flows, as well as build connectors. Platform deployment is capable to virtually any environment, including Docker containers and Kubernetes clusters on AWS, Azure, GCP and on-premises. All APIs can be managed, monitored and scaled securely from a single place. Development can be jumpstarted using pre-built APIs, connectors, templates, accelerators and other integration assets. MuleSoft operates as a wholly-owned subsidiary of Salesforce.com, Inc.

Parent Salesforce offers health benefits to MuleSoft employees.

FINANCIAL DATA: Note: Data for latest year may not have been available at press time.

In U.S. $	2022	2021	2020	2019	2018	2017
Revenue	480,300,000	473,141,025	463,863,750	452,550,000	431,000,000	296,456,000
R&D Expense						
Operating Income						
Operating Margin %						
SGA Expense						
Net Income						
Operating Cash Flow						
Capital Expenditure						
EBITDA						
Return on Assets %						
Return on Equity %						
Debt to Equity						

CONTACT INFORMATION:

Phone: 415-229-2009   Fax:
Toll-Free:
Address: 415 Mission St., San Francisco, CA 94105 United States

STOCK TICKER/OTHER:

Stock Ticker: Subsidiary   Exchange:
Employees: 1,400   Fiscal Year Ends:
Parent Company: Salesforce.com Inc

SALARIES/BONUSES:

Top Exec. Salary: $ Bonus: $
Second Exec. Salary: $ Bonus: $

OTHER THOUGHTS:

Estimated Female Officers or Directors:
Hot Spot for Advancement for Women/Minorities:

MyHeritage Ltd

www.myheritage.com

NAIC Code: 519130

TYPES OF BUSINESS:

Online Genealogy
Heritage Social Networking Platform
Family Tree Building
Heritage Information, Data and Photos
DNA Testing
Genealogy Tools
Matching Software and Technology

BRANDS/DIVISIONS/AFFILIATES:

MyHeritage.com
Family Tree Builder

CONTACTS: *Note: Officers with more than one job title may be intentionally listed here more than once.*

Gilad Japhet, CEO
Ran Michnowsky, VP-Operations
Smadar Levi, CFO
Aaron Godfrey, CMO
Neta Langer Levitan, Chief People Officer
Sagi Bashari, CTO
Uri Gonen, Sr. VP-Prod. Mgmt.
Russ Wilding, Chief Content Officer
Roger Bell, VP-Prod.
Noah Tutak, Gen. Mgr.-USA
Ran Peled, Chief Architect
Russ Wilding, Chief Content Officer

GROWTH PLANS/SPECIAL FEATURES:

MyHeritage Ltd. owns and manages MyHeritage.com, a private social networking site which allows family members to connect with one another and upload and share family trees, events, videos and messages. The firm offers a series of tools and software which allow its 104 million worldwide users to update and maintain their family profiles (as of January 2024). Family Tree Builder, a free windows software, provides tools for building geographical maps of family members' and ancestors' locations, photo albums, family charts, a report generator, tools for building family member profiles and making timelines, a digital scrapbook, a family statistic compiler and an automatic historical record search and match from international historical records. Family Tree Builder is available in more than 42 languages and allows users to choose from Gregorian, Hebrew and French Revolutionary calendars. Users can upload files created in Family Tree Builder directly onto their MyHeritage.com profile for other family members to see. The genealogy tools offered by the firm allow users to cross compare their family trees with the other users on MyHeritage.com for matches using the firm's proprietary smart match technology. Users can confirm or reject matches pulled up by the matching technology and connect with possible family members through their MyHeritage.com accounts. The company comprises a global search engine that retrieves and delivers historical records of births, deaths, marriages, immigration, census and original documents. The search engine utilizes semantics analysis to find matches for family trees in newspapers, books and other free text documents. MyHeritage offers DNA testing through the maternal and paternal lines to find family matches using autosomal DNA.

FINANCIAL DATA: *Note: Data for latest year may not have been available at press time.*

In U.S. $	2022	2021	2020	2019	2018	2017
Revenue	187,200,000	180,000,000	177,581,250	173,250,000	165,000,000	133,000,000
R&D Expense						
Operating Income						
Operating Margin %						
SGA Expense						
Net Income						
Operating Cash Flow						
Capital Expenditure						
EBITDA						
Return on Assets %						
Return on Equity %						
Debt to Equity						

CONTACT INFORMATION:

Phone: 972-3-6280000   Fax: 972-3-6280003
Toll-Free:
Address: 3 Ariel Sharon St., Fl. 4, Or Yehuda, 60250 Israel

STOCK TICKER/OTHER:

Stock Ticker: Private   Exchange:
Employees: 450   Fiscal Year Ends:
Parent Company:

SALARIES/BONUSES:

Top Exec. Salary: $ Bonus: $
Second Exec. Salary: $ Bonus: $

OTHER THOUGHTS:

Estimated Female Officers or Directors: 1
Hot Spot for Advancement for Women/Minorities:

Myspace LLC

www.myspace.com

NAIC Code: 519130

TYPES OF BUSINESS:

Social Networking
Online Content Distribution-Audio & Video
Music Social Networking Platform
Entertainment Distribution
Content Sharing
Social Media Platform

BRANDS/DIVISIONS/AFFILIATES:

Viant Technology LLC

GROWTH PLANS/SPECIAL FEATURES:

Myspace, LLC is an internet-based music social networking platform with access to millions of songs, photos, personal profiles, blogs and videos. The Myspace website and mobile app enable users such as individuals, bands, comedians and filmmakers, to create and customize content-rich digital profile pages, share user-generated video, participate in user groups and communicate with each through various technologies, including instant messaging. In addition, Myspace provides a way for artists to connect with their fan base, and allows users to discover new music, films and other media. The Myspace mobile app features a tool for users to create and edit gif images and post them to their Myspace stream. It also allows users to stream available live streams of concerts. Myspace is owned by Viant Technology LLC.

CONTACTS: Note: Officers with more than one job title may be intentionally listed here more than once.

Tim Vanderhook, CEO
Roger Mincheff, Pres.
Tim Vanderhook, CEO-Specific Media

FINANCIAL DATA: Note: Data for latest year may not have been available at press time.

In U.S. $	2022	2021	2020	2019	2018	2017
Revenue						
R&D Expense						
Operating Income						
Operating Margin %						
SGA Expense						
Net Income						
Operating Cash Flow						
Capital Expenditure						
EBITDA						
Return on Assets %						
Return on Equity %						
Debt to Equity						

CONTACT INFORMATION:

Phone: 310-969-7400   Fax:
Toll-Free:
Address: 407 N. Maple Dr., Beverly Hills, CA 90210 United States

STOCK TICKER/OTHER:

Stock Ticker: Subsidiary   Exchange:
Employees: 150   Fiscal Year Ends: 12/31
Parent Company: Viant Technology LLC

SALARIES/BONUSES:

Top Exec. Salary: $ Bonus: $
Second Exec. Salary: $ Bonus: $

OTHER THOUGHTS:

Estimated Female Officers or Directors:
Hot Spot for Advancement for Women/Minorities: Y

Sales, profits and employees may be estimates. Financial information, benefits and other data can change quickly and may vary from those stated here.

Namely Inc

www.namely.com

NAIC Code: 511210Q

TYPES OF BUSINESS:

Computer Software: Accounting, Banking & Financial
Cloud Business Software
Human Resource Management Solutions
Employee Benefits Solutions
Payroll Data Solutions
Employee Engagement Solutions
Time and Attendance Solutions

BRANDS/DIVISIONS/AFFILIATES:

GROWTH PLANS/SPECIAL FEATURES:

Namely, Inc. provides a cloud-based platform for mid-market companies regarding the management of human resources, benefits and payroll data. These mid-sized companies range from 50 to 1,000 employees, and span a wide range of industries. The Namely platform is a single system of record and spans areas such as human resources, benefits administration, compliance, attracting and retaining talent, payroll and time/hours worked. Through its HR analytics, data can be turned into business results via strategic analytics tools. Enhanced services include outsourced managed payroll and employee benefits consulting and brokerage.

Namely offers its employees comprehensive health benefits, a 401(k), savings and spending accounts and other plans, programs and perks.

CONTACTS: Note: Officers with more than one job title may be intentionally listed here more than once.

Elisa Steele, CEO

FINANCIAL DATA: Note: Data for latest year may not have been available at press time.

In U.S. $	2022	2021	2020	2019	2018	2017
Revenue	41,600,000	40,000,000	51,841,500	54,570,000	51,000,000	39,000,000
R&D Expense						
Operating Income						
Operating Margin %						
SGA Expense						
Net Income						
Operating Cash Flow						
Capital Expenditure						
EBITDA						
Return on Assets %						
Return on Equity %						
Debt to Equity						

CONTACT INFORMATION:

Phone: 347 263-7044   Fax:
Toll-Free: 855-626-3591
Address: 195 Broadway, Fl. 15, New York, NY 10007 United States

STOCK TICKER/OTHER:

Stock Ticker: Private   Exchange:
Employees: 260   Fiscal Year Ends:
Parent Company:

SALARIES/BONUSES:

Top Exec. Salary: $ Bonus: $
Second Exec. Salary: $ Bonus: $

OTHER THOUGHTS:

Estimated Female Officers or Directors:
Hot Spot for Advancement for Women/Minorities:

Naver Corporation

www.navercorp.com

NAIC Code: 519130

TYPES OF BUSINESS:

Online Portal
Online Game Portal
Online Advertising
Search Engine
Technology
Internet

GROWTH PLANS/SPECIAL FEATURES:

Naver has been the leading search portal in South Korea for many years. The company has also been evolving into an internet platform providing a variety of internet services, such as news, a dictionary, maps, digital comic content, social networking, e-commerce, videos, fintech services based on online payments, and Cloud services. Naver was also the incubator of Line Yahoo, the leading mobile messaging app in Japan, Taiwan, Thailand, and Indonesia, which merged with Z Holdings (Yahoo Japan), with Naver now owning 32.5% of the merged entity renamed LY. Snow, the Snapchat-like mobile app launched in 2015, has also been well received in South Korea, Japan, and other Asian countries.

BRANDS/DIVISIONS/AFFILIATES:

Naver.com
Naver Dictionary
LINE
SNOW
V LIVE
Papago
WHALE
Clova

CONTACTS: *Note: Officers with more than one job title may be intentionally listed here more than once.*

Seong-sook Han, CEO

FINANCIAL DATA: *Note: Data for latest year may not have been available at press time.*

In U.S. $	2022	2021	2020	2019	2018	2017
Revenue	6,237,019,000	5,172,882,000	4,024,542,000	3,305,315,000	4,239,087,000	3,549,808,000
R&D Expense						
Operating Income	989,919,600	1,005,712,000	922,146,100	876,380,400	715,150,500	894,713,700
Operating Margin %	.16%	.19%	.23%	.27%	.17%	.25%
SGA Expense	3,464,317,000	2,646,277,000	1,986,942,000	1,503,311,000	2,189,767,000	1,662,540,000
Net Income	576,851,100	12,511,740,000	760,337,500	442,393,100	492,289,500	586,425,500
Operating Cash Flow	1,102,766,000	1,047,009,000	1,098,078,000	1,029,511,000	738,652,000	713,215,200
Capital Expenditure	573,795,600	611,418,600	656,848,400	388,207,600	441,071,100	381,835,500
EBITDA	1,302,263,000	1,976,562,000	1,631,703,000	1,446,039,000	1,051,984,000	1,064,269,000
Return on Assets %	.02%	.65%	.07%	.05%	.07%	.11%
Return on Equity %	.03%	1.07%	.15%	.11%	.13%	.18%
Debt to Equity	.12%	.14%	0.033	0.234	.15%	0.01

CONTACT INFORMATION:

Phone: 82-1588-3830   Fax: 82-31-784-1000
Toll-Free:
Address: 6, Buljeong-ro, Bundang-gu, Gyeonggi-do, Bundang-gu, Gyeonggi-do 463-867 South Korea

STOCK TICKER/OTHER:

Stock Ticker: NHNCF   Exchange: PINX
Employees: 2,501   Fiscal Year Ends: 12/31
Parent Company:

SALARIES/BONUSES:

Top Exec. Salary: $ Bonus: $
Second Exec. Salary: $ Bonus: $

OTHER THOUGHTS:

Estimated Female Officers or Directors:
Hot Spot for Advancement for Women/Minorities:

NaviSite LLC

www.navisite.com

NAIC Code: 519130

TYPES OF BUSINESS:

Web Site Hosting
Managed Cloud Services
Application Services
Cloud Marketplace Solutions
Data Intelligence Services
Automation Services
Infrastructure Services
Security and Supply Chain Services

BRANDS/DIVISIONS/AFFILIATES:

RDX

CONTACTS: *Note: Officers with more than one job title may be intentionally listed here more than once.*

Mark Clayman, CEO
Gina Murphy, Pres.
Jeff Nachbor, CFO
Bindu Crandall, CMO
Aaron Boissonnault, CIO
Chris Patterson, VP-Prod. Mgmt.
Michael Poole, Sr. VP-Worldwide Delivery
Peter Salamanca, COO

GROWTH PLANS/SPECIAL FEATURES:

NaviSite, LLC is a modem managed cloud service provider, serving the business needs of primarily mid-market and small enterprise customers. The company's services are grouped into eight categories, including application services, cloud marketplaces, cloud services, data intelligence and automation, database services, employee and payroll, infrastructure services, security services and supply chain. NaviSite provides the people, skills, solutions, capabilities and public cloud expertise to help its customers navigate information technology (IT) and accelerate IT transformation across every part of the technology stack, from cloud migration and management to infrastructure, enterprise application and data management services. Industry sectors served by NaviSite include healthcare, life sciences, manufacturing, independent software vendor (ISV) and software-as-a-service (SaaS). Based in Massachusetts, USA, the firm has international office locations in the U.K. and India. NaviSite operates as a subsidiary of RDX, an independent cloud, database and application managed service provider.

FINANCIAL DATA: *Note: Data for latest year may not have been available at press time.*

In U.S. $	2022	2021	2020	2019	2018	2017
Revenue						
R&D Expense						
Operating Income						
Operating Margin %						
SGA Expense						
Net Income						
Operating Cash Flow						
Capital Expenditure						
EBITDA						
Return on Assets %						
Return on Equity %						
Debt to Equity						

CONTACT INFORMATION:

Phone: 978-682-8300   Fax: 978-688-8100
Toll-Free: 888-298-8222
Address: 400 Minuteman Rd., Andover, MA 01810 United States

STOCK TICKER/OTHER:

Stock Ticker: Private   Exchange:
Employees: 700   Fiscal Year Ends: 07/31
Parent Company:

SALARIES/BONUSES:

Top Exec. Salary: $ Bonus: $
Second Exec. Salary: $ Bonus: $

OTHER THOUGHTS:

Estimated Female Officers or Directors: 2
Hot Spot for Advancement for Women/Minorities: Y

Net2Phone Inc

www.net2phone.com

NAIC Code: 517311

TYPES OF BUSINESS:

VoIP Service Providers
Retail Voice Over Internet Protocol (VoIP)
Cloud Telephone Products and Services
Cloud PBX
Contact Center Services
SIP Trunking Services
Platform Integrations
Unite

BRANDS/DIVISIONS/AFFILIATES:

IDT Corporation

CONTACTS: Note: Officers with more than one job title may be intentionally listed here more than once.

Jonah Fink, CEO
Zali Ritholtz, COO
Darin Zaga, VP-Finance
Denise D'Arienzo, VP-Mktg. & Sales
Dan Leubitz, VP-Product
Jeffrey Skelton, CTO
Arunim Devroy, VP-Engineering

GROWTH PLANS/SPECIAL FEATURES:

Net2Phone, Inc. is a provider of retail voice over internet protocol (VoIP) cloud telephone products, solutions and services. The company's cloud services products include unified communications, business phone system, cloud contact center, omnichannel contact center, cloud call center, sip trunking and cloud pbx for business. Cloud PBX is an internet phone solution via Net2Phone's unified cloud PBX platform, with advanced features such as real-time analytics, video conferencing, unlimited calling and more. UContact is an omnichannel cloud contact-center-as-a-service solution that helps contact centers to manage all voice and digital interactions, across all channels, from a single screen. SIP trunking combines voice and data into a single unified communications solution with an integration from Net2Phone, a global SIP trunk provider. The SIP trunking solution can be integrated without replacing any existing equipment. Teams integration is provided through Microsoft Teams' platform and enables users to experience Net2Phone's cloud PBX system directly inside Microsoft Teams. Net2Phone's unified communication features span web calling, international calling, video conferencing, auto attendant, analytics, business text messaging, call recording, ring groups, receptionist console, mobile app, welcome menu, Google Chrome extension and more. Industries served by Net2Phone include education, hospitality, HVAC, law offices, property managers, real estate, car dealerships, accounting, healthcare, government/municipalities, business-to-business companies, business-to-consumer companies and more. Net2Phone serves businesses of all sizes, from small to mid-market to enterprise. The firm is a subsidiary of IDT Corporation, a holding company with strong interest in telecommunications.

FINANCIAL DATA: Note: Data for latest year may not have been available at press time.

In U.S. $	2022	2021	2020	2019	2018	2017
Revenue	58,654,451	43,897,000	31,781,000	47,264,000	34,857,000	29,450,000
R&D Expense						
Operating Income						
Operating Margin %						
SGA Expense						
Net Income						
Operating Cash Flow						
Capital Expenditure						
EBITDA						
Return on Assets %						
Return on Equity %						
Debt to Equity						

CONTACT INFORMATION:

Phone: 973 438-3111   Fax:
Toll-Free: 866-978-8260
Address: 520 Broad St., Newark, NJ 07102 United States

STOCK TICKER/OTHER:

Stock Ticker: Subsidiary   Exchange:
Employees: 800   Fiscal Year Ends: 07/31
Parent Company: IDT Corporation

SALARIES/BONUSES:

Top Exec. Salary: $ Bonus: $
Second Exec. Salary: $ Bonus: $

OTHER THOUGHTS:

Estimated Female Officers or Directors:
Hot Spot for Advancement for Women/Minorities:

NetEase Inc

NAIC Code: 519130

TYPES OF BUSINESS:

Internet Portal
Online Gaming
Ecommerce
Online Education
Technology
Live Video Streaming
Music Streaming

BRANDS/DIVISIONS/AFFILIATES:

Fantasy Westward Journey
New Westward Journey
Yanxuan
Youdao

GROWTH PLANS/SPECIAL FEATURES:

NetEase, which started on an internet portal service in 1997, is a leading online services provider in China. Its key services include online/mobile games, cloud music, media, advertising, email, live streaming, online education, and e-commerce. The company develops and operates some of the China's most popular PC client and mobile games, and it partners with global leading game developers, such as Blizzard Entertainment and Mojang (a Microsoft subsidiary).

CONTACTS: *Note: Officers with more than one job title may be intentionally listed here more than once.*

William Ding, CEO
Zhaoxuan Yang, CFO

FINANCIAL DATA: *Note: Data for latest year may not have been available at press time.*

In U.S. $	2022	2021	2020	2019	2018	2017
Revenue	13,269,680,000	12,047,200,000	10,130,380,000	8,146,584,000	7,037,854,000	6,110,831,000
R&D Expense	2,068,100,000	1,935,669,000	1,425,952,000	1,156,950,000	1,014,654,000	572,295,100
Operating Income	2,699,238,000	2,257,604,000	1,999,258,000	1,896,430,000	1,372,041,000	1,787,004,000
Operating Margin %		.19%	.20%	.23%	.19%	.29%
SGA Expense	2,488,829,000	2,265,947,000	1,935,617,000	1,285,967,000	1,373,829,000	1,084,511,000
Net Income	2,796,738,000	2,318,079,000	1,658,817,000	2,920,490,000	846,052,200	1,472,509,000
Operating Cash Flow	3,810,453,000	3,427,815,000	3,422,513,000	2,367,532,000	1,844,893,000	1,634,956,000
Capital Expenditure	363,520,400	427,674,900	452,493,400	457,759,800	940,252,700	337,264,500
EBITDA	3,092,287,000	2,708,068,000	2,474,757,000	2,255,866,000	1,655,342,000	1,895,885,000
Return on Assets %		.11%	.09%	.21%	.08%	.17%
Return on Equity %		.19%	.17%	.40%	.14%	.26%
Debt to Equity		.02%	0.006	0.005		

CONTACT INFORMATION:

Phone: 86 10-8255-8163   Fax: 8610-8261-7823
Toll-Free:
Address: Bldg. 7, No. 10 Zibeiwang East Rd., Haidian Dist., Beijing, Beijing 100193 China

STOCK TICKER/OTHER:

Stock Ticker: NTES
Employees: 31,119
Parent Company:

Exchange: NAS
Fiscal Year Ends: 12/31

SALARIES/BONUSES:

Top Exec. Salary: $ Bonus: $
Second Exec. Salary: $ Bonus: $

OTHER THOUGHTS:

Estimated Female Officers or Directors:
Hot Spot for Advancement for Women/Minorities:

Netflix Inc

NAIC Code: 515210

TYPES OF BUSINESS:
Streaming Movies and TV Shows
Movie and Film Rental Services
Television Content
Documentary Content
Feature Films

BRANDS/DIVISIONS/AFFILIATES:

GROWTH PLANS/SPECIAL FEATURES:
Netflix's relatively simple business model involves only one business, its streaming service. It has the biggest television entertainment subscriber base in both the United States and the collective international market, with almost 250 million subscribers globally. Netflix has exposure to nearly the entire global population outside of China. The firm has traditionally avoided live programming or sports content, instead focusing on on-demand access to episodic television, movies, and documentaries. The firm recently began introducing ad-supported subscription plans, giving the firm exposure to the advertising market in addition to the subscription fees that have historically accounted for nearly all its revenue.

CONTACTS:
Note: Officers with more than one job title may be intentionally listed here more than once.

Spencer Neumann, CFO
Reed Hastings, Chairman of the Board
David Hyman, Chief Legal Officer
Bozoma John, Chief Marketing Officer
Ted Sarandos, Co-CEO
Greg Peters, COO
Rachel Whetstone, Other Executive Officer
Jessica Neal, Other Executive Officer

FINANCIAL DATA:
Note: Data for latest year may not have been available at press time.

In U.S. $	2022	2021	2020	2019	2018	2017
Revenue	31,615,550,000	29,697,840,000	24,996,060,000	20,156,450,000	15,794,340,000	
R&D Expense	2,711,041,000	2,273,885,000	1,829,600,000	1,545,149,000	1,221,814,000	
Operating Income	5,632,831,000	6,194,509,000	4,585,289,000	2,604,254,000	1,605,226,000	
Operating Margin %	.18%	.21%	.18%	.13%	.10%	
SGA Expense	4,103,393,000	3,896,767,000	3,304,848,000	3,566,831,000	2,999,763,000	
Net Income	4,491,924,000	5,116,228,000	2,761,395,000	1,866,916,000	1,211,242,000	
Operating Cash Flow	2,026,257,000	392,610,000	2,427,077,000	-2,887,322,000	-2,680,479,000	
Capital Expenditure	407,729,000	524,585,000	497,923,000	253,035,000	173,946,000	
EBITDA	20,332,960,000	19,044,500,000	15,507,910,000	12,008,080,000	9,262,196,000	
Return on Assets %	.10%	.12%	.08%	.06%	.05%	
Return on Equity %	.25%	.38%	.30%	.29%	.27%	
Debt to Equity	.69%	.93%	1.429	1.947	1.98%	

CONTACT INFORMATION:
Phone: 408 540-3700   Fax: 408 540-3737
Toll-Free: 1-877-742-1480
Address: 100 Winchester Cir., Los Gatos, CA 95032 United States

STOCK TICKER/OTHER:
Stock Ticker: NFLX   Exchange: NAS
Employees: 13,000   Fiscal Year Ends: 12/31
Parent Company:

SALARIES/BONUSES:
Top Exec. Salary: $20,000,000   Bonus: $
Second Exec. Salary: $16,000,000 Bonus: $

OTHER THOUGHTS:
Estimated Female Officers or Directors: 3
Hot Spot for Advancement for Women/Minorities: Y

NetScout Systems Inc

www.netscout.com

NAIC Code: 511210B

TYPES OF BUSINESS:

Computer Software, Network Management (IT), System Testing & Storage
Digital Cyber Security
Digital Business Network Security Solutions
Cyber Threat Solutions
Technologies
Business Transformation Solutions
Digital Transformation Solutions
Software Security Solutions

BRANDS/DIVISIONS/AFFILIATES:

Ngenius
Omnis
Arbor
Spectra

GROWTH PLANS/SPECIAL FEATURES:

NetScout Systems Inc is a provider of service assurance and cybersecurity solutions to enterprise and government networks. It bases its solutions on proprietary adaptive service intelligence technology, which helps customers monitor and identify performance issues and provides insight into network-based security threats. These solutions also deliver real-time and historical information, which provides insight to restore service and understand the quality of user experience. The company derives revenue primarily from the sale of network management tools and security solutions. Its geographical regions include USA, Europe, Asia, and Rest of the World.

CONTACTS: *Note: Officers with more than one job title may be intentionally listed here more than once.*

Anil Singhal, CEO
Jean Bua, CFO
Michael Szabados, COO
John Downing, Executive VP, Divisional

FINANCIAL DATA: *Note: Data for latest year may not have been available at press time.*

In U.S. $	2022	2021	2020	2019	2018	2017
Revenue	855,575,000	831,282,000	891,820,000	909,918,000	986,787,000	
R&D Expense	171,131,000	179,163,000	188,294,000	203,588,000	215,076,000	
Operating Income	48,634,000	37,192,000	20,312,000	-7,544,000	1,151,000	
Operating Margin %	.06%	.04%	.02%	-.01%	.00%	
SGA Expense	361,883,000	331,699,000	376,517,000	385,442,000	422,015,000	
Net Income	35,874,000	19,352,000	-2,754,000	-73,324,000	79,812,000	
Operating Cash Flow	296,013,000	213,921,000	225,023,000	149,838,000	222,454,000	
Capital Expenditure	10,400,000	16,523,000	19,922,000	23,526,000	16,594,000	
EBITDA	146,724,000	139,011,000	138,625,000	71,109,000	147,477,000	
Return on Assets %	.01%	.01%	.00%	-.02%	.02%	
Return on Equity %	.02%	.01%	.00%	-.04%	.04%	
Debt to Equity	.20%	.21%	0.269	0.266	.29%	

CONTACT INFORMATION:

Phone: 978 614-4000   Fax: 978 614-4004
Toll-Free: 800-357-7666
Address: 310 Littleton Rd., Westford, MA 01886 United States

STOCK TICKER/OTHER:

Stock Ticker: NTCT   Exchange: NAS
Employees: 2,355   Fiscal Year Ends: 03/31
Parent Company:

SALARIES/BONUSES:

Top Exec. Salary: $594,825   Bonus: $
Second Exec. Salary: $423,500   Bonus: $

OTHER THOUGHTS:

Estimated Female Officers or Directors: 2
Hot Spot for Advancement for Women/Minorities:

Netskope Inc

www.netskope.com

NAIC Code: 511210E

TYPES OF BUSINESS:

Computer Software: Network Security, Managed Access, Digital ID,
Cybersecurity & Anti-Virus
Cloud Access
Online Security Solutions
Software-as-a-Service Platform
Cloud Applications
SD-WAN Products
Real-Time Visibility Platform

BRANDS/DIVISIONS/AFFILIATES:

Cloud XD
Infiot

CONTACTS: Note: Officers with more than one job title may be intentionally listed here more than once.

Sanjay Beri, CEO
Krishna Narayanaswamy, CTO
Drew Del Matto, CFO
John Martin, Chief Product Officer
Marilyn Milller, Chief People Officer
Mike Anderson, CIO
Lamont Orange, Chief Information Security Officer

GROWTH PLANS/SPECIAL FEATURES:

Netskope, Inc. is a cloud access security broker. The firm provides a software-as-a-service (SaaS) platform that helps companies find, understand and use cloud applications relevant to them. Netskope's platform enables the discovery and monitoring of various known or unknown cloud applications running in their organizations, draw analytics from that data and provide policy enforcement, all in real-time. The company's patented Cloud XD technology eliminates blind spots by quickly targeting and controlling activities across thousands of cloud services and millions of websites. Once connected with Netskope, cloud app traffic is steered to its private cloud tenant via flexible deployment options. This enables Netskope users to perform the analysis and policy enforcement on the traffic, and therefore strengthening data security in the cloud. The company also offers an appliance that can be deployed on premises. This ensures that all cloud traffic processing happens inside those data centers and the security metadata is physically constrained to the Netskope appliance. The company has more than 40 patents. Its products are grouped into three categories: security service Edge products, to protect against advanced and cloud-enabled threats and safeguard data across all vectors; borderless software-defined wide area network (SD-WAN), for providing secure, high-performance access to all remote users, device, site and cloud; and Secure Access Service Edge, which combines Netskope's market-leading Intelligent SSE with its next-generation Borderless SD-WAN to provide a cloud-native, fully-converged and single-vendor SASE solution..

FINANCIAL DATA: Note: Data for latest year may not have been available at press time.

In U.S. $	2022	2021	2020	2019	2018	2017
Revenue						
R&D Expense						
Operating Income						
Operating Margin %						
SGA Expense						
Net Income						
Operating Cash Flow						
Capital Expenditure						
EBITDA						
Return on Assets %						
Return on Equity %						
Debt to Equity						

CONTACT INFORMATION:

Phone: 650 281-9636   Fax:
Toll-Free: 800-979-6988
Address: 2445 Augustine Dr., Fl. 3, Santa Clara, CA 95054 United States

STOCK TICKER/OTHER:

Stock Ticker: Private   Exchange:
Employees: 1,000   Fiscal Year Ends:
Parent Company:

SALARIES/BONUSES:

Top Exec. Salary: $ Bonus: $
Second Exec. Salary: $ Bonus: $

OTHER THOUGHTS:

Estimated Female Officers or Directors:
Hot Spot for Advancement for Women/Minorities:

Neustar Inc

www.home.neustar

NAIC Code: 518210

TYPES OF BUSINESS:

Clearinghouse Services
Data Analytics
Marketing Software
Fraud and Risk Solutions
Marketing Brand Connectivity Solutions
Communication Solutions
Professional Services
Advisory and Training Services

BRANDS/DIVISIONS/AFFILIATES:

TransUnion LLC
Marketing Solutions
Fraud Solutions
Communications Solutions

CONTACTS: *Note: Officers with more than one job title may be intentionally listed here more than once.*

Chris Cartwright, CEO-Corp.
Leonard Kennedy, General Counsel
Brian Foster, Senior VP, Divisional
Venkat Achanta, Senior VP, Divisional
Steve Edwards, Senior VP, Divisional
Henry (Hank) Skorny, Senior VP, Divisional

GROWTH PLANS/SPECIAL FEATURES:

Neustar, Inc., owned by TransUnion LLC, provides data analytics and modeling software that help marketers send timely and relevant messages to target audiences. The firm's solutions are grouped into four categories: marketing, fraud, communications and professional services. Marketing solutions encompass customer analytics, customer experience, customer intelligence and advertising advisory, as well as marketing connectivity between brands, publishers and consumers through its Fabrick platform. Fraud solutions span digital identity risk, in-bound authentication solutions, phone takeover risk, IP geolocation and VPN/proxy decisioning data, and IP address and identity. Communications solutions by Neustar help simplify, streamline and speed how connectivity is delivered and include trusted call solutions, contact center solutions, carrier provisioning solutions, global numbering insights and business identity protection. Professional services by Neustar include marketing advisory services, communications professional services, applied expertise via data audits, merger integration services, numbering resource utilization/forecast (NRUF) generation services, business and performance analytics, staff augmentation, staff training, test support services and evaluating existing practices and processes to improve revenue recovery. Industries served by Neustar include retail, consumer packaged goods, quick service restaurant, financial services, insurance, automotive, travel/hospitality, communications and technology, and government. Headquartered in Virginia, Neustar has additional offices throughout the U.S., as well as in India, Costa Rica and the U.K. In 2023, parent TransUnion rebranded Neustar's marketing, fraud and communications services into three new units: Marketing Solutions, Fraud Solutions and Communications Solutions.

Neustar offers its employees comprehensive health benefits, a 401(k), flexible spending accounts, life and disability insurance, tuition assistance and more.

FINANCIAL DATA: *Note: Data for latest year may not have been available at press time.*

In U.S. $	2022	2021	2020	2019	2018	2017
Revenue	621,000,000	575,000,000	420,000,000	400,000,000		
R&D Expense						
Operating Income						
Operating Margin %						
SGA Expense						
Net Income						
Operating Cash Flow						
Capital Expenditure						
EBITDA						
Return on Assets %						
Return on Equity %						
Debt to Equity						

CONTACT INFORMATION:

Phone: 571 434-5400   Fax: 571 434-5401
Toll-Free: 855-683-2677
Address: 1906 Reston Metro Plz., Ste. 500, Reston, VA 20190 United States

STOCK TICKER/OTHER:

Stock Ticker: Subsidiary
Employees: 1,988
Parent Company: TransUnion LLC

Exchange:
Fiscal Year Ends: 12/31

SALARIES/BONUSES:

Top Exec. Salary: $ Bonus: $
Second Exec. Salary: $ Bonus: $

OTHER THOUGHTS:

Estimated Female Officers or Directors:
Hot Spot for Advancement for Women/Minorities:

Sales, profits and employees may be estimates. Financial information, benefits and other data can change quickly and may vary from those stated here.

New York Times Company (The)

www.nytco.com

NAIC Code: 511110

TYPES OF BUSINESS:

Newspaper Publishing
Newspaper Distribution
Newsprint & Paper Manufacturing
Digital Publishing

BRANDS/DIVISIONS/AFFILIATES:

New York Times (The)

GROWTH PLANS/SPECIAL FEATURES:

New York Times Co is an American media company known for publishing its flagship newspaper, The New York Times. The company also operates the International New York Times newspaper, as well as digital properties such as nytimes and various smartphone applications. Circulation of The New York Times is the source of revenue for the company, followed by print and digital advertising and its paid digital-only subscription to The New York Times. The company has a daily print circulation of over 3,00,000 and 7,40,000 on Sundays. The source of growth for The New York Times is its digital subscription service, which has over 1,000,000 paid users.

CONTACTS: *Note: Officers with more than one job title may be intentionally listed here more than once.*

Meredith Kopit Levien, CEO
Roland Caputo, CFO
A. Sulzberger, Chairman of the Board
R. Benten, Chief Accounting Officer
David Perpich, Director
Diane Brayton, Executive VP
Jacqueline Welch, Executive VP

FINANCIAL DATA: *Note: Data for latest year may not have been available at press time.*

In U.S. $	2022	2021	2020	2019	2018	2017
Revenue	2,308,321,000	2,074,877,000	1,783,639,000	1,812,184,000	1,748,598,000	1,675,639,000
R&D Expense	204,185,000	160,871,000	133,384,000	106,415,000	84,098,000	
Operating Income	255,737,000	271,865,000	176,256,000	177,545,000	185,316,000	182,361,000
Operating Margin %	.11%	.13%	.10%	.10%	.11%	.11%
SGA Expense	556,812,000	545,071,000	452,551,000	479,404,000	472,289,000	815,065,000
Net Income	173,905,000	219,971,000	100,103,000	139,966,000	125,684,000	4,296,000
Operating Cash Flow	150,687,000	269,098,000	297,933,000	189,898,000	157,117,000	86,712,000
Capital Expenditure	36,961,000	34,637,000	34,451,000	45,441,000	77,487,000	84,753,000
EBITDA	329,373,000	358,260,000	186,863,000	259,364,000	262,784,000	199,570,000
Return on Assets %	.07%	.09%	.05%	.07%	.06%	.00%
Return on Equity %	.11%	.15%	.08%	.13%	.13%	.00%
Debt to Equity	.04%	.04%	0.04	0.047		0.279

CONTACT INFORMATION:

Phone: 212 556-1234   Fax:
Toll-Free:
Address: 620 Eighth Ave., New York, NY 10018 United States

STOCK TICKER/OTHER:

Stock Ticker: NYT   Exchange: NYS
Employees: 5,800   Fiscal Year Ends: 12/31
Parent Company:

SALARIES/BONUSES:

Top Exec. Salary: $938,366   Bonus: $
Second Exec. Salary: Bonus: $
$647,289

OTHER THOUGHTS:

Estimated Female Officers or Directors: 6
Hot Spot for Advancement for Women/Minorities: Y

Newegg Commerce Inc

www.newegg.com

NAIC Code: 454110

TYPES OF BUSINESS:

Online Retail-Computers & Electronics
Ecommerce
Retail
Logistics
Computer Products
Distribution

GROWTH PLANS/SPECIAL FEATURES:

Newegg Commerce Inc is an e-commerce company offering direct sales and an online marketplace platform for IT computer components, consumer electronics, entertainment, smart home and gaming products and provides certain third-party logistics services globally.

BRANDS/DIVISIONS/AFFILIATES:

Newegg.com
newegg.ca
newegg.com.cn
NeweggBusiness.com
Rosewill Inc
GameCrate.com
Newegg Logistics

CONTACTS: *Note: Officers with more than one job title may be intentionally listed here more than once.*

Anthony Chow, CEO
Robert Chang, CFO
Zhitao He, Chairman of the Board
Montaque Hou, Chief Technology Officer
Jamie Spannos, COO
Matt Strathman, General Counsel

FINANCIAL DATA: *Note: Data for latest year may not have been available at press time.*

In U.S. $	2022	2021	2020	2019	2018	2017
Revenue	1,720,273,000	2,376,225,000	2,114,872,000	1,533,928,000		
R&D Expense						
Operating Income	-49,538,000	33,512,000	23,390,000	-36,004,000		
Operating Margin %		.01%	.01%			
SGA Expense	266,164,000	292,464,000	250,239,000	229,192,000		
Net Income	-57,429,000	36,262,000	30,426,000	-16,991,000		
Operating Cash Flow	20,480,000	-53,286,000	84,512,000	-10,077,000		
Capital Expenditure	9,190,000	13,839,000	6,156,000	10,283,000		
EBITDA	-31,622,000	41,917,000	42,122,000	1,251,000		
Return on Assets %		.06%	.05%			
Return on Equity %		.23%	.24%			
Debt to Equity		.47%	0.323			

CONTACT INFORMATION:

Phone: 626-271-9700   Fax: 626-271-9403
Toll-Free: 800-390-1119
Address: 17560 Rowland St., City of Industry, CA 91748 United States

STOCK TICKER/OTHER:

Stock Ticker: NEGG   Exchange: NAS
Employees: 1,355   Fiscal Year Ends: 12/31
Parent Company:

SALARIES/BONUSES:

Top Exec. Salary: $ Bonus: $
Second Exec. Salary: $ Bonus: $

OTHER THOUGHTS:

Estimated Female Officers or Directors:
Hot Spot for Advancement for Women/Minorities:

Newfold Digital Inc

newfold.com

NAIC Code: 518210

TYPES OF BUSINESS:

Web Hosting Products & Services
Web Design Services
Search Engine Optimization
Web Hosting
Ecommerce
Domain Name

BRANDS/DIVISIONS/AFFILIATES:

Web.com Group Inc
Endurance Web Presence
Web.com
Network Solutions
Register.com
Name Jet
Bluehost Inc
Freeparking Ltd

CONTACTS: *Note: Officers with more than one job title may be intentionally listed here more than once.*

Sharon Rowlands, CEO
Ed Jay, Pres.
Christina Clohecy, CFO
Paula Drum, CMO
Deb Myers, Chief People Officer
Michael Bouchet, CIO
Roseann Duran, Executive VP
Anuj Saxena, CTO

GROWTH PLANS/SPECIAL FEATURES:

Newfold Digital, Inc. is a result of the combination of Web.com Group, Inc. and Endurance Web Presence and is a web technology company servicing millions of business customers worldwide. The firm's portfolio of brands includes Web.com, Network Solutions, Register.com, Name Jet, Bluehost Inc., and Freeparking Ltd. Web.com offers website, marketing, web hosting, web security, business email and other web-related solutions and services, including website and app building. Network Solutions helps small businesses to begin marketing themselves on the web, offering a full range of web-related services including domains, building websites and ecommerce platforms, and online marketing and information technology services. Register.com is a leading provider of global domain name registration, website design and management services. The platform is also a business web hosting provider. NameJet is a premier aftermarket domain name service. Bluehost, Inc. is a web hosting solutions company. Freeparking Ltd. offers domain name services, website building, web and email hosting and other services. Additional brands of Newfold Digital include HostGator, Domain.com, Crazydomains.com, sitebeat, resellerclub, iPage, BigRock, Sitebuilder.com, Vodien 24/7 cloud hosting, LogicBoxes, BuyDomains.com and Snap[NAMES].

FINANCIAL DATA: *Note: Data for latest year may not have been available at press time.*

In U.S. $	2022	2021	2020	2019	2018	2017
Revenue	901,243,200	866,580,000	833,250,000	825,000,000	798,000,000	749,260,992
R&D Expense						
Operating Income						
Operating Margin %						
SGA Expense						
Net Income				55,795,611	54,701,580	53,629,000
Operating Cash Flow						
Capital Expenditure						
EBITDA						
Return on Assets %						
Return on Equity %						
Debt to Equity						

CONTACT INFORMATION:

Phone: 904 680-6600   Fax: 904 880-0350
Toll-Free:
Address: 5335 Gate Pkwy., Jacksonville, FL 32256 United States

STOCK TICKER/OTHER:

Stock Ticker: Private   Exchange:
Employees: 3,600   Fiscal Year Ends: 12/31
Parent Company: Siris Capital Group LLC

SALARIES/BONUSES:

Top Exec. Salary: $ Bonus: $
Second Exec. Salary: $ Bonus: $

OTHER THOUGHTS:

Estimated Female Officers or Directors: 3
Hot Spot for Advancement for Women/Minorities: Y

News Corporation

www.newscorp.com

NAIC Code: 511110

TYPES OF BUSINESS:

Newspaper Publishing
Magazine & Book Publishing
Advertising Services
Online Media
Sports Broadcasting
Business Information
Financial Information

BRANDS/DIVISIONS/AFFILIATES:

REA Group Limited
NXE Australia Pty Limited
Dow Jones
Wall Street Journal (The)
HarperCollins Publishers Limited
News Corp Australia
New York Post (The)
talkSPORT

CONTACTS: *Note: Officers with more than one job title may be intentionally listed here more than once.*

Robert Thomson, CEO
Susan Panuccio, CFO
David Pitofsky, Chief Compliance Officer
Lachlan Murdoch, Co-Chairman of the Board
Keith Murdoch, Co-Chairman of the Board

GROWTH PLANS/SPECIAL FEATURES:

News Corporation is a diversified media conglomerate with significant presence in the U.S, the U.K., and Australia. Key mastheads include The Wall Street Journal, Herald Sun, and The Times. The company also has a strong presence in the Australian pay-TV market through Fox Sports, Foxtel, and associated streaming platforms (all 65%-owned), while its 61%-owned REA Group is the dominant real estate classified business in Australia. In addition, it owns HarperCollins, one of the largest book publishers in the world, and also has a substantial digital property advertising business (Move) in the U.S.

FINANCIAL DATA: *Note: Data for latest year may not have been available at press time.*

In U.S. $	2022	2021	2020	2019	2018	2017
Revenue	10,385,000,000	9,358,000,000	9,008,000,000	10,074,000,000	9,024,000,000	
R&D Expense						
Operating Income	981,000,000	593,000,000	369,000,000	585,000,000	599,000,000	
Operating Margin %	.09%	.06%	.04%	.06%	.07%	
SGA Expense	3,592,000,000	3,254,000,000	2,995,000,000	3,191,000,000	3,049,000,000	
Net Income	623,000,000	330,000,000	-1,269,000,000	155,000,000	-1,514,000,000	
Operating Cash Flow	1,354,000,000	1,237,000,000	780,000,000	928,000,000	757,000,000	
Capital Expenditure	499,000,000	390,000,000	438,000,000	572,000,000	364,000,000	
EBITDA	1,599,000,000	1,183,000,000	-855,000,000	1,072,000,000	1,071,000,000	
Return on Assets %	.04%	.02%	-.08%	.01%	-.10%	
Return on Equity %	.08%	.04%	-.15%	.02%	-.15%	
Debt to Equity	.45%	.41%	0.307	0.11	.16%	

CONTACT INFORMATION:

Phone: 212 852-7000   Fax:
Toll-Free:
Address: 1211 Avenue of the Americas, New York, NY 10036 United States

STOCK TICKER/OTHER:

Stock Ticker: NWS
Employees: 25,000
Parent Company:

Exchange: NAS
Fiscal Year Ends: 06/30

SALARIES/BONUSES:

Top Exec. Salary: $3,000,000   Bonus: $
Second Exec. Salary: $1,540,000   Bonus: $

OTHER THOUGHTS:

Estimated Female Officers or Directors: 6
Hot Spot for Advancement for Women/Minorities: Y

NTT DOCOMO Inc

www.nttdocomo.co.jp/english

NAIC Code: 517312

TYPES OF BUSINESS:

Mobile Telephone Service
Mobile
5G
Telecommunications
Tablets
Data Communication
Advanced Wireless Networks
LTE Networks

BRANDS/DIVISIONS/AFFILIATES:

Nippon Telegraph and Telephone Corporation (NTT)
docomo

GROWTH PLANS/SPECIAL FEATURES:

NTT DOCOMO, Inc. is a leading telecommunications company in Japan. The firm serves more than 87 million customers in Japan via advanced wireless networks, including long-term evolution (LTE) and LTE-advanced networks. NTT DOCOMO is a world-leading developer of 5G networks, deploying the network and network function virtualization (NFV) and other related technologies during the early-2020s. Outside Japan, NTT DOCOMO provides technical and operational expertise to mobile operators and other partner companies, and contributes to the global standardization of new mobile technologies. Products by NTT DOCOMO include iPhones, iPads, docomo 4G and 5G smartphones, docomo tablets and other phones, watches, data communications products, drivers support products and more. The parent company of the firm is Nippon Telegraph and Telephone Corporation (NTT).

CONTACTS:
Note: Officers with more than one job title may be intentionally listed here more than once.

Motoyuki Ii, CEO
Seizo Onoe, CTO
Fumio Iwasaki, Sr. Exec. VP
Tsutomu Shindou, Exec. VP
Takashi Tanaka, Exec. VP
Kazuhiro Yoshizawa, Exec. VP

FINANCIAL DATA: *Note: Data for latest year may not have been available at press time.*

In U.S. $	2022	2021	2020	2019	2018	2017
Revenue	49,695,675,640	42,874,999,988	43,134,016,602	46,076,108,800	45,396,140,032	42,620,825,600
R&D Expense						
Operating Income						
Operating Margin %						
SGA Expense						
Net Income	8,972,124,044	8,286,093,708	5,485,300,000	6,339,808,768	7,086,691,328	6,066,396,160
Operating Cash Flow						
Capital Expenditure						
EBITDA						
Return on Assets %						
Return on Equity %						
Debt to Equity						

CONTACT INFORMATION:

Phone: 81 351561111   Fax: 81 351560271
Toll-Free:
Address: 2-11-1, Nagata-cho, Chiyoda-ku, Tokyo, 100-6150 Japan

STOCK TICKER/OTHER:

Stock Ticker: Subsidiary   Exchange:
Employees: 38,000   Fiscal Year Ends: 03/31
Parent Company: Nippon Telegraph and Telephone Corporation (NTT)

SALARIES/BONUSES:

Top Exec. Salary: $ Bonus: $
Second Exec. Salary: $ Bonus: $

OTHER THOUGHTS:

Estimated Female Officers or Directors:
Hot Spot for Advancement for Women/Minorities:

Nutanix Inc

NAIC Code: 511210B

www.nutanix.com

TYPES OF BUSINESS:

Computer Software: Network Management (IT), System Testing & Storage
Enterprise Cloud Platform
Software Solutions
Cloud Services
Multi-Cloud Solutions
Cloud Infrastructure
Cloud Management
Storage

BRANDS/DIVISIONS/AFFILIATES:

GROWTH PLANS/SPECIAL FEATURES:

Nutanix Inc provides native hybrid cloud capabilities for businesses. The company offers Enterprise Cloud Platform to businesses for various uses such as web-scale engineering and consumer-grade design, virtualization, and storage into a resilient, and software-defined solution. Geographically, it derives a majority of revenue from the United States and also has a presence in Europe, the Middle East, Asia Pacific, Africa, and other regions.

CONTACTS: *Note: Officers with more than one job title may be intentionally listed here more than once.*

Rajiv Ramaswami, CEO
Duston Williams, CFO
Virginia Gambale, Chairman of the Board
Aaron Boynton, Chief Accounting Officer
Tyler Wall, Chief Legal Officer
David Sangster, COO
Christopher Kaddaras, Other Executive Officer

FINANCIAL DATA: *Note: Data for latest year may not have been available at press time.*

In U.S. $	2022	2021	2020	2019	2018	2017
Revenue	1,580,796,000	1,394,364,000	1,307,682,000	1,236,143,000	1,155,457,000	
R&D Expense	572,999,000	558,008,000	553,978,000	500,719,000	313,777,000	
Operating Income	-458,852,000	-662,111,000	-828,921,000	-598,041,000	-280,408,000	
Operating Margin %	- .29%	- .47%	- .63%	- .48%	- .24%	
SGA Expense	1,145,493,000	1,206,561,000	1,295,936,000	1,029,337,000	736,058,000	
Net Income	-798,946,000	-1,035,589,000	-872,883,000	-621,179,000	-297,161,000	
Operating Cash Flow	67,543,000	-99,810,000	-159,885,000	42,168,000	92,540,000	
Capital Expenditure	49,058,000	58,647,000	89,488,000	118,452,000	62,372,000	
EBITDA	-630,996,000	-842,797,000	-730,136,000	-506,136,000	-230,106,000	
Return on Assets %	- .34%	- .51%	- .49%	- .37%	- .25%	
Return on Equity %				-2.42%	-1.09%	
Debt to Equity				2.455	1.31%	

CONTACT INFORMATION:

Phone: 855-688-2649   Fax: 408-916-4039
Toll-Free:
Address: 1740 Technology Dr., Ste. 150, San Jose, CA 95110 United States

STOCK TICKER/OTHER:

Stock Ticker: NTNX
Employees: 6,450
Parent Company:

Exchange: NAS
Fiscal Year Ends: 07/31

SALARIES/BONUSES:

Top Exec. Salary: $800,010   Bonus: $
Second Exec. Salary: $475,010   Bonus: $

OTHER THOUGHTS:

Estimated Female Officers or Directors:
Hot Spot for Advancement for Women/Minorities:

Ocado Group PLC

www.ocado.com

NAIC Code: 454110

TYPES OF BUSINESS:
Online Grocery Shopping
Ecommerce
Grocery
Home Delivery
Technology
Robotics
Automation
Warehouse

BRANDS/DIVISIONS/AFFILIATES:
Ocado Smart Platform
Ocado.com
Ocado Retail Limited
Ocado Engineering

GROWTH PLANS/SPECIAL FEATURES:
Ocado, one of the largest pure online grocers in the world, operates in two divisions. Ocado Retail is the group's online grocery business in the United Kingdom, a joint venture with Marks & Spencer; it offers an extensive product range of over 55,000 items via its Ocado.com website and holds more than 15% of the U.K. online grocery market and approximately 2% of the total U.K. grocery market. Ocado Solutions is built on the Ocado Smart Platform, a modular, automated online retail fulfillment and delivery solution that involves the provision of software, fulfillment infrastructure, and support services to corporate clients for a variety of one-time and ongoing costs. OSP has allowed the company to work with some of the world's largest grocers, including Ocado's retail operation.

CONTACTS: Note: Officers with more than one job title may be intentionally listed here more than once.
Tim Steiner, CEO
Neill Abrams, Dir.-Legal & Bus. Affairs
Mark Richardson, Dir.-Oper.
Jason Gissing, Dir.-Commercial

FINANCIAL DATA: Note: Data for latest year may not have been available at press time.

In U.S. $	2022	2021	2020	2019	2018	2017
Revenue	3,173,188,000	3,153,623,000	2,943,449,000	2,217,369,000	2,018,177,000	1,836,026,000
R&D Expense						
Operating Income	-679,626,300	-287,679,900	-146,049,000	-282,251,900	-58,697,300	-11,108,310
Operating Margin %	-.21%	-.09%	-.05%	-.13%	-.03%	-.01%
SGA Expense	2,007,069,000	1,579,778,000	1,249,811,000	1,118,404,000	823,655,600	696,667,500
Net Income	-574,981,000	-281,747,000	-169,527,900	-268,997,700	-56,677,600	-10,477,150
Operating Cash Flow	9,972,229	-20,196,920	284,524,100	65,261,290	162,080,300	149,331,000
Capital Expenditure	992,047,400	871,875,800	570,310,500	328,326,100	214,718,500	228,351,400
EBITDA	-95,556,670	154,885,100	217,748,000	62,357,980	77,758,140	96,692,740
Return on Assets %	-.10%	-.05%	-.04%	-.12%	-.04%	-.01%
Return on Equity %	-.27%	-.13%	-.10%	-.27%	-.11%	-.03%
Debt to Equity	1.00%	1.12%	0.77	0.533	.61%	1.417

CONTACT INFORMATION:
Phone: 44-1707-228080   Fax: 44-1707-227999
Toll-Free:
Address: Apollo Court, 2 Bishop Sq., Hatfield Bus. Park, Hatfield, Hertfordshire AL10 9EX United Kingdom

STOCK TICKER/OTHER:
Stock Ticker: OCDGF
Employees: 21,399
Parent Company:

Exchange: PINX
Fiscal Year Ends: 11/30

SALARIES/BONUSES:
Top Exec. Salary: $953,042   Bonus: $
Second Exec. Salary: $710,679   Bonus: $

OTHER THOUGHTS:
Estimated Female Officers or Directors: 2
Hot Spot for Advancement for Women/Minorities:

Sales, profits and employees may be estimates. Financial information, benefits and other data can change quickly and may vary from those stated here.

OfferUp Inc

NAIC Code: 519130

TYPES OF BUSINESS:

Online Classified Ads Platform
Ecommerce Platform
Secondhand Buy and Sell
Automobile Dealership Platform

BRANDS/DIVISIONS/AFFILIATES:

GROWTH PLANS/SPECIAL FEATURES:

OfferUp, Inc. operates an online and mobile ecommerce platform that allows individuals to sell items. Users take a photo of the item, upload it to the website/app and promote it for sale. Once the app is downloaded, consumers interested in purchasing items can browse the listings in order to find deals. If interested, the potential buyer sends a chat message securely through the app without giving away personal information. Notifications are sent in real-time when a buyer or seller sends a message. User profiles are also provided, describing buyers and sellers, along with ratings that are applied once transactions are complete. OfferUp is free to download. Identification verification is validated through the app as well. In addition, OfferUp has a verified automobile dealer program that enables dealers to upload their vehicles for sale on the platform. OfferUp has more than 20 million monthly active users.

CONTACTS: *Note: Officers with more than one job title may be intentionally listed here more than once.*

Todd Dunlap, CEO

FINANCIAL DATA: *Note: Data for latest year may not have been available at press time.*

In U.S. $	2022	2021	2020	2019	2018	2017
Revenue						
R&D Expense						
Operating Income						
Operating Margin %						
SGA Expense						
Net Income						
Operating Cash Flow						
Capital Expenditure						
EBITDA						
Return on Assets %						
Return on Equity %						
Debt to Equity						

CONTACT INFORMATION:

Phone: 844-633-3787   Fax:
Toll-Free:
Address: 1745 114th Ave. SE, Bellevue, WA 98004 United States

STOCK TICKER/OTHER:

Stock Ticker: Private   Exchange:
Employees: 240   Fiscal Year Ends:
Parent Company:

SALARIES/BONUSES:

Top Exec. Salary: $ Bonus: $
Second Exec. Salary: $ Bonus: $

OTHER THOUGHTS:

Estimated Female Officers or Directors:
Hot Spot for Advancement for Women/Minorities:

OneSpan Inc

www.onespan.com

NAIC Code: 511210E

TYPES OF BUSINESS:

Computer Software: Network Security, Managed Access, Digital ID, Cybersecurity & Anti-Virus
Identity Security
Authentication
Anti-Fraud Services
Agreement Automation

BRANDS/DIVISIONS/AFFILIATES:

GROWTH PLANS/SPECIAL FEATURES:

OneSpan Inc is a provider of information technology security solutions for banking and financial services and application security markets. Its solutions secure and manage access to digital assets and protect online transactions, via mobile devices and in-person. Authentication and anti-fraud solutions are the organization's primary product offerings and include multifactor authentication and virtual private network access capabilities. The company derives revenues from hardware and license fees, maintenance and support fees, and subscription fees. A large majority of the firm's revenue is generated in Europe, Middle East and Africa, and the rest in the United States and Asia-Pacific region.

CONTACTS: Note: Officers with more than one job title may be intentionally listed here more than once.

Steven Worth, CEO
Jan van Gaalen, CFO
Alfred Nietzel, Chairman of the Board
John Bosshart, Chief Accounting Officer

FINANCIAL DATA: Note: Data for latest year may not have been available at press time.

In U.S. $	2022	2021	2020	2019	2018	2017
Revenue	219,006,000	214,481,000	215,691,000	253,484,000	211,336,000	193,291,000
R&D Expense	41,735,000	47,414,000	41,194,000	42,463,000	32,197,000	23,119,000
Operating Income	-13,805,000	-26,128,000	-5,258,000	14,189,000	-920,000	6,192,000
Operating Margin %	-.06%	-.12%	-.02%	.06%	.00%	.03%
SGA Expense	116,501,000	115,761,000	103,001,000	101,716,000	105,394,000	96,394,000
Net Income	-14,434,000	-30,584,000	-5,455,000	7,864,000	3,044,000	-22,399,000
Operating Cash Flow	-5,786,000	-2,745,000	14,922,000	18,244,000	1,226,000	17,627,000
Capital Expenditure	5,025,000	2,204,000	3,234,000	7,453,000	3,685,000	3,088,000
EBITDA	-6,739,000	-17,202,000	6,745,000	25,734,000	11,218,000	16,793,000
Return on Assets %	-.04%	-.09%	-.01%	.02%	.01%	-.07%
Return on Equity %	-.07%	-.13%	-.02%	.03%	.01%	-.09%
Debt to Equity	.04%	.05%	0.048	0.043		

CONTACT INFORMATION:

Phone: 312 766-4001   Fax:
Toll-Free:
Address: 121 West Wacker Dr., Ste. 2050, Chicago, IL 60601 United States

STOCK TICKER/OTHER:

Stock Ticker: OSPN
Employees: 790
Parent Company:

Exchange: NAS
Fiscal Year Ends: 12/31

SALARIES/BONUSES:

Top Exec. Salary: $526,091   Bonus: $
Second Exec. Salary: $480,000   Bonus: $

OTHER THOUGHTS:

Estimated Female Officers or Directors:
Hot Spot for Advancement for Women/Minorities:

OneWeb Ltd

NAIC Code: 517410

www.oneweb.world

TYPES OF BUSINESS:
Satellite Telecommunication Services (Including Satellite Telephone Companies)
Satellites
Global Communications Network
Internet Connectivity Services
User Terminals
Satellite Design and Build

BRANDS/DIVISIONS/AFFILIATES:
UK Department for Business Energy and Industrial
Bharthi Group

CONTACTS: *Note: Officers with more than one job title may be intentionally listed here more than once.*
Neil Masterson, CEO

GROWTH PLANS/SPECIAL FEATURES:
OneWeb Ltd. has been building a global communications network in space for the delivery of high-throughput, high-speed services capable of connecting everywhere and to everyone. The firm's advanced, low-Earth-orbit satellite constellation is referred to as OneWeb. OneWeb's network enables connectivity solutions for maritime, aviation, enterprise and government entities and is able to cover cell site backhaul. The company powers digital transformation and offers tailored networking solutions for any need, at any level. OneWeb satellites orbit relatively close to the Earth, allowing for better internet access speeds. As they orbit, they interlock with each other electronically to create coverage over the entire planet. Small, low-cost user terminals communicate with the satellite network and provide wireless internet access. The terminals provide connectivity with no change in latency (speed) during satellite handovers in order to ensure continuous quality of voice, gaming and web surfing experience. User terminals consist of a satellite antenna, a receiver and a customer network exchange unit (CNX). The CNX connects the user terminal to the customer's network which in turn connects to end-user devices such as laptops, smartphones, sensors and more. OneWeb units contain on-board propulsion and state-of-the-art positioning GPS sensors that ground-track their placement within meters. The propulsion systems perform maneuvers for steering clear of space debris. When a OneWeb satellite nears the end of its service life, it will de-orbit automatically. Headquartered in London, UK, OneWeb has an international office in Virginia, USA. The firm is owned by the UK government, Bharti Group and Eutelsat, with additional investments from SoftBank and Hughes Network Group, among others.

FINANCIAL DATA: *Note: Data for latest year may not have been available at press time.*

In U.S. $	2022	2021	2020	2019	2018	2017
Revenue	9,600,000	3,000,000	26,520,760	75,773,600	216,496,000	81,254,000
R&D Expense						
Operating Income						
Operating Margin %						
SGA Expense						
Net Income	-389,800,000	370,800,000			-213,184,000	-73,857,000
Operating Cash Flow						
Capital Expenditure						
EBITDA						
Return on Assets %						
Return on Equity %						
Debt to Equity						

CONTACT INFORMATION:
Phone: 44 20 3727 1160   Fax:
Toll-Free:
Address: 195 Wood Ln., W., Works Bldg., Fl.3, London, W12 7FQ United Kingdom

STOCK TICKER/OTHER:
Stock Ticker: Subsidiary   Exchange:
Employees: 600   Fiscal Year Ends: 03/31
Parent Company: UK Department for Business Energy and Industrial

SALARIES/BONUSES:
Top Exec. Salary: $ Bonus: $
Second Exec. Salary: $ Bonus: $

OTHER THOUGHTS:
Estimated Female Officers or Directors:
Hot Spot for Advancement for Women/Minorities:

Onstream Media Corporation

www.onstreammedia.com

NAIC Code: 541810E

TYPES OF BUSINESS:
Online Video Management Services
Online Media Communications Service
Live and On-Demand Media Communications
Audio and Video Communications
Webcasting and Web Conferencing Solutions
Content Publishing Solutions
Digital Media Services
Digital Media Tools

BRANDS/DIVISIONS/AFFILIATES:
Onstream Digital Media Services Platform

CONTACTS: Note: Officers with more than one job title may be intentionally listed here more than once.
Randy Selman, CEO
Alan M. Saperstein, COO
David Glassman, CMO
Clifford Friedland, Sr. VP-Bus. Dev.
Clifford Friedland, Senior VP, Divisional

GROWTH PLANS/SPECIAL FEATURES:
Onstream Media Corporation is an online service provider of live and on-demand media communications through its Onstream Digital Media-Services Platform. The firm specializes in online audio/video corporate communications; therefore, its digital-asset-management active server pages technology provides the tools for webcasting, web conferencing and content-publishing. Onstream Media's digital media services are used by many Fortune 100 company executives to broadcast their announcements in sales, marketing, communications, investor relations, human resources and training. Onstream Media's tools facilitate the integration of data, video and voice to offer media management and online communication services across multiple global geographies and platforms. The company's goal is to free customers from the need to build, manage and operate their own media asset-management infrastructures by providing capabilities that allow users to search, access, share and distribute within a secure, hosted platform. Industries served by Onstream Media include associations, accounting, investors/IR, education, legal, health sciences, technology, media/entertainment, government and publishing.

Onstream Media offers its employees comprehensive health benefits, a 401(k), and life and disability insurance plans.

FINANCIAL DATA: Note: Data for latest year may not have been available at press time.

In U.S. $	2022	2021	2020	2019	2018	2017
Revenue	19,400,000	17,041,342	16,385,906	15,986,250	15,225,000	14,500,000
R&D Expense						
Operating Income						
Operating Margin %						
SGA Expense						
Net Income						
Operating Cash Flow						
Capital Expenditure						
EBITDA						
Return on Assets %						
Return on Equity %						
Debt to Equity						

CONTACT INFORMATION:
Phone: 954 917-6655   Fax: 954-917-0575
Toll-Free: 877-932-3400
Address: 1451 W. Cypress Creek Rd., Ste. 204, Fort Lauderdale, FL 33309 United States

STOCK TICKER/OTHER:
Stock Ticker: Private   Exchange:
Employees: 82   Fiscal Year Ends: 09/30
Parent Company:

SALARIES/BONUSES:
Top Exec. Salary: $ Bonus: $
Second Exec. Salary: $ Bonus: $

OTHER THOUGHTS:
Estimated Female Officers or Directors:
Hot Spot for Advancement for Women/Minorities:

Open Text Corporation

www.opentext.com

NAIC Code: 511210L

TYPES OF BUSINESS:

Enterprise Content Management
Enterprise Information Management
Cloud Hosting
Internet of Things
Artificial Intelligence
IT Security
Analytics

BRANDS/DIVISIONS/AFFILIATES:

GROWTH PLANS/SPECIAL FEATURES:

Open Text Corp grew out of a technology project involving the Oxford English Dictionary at Canada's University of Waterloo in the mid-1980s. Its software allows clients to archive, aggregate, retrieve, and search unstructured information (such as documents, e-mail, and presentations). The OpenText Information Management platform and services provide secure and scalable solutions for global enterprises, SMBs, governments, and consumers around the world. It also accelerates transformations with intelligent tools and services. The company is based in Ontario, Canada.

Open Text offers employees comprehensive benefits.

CONTACTS: Note: Officers with more than one job title may be intentionally listed here more than once.

Mark Barrenechea, CEO
Muhi Majzoub, Exec. VP
Madhu Ranganathan, CFO
Howard Rosen, Chief Accounting Officer
Renee McKenzie, Chief Information Officer
Gordon Davies, Chief Legal Officer
Lou Blatt, Chief Marketing Officer
P. Jenkins, Director
James McGourlay, Executive VP, Divisional
Paul Duggan, Executive VP, Divisional
Simon Harrison, Executive VP, Divisional
Prentiss Donohue, Executive VP, Divisional
Kristina Lengyel, Executive VP, Divisional
Brian Sweeney, Executive VP
Douglas Parker, Senior VP, Divisional

FINANCIAL DATA: Note: Data for latest year may not have been available at press time.

In U.S. $	2022	2021	2020	2019	2018	2017
Revenue	3,493,844,000	3,386,115,000				
R&D Expense	440,448,000	421,447,000				
Operating Income	691,646,000	742,651,000				
Operating Margin %	.20%	.22%				
SGA Expense	994,203,000	885,742,000				
Net Income	397,090,000	310,672,000				
Operating Cash Flow	981,810,000	876,120,000				
Capital Expenditure	93,109,000	63,675,000				
EBITDA	1,171,533,000	1,317,021,000				
Return on Assets %	.04%	.03%				
Return on Equity %	.10%	.08%				
Debt to Equity	1.09%	.93%				

CONTACT INFORMATION:

Phone: 519 888-7111　　　　Fax: 519 888-0677
Toll-Free: 800-499-6544
Address: 275 Frank Tompa Dr., Waterloo, ON N2L 0A1 Canada

STOCK TICKER/OTHER:

Stock Ticker: OTEX　　　　　　　　Exchange: NAS
Employees: 24,100　　　　　　　　Fiscal Year Ends: 06/30
Parent Company:

SALARIES/BONUSES:

Top Exec. Salary: $950,000　　　　Bonus: $
Second Exec. Salary:　　　　　　　Bonus: $
$688,750

OTHER THOUGHTS:

Estimated Female Officers or Directors: 4
Hot Spot for Advancement for Women/Minorities: Y

OpenTable Inc

www.opentable.com

NAIC Code: 519130

TYPES OF BUSINESS:

Restaurant Reservations Online
Restaurant Reservations
Online and Mobile App Reservation Solutions
Software and Digital Technology
Marketing Solutions
Customer Review Portal
Venue Software and Hardware
Installation and Training Services

BRANDS/DIVISIONS/AFFILIATES:

Bookings Holdings Inc
OpenTable.com
Guestcenter
Venga
Connect

GROWTH PLANS/SPECIAL FEATURES:

OpenTable, Inc. offers free, real-time online reservations for diners and reservation and guest management solutions for restaurants. The company's solutions include its real-time restaurant reservation website for diners, OpenTable.com. The OpenTable network includes more than 50,000 restaurants in all 50 U.S. states as well as internationally, with bookable restaurants in over 20 other countries. International teams and offices include the U.K. (opentable.co.uk), Japan (opentable.jp), Mexico (opentable.com.mx) and Australia (opentable.com.au), among others. The company seats more than 1 billion diners each year, and diners often submit restaurant reviews. While OpenTable's service is free to diners, it collects fees from restaurants, such as: installation fees for onsite installation and training, a fee for each restaurant guest seated through online reservations and a monthly subscription payment for the use of the company's software and hardware. OpenTable operates as a subsidiary of Booking Holdings, Inc.

CONTACTS: Note: Officers with more than one job title may be intentionally listed here more than once.

Debby Soo, CEO
Jocelyn Mangan, Sr. VP-Prod. Mgmt.
John Orta, General Counsel
Joel Brown, Sr. VP-Oper.
Douglas Boake, Sr. VP-Bus. Dev.
Michael Dodson, Sr. VP-Sales
Michael Xenakis, Managing Dir.-OpenTable Europe Ltd.
Elizabeth Casey, VP-Restaurant Prod.
Catherine Porter, VP-Intl. Dev.

FINANCIAL DATA: Note: Data for latest year may not have been available at press time.

In U.S. $	2022	2021	2020	2019	2018	2017
Revenue	420,000,000	400,000,000	349,125,000	367,500,000	350,000,000	331,000,000
R&D Expense						
Operating Income						
Operating Margin %						
SGA Expense						
Net Income						
Operating Cash Flow						
Capital Expenditure						
EBITDA						
Return on Assets %						
Return on Equity %						
Debt to Equity						

CONTACT INFORMATION:

Phone: 415 344-4200   Fax:
Toll-Free: 800-6736-8225
Address: 1 Montgomery St., Ste. 700, San Francisco, CA 94104 United States

STOCK TICKER/OTHER:

Stock Ticker: Subsidiary   Exchange:
Employees: 1,900   Fiscal Year Ends: 12/31
Parent Company: Booking Holdings Inc

SALARIES/BONUSES:

Top Exec. Salary: $ Bonus: $
Second Exec. Salary: $ Bonus: $

OTHER THOUGHTS:

Estimated Female Officers or Directors: 6
Hot Spot for Advancement for Women/Minorities: Y

Optimizely Inc

www.optimizely.com

NAIC Code: 511210G

TYPES OF BUSINESS:

Online Advertising Optimization Platform
Digital Experience Software
Personalization Capabilities
Technology
Tools and Insights
Content Cloud Solutions
Commerce Cloud Solutions
Intelligence Cloud Solutions

BRANDS/DIVISIONS/AFFILIATES:

Insight Partners
Content Cloud
Commerce Cloud
Intelligence Cloud

CONTACTS: *Note: Officers with more than one job title may be intentionally listed here more than once.*

Alex Atzberger, CEO
Rupali Jain, Chief Product Officer
Myles Johnson, CFO
Shafqat Islam, CMO
Laura Thiele, Chief People Officer
Peter Yeung, CIO
Aniel Sud, CTO

GROWTH PLANS/SPECIAL FEATURES:

Optimizely, Inc. offers a digital experience platform that provides teams with related tools and insights for creating and optimizing personalized experiences. The firm has three main products which include orchestrate: plan campaigns, create content, and seamlessly collaborate across teams; experiment: run tests, uncover insights, and continuously refine every customer interaction; monetize: deliver modern, relevant commerce experiences your customers will love. Users can create through the firm's content, commerce, intelligence and experimentation capabilities. The digital experience platform is an open, extensible solution that provides a foundation behind every touchpoint, including content management, approval workflows, media management, authoring, layout, project management, business-to-business (B2B), business-to-customer, targeting, catalog management, customer-specific pricing, web testing, email, data, recommendations and more. Optimizely's customer-centric digital experience platform consists of its Content Cloud, Commerce Cloud and Intelligence Cloud product lines. Optimizely is owned by venture capital and private equity firm Insight Partners.

FINANCIAL DATA: *Note: Data for latest year may not have been available at press time.*

In U.S. $	2022	2021	2020	2019	2018	2017
Revenue						
R&D Expense						
Operating Income						
Operating Margin %						
SGA Expense						
Net Income						
Operating Cash Flow						
Capital Expenditure						
EBITDA						
Return on Assets %						
Return on Equity %						
Debt to Equity						

CONTACT INFORMATION:

Phone: 603-594-0249   Fax:
Toll-Free:
Address: 119 Fifth Ave., Fl. 7, New York, NY 10003 United States

STOCK TICKER/OTHER:

Stock Ticker: Private   Exchange:
Employees: 400   Fiscal Year Ends:
Parent Company: Insight Partners

SALARIES/BONUSES:

Top Exec. Salary: $ Bonus: $
Second Exec. Salary: $ Bonus: $

OTHER THOUGHTS:

Estimated Female Officers or Directors:
Hot Spot for Advancement for Women/Minorities:

Oracle Corporation

www.oracle.com

NAIC Code: 511210H

TYPES OF BUSINESS:

Computer Software, Data Base & File Management
Enterprise Software
Servers
Operating Systems
Infrastructure Technologies
Software
Cloud Deployment

BRANDS/DIVISIONS/AFFILIATES:

GROWTH PLANS/SPECIAL FEATURES:

Oracle provides database technology and enterprise resource planning, or ERP, software to enterprises around the world. Founded in 1977, Oracle pioneered the first commercial SQL-based relational database management system. Today, Oracle has 430,000 customers in 175 countries, supported by its base of 136,000 employees.

Oracle offers employees health, life and disability benefits, a 401(k) plan and an employee stock purchase plan.

CONTACTS: *Note: Officers with more than one job title may be intentionally listed here more than once.*

Safra Catz, CEO
Lawrence Ellison, Chairman of the Board
Jeffrey Henley, Director
Dorian Daley, Executive VP
Edward Screven, Executive VP
Lawrence J. Ellison, Chmn.

FINANCIAL DATA: *Note: Data for latest year may not have been available at press time.*

In U.S. $	2022	2021	2020	2019	2018	2017
Revenue	42,440,000,000	40,479,000,000	39,068,000,000	39,506,000,000	39,383,000,000	
R&D Expense	7,219,000,000	6,527,000,000	6,067,000,000	6,026,000,000	6,084,000,000	
Operating Income	15,830,000,000	15,782,000,000	14,202,000,000	14,022,000,000	13,904,000,000	
Operating Margin %	.26%	.39%	.36%	.35%	.35%	
SGA Expense	9,364,000,000	8,935,999,000	9,275,000,000	9,774,000,000	9,715,000,000	
Net Income	6,717,000,000	13,746,000,000	10,135,000,000	11,083,000,000	3,587,000,000	
Operating Cash Flow	9,539,000,000	15,887,000,000	13,139,000,000	14,551,000,000	15,386,000,000	
Capital Expenditure	4,511,000,000	2,135,000,000	1,564,000,000	1,660,000,000	1,736,000,000	
EBITDA	13,526,000,000	18,411,000,000	17,026,000,000	17,269,000,000	17,234,000,000	
Return on Assets %	.06%	.11%	.09%	.09%	.03%	
Return on Equity %		1.59%	.60%	.33%	.07%	
Debt to Equity		14.51%	5.733	2.372	1.21%	

CONTACT INFORMATION:

Phone: 737-867-1000   Fax:
Toll-Free:
Address: 2300 Oracle Way, Austin, TX 78741 United States

STOCK TICKER/OTHER:

Stock Ticker: ORCL   Exchange: NYS
Employees: 164,000   Fiscal Year Ends: 05/31
Parent Company:

SALARIES/BONUSES:

Top Exec. Salary: $557,765   Bonus: $650,000
Second Exec. Salary: $950,000   Bonus: $

OTHER THOUGHTS:

Estimated Female Officers or Directors: 6
Hot Spot for Advancement for Women/Minorities: Y

Oracle NetSuite

www.netsuite.com

NAIC Code: 511210H

TYPES OF BUSINESS:

Business Management Application Suites
Enterprise Resource Planning
Customer Relationship Management
Ecommerce
Automation
Marketing
Analytics and Reporting
Business Intelligence

BRANDS/DIVISIONS/AFFILIATES:

Oracle Corporation

CONTACTS: *Note: Officers with more than one job title may be intentionally listed here more than once.*

Evan Goldberg, Exec. VP-Global Business
Sam Levy, Sr. VP-Sales
Douglas Solomon, General Counsel
Marc Huffman, President, Divisional

GROWTH PLANS/SPECIAL FEATURES:

Oracle NetSuite is a global business unit of Oracle Corporation and a leading vendor of cloud-based financials, enterprise resource planning (ERP) and omnichannel commerce software. The firm's solutions are used by more than 32,000 business customers worldwide. Oracle NetSuite's cloud ERP, customer relationship management (CRM) and ecommerce products enable customers to manage their back-office, front-office and web operations in a single application. Products by the company also include global business management, human capital management, professional services automation, omnichannel commerce, accounting software, platform, infrastructure, email marketing, analytics and reporting, and business intelligence. Industries served by the company include advertising and digital marketing agencies, apparel/footwear/accessories, campus store, consulting, education, energy, financial services, food and beverage, health and beauty, healthcare, IT services, manufacturing, media and publishing, nonprofit, professional services, restaurants, hospitality, retail, software and technology companies, transportation, logistics and wholesale distribution. Oracle NetSuite is headquartered in Texas, USA, and has offices throughout North and South America, Europe, the U.K., the Middle East, Asia and Oceania.

FINANCIAL DATA: *Note: Data for latest year may not have been available at press time.*

In U.S. $	2022	2021	2020	2019	2018	2017
Revenue	1,144,000,000	1,100,000,000	1,008,291,375	960,277,500	914,550,000	871,000,000
R&D Expense						
Operating Income						
Operating Margin %						
SGA Expense						
Net Income						
Operating Cash Flow						
Capital Expenditure						
EBITDA						
Return on Assets %						
Return on Equity %						
Debt to Equity						

CONTACT INFORMATION:

Phone: 877-638-7848   Fax:
Toll-Free:
Address: 2300 Oracle Way, Austin, TX 78741 United States

STOCK TICKER/OTHER:

Stock Ticker: Subsidiary   Exchange:
Employees: 3,357   Fiscal Year Ends: 12/31
Parent Company: Oracle Corporation

SALARIES/BONUSES:

Top Exec. Salary: $ Bonus: $
Second Exec. Salary: $ Bonus: $

OTHER THOUGHTS:

Estimated Female Officers or Directors: 3
Hot Spot for Advancement for Women/Minorities: Y

Sales, profits and employees may be estimates. Financial information, benefits and other data can change quickly and may vary from those stated here.

Orbitz LLC

NAIC Code: 561510

www.orbitz.com

TYPES OF BUSINESS:

Online Reservation Systems
Discount Travel & Accommodations
Ecommerce
Online Booking

BRANDS/DIVISIONS/AFFILIATES:

Expedia Group Inc
Orbitz Rewards
Orbucks

GROWTH PLANS/SPECIAL FEATURES:

Orbitz, LLC, a subsidiary of Expedia Group, Inc., is a global online travel company that uses technology to enable leisure and business travelers to search for, plan and book a broad range of travel products and services. Travel products include air travel, hotels, vacation packages, car rentals, cruises and travel insurance as well as destination services, such as ground transportation, event tickets and tours, through a portfolio of websites. For customers, the firm offers access to travel inventory from a broad base of suppliers. For suppliers, the company represents a distribution channel that reaches millions of potential customers. Orbitz Rewards enables users to earn Orbucks the moment they book and redeem them on hotels worldwide. Other rewards include hotel perks, TSA pre-check and more.

CONTACTS: *Note: Officers with more than one job title may be intentionally listed here more than once.*

Ariane Gorin, CEO- Corp.
Michael Randolfi, CFO
Scott Forbes, Director
James Rogers, General Counsel
Guillaume Cussac, Managing Director, Divisional
Chris Brown, Other Executive Officer
Samuel Fulton, Senior VP, Divisional
Barry Diller, Chmn.-Corp.

FINANCIAL DATA: *Note: Data for latest year may not have been available at press time.*

In U.S. $	2022	2021	2020	2019	2018	2017
Revenue	932,000,000	562,224,000	432,480,000	848,000,000	840,000,000	800,000,000
R&D Expense						
Operating Income						
Operating Margin %						
SGA Expense						
Net Income						
Operating Cash Flow						
Capital Expenditure						
EBITDA						
Return on Assets %						
Return on Equity %						
Debt to Equity						

CONTACT INFORMATION:

Phone: 312 894-5000   Fax: 312 894-5001
Toll-Free: 888-656-4546
Address: 500 W. Madison St., Ste. 1000, Chicago, IL 60661 United States

STOCK TICKER/OTHER:

Stock Ticker: Subsidiary   Exchange:
Employees: 1,530   Fiscal Year Ends: 12/31
Parent Company: Expedia Group Inc

SALARIES/BONUSES:

Top Exec. Salary: $ Bonus: $
Second Exec. Salary: $ Bonus: $

OTHER THOUGHTS:

Estimated Female Officers or Directors:
Hot Spot for Advancement for Women/Minorities:

Sales, profits and employees may be estimates. Financial information, benefits and other data can change quickly and may vary from those stated here.

Ozon Holdings PLC

NAIC Code: 454110

TYPES OF BUSINESS:

Online Retail Store
Ecommerce
Consumer Products
Travel Booking
Distribution
eBooks
Online Payments
Innovative Technology

BRANDS/DIVISIONS/AFFILIATES:

Ozon.ru
Ozon Travel
ozon.ru/travel/

GROWTH PLANS/SPECIAL FEATURES:

Ozon Holdings PLC is a multi-category e-commerce platform. It provides customers with the widest selection of goods and door delivery across Russia's 11 time zones. The firm operates in two segments. The Ozon.ru segment engages in sales of multi-category consumer products through Ozon mobile app and Ozon website. The Ozon Travel segment comprises sales of airline and train tickets through the Ozon.Travel mobile app and ozon.ru/travel/ website.

CONTACTS: Note: Officers with more than one job title may be intentionally listed here more than once.

Alexander Shulgin, CEO
Daniil Fedorov, CFO

FINANCIAL DATA: Note: Data for latest year may not have been available at press time.

In U.S. $	2022	2021	2020	2019	2018	2017
Revenue	3,784,800,000	2,440,799,744	1,687,419,008	823,173,312	500,005,376	374,591,000
R&D Expense						
Operating Income						
Operating Margin %						
SGA Expense						
Net Income	-794,700,000	-777,634,752	-360,025,856	-265,192,080	-76,048,648	
Operating Cash Flow						
Capital Expenditure						
EBITDA						
Return on Assets %						
Return on Equity %						
Debt to Equity						

CONTACT INFORMATION:

Phone: 357 22-360000   Fax:
Toll-Free:
Address: Arch. Makariou III, 2-4, Capital Center, 9/Fl, Nicosia, 1065 Cyprus

STOCK TICKER/OTHER:

Stock Ticker: OZON   Exchange: Moscow
Employees: 49,889   Fiscal Year Ends: 12/31
Parent Company:

SALARIES/BONUSES:

Top Exec. Salary: $ Bonus: $
Second Exec. Salary: $ Bonus: $

OTHER THOUGHTS:

Estimated Female Officers or Directors: 1
Hot Spot for Advancement for Women/Minorities: Y

PagerDuty Inc

www.pagerduty.com

NAIC Code: 511210C

TYPES OF BUSINESS:

Computer Software, Telecom, Communications & VOIP
Alarm Service
Dispatching Service
DevOps Monitoring
Information Technology
Cloud Transformation
Enterprise Security

BRANDS/DIVISIONS/AFFILIATES:

Rundeck

GROWTH PLANS/SPECIAL FEATURES:

PagerDuty is a digital operations management platform that manages urgent and mission-critical work for a modern, digital business. Its platform harnesses digital signals from virtually any software-enabled system or device, combines it with human response data, and orchestrates teams to take the right actions in real-time. The product offerings of the company include DEVOPS, AIOPS, PROCESS AUTOMATION and BUSINESS OPERATIONS.

PagerDuty offers its employees medical coverage, paid time off, career development programs and a variety of company perks.

CONTACTS: Note: Officers with more than one job title may be intentionally listed here more than once.

Jennifer Tejada, CEO
Owen Howard Wilson, CFO
Alexandru Solomon, Chief Technology Officer
David Justice, Executive VP
Stacey Giamalis, General Counsel

FINANCIAL DATA: Note: Data for latest year may not have been available at press time.

In U.S. $	2022	2021	2020	2019	2018	2017
Revenue	281,396,000	213,556,000	166,351,000	117,823,000	79,630,000	
R&D Expense	95,690,000	64,566,000	49,011,000	38,858,000	33,532,000	
Operating Income	-101,711,000	-66,282,000	-55,559,000	-42,321,000	-38,316,000	
Operating Margin %	-.36%	-.31%	-.33%	-.36%		
SGA Expense	239,056,000	184,586,000	148,320,000	104,031,000	71,697,000	
Net Income	-107,455,000	-68,903,000	-50,339,000	-40,741,000	-38,149,000	
Operating Cash Flow	-6,021,000	10,095,000	-173,000	-5,608,000	-11,836,000	
Capital Expenditure	6,810,000	4,848,000	5,174,000	4,119,000	822,000	
EBITDA	-94,970,000	-58,278,000	-47,327,000	-38,348,000	-35,917,000	
Return on Assets %	-.13%	-.11%	-.16%	-.29%		
Return on Equity %	-.34%	-.20%	-.42%			
Debt to Equity	1.13%	.67%				

CONTACT INFORMATION:

Phone: 650-989-2965   Fax:
Toll-Free: 866-935-1337
Address: 600 Townsend St., Ste. 200, San Francisco, CA 94103 United States

STOCK TICKER/OTHER:

Stock Ticker: PD   Exchange: NYS
Employees: 1,166   Fiscal Year Ends: 01/31
Parent Company:

SALARIES/BONUSES:

Top Exec. Salary: $586,667   Bonus: $
Second Exec. Salary: $450,735   Bonus: $

OTHER THOUGHTS:

Estimated Female Officers or Directors:
Hot Spot for Advancement for Women/Minorities:

Pandora Media LLC

NAIC Code: 515111

www.pandora.com

TYPES OF BUSINESS:

Radio Networks, Traditional, Satellite and Online
Music Streaming
Podcast Streaming
Personalized Listening
Technology
Mobile App
Online
Streaming Integration

BRANDS/DIVISIONS/AFFILIATES:

Sirius XM Holdings Inc
Music Genome Project
Podcast Genome Project

GROWTH PLANS/SPECIAL FEATURES:

Pandora Media, LLC is a music streaming and podcast discovery platform, providing personalized listening experiences to approximately 50 million users each month. Pandora's platform consists of its proprietary Music Genome Project and Podcast Genome Project technology via mobile app, website and integrations with over 2,000 connected products. Pandora also offers a digital audio advertising platform, enabling marketers and businesses to connect with listeners. Price plans include free, Pandora Plus without ads and other features for about $5 per month, and Pandora Premium for making/sharing playlists among other features for about $10 per month. Pandora operates as a subsidiary of Sirius XM Holdings, Inc.

CONTACTS: Note: Officers with more than one job title may be intentionally listed here more than once.

Roger Lynch, CEO
Karen Walker, Chief Accounting Officer
Gregory Maffei, Director
Roger Lynch, Director
Stephen Bene, General Counsel
Kristen Robinson, Other Executive Officer
John Trimble, Other Executive Officer
Christopher Phillips, Other Executive Officer

FINANCIAL DATA: Note: Data for latest year may not have been available at press time.

In U.S. $	2022	2021	2020	2019	2018	2017
Revenue	1,576,000,000	1,542,000,000	1,698,000,000	1,617,160,266	1,540,152,634	1,466,812,032
R&D Expense						
Operating Income						
Operating Margin %						
SGA Expense						
Net Income						
Operating Cash Flow						
Capital Expenditure						
EBITDA						
Return on Assets %						
Return on Equity %						
Debt to Equity						

CONTACT INFORMATION:

Phone: 510 451-4100   Fax:
Toll-Free:
Address: 2100 Franklin St. #700, Oakland, CA 94612 United States

STOCK TICKER/OTHER:

Stock Ticker: Subsidiary   Exchange:
Employees: 2,500   Fiscal Year Ends: 12/31
Parent Company: Sirius XM Holdings Inc

SALARIES/BONUSES:

Top Exec. Salary: $ Bonus: $
Second Exec. Salary: $ Bonus: $

OTHER THOUGHTS:

Estimated Female Officers or Directors: 5
Hot Spot for Advancement for Women/Minorities: Y

Sales, profits and employees may be estimates. Financial information, benefits and other data can change quickly and may vary from those stated here.

Paramount Streaming
www.paramount.com/brand/paramount-streaming

NAIC Code: 519130

TYPES OF BUSINESS:
Online Content
Web Site Management
Music Downloads
Entertainment News
Recipes

BRANDS/DIVISIONS/AFFILIATES:
Paramount Global
CBS Interactive Inc
Paramount+
CBSN
CBS.com
CBSNews.com
CBSSports.com
Pluto TV

CONTACTS: *Note: Officers with more than one job title may be intentionally listed here more than once.*
Robert M. Bakish, CEO
Naveen Chopra, CFO
Nancy Phillips, Exec. VP-Human Resources
Phil Wiser, CTO
Rosabel Tao, Sr. VP-Comm.
David Rice, Sr. VP-CBS Interactive Games
Jason Kint, Sr. VP-Interactive

GROWTH PLANS/SPECIAL FEATURES:
Paramount Streaming, formerly ViacomCBS Streaming and CBS Interactive, Inc., handles the online content operations of its parent company, Paramount Global. The firm delivers information and entertainment in the fields of technology, entertainment, sports and news. Paramount+ is a digital subscription, video-on-demand and live streaming service, and offers the 24/7 digital news network, CBSN. Paramount's streaming's additional sites include DirecTV Stream, Philo, Hulu with Live TV, Sling TV, Fubo TV, DirecTV Stream Ultimate, Fubo TV Elite, Vidgo, or Spectrum TV Choice., featuring both original films and television series. Paramount is headquartered in Manhattan, New York, with additional offices in California, Florida, Kentucky and Tennessee, USA, as well as in Canada, the U.K, Australia and Singapore.

FINANCIAL DATA: *Note: Data for latest year may not have been available at press time.*

In U.S. $	2022	2021	2020	2019	2018	2017
Revenue						
R&D Expense						
Operating Income						
Operating Margin %						
SGA Expense						
Net Income						
Operating Cash Flow						
Capital Expenditure						
EBITDA						
Return on Assets %						
Return on Equity %						
Debt to Equity						

CONTACT INFORMATION:
Phone: 415-344-2000   Fax:
Toll-Free:
Address: 235 Second St., San Francisco, CA 94105 United States

STOCK TICKER/OTHER:
Stock Ticker: Subsidiary   Exchange:
Employees: 2,080   Fiscal Year Ends:
Parent Company: Paramount Global

SALARIES/BONUSES:
Top Exec. Salary: $ Bonus: $
Second Exec. Salary: $ Bonus: $

OTHER THOUGHTS:
Estimated Female Officers or Directors: 2
Hot Spot for Advancement for Women/Minorities: Y

PayPal Holdings Inc

www.paypal.com

NAIC Code: 522320

TYPES OF BUSINESS:

Payment Processing-Intermediary
Online Payment Systems
Web-Enabled Payments
Online Auction Technology
Credit Cards
Debit Cards
Account Management
Money Transfer

BRANDS/DIVISIONS/AFFILIATES:

PayPal
PayPal Credit
Braintree
Venmo
Xoom
iZettle
Hyperwallet
Honey

CONTACTS: *Note: Officers with more than one job title may be intentionally listed here more than once.*

Daniel Schulman, CEO
John Rainey, CFO
John Donahoe, Chairman of the Board
Jeffrey Karbowski, Chief Accounting Officer
Louise Pentland, Chief Legal Officer
Aaron Karczmer, Chief Risk Officer
Jonathan Auerbach, Chief Strategy Officer
Sripada Shivananda, Chief Technology Officer
Peggy Alford, Executive VP, Divisional
Mark Britto, Executive VP

GROWTH PLANS/SPECIAL FEATURES:

PayPal was spun off from eBay in 2015 and provides electronic payment solutions to merchants and consumers, with a focus on online transactions. The company had 426 million active accounts at the end of 2023. The company also owns Venmo, a person-to-person payment platform.

FINANCIAL DATA: *Note: Data for latest year may not have been available at press time.*

In U.S. $	2022	2021	2020	2019	2018	2017
Revenue	27,518,000,000	25,371,000,000	21,454,000,000	17,772,000,000	15,451,000,000	
R&D Expense	3,253,000,000	3,038,000,000	2,642,000,000	2,085,000,000	1,831,000,000	
Operating Income	4,044,000,000	4,324,000,000	3,428,000,000	2,790,000,000	2,503,000,000	
Operating Margin %	.15%	.17%	.16%	.16%	.16%	
SGA Expense	4,356,000,000	4,559,000,000	3,931,000,000	3,112,000,000	2,855,000,000	
Net Income	2,419,000,000	4,169,000,000	4,202,000,000	2,459,000,000	2,057,000,000	
Operating Cash Flow	5,813,000,000	5,797,000,000	6,219,000,000	4,071,000,000	5,480,000,000	
Capital Expenditure	706,000,000	908,000,000	866,000,000	704,000,000	823,000,000	
EBITDA	4,987,000,000	5,596,000,000	6,463,000,000	4,025,000,000	3,229,000,000	
Return on Assets %	.03%	.06%	.07%	.05%	.05%	
Return on Equity %	.12%	.20%	.23%	.15%	.13%	
Debt to Equity	.51%	.37%	0.447	0.294		

CONTACT INFORMATION:

Phone: 408-967-1000   Fax: 650-864-8001
Toll-Free:
Address: 2211 N. First St., San Jose, CA 95131 United States

STOCK TICKER/OTHER:

Stock Ticker: PYPL   Exchange: NAS
Employees: 29,900   Fiscal Year Ends: 12/31
Parent Company:

SALARIES/BONUSES:

Top Exec. Salary: $302,885   Bonus: $4,000,000
Second Exec. Salary: Bonus: $1,035,000
$534,231

OTHER THOUGHTS:

Estimated Female Officers or Directors: 1
Hot Spot for Advancement for Women/Minorities: Y

Paysafe Limited

www.paysafe.com

NAIC Code: 522320

TYPES OF BUSINESS:

Online Payment Systems
Payment Software
Payment Equipment

BRANDS/DIVISIONS/AFFILIATES:

Paysafe
Paysafecash
paysafecard
Skrill
NETELLER
Income Access

GROWTH PLANS/SPECIAL FEATURES:

Paysafe Ltd is an integrated payments platform. Its core purpose is to enable businesses and consumers to connect and transact seamlessly through capabilities in payment processing, digital wallet, and online cash solutions. The company provides payment solutions through three primary lines of business: Integrated Processing, Digital Wallet, and eCash Solutions. It derives a majority of revenue from the USA followed by Germany, the UK, and all other countries.

CONTACTS: *Note: Officers with more than one job title may be intentionally listed here more than once.*

Philip McHugh, CEO
Danny Chazonoff, COO
Ismail (Izzy) Dawood, CFO
Louise Clements, CMO
Nick Walker, Chief Human Resources Officer
Roy Aston, CIO
William P. Foley, II, Chmn.

FINANCIAL DATA: *Note: Data for latest year may not have been available at press time.*

In U.S. $	2022	2021	2020	2019	2018	2017
Revenue	1,496,137,000	1,487,013,000	1,426,489,000	1,418,140,000	1,140,662,000	
R&D Expense						
Operating Income	80,778,000	80,756,000	157,603,000	186,510,000	173,731,000	
Operating Margin %	.05%	.05%	.11%	.13%		
SGA Expense	534,515,000	545,107,000	465,897,000	443,064,000	341,960,000	
Net Income	-1,862,655,000	-110,954,000	-126,715,000	-110,198,000	-39,711,000	
Operating Cash Flow	924,078,000	224,468,000	409,109,000	289,047,000	-27,290,000	
Capital Expenditure	150,046,000	147,749,000	86,919,000	160,103,000	92,899,000	
EBITDA	-1,521,339,000	231,761,000	248,595,000	326,186,000	364,296,000	
Return on Assets %	- .28%	- .02%	- .02%	- .02%		
Return on Equity %	-1.09%	- .05%	- .06%	- .05%		
Debt to Equity	3.10%	1.08%	1.708	1.559		

CONTACT INFORMATION:

Phone: 44 02038849226   Fax:
Toll-Free:
Address: 25 Canada Sq., Fl. 27, London, E14 5LQ United Kingdom

STOCK TICKER/OTHER:

Stock Ticker: PSFE   Exchange: NYS
Employees: 3,300   Fiscal Year Ends: 12/31
Parent Company:

SALARIES/BONUSES:

Top Exec. Salary: $ Bonus: $
Second Exec. Salary: $ Bonus: $

OTHER THOUGHTS:

Estimated Female Officers or Directors:
Hot Spot for Advancement for Women/Minorities:

PDD Holdings Inc

investor.pddholdings.com

NAIC Code: 454110

TYPES OF BUSINESS:

Electronic Shopping
eCommerce
Team Purchasing

BRANDS/DIVISIONS/AFFILIATES:

Pinduoduo
TEMU

GROWTH PLANS/SPECIAL FEATURES:

PDD Holdings (Nasdaq: PDD) is a multinational commerce group that owns and operates a portfolio of businesses. PDD Holdings aims to bring more businesses and people into the digital economy so that local communities and small businesses can benefit from the increased productivity and new opportunities. PDD Holdings has built a network of sourcing, logistics, and fulfilment capabilities, that support its underlying businesses.

CONTACTS: *Note: Officers with more than one job title may be intentionally listed here more than once.*

Zheng Huang, CEO
Junyun Xiao, Sr. VP-Oper.
Lei Chen, CTO

FINANCIAL DATA: *Note: Data for latest year may not have been available at press time.*

In U.S. $	2022	2021	2020	2019	2018	2017
Revenue	17,953,710,000	12,919,580,000	8,181,062,000	4,144,981,000	1,804,204,000	239,837,700
R&D Expense	1,428,061,000	1,236,622,000	947,710,100	532,234,800	153,475,300	17,764,410
Operating Income	4,180,739,000	948,412,600	-1,289,941,000	-1,174,137,000	-1,485,133,000	-80,546,210
Operating Margin %		.07%	-.16%	-.28%	-.82%	-.34%
SGA Expense	8,018,352,000	6,372,817,000	5,872,179,000	3,915,202,000	2,736,345,000	203,219,100
Net Income	4,336,976,000	1,068,314,000	-987,326,800	-958,154,400	-1,405,014,000	-72,211,520
Operating Cash Flow	6,670,589,000	3,958,114,000	3,877,477,000	2,038,116,000	1,068,211,000	1,332,022,000
Capital Expenditure	87,420,890	452,045,800	5,919,498	3,772,879	3,758,440	1,226,777
EBITDA	5,391,404,000	1,723,163,000	-784,608,100	-844,261,200	-1,336,669,000	-71,900,050
Return on Assets %		.05%	-.06%	-.12%	-.36%	-.07%
Return on Equity %		.11%	-.17%	-.32%	-1.16%	
Debt to Equity		.16%	0.247	0.229		

CONTACT INFORMATION:

Phone: 353 1-5397938   Fax:
Toll-Free:
Address: 25 Saint Stephen's Green, Fl. 1, Dublin 2, D02 XF99 Ireland

STOCK TICKER/OTHER:

Stock Ticker: PDD   Exchange: NAS
Employees: 12,992   Fiscal Year Ends: 12/31
Parent Company:

SALARIES/BONUSES:

Top Exec. Salary: $ Bonus: $
Second Exec. Salary: $ Bonus: $

OTHER THOUGHTS:

Estimated Female Officers or Directors:
Hot Spot for Advancement for Women/Minorities:

Perficient Inc

NAIC Code: 541512

www.perficient.com

TYPES OF BUSINESS:

Consulting-On-Site Technical Services
Middleware
Web Services
Content Management Software
Enterprise Portal Services
IT Outsourcing

GROWTH PLANS/SPECIAL FEATURES:

Perficient Inc provides a variety of information technology and consulting services that focus on digital experience, business optimization, and IT solutions. The company's services include big data analytics, technology platform implementations, enterprise content management, portals and collaboration, management consulting, custom applications, business integration, business process management, and customer relationship management. It serves the healthcare, financial services, retail, and electronics industries. The vast majority of the company's revenue comes from the United States.

BRANDS/DIVISIONS/AFFILIATES:

Sundog Interactive Inc
MedTouch LLC
Productora de Software SAS
Catalyst Networks Inc

CONTACTS: *Note: Officers with more than one job title may be intentionally listed here more than once.*

Jeffrey Davis, CEO
Paul Martin, CFO
Thomas Hogan, COO

FINANCIAL DATA: *Note: Data for latest year may not have been available at press time.*

In U.S. $	2022	2021	2020	2019	2018	2017
Revenue	905,062,000	761,027,000	612,133,000	565,527,000	498,375,000	485,261,000
R&D Expense						
Operating Income	148,195,000	109,944,000	68,448,000	56,529,000	39,632,000	33,574,000
Operating Margin %	.16%	.14%	.11%	.10%	.08%	.07%
SGA Expense	171,128,000	152,419,000	134,675,000	134,187,000	118,484,000	108,192,000
Net Income	104,392,000	52,091,000	30,181,000	37,125,000	24,559,000	18,581,000
Operating Cash Flow	118,068,000	84,916,000	117,960,000	77,965,000	68,580,000	55,221,000
Capital Expenditure	9,899,000	10,204,000	6,731,000	9,256,000	4,648,000	4,322,000
EBITDA	177,151,000	106,386,000	78,744,000	75,957,000	60,060,000	53,321,000
Return on Assets %	.11%	.06%	.04%	.06%	.05%	.04%
Return on Equity %	.27%	.14%	.08%	.10%	.07%	.05%
Debt to Equity	1.01%	.96%	0.54	0.379	.34%	0.15

CONTACT INFORMATION:

Phone: 314 930-2900   Fax: 512 531-6011
Toll-Free:
Address: 555 Maryville University Dr., Ste. 600, Saint Louis, MO 63141 United States

STOCK TICKER/OTHER:

Stock Ticker: PRFT   Exchange: NAS
Employees: 6,893   Fiscal Year Ends: 12/31
Parent Company:

SALARIES/BONUSES:

Top Exec. Salary: $650,000   Bonus: $
Second Exec. Salary: $513,333   Bonus: $

OTHER THOUGHTS:

Estimated Female Officers or Directors: 2
Hot Spot for Advancement for Women/Minorities:

Performics Inc

www.performics.com

NAIC Code: 541810E

TYPES OF BUSINESS:

Marketing Software
Search Engine Marketing
Affiliate Marketing Services
Data Feed Marketing
Online Lead Generation
Consumer Insights
Search Technologies
Marketing Consulting Services

BRANDS/DIVISIONS/AFFILIATES:

Publicis Groupe SA
PFX Consulting

CONTACTS: *Note: Officers with more than one job title may be intentionally listed here more than once.*

Michael Kahn, CEO
Patricia Powel, CFO
Craig Greenfield, COO
Jon Wegman, VP-Strategy & Planning
Lindsay Landsberg, Sr. VP-Bus. Dev.
Dona Ross, Sr. VP-Client Services
Luis Barreiro, Global Comm. Coordinator
Carrie Anger, Dir.-Acct.
Karishma Kiri, Sr. VP
Craig Greenfield, Exec. VP-Global Managing Dir.
Vidur Luthra, CEO-Resultrix
Frederic Joseph, CEO-EMEA

GROWTH PLANS/SPECIAL FEATURES:

Performics, Inc., a division of Publicis Groupe SA, provides performance-based marketing services and technologies for large, multi-channel retail companies. Performics utilizes its account managers, advanced market expertise and proprietary tracking and reporting technology platform to help clients acquire and retain online customers. Search engine marketing includes keyword management, paid listings, pay-per-click (PPC), paid inclusion and natural search optimization solutions. Performics collaborates with global brands, performing across paid, owned and earned media. The firm's services are divided into six groups: performance media, performance content, planning and insights, analytics and technology, performance solutions and PFX Consulting. Performance media includes media planning and optimization, buying, affiliate marketing, feeds, marketplace and digital co-operation. Performance content includes content strategy, creative development, content distribution, optimization and search engine optimization. Planning and insights include consumer insights, communications planning, competitive intelligence and strategic research. Analytics and technology includes business intelligence, data management personalization, cross-channel attribution modeling and predictive analysis. Performance solutions span intent-based marketing, web-based search optimization, bench tools, direct-commerce marketplace management, conversion optimization, conversation-to-commerce (C2C), performance-based local listings and discovering new consumers. Last, PFX Consulting is the company's marketing consultancy, focused on aiding brands in their business transformation via proprietary processes, products and analytical tools. Performics is based in the U.S., with offices throughout the Americas, Europe, the Middle East, Africa and Asia Pacific.

FINANCIAL DATA: *Note: Data for latest year may not have been available at press time.*

In U.S. $	2022	2021	2020	2019	2018	2017
Revenue						
R&D Expense						
Operating Income						
Operating Margin %						
SGA Expense						
Net Income						
Operating Cash Flow						
Capital Expenditure						
EBITDA						
Return on Assets %						
Return on Equity %						
Debt to Equity						

CONTACT INFORMATION:

Phone: 312-739-0222   Fax: 312-739-0223
Toll-Free: 800-615-6126
Address: 35 W. Wacker, Fl. 15, Chicago, IL 60601 United States

STOCK TICKER/OTHER:

Stock Ticker: Subsidiary   Exchange:
Employees: 3,400   Fiscal Year Ends: 12/31
Parent Company: Publicis Groupe SA

SALARIES/BONUSES:

Top Exec. Salary: $ Bonus: $
Second Exec. Salary: $ Bonus: $

OTHER THOUGHTS:

Estimated Female Officers or Directors: 1
Hot Spot for Advancement for Women/Minorities:

Perplexity AI

www.perplexity.ai

NAIC Code: 519130

TYPES OF BUSINESS:
Internet Search Engines, Online Publishing, Sharing, Gig and Consumer Services, Online Radio, TV and Entertainment Sites and Social Media

GROWTH PLANS/SPECIAL FEATURES:
Perplexity AI is an artificial intelligence (AI) company that aims at providing a straightforward and advertisement free search engine that is driven by AI. The firm's emphasis on natural language processing (NLP) and machine learning offer easily understood and usable answers to user queries. Perplexity AI was founded by former Google staffers Andy Konwinski, Aravind Srinivas, Denis Yarats and Johnny Ho.

BRANDS/DIVISIONS/AFFILIATES:

CONTACTS: Note: Officers with more than one job title may be intentionally listed here more than once.
Aravind Srinivas, CEO

FINANCIAL DATA: Note: Data for latest year may not have been available at press time.

In U.S. $	2022	2021	2020	2019	2018	2017
Revenue						
R&D Expense						
Operating Income						
Operating Margin %						
SGA Expense						
Net Income						
Operating Cash Flow						
Capital Expenditure						
EBITDA						
Return on Assets %						
Return on Equity %						
Debt to Equity						

CONTACT INFORMATION:
Phone: 707 641-2519   Fax:
Toll-Free:
Address: 341 Moultrie St., San Francisco, CA 94110 United States

STOCK TICKER/OTHER:
Stock Ticker: Private   Exchange:
Employees: Fiscal Year Ends:
Parent Company:

SALARIES/BONUSES:
Top Exec. Salary: $ Bonus: $
Second Exec. Salary: $ Bonus: $

OTHER THOUGHTS:
Estimated Female Officers or Directors:
Hot Spot for Advancement for Women/Minorities:

Photobucket Inc

NAIC Code: 519130

TYPES OF BUSINESS:

Online Photo Sharing
Digital Media Hosting
Image Storage
Image Editing
Image Add-ons
Personalized Gifts
Image Filters
Image Printing

BRANDS/DIVISIONS/AFFILIATES:

Photobucket.com

CONTACTS: *Note: Officers with more than one job title may be intentionally listed here more than once.*

Ted Leonard, CEO
Tom Munro, Pres.
Jim Goss, VP-Oper.
Erin Robinson, VP-Finance
Darren Kelly, Chief Revenue Officer

GROWTH PLANS/SPECIAL FEATURES:

Photobucket, Inc. is a visual media company that hosts various formats of digital content through its Photobucket.com website and mobile app. Monthly and annual plans offer 1 terabyte (TB) of storage with mobile auto backup, album creation, sorting tools, compression-free guarantee and carbon-neutral memory management for 5$ a month ($50 annually) or users can spend $8 a month ($80 annually) to add group sharing, personal/social sharing, photo editing tools, video playback. Users have access to all their photos on all their devices at any time, whether Android or iOS. Photos can be backed up automatically and shared on social platforms. A single image upload can be used on various forums, websites, blogs or marketplaces without the need to upload it over and over again. Photo filters are available, as well as cropping tools and other features for editing and personalizing images. Photobucket's platform encompasses intuitive privacy settings. Available products by Photobucket include canvas prints of uploaded photos, as well as enlargements, greeting cards, photo books and photo gifts.

FINANCIAL DATA: *Note: Data for latest year may not have been available at press time.*

In U.S. $	2022	2021	2020	2019	2018	2017
Revenue						
R&D Expense						
Operating Income						
Operating Margin %						
SGA Expense						
Net Income						
Operating Cash Flow						
Capital Expenditure						
EBITDA						
Return on Assets %						
Return on Equity %						
Debt to Equity						

CONTACT INFORMATION:

Phone: 303-226-6800   Fax: 303-395-1165
Toll-Free:
Address: 2399 Black St., Ste. 160, Denver, CO 80201 United States

STOCK TICKER/OTHER:

Stock Ticker: Private   Exchange:
Employees: 10   Fiscal Year Ends: 12/31
Parent Company:

SALARIES/BONUSES:

Top Exec. Salary: $ Bonus: $
Second Exec. Salary: $ Bonus: $

OTHER THOUGHTS:

Estimated Female Officers or Directors: 1
Hot Spot for Advancement for Women/Minorities: Y

Piksel Inc

www.piksel.com

NAIC Code: 511210F

TYPES OF BUSINESS:

Computer Software, Multimedia, Graphics & Publishing
Business IT Development
Business Transformation Solutions
Technical Design and Development Services
Technology Integration and Implementation
Technology Support Services
Mobile App Creation
Data and Analytics

BRANDS/DIVISIONS/AFFILIATES:

CONTACTS: Note: Officers with more than one job title may be intentionally listed here more than once.

Laura Bertolotti, Managing Dir.
Mark Portu, Chief Product Officer
Ralf Tillmann, Chief Strategy Officer
Kevin Joyce, Chief Commercial Officer

GROWTH PLANS/SPECIAL FEATURES:

Piksel, Inc. develops and supports information technology (IT) solutions. The firm's products and expertise in technological transformation helps organizations increase efficiency, productivity and customer satisfaction. Piksel supports customers in moving existing systems and processes to modern software architectures, and provides user experience, video management, revenue assurance, technical consultancy, cloud solutions, application management, digital channels, mobile development, digital living and e-commerce development. The company's solutions extend digital channels for engaging and reaching users; enables organizations to develop modern and innovative mobile apps; can use network-connected devices to collect data for massive machine learning applications; can be used for developing customer experience platforms to increase loyalty and sales; for connecting services to customers; for delivering online video services at scale; and for supporting customer billing processes, including identifying/correcting/preventing inaccuracies to avoid loss of revenue. Based in Italy, Piksel has offices in Milan and Catania.

FINANCIAL DATA: Note: Data for latest year may not have been available at press time.

In U.S. $	2022	2021	2020	2019	2018	2017
Revenue	70,000,000	68,000,000	66,161,260	60,146,600	53,992,400	60,727,400
R&D Expense						
Operating Income						
Operating Margin %						
SGA Expense						
Net Income				396,978,000	-8,337,900	-4,970,120
Operating Cash Flow						
Capital Expenditure						
EBITDA						
Return on Assets %						
Return on Equity %						
Debt to Equity						

CONTACT INFORMATION:

Phone: 39 02-842-781   Fax:
Toll-Free:
Address: Via Ernesto Breda, 176, Milan, 20126 Italy

STOCK TICKER/OTHER:

Stock Ticker: Private   Exchange:
Employees: 800   Fiscal Year Ends: 12/31
Parent Company:

SALARIES/BONUSES:

Top Exec. Salary: $ Bonus: $
Second Exec. Salary: $ Bonus: $

OTHER THOUGHTS:

Estimated Female Officers or Directors:
Hot Spot for Advancement for Women/Minorities:

Ping An Healthcare and Technology Company Limited

www.pagd.net
NAIC Code: 519130

TYPES OF BUSINESS:
Health Care Internet Portals
Healthcare Consultation

BRANDS/DIVISIONS/AFFILIATES:
Ping An Good Doctor
Health Guard 360

GROWTH PLANS/SPECIAL FEATURES:
Ping An Healthcare and Technology is the parent of Ping An Good Doctor, or PAGD, an online platform offering healthcare services in the form of a health maintenance organization, or HMO, model that provides commercial healthcare services and offers healthcare checkup, healthcare management, and corporate reimbursement for a fee. The company leverages the network of health providers from its parent Ping An Group, where it enters into contracts with physicians, hospitals, and specialists to offer their services to HMO participants. Other than commercial healthcare premium services, PAGD offers online consultations and prescription e-commerce online to individuals. The platform has 978 corporate clients and 43 million paying users. PAGD is 38.43% owned by its parent company.

CONTACTS: *Note: Officers with more than one job title may be intentionally listed here more than once.*
Weiho Fang, CEO

FINANCIAL DATA: *Note: Data for latest year may not have been available at press time.*

In U.S. $	2022	2021	2020	2019	2018	2017
Revenue	847,071,700	1,008,569,000	944,180,500	696,575,700	459,006,400	256,882,100
R&D Expense						
Operating Income	-162,862,200	-251,596,000	-92,992,620	-147,364,500	-178,868,400	-111,129,300
Operating Margin %		-.25%	-.10%	-.21%	-.39%	-.43%
SGA Expense	392,431,400	495,502,000	358,050,800	313,807,900	307,094,000	197,227,800
Net Income	-83,550,240	-211,524,200	-130,430,600	-100,917,200	-125,367,800	-137,741,600
Operating Cash Flow	-111,472,200	-192,933,900	-151,579,600	-69,335,940	-149,231,000	-66,549,590
Capital Expenditure	4,735,626	12,260,070	10,061,880	18,292,740	27,181,340	1,659,539
EBITDA	-55,886,770	-179,573,000	-105,278,900	-79,100,780	-119,276,900	-129,394,200
Return on Assets %		-.08%	-.06%	-.06%	-.10%	-.20%
Return on Equity %		-.10%	-.07%	-.07%	-.13%	-.31%
Debt to Equity		.01%	0.002	0.005		

CONTACT INFORMATION:
Phone: Fax: 86 21 3863 3719
Toll-Free:
Address: 166 Kaibin Rd., Block B, Fl. 17-19, Ping Ann Bldg., Shanghai, Shanghai 200032 China

STOCK TICKER/OTHER:
Stock Ticker: PIAHY Exchange: PINX
Employees: 2,556 Fiscal Year Ends: 12/31
Parent Company:

SALARIES/BONUSES:
Top Exec. Salary: $ Bonus: $
Second Exec. Salary: $ Bonus: $

OTHER THOUGHTS:
Estimated Female Officers or Directors:
Hot Spot for Advancement for Women/Minorities:

Pinterest Inc

www.pinterest.com

NAIC Code: 519130

TYPES OF BUSINESS:

Online Idea Sharing Site
Social Media Platform
Online Photo Sharing
Online Video Sharing
Project Management Platform

BRANDS/DIVISIONS/AFFILIATES:

Pinterest.com
Pinterest Lens
Vochi

GROWTH PLANS/SPECIAL FEATURES:

Pinterest is an online product and idea discovery platform that helps users gather ideas on everything from recipes to cook to destinations to travel to. Founded in 2010, the platform consists of a largely female audience, at roughly two thirds of its 498 million monthly active users. The company generates revenue by selling digital ads and is now rolling out more in-platform e-commerce features.

Employee benefits offered.

CONTACTS: *Note: Officers with more than one job title may be intentionally listed here more than once.*

Benjamin Silbermann, CEO
Todd Morgenfeld, CFO
Andrea Acosta, Chief Accounting Officer
Evan Sharp, Co-Founder
Christine Flores, General Counsel
Naveen Gavini, Other Corporate Officer

FINANCIAL DATA: *Note: Data for latest year may not have been available at press time.*

In U.S. $	2022	2021	2020	2019	2018	2017
Revenue	2,802,574,000	2,578,027,000	1,692,658,000	1,142,761,000	755,932,000	
R&D Expense	948,980,000	780,264,000	606,194,000	1,207,059,000	251,662,000	
Operating Income	-101,677,000	326,187,000	-142,504,000	-1,388,866,000	-74,721,000	
Operating Margin %	-.04%	.13%	-.08%	-1.22%	-.10%	
SGA Expense	1,276,674,000	942,256,000	779,610,000	965,665,000	337,407,000	
Net Income	-96,047,000	316,438,000	-128,323,000	-1,361,371,000	-62,974,000	
Operating Cash Flow	469,202,000	752,907,000	28,826,000	657,000	-60,369,000	
Capital Expenditure	28,984,000	9,031,000	17,401,000	33,783,000	22,194,000	
EBITDA	-55,188,000	353,687,000	-89,397,000	-1,330,911,000	-40,710,000	
Return on Assets %	-.03%	.10%	-.05%	-.77%	-.05%	
Return on Equity %	-.03%	.12%	-.06%	-1.91%		
Debt to Equity	.05%	.07%	0.062	0.086		

CONTACT INFORMATION:

Phone: 415-762-7100   Fax:
Toll-Free:
Address: 505 Brannan St., San Francisco, CA 94107 United States

STOCK TICKER/OTHER:

Stock Ticker: PINS   Exchange: NYS
Employees: 3,987   Fiscal Year Ends: 12/31
Parent Company:

SALARIES/BONUSES:

Top Exec. Salary: $53,030   Bonus: $500,000
Second Exec. Salary: $393,417   Bonus: $

OTHER THOUGHTS:

Estimated Female Officers or Directors:
Hot Spot for Advancement for Women/Minorities: Y

Sales, profits and employees may be estimates. Financial information, benefits and other data can change quickly and may vary from those stated here.

Planet Labs PBC

NAIC Code: 517410

www.planet.com

TYPES OF BUSINESS:

Satellite Telecommunication Services (Including Satellite Telephone Companies)
Satellite Design and Manufacture
Satellite Imagery
Mapping
Whole-Earth Imaging Datasets
Analytics
Machine Learning
Cloud-based Platform

BRANDS/DIVISIONS/AFFILIATES:

GROWTH PLANS/SPECIAL FEATURES:

Planet Labs PBC is an Earth-imaging company. The company provides daily satellite data that helps businesses, governments, researchers, and journalists understand the physical world and take action.

Planet Labs offers its employees comprehensive health benefits, learning/tuition reimbursement and company perks.

CONTACTS: *Note: Officers with more than one job title may be intentionally listed here more than once.*

Will Marshall, CEO
Kevin Weil, Pres.-Product & Business
Ashley Fieglein Johnson, CFO
Rosanne Saccone, CMO
Kristi Erickson, Chief People Officer
Robbie Schingler, Chief Strategy Officer
Brian Hernacki, Sr. VP-Software

FINANCIAL DATA: *Note: Data for latest year may not have been available at press time.*

In U.S. $	2022	2021	2020	2019	2018	2017
Revenue	131,209,000	113,168,000	95,736,000			
R&D Expense	66,684,000	43,825,000	37,871,000			
Operating Income	-128,051,000	-87,442,000	-106,460,000			
Operating Margin %	- .98%	- .77%				
SGA Expense	109,589,000	69,402,000	61,932,000			
Net Income	-137,124,000	-127,103,000	-123,714,000			
Operating Cash Flow	-42,211,000	-4,027,000	-33,687,000			
Capital Expenditure	14,931,000	30,126,000	24,101,000			
EBITDA	-81,199,000	-54,371,000	-39,009,000			
Return on Assets %	- .22%	- .33%				
Return on Equity %	- .36%	- .78%				
Debt to Equity		1.45%				

CONTACT INFORMATION:

Phone: 415 829-3313   Fax:
Toll-Free:
Address: 645 Harrison St., Fl. 4, San Francisco, CA 94107 United States

STOCK TICKER/OTHER:

Stock Ticker: PL   Exchange: NYS
Employees: 1,100   Fiscal Year Ends: 01/31
Parent Company:

SALARIES/BONUSES:

Top Exec. Salary: $400,000   Bonus: $
Second Exec. Salary: Bonus: $
$370,000

OTHER THOUGHTS:

Estimated Female Officers or Directors:
Hot Spot for Advancement for Women/Minorities:

PoF (Plentyoffish Media ULC)

www.pof.com

NAIC Code: 511210G

TYPES OF BUSINESS:
Computer Software, Electronic Games, Apps & Entertainment
Online Dating Platform
Mobile App Dating Platform
Match-Making Technology

BRANDS/DIVISIONS/AFFILIATES:
Match Group Inc

GROWTH PLANS/SPECIAL FEATURES:
Plentyoffish Media ULC operates Plenty of Fish (PoF), a dating platform. Every day, over 3 million people utilize PoF to help them connect with and meet someone. Established in Vancouver, Canada in 2003, PoF began as a free dating site and was later acquired by Match Group, Inc. As of early-2024, the company is available in 11 languages and more than 20 countries on web, iOS and Android devices. PoF members are encouraged to represent themselves truthfully; therefore, images that are heavily edited or use filters are removed. Memes and images that contain overlaid text or watermarks are also not allowed. Members are matched according to their likes, dislikes, hobbies, lifestyle, ambitions and other shared information. Members can learn who picked them from PoF.

PoF offers its employees health benefits, an employee stock purchase plan and other company plans, options and perks.

CONTACTS:
Note: Officers with more than one job title may be intentionally listed here more than once.

Bernard Kim, CEO- Corp.

FINANCIAL DATA:
Note: Data for latest year may not have been available at press time.

In U.S. $	2022	2021	2020	2019	2018	2017
Revenue						
R&D Expense						
Operating Income						
Operating Margin %						
SGA Expense						
Net Income						
Operating Cash Flow						
Capital Expenditure						
EBITDA						
Return on Assets %						
Return on Equity %						
Debt to Equity						

CONTACT INFORMATION:
Phone: 604-688-8848   Fax:
Toll-Free:
Address: 142-757 West Hastings, PMB 670, Vancouver, BC V6C 1A1 Canada

STOCK TICKER/OTHER:
Stock Ticker: Subsidiary   Exchange:
Employees: Fiscal Year Ends:
Parent Company: Match Group Inc

SALARIES/BONUSES:
Top Exec. Salary: $ Bonus: $
Second Exec. Salary: $ Bonus: $

OTHER THOUGHTS:
Estimated Female Officers or Directors:
Hot Spot for Advancement for Women/Minorities:

Sales, profits and employees may be estimates. Financial information, benefits and other data can change quickly and may vary from those stated here.

PointClickCare

www.pointclickcare.com

NAIC Code: 511210D

TYPES OF BUSINESS:

Computer Software, Healthcare & Biotechnology
Cloud Healthcare Software
Senior Care Software Solutions
Healthcare Collaboration Solutions
Healthcare Management
Analytics
Care Insights
Care Documentation Solutions

BRANDS/DIVISIONS/AFFILIATES:

Audacious Inquiry

CONTACTS: Note: Officers with more than one job title may be intentionally listed here more than once.

Dave Wessinger, CEO
B.J. Boyle, Chief Product Officer
James Yersh, CFO
Annie McBride, CMO
Orysia Semotiuk, Chief People Officer
Bill McQuaide, Chief Transformation Officer
Betsy S. Atkins, Chmn.

GROWTH PLANS/SPECIAL FEATURES:

PointClickCare provides a cloud-based platform that supports a large network of senior care providers in the skilled nursing facility, senior living community and home health agency markets. The company's technology seamlessly connects providers across the senior care continuum, enabling person-centered care, with an emphasis on quality and outcomes. Products offered by PointClickCare include a skilled nursing core platform, analytics, care insights, infection prevention and control, market insights, performance insights, automated care messaging, connection to a national-level health data network, integrated direct messaging, secure conversations, care insights, care documentation and service delivery, integrated medication management, nutrition management, point-of-care access, practitioner engagement, skin and wound care, medication administration record maintenance, eligibility verification and many more. Industry solutions include nursing, senior living, providers, health plans, hospital associations, health information exchange (HIE), federal government, state government, life sciences, continuing care retirement communities (CCRC), pharmacy and group home. PointClickCare is headquartered in Ontario, Canada, with additional offices in both Canada and the U.S.

PointClickCare offers its employees a flexible work model, including work from home and remote.

FINANCIAL DATA: Note: Data for latest year may not have been available at press time.

In U.S. $	2022	2021	2020	2019	2018	2017
Revenue	196,365,000	188,811,909	179,820,866	175,649,198	167,284,950	159,319,000
R&D Expense						
Operating Income						
Operating Margin %						
SGA Expense						
Net Income						
Operating Cash Flow						
Capital Expenditure						
EBITDA						
Return on Assets %						
Return on Equity %						
Debt to Equity						

CONTACT INFORMATION:

Phone: 905-858-8885   Fax: 905-858-2248
Toll-Free: 800-277-5889
Address: 5570 Explorer Dr., Mississauga, ON L4W 0C4 Canada

STOCK TICKER/OTHER:

Stock Ticker: Private   Exchange:
Employees: 1,450   Fiscal Year Ends: 10/31
Parent Company:

SALARIES/BONUSES:

Top Exec. Salary: $ Bonus: $
Second Exec. Salary: $ Bonus: $

OTHER THOUGHTS:

Estimated Female Officers or Directors: 2
Hot Spot for Advancement for Women/Minorities: Y

Polished.com Inc

investor.polished.com/overview/default.aspx

NAIC Code: 454110

TYPES OF BUSINESS:

Online Sales, B2C Ecommerce, Sharing Economy Platforms

BRANDS/DIVISIONS/AFFILIATES:

GROWTH PLANS/SPECIAL FEATURES:

Polished.com Inc is an e-commerce destination for home furnishings, appliances, furniture, home goods, and related products. It sells various products such as refrigerators, ranges, ovens, dishwashers, microwaves, freezers, washers, and dryers. The firm's brand portfolio consists of Bosch, Whirlpool, GE, Maytag, LG, Samsung, Sharp, and Kitchen Aid, among others.

CONTACTS: *Note: Officers with more than one job title may be intentionally listed here more than once.*

John (Rick) Bunka, Interim CEO
Robert (Bob) Barry, Interim CFO
Jody Rusnak, Chief Merchandising & Brand Innovation Officer

FINANCIAL DATA: *Note: Data for latest year may not have been available at press time.*

In U.S. $	2022	2021	2020	2019	2018	2017
Revenue	534,474,000	345,725,000	55,134,000		56,307,960	
R&D Expense						
Operating Income	-426,000	12,582,000	-12,626,000		3,258,949	
Operating Margin %		.06%				
SGA Expense	78,487,000	50,664,000	19,331,000		7,599,488	
Net Income	-125,965,000	-7,582,000	-21,568,000		2,005,378	
Operating Cash Flow	-46,681,000	-18,328,000	5,409,000		442,074	
Capital Expenditure	1,420,000	1,899,000	113,000			
EBITDA	-118,978,000	2,759,000	-19,449,000		2,045,166	
Return on Assets %		.04%				
Return on Equity %		.08%				
Debt to Equity		.30%				

CONTACT INFORMATION:

Phone: 888 768-1710   Fax:
Toll-Free:
Address: 13850 Manchester Road, St. Louis, MO 63011 United States

STOCK TICKER/OTHER:

Stock Ticker: POL   Exchange: ASE
Employees: 391   Fiscal Year Ends: 12/31
Parent Company:

SALARIES/BONUSES:

Top Exec. Salary: $310,961   Bonus: $
Second Exec. Salary: Bonus: $
$306,308

OTHER THOUGHTS:

Estimated Female Officers or Directors:
Hot Spot for Advancement for Women/Minorities:

Poshmark Inc

poshmark.com

NAIC Code: 454110

TYPES OF BUSINESS:

Electronic Shopping
Ecommerce
Apparel
Home
Beauty
Used
New
Payment Platform

BRANDS/DIVISIONS/AFFILIATES:

GROWTH PLANS/SPECIAL FEATURES:

Poshmark is one of the largest players in a quickly growing e-commerce resale space, connecting over 100 million registered users on a platform that sells men's and women's apparel, accessories, shoes, and more recently consumer electronics and pet products. The marketplace operates the U.S. and Canada with a capital-light, peer-to-peer model that dovetails nicely with prevailing trends toward social commerce, apparel resale and an ongoing pivot toward the e-commerce channel. Since its inception, the seller community has sold over 300 million items on the platform, earning over $6 billion.

CONTACTS: *Note: Officers with more than one job title may be intentionally listed here more than once.*

Manish Chandra, CEO
Chetan Pungaliya, Sr. VP-Eng.
Kapil Agrawal, CFO
Tracy Sun, Sr. VP-New Markets
Gautam Golwala, CTO

FINANCIAL DATA: *Note: Data for latest year may not have been available at press time.*

In U.S. $	2022	2021	2020	2019	2018	2017
Revenue	339,050,000	326,008,992	261,600,992	204,983,008	148,304,992	100,000,000
R&D Expense						
Operating Income						
Operating Margin %						
SGA Expense						
Net Income		-98,329,000	18,846,000	-47,724,000	-14,475,000	
Operating Cash Flow						
Capital Expenditure						
EBITDA						
Return on Assets %						
Return on Equity %						
Debt to Equity						

CONTACT INFORMATION:

Phone: 650-262-4771   Fax:
Toll-Free:
Address: 203 Redwood Shores Pkwy, 8/Fl, Redwood City, CA 94065 United States

STOCK TICKER/OTHER:

Stock Ticker: Subsidiary   Exchange:
Employees: 750   Fiscal Year Ends: 12/31
Parent Company: Naver Corp

SALARIES/BONUSES:

Top Exec. Salary: $ Bonus: $
Second Exec. Salary: $ Bonus: $

OTHER THOUGHTS:

Estimated Female Officers or Directors:
Hot Spot for Advancement for Women/Minorities:

Sales, profits and employees may be estimates. Financial information, benefits and other data can change quickly and may vary from those stated here.

Princess Polly Group Pty Ltd

us.princesspolly.com

NAIC Code: 454110

TYPES OF BUSINESS:

Online Sales, B2C Ecommerce, Sharing Economy Platforms
Women's Clothing Retail

BRANDS/DIVISIONS/AFFILIATES:

GROWTH PLANS/SPECIAL FEATURES:

Princess Polly is an Australian-based online women's fashion retailer and was founded in 2010 in Queensland, Australia. The firm owns an e-commerce site where it sells women's clothing in categories such as dresses, tops, rompers/jumpsuits, bottoms, jackets, lingerie, sweaters/sweatshirts, lower impact, swim, curve, tall, petite and edits. Princess Polly has headquarters in Queensland, Australia and California, USA after it expanded to the U.S. market in 2018 with the backing of A.K.A. Brands.

CONTACTS:
Note: Officers with more than one job title may be intentionally listed here more than once.

Eirin Bryett, CEO

FINANCIAL DATA:
Note: Data for latest year may not have been available at press time.

In U.S. $	2022	2021	2020	2019	2018	2017
Revenue	40,000,000					
R&D Expense						
Operating Income						
Operating Margin %						
SGA Expense						
Net Income						
Operating Cash Flow						
Capital Expenditure						
EBITDA						
Return on Assets %						
Return on Equity %						
Debt to Equity						

CONTACT INFORMATION:

Phone: 61 7-5610-2516   Fax:
Toll-Free:
Address: P.O. BOX 5984, Gold Coast MC, QLD 9726 Australia

STOCK TICKER/OTHER:

Stock Ticker: Subsidiary   Exchange:
Employees: Fiscal Year Ends:
Parent Company: a.k.a. Brands Holding Corp

SALARIES/BONUSES:

Top Exec. Salary: $ Bonus: $
Second Exec. Salary: $ Bonus: $

OTHER THOUGHTS:

Estimated Female Officers or Directors:
Hot Spot for Advancement for Women/Minorities:

Procore Technologies Inc

NAIC Code: 511210N

www.procore.com

TYPES OF BUSINESS:

Computer Software, Product Lifecycle, Engineering, Design & CAD
Cloud Software
Construction Management

GROWTH PLANS/SPECIAL FEATURES:

Procore Technologies Inc is a cloud-based construction management software company. It generates revenue through subscriptions for access to its software products. The company's products include Design Coordination, BIM, Field Productivity, Project Financials, Invoice Management, Portfolio Financials, Capital Planning, Accounting Integrations, and Analytics.

Procore offers its employees comprehensive health benefits, retirement plans and employee enrichment programs.

BRANDS/DIVISIONS/AFFILIATES:

Procore

CONTACTS: Note: Officers with more than one job title may be intentionally listed here more than once.

Craig Courtemanche, CEO
Paul Lyandres, CFO
William Fleming, Chief Accounting Officer
Benjamin Singer, Chief Legal Officer
Sam Crigman, Chief Technology Officer
Patricia Wadors, Other Executive Officer
Steve Zahm, Other Executive Officer
Dennis Lyandres, Other Executive Officer

FINANCIAL DATA: Note: Data for latest year may not have been available at press time.

In U.S. $	2022	2021	2020	2019	2018	2017
Revenue	720,203,000	514,821,000	400,291,000	289,194,000	186,396,000	112,251,000
R&D Expense	270,982,000	237,290,000	124,661,000	87,022,000	55,950,000	39,762,000
Operating Income	-290,454,000	-285,927,000	-58,530,000	-82,624,000	-55,043,000	-55,128,000
Operating Margin %	-.40%	-.56%	-.15%	-.29%	-.30%	
SGA Expense	591,259,000	465,146,000	262,497,000	231,630,000	148,088,000	102,264,000
Net Income	-286,931,000	-265,165,000	-96,167,000	-83,107,000	-56,671,000	-55,540,000
Operating Cash Flow	12,608,000	36,730,000	21,853,000	-7,004,000	-21,103,000	-24,660,000
Capital Expenditure	49,430,000	27,631,000	18,966,000	27,990,000	21,832,000	9,117,000
EBITDA	-221,291,000	-250,219,000	-68,813,000	-67,225,000	-46,773,000	-49,662,000
Return on Assets %	-.17%	-.21%	-.15%	-.21%	-.21%	
Return on Equity %	-.25%	-.58%				
Debt to Equity	.07%	.07%				

CONTACT INFORMATION:

Phone: 866-477-6267   Fax: 866-281-2906
Toll-Free:
Address: 6309 Carpinteria Ave., Carpinteria, CA 93013 United States

STOCK TICKER/OTHER:

Stock Ticker: PCOR   Exchange: NYS
Employees: 3,568   Fiscal Year Ends: 12/31
Parent Company:

SALARIES/BONUSES:

Top Exec. Salary: $517,500   Bonus: $
Second Exec. Salary: $297,917   Bonus: $200,000

OTHER THOUGHTS:

Estimated Female Officers or Directors:
Hot Spot for Advancement for Women/Minorities:

Progress Software Corporation

web.progress.com

NAIC Code: 511210I

TYPES OF BUSINESS:
Software, Application Development & Integration
Consulting & Technical Support Services
Data Connectivity Products
Data Management Software

BRANDS/DIVISIONS/AFFILIATES:
Progress OpenEdge
Progress DataDirect
Progress DataDirect Hybrid Data Pipeline
NativeChat
NativeScript
Telerik
Corticon
Kemp

CONTACTS: Note: Officers with more than one job title may be intentionally listed here more than once.
Yogesh Gupta, CEO
Anthony Folger, CFO
John Egan, Chairman of the Board
Tony Murphy, Chief Information Officer
Stephen Faberman, Chief Legal Officer
Loren Jarrett, General Manager, Divisional
Sundar Subramanian, General Manager, Divisional
Kathryn Kulikoski, Other Corporate Officer
Jeremy Segal, Senior VP, Divisional
John Ainsworth, Senior VP, Divisional
Gary Quinn, Senior VP, Divisional
Jennifer Ortiz, Vice President, Divisional

GROWTH PLANS/SPECIAL FEATURES:
Progress Software Corporation is a provider of cloud-based security solutions to large-and mid-sized organizations in a wide range of industries. Its product includes OpenEdge; Chef; Developer Tools; Kemp LoadMaster; MOVEit; DataDirect; WhatsUp Gold; Sitefinity; Flowmon and Corticon. The company derives revenue from perpetual licenses to its products, but some products also use term licensing models. Its cloud-based offerings use a subscription-based model. A majority of the firm's revenue is generated in the United States and it also has presence in Canada, the Middle East, and Africa (EMEA), Latin America, and Asia Pacific.

FINANCIAL DATA: Note: Data for latest year may not have been available at press time.

In U.S. $	2022	2021	2020	2019	2018	2017
Revenue	602,013,000	531,313,000	442,150,000	413,298,000	378,981,000	
R&D Expense	114,568,000	103,338,000	88,599,000	88,572,000	79,739,000	
Operating Income	127,445,000	126,512,000	117,271,000	72,169,000	75,470,000	
Operating Margin %	.21%	.24%	.27%	.17%	.20%	
SGA Expense	218,636,000	191,018,000	154,117,000	155,061,000	143,558,000	
Net Income	95,069,000	78,420,000	79,722,000	26,400,000	49,670,000	
Operating Cash Flow	192,160,000	178,530,000	144,847,000	128,484,000	121,352,000	
Capital Expenditure	6,090,000	4,654,000	6,517,000	3,998,000	7,250,000	
EBITDA	207,777,000	168,563,000	141,570,000	95,087,000	110,447,000	
Return on Assets %	.07%	.07%	.08%	.03%	.07%	
Return on Equity %	.23%	.21%	.24%	.08%	.14%	
Debt to Equity	1.57%	1.35%	1.131	0.86	.34%	

CONTACT INFORMATION:
Phone: 781 280-4000   Fax: 781 280-4095
Toll-Free: 800-477-6473
Address: 14 Oak Park, Bedford, MA 01730 United States

STOCK TICKER/OTHER:
Stock Ticker: PRGS
Employees: 2,284
Parent Company:

Exchange: NAS
Fiscal Year Ends: 11/30

SALARIES/BONUSES:
Top Exec. Salary: $575,000   Bonus: $
Second Exec. Salary: Bonus: $
$414,423

OTHER THOUGHTS:
Estimated Female Officers or Directors: 2
Hot Spot for Advancement for Women/Minorities: Y

ProQuest LLC

NAIC Code: 519130

www.proquest.com

TYPES OF BUSINESS:

Online Database of News and Information
Dissertation Publishing
Streaming Videos
eBook Platforms
Content Discovery Systems
Library Tools
Primary Research Collections
News Collections

BRANDS/DIVISIONS/AFFILIATES:

Clarivate plc
Summon
RefWorks
Pivot
Intota
Ex Libris

CONTACTS: *Note: Officers with more than one job title may be intentionally listed here more than once.*

Jonathan Gear, CEO
Jonathan Collins, CFO
Julie Wilson, Chief People Officer
Bill Graff, CIO
Kevin A. Norris, General Counsel
Tim Wahlberg, Sr. VP
Simon Beale, Sr. VP
Kevin Sayar, Sr. VP
Rafael Sidi, Sr. VP

GROWTH PLANS/SPECIAL FEATURES:

ProQuest, LLC serves researchers and librarians throughout the world by offering a portfolio of assets, such as content, technologies and deep expertise. ProQuest's wide range of content includes 90,000 authoritative sources and 6 billion digital pages that span six centuries. It includes a world-leading collection of dissertations and theses; 20 million pages and three centuries of global, national, regional and specialty newspapers; more than 450,000 eBooks; rich aggregated collections of the world's most important scholarly journals and periodicals; and unique vaults of digitized historical collections from great libraries and museums, as well as organizations as varied as the Royal Archives, the Associated Press and the National Association for the Advancement of Colored People. This content allows the research of virtually any topic from multiple perspectives and across multiple formats. For librarians, ProQuest provides practical and interoperable software-as-a-service solutions for the acquisition, assessment, management and marketing of their information collections. ProQuest's aggregation solutions abstract and index content, with historical collections being preserved and digitized into archival collections. The company's Summon discovery service enables patrons to search their library's collection through a single online portal; RefWorks provides students and faculty with a digital space for collaboration and management of all their research; Pivot is a resource that matches funding and collaborators with researchers; and Intota is a management platform that enables libraries to shift from print to digital formats. Additionally, Ex Libris, a ProQuest subsidiary, is a leading global provider of cloud-based solutions that enable institutions and their individual users to create, manage, and share knowledge. ProQuest is headquartered in Michigan, with offices throughout the world. ProQuest is a subsidiary of Clarivate plc, a provider of information and insights regarding innovation.

FINANCIAL DATA: *Note: Data for latest year may not have been available at press time.*

In U.S. $	2022	2021	2020	2019	2018	2017
Revenue	634,400,000	610,000,000	604,012,500	619,500,000	590,000,000	572,000,000
R&D Expense						
Operating Income						
Operating Margin %						
SGA Expense						
Net Income						
Operating Cash Flow						
Capital Expenditure						
EBITDA						
Return on Assets %						
Return on Equity %						
Debt to Equity						

CONTACT INFORMATION:

Phone: 734-761-4700   Fax:
Toll-Free: 800-521-0600
Address: 789 E. Eisenhower Pkwy., Ann Arbor, MI 48108 United States

STOCK TICKER/OTHER:

Stock Ticker: Subsidiary   Exchange:
Employees: 2,450   Fiscal Year Ends:
Parent Company: Clarivate plc

SALARIES/BONUSES:

Top Exec. Salary: $ Bonus: $
Second Exec. Salary: $ Bonus: $

OTHER THOUGHTS:

Estimated Female Officers or Directors: 1
Hot Spot for Advancement for Women/Minorities:

Sales, profits and employees may be estimates. Financial information, benefits and other data can change quickly and may vary from those stated here.

PSI Capital Inc

www.psi-capital.com

NAIC Code: 454110

TYPES OF BUSINESS:

Online Retail-Music Downloads
Music Portal
Music Merchandise
Digital Rights Digital Rights Management

BRANDS/DIVISIONS/AFFILIATES:

ARTISTdirect
ARTISTdirect Opportunity Fund
Ticket Fairy (The)
Venga
Rubicon Entertainment
Drama Club
World Armwrestling League

CONTACTS: *Note: Officers with more than one job title may be intentionally listed here more than once.*

James A. Graf, CEO
Augustine Wong, Pres.
Rene Rousselet, Principal Acct. Officer
Frederick W. Field, CEO-Artistdirect Records LLC
Laura Laytham, Sr. VP

GROWTH PLANS/SPECIAL FEATURES:

PSI Capital, Inc. owns and operates ARTISTdirect, an online platform for the music industry. The ArtistDirect.com website offers multimedia music content, including news, artists and videos. News categories include the latest music, live show reviews and specific music by genre. Specific information about bands and artists are available, as well as music videos. Genres include, but are not limited to, pop, hip hop, R&B, soul, rock, country, hard rock, alternative rock, indie rock, electronica, punk, jazz, Latin, blues, new age and gospel. The Singer/Songwriter category highlights an ARTIST of the week, offers exclusive interviews and much more. ArtistDirectInterviews.com offers exclusive interviews with established and emerging artists from all over the world. ARTISTdirect offers free downloads as well as ecommerce options, and is available on web and mobile application across any device. ARTISTdirect serves as the catalyst for the $25 million ARTISTdirect Opportunity Fund, which was established to invest in high-growth ventures operating in compelling niches in the broader music industry ecosystem. Targeted sectors are engaged in new technology and include music rights, licensing and royalty payments, as well as fan-related big data, ticketing and related commerce and logistics capabilities. Current investments include The Ticket Fairy, Venga, Rubicon Entertainment, Drama Club and the World Armwrestling League.

FINANCIAL DATA: *Note: Data for latest year may not have been available at press time.*

In U.S. $	2022	2021	2020	2019	2018	2017
Revenue						
R&D Expense						
Operating Income						
Operating Margin %						
SGA Expense						
Net Income						
Operating Cash Flow						
Capital Expenditure						
EBITDA						
Return on Assets %						
Return on Equity %						
Debt to Equity						

CONTACT INFORMATION:

Phone: 323-569-8698   Fax:
Toll-Free:
Address: 1450 2nd St., Santa Monica, CA 90401 United States

STOCK TICKER/OTHER:

Stock Ticker: Private   Exchange:
Employees: 70   Fiscal Year Ends: 12/31
Parent Company:

SALARIES/BONUSES:

Top Exec. Salary: $ Bonus: $
Second Exec. Salary: $ Bonus: $

OTHER THOUGHTS:

Estimated Female Officers or Directors:
Hot Spot for Advancement for Women/Minorities:

Publicis Sapient

NAIC Code: 541512

www.publicissapient.com

TYPES OF BUSINESS:

IT Consulting
Digital Transformation Solutions
Consulting and Technology Services
Customer Engagement and Analytics
Commerce Solutions
Technology Modernization
Business Innovation
Artificial Intelligence

BRANDS/DIVISIONS/AFFILIATES:

Publicis Groupe SA
Changi Consulting

CONTACTS: *Note: Officers with more than one job title may be intentionally listed here more than once.*

Nigel Vaz, CEO
Nathalie Le Bos, CFO
Teresa Barreira, CMO
Kameshwari Rao, Chief People Officer
Alan Wexler, Executive VP
J. Moore, Founder
Joseph LaSala, General Counsel
Harry Register, Managing Director, Divisional
Christian Oversohl, Managing Director, Geographical
Laurie MacLaren, Senior VP, Divisional

GROWTH PLANS/SPECIAL FEATURES:

Publicis Sapient, a subsidiary of Publicis Groupe SA, is a business consulting and technology services firm focused on digital transformation and the dynamics of an always-on world. The firm's platform is designed to help clients reimagine core business activities via transformation to drive growth and improve operating efficiency. Solutions offered include: generative ai, experience transformation, customer engagement, digital commerce, digital engineering, cloud and infrastructure, application and infrastructure management services and innovation. Services offered by Publicis Sapient include customer experience and design, data and artificial intelligence, enterprise platforms, product management, strategy and consulting, technology and engineering. The firm serves a wide range of industries, including consumer products, energy and commodities, financial services, health, public sector, retail, telecom, media and technology, transportation and mobility, travel and hospitality. Based in the USA, the firm has more than 53 offices in 20 countries worldwide.

FINANCIAL DATA: *Note: Data for latest year may not have been available at press time.*

In U.S. $	2022	2021	2020	2019	2018	2017
Revenue	2,085,000,000	1,950,000,000	1,877,871,996	1,805,646,150	1,765,050,000	1,681,000,000
R&D Expense						
Operating Income						
Operating Margin %						
SGA Expense						
Net Income						
Operating Cash Flow						
Capital Expenditure						
EBITDA						
Return on Assets %						
Return on Equity %						
Debt to Equity						

CONTACT INFORMATION:

Phone: 617 621-0200   Fax: 617 621-1300
Toll-Free: 877-454-9860
Address: 40 Water St., Boston, MA 02109 United States

STOCK TICKER/OTHER:

Stock Ticker: Subsidiary   Exchange:
Employees: 20,000   Fiscal Year Ends: 12/31
Parent Company: Publicis Groupe SA

SALARIES/BONUSES:

Top Exec. Salary: $ Bonus: $
Second Exec. Salary: $ Bonus: $

OTHER THOUGHTS:

Estimated Female Officers or Directors: 2
Hot Spot for Advancement for Women/Minorities:

Qualtrics International Inc

www.qualtrics.com

NAIC Code: 511210J

TYPES OF BUSINESS:

Computer Software, Data Base & File Management
Software Development
Experience Management Solutions
Behavior Analysis
Predictive Intelligence Engine
Machine Learning
Artificial Intelligence

BRANDS/DIVISIONS/AFFILIATES:

XM Platform

GROWTH PLANS/SPECIAL FEATURES:

Qualtrics International, Inc. is a software technology company based in the United States. It develops artificial intelligence (AI) software used by almost 20,000 organizations worldwide. Its XM Platform is purpose-built to help organizations collect feedback and data across four vital signs of a business: customers, employees, brand and product. The firm derives revenue from sales of subscriptions to access its XM Platform, research services and professional services. Qualtrics is headquartered in Provo, Utah and Seattle, Washington, and has offices around the world.

CONTACTS:
Note: Officers with more than one job title may be intentionally listed here more than once.

Zig Serafin, CEO
Robert Bachman, CFO
Ryan Smith, Chairman of the Board
John Thimsen, Chief Technology Officer
Bill McMurray, Other Executive Officer
Chris Beckstead, President
Brad Anderson, President, Divisional

FINANCIAL DATA:
Note: Data for latest year may not have been available at press time.

In U.S. $	2022	2021	2020	2019	2018	2017
Revenue	1,458,627,968	1,075,664,000	763,521,984	591,155,008	401,908,000	289,903,000
R&D Expense						
Operating Income						
Operating Margin %						
SGA Expense						
Net Income	-1,061,478,016	-1,059,145,984	-272,502,016	-1,007,633,024	-37,308,000	2,556,000
Operating Cash Flow						
Capital Expenditure						
EBITDA						
Return on Assets %						
Return on Equity %						
Debt to Equity						

CONTACT INFORMATION:

Phone: 385 203-4999   Fax:
Toll-Free: 800-340-9194
Address: 333 W. River Park Dr., Provo, UT 84604 United States

STOCK TICKER/OTHER:

Stock Ticker: Private   Exchange:
Employees: 4,808   Fiscal Year Ends:
Parent Company: Silver Lake Technology Management LLC

SALARIES/BONUSES:

Top Exec. Salary: $ Bonus: $
Second Exec. Salary: $ Bonus: $

OTHER THOUGHTS:

Estimated Female Officers or Directors:
Hot Spot for Advancement for Women/Minorities:

Sales, profits and employees may be estimates. Financial information, benefits and other data can change quickly and may vary from those stated here.

Quotient Technology Inc

www.quotient.com

NAIC Code: 541810E

TYPES OF BUSINESS:

Online Coupon Advertising & Distribution

BRANDS/DIVISIONS/AFFILIATES:

Neptune Retail Solutions
Shopmium

CONTACTS: Note: Officers with more than one job title may be intentionally listed here more than once.

Steven Boal, CEO
Pamela Strayer, CFO
Connie Chen, General Counsel
Scott Raskin, President

GROWTH PLANS/SPECIAL FEATURES:

Quotient Technology Inc is a promotions and media technology company that delivers targeted digital promotions and media for advertisers and retailers to reach consumers and drive action. Using the company's platforms and suite of omnichannel solutions, advertisers can plan, target, deliver and measure performance marketing and brand marketing to impact sales. Quotient 's network includes the digital properties of retail partners, non-retail publisher partners and CPG customers, social media platforms, its consumer brand, Shopmium, and its digital out-of-home properties. This network provides the firm with proprietary and licensed data, including retailers' in-store point-of-sale shopper data, first-party consumer behavior and purchase intent data, and location intelligence. In September 2023, Quotient was acquired by Neptune Retail Solutions, a leading omnichannel retail marketing company in the U.S. & Canada.

Quotient offers its employees comprehensive health benefits, 401(k) and company perks.

FINANCIAL DATA: Note: Data for latest year may not have been available at press time.

In U.S. $	2022	2021	2020	2019	2018	2017
Revenue	288,766,016	521,494,016	445,887,008	436,160,000	386,958,016	322,115,008
R&D Expense						
Operating Income						
Operating Margin %						
SGA Expense						
Net Income	-76,511,000	-45,568,000	-65,381,000	-37,057,000	-28,318,000	-15,077,000
Operating Cash Flow						
Capital Expenditure						
EBITDA						
Return on Assets %						
Return on Equity %						
Debt to Equity						

CONTACT INFORMATION:

Phone: 650-605-4600   Fax: 650-605-4700
Toll-Free:
Address: 400 Logue Ave., Mountain View, CA 94043 United States

STOCK TICKER/OTHER:

Stock Ticker: Subsidiary   Exchange:
Employees: 1,162   Fiscal Year Ends: 12/31
Parent Company: Neptune Retail Solutions

SALARIES/BONUSES:

Top Exec. Salary: $ Bonus: $
Second Exec. Salary: $ Bonus: $

OTHER THOUGHTS:

Estimated Female Officers or Directors: 1
Hot Spot for Advancement for Women/Minorities:

Qurate Retail Inc

www.qurateretailgroup.com

NAIC Code: 454110

TYPES OF BUSINESS:

Online and Internet Businesses
Ecommerce
Interactive Shopping
Live Broadcasts
Pre-Recorded Programming
Catalog Shopping
Retail and Outlet Stores
Merchandise

BRANDS/DIVISIONS/AFFILIATES:

QVC Inc
HSN Inc
Cornerstone Brands Inc
zulily llc
Frontgate
Ballard Designs
Grandin Road
Garnet Hill

GROWTH PLANS/SPECIAL FEATURES:

Qurate Retail Inc, through its subsidiaries, is engaged in the video and online commerce industries. Its segments include QxH, which includes QVC U.S. and HSN market and sell a wide variety of consumer products in the United States, primarily using their televised shopping programs and via the Internet through their websites and mobile applications; QVC International segment markets and sells a wide variety of consumer products in several foreign countries, primarily using its televised shopping programs and via the Internet through its international websites and mobile applications; and Zulily markets and sells a wide variety of consumer products in the United States and several foreign countries. Its geographical segments include the U.S, Japan, Germany, and Other countries.

CONTACTS: *Note: Officers with more than one job title may be intentionally listed here more than once.*

Michael George, CEO
Brian Wendling, CFO
Gregory Maffei, Chairman of the Board
Renee Wilm, Chief Administrative Officer
Albert Rosenthaler, Other Executive Officer

FINANCIAL DATA: *Note: Data for latest year may not have been available at press time.*

In U.S. $	2022	2021	2020	2019	2018	2017
Revenue	12,106,000,000	14,044,000,000	14,177,000,000	13,458,000,000	14,070,000,000	10,404,000,000
R&D Expense						
Operating Income	948,000,000	1,471,000,000	1,572,000,000	1,351,000,000	1,357,000,000	1,043,000,000
Operating Margin %	.08%	.10%	.11%	.10%	.10%	.10%
SGA Expense	1,945,000,000	1,930,000,000	1,885,000,000	1,758,000,000	1,897,000,000	1,188,000,000
Net Income	-2,594,000,000	340,000,000	1,196,000,000	-456,000,000	916,000,000	2,441,000,000
Operating Cash Flow	194,000,000	1,225,000,000	2,455,000,000	1,284,000,000	1,273,000,000	1,490,000,000
Capital Expenditure	313,000,000	431,000,000	313,000,000	459,000,000	415,000,000	255,000,000
EBITDA	-1,371,000,000	1,643,000,000	2,021,000,000	358,000,000	1,901,000,000	2,130,000,000
Return on Assets %	-.18%	.02%	.07%	-.03%	.03%	.06%
Return on Equity %	-1.59%	.11%	.28%	-.09%	.09%	.16%
Debt to Equity	14.67%	2.10%	1.441	1.21	1.06%	0.757

CONTACT INFORMATION:

Phone: 720 875-5300   Fax:
Toll-Free:
Address: 12300 Liberty Blvd., Englewood, CO 80112 United States

STOCK TICKER/OTHER:

Stock Ticker: QRTEA   Exchange: NAS
Employees: 24,600   Fiscal Year Ends: 12/31
Parent Company:

SALARIES/BONUSES:

Top Exec. Salary: $1,250,000   Bonus: $
Second Exec. Salary: Bonus: $
$390,000

OTHER THOUGHTS:

Estimated Female Officers or Directors: 1
Hot Spot for Advancement for Women/Minorities:

Rackspace Technology Inc

www.rackspace.com

NAIC Code: 517311

TYPES OF BUSINESS:

Web Hosting Services
Data Centers
Cloud Computing Services
Server Farms

BRANDS/DIVISIONS/AFFILIATES:

Apollo Global Management LLC
Onica

GROWTH PLANS/SPECIAL FEATURES:

Rackspace Technology Inc is an end-to-end multi cloud technology services company. It designs, builds and operates its customers' cloud environments across all technology platforms, irrespective of technology stack or deployment model. The company's solutions include Application Services; Data; Colocation; Managed Cloud; Managed Hosting; Professional Services; and Security & Compliance. It operates in three reportable segments Multicloud Services; Apps & Cross-Platform; and OpenStack Public Cloud. It generates revenue through the sale of consumption-based contracts for its services offerings and from the sale of professional services related to designing and building custom solutions.

CONTACTS:
Note: Officers with more than one job title may be intentionally listed here more than once.

Kevin Jones, CEO
Amar Maletira, CFO
David Sambur, Chairman of the Board
Mark Marino, Chief Accounting Officer
Holly Windham, Chief Legal Officer
Zarina Stanford, Chief Marketing Officer
Tolga Tarhan, Chief Technology Officer
Subroto Mukerji, COO
John McCabe, Executive VP, Geographical
Sandeep Bhargava, Managing Director, Geographical
Martin Blackburn, Managing Director, Geographical
Neil Emerson, Other Executive Officer
Thomas Wolf, Senior VP, Divisional

FINANCIAL DATA:
Note: Data for latest year may not have been available at press time.

In U.S. $	2022	2021	2020	2019	2018	2017
Revenue	3,122,300,000	3,009,500,000	2,707,100,000	2,438,100,000	2,452,800,000	2,144,700,000
R&D Expense						
Operating Income	1,600,000	30,000,000	24,700,000	99,500,000	57,800,000	-122,800,000
Operating Margin %	.00%	.01%	.01%	.04%	.02%	
SGA Expense	855,300,000	906,800,000	959,700,000	911,700,000	949,300,000	942,200,000
Net Income	-804,800,000	-218,300,000	-245,800,000	-102,300,000	-470,600,000	-59,900,000
Operating Cash Flow	246,700,000	370,800,000	116,700,000	292,900,000	429,800,000	291,700,000
Capital Expenditure	80,400,000	108,400,000	116,500,000	198,000,000	294,300,000	189,500,000
EBITDA	-241,600,000	446,700,000	493,300,000	774,100,000	391,600,000	620,600,000
Return on Assets %	-.14%	-.03%	-.04%	-.02%	-.08%	
Return on Equity %	-.82%	-.16%	-.22%	-.11%	-.52%	
Debt to Equity	5.94%	2.89%	2.797	4.757	4.65%	

CONTACT INFORMATION:

Phone: 210 312-4000   Fax: 210 312-4300
Toll-Free: 800-961-2888
Address: 1 Fanatical Pl., City of Windcrest, San Antonio, TX 78218
United States

STOCK TICKER/OTHER:

Stock Ticker: RXT   Exchange: NAS
Employees: 6,800   Fiscal Year Ends: 12/31
Parent Company: Apollo Global Management LLC

SALARIES/BONUSES:

Top Exec. Salary: $795,173   Bonus: $821,910
Second Exec. Salary: Bonus: $954,375
$525,000

OTHER THOUGHTS:

Estimated Female Officers or Directors: 1
Hot Spot for Advancement for Women/Minorities:

Radware Ltd

www.radware.com

NAIC Code: 511210B

TYPES OF BUSINESS:

Computer Software: Network Management (IT), System Testing & Storage
Internet Security Software
Ecommerce Software
Connectivity Software
Cloud Solutions

GROWTH PLANS/SPECIAL FEATURES:

Radware Ltd develops and sells a broad portfolio of network products including physical and virtual application delivery controllers, web application firewalls, intrusion prevention systems, and other security products geared toward large enterprise and service provider segments. It offers an infrastructure that supports our DDoS scrubbing center services, WAF and bot management cloud-based services. In addition, It provides other services through the cloud, such as Cloud Workload Protect and Content Delivery Network.

BRANDS/DIVISIONS/AFFILIATES:

RAD Group
Application Delivery Controller
DefensePro
AppWall
DefenseFlow
Alteon
LinkProof
FastView

CONTACTS: Note: Officers with more than one job title may be intentionally listed here more than once.

Roy Zisapel, CEO
Gabi Malka, COO
Yoav Gazelle, VP-Int'l Sales
Riki Goldriech, VP-Global Human Resources
David Aviv, CTO
Gadi Meroz, General Counsel
David Aviv, VP-Advanced Svcs.
Gilad Zlotkin, VP-Virtualization & Management
Terence Ying, VP-Asia Pacific
Yehuda Zisapel, Chmn.
Yoav Gazelle, VP-EMEA, Central & Latin America
Christina Aruza, VP-Corporate Mktg.

FINANCIAL DATA: Note: Data for latest year may not have been available at press time.

In U.S. $	2022	2021	2020	2019	2018	2017
Revenue	293,426,000	286,496,000	250,027,000	252,072,000	234,404,000	211,369,000
R&D Expense	86,562,000	74,098,000	66,836,000	61,841,000	57,674,000	59,003,000
Operating Income	-3,339,000	18,225,000	6,168,000	16,917,000	7,524,000	-6,671,000
Operating Margin %		.06%	.02%	.07%	.03%	- .03%
SGA Expense	156,319,000	141,727,000	131,939,000	128,140,000	127,531,000	126,321,000
Net Income	-166,000	7,811,000	9,636,000	22,566,000	11,735,000	-7,493,000
Operating Cash Flow	32,148,000	71,774,000	63,865,000	52,852,000	49,251,000	31,462,000
Capital Expenditure	8,814,000	5,603,000	8,671,000	8,155,000	8,869,000	7,210,000
EBITDA	8,353,000	28,421,000	16,727,000	28,200,000	17,306,000	4,561,000
Return on Assets %		.01%	.02%	.04%	.02%	- .02%
Return on Equity %		.02%	.02%	.06%	.03%	- .02%
Debt to Equity		.06%	0.064		0.035	

CONTACT INFORMATION:

Phone: 972 37668666   Fax: 972-3-7668982
Toll-Free:
Address: 22 Raoul Wallenberg St., Tel Aviv, 6971917 Israel

STOCK TICKER/OTHER:

Stock Ticker: RDWR   Exchange: NAS
Employees: 419   Fiscal Year Ends: 12/31
Parent Company:

SALARIES/BONUSES:

Top Exec. Salary: $452,000   Bonus: $382,000
Second Exec. Salary: $239,000   Bonus: $228,000

OTHER THOUGHTS:

Estimated Female Officers or Directors: 3
Hot Spot for Advancement for Women/Minorities: Y

Sales, profits and employees may be estimates. Financial information, benefits and other data can change quickly and may vary from those stated here.

Rakuten (Ebates Inc)

www.rakuten.com

NAIC Code: 454110

TYPES OF BUSINESS:

Consumer Electronics, Online Retail
Book, Game, DVD, VHS & Music Sales
Software & Accessories Sales
Music Downloads
Social Networking
Jewelry and Watches
Household Items

BRANDS/DIVISIONS/AFFILIATES:

Rakuten Group Inc
Ebates Inc
Ebates Performance Marketing Inc
Rakuten Rewards

CONTACTS: *Note: Officers with more than one job title may be intentionally listed here more than once.*

Anit Patel, CEO
Adrienne Down Coulson, COO
Greg Kaplan, CFO
Dana Marineau, CMO
Joe Molnar, CTO
Jane Chun, VP-Sales
Hiroshi Mikitani, Chmn. & CEO-Rakuten, Inc.
Fumio Kobayashi, Chief Marketplace Officer
Kristen Gall, Pres.

GROWTH PLANS/SPECIAL FEATURES:

Ebates, Inc. does business as Rakuten, offering a shopping reward program that offers cash back on products and services to its over 20 million members throughout the U.S. More than 3,500 retail and ecommerce stores are within the Rakuten cash back program and may also offer coupons and deals. How shopping works: download the Rakuten app, browser extension or Rakuten.com website; choose a store; shop; and receive a cash back payment every three months via check of PayPal. The partner stores pay Rakuten for sending them shoppers, and that money is shared with Rakuten members as a cash back reward. Stores can activate cash back directly on their websites and apply coupons, and members can earn extra during exclusive app events. Push notifications are available. Personalized shopping can be set up by choosing favored stores. Popular product categories include baby and toddler, clothing, accessories, electronics, travel and vacations, health and beauty, shoes, home and garden, and food/restaurants/beverages. By linking store offers to credit cards, members can earn in-store cash back. Referring others to Rakuten enables members to earn a cash back bonus. Subsidiary Ebates Performance Marketing, Inc. does business as Rakuten Rewards. All trademarks are proprietary to Ebates, Inc., which is ultimately the subsidiary of Rakuten Group, Inc. based in Japan. International partner sites are available in Canada, Japan and France, with other partner sites including Cartera and ShopStyle.

FINANCIAL DATA: *Note: Data for latest year may not have been available at press time.*

In U.S. $	2022	2021	2020	2019	2018	2017
Revenue						
R&D Expense						
Operating Income						
Operating Margin %						
SGA Expense						
Net Income						
Operating Cash Flow						
Capital Expenditure						
EBITDA						
Return on Assets %						
Return on Equity %						
Debt to Equity						

CONTACT INFORMATION:

Phone: 949-389-2000   Fax:
Toll-Free:
Address: 800 Concar Dr., Ste. 175, San Mateo, CA 94402 United States

STOCK TICKER/OTHER:

Stock Ticker: Subsidiary   Exchange:
Employees: 115   Fiscal Year Ends: 12/31
Parent Company: Rakuten Group Inc

SALARIES/BONUSES:

Top Exec. Salary: $ Bonus: $
Second Exec. Salary: $ Bonus: $

OTHER THOUGHTS:

Estimated Female Officers or Directors: 4
Hot Spot for Advancement for Women/Minorities: Y

Rakuten Inc

www.rakuten.co.jp

NAIC Code: 454110

TYPES OF BUSINESS:

E-Commerce
Internet Marketing
Ecommerce
Communications
FinTech
Advertising
Investment

BRANDS/DIVISIONS/AFFILIATES:

Rakuten Travel
Rakuten GORA
Rakuten Mobile
Rakuten Energy
Rakuten Card
Rakuten Bank
Rakuten Recipe
Rakuten Capital

GROWTH PLANS/SPECIAL FEATURES:

Rakuten is a leading e-commerce and fintech service provider in Japan. It has built up a comprehensive Rakuten ecosystem in Japan, including Rakuten Ichiba for e-commerce, Rakuten Travel, Rakuten Card, Rakuten Bank, Rakuten Securities, and decided to become the fourth mobile network operator in Japan, started its full service in April 2020. Mergers and acquisitions in internet and e-finance businesses have driven growth. The loyalty program, Rakuten Super Points, has encouraged cross-use of services in its ecosystem. About 80% of its revenue is generated from the Japanese market.

CONTACTS:
Note: Officers with more than one job title may be intentionally listed here more than once.

Hiroshi Mikitani, CEO
Kentaro Hyakuno, COO
Kenji Hirose, CFO
Naho Kono, CMO
Yasufumi Hirai, CIO
Atsushi Kunishige, Exec. VP
Masatada Kobayashi, Sr. Exec. Officer
Hiroaki Yasutake, Sr. Exec. Officer
Kazunori Takeda, Sr. Exec. Officer
Hiroshi Mikitani, Chmn.

FINANCIAL DATA:
Note: Data for latest year may not have been available at press time.

In U.S. $	2022	2021	2020	2019	2018	2017
Revenue	13,155,720,000	11,476,200,000	9,932,498,000	8,624,990,000	7,516,428,000	6,445,030,000
R&D Expense						
Operating Income	-2,483,176,000	-1,328,798,000	-640,419,500	496,407,200	1,162,969,000	1,019,114,000
Operating Margin %		-.12%	-.06%	.06%	.15%	.16%
SGA Expense						
Net Income	-2,544,537,000	-913,233,700	-779,286,700	-217,601,600	970,923,200	754,625,000
Operating Cash Flow	-1,760,214,000	3,976,355,000	7,106,385,000	2,172,195,000	993,667,300	1,105,860,000
Capital Expenditure	2,998,526,000	2,802,188,000	2,627,720,000	1,414,179,000	597,653,900	535,665,300
EBITDA	103,109,700	159,441,200	546,576,800	483,400,800	1,651,283,000	1,335,997,000
Return on Assets %		-.01%	-.01%	.00%	.02%	.02%
Return on Equity %		-.16%	-.17%	-.04%	.20%	.16%
Debt to Equity		3.11%	4.086	2.348	1.59%	1.487

CONTACT INFORMATION:

Phone: 8150-5581-6910   Fax:
Toll-Free:
Address: 1-14-1 Tamagawa, Setagaya-ku, Tokyo, 158-0094 Japan

STOCK TICKER/OTHER:

Stock Ticker: RKUNF   Exchange: PINX
Employees: 17,214   Fiscal Year Ends: 12/31
Parent Company:

SALARIES/BONUSES:

Top Exec. Salary: $ Bonus: $
Second Exec. Salary: $ Bonus: $

OTHER THOUGHTS:

Estimated Female Officers or Directors:
Hot Spot for Advancement for Women/Minorities:

Rakuten Marketing LLC

rakutenadvertising.com

NAIC Code: 541810E

TYPES OF BUSINESS:

Affiliate Marketing Network
Market Research Services
Web Analytics and Data Insight Software
Commission Tracking Software
Advertising
Digital Marketing Solutions
Integrated Advertising Strategies
Paid Search Advertising

BRANDS/DIVISIONS/AFFILIATES:

Rakuten Inc
Rakuten Advertising

CONTACTS: *Note: Officers with more than one job title may be intentionally listed here more than once.*

Nick Stamos, CEO
Vincent Karachira, COO
Cindy Curry, CFO
Reginald Rasch, General Counsel
Yuichi Ishizumi Yuichi Ishizumi, Pres.

GROWTH PLANS/SPECIAL FEATURES:

Rakuten Marketing, LLC does business as Rakuten Advertising offers integrated online solutions that enable marketers to utilize digital marketing strategies. Integrated advertising strategies enhance performance across channels and provide consumer journey and data insights for driving performance. Affiliate marketing strategies promote discovery and engage shoppers across the entire consumer journey. It connects advertisers with publishers to reach new audiences and influence repeat purchases. Rakuten Advertising's data-driven display advertising strategies enable marketers to accurately identify consumers in the areas they spend their time and money, and does so across screens, social media and traditional publishers. Its team of experts engage in developing specific digital marketing strategies for its clients so they can receive incremental revenue. To Rakuten Advertising, as clients increase their customer footprint, sales will increase as well. Last, Rakuten Advertising's paid search advertising strategy reaches consumers across the funnel. Customers become engaged via product listing ads as they shop across platforms. Rakuten Advertising's advanced bidding algorithms and unique data optimize this marketing strategy and save costs. Rakuten Marketing is a subsidiary of Rakuten Group, Inc.

FINANCIAL DATA: *Note: Data for latest year may not have been available at press time.*

In U.S. $	2022	2021	2020	2019	2018	2017
Revenue						
R&D Expense						
Operating Income						
Operating Margin %						
SGA Expense						
Net Income						
Operating Cash Flow						
Capital Expenditure						
EBITDA						
Return on Assets %						
Return on Equity %						
Debt to Equity						

CONTACT INFORMATION:

Phone: 949-389-2000   Fax:
Toll-Free:
Address: 800 Concar Dr., Ste. 175, San Mateo, CA 94402 United States

STOCK TICKER/OTHER:

Stock Ticker: Subsidiary   Exchange:
Employees: 730   Fiscal Year Ends: 06/30
Parent Company: Rakuten Group Inc

SALARIES/BONUSES:

Top Exec. Salary: $ Bonus: $
Second Exec. Salary: $ Bonus: $

OTHER THOUGHTS:

Estimated Female Officers or Directors: 2
Hot Spot for Advancement for Women/Minorities:

REA Group Ltd

NAIC Code: 519130

www.rea-group.com

TYPES OF BUSINESS:
Online Real Estate
Digital Advertising
Real Estate Search
Property Data

GROWTH PLANS/SPECIAL FEATURES:
REA Group is a technology company operating in the real estate sector. REA Group's primary business is a online listings platform for residential real estate, www.realestate.com.au, which is the largest residential real estate listings platform in Australia, at around three times the size of number two, www.domain.com.au, owned by Domain Group. REA Group is majority-owned by News Corp (ASX:NWS), while Domain is majority-owned by rival media company Nine Entertainment (ASX:NEC). REA Group's other businesses include adjacent markets and services, and investments in online listings platforms in Asia.

BRANDS/DIVISIONS/AFFILIATES:
realestate.com.au
Flatmates.com.au
hometrack
iproperty.com.my
squarefoot.com.hk
proptiger.com
Move Inc
realtor.com

CONTACTS: Note: Officers with more than one job title may be intentionally listed here more than once.
Owen Wilson, CEO
Kul Singh, Chief Sales Officer
Janelle Hopkins, CFO
Melina Cruickshank, CMO
Mary Lemonis, Chief People Officer
Tomas Varsavsky, CTO
Hamish McLennan, Chmn.

FINANCIAL DATA: Note: Data for latest year may not have been available at press time.

In U.S. $	2022	2021	2020	2019	2018	2017
Revenue	921,829,200	649,275,500	569,512,100	607,959,700	560,160,100	
R&D Expense						
Operating Income	358,230,800	295,318,000	260,413,800	294,324,700	272,890,900	
Operating Margin %	.39%	.45%	.46%	.48%	.49%	
SGA Expense	274,921,300	215,355,700	189,801,600	204,517,700	198,394,100	
Net Income	248,507,700	208,388,000	72,571,610	67,808,110	163,247,200	
Operating Cash Flow						
Capital Expenditure	61,351,950	43,227,290	47,372,100	43,889,890	38,273,280	
EBITDA	419,259,900	360,245,800	207,146,100	204,431,200	286,588,500	
Return on Assets %	.16%	.16%	.07%	.06%	.15%	
Return on Equity %	.32%	.33%	.13%	.11%	.29%	
Debt to Equity	.37%	.46%	0.29	0.077	.33%	

CONTACT INFORMATION:
Phone: 61 3-9897-1121 Fax: 61 3-9897-1114
Toll-Free:
Address: 511 Church St., Richmond, VIC 3121 Australia

STOCK TICKER/OTHER:
Stock Ticker: RPGRY Exchange: PINX
Employees: 3,000 Fiscal Year Ends: 06/30
Parent Company:

SALARIES/BONUSES:
Top Exec. Salary: $ Bonus: $
Second Exec. Salary: $ Bonus: $

OTHER THOUGHTS:
Estimated Female Officers or Directors:
Hot Spot for Advancement for Women/Minorities: Y

RealNetworks LLC

www.realnetworks.com

NAIC Code: 511210F

TYPES OF BUSINESS:
Computer Software, Multimedia, Graphics & Publishing
Computer Software-Streaming Audio & Video
Online Retail-Digital Media
Natural Language Processing Solutions
Image Technology
Mobile Carrier Services
Online Games
Video Downloads and Sharing

BRANDS/DIVISIONS/AFFILIATES:
SAFR
KONTXT
RealMedia HD
Mobile Carrier Services
Ringback
GameHouse
RealPlayer
RealTimes

CONTACTS: *Note: Officers with more than one job title may be intentionally listed here more than once.*
Chris Wheaton, Pres.
Michael Parham, General Counsel

GROWTH PLANS/SPECIAL FEATURES:
RealNetworks LLC creates a new generation of products that employ artificial intelligence and machine learning to enhance and secure daily lives. Real's portfolio includes SAFR, the computer vision platform for live video; KONTXT, an NLP (Natural Language Processing) platform for text and multi-media analysis; RealMedia HD, a technology that offers consumers innovative streaming technology that delivers image quality for a high-definition (up to 8K) experience on mobile devices; Mobile Carrier Services, offering mobile messaging services and Ringback solutions for mobile carriers; GameHouse, offering online casual games developed with original stories; RealPlayer, a video download that is compatible with websites such as YouTube, Vimeo, Facebook and Instagram, among many others; and RealTimes, for creating video stories from photos and videos, and can be shared, enhanced with effects and music.

RealNetworks offers its employees comprehensive health benefits, an employee assistance program, a 401(k), life and accident insurance and company perks.

FINANCIAL DATA: *Note: Data for latest year may not have been available at press time.*

In U.S. $	2022	2021	2020	2019	2018	2017
Revenue	47,865,400	58,183,000	68,062,000	65,802,000	69,510,000	78,718,000
R&D Expense						
Operating Income						
Operating Margin %						
SGA Expense						
Net Income		-21,981,000	-4,852,000	-20,001,000	-24,989,000	-16,305,000
Operating Cash Flow						
Capital Expenditure						
EBITDA						
Return on Assets %						
Return on Equity %						
Debt to Equity						

CONTACT INFORMATION:
Phone: 206 674-2700   Fax: 206 674-2699
Toll-Free:
Address: 1501 First Ave. S., Ste. 600, Seattle, WA 98134 United States

STOCK TICKER/OTHER:
Stock Ticker: Private   Exchange:
Employees: 281   Fiscal Year Ends: 12/31
Parent Company:

SALARIES/BONUSES:
Top Exec. Salary: $ Bonus: $
Second Exec. Salary: $ Bonus: $

OTHER THOUGHTS:
Estimated Female Officers or Directors:
Hot Spot for Advancement for Women/Minorities:

RealPage Inc

www.realpage.com

NAIC Code: 511210H

TYPES OF BUSINESS:

Online Real Estate Management Services
Property Management Technology
Real Estate Platform
Cloud Solutions
Property Marketing Solutions
Applicant Screening Solutions
Resident Services

BRANDS/DIVISIONS/AFFILIATES:

Thomas Bravo LP
Knock Inc

GROWTH PLANS/SPECIAL FEATURES:

RealPage, Inc. provides a technology platform for real estate owners and managers. The platform enables users to gain transparency in asset performance, leverage data insights and monetize space. Types of properties include affordable, commercial, military, multifamily, senior, single family and student. RealPage also provides commercial and mixed-use property management solutions. The firm's products are cloud-based, and available online and through mobile devices. Its services are used for compliance through compliance services; vendor services with credentialing, vendor marketplace and vendor catalog/eInvoices; integrations, realpartners, professional services, realpage exchange, realpage training and support services. Operations includes resident technology and smartsource IT and financial includes billing services and smartsource accounting RealPage currently serves over 24 million units worldwide from offices in North America, Europe and Asia. The company operates as a subsidiary of Thoma Bravo LP.

CONTACTS: *Note: Officers with more than one job title may be intentionally listed here more than once.*

Dana Jones, CEO
Vinit Doshi, COO
Akash Raj, CFO
Brandon Bible, Chief Sales Officer
Lynnelle Long, Chief People Officer
Lance French, CIO
Ashley Chaffin Glover, Executive VP
William Chaney, Executive VP
Evan Davies, CTO

FINANCIAL DATA: *Note: Data for latest year may not have been available at press time.*

In U.S. $	2022	2021	2020	2019	2018	2017
Revenue	1,500,000,000	1,200,000,000	1,200,000,000	988,136,000	869,480,000	670,963,008
R&D Expense						
Operating Income						
Operating Margin %						
SGA Expense						
Net Income			46,300,000	58,208,000	34,725,000	377,000
Operating Cash Flow						
Capital Expenditure						
EBITDA						
Return on Assets %						
Return on Equity %						
Debt to Equity						

CONTACT INFORMATION:

Phone: 972 820-3000 Fax:
Toll-Free: 877-325-7243
Address: 2201 Lakeside Blvd., Richardson, TX 75082-4305 United States

STOCK TICKER/OTHER:

Stock Ticker: Private Exchange:
Employees: 7,000 Fiscal Year Ends: 12/31
Parent Company: Thoma Bravo LP

SALARIES/BONUSES:

Top Exec. Salary: $ Bonus: $
Second Exec. Salary: $ Bonus: $

OTHER THOUGHTS:

Estimated Female Officers or Directors: 6
Hot Spot for Advancement for Women/Minorities: Y

Red Hat Inc

NAIC Code: 511210I

TYPES OF BUSINESS:

Computer Software-Linux Operating Systems
Open-Source Software
Enterprise Automation Technology
Enterprise Hybrid Cloud
Application Management
Technology Innovation and Implementation
Cloud Container Deployment Solutions
Kubernetes Container Platform

BRANDS/DIVISIONS/AFFILIATES:

International Business Machines Corporation (IBM)
Red Hat Ansible Automation Platform
Red Hat Enterprise Linux
Red Hat OpenShift Container Storage
Red Hat OpenShift Container Platform
Red Hat OpenStack Platform

CONTACTS: *Note: Officers with more than one job title may be intentionally listed here more than once.*

Matt Hicks, CEO
Eric Shander, CFO
Arun Oberoi, Executive VP, Divisional
Michael Cunningham, Executive VP
DeLisa Alexander, Executive VP
Paul Cormier, President, Divisional

GROWTH PLANS/SPECIAL FEATURES:

Red Hat, Inc. is a provider of open-source software solutions. Founded in 1993, the firm's Red Hat Ansible Automation Platform is a foundation for building and operating automation across an organization. It comes with all the tools needed to implement enterprise-wide automation. Red Hat Enterprise Linux is the company's foundation for an enterprise hybrid cloud. It is an opensource operating system from which enterprises can scale existing apps and roll out emerging technologies across bare-metal, virtual, container and other types of cloud environments. Red Hat OpenShift Container Storage is a software-defined storage for hybrid cloud and multi-cloud container deployments. Red Hat OpenShift Ansible Automation Platform is a foundation for implementing enterprise wide automation. Red Hat Cloud Services include hosted and managed platform, application, and data services that streamline the hybrid cloud experience and is available on Amazon Web Services, Microsoft Azure, Google Cloud and IBM Cloud. Red Hat also offers related tools for customers, partners and developers, and its website provides a resource library for information purposes. Red Hat is owned by the multinational information technology company IBM.

FINANCIAL DATA: *Note: Data for latest year may not have been available at press time.*

In U.S. $	2022	2021	2020	2019	2018	2017
Revenue	3,483,000,000	3,447,600,000	3,315,000,000	3,400,000,000	2,920,461,056	2,411,802,880
R&D Expense						
Operating Income						
Operating Margin %						
SGA Expense						
Net Income						
Operating Cash Flow						
Capital Expenditure						
EBITDA						
Return on Assets %						
Return on Equity %						
Debt to Equity						

CONTACT INFORMATION:

Phone: 919 754-4950   Fax: 919 754-3701
Toll-Free: 888-733-4281
Address: 100 E. Davie St., Raleigh, NC 27601 United States

STOCK TICKER/OTHER:

Stock Ticker: Subsidiary   Exchange:
Employees: 10,500   Fiscal Year Ends: 02/28
Parent Company: International Business Machines Corporation (IBM)

SALARIES/BONUSES:

Top Exec. Salary: $ Bonus: $
Second Exec. Salary: $ Bonus: $

OTHER THOUGHTS:

Estimated Female Officers or Directors: 3
Hot Spot for Advancement for Women/Minorities: Y

Reformation (LYMI Inc)

www.thereformation.com

NAIC Code: 454110

TYPES OF BUSINESS:

Electronic Shopping
Apparel Design and Manufacture
Sustainable Materials
Ecommerce
Made-to-Order
Repurposed Vintage Clothing
Recyclable Materials
Retail Stores

BRANDS/DIVISIONS/AFFILIATES:

Permira Advisers Limited
Reformation

CONTACTS: Note: Officers with more than one job title may be intentionally listed here more than once.

Yael Aflalo, CEO

GROWTH PLANS/SPECIAL FEATURES:

LYMI, Inc. does business as Reformation and designs and manufactures clothes for women, from petite to plus-size. The firm's fashion is designed and ready in about 30-to-40 days. All pieces are made from sustainable materials, deadstock fabrics and repurposed vintage clothing. Many of the company's garments are made with TENCEL, a semi-synthetic fiber manufactured from Eucalyptus trees. Other fabrics are made from: TENCEL Lyocell, made by Austrian company Lenzing, a regenerated cellulose fiber with properties nearly identical to cotton, and also made from renewable wood materials; TENCEL X REFIBRA, which combines up to 30% of recycled cotton waste with wood pulp; linen, which is made from flax; TENCEL Modal, a wood-based fiber; Viscose, a man-made fiber from plant material; and recycled materials such as cashmere, deadstock and vintage clothing. About 5% of LYMI's fabrics are deadstock, meaning they are given a second life; and about 2%-5% are made from vintage clothing purchased from wholesalers throughout the U.S and repurposed into new pieces. Apparel includes dresses, tops, wedding/party attire, jeans, bottoms, outerwear, sweaters, shoes and more. The Reformation site has a link for new items and a link for current sales. Reformation is majority-owned by Permira Advisers Limited, a private investment firm. Reformation has brick and mortar stores throughout the U.S., including California, New York, Massachusetts, Washington DC, Washington, Oregon, Texas, Illinois, Georgia, Hawaii and Florida, as well as internationally in Canada and the U.K.

FINANCIAL DATA: Note: Data for latest year may not have been available at press time.

In U.S. $	2022	2021	2020	2019	2018	2017
Revenue	94,100,000	91,485,000	85,500,000	150,000,000	105,000,000	100,000,000
R&D Expense						
Operating Income						
Operating Margin %						
SGA Expense						
Net Income						
Operating Cash Flow						
Capital Expenditure						
EBITDA						
Return on Assets %						
Return on Equity %						
Debt to Equity						

CONTACT INFORMATION:

Phone: 213-746-6339   Fax:
Toll-Free:
Address: 2263 E. Vernon Ave., Vernon, CA 90058 United States

STOCK TICKER/OTHER:

Stock Ticker: Private   Exchange:
Employees: 550   Fiscal Year Ends:
Parent Company: Permira Advisers Limited

SALARIES/BONUSES:

Top Exec. Salary: $ Bonus: $
Second Exec. Salary: $ Bonus: $

OTHER THOUGHTS:

Estimated Female Officers or Directors:
Hot Spot for Advancement for Women/Minorities:

Sales, profits and employees may be estimates. Financial information, benefits and other data can change quickly and may vary from those stated here.

Register.com Inc

NAIC Code: 518210

TYPES OF BUSINESS:

Domain Name Registration Services
Website Domain Search Services
Internet Site Support Services
Website Name
Web Hosting
Ecommerce Solutions
Marketing Services
IT Support Services

BRANDS/DIVISIONS/AFFILIATES:

Newfold Digital Inc
MyTime Support

CONTACTS: *Note: Officers with more than one job title may be intentionally listed here more than once.*

Sharon Rowlands, CEO-Newfold Digital
Alexander Ross, Sr. VP-Sales & Svcs.

GROWTH PLANS/SPECIAL FEATURES:

Register.com, Inc., a subsidiary of Newfold Digital, Inc., is a leading provider of global domain name registration and other internet services for small- and medium-sized businesses, large corporations and individual consumers. Register.com has active domain names under management. The company also allows users to transfer their previously existing domain name to Register.com. Register.com's products are grouped into: domains, including .com, .org, .net, .info, .business, .guru, .company, .club, .nyc and more; websites, featuring do-it-myself, do-it-for-me, ecommerce and a call center option; hosting, including hosting packages, hosting help and security solutions; email, including web hosting packages and security solutions; and online marketing/ecommerce, including local business listings, premium services, search engine optimization, pay-per-click advertising, lead stream, take-a-payment and more. Information technology support is also provided by Register.com through its MyTime Support products, which include website support as well as entire office technical support.

FINANCIAL DATA: *Note: Data for latest year may not have been available at press time.*

In U.S. $	2022	2021	2020	2019	2018	2017
Revenue						
R&D Expense						
Operating Income						
Operating Margin %						
SGA Expense						
Net Income						
Operating Cash Flow						
Capital Expenditure						
EBITDA						
Return on Assets %						
Return on Equity %						
Debt to Equity						

CONTACT INFORMATION:

Phone: Fax:
Toll-Free: 855 897-1721
Address: 5335 Gate Pkwy., Jacksonville, FL 32256 United States

STOCK TICKER/OTHER:

Stock Ticker: Subsidiary   Exchange:
Employees: 490   Fiscal Year Ends: 12/31
Parent Company: Newfold Digital Inc

SALARIES/BONUSES:

Top Exec. Salary: $ Bonus: $
Second Exec. Salary: $ Bonus: $

OTHER THOUGHTS:

Estimated Female Officers or Directors:
Hot Spot for Advancement for Women/Minorities:

Rent the Runway Inc

www.renttherunway.com

NAIC Code: 454110

TYPES OF BUSINESS:
Online Rental of Luxury Apparel and Accessories

BRANDS/DIVISIONS/AFFILIATES:

GROWTH PLANS/SPECIAL FEATURES:
Rent the Runway Inc is an e-commerce platform that allows users to rent, subscribe, or buy designer apparel and accessories.

Benefits for qualified employees at all levels include paid bereavement leave, paid family and parental sick leave and sabbatical packages. The main plant and logistics center is in New Jersey.

CONTACTS: *Note: Officers with more than one job title may be intentionally listed here more than once.*
Jennifer Hyman, CEO
Scarlett O'Sullivan, CFO
Larry Steinberg, Chief Technology Officer
Anushka Salinas, COO
Cara Schembri, General Counsel
Sarah Tam, Other Executive Officer
Brian Donato, Other Executive Officer
Andrea Alexander, Other Executive Officer

FINANCIAL DATA: *Note: Data for latest year may not have been available at press time.*

In U.S. $	2022	2021	2020	2019	2018	2017
Revenue	203,300,000	157,500,000				
R&D Expense	45,300,000	37,700,000				
Operating Income	-125,900,000	-130,500,000				
Operating Margin %	-.62%	-.83%				
SGA Expense	130,900,000	85,300,000				
Net Income	-211,800,000	-171,100,000				
Operating Cash Flow	-42,300,000	-42,800,000				
Capital Expenditure	41,100,000	78,700,000				
EBITDA	-34,800,000	-18,500,000				
Return on Assets %	-.55%	-.57%				
Return on Equity %						
Debt to Equity	4.32%					

CONTACT INFORMATION:
Phone: 646-832-3582   Fax:
Toll-Free: 800-509-0842
Address: 163 Varick St., Fl. 4, New York, NY 10013 United States

STOCK TICKER/OTHER:
Stock Ticker: RENT   Exchange: NAS
Employees: 1,015   Fiscal Year Ends: 01/31
Parent Company:

SALARIES/BONUSES:
Top Exec. Salary: $650,000   Bonus: $
Second Exec. Salary: Bonus: $
$600,000

OTHER THOUGHTS:
Estimated Female Officers or Directors: 3
Hot Spot for Advancement for Women/Minorities: Y

Sales, profits and employees may be estimates. Financial information, benefits and other data can change quickly and may vary from those stated here.

Revolve Group Inc

NAIC Code: 454110

www.revolve.com

TYPES OF BUSINESS:

Online Clothing Retailer
Online Fashion Retail
Ecommerce

BRANDS/DIVISIONS/AFFILIATES:

GROWTH PLANS/SPECIAL FEATURES:

The Revolve Group is an emerging e-commerce retailer, selling women's dresses, handbags, shoes, beauty products, and incidentals across its marketplace properties, Revolve and FWRD. The platform is built to suit the "next-generation customer," emphasizing mobile commerce, influencer marketing, and occupying an aspirational but attainable luxury niche. With $1.1 billion in 2022 net sales, the firm sits just outside the top 30 apparel retailers (by sales) in the U.S., but has consistently generated top-line growth north of 20%-25% as the industry continues to favor digital channels. Revolve generates approximately 20% of sales from private-label offerings, while focusing on building an inventory of unique products from emerging fashion brands with less than $10 million in annual sales.

CONTACTS: *Note: Officers with more than one job title may be intentionally listed here more than once.*

Jesse Timmermans, CFO
Michael Karanikolas, Chairman of the Board
Michael Mente, Co-CEO

FINANCIAL DATA: *Note: Data for latest year may not have been available at press time.*

In U.S. $	2022	2021	2020	2019	2018	2017
Revenue	1,101,416,000	891,390,000	580,649,000	600,993,000	498,739,000	399,597,000
R&D Expense						
Operating Income	73,140,000	105,291,000	61,066,000	48,098,000	41,798,000	20,522,000
Operating Margin %	.07%	.12%	.11%	.08%	.08%	
SGA Expense	487,379,000	363,210,000	227,743,000	254,442,000	210,216,000	163,710,000
Net Income	58,697,000	99,840,000	56,790,000	35,667,000	30,685,000	5,347,000
Operating Cash Flow	23,436,000	62,313,000	73,773,000	46,057,000	26,655,000	16,479,000
Capital Expenditure	5,167,000	2,195,000	2,324,000	12,455,000	3,045,000	2,262,000
EBITDA	77,931,000	109,799,000	65,893,000	52,050,000	44,665,000	23,371,000
Return on Assets %	.11%	.25%	.21%	- .03%	.21%	
Return on Equity %	.17%	.39%	.34%	- .05%	.62%	
Debt to Equity	.05%	.01%				

CONTACT INFORMATION:

Phone: 562-677-9480   Fax:
Toll-Free:
Address: 12889 Moore St., Cerritos, CA 90703 United States

STOCK TICKER/OTHER:

Stock Ticker: RVLV   Exchange: NYS
Employees: 1,384   Fiscal Year Ends: 12/31
Parent Company:

SALARIES/BONUSES:

Top Exec. Salary: $561,313   Bonus: $
Second Exec. Salary: Bonus: $
$451,236

OTHER THOUGHTS:

Estimated Female Officers or Directors:
Hot Spot for Advancement for Women/Minorities:

Rocket Internet SE

NAIC Code: 519130

TYPES OF BUSINESS:

Internet Search Web Sites
Ecommerce

BRANDS/DIVISIONS/AFFILIATES:

GROWTH PLANS/SPECIAL FEATURES:

Rocket Internet SE is a German company which provides software solutions. The company identifies proven internet and mobile business models and builds these either independently or invests in already existing companies. The company targets mainly new, underserved or untapped markets, in which new companies will be scaled to market leadership positions. It is focused on online business models to satisfy consumer needs across eCommerce, marketplace and financial technology sectors. Rocket Internet has a flexible and scalable technology platform, which enables realizing several new projects per year in its five target regions Europe, Africa and Middle-East, Asia-Pacific, Russia and Commonwealth of the Independent States and Latin America.

CONTACTS: Note: Officers with more than one job title may be intentionally listed here more than once.

Oliver Samwer, CEO
Jacob Bro, Global Chief Prod. Officer
Franziska Leonhardt, General Counsel
Patrick Fink, Global Head-Bus. Intelligence
Andreas Winiarski, Global Head-Public Rel.
Arnt Jeschke, Managing Dir.-Berlin
Eyad Alkassar, Managing Dir.-Middle East
Eduardo Goes, Managing Dir.-Latin America
Ian Marsh, Managing Dir.-U.K.
Marcus Englert, Chmn.
Don Phan, Managing Dir.-Vietnam

FINANCIAL DATA: Note: Data for latest year may not have been available at press time.

In U.S. $	2022	2021	2020	2019	2018	2017
Revenue	131,040,000	126,000,000	73,482,435	68,630,048	50,142,864	44,034,700
R&D Expense						
Operating Income						
Operating Margin %						
SGA Expense						
Net Income				291,040,352	227,449,824	-7,156,040
Operating Cash Flow						
Capital Expenditure						
EBITDA						
Return on Assets %						
Return on Equity %						
Debt to Equity						

CONTACT INFORMATION:

Phone: 49-30-300131800   Fax:
Toll-Free:
Address: Charlottenstrasse 4, Berlin, 10969 Germany

STOCK TICKER/OTHER:

Stock Ticker: Private
Employees: 400
Parent Company:

Exchange:
Fiscal Year Ends: 12/31

SALARIES/BONUSES:

Top Exec. Salary: $ Bonus: $
Second Exec. Salary: $ Bonus: $

OTHER THOUGHTS:

Estimated Female Officers or Directors: 2
Hot Spot for Advancement for Women/Minorities:

Rogers Communications Inc

www.rogers.com

NAIC Code: 517311

TYPES OF BUSINESS:

Cable TV Service
Internet Services
Wireless Phone Service
5G Technology
Wireless Services
Connected Home
Internet of Things
Media Services

BRANDS/DIVISIONS/AFFILIATES:

Rogers
Fido
chatr

GROWTH PLANS/SPECIAL FEATURES:

Rogers Communications is the largest wireless service provider in Canada, with its more than 11 million subscribers equating to one third of the total Canadian market. Its wireless business accounted for more than half of total revenue and has increasingly been providing a bigger portion of total company sales over the last several years. Rogers' cable segment, which provides about 35% of total revenue after acquiring Shaw, offers home internet, television, and landline phone service to consumers and businesses. Remaining sales come from Rogers' media unit, which owns and operates various television and radio stations and the Toronto Blue Jays. Rogers' significant exposure to sports also includes ownership stakes in the Toronto Maple Leafs, Raptors, FC, and Argonauts.

CONTACTS:
Note: Officers with more than one job title may be intentionally listed here more than once.

Alan Horn, CEO, Subsidiary
Jordan Banks, Pres., Divisional
Joseph Natale, CEO
Anthony Staffieri, CFO
Edward Rogers, Chairman of the Board
Jorge Fernandes, Chief Information Officer
Graeme McPhail, Chief Legal Officer
Melinda Rogers-Hixon, Deputy Chairman
Philip Lind, Director
Lisa Durocher, Executive VP, Divisional
James Reid, Other Executive Officer
Eric Agius, Other Executive Officer
Sevaun Palvetzian, Other Executive Officer
Dean Prevost, President, Divisional
Brent Johnston, President, Divisional

FINANCIAL DATA:
Note: Data for latest year may not have been available at press time.

In U.S. $	2022	2021	2020	2019	2018	2017
Revenue	11,321,670,000	10,776,770,000	10,233,330,000	11,084,150,000	11,101,060,000	10,566,450,000
R&D Expense						
Operating Income	2,806,886,000	2,428,174,000	2,381,846,000	2,738,497,000	2,773,795,000	2,470,824,000
Operating Margin %	.25%	.23%	.23%	.25%	.25%	.23%
SGA Expense						
Net Income	1,235,412,000	1,145,698,000	1,170,700,000	1,502,350,000	1,514,115,000	1,356,747,000
Operating Cash Flow	3,303,993,000	3,059,851,000	3,177,510,000	3,328,260,000	3,153,243,000	2,895,865,000
Capital Expenditure	2,295,808,000	2,089,906,000	1,742,078,000	2,108,290,000	2,091,377,000	1,834,734,000
EBITDA	4,655,592,000	4,115,100,000	4,199,666,000	4,499,695,000	4,257,025,000	4,022,444,000
Return on Assets %	.03%	.04%	.04%	.06%	.07%	.06%
Return on Equity %	.16%	.15%	.17%	.23%	.26%	.27%
Debt to Equity	3.13%	1.78%	1.912	1.855	1.64%	1.693

CONTACT INFORMATION:

Phone: 416 935-2303   Fax: 416 935-3548
Toll-Free:
Address: 333 Bloor St. E., Fl. 10, Toronto, ON M4W 1G9 Canada

STOCK TICKER/OTHER:

Stock Ticker: RCI   Exchange: NYS
Employees: 25,300   Fiscal Year Ends: 12/31
Parent Company:

SALARIES/BONUSES:

Top Exec. Salary: $1,376,538   Bonus: $
Second Exec. Salary: Bonus: $
$700,904

OTHER THOUGHTS:

Estimated Female Officers or Directors: 6
Hot Spot for Advancement for Women/Minorities: Y

Ruhnn Holding Limited

www.ruhnn.com

NAIC Code: 519130

TYPES OF BUSINESS:

Internet Publishing and Broadcasting and Web Search Portals
Ecommerce Branding
Marketing Solutions
Influencer Training System
Personalized Advertising
Online Customization Tools
Ecommerce Transformation

BRANDS/DIVISIONS/AFFILIATES:

RUNION Holding Limited

GROWTH PLANS/SPECIAL FEATURES:

Ruhnn Holding Limited provides an ecommerce celebrity incubation and marketing platform. The site encompasses an influencer training system for product and branding purposes. Business introduction services includes positioning and content planting, personalized advertising with customization tools, and brand conversion to ecommerce platforms. Ruhnn Holding is privately owned by RUNION Holding Limited.

CONTACTS: Note: Officers with more than one job title may be intentionally listed here more than once.

Lei Sun, CEO

FINANCIAL DATA: Note: Data for latest year may not have been available at press time.

In U.S. $	2022	2021	2020	2019	2018	2017
Revenue	197,943,000	190,329,360	183,009,000	162,522,896	140,843,424	81,417,696
R&D Expense						
Operating Income						
Operating Margin %						
SGA Expense						
Net Income			-13,810,000	-10,886,940	-15,458,824	-7,802,715
Operating Cash Flow						
Capital Expenditure						
EBITDA						
Return on Assets %						
Return on Equity %						
Debt to Equity						

CONTACT INFORMATION:

Phone: 86 571-8602-3171   Fax:
Toll-Free:
Address: Fl. 11, Bldg. 2, Lvgu Chuangzhi Ctr., 788 Hong Pu Rd., Jianggan Dist., Hangzhou, Zhejiang 310016 China

STOCK TICKER/OTHER:

Stock Ticker: Private   Exchange:
Employees: 780   Fiscal Year Ends: 03/31
Parent Company: RUNION Holding Limited

SALARIES/BONUSES:

Top Exec. Salary: $ Bonus: $
Second Exec. Salary: $ Bonus: $

OTHER THOUGHTS:

Estimated Female Officers or Directors:
Hot Spot for Advancement for Women/Minorities:

Sales, profits and employees may be estimates. Financial information, benefits and other data can change quickly and may vary from those stated here.

Sabre Corporation

www.sabre-holdings.com

NAIC Code: 561510

TYPES OF BUSINESS:

Travel Reservations System for Airlines
Travel Marketing Solutions
Distribution & Technology Solutions
Consulting Services

GROWTH PLANS/SPECIAL FEATURES:

Sabre holds the number-two air booking volume share in the global distribution system industry. The travel solutions segment represented 91% of total 2023 revenue, split between distribution (78% of segment sales) and airline IT solutions (22%) revenue. The company also has a growing hotel IT solutions division (9% of revenue). Transaction fees, which are mostly tied to volume and not price, account for the bulk of sales and profits.

BRANDS/DIVISIONS/AFFILIATES:

SabreSonic
Sabre AirVision Marketing & Planning
Sabre AirCentre Enterprise
SynXis
SynXis Property Manager Solutions

CONTACTS: Note: Officers with more than one job title may be intentionally listed here more than once.

Sean Menke, CEO
Douglas Barnett, CFO
Karl Peterson, Chairman of the Board
Jami Kindle, Chief Accounting Officer
David Moore, Chief Technology Officer
Wade Jones, Executive VP
Cem Tanyel, Executive VP
Roshan Mendis, Executive VP
Shawn Williams, Executive VP
Scott Wilson, Executive VP
Dave Shirk, Executive VP

FINANCIAL DATA: Note: Data for latest year may not have been available at press time.

In U.S. $	2022	2021	2020	2019	2018	2017
Revenue	2,537,015,000	1,688,875,000	1,334,100,000	3,974,988,000	3,866,956,000	
R&D Expense						
Operating Income	-261,060,000	-665,487,000	-988,039,000	363,417,000	562,016,000	
Operating Margin %	-.10%	-.39%	-.74%	.09%	.15%	
SGA Expense	661,159,000	610,078,000	586,406,000	600,210,000	551,923,000	
Net Income	-435,448,000	-928,469,000	-1,282,339,000	158,592,000	337,531,000	
Operating Cash Flow	-279,717,000	-418,152,000	-773,177,000	578,877,000	722,902,000	
Capital Expenditure	69,494,000	54,302,000	65,420,000	115,166,000	283,940,000	
EBITDA	56,431,000	-418,384,000	-715,411,000	770,650,000	968,774,000	
Return on Assets %	-.09%	-.17%	-.22%	.03%	.06%	
Return on Equity %			-2.12%	.17%	.41%	
Debt to Equity			17.315	3.527	3.45%	

CONTACT INFORMATION:

Phone: 682-605-1000   Fax:
Toll-Free:
Address: 3150 Sabre Dr., Southlake, TX 76092 United States

STOCK TICKER/OTHER:

Stock Ticker: SABR   Exchange: NAS
Employees: 7,461   Fiscal Year Ends: 12/31
Parent Company:

SALARIES/BONUSES:

Top Exec. Salary: $1,000,000   Bonus: $
Second Exec. Salary: Bonus: $
$750,000

OTHER THOUGHTS:

Estimated Female Officers or Directors: 1
Hot Spot for Advancement for Women/Minorities:

Sage Intacct Inc

www.sageintacct.com

NAIC Code: 511210Q

TYPES OF BUSINESS:

Computer Software: Accounting, Banking & Financial
Finance and Accounting Software
Cloud-Based Software Development
Industry-Specific Dashboards
Financial Management Solutions
Software-as-a-Service (SaaS)
Integration Technology
Application Programming Interface (API)

BRANDS/DIVISIONS/AFFILIATES:

Sage Group plc (The)

CONTACTS: Note: Officers with more than one job title may be intentionally listed here more than once.

Steve Hare, CEO
Jonathan Howell, CFO
Cath Keers, CMO
Amanda Cusdin, Chief People Officer
Aaron Harris, CTO
Andrew Duff, Chmn.

GROWTH PLANS/SPECIAL FEATURES:

Sage Intacct, Inc. provides cloud-based accounting software and financial management solutions for small- and medium-sized businesses. The firm's accounting and financial products include industry-specific dashboards for decision-making purposes. Sage Intacct's many wide range of products address accounts payable and receivable, cash management, intelligent general ledger, order management, purchasing, collaboration, interactive visuals, software-as-a-service (SaaS) intelligence, contract and subscription billing, project costing/billing, revenue reconciliation, sales and use tax, spend management, time and expense management, vendor payment services, inventory management and more. The company's platform comprises built-in tools for unique business needs, and include platform services, Salesforce integration and a web services application programming interface (API). Sage Intacct serves many industry customers, including accountants and CPA firms, biotech and life sciences, construction and real estate, financial services, franchises, healthcare, hospitality, nonprofits, professional services, retail, SaaS and wholesale distribution, among others. Sage Intacct is based in California, USA, with international offices in India and Romania. It operates as a wholly-owned subsidiary of The Sage Group plc.

FINANCIAL DATA: Note: Data for latest year may not have been available at press time.

In U.S. $	2022	2021	2020	2019	2018	2017
Revenue	195,771,000	188,241,040	181,001,000	156,081,000	118,019,000	70,000,000
R&D Expense						
Operating Income						
Operating Margin %						
SGA Expense						
Net Income						
Operating Cash Flow						
Capital Expenditure						
EBITDA						
Return on Assets %						
Return on Equity %						
Debt to Equity						

CONTACT INFORMATION:

Phone: 408-878-0900   Fax: 408-878-0910
Toll-Free: 877-968-0600
Address: 300 Park Ave., Ste,1400, San Jose, CA 95110 United States

STOCK TICKER/OTHER:

Stock Ticker: Subsidiary   Exchange:
Employees: 450   Fiscal Year Ends:
Parent Company: Sage Group plc (The)

SALARIES/BONUSES:

Top Exec. Salary: $ Bonus: $
Second Exec. Salary: $ Bonus: $

OTHER THOUGHTS:

Estimated Female Officers or Directors:
Hot Spot for Advancement for Women/Minorities:

Salesforce Inc

www.salesforce.com

NAIC Code: 511210K

TYPES OF BUSINESS:

Software, Sales & Marketing Automation
Customer Relationship Management Software
Software Subscription Services

BRANDS/DIVISIONS/AFFILIATES:

Sales Cloud
Service Cloud
Marketing Cloud
Community Cloud
Industries
IoT Cloud
Tableau Software Inc
myTrailhead

CONTACTS: *Note: Officers with more than one job title may be intentionally listed here more than once.*

Marc Benioff, CEO
Amy Weaver, CFO
Joe Allanson, Chief Accounting Officer
Parker Harris, Chief Technology Officer
Bret Taylor, Co-President
Brent Hyder, Co-President
Srinivas Tallapragada, Co-President
Gavin Patterson, Co-President

GROWTH PLANS/SPECIAL FEATURES:

Salesforce Inc provides enterprise cloud computing solutions. The company offers customer relationship management technology that brings companies and customers together. Its Customer 360 platform helps the group to deliver a single source of truth, connecting customer data across systems, apps, and devices to help companies sell, service, market, and conduct commerce. It also offers Service Cloud for customer support, Marketing Cloud for digital marketing campaigns, Commerce Cloud as an e-commerce engine, the Salesforce Platform, which allows enterprises to build applications, and other solutions, such as MuleSoft for data integration.

FINANCIAL DATA: *Note: Data for latest year may not have been available at press time.*

In U.S. $	2022	2021	2020	2019	2018	2017
Revenue	26,492,000,000	21,252,000,000	17,098,000,000	13,282,000,000	10,540,000,000	
R&D Expense	4,465,000,000	3,598,000,000	2,766,000,000	1,886,000,000	1,553,000,000	
Operating Income	548,000,000	455,000,000	463,000,000	535,000,000	454,000,000	
Operating Margin %	.02%	.02%	.03%	.04%	.04%	
SGA Expense	14,453,000,000	11,761,000,000	9,634,000,000	7,410,000,000	5,760,000,000	
Net Income	1,444,000,000	4,072,000,000	126,000,000	1,110,000,000	360,000,000	
Operating Cash Flow	6,000,000,000	4,801,000,000	4,331,000,000	3,398,000,000	2,738,000,000	
Capital Expenditure	717,000,000	710,000,000	643,000,000	595,000,000	534,000,000	
EBITDA	3,846,000,000	3,301,000,000	2,598,000,000	1,517,000,000	1,238,000,000	
Return on Assets %	.02%	.07%	.00%	.04%	.02%	
Return on Equity %	.03%	.11%	.01%	.09%	.04%	
Debt to Equity	.23%	.13%	0.151	0.203	.07%	

CONTACT INFORMATION:

Phone: 415 901-7000   Fax: 415 901-7040
Toll-Free:
Address: Salesforce Tower, 415 Mission St., 3/Fl, San Francisco, CA 94105 United States

STOCK TICKER/OTHER:

Stock Ticker: CRM
Employees: 79,390
Parent Company:

Exchange: NYS
Fiscal Year Ends: 01/31

SALARIES/BONUSES:

Top Exec. Salary: $900,000   Bonus: $2,500,000
Second Exec. Salary: $1,550,000   Bonus: $3,750

OTHER THOUGHTS:

Estimated Female Officers or Directors: 4
Hot Spot for Advancement for Women/Minorities: Y

Salon.com LLC

www.salon.com

NAIC Code: 519130

TYPES OF BUSINESS:
Online News & Media
Digital Publication Platform
News Publications
Political Publications
Culture and Entertainment
Health and Science
Email Newsletters
Mobile Apps

BRANDS/DIVISIONS/AFFILIATES:
Salon.com
Salon TV
Salon Talks

GROWTH PLANS/SPECIAL FEATURES:
Salon.com, LLC operates an independent digital publication platform that primarily offers news and politics through a progressive, non-partisan editorial lens. Other publication topics include culture, entertainment, science, health and food. Salon.com offers original reporting, news analysis, investigation findings, commentary, criticism, essays and in-depth interviews. The company's journalism is distributed across Salon.com, Salon TV, social media, news platforms, email newsletters and mobile apps. Salon's content includes flagship Salon Talks show and other Salon TV programming, which reach approximately 10 million monthly unique visitors. Salon's publications are offered free of charge, but subscribers receive ad-free content.

CONTACTS:
Note: Officers with more than one job title may be intentionally listed here more than once.

Drew Schoentrup, CEO
Norman Blashka, CFO
David Talbot, Founder
Joan Walsh, Other Corporate Officer
Benjamin Zagorski, Vice President, Divisional

FINANCIAL DATA:
Note: Data for latest year may not have been available at press time.

In U.S. $	2022	2021	2020	2019	2018	2017
Revenue						
R&D Expense						
Operating Income						
Operating Margin %						
SGA Expense						
Net Income						
Operating Cash Flow						
Capital Expenditure						
EBITDA						
Return on Assets %						
Return on Equity %						
Debt to Equity						

CONTACT INFORMATION:
Phone: 415-645-9200   Fax: 415 645-9204
Toll-Free:
Address: 22 4th St., Fl. 15, San Francisco, CA 94103 United States

SALARIES/BONUSES:
Top Exec. Salary: $ Bonus: $
Second Exec. Salary: $ Bonus: $

STOCK TICKER/OTHER:
Stock Ticker: Private   Exchange:
Employees: 44   Fiscal Year Ends: 03/31
Parent Company:

OTHER THOUGHTS:
Estimated Female Officers or Directors: 3
Hot Spot for Advancement for Women/Minorities: Y

SAP Ariba
www.ariba.com

NAIC Code: 511210Q

TYPES OF BUSINESS:
Computer Software: Accounting, Banking & Financial
Cloud Procurement & Logistics Solutions
Business Process Software
Consulting Services
Business Collaboration Solutions
Buying and Selling Solutions
Sourcing and Supply Chain Solutions
Procurement, and Integration Solutions

BRANDS/DIVISIONS/AFFILIATES:
SAP SE
Ariba Network

CONTACTS: Note: Officers with more than one job title may be intentionally listed here more than once.
Christian Klein, CEO-Corp.
Dominik Asam, CFO-Corp.
Gina Vargiu-Breuer, chief People Officer-Corp.
Juergen Mueller, CTO-Corp.
Matthew Zack, Sr. VP-Corp. Dev.
Charles Jackson, Exec. VP
Hasso Plattner, Chmn.-Corp.
Michael J. Arenth, Sr. VP-Global Customer Mgmt.

GROWTH PLANS/SPECIAL FEATURES:
SAP Ariba provides cloud procurement solutions for buyers and suppliers. The firm is a subsidiary of SAP SE. The company's cloud based Ariba Network is a business network where customers can collaborate with any company, anytime, anywhere. This collaborative business community provides potential buying or selling opportunities. Solutions offered by the firm include supplier management, strategic sourcing, supply chain, procurement, financial supply chain, platform solutions, integration solutions and services for buyers. SAP Ariba is open to all systems and all types of goods and services. It offers an end-to-end automated system that removes complexity and allows buyers and suppliers to manage everything from contracts to payments all in one place. Ariba's website offers resources, demos and explanations about its network, solutions and capabilities. Key industries served by SAP Ariba include automotive, banking, chemicals, consumer products, energy and natural resources, insurance and public sector.

FINANCIAL DATA: Note: Data for latest year may not have been available at press time.

In U.S. $	2022	2021	2020	2019	2018	2017
Revenue	1,670,000,000	1,493,490,653	1,675,400,000	1,460,450,000	1,336,280,000	1,351,890,000
R&D Expense						
Operating Income						
Operating Margin %						
SGA Expense						
Net Income		565,956,534	483,322,000	372,018,000	243,317,000	195,870,000
Operating Cash Flow						
Capital Expenditure						
EBITDA						
Return on Assets %						
Return on Equity %						
Debt to Equity						

CONTACT INFORMATION:
Phone: 650-849-4000   Fax:
Toll-Free:
Address: 3420 Hillview Ave., Palo Alto, CA 94304 United States

STOCK TICKER/OTHER:
Stock Ticker: Subsidiary   Exchange:
Employees: 1,800   Fiscal Year Ends: 12/31
Parent Company: SAP SE

SALARIES/BONUSES:
Top Exec. Salary: $ Bonus: $
Second Exec. Salary: $ Bonus: $

OTHER THOUGHTS:
Estimated Female Officers or Directors:
Hot Spot for Advancement for Women/Minorities:

SAP SE

www.sap.com

NAIC Code: 511210H

TYPES OF BUSINESS:

Computer Software, Business Management & ERP
Consulting & Training Services
Hosting Services
Software Licensing
Software Development

GROWTH PLANS/SPECIAL FEATURES:

Founded in 1972 by former IBM employees, SAP provides database technology and enterprise resource planning software to enterprises around the world. Across more than 180 countries, the company serves 440,000 customers, approximately 80% of which are small- to medium-size enterprises.

SAP offers medical, dental, vision and life insurance; a 401(k) and spending/saving accounts.

BRANDS/DIVISIONS/AFFILIATES:

SAP HANA

CONTACTS: *Note: Officers with more than one job title may be intentionally listed here more than once.*

Christian Klein, CEO
Luka Mucic, CFO
Sabine Bendiek, Chief People Officer
Juergen Mueller, CTO
Luca Mucic, Head-Global Finance
Jim Hagemann Snabe, Co-CEO
Bernd Leukert, Head- Application Innovation

FINANCIAL DATA: *Note: Data for latest year may not have been available at press time.*

In U.S. $	2022	2021	2020	2019	2018	2017
Revenue	33,323,620,000	30,053,970,000	29,509,930,000	29,742,010,000	26,670,980,000	25,324,910,000
R&D Expense	6,655,872,000	5,602,332,000	4,807,858,000	4,632,988,000	3,911,917,000	3,618,307,000
Operating Income	5,189,983,000	5,196,460,000	7,147,021,000	6,048,143,000	6,177,676,000	5,462,003,000
Operating Margin %	.16%	.17%	.24%	.20%	.23%	.22%
SGA Expense	11,890,110,000	10,725,390,000	9,134,283,000	10,062,610,000	8,504,965,000	8,634,499,000
Net Income	2,465,458,000	5,673,575,000	5,553,756,000	3,584,844,000	4,407,383,000	4,326,425,000
Operating Cash Flow	6,096,718,000	6,718,480,000	7,766,623,000	3,772,668,000	4,643,782,000	5,446,891,000
Capital Expenditure	943,436,900	863,557,800	880,829,000	881,908,400	1,573,834,000	1,376,295,000
EBITDA	7,762,306,000	10,331,390,000	10,522,450,000	7,617,659,000	7,966,321,000	7,112,478,000
Return on Assets %	.03%	.08%	.09%	.06%	.09%	.09%
Return on Equity %	.06%	.15%	.17%	.11%	.15%	.15%
Debt to Equity	.22%	.28%	0.458	0.362	.37%	0.196

CONTACT INFORMATION:

Phone: 49 6227747474   Fax: 49 6227757575
Toll-Free: 800-872-1727
Address: Dietmar-Hopp-Allee 16, Walldorf, 69190 Germany

STOCK TICKER/OTHER:

Stock Ticker: SAP   Exchange: NYS
Employees: 111,961   Fiscal Year Ends: 12/31
Parent Company:

SALARIES/BONUSES:

Top Exec. Salary: $1,241,364   Bonus: $
Second Exec. Salary: Bonus: $
$755,613

OTHER THOUGHTS:

Estimated Female Officers or Directors: 4
Hot Spot for Advancement for Women/Minorities: Y

Sales, profits and employees may be estimates. Financial information, benefits and other data can change quickly and may vary from those stated here.

Sea Limited

NAIC Code: 511210M

TYPES OF BUSINESS:

Online Marketplace Tools
Ecommerce

BRANDS/DIVISIONS/AFFILIATES:

Garena
Shopee
SeaMoney
AirPay
ShopeePay
ShopeePayLater

GROWTH PLANS/SPECIAL FEATURES:

Sea operates Southeast Asia's largest e-commerce company, Shopee, in terms of gross merchandise value and number of transactions. Sea started as a gaming business, Garena, but in 2015 expanded into e-commerce, which is now the main growth driver. Shopee is a hybrid C2C and B2C marketplace platform operating in eight core markets. Indonesia accounts for 35% of GMV, with the rest split mainly among Taiwan, Vietnam, Thailand, Malaysia, and the Philippines. For Garena, Free Fire was the most downloaded game in January 2022 and accounted for 74% of gaming revenue in 2021. Sea's third business, SeaMoney, provides mostly credit lending.

CONTACTS:
Note: Officers with more than one job title may be intentionally listed here more than once.

Forrest Li, CEO
Gang Ye, COO
Tony Hou, CFO

FINANCIAL DATA:
Note: Data for latest year may not have been available at press time.

In U.S. $	2022	2021	2020	2019	2018	2017
Revenue	12,449,700,000	9,955,190,000	4,375,664,000	2,175,378,000	826,968,000	414,190,000
R&D Expense	1,376,501,000	831,703,000	353,785,000	156,634,000	67,529,000	29,323,000
Operating Income	-1,132,565,000	-1,583,060,000	-1,303,325,000	-891,232,000	-988,768,000	-502,356,000
Operating Margin %		-.16%	-.30%	-.41%	-1.20%	-1.21%
SGA Expense	4,706,835,000	4,817,611,000	2,430,581,000	1,355,408,000	945,796,000	563,842,000
Net Income	-1,651,421,000	-2,046,759,000	-1,618,056,000	-1,462,799,000	-961,241,000	-560,485,000
Operating Cash Flow	-1,055,692,000	208,649,000	555,868,000	69,865,000	-495,220,000	-259,228,000
Capital Expenditure	976,283,000	807,176,000	357,054,000	247,098,000	178,485,000	79,746,000
EBITDA	-1,026,793,000	-1,299,276,000	-1,178,634,000	-1,198,779,000	-843,857,000	-481,086,000
Return on Assets %		-.14%	-.21%	-.39%	-.46%	-.45%
Return on Equity %		-.38%	-.71%	-3.18%	-8.51%	-3.26%
Debt to Equity		.54%	0.597	1.296		1.55

CONTACT INFORMATION:

Phone: 65-6270-8100   Fax:
Toll-Free:
Address: 1 Fusionopolis Pl., #17-10, Galaxis Bldg., Singapore, 138522 Singapore

STOCK TICKER/OTHER:

Stock Ticker: SE
Employees: 63,800
Parent Company:

Exchange: NYS
Fiscal Year Ends: 12/31

SALARIES/BONUSES:

Top Exec. Salary: $ Bonus: $
Second Exec. Salary: $ Bonus: $

OTHER THOUGHTS:

Estimated Female Officers or Directors:
Hot Spot for Advancement for Women/Minorities:

Seek Limited

NAIC Code: 519130

www.seek.com.au

TYPES OF BUSINESS:
Online Marketplace
Online Jobs Listings

GROWTH PLANS/SPECIAL FEATURES:
Seek is a technology company operating in the employment segment. Seek's primary business is an online listings platform for employment, www.seek.com.au, which is the largest online listings platform for employment in Australia and New Zealand. Seek also owns and operates employment listings platforms in Southeast Asia and Latin America and operates an investment business in employment listings platforms and other employment related businesses.

BRANDS/DIVISIONS/AFFILIATES:

CONTACTS: *Note: Officers with more than one job title may be intentionally listed here more than once.*
Andrew Bassat, CEO
Ian Narev, COO
Geoff Roberts, CFO
Graham Goldsmith, Chmn.

FINANCIAL DATA: *Note: Data for latest year may not have been available at press time.*

In U.S. $	2022	2021	2020	2019	2018	2017
Revenue	721,046,800	491,009,400	1,018,701,000	992,803,700	836,001,000	
R&D Expense						
Operating Income	248,378,500	146,082,200	154,929,800	243,276,600	205,561,300	
Operating Margin %	.34%	.30%	.15%	.25%	.25%	
SGA Expense	350,804,000	252,188,800	499,340,300	542,286,700	477,059,900	
Net Income	109,012,700	485,778,300	-72,136,980	116,439,500	34,357,090	
Operating Cash Flow						
Capital Expenditure	85,828,150	89,057,200	81,178,320	80,790,830	73,364,020	
EBITDA	309,730,500	171,850,000	105,008,700	281,702,300	184,249,600	
Return on Assets %	.04%	.17%	-.03%	.04%	.01%	
Return on Equity %	.09%	.52%	-.09%	.13%	.04%	
Debt to Equity	.85%	.66%	1.694	1.048	.91%	

CONTACT INFORMATION:
Phone: 61 3 8517 4100   Fax: 61 3 9510 7244
Toll-Free:
Address: Level 6, 541 St Kilda Rd., Melbourne, VIC 3004 Australia

STOCK TICKER/OTHER:
Stock Ticker: SKLTY   Exchange: PINX
Employees: 2,659   Fiscal Year Ends: 06/30
Parent Company:

SALARIES/BONUSES:
Top Exec. Salary: $ Bonus: $
Second Exec. Salary: $ Bonus: $

OTHER THOUGHTS:
Estimated Female Officers or Directors:
Hot Spot for Advancement for Women/Minorities:

Segment.io Inc
NAIC Code: 511210J

TYPES OF BUSINESS:
Computer Software, Data Base & File Management
Customer Data Platform
Single Application Program Interface
Data Analytics
Product Marketing Solutions
Product Data
Data Management
Product and Marketing Campaigns

BRANDS/DIVISIONS/AFFILIATES:
Twilio Inc
Twilio Engage

CONTACTS: *Note: Officers with more than one job title may be intentionally listed here more than once.*
Khozema Shipchandler, CEO-Corp.

GROWTH PLANS/SPECIAL FEATURES:
Segment.io, Inc. provides a platform for collecting, cleaning and activating data, serving businesses across a range of industries, from startups to enterprises. The Segment platform collects events from the company's websites and mobile apps and provides a complete data toolkit to every team. Marketing teams can personalize customer experiences in real-time; product data offers analytics for decision-making purposes; and the single platform enables engineers to collect and manage data. Products by Segment include: connections, for integrating web and mobile app data through a single application programming interface (API); protocols, for protecting data; profiles, for a complete view of customers; and Twilio Engage, for designing personalized omnichannel product/marketing campaigns. Segment primarily serves the retail, business-to-business, financial services, media, marketplace, mobile and healthcare industries. The firm's website offers documentation regarding integrating Segment products and tools, as well as other related resources. Prices range from free to $120/month for teams to custom pricing for businesses. Segment.io operates as a subsidiary of Twilio, Inc.

FINANCIAL DATA: *Note: Data for latest year may not have been available at press time.*

In U.S. $	2022	2021	2020	2019	2018	2017
Revenue						
R&D Expense						
Operating Income						
Operating Margin %						
SGA Expense						
Net Income						
Operating Cash Flow						
Capital Expenditure						
EBITDA						
Return on Assets %						
Return on Equity %						
Debt to Equity						

CONTACT INFORMATION:
Phone: 415-213-2870   Fax:
Toll-Free:
Address: 100 California St., Ste. 700, San Francisco, CA 94111 United States

STOCK TICKER/OTHER:
Stock Ticker: Subsidiary   Exchange:
Employees: 550   Fiscal Year Ends:
Parent Company: Twilio Inc

SALARIES/BONUSES:
Top Exec. Salary: $ Bonus: $
Second Exec. Salary: $ Bonus: $

OTHER THOUGHTS:
Estimated Female Officers or Directors:
Hot Spot for Advancement for Women/Minorities:

SendGrid Inc

sendgrid.com

NAIC Code: 511210F

TYPES OF BUSINESS:

Computer Software, Multimedia, Graphics & Publishing
Email Delivery Services
Cloud-based Delivery Platform
Application Program Interface Solution
Software Integration
Marketing Solutions

BRANDS/DIVISIONS/AFFILIATES:

Twilio Inc
Twilio SendGrid

CONTACTS:
Note: Officers with more than one job title may be intentionally listed here more than once.

Sameer Dholakia, CEO

GROWTH PLANS/SPECIAL FEATURES:

SendGrid, Inc. does business as Twilio SendGrid and provides a cloud-based platform that solves challenges of email delivery on behalf of its customers, from startups to marketers to enterprises. Many application emails do not get delivered, so SendGrid's app was designed for this kind of deliverability. Today, Twilio SendGrid is responsible for sending more than 100 billion emails for companies every month, globally. The firm's application program interface (API) email solution integrates with its customer's business application (whether content management system, framework, CRM or own code) and their email delivery begins via simple mail transfer protocol (SMTP) or API within five minutes or less. SendGrid secures email delivery with two-factor authentication, multi-user credentials, API key permissions, internet protocol (IP) access management and more. The firm's single platform can be shared with business' entire team for all its email sending needs. Text messages can also be programmed globally with the API. Marketers can send (templates are provided), well-targeted marketing campaigns with Twilio SendGrid's marketing solution. This product provides 24/7 support and step-by-step resources, as well as the ability to design A/B tests with a select number of subject lines or content variations. Campaign accounts are safeguarded with Twilio SendGrid's internet service provider monitoring systems, and users can manage recipients, scheduling, content and testing all from one viewpoint. SendGrid's marketing campaign solution enables teams to define segments based on customer data and campaign engagement, add contacts to relative segments, and create static lists for groups of contacts to be managed manually. Key metrics such as track sends, delivery rates, bounces, spam reports, link clicks, opens and unsubscribes can be easily applied. SendGrid operates as a subsidiary of Twilio, Inc.

Parent Twilio offers employees comprehensive health benefits, a retirement savings plan, remote work and other plans, programs and company perks.

FINANCIAL DATA:
Note: Data for latest year may not have been available at press time.

In U.S. $	2022	2021	2020	2019	2018	2017
Revenue	215,000,000	197,997,800	190,382,500	177,100,000	117,482,400	111,888,000
R&D Expense						
Operating Income						
Operating Margin %						
SGA Expense						
Net Income						
Operating Cash Flow						
Capital Expenditure						
EBITDA						
Return on Assets %						
Return on Equity %						
Debt to Equity						

CONTACT INFORMATION:

Phone: 303 552-0653   Fax:
Toll-Free: 888-985-8363
Address: 1801 California St., Ste. 500, Denver, CO 80202 United States

STOCK TICKER/OTHER:

Stock Ticker: Subsidiary   Exchange:
Employees: 415   Fiscal Year Ends:
Parent Company: Twilio Inc

SALARIES/BONUSES:

Top Exec. Salary: $ Bonus: $
Second Exec. Salary: $ Bonus: $

OTHER THOUGHTS:

Estimated Female Officers or Directors:
Hot Spot for Advancement for Women/Minorities:

Sales, profits and employees may be estimates. Financial information, benefits and other data can change quickly and may vary from those stated here.

ServiceMax Inc

NAIC Code: 511210H

TYPES OF BUSINESS:

Computer Software, Business Management & ERP
Cloud-based Field Service Management Solutions
Contract Management
Schedule Management
Parts Management Solutions
Mobile Capabilities
Internet of Things
Data Analytics

BRANDS/DIVISIONS/AFFILIATES:

PTC
ServiceMax Asset 360 for Salesforce
ServiceMax Core
ServiceMax Field FX
ServiceMax Engage
Zinc Intelligent Remote Service

CONTACTS: *Note: Officers with more than one job title may be intentionally listed here more than once.*

Neil Barua, CEO-Corp.

GROWTH PLANS/SPECIAL FEATURES:

ServiceMax, Inc. develops and provides innovative field service management and real-time communication solutions that minimize unplanned downtime for a range of industries. ServiceMax's Asset 360 for Salesforce product delivers visibility into a company's service operation to maximize equipment uptime, reduce costs and add outcome-based service models. Asset 360 offers warranty and contract management, contractor management, proactive maintenance, mobile technician app, field service analytics, returns and repair, remote service app, service processing management, scheduling and other solutions. ServiceMax Core offers field service management software for asset-centric industries. Core's features, services and integrations help customers improve asset uptime, boost technician productivity via mobile tools, and deliver metrics for decision-making purposes. ServiceMax FieldFX is a field service management product for oil and gas companies, enabling them to connect to the office from anywhere, any time. ServiceMax Engage is a turnkey mobile app that connects service organizations with end customers to improve customer experience and asset data quality. Engage customers primarily consist of business owners and business operators. ServiceMax's Zinc Intelligent Remote Service connects service teams with people and information needed to get jobs accomplished, in real-time. Industries served by ServiceMax include medical device manufacturing, equipment dealers, industrial equipment manufacturing, oil and gas, power and utilities, building and construction equipment, telecommunications, high-tech manufacturing, mining and rail transportation. Based in California, USA, the firm has global offices in India. ServiceMax is majority owned by PTC (formerly know as Parametric Technology Corporation).

ServiceMax offers employee health and retirement benefits.

FINANCIAL DATA: *Note: Data for latest year may not have been available at press time.*

In U.S. $	2022	2021	2020	2019	2018	2017
Revenue	82,000,000	80,000,000	75,245,625	77,175,000	73,500,000	70,000,000
R&D Expense						
Operating Income						
Operating Margin %						
SGA Expense						
Net Income						
Operating Cash Flow						
Capital Expenditure						
EBITDA						
Return on Assets %						
Return on Equity %						
Debt to Equity						

CONTACT INFORMATION:

Phone: 925-965-7859   Fax: 925-391-3516
Toll-Free: 800-756-4960
Address: 4450 Rosewood Dr., #200, Pleasanton, CA 94588 United States

STOCK TICKER/OTHER:

Stock Ticker: Subsidiary   Exchange:
Employees: 620   Fiscal Year Ends:
Parent Company: PTC

SALARIES/BONUSES:

Top Exec. Salary: $ Bonus: $
Second Exec. Salary: $ Bonus: $

OTHER THOUGHTS:

Estimated Female Officers or Directors:
Hot Spot for Advancement for Women/Minorities:

ServiceNow Inc

www.service-now.com

NAIC Code: 511210B

TYPES OF BUSINESS:

Computer Software: Network Management (IT), System Testing & Storage
Cloud-Based Workflow Software

BRANDS/DIVISIONS/AFFILIATES:

Loom Systems Ltd
Rupert Labs Inc
Passage AI
Sweagle NV

GROWTH PLANS/SPECIAL FEATURES:

ServiceNow Inc provides software solutions to structure and
automate various business processes via a SaaS delivery
model. The company primarily focuses on the IT function for
enterprise customers. ServiceNow began with IT service
management, expanded within the IT function, and more
recently directed its workflow automation logic to functional
areas beyond IT, notably customer service, HR service
delivery, and security operations. ServiceNow also offers an
application development platform as a service.

CONTACTS: Note: Officers with more than one job title may be intentionally listed here more than once.

William Mcdermott, CEO
Gina Mastantuono, CFO
Frederic Luddy, Chairman of the Board
Fay Goon, Chief Accounting Officer
Russell Elmer, General Counsel
Kevin Haverty, Other Executive Officer
Chirantan Desai, Other Executive Officer

FINANCIAL DATA: Note: Data for latest year may not have been available at press time.

In U.S. $	2022	2021	2020	2019	2018	2017
Revenue	7,245,000,000	5,896,000,000	4,519,000,000	3,460,000,000	2,608,816,000	
R&D Expense	1,768,000,000	1,397,000,000	1,024,000,000	749,000,000	529,501,000	
Operating Income	355,000,000	257,000,000	199,000,000	42,000,000	-42,426,000	
Operating Margin %	.05%	.04%	.04%	.01%	-.02%	
SGA Expense	3,549,000,000	2,889,000,000	2,309,000,000	1,873,000,000	1,499,083,000	
Net Income	325,000,000	230,000,000	119,000,000	627,000,000	-26,704,000	
Operating Cash Flow	2,723,000,000	2,191,000,000	1,786,000,000	1,236,000,000	811,089,000	
Capital Expenditure	550,000,000	392,000,000	432,000,000	338,000,000	248,862,000	
EBITDA	859,000,000	729,000,000	519,000,000	352,000,000	163,313,000	
Return on Assets %	.03%	.02%	.02%	.13%	-.01%	
Return on Equity %	.07%	.07%	.05%	.39%	-.03%	
Debt to Equity	.42%	.55%	0.728	0.507	.60%	

CONTACT INFORMATION:

Phone: 408-501-8550   Fax:
Toll-Free:
Address: 2225 Lawson Ln., Santa Clara, CA 95054 United States

STOCK TICKER/OTHER:

Stock Ticker: NOW   Exchange: NYS
Employees: 22,668   Fiscal Year Ends: 12/31
Parent Company:

SALARIES/BONUSES:

Top Exec. Salary: $1,166,667   Bonus: $
Second Exec. Salary: Bonus: $
$930,035

OTHER THOUGHTS:

Estimated Female Officers or Directors:
Hot Spot for Advancement for Women/Minorities:

Shaw Communications Inc

www.shaw.ca

NAIC Code: 517311

TYPES OF BUSINESS:

Cable TV Service
Internet Service Provider
Satellite Services
Digital and Phone Services
Television Connectivity Services
Business Connectivity Solutions
Wireless Solutions and Services

BRANDS/DIVISIONS/AFFILIATES:

Shaw
Shaw Direct
Shaw Business
Freedom

GROWTH PLANS/SPECIAL FEATURES:

Shaw Communications is a Canadian cable company that is one of the biggest providers of internet, television, and landline telephone services in Western Canada. Shaw's products and services are divided into three areas. The firm's residential internet, TV and mobile services are offered under the Shaw brand. Shaw Direct is a leading Canadian licensed satellite video service provider. Shaw Business offers business internet, TV and mobile services. In April of 2023, the firm was acquired by Rogers Communications Inc.

CONTACTS: *Note: Officers with more than one job title may be intentionally listed here more than once.*

Tony Staffieri, CEO-Rogers Communications Inc
Trevor English, CFO
Dan Markou, Executive VP
Paul Mcaleese, President
Paul Deverell, President, Divisional
Katherine Emberly, President, Divisional

FINANCIAL DATA: *Note: Data for latest year may not have been available at press time.*

In U.S. $	2022	2021	2020	2019	2018	2017
Revenue	3,984,174,592	4,028,784,640	4,205,491,200	3,905,193,472	4,112,890,624	3,482,665,216
R&D Expense						
Operating Income						
Operating Margin %						
SGA Expense						
Net Income	558,720,512	721,071,232	535,117,056	534,587,328	47,103,156	607,076,608
Operating Cash Flow						
Capital Expenditure						
EBITDA						
Return on Assets %						
Return on Equity %						
Debt to Equity						

CONTACT INFORMATION:

Phone: 403 750-4500   Fax: 403 750-4501
Toll-Free: 888-472-2222
Address: 630 - 3rd Avenue S.W., Calgary, AB T2P 4L4 Canada

STOCK TICKER/OTHER:

Stock Ticker: Subsidiary   Exchange:
Employees: 9,500   Fiscal Year Ends: 08/31
Parent Company: Rogers Communications Inc

SALARIES/BONUSES:

Top Exec. Salary: $ Bonus: $
Second Exec. Salary: $ Bonus: $

OTHER THOUGHTS:

Estimated Female Officers or Directors: 3
Hot Spot for Advancement for Women/Minorities: Y

SHEIN

NAIC Code: 454110

TYPES OF BUSINESS:

Electronic Shopping
Ecommerce Retailing
On-Demand Manufacturing
Innovative Technology
Integrated Supply Chain Solutions
Global Ordering and Shipping
Shipment Tracking
Online Marketing

BRANDS/DIVISIONS/AFFILIATES:

Roadget Business Pte
Guangzhou Shein International
Misguided
Forever 21

CONTACTS: Note: Officers with more than one job title may be intentionally listed here more than once.

Chris XU, CEO

GROWTH PLANS/SPECIAL FEATURES:

SHEIN, founded in Nanjing, China and part of the holding company Roadget Business Pte, is a global fashion and lifestyle ecommerce retailer that offers women's wear, men's apparel, children's apparel, accessories, shoes, bags and other fashion and beauty/care items. The company utilizes on-demand manufacturing technology to connect suppliers to its integrated supply chain, primarily in plants within China. This enables SHEIN to reduce inventory waste and deliver products at extremely affordable prices to consumers throughout the world. Apparel categories include dresses, tops, two-piece outfits, jumpsuits and bodysuits, bottoms, denim, suits, separates, sweatshirts, sweaters/cardigans, outerwear, beachwear, intimates, sleep and lounge wear, maternity and nursing wear, activewear, wedding attire and collection lines. SHEIN is based in China, and has additional operations in Singapore and California, USA, as well as other global markets. The firm sells products to more than 150 countries. SHEIN utilizes a digital-first model, reaching customers via mobile devices, online and on social media platforms. It offers customer support for shipping, tracking, returns and online payments.

FINANCIAL DATA: Note: Data for latest year may not have been available at press time.

In U.S. $	2022	2021	2020	2019	2018	2017
Revenue	23,800,000,000	15,500,000,000	11,000,000,000	7,500,000,000		
R&D Expense						
Operating Income						
Operating Margin %						
SGA Expense						
Net Income		800,000,000				
Operating Cash Flow						
Capital Expenditure						
EBITDA						
Return on Assets %						
Return on Equity %						
Debt to Equity						

CONTACT INFORMATION:

Phone: 659-862-4700   Fax:
Toll-Free:
Address: 7 Temasek Blvd., #12-07, Guangzhou, Guangdong 03987 China

STOCK TICKER/OTHER:

Stock Ticker: Private
Employees: 10,000
Parent Company:

Exchange:
Fiscal Year Ends:

SALARIES/BONUSES:

Top Exec. Salary: $ Bonus: $
Second Exec. Salary: $ Bonus: $

OTHER THOUGHTS:

Estimated Female Officers or Directors:
Hot Spot for Advancement for Women/Minorities:

Sales, profits and employees may be estimates. Financial information, benefits and other data can change quickly and may vary from those stated here.

Shopify Inc

NAIC Code: 511210K

TYPES OF BUSINESS:

Ecommerce Site Platform
Online Marketing Tools
Warehouse Automation Technologies
Online Payments Platform
Working Capital for Small Businesses

BRANDS/DIVISIONS/AFFILIATES:

Shopify Plus
www.shopify.com/plus
Shop Pay
Shopify Capital

GROWTH PLANS/SPECIAL FEATURES:

Shopify offers an e-commerce platform primarily to small and medium-size businesses. The firm has two segments. The subscription solutions segment allows Shopify merchants to conduct e-commerce on a variety of platforms, including the company's website, physical stores, pop-up stores, kiosks, social networks (Facebook), and Amazon. The merchant solutions segment offers add-on products for the platform that facilitate e-commerce and include Shopify Payments, Shopify Shipping, and Shopify Capital.

The company is largely remote-work based.

CONTACTS: Note: Officers with more than one job title may be intentionally listed here more than once.

Tobias Lutke, CEO
Amy Shapero, CFO
Joseph Frasca, Chief Legal Officer
Jean-Michel Lemieux, Chief Technology Officer
Toby Shannan, COO
Brittany Forsyth, Other Executive Officer
Craig Miller, Other Executive Officer
Harley Finkelstein, President

FINANCIAL DATA: Note: Data for latest year may not have been available at press time.

In U.S. $	2022	2021	2020	2019	2018	2017
Revenue	5,600,000,000	4,611,856,000				
R&D Expense	1,503,000,000	854,383,000				
Operating Income	-822,000,000	268,643,000				
Operating Margin %	-.15%	.06%				
SGA Expense	1,938,000,000	1,276,401,000				
Net Income	-3,460,000,000	2,914,659,000				
Operating Cash Flow	-136,000,000	535,711,000				
Capital Expenditure	50,000,000	50,788,000				
EBITDA	-729,000,000	3,208,050,000				
Return on Assets %	-.29%	.28%				
Return on Equity %	-.36%	.33%				
Debt to Equity	.17%	.10%				

CONTACT INFORMATION:

Phone: 613-241-2828   Fax:
Toll-Free:
Address: 151 O'Connor St., Ground Floor, Ottawa, ON K2P 2L8 Canada

STOCK TICKER/OTHER:

Stock Ticker: SHOP   Exchange: NYS
Employees: 11,600   Fiscal Year Ends: 12/31
Parent Company:

SALARIES/BONUSES:

Top Exec. Salary: $551,523   Bonus: $
Second Exec. Salary: $488,628   Bonus: $

OTHER THOUGHTS:

Estimated Female Officers or Directors:
Hot Spot for Advancement for Women/Minorities:

Shopping.com Ltd

NAIC Code: 454110

TYPES OF BUSINESS:

Online Comparison Shopping
Online Consumer Reviews
Online Shopping
Price Comparison
Ecommerce
Product Information

BRANDS/DIVISIONS/AFFILIATES:

eBay Inc
Shopping.com

CONTACTS: *Note: Officers with more than one job title may be intentionally listed here more than once.*

Venky Natarajan, Global Head-Prod.
Bridget Davies, Managing Dir.-Global Bus.
Stephen Howard-Sarin, Sr. Dir.-North America Display Advertising
Paul S. Pressler, Chmn.-eBay

GROWTH PLANS/SPECIAL FEATURES:

Shopping.com Ltd., part of eBay, Inc.'s commerce network, provides an online price comparison shopping service for consumers and retailers. Shopping.com reaches hundreds of millions of shoppers each month through a single advertisement. The company also offers web-navigation tools as well as product reviews. Product categories include automotive parts, clothing and accessories, computers, electronics, flowers and gifts, health and beauty, home and garden, jewelry and watches, kids and family, magazine and subscriptions, media, musical instruments and accessories, office, sports and outdoors and video games. Shopping.com provides retailers with highest high conversion to sales rate; its efficient presentation of product information via the internet enables quick consumer purchase decisions. Features of the website include the ability to shop for brands and listings of its most popular items. The firm has operations in the U.S., France, Germany, United Kingdom, Italy, Spain, Netherlands, Poland, Austria, Ireland and Switzerland, and is a leading ecommerce destination worldwide.

FINANCIAL DATA: *Note: Data for latest year may not have been available at press time.*

In U.S. $	2022	2021	2020	2019	2018	2017
Revenue						
R&D Expense						
Operating Income						
Operating Margin %						
SGA Expense						
Net Income						
Operating Cash Flow						
Capital Expenditure						
EBITDA						
Return on Assets %						
Return on Equity %						
Debt to Equity						

CONTACT INFORMATION:

Phone: 408-376-7400   Fax: 408-516-8811
Toll-Free:
Address: 2025 Hamilton Ave., San Jose, CA 95125 United States

STOCK TICKER/OTHER:

Stock Ticker: Subsidiary   Exchange:
Employees: 200   Fiscal Year Ends: 12/31
Parent Company: eBay Inc

SALARIES/BONUSES:

Top Exec. Salary: $ Bonus: $
Second Exec. Salary: $ Bonus: $

OTHER THOUGHTS:

Estimated Female Officers or Directors: 2
Hot Spot for Advancement for Women/Minorities:

Sales, profits and employees may be estimates. Financial information, benefits and other data can change quickly and may vary from those stated here.

Shutterfly LLC

www.shutterfly.com

NAIC Code: 519130

TYPES OF BUSINESS:

Online Photographic Service
Personalized Products
Photo Keepsakes
Custom Stationery
Professional Photography
Photographic and Video Equipment Rental
Business Marketing Solutions and Technology
Business Document Management

BRANDS/DIVISIONS/AFFILIATES:

Apollo Global Management Inc
Shutterfly
Spoonflower
Snapfish
Lifetouch
BorrowLenses
Shutterfly Business Solutions

CONTACTS: Note: Officers with more than one job title may be intentionally listed here more than once.

Sally Pofcher, CEO
Dwayne Black, COO
William Lansing, Chairman of the Board
Jan Paul Teuwen, CFO
Bree Casart, CMO
Mandy Clark, Chief Human Resources Officer
Moudy Elbayadi, CTO
Ishantha Lokuge, Other Executive Officer
Tracy Layney, Other Executive Officer
James Hilt, President, Divisional
Scott Arnold, President, Divisional
Christopher North, President
Dennis Gregory Hintz, Senior VP, Divisional
Michael Pope, Senior VP
Lisa Blackwood-Kapral, Vice President

GROWTH PLANS/SPECIAL FEATURES:

Shutterfly, LLC comprises a family of brands that together make up an ecommerce and manufacturing platform for personalized products and custom design. The Shutterfly brand offers personalized photos and services that allow users to create keepsakes, photo books and custom stationery such as cars and announcements. Spoonflower is a global marketplace for connecting makers and consumers with artists. Consumers can either design their own patterns on premium fabric, wallpaper and home goods, or shop from an ecommerce marketplace. Snapfish enables users to create memories through a range of products, including drinkware, home decorations, photo books, prints and more. Lifetouch is a professional photography company that primarily serves schools for occasions such as annual school pictures (pre-school through high school), graduation pictures and sports and events coverage, as well as family pictures and portraits. BorrowLenses is an online destination for high-quality photographic and video equipment rentals, offering gear, shipping, pickup and return options. Users can also try before they purchase through the BorrowLenses platform. Tinyprints allows customer to print small birth announcements, invitations, stationery and holiday cards. Last, Shutterfly Business Solutions enable businesses to reach the global market via technology and project management tools. Business program packages offer ways to launch initiatives by utilizing global assets, leverage customer-level targeting through CRM-based strategies, obtain complex logic-based marketing support across multiple markets simultaneously, managing brand standards securely, and storing and billing documents in a centralized administration environment. Shutterfly is majority-owned by Apollo Global Management, Inc.

Shutterfly offers its employees health and wellness benefits, tradition and Roth 401(k) retirement plans and employee perks.

FINANCIAL DATA: Note: Data for latest year may not have been available at press time.

In U.S. $	2022	2021	2020	2019	2018	2017
Revenue	3,536,000,000	3,400,000,000	2,008,413,258	2,059,911,034	1,961,820,032	1,190,201,984
R&D Expense						
Operating Income						
Operating Margin %						
SGA Expense						
Net Income						
Operating Cash Flow						
Capital Expenditure						
EBITDA						
Return on Assets %						
Return on Equity %						
Debt to Equity						

CONTACT INFORMATION:

Phone: 650 610-5200   Fax:
Toll-Free: 877-284-9610
Address: 10 Almaden Blvd., San Jose, CA 95113 United States

STOCK TICKER/OTHER:

Stock Ticker: Subsidiary   Exchange:
Employees: 2,100   Fiscal Year Ends: 12/31
Parent Company: Apollo Global Management Inc

SALARIES/BONUSES:

Top Exec. Salary: $ Bonus: $
Second Exec. Salary: $ Bonus: $

OTHER THOUGHTS:

Estimated Female Officers or Directors: 2
Hot Spot for Advancement for Women/Minorities:

SINA Corporation

NAIC Code: 519130

english.sina.com

TYPES OF BUSINESS:
Internet Portal-Chinese
Email & Messaging Services
Search Engine
Online Games
Wireless Services
Online Auctions & Retail
Online News
Apps

BRANDS/DIVISIONS/AFFILIATES:
SINA Group Holding Co Ltd
SINA.com Technology (China) Co Ltd
Beijing New Media Information Technology Co Ltd
Beijing SINA Advertising Co Ltd
SINA (Shanghai) Management Co Ltd
Shanghai SINA Advertising Co Ltd
Weibo Internet Technology (China) Co Ltd
Starshining Mobile Technology (China) Ltd

CONTACTS: *Note: Officers with more than one job title may be intentionally listed here more than once.*
Charles Chao, CEO
Gaofei Wang, Sr. VP
Tong Chen, Exec. VP

GROWTH PLANS/SPECIAL FEATURES:

SINA Corporation is an online media company and mobile value-added services provider based in China. The firm's business is maintained primarily through its wholly-owned subsidiaries SINA.com Technology (China) Co., Ltd.; Starshining Mobile Technology (China) Ltd.; Beijing New Media Information Technology Co., Ltd.; Beijing SINA Advertising Co., Ltd.; SINA (Shanghai) Management Co., Ltd.; Shanghai SINA Advertising Co., Ltd.; and Weibo Internet Technology (China) Co., Ltd. SINA Corporation provides services such as online portals, blogs, video and music streaming, online games, classified listings and ecommerce through SINA.com, SINA.cn and Weibo.com. SINA.com is an online brand advertising property in China, providing Chinese language online news and content as well as such advertising product offerings as banner, button and text-link advertisements that appear on pages within the SINA network. SINA.com has portals in mainland China, Taiwan, Hong Kong and North America and consists of various regional, interest-based channels such as SINA News, SINA Entertainment, SINA Technology, SINA Video, SINA Sports, SINA Auto and SINA Finance, among others. SINA.cn provides entertainment and information from the SINA portal for mobile users. Weibo.com offers microblogging and social networking services, allowing users to connect 24/7 via a third-party mobile platform. SINA generates the majority of its revenue from online advertising, mobile value-added services and fee-based offerings. SINA operates as a subsidiary of SINA Group Holding Co. Ltd.

FINANCIAL DATA: *Note: Data for latest year may not have been available at press time.*

In U.S. $	2022	2021	2020	2019	2018	2017
Revenue	2,833,817,132	2,673,412,389	2,595,546,009	2,162,955,008	2,108,327,040	1,583,884,032
R&D Expense						
Operating Income						
Operating Margin %						
SGA Expense						
Net Income				-70,542,000	125,562,000	156,568,992
Operating Cash Flow						
Capital Expenditure						
EBITDA						
Return on Assets %						
Return on Equity %						
Debt to Equity						

CONTACT INFORMATION:
Phone: 86 10-8262-8881   Fax: 8610-8260-7166
Toll-Free:
Address: No. 8 SINA Plaza, Ctyd. 10, W. Xibeiwang E. Rd., H, Shanghai, Shanghai 100193 China

STOCK TICKER/OTHER:
Stock Ticker: Private   Exchange:
Employees: 8,300   Fiscal Year Ends: 12/31
Parent Company: SINA Group Holding Co Ltd

SALARIES/BONUSES:
Top Exec. Salary: $ Bonus: $
Second Exec. Salary: $ Bonus: $

OTHER THOUGHTS:
Estimated Female Officers or Directors:
Hot Spot for Advancement for Women/Minorities:

Sisense Inc

NAIC Code: 511210H

TYPES OF BUSINESS:

Computer Software, Business Management & ERP
Business Analytics
Artificial Intelligence
Business Intelligence
Software
Data Platform
Business Strategy Solutions

BRANDS/DIVISIONS/AFFILIATES:

GROWTH PLANS/SPECIAL FEATURES:

Sisense, Inc. provides an artificial intelligence (AI)-driven platform that offers analytics so that businesses can make strategic and swift decisions for their company and customers. Platforms offered by the firm include Sisense Platform, Fusion Embed and Fusion Compose SDK. Global companies rely on Sisense for: embedding white-labeled analytic experiences into customer applications and workflows; customizing how and where it is best to access analyzed data; and forming business strategy via cloud innovation. Primary business departments that use Sisense solutions include finance, marketing, customer service, human resources and information technology (IT). Industries served include healthcare, manufacturing, financial services, retail, technology, pharmaceutical and life sciences. Resources offered on the Sisense website include an online community, a support portal, whitepapers and webinars.

CONTACTS: Note: Officers with more than one job title may be intentionally listed here more than once.

Ariel Katz, CEO
Kristina Agassi, COO
Alyssa Shadinger, VP- Finance
Scott Castle, SVP- Customer Care
Vicki Nichamov, VP-People
Amir Orad, Chmn.

FINANCIAL DATA: Note: Data for latest year may not have been available at press time.

In U.S. $	2022	2021	2020	2019	2018	2017
Revenue						
R&D Expense						
Operating Income						
Operating Margin %						
SGA Expense						
Net Income						
Operating Cash Flow						
Capital Expenditure						
EBITDA						
Return on Assets %						
Return on Equity %						
Debt to Equity						

CONTACT INFORMATION:

Phone: 212-608-4041   Fax:
Toll-Free:
Address: 1359 Broadway, Fl. 4, New York, NY 10018 United States

STOCK TICKER/OTHER:

Stock Ticker: Private   Exchange:
Employees: 250   Fiscal Year Ends:
Parent Company:

SALARIES/BONUSES:

Top Exec. Salary: $ Bonus: $
Second Exec. Salary: $ Bonus: $

OTHER THOUGHTS:

Estimated Female Officers or Directors:
Hot Spot for Advancement for Women/Minorities:

SK Telecom Co Ltd

www.sktelecom.com

NAIC Code: 517312

TYPES OF BUSINESS:

Wireless Telecommunications Services
Multimedia Broadcasting
Online Shopping
Internet of Things
Telecommunications

BRANDS/DIVISIONS/AFFILIATES:

Eleven Street
SK Hynix Inc
KEB HanaCard Co Ltd
Content Wavve

GROWTH PLANS/SPECIAL FEATURES:

SK Telecom is South Korea's largest wireless telecom operator, with 31 million mobile customers. The firm also owns SK Broadband (formerly Hanaro Telecom), which has 6.9 million broadband customers and 9.5 million pay TV customers (6.8 million IPTV and 2.7 million Cable TV). While the firm also purchased stakes in businesses in security and semiconductor memory production as well as developing e-commerce and internet platform businesses, these were all spun off into the separate, SK Square business in November 2021. The company was formed after SK Group purchased KT's mobile business in 1994.

CONTACTS: Note: Officers with more than one job title may be intentionally listed here more than once.

Jung-Ho Park, CEO
Young Sang Ryu, Dir.-Mobile Network Oper.
Dong Seob Jee, Head-Corp. Vision Dept.
Young Tae Kim, Exec. Dir.
Daesik Cho, Chmn.

FINANCIAL DATA: Note: Data for latest year may not have been available at press time.

In U.S. $	2022	2021	2020	2019	2018	2017
Revenue	13,130,220,000	12,708,060,000	12,206,640,000	11,697,280,000	12,803,190,000	13,293,380,000
R&D Expense	258,632,000	263,827,200	267,990,500	245,875,800	294,150,000	299,917,300
Operating Income	1,258,807,000	1,115,912,000	982,151,100	828,328,100	945,492,700	1,128,743,000
Operating Margin %		.09%	.08%	.07%	.07%	.08%
SGA Expense	6,370,977,000	6,171,061,000	5,834,243,000	5,473,627,000	6,316,418,000	6,467,156,000
Net Income	692,287,300	1,826,718,000	1,141,433,000	674,303,300	2,373,297,000	1,972,631,000
Operating Cash Flow	3,914,653,000	3,817,504,000	4,417,373,000	3,061,561,000	3,287,363,000	2,925,619,000
Capital Expenditure	2,311,486,000	2,510,292,000	2,798,115,000	2,668,457,000	2,500,565,000	2,171,250,000
EBITDA	4,036,398,000	4,637,750,000	4,070,098,000	3,895,986,000	5,741,966,000	5,273,241,000
Return on Assets %		.06%	.03%	.02%	.08%	.08%
Return on Equity %		.14%	.06%	.04%	.15%	.15%
Debt to Equity		.74%	0.453	0.442	.38%	0.326

CONTACT INFORMATION:

Phone: 82 2-6100-2114   Fax: 82-2-6110-7830
Toll-Free:
Address: SK T-Tower, 65, Eulji-ro, Jung-gu, Seoul, 100-999 South Korea

STOCK TICKER/OTHER:

Stock Ticker: SKM
Employees: 26,053
Parent Company:

Exchange: NYS
Fiscal Year Ends: 12/31

SALARIES/BONUSES:

Top Exec. Salary: $ Bonus: $
Second Exec. Salary: $ Bonus: $

OTHER THOUGHTS:

Estimated Female Officers or Directors:
Hot Spot for Advancement for Women/Minorities:

Sales, profits and employees may be estimates. Financial information, benefits and other data can change quickly and may vary from those stated here.

Skype Technologies Sarl

www.skype.com

NAIC Code: 511210C

TYPES OF BUSINESS:

Computer Software: Telecom, Communications & VOIP
Voice and Video Communication Services
Video Calling Services
Online and Mobile Applications
Call Recording and Live Subtitle Solutions
Group Communication Solutions
Text Messaging and Content Sharing Solutions
Subscription Services

BRANDS/DIVISIONS/AFFILIATES:

Microsoft Corporation

CONTACTS: *Note: Officers with more than one job title may be intentionally listed here more than once.*

Satya Nadella, CEO-Microsoft

GROWTH PLANS/SPECIAL FEATURES:

Skype Technologies Sarl, a subsidiary of Microsoft Corporation, offers software capabilities that enable users to make free audio and video calls. The firm's proprietary online software and mobile applications help people stay connected not only through calls, but also via instant messaging and photo- and file-sharing in real-time. Additional features by Skype include call recording, live subtitles and end-to-end encryption for private conversations. Compatible devices for Skyping include phones, desktop computers, tablets, the internet, Alexa and Xbox. Audio conferencing is also available through Skype, with the ability to host up to 100 people, as well as to record the calls and offer live captions and subtitles. Skype numbers are available for purchase in several countries and regions, and can be used across devices. For those not on Skype, landlines and mobiles anywhere in the world pay a low rate using Skype Credit or through Skype's subscription options. Skype numbers are available in 25 countries and regions for a flat fee for unlimited incoming calls.

FINANCIAL DATA: *Note: Data for latest year may not have been available at press time.*

In U.S. $	2022	2021	2020	2019	2018	2017
Revenue						
R&D Expense						
Operating Income						
Operating Margin %						
SGA Expense						
Net Income						
Operating Cash Flow						
Capital Expenditure						
EBITDA						
Return on Assets %						
Return on Equity %						
Debt to Equity						

CONTACT INFORMATION:

Phone: 352 26-20-15-82   Fax: 352-26-27-05-88
Toll-Free:
Address: 23-29 Rives de Clausen, Luxembourg, L-2165 Luxembourg

STOCK TICKER/OTHER:

Stock Ticker: Subsidiary   Exchange:
Employees: 1,400   Fiscal Year Ends: 12/31
Parent Company: Microsoft Corporation

SALARIES/BONUSES:

Top Exec. Salary: $ Bonus: $
Second Exec. Salary: $ Bonus: $

OTHER THOUGHTS:

Estimated Female Officers or Directors: 1
Hot Spot for Advancement for Women/Minorities: Y

Slack Technologies LLC

NAIC Code: 511210C

TYPES OF BUSINESS:

Computer Software, Telecom, Communications & VOIP
Business Collaboration Software Development
Digital Communication Platform
Business Organization Solutions
Business Team Communication Solutions
Software Integration Solutions
Custom App Integration Solutions
Disabled User Communication Solutions

BRANDS/DIVISIONS/AFFILIATES:

Salesforce Inc
Slack

CONTACTS: Note: Officers with more than one job title may be intentionally listed here more than once.

Denise Dresser, CEO
Sarah Walker, COO
Allen Shim, CFO
Parker Harris, CTO
David Schellhase, General Counsel
Tamar Yehoshua, Other Executive Officer
Robert Frati, Senior VP, Divisional

GROWTH PLANS/SPECIAL FEATURES:

Slack Technologies, LLC is a computer software firm that operates Slack, a digital platform that enables team communications through a single hub. More than 150 countries have daily active users in Slack, and more than 200,000 customers pay for a Slack subscription. The Slack platform features: channels for staying organized via centralized spaces for conversations, files, tools and more; Slack Connect, for collaborating with teams at other companies; message-sending similar to text messages; huddle/group messages, with video clip capabilities; and a variety of accessibility features for users, including disabled individuals. Slack's solutions are utilized by a wide range of team types, including engineering, IT, customer service, sales, project management, human resources, marketing and security. Slack can adapt to fit the needs of its group users. The platform enables software integration and custom app integration. Slack offers a free service and a range of subscription services for small teams up to enterprises. Headquartered in California, USA, Slack has additional offices in the U.S., Canada, Latin America, Caribbean, Europe, Middle East, Africa and Asia Pacific. Slack Technologies operates as a subsidiary of Salesforce, Inc.

Through parent Salesforce, Slack offers its employees health coverage and family planning programs.

FINANCIAL DATA: Note: Data for latest year may not have been available at press time.

In U.S. $	2022	2021	2020	2019	2018	2017
Revenue	681,864,453	655,638,896	630,422,016	400,552,000	220,544,000	105,153,000
R&D Expense						
Operating Income						
Operating Margin %						
SGA Expense						
Net Income			-571,057,984	-140,683,008	-140,084,992	-146,864,000
Operating Cash Flow						
Capital Expenditure						
EBITDA						
Return on Assets %						
Return on Equity %						
Debt to Equity						

CONTACT INFORMATION:

Phone: 415 630-7943   Fax:
Toll-Free:
Address: 500 Howard St., San Francisco, CA 94105 United States

STOCK TICKER/OTHER:

Stock Ticker: Subsidiary   Exchange:
Employees: 2,545   Fiscal Year Ends: 01/31
Parent Company: Salesforce Inc

SALARIES/BONUSES:

Top Exec. Salary: $ Bonus: $
Second Exec. Salary: $ Bonus: $

OTHER THOUGHTS:

Estimated Female Officers or Directors:
Hot Spot for Advancement for Women/Minorities:

Smartsheet Inc

www.smartsheet.com

NAIC Code: 511210H

TYPES OF BUSINESS:

Computer Software, Business Management & ERP
Cloud Software
Workplace Collaboration
Workplace Automation

BRANDS/DIVISIONS/AFFILIATES:

GROWTH PLANS/SPECIAL FEATURES:

Smartsheet is a provider of collaborative work management software delivered via a cloud-based, software-as-a-service model. The firm's solution offers scalable, dynamic tools to improve the efficiency of project and process management across countless use cases. Smartsheet's offering supports workflow management across teams, provides real-time visibility into projects, and reporting and automation capabilities. The firm generates revenue via software subscriptions on a per-user basis, and incremental charges for added platform capabilities.

CONTACTS: Note: Officers with more than one job title may be intentionally listed here more than once.

Mark Mader, CEO
Pete Godbole, CFO
Geoffrey Barker, Chairman of the Board
Jolene Marshalll, Chief Legal Officer
Andrew Bennett, Chief Marketing Officer
Anna Griffin, Chief Marketing Officer
Gene Farrell, Chief Strategy Officer
Praerit Garg, Chief Technology Officer
Brent Frei, Co-Founder
Stephen Branstetter, COO
Michael Arntz, Executive VP, Divisional
Megan Hansen, Other Executive Officer

FINANCIAL DATA: Note: Data for latest year may not have been available at press time.

In U.S. $	2022	2021	2020	2019	2018	2017
Revenue	550,832,000	385,513,000	270,882,000	177,722,000	111,253,000	
R&D Expense	165,440,000	118,722,000	95,469,000	58,841,000	37,590,000	
Operating Income	-170,036,000	-120,472,000	-103,774,000	-55,084,000	-48,978,000	
Operating Margin %	- .31%	- .31%	- .38%	- .31%	- .44%	
SGA Expense	438,955,000	301,724,000	226,287,000	140,116,000	100,959,000	
Net Income	-171,097,000	-114,979,000	-95,940,000	-53,885,000	-49,106,000	
Operating Cash Flow	-3,512,000	-15,648,000	-10,870,000	-2,855,000	-13,581,000	
Capital Expenditure	17,300,000	11,784,000	11,852,000	8,784,000	9,481,000	
EBITDA	-148,271,000	-103,217,000	-90,325,000	-47,380,000	-44,902,000	
Return on Assets %	- .18%	- .13%	- .17%	- .25%	- .62%	
Return on Equity %	- .33%	- .22%	- .28%	-1.25%		
Debt to Equity	.12%	.14%	0.096	0.013		

CONTACT INFORMATION:

Phone: 425 283-1870   Fax:
Toll-Free: 844-324-2360
Address: 10500 N.E. 8th St., Ste. 1300, Bellevue, WA 98004-4357
United States

STOCK TICKER/OTHER:

Stock Ticker: SMAR   Exchange: NYS
Employees: 3,191   Fiscal Year Ends: 01/31
Parent Company:

SALARIES/BONUSES:

Top Exec. Salary: $540,135   Bonus: $
Second Exec. Salary: Bonus: $
$411,077

OTHER THOUGHTS:

Estimated Female Officers or Directors:
Hot Spot for Advancement for Women/Minorities:

SMS Assist LLC

NAIC Code: 511210H

TYPES OF BUSINESS:

Software Platform for Property Mangers
Contractor Referral Software
Property Management
Services Transparency Technology
Data Analytics
Communication and Collaboration
Training Services

BRANDS/DIVISIONS/AFFILIATES:

SMS Assist LLC
ONE by Lessen
SMS University

CONTACTS: *Note: Officers with more than one job title may be intentionally listed here more than once.*

Jay McKee, CEO
Maureen Ehrenberg, Pres.
Arvind Bobra, CFO
Cynthia Bowers, Chief People Officer
Jianqing Zhao, CTO

GROWTH PLANS/SPECIAL FEATURES:

Lessen. Formerly SMS Assist LLC, provides a proprietary technology platform for the multi-site property management market. The platform is utilized by a network of more than 30,000 qualified venders and serves over 280,000 properties. Lessen offers services to both commercial and residential property owners as well as venders. Both commercial and residential clients can use ONE by Lessen which integrates Lessen clients, affiliates and employees on one proprietary technology platform. This results in clients receiving real-time visibility, actionable big data analytics, transparency and savings; affiliates benefiting from improved communication, streamlined administration and increased sales growth; and Lessen having superior communication, visibility and management of all stakeholders in the value chain. For venders the company provides referrals to contractors for services such as exterior maintenance, facilities maintenance, interior maintenance, property management services and residential property services by becoming an affiliate.

SMS Assist offers its employees group benefits, continuing education, amenities, competitive salaries and advancement opportunities.

FINANCIAL DATA: *Note: Data for latest year may not have been available at press time.*

In U.S. $	2022	2021	2020	2019	2018	2017
Revenue						
R&D Expense						
Operating Income						
Operating Margin %						
SGA Expense						
Net Income						
Operating Cash Flow						
Capital Expenditure						
EBITDA						
Return on Assets %						
Return on Equity %						
Debt to Equity						

CONTACT INFORMATION:

Phone: 312-698-7000   Fax:
Toll-Free:
Address: 130 E. Randolph St., Ste. 200, Chicago, IL 60601 United States

STOCK TICKER/OTHER:

Stock Ticker: Private   Exchange:
Employees: 9,950   Fiscal Year Ends:
Parent Company:

SALARIES/BONUSES:

Top Exec. Salary: $ Bonus: $
Second Exec. Salary: $ Bonus: $

OTHER THOUGHTS:

Estimated Female Officers or Directors: 2
Hot Spot for Advancement for Women/Minorities: Y

Snap Inc (Snapchat)

NAIC Code: 519130

www.snapchat.com

TYPES OF BUSINESS:

Social Media
Advertising Services
Camera App
Social Platform

BRANDS/DIVISIONS/AFFILIATES:

Snapchat
Snaps
Friends Page
Stories
Discover
Snap Map
Memories
Spectacles

CONTACTS: *Note: Officers with more than one job title may be intentionally listed here more than once.*

Evan Spiegel, CEO
Derek Andersen, CFO
Michael Lynton, Chairman of the Board
Rebecca Morrow, Chief Accounting Officer
Jared Grusd, Chief Strategy Officer
Robert Murphy, Chief Technology Officer
Michael OSullivan, General Counsel
Jeremi Gorman, Other Executive Officer
Jerry Hunter, Senior VP, Divisional

GROWTH PLANS/SPECIAL FEATURES:

Snap, which refers to itself as a camera company, has one of the most popular social networking apps, Snapchat, in developed regions such as North America and Europe. Snap generates nearly all its revenue from advertising with 70% coming from North America. The firm is headquartered in Venice, California.

FINANCIAL DATA: *Note: Data for latest year may not have been available at press time.*

In U.S. $	2022	2021	2020	2019	2018	2017
Revenue	4,601,847,000	4,117,048,000	2,506,626,000	1,715,534,000	1,180,446,000	
R&D Expense	2,109,800,000	1,565,467,000	1,101,561,000	883,509,000	772,185,000	
Operating Income	-1,395,306,000	-702,069,000	-862,072,000	-1,103,328,000	-1,268,450,000	
Operating Margin %	- .30%	- .17%	- .34%	- .64%	-1.07%	
SGA Expense	2,072,011,000	1,503,404,000	1,084,632,000	1,039,515,000	877,846,000	
Net Income	-1,429,653,000	-487,955,000	-944,839,000	-1,033,660,000	-1,255,911,000	
Operating Cash Flow	184,614,000	292,880,000	-167,644,000	-304,958,000	-689,924,000	
Capital Expenditure	129,306,000	69,875,000	57,832,000	36,478,000	120,242,000	
EBITDA	-1,177,065,000	-337,554,000	-742,213,000	-921,028,000	-1,157,822,000	
Return on Assets %	- .18%	- .08%	- .21%	- .31%	- .41%	
Return on Equity %	- .45%	- .16%	- .41%	- .45%	- .47%	
Debt to Equity	1.60%	.68%	0.842	0.529		

CONTACT INFORMATION:

Phone: 310-399-3339   Fax:
Toll-Free:
Address: 2772 Donald Douglas Loop N., Santa Monica, CA 90405 United States

STOCK TICKER/OTHER:

Stock Ticker: SNAP   Exchange: NYS
Employees: 5,288   Fiscal Year Ends: 12/31
Parent Company:

SALARIES/BONUSES:

Top Exec. Salary: $538,462   Bonus: $375,000
Second Exec. Salary: $855,770   Bonus: $

OTHER THOUGHTS:

Estimated Female Officers or Directors:
Hot Spot for Advancement for Women/Minorities:

Snapdeal

NAIC Code: 454110

www.snapdeal.com

TYPES OF BUSINESS:

Electronic Shopping
Ecommerce
Online Retailing
Mobile App Retailing
Payment Technology Solutions
eGifts

GROWTH PLANS/SPECIAL FEATURES:

Snapdeal is an online marketplace based in New Delhi, India, and owned by Snapdeal Private Limited. Snapdeal is one of the largest ecommerce sites in the country. The platform is comprised of sellers in over 2,500 cities and towns throughout the country. Top categories include apparel (men, women & children), home and kitchen, toys, health and beauty, baby care, stationery, food and household essentials, with other categories spanning automotives, mobile, electronics, sports and outdoor, computers and gaming, books, media and music. Manufacturers, wholesalers, distributors and retailers can register and sell authorized products via website and/or mobile app. Snapdeal services for sellers include receiving orders, servicing the orders received and the reception of payments. The company's payment solutions are secure, offering 100% payment protection technology. Sellers pay a small commission for what they sell. Seller subscriptions can be cancelled at any time.

BRANDS/DIVISIONS/AFFILIATES:

Snapdeal Private Limited

CONTACTS: Note: Officers with more than one job title may be intentionally listed here more than once.

Himanshu Chakrawarti, CEO

FINANCIAL DATA: Note: Data for latest year may not have been available at press time.

In U.S. $	2022	2021	2020	2019	2018	2017
Revenue	131,683,000	126,617,920	121,748,000	132,999,000	82,381,500	198,956,000
R&D Expense						
Operating Income						
Operating Margin %						
SGA Expense						
Net Income			-35,913,100	-26,734,900	-94,233,700	-715,984,000
Operating Cash Flow						
Capital Expenditure						
EBITDA						
Return on Assets %						
Return on Equity %						
Debt to Equity						

CONTACT INFORMATION:

Phone: 91-9212692126   Fax:
Toll-Free:
Address: Fl. 6, Cyberscape, Sector 59, Golf Course Extension Rd., Gurugram, Haryana, 122002 India

STOCK TICKER/OTHER:

Stock Ticker: Private   Exchange:
Employees: 7,000   Fiscal Year Ends: 03/31
Parent Company: Snapdeal Private Limited

SALARIES/BONUSES:

Top Exec. Salary: $ Bonus: $
Second Exec. Salary: $ Bonus: $

OTHER THOUGHTS:

Estimated Female Officers or Directors:
Hot Spot for Advancement for Women/Minorities:

Sales, profits and employees may be estimates. Financial information, benefits and other data can change quickly and may vary from those stated here.

SoftBank Group Corp

NAIC Code: 517311

TYPES OF BUSINESS:
Telecommunications Services
Investment
Managed Funds
Technology
Artificial Intelligence
Robotics
Smartphone Payment
Electricity

BRANDS/DIVISIONS/AFFILIATES:
SoftBank Group Capital Limited
SB Northstar LP
SoftBank Investment Advisers
SoftBank Vision Fund LP
Z Holdings
Arm Limited
Fortress Investment Group LLC
PayPay Corporation

GROWTH PLANS/SPECIAL FEATURES:
SoftBank is a Japan-based telecom and e-commerce conglomerate that has expanded mainly through acquisitions, and its key assets include a 40%-owned mobile and fixed broadband telecom operator business in Japan. It also owns 90% of semiconductor chip designer ARM Holdings following the 2023 IPO of this business, and has a vast portfolio of mainly internet- and e-commerce-focused early stage investments. It is also general partner of the $100 billion SoftBank Vision Fund 1 and sole investor in SoftBank Vision Fund 2, both of which primarily invest in pre-IPO internet companies.

CONTACTS: Note: Officers with more than one job title may be intentionally listed here more than once.
Masayoshi Shon, CEO
Marcelo Claure, COO
Ken Miyauchi, COO-SOFTBANK MOBILE Corp.
Ronald D. Fisher, Pres., SOFTBANK Holdings, Inc.
Masayoshi Son, Chmn.

FINANCIAL DATA: Note: Data for latest year may not have been available at press time.

In U.S. $	2022	2021	2020	2019	2018	2017
Revenue	42,455,350,000	38,406,250,000	35,750,170,000	41,581,980,000	62,498,820,000	
R&D Expense						
Operating Income	4,871,280,000	4,117,781,000	4,057,410,000	12,947,560,000	8,897,054,000	
Operating Margin %	.11%	.11%	.11%	.31%	.14%	
SGA Expense	17,412,790,000	15,500,550,000	14,057,850,000	12,735,610,000	17,419,210,000	
Net Income	-11,655,480,000	34,037,530,000	-6,561,733,000	9,629,932,000	7,089,912,000	
Operating Cash Flow	18,598,300,000	3,802,638,000	7,628,334,000	7,996,725,000	7,428,694,000	
Capital Expenditure	5,698,484,000	4,414,322,000	8,410,849,000	9,314,358,000	7,266,365,000	
EBITDA	2,493,289,000	46,600,810,000	16,346,100,000	25,376,830,000	16,968,640,000	
Return on Assets %	-.04%	.12%	-.03%	.04%	.04%	
Return on Equity %	-.17%	.62%	-.14%	.22%	.24%	
Debt to Equity	1.50%	1.16%	1.763	1.601	2.67%	

CONTACT INFORMATION:
Phone: 81 3-6889-2000 Fax:
Toll-Free:
Address: 1-9-1 Higashi-shimbashi, Tokyo, 105-7303 Japan

STOCK TICKER/OTHER:
Stock Ticker: SFTBY
Employees: 92,069
Parent Company:

Exchange: PINX
Fiscal Year Ends: 03/31

SALARIES/BONUSES:
Top Exec. Salary: $ Bonus: $
Second Exec. Salary: $ Bonus: $

OTHER THOUGHTS:
Estimated Female Officers or Directors:
Hot Spot for Advancement for Women/Minorities:

Sogou Inc

NAIC Code: 519130

TYPES OF BUSINESS:

Search Engine
Search Engine
Ecommerce Platform
Product and Price Comparison
Brand Exposure
Data Collection
Consumer Behavior Analytics
User Experience Technology

BRANDS/DIVISIONS/AFFILIATES:

Tencent Holdings Ltd
Sogou
WeChat

GROWTH PLANS/SPECIAL FEATURES:

Sogou, Inc. is a technology company that offers a Chinese search engine marketing platform. Online shoppers can research products online before buying. Sogou attracts millions of users daily. The company offers retail partners ecommerce tools to sell their products and increase brand exposure. Sogou.com integrates social content such as WeChat into its search results and allows brands to add widgets that can show product images and links. In return, WeChat can collect information about consumers, including shopping history, spending habits and more, to strategically enhance data and user experiences. Sogou is an indirect, wholly owned subsidiary of Tencent Holdings Ltd.

CONTACTS: Note: Officers with more than one job title may be intentionally listed here more than once.

Ma Huateng, CEO

FINANCIAL DATA: Note: Data for latest year may not have been available at press time.

In U.S. $	2022	2021	2020	2019	2018	2017
Revenue	967,200,000	930,000,000	924,664,000	1,172,252,032	1,124,157,952	908,356,992
R&D Expense						
Operating Income						
Operating Margin %						
SGA Expense						
Net Income			-108,221,000	89,105,000	98,781,000	82,200,000
Operating Cash Flow						
Capital Expenditure						
EBITDA						
Return on Assets %						
Return on Equity %						
Debt to Equity						

CONTACT INFORMATION:

Phone: 86 10-6272-6666   Fax: 86 1062726588
Toll-Free:
Address: Level 15, No.1 Unit Zhongguancun, Haidian Distr., Beijing, Beijing 100084 China

STOCK TICKER/OTHER:

Stock Ticker: Subsidiary   Exchange:
Employees: 3,000   Fiscal Year Ends:
Parent Company: Tencent Holdings Limited

SALARIES/BONUSES:

Top Exec. Salary: $ Bonus: $
Second Exec. Salary: $ Bonus: $

OTHER THOUGHTS:

Estimated Female Officers or Directors:
Hot Spot for Advancement for Women/Minorities:

Sohu.com Limited

NAIC Code: 519130

TYPES OF BUSINESS:

Internet Portal-Chinese
Internet Service Provider
Online Gaming Portal
Real Estate Services
Wireless Media Content
Search Engine-Chinese
Apps

BRANDS/DIVISIONS/AFFILIATES:

Sohu
Sogou Inc
Changyou.com Limited

GROWTH PLANS/SPECIAL FEATURES:

Sohu.com Ltd provides online media, games, and search products and services on PCs and mobile devices in China. The company operates in Sohu and Changyou segments. Sohu is a Chinese language online media content and services provider. Changyou is involved in the development, operation, and licensing of online games for PCs and mobile devices, which include massively multiplayer online role-playing games, casual games, strategy games. In addition, it operates focus.cn, which provides online real estate information and services; and 17173.com website, which provides news, electronic forums, online videos, and other online game information services to game players, as well as offers mobile game distribution services. It generates maximum revenue from the Changyou segment.

CONTACTS:
Note: Officers with more than one job title may be intentionally listed here more than once.

Zhang Chaoyang, CEO
Belinda Wang, Co-Pres.
Lu Yangfeng, CFO
Gang Fang, VP-Prod.
Xuemei (Sherry) Zhang, VP-Admin.
Lili Cui, VP-Brand Advertising Sales
Ye Deng, VP
Zhang Chaoyang, Chmn.

FINANCIAL DATA:
Note: Data for latest year may not have been available at press time.

In U.S. $	2022	2021	2020	2019	2018	2017
Revenue	733,872,000	835,576,000	749,890,000	673,803,000	690,175,000	1,769,589,000
R&D Expense	260,772,000	268,863,000	241,941,000	234,852,000	246,155,000	412,173,000
Operating Income	8,687,000	102,717,000	85,468,000	-57,282,000	-146,681,000	-100,156,000
Operating Margin %		.12%	.11%	-.09%	-.21%	-.06%
SGA Expense	282,400,000	264,570,000	217,141,000	259,256,000	307,027,000	509,464,000
Net Income	-17,343,000	927,725,000	-86,112,000	-149,336,000	-160,082,000	-554,526,000
Operating Cash Flow	32,242,000	-62,278,000	95,207,000	210,590,000	84,025,000	187,687,000
Capital Expenditure	23,841,000	42,207,000	33,780,000	65,664,000	121,534,000	144,363,000
EBITDA	71,903,000	175,023,000	142,785,000	11,366,000	-28,181,000	50,383,000
Return on Assets %		.37%	-.03%	-.05%	-.05%	-.19%
Return on Equity %		1.13%	-.22%	-.29%	-.24%	-.64%
Debt to Equity			0.265		.51%	0.163

CONTACT INFORMATION:

Phone: 86 10 6272-6666   Fax:
Toll-Free:
Address: Level 18 Media Plaza, Block 3, No. 2 Kexueyuan S., Beijing, Beijing 100190 China

STOCK TICKER/OTHER:

Stock Ticker: SOHU   Exchange: NAS
Employees: 4,900   Fiscal Year Ends: 12/31
Parent Company:

SALARIES/BONUSES:

Top Exec. Salary: $602,664   Bonus: $
Second Exec. Salary: $361,598   Bonus: $

OTHER THOUGHTS:

Estimated Female Officers or Directors: 5
Hot Spot for Advancement for Women/Minorities: Y

Solo Brands Inc

solobrands.com

NAIC Code: 454110

TYPES OF BUSINESS:

Online Sales, B2C Ecommerce, Sharing Economy Platforms

BRANDS/DIVISIONS/AFFILIATES:

GROWTH PLANS/SPECIAL FEATURES:

Solo Brands Inc is a Direct-To-Consumer (DTC) platform. It operates four premium outdoor lifestyle brands Solo Stove, Oru, ISLE, and Chubbies apparel. Solo Stove offers portable, low-smoke fire pits, grills, and camping stoves for backyard and outdoor use in different sizes, fire pit bundles, gear kits, stoves, cookware, dinnerware, and a variety of clothing and accessories. Oru offers a flagship line of lightweight, foldable kayaks. ISLE produces high-quality stand-up paddle boards with colorful designs that are engineered to accommodate every skill level, style, and interest. Chubbies is a fun-loving, premium apparel brand that offers well-fitted comfortable clothing. Solo Brands distributes its products through individual brand websites and other partners.

CONTACTS: Note: Officers with more than one job title may be intentionally listed here more than once.

John Merris, CEO
Matthew Webb, COO
Somer Webb, CFO
Tom Montgomery, Chief Digital Officer
Matthew-Guy Hamliton, Chmn.

FINANCIAL DATA: Note: Data for latest year may not have been available at press time.

In U.S. $	2022	2021	2020	2019	2018	2017
Revenue	517,627,000	403,717,000	127,444,000	39,852,000		
R&D Expense						
Operating Income	30,953,000	68,863,000	16,145,000	-28,665,000		
Operating Margin %	.06%	.17%	.13%			
SGA Expense	259,048,000	159,524,000	38,920,000	16,369,000		
Net Income	-4,945,000	48,654,000	21,475,000	-29,540,000		
Operating Cash Flow	32,395,000	-10,246,000	31,413,000	-19,817,000		
Capital Expenditure	9,241,000	10,645,000	960,000	118,000		
EBITDA	55,545,000	87,091,000	21,602,000	-27,842,000		
Return on Assets %	-.01%	.02%	.07%			
Return on Equity %	-.01%	.03%	.11%			
Debt to Equity	.30%	.35%	0.22			

CONTACT INFORMATION:

Phone: 817 900-2664 Fax:
Toll-Free:
Address: 1070 S. Kimball Ave., Southlake, TX 76092 United States

STOCK TICKER/OTHER:

Stock Ticker: DTC Exchange: NYS
Employees: 350 Fiscal Year Ends: 12/31
Parent Company:

SALARIES/BONUSES:

Top Exec. Salary: $650,000 Bonus: $487,500
Second Exec. Salary: $315,385 Bonus: $225,000

OTHER THOUGHTS:

Estimated Female Officers or Directors:
Hot Spot for Advancement for Women/Minorities:

Sales, profits and employees may be estimates. Financial information, benefits and other data can change quickly and may vary from those stated here.

Sopra Steria Group SA

NAIC Code: 541512

www.soprasteria.com/en

TYPES OF BUSINESS:

IT Consulting
Business Strategy Consulting
Business Process Outsourcing

GROWTH PLANS/SPECIAL FEATURES:

Sopra Steria Group SA is a French technology company offering consulting, digital services, systems integration, software development, business process services, infrastructure management and cybersecurity services. Industries served include aerospace, defense & security, energy & utilities, financial services, insurance & social, government, retail, telecommunication/media & entertainment and transportation. In March 2023, Sopra Steria agreed to acquire Dutch communications firm Ordina NV for approximately $555 million. That same month, the company completed the acquisition of Belgian digital consultancy and services company Tobania. Sopra Steria has operations in 30 countries worldwide.

BRANDS/DIVISIONS/AFFILIATES:

Ordina NV
Tobania

CONTACTS:
Note: Officers with more than one job title may be intentionally listed here more than once.

Cyril Malarge, CEO
Laurent Giovachini, Deputy CEO
Christian Levi, Head-Sopra Consulting

FINANCIAL DATA:
Note: Data for latest year may not have been available at press time.

In U.S. $	2022	2021	2020	2019	2018	2017
Revenue	5,445,479,988	5,302,802,720	5,235,864,296	4,521,629,184	4,625,001,472	4,551,880,000
R&D Expense						
Operating Income						
Operating Margin %						
SGA Expense						
Net Income	265,805,010	219,119,400	146,037,736	163,468,000	141,280,896	205,314,000
Operating Cash Flow						
Capital Expenditure						
EBITDA						
Return on Assets %						
Return on Equity %						
Debt to Equity						

CONTACT INFORMATION:

Phone: 33-1-40-67-29-29   Fax:
Toll-Free:
Address: 6 Ave. Kleber, Paris, 75016 France

STOCK TICKER/OTHER:

Stock Ticker: SOP
Employees: 55,000
Parent Company:

Exchange: Paris
Fiscal Year Ends: 12/31

SALARIES/BONUSES:

Top Exec. Salary: $ Bonus: $
Second Exec. Salary: $ Bonus: $

OTHER THOUGHTS:

Estimated Female Officers or Directors: 1
Hot Spot for Advancement for Women/Minorities:

Spotify Technology SA

NAIC Code: 515111

www.spotify.com

TYPES OF BUSINESS:
Radio Networks, Traditional, Satellite and Online
Audio Streaming Services
Online and Offline Streaming
Music Media
Podcast Media

GROWTH PLANS/SPECIAL FEATURES:
Spotify, headquartered in Stockholm, Sweden, is one of the world's largest music streaming service providers, with 602 million total listeners. The firm monetizes its users through a paid subscription model, referred to as its premium service, and an ad-based model, referred to as its ad-supported service. Revenue from premium and ad-supported services represented 86% and 14% of Spotify's 2023 total revenue, respectively.

BRANDS/DIVISIONS/AFFILIATES:
Podz Inc
Betty Labs Incorporated

CONTACTS: *Note: Officers with more than one job title may be intentionally listed here more than once.*
Daniel Ek, CEO
Gustav Soderstrom, Chief Prod. Officer
Angela Watts, VP-Global Comm.
Ken Parks, Managing Dir.-USA
Stefan Zilch, Country Mgr.-Germany, Austria & Switzerland
Steve Savoca, Head-Content
Kate Vale, Managing Dir.-Australia & New Zealand
Jeff Levick, Chief Int'l Officer

FINANCIAL DATA: *Note: Data for latest year may not have been available at press time.*

In U.S. $	2022	2021	2020	2019	2018	2017
Revenue	12,658,680,000	10,436,100,000	8,506,044,000	7,301,382,000	5,676,813,000	
R&D Expense	1,497,193,000	984,455,900	903,497,300	663,860,100	532,167,500	
Operating Income	-711,355,800	101,468,000	-316,278,000	-78,799,650	-46,416,230	
Operating Margin %	-.06%	.01%	-.04%	-.01%	-.01%	
SGA Expense	2,372,625,000	1,710,924,000	1,587,867,000	1,273,748,000	974,740,900	
Net Income	-464,162,300	-36,701,210	-627,158,800	-200,777,200	-84,196,890	
Operating Cash Flow	49,654,580	389,680,500	279,576,800	618,523,300	371,329,900	
Capital Expenditure	26,986,180	91,753,020	84,196,890	145,725,400	134,930,900	
EBITDA	-152,202,100	460,924,000	-587,219,300	-1,079,447	-145,725,400	
Return on Assets %	-.06%	-.01%	-.10%	-.04%	-.02%	
Return on Equity %	-.19%	-.01%	-.24%	-.09%	-.07%	
Debt to Equity	.70%	.84%	0.206	0.305		

CONTACT INFORMATION:
Phone: 46-70-220-4607   Fax:
Toll-Free:
Address: 42-44, Ave. de la Gare, Luxembourg City, L-1610 Luxembourg

STOCK TICKER/OTHER:
Stock Ticker: SPOT   Exchange: NYS
Employees: 8,359   Fiscal Year Ends: 12/31
Parent Company:

SALARIES/BONUSES:
Top Exec. Salary: $860,000   Bonus: $
Second Exec. Salary: Bonus: $
$600,000

OTHER THOUGHTS:
Estimated Female Officers or Directors: 2
Hot Spot for Advancement for Women/Minorities:

Sprinklr Inc

NAIC Code: 511210F

TYPES OF BUSINESS:
Computer Software, Multimedia, Graphics & Publishing
Enterprise Software
Marketing
Social Media
Customer Relations
Collaboration

GROWTH PLANS/SPECIAL FEATURES:
Sprinklr Inc is engaged in providing enterprise software that enables every customer-facing function across the front office, from Customer Care to Marketing, to collaborate across internal silos, and communicate across digital channels. Its products include Modern Marketing and Advertising, Morden Research, Modern Care, Core Platform, and Developer portal among others.

BRANDS/DIVISIONS/AFFILIATES:
Sprinklr Core Platform

CONTACTS: *Note: Officers with more than one job title may be intentionally listed here more than once.*
Ragy Thomas, CEO
Christopher Lynch, CFO
Pavitar Singh, Chief Technology Officer
Vivek Kundra, COO
Carlos Dominguez, Director
Daniel Haley, General Counsel
Wilson Conn, Other Executive Officer
Luca Lazzaron, Other Executive Officer
Diane Adams, Other Executive Officer

FINANCIAL DATA: *Note: Data for latest year may not have been available at press time.*

In U.S. $	2022	2021	2020	2019	2018	2017
Revenue	492,394,000	386,930,000	324,276,000			
R&D Expense	60,591,000	40,280,000	32,481,000			
Operating Income	-87,470,000	-25,577,000	-35,529,000			
Operating Margin %	-.18%	-.07%				
SGA Expense	371,722,000	250,145,000	204,165,000			
Net Income	-111,470,000	-37,970,000	-39,754,000			
Operating Cash Flow	-32,922,000	7,311,000	18,966,000			
Capital Expenditure	12,406,000	6,484,000	5,166,000			
EBITDA	-79,412,000	-19,887,000	-31,113,000			
Return on Assets %	-.15%	-.09%				
Return on Equity %	-.78%					
Debt to Equity						

CONTACT INFORMATION:
Phone: 917-933-7800   Fax:
Toll-Free:
Address: 29 West 35th St., 7/Fl, New York, NY 10001 United States

STOCK TICKER/OTHER:
Stock Ticker: CXM   Exchange: NYS
Employees: 3,511   Fiscal Year Ends: 01/31
Parent Company:

SALARIES/BONUSES:
Top Exec. Salary: $536,666   Bonus: $
Second Exec. Salary: Bonus: $
$458,333

OTHER THOUGHTS:
Estimated Female Officers or Directors:
Hot Spot for Advancement for Women/Minorities:

Squarespace Inc

www.squarespace.com

NAIC Code: 541511

TYPES OF BUSINESS:

Internet Page Design Services, Custom
Website Building
Email Campaigns
Advertising

BRANDS/DIVISIONS/AFFILIATES:

GROWTH PLANS/SPECIAL FEATURES:

Squarespace is a provider of subscription-based website-building software and hosting services primarily servicing entrepreneurs and micro businesses. The company offers a range of add-on and standalone tools, including scheduling functionality, email marketing, member areas for paid content, and design tools for social media and video content. Following the 2021 acquisition of Tock, Squarespace has expanded into servicing hospitality customers with reservation, take-out, and event management software.

Squarespace offers its employees medical, dental and vision coverage; parental leave; and 401(k).

CONTACTS: *Note: Officers with more than one job title may be intentionally listed here more than once.*

Anthony Casalena, CEO
Marcela Martin, CFO
Courtenay OConnor, General Counsel
Paul Gubbay, Other Executive Officer

FINANCIAL DATA: *Note: Data for latest year may not have been available at press time.*

In U.S. $	2022	2021	2020	2019	2018	2017
Revenue	866,972,000	784,038,000	621,149,000	484,751,000		
R&D Expense	227,297,000	190,371,000	167,906,000	107,645,000		
Operating Income	13,349,000	-240,874,000	40,220,000	61,340,000		
Operating Margin %	.02%	-.31%	.06%			
SGA Expense	473,671,000	707,910,000	314,686,000	233,856,000		
Net Income	-252,221,000	-249,149,000	30,588,000	58,152,000		
Operating Cash Flow	164,219,000	123,157,000	150,030,000	102,333,000		
Capital Expenditure	11,543,000	11,021,000	4,712,000	8,217,000		
EBITDA	-175,167,000	-201,523,000	54,245,000	83,464,000		
Return on Assets %	-.31%	-.41%	-.79%			
Return on Equity %						
Debt to Equity						

CONTACT INFORMATION:

Phone: 646-580-3456   Fax:
Toll-Free:
Address: 225 Varick St., Fl. 12, New York, NY 10014 United States

STOCK TICKER/OTHER:

Stock Ticker: SQSP   Exchange: NYS
Employees: 1,800   Fiscal Year Ends: 12/31
Parent Company:

SALARIES/BONUSES:

Top Exec. Salary: $620,833   Bonus: $
Second Exec. Salary: $153,409   Bonus: $300,000

OTHER THOUGHTS:

Estimated Female Officers or Directors:
Hot Spot for Advancement for Women/Minorities:

Sales, profits and employees may be estimates. Financial information, benefits and other data can change quickly and may vary from those stated here.

Stamps.com Inc

www.stamps.com

NAIC Code: 454110

TYPES OF BUSINESS:

Postage Stamps, Online Retail
Online Shipping Services
Online Postage Services
Postal and Shipping Labels
Shipping Tacking Services
Postage Reporting Services

BRANDS/DIVISIONS/AFFILIATES:

Thoma Bravo
Auctane

GROWTH PLANS/SPECIAL FEATURES:

Stamps.com, Inc. offers internet-based postage and shipping solutions in the U.S. Postage and shipping labels can be created from one's own devices, such as a computer, mobile phone and printer. The company primarily serves small businesses, home offices and online retailers, and currently has PC Postage partnerships with Avery, Microsoft, HP, the U.S. Postal Service and others. Stamps.com is approximately 50% cheaper than traditional postage meters and allows for tracking and reporting of postage expenditures. Products offered include small office mailers, online sellers, warehouse shippers, corporate postage solutions and related supplies. Support services include an online learning center, how-to videos, frequently asked questions/answers, software download, system status and more. Stamps.com is owned by Chicago-based private equity firm Thoma Bravo.

Stamps.com offers its employees comprehensive health benefits, a 401(k), education reimbursement and a variety of assistance programs and company perks.

CONTACTS:
Note: Officers with more than one job title may be intentionally listed here more than once.

Nathan Jones, CEO
Kate May, CEO, Subsidiary
Jonathan Bourgoine, Chief Technology Officer
Katie May, Director
John Clem, Other Executive Officer
Steve Rifai, Other Executive Officer
Amine Khechfe, Other Executive Officer
Matthew Lipson, Other Executive Officer

FINANCIAL DATA:
Note: Data for latest year may not have been available at press time.

In U.S. $	2022	2021	2020	2019	2018	2017
Revenue	819,831,000	788,299,233	757,980,032	571,849,984	586,929,984	468,708,992
R&D Expense						
Operating Income						
Operating Margin %						
SGA Expense						
Net Income			178,664,992	59,229,000	168,642,000	150,603,008
Operating Cash Flow						
Capital Expenditure						
EBITDA						
Return on Assets %						
Return on Equity %						
Debt to Equity						

CONTACT INFORMATION:

Phone: 310 482-5800   Fax:
Toll-Free: 1-855-889-7867
Address: 1990 E. Grand Ave., El Segundo, CA 90245 United States

STOCK TICKER/OTHER:

Stock Ticker: Private   Exchange:
Employees: 1,500   Fiscal Year Ends: 12/31
Parent Company: Thoma Bravo LP

SALARIES/BONUSES:

Top Exec. Salary: $ Bonus: $
Second Exec. Salary: $ Bonus: $

OTHER THOUGHTS:

Estimated Female Officers or Directors:
Hot Spot for Advancement for Women/Minorities:

Steel Connect Inc

steelconnectinc.com

NAIC Code: 511210A

TYPES OF BUSINESS:
Computer Software, Supply Chain & Logistics
Supply Chain Management
Direct Marketing Solutions

GROWTH PLANS/SPECIAL FEATURES:
Steel Connect Inc is a diversified holding company. The company's operating segment include Direct Marketing and Supply Chain. It generates maximum revenue from the Direct Marketing segment. Geographically, it derives a majority of revenue from the United States and also has a presence in China; Netherlands, and others. The company serves clients in various industries including consumer electronics, communications, computing, software, storage, and retail industries.

BRANDS/DIVISIONS/AFFILIATES:
ModusLink Corporation
IWCO Direct Inc

CONTACTS: *Note: Officers with more than one job title may be intentionally listed here more than once.*
John Ashe, CEO, Subsidiary
Fawaz Khalil, CEO, Subsidiary
Warren Lichtenstein, CEO
Jason Wong, CFO
Joseph Sherk, Chief Accounting Officer
Glen Kassan, Director

FINANCIAL DATA: *Note: Data for latest year may not have been available at press time.*

In U.S. $	2022	2021	2020	2019	2018	2017
Revenue	203,272,000	226,256,000	782,813,000	819,830,000	645,258,000	
R&D Expense						
Operating Income	1,163,000	-1,570,000	32,443,000	-24,794,000	-20,998,000	
Operating Margin %	.01%	-.01%	.04%	-.03%	-.03%	
SGA Expense	40,373,000	49,274,000	103,261,000	144,078,000	101,972,000	
Net Income	-10,968,000	-44,391,000	-5,284,000	-66,727,000	36,715,000	
Operating Cash Flow	-3,134,000	-8,110,000	71,624,000	20,849,000	10,002,000	
Capital Expenditure	1,485,000	1,217,000	12,070,000	14,539,000	18,423,000	
EBITDA	7,472,000	3,020,000	84,932,000	32,356,000	31,672,000	
Return on Assets %	-.03%	-.06%	-.01%	-.09%	.06%	
Return on Equity %		-1.69%	-.15%	-.86%	.41%	
Debt to Equity		2.91%	8.536	7.135	3.69%	

CONTACT INFORMATION:
Phone: 914-461-1276   Fax:
Toll-Free:
Address: 2000 Midway Ln, Smyrna, TN 37167 United States

STOCK TICKER/OTHER:
Stock Ticker: STCN   Exchange: NAS
Employees: 1,000   Fiscal Year Ends: 07/31
Parent Company:

SALARIES/BONUSES:
Top Exec. Salary: $325,000   Bonus: $169,000
Second Exec. Salary: $ Bonus: $

OTHER THOUGHTS:
Estimated Female Officers or Directors: 2
Hot Spot for Advancement for Women/Minorities:

Stitch Fix Inc

NAIC Code: 454110

www.stitchfix.com

TYPES OF BUSINESS:

Subscription-Based Apparel Selection
Personal Shopping Services Online
Men's Apparel
Women's Apparel
Ecommerce

BRANDS/DIVISIONS/AFFILIATES:

GROWTH PLANS/SPECIAL FEATURES:

Stitch Fix Inc offers personal style services for men and women. The company engages in delivering one-to-one personalization to clients through the combination of data science and human judgment. It provides a shipment service called A FIX where the stylist's hand selects items from several merchandise with analysis of client and merchandise data to provide a personalized shipment of apparel, shoes, and accessories suited to the client's needs. The company offers products across categories, brands, product types, and price points including Women's, Petite, Maternity, Men's, and Plus. It also offers various product types, including denim, dresses, blouses, skirts, shoes, jewelry, and handbags, and sells merchandise across various ranges of price points.

CONTACTS: *Note: Officers with more than one job title may be intentionally listed here more than once.*

Elizabeth Spaulding, CEO
Dan Jedda, CFO
Katrina Lake, Chairman of the Board
Sarah Barkema, Chief Accounting Officer
Scott Darling, Chief Legal Officer

FINANCIAL DATA: *Note: Data for latest year may not have been available at press time.*

In U.S. $	2022	2021	2020	2019	2018	2017
Revenue	2,072,812,000	2,101,258,000	1,711,733,000	1,577,558,000	1,226,505,000	
R&D Expense						
Operating Income	-208,045,000	-63,361,000	-51,664,000	23,495,000	43,024,000	
Operating Margin %	- .10%	- .03%	- .03%	.01%	.04%	
SGA Expense	1,116,519,000	1,010,997,000	805,874,000	679,634,000	492,998,000	
Net Income	-207,121,000	-8,876,000	-67,117,000	36,881,000	44,900,000	
Operating Cash Flow	55,395,000	-15,675,000	42,877,000	78,594,000	72,178,000	
Capital Expenditure	46,351,000	35,256,000	30,207,000	30,825,000	16,565,000	
EBITDA	-170,860,000	-33,432,000	-29,047,000	37,826,000	53,566,000	
Return on Assets %	- .26%	- .01%	- .10%	.07%	.10%	
Return on Equity %	- .53%	- .02%	- .17%	.10%	.19%	
Debt to Equity	.44%	.26%	0.35			

CONTACT INFORMATION:

Phone: 415-882-7765   Fax:
Toll-Free:
Address: 1 Montgomery St., Ste. 1500, San Francisco, CA 94104 United States

STOCK TICKER/OTHER:

Stock Ticker: SFIX   Exchange: NAS
Employees: 5,860   Fiscal Year Ends: 07/31
Parent Company:

SALARIES/BONUSES:

Top Exec. Salary: $588,941   Bonus: $
Second Exec. Salary: $479,326   Bonus: $17,000

OTHER THOUGHTS:

Estimated Female Officers or Directors:
Hot Spot for Advancement for Women/Minorities:

Stripe Inc

NAIC Code: 522320

TYPES OF BUSINESS:

Credit Card Processing -Intermediary
Digital Payment Solutions
Payments Technology and Software
Ecommerce Solutions
Revenue and Financial Management Products
Banking-as-a-Service Products
Invoicing and Billing Management
Credit Card Creation and Issuing

BRANDS/DIVISIONS/AFFILIATES:

CONTACTS: Note: Officers with more than one job title may be intentionally listed here more than once.

Patrick Collison, CEO
John Collison, Pres.
Eileen O'mara, Chief Revenue Officer
Jeff Titterton, CMO
David Singleton, CTO

GROWTH PLANS/SPECIAL FEATURES:

Stripe, Inc. is a technology company that develops and offers payments software for businesses, including digital payments. The Stripe platform is built for startups to enterprises so they can accept payments and manage their businesses online. The firm serves companies in over 45 countries and offers more than 135 currencies and payment methods. Stripe's products are grouped into three categories, global payments, revenue and financial management, and banking-as-a-service (BaaS). Global payments products include online payments, pre-built payment checkout, customizable payments, no-code payment links, fraud and risk management, payments for platforms, billing, invoicing, in-person terminal payments, financial linked-account data capabilities and online identity verification. Revenue and financial management products include subscription billing management, invoicing, sales tax and VAT automation, automated revenue recognition, custom reports, data warehouse sync capabilities, startup incorporation, and climate carbon removal technologies for climate change support. Last, BaaS products include payments for platforms, business capital financing, credit card creation and issuing, and BaaS. Product and tool integration services are offered to developers, as well as application programming interface (API) resources and related information. Stripe is dual headquartered in San Francisco and Dublin, with offices in London, Paris, Singapore, Tokyo and more.

FINANCIAL DATA: Note: Data for latest year may not have been available at press time.

In U.S. $	2022	2021	2020	2019	2018	2017
Revenue	25,000,000,000	12,000,000,000	7,400,000,000	1,350,000,000	800,000,000	790,500,000
R&D Expense						
Operating Income						
Operating Margin %						
SGA Expense						
Net Income						
Operating Cash Flow						
Capital Expenditure						
EBITDA						
Return on Assets %						
Return on Equity %						
Debt to Equity						

CONTACT INFORMATION:

Phone: 650 427-9276   Fax:
Toll-Free: 888-963-8955
Address: 510 Townsend St., San Francisco, CA 94103-4918 United States

STOCK TICKER/OTHER:

Stock Ticker: Private   Exchange:
Employees: 8,000   Fiscal Year Ends: 12/31
Parent Company:

SALARIES/BONUSES:

Top Exec. Salary: $ Bonus: $
Second Exec. Salary: $ Bonus: $

OTHER THOUGHTS:

Estimated Female Officers or Directors: 2
Hot Spot for Advancement for Women/Minorities: Y

Student Advantage LLC

www.shopandtravelusa.com/sa-mobile

NAIC Code: 541800

TYPES OF BUSINESS:

Marketing Services
Discount Service Company
Services for College Student Marketing
Discount Student Card
Student Travel Savings
Student Deals via Mobile App
Student Payment Solutions
Payments and Discount Technology

BRANDS/DIVISIONS/AFFILIATES:

Roper Technologies Inc
Student Advantage Discount Card
Local Merchant
My Deals

CONTACTS: *Note: Officers with more than one job title may be intentionally listed here more than once.*

Neil Hunn, CEO-Corp.
Sami Takieddine, Dir.-Oper., Atlanta
Shawn McCarthy, VP-Wide Area Commerce Solutions

GROWTH PLANS/SPECIAL FEATURES:

Student Advantage, LLC, a subsidiary of Roper Technologies, Inc., is a discount service company for the college market. Student Advantage works with universities, colleges and campus organizations, along with thousands of discount locations, to provide students with discounted purchases at their campuses, in stores throughout the country and online. The firm connects with students via website, mobile app and the Student Advantage Discount Card, all of which provides students with discounts from partnering discount locations. Student Advantage has partners across a vast number of industries, offering 350,000 discounts nationwide. There are three savings categories: travel savings, SA (Student Advantage) mobile discounts and traditional discounts. The travel category offers discounts on flights, car rentals and hotel reservations with more than 500,000 hotels and car rental locations. Members get $100 worth of travel credits that go toward a stay at over 400,000 nationwide hotels. SA mobile discounts work through the My Deals mobile app. This allows students to redeem deals directly from a mobile device, including categories like automotive, dining and food, entertainment and recreation, gold, health and beauty, home and garden, hotel, movies, services and shopping. Traditional discount provides university-specific ID cards, allowing students to save money and universities to generate extra income. Student Advantage's Local Merchant programs enable students to use their Discount Cards as a method of payment for off-campus dining, shopping and other purchase needs. Dedicated emails can be sent to Student Advantage cardholders from discount partners, offering information on upcoming deals. A one-year memberships costs $30.

FINANCIAL DATA: *Note: Data for latest year may not have been available at press time.*

In U.S. $	2022	2021	2020	2019	2018	2017
Revenue						
R&D Expense						
Operating Income						
Operating Margin %						
SGA Expense						
Net Income						
Operating Cash Flow						
Capital Expenditure						
EBITDA						
Return on Assets %						
Return on Equity %						
Debt to Equity						

CONTACT INFORMATION:

Phone: 844-462-2673   Fax:
Toll-Free: 800-333-2920
Address: 950 Danby Rd., Ste. 100C, Ithaca, NY 14850 United States

STOCK TICKER/OTHER:

Stock Ticker: Subsidiary   Exchange:
Employees: 450   Fiscal Year Ends: 12/31
Parent Company: Roper Technologies Inc

SALARIES/BONUSES:

Top Exec. Salary: $ Bonus: $
Second Exec. Salary: $ Bonus: $

OTHER THOUGHTS:

Estimated Female Officers or Directors:
Hot Spot for Advancement for Women/Minorities:

SugarCRM Inc

www.sugarcrm.com

NAIC Code: 511210K

TYPES OF BUSINESS:

Customer Relationship Management Software
Software Development
Customer Relationship Management
Artificial Intelligence
Automated Data Capture
Real-Time Information Retrieval
Integrated Tools
Training and Support Services

BRANDS/DIVISIONS/AFFILIATES:

GROWTH PLANS/SPECIAL FEATURES:

SugarCRM, Inc. provides customer relationship management (CRM) software solutions for businesses. The firm's Sugar Sell platform offers customer historical records, artificial intelligence (AI)-based predictions, automated data capture for real-time information retrieval, and integrated CRM tools. Sugar Market is a marketing automation platform designed for creating campaigns, engaging one-to-one at scale, predicting needs and understanding what is/isn't working marketing-wise. Sugar Serve is a platform for creating better customer experiences, retaining customers and driving growth. Sugar Enterprise is an on-premises CRM deployment platform that is customizable and enables enterprises to have complete control over the technology stack. SugarCRM offers a range of pricing plans for specific use purposes, and also provides product support, training and certification services. Companies in over 120 countries rely on the Sugar platform.

CONTACTS: *Note: Officers with more than one job title may be intentionally listed here more than once.*

Craig Charlton, CEO
Clint Oram, Chief Strategy Officer
Matt Quilter, CFO
Clare Dorrian, CMO
Shana Sweeney, Chief Human Resources Officer
Zac Sprackett, CTO
Lila Tretikov, Chief Prod. Officer
Patricia Timm, General Counsel
S. Zachariah Sprackett, VP-Oper.
Majed Itani, VP-Dev.
Craig A. Lewis, Sr. VP-Global Svcs. & Channel Dev.
Chris Pennington, Chief Customer Officer
Glenn Cross, Exec. VP-Worldwide Field Oper.

FINANCIAL DATA: *Note: Data for latest year may not have been available at press time.*

In U.S. $	2022	2021	2020	2019	2018	2017
Revenue	348,795,720	335,380,500	322,481,250	330,750,000	315,000,000	300,000,000
R&D Expense						
Operating Income						
Operating Margin %						
SGA Expense						
Net Income						
Operating Cash Flow						
Capital Expenditure						
EBITDA						
Return on Assets %						
Return on Equity %						
Debt to Equity						

CONTACT INFORMATION:

Phone: 408-454-6900   Fax: 408-873-2872
Toll-Free: 877-842-7276
Address: 10050 N. Wolfe Rd., SW2-130, Cupertino, CA 95014 United States

STOCK TICKER/OTHER:

Stock Ticker: Private   Exchange:
Employees: 475   Fiscal Year Ends:
Parent Company:

SALARIES/BONUSES:

Top Exec. Salary: $ Bonus: $
Second Exec. Salary: $ Bonus: $

OTHER THOUGHTS:

Estimated Female Officers or Directors: 2
Hot Spot for Advancement for Women/Minorities: Y

Sales, profits and employees may be estimates. Financial information, benefits and other data can change quickly and may vary from those stated here.

Sumo Logic Inc

www.sumologic.com

NAIC Code: 511210J

TYPES OF BUSINESS:

Computer Software, Data Base & File Management

BRANDS/DIVISIONS/AFFILIATES:

Francisco Partners Management LP
Sumo Logic SaaS Log Analytics Platform

GROWTH PLANS/SPECIAL FEATURES:

Sumo Logic Inc is a software company that develops software which enables organizations of all sizes to address the challenges and opportunities presented by digital transformation, modern applications, and cloud computing. The firm's Sumo Logic SaaS Log Analytics Platform enables organizations to automate the collection, ingestion, and analysis of application, infrastructure, security, and IoT data. The solutions provided are in the categories of Operations Intelligence, Security Intelligence, and Business Intelligence. The company caters its solutions to the public, education, gaming, retail, financial services, and fintech sectors. In May 2023, Sumo Logic was taken private by the investment firm Francisco Partners Management LP.

Sumo Logic offers its employees health benefits and company perks.

CONTACTS: *Note: Officers with more than one job title may be intentionally listed here more than once.*

Joe Kim, CEO
Stewart Grierson, COO
Jennifer McCord, Chief Accounting Officer
Jennifer McCord, CFO
Liz Shulof, CMO
Sophie Kitson, Chief Human Resources Officer
Tej Redkar, Chief Product Officer
Katherine Haar, General Counsel
Steven Fitz, Other Executive Officer
Lynne Doherty McDonald, President, Divisional
Raymond Yue, Vice President, Divisional
Paul Thomas, Vice President, Divisional

FINANCIAL DATA: *Note: Data for latest year may not have been available at press time.*

In U.S. $	2022	2021	2020	2019	2018	2017
Revenue	242,124,992	202,636,992	155,056,000	103,642,000	67,828,000	
R&D Expense						
Operating Income						
Operating Margin %						
SGA Expense						
Net Income	-123,365,000	-80,297,000	-92,137,000	-47,789,000	-32,435,000	
Operating Cash Flow						
Capital Expenditure						
EBITDA						
Return on Assets %						
Return on Equity %						
Debt to Equity						

CONTACT INFORMATION:

Phone: 650-810-8700   Fax: 650-961-1711
Toll-Free: 855-564-7866
Address: 305 Main St., Redwood City, CA 94063 United States

SALARIES/BONUSES:

Top Exec. Salary: $ Bonus: $
Second Exec. Salary: $ Bonus: $

STOCK TICKER/OTHER:

Stock Ticker: Private   Exchange:
Employees: 983   Fiscal Year Ends: 01/31
Parent Company: Francisco Partners Management LP

OTHER THOUGHTS:

Estimated Female Officers or Directors:
Hot Spot for Advancement for Women/Minorities:

Suning.com Co Ltd

www.suning.com

NAIC Code: 454110

TYPES OF BUSINESS:

Electronic Shopping
Ecommerce
Retail Stores
Consumer Goods
Delivery Network
Trucks
Logistics
Warehousing

BRANDS/DIVISIONS/AFFILIATES:

Yifuboa
Suning Payment

CONTACTS: Note: Officers with more than one job title may be intentionally listed here more than once.

Zhang Jindong, Chmn.

GROWTH PLANS/SPECIAL FEATURES:

Suning.com Co., Ltd. is an ecommerce China-based retailer that offers household appliances, digital products and communication products, as well as consumer goods such as personal care items and non-perishable food and beverages. The products are sent from retailers directly to the user's address. Tens of thousands of stores and service terminals utilize Suning.com to serve customers throughout the country. Suning engages in three business units: retail, finance and logistics. The retail business engages in the retail of mobile phones, cameras, TVs, portable electronics, refrigerators, office supplies, men and women's clothing, luggage, jewelry, clocks, shoes, watches, books, children's books, washing machine, kitchen and bathroom, computers, computer accessories, food and drink, toys, cleaning products, air conditioning units, car and motorcycles, car and motorcycle parts, exercise equipment, pet supplies, smart technology, makeup, home textiles, used cars, art supplies, medical supplies, health products, foreign products and more. The finance segment provides small and medium sized businesses with quality and comprehensive financial services. Services include payment, supply chain financing, consumer finance, investment and wealth management, crowd funding, insurance, investments and pre-paid cards. Customers must set up an account through Yifuboa, also known as Suning Payment, to pay for items on the site. The logistics segment provides logistics services throughout the entire supply chain process focusing on efficiency, customer experience, management and innovation. The segment has five warehouses focusing on the cloud and robotics and engages in the creation of unmanned vehicles and heavy trucks, but also utilizes thousands of truck drivers within its delivery network.

FINANCIAL DATA: Note: Data for latest year may not have been available at press time.

In U.S. $	2022	2021	2020	2019	2018	2017
Revenue	10,305,143,000	20,158,616,980	38,652,900,000	38,527,500,000	35,613,600,000	28,855,700,000
R&D Expense						
Operating Income						
Operating Margin %						
SGA Expense						
Net Income	-2,341,945,000	270,782,169	-820,851,000	1,333,690,000	1,838,130,000	1,457,620,000
Operating Cash Flow						
Capital Expenditure						
EBITDA						
Return on Assets %						
Return on Equity %						
Debt to Equity						

CONTACT INFORMATION:

Phone: 86 25-8441-8888   Fax:
Toll-Free:
Address: No. 1 Suning St., Xuanwu Dist., Nanjing, Jiangsu 210042 China

STOCK TICKER/OTHER:

Stock Ticker: 2024
Employees: 35,583
Parent Company:

Exchange: Shenzhen
Fiscal Year Ends: 12/31

SALARIES/BONUSES:

Top Exec. Salary: $ Bonus: $
Second Exec. Salary: $ Bonus: $

OTHER THOUGHTS:

Estimated Female Officers or Directors:
Hot Spot for Advancement for Women/Minorities:

Sales, profits and employees may be estimates. Financial information, benefits and other data can change quickly and may vary from those stated here.

SurveyMonkey Inc

www.surveymonkey.com

NAIC Code: 519130

TYPES OF BUSINESS:

Tools for Online Surveys
Survey Software
Online Platform
Mobile Platform

BRANDS/DIVISIONS/AFFILIATES:

Symphony Technology Group
Momentive Global Inc

GROWTH PLANS/SPECIAL FEATURES:

SurveyMonkey, Inc., formerly Momentive Global Inc., is engaged in providing survey software products and purpose-built solutions that enable organizations to engage with their key constituents, including their customers, employees and the markets they serve. It offers a cloud-based SaaS platform that helps individuals and organizations design and distribute surveys. Products offered by the company enable individuals and organizations of all sizes to collect and analyze People Powered Data. In June 2023, the firm was acquired by private equity firm Symphony Technology Group.

CONTACTS: Note: Officers with more than one job title may be intentionally listed here more than once.

Eric Johnson, CEO
Antoine Andrews, Chief Diversity & Social Impact Officer
Justin Coulombe, CFO
Rich Sullivan, CFO
Becky Cantieri, Chief People Officer
Robin Ducot, Chief Technology Officer
David Ebersman, Director
Rebecca Cantieri, Other Executive Officer
John Schoenstein, Other Executive Officer
Thomas Hale, President

FINANCIAL DATA: Note: Data for latest year may not have been available at press time.

In U.S. $	2022	2021	2020	2019	2018	2017
Revenue	480,916,992	443,785,984	375,609,984	307,420,992	254,324,000	218,772,992
R&D Expense						
Operating Income						
Operating Margin %						
SGA Expense						
Net Income	-89,891,000	-123,249,000	-91,581,000	-73,859,000	-154,740,000	-24,010,000
Operating Cash Flow						
Capital Expenditure						
EBITDA						
Return on Assets %						
Return on Equity %						
Debt to Equity						

CONTACT INFORMATION:

Phone: 650-543-8400   Fax:
Toll-Free:
Address: One Curiosity Way, San Mateo, CA 94403 United States

STOCK TICKER/OTHER:

Stock Ticker: Private   Exchange:
Employees: 1,400   Fiscal Year Ends: 12/31
Parent Company: Symphony Technology Group

SALARIES/BONUSES:

Top Exec. Salary: $ Bonus: $
Second Exec. Salary: $ Bonus: $

OTHER THOUGHTS:

Estimated Female Officers or Directors: 5
Hot Spot for Advancement for Women/Minorities: Y

Switch Inc

www.switch.com

NAIC Code: 518210

TYPES OF BUSINESS:
Data Processing, Hosting, and Related Services

GROWTH PLANS/SPECIAL FEATURES:
Switch Inc, owned by DigitalBridge Group, Inc. and IFM Investors, is a U.S.-based technology infrastructure company. The firm is engaged in designing, constructing, and operating hyper-scale data centers. Switch has developed patented technologies that have redefined data center space and cooling, allowing customers to deploy high-density and scalable IT architectures to support demanding and critical workloads. Switch owns and operates primary campus locations called PRIMES. These PRIMES are The Core Campus in Vegas, Nevada; The Citadel Campus near Reno, Nevada; The Pyramid Campus in Grand Rapids, Michigan; The Keep Campus in Atlanta, Georgia; and The Rock Campus in Austin, Texas.

BRANDS/DIVISIONS/AFFILIATES:
DigitalBridge Group Inc
IFM Investors
PRIMES

CONTACTS:
Note: Officers with more than one job title may be intentionally listed here more than once.

Rob Roy, CEO
Rob Roy, Chairman of the Board
Madonna Park, CFO
Teresa Borden, Other Executive Officer

FINANCIAL DATA:
Note: Data for latest year may not have been available at press time.

In U.S. $	2022	2021	2020	2019	2018	2017
Revenue	615,700,000	592,044,992	511,547,008	462,310,016	405,860,000	378,275,000
R&D Expense						
Operating Income						
Operating Margin %						
SGA Expense						
Net Income		5,412,000	15,539,000	8,917,000	4,052,000	-8,580,000
Operating Cash Flow						
Capital Expenditure						
EBITDA						
Return on Assets %						
Return on Equity %						
Debt to Equity						

CONTACT INFORMATION:
Phone: 702-444-4111   Fax:
Toll-Free:
Address: 7135 S. Decatur Blvd., Las Vegas, NV 89118 United States

STOCK TICKER/OTHER:
Stock Ticker: Private   Exchange:
Employees: 830   Fiscal Year Ends: 12/31
Parent Company: DigitalBridge Group Inc

SALARIES/BONUSES:
Top Exec. Salary: $ Bonus: $
Second Exec. Salary: $ Bonus: $

OTHER THOUGHTS:
Estimated Female Officers or Directors:
Hot Spot for Advancement for Women/Minorities:

Sales, profits and employees may be estimates. Financial information, benefits and other data can change quickly and may vary from those stated here.

Symphony Technology Group
NAIC Code: 511210H

TYPES OF BUSINESS:
Enterprise Management Software
Technology Business Investments
Innovative Software
Data Technology
Analytics Technology

BRANDS/DIVISIONS/AFFILIATES:
BRADY.
eProductivity Software
Dodge Construction Network
escalent
jobrapido
Skyhigh Security
Trellix
STG Exited Investments

CONTACTS: *Note: Officers with more than one job title may be intentionally listed here more than once.*
Stephen Henkenmeier, CFO
Chris Langone, VP-Bus. Dev.
Mattias Derynck, VP-Investor Rel.
Stephen Combs, Chief Recruiting Officer
William Chisholm, Managing Dir.
Pallab Chatterjee, Managing Dir.
J.T.Treadwell, Managing Dir.
Mahinder Mathrani, Managing Dir.-STG India

GROWTH PLANS/SPECIAL FEATURES:
Symphony Technology Group (STG) is a private equity firm with a focus on innovative software, data and analytics to mid-market companies. STG seeks to find, transform and build technology companies in partnership with their management teams. STG's global portfolio of companies include Accelerated Technology, alveo, Cadmium, CAI, CaseWorthy Cletra Dodge Construction, eProductivity Software, escalent, extendearetail, fishbowl, govini, jobrapido, netwitness, nomis, Onclusive, OUTSEER, QUOR, REDSEAL, RSA, SAI360, Sciforma, Skyhigh security, SurveyMonkey, Symphony Talent, Traceone, Trellix and wrike. Symphony Technology Group is based in California, USA, with international locations in Italy and India.

FINANCIAL DATA: *Note: Data for latest year may not have been available at press time.*

In U.S. $	2022	2021	2020	2019	2018	2017
Revenue	3,120,000,000	3,000,000,000	2,998,125,000	2,925,000,000	2,900,000,000	2,800,000,000
R&D Expense						
Operating Income						
Operating Margin %						
SGA Expense						
Net Income						
Operating Cash Flow						
Capital Expenditure						
EBITDA						
Return on Assets %						
Return on Equity %						
Debt to Equity						

CONTACT INFORMATION:
Phone: 650-935-9500   Fax: 650-935-9501
Toll-Free:
Address: 1300 El Camino Real, Ste. 300, Menlo Park, CA 94025 United States

STOCK TICKER/OTHER:
Stock Ticker: Private   Exchange:
Employees: 15,250   Fiscal Year Ends: 12/31
Parent Company:

SALARIES/BONUSES:
Top Exec. Salary: $ Bonus: $
Second Exec. Salary: $ Bonus: $

OTHER THOUGHTS:
Estimated Female Officers or Directors:
Hot Spot for Advancement for Women/Minorities:

Taboola Inc

www.taboola.com

NAIC Code: 541810E

TYPES OF BUSINESS:

Advertising/Marketing--Online
Content Discovery Platform
Open Web Advertising
Artificial Intelligence

BRANDS/DIVISIONS/AFFILIATES:

GROWTH PLANS/SPECIAL FEATURES:

Taboola.com Ltd is a technology company that powers recommendations across the Open Web with an artificial intelligence-based, algorithmic engine. It partners with websites, devices, and mobile apps, collectively referred to as digital properties, to recommend editorial content and advertisements on the Open Web. Geographically it serves Israel, the United Kingdom, Germany, France, Rest of the world whilst it generates the majority of its revenue from the United States.

CONTACTS: *Note: Officers with more than one job title may be intentionally listed here more than once.*

Adam Singolda, CEO
Stephen Walker, CFO
Zvi Limon, Chairman of the Board
Lior Golan, Chief Technology Officer
Eldad Maniv, COO
Kristy Sundjaja, Senior VP, Divisional

FINANCIAL DATA: *Note: Data for latest year may not have been available at press time.*

In U.S. $	2022	2021	2020	2019	2018	2017
Revenue	1,401,150,000	1,378,458,000	1,188,893,000	1,093,830,000	909,246,000	
R&D Expense	129,276,000	117,933,000	99,423,000	84,710,000	73,024,000	
Operating Income	-13,665,000	-13,265,000	26,193,000	-19,636,000	17,333,000	
Operating Margin %	-.01%	-.01%	.02%	-.02%		
SGA Expense	348,642,000	336,403,000	193,881,000	166,895,000	143,873,000	
Net Income	-11,975,000	-24,948,000	8,493,000	-28,025,000	10,661,000	
Operating Cash Flow	53,484,000	63,521,000	139,087,000	18,056,000	76,977,000	
Capital Expenditure	34,914,000	39,070,000	17,774,000	44,328,000	32,157,000	
EBITDA	77,556,000	39,846,000	60,150,000	19,728,000	52,605,000	
Return on Assets %	-.01%	-.03%	-.03%	-.10%		
Return on Equity %	-.01%	-.09%	-.54%	-6.77%		
Debt to Equity	.34%	.45%	1.352	8.67		

CONTACT INFORMATION:

Phone: 212-206-7663   Fax:
Toll-Free:
Address: 16 Madison Square W., 7/Fl, New York, NY 10010 United States

STOCK TICKER/OTHER:

Stock Ticker: TBLA   Exchange: NAS
Employees: 1,815   Fiscal Year Ends: 12/31
Parent Company:

SALARIES/BONUSES:

Top Exec. Salary: $ Bonus: $
Second Exec. Salary: $ Bonus: $

OTHER THOUGHTS:

Estimated Female Officers or Directors:
Hot Spot for Advancement for Women/Minorities:

Talkdesk Inc

www.talkdesk.com

NAIC Code: 511210K

TYPES OF BUSINESS:

Computer Software, Sales & Customer Relationship Management
Cloud Business Software
Customer Experience Solutions
Workplace Optimization
Call Center Software
Artificial Intelligence
Platform and Cloud Products
Business Analytics

BRANDS/DIVISIONS/AFFILIATES:

CONTACTS: *Note: Officers with more than one job title may be intentionally listed here more than once.*

Tiago Paiva, CEO
William Welch, Pres.
Sydney Carey, CFO
Neville Letzerich, CMO
Shauna Geraghty, Sr. VP-People & Oper.
Graham Smith, Chmn.

GROWTH PLANS/SPECIAL FEATURES:

Talkdesk, Inc. provides cloud-based call center software solutions for businesses. The company's solutions enable users to optimize calls and adapt to the evolving needs of work teams, employees and customers. The software can provide an overview of employees and repeat customers via information obtained from various departments within the database, including customer relations management, helpdesk, back office, connected social/networking sites and more. Talkdesk's products are grouped into categories such as contact center software, self-service experience, omnichannel engagement, workforce engagement management, employee collaboration and customer experience analytics, as well as various platform and cloud offerings. The firm's solutions span a range of industries, including communications, media, internet, financial services, insurance, government, education, healthcare, life sciences, retail, consumer goods, transportation and hospitality. Talkdesk is headquartered in California, with employees located in nearly 19 countries.

FINANCIAL DATA: *Note: Data for latest year may not have been available at press time.*

In U.S. $	2022	2021	2020	2019	2018	2017
Revenue						
R&D Expense						
Operating Income						
Operating Margin %						
SGA Expense						
Net Income						
Operating Cash Flow						
Capital Expenditure						
EBITDA						
Return on Assets %						
Return on Equity %						
Debt to Equity						

CONTACT INFORMATION:

Phone: 415 801-4869   Fax:
Toll-Free: 844-332-2859
Address: 201 Spear St., Ste. 1100, San Francisco, CA 94105 United States

STOCK TICKER/OTHER:

Stock Ticker: Private   Exchange:
Employees: 300   Fiscal Year Ends:
Parent Company:

SALARIES/BONUSES:

Top Exec. Salary: $ Bonus: $
Second Exec. Salary: $ Bonus: $

OTHER THOUGHTS:

Estimated Female Officers or Directors:
Hot Spot for Advancement for Women/Minorities:

Sales, profits and employees may be estimates. Financial information, benefits and other data can change quickly and may vary from those stated here.

Tantan (Tantan Cultural Development Beijing Co Ltd)
tantanapp.com/en
NAIC Code: 511210G

TYPES OF BUSINESS:
Computer Software, Electronic Games, Apps & Entertainment
Dating App
Online Dating Platform
Live Group Features
Voice Enablement
Video Upload
Technology

BRANDS/DIVISIONS/AFFILIATES:

GROWTH PLANS/SPECIAL FEATURES:
Yay Media Labs Limited operates Tantan, an online dating platform primarily serving the Asian market. Tantan allows users to browse profiles based on location, distance and gender preferences, and to swipe right if interested and swipe left if not interested. When users are interested in each other, it is considered a match, and chats, notifications and messages then become available between them. Messages from random people are not transmitted. A user's dating profile can also be private by choosing to hide their contacts. Tantan features live group chats, text, voice and video. Approximately 300 million registered users and more than 10 million matches take place on Tantan daily.

CONTACTS: *Note: Officers with more than one job title may be intentionally listed here more than once.*
Yu Wang, CEO

FINANCIAL DATA: *Note: Data for latest year may not have been available at press time.*

In U.S. $	2022	2021	2020	2019	2018	2017
Revenue						
R&D Expense						
Operating Income						
Operating Margin %						
SGA Expense						
Net Income						
Operating Cash Flow						
Capital Expenditure						
EBITDA						
Return on Assets %						
Return on Equity %						
Debt to Equity						

CONTACT INFORMATION:
Phone: 86 10 5869-9811   Fax:
Toll-Free:
Address: 507, Soho 2D, Guanghua Rd., Chaoyang Dist., Beijing, Beijing 100020 China

STOCK TICKER/OTHER:
Stock Ticker: Private   Exchange:
Employees: Fiscal Year Ends:
Parent Company:

SALARIES/BONUSES:
Top Exec. Salary: $ Bonus: $
Second Exec. Salary: $ Bonus: $

OTHER THOUGHTS:
Estimated Female Officers or Directors:
Hot Spot for Advancement for Women/Minorities:

Tata Consultancy Services Limited (TCS)   www.tcs.com

NAIC Code: 541512

TYPES OF BUSINESS:

IT Consulting
Software Consultancy
Analytics and Insight Services
Blockchain Services
Cybersecurity Services
Automation and Artificial Intelligence
Cloud Consulting
Internet of Things

BRANDS/DIVISIONS/AFFILIATES:

Tata Group
TCS BaNCS

CONTACTS: *Note: Officers with more than one job title may be intentionally listed here more than once.*

K. Krithivasan, CEO
N.G. Subramaniam, COO
Samir Seksaria, CFO
Milind Lakkad, Exec. VP-Global Human Resources
N. Chandrasekaran, Chmn.

GROWTH PLANS/SPECIAL FEATURES:

Tata Consultancy Services Limited (TCS) is one of India's largest consulting companies and one of Asia's largest independent software and services organizations, with a presence in 131 countries. The firm is part of the Tata Group, an Asian conglomerate with interests in Banking, capital markets, consumer goods and distribution, communications, media and information services, education, energy, resources and utilities, healthcare, high tech, insurance life sciences, manufacturing, public services, retail and travel/logistics. TCS offers a range of services, including cloud, cognitive business operations, consulting, cybersecurity, data and analytics, enterprise solutions, internet of things (IoT) and digital engineering, network solutions and services, TCS interactive and sustainability services. The company's TCS BaNCS core banking software suite is used by retail banks, and includes functions for universal banking, core banking, payments, wealth management, foreign exchange, compliance and many more operations. Other industries served by TCS include capital markets, consumer goods and distribution, communication, media, technology, education, energy, utilities, hi-tech, information services, insurance, life sciences and healthcare, manufacturing, retail, travel, transportation and hospitality. The firm has formed alliances with leading technology companies, academic institutions and consulting firms to provide customers with expertise in technology fields in which it does not specialize. Development of new strategies and technologies occurs in TCS' global centers of excellence, located in several nations. TCS has offices throughout North America (with a regional headquarters in New York City), some of which are development centers and centers of excellence.

FINANCIAL DATA: *Note: Data for latest year may not have been available at press time.*

In U.S. $	2022	2021	2020	2019	2018	2017
Revenue	25,700,000,000	22,803,318,123	21,470,898,933	23,219,300,000	19,090,000,000	18,094,166,016
R&D Expense						
Operating Income						
Operating Margin %						
SGA Expense						
Net Income	2,379,843,586	4,437,972,666	4,312,628,111	4,663,800,000	4,730,000,000	4,032,327,168
Operating Cash Flow						
Capital Expenditure						
EBITDA						
Return on Assets %						
Return on Equity %						
Debt to Equity						

CONTACT INFORMATION:

Phone: 91 22-6778-9999   Fax: 91-22-6630-3672
Toll-Free:
Address: TCS House, Raveline St., Mumbai, 400 001 India

STOCK TICKER/OTHER:

Stock Ticker: 532540   Exchange: Bombay
Employees: 592,000   Fiscal Year Ends: 03/31
Parent Company: Tata Group

SALARIES/BONUSES:

Top Exec. Salary: $ Bonus: $
Second Exec. Salary: $ Bonus: $

OTHER THOUGHTS:

Estimated Female Officers or Directors:
Hot Spot for Advancement for Women/Minorities:

Teespring Inc (dba SPRING)

NAIC Code: 454110

teespring.com

TYPES OF BUSINESS:
Electronic Shopping
Ecommerce
Product Design
Crowd Funding

BRANDS/DIVISIONS/AFFILIATES:
Amaze Software Inc

CONTACTS: Note: Officers with more than one job title may be intentionally listed here more than once.
Chris Lamontagne, CEO

GROWTH PLANS/SPECIAL FEATURES:
Teespring, Inc. operates the SPRING ecommerce platform established to enable anyone to design and sell products. The company was founded in 2011 by two Brown University students who developed a website in mere hours to sell commemorative shirts in lieu of the closing of their favorite local bar. The site was designed to accept prepaid orders before printing anything and therefore bypassing heavy upfront production costs. Obtaining hundreds of orders within hours, the concept and site was then launched, allowing anyone to create a crowdfunding campaign for custom apparel. The SPRING platform provides tools to create unique designs, print them on the merchandise offered and then sell them without the restrictions usually associated with starting an online store. The platform sells the items in campaigns (or limited edition runs) so they can be printed in bulk. Merchandise includes t-shirts, hoodies, sweatshirts and sportswear, as well as many other items such as stickers and tapestries. Merchandise is shipped from Teespring's Kentucky facility. Popular categories at the teespring.com site include age, family, hobbies and animals. Purchasing from SPRING supports the independent creators and the causes they care about. Teespring is a subsidiary of Amaze Software, Inc.

FINANCIAL DATA: Note: Data for latest year may not have been available at press time.

In U.S. $	2022	2021	2020	2019	2018	2017
Revenue	165,000,000	165,000,000	161,240,625	165,375,000	157,500,000	150,000,000
R&D Expense						
Operating Income						
Operating Margin %						
SGA Expense						
Net Income						
Operating Cash Flow						
Capital Expenditure						
EBITDA						
Return on Assets %						
Return on Equity %						
Debt to Equity						

CONTACT INFORMATION:
Phone: 855-833-7774   Fax:
Toll-Free:
Address: 2430 3rd St., San Francisco, CA 94107 United States

STOCK TICKER/OTHER:
Stock Ticker: Private   Exchange:
Employees: 312   Fiscal Year Ends:
Parent Company: Amaze Software Inc

SALARIES/BONUSES:
Top Exec. Salary: $ Bonus: $
Second Exec. Salary: $ Bonus: $

OTHER THOUGHTS:
Estimated Female Officers or Directors:
Hot Spot for Advancement for Women/Minorities:

TEGNA Inc

NAIC Code: 515120

www.tegna.com

TYPES OF BUSINESS:

Television Broadcasting
Internet Broadcasting
Television Stations
Radio Stations
Digital Platforms
Campaign Services and Solutions

BRANDS/DIVISIONS/AFFILIATES:

True Crime Network
Quest
TEGNA Marketing Solutions
Locked On

GROWTH PLANS/SPECIAL FEATURES:

Tegna Inc is a media company with a portfolio of broadcast stations and digital sites. The firm has around 64 television stations and 2 radio stations in approximately 51 U.S markets. The company owns multicast networks of True Crime Network, Twist and Quest. Each television station also has a robust digital presence across online, mobile, connected television and social platforms, reaching consumers on all devices and platforms they use to consume news content. It generates key revenue from advertising and marketing services, subscription, political advertising, and other services.

CONTACTS: *Note: Officers with more than one job title may be intentionally listed here more than once.*

David Lougee, CEO
Victoria Harker, CFO
Howard Elias, Chairman of the Board
Clifton McClelland, Chief Accounting Officer
Lynn Beall, COO, Divisional
Akinyale Harrison, General Counsel

FINANCIAL DATA: *Note: Data for latest year may not have been available at press time.*

In U.S. $	2022	2021	2020	2019	2018	2017
Revenue	3,279,245,000	2,991,093,000	2,937,780,000	2,299,497,000	2,207,282,000	1,903,026,000
R&D Expense						
Operating Income	990,309,000	799,909,000	861,027,000	553,683,000	686,775,000	550,331,000
Operating Margin %	.30%	.27%	.29%	.24%	.31%	.29%
SGA Expense	474,638,000	464,573,000	438,896,000	406,948,000	367,787,000	342,339,000
Net Income	629,909,000	477,001,000	481,830,000	286,235,000	405,665,000	273,744,000
Operating Cash Flow	812,151,000	501,612,000	805,136,000	297,473,000	527,209,000	389,429,000
Capital Expenditure	51,333,000	63,076,000	45,499,000	88,356,000	65,230,000	76,886,000
EBITDA	1,128,667,000	927,180,000	981,920,000	691,756,000	787,559,000	657,507,000
Return on Assets %	.09%	.07%	.07%	.05%	.08%	.04%
Return on Equity %	.23%	.21%	.26%	.20%	.35%	.17%
Debt to Equity	1.03%	1.32%	1.775	2.694	2.20%	3.022

CONTACT INFORMATION:

Phone: 703-873-6600   Fax:
Toll-Free:
Address: 8350 Broad St., Ste. 2000, Tysons, VA 22102-5151 United States

STOCK TICKER/OTHER:

Stock Ticker: TGNA   Exchange: NYS
Employees: 6,300   Fiscal Year Ends: 12/31
Parent Company:

SALARIES/BONUSES:

Top Exec. Salary: $975,000   Bonus: $1,267,500
Second Exec. Salary: $722,500   Bonus: $730,000

OTHER THOUGHTS:

Estimated Female Officers or Directors:
Hot Spot for Advancement for Women/Minorities:

Telecomunicaciones de Puerto Rico Inc

www.claropr.com

NAIC Code: 517311

TYPES OF BUSINESS:

Local Exchange Carrier
Telecommunication Services
Mobile and Home Telecommunications
Prepaid and Postpaid Services
Mobile Internet
Deaf Telecommunication Services
Television Broadcasting Services
Mobile and Fixed Telephone Services

BRANDS/DIVISIONS/AFFILIATES:

America Movil SAB de CV
Claro Puerto Rico

GROWTH PLANS/SPECIAL FEATURES:

Telecomunicaciones de Puerto Rico, Inc. is a subsidiary of America Movil SAB de CV that does business as Claro Puerto Rico, and is a leading telecommunication services company in Puerto Rico. Claro Puerto Rico offers mobile and home telecommunication services. Mobile services include prepaid, postpaid (no contract), mobile internet, roaming, deaf community, clear protection, updating services, switching services and eSIM. Home services span Macbook Pro, 2, internet,, claroTV+ and fixed telephone. Universal telecommunication services is also provided, including Wi-Fi hotspot services. Additional payment services by Claro Puerto Rico include paying through mobile apps, banks or ATMs.

CONTACTS:
Note: Officers with more than one job title may be intentionally listed here more than once.

Christina Lambert, CEO

FINANCIAL DATA:
Note: Data for latest year may not have been available at press time.

In U.S. $	2022	2021	2020	2019	2018	2017
Revenue	1,001,669,760	963,144,000	926,100,000	882,000,000	840,000,000	800,000,000
R&D Expense						
Operating Income						
Operating Margin %						
SGA Expense						
Net Income						
Operating Cash Flow						
Capital Expenditure						
EBITDA						
Return on Assets %						
Return on Equity %						
Debt to Equity						

CONTACT INFORMATION:

Phone: 787 792-6052   Fax: 787-282-0958
Toll-Free: 800-781-1314
Address: 1515 FD Roosevelt Ave., Guaynabo, 00968 Puerto Rico

STOCK TICKER/OTHER:

Stock Ticker: Private   Exchange:
Employees: 4,600   Fiscal Year Ends: 12/31
Parent Company: America Movil SAB de CV

SALARIES/BONUSES:

Top Exec. Salary: $ Bonus: $
Second Exec. Salary: $ Bonus: $

OTHER THOUGHTS:

Estimated Female Officers or Directors: 1
Hot Spot for Advancement for Women/Minorities:

Sales, profits and employees may be estimates. Financial information, benefits and other data can change quickly and may vary from those stated here.

Telenor ASA

NAIC Code: 517312

www.telenor.com

TYPES OF BUSINESS:

Mobile Telephone Services
Fixed-Line Telephone Services
Cable Services
Satellite Communications
Satellite Television Broadcasting
Internet of Things

GROWTH PLANS/SPECIAL FEATURES:

Telenor is an international provider of telecom, data, and media communication services. It is the incumbent dominant telecom operator in Norway and the Norwegian government holds a stake of more than 50% in the firm. Telenor also operates in other Nordic countries and owns several businesses in Asia. Most of Telenor's operations are mobile businesses, although it also has some fixed-line operations in Nordic European countries.

BRANDS/DIVISIONS/AFFILIATES:

Telenor Norway
Telenor Sweden
Telenor Denmark
DNA
dtac
Digi
Grameenphone
Telenor Pakistan

CONTACTS: *Note: Officers with more than one job title may be intentionally listed here more than once.*

Sigve Brekke, CEO
Tone Hegland Bachke, CFO
Cecilie Blydt Heuch, Chief People Officer
Ruza Sabanovic, CTO
Morten Karlsen Sorby, Head-Strategy & Regulatory Affairs
Rolv-Erik Spilling, Exec. VP
Hilde M. Tonne, Exec. VP
Berit Svendsen, Exec. VP
Bjorn Magnus Kopperud, Acting Head-Central & Eastern European Oper.
Gunn Waersted, Chmn.
Sigve Brekke, Head-Asia Oper.

FINANCIAL DATA: *Note: Data for latest year may not have been available at press time.*

In U.S. $	2022	2021	2020	2019	2018	2017
Revenue	9,299,271,000	9,130,020,000	10,886,050,000	10,681,750,000	9,954,187,000	10,531,860,000
R&D Expense						
Operating Income	1,795,500,000	1,824,162,000	2,263,498,000	2,376,833,000	1,988,620,000	2,267,915,000
Operating Margin %		.20%	.21%	.22%	.20%	.22%
SGA Expense	762,048,800	732,258,600	650,687,700	731,976,600	706,133,300	950,470,100
Net Income	4,220,730,000	143,594,800	1,629,632,000	730,473,000	1,384,356,000	1,126,111,000
Operating Cash Flow	3,685,914,000	3,972,540,000	4,118,014,000	3,216,036,000	3,420,151,000	3,826,972,000
Capital Expenditure	1,813,543,000	1,827,545,000	1,785,538,000	2,066,150,000	1,974,523,000	1,936,557,000
EBITDA	3,908,355,000	4,752,444,000	5,335,188,000	4,713,256,000	3,822,649,000	4,169,795,000
Return on Assets %		.01%	.07%	.04%	.07%	.06%
Return on Equity %		.05%	.45%	.18%	.28%	.22%
Debt to Equity		4.38%	3.495	3.04	1.12%	0.888

CONTACT INFORMATION:

Phone: 47 81077000   Fax: 47 67890000
Toll-Free:
Address: Snaroyveien 30, Fornebu, N-1360 Norway

STOCK TICKER/OTHER:

Stock Ticker: TELNY   Exchange: PINX
Employees: 14,000   Fiscal Year Ends: 12/31
Parent Company:

SALARIES/BONUSES:

Top Exec. Salary: $ Bonus: $
Second Exec. Salary: $ Bonus: $

OTHER THOUGHTS:

Estimated Female Officers or Directors: 6
Hot Spot for Advancement for Women/Minorities: Y

Telephone and Data Systems Inc (TDS)

www.tdsinc.com

NAIC Code: 517311

TYPES OF BUSINESS:

Local Telephone Service
Cellular Telephone Services
Internet Access
Printing Services
Long-Distance Telephone Service
Data Networks
Broadband Service

BRANDS/DIVISIONS/AFFILIATES:

United States Cellular Corporation
TDS Telecommunications Corporation
OneNeck
Suttle-Straus Inc

GROWTH PLANS/SPECIAL FEATURES:

Telephone and Data Systems Inc is a diversified telecommunications operator that provides mobile, telephone, and broadband services. The company's segments include UScellular and TDS Telecom. It generates maximum revenue from the UScellular segment.

TDS offers its employees comprehensive health benefits, life and disability insurance, 401(k) and assistance programs.

CONTACTS: Note: Officers with more than one job title may be intentionally listed here more than once.

James Butman, CEO, Subsidiary
Laurent Therivel, CEO, Subsidiary
Leroy Carlson, CEO
Peter Sereda, CFO
Walter Carlson, Chairman of the Board
Anita Kroll, Chief Accounting Officer
Jane McCahon, Secretary
Daniel DeWitt, Senior VP, Divisional
Scott Williamson, Senior VP, Divisional
Joseph Hanley, Senior VP, Divisional
Kurt Thaus, Senior VP, Divisional

FINANCIAL DATA: Note: Data for latest year may not have been available at press time.

In U.S. $	2022	2021	2020	2019	2018	2017
Revenue	5,413,000,000	5,329,000,000	5,225,000,000	5,176,000,000	5,109,000,000	
R&D Expense						
Operating Income	151,000,000	285,000,000	281,000,000	190,000,000	196,000,000	
Operating Margin %	.03%	.05%	.05%	.04%	.04%	
SGA Expense	1,768,000,000	1,677,000,000	1,681,000,000	1,717,000,000	1,694,000,000	
Net Income	62,000,000	156,000,000	226,000,000	121,000,000	135,000,000	
Operating Cash Flow	1,155,000,000	1,103,000,000	1,532,000,000	1,016,000,000	1,017,000,000	
Capital Expenditure	1,775,000,000	2,459,000,000	1,368,000,000	962,000,000	778,000,000	
EBITDA	1,228,000,000	1,348,000,000	1,365,000,000	1,308,000,000	1,276,000,000	
Return on Assets %	.00%	.01%	.02%	.01%	.01%	
Return on Equity %	.00%	.02%	.05%	.03%	.03%	
Debt to Equity	.97%	.80%	0.908	0.698	.53%	

CONTACT INFORMATION:

Phone: 312 630-1900   Fax: 312-630-1908
Toll-Free:
Address: 30 N. LaSalle St., Ste. 4000, Chicago, IL 60602 United States

STOCK TICKER/OTHER:

Stock Ticker: TDS   Exchange: NYS
Employees: 9,300   Fiscal Year Ends: 12/31
Parent Company:

SALARIES/BONUSES:

Top Exec. Salary: $1,352,700   Bonus: $1,046,500
Second Exec. Salary: Bonus: $750,867
$824,887

OTHER THOUGHTS:

Estimated Female Officers or Directors: 5
Hot Spot for Advancement for Women/Minorities: Y

Tellabs Inc

www.tellabs.com

NAIC Code: 334210

TYPES OF BUSINESS:

Wireline & Wireless Products & Services
Fiber-Based Technology Innovation
Broadband Support
Passive Optical Local Area Network Solutions
Copper and Fiber Connectivity Solutions

BRANDS/DIVISIONS/AFFILIATES:

Marlin Equity Partners LLC

CONTACTS: Note: Officers with more than one job title may be intentionally listed here more than once.

Rich Schroder, CEO
Norm Burke, CFO
Karen Leos, VP-Global Sales
Tom Dobozy, VP-Engineering
James M. Sheehan, Chief Admin. Officer
James M. Sheehan, General Counsel
John M. Brots, Exec. VP-Global Oper.
Kenneth G. Craft, Exec. VP-Product Dev.

GROWTH PLANS/SPECIAL FEATURES:

Tellabs, Inc. innovates fiber-based technologies to offer products and solutions that support broadband access for service providers and passive optical local area networks (LANs) across all enterprise industries. Tellabs 1000 MSAP is a broadband digital loop carrier platform that converges legacy copper and modern fiber connectivity. Tellabs Optical LAN is an enterprise centric solution that offers a means of designing and operating networks inside buildings and across extended campuses. Solutions offered through these products a passive optical network: passive optical networking, passive optical LAN, operational efficiencies, sustainability, reliability, security, wireless, innovations; network modernization: 911 redundancy, broadband stimulus, broadband DSL, broadband ethernet, class-5 switch replace, narrowband services, broadband transport, 1/0 DCS and D4 replace for network optimization. Industries served include enterprise, education, government, healthcare, hospitality, transportation, manufacturing and service providers. Tellabs is a subsidiary of Marlin Equity Partners, LLC.

FINANCIAL DATA: Note: Data for latest year may not have been available at press time.

In U.S. $	2022	2021	2020	2019	2018	2017
Revenue	1,660,000,000	1,640,000,000	1,610,256,375	1,533,577,500	1,460,550,000	1,391,000,000
R&D Expense						
Operating Income						
Operating Margin %						
SGA Expense						
Net Income						
Operating Cash Flow						
Capital Expenditure						
EBITDA						
Return on Assets %						
Return on Equity %						
Debt to Equity						

CONTACT INFORMATION:

Phone: 972 588-7000   Fax:
Toll-Free:
Address: 4240 International Pkwy, St. 105, Carrollton, TX 75007 United States

STOCK TICKER/OTHER:

Stock Ticker: Private   Exchange:
Employees: 9,400   Fiscal Year Ends: 12/31
Parent Company: Marlin Equity Partners LLC

SALARIES/BONUSES:

Top Exec. Salary: $ Bonus: $
Second Exec. Salary: $ Bonus: $

OTHER THOUGHTS:

Estimated Female Officers or Directors: 1
Hot Spot for Advancement for Women/Minorities: Y

Temu

NAIC Code: 454110

TYPES OF BUSINESS:

Electronic Shopping

BRANDS/DIVISIONS/AFFILIATES:

PDD Holdings Inc

CONTACTS: *Note: Officers with more than one job title may be intentionally listed here more than once.*

Lei Chen, CEO- Corp.

GROWTH PLANS/SPECIAL FEATURES:

TEMU is an e-commerce platform established in the USA in 2022, owned by PDD Holdings, Inc. The firm operates as an online marketplace, connecting sellers predominantly from China with Western customers and focuses on providing low-priced goods across various categories. Products include home/kitchen, women's clothing, women's curve clothing, women's shoes, women's lingerie/lounge, men's clothing, men's shoes, men's big/tall, men's underwear/sleepwear, sports/outdoors, jewelry/accessories, beauty/health, toys/games, automotive, kids' fashion, kids' shoes, baby/maternity, bags/luggage, patio, lawn/garden, arts, crafts/sewing and electronics. The platform enables sellers to offer their products directly to consumers without intermediate distributors, contributing to the affordability of the items. Temu works with leading package carriers like UPS, FedEx and USPS to ensure that all orders are delivered promptly and securely to customers.

FINANCIAL DATA: *Note: Data for latest year may not have been available at press time.*

In U.S. $	2022	2021	2020	2019	2018	2017
Revenue						
R&D Expense						
Operating Income						
Operating Margin %						
SGA Expense						
Net Income						
Operating Cash Flow						
Capital Expenditure						
EBITDA						
Return on Assets %						
Return on Equity %						
Debt to Equity						

CONTACT INFORMATION:

Phone: Fax:
Toll-Free: 888 480-8368
Address: 31 St. James Ave., Ste. 355, Boston, MA 02116 United States

STOCK TICKER/OTHER:

Stock Ticker: Subsidiary   Exchange:
Employees: Fiscal Year Ends:
Parent Company: PDD Holdings Inc

SALARIES/BONUSES:

Top Exec. Salary: $ Bonus: $
Second Exec. Salary: $ Bonus: $

OTHER THOUGHTS:

Estimated Female Officers or Directors:
Hot Spot for Advancement for Women/Minorities:

Tencent Holdings Limited

www.tencent.com

NAIC Code: 519130

TYPES OF BUSINESS:

Websites and Services
Instant Messaging
Electronic Games
Value-added Services
Software
Advertising
Social Networking
Online Search Engine

BRANDS/DIVISIONS/AFFILIATES:

Weixin
QQ
WeChat
Tencent Games
Tencent Music Entertainment Group
Weixin Pay
Tencent Blockchain
Tencent Mobile Manager

CONTACTS: *Note: Officers with more than one job title may be intentionally listed here more than once.*

Huateng (Pony) Ma, CEO
Chi Ping (Martin) Lau, Pres.
John Lo, CFO
Yuxin (Mark) Ren, COO
Chenye (Daniel) Xu, CIO
Zhidong Zhang, CTO
Shan Lu, Pres., Tech. & Eng. Group
James Mitchell, Chief Strategy Officer
Seng Yee Lau, Pres., Online Media Bus.
Taosang Tong, Pres., Social Network Group
Yuxin (Mark) Ren, Pres., Interactive Entertainment Bus.
Xiaoguang (Free) Wu, Sr. Exec. VP
Huateng (Pony) Ma, Chmn.
David Wallerstein, Sr. Exec. VP-Intl Bus.

GROWTH PLANS/SPECIAL FEATURES:

Tencent is arguably the most influential internet firm in China as one can hardly go by a day without using its products. Tencent is the world's largest video game vendor and owns the world's top-grossing mobile game--Honor of Kings. Tencent also runs China's largest social media super app--WeChat. The app is now part of the fabric of life for Chinese people who use it to chat, shop, watch videos, play games, order food and taxis, and more. Equally as impressive as its own portfolio, Tencent is also among the world's largest venture capital and investment corporations. The firm is now one of the largest shareholders in leading tech companies like Meituan, JD, DiDi, Snap, PDD, Kuaishou, Epic Games, and more.

FINANCIAL DATA: *Note: Data for latest year may not have been available at press time.*

In U.S. $	2022	2021	2020	2019	2018	2017
Revenue	76,259,570,000	77,024,980,000	66,291,340,000	51,883,140,000	43,000,320,000	32,695,720,000
R&D Expense						
Operating Income	15,668,530,000	17,105,710,000	17,611,770,000	13,332,690,000	10,727,730,000	9,652,635,000
Operating Margin %		.22%	.27%	.26%	.25%	.30%
SGA Expense	18,691,810,000	17,937,680,000	13,941,750,000	10,291,940,000	9,042,341,000	6,972,455,000
Net Income	25,886,360,000	30,916,540,000	21,981,460,000	12,831,580,000	10,825,090,000	9,833,743,000
Operating Cash Flow	20,089,800,000	24,090,810,000	26,694,400,000	20,433,450,000	15,255,910,000	14,595,910,000
Capital Expenditure	6,992,670,000	8,548,659,000	9,158,403,000	7,836,741,000	7,434,232,000	4,401,050,000
EBITDA	38,700,470,000	43,131,780,000	32,762,410,000	22,244,940,000	18,373,740,000	15,798,620,000
Return on Assets %		.15%	.14%	.11%	.12%	.15%
Return on Equity %		.30%	.28%	.25%	.27%	.33%
Debt to Equity		.37%	0.347	0.453	.43%	0.435

CONTACT INFORMATION:

Phone: 86 755-8601-3388   Fax: 86 75586013399
Toll-Free:
Address: No. 33, Haitian Second Rd., Nanshan Dist., Shenzhen, Guangdong 518054 China

STOCK TICKER/OTHER:

Stock Ticker: TCEHY   Exchange: PINX
Employees: 108,436   Fiscal Year Ends: 12/31
Parent Company:

SALARIES/BONUSES:

Top Exec. Salary: $ Bonus: $
Second Exec. Salary: $ Bonus: $

OTHER THOUGHTS:

Estimated Female Officers or Directors:
Hot Spot for Advancement for Women/Minorities:

Tencent Music Entertainment Group

www.qq.com

NAIC Code: 515111

TYPES OF BUSINESS:
Radio Networks
Online Music Platforms and Services
Music Discovery
Music Video Content
Live Music Performances
Short Music Videos
Online Karaoke
Online Performances

BRANDS/DIVISIONS/AFFILIATES:
Tencent Holdings Limited
QQ Music
Kugou Music
Kuwo Music
WeSing
Weixin/WeChat
QQ

CONTACTS: Note: Officers with more than one job title may be intentionally listed here more than once.
Pang Kar Shun Cussion, CEO
Zhenyu Xie, Pres.
Min Hu, CFO

GROWTH PLANS/SPECIAL FEATURES:
TME is the largest online music service provider in China. It was founded in 2016 with the business combination of QQ Music (founded in 2005), Kuwo Music (founded in 2005) and Kugou Music (founded in 2004) streaming platforms. Tencent is the largest shareholder of TME with over 50% shares and over 90% voting rights held. TME also provides social entertainment services, including music live audio/video broadcasts and online concert services through the three platforms mentioned above, and online karaoke through an independent platform WeSing.

FINANCIAL DATA: Note: Data for latest year may not have been available at press time.

In U.S. $	2022	2021	2020	2019	2018	2017
Revenue	3,897,055,000	4,296,539,000	4,008,993,000	3,497,573,000	2,610,734,000	1,510,059,000
R&D Expense						
Operating Income	485,705,200	427,673,600	546,074,600	558,451,000	461,640,000	193,347,000
Operating Margin %		.10%	.14%	.16%	.18%	.13%
SGA Expense	764,174,400	919,567,000	766,787,200	652,374,100	546,212,100	334,713,000
Net Income	505,645,000	416,534,800	571,377,500	547,587,300	252,066,100	182,345,700
Operating Cash Flow	1,028,754,000	720,444,400	671,763,900	852,596,900	774,488,100	343,789,100
Capital Expenditure	144,804,000	379,268,100	68,895,340	39,329,470	19,802,250	10,588,700
EBITDA	776,688,300	653,611,800	763,899,300	713,843,600	331,000,100	271,730,900
Return on Assets %		.04%	.07%	.08%	.05%	.05%
Return on Equity %		.06%	.09%	.10%	.06%	.06%
Debt to Equity		.10%	0.103	0.002		

CONTACT INFORMATION:
Phone: 86-755-8601-3388   Fax:
Toll-Free:
Address: Fl. 17, Matsunichi Bldg., Kejizhongyi Rd., Nanshan Dist.,, Shenzhen, Guangdong 518057 China

STOCK TICKER/OTHER:
Stock Ticker: TME   Exchange: NYS
Employees: 5,805   Fiscal Year Ends: 12/31
Parent Company: Tencent Holdings Limited

SALARIES/BONUSES:
Top Exec. Salary: $ Bonus: $
Second Exec. Salary: $ Bonus: $

OTHER THOUGHTS:
Estimated Female Officers or Directors:
Hot Spot for Advancement for Women/Minorities:

Teradata Corporation

www.teradata.com

NAIC Code: 511210J

TYPES OF BUSINESS:

Data Warehousing
Database & Data Mining Software
Consulting Services

BRANDS/DIVISIONS/AFFILIATES:

Vantage
Vantage Analyst
Vantage Customer Experience
DataDNA

GROWTH PLANS/SPECIAL FEATURES:

Teradata Corp provides analytic data products and related services. The Company operates in data and analytics, which captures, integrates, stores, manages, and analyzes data of all types to answer business questions and deliver insight; and marketing applications, which offer marketing management products to help businesses win customer loyalty. Its solutions include components such as data warehousing, Asset optimization, Fraud prevention, Product innovation, and risk mitigation. A majority of the firm's revenue is generated in the United States.

CONTACTS: Note: Officers with more than one job title may be intentionally listed here more than once.

Stephen McMillan, CEO
Claire Bramley, CFO
Michael Gianoni, Chairman of the Board
Margaret Treese, Chief Legal Officer
Martyn Etherington, Chief Marketing Officer
Daniel Harrington, Other Executive Officer
Kathleen Cullen-Cote, Other Executive Officer
Hillary Ashton, Other Executive Officer
Todd Cione, Other Executive Officer

FINANCIAL DATA: Note: Data for latest year may not have been available at press time.

In U.S. $	2022	2021	2020	2019	2018	2017
Revenue	1,795,000,000	1,917,000,000	1,836,000,000	1,899,000,000	2,164,000,000	2,156,000,000
R&D Expense	313,000,000	309,000,000	334,000,000	327,000,000	317,000,000	305,000,000
Operating Income	118,000,000	231,000,000	16,000,000	10,000,000	43,000,000	68,000,000
Operating Margin %	.07%	.12%	.01%	.01%	.02%	.03%
SGA Expense	650,000,000	646,000,000	669,000,000	618,000,000	666,000,000	651,000,000
Net Income	33,000,000	147,000,000	129,000,000	-20,000,000	30,000,000	-67,000,000
Operating Cash Flow	419,000,000	463,000,000	267,000,000	148,000,000	364,000,000	324,000,000
Capital Expenditure	16,000,000	31,000,000	51,000,000	59,000,000	160,000,000	87,000,000
EBITDA	225,000,000	367,000,000	175,000,000	163,000,000	179,000,000	211,000,000
Return on Assets %	.02%	.07%	.06%	-.01%	.01%	-.03%
Return on Equity %	.09%	.34%	.39%	-.05%	.05%	-.08%
Debt to Equity	2.18%	.86%	1.273	2.164	1.03%	0.716

CONTACT INFORMATION:

Phone: 866 548-8348   Fax:
Toll-Free:
Address: 17095 Via Del Campo, San Diego, CA 92127 United States

STOCK TICKER/OTHER:

Stock Ticker: TDC   Exchange: NYS
Employees: 7,000   Fiscal Year Ends: 12/31
Parent Company:

SALARIES/BONUSES:

Top Exec. Salary: $800,000   Bonus: $
Second Exec. Salary: $500,000   Bonus: $

OTHER THOUGHTS:

Estimated Female Officers or Directors: 2
Hot Spot for Advancement for Women/Minorities: Y

TheRealReal Inc

www.therealreal.com

NAIC Code: 454110

TYPES OF BUSINESS:

Electronic Shopping
Consignment Store for Luxury Goods
Ecommerce
Software
Pre-Owned Goods

BRANDS/DIVISIONS/AFFILIATES:

GROWTH PLANS/SPECIAL FEATURES:

The RealReal is the largest luxury resale platform in the U.S., generating $1.8 billion in 2022 gross merchandise volume and addressing a niche (personal luxury resale) that had previously been serviced by inefficient upscale boutiques and local pawn shops. The firm generates revenue via consignment and first-party sales on its online marketplace, and through direct sales across its brick-and-mortar footprint. With a hands-on approach that actively sources inventory and authenticates every item on its platform, The RealReal is able to justify much higher take rates than peers, working out to roughly 35% of net merchandise value, which excludes returns, cancellations, and first-party sales.

CONTACTS: *Note: Officers with more than one job title may be intentionally listed here more than once.*

Julie Wainwright, CEO
Matt Gustke, CFO
Steve Lo, Chief Accounting Officer
Todd Suko, Chief Legal Officer
Arnie Katz, Chief Technology Officer
Rati Levesque, COO

FINANCIAL DATA: *Note: Data for latest year may not have been available at press time.*

In U.S. $	2022	2021	2020	2019	2018	2017
Revenue	603,493,000	467,692,000	299,949,000	316,354,000	213,732,000	137,521,000
R&D Expense						
Operating Income	-188,707,000	-201,519,000	-171,706,000	-100,105,000	-73,904,000	-51,784,000
Operating Margin %	-.31%	-.43%	-.57%	-.32%	-.35%	
SGA Expense	258,288,000	239,167,000	195,465,000	158,397,000	105,893,000	80,746,000
Net Income	-196,445,000	-236,107,000	-175,832,000	-98,429,000	-75,765,000	-52,308,000
Operating Cash Flow	-91,557,000	-142,151,000	-134,419,000	-54,490,000	-47,195,000	-38,574,000
Capital Expenditure	36,922,000	47,437,000	26,931,000	34,028,000	19,116,000	14,120,000
EBITDA	-158,132,000	-190,989,000	-151,622,000	-84,206,000	-65,224,000	-45,855,000
Return on Assets %	-.29%	-.35%	-.33%	-.34%	-.80%	
Return on Equity %		-1.79%	-.67%	-2.56%		
Debt to Equity		6.72%	1.382			

CONTACT INFORMATION:

Phone: 855-435-5893   Fax:
Toll-Free: 800 215-0566
Address: 55 Francisco St., Ste. 600, San Francisco, CA 94133 United States

STOCK TICKER/OTHER:

Stock Ticker: REAL
Employees: 3,468
Parent Company:

Exchange: NAS
Fiscal Year Ends: 12/31

SALARIES/BONUSES:

Top Exec. Salary: $425,000   Bonus: $1,000,000
Second Exec. Salary: $417,308   Bonus: $250,000

OTHER THOUGHTS:

Estimated Female Officers or Directors:
Hot Spot for Advancement for Women/Minorities:

Sales, profits and employees may be estimates. Financial information, benefits and other data can change quickly and may vary from those stated here.

TheStreet Inc

www.thestreet.com

NAIC Code: 519130

TYPES OF BUSINESS:

Online Financial Information
Digital Financial Media
Investing Information and News
Financial News
Financial Market Analysis
Digital Financial Services and Tools
Digital Information Platform
Subscription

BRANDS/DIVISIONS/AFFILIATES:

Arena Group Holdings Inc (The)
TheStreet Smarts
Action Alert Plus
Real Money
Crypto Investor
Real Money Pro
Qant Ratings
Retirement Daily

CONTACTS: *Note: Officers with more than one job title may be intentionally listed here more than once.*

Lawrence Kramer, Chairman of the Board
James Cramer, Founder
Rachelle Zorn, President, Divisional
Jeffrey Davis, President, Divisional
Ross Levinsohn, Chmn.-Corp.

GROWTH PLANS/SPECIAL FEATURES:

TheStreet, Inc. is a digital financial media company that reports on the latest investment trends. The firm provides financial news and related information to investors and institutions worldwide and produces business news and market analysis for individual investors. TheStreet's suite of digital services provide tools and insight in regards to making financial decisions. The company offers editorials through its subscription platform, which is offered through its mobile-friendly content management system, social, video and monetization technology. TheStreet.com site offers subject categories such as technology, retail, investing, personal finance, retirement, cryptocurrency, markets, entertainment economics, breaking news, deals and more. Three types of subscription services are offered by TheStreet, each with a 14-day free trial, with annual rates including $34.99/yr., $49.99/yr., $199.99/yr. and $799.99/yr. Premium subscription products are currently (as February 2024) categorized into the following headings: TheStreet Smarts, Action Alert Plus, Real Money Pro, Crypto Investor, Real Money Pro, Quant Ratings, Retirement Daily, chairman's club and Top Stocks. TheStreet is a subsidiary of The Arena Group Holdings, Inc., a data-driven media company.

FINANCIAL DATA: *Note: Data for latest year may not have been available at press time.*

In U.S. $	2022	2021	2020	2019	2018	2017
Revenue	76,500,000	72,000,000	64,981,489	54,151,241	53,089,452	62,469,392
R&D Expense						
Operating Income						
Operating Margin %						
SGA Expense						
Net Income						
Operating Cash Flow						
Capital Expenditure						
EBITDA						
Return on Assets %						
Return on Equity %						
Debt to Equity						

CONTACT INFORMATION:

Phone: 212 321-5000   Fax: 212 321-5016
Toll-Free: 866-321-8726
Address: 14 Wall St., Fl. 15, New York, NY 10005 United States

STOCK TICKER/OTHER:

Stock Ticker: Subsidiary   Exchange:
Employees: 650   Fiscal Year Ends: 12/31
Parent Company: Arena Group Holdings Inc (The)

SALARIES/BONUSES:

Top Exec. Salary: $ Bonus: $
Second Exec. Salary: $ Bonus: $

OTHER THOUGHTS:

Estimated Female Officers or Directors: 4
Hot Spot for Advancement for Women/Minorities: Y

Thomson Reuters Corporation

www.thomsonreuters.com

NAIC Code: 511120A

TYPES OF BUSINESS:

Information Services & Software
Legal & Regulatory Information Services
Financial Information & Technology
New Business Exploration
Scientific Data Tools
Artificial Intelligence

BRANDS/DIVISIONS/AFFILIATES:

GROWTH PLANS/SPECIAL FEATURES:

Thomson Reuters is the result of the $17.6 billion megamerger of Canada's Thomson and the United Kingdom's Reuters Group in 2008. In 2021, Thomson Reuters completed the sale of Refinitiv to LSE Group. Thomson Reuters' three largest segments are its legal professionals, Tax and accounting, and corporates segments. Legal professionals is about 42% of the firm's revenue and 47% of the firm's adjusted EBITDA. Tax and accounting makes up about 20%-25% of the firm's revenue and EBITDA. Corporates, which consists of legal professionals and tax and accounting products sold to corporations, also makes up about 20%-25% of the firm's revenue and EBITDA. Thomson Reuters' smaller segments include its Reuters news business and global print business.

CONTACTS: Note: Officers with more than one job title may be intentionally listed here more than once.

Steve Hasker, CEO
Michael Friedenberg, Pres., Divisional
Michael Eastwood, CFO
David Thomson, Chairman of the Board
Thomas Kim, Chief Legal Officer
Kirsty Roth, Chief Technology Officer
Brian Peccarelli, COO, Divisional
David Binet, Deputy Chairman
Mary-Alice Vuicic, Other Executive Officer
David Wong, Other Executive Officer
Paul Fischer, President, Divisional
Sunil Pandita, President, Divisional
Charlotte Rushton, President, Divisional

FINANCIAL DATA: Note: Data for latest year may not have been available at press time.

In U.S. $	2022	2021	2020	2019	2018	2017
Revenue	6,627,000,000	6,348,000,000	5,984,000,000	5,906,000,000	5,501,000,000	5,297,000,000
R&D Expense						
Operating Income	1,815,000,000	1,234,000,000	1,919,000,000	1,199,000,000	775,000,000	1,034,000,000
Operating Margin %	.27%	.19%	.32%	.20%	.14%	.20%
SGA Expense	1,622,000,000	1,624,000,000	1,466,000,000	1,717,000,000	1,391,000,000	1,465,000,000
Net Income	1,338,000,000	5,689,000,000	1,122,000,000	1,564,000,000	3,933,000,000	1,395,000,000
Operating Cash Flow	1,915,000,000	1,773,000,000	1,745,000,000	702,000,000	2,062,000,000	2,029,000,000
Capital Expenditure	595,000,000	487,000,000	504,000,000	505,000,000	576,000,000	519,000,000
EBITDA	3,010,000,000	2,025,000,000	2,757,000,000	1,895,000,000	1,450,000,000	1,476,000,000
Return on Assets %	.06%	.28%	.06%	.09%	.18%	.05%
Return on Equity %	.10%	.48%	.12%	.17%	.36%	.11%
Debt to Equity	.26%	.28%	0.382	0.283	.35%	0.415

CONTACT INFORMATION:

Phone: 416-687-7500   Fax:
Toll-Free:
Address: 333 Bay St., Ste. 300, Toronto, ONT M5H 2R2 Canada

STOCK TICKER/OTHER:

Stock Ticker: TRI   Exchange: NYS
Employees: 25,200   Fiscal Year Ends: 12/31
Parent Company:

SALARIES/BONUSES:

Top Exec. Salary: $1,146,685   Bonus: $
Second Exec. Salary: Bonus: $
$750,000

OTHER THOUGHTS:

Estimated Female Officers or Directors: 2
Hot Spot for Advancement for Women/Minorities: Y

Sales, profits and employees may be estimates. Financial information, benefits and other data can change quickly and may vary from those stated here.

Thumbtack Inc

NAIC Code: 519130

TYPES OF BUSINESS:

Online Freelance Work Arrangement Services
Online and Mobile Hire Platform
Job Tasks
Software and Innovative Technology
Professional Services

BRANDS/DIVISIONS/AFFILIATES:

CONTACTS: *Note: Officers with more than one job title may be intentionally listed here more than once.*

Marco Zappacosta, CEO

GROWTH PLANS/SPECIAL FEATURES:

Thumbtack, Inc. operates a platform that connects users with qualified professionals that help them get whatever it is they need done. Jobs and tasks can include painting or remodeling a home, learning a new language, tutoring, disc jockeying an event, photographing weddings, catering, helping someone move and more. There are more than 500 different categories on the Thumbtack web and mobile platform. How it works: users answer questions about what is needed; Thumbtack takes those details and matches them with related professionals (keeping email and phone number private during the process); users compare the listed professionals, who have paid to send a custom quote; and hire the preferred professional. Along with the listed quote, each professional includes customer reviews, contact information, business profile and a customized message. When professionals register on the marketplace, they each describe the kind of jobs sought, how far they are willing to drive, as well as what projects they can work on and when they are available, in real-time. The firm's proprietary platform matches professionals with customers that fit and sends customer job prompts. If interested, each professional presents a quote in response to the request. Thumbtack's network comprises professionals throughout the U.S. Thumbtack also offers a membership plan for $49 a year and includes a $10,000 money-back guarantee, 20% off on on-demand bookings and additional support from home specialists.

Thumbtack offers its employees career development and physical/emotional wellness benefits.

FINANCIAL DATA: *Note: Data for latest year may not have been available at press time.*

In U.S. $	2022	2021	2020	2019	2018	2017
Revenue	205,000,000	195,000,000	185,000,000	155,000,000	101,850,000	97,000,000
R&D Expense						
Operating Income						
Operating Margin %						
SGA Expense						
Net Income						
Operating Cash Flow						
Capital Expenditure						
EBITDA						
Return on Assets %						
Return on Equity %						
Debt to Equity						

CONTACT INFORMATION:

Phone: 415 779-2191   Fax:
Toll-Free:
Address: 1355 Market St., San Francisco, CA 94103 United States

STOCK TICKER/OTHER:

Stock Ticker: Private   Exchange:
Employees: 550   Fiscal Year Ends:
Parent Company:

SALARIES/BONUSES:

Top Exec. Salary: $ Bonus: $
Second Exec. Salary: $ Bonus: $

OTHER THOUGHTS:

Estimated Female Officers or Directors:
Hot Spot for Advancement for Women/Minorities:

TIBCO Software Inc

www.tibco.com

NAIC Code: 511210H

TYPES OF BUSINESS:

Computer Software, Business Process
Data Management Software
Technology Software Solutions
Business Analytics and Insights
Platform Integration Solutions
Data Access and Management

BRANDS/DIVISIONS/AFFILIATES:

Vista Equity Partners
Elliott Investment Management LP
Evergreen Coast Capital Corp
Cloud Software Group

GROWTH PLANS/SPECIAL FEATURES:

TIBCO Software, Inc. provides technology software solutions that unlock data for making fast and smart business decisions. The firm's connected intelligent platform seamlessly connects any application or data source, intelligently unifies data for enhanced access, trust and control; and predicts outcomes in real-time at scale. TIBCO Software's solutions serve industries including banking, credit union, energy, government, healthcare, insurance, law enforcement, manufacturing, retail, travel/transportation and telecommunications. Vista Equity Partners and Evergreen Coast Capital Corp., an affiliate of Elliott Investment Management LP acquired Citrix Systems, Inc. and combined it with TIBCO Software. As a result of the transaction, Citrix and TIBCO became business units within the Cloud Software Group, a newly formed joint venture between Vista Equity and Evergreen.

CONTACTS: Note: Officers with more than one job title may be intentionally listed here more than once.

Tom Krause, CEO-Cloud Software Group
Thomas Laffey, Executive VP, Divisional
Ram Menon, Executive VP
William Hughes, Executive VP
R. Bradley, President
John Ederer, Vice President, Divisional

FINANCIAL DATA: Note: Data for latest year may not have been available at press time.

In U.S. $	2022	2021	2020	2019	2018	2017
Revenue	1,369,470,374	1,316,798,437	1,254,093,750	1,286,250,000	1,225,000,000	1,100,000,000
R&D Expense						
Operating Income						
Operating Margin %						
SGA Expense						
Net Income						
Operating Cash Flow						
Capital Expenditure						
EBITDA						
Return on Assets %						
Return on Equity %						
Debt to Equity						

CONTACT INFORMATION:

Phone: 650 846-1000   Fax: 650 846-1005
Toll-Free: 800-420-8450
Address: 3307 Hillview Ave., Palo Alto, CA 94304 United States

STOCK TICKER/OTHER:

Stock Ticker: Private   Exchange:
Employees: 4,200   Fiscal Year Ends: 11/30
Parent Company: Cloud Software Group

SALARIES/BONUSES:

Top Exec. Salary: $ Bonus: $
Second Exec. Salary: $ Bonus: $

OTHER THOUGHTS:

Estimated Female Officers or Directors: 2
Hot Spot for Advancement for Women/Minorities:

TikTok (ByteDance Ltd)

bytedance.com

NAIC Code: 519130

TYPES OF BUSINESS:

Video Sharing OnlineShort Form)
On-App Merchandising, Advertising and Ecommerce
Artificial Intelligence
Online App Creation
Content Discovery and Creation
Video Sharing (Short Form)
Social Networking
Data Tools

BRANDS/DIVISIONS/AFFILIATES:

Toutiao
TikTok
Helo
Douyin
Xigua Video
Lark
BytePlus
Tech for Good

CONTACTS: *Note: Officers with more than one job title may be intentionally listed here more than once.*

Rubo Liang, Chmn.

GROWTH PLANS/SPECIAL FEATURES:

TikTok's parent firm, ByteDance, founded in 2012, designs and produces mobile-first products powered by machine learning technology. The firm desires to not just deliver information but to serve as a creative hub that hosts and serves product creators. ByteDance's flagship product is TikTok, a global short-form video platform and social network. Other important products include Toutiao, a content discovery and creation platform in China; Helo, a social media platform in India, made for sharing content; Douyin, a Chinese destination for short-form mobile videos; Xigua Video, a video app for the China market; Lark, which combines a multitude of essential collaboration tools in a single interconnected platform, including chat, calendar, creation, cloud storage and app center; BytePlus, an intelligent services platform ranging from data analytics tools to computer vision software, to help businesses reach their potential; and Tech for Good, which works with non-profits to provide the tools and guidance to raise awareness for their causes on ByteDance's platform. The company's artificial intelligence (AI) technology is at the heart of all its content platforms. ByteDance builds intelligent machines capable of understanding and analyzing texts, images and videos using natural language processing and computer vision technology. Then it uses large-scale machine learning and deep learning algorithms to serve users with the content they will find most interesting. The AI cycle optimizes every stage of the content lifecycle, including creation, moderation, curation, recommendation and interaction. ByteDance and its affiliated companies have been granted and awarded a number of patents and designs by China, U.S. and European patent offices. Its technologies cover machine vision, image processing, mobile internet, multimedia interactivity, big data analysis, data storage and compression, audio and video processing and natural language processing.

FINANCIAL DATA: *Note: Data for latest year may not have been available at press time.*

In U.S. $	2022	2021	2020	2019	2018	2017
Revenue	80,000,000,000	60,000,000,000	34,300,000,000	17,200,000,000	7,200,000,000	
R&D Expense						
Operating Income						
Operating Margin %						
SGA Expense						
Net Income	40,000,000,000	28,000,000,000	19,000,000,000	3,000,000,000		
Operating Cash Flow						
Capital Expenditure						
EBITDA						
Return on Assets %						
Return on Equity %						
Debt to Equity						

CONTACT INFORMATION:

Phone: 86 10-5873-4313   Fax:
Toll-Free:
Address: 3000 El Bldg., Fl. 2, 4 Camino Real, Beijing, Beijing 100089 China

STOCK TICKER/OTHER:

Stock Ticker: Private   Exchange:
Employees: 150,000   Fiscal Year Ends:
Parent Company:

SALARIES/BONUSES:

Top Exec. Salary: $ Bonus: $
Second Exec. Salary: $ Bonus: $

OTHER THOUGHTS:

Estimated Female Officers or Directors:
Hot Spot for Advancement for Women/Minorities:

Tinder Inc

www.tinder.com

NAIC Code: 511210G

TYPES OF BUSINESS:

Computer Software, Electronic Games, Apps & Entertainment
Online Dating App
Online Dating Website
Location-Based Technology
Match-Making Platform

BRANDS/DIVISIONS/AFFILIATES:

Match Group Inc
Tinder University

CONTACTS: Note: Officers with more than one job title may be intentionally listed here more than once.

Faye Iosotaluno, CEO

GROWTH PLANS/SPECIAL FEATURES:

Tinder, Inc. operates Tinder, an online match-making platform. People are matched for several reasons, such as to make friends, for a date, for romance or other purpose. The Tinder site is available in 190 countries and more than 40 languages. Tinder's platform is location-based and provides users the ability to use a swiping motion to like (swiping right) or dislike (swipe left) other users. If two parties have swiped right/liked each other, they can then text message through the app. Information about individuals is available via pictures and a short biography. Tinder University is a college student only feature. For safety purposes across its platforms, Tinder features include a panic button for when on a date or meeting, which transmits location data, and emergency services can be called. Before going to a meeting, users are required to take selfies to prove that their photos in Tinder profiles match their real identities. Users can pay to make use of the Tinder Gold and Tinder Platinum services that remove ads, see those who swiped right on them faster and send Super Likes, which immediately notify the person that they have been swiped right. Tinder, Inc. operates as a subsidiary of Match Group, Inc.

FINANCIAL DATA: Note: Data for latest year may not have been available at press time.

In U.S. $	2022	2021	2020	2019	2018	2017
Revenue	1,790,000,000	1,649,000,000	1,080,000,000	1,200,000,000	800,000,000	
R&D Expense						
Operating Income						
Operating Margin %						
SGA Expense						
Net Income						
Operating Cash Flow						
Capital Expenditure						
EBITDA						
Return on Assets %						
Return on Equity %						
Debt to Equity						

CONTACT INFORMATION:

Phone: Fax: 214 853-4309
Toll-Free:
Address: 8899 Beverly Blvd., Los Angeles, CA 90069 United States

STOCK TICKER/OTHER:

Stock Ticker: Subsidiary   Exchange:
Employees: Fiscal Year Ends:
Parent Company: Match Group Inc

SALARIES/BONUSES:

Top Exec. Salary: $ Bonus: $
Second Exec. Salary: $ Bonus: $

OTHER THOUGHTS:

Estimated Female Officers or Directors:
Hot Spot for Advancement for Women/Minorities:

T-Mobile US Inc

www.t-mobile.com

NAIC Code: 517312

TYPES OF BUSINESS:

Mobile Phone and Wireless Services
Wireless Services
Cellular
Mobile Devices
5G

BRANDS/DIVISIONS/AFFILIATES:

Deutsche Telekom AG
T-Mobile International AG
T-Mobile
Metro by T-Mobile
Sprint Corporation

GROWTH PLANS/SPECIAL FEATURES:

Deutsche Telekom merged its T-Mobile USA unit with prepaid specialist MetroPCS in 2013, and that firm merged with Sprint in 2020, creating the second-largest wireless carrier in the U.S. T-Mobile now serves 76 million postpaid and 22 million prepaid phone customers, equal to around 30% of the U.S. retail wireless market. The firm entered the fixed-wireless broadband market aggressively in 2021 and now serves nearly 5 million residential and business customers. In addition, T-Mobile provides wholesale services to resellers.

CONTACTS: Note: Officers with more than one job title may be intentionally listed here more than once.

G. Sievert, CEO
Peter Osvaldik, CFO
Timotheus Hottges, Chairman of the Board
Dara Bazzano, Chief Accounting Officer
Matthew Staneff, Chief Marketing Officer
Peter Ewens, Executive VP, Divisional
David Miller, Executive VP
Deeanne King, Executive VP
Neville Ray, President, Divisional

FINANCIAL DATA: Note: Data for latest year may not have been available at press time.

In U.S. $	2022	2021	2020	2019	2018	2017
Revenue	79,571,000,000	80,118,000,000	68,397,000,000	44,998,000,000	43,310,000,000	
R&D Expense						
Operating Income	8,107,000,000	6,892,000,000	7,054,000,000	5,722,000,000	5,309,000,000	
Operating Margin %	.10%	.09%	.10%	.13%	.12%	
SGA Expense	21,607,000,000	20,238,000,000	18,926,000,000	14,139,000,000	13,161,000,000	
Net Income	2,590,000,000	3,024,000,000	3,064,000,000	3,468,000,000	2,888,000,000	
Operating Cash Flow	16,781,000,000	13,917,000,000	8,640,000,000	6,824,000,000	3,899,000,000	
Capital Expenditure	17,301,000,000	21,692,000,000	12,367,000,000	7,358,000,000	5,668,000,000	
EBITDA	20,161,000,000	23,076,000,000	20,382,000,000	12,354,000,000	11,760,000,000	
Return on Assets %	.01%	.01%	.02%	.04%	.04%	
Return on Equity %	.04%	.04%	.07%	.13%	.12%	
Debt to Equity	1.41%	1.39%	1.449	1.279	.49%	

CONTACT INFORMATION:

Phone: 425 378-4000   Fax: 425-378-4040
Toll-Free: 800-318-9270
Address: 12920 SE 38th St., Bellevue, WA 98006-1350 United States

STOCK TICKER/OTHER:

Stock Ticker: TMUS   Exchange: NAS
Employees: 67,000   Fiscal Year Ends: 12/31
Parent Company: Deutsche Telekom AG

SALARIES/BONUSES:

Top Exec. Salary: $1,664,285   Bonus: $
Second Exec. Salary: Bonus: $
$950,000

OTHER THOUGHTS:

Estimated Female Officers or Directors:
Hot Spot for Advancement for Women/Minorities:

Total System Services LLC (TSYS)

www.tsys.com

NAIC Code: 522320

TYPES OF BUSINESS:

Credit Card Processing
Payment Solutions
Card Issuance
Cloud-Native Payments Platform
Configurable Payments Solutions
Digital Onboarding
Payment Processing
Risk and Fraud Payments Management

BRANDS/DIVISIONS/AFFILIATES:

Global Payments Inc

GROWTH PLANS/SPECIAL FEATURES:

Total System Services, LLC (TSYS) is a global builder and provider of seamless, secure and innovative solutions to payment card issuers, financial institutions, Fintechs and retail companies worldwide. TSYS' payments platform is cloud-native and configurable, and includes digital onboarding, activations, loyalty and rewards, authentication, payment processing, data and portfolio analytics, risk and fraud management, service and customer relations management. Solutions by TSYS include virtual card issuance, re-platforming through cloud native/API/configurable programs, adding new customer services, launching greenfield digital card programs, scaling card programs, optimizing commercial issuance and creating new solutions via technologies. TSYS operates as a subsidiary of Global Payments, Inc., a pure play payments technology firm.

CONTACTS:
Note: Officers with more than one job title may be intentionally listed here more than once.

Paul Todd, CFO
G. Griffith, Secretary
M. Troy Woods, Chmn.

FINANCIAL DATA:
Note: Data for latest year may not have been available at press time.

In U.S. $	2022	2021	2020	2019	2018	2017
Revenue	4,264,000,000	4,100,000,000	4,205,200,000	4,911,892,000	4,028,210,944	4,927,965,184
R&D Expense						
Operating Income						
Operating Margin %						
SGA Expense						
Net Income				469,276,000	576,656,000	586,185,024
Operating Cash Flow						
Capital Expenditure						
EBITDA						
Return on Assets %						
Return on Equity %						
Debt to Equity						

CONTACT INFORMATION:

Phone: 844-663-8797   Fax:
Toll-Free:
Address: One TSYS Way, Columbus, GA 31901-4222 United States

STOCK TICKER/OTHER:

Stock Ticker: Subsidiary   Exchange:
Employees: 11,500   Fiscal Year Ends: 12/31
Parent Company: Global Payments Inc

SALARIES/BONUSES:

Top Exec. Salary: $ Bonus: $
Second Exec. Salary: $ Bonus: $

OTHER THOUGHTS:

Estimated Female Officers or Directors: 3
Hot Spot for Advancement for Women/Minorities: Y

TradeStation Group Inc

www.tradestation.com

NAIC Code: 523120

TYPES OF BUSINESS:

Online Stock Brokerage
Financial Information
Stock Trading Software
Foreign Exchange Transactions
Futures Commission Merchant

BRANDS/DIVISIONS/AFFILIATES:

Monex Group Inc
TradeStation Securities inc
TradeStation Crypto Inc
TradeStation Technologies inc
TradeStation
You Can Trade Inc

CONTACTS: *Note: Officers with more than one job title may be intentionally listed here more than once.*

John Bartleman, CEO
Takashi Oyagi, Chief Strategic Officer
Greg Vance, CFO
Peter Korotkiy, Chief Brokerage Officer
Michael Fisch, CTO
Marc J. Stone, Chief Legal Officer
William P. Cahill, VP-Brokerage Oper.
Takashi Oyagi, Chief Strategic Officer
Edward Codispoti, VP-Finance
Marc J. Stone, Chief Legal Officer

GROWTH PLANS/SPECIAL FEATURES:

TradeStation Group, Inc. is an online brokerage firm operating through its wholly-owned subsidiaries, including TradeStation Securities, Inc.; TradeStation Crypto, Inc.; and TradeStation Technologies, Inc. Together, the group provides products and services under the TradeStation brand and trademark. Trading products include stocks, exchange traded funds (ETFs), an initial public offer (IPO) trading platform, options, futures, futures options, cryptocurrency and mutual funds. Platforms and tools offered by TradeStation include desktop, web trading, mobile apps, simulated trading, order execution, a web application programming interface (API), and a trading app store, among others. In addition, wholly-owned You Can Trade, Inc. offers an online media publication service that provides investment educational content, ideas and demonstrations, and does not provide investment or trading advice, research or recommendations. You Can Trade operates under its own brand and trademarks. TradeStation itself operates as a wholly-owned subsidiary of Japanese online financial services provider, Monex Group, Inc. Headquartered in Florida, TradeStation Group has additional offices in Illinois, New York and Texas.

TradeStation offers its employees comprehensive health benefits, life and disability insurance, retirement savings plans, and a variety of employee assistance plans and programs.

FINANCIAL DATA: *Note: Data for latest year may not have been available at press time.*

In U.S. $	2022	2021	2020	2019	2018	2017
Revenue	142,000,000	218,652,000	188,639,000	181,131,000	188,196,000	167,752,000
R&D Expense						
Operating Income						
Operating Margin %						
SGA Expense						
Net Income		23,790,000	10,277,000	18,596,000	2,649,000	-4,103,000
Operating Cash Flow						
Capital Expenditure						
EBITDA						
Return on Assets %						
Return on Equity %						
Debt to Equity						

CONTACT INFORMATION:

Phone: 954-652-7000   Fax: 954-652-7300
Toll-Free: 800-556-2022
Address: 8050 SW 10th St., Ste. 2000, Plantation, FL 33324 United States

STOCK TICKER/OTHER:

Stock Ticker: Subsidiary
Employees: 700
Parent Company: Monex Group Inc

Exchange:
Fiscal Year Ends: 03/31

SALARIES/BONUSES:

Top Exec. Salary: $ Bonus: $
Second Exec. Salary: $ Bonus: $

OTHER THOUGHTS:

Estimated Female Officers or Directors:
Hot Spot for Advancement for Women/Minorities:

Travelport Worldwide Limited

www.travelport.com

NAIC Code: 561510

TYPES OF BUSINESS:

Online Travel Reservation Systems
Travel Distribution Services & Solutions
Consumer Travel Reservation Sites
Application Programming Interfaces
Merchandising Solutions

BRANDS/DIVISIONS/AFFILIATES:

Siris Capital Group LLC
Evergreen Coast Capital Corporation
Travelport+
MyTravelport

GROWTH PLANS/SPECIAL FEATURES:

Travelport Worldwide Limited is a technology company that operates a travel commerce platform. This business-to-business (B2B) platform provides distribution, technology, payment and other solutions for the global travel and tourism industry. It facilitates travel commerce by connecting travel providers with online and offline travel buyers. Travelport has a leadership position in airline merchandising, hotel content and distribution, car rental, mobile commerce and B2B payment solutions. The firm also provides IT services to airlines, such as shopping, ticketing, departure control, application programming interfaces (APIs) and other solutions. Product lines include Travelport+ and MyTravelport. Travelport is represented in approximately 180 countries and territories. The firm is a joint venture of Siris Capital Group, LLC and Elliot management.

CONTACTS: Note: Officers with more than one job title may be intentionally listed here more than once.

Greg Webb, CEO
John Elieson, COO
Douglas Steenland, Chmn.
Nick Bray, CFO
Jen Catto, CMO
Phil Donnelly, Chief People Officer
Bates Turpen, CIO
Terence Conley, Executive VP, Divisional
Philip Emery, Executive VP
Thomas Murphy, Executive VP
Matthew Minetola, Executive VP
Kurt Ekert, Executive VP
Gordon Wilson, President
Rochelle Boas, Secretary
Bryan Conway, Senior VP
Christopher Roberts, Vice President, Divisional
Kate Aldridge, Vice President, Divisional
John Swainson, Chmn.

FINANCIAL DATA: Note: Data for latest year may not have been available at press time.

In U.S. $	2022	2021	2020	2019	2018	2017
Revenue	1,950,033,370	1,875,032,087	1,500,025,670	2,678,617,267	2,551,064,064	2,447,279,104
R&D Expense						
Operating Income						
Operating Margin %						
SGA Expense						
Net Income				76,259,400	72,628,000	142,463,008
Operating Cash Flow						
Capital Expenditure						
EBITDA						
Return on Assets %						
Return on Equity %						
Debt to Equity						

CONTACT INFORMATION:

Phone: 770-563-7400   Fax:
Toll-Free:
Address: Axis One, Axis Park 10 Hurricane Way Langley, Berkshire, SL3 8AG United Kingdom

STOCK TICKER/OTHER:

Stock Ticker: Joint Venture   Exchange:
Employees: 3,750   Fiscal Year Ends: 12/31
Parent Company: Siris Capital Group LLC

SALARIES/BONUSES:

Top Exec. Salary: $ Bonus: $
Second Exec. Salary: $ Bonus: $

OTHER THOUGHTS:

Estimated Female Officers or Directors: 2
Hot Spot for Advancement for Women/Minorities: Y

Sales, profits and employees may be estimates. Financial information, benefits and other data can change quickly and may vary from those stated here.

Travelscape LLC (Travelocity.com)

www.travelocity.com

NAIC Code: 561510

TYPES OF BUSINESS:

Online Travel Services
Online Reservations
Retail Travel Service Kiosks
Corporate Travel Agency
Vacation Planning
Group and Meeting Booking

BRANDS/DIVISIONS/AFFILIATES:

Expedia Group Inc
Travelscape LLC
Ortbitz

GROWTH PLANS/SPECIAL FEATURES:

Travelocity.com is a leading provider of online travel services for business and leisure travelers. The firm operates as a subsidiary of Travelscape, LLC, itself a wholly-owned subsidiary of Expedia Group, Inc. Travelocity provides access to vacation packages, domestic and international flights, hotel accommodations, rental car companies and cruises, as well as last-minute packages at discounted prices. Airlines and hotels can be searched and booked through Travelocity's online and mobile platforms. Additionally, Travelocity has a customer care unit staffed by representatives able to answer questions, change travel arrangements and handle travel-related emergencies 24-hours-a-day. Services also include arrangements for groups and meetings. Travelocity and the Travelocity logo are trademarks of Travelscape, LLC.

CONTACTS: Note: Officers with more than one job title may be intentionally listed here more than once.

Carl Sparks, Pres.
Jonathan Perkel, General Counsel
Stephen Dumaine, Sr. VP-Global Strategy & Prod. Innovation
Yannis Karnis, Pres., Travelocity Business
Noreen Henry, Sr. VP-Global Partner Svcs.
Roshan Mendis, Pres., Travelocity North America & Zuji
Scott Quigley, VP-Sales & Customer Care
Barry Diller, Chmn.-Corp.

FINANCIAL DATA: Note: Data for latest year may not have been available at press time.

In U.S. $	2022	2021	2020	2019	2018	2017
Revenue						
R&D Expense						
Operating Income						
Operating Margin %						
SGA Expense						
Net Income						
Operating Cash Flow						
Capital Expenditure						
EBITDA						
Return on Assets %						
Return on Equity %						
Debt to Equity						

CONTACT INFORMATION:

Phone: 682-605-1000   Fax: 972-582-2346
Toll-Free: 888-872-8356
Address: 5400 LBJ Fwy., Ste. 500, Dallas, TX 75240 United States

STOCK TICKER/OTHER:

Stock Ticker: Subsidiary   Exchange:
Employees: 1,600   Fiscal Year Ends: 12/31
Parent Company: Expedia Group Inc

SALARIES/BONUSES:

Top Exec. Salary: $ Bonus: $
Second Exec. Salary: $ Bonus: $

OTHER THOUGHTS:

Estimated Female Officers or Directors:
Hot Spot for Advancement for Women/Minorities:

Travelzoo Inc

www.travelzoo.com

NAIC Code: 561510

TYPES OF BUSINESS:

Travel Services-Online
Internet Media
Travel Information
Entertainment Deals
Website Operations
Travel Deals
Advertising & Marketing Services
Flight Deal Subscriptions

BRANDS/DIVISIONS/AFFILIATES:

Azzurro Capital Inc
Travelzoo Top 20
Local Deals
Getaway
Travelzoo Network
Jacks Flight Club

GROWTH PLANS/SPECIAL FEATURES:

Travelzoo acts as a publisher of travel and entertainment offers. It operates in three segments. Travelzoo North America segment consists of operations in Canada and the U.S.; Travelzoo Europe segment consists of operations in France, Germany, Spain, and the U.K.; and Jack's Flight Club segment consists of subscription revenue from premium members to access and receive flight deals from Jack's Flight Club via email or via Android or Apple mobile applications. It derives its revenue through advertising fees including listing fees paid by travel, entertainment, and local businesses to advertise their offers on the company's media properties. Most of the company's revenue is derived from North America.

CONTACTS:
Note: Officers with more than one job title may be intentionally listed here more than once.

Holger Bartel, CEO
Michele Huiban, CFO
Ralph Bartel, Chairman of the Board
Lisa Su, Chief Accounting Officer
Christina Ciocca, Director

FINANCIAL DATA:
Note: Data for latest year may not have been available at press time.

In U.S. $	2022	2021	2020	2019	2018	2017
Revenue	70,599,000	62,712,000	53,601,000	104,925,000	111,322,000	106,524,000
R&D Expense	2,064,000	2,590,000	3,081,000	6,709,000	8,993,000	9,224,000
Operating Income	7,557,000	-1,313,000	-11,153,000	17,041,000	8,238,000	4,545,000
Operating Margin %		- .02%	- .21%	.16%	.07%	.04%
SGA Expense	50,975,000	50,047,000	51,110,000	69,740,000	81,823,000	79,846,000
Net Income	6,634,000	911,000	-13,423,000	4,155,000	4,661,000	3,530,000
Operating Cash Flow	-23,121,000	-8,083,000	47,019,000	11,236,000	5,317,000	2,076,000
Capital Expenditure	1,511,000	29,000	253,000	474,000	752,000	738,000
EBITDA	9,746,000	507,000	-8,839,000	18,359,000	10,066,000	6,620,000
Return on Assets %		.01%	- .17%	.08%	.10%	.07%
Return on Equity %			-2.10%	.33%	.34%	.23%
Debt to Equity			6.128	0.729		

CONTACT INFORMATION:

Phone: 212 484-4900   Fax: 212 521-4230
Toll-Free:
Address: 590 Madison Ave., Fl. 35, New York, NY 10022 United States

STOCK TICKER/OTHER:

Stock Ticker: TZOO   Exchange: NAS
Employees: 237   Fiscal Year Ends: 12/31
Parent Company: Azzurro Capital Inc

SALARIES/BONUSES:

Top Exec. Salary: $450,000   Bonus: $100,000
Second Exec. Salary: $335,000   Bonus: $

OTHER THOUGHTS:

Estimated Female Officers or Directors: 2
Hot Spot for Advancement for Women/Minorities: Y

Sales, profits and employees may be estimates. Financial information, benefits and other data can change quickly and may vary from those stated here.

Trend Micro Inc

NAIC Code: 511210E

TYPES OF BUSINESS:

Computer Software: Network Security, Managed Access, Digital ID,
Cybersecurity & Anti-Virus
Antivirus Software

GROWTH PLANS/SPECIAL FEATURES:

Trend Micro provides antivirus and other security products that
protect the flow of information on PCs, file servers, e-mail
servers, and the Internet gateway. Sales have averaged 75%
annual growth over the past decade. Customers include British
Airways, Merrill Lynch, Microsoft, Pacific Bell, and
governmental agencies in the United States and Japan.

BRANDS/DIVISIONS/AFFILIATES:

XGen

CONTACTS: *Note: Officers with more than one job title may be intentionally listed here more than once.*

Eva Chen, CEO
Kevin Simzer, COO
Mahendra Negi, CFO
Leah MacMillan, CMO
Max Cheng, CIO
Raimund Genes, CTO
Steve Quane, Chief Product Officer
Felix Sterling, General Counsel
Wael Mohamed, Exec. VP-Corporate Strategy & Global Field Oper.
Jenny Chang, Chief Cultural Officer
Mitchel Chang, Sr. VP-Global Tech. Support
Oscar Chang, Chief Dev. Officer
Steve Chang, Chmn.
Oscar Chang, Exec. VP-Greater China Sales
Akihiko Omikawa, Gen. Manager-Japan Region & Consumer Business Unit

FINANCIAL DATA: *Note: Data for latest year may not have been available at press time.*

In U.S. $	2022	2021	2020	2019	2018	2017
Revenue	1,527,163,000	1,298,998,000	1,187,781,000	1,127,280,000	1,094,627,000	1,015,477,000
R&D Expense						
Operating Income	213,862,100	297,803,400	269,299,800	257,166,800	244,549,400	248,671,100
Operating Margin %		.23%	.23%	.23%	.22%	.24%
SGA Expense						
Net Income	203,646,700	261,813,900	183,591,200	190,701,700	193,212,900	175,313,700
Operating Cash Flow	388,302,400	377,138,500	370,607,900	307,820,900	340,917,000	320,144,900
Capital Expenditure	143,159,300	128,201,300	80,795,400	72,961,520	84,807,870	83,443,080
EBITDA	458,056,700	500,037,500	424,046,200	365,101,000	362,391,900	348,355,100
Return on Assets %		.10%	.07%	.08%	.08%	.08%
Return on Equity %		.19%	.14%	.15%	.16%	.15%
Debt to Equity						

CONTACT INFORMATION:

Phone: 81 3-5334-3618   Fax: 81-3-5334-4008
Toll-Free: 800-228-5651
Address: Shibuya-ku, 2-1-1 Shinjuku Maynds Tower, Tokyo, 151-0053
Japan

STOCK TICKER/OTHER:

Stock Ticker: TMICF   Exchange: PINX
Employees: 6,562   Fiscal Year Ends: 12/31
Parent Company:

SALARIES/BONUSES:

Top Exec. Salary: $ Bonus: $
Second Exec. Salary: $ Bonus: $

OTHER THOUGHTS:

Estimated Female Officers or Directors: 3
Hot Spot for Advancement for Women/Minorities: Y

Trip.com Group Limited

www.trip.com

NAIC Code: 561510

TYPES OF BUSINESS:

Online Hotel & Flight Booking
Travel Booking
Online Booking

BRANDS/DIVISIONS/AFFILIATES:

Skyscanner
Ctrip

GROWTH PLANS/SPECIAL FEATURES:

Trip.com is the largest online travel agent in China and is positioned to benefit from the country's rising demand for higher-margin outbound travel as passport penetration is only 12% in China. The company generated about 78% of sales from accommodation reservations and transportation ticketing in 2020. The rest of revenue comes from package tours and corporate travel. Prior to the pandemic in 2019, the company generated 25% of revenue from international business, which is important to its margin expansion. Most of sales come from websites and mobile platforms, while the rest come from call centers. The competes in a crowded OTA industry in China, including Meituan, Alibaba-backed Fliggy, Tongcheng, and Qunar. The company was founded in 1999 and listed on the Nasdaq in December 2003.

CONTACTS:
Note: Officers with more than one job title may be intentionally listed here more than once.

Jane Sun, CEO
Cindy Xiaofan Wang, CFO
James Liang, Chmn.

FINANCIAL DATA:
Note: Data for latest year may not have been available at press time.

In U.S. $	2022	2021	2020	2019	2018	2017
Revenue	2,755,676,000	2,753,475,000	2,518,736,000	4,904,633,000	4,258,172,000	3,684,869,000
R&D Expense	1,147,018,000	1,236,541,000	1,054,332,000	1,467,292,000	1,322,900,000	1,135,742,000
Operating Income	97,086,040	-118,401,000	-113,037,800	693,078,800	358,228,200	404,708,500
Operating Margin %		-.04%	-.04%	.14%	.08%	.11%
SGA Expense	975,948,400	1,078,673,000	1,105,763,000	1,730,497,000	1,707,394,000	1,501,121,000
Net Income	192,934,400	-75,633,600	-446,513,300	964,122,100	152,917,400	296,346,200
Operating Cash Flow	363,178,800	340,351,200	-525,722,300	1,008,402,000	978,423,700	972,098,000
Capital Expenditure	68,482,780	78,521,420	73,158,320	114,688,000	97,361,070	67,932,720
EBITDA	748,085,100	344,751,700	282,869,700	1,679,616,000	606,581,400	782,876,500
Return on Assets %		.00%	-.02%	.04%	.01%	.01%
Return on Equity %		-.01%	-.03%	.07%	.01%	.03%
Debt to Equity		.10%	0.233	0.196	.28%	0.344

CONTACT INFORMATION:

Phone: 86 21-3406-4880   Fax: 86 2152510000
Toll-Free:
Address: 968 Jin Zhong Rd., Shanghai, Shanghai 200335 China

STOCK TICKER/OTHER:

Stock Ticker: TCOM   Exchange: NAS
Employees: 32,202   Fiscal Year Ends: 12/31
Parent Company:

SALARIES/BONUSES:

Top Exec. Salary: $ Bonus: $
Second Exec. Salary: $ Bonus: $

OTHER THOUGHTS:

Estimated Female Officers or Directors:
Hot Spot for Advancement for Women/Minorities: Y

TripAdvisor Inc

www.tripadvisor.com

NAIC Code: 561510

TYPES OF BUSINESS:

Online Travel Information
Online Travel Platform
Mobile Travel Platform
Travel Reviews
Trip Planning Tools

BRANDS/DIVISIONS/AFFILIATES:

Business Advantage
tripadvisor.com
www.bokun.io
www.cruisecritic.com
www.flipkey.com
www.thefork.com
www.helloreco.com
www.holidaylettings.co.uk

GROWTH PLANS/SPECIAL FEATURES:

Tripadvisor is the world's leading travel metasearch company. Its platform offers 1 billion reviews and information on about 8 million accommodations, restaurants, experiences, airlines, and cruises. In 2022, 65% of revenue came from the company's core segment, which includes hotel revenue generated through advertising on its metasearch platform. Viator, its experiences brand, was 33% of sales in 2022, and TheFork, its dining brand, represented 8% of revenue (about 6% of sales were intersegment, which are eliminated from consolidated revenue).

TripAdvisor offers its employees comprehensive benefits, which vary by location.

CONTACTS: Note: Officers with more than one job title may be intentionally listed here more than once.

Ernst Teunissen, CEO, Subsidiary
Stephen Kaufer, CEO
Gregory Maffei, Chairman of the Board
Geoffrey Gouvalaris, Chief Accounting Officer
Seth Kalvert, Chief Legal Officer
Lindsay Nelson, Other Executive Officer
Kanika Soni, Other Executive Officer

FINANCIAL DATA: Note: Data for latest year may not have been available at press time.

In U.S. $	2022	2021	2020	2019	2018	2017
Revenue	1,492,000,000	902,000,000	604,000,000	1,560,000,000	1,615,000,000	
R&D Expense						
Operating Income	101,000,000	-131,000,000	-285,000,000	188,000,000	183,000,000	
Operating Margin %	.07%	-.15%	-.47%	.12%	.11%	
SGA Expense	956,000,000	636,000,000	489,000,000	859,000,000	955,000,000	
Net Income	20,000,000	-148,000,000	-289,000,000	126,000,000	113,000,000	
Operating Cash Flow	400,000,000	108,000,000	-194,000,000	424,000,000	405,000,000	
Capital Expenditure	56,000,000	54,000,000	55,000,000	83,000,000	61,000,000	
EBITDA	208,000,000	-29,000,000	-209,000,000	327,000,000	301,000,000	
Return on Assets %	.01%	-.07%	-.15%	.06%	.05%	
Return on Equity %	.02%	-.18%	-.28%	.10%	.08%	
Debt to Equity	1.06%	1.17%	0.686	0.122	.06%	

CONTACT INFORMATION:

Phone: 781-800-5000   Fax:
Toll-Free:
Address: 400 1st Ave., Needham, MA 02494 United States

STOCK TICKER/OTHER:

Stock Ticker: TRIP   Exchange: NAS
Employees: 3,100   Fiscal Year Ends: 12/31
Parent Company:

SALARIES/BONUSES:

Top Exec. Salary: $548,000   Bonus: $1,071,449
Second Exec. Salary: Bonus: $500,000
$387,692

OTHER THOUGHTS:

Estimated Female Officers or Directors: 4
Hot Spot for Advancement for Women/Minorities: Y

trivago NV

company.trivago.com

NAIC Code: 561510

TYPES OF BUSINESS:
Online Reservation Systems

BRANDS/DIVISIONS/AFFILIATES:
trivago.com
weekengo GmbH
weekend.com

GROWTH PLANS/SPECIAL FEATURES:
trivago NV is a hotel search company focused on reshaping the way travelers search for and compare hotels while enabling hotel advertisers to grow their businesses by providing access to a broad audience of travelers through the company's websites and apps. The platform allows travelers to make informed decisions by personalizing their hotel search and providing access to a deep supply of hotel information and prices. The company operates in three operating segments namely the Americas, Developed Europe, and the Rest of the World. It derives a majority of revenue from the Developed Europe segment. The Developed Europe segment is comprised of Austria, Belgium, Denmark, Finland, France, Germany, Ireland, Italy, Luxembourg, Malta, the Netherlands, Norway, Portugal, Spain, Sweden, and others.

CONTACTS:
Note: Officers with more than one job title may be intentionally listed here more than once.

Rolf Schromgens, CEO

FINANCIAL DATA:
Note: Data for latest year may not have been available at press time.

In U.S. $	2022	2021	2020	2019	2018	2017
Revenue	577,508,600	390,182,400	268,697,100	905,242,900	987,495,600	1,117,641,000
R&D Expense						
Operating Income	69,494,820	10,849,530	-48,610,750	41,181,990	-20,688,690	-21,986,180
Operating Margin %	.12%	.03%	-.18%	.05%	-.02%	-.02%
SGA Expense	434,883,400	310,237,500	236,604,000	776,876,000	928,280,400	1,073,369,000
Net Income	-137,325,100	11,554,400	-264,872,600	18,524,390	-23,196,240	-13,472,580
Operating Cash Flow	71,532,810	35,120,900	8,497,409	80,117,660	-4,948,187	-9,197,970
Capital Expenditure	4,291,883	4,081,390	5,938,040	8,653,929	26,747,620	18,743,520
EBITDA	-123,126,100	34,572,540	-261,238,100	53,655,000	-6,015,760	-7,283,031
Return on Assets %	-.17%	.01%	-.25%	.02%	-.02%	-.01%
Return on Equity %	-.20%	.02%	-.31%	.02%	-.03%	-.02%
Debt to Equity	.07%	.07%	0.129	0.106		

CONTACT INFORMATION:
Phone: 49-211-54056110   Fax:
Toll-Free:
Address: Bennigsen-Platz 1, Dusseldorf, 40474 Germany

STOCK TICKER/OTHER:
Stock Ticker: TRVG   Exchange: NAS
Employees: 709   Fiscal Year Ends: 12/31
Parent Company:

SALARIES/BONUSES:
Top Exec. Salary: $539,724   Bonus: $33,463
Second Exec. Salary: $539,724   Bonus: $

OTHER THOUGHTS:
Estimated Female Officers or Directors:
Hot Spot for Advancement for Women/Minorities:

Sales, profits and employees may be estimates. Financial information, benefits and other data can change quickly and may vary from those stated here.

TrueCar Inc

www.truecar.com

NAIC Code: 519130

TYPES OF BUSINESS:

Internet Publishing and Broadcasting and Web Search Portals
Automobile Ecommerce
Vehicle Search
Vehicle Trade-In
Automobile Financing
Automobile Insurance
Analytics
Digital Technology

BRANDS/DIVISIONS/AFFILIATES:

TrueCar Certified Dealer
TrueCar Deal Builder
TrueCar Dealer Solutions Inc

GROWTH PLANS/SPECIAL FEATURES:

TrueCar Inc is a data-driven online platform operating on common technology infrastructure, powered by proprietary data and analytics. It also customizes and operates its platform for affinity group marketing partners, including financial institutions like PenFed and American Express; membership-based organizations like Consumer Reports, AARP, Sam's Club, and AAA; and employee buying programs for large enterprises such as IBM and Walmart. The company enables users to obtain market-based pricing data on new and used cars, and to connect with its network of TrueCar Certified Dealers.

CONTACTS:
Note: Officers with more than one job title may be intentionally listed here more than once.

Michael Darrow, CEO
Jantoon Reigersman, CFO
Christopher Claus, Chairman of the Board
Charles Thomas, Chief Accounting Officer
Simon Smith, Executive VP, Divisional
Jeffrey Swart, Executive VP
Beth Mach, Other Executive Officer

FINANCIAL DATA:
Note: Data for latest year may not have been available at press time.

In U.S. $	2022	2021	2020	2019	2018	2017
Revenue	161,524,000	231,698,000	278,678,000	335,046,000	335,089,000	323,149,000
R&D Expense	46,090,000	41,432,000	44,930,000	56,114,000	60,251,000	59,070,000
Operating Income	-65,920,000	-33,478,000	-10,252,000	-60,856,000	-33,064,000	-33,663,000
Operating Margin %	-.41%	-.14%	-.04%	-.18%	-.10%	-.10%
SGA Expense	148,621,000	185,226,000	201,904,000	291,295,000	263,970,000	247,043,000
Net Income	-118,685,000	-38,329,000	76,544,000	-54,890,000	-28,321,000	-32,849,000
Operating Cash Flow	-29,137,000	14,194,000	39,117,000	20,344,000	24,833,000	22,118,000
Capital Expenditure	11,680,000	10,689,000	10,277,000	10,181,000	16,116,000	19,809,000
EBITDA	-45,460,000	-12,904,000	15,528,000	-34,215,000	-12,479,000	-9,931,000
Return on Assets %	-.37%	-.09%	.17%	-.13%	-.07%	-.10%
Return on Equity %	-.45%	-.11%	.22%	-.16%	-.09%	-.12%
Debt to Equity	.09%	.08%	0.084	0.113	.07%	0.093

CONTACT INFORMATION:

Phone: 424 258-8000   Fax:
Toll-Free: 800-200-2000
Address: 120 Broadway, Ste. 200, Santa Monica, CA 90401 United States

STOCK TICKER/OTHER:

Stock Ticker: TRUE
Employees: 441
Parent Company:

Exchange: NAS
Fiscal Year Ends: 12/31

SALARIES/BONUSES:

Top Exec. Salary: $590,000   Bonus: $
Second Exec. Salary: $443,750   Bonus: $

OTHER THOUGHTS:

Estimated Female Officers or Directors:
Hot Spot for Advancement for Women/Minorities:

Tucows Inc

www.tucowsinc.com

NAIC Code: 518210

TYPES OF BUSINESS:
Domain Name Registry Services
Digital Web Certificates
Software

BRANDS/DIVISIONS/AFFILIATES:
Ting
www.ting.com
Hover.com
eNom
Ascio Technologies
Cedar Holdings Group
Platypus
EPAG

CONTACTS: Note: Officers with more than one job title may be intentionally listed here more than once.
Elliot Noss, CEO
Davinder Singh, CFO
Bret Fausett, Chief Legal Officer
Jill Szuchmacher, Chief Strategy Officer
Hanno Liem, Chief Technology Officer
Allen Karp, Co-Chairman of the Board
Robin Chase, Co-Chairman of the Board
David Woroch, Executive VP, Divisional
Michael Goldstein, Other Executive Officer
Ross Rader, Other Executive Officer
Jessica Johannson, Other Executive Officer
Justin Reilly, Other Executive Officer

GROWTH PLANS/SPECIAL FEATURES:
Tucows Inc provides us consumers and small businesses with mobile phone services nationally and high-speed fixed Internet access in selected towns. The Company offers Mobile Service Enabler (MSE) solutions, as well as professional services to other retail mobile providers. The Company is also a global distributor of Internet services, including domain name registration, digital certificates, and email. It provides these services primarily through a global Internet-based distribution network of Internet Service Providers, web hosting companies, and other providers of Internet services to end-users. It operates in three segments: Domain Services, Mobile Services, and Fiber Internet Services. It generates the majority of its revenue from Domain Services.

FINANCIAL DATA: Note: Data for latest year may not have been available at press time.

In U.S. $	2022	2021	2020	2019	2018	2017
Revenue	321,142,000	304,337,000	311,202,000	337,145,000	346,013,000	329,421,000
R&D Expense	14,187,000	14,310,000	12,427,000	9,717,000	8,748,000	7,258,000
Operating Income	-31,201,000	-7,816,000	7,948,000	29,215,000	29,578,000	27,095,000
Operating Margin %	-.10%	-.03%	.03%	.09%	.09%	.08%
SGA Expense	84,782,000	61,841,000	54,542,000	52,150,000	50,773,000	43,017,000
Net Income	-27,571,000	3,364,000	5,775,000	15,398,000	17,135,000	22,327,000
Operating Cash Flow	19,876,000	29,637,000	36,081,000	40,381,000	37,209,000	31,896,000
Capital Expenditure	137,492,000	73,949,000	44,509,000	47,636,000	28,484,000	15,877,000
EBITDA	26,249,000	39,880,000	38,423,000	48,634,000	44,807,000	39,769,000
Return on Assets %	-.05%	.01%	.01%	.04%	.05%	.09%
Return on Equity %	-.26%	.03%	.06%	.18%	.24%	.46%
Debt to Equity	2.60%	1.76%	1.25	1.305	.58%	0.974

CONTACT INFORMATION:
Phone: 416 535-0123   Fax: 416 531-5584
Toll-Free: 800-371-6992
Address: 96 Mowat Ave., Toronto, ON M6K 3M1 Canada

STOCK TICKER/OTHER:
Stock Ticker: TCX   Exchange: NAS
Employees: 1,100   Fiscal Year Ends: 12/31
Parent Company:

SALARIES/BONUSES:
Top Exec. Salary: $603,031   Bonus: $361,818
Second Exec. Salary: $409,156   Bonus: $281,452

OTHER THOUGHTS:
Estimated Female Officers or Directors: 1
Hot Spot for Advancement for Women/Minorities:

Tujia Online Information Technology (Beijing) Co Ltd

www.tujia.com
NAIC Code: 561510

TYPES OF BUSINESS:

Online Homestay Reservations
Room Rental Reservations
Home Rental
Online Booking

BRANDS/DIVISIONS/AFFILIATES:

CONTACTS: *Note: Officers with more than one job title may be intentionally listed here more than once.*

Gang Chen, CEO

GROWTH PLANS/SPECIAL FEATURES:

Tujia Online Information Technology (Beijing) Co., Ltd. operates Tujia, an online short-term home rental platform in China. Tujia offers destinations in China and overseas. The platform's online listings include accommodation products and extension services such as homestays, apartments, villas and more. Short-term rentals primarily serve the vacation traveler's accommodation needs, but are also used by business travelers, group travelers, holiday gatherings and more. Users can book via online or mobile channels, as well as WeChat and telephone. Tujia takes care of verifying that the listed properties are what and where they say they are, and provides tenants with an advanced payment guarantee fund. Tujia members also receive benefits of the local culture, as well as discounts at nearby coffee houses, attractions and more. The company welcomes landlords who have idle houses to rent/share, as well as new-home builders desiring to share a portion of their rooms for advertising/accommodation purposes. Owners and landlords publish their homes on Tujia's multiple website portals for free. The company also guides landlords through the process for a worry-free, seamless process. Tujia has signed contracts with government agencies in China, as well as partnership agreements with top-tier real estate development companies.

FINANCIAL DATA: *Note: Data for latest year may not have been available at press time.*

In U.S. $	2022	2021	2020	2019	2018	2017
Revenue						
R&D Expense						
Operating Income						
Operating Margin %						
SGA Expense						
Net Income						
Operating Cash Flow						
Capital Expenditure						
EBITDA						
Return on Assets %						
Return on Equity %						
Debt to Equity						

CONTACT INFORMATION:

Phone: 86 10-5975-6798   Fax: 86-10-5975-6717
Toll-Free:
Address: 10 Jiuxianqiao Rd., Chaoyang Dist., Beijing, Beijing 100015 China

STOCK TICKER/OTHER:

Stock Ticker: Private   Exchange:
Employees: Fiscal Year Ends:
Parent Company:

SALARIES/BONUSES:

Top Exec. Salary: $ Bonus: $
Second Exec. Salary: $ Bonus: $

OTHER THOUGHTS:

Estimated Female Officers or Directors:
Hot Spot for Advancement for Women/Minorities:

Twilio Inc

www.twilio.com

NAIC Code: 511210C

TYPES OF BUSINESS:

Computer Software: Telecom, Communications & VOIP
Cloud Communications Platform
Software Applications
Application Programming Interfaces
Software Communications
Customer Data Software

BRANDS/DIVISIONS/AFFILIATES:

Twilio
Super Network
Segment
Segment io Inc

GROWTH PLANS/SPECIAL FEATURES:

Twilio is a cloud-based communications platform-as-a-service company offering communication building blocks that allow for a fully customized customer engagement experience spanning voice, video, chat, and SMS messaging. It does this through various application programming interfaces and prebuilt solution applications aimed at improving customer engagement. The company leverages its Super Network, a global network of carrier relationships, to facilitate high-speed, cost-effective communication.

Employees of Twilio receive medical, dental and vision insurance; a 401(k) plan; and pre-tax commuter benefits..

CONTACTS: Note: Officers with more than one job title may be intentionally listed here more than once.

Jeff Lawson, CEO
Khozema Shipchandler, CFO
Karyn Smith, General Counsel
Chee Chew, Other Executive Officer

FINANCIAL DATA: Note: Data for latest year may not have been available at press time.

In U.S. $	2022	2021	2020	2019	2018	2017
Revenue	3,826,321,000	2,841,839,000	1,761,776,000	1,134,468,000	650,067,000	399,020,000
R&D Expense	1,079,081,000	789,219,000	530,548,000	391,355,000	171,358,000	120,739,000
Operating Income	-1,030,950,000	-915,584,000	-492,901,000	-369,785,000	-115,235,000	-66,074,000
Operating Margin %	-.27%	-.32%	-.28%	-.33%	-.18%	-.17%
SGA Expense	1,765,446,000	1,517,078,000	878,014,000	587,347,000	293,103,000	161,460,000
Net Income	-1,256,145,000	-949,900,000	-490,979,000	-307,063,000	-121,949,000	-63,708,000
Operating Cash Flow	-254,368,000	-58,192,000	32,654,000	14,048,000	7,983,000	-3,255,000
Capital Expenditure	80,182,000	90,021,000	59,133,000	67,290,000	24,655,000	26,818,000
EBITDA	-751,823,000	-657,206,000	-343,241,000	-259,355,000	-89,140,000	-47,310,000
Return on Assets %	-.10%	-.08%	-.07%	-.10%	-.16%	-.15%
Return on Equity %	-.12%	-.10%	-.08%	-.13%	-.31%	-.18%
Debt to Equity	.11%	.11%	0.065	0.142	1.00%	

CONTACT INFORMATION:

Phone: 415-390-2337   Fax:
Toll-Free:
Address: 101 Spear St., Fl. 1, San Francisco, CA 94105 United States

STOCK TICKER/OTHER:

Stock Ticker: TWLO
Employees: 8,156
Parent Company:

Exchange: NYS
Fiscal Year Ends: 12/31

SALARIES/BONUSES:

Top Exec. Salary: $1,100,000   Bonus: $
Second Exec. Salary: $900,000   Bonus: $

OTHER THOUGHTS:

Estimated Female Officers or Directors: 2
Hot Spot for Advancement for Women/Minorities:

Uber Technologies Inc

NAIC Code: 561599

TYPES OF BUSINESS:

Ride Sharing and Car Sharing Platform
Freight Truck Dispatch Service
Restaurant Meal Delivery Service
Transportation Marketplace Technologies
Self-Driving Truck Technologies
Self-Driving Car Technologies

BRANDS/DIVISIONS/AFFILIATES:

UberEATS
Uber Freight
JUMP Bikes
Uber for Business
Postmates

GROWTH PLANS/SPECIAL FEATURES:

Uber Technologies is a technology provider that matches riders with drivers, hungry people with restaurants and food delivery service providers, and shippers with carriers. The firm's on-demand technology platform could eventually be used for additional products and services, such as autonomous vehicles, delivery via drones, and Uber Elevate, which, as the firm refers to it, provides "aerial ride-sharing." Uber Technologies is headquartered in San Francisco and operates in over 63 countries with over 150 million users who order rides or food at least once a month. Approximately 56% of its gross revenue comes from ridesharing and 31% from food delivery.

CONTACTS: *Note: Officers with more than one job title may be intentionally listed here more than once.*

Dara Khosrowshahi, CEO
Nelson Chai, CFO
Ronald Sugar, Chairman of the Board
Glen Ceremony, Chief Accounting Officer
Tony West, Chief Legal Officer
Nikki Krishnamurthy, Other Executive Officer
Jill Hazelbaker, Senior VP, Divisional

FINANCIAL DATA: *Note: Data for latest year may not have been available at press time.*

In U.S. $	2022	2021	2020	2019	2018	2017
Revenue	31,877,000,000	17,455,000,000	11,139,000,000	13,000,000,000	10,433,000,000	
R&D Expense	2,798,000,000	2,054,000,000	2,205,000,000	4,836,000,000	1,505,000,000	
Operating Income	-1,832,000,000	-3,834,000,000	-4,863,000,000	-8,596,000,000	-3,033,000,000	
Operating Margin %	- .06%	- .22%	- .44%	- .66%	- .29%	
SGA Expense	7,892,000,000	7,105,000,000	6,249,000,000	7,925,000,000	5,233,000,000	
Net Income	-9,141,000,000	-496,000,000	-6,768,000,000	-8,506,000,000	997,000,000	
Operating Cash Flow	642,000,000	-445,000,000	-2,745,000,000	-4,321,000,000	-1,541,000,000	
Capital Expenditure	252,000,000	298,000,000	616,000,000	588,000,000	558,000,000	
EBITDA	-7,914,000,000	360,000,000	-5,913,000,000	-7,402,000,000	2,386,000,000	
Return on Assets %	- .26%	- .01%	- .21%	- .31%		
Return on Equity %	- .84%	- .04%	- .51%	-2.50%		
Debt to Equity	1.49%	.76%	0.742	0.52		

CONTACT INFORMATION:

Phone: 415-986-2715   Fax: 415-986-2104
Toll-Free:
Address: 1455 Market St., Ste. 400, San Francisco, CA 94103 United States

STOCK TICKER/OTHER:

Stock Ticker: UBER
Employees: 32,800
Parent Company:

Exchange: NYS
Fiscal Year Ends: 12/31

SALARIES/BONUSES:

Top Exec. Salary: $1,000,000   Bonus: $
Second Exec. Salary: $800,000   Bonus: $

OTHER THOUGHTS:

Estimated Female Officers or Directors: 1
Hot Spot for Advancement for Women/Minorities:

United Internet AG

www.unitedinternet.de

NAIC Code: 517311

TYPES OF BUSINESS:
Internet Service Provider
Online Advertising Services
Internet Service Provider

BRANDS/DIVISIONS/AFFILIATES:
1&1
GMX
WEB.DE
Home.pl
IONOS
united-domains
Arsys
World4You

GROWTH PLANS/SPECIAL FEATURES:
United Internet AG is a telecommunications provider that operates through two segments: access and applications. The access segment earns revenue by providing broadband and mobile services to homes, individuals, and small to midsize enterprises. The applications segment generates revenue from marketing services, managed services, and personal information management. The customer segment is the same as the access segment. The company owns fiber and data center infrastructure. United Internet generates the vast majority of its revenue in Germany.

CONTACTS: *Note: Officers with more than one job title may be intentionally listed here more than once.*
Ralph Dommermuth, CEO
Martin Mildner, CFO
Markt Schwaben, Chmn.

FINANCIAL DATA: *Note: Data for latest year may not have been available at press time.*

In U.S. $	2022	2021	2020	2019	2018	2017
Revenue	6,384,998,000	6,094,750,000	5,793,662,000	5,606,749,000	5,508,286,000	4,540,481,000
R&D Expense						
Operating Income	968,799,600	986,009,200	717,257,100	941,431,300	987,473,000	748,082,900
Operating Margin %		.16%	.12%	.17%	.18%	.16%
SGA Expense	645,522,400	571,719,600	486,715,200	489,545,500	454,859,700	451,789,700
Net Income	396,368,700	449,560,600	313,631,200	457,617,600	203,793,200	700,762,000
Operating Cash Flow	644,987,100	958,153,000	999,289,700	894,784,100	520,595,800	783,677,600
Capital Expenditure	735,511,600	312,777,400	482,548,500	272,858,400	293,351,600	252,029,300
EBITDA	1,328,851,000	1,385,550,000	1,152,313,000	1,390,628,000	1,061,916,000	1,321,490,000
Return on Assets %		.04%	.03%	.05%	.02%	.11%
Return on Equity %		.09%	.07%	.10%	.05%	.25%
Debt to Equity		.43%	0.326	0.419	.42%	0.447

CONTACT INFORMATION:
Phone: 49 2602961631   Fax: 49 2602961013
Toll-Free:
Address: Elgendorfer Strasse 57, Montabaur, RP 56410 Germany

STOCK TICKER/OTHER:
Stock Ticker: UDIRY   Exchange: PINX
Employees: 10,474   Fiscal Year Ends: 12/31
Parent Company:

SALARIES/BONUSES:
Top Exec. Salary: $ Bonus: $
Second Exec. Salary: $ Bonus: $

OTHER THOUGHTS:
Estimated Female Officers or Directors:
Hot Spot for Advancement for Women/Minorities:

United Online Inc

www.untd.com

NAIC Code: 517311

TYPES OF BUSINESS:

Internet Service Provider
Internet Services
Media Advertising Services
Dial-up Services
DSL Services
Email Services
Data Protection
Email and Web Hosting Services

BRANDS/DIVISIONS/AFFILIATES:

B Riley Financial Inc
NetZero
Juno
NetZero HiSpeed
Juno Turbo
NetZero DataShield WiFi

CONTACTS: *Note: Officers with more than one job title may be intentionally listed here more than once.*

Edward Zinser, CFO
Howard Phanstiel, Director
Mark Harrington, Executive VP
Shahir Fakiri, General Manager, Divisional
Howard G. Phanstiel, Chmn.

GROWTH PLANS/SPECIAL FEATURES:

United Online, Inc., a subsidiary of B. Riley Financial, Inc., provides consumer products and internet and media services over the internet. These products feature value-priced internet access through the NetZero and Juno brands. The brands offer a full range of low-priced dial-up and digital subscriber line (DSL) internet access services. Types of nationwide dial-up services include: Free, providing 10 hours of access each month and includes NetZero email; Basic, providing unlimited access along with email and spam protection; Accelerated (NetZero HiSpeed or Juno Turbo), enabling users to surf the web at up to five times the speed of standard dial-up; and Toll-Free, enabling customers who live in hard-to-serve areas to connect to the internet through a toll-free 800 access number. DSL service from NetZero and Juno is available in select cities and delivers broadband internet directly to the home; and also receive North Antivirus online, MegaMail with built-in spam and email virus protection. United Online's communications division offers email and web-hosting services. This division's NetZero DataShield WiFi security service encrypts and protects users' data when they connect to the internet via WiFi connections, including public WiFi hubs. Services for advertisers include a full suite of display, search, email and text-link opportunities across the company's internet properties.

FINANCIAL DATA: *Note: Data for latest year may not have been available at press time.*

In U.S. $	2022	2021	2020	2019	2018	2017
Revenue	204,584,640	196,716,000	189,150,000	194,000,000	193,000,000	191,000,000
R&D Expense						
Operating Income						
Operating Margin %						
SGA Expense						
Net Income						
Operating Cash Flow						
Capital Expenditure						
EBITDA						
Return on Assets %						
Return on Equity %						
Debt to Equity						

CONTACT INFORMATION:

Phone: 818 287-3000   Fax: 818 287-3001
Toll-Free:
Address: 21301 Burbank Blvd., Woodland Hills, CA 91367 United States

STOCK TICKER/OTHER:

Stock Ticker: Subsidiary   Exchange:
Employees: 625   Fiscal Year Ends: 12/31
Parent Company: B Riley Financial Inc

SALARIES/BONUSES:

Top Exec. Salary: $ Bonus: $
Second Exec. Salary: $ Bonus: $

OTHER THOUGHTS:

Estimated Female Officers or Directors:
Hot Spot for Advancement for Women/Minorities:

US Interactive Inc

www.usinteractive.com

NAIC Code: 511210K

TYPES OF BUSINESS:

CRM Software
Software Development
Customer Management Applications
Integrated Technology Solutions
Online Connectivity

BRANDS/DIVISIONS/AFFILIATES:

USI Customer Management Platform
eViews
e2e Hub

CONTACTS: *Note: Officers with more than one job title may be intentionally listed here more than once.*

Sunil Mathur, CEO

GROWTH PLANS/SPECIAL FEATURES:

U.S. Interactive, Inc. (USI) is a software and services organization that develops and deploys internet-based customer management applications for communications and next generation service providers. The company has domestic and international offices, with locations on the east and west coasts of the U.S.; Mumbai, India; and Munich, Germany. The firm's USI Customer Management Platform is an integrated technology platform developed by the company and its affiliates. The platform is made up of three components: eViews, e2e Hub and connectors. eViews are the applications component of the U.S. Interactive platform for customer management services. These applications deliver a single, unified web-based view of the customer across order management, billing and customer service. e2e (enterprise-to-enterprise) Hub is the infrastructure that supports eViews. Connectors are the USI applications that integrate the commercial software of its affiliates. USI's customer base includes ISPs/ASPs (internet service providers/application service providers), CLECs (competitive local exchange carriers), broadband service and digital media providers and wireless carriers. The firm partners with companies that have quality products and services to provide technology options for its clients. Primary partners include BEA Systems, an e-business infrastructure software company; Portal, an integrated billing and e-CRM (electronic customer relationship management) solutions firm for communications and next-generation service providers; Commerce One, an e-marketplace company; IBM, an information technology company; Sun Microsystems, a technology sharing and marketing support company; and Vignette Corporation, which develops internet applications that enable businesses to use the web for publishing and commerce. Headquartered in California, USA, USI has an international office in Toronto, Canada.

FINANCIAL DATA: *Note: Data for latest year may not have been available at press time.*

In U.S. $	2022	2021	2020	2019	2018	2017
Revenue						
R&D Expense						
Operating Income						
Operating Margin %						
SGA Expense						
Net Income						
Operating Cash Flow						
Capital Expenditure						
EBITDA						
Return on Assets %						
Return on Equity %						
Debt to Equity						

CONTACT INFORMATION:

Phone: 408-863-7500   Fax: 408-863-7501
Toll-Free:
Address: 2005 De La Cruz Blvd, Ste. 195, Santa Clara, CA 95050 United States

STOCK TICKER/OTHER:

Stock Ticker: Private   Exchange:
Employees: 700   Fiscal Year Ends: 12/31
Parent Company:

SALARIES/BONUSES:

Top Exec. Salary: $ Bonus: $
Second Exec. Salary: $ Bonus: $

OTHER THOUGHTS:

Estimated Female Officers or Directors:
Hot Spot for Advancement for Women/Minorities:

Ushahidi Inc

NAIC Code: 511210M

www.ushahidi.com

TYPES OF BUSINESS:

Visualization Software
Open Source Information Software
Data Collection
Data Retrieval
Software Development
Innovative Technology

BRANDS/DIVISIONS/AFFILIATES:

Ushahidi Platform
TenFour
BRCK
SMSsync
CrisisNET

CONTACTS: *Note: Officers with more than one job title may be intentionally listed here more than once.*

Angela Oduor Lungati, CEO
Jon Shuler, R&D Manager
Sharon Rutto, Quality Assurance Engineer
Esther Ondigo, Admin. Assistant
Erik Hersman, Dir.-Oper.
Erik Hersman, Dir.-Strategy
Limo Taboi, Dir.-Finance
Nathaniel Manning, Dir.-Bus. Dev.
Linda Kamau, Developer
Emmanuel Kala, Developer
Angel Odour, Developer
Daudi Were, Project Dir.-Africa

GROWTH PLANS/SPECIAL FEATURES:

Ushahidi, Inc. is a nonprofit software company that develops opensource software for data collection, visualization and interactive mapping. Ushahidi, meaning testimony in Swahili, is based on crowdsourcing concepts and seeks to make information regarding elections, crisis and other geopolitical events more widely available and transparent. Ushahidi designs its products and initiatives with a global perspective. Combining eyewitness reports delivered by text message, email or over the web with media information and geographical mapping tools, the Ushahidi Platform facilitates the democratization of information. The platform was initially developed to respond to information challenges following reports of violence in the aftermath of presidential elections in Kenya in 2008. It has since been used to compile information on elections in countries such as India, Mexico, Lebanon and Afghanistan; protest movements in the Middle East; and post-natural disasters in Haiti, Chile, Japan, Russia and the U.S. The Ushahidi Platform collects the submitted data, manages the data, offers data visualization features, provides automated alerts about changes and updates, and encompasses capabilities for building and scaling for deployments. For individuals, Ushahidi offers a one-month free demo plan and then charges a monthly subscription fee. Enterprises contact Ushahidi for a price rate whether for a single deployment of multiple deployments.

FINANCIAL DATA: *Note: Data for latest year may not have been available at press time.*

In U.S. $	2022	2021	2020	2019	2018	2017
Revenue			1,658,402	1,727,503	2,217,785	3,520,014
R&D Expense						
Operating Income						
Operating Margin %						
SGA Expense						
Net Income				282,673	-490,067	362,907
Operating Cash Flow						
Capital Expenditure						
EBITDA						
Return on Assets %						
Return on Equity %						
Debt to Equity						

CONTACT INFORMATION:

Phone: 407 427-0412   Fax:
Toll-Free:
Address: 12472 Lake Underhill Rd., #330, Orlando, FL 32828 United States

STOCK TICKER/OTHER:

Stock Ticker: Nonprofit
Employees: 30
Parent Company:

Exchange:
Fiscal Year Ends: 12/31

SALARIES/BONUSES:

Top Exec. Salary: $ Bonus: $
Second Exec. Salary: $ Bonus: $

OTHER THOUGHTS:

Estimated Female Officers or Directors: 6
Hot Spot for Advancement for Women/Minorities: Y

VANCL

www.vancl.com

NAIC Code: 454110

TYPES OF BUSINESS:

Electronic Shopping
Ecommerce
Apparel
Ecommerce Technology
Payments Technology
Home Goods

GROWTH PLANS/SPECIAL FEATURES:

VANCL is a Chinese ecommerce platform developed and operated by Fanke Eslite (Beijing) Technology Co., Ltd. VANCL offers apparel, accessories, footwear, wallets, luggage and home accessories for men, women and children. VANCL began as an ecommerce specialty site for Fanke-branded t-shirts for men. Fanke Eslite developed and produced the Fanke Ironing Shirt under the theme of One Shirt, comprising technology for an anti-wrinkle, high-quality fashion shirt. As an ecommerce retailer, VANCL has since expanded its portfolio of merchandise to include consumers of all ages, as well as products by designers from around the globe.

BRANDS/DIVISIONS/AFFILIATES:

Fanke Eslite (Beijing) Technology Co Ltd
Fanke Ironing Shirt

CONTACTS: Note: Officers with more than one job title may be intentionally listed here more than once.

Chen Nian, CEO

FINANCIAL DATA: Note: Data for latest year may not have been available at press time.

In U.S. $	2022	2021	2020	2019	2018	2017
Revenue						
R&D Expense						
Operating Income						
Operating Margin %						
SGA Expense						
Net Income						
Operating Cash Flow						
Capital Expenditure						
EBITDA						
Return on Assets %						
Return on Equity %						
Debt to Equity						

CONTACT INFORMATION:

Phone: 86 10-5769-5159   Fax: 86-10-59763401
Toll-Free:
Address: No. 20, Middle East 3rd Ring Rd., Bldg. A Landgent, Beijing, Beijing 100022 China

STOCK TICKER/OTHER:

Stock Ticker: Private   Exchange:
Employees: 165   Fiscal Year Ends:
Parent Company:

SALARIES/BONUSES:

Top Exec. Salary: $ Bonus: $
Second Exec. Salary: $ Bonus: $

OTHER THOUGHTS:

Estimated Female Officers or Directors:
Hot Spot for Advancement for Women/Minorities:

Sales, profits and employees may be estimates. Financial information, benefits and other data can change quickly and may vary from those stated here.

Veeam Software

NAIC Code: 511210B

TYPES OF BUSINESS:

Computer Software: Network Management (IT), System Testing & Storage
Data Backup Solutions
Data Recovery Solutions
Data Management Solutions
Data Protection
Software Development
Software-as-a-Service

BRANDS/DIVISIONS/AFFILIATES:

Insight Partners

GROWTH PLANS/SPECIAL FEATURES:

Veeam Software, Inc. offers backup, recovery and data management solutions that provide data protection through a single platform for cloud, virtual, physical, software-as-a-service (SaaS) and Kubernetes environments. The Veeam Platform enables businesses to modernize their data protection and to manage all workloads. It is a complete data protection solution for all data, whether data is deployed on-premises, in the cloud, through backup-as-a-service (BaaS) or disaster-recovering-as-a-service (DRaaS). The company's solutions are for enterprises, small businesses and service providers. Industries served primarily include financial services, insurance, healthcare and educational institutions. Veeam also offers free tools on its website, including product downloads. Headquartered in the U.S., the company has offices across the Americas, EMEA and Asia-Pacific. Veeam Software is privately-owned by software investor Insight Partners.

CONTACTS:
Note: Officers with more than one job title may be intentionally listed here more than once.

Anand Eswaran, CEO
Matthew Bishop, COO
Dustin Driggs, CFO
Rick Jackson, CMO
Kacy Hassack, Chief People Officer
Gil Vega, Chief Information Security Officer
Nate Kurtz, CIO

FINANCIAL DATA:
Note: Data for latest year may not have been available at press time.

In U.S. $	2022	2021	2020	2019	2018	2017
Revenue						
R&D Expense						
Operating Income						
Operating Margin %						
SGA Expense						
Net Income						
Operating Cash Flow						
Capital Expenditure						
EBITDA						
Return on Assets %						
Return on Equity %						
Debt to Equity						

CONTACT INFORMATION:

Phone: 41 41-766-71-31   Fax:
Toll-Free: 800-691-1991
Address: Lindenstrasse 16, Baar, Zug 43240 Switzerland

STOCK TICKER/OTHER:

Stock Ticker: Private   Exchange:
Employees: 4,500   Fiscal Year Ends:
Parent Company: Insight Partners

SALARIES/BONUSES:

Top Exec. Salary: $ Bonus: $
Second Exec. Salary: $ Bonus: $

OTHER THOUGHTS:

Estimated Female Officers or Directors:
Hot Spot for Advancement for Women/Minorities:

Sales, profits and employees may be estimates. Financial information, benefits and other data can change quickly and may vary from those stated here.

Veepee

www.veepee.com

NAIC Code: 454110

TYPES OF BUSINESS:

Electronic Shopping
Ecommerce
Flash Sales
Online Payments Solution
Product Delivery Solutions
Return and Refund Services
Ecommerce Platform Technology

BRANDS/DIVISIONS/AFFILIATES:

vente-privee
privalia
vente-exclusive
zlotewyprzedaze
e-boutich
designer & friends

GROWTH PLANS/SPECIAL FEATURES:

Veepee is an international ecommerce company that specializes in the flash sales industry. Flash sales are products sold at greatly reduced prices, with the sale lasting for only a short period of time. Veepeesale owns several trademarked brands, including vente-privee, privalia, vente-exclusive, zlotewyprzedaze, e-boutich, and designers & friends. These ecommerce brands offer a wide range of products such as apparel, accessories, music, homewares, wine, toys, sports equipment, high-tech devices and more. Payment solutions are provided on the platforms, as well as delivery information, after-sales service, returns and refunds. The retailer's online and mobile platform operates in France, Germany, Italy, England, Spain, Austria, Switzerland, Poland, Denmark, Belgium, Luxembourg and the Netherlands.

CONTACTS:
Note: Officers with more than one job title may be intentionally listed here more than once.

Jacques-Antoine Granjon, CEO
Timothy Quinn, VP-Finance
Katherine Wu Brady, CEO-Vente-Privee USA LLC

FINANCIAL DATA:
Note: Data for latest year may not have been available at press time.

In U.S. $	2022	2021	2020	2019	2018	2017
Revenue	3,842,964,000	3,421,280,000	3,856,875,750	3,955,770,000	3,767,400,000	3,588,000,000
R&D Expense						
Operating Income						
Operating Margin %						
SGA Expense						
Net Income						
Operating Cash Flow						
Capital Expenditure						
EBITDA						
Return on Assets %						
Return on Equity %						
Debt to Equity						

CONTACT INFORMATION:

Phone: 4141-766   Fax:
Toll-Free: 877-453-3909
Address: 249 Avenue du President Wilson, Saint-Denis, 93210 France

STOCK TICKER/OTHER:

Stock Ticker: Private   Exchange:
Employees: 5,500   Fiscal Year Ends: 12/31
Parent Company:

SALARIES/BONUSES:

Top Exec. Salary: $ Bonus: $
Second Exec. Salary: $ Bonus: $

OTHER THOUGHTS:

Estimated Female Officers or Directors: 2
Hot Spot for Advancement for Women/Minorities:

Veon Ltd

NAIC Code: 517312

TYPES OF BUSINESS:

Cell Phone Service
Wireless Internet Service
IPTV
Fixed-Line Telephony
Digital

BRANDS/DIVISIONS/AFFILIATES:

Veon
Beeline
Kyivstar
banglalink
Jazz
Djezzy

GROWTH PLANS/SPECIAL FEATURES:

VEON Ltd is a global provider of connectivity and internet services. The company provides its customers with voice, fixed broadband, data, and digital services. Currently, the company offers services to customers in the following countries: Pakistan, Ukraine, Kazakhstan, Bangladesh, Uzbekistan, and Kyrgyzstan. The reportable segments currently consist of the following five segments: Pakistan, Ukraine, Kazakhstan, Bangladesh, and Uzbekistan. The company provides services under the Beeline, Kyivstar, banglalink and Jazz brands.

CONTACTS: Note: Officers with more than one job title may be intentionally listed here more than once.

Sergi Herrero, Co-CEO
Kaan Terzioglu, Co-CEO
Serkan Okandan, CFO
Jeffrey D. McGhie, General Counsel
Dmitry G. Kromsky, Head-CIS Bus. Unit
Anton Kudryashov, Head-Russia Bus. Unit
Ahmed Abou Doma, Head-Africa & Asia Bus. Unit
Romano Righetti, Group Chief Regulatory Officer
Gennady Gazin, Chmn.
Maximo Ibarra, Head-Italy

FINANCIAL DATA: Note: Data for latest year may not have been available at press time.

In U.S. $	2022	2021	2020	2019	2018	2017
Revenue	3,755,000,000	3,850,000,000	3,482,000,000	8,089,000,000	9,086,000,000	9,474,000,000
R&D Expense						
Operating Income	997,000,000	1,055,000,000	917,000,000	2,070,000,000	1,501,000,000	1,618,000,000
Operating Margin %		.19%	.20%	.26%	.17%	.17%
SGA Expense	1,475,000,000	1,462,000,000	1,360,000,000	2,529,000,000	3,418,000,000	3,470,000,000
Net Income	-162,000,000	674,000,000	-349,000,000	621,000,000	582,000,000	-505,000,000
Operating Cash Flow	2,557,000,000	2,638,000,000	2,443,000,000	2,948,000,000	2,515,000,000	2,475,000,000
Capital Expenditure	1,010,000,000	858,000,000	682,000,000	1,582,000,000	1,948,000,000	2,037,000,000
EBITDA	2,163,000,000	1,881,000,000	1,734,000,000	3,873,000,000	3,260,000,000	3,357,000,000
Return on Assets %		.04%	- .02%	.04%	.03%	- .02%
Return on Equity %		1.80%	- .50%	.25%	.15%	- .10%
Debt to Equity		16.05%	54.184	6.329	1.79%	2.393

CONTACT INFORMATION:

Phone: 31 207977200   Fax: 31 207977201
Toll-Free:
Address: Claude Debussylaan 88, Amsterdam, 1082 MD Netherlands

STOCK TICKER/OTHER:

Stock Ticker: VEON   Exchange: NAS
Employees: 16,422   Fiscal Year Ends: 12/31
Parent Company:

SALARIES/BONUSES:

Top Exec. Salary: $6,155,568   Bonus: $6,124,678
Second Exec. Salary: Bonus: $4,215,842
$1,398,993

OTHER THOUGHTS:

Estimated Female Officers or Directors: 1
Hot Spot for Advancement for Women/Minorities:

Veracode Inc

www.veracode.com

NAIC Code: 511210E

TYPES OF BUSINESS:

Computer Software: Network Security, Managed Access, Digital ID,
Cybersecurity & Anti-Virus
Security Software
Cloud Solutions
Application Security Solutions
Web and Mobile Application Creation
Automation Solutions
Technical Support Services
Security Testing Solutions

BRANDS/DIVISIONS/AFFILIATES:

Thoma Bravo LP

CONTACTS: Note: Officers with more than one job title may be intentionally listed here more than once.

Sam King, CEO
Brian Roche, Chief Product Officer
David Forlizzi, CFO
Alexandra Gobbi, CMO
Alison Bayiates, Chief People Officer
Chris Wysopal, CTO

GROWTH PLANS/SPECIAL FEATURES:

Veracode, Inc. provides cloud-based application security software solutions and services. The company's unified platform enables organizations to assess and improve the security of applications from inception through production. By doing so, these organizations can confidently innovate with the web and mobile applications they build, buy and assemble, as well as the components they integrate into their environments. Veracode is comprised of a powerful combination of automation, process and speed, and seamlessly integrates application security into software development. Without the need for additional staff or equipment, Veracode customers connect quickly, see results and prove value on day one, and consistently see improvement over time. The company's services include application security consulting, technical support, manual penetration testing, developer training, security program management, customer success packages and DevOps penetration test. Products by the firm include an application security platform, static analysis, software composition analysis, dynamic analysis, vendor application security testing and developer training. Veracode's corporate headquarters are in Massachusetts, USA, and its EMEA headquarters are located in London, UK. The firm is a subsidiary of Thoma Bravo LP, a leading private equity investment firm.

FINANCIAL DATA: Note: Data for latest year may not have been available at press time.

In U.S. $	2022	2021	2020	2019	2018	2017
Revenue						
R&D Expense						
Operating Income						
Operating Margin %						
SGA Expense						
Net Income						
Operating Cash Flow						
Capital Expenditure						
EBITDA						
Return on Assets %						
Return on Equity %						
Debt to Equity						

CONTACT INFORMATION:

Phone: 339-674-2500   Fax: 339-674-2502
Toll-Free:
Address: 65 Blue Sky Dr., Burlington, MA 01803 United States

STOCK TICKER/OTHER:

Stock Ticker: Private   Exchange:
Employees: 550   Fiscal Year Ends:
Parent Company: Thoma Bravo LP

SALARIES/BONUSES:

Top Exec. Salary: $ Bonus: $
Second Exec. Salary: $ Bonus: $

OTHER THOUGHTS:

Estimated Female Officers or Directors: 2
Hot Spot for Advancement for Women/Minorities: Y

Sales, profits and employees may be estimates. Financial information, benefits and other data can change quickly and may vary from those stated here.

VeriFone Inc

www.verifone.com

NAIC Code: 522320

TYPES OF BUSINESS:

Payment & Transaction Processing
Electronic Payment Device Solutions
Electronic Payment Technologies
Point of Sale Payment Systems
Software and Cloud-Based Solutions
Unattended POS Solutions
Digital Commerce and Ecommerce
Managed Services

BRANDS/DIVISIONS/AFFILIATES:

Francisco Partners
British Columbia Investment Management Corporation

CONTACTS: *Note: Officers with more than one job title may be intentionally listed here more than once.*

Himanshu Patel, CEO
Tom Weikart, Exec. VP- Global Operations
John Tracy, CFO
Peyton O'Connor, Exec. VP-Human Resources
Bruce Gureck, Exec. VP-Engineering & Product
Alex Hart, Director
Glen Robson, Executive VP, Divisional
Vin D'Agostino, Executive VP

GROWTH PLANS/SPECIAL FEATURES:

VeriFone, Inc. designs and markets electronic payment technologies and services. The firm focuses on point of sale (POS) payment systems, making it easier for brands to create their customer journeys through software applications with business needs and consumer lifestyles in mind. VeriFone connects merchants through its cloud-based suite of services. Industry solutions include retail, hospitality, banking, petroleum & convenience, transportation & travel, digital, acquiring, vending and ticketing. The firm's products include platforms and enhancements. Platforms offered include payment devices, global ecommerce, payment processing, omnichannel, acquiring services and managed services. Enhancements provided include payment gateway, device management, hosted checkout, advanced payment methods, fraud management/compliance, tokenization, reporting & analytics, subscription billing and self-service onboarding. VeriFone is owned by Francisco Partners and British Columbia Investment Management Corporation (BCI).

VeriFone offers its employees health and wellness benefits, retirement and income protection benefits, career planning opportunities and other employee plans and programs.

FINANCIAL DATA: *Note: Data for latest year may not have been available at press time.*

In U.S. $	2022	2021	2020	2019	2018	2017
Revenue	1,800,000,000	1,801,689,081	1,637,899,165	1,688,555,840	1,777,427,200	1,870,976,000
R&D Expense						
Operating Income						
Operating Margin %						
SGA Expense						
Net Income						
Operating Cash Flow						
Capital Expenditure						
EBITDA						
Return on Assets %						
Return on Equity %						
Debt to Equity						

CONTACT INFORMATION:

Phone: 408 232-7800   Fax: 408 232-7811
Toll-Free: 800-837-4366
Address: 2744 N. University Dr., Coral Springs, FL 33065 United States

STOCK TICKER/OTHER:

Stock Ticker: Private   Exchange:
Employees: 6,000   Fiscal Year Ends: 10/31
Parent Company: Francisco Partners

SALARIES/BONUSES:

Top Exec. Salary: $ Bonus: $
Second Exec. Salary: $ Bonus: $

OTHER THOUGHTS:

Estimated Female Officers or Directors: 2
Hot Spot for Advancement for Women/Minorities: Y

Verio Inc

NAIC Code: 517312

TYPES OF BUSINESS:
Internet Service Provider
Domain Name Registration
Website Hosting
Domain Extensions
Website Management Services
Ecommerce Services
Marketing Services
Data Centers

BRANDS/DIVISIONS/AFFILIATES:
Nippon Telegraph and Telephone Corporation (NTT)
NTT Communications

CONTACTS: *Note: Officers with more than one job title may be intentionally listed here more than once.*
Hideyuki Yamasawa, CEO
Fred Martin, Sr. VP-Oper.
Tomoyuki Sakae, VP-Corp. Svcs.
William Gunther, VP-Systems Dev. & Architecture
Fred Martin, Sr. VP-Customer Service
Fred White, VP-Product Mgmt.
Wataru Imajuku, VP-Global Service Dev. & Japanese Sales

GROWTH PLANS/SPECIAL FEATURES:
Verio, Inc. offers shared website hosting solutions, domain name registration, virtual private server (VPS) hosting and other online services to individuals and small-to-medium-sized businesses. The company's hosting plans include free site-building software, as well as access to more than 200 other tools and services. Domain name registrations have hundreds of new domains available, as well as pre-registration services for soon-to-be-released domain extensions. Domain name Trademark capabilities are also available. Verio offers secure customer data and payments with SSL Certificates to enhance customer confidence from the business' website, to help boost Google rankings and utilizing encryption at lower costs. Email services through Microsoft offers businesses the latest in business-class email management and collaboration, including email, calendar, contact and task management from anywhere, any time. Verio's marketing services provide solutions for generating more traffic to the business' website, including design services, marketing services, Google Workspace, search engine optimization, search engine marketing, email marketing and more. Marketing strategies include website, advertising and website traffic management and analytics. As of March 2024, Verio is partnering with Web.com to offer website, ecommerce and online marketing solutions. Verio operates as a wholly-owned subsidiary of NTT Communications, which itself is a subsidiary of Nippon Telegraph and Telephone Corporation.

FINANCIAL DATA: *Note: Data for latest year may not have been available at press time.*

In U.S. $	2022	2021	2020	2019	2018	2017
Revenue						
R&D Expense						
Operating Income						
Operating Margin %						
SGA Expense						
Net Income						
Operating Cash Flow						
Capital Expenditure						
EBITDA						
Return on Assets %						
Return on Equity %						
Debt to Equity						

CONTACT INFORMATION:
Phone: 855 765-0425   Fax:
Toll-Free:
Address: 5335 Gate Pkwy., Fl. 2, Jacksonville, FL 32256 United States

STOCK TICKER/OTHER:
Stock Ticker: Subsidiary   Exchange:
Employees: 2,000   Fiscal Year Ends: 03/31
Parent Company: Nippon Telegraph and Telephone Corporation (NTT)

SALARIES/BONUSES:
Top Exec. Salary: $ Bonus: $
Second Exec. Salary: $ Bonus: $

OTHER THOUGHTS:
Estimated Female Officers or Directors:
Hot Spot for Advancement for Women/Minorities:

VeriSign Inc

www.verisigninc.com

NAIC Code: 511210E

TYPES OF BUSINESS:

Computer Software: Network Security, Managed Access, Digital ID,
Cybersecurity & Anti-Virus
Domain Name Registration

BRANDS/DIVISIONS/AFFILIATES:

Registry Services
Security Services

GROWTH PLANS/SPECIAL FEATURES:

Verisign is the sole authorized registry for several generic top-level domains, including the widely utilized .com and .net top-level domains. The company operates critical internet infrastructure to support the domain name system, including operating two of the world's 13 root servers that are used to route internet traffic. In 2018, the firm sold off its Security Services business, signaling a renewed focus on the core registry business.

Employees of VeriSign receive a flexible benefits package that includes health, dental, vision, disability and life insurance; flexible spending accounts; a 401(k); an employee assistance program; a group legal plan; domestic partner coverage; tuition ass

CONTACTS: Note: Officers with more than one job title may be intentionally listed here more than once.

D. Bidzos, CEO
George Kilguss, CFO
Todd Strubbe, COO
Thomas Indelicarto, Executive VP

FINANCIAL DATA: Note: Data for latest year may not have been available at press time.

In U.S. $	2022	2021	2020	2019	2018	2017
Revenue	1,424,900,000	1,327,600,000	1,265,052,000	1,231,661,000	1,214,969,000	
R&D Expense	85,700,000	80,500,000	74,671,000	60,805,000	57,884,000	
Operating Income	943,100,000	866,800,000	824,201,000	806,127,000	767,392,000	
Operating Margin %	.66%	.65%	.65%	.65%	.63%	
SGA Expense	195,400,000	188,400,000	186,003,000	184,262,000	197,559,000	
Net Income	673,800,000	784,800,000	814,888,000	612,299,000	582,489,000	
Operating Cash Flow	831,100,000	807,200,000	730,183,000	753,892,000	697,767,000	
Capital Expenditure	27,400,000	53,000,000	43,395,000	40,316,000	37,007,000	
EBITDA	1,002,400,000	913,400,000	886,740,000	895,717,000	889,197,000	
Return on Assets %	.36%	.42%	.45%	.32%	.24%	
Return on Equity %						
Debt to Equity						

CONTACT INFORMATION:

Phone: 703 948-3200 Fax:
Toll-Free: 800-922-4917
Address: 12061 Bluemont Way, Reston, VA 20190 United States

STOCK TICKER/OTHER:

Stock Ticker: VRSN Exchange: NAS
Employees: 917 Fiscal Year Ends: 12/31
Parent Company:

SALARIES/BONUSES:

Top Exec. Salary: $946,154 Bonus: $
Second Exec. Salary: $587,692 Bonus: $

OTHER THOUGHTS:

Estimated Female Officers or Directors:
Hot Spot for Advancement for Women/Minorities:

Verizon Communications Inc

www.verizon.com

NAIC Code: 517312

TYPES OF BUSINESS:

Mobile Phone and Wireless Services
Communications Services
Mobile Services
Home Services
Business Services
Network Technologies
Wireless
Wireline

BRANDS/DIVISIONS/AFFILIATES:

Verizon Consumer Group
Verizon Business Group
Verizon Fios

GROWTH PLANS/SPECIAL FEATURES:

Wireless services account for about 70% of Verizon Communications' total service revenue and nearly all of its operating income. The firm serves about 93 million postpaid and 21 million prepaid phone customers (following the acquisition of Tracfone) via its nationwide network, making it the largest U.S. wireless carrier. Fixed-line telecom operations include local networks in the Northeast, which reach about 25 million homes and businesses and serve about 8 million broadband customers. Verizon also provides telecom services nationwide to enterprise customers, often using a mixture of its own and other carriers' networks.

Verizon offers comprehensive employee benefits.

CONTACTS: Note: Officers with more than one job title may be intentionally listed here more than once.

Ronan Dunne, CEO, Divisional
Tami Erwin, CEO, Divisional
Hans Vestberg, CEO
Matthew Ellis, CFO
Anthony Skiadas, Chief Accounting Officer
Craig Silliman, Chief Administrative Officer
Rima Qureshi, Chief Strategy Officer
Kyle Malady, Chief Technology Officer
Christine Pambianchi, Executive VP

FINANCIAL DATA: Note: Data for latest year may not have been available at press time.

In U.S. $	2022	2021	2020	2019	2018	2017
Revenue	136,835,000,000	133,613,000,000	128,292,000,000	131,868,000,000	130,863,000,000	
R&D Expense						
Operating Income	30,467,000,000	32,448,000,000	28,798,000,000	30,564,000,000	26,869,000,000	
Operating Margin %	.22%	.24%	.22%	.23%	.21%	
SGA Expense	30,136,000,000	28,658,000,000	31,573,000,000	29,896,000,000	31,083,000,000	
Net Income	21,256,000,000	22,065,000,000	17,801,000,000	19,265,000,000	15,528,000,000	
Operating Cash Flow	37,141,000,000	39,539,000,000	41,768,000,000	35,746,000,000	34,339,000,000	
Capital Expenditure	26,740,000,000	67,882,000,000	22,088,000,000	18,837,000,000	18,087,000,000	
EBITDA	48,983,000,000	49,111,000,000	44,934,000,000	44,145,000,000	41,859,000,000	
Return on Assets %	.06%	.06%	.06%	.07%	.06%	
Return on Equity %	.25%	.29%	.28%	.34%	.32%	
Debt to Equity	1.78%	2.04%	2.081	1.94	1.99%	

CONTACT INFORMATION:

Phone: 212 395-1000   Fax:
Toll-Free: 800-837-4966
Address: 1095 Avenue of the Americas, New York, NY 10036 United States

STOCK TICKER/OTHER:

Stock Ticker: VZ   Exchange: NYS
Employees: 117,100   Fiscal Year Ends: 12/31
Parent Company:

SALARIES/BONUSES:

Top Exec. Salary: $1,500,000   Bonus: $
Second Exec. Salary: $950,000   Bonus: $

OTHER THOUGHTS:

Estimated Female Officers or Directors: 5
Hot Spot for Advancement for Women/Minorities: Y

Sales, profits and employees may be estimates. Financial information, benefits and other data can change quickly and may vary from those stated here.

VerticalResponse Inc

www.verticalresponse.com

NAIC Code: 541810E

TYPES OF BUSINESS:

Direct Marketing Software
Email & Postcard Marketing
Email Management
Design Services
Survey Creation and Management
Marketing Software Solutions

BRANDS/DIVISIONS/AFFILIATES:

Deluxe Corporation

CONTACTS: *Note: Officers with more than one job title may be intentionally listed here more than once.*

Andy Mentges, CEO
Janine Popick, Pres.
David Williams, Sr. VP-Prod. & Mktg.
Joshua Feinberg, VP-Platform Mgmt.

GROWTH PLANS/SPECIAL FEATURES:

VerticalResponse, Inc. provides self-service email and social media marketing software solutions designed for reaching customers. The company's solutions enable users to create, send and track emails and social posts that look professional across every device. Customizable templates are provided, with easy drag-and-drop editor features. Text, images, brand colors, logos and social buttons can be added to create attractive emails. Website visitors can be turned into email subscribers through VerticalResponse tools such as adding a sign-up form to websites or sharing a link on social media. Other features include automated follow-up emails, advanced analytics reporting, landing page builder, A/B subject line testing, test kits for nearly 60 different devices, surveys and more. VerticalResponse offers a free, 60-day trial period with no commitment. Email marketing plans include Basic, for $11 a month; and Pro at $16/month. Prices are subject to change based on a customer's email list size. VerticalResponse also offers an email pay-as-you-go option. Survey plans include a free plan that never expires and includes core features such as surveys with up to 10 questions each, up to 100 respondents and basic reporting/analytics; and Basic, for $19 a month that allows for unlimited asked questions and responses, removes VerticalResponse branding, can randomize questions and incorporate skip logic. VerticalResponse provides free articles and webinars on its website, and offers businesses marketing advice and strategies on its blog. The firm is a subsidiary of Deluxe Corporation.

VerticalResponse offers its employees comprehensive benefits, short- and long-term disability, life insurance, a 401(k), learning and development opportunities, personal discounts and other company plans, programs and perks.

FINANCIAL DATA: *Note: Data for latest year may not have been available at press time.*

In U.S. $	2022	2021	2020	2019	2018	2017
Revenue						
R&D Expense						
Operating Income						
Operating Margin %						
SGA Expense						
Net Income						
Operating Cash Flow						
Capital Expenditure						
EBITDA						
Return on Assets %						
Return on Equity %						
Debt to Equity						

CONTACT INFORMATION:

Phone: Fax:
Toll-Free: 866-683-7842
Address: 111 2nd Ave. NE, Ste. 1500, St. Petersburg, FL 33701 United States

STOCK TICKER/OTHER:

Stock Ticker: Subsidiary
Employees: 120
Parent Company: Deluxe Corporation

Exchange:
Fiscal Year Ends: 12/31

SALARIES/BONUSES:

Top Exec. Salary: $ Bonus: $
Second Exec. Salary: $ Bonus: $

OTHER THOUGHTS:

Estimated Female Officers or Directors:
Hot Spot for Advancement for Women/Minorities:

Sales, profits and employees may be estimates. Financial information, benefits and other data can change quickly and may vary from those stated here.

viagogo Entertainment Inc

www.viagogo.com

NAIC Code: 561599

TYPES OF BUSINESS:

Ticket Agency
Ticket Re-sale Platform
Online Website
Mobile App
Live Event Tickets
Payment Technology
Ticket Transfer

BRANDS/DIVISIONS/AFFILIATES:

StubHub Holdings

GROWTH PLANS/SPECIAL FEATURES:

Viagogo Entertainment, Inc. operates a global online platform, viagogo, for selling and purchasing tickets to live sport, music and entertainment events throughout the world. On the viagogo website or mobile app, users search for tickets either by entering the name of an event, a venue or preferred city. Prices are set by sellers and may either be below or above face value, and purchases span many global currencies. The viagogo platform helps ticket sellers ranging from individuals with a spare ticket to large multi-national event organizers aiming to reach a global audience. viagogo delivers the tickets to any country in the world. viagogo is owned by StubHub Holdings, which also owns the StubHub ticket exchange and resale platform.

CONTACTS: *Note: Officers with more than one job title may be intentionally listed here more than once.*

Eric Baker, CEO

FINANCIAL DATA: *Note: Data for latest year may not have been available at press time.*

In U.S. $	2022	2021	2020	2019	2018	2017
Revenue						
R&D Expense						
Operating Income						
Operating Margin %						
SGA Expense						
Net Income						
Operating Cash Flow						
Capital Expenditure						
EBITDA						
Return on Assets %						
Return on Equity %						
Debt to Equity						

CONTACT INFORMATION:

Phone: 866-961-3071   Fax:
Toll-Free:
Address: 160 Greentree Dr., Ste. 101, Dover, DE 19904 United States

STOCK TICKER/OTHER:

Stock Ticker: Private   Exchange:
Employees: Fiscal Year Ends:
Parent Company: StubHub Holdings

SALARIES/BONUSES:

Top Exec. Salary: $ Bonus: $
Second Exec. Salary: $ Bonus: $

OTHER THOUGHTS:

Estimated Female Officers or Directors:
Hot Spot for Advancement for Women/Minorities:

Vibrant Media Inc

www.vibrantmedia.com

NAIC Code: 541810E

TYPES OF BUSINESS:

Online Advertising
Advertising Solutions
Contextual Advertising
Digital Advertising Solutions
Standard and Custom Context Ads
Audience Targeting
Interactive Advertising Bureau Displays
Editorial Advertising Content Solutions

BRANDS/DIVISIONS/AFFILIATES:

Quintesse

CONTACTS: *Note: Officers with more than one job title may be intentionally listed here more than once.*

Doug Stevenson, CEO
Jeff Babka, Chief Admin. Officer
Julie R. Fenster, VP-Corp. Counsel
Brian White, Sr. VP-Publisher Solutions & Ad Oper.
Ariff Quli, Sr. VP-Sales Oper. & Global Accounts
Nicole Stein, Sr. VP-Sales, East Region
Will Kunkel, VP-Global Creative

GROWTH PLANS/SPECIAL FEATURES:

Vibrant Media, Inc. develops and offers contextual advertising services. The company's digital solutions are delivered across devices. For advertisers, Vibrant's contextual technology enables advertisers and agencies to deliver brand experiences relevant to people in real-time. Through its exclusive contextual network and precise targeting across the global bidstream, the firm's Quintesse demand side platform addresses the full range of agencies and marketers' privacy-safe contextual data and advertising needs. Targeting options include standard or custom context, topic-based or search-intent audience targeting. Creative options include interactive advertising bureau (IAB) display, rich media, video and native; and activation occurs through a critical path method (CPM) via direct IO or programmatic techniques. For publishers, Vibrant Media offers revenue solutions through existing text and image editorial content. Publishers would have control to select and block certain sections, pages and content areas; to sell inventory on a blind bases via key words and verticals; to avoid monetizing inappropriate content; to maximize the number of links and/or ads per page; to customize the look and feel of in-text hyperlinks; and to block certain advertisers. Vibrant Media uses natural language processing (NLP) and computational linguistics to offer content so that brands can scale campaigns using inventory from across the global bidstream, uniquely relevant to their messaging. Headquartered in New York City, the firm has additional offices in San Francisco, Chicago, London, Hamburg and Dusseldorf.

FINANCIAL DATA: *Note: Data for latest year may not have been available at press time.*

In U.S. $	2022	2021	2020	2019	2018	2017
Revenue						
R&D Expense						
Operating Income						
Operating Margin %						
SGA Expense						
Net Income						
Operating Cash Flow						
Capital Expenditure						
EBITDA						
Return on Assets %						
Return on Equity %						
Debt to Equity						

CONTACT INFORMATION:

Phone: 646-312-6100   Fax:
Toll-Free:
Address: 300 Park Ave., Fl. 12, New York, NY 10022 United States

STOCK TICKER/OTHER:

Stock Ticker: Private   Exchange:
Employees: 209   Fiscal Year Ends: 12/31
Parent Company:

SALARIES/BONUSES:

Top Exec. Salary: $ Bonus: $
Second Exec. Salary: $ Bonus: $

OTHER THOUGHTS:

Estimated Female Officers or Directors: 3
Hot Spot for Advancement for Women/Minorities: Y

Vimeo Inc

www.vimeo.com

NAIC Code: 519130

TYPES OF BUSINESS:
Online Video Sharing Services
Online Sharing
For Hire Marketplace
Enterprise Video Sharing
User Creations
Video Sharing Instruction

BRANDS/DIVISIONS/AFFILIATES:
IAC/InterActiveCorp
Vimeo Enterprise
Vimeo Create

GROWTH PLANS/SPECIAL FEATURES:
Vimeo Inc is the all-in-one video software solution, providing the full breadth of video tools through a software-as-a-service model. The company's comprehensive and cloud-based tools empower its users to create, collaborate and communicate with video on a single, turnkey platform. The company derives its revenue from SaaS subscription fees paid by customers for subscription plans.

Vimeo offers its employees medical and dental benefits, 401(k), tuition reimbursement and a variety of employee assistance plans.

CONTACTS:
Note: Officers with more than one job title may be intentionally listed here more than once.

Anjali Sud, CEO
Narayan Menon, CFO
Joseph Levin, Chairman of the Board
Harris Beber, Chief Marketing Officer
Courtney Sanchez, COO
Michael Cheah, General Counsel
Kathleen Barrett, Other Corporate Officer
Mark Kornfilt, Other Executive Officer
Josh Normand, Senior VP, Divisional

FINANCIAL DATA:
Note: Data for latest year may not have been available at press time.

In U.S. $	2022	2021	2020	2019	2018	2017
Revenue	433,028,000	391,678,000	283,218,000	196,015,000		
R&D Expense	127,661,000	105,586,000	64,238,000	46,946,000		
Operating Income	-82,938,000	-61,016,000	-40,777,000	-60,253,000		
Operating Margin %	-.19%	-.16%	-.14%			
SGA Expense	277,412,000	237,802,000	155,476,000	121,526,000		
Net Income	-79,591,000	-52,767,000	-50,628,000	-75,577,000		
Operating Cash Flow	-37,071,000	15,954,000	13,861,000	-27,178,000		
Capital Expenditure	802,000	445,000	844,000	2,801,000		
EBITDA	-69,876,000	-44,006,000	-25,480,000	-56,563,000		
Return on Assets %	-.13%	-.10%	-.16%			
Return on Equity %	-.22%	-.23%	-.93%			
Debt to Equity			0.588			

CONTACT INFORMATION:
Phone: 212-314-7300   Fax:
Toll-Free:
Address: 555 W. 18th St., New York, NY 10011 United States

STOCK TICKER/OTHER:
Stock Ticker: VMEO   Exchange: NAS
Employees: 1,236   Fiscal Year Ends: 12/31
Parent Company:

SALARIES/BONUSES:
Top Exec. Salary: $600,000   Bonus: $300,000
Second Exec. Salary: $450,000   Bonus: $225,000

OTHER THOUGHTS:
Estimated Female Officers or Directors: 1
Hot Spot for Advancement for Women/Minorities:

Vipshop Holdings Limited

NAIC Code: 454110

ir.vip.com/investor-overview

TYPES OF BUSINESS:

Electronic Shopping

BRANDS/DIVISIONS/AFFILIATES:

vipshop.com
vip.com
lefeng.com

GROWTH PLANS/SPECIAL FEATURES:

Vipshop Holdings Ltd is an online discount retailer for brands in China. The company offers branded products to consumers in China through flash sales on its vipshop.com, vip.com and lefeng.com websites. Flash sales represent an online retail format combining the advantages of e-commerce and discount sales through selling a finite quantity of discounted products or services online for a limited period of time. It deals in wide range of products and services for consumers specializing in branded cosmetics, apparel, healthcare products, food and other consumer products. Its operating segment includes Vip.com and Shan Shan Outlets. The company generates maximum revenue from Vip.com segment.

CONTACTS: Note: Officers with more than one job title may be intentionally listed here more than once.

Eric Ya Shen, CEO
Arthur Xiaobo Hong, COO
David Cui, CFO
Yizhi Tang, Sr. VP-Logistics
Daniel Kao, CTO

FINANCIAL DATA: Note: Data for latest year may not have been available at press time.

In U.S. $	2022	2021	2020	2019	2018	2017
Revenue	14,185,080,000	16,097,530,000	14,007,140,000	12,788,190,000	11,623,360,000	10,026,580,000
R&D Expense						
Operating Income	824,378,300	743,536,400	786,407,600	681,424,300	318,944,800	360,490,800
Operating Margin %		.05%	.06%	.05%	.03%	.04%
SGA Expense	2,219,979,000	2,536,987,000	2,218,550,000	2,237,930,000	2,118,417,000	1,943,708,000
Net Income	866,185,700	643,720,800	812,298,900	552,377,200	292,741,500	268,108,000
Operating Cash Flow	1,446,622,000	927,494,000	1,625,496,000	1,690,092,000	790,130,200	134,937,400
Capital Expenditure	426,654,500	492,119,600	312,421,100	588,246,900	494,099,600	340,156,400
EBITDA	1,308,442,000	982,860,800	1,131,203,000	822,249,300	522,085,200	514,375,700
Return on Assets %		.08%	.11%	.09%	.05%	.06%
Return on Equity %		.15%	.23%	.21%	.13%	.19%
Debt to Equity		.03%	0.048	0.067		0.286

CONTACT INFORMATION:

Phone: 86 20-2233-0732   Fax:
Toll-Free:
Address: No. 20 Huahai St., Liwan Distr., Guangzhou, Guangdong 510370 China

STOCK TICKER/OTHER:

Stock Ticker: VIPS
Employees: 6,815
Parent Company:

Exchange: NYS
Fiscal Year Ends: 12/31

SALARIES/BONUSES:

Top Exec. Salary: $ Bonus: $
Second Exec. Salary: $ Bonus: $

OTHER THOUGHTS:

Estimated Female Officers or Directors:
Hot Spot for Advancement for Women/Minorities:

VitaCost.com Inc

www.vitacost.com

NAIC Code: 454110

TYPES OF BUSINESS:

Online Vitamin Sales
Ecommerce
Wellness Products
Vitamins
Supplements
Herbs and Botanicals
Diet Products
Health and Nutrition Information

BRANDS/DIVISIONS/AFFILIATES:

Kroger Company (The)
Vitacost
Synergy
ROOT2

GROWTH PLANS/SPECIAL FEATURES:

VitaCost.com, Inc., a subsidiary of The Kroger Company, is an online retailer and direct marketer of health and wellness products. The firm's foods and products are priced up to 50% lower than manufacturers' suggested retail prices. Product categories include vitamins, supplements, food and beverages, beauty and personal care, sports and fitness, herbs and botanicals, household and family essentials, diet products and professional supplements. VitaCost.com offers approximately 30,000 items from over 1,600 third-party brands. Vitacost.com also sells items under its own brand names, including: Vitacost everyday formulas, Synergy multivitamins and essential fatty acid supplementations (EFAS), and ROOT2 premium supplements. The company markets through its website, mobile app and direct mail catalogs. VitaCost.com operates a brick-and-mortar store in Las Vegas. Free eBooks are offered on VitaCost.com for those wanting to learn about specialty diets and health concerns, as well as related recipes.

CONTACTS: Note: Officers with more than one job title may be intentionally listed here more than once.

Jeffrey Horowitz, CEO
Mary L. Marbach, General Counsel
Kathleen M. Reed, Dir.-Investor Rel.

FINANCIAL DATA: Note: Data for latest year may not have been available at press time.

In U.S. $	2022	2021	2020	2019	2018	2017
Revenue	487,000,000	486,999,450	490,612,500	467,250,000	445,000,000	432,000,000
R&D Expense						
Operating Income						
Operating Margin %						
SGA Expense						
Net Income						
Operating Cash Flow						
Capital Expenditure						
EBITDA						
Return on Assets %						
Return on Equity %						
Debt to Equity						

CONTACT INFORMATION:

Phone: 561-982-4180   Fax:
Toll-Free: 1-800-381-0759
Address: 5400 Broken Sound Blvd. NW, Ste. 500, Boca Raton, FL 33487 United States

STOCK TICKER/OTHER:

Stock Ticker: Subsidiary   Exchange:
Employees: 800   Fiscal Year Ends: 12/31
Parent Company: Kroger Company (The)

SALARIES/BONUSES:

Top Exec. Salary: $ Bonus: $
Second Exec. Salary: $ Bonus: $

OTHER THOUGHTS:

Estimated Female Officers or Directors: 2
Hot Spot for Advancement for Women/Minorities: Y

VK Company Limited

NAIC Code: 519130

TYPES OF BUSINESS:

Internet Web Site Holding Company
Online Platform
Digital Services
Communication Solutions
Online Gaming
Ecommerce
Food Order and Delivery
Payment Solutions

BRANDS/DIVISIONS/AFFILIATES:

@mail.ru
am.ru
DonationAlerts
GeekBrains
maps.me
samokat
vatera.hu

GROWTH PLANS/SPECIAL FEATURES:

VK Company Limited is a Russian company that offers multiple services online through a single-user VK account. The VK ecosystem enables users to communicate, play online games, sell and purchase goods and services, order food, order a taxi, find a job or employees, receive professional training for new skills and obtain information about innovative developments and more. The VK platform is comprised of a voice assistant, universal user account, micro apps and payment solutions. For businesses, VK offers a range of digital solutions spanning business processes, from online promotion to cloud services. Just a few of the many brands within VK include @mail.ru, am.ru, DonationAlerts, GeekBrains, maps.me, samokat and vatera.hu.

CONTACTS: *Note: Officers with more than one job title may be intentionally listed here more than once.*

Vladimir Kiriyenko, CEO
Gregory Finger, Pres.
Verdi Israelian, Head-Russian Oper.

FINANCIAL DATA: *Note: Data for latest year may not have been available at press time.*

In U.S. $	2022	2021	2020	2019	2018	2017
Revenue	1,335,342,660	1,597,861,600	1,354,120,000	1,552,110,000	952,373,000	868,063,000
R&D Expense						
Operating Income						
Operating Margin %						
SGA Expense						
Net Income	-42,940,752	-207,866,482	-285,877,000	304,048,000	-116,163,000	39,557,500
Operating Cash Flow						
Capital Expenditure						
EBITDA						
Return on Assets %						
Return on Equity %						
Debt to Equity						

CONTACT INFORMATION:

Phone: 44-203-178-2601   Fax:
Toll-Free:
Address: Leningradsky Prospekt 39, Bldg 79, Moscow, 125167 Russia

STOCK TICKER/OTHER:

Stock Ticker: VKCO   Exchange: London
Employees: 10,000   Fiscal Year Ends: 12/31
Parent Company: USM Holdings

SALARIES/BONUSES:

Top Exec. Salary: $ Bonus: $
Second Exec. Salary: $ Bonus: $

OTHER THOUGHTS:

Estimated Female Officers or Directors:
Hot Spot for Advancement for Women/Minorities:

Vodafone Group plc

www.vodafone.com

NAIC Code: 517312

TYPES OF BUSINESS:
Cell Phone Service
Mobile Communications
Fixed Communications
Unified Communications
Cloud Hosting
Internet of Things
Carrier Services

BRANDS/DIVISIONS/AFFILIATES:
TPG Telecom

GROWTH PLANS/SPECIAL FEATURES:
Vodafone operates mobile and fixed-line networks and businesses in more than 20 countries. Its largest market is Germany, where it is the second mobile operator after Deutsche Telekom and owns a cable network after acquiring Kabel Deutschland in 2013 and Liberty Global Germany in 2019. In the U.K. and Italy, it acts as a mobile operator, while in Spain it offers converged services after the acquisition of cable operator Ono in 2014. Vodafone also has operations in several Central European and African countries, which combined represent around one third of revenue.

CONTACTS: *Note: Officers with more than one job title may be intentionally listed here more than once.*
Nick Read, CEO
Margherita Della Valle, CFO
Ahmed Essam, Chief Commercial Operations Officer
Leanne Wood, Chief Human Resources Officer
Johan Wibergh, Group Technology Officer
Rosemary Martin, General Counsel
Warren Finegold, Dir.-Strategy & Bus. Dev.
Matthew Kirk, Dir.-External Affairs
Morten Lundal, Chief Commercial Officer
Philipp Humm, CEO-Northern & Central Europe
Paulo Bertoluzzo, CEO-Southern Europe
Nick Jeffery, Dir-Group Enterprises
Gerard Kleisterlee, Chmn.
Nick Read, CEO-Asia-Pacific, Africa & Middle East Region

FINANCIAL DATA: *Note: Data for latest year may not have been available at press time.*

In U.S. $	2022	2021	2020	2019	2018	2017
Revenue	49,201,210,000	47,289,510,000	48,547,060,000	47,135,150,000	50,270,940,000	
R&D Expense						
Operating Income	6,460,492,000	5,849,525,000	9,659,974,000	4,379,317,000	5,274,180,000	
Operating Margin %	.13%	.12%	.20%	.09%	.10%	
SGA Expense	9,791,666,000	9,576,856,000	10,388,600,000	10,039,940,000	9,852,115,000	
Net Income	2,414,724,000	63,687,390	-993,091,500	-8,657,166,000	2,632,772,000	
Operating Cash Flow	19,517,490,000	18,582,690,000	18,759,710,000	14,011,230,000	14,680,480,000	
Capital Expenditure	9,779,792,000	9,326,424,000	8,209,197,000	8,798,575,000	8,811,528,000	
EBITDA	21,978,630,000	22,675,950,000	18,895,720,000	9,493,738,000	16,719,560,000	
Return on Assets %	.01%	.00%	-.01%	-.06%	.02%	
Return on Equity %	.04%	.00%	-.01%	-.12%	.03%	
Debt to Equity	1.06%	1.06%	1.025	0.782	.49%	

CONTACT INFORMATION:
Phone: 44 163533251   Fax: 44 1635238080
Toll-Free:
Address: Vodafone House, The Connection, Newbury, Berkshire RG14 2FN United Kingdom

STOCK TICKER/OTHER:
Stock Ticker: VOD   Exchange: NAS
Employees: 98,103   Fiscal Year Ends: 03/31
Parent Company:

SALARIES/BONUSES:
Top Exec. Salary: $1,017,420   Bonus: $1,522,343
Second Exec. Salary: $1,013,633   Bonus: $1,141,126

OTHER THOUGHTS:
Estimated Female Officers or Directors: 2
Hot Spot for Advancement for Women/Minorities: Y

Sales, profits and employees may be estimates. Financial information, benefits and other data can change quickly and may vary from those stated here.

Vonage Holdings Corp

www.vonage.com

NAIC Code: 517311

TYPES OF BUSINESS:

VOIP Telecommunications
Unified Communications
Cloud-based communications
VOIP Phone Systems
API Platforms

BRANDS/DIVISIONS/AFFILIATES:

CONTACTS: *Note: Officers with more than one job title may be intentionally listed here more than once.*

Rory Read, CEO
Jay Bellissimo, COO
Stephen Lasher, CFO
Joy Corso, CMO
Tracey Leahy, Chief People Officer
Joy Corso, Chief Marketing Officer
Sanjay Macwan, CIO
Jay Bellissimo, COO
Savinay Berry, Executive VP, Divisional
Susan Quackenbush, Other Executive Officer
Sanjay Macwan, Other Executive Officer
Omar Javaid, Other Executive Officer
Rodolpho Cardenuto, President, Divisional

GROWTH PLANS/SPECIAL FEATURES:

Vonage Holdings Corp is a North American technology company that provides cloud-based communication services to businesses and consumers. For businesses, the company provides unified communications (as a service), which consists of integrated voice, text, video, data, and mobile applications over Voice over Internet Protocol network. It also offers an API platform that allows consumers to integrate communication features into their own websites. Its reportable operating segments include Vonage Communications Platform and Consumer. For consumer service customers, there is a home telephone replacement service. This can include services such as voicemail, call waiting, and call forwarding. This service is delivered over the Internet. The company generates most of its revenue within the United States.

Vonage offers its employees many benefits, including comprehensive medical, dental & vision coverage, paid leave, tuition reimbursement, retirement plans, parental leave, auto, home & pet insurances, health savings accounts and more.

FINANCIAL DATA: *Note: Data for latest year may not have been available at press time.*

In U.S. $	2022	2021	2020	2019	2018	2017
Revenue	1,435,320,000	1,409,015,040	1,247,933,952	1,189,346,048	1,048,782,016	1,002,286,016
R&D Expense						
Operating Income						
Operating Margin %						
SGA Expense						
Net Income		-24,497,000	-36,212,000	-19,482,000	35,728,000	-33,933,000
Operating Cash Flow						
Capital Expenditure						
EBITDA						
Return on Assets %						
Return on Equity %						
Debt to Equity						

CONTACT INFORMATION:

Phone: 732 528-2600   Fax: 732 287-9119
Toll-Free: 800-980-1455
Address: 23 Main St., Holmdel, NJ 07733 United States

STOCK TICKER/OTHER:

Stock Ticker: Subsidiary   Exchange:
Employees: 2,100   Fiscal Year Ends: 12/31
Parent Company: LM Ericsson Telephone Company (Ericsson)

SALARIES/BONUSES:

Top Exec. Salary: $ Bonus: $
Second Exec. Salary: $ Bonus: $

OTHER THOUGHTS:

Estimated Female Officers or Directors: 1
Hot Spot for Advancement for Women/Minorities:

WalkMe Inc

NAIC Code: 511210K

TYPES OF BUSINESS:

Computer Software, Sales & Customer Relationship Management
Digital Adoption Platform
No-Code Software
Business Measurement
Business Analytics
Digital Transformation
New Business Process Solutions
Artificial Intelligence, Business Integrations

BRANDS/DIVISIONS/AFFILIATES:

WalkMe Ltd
WalkMe Digital Adoption Platform

CONTACTS: *Note: Officers with more than one job title may be intentionally listed here more than once.*

Dan Adika, CEO
Hagit Ynon, CFO
Adriel Sanchex, CMO
Chelsea Pyrzenskl, Chief People Officer
Michele Bettencourt, Chmn.

GROWTH PLANS/SPECIAL FEATURES:

WalkMe, Inc. offers the WalkMe Digital Adoption Platform (DAP), a no-code software platform that enables organizations to measure and act on data analytics. DAP provides business executives with visibility across the tech stack and the insights needed to ultimately maximize digital transformation strategies. Its dashboard management software displays system usage, user productivity, digital experience analytics, tracked events, funnels, session streaming and session playback. Its code-free editor proactively guides users to complete any business process across single or multiple applications via strategically placed and personalized content. Digital transformation implements digital technologies, which enables businesses to create new or modify existing business processes. The transformation can lead to new business models and revenue streams. Technology used by WalkMe artificial intelligence (AI), Deepui technology, omnichannel, integrations, enterprise-grade security. Solutions span industries such as telecommunications, retail/ecommerce, public sector, banking & financial institutions, healthcare institutions. WalkMe is the U.S. subsidiary of WalkMe Ltd., based in Israel.

FINANCIAL DATA: *Note: Data for latest year may not have been available at press time.*

In U.S. $	2022	2021	2020	2019	2018	2017
Revenue						
R&D Expense						
Operating Income						
Operating Margin %						
SGA Expense						
Net Income						
Operating Cash Flow						
Capital Expenditure						
EBITDA						
Return on Assets %						
Return on Equity %						
Debt to Equity						

CONTACT INFORMATION:

Phone: 415 830-8150   Fax:
Toll-Free: 855-492-5563
Address: 71 Stevenson St., Fl. 20, San Francisco, CA 94105 United States

STOCK TICKER/OTHER:

Stock Ticker: Subsidiary   Exchange:
Employees: 300   Fiscal Year Ends: 12/31
Parent Company: WalkMe Ltd

SALARIES/BONUSES:

Top Exec. Salary: $ Bonus: $
Second Exec. Salary: $ Bonus: $

OTHER THOUGHTS:

Estimated Female Officers or Directors: 2
Hot Spot for Advancement for Women/Minorities: Y

Walt Disney Company (The)

corporate.disney.go.com

TYPES OF BUSINESS:
Cable TV Networks, Broadcasting & Entertainment
Film Media
Television Media
Content Production and Distribution
Content Sales and Licensing
Theme Parks, Resorts & Cruise Lines
Book and Comic Book Publishing
Branded Merchandise

BRANDS/DIVISIONS/AFFILIATES:
Disney
ESPN
Freeform
National Geographic
A+E Television Networks
Disney+
Star+
Disney Cruise Line

CONTACTS: *Note: Officers with more than one job title may be intentionally listed here more than once.*
Robert Chapek, CEO
Christine Mccarthy, CFO
Robert Iger, Chairman of the Board
Brent Woodford, Executive VP, Divisional
Alan Braverman, General Counsel
Paul Richardson, Other Executive Officer
Zenia Mucha, Senior Executive VP, Divisional

GROWTH PLANS/SPECIAL FEATURES:
Disney operates in three global business segments: entertainment, sports, and experiences. Entertainment and experiences both benefit from franchises and characters the firm has created over the course of a century. Entertainment includes the ABC broadcast network, several cable television networks, and the Disney+ and Hulu streaming services. Within the segment, Disney also engages in movie and television production and distribution, with content licensed to movie theaters, other content providers, or, increasingly, kept in-house for use on Disney's own streaming platform and television networks. The sports segment houses ESPN and the ESPN+ streaming service. Experiences contains Disney's theme parks and vacation destinations, and also benefits from merchandise licensing.

FINANCIAL DATA: *Note: Data for latest year may not have been available at press time.*

In U.S. $	2022	2021	2020	2019	2018	2017
Revenue	82,722,000,000	67,418,000,000	65,388,000,000	69,607,000,000	59,434,000,000	
R&D Expense						
Operating Income	6,770,000,000	3,659,000,000	3,794,000,000	11,830,000,000	14,837,000,000	
Operating Margin %	.08%	.05%	.06%	.17%	.25%	
SGA Expense	16,388,000,000	13,517,000,000	12,369,000,000	11,549,000,000	8,860,000,000	
Net Income	3,145,000,000	1,995,000,000	-2,864,000,000	11,054,000,000	12,598,000,000	
Operating Cash Flow	6,010,000,000	5,567,000,000	7,618,000,000	6,606,000,000	14,295,000,000	
Capital Expenditure	4,943,000,000	3,578,000,000	4,022,000,000	4,876,000,000	4,465,000,000	
EBITDA	11,997,000,000	9,078,000,000	5,093,000,000	19,068,000,000	18,314,000,000	
Return on Assets %	.02%	.01%	- .01%	.08%	.13%	
Return on Equity %	.03%	.02%	- .03%	.16%	.28%	
Debt to Equity	.51%	.58%	0.668	0.429	.35%	

CONTACT INFORMATION:
Phone: 818 5601000   Fax:
Toll-Free:
Address: 500 S. Buena Vista St., Burbank, CA 91521 United States

STOCK TICKER/OTHER:
Stock Ticker: DIS   Exchange: NYS
Employees: 225,000   Fiscal Year Ends: 09/30
Parent Company:

SALARIES/BONUSES:
Top Exec. Salary: $489,500   Bonus: $2,750,000
Second Exec. Salary: Bonus: $2,000,000
$870,000

OTHER THOUGHTS:
Estimated Female Officers or Directors: 7
Hot Spot for Advancement for Women/Minorities: Y

Sales, profits and employees may be estimates. Financial information, benefits and other data can change quickly and may vary from those stated here.

Warby Parker Inc

www.warbyparker.com

NAIC Code: 446130

TYPES OF BUSINESS:

Eyeglasses Sales Online and Retail

GROWTH PLANS/SPECIAL FEATURES:

Warby Parker Inc is engaged in designing and developing designer prescription glasses and contacts to eye exams and vision tests. Brand that operates at the intersection of design, technology, healthcare, and social enterprise. The company primarily derives revenue from the sales of eyewear products, optical services, and accessories. The firm sells products and services through its stores, website, and mobile apps. Revenue generated from eyewear products includes the sales of prescription and non-prescription optical glasses and sunglasses, contact lenses, eyewear accessories, and expedited shipping charges.

BRANDS/DIVISIONS/AFFILIATES:

Warby Parker

CONTACTS: Note: Officers with more than one job title may be intentionally listed here more than once.

Steven Miller, CFO
Neil Blumenthal, Co-CEO
David Gilboa, Co-CEO

FINANCIAL DATA: Note: Data for latest year may not have been available at press time.

In U.S. $	2022	2021	2020	2019	2018	2017
Revenue	598,112,000	540,798,000	393,719,000	370,463,000		
R&D Expense						
Operating Income	-111,203,000	-143,661,000	-55,632,000	-1,663,000		
Operating Margin %	- .19%	- .27%	- .14%			
SGA Expense	452,265,000	461,410,000	287,567,000	224,771,000		
Net Income	-110,393,000	-144,271,000	-55,919,000			
Operating Cash Flow	10,370,000	-31,994,000	32,758,000	21,394,000		
Capital Expenditure	60,181,000	48,513,000	20,070,000	32,632,000		
EBITDA	-79,339,000	-122,110,000	-37,869,000	12,853,000		
Return on Assets %	- .22%	- .36%	- .18%			
Return on Equity %	- .39%	-3.58%				
Debt to Equity	.53%					

CONTACT INFORMATION:

Phone: 646-517-5223   Fax:
Toll-Free:
Address: 161 Ave. of the Americas, New York, NY 10013 United States

STOCK TICKER/OTHER:

Stock Ticker: WRBY   Exchange: NYS
Employees: 3,032   Fiscal Year Ends: 12/31
Parent Company:

SALARIES/BONUSES:

Top Exec. Salary: $500,000   Bonus: $
Second Exec. Salary: Bonus: $
$500,000

OTHER THOUGHTS:

Estimated Female Officers or Directors:
Hot Spot for Advancement for Women/Minorities:

WatchGuard Technologies Inc

www.watchguard.com

NAIC Code: 511210E

TYPES OF BUSINESS:

Computer Software: Network Security, Managed Access, Digital ID,
Cybersecurity & Anti-Virus
Firewall & VPN Appliances
Unified Cybersecurity Solutions
Network Security Solutions
Multi-Factor Authentication Solutions
Cloud Management Solutions
Wi-Fi Security Solutions
Endpoint Security Solutions

BRANDS/DIVISIONS/AFFILIATES:

Vector Capital

CONTACTS: *Note: Officers with more than one job title may be intentionally listed here more than once.*

Prakash Panjwani, CEO
Simon Yeo, Sr. VP-Operations
Katy Coffey, CFO
Michelle Welch, CMO
Shane Watkins, Sr. VP-Global Human Resources
Sin-Yaw Wang, VP-Eng.
Dave R. Taylor, VP-Corp. Strategy
Jon Bickford, VP-Sales, U.S.
Shari McLaren, VP-Customer Svcs. & Support
Philippe Ortodoro, VP-Sales, EMEA
Jack Waters, Sr. VP-Engineering
Scott Robertson, VP-Sales, Asia Pacific

GROWTH PLANS/SPECIAL FEATURES:

WatchGuard Technologies, Inc. develops and implements network security services, and is a global leader in unified cybersecurity. The company's Unified Security Platform is designed for managed service providers to deliver security that increases their business scale and velocity while also improving operational efficiency. WatchGuard's products and services are grouped into five categories: network security, offering security services, firewall appliances, cloud and virtual firewalls, network security management, and reporting and visibility; multi-factor authentication, including authentication service, cloud management, mobile app and hardware token; secure Wi-Fi, including wireless access points, Wi-Fi in the WatchGuard cloud, reporting and visibility, and tabletop Wi-Fi appliances; endpoint security, including protection and detection response, security modules, security operations center and DNS-level protection; and technology ecosystem, offering a wide range of product integrations for smart security purposes. The firm is majority owned by Vector Capital.

FINANCIAL DATA: *Note: Data for latest year may not have been available at press time.*

In U.S. $	2022	2021	2020	2019	2018	2017
Revenue						
R&D Expense						
Operating Income						
Operating Margin %						
SGA Expense						
Net Income						
Operating Cash Flow						
Capital Expenditure						
EBITDA						
Return on Assets %						
Return on Equity %						
Debt to Equity						

CONTACT INFORMATION:

Phone: 206 613-6600   Fax: 206-521-8342
Toll-Free: 800-734-9905
Address: 505 5th Ave. S., Ste. 500, Seattle, WA 98104 United States

STOCK TICKER/OTHER:

Stock Ticker: Private   Exchange:
Employees: 1,200   Fiscal Year Ends: 12/31
Parent Company: Vector Capital

SALARIES/BONUSES:

Top Exec. Salary: $ Bonus: $
Second Exec. Salary: $ Bonus: $

OTHER THOUGHTS:

Estimated Female Officers or Directors: 2
Hot Spot for Advancement for Women/Minorities: Y

Wayfair LLC

www.wayfair.com

NAIC Code: 454110

TYPES OF BUSINESS:

Online Furniture Store

GROWTH PLANS/SPECIAL FEATURES:

Wayfair engages in e-commerce in the United States (86% of 2022 sales), Canada, the United Kingdom, Germany, and Ireland. At the end of 2022, the firm offered more than 40 million products from more than 20,000 suppliers under the brands Wayfair, Joss & Main, AllModern, Birch Lane, and Perigold. Its offerings include furniture, everyday and seasonal decor, decorative accents, housewares, and other home goods. Wayfair was founded in 2002 and began trading publicly in 2014.

BRANDS/DIVISIONS/AFFILIATES:

CastleGate
Wayfair
Joss & Main
AllModern
Perigold
Birch Lane

CONTACTS: *Note: Officers with more than one job title may be intentionally listed here more than once.*

Niraj Shah, CEO
Michael Fleisher, CFO
James Miller, Chief Technology Officer
Steven Conine, Co-Chairman of the Board
Thomas Netzer, COO
Steve Oblak, Other Executive Officer

FINANCIAL DATA: *Note: Data for latest year may not have been available at press time.*

In U.S. $	2022	2021	2020	2019	2018	2017
Revenue	12,218,000,000	13,708,000,000	14,145,000,000	9,127,000,000	6,779,174,000	4,720,895,000
R&D Expense						
Operating Income	-1,314,000,000	-82,000,000	360,000,000	-930,000,000	-473,279,000	-235,453,000
Operating Margin %	-.11%	-.01%	.03%	-.10%	-.07%	-.05%
SGA Expense	4,098,000,000	3,393,000,000	3,242,000,000	2,720,000,000	1,799,956,000	1,184,760,000
Net Income	-1,331,000,000	-131,000,000	185,000,000	-985,000,000	-504,080,000	-244,614,000
Operating Cash Flow	-674,000,000	410,000,000	1,417,000,000	-197,000,000	84,861,000	33,634,000
Capital Expenditure	458,000,000	280,000,000	335,000,000	401,000,000	221,955,000	146,879,000
EBITDA	-921,000,000	224,000,000	637,000,000	-735,000,000	-349,941,000	-148,433,000
Return on Assets %	-.33%	-.03%	.05%	-.41%	-.32%	-.25%
Return on Equity %						-15.75%
Debt to Equity						

CONTACT INFORMATION:

Phone: 866-263-8325   Fax:
Toll-Free: 877-929-3247
Address: 4 Copley Pl., Fl. 7, Boston, MA 02116 United States

STOCK TICKER/OTHER:

Stock Ticker: W   Exchange: NYS
Employees: 15,745   Fiscal Year Ends: 12/31
Parent Company:

SALARIES/BONUSES:

Top Exec. Salary: $236,539   Bonus: $13,462
Second Exec. Salary: $236,539   Bonus: $13,462

OTHER THOUGHTS:

Estimated Female Officers or Directors: 5
Hot Spot for Advancement for Women/Minorities: Y

WebMD Health Corp

www.webmd.com

NAIC Code: 519130

TYPES OF BUSINESS:

Health Care Internet Portals
Health Information Platform
Online Health Solutions
Health Coaching
Health Professional Collaboration
Health Websites and Mobile Apps
Health Magazine

BRANDS/DIVISIONS/AFFILIATES:

KKR & Co Inc
Internet Brands Inc
WebMD.com
WebMD Health Services
WebMD Consumer
WebMD Professional
WebMD Magazine
Medscape

CONTACTS: *Note: Officers with more than one job title may be intentionally listed here more than once.*

Robert N. Brisco, CEO
Martin Wygod, Chairman of the Board
Michael Glick, Executive VP
Douglas Wamsley, Executive VP
Steven Zatz, President

GROWTH PLANS/SPECIAL FEATURES:

WebMD Health Corp. provides health information services to consumers, physicians, health care professionals, employers and health plans through its public and private online portals, mobile platforms and publications. WebMD.com (also known as WebMD Health) is the company's primary public portal for consumers. Other sites within the public division include MedicineNe.com, RxList.com, eMedicineHealth.com and Medscape, which provide health and wellness content, tools and services, all of which are free of charge. WebMD Health Services provides wellness services and solutions that help employers and health plans improve the health of their employees and plan participants. Other services include health coaching and condition management services on a per-participant basis. WebMD Wellness at Your Side is WebMD Health's mobile app. The WebMD Consumer network offers online news articles and features, special reports, interactive guides, videos, self-assessment questionnaires, community forums and reference resources. Its programming caters to all health-related interests. WebMD Consumer mobile apps and solutions include WebMD app, WebMD Magazine app, WebMD Pregnancy app, WebMD Baby app and WebMD Allergy app. It also includes the WebMD.com, MedicineNet.com, eMedicineHealth.com and RxList.com sites. The WebMD Professional network consists of: Medscape, a source of clinical news, medical information and point-of-care tools for physicians, nurse practitioners and other healthcare professionals; and Medscape Education (Medscape.org), which offers thousands of free continuing medical education and other educational programs for physicians, nurses and other healthcare professionals. Professional mobile apps and solutions include Medscape app, Medscape MedPulse app, Medscape CME & Education app and Medscape Consult. Last, WebMD Magazine is offered in print and free to physicians in the U.S. for use in their office waiting rooms. The magazine is offered online for WebMD members. WebMD is a subsidiary of Internet Brands, Inc., itself a subsidiary of KKR & Co., Inc.

FINANCIAL DATA: *Note: Data for latest year may not have been available at press time.*

In U.S. $	2022	2021	2020	2019	2018	2017
Revenue	922,504,156	887,023,227	852,906,949	816,178,899	777,313,237	740,298,321
R&D Expense						
Operating Income						
Operating Margin %						
SGA Expense						
Net Income						
Operating Cash Flow						
Capital Expenditure						
EBITDA						
Return on Assets %						
Return on Equity %						
Debt to Equity						

CONTACT INFORMATION:

Phone: 212-624-3700   Fax:
Toll-Free:
Address: 395 Hudson St., Fl. 3, New York, NY 10011 United States

STOCK TICKER/OTHER:

Stock Ticker: Subsidiary   Exchange:
Employees: 1,815   Fiscal Year Ends: 12/31
Parent Company: KKR & Co Inc

SALARIES/BONUSES:

Top Exec. Salary: $ Bonus: $
Second Exec. Salary: $ Bonus: $

OTHER THOUGHTS:

Estimated Female Officers or Directors: 1
Hot Spot for Advancement for Women/Minorities: Y

Westell Technologies Inc

www.westell.com

NAIC Code: 334210

TYPES OF BUSINESS:

Telecommunications Equipment-High-Speed Data Transmission
Distributed Antenna Systems
Digital Repeaters
Passive System Components
Remote Units
Integrated Cabinets
Power Distribution
Fiber Network Connectivity

BRANDS/DIVISIONS/AFFILIATES:

GROWTH PLANS/SPECIAL FEATURES:

Westell Technologies Inc is a provider of wireless network infrastructure solutions. It is organized into the following operating segments, In-Building Wireless (IBW), Intelligent Site Management (ISM), and Communications Network Solutions (CNS). IBW segment solutions enable cellular and public safety coverage in stadiums, arenas, malls, buildings, and other indoor areas not served well or at all by the existing macro outdoor cellular network. ISM segment solutions include a suite of remote units, which provide machine-to-machine communications that enable operators to remotely monitor, manage, and control physical site infrastructure and support systems. The majority of revenue is derived from the CNS segment Geographically, it derives a majority of revenue from the USA.

Westell offers its employees comprehensive medical benefits, a 401(k) plan and paid time off.

CONTACTS:
Note: Officers with more than one job title may be intentionally listed here more than once.

Thomas Minichiello, CFO
Kirk Brannock, Chairman of the Board
Alfred John, President
Jesse Swartwood, Senior VP, Divisional

FINANCIAL DATA:
Note: Data for latest year may not have been available at press time.

In U.S. $	2022	2021	2020	2019	2018	2017
Revenue		29,947,000	29,956,000	43,570,000	58,577,000	62,965,000
R&D Expense		4,032,000	5,346,000	6,790,000	7,375,000	12,367,000
Operating Income		-4,156,000	-9,281,000	-6,902,000	-1,289,000	-11,717,000
Operating Margin %		-.14%	-.31%	-.16%	-.02%	-.19%
SGA Expense		9,293,000	12,349,000	15,041,000	14,892,000	18,335,000
Net Income		-2,734,000	-10,102,000	-11,382,000	31,000	-15,941,000
Operating Cash Flow		95,000	-2,272,000	-760,000	6,945,000	-7,011,000
Capital Expenditure		72,000	2,135,000	290,000	408,000	596,000
EBITDA		-2,862,000	-7,381,000	-2,876,000	3,668,000	-5,573,000
Return on Assets %		-.08%	-.23%	-.21%	.00%	-.21%
Return on Equity %		-.10%	-.28%	-.24%	.00%	-.27%
Debt to Equity		.16%	0.008			

CONTACT INFORMATION:

Phone: 630 898-2500   Fax: 630 375-4931
Toll-Free:
Address: 750 North Commons Drive, Aurora, IL 60504 United States

STOCK TICKER/OTHER:

Stock Ticker: WSTL   Exchange: PINX
Employees: 102   Fiscal Year Ends: 03/31
Parent Company:

SALARIES/BONUSES:

Top Exec. Salary: $253,962   Bonus: $
Second Exec. Salary: $225,000   Bonus: $

OTHER THOUGHTS:

Estimated Female Officers or Directors: 2
Hot Spot for Advancement for Women/Minorities:

WhatsApp LLC

NAIC Code: 511210C

TYPES OF BUSINESS:

Computer Software: Telecom, Communications & VOIP
Online and Mobile Message Platform
Document Sharing
Digital Media
End-to-End Encryption and Privacy Controls
Video Calling
Voice Calling
Business Collaboration Solutions

BRANDS/DIVISIONS/AFFILIATES:

Meta Platforms Inc
WhatsApp Business

CONTACTS: *Note: Officers with more than one job title may be intentionally listed here more than once.*

Brian Acton, Co-Founder
Mark Zuckerberg, Chmn.-Corp.

GROWTH PLANS/SPECIAL FEATURES:

WhatsApp, LLC, a subsidiary of Meta Platforms, Inc., offers a cross-platform mobile messaging service for mobile and web applications. Since WhatsApp uses a customized version of the open standard Extensible Messaging and Presence Protocol, it is not only supported by various digital platforms, it also allows them to communicate with each other via the use of the app's client-server system architecture. By using the app to message another app user, the client is able to exchange messages without having to pay the short message service fee usually applicable when sending a message over the phone. In addition to basic text messages, users can send video and audio messages, images, documents and their location, as well as engage in voice and video calls using the apps' integrated mapping features. The app offers group calls and group video calls. WhatsApp features include end-to-end encryption and privacy controls. WhatsApp Business is a free app through which businesses can interact with customers. The app's tools can be used to automate, sort and quickly respond to messages. WhatsApp has over 2 billion active users in over 180 countries.

FINANCIAL DATA: *Note: Data for latest year may not have been available at press time.*

In U.S. $	2022	2021	2020	2019	2018	2017
Revenue						
R&D Expense						
Operating Income						
Operating Margin %						
SGA Expense						
Net Income						
Operating Cash Flow						
Capital Expenditure						
EBITDA						
Return on Assets %						
Return on Equity %						
Debt to Equity						

CONTACT INFORMATION:

Phone: 650 543-4800   Fax:
Toll-Free:
Address: 1601 Willow Rd., Menlo Park, CA 94025 United States

STOCK TICKER/OTHER:

Stock Ticker: Subsidiary   Exchange:
Employees: 55   Fiscal Year Ends:
Parent Company: Meta Platforms Inc

SALARIES/BONUSES:

Top Exec. Salary: $ Bonus: $
Second Exec. Salary: $ Bonus: $

OTHER THOUGHTS:

Estimated Female Officers or Directors:
Hot Spot for Advancement for Women/Minorities:

Whitepages Inc

www.whitepages.com

NAIC Code: 519130

TYPES OF BUSINESS:

Online Directory
Open Web Search
Online Yellow & White Pages
People Search Directory Platform
Phone Number and Address Directory
Business Location Directory
Background Check Search
Rental Application Screening

BRANDS/DIVISIONS/AFFILIATES:

Whitepages Smartcheck
Whitepages TenantCheck
411.com

GROWTH PLANS/SPECIAL FEATURES:

Whitepages, Inc. provides open search web properties to help verify identities worldwide. The company's platform serves more than 30 million monthly users. The directory technology platform enables people to search for people, phone numbers, addresses and businesses. Whitepages SmartCheck is a comprehensive background check platform for information on criminal history and other types of personal records across all 50 U.S. states. Whitepages TenantCheck is designed specifically for screening rental applications. 411.com is another comprehensive search site by Whitepages, for contact information on people, including reverse phone and reverse address lookup capabilities.

Whitepages offers its employees comprehensive health benefits, life and disability insurance, a 401(k) and a variety of employee assistance programs and company perks.

CONTACTS: Note: Officers with more than one job title may be intentionally listed here more than once.

Leigh McMillan, CEO
Nadine Thisselle, VP-Finance & Oper.
Divina Sequi, VP-Finance & Accounting
Cam Nguyen, VP-Product
Eric Merritt, VP-Engineering
Suki Hayre, VP-Admin.
Suki Hayre, VP-Finance
Craig Paris, Chief Revenue Officer
Alex Algard, Chmn.

FINANCIAL DATA: Note: Data for latest year may not have been available at press time.

In U.S. $	2022	2021	2020	2019	2018	2017
Revenue						
R&D Expense						
Operating Income						
Operating Margin %						
SGA Expense						
Net Income						
Operating Cash Flow						
Capital Expenditure						
EBITDA						
Return on Assets %						
Return on Equity %						
Debt to Equity						

CONTACT INFORMATION:

Phone: 206-973-5100   Fax: 206-621-1375
Toll-Free:
Address: 2033 6th Ave., Ste. 110, Seattle, WA 98121 United States

STOCK TICKER/OTHER:

Stock Ticker: Private   Exchange:
Employees: 165   Fiscal Year Ends: 12/31
Parent Company:

SALARIES/BONUSES:

Top Exec. Salary: $ Bonus: $
Second Exec. Salary: $ Bonus: $

OTHER THOUGHTS:

Estimated Female Officers or Directors: 5
Hot Spot for Advancement for Women/Minorities: Y

Wikimedia Foundation

www.wikimediafoundation.org

NAIC Code: 519130

TYPES OF BUSINESS:

Online Dictionary
Online Encyclopedia
Online Educational Content

BRANDS/DIVISIONS/AFFILIATES:

Wikipedia
Wikiversity
Wikibooks
Wikisource
Wikiquote
Wikinews
MediaWiki
Wikidata

CONTACTS: *Note: Officers with more than one job title may be intentionally listed here more than once.*

Maryana Iskander, CEO
Erik Moller, VP-Eng. & Prod. Dev.
Garfield Byrd, Chief Admin. Officer
Geoff Brigham, General Counsel
Frank Schulenburg, Sr. Dir.-Program Dev.
Lisa Seitz-Gruwell, Chief Revenue Officer
Anasuya Sengupta, Sr. Dir.-Grantmaking

GROWTH PLANS/SPECIAL FEATURES:

Wikimedia Foundation is a nonprofit charitable organization that operates Wikipedia, a free online encyclopedia that contains more than 100 million media files and is offered in approximately 300 languages. The foundation also administers a number of other resources, including: Wikiversity, a source for tutorials and learning development; Wikibooks, a source for free content textbooks; Wikisource, a collection of published texts; Wikiquote, a collection of quotations; Wikinews, a source for news entries written in the style of news stories; Wikispecies, a comprehensive catalog of species aimed at scientists; MediaWiki, a software application engine that manages Wiki content; Wiktionary, a dictionary and thesaurus; Wikivoyage, a free travel guide; Wikidata, a free knowledge base; and Wikimedia Commons, a collection of images and other media. Article contribution and editing of Wiki content is open to anyone, from anonymous volunteers to highly specialized professionals. The aim of the foundation is to foster the collection and development of educational content by people all over the world and to provide a free and public domain for the issuing of information. Because Wikipedia owns all the servers that run each project, the sites feature no advertisements. Wikimedia is run by a staff with the help of numerous volunteers either contributing content, participating through committees or acting as interns. The foundation relies heavily on donations from individuals, but also receives money from grants and fundraising. Wikimedia has chapters in many different countries that support the aims of Wikimedia, but do not share control of Wikimedia sites.

Wikimedia Foundation offers its employees comprehensive health benefits, retirement options and a variety of employee assistance programs.

FINANCIAL DATA: *Note: Data for latest year may not have been available at press time.*

In U.S. $	2022	2021	2020	2019	2018	2017
Revenue	154,686,521	162,886,686	129,234,327	120,067,266	104,505,783	91,242,418
R&D Expense						
Operating Income						
Operating Margin %						
SGA Expense						
Net Income	8,173,996	50,861,811	14,674,300	30,691,855	21,619,373	22,105,660
Operating Cash Flow						
Capital Expenditure						
EBITDA						
Return on Assets %						
Return on Equity %						
Debt to Equity						

CONTACT INFORMATION:

Phone: 415-839-6885   Fax: 415-882-0495
Toll-Free:
Address: 1 Montgomery St., Ste. 1600, San Francisco, CA 94104 United States

STOCK TICKER/OTHER:

Stock Ticker: Nonprofit   Exchange:
Employees: 550   Fiscal Year Ends: 06/30
Parent Company:

SALARIES/BONUSES:

Top Exec. Salary: $ Bonus: $
Second Exec. Salary: $ Bonus: $

OTHER THOUGHTS:

Estimated Female Officers or Directors:
Hot Spot for Advancement for Women/Minorities:

Windstream Holdings Inc
investor.windstream.com/home/default.aspx

NAIC Code: 517311

TYPES OF BUSINESS:
Telephone Service--Local Exchange Carrier & Diversified
Network Communications
Network Software Solutions
Managed Communications Services
SD-WAN and UCaaS Services
Broadband and Bandwidth Services
Wireless Services
High-Speed Internet Services

BRANDS/DIVISIONS/AFFILIATES:
Kinetic by Windstream
windstream.com
windstreamenterprise.com

GROWTH PLANS/SPECIAL FEATURES:
Windstream Holdings, Inc. is a privately-owned communications and software company. The firm offers managed communications services, including software-defined wide area network (SD-WAN) and unified-communications-as-a-service (UCaaS), as well as high-capacity bandwidth and transport services to businesses across the U.S. Its Kinetic by Windstream business provides premium broadband, entertainment and security services through an enhanced fiber network and 5G fixed wireless service to consumers and small/medium sized businesses primarily in rural areas within 18 states. Kinetic's services include high-speed internet plans for residential applications. Websites of Windstream Holdings include windstream.com and windstreamenterprise.com

CONTACTS:
Note: Officers with more than one job title may be intentionally listed here more than once.

Paul Sunu, CEO
Robert Gunderman, CFO
Alan Wells, Director
Kristi Moody, General Counsel
Jeffery Small, President, Divisional
Layne Levine, President, Divisional

FINANCIAL DATA:
Note: Data for latest year may not have been available at press time.

In U.S. $	2022	2021	2020	2019	2018	2017
Revenue	5,200,000,000	5,000,000,000	4,987,515,000	5,115,400,000	5,713,099,776	5,852,899,840
R&D Expense						
Operating Income						
Operating Margin %						
SGA Expense						
Net Income				-3,517,000,000	-723,000,000	-2,116,600,064
Operating Cash Flow						
Capital Expenditure						
EBITDA						
Return on Assets %						
Return on Equity %						
Debt to Equity						

CONTACT INFORMATION:
Phone: 501 748-7000		Fax:
Toll-Free: 866-445-5880
Address: 4001 N. Rodney Parkham Rd., Little Rock, AR 72212 United States

STOCK TICKER/OTHER:
Stock Ticker: Private
Employees: 11,080
Parent Company:

Exchange:
Fiscal Year Ends: 12/31

SALARIES/BONUSES:
Top Exec. Salary: $		Bonus: $
Second Exec. Salary: $		Bonus: $

OTHER THOUGHTS:
Estimated Female Officers or Directors:
Hot Spot for Advancement for Women/Minorities:

Wipro Limited

www.wipro.com

NAIC Code: 541512

TYPES OF BUSINESS:

IT Consulting
Computer Hardware & Software Design
Hydraulic Equipment
Medical Electronics
Lighting Equipment
Soaps & Toiletries

GROWTH PLANS/SPECIAL FEATURES:

Wipro is a leading global IT services provider, with 175,000 employees. Based in Bengaluru, this India IT services firm leverages its offshore outsourcing model to derive over half of its revenue (57%) from North America. The company offers traditional IT services offerings: consulting, managed services, and cloud infrastructure services as well as business process outsourcing as a service.

BRANDS/DIVISIONS/AFFILIATES:

Cloud Studios
METRO-NOM GMBH
METRO Systems Romania SRL

CONTACTS: Note: Officers with more than one job title may be intentionally listed here more than once.

Abidali Z. Neemuchwala, CEO
Bhanumurthy B. M., Pres.
Jatin Dalal, CFO
MIlan Rao, Pres.-Mktg., Innovation & Tech.
Saurabh Govil, Chief Human Resources Officer
Sangita Singh, Sr. VP- Health Care & Life Sciences
Nitin Parab, Sr. VP-Global Technology
N.S. Bala, Sr. VP-Mfg. & High Tech.
Inderpreet Sawhney, Sr. VP
Rishad Premji, Chief Strategy Officer
Ayan Mukerji, Sr. VP-Media & Telecom
Vineet Agrawal, Pres., Wipro Consumer Care & Lighting
Anurag Behar, Chief Sustainability Officer
Alexis Samuel, Chief Process Officer
Rajat Mathur Rajat Mathur Rajat Mathur, Chief Sales & Oper. Officer-Growth Markets
Rishad Premji, Chmn.
Ulrich Meister, Sr. VP-Continental Europe

FINANCIAL DATA: Note: Data for latest year may not have been available at press time.

In U.S. $	2022	2021	2020	2019	2018	2017
Revenue	9,559,894,000	7,486,953,000	7,375,778,000	7,081,016,000	6,585,769,000	
R&D Expense						
Operating Income	1,642,977,000	1,451,122,000	1,239,639,000	1,168,737,000	1,000,863,000	
Operating Margin %	.17%	.19%	.17%	.17%	.15%	
SGA Expense	1,133,806,000	919,639,500	879,076,000	972,519,400	924,522,600	
Net Income	1,476,903,000	1,304,726,000	1,175,059,000	1,088,190,000	967,926,500	
Operating Cash Flow	1,339,186,000	1,783,414,000	1,216,456,000	1,405,893,000	1,018,111,000	
Capital Expenditure	243,586,100	236,624,100	284,004,500	275,350,300	264,339,200	
EBITDA	2,266,416,000	2,066,379,000	1,795,017,000	1,698,262,000	1,535,621,000	
Return on Assets %	.13%	.13%	.12%	.11%	.10%	
Return on Equity %	.20%	.19%	.17%	.17%	.16%	
Debt to Equity	.11%	.04%	0.031	0.05	.09%	

CONTACT INFORMATION:

Phone: 91 8028440055   Fax: 91 8028440256
Toll-Free:
Address: Doddakannelli, Sarjapur Rd., Bengaluru, Karnataka 560035 India

STOCK TICKER/OTHER:

Stock Ticker: WIT   Exchange: NYS
Employees: 250,000   Fiscal Year Ends: 03/31
Parent Company:

SALARIES/BONUSES:

Top Exec. Salary: $1,602,506   Bonus: $1,306,153
Second Exec. Salary: $861,620   Bonus: $

OTHER THOUGHTS:

Estimated Female Officers or Directors: 3
Hot Spot for Advancement for Women/Minorities: Y

Wish.com (ContextLogic Inc)

www.wish.com

NAIC Code: 454110

TYPES OF BUSINESS:
Electronic Shopping
Ecommerce
Merchants

GROWTH PLANS/SPECIAL FEATURES:
ContextLogic Inc is an online shopping store. The store provides personalized products, clothing products, accessories, gaming products and equipment, cosmetics, plastic products, mobile covers, and other products. Geographically, it derives a majority of revenue from Europe and also has a presence in North America; South America, and other countries.

BRANDS/DIVISIONS/AFFILIATES:
ContextLogic Inc

CONTACTS: *Note: Officers with more than one job title may be intentionally listed here more than once.*
Peter Szulczewski, CEO
Brett Just, Chief Accounting Officer
Jennifer Oliver, Co-CFO
Devang Shah, General Counsel
Pai Liu, Vice President, Divisional
Thomas Chuang, Vice President, Divisional

FINANCIAL DATA: *Note: Data for latest year may not have been available at press time.*

In U.S. $	2022	2021	2020	2019	2018	2017
Revenue	571,000,000	2,085,000,000	2,541,000,000	1,901,000,000	1,728,000,000	1,101,000,000
R&D Expense	194,000,000	208,000,000	222,000,000	74,000,000	45,000,000	28,000,000
Operating Income	-398,000,000	-367,000,000	-631,000,000	-144,000,000	-223,000,000	-147,000,000
Operating Margin %	-.70%	-.18%	-.25%	-.08%	-.13%	
SGA Expense	370,000,000	1,267,000,000	2,003,000,000	1,528,000,000	1,628,000,000	1,015,000,000
Net Income	-384,000,000	-361,000,000	-745,000,000	-129,000,000	-208,000,000	-207,000,000
Operating Cash Flow	-422,000,000	-951,000,000		-60,000,000	-94,000,000	146,000,000
Capital Expenditure	2,000,000	2,000,000	2,000,000	11,000,000	20,000,000	12,000,000
EBITDA	-392,000,000	-358,000,000	-619,000,000	-134,000,000	-215,000,000	-143,000,000
Return on Assets %	-.37%	-.20%	-.40%	-.11%	-.17%	
Return on Equity %	-.59%	-.39%				
Debt to Equity	.03%	.02%	0.037			

CONTACT INFORMATION:
Phone: 415 432-7323   Fax:
Toll-Free: 800-266-0172
Address: 1 Sansome St., 40/Fl, San Francisco, CA 94104 United States

STOCK TICKER/OTHER:
Stock Ticker: WISH   Exchange: NAS
Employees: 886   Fiscal Year Ends: 12/31
Parent Company:

SALARIES/BONUSES:
Top Exec. Salary: $77,083   Bonus: $425,000
Second Exec. Salary: $450,000   Bonus: $

OTHER THOUGHTS:
Estimated Female Officers or Directors:
Hot Spot for Advancement for Women/Minorities:

Sales, profits and employees may be estimates. Financial information, benefits and other data can change quickly and may vary from those stated here.

Workday Inc

www.workday.com

NAIC Code: 511210H

TYPES OF BUSINESS:

Human Resources Software
Enterprise Financial Planning Software (ERF)
Analytics Software

BRANDS/DIVISIONS/AFFILIATES:

Scout REP
Workday Strategic Sourcing

GROWTH PLANS/SPECIAL FEATURES:

Workday is a software company that offers human capital management, or HCM, financial management, and business planning solutions. Known for being a cloud-only software provider, Workday is headquartered in Pleasanton, California. Founded in 2005, Workday now employs over 12,000 employees.

Workday offers its employees health plans, retirement plans and employee assistance programs.

CONTACTS: *Note: Officers with more than one job title may be intentionally listed here more than once.*

Robynne Sisco, CFO
Thomas Bogan, Vice Chairman, Divisional
David Duffield, Chairman Emeritus
Aneel Bhusri, Chairman of the Board
Richard Sauer, Chief Legal Officer
Christine Cefalo, Chief Marketing Officer
Luciano Gomez, Co-CEO
James Bozzini, COO
Doug Robinson, Co-President
George Still, Director
Sayan Chakraborty, Executive VP, Divisional
Pete Schlampp, Executive VP, Divisional
Leighanne Levensaler, Executive VP, Divisional
Emily McEvilly, Other Executive Officer
Ashley Goldsmith, Other Executive Officer
Barbara Larson, Senior VP, Divisional
Michael Stankey, Vice Chairman

FINANCIAL DATA: *Note: Data for latest year may not have been available at press time.*

In U.S. $	2022	2021	2020	2019	2018	2017
Revenue	5,138,798,000	4,317,996,000	3,627,206,000	2,822,180,000	2,143,050,000	
R&D Expense	1,879,220,000	1,721,222,000	1,549,906,000	1,211,832,000	910,584,000	
Operating Income	-116,450,000	-248,599,000	-502,230,000	-463,284,000	-303,223,000	
Operating Margin %	-.02%	-.06%	-.14%	-.16%	-.14%	
SGA Expense	1,947,933,000	1,647,241,000	1,514,272,000	1,238,682,000	906,276,000	
Net Income	29,373,000	-282,431,000	-480,674,000	-418,258,000	-321,222,000	
Operating Cash Flow	1,650,704,000	1,268,441,000	864,598,000	606,658,000	465,727,000	
Capital Expenditure	272,274,000	256,330,000	244,544,000	212,957,000	152,536,000	
EBITDA	376,507,000	87,329,000	-147,484,000	-165,432,000	-134,514,000	
Return on Assets %	.00%	-.04%	-.08%	-.08%	-.08%	
Return on Equity %	.01%	-.10%	-.22%	-.24%	-.22%	
Debt to Equity	.18%	.32%	0.506	0.496	.73%	

CONTACT INFORMATION:

Phone: 925-951-9000   Fax:
Toll-Free: 877-967-5329
Address: 6230 Stoneridge Mall Rd., Ste. 200, Pleasanton, CA 94588 United States

STOCK TICKER/OTHER:

Stock Ticker: WDAY   Exchange: NAS
Employees: 17,700   Fiscal Year Ends: 01/31
Parent Company:

SALARIES/BONUSES:

Top Exec. Salary: $607,791   Bonus: $521,136
Second Exec. Salary: $515,000 Bonus: $231,000

OTHER THOUGHTS:

Estimated Female Officers or Directors: 2
Hot Spot for Advancement for Women/Minorities:

Sales, profits and employees may be estimates. Financial information, benefits and other data can change quickly and may vary from those stated here.

X Corp (Twitter)

www.twitter.com

NAIC Code: 519130

TYPES OF BUSINESS:

Real-Time Short Messaging
Open Distribution Platform
Artificial Intelligence
Online and Mobile Application
Text, Image and Video Content Sharing
Advertising
Licensing
Subscription Features

BRANDS/DIVISIONS/AFFILIATES:

Twitter
Twitter Blue
Tweets
X Corp.

GROWTH PLANS/SPECIAL FEATURES:

X Corp., formerly known as Twitter, Inc., was renamed in July 2023, a few months after it was taken private by Elon Musk and several partners. The company is the developer and operator of an open distribution platform (Twitter) for conversing via short-form text (Tweets), image and video content. Users can choose to pay for a subscription and gain access to features such as exclusive posts, subscriber badges, tabs, links, community only replies and more. Its users can create different social networks based on their interests. X generates revenue from advertising (90%), and by licensing the user data it compiles (10%). Developer and business resources are provided on the firm's website, as well as a help center, information on how to use X, managing an account, creating preferences and accessing rules/policies.

CONTACTS: Note: Officers with more than one job title may be intentionally listed here more than once.

Linda Yaccarino, CEO

FINANCIAL DATA: Note: Data for latest year may not have been available at press time.

In U.S. $	2022	2021	2020	2019	2018	2017
Revenue	3,000,000,000	5,077,481,984	3,716,348,928	3,459,329,024	3,042,359,040	2,443,299,072
R&D Expense						
Operating Income						
Operating Margin %						
SGA Expense						
Net Income		-221,408,992	-1,135,625,984	1,465,659,008	1,205,596,032	-108,063,000
Operating Cash Flow						
Capital Expenditure						
EBITDA						
Return on Assets %						
Return on Equity %						
Debt to Equity						

CONTACT INFORMATION:

Phone: 415 222-9670   Fax: 415-222-0922
Toll-Free:
Address: 1355 Market St., Ste. 900, San Francisco, CA 94103 United States

STOCK TICKER/OTHER:

Stock Ticker: Private   Exchange:
Employees: 1,950   Fiscal Year Ends: 12/31
Parent Company:

SALARIES/BONUSES:

Top Exec. Salary: $ Bonus: $
Second Exec. Salary: $ Bonus: $

OTHER THOUGHTS:

Estimated Female Officers or Directors: 2
Hot Spot for Advancement for Women/Minorities: Y

Sales, profits and employees may be estimates. Financial information, benefits and other data can change quickly and may vary from those stated here.

Xaxis LLC

NAIC Code: 541810E

TYPES OF BUSINESS:

Internet Advertising
Media Advertising Solutions
Artificial Intelligence
Audience Targeting Solutions
Digital Video and Audio Solutions
Managed Programmatic Services

BRANDS/DIVISIONS/AFFILIATES:

WPP plc
GroupM

GROWTH PLANS/SPECIAL FEATURES:

Xaxis, LLC is a global provider of outcome media solutions for the advertising industry. The firm combines brand-safe media access, programmatic expertise and visible data with proprietary artificial intelligence (AI) technology to help global brands achieve the outcomes they seek from their digital media investments. Xaxis' proprietary audience targeting and verification capabilities enable its video, audio digital and display solutions to reach the right audience across premium, brand-safe placements in instream, outstream, YouTube, over-the-top (OTT), voice-sharing, digital mobile and web supply. The company's solutions span media, creative studios, omnichannel and ecommerce. Xaxis offers managed programmatic services across North America, Europe, Asia Pacific, Latin America, the Middle East and Africa. The firm is headquartered in the U.S., with international headquarters located in London and Singapore. Xaxis is part of GroupM and WPP plc.

CONTACTS: *Note: Officers with more than one job title may be intentionally listed here more than once.*

Nicolas Bidon, CEO
Matt Haies, VP
Irene Bondar, Exec. VP-Global Client Oper.
Rob Schneider, Sr. VP-Corp. Strategy & Platform Dev.
Nicolle Pangis, Pres., Real Media Group

FINANCIAL DATA: *Note: Data for latest year may not have been available at press time.*

In U.S. $	2022	2021	2020	2019	2018	2017
Revenue	1,910,000,000	1,700,000,000	1,261,039,500	948,150,000	903,000,000	860,000,000
R&D Expense						
Operating Income						
Operating Margin %						
SGA Expense						
Net Income						
Operating Cash Flow						
Capital Expenditure						
EBITDA						
Return on Assets %						
Return on Equity %						
Debt to Equity						

CONTACT INFORMATION:

Phone: 646-259-4200   Fax:
Toll-Free:
Address: 175 Greenwich St., Fl. 30, 3 World Trade Center, New York, NY 10007 United States

STOCK TICKER/OTHER:

Stock Ticker: Subsidiary   Exchange:
Employees: 1,800   Fiscal Year Ends: 12/31
Parent Company: GroupM Nexus

SALARIES/BONUSES:

Top Exec. Salary: $ Bonus: $
Second Exec. Salary: $ Bonus: $

OTHER THOUGHTS:

Estimated Female Officers or Directors:
Hot Spot for Advancement for Women/Minorities:

Yahoo Inc

www.yahooinc.com

NAIC Code: 519130

TYPES OF BUSINESS:

Online Content Provider
Media Platform
Media Technology
Business Solutions
Mobile Apps
Websites and Social Platforms
User Experience Solutions
Analytics Solutions

BRANDS/DIVISIONS/AFFILIATES:

Apollo Global Management Inc
Yahoo!
Yahoo! Sports
Yahoo! Finance
Yahoo! Mail
Yahoo! News
Yahoo! Life
Yahoo! Entertainment

CONTACTS: Note: Officers with more than one job title may be intentionally listed here more than once.

Jim Lanzone, CEO
Julie Jacobs, Executive VP
Bob Lord, President
Susan Lyne, President, Subsidiary

GROWTH PLANS/SPECIAL FEATURES:

Yahoo, Inc. designs and operates media, technology and business platforms that connect millions of people worldwide. The company's Yahoo! platforms consist of apps and sites such as Yahoo! Sports, Yahoo! Finance, Yahoo! Fantasy, Yahoo! Mail, Yahoo! News, Yahoo! Life, Yahoo! Entertainment and Yahoo! Sportsbook. Other brands include TechCrunch, offering breaking technology news: Aol., a hub for news, entertainment, human interests stories and more; Engadget, a multilingual technology blog network; autoblog, offering vehicle news, reviews and videos; In The Know, a youth culture in 90 seconds or less platform; rivals, for college football and basketball fans to read highlights, interviews and rankings; Makers, a story-telling platform by female leaders; Built By Girls, a community for next-generation females and non-binary leaders; and Flurry, a mobile app analytics solution. Yahoo's business solutions include data, insights and technology, as well as innovative consumer experience tools that help businesses connect with consumers. Based in the U.S., Yahoo! has office locations across North and South America, Europe and Asia Pacific. Yahoo! operates as a subsidiary of Apollo Global Management, Inc.

FINANCIAL DATA: Note: Data for latest year may not have been available at press time.

In U.S. $	2022	2021	2020	2019	2018	2017
Revenue	1,491,110,720	1,748,448,000	1,681,200,000	1,868,000,000	2,100,000,000	2,050,000,000
R&D Expense						
Operating Income						
Operating Margin %						
SGA Expense						
Net Income						
Operating Cash Flow						
Capital Expenditure						
EBITDA						
Return on Assets %						
Return on Equity %						
Debt to Equity						

CONTACT INFORMATION:

Phone: 212 652-6400   Fax:
Toll-Free:
Address: 770 Broadway, Fl 4-6, 9, New York, NY 10003-9562 United States

STOCK TICKER/OTHER:

Stock Ticker: Subsidiary   Exchange:
Employees: 10,600   Fiscal Year Ends: 12/31
Parent Company: Apollo Global Management Inc

SALARIES/BONUSES:

Top Exec. Salary: $ Bonus: $
Second Exec. Salary: $ Bonus: $

OTHER THOUGHTS:

Estimated Female Officers or Directors: 7
Hot Spot for Advancement for Women/Minorities: Y

Yandex NV

NAIC Code: 519130

www.yandex.com

TYPES OF BUSINESS:

Online Search Engine
Online Payment System
Investment Company
On Demand Transportation
Media Services
Ticketing

BRANDS/DIVISIONS/AFFILIATES:

yandex.ru
MatrixNet
Yandex.Market
Yandex.Taxi
Auto.ru
Yandex.Jobs
KinoPoisk
Yandex Zen

GROWTH PLANS/SPECIAL FEATURES:

Yandex NV is an internet and technology company and operating internet search engines in Russia. It builds products and services powered by machine learning. The company operates through the following segments namely, Search and Portal; E-commerce, Mobility and Delivery; Plus and Entertainment Services; Classifieds; Media Services; Classifieds, and Other Business units. The search and Portal segment offers services in Russia, Belarus, and Kazakhstan which generates most of the revenue.

CONTACTS: *Note: Officers with more than one job title may be intentionally listed here more than once.*

Arkady Volozh, CEO
Gregory Abovsky, CFO
Elena Bunina, Dir.-Human Resources
Mikhail Parakhin, CTO
Dmitry Ivanov, Chief Product Officer
Anya Barski, VP-Eng.
Ekaterina Fadeeva, Chief Legal Officer
Mikhail Fadeev, Chief Systems Oper. Officer
Alexey Mazurov, Chief Dev. Officer
Dina Litvinova, Head-Press Svcs.
Katya Zhukova, Head-Investor Rel.
Dmitry Barsukov, Dir.-Corp. Finance
Elena Kolmanovskaya, Chief Editor
Anya Barski, CEO-Yandex Labs
Maxim Kiselev, Dir.-Bus. Dev.
Jane Zavalishina, CEO-Yandex.Money
John Boynton, Chmn.

FINANCIAL DATA: *Note: Data for latest year may not have been available at press time.*

In U.S. $	2022	2021	2020	2019	2018	2017
Revenue	5,422,221,000	3,701,824,000	2,269,335,000	1,822,907,000	1,326,789,000	977,539,900
R&D Expense	751,213,400	503,674,100	377,685,400	303,580,500	234,672,400	196,081,700
Operating Income	137,566,900	-137,993,000	162,874,800	263,181,400	216,619,000	133,471,900
Operating Margin %		-.04%	.07%	.14%	.16%	.14%
SGA Expense	1,788,619,000	1,277,597,000	653,879,400	522,735,600	376,303,100	282,232,500
Net Income	410,175,200	-152,460,600	256,851,900	131,912,900	477,929,600	95,629,590
Operating Cash Flow	433,279,600	96,585,780	338,866,100	461,248,300	293,218,300	247,071,700
Capital Expenditure	539,957,400	463,763,500	255,168,100	213,511,400	294,372,000	128,763,700
EBITDA	1,329,876,000	397,110,700	719,835,800	498,196,800	739,915,900	315,595,300
Return on Assets %		-.03%	.06%	.05%	.24%	.08%
Return on Equity %		-.05%	.10%	.07%	.35%	.12%
Debt to Equity		.49%	0.306	0.056	.07%	

CONTACT INFORMATION:

Phone: 31-20-206-6970   Fax: 31-20-446-6372
Toll-Free:
Address: Schiphol Boulevard 165, Shiphol, 1118 BG Netherlands

STOCK TICKER/OTHER:

Stock Ticker: YNDX   Exchange: NAS
Employees: 20,850   Fiscal Year Ends: 12/31
Parent Company:

SALARIES/BONUSES:

Top Exec. Salary: $ Bonus: $
Second Exec. Salary: $ Bonus: $

OTHER THOUGHTS:

Estimated Female Officers or Directors: 8
Hot Spot for Advancement for Women/Minorities: Y

Sales, profits and employees may be estimates. Financial information, benefits and other data can change quickly and may vary from those stated here.

Yardi Systems Inc

NAIC Code: 511210H

TYPES OF BUSINESS:

Computer Software, Business Management & ERP
Real Estate Software
Real Estate Listing Management
Housing Platform
Commercial Property Platform
Property Management Software
Search Engine Marketing
Ecommerce

BRANDS/DIVISIONS/AFFILIATES:

Yardi Breeze
Yardi Kube
RentCafe.com
CommercialCafe
PropertyShark
CondoCafe
StorageCafe
VendorCafe

CONTACTS: Note: Officers with more than one job title may be intentionally listed here more than once.

Anant Yardi, CEO
Jay Shobe, Sr. VP-Finance & Cloud Svcs.
Terri Dowen, Sr. VP-Sales
Sally Parks, VP-Human Resources

GROWTH PLANS/SPECIAL FEATURES:

Yardi Systems, Inc. provides software for the real estate industry. The company works from over 40 offices throughout North America, Europe, the Middle East, Asia and Australia. Yardi's web-based, fully integrated end-to-end platform offers mobile access for large portfolios to manage operations, execute leasing, run analytics and provide innovative resident, tenant and investor services. It is applicable for real estate environments such as residential, affordable housing, senior housing, condo, co-op and homeowner's association (HOA), military housing, social housing, student housing, commercial, airports, government, ports and parks and recreation. Breeze is an online platform comprised of software-as-a-service (SaaS) property management software for small-to-mid-size companies and owners of single-family homes, multi-family and commercial properties. It streamlines property management and accounting with rental property management software that features a single database and works with any browser. Services offered by Yardi include client services, technical support, training, implementation, search engine marketing, SaaS and consulting. Yardi companies and affiliates include: Yardi Kube, a single platform solution for coworking and shared workspace operators, designed to help business growth, eliminate third party integrations and save time; RentCafe.com, providing an online apartment search platform; CommercialCafe, a platform for commercial listings and co-working spaces; Point2, a real estate marketplace for connecting buyers and sellers; and PropertyShark, a real estate data source that offers property data such as owner names, foreclosures, property description, zoning, value and more. Other subsidiary and affiliate brands include CondoCafe, StorageCafe, VendorCafe, Yardi Marketplace, Yardi Matrix, ALMSA, Commercial Property Executive, Yardi Corom, Planimetron, CommercialEdge and more.

FINANCIAL DATA: Note: Data for latest year may not have been available at press time.

In U.S. $	2022	2021	2020	2019	2018	2017
Revenue						
R&D Expense						
Operating Income						
Operating Margin %						
SGA Expense						
Net Income						
Operating Cash Flow						
Capital Expenditure						
EBITDA						
Return on Assets %						
Return on Equity %						
Debt to Equity						

CONTACT INFORMATION:

Phone: 805-699-2040   Fax: 805-699-2044
Toll-Free: 800-866-1124
Address: 430 S. Fairview Ave., Santa Barbara, CA 93117 United States

STOCK TICKER/OTHER:

Stock Ticker: Private   Exchange:
Employees: 7,500   Fiscal Year Ends:
Parent Company:

SALARIES/BONUSES:

Top Exec. Salary: $ Bonus: $
Second Exec. Salary: $ Bonus: $

OTHER THOUGHTS:

Estimated Female Officers or Directors:
Hot Spot for Advancement for Women/Minorities:

Sales, profits and employees may be estimates. Financial information, benefits and other data can change quickly and may vary from those stated here.

Yelp Inc

NAIC Code: 519130

www.yelp.com

TYPES OF BUSINESS:

Online Community-Business Reviews
Advertising Services
Users Ratings

BRANDS/DIVISIONS/AFFILIATES:

Yelp.com
Yelp Reservations

GROWTH PLANS/SPECIAL FEATURES:

Yelp Inc operates in the online content market based in the United States. It provides a web-based platform and mobile application to bridge the gap between businesses and consumers. The platform assists consumers through product reviews, tips, photos and videos thereby enabling them in making better buying decisions and posting their feedbacks. Its products and services includes Advertising Products and Business Page Products. In addition, it also lets the buyers directly transact with businesses directly through its platform. Yelp generates revenue mainly from the sale of advertising on its website and mobile app to businesses. The company generates majority of the revenue from United States.

CONTACTS: *Note: Officers with more than one job title may be intentionally listed here more than once.*

Jeremy Stoppelman, CEO
David Schwarzbach, CFO
Diane Irvine, Chairman of the Board
Laurence Wilson, Chief Administrative Officer
Sam Eaton, Chief Technology Officer
Joseph Nachman, COO
Vivek Patel, Other Executive Officer
Miriam Warren, Other Executive Officer
Carolyn Patterson, Other Executive Officer
James Miln, Senior VP, Divisional

FINANCIAL DATA: *Note: Data for latest year may not have been available at press time.*

In U.S. $	2022	2021	2020	2019	2018	2017
Revenue	1,193,506,000	1,031,839,000	872,933,000	1,014,194,000	942,773,000	850,847,000
R&D Expense	305,561,000	276,473,000	232,561,000	230,440,000	212,319,000	175,787,000
Operating Income	58,353,000	31,546,000	-34,933,000	35,511,000	25,897,000	16,213,000
Operating Margin %	.05%	.03%	-.04%	.04%	.03%	.02%
SGA Expense	679,035,000	590,040,000	567,510,000	636,477,000	603,878,000	547,131,000
Net Income	36,347,000	39,671,000	-19,424,000	40,881,000	55,350,000	152,995,000
Operating Cash Flow	192,309,000	212,655,000	176,701,000	204,782,000	160,187,000	167,647,000
Capital Expenditure	31,979,000	28,282,000	38,131,000	37,522,000	44,972,000	30,245,000
EBITDA	103,205,000	87,229,000	15,676,000	84,867,000	68,704,000	57,411,000
Return on Assets %	.04%	.04%	-.02%	.04%	.05%	.14%
Return on Equity %	.05%	.05%	-.02%	.04%	.05%	.16%
Debt to Equity	.12%	.17%	0.174	0.231		

CONTACT INFORMATION:

Phone: 415 908-3801   Fax:
Toll-Free:
Address: 140 New Montgomery St., 9/Fl, San Francisco, CA 94105 United States

STOCK TICKER/OTHER:

Stock Ticker: YELP
Employees: 4,900
Parent Company:

Exchange: NYS
Fiscal Year Ends: 12/31

SALARIES/BONUSES:

Top Exec. Salary: $398,077   Bonus: $625,000
Second Exec. Salary: $500,000   Bonus: $

OTHER THOUGHTS:

Estimated Female Officers or Directors: 5
Hot Spot for Advancement for Women/Minorities: Y

YOOX Net-A-Porter Group SpA (YNAP)

www.ynap.com

NAIC Code: 454110

TYPES OF BUSINESS:

Online Apparel Sales
Ecommerce
High-End Retail
Apparel
Accessories
Websites
Furniture and Home Design Products
Home Art Products

BRANDS/DIVISIONS/AFFILIATES:

Net-A-Porter
Mr Porter
Outnet (The)
YOOX
Home Decor + Art

GROWTH PLANS/SPECIAL FEATURES:

YOOX Net-A-Porter Group SpA (YNAP) is an Italy-based online mail order retailer of men's and women's multi-brand clothing and accessories. YNAP was established by the 2015 merger between YOOX Group and The Net-A-Porter Group, each of which were premier online luxury fashion retailers. YNAP offers style-conscious customers around the world a high-end online retail experience through its net-a-porter.com, mrporter.com, yoox.com and theoutnet.com websites. The company is made up of four multi-brand online stores, including Net-A-Porter, Mr. Porter, The Outnet and YOOX. In addition, YOOX Net-A-Porter's online flagship stores partner with world-leading luxury brands to expand product reach. YNAP serves more than 5.3 million customers in 170 countries, and operates global offices, distribution centers, digital production facilities, customer care centers and more.

CONTACTS:
Note: Officers with more than one job title may be intentionally listed here more than once.

Alison Loehnis, Interim CEO
Mirko Nobili, COO
Paola Agasso, CFO
Matt Lindsey, Chief Product Officer
Paolo Inga, Dir.-Human Resources
Gabriele Tazzari, Dir.-R&D
Pete Marsden, CTO
Gabriele Tazzari, Dir.-Strategy, Governance & Innovation
Paolo Mascio, Dir.-Online Stores
Silvia Scagnelli, Mgr.-Investor Rel.
Alessandra Rossi, Dir.-Commercial
Alberto Grignolo, Gen. Mgr.
Davide di Dario, Dir.-Demand Planning
Marc-OliverSchmiedle, Chief Growth Officer
Luca Martines, Dir.-Asia Pacific

FINANCIAL DATA:
Note: Data for latest year may not have been available at press time.

In U.S. $	2022	2021	2020	2019	2018	2017
Revenue	1,580,000,000	1,529,073,002	1,470,262,502	2,491,970,342	2,373,305,088	2,260,290,560
R&D Expense						
Operating Income						
Operating Margin %						
SGA Expense						
Net Income						
Operating Cash Flow						
Capital Expenditure						
EBITDA						
Return on Assets %						
Return on Equity %						
Debt to Equity						

CONTACT INFORMATION:

Phone: 39028-311-2811   Fax: 39028-311-2821
Toll-Free:
Address: Via Morimondo 17, Milan, 20143 Italy

STOCK TICKER/OTHER:

Stock Ticker: Private   Exchange:
Employees: 4,703   Fiscal Year Ends: 12/31
Parent Company:

SALARIES/BONUSES:

Top Exec. Salary: $ Bonus: $
Second Exec. Salary: $ Bonus: $

OTHER THOUGHTS:

Estimated Female Officers or Directors: 4
Hot Spot for Advancement for Women/Minorities: Y

Sales, profits and employees may be estimates. Financial information, benefits and other data can change quickly and may vary from those stated here.

Youku Tudou Inc

www.youku.com

NAIC Code: 519130

TYPES OF BUSINESS:

Online Video Service
Mobile Broadcasting
Video Production
Advertising Services
Television Series
Movies, Variety Shows and Documentaries
Children's Programming and Education
Technology Information and Games

BRANDS/DIVISIONS/AFFILIATES:

Alibaba Group Holding Limited
Youku
Tudou

GROWTH PLANS/SPECIAL FEATURES:

Youku Tudou, Inc. is a multi-screen entertainment and media company in China. The firm operates an internet television platform that enables users to search, view and share high-quality video content quickly and easily across multiple devices. The Youku platform has multiple content formats such as copyright, self-made, co-production, self-channel and live broadcasts. The Youku and Tudou brands are among the most recognized online video brands in the country. Types of entertainment media spans TV series, movies, variety shows, children's programming, documentaries, public welfare information, sports car, technology, animation, fashion, parent-child, education, games and more. Youku Tudou operates as a wholly owned subsidiary of Alibaba Group Holding Ltd.

CONTACTS: *Note: Officers with more than one job title may be intentionally listed here more than once.*

Victor Wing Cheung Koo, CEO
Sunny Xiangyang Zhu, Chief Content Officer
Frank Ming Wei, Sr. VP
Weidong Yang, Sr. VP
Zhou Yu, Sr. VP

FINANCIAL DATA: *Note: Data for latest year may not have been available at press time.*

In U.S. $	2022	2021	2020	2019	2018	2017
Revenue	1,280,000,000	1,274,818,125	1,237,687,500	1,207,500,000	1,150,000,000	1,050,000,000
R&D Expense						
Operating Income						
Operating Margin %						
SGA Expense						
Net Income						
Operating Cash Flow						
Capital Expenditure						
EBITDA						
Return on Assets %						
Return on Equity %						
Debt to Equity						

CONTACT INFORMATION:

Phone: 86 10-5885-1881   Fax: 86-10-5970-8818
Toll-Free: 400-810-0580
Address: Bldg. 4, Dist. 4, Wangjing East Park, Chaoyang Dist., Beijing, Beijing 100102 China

STOCK TICKER/OTHER:

Stock Ticker: Subsidiary   Exchange:
Employees: 2,800   Fiscal Year Ends: 12/31
Parent Company: Alibaba Group Holding Ltd

SALARIES/BONUSES:

Top Exec. Salary: $ Bonus: $
Second Exec. Salary: $ Bonus: $

OTHER THOUGHTS:

Estimated Female Officers or Directors:
Hot Spot for Advancement for Women/Minorities:

Sales, profits and employees may be estimates. Financial information, benefits and other data can change quickly and may vary from those stated here.

YouTube LLC

www.youtube.com

NAIC Code: 519130

TYPES OF BUSINESS:

Online Video Services
Video Subscriptions
Online Video Advertising Services
Video Sharing
User-Generated Content

BRANDS/DIVISIONS/AFFILIATES:

Alphabet Inc
Google LLC
YouTube Select
YouTube Premium
YouTube Music
YouTube Go
YouTube Studio
YouTube TV

CONTACTS: Note: Officers with more than one job title may be intentionally listed here more than once.

Neal Mohan, CEO
Mary Ellen Coe, Chief Business Officer
Danielle Tiedt, CMO
Hunter Walk, Head-Product
Kevin Donahue, VP-Content
Julie Supan, Sr. Dir.-Mktg.

GROWTH PLANS/SPECIAL FEATURES:

YouTube, LLC, a subsidiary of Alphabet, Inc.'s Google LLC, is a leading online video-sharing site, featuring significant amounts of user-generated content. More than 500 hours of video content is uploaded to YouTube every minute. The site has more than 2.7 billion users, is localized in over 100 countries and can be accessed in 80 languages. YouTube derives most of its revenue through in-video advertising, sponsorships and brand channels. Advertisers have the option of purchasing promoted videos, which offer more visibility; 24-hour video banner ads on the website's homepage; the ability to hand-pick videos to advertise against; mobile advertisements; and the ability to advertise with content partners. YouTube allows producers of original content that targets a wide audience to upload ad-supported videos, rentals, high quality content and live-streaming videos. Advertisers can track the impact of these advertisements via page views, video popularity, demographics and audience attention. YouTube is also available through a variety of mobile devices. YouTube Select provides relevant content lineups and programs tailored to unique marketing needs for businesses. YouTube Premium is a monthly subscription that enables users to watch without seeing ads on most types of videos. YouTube Music is a music streaming service. YouTube Go is an app that makes it easier to access YouTube via mobile devices in emerging markets. YouTube Studio is for creators, where they can manage their presence, grow their channels, interact with audiences and earn money. YouTube TV is a live TV streaming service, offering more than 100 live TV channels of entertainment, news, live sports and more. YouTube Kids is a children's video app with curated selections of content, parental control features and more.

Alphabet offers employees health benefits, retirement plans and a variety of employee assistance programs.

FINANCIAL DATA: Note: Data for latest year may not have been available at press time.

In U.S. $	2022	2021	2020	2019	2018	2017
Revenue	29,200,000,000	28,845,000,000	19,772,000,000	15,149,000,000	15,000,000,000	13,250,000,000
R&D Expense						
Operating Income						
Operating Margin %						
SGA Expense						
Net Income						
Operating Cash Flow						
Capital Expenditure						
EBITDA						
Return on Assets %						
Return on Equity %						
Debt to Equity						

CONTACT INFORMATION:

Phone: 650-253-0000 Fax: 650-253-0001
Toll-Free:
Address: 901 Cherry Ave., San Bruno, CA 94066 United States

STOCK TICKER/OTHER:

Stock Ticker: Subsidiary Exchange:
Employees: 11,000 Fiscal Year Ends: 12/31
Parent Company: Alphabet Inc

SALARIES/BONUSES:

Top Exec. Salary: $ Bonus: $
Second Exec. Salary: $ Bonus: $

OTHER THOUGHTS:

Estimated Female Officers or Directors: 2
Hot Spot for Advancement for Women/Minorities:

Zalando SE

NAIC Code: 454110

www.zalando.de

TYPES OF BUSINESS:
Electronic Shopping
Ecommerce
Apparel
Home Products

BRANDS/DIVISIONS/AFFILIATES:
Zalando
Zalando Lounge
Zalon
Zalando Marketing Solutions
Zalando Partner Solutions
Offprice
Fision

GROWTH PLANS/SPECIAL FEATURES:
Zalando, founded in 2008, is Europe's biggest pure-play online fashion platform. Zalando is present in 25 European countries, and its major market is the DACH region, comprising Germany, Austria, and Switzerland, which accounts for around 40% of revenue. The company commands around 4% of European apparel sales and 12% market share in European online apparel sales. It has 12 fulfilment centers and presents over 7,000 brands on its platform. In 2022, Zalando had over 50 million active users (more than 10% of the population in countries where the firm has a presence) and over 7 billion site visits.

CONTACTS: Note: Officers with more than one job title may be intentionally listed here more than once.
Robert Gentz, Co-CEO
David Schneider, Co-CEO
Rubin Ritter, Co-CEO
Jim Freeman, CTO
David Schroder, CFO

FINANCIAL DATA: Note: Data for latest year may not have been available at press time.

In U.S. $	2022	2021	2020	2019	2018	2017
Revenue	11,166,670,000	11,176,600,000	8,616,148,000	6,997,517,000	5,815,954,000	4,845,639,000
R&D Expense						
Operating Income	87,435,230	458,441,200	396,157,200	178,864,400	128,670,100	202,504,300
Operating Margin %	.01%	.04%	.05%	.03%	.02%	.04%
SGA Expense	1,376,187,000	1,428,648,000	1,057,966,000	886,334,200	2,340,350,000	1,914,616,000
Net Income	18,134,710	253,130,400	244,063,000	107,620,900	55,483,590	111,291,000
Operating Cash Flow	496,437,800	665,155,400	569,300,500	353,195,100	229,706,400	209,088,900
Capital Expenditure	379,533,700	359,348,000	269,969,800	330,850,600	300,518,100	263,277,200
EBITDA	446,783,200	700,561,300	638,708,900	399,719,300	224,525,000	270,401,500
Return on Assets %	.00%	.04%	.04%	.03%	.02%	.04%
Return on Equity %	.01%	.11%	.12%	.06%	.03%	.07%
Debt to Equity	.72%	.66%	0.612	0.287	.00%	0.005

CONTACT INFORMATION:
Phone: 49-030-200088400   Fax:
Toll-Free:
Address: Valeska-Gert-Strabe 5, Berlin, 10243 Germany

STOCK TICKER/OTHER:
Stock Ticker: ZLNDY
Employees: 17,043
Parent Company:

Exchange: PINX
Fiscal Year Ends: 12/31

SALARIES/BONUSES:
Top Exec. Salary: $ Bonus: $
Second Exec. Salary: $ Bonus: $

OTHER THOUGHTS:
Estimated Female Officers or Directors:
Hot Spot for Advancement for Women/Minorities:

Zappos.com LLC

www.zappos.com

NAIC Code: 454110

TYPES OF BUSINESS:

Online Shoes Retailing
Ecommerce Retailing
Software Development
Payment Solutions
Technology
Apparel
Housewares
Merchandising Strategies

BRANDS/DIVISIONS/AFFILIATES:

Amazon.com Inc
Zappos Gift Cards Inc
Zappos Insights inc
Zappos Merchandising Inc
6pm.com LLC

GROWTH PLANS/SPECIAL FEATURES:

Zappos.com, LLC, a subsidiary of Amazon.com, Inc., is an online and mobile app retailer of shoes, handbags and other accessories, offering millions of products from a wide variety of footwear and apparel brands. The platform's inventory includes shoes, bags and handbags, clothing, beauty products, eyewear, sporting goods, housewares, watches and more. Due to massive growth, the firm operates through several divisions and companies under the Zappos family umbrella, including solutions such as finance, accounting, help desk, human resources, information technology, legal and training. The Pipeline team provides a training class on Zappos and teaches classes in management, Microsoft Office and more. The IP division provides website software development, project management, marketing and content and creative services to the Zappos family of companies and follows customer experience trends.

Zappos.com offers its employees comprehensive health and retirement benefits.

CONTACTS:
Note: Officers with more than one job title may be intentionally listed here more than once.

Scott Schaefer, CEO

FINANCIAL DATA:
Note: Data for latest year may not have been available at press time.

In U.S. $	2022	2021	2020	2019	2018	2017
Revenue	4,950,000,000	4,944,447,900	4,120,373,250	3,098,025,000	2,950,500,000	2,810,000,000
R&D Expense						
Operating Income						
Operating Margin %						
SGA Expense						
Net Income						
Operating Cash Flow						
Capital Expenditure						
EBITDA						
Return on Assets %						
Return on Equity %						
Debt to Equity						

CONTACT INFORMATION:

Phone: 702-943-7777   Fax: 702-943-7778
Toll-Free: 800-927-7671
Address: 400 E. Stewart Ave., Las Vegas, NV 89101 United States

STOCK TICKER/OTHER:

Stock Ticker: Subsidiary   Exchange:
Employees: 1,500   Fiscal Year Ends: 12/31
Parent Company: Amazon.com Inc

SALARIES/BONUSES:

Top Exec. Salary: $ Bonus: $
Second Exec. Salary: $ Bonus: $

OTHER THOUGHTS:

Estimated Female Officers or Directors:
Hot Spot for Advancement for Women/Minorities:

Zillow Group Inc

NAIC Code: 519130

TYPES OF BUSINESS:

Online Real Estate Information
Real Estate Platform
Mortgage Loans
Artificial Intelligence
Machine Learning
Broker

BRANDS/DIVISIONS/AFFILIATES:

Zillow
Trulia
StreetEasy
HotPads
OutEast.com
Zestimates
Mortech
dotloop

GROWTH PLANS/SPECIAL FEATURES:

Zillow Group Inc is an Internet-based real estate company that offers its customers an on-demand experience for selling, buying, renting, or financing with transparency and ease The group works with real estate agents, brokers, builders, property managers, and landlords to pair technology with top-notch service. The group operates in three segments namely the Internet, Media & Technology (IMT) segment, the Mortgages segment, and the Homes segment.

CONTACTS: Note: Officers with more than one job title may be intentionally listed here more than once.

Richard Barton, CEO
Allen Parker, CFO
Lloyd Frink, Chairman of the Board
Jennifer Rock, Chief Accounting Officer
Aimee Johnson, Chief Marketing Officer
David Beitel, Chief Technology Officer
Jeremy Wacksman, COO
Bradley Owens, General Counsel
Dan Spaulding, Other Executive Officer
Errol Samuelson, Other Executive Officer
Stanley Humphries, Other Executive Officer
Arik Prawer, President, Divisional
Susan Daimler, President, Divisional

FINANCIAL DATA: Note: Data for latest year may not have been available at press time.

In U.S. $	2022	2021	2020	2019	2018	2017
Revenue	1,958,000,000	2,132,000,000	3,339,817,000	2,742,837,000	1,333,554,000	
R&D Expense	498,000,000	421,000,000	390,172,000	350,923,000	410,818,000	
Operating Income	-69,000,000	259,000,000	35,412,000	-246,835,000	-45,628,000	
Operating Margin %	-.04%	.12%	.01%	-.09%	-.03%	
SGA Expense	1,162,000,000	1,129,000,000	1,047,841,000	1,094,650,000	814,774,000	
Net Income	-101,000,000	-528,000,000	-162,115,000	-305,361,000	-119,858,000	
Operating Cash Flow	4,504,000,000	-3,177,000,000	424,197,000	-612,174,000	3,850,000	
Capital Expenditure	140,000,000	105,000,000	108,517,000	86,635,000	78,535,000	
EBITDA	130,000,000	382,000,000	119,958,000	-97,218,000	-10,314,000	
Return on Assets %	-.01%	-.06%	-.02%	-.06%	-.03%	
Return on Equity %	-.02%	-.10%	-.04%	-.09%	-.04%	
Debt to Equity	.40%	.27%	0.384	0.513	.21%	

CONTACT INFORMATION:

Phone: 206 470-7000   Fax:
Toll-Free:
Address: 1301 Second Ave., Fl. 31, Seattle, WA 98101 United States

STOCK TICKER/OTHER:

Stock Ticker: Z   Exchange: NAS
Employees: 5,724   Fiscal Year Ends: 12/31
Parent Company:

SALARIES/BONUSES:

Top Exec. Salary: $702,647   Bonus: $
Second Exec. Salary: Bonus: $
$689,736

OTHER THOUGHTS:

Estimated Female Officers or Directors: 2
Hot Spot for Advancement for Women/Minorities: Y

Sales, profits and employees may be estimates. Financial information, benefits and other data can change quickly and may vary from those stated here.

ZipRecruiter Inc

www.ziprecruiter.com

NAIC Code: 519130

TYPES OF BUSINESS:

Online Jobs Site
Job Recruitment Platform
Cloud

GROWTH PLANS/SPECIAL FEATURES:

ZipRecruiter Inc is an online employment marketplace. It was founded to make meaningful connections between job seekers and employers. It connects millions of job seekers with companies of all sizes.

ZipRecruiter offers its employees comprehensive benefits, 401(k) and company perks.

BRANDS/DIVISIONS/AFFILIATES:

ZipAlerts
ZipPost

CONTACTS: *Note: Officers with more than one job title may be intentionally listed here more than once.*

Marguerite Bui, Assistant General Counsel
Ian Siegel, CEO
David Travers, CFO
Amy Garefis, Chief Accounting Officer
Boris Shimanovsky, Chief Technology Officer
Qasim Saifee, COO
Ryan Sakamoto, General Counsel
Renata Dionello, Other Executive Officer
Ryan Eberhard, Other Executive Officer
Timothy Yarbrough, Other Executive Officer
Erich Gazaui, Senior VP, Divisional
Jennifer Ringel, Senior VP, Divisional
Yaniv Shalev, Senior VP, Divisional
Elliot Wilson, Senior VP, Divisional

FINANCIAL DATA: *Note: Data for latest year may not have been available at press time.*

In U.S. $	2022	2021	2020	2019	2018	2017
Revenue	904,649,000	741,141,000	418,142,000	429,559,000		
R&D Expense	127,737,000	110,470,000	69,408,000	65,410,000		
Operating Income	97,228,000	-8,392,000	64,432,000	-6,318,000		
Operating Margin %	.11%	- .01%	.15%			
SGA Expense	593,386,000	559,449,000	230,139,000	315,689,000		
Net Income	61,494,000	3,600,000	86,048,000	-6,349,000		
Operating Cash Flow	128,808,000	144,136,000	88,013,000	-2,135,000		
Capital Expenditure	10,544,000	13,336,000	7,373,000	10,364,000		
EBITDA	113,264,000	1,103,000	75,323,000	3,758,000		
Return on Assets %	.11%	.01%	.38%			
Return on Equity %	.47%	.02%				
Debt to Equity	19.38%	.08%				

CONTACT INFORMATION:

Phone: 310 496-1311   Fax:
Toll-Free: 800-557-9015
Address: 1453 Third St. Promenade, Ste. 335, Santa Monica, CA 90401 United States

STOCK TICKER/OTHER:

Stock Ticker: ZIP   Exchange: NYS
Employees: 1,400   Fiscal Year Ends: 12/31
Parent Company:

SALARIES/BONUSES:

Top Exec. Salary: $550,000   Bonus: $
Second Exec. Salary: $430,000   Bonus: $

OTHER THOUGHTS:

Estimated Female Officers or Directors:
Hot Spot for Advancement for Women/Minorities:

Zoho Corporation Pvt Ltd

NAIC Code: 511210H

www.zoho.com

TYPES OF BUSINESS:

Enterprise Management Software
Enterprise Information Technology
Cloud Solutions
Management Software
Mobile Apps
App Customization Tools

GROWTH PLANS/SPECIAL FEATURES:

Zoho Corporation Pvt. Ltd. provides cloud-based enterprise information technology (IT) management software. The company's single platform, Zoho One, enables users to run a business completely from the cloud. Zoho's mobile apps are engineered for ease, speed and enhanced functionality to manage businesses from anywhere, anytime. Users can customize apps with Zoho's creator tool; manage the entire recruitment process through the app; create online reports via intelligent analytics; manage email campaigns; offer live chat to increase sales; improve customer service; manage invoices, track payments and upload expense receipts; invoice; and access and update expenses as well as inventory. The firm's more than 55 apps cover sales and marketing, email, collaboration, workplace, business process, finance, IT, business intelligence, help desk, customer relations management, human resources solutions and mapping/routing solutions, as well as customized solutions. Based in India, the firm has offices in the U.S., Canada, India, Japan, China, Singapore, Mexico, Brazil, Australia, Netherlands, South Africa, Saudi Arabia, Egypt, Kenya, Nigeria, U.K. and United Arab Emirates.

BRANDS/DIVISIONS/AFFILIATES:

Zoho One

CONTACTS: Note: Officers with more than one job title may be intentionally listed here more than once.

Sridhar Vembu, CEO

FINANCIAL DATA: Note: Data for latest year may not have been available at press time.

In U.S. $	2022	2021	2020	2019	2018	2017
Revenue	925,216,000	697,000,000	582,955,000	490,140,000	381,393,000	270,678,000
R&D Expense						
Operating Income						
Operating Margin %						
SGA Expense						
Net Income		255,700,000	106,445,000	74,167,800	62,720,000	43,968,200
Operating Cash Flow						
Capital Expenditure						
EBITDA						
Return on Assets %						
Return on Equity %						
Debt to Equity						

CONTACT INFORMATION:

Phone: 91 44-67447070   Fax: 91 44-67447172
Toll-Free:
Address: Estancia IT Park, Plot #140 & 151, GST Rd., Vallancherry Village, Kanchipuram District 603 202 India

STOCK TICKER/OTHER:

Stock Ticker: Private
Employees: 15,000
Parent Company:

Exchange:
Fiscal Year Ends: 03/31

SALARIES/BONUSES:

Top Exec. Salary: $ Bonus: $
Second Exec. Salary: $ Bonus: $

OTHER THOUGHTS:

Estimated Female Officers or Directors:
Hot Spot for Advancement for Women/Minorities:

Zoom Video Communications Inc

zoom.us

NAIC Code: 511210C

TYPES OF BUSINESS:
Computer Software, Telecom, Communications & VOIP

GROWTH PLANS/SPECIAL FEATURES:
Zoom Video Communications provides a communications platform that connects people through video, voice, chat, and content sharing. The company's cloud-native platform enables face-to-face video and connects users across various devices and locations in a single meeting. Zoom, which was founded in 2011 and is headquartered in San Jose, California, serves companies of all sizes from all industries around the world.

BRANDS/DIVISIONS/AFFILIATES:
Zoom
Zoom Room

CONTACTS: Note: Officers with more than one job title may be intentionally listed here more than once.
Eric Yuan, CEO
Kelly Steckelberg, CFO
Shane Crehan, Chief Accounting Officer
Aparna Bawa, Chief Legal Officer
Janine Pelosi, Chief Marketing Officer
Ryan Azus, Other Executive Officer
Velchamy Sankarlingam, President, Divisional

FINANCIAL DATA: Note: Data for latest year may not have been available at press time.

In U.S. $	2022	2021	2020	2019	2018	2017
Revenue	4,099,864,000	2,651,368,000	622,658,000	330,517,000	151,478,000	
R&D Expense	362,990,000	164,080,000	67,079,000	33,014,000	15,733,000	
Operating Income	1,063,591,000	659,848,000	12,696,000	6,167,000	-4,833,000	
Operating Margin %	.26%	.25%	.02%	.02%	- .03%	
SGA Expense	1,618,729,000	1,005,451,000	427,487,000	230,335,000	109,798,000	
Net Income	1,375,639,000	672,316,000	25,305,000	7,584,000	-3,822,000	
Operating Cash Flow	1,605,266,000	1,471,177,000	151,892,000	51,332,000	19,426,000	
Capital Expenditure	145,608,000	85,815,000	38,225,000	30,450,000	9,738,000	
EBITDA	1,111,779,000	688,705,000	29,145,000	13,175,000	-2,047,000	
Return on Assets %	.21%	.20%	.03%	.03%	- .04%	
Return on Equity %	.29%	.29%	.04%	.11%		
Debt to Equity	.01%	.02%	0.078			

CONTACT INFORMATION:
Phone: 650 397-6096   Fax:
Toll-Free: 888-799-9666
Address: 55 Almaden Blvd., Fl. 6, San Jose, CA 95113 United States

STOCK TICKER/OTHER:
Stock Ticker: ZM
Employees: 8,484
Parent Company:

Exchange: NAS
Fiscal Year Ends: 01/31

SALARIES/BONUSES:
Top Exec. Salary: $451,731   Bonus: $
Second Exec. Salary: $426,923   Bonus: $

OTHER THOUGHTS:
Estimated Female Officers or Directors:
Hot Spot for Advancement for Women/Minorities:

Sales, profits and employees may be estimates. Financial information, benefits and other data can change quickly and may vary from those stated here.

Zozo Inc
NAIC Code: 454110

corp.zozo.com

TYPES OF BUSINESS:
Electronic Shopping
Ecommerce
Retail
Fashion
Cosmetics
Online Marketing
Website Development

BRANDS/DIVISIONS/AFFILIATES:
ZOZOTOWN
ZOZO Group
ZOZO Technologies Inc
ZOZOUSED Inc
aratana Inc
ZOZO Research
aratana gateway
Yahoo Japan Corp

GROWTH PLANS/SPECIAL FEATURES:
Zozo was established in 1998 by Yusaku Maezawa (founder and former CEO), and its main business is Zozotown, the largest fashion e-commerce platform in Japan. Zozotown's business consists mainly of consignment sales, where each brand's products are stocked in Zozotown's logistics bases, and brands open their shops on Zozotown as tenants. As of 2022, Zozotown sold clothing from over 8,500 brands and boasted about 9.3 million annual active users. In 2019, Zozo was acquired by Z Holdings. Since then, Zozo also sells through the Yahoo-owned general e-commerce site PayPay Mall.

CONTACTS: Note: Officers with more than one job title may be intentionally listed here more than once.
Kotaro Sawada, CEO
Masahiro Ito, COO
Koji Yanagisawa, CFO

FINANCIAL DATA: Note: Data for latest year may not have been available at press time.

In U.S. $	2022	2021	2020	2019	2018	2017
Revenue	1,134,131,000	1,005,643,000				
R&D Expense						
Operating Income	338,883,500	301,276,800				
Operating Margin %	.30%	.30%				
SGA Expense	340,712,300	294,384,600				
Net Income	235,371,200	211,078,000				
Operating Cash Flow	272,240,900	305,644,100				
Capital Expenditure	9,116,778	22,873,830				
EBITDA	353,077,200	315,006,500				
Return on Assets %	.27%	.28%				
Return on Equity %	.62%	.69%				
Debt to Equity						

CONTACT INFORMATION:
Phone: 81 43 2135171   Fax:
Toll-Free:
Address: WBG Maribu West 15th-16th Floor, Chiba, 261-7116 Japan

STOCK TICKER/OTHER:
Stock Ticker: SATLF   Exchange: PINX
Employees: 3,392   Fiscal Year Ends: 03/30
Parent Company: Yahoo Japan Corp

SALARIES/BONUSES:
Top Exec. Salary: $ Bonus: $
Second Exec. Salary: $ Bonus: $

OTHER THOUGHTS:
Estimated Female Officers or Directors:
Hot Spot for Advancement for Women/Minorities:

Zscaler Inc

www.zscaler.com

NAIC Code: 511210E

TYPES OF BUSINESS:

Computer Software, Network Security, Managed Access, Digital ID, Cybersecurity & Anti-Virus

GROWTH PLANS/SPECIAL FEATURES:

Zscaler is a software-as-a-service, or SaaS, firm focusing on providing cloud-native cybersecurity solutions to primarily enterprise customers. Zscaler's offerings can be broadly partitioned into Zscaler Internet Access, which provides secure access to external applications, and Zscaler Private Access, which provides secure access to internal applications. The firm is headquartered in San Jose, California, and went public in 2018.

BRANDS/DIVISIONS/AFFILIATES:

Zscaler Internet Access
Zscaler Private Access
Zscaler App
Edgewise Networks

CONTACTS: Note: Officers with more than one job title may be intentionally listed here more than once.

Eileen Naughton,
Jagtar Chaudhry, CEO
Remo Canessa, CFO
Robert Schlossman, Chief Legal Officer
Amit Sinha, Chief Technology Officer
Dalibor Rajic, Other Executive Officer

FINANCIAL DATA: Note: Data for latest year may not have been available at press time.

In U.S. $	2022	2021	2020	2019	2018	2017
Revenue	1,090,946,000	673,100,000	431,269,000	302,836,000	190,174,000	
R&D Expense	289,139,000	174,653,000	97,879,000	61,969,000	39,379,000	
Operating Income	-327,429,000	-207,396,000	-113,956,000	-35,313,000	-34,624,000	
Operating Margin %	-.30%	-.31%	-.26%	-.12%	-.18%	
SGA Expense	886,250,000	555,199,000	351,613,000	216,511,000	147,544,000	
Net Income	-390,278,000	-262,029,000	-115,116,000	-28,655,000	-33,646,000	
Operating Cash Flow	321,912,000	202,040,000	79,317,000	58,027,000	17,307,000	
Capital Expenditure	90,580,000	58,297,000	51,809,000	30,162,000	15,170,000	
EBITDA	-277,585,000	-167,356,000	-86,832,000	-16,606,000	-24,321,000	
Return on Assets %	-.15%	-.13%	-.09%	-.05%	-.13%	
Return on Equity %	-.71%	-.52%	-.29%	-.10%	-.90%	
Debt to Equity	1.78%	1.79%	1.835			

CONTACT INFORMATION:

Phone: 408-533-0288   Fax:
Toll-Free:
Address: 110 Rose Orchard Way, San Jose, CA 95134 United States

STOCK TICKER/OTHER:

Stock Ticker: ZS   Exchange: NAS
Employees: 5,962   Fiscal Year Ends: 07/31
Parent Company:

SALARIES/BONUSES:

Top Exec. Salary: $430,000   Bonus: $
Second Exec. Salary: Bonus: $
$430,000

OTHER THOUGHTS:

Estimated Female Officers or Directors:
Hot Spot for Advancement for Women/Minorities:

Zuora Inc

NAIC Code: 522320

TYPES OF BUSINESS:

Recurring Billing Software Tools
Subscription Management Tools
Online Billing and Subscription Tools
Games and Apps Subscription Tools

BRANDS/DIVISIONS/AFFILIATES:

Zuora
Zuora Billing
Zuora Revenue
Zuora CPQ
Zuora Collect
Zuora Central Platform

GROWTH PLANS/SPECIAL FEATURES:

Zuora Inc provides cloud-based software on a subscription basis that enables companies in various industries to launch, manage, and transform into a subscription business. The firm offers Zuora Central platform that acts as an intelligent subscription management hub that automates the subscription order-to-cash process, including quoting, billing, collections, analytics, and revenue recognition. Its products include Zuora Billing, Zuora CPQ, and Zuora Collect. Zuora caters to various industries comprising software, hardware, media, transportation, construction, healthcare, education, retail, Internet of Things, and others worldwide. Geographically, it derives a majority of its revenue from the United States.

CONTACTS: Note: Officers with more than one job title may be intentionally listed here more than once.

Tien Tzuo, CEO
Todd McElhatton, CFO
Jennifer Pileggi, General Counsel
Robert Traube, Other Executive Officer
Sri Srinivasan, Other Executive Officer
Brent Cromley, Senior VP, Divisional

FINANCIAL DATA: Note: Data for latest year may not have been available at press time.

In U.S. $	2022	2021	2020	2019	2018	2017
Revenue	346,738,000	305,420,000	276,057,000	234,989,000	171,106,000	
R&D Expense	83,219,000	76,795,000	74,398,000	54,417,000	38,639,000	
Operating Income	-96,176,000	-73,862,000	-85,665,000	-70,417,000	-38,078,000	
Operating Margin %	- .28%	- .24%	- .31%	- .30%	- .22%	
SGA Expense	219,589,000	171,717,000	153,143,000	134,399,000	90,639,000	
Net Income	-99,425,000	-73,174,000	-83,394,000	-72,741,000	-39,377,000	
Operating Cash Flow	18,686,000	11,286,000	-3,590,000	-23,581,000	-24,776,000	
Capital Expenditure	10,125,000	13,144,000	21,424,000	13,412,000	4,698,000	
EBITDA	-79,416,000	-55,659,000	-73,799,000	-62,189,000	-31,528,000	
Return on Assets %	- .23%	- .18%	- .23%	- .30%	- .29%	
Return on Equity %	- .58%	- .43%	- .48%	- .70%	- .96%	
Debt to Equity	.27%	.32%	0.415	0.058	.46%	

CONTACT INFORMATION:

Phone: 888-976-9056   Fax:
Toll-Free:
Address: 101 Redwood Shores Pkwy., Redwood City, CA 94065 United States

STOCK TICKER/OTHER:

Stock Ticker: ZUO
Employees: 1,549
Parent Company:

Exchange: NYS
Fiscal Year Ends: 01/31

SALARIES/BONUSES:

Top Exec. Salary: $500,000   Bonus: $
Second Exec. Salary: $450,000   Bonus: $

OTHER THOUGHTS:

Estimated Female Officers or Directors:
Hot Spot for Advancement for Women/Minorities:

Zynga Inc

www.zynga.com

NAIC Code: 511210G

TYPES OF BUSINESS:
Computer Software, Electronic Games, Apps & Entertainment
Social Game Development
Social Game Operation
Mobile and Online Games
Advertising Services

BRANDS/DIVISIONS/AFFILIATES:
Take-Two Interactive Software Inc
FarmVille 3
Harry Potter Puzzles & Spells
Game of Thrones Slots Casino
Words with Friends 2
Zynga Poker
CSR 2
Chartboost

CONTACTS: *Note: Officers with more than one job title may be intentionally listed here more than once.*
Frank Gibeau, Pres.
Gerard Griffin, CFO
Jeffrey Ryan, Other Executive Officer
Bernard Kim, President, Divisional

GROWTH PLANS/SPECIAL FEATURES:
Zynga, Inc. develops, markets, and operates social games as live services played on mobile platforms and social networking sites, such as Facebook. Zynga generates revenue through game downloads, in-games sales of virtual goods, and advertising services. Zynga's global reach spans more than 175 countries and regions. Featured games include: FarmVille 3, a nature experience where players harvest crops and raise animals; Harry Potter Puzzles & Spells, offering an enchanted experience of casting spells, outsmarting challenges and exploring the world of wizarding; Game of Thrones Slots Casino, an immersive slot machine game for testing skills through various kingdoms; Words with Friends 2, a mobile word game; Zynga Poker, a digital poker competition game against millions of other users 24/7/365; CSR 2, a drag racing game for competing against live players across the world via custom-built supercars; and Merge Dragons, a game that enables users to merge all sorts of things in the world and evolve them into other things. Additional popular game franchises include Empires & Puzzles, Golf Rival, Hair Challenge, High Heels!, Toon Blast, Toy Blast and more. Chartboost is the company's mobile advertising and monetization platform. Headquartered in California, Zynga has locations in North America, Europe and Asia.

Zynga offers its employees comprehensive health benefits

FINANCIAL DATA: *Note: Data for latest year may not have been available at press time.*

In U.S. $	2022	2021	2020	2019	2018	2017
Revenue	2,159,200,000	2,800,000,000	1,974,800,000	1,321,659,008	907,208,000	861,390,016
R&D Expense						
Operating Income						
Operating Margin %						
SGA Expense						
Net Income		-104,200,000	-429,400,000	41,925,000	15,457,000	26,639,000
Operating Cash Flow						
Capital Expenditure						
EBITDA						
Return on Assets %						
Return on Equity %						
Debt to Equity						

CONTACT INFORMATION:
Phone: 415 703-0130   Fax:
Toll-Free: 800 762-2530
Address: 1200 Park Pl., San Mateo, CA 94403 United States

STOCK TICKER/OTHER:
Stock Ticker: Subsidiary   Exchange:
Employees: 2,245   Fiscal Year Ends: 12/31
Parent Company: Take-Two Interactive Software Inc

SALARIES/BONUSES:
Top Exec. Salary: $ Bonus: $
Second Exec. Salary: $ Bonus: $

OTHER THOUGHTS:
Estimated Female Officers or Directors: 2
Hot Spot for Advancement for Women/Minorities:

ADDITIONAL INDEXES

CONTENTS:

INDEX OF FIRMS NOTED AS HOT SPOTS FOR ADVANCEMENT FOR WOMEN & MINORITIES

Accenture plc
Adobe Inc
AG Interactive Inc
Airbnb Inc
Akamai Technologies Inc
Alibaba Group Holding Limited
Alibris Inc
Alphabet Inc (Google)
Altice USA Inc
Amadeus IT Group SA
Amazon.com Inc
American Greetings Corporation LLC
ASOS plc
AT&T Inc
Atos SE
Audible Inc
Automatic Data Processing Inc (ADP)
Avantax Inc
Beyond Inc
Bloomberg LP
Blue Nile Inc
BMC Software Inc
Booking Holdings Inc
Boursorama
Brightcove Inc
Campaign Monitor Pty Ltd
CareerBuilder LLC
Charles Schwab Corporation (The)
Check Point Software Technologies Ltd
China Mobile Limited
Cincinnati Bell Inc (altafiber)
Cisco Systems Inc
Comcast Corporation
CoreSite an American Tower Company
CoStar Group Inc
Cox Communications Inc
Craigslist Inc
Critical Mass Inc
CyberSource Corporation
D&B Hoovers
Deem Inc
Dell Technologies Inc
Digital River Inc
Digitas
DirecTV LLC (DIRECTV)
Dotdash Meredith
Dow Jones & Company Inc
eBay Inc
Elavon Inc
Endeavor Streaming
Equinix Inc
E-Trade from Morgan Stanley
Etsy Inc

Eventbrite Inc
Evernote Corporation
Everyday Health Inc
F5 Inc
FactSet Research Systems Inc
Fandango Inc
Forrester Research Inc
Fredericks of Hollywood
Frontier Communications Corporation
Gainsight Inc
Gartner Inc
Gen Digital Inc
Global Payments Inc
GoDaddy Inc
Grubhub Inc
Honest Company Inc (The)
Hootsuite Inc
Hotwire Inc
Huawei Technologies Co Ltd
Hulu LLC
IAC/InterActiveCorp
iCrossing Inc
Infosys Limited
Instacart (Maplebear Inc)
Internap Corporation
International Business Machines Corporation (IBM)
Intuit Inc
JAGGAER
Juniper Networks Inc
KAYAK
Kickstarter PBC
Leaf Group Ltd
Liberty Global plc
LifeWay Christian Resources
LinkedIn Corporation
Lionbridge Technologies LLC
LiveRamp Holdings Inc
LiveWorld Inc
LivingSocial LLC
Lumen Technologies Inc
Macquarium Inc
MarketWatch Inc
McAfee Corp
Medallia Inc
MediaPlatform Inc
Meta Platforms Inc (Facebook)
Microsoft Corporation
MKTG Sports + Entertainment
Moatable Inc
Monster Worldwide Inc
Myspace LLC
NaviSite LLC
Netflix Inc
New York Times Company (The)
Newfold Digital Inc
News Corporation
Open Text Corporation
OpenTable Inc

Oracle Corporation
Oracle NetSuite
Ozon Holdings PLC
Pandora Media LLC
Paramount Streaming
PayPal Holdings Inc
Photobucket Inc
Pinterest Inc
PointClickCare
Progress Software Corporation
Radware Ltd
Rakuten (Ebates Inc)
REA Group Ltd
RealPage Inc
Red Hat Inc
Rent the Runway Inc
Rogers Communications Inc
Salesforce Inc
Salon.com LLC
SAP SE
Shaw Communications Inc
Skype Technologies Sarl
SMS Assist LLC
Sohu.com Limited
Stripe Inc
SugarCRM Inc
SurveyMonkey Inc
Telenor ASA
Telephone and Data Systems Inc (TDS)
Tellabs Inc
Teradata Corporation
TheStreet Inc
Thomson Reuters Corporation
Total System Services LLC (TSYS)
Travelport Worldwide Limited
Travelzoo Inc
Trend Micro Inc
Trip.com Group Limited
TripAdvisor Inc
Ushahidi Inc
Veracode Inc
VeriFone Inc
Verizon Communications Inc
Vibrant Media Inc
VitaCost.com Inc
Vodafone Group plc
WalkMe Inc
Walt Disney Company (The)
WatchGuard Technologies Inc
Wayfair LLC
WebMD Health Corp
Whitepages Inc
Wipro Limited
X Corp (Twitter)
Yahoo Inc
Yandex NV
Yelp Inc
YOOX Net-A-Porter Group SpA (YNAP)

Zillow Group Inc

INDEX OF SUBSIDIARIES, BRAND NAMES AND AFFILIATIONS

INDEX OF SUBSIDIARIES, BRAND NAMES AND AFFILIATIONS, CONT.

INDEX OF SUBSIDIARIES, BRAND NAMES AND AFFILIATIONS, CONT.

INDEX OF SUBSIDIARIES, BRAND NAMES AND AFFILIATIONS, CONT.

INDEX OF SUBSIDIARIES, BRAND NAMES AND AFFILIATIONS, CONT.

INDEX OF SUBSIDIARIES, BRAND NAMES AND AFFILIATIONS, CONT.

INDEX OF SUBSIDIARIES, BRAND NAMES AND AFFILIATIONS, CONT.

hStream; **HealthStream Inc**
Huaewi; **Huawei Technologies Co Ltd**
Hulu + Live TV; **Hulu LLC**
Hulu Originals; **Hulu LLC**
Hyperblock; **Anaplan Inc**
Hyperwallet; **PayPal Holdings Inc**
i24NEWS; **Altice USA Inc**
IAC/InterActiveCorp; **Dotdash Meredith**
IAC/InterActiveCorp; **Vimeo Inc**
IberLibros.com; **AbeBooks Inc**
Ibibo Group Holdings (Singapore) Pte Ltd; **MakeMyTrip Limited**
Ibibo Group Private Limited; **MakeMyTrip Limited**
IBM; **International Business Machines Corporation (IBM)**
iControl; **AutoWeb Inc**
IDComply; **Geocomply Solutions Inc**
Idera Inc; **Embarcadero Inc**
IDT Corporation; **Net2Phone Inc**
IFM Investors; **Switch Inc**
IGN; **Consensus Cloud Solutions Inc**
IGTV; **Instagram**
Illumio CloudSecure; **Illumio**
Illumio Core; **Illumio**
Illumio Edge; **Illumio**
i-mercury Capital Inc; **mixi Inc**
INAP; **Internap Corporation**
Income Access; **Paysafe Limited**
InDemand; **Indiegogo Inc**
Industries; **Salesforce Inc**
Infinity-Vision; **Check Point Software Technologies Ltd**
Infiot; **Netskope Inc**
Infosys BPM; **Infosys Limited**
Infosys Consulting; **Infosys Limited**
Infosys Public Services; **Infosys Limited**
Infrastructure Solutions Group; **Dell Technologies Inc**
InMobi University; **InMobi Pte Ltd**
INNOVATE Corp; **INNOVATE Corp**
inSided; **Gainsight Inc**
InsideSales; **InsideSales**
Insight Partners; **Optimizely Inc**
Insight Partners; **Veeam Software**
Instacart Connect; **Instacart (Maplebear Inc)**
Instacart Platform; **Instacart (Maplebear Inc)**
Instacart+; **Instacart (Maplebear Inc)**
Instagram; **Meta Platforms Inc (Facebook)**
Instagram Stories; **Instagram**
Instapro; **Angi Inc**
Instashop; **Delivery Hero SE**
Intelligence Cloud; **Optimizely Inc**
INterBase; **Embarcadero Inc**
Internap Holding LLC; **Internap Corporation**
International Business Exchange (IBX); **Equinix Inc**
International Business Machines Corporation (IBM); **Red Hat Inc**

Internet Brands; **MH Sub I LLC (dba Internet Brands)**
Internet Brands Inc; **WebMD Health Corp**
Intota; **ProQuest LLC**
Intuit Inc; **Intuit MailChimp (The Rocket Science Group LLC)**
Intuit MailChimp; **Intuit MailChimp (The Rocket Science Group LLC)**
Investopedia; **Dotdash Meredith**
Invoice2go; **Bill.com Holdings Inc**
IONOS; **United Internet AG**
iOS; **Apple Inc**
IoT Cloud; **Salesforce Inc**
iPad; **Apple Inc**
iPhone; **Apple Inc**
iproperty.com.my; **REA Group Ltd**
IPVanish; **Consensus Cloud Solutions Inc**
iQIYI; **Baidu Inc**
ITC Bangkok Co Ltd; **MakeMyTrip Limited**
ITI Neovision; **Liberty Global plc**
ITV; **Liberty Global plc**
IWCO Direct Inc; **Steel Connect Inc**
iZettle; **PayPal Holdings Inc**
j2 Global Inc; **Everyday Health Inc**
Jacks Flight Club; **Travelzoo Inc**
JAGGAER ONE; **JAGGAER**
Jazz; **Veon Ltd**
Jetcost; **lastminute.com NV (lm group)**
Jio; **Jio (Reliance Jio Infocomm Ltd)**
JioFi; **Jio (Reliance Jio Infocomm Ltd)**
JioFiber; **Jio (Reliance Jio Infocomm Ltd)**
JLL Partners; **MedeAnalytics Inc**
jobrapido; **Symphony Technology Group**
Joss & Main; **Wayfair LLC**
JP Morgan Payments; **Linden Research Inc (Linden Lab)**
Jumia; **Jumia Technologies AG**
JumiaPay; **Jumia Technologies AG**
JUMP Bikes; **Uber Technologies Inc**
Juno; **United Online Inc**
Juno Turbo; **United Online Inc**
Just Eat Takeaway.com NV; **Grubhub Inc**
justWink; **AG Interactive Inc**
Kaixin Auto Group; **Moatable Inc**
Karen Millen; **Boohoo.com PLC**
KAYAK; **Booking Holdings Inc**
KAYAK Trips; **KAYAK**
KAYAK.com; **KAYAK**
KEB HanaCard Co Ltd; **SK Telecom Co Ltd**
Kelley Blue Book; **Cox Automotive Inc**
Kemp; **Progress Software Corporation**
Khoros Platform; **Khoros LLC**
Kibo Commerce; **Kibo Software Inc**
Kindle Direct Publishing; **Amazon.com Inc**
Kinetic by Windstream; **Windstream Holdings Inc**
KinoPoisk; **Yandex NV**
KKR & Co Inc; **BMC Software Inc**

INDEX OF SUBSIDIARIES, BRAND NAMES AND AFFILIATIONS, CONT.

INDEX OF SUBSIDIARIES, BRAND NAMES AND AFFILIATIONS, CONT.

INDEX OF SUBSIDIARIES, BRAND NAMES AND AFFILIATIONS, CONT.

INDEX OF SUBSIDIARIES, BRAND NAMES AND AFFILIATIONS, CONT.

INDEX OF SUBSIDIARIES, BRAND NAMES AND AFFILIATIONS, CONT.

ServiceMax Core; **ServiceMax Inc**
ServiceMax Engage; **ServiceMax Inc**
ServiceMax Field FX; **ServiceMax Inc**
SFIDANTE Inc; **mixi Inc**
Shanghai SINA Advertising Co Ltd; **SINA Corporation**
SharePoint; **Microsoft Corporation**
Shaw; **Shaw Communications Inc**
Shaw Business; **Shaw Communications Inc**
Shaw Direct; **Shaw Communications Inc**
Shop Hulu; **Hulu LLC**
Shop Pay; **Shopify Inc**
Shopee; **Sea Limited**
ShopeePay; **Sea Limited**
ShopeePayLater; **Sea Limited**
Shopify Capital; **Shopify Inc**
Shopify Plus; **Shopify Inc**
Shopinvest Group (The); **3 Suisses**
ShopKeep Inc; **Lightspeed Commerce Inc**
Shopmium; **Quotient Technology Inc**
Shopping.com; **Shopping.com Ltd**
Shoptime; **Americanas SA**
SHOWROOM; **DeNA Co Ltd**
Shutterfly; **Shutterfly LLC**
Shutterfly Business Solutions; **Shutterfly LLC**
Signal Sciences; **Fastly Inc**
Signet Jewelers Ltd; **Blue Nile Inc**
Simplenote; **Automattic Inc**
Sims (The); **Electronic Arts Inc (EA)**
SINA (Shanghai) Management Co Ltd; **SINA Corporation**
SINA Group Holding Co Ltd; **SINA Corporation**
SINA.com Technology (China) Co Ltd; **SINA Corporation**
Siris Capital Group LLC; **Digital River Inc**
Siris Capital Group LLC; **Travelport Worldwide Limited**
Sirius XM Holdings Inc; **Pandora Media LLC**
Sistema JSGC; **Mobile TeleSystems PJSC**
Site Factory; **Acquia Inc**
Site Studio; **Acquia Inc**
SK Hynix Inc; **SK Telecom Co Ltd**
SkillSurvey; **iCIMS Inc**
Skrill; **Paysafe Limited**
Sky Limited; **Comcast Corporation**
Sky News; **Comcast Corporation**
Sky Sports; **Comcast Corporation**
Skyhigh Security; **Symphony Technology Group**
Skype for Business; **Microsoft Corporation**
Skyscanner; **Trip.com Group Limited**
Slack; **Slack Technologies LLC**
SmartScan; **Expensify Inc**
SmashUps; **AG Interactive Inc**
SmashUps; **American Greetings Corporation LLC**
SMS Assist LLC; **SMS Assist LLC**
SMS University; **SMS Assist LLC**
SMSsync; **Ushahidi Inc**
Snap Map; **Snap Inc (Snapchat)**
Snapchat; **Snap Inc (Snapchat)**

Snapdeal Private Limited; **Snapdeal**
Snapfish; **Shutterfly LLC**
Snaps; **Snap Inc (Snapchat)**
SNOW; **Naver Corporation**
Societe Generale Group; **Boursorama**
society6; **Leaf Group Ltd**
SoftBank Group Capital Limited; **SoftBank Group Corp**
SoftBank Investment Advisers; **SoftBank Group Corp**
SoftBank Vision Fund LP; **SoftBank Group Corp**
Sogou; **Sogou Inc**
Sogou Inc; **Sohu.com Limited**
Sohu; **Sohu.com Limited**
Sou Barato; **Americanas SA**
Southern Baptist Convention; **LifeWay Christian Resources**
Spectacles; **Snap Inc (Snapchat)**
Spectra; **NetScout Systems Inc**
Spectrum; **Charter Communications Inc**
Spectrum Community Solutions; **Charter Communications Inc**
Spectrum Enterprise Solutions; **Charter Communications Inc**
Spectrum Internet Gig; **Charter Communications Inc**
Spectrum Mobile; **Charter Communications Inc**
Spectrum Reach; **Charter Communications Inc**
Spectrum TV; **Charter Communications Inc**
Spectrum Voice; **Charter Communications Inc**
Spoonflower; **Shutterfly LLC**
Sprinklr Core Platform; **Sprinklr Inc**
Sprint Corporation; **T-Mobile US Inc**
squarefoot.com.hk; **REA Group Ltd**
SRX; **Juniper Networks Inc**
SS&C Intralinks; **Intralinks Inc**
SS&C Technologies Holdings Inc; **Intralinks Inc**
STAR; **Fiserv Inc**
Star+; **Walt Disney Company (The)**
Starshining Mobile Technology (China) Ltd; **SINA Corporation**
steapandcheap.com; **BackCountry.com LLC**
STG Exited Investments; **Symphony Technology Group**
StorageCafe; **Yardi Systems Inc**
Stories; **Snap Inc (Snapchat)**
STR; **CoStar Group Inc**
Straight Talk; **America Movil SAB de CV**
Strategic Investment Office; **DeNA Co Ltd**
StreetEasy; **Zillow Group Inc**
STRIVE; **Gree Inc**
StubHub Holdings; **viagogo Entertainment Inc**
Student Advantage Discount Card; **Student Advantage LLC**
Submarino; **Americanas SA**
Suddenlink; **Altice USA Inc**
Summon; **ProQuest LLC**
Sumo Logic SaaS Log Analytics Platform; **Sumo Logic Inc**
Sundog Interactive Inc; **Perficient Inc**

INDEX OF SUBSIDIARIES, BRAND NAMES AND AFFILIATIONS, CONT.

INDEX OF SUBSIDIARIES, BRAND NAMES AND AFFILIATIONS, CONT.

INDEX OF SUBSIDIARIES, BRAND NAMES AND AFFILIATIONS, CONT.

INDEX OF SUBSIDIARIES, BRAND NAMES AND AFFILIATIONS, CONT.

Zoom Room; **Zoom Video Communications Inc**
ZOZO Group; **Zozo Inc**
ZOZO Research; **Zozo Inc**
ZOZO Technologies Inc; **Zozo Inc**
ZOZOTOWN; **Zozo Inc**
ZOZOUSED Inc; **Zozo Inc**
Zscaler App; **Zscaler Inc**
Zscaler Internet Access; **Zscaler Inc**
Zscaler Private Access; **Zscaler Inc**
zulily llc; **Qurate Retail Inc**
Zuora; **Zuora Inc**
Zuora Billing; **Zuora Inc**
Zuora Central Platform; **Zuora Inc**
Zuora Collect; **Zuora Inc**
Zuora CPQ; **Zuora Inc**
Zuora Revenue; **Zuora Inc**
ZVAB.com; **AbeBooks Inc**
Zynga Poker; **Zynga Inc**

INDEX OF SUBSIDIARIES, BRAND NAMES AND AFFILIATIONS, CONT.

A Short E-Commerce & Internet Business Glossary

2FA: See "Two-Factor Authentication (2FA)."

3G: Short for third generation, this term refers to relatively high-speed enhancements to wireless service. 3G has been largely replaced by newer, more advanced 4G and higher technologies.

3GPP: Third Generation Partnership Project. It is an organization set up to create and monitor advanced 3G wireless standards.

3PF: See "Third-Party Fulfillment (3PF)."

3PL: See "Third-Party Logistics (3PL)."

4G: An advancement in speed and capabilities over 3G wireless networks. 4G not only features relatively high data transfer speeds, it also has an enhanced ability to support interactive multimedia, internet access, mobile video and other vital tasks. It may eventually be surpassed by 5G, 6G and other more advanced networks.

4PL: See "Fourth-Party Logistics (4PL)."

5G: A wireless technology that can provide high download speeds of one gigabyte per second (Gbps) to 20 Gbps and more. The first specifications for 5G were agreed to by the global wireless industry from 2017 to 2019. While certain 5G features can be used to boost speeds of earlier 4G networks, a true rollout required major investment in new cellular infrastructure and systems.

802.11: See "Wi-Fi."

802.11n (MIMO): Multiple Input Multiple Output. MIMO is a standard in the series of 802.11 Wi-Fi specifications for wireless networks. It can provide very high speed network access. 802.11n also boasts better operating distances than many networks. MIMO uses spectrum more efficiently without any loss of reliability. The technology is based on several different antennas all tuned to the same channel, each transmitting a different signal. Advancements include MU-MIMO (Multi-User MIMO) and OFDMA (Orthogonal Frequency-Division Multiple Access), each of which improves network throughput.

802.15: See "Ultrawideband (UWB)." For 802.15.1, see "Bluetooth."

802.16: See "WiMAX."

Active Server Page (ASP): A web page that includes one or more embedded programs, usually written in Java or Visual Basic code. See "Java."

Active X: A set of technologies developed by Microsoft Corporation for sharing information across different applications.

ADM: The application, development and maintenance of software.

ADN: See "Advanced Digital Network (ADN)."

Advanced Digital Network (ADN): See "Integrated Digital Network (IDN)."

Advertising: Advertising generally refers to paid insertions of messages, video, audio and/or graphics into any type of media that accepts a fee for this service. This can include traditional mass media, such as radio, billboards, direct mail, television, newspapers and magazines, as well as digital media, including emails, websites and blogs. Another type of paid advertising is the payment of fees to influencers who write favorably about a company, product or service within a blog, social media post or other medium controlled by the influencer. A third type of paid advertising is product placement. A good example of product placemeent is paying a film producer to feature a certain product within a scene is a movie. Other types of messaging often encompass marketing, as opposed to advertising, such as public relations campaigns.

AI: See "Artificial Intelligence (AI)."

Ajax: Asynchronous JavaScript and XML. It is a technology that enables web page data to update within a browser on a continuous basis, thus updating the page on the fly. This means that applications that reside on the Internet, such as instant messaging, can appear to run so quickly that they seem like programs that are local to a user's computer. An example is Google Inc.'s Google Maps, launched in 2005. During that year, Microsoft also announced services that will run via Ajax.

Ambient Backscatter: Ambient Backscatter converts wireless signals into both a source of power and a communication medium. It enables battery-free devices to communicate by backscattering existing wireless signals. Backscatter communication is vastly more power-efficient than traditional radio communication. Since it leverages the ambient RF signals that are already around us, it does not require a dedicated power source.

Analog: A form of transmitting information characterized by continuously variable quantities. Digital transmission, in contrast, is characterized by discrete bits of information in numerical steps. An analog signal responds to changes in light, sound, heat and pressure.

Analytics: Generally refers to the deep examination of massive amounts of data, often on a continual or real-time basis. The goal is to discover deeper insights, make recommendations or generate predictions. Advanced analytics includes such techniques as big data, predictive analytics, text analytics, data mining, forecasting, optimization and simulation.

ANSI: American National Standards Institute. Founded in 1918, ANSI is a private, non-profit organization that administers and coordinates the U.S. voluntary standardization and conformity assessment system. Its mission is to enhance both the global competitiveness of U.S. business and the quality of U.S. life by promoting and facilitating voluntary consensus standards and conformity assessment systems, and safeguarding their integrity. See www.ansi.org.

API: See "Application Programming Interface (API)."

Applets: Small, object-based applications written in Java that net browsers can download from the Internet on an as-needed basis. These may be software, accessories (such as spell checkers or calculators), information-packed databases or other items. See "Object Technology."

Application Programming Interface (API): A set of protocols, routines and tools used by computer programmers as a way of setting common definitions regarding how one piece of software communicates with another.

Application Service Provider (ASP): A web site that enables utilization of software and databases that reside permanently on a service company's remote web server, rather than having to be downloaded to the user's computer. Advantages include the ability for multiple remote users to access the same tools over the Internet and the fact that the ASP provider is responsible for developing and maintaining the software. (ASP is also an acronym for "active server page," which is not related.) For the latest developments in ASP, see "Software as a Service (SaaS)."

Applications: Computer programs and systems that allow users to interface with a computer and that collect, manipulate, summarize and report data and information. Also, see "Apps."

Applied Research: The application of compounds, processes, materials or other items discovered during basic research to practical uses. The goal is to move discoveries along to the final development phase.

Apps: Short for applications, apps are small software programs designed to run primarily on mobile devices such as smartphones and tablets. Also known as "mobile apps."

Archie: This software tool can be used to find files stored on anonymous FTP sites, as long as the user knows the file name or a sub-string of the file name that is being searched for. See "File Transfer Protocol (FTP)."

ARPANet: Advanced Research Projects Agency Network. The forefather of the Internet, ARPANet was developed during the latter part of the 1960s by the United States Department of Defense.

ARPU: See "Average Revenue Per User (ARPU)."

Artificial Intelligence (AI): The use of computer technology to perform functions somewhat like those normally associated with human intelligence, such as reasoning, learning and self-improvement.

ASCII: American Standard Code for Information Exchange. There are 128 standard ASCII codes that represent all Latin letters, numbers and punctuation. Each ASCII code is represented by a seven-digit binary number, such as 0000000 or 0000111. This code is accepted as a standard throughout the world.

Asia Pacific Advisory Committee (APAC): A multi-country committee representing the Asia and Pacific region.

ASP: See "Application Service Provider (ASP)."

Asymmetrical Digital Subscriber Line (ADSL): High-speed technology that enables the transfer of data over existing copper phone lines, allowing more bandwidth downstream than upstream.

Asynchronous Communications: A stream of data routed through a network as generated instead of in organized message blocks. Most personal computers use this format to send data.

Asynchronous Transfer Mode (ATM): A digital switching and transmission technology based on high speed. ATM allows voice, video and data signals to be sent over a single telephone line at speeds from 25 million to 1 billion bits per second (bps). This digital ATM speed is much faster than traditional analog phone lines, which allow no more than 2 million bps. See "Broadband."

Augmented Reality (AR): A technology utilizing software, apps and specialized hardware such as AR glasses to provide overlays of digital content into real-life environments and objects. This enriches the user experience and turns a screen into an interactive learning environment. While AR can be used for entertainment, it is of high value in guiding manufacturing workers, technicians and surgeons in their tasks. AR is boosted by technologies such as digital cameras, GPS, AI and the internet of things.

Automated Ad Buying: The purchase of advertising using high-speed, algorithmic programs that match ads to desired audiences based on consumer habits such as previous purchases, favored web sites and social media activity.

Average Revenue Per User (ARPU): A measure of the average monthly billing revenue of a service, such as a wireless service subscription, on a per user basis.

B2B: See "Business-to-Business."

B2C: See "Business-to-Consumer."

B2E: See "Business-to-Employee."

B2G: See "Business-to-Government."

Baby Boomer: Generally refers to people born from 1946 to 1964. In the U.S., the initial number of Baby Boomers totaled about 78 million. The term evolved to describe the children of soldiers and war industry workers who were involved in World War II and who began forming families after the war's end. In 2011, the oldest Baby Boomers began reaching the traditional retirement age of 65.

Backbone: Traditionally the part of a communications network that carries the heaviest traffic: the high-speed line or series of connections that forms a large pathway within a network or within a region. The combined networks of AT&T, MCI and other large telecommunications companies make up the backbone of the Internet.

Back-Office: Generally considered to include such areas as accounting, human resources, call centers, financial transaction processing. A back-office application is a software program designed to handle back-office tasks. Also, see "Business Process Outsourcing (BPO)."

Bandwidth: The data transmission capacity of a network, measured in the amount of data (in bits and bauds) it can transport in one second. A full page of text is about 15,000 to 20,000 bits. Full-motion, full-screen video requires about 10 million bits per second, depending on compression.

Basic Research: Attempts to discover compounds, materials, processes or other items that may be largely or entirely new and/or unique. Basic research may start with a theoretical concept that has yet to be proven. The goal is to create discoveries that can be moved along to applied research. Basic research is sometimes referred to as "blue sky" research.

Baud: Refers to how many times the carrier signal in a modem switches value per second or how many bits a modem can send and receive in a second.

Beam: The coverage and geographic service area offered by a satellite transponder. A global beam effectively covers one-third of the earth's surface. A spot beam provides a very specific high-powered downlink pattern that is limited to a particular geographical area to which it may be steered or pointed.

Behavioral Targeting: An advertising method that attempts to target ads to individual consumers based on their history of activities or purchases.

Big Data: The massive sets of data that are generated and captured to a growing extent by a wide variety of enterprises. For example, the digitization of health care records is creating big data sets. Likewise, consumer activities on an extremely popular website like Facebook create big data sets. A growing trend will be the generation of big data sets by remote wireless sensors. The challenges created by big data include the steps of data capture, storage, visualization and analysis. The opportunities include targeted online advertising: greater efficiency in health care, energy, business and industry, as well as intelligent transportation systems and better outcomes in health care.

Binhex: A means of changing non-ASCII (or non-text) files into text/ASCII files so that they can be used, for example, as e-mail.

Biometrics: The use of a user's physical attributes to enable login to a network or account. Biometrics may include iris scans, fingerprints, facial images or other features, rather than relying on passwords or PIN codes that can be more easily hacked.

Bit: A single digit number, either a one or a zero, which is the smallest unit of computerized data.

Bitcoin: A digital (virtual) cryptocurrency launched in 2009. Bitcoin utilizes blockchain technologies. See "Cryptocurrency."

Bits Per Second (Bps): An indicator of the speed of data movement.

Blockchain: A technology that records ownership of Bitcoin and similar cryptocurrencies. Records of transactions made in these cryptocurrencies are maintained across multiple computers linked in a peer-to-peer network.

Blog (Web Log): A web site consisting of a personal journal, news coverage, special-interest content or other data that is posted on the Internet, frequently updated and intended for public viewing by anyone who might be interested in the author's thoughts. Short for "web log," blog content is frequently distributed via RSS (Real Simple Syndication). Blog content has evolved to include video files (VLOGs)

and audio files (Podcasting) as well as text. Also, see "Real Simple Syndication (RSS)," "Video Blog (VLOG)," "Moblog": "Podcasting," and "User Generated Content (UGC)."

Bluetooth: An industry standard for a technology that enables wireless, short-distance infrared connections between devices such as cell phone headsets, Palm Pilots or PDAs, laptops, printers and Internet appliances.

BPL: See "Broadband Over Power Lines (BPL)."

BPO: See "Business Process Outsourcing (BPO)."

Bps: See "Bits Per Second (Bps)."

Brand Marketing: A marketing strategy that places a focus on the brand name of a product, service or firm in order to eventually enhance the brand's market share, increase sales, establish credibility, improve satisfaction, raise the profile of the firm and increase profits. Public relations and special events are common methods of brand marketing. In contrast, performance marketing is focused on getting the consumer of a message to take a specific action, such as a click on a link.

Branding: A marketing strategy that places a focus on the brand name of a product, service or firm in order to increase the brand's market share, increase sales, establish credibility, improve satisfaction, raise the profile of the firm and increase profits. Also, see "Brand."

Broadband: The high-speed transmission range for telecommunications and computer data. Broadband generally refers to any transmission at 2 million bps (bits per second) or higher (much higher than analog speed). A broadband network can carry voice, video and data all at the same time. Internet users enjoying broadband access typically connect to the Internet via DSL line, cable modem or T1 line. Several wireless methods offer broadband as well.

Broadband Over Power Lines (BPL): Refers to the use of standard electric power lines to provide fast Internet service. Internet data is converted into radio frequency signals, which are not affected by electricity. Subscribers utilize special modems.

Browser: A program that allows a user to read Internet text or graphics and to navigate from one page to another. The most popular browsers are Microsoft Internet Explorer and Netscape Navigator. Firefox is an open source browser introduced in 2005 that is rapidly gaining popularity.

Buffer: A location for temporarily storing data being sent or received. It is usually located between two devices that have different data transmission rates.

Business Process Outsourcing (BPO): The process of hiring another company to handle business activities. BPO is one of the fastest-growing segments in the offshoring sector. Services include human resources management, billing and purchasing and call centers, as well as many types of customer service or marketing activities, depending on the industry involved. Also, see "Knowledge Process Outsourcing (KPO)" and Business Transformation Outsourcing (BTO)."

Business Transformation Outsourcing (BTO): A segment within outsourcing in which the client company revamps its business processes with the goal of transforming its business by following a collaborative approach with its outsourced services provider.

Business-to-Business: An organization focused on selling products, services or data to commercial customers rather than individual consumers. Also known as B2B.

Business-to-Consumer: An organization focused on selling products, services or data to individual consumers rather than commercial customers. Also known as B2C.

Business-to-Employee: A corporate communications system, such as an intranet, aimed at conveying information from a company to its employees. Also known as B2E.

Business-to-Government: An organization focused on selling products, services or data to government units rather than commercial businesses or consumers. Also known as B2G.

Byte: A set of eight bits that represent a single character.

Cable Modem: An interface between a cable television system and a computer or router. Most cable modems are external devices that connect to the PC

through a standard 10Base-T Ethernet card and twisted-pair wiring. External Universal Serial Bus (USB) modems and internal PCI modem cards are also available.

Caching: A method of storing data in a temporary location closer to the user so that it can be retrieved quickly when requested.

CAFTA-DR: See "Central American-Dominican Republic Free Trade Agreement (CAFTA-DR)."

Capability Maturity Model (CMM): A global process management standard for software development established by the Software Engineering Institute at Carnegie Mellon University.

Captive Offshoring: Used to describe a company-owned offshore operation. For example, Microsoft owns and operates significant captive offshore research and development centers in China and elsewhere that are offshore from Microsoft's U.S. home base. Also see "Offshoring."

Carrier: In communications, the basic radio, television or telephony center of transmit signal. The carrier in an analog signal is modulated by varying volume or shifting frequency up or down in relation to the incoming signal. Satellite carriers operating in the analog mode are usually frequency-modulated.

CATV: Cable television.

CDMA: See "Code Division Multiple Access (CDMA)."

CDP: See "Customer Data Platform (CDP)."

Central American-Dominican Republic Free Trade Agreement (CAFTA-DR): A trade agreement signed into law in 2005 that aimed to open up the Central American and Dominican Republic markets to American goods. Member nations include Guatemala, Nicaragua, Costa Rica, El Salvador, Honduras and the Dominican Republic. Before the law was signed, products from those countries could enter the U.S. almost tariff-free, while American goods heading into those countries faced stiff tariffs. The goal of this agreement was to create U.S. jobs while at the same time offering the non-U.S. member citizens a chance for a better quality of life through access to U.S.-made goods.

Central Processing Unit (CPU): The part of a computer that interprets and executes instructions. It is composed of an arithmetic logic unit, a control unit and a small amount of memory.

CGI: See "Common Gateway Interface (CGI)."

CGI-BIN: The frequently used name of a directory on a web server where CGI programs exist.

Channel Definition Format (CDF): Used in Internet-based broadcasting. With this format, a channel serves as a web site that also sends an information file about that specific site. Users subscribe to a channel by downloading the file.

Chat Bot: Like a voice assistant, chat bots are services accessed through a digital chat interface. A chat bot is intended to enable a website to interface in a non-human manner to provide instant service to customers and visitors. Chat bots can be connected to artificial intelligence in order to provide reasonable answers to common customer questions or needs. ChatterBot is a dialog engine for creating chatbots.

CIAM: Customer Identity and Access Management.

Click Through: In advertising on the Internet, click through refers to how often viewers respond to an ad by clicking on it. Also known as click rate.

Client/Server: In networking, a way of running a large computer setup. The server is the host computer that acts as the central holding ground for files, databases and application software. The clients are all of the PCs connected to the network that share data with the server. This represents a vast change from past networks, which were connected to expensive, complicated "mainframe" computers.

Cloud: Refers to the use of outsourced servers to store and access data, as opposed to computers owned or managed by one organization. Firms that offer cloud services for a fee run clusters of servers networked together, often based on open standards. Such cloud networks can consist of hundreds or even thousands of computers. Cloud services enable a client company to immediately increase computing capability without any investment in physical infrastructure. (The word "cloud" is also broadly used to describe any data or application that runs via the Internet.) The concept of cloud is also increasingly linked with software as a service.

Cloud Computing: See "Cloud."

Code Division Multiple Access (CDMA): A cellular telephone multiple-access scheme whereby stations use spread-spectrum modulations and orthogonal codes to avoid interfering with one another. IS-95 (also known as CDMAOne) is the 2G CDMA standard. CDMA2000 is the 3G standard. CDMA in the 1xEV-DO standard offers data transfer speeds up to 2.4 Mbps. CDMA 1xRTT is a slower standard offering speeds of 144 kbps.

Codec: Hardware or software that converts analog to digital and digital to analog (in both audio and video formats). Codecs can be found in digital telephones, set-top boxes, computers and videoconferencing equipment. The term is also used to refer to the compression of digital information into a smaller format.

Co-Location: Refers to the hosting of computer servers at locations operated by service organizations. Co-location is offered by firms that operate specially designed co-location centers with high levels of security, extremely high-speed telecommunication lines for Internet connectivity and reliable backup electrical power systems in case of power failure, as well as a temperature-controlled environment for optimum operation of computer systems.

Commerce Chain Management (CCM): Refers to Internet-based tools to facilitate sales, distribution, inventory management and content personalization in the e-commerce industry. Also see "Supply Chain."

Common Gateway Interface (CGI): A set of guidelines that determines the manner in which a web server receives and sends information to and from software on the same machine.

Competitive Local Exchange Carrier (CLEC): A newer company providing local telephone service that competes against larger, traditional firms known as ILECs (incumbent local exchange carriers).

Compression: A technology in which a communications signal is squeezed so that it uses less bandwidth (or capacity) than it normally would. This saves storage space and shortens transfer time. The original data is decompressed when read back into memory.

Computer-Assisted Software Engineering (CASE): The application of computer technology to systems development activities, techniques and methodologies. Sometimes referred to as "computer-aided systems engineering."

Consumer Valuation: See "Buying Power Score."

Contract Manufacturing: A business arrangement whereby a company manufactures products that will be sold under the brand names of its client companies. For example, a large number of consumer electronics, such as laptop computers, are manufactured by contract manufacturers for leading brand-name computer companies such as Dell and Apple. Many other types of products, such as shoes and apparel, are made under contract manufacturing. Also see "Original Equipment Manufacturer (OEM)" and "Original Design Manufacturer (ODM)."

Cookie: A piece of information sent to a web browser from a web server that the browser software saves and then sends back to the server upon request. Cookies are used by web site operators to track the actions of users returning to the site.

Cost Per Click (CPC): Online advertising that is billed on a response basis. An advertiser sells a banner ad and is paid by the number of users who click on the ad.

Cost Per Thousand (CPM): A charge for advertising calculated on a fixed amount multiplied by the number of users who view an ad, computed in thousands.

CPC: See "Cost Per Click (CPC)."

CPM: See "Cost Per Thousand (CPM)."

CRM: See "Customer Relationship Management (CRM)."

Crowdsourcing: A method of gathering data that capitalizes on users of a web site or database to find and post the data. Wikipedia is a well known example.

Cryptocurrency: A digital (virtual) currency that is encrypted for security. Cryptocurrencies are housed within decentralized systems based on blockchain technology. Bitcoin is a leading example.

Customer Data Platform (CDP): Somewhat similar to a CRM (Customer Relationship Management) software platform, CDPs are generally deeply integrated with digital marketing efforts and typically contain more information regarding how the customer was acquired (e.g., what advertisement did the customer respond to or click on) and the customer's path through a company's digital marketing (e.g., what product pages did the customer look at on a company's web site).

Customer Relationship Management (CRM): Refers to the automation, via sophisticated software, of business processes involving existing and prospective customers. CRM may cover aspects such as sales (contact management and contact history), marketing (campaign management and telemarketing) and customer service (call center history and field service history). Well known providers of CRM software include Salesforce, which delivers via a Software as a Service model (see "Software as a Service (Saas)"), Microsoft and Oracle.

Cyberspace: Refers to the entire realm of information available through computer networks and the Internet.

Data Base Management System (DBMS): A software system used to store, retrieve and manipulate data in an organized fashion. Usually consists of dictionary, manipulation, security and access components.

Data Mining: Analyzing large sets of data in order to find patterns. Machine learning is often utilized.

Data Over Cable Service Interface Specification (DOCSIS): A set of standards for transferring data over cable television. DOCSIS 3.0 will enable very high-speed Internet access that may eventually reach 160 Mbps.

Datanets: Private networks of land-based telephone lines, satellites or wireless networks that allow corporate users to send data at high speeds to remote locations while bypassing the speed and cost constraints of traditional telephone lines.

DBMS: See "Data Base Management System (DBMS)."

DDOS: See "Distributed Denial-of-Service (DDOS)."

Decentralized Finance (DeFI): The use of a blockchain network to deliver financial products and track their ownership. This enables buyers, lenders and sellers of financial products to transact directly with each other (peer-to-peer), rather than going through a middleman such as a traditional financial institution.

Dedicated Internet Access (DIA): A high speed Internet service with dedicated access from the carrier to the customer.

DeFI: See "Decentralized Finance (DeFI)."

Demographics: The breakdown of the population into statistical categories such as age, income, education and sex.

Digital: The transmission of a signal by reducing all of its information to ones and zeros and then regrouping them at the reception end. Digital transmission vastly improves the carrying capacity of the spectrum while reducing noise and distortion of the transmission.

Digital ID: Data that can confirm the identity of the user of a network, shopping cart or online system.

Digital Local Telephone Switch: A computer that interprets signals (dialed numbers) from a telephone caller and routes calls to their proper destinations. A digital switch also provides a variety of calling features not available in older analog switches, such as call waiting.

Digital Millennium Copyright Act: A U.S. law created in 1998. It was written in response to the rapid growth of content on the Internet. The act contains a "safe harbor" provision that enables Internet site publishers to promptly eliminate most faults or penalties of infringement if they promptly remove online content when notified by the proper owners of that content's copyright.

Digital Rights Management (DRM): Restrictions placed on the use of digital content by copyright holders and hardware manufacturers. DRM for Apple, Inc.'s iTunes, for example, allows downloaded music to be played only on Apple's iPod player and iPhones, per agreement with music production companies Universal Music Group, SonyBMG, Warner Music and EMI.

Digital Subscriber Line (DSL): A broadband (high-speed) Internet connection provided via telecommunications systems. These lines are a cost-effective means of providing homes and small businesses with relatively fast Internet access. Common variations include ADSL and SDSL. DSL competes with cable modem access and wireless access.

Digital Transformation (DX): The implementation of digital technologies into as many areas of a business as reasonably possible Goals may include: to fundamentally change how the enterprise operates: how data is gathered and tracked: how innovation is launched: and how value is delivered to customers. The hoped-for result is to create new operating efficiencies and develop new revenue or profit opportunities, while better positioning the enterprise for the future. Also abbreviated as DX or DT.

Digital Wallet: An app that enables a consumer to store encrypted bank account, debit card and credit card information. A technology called tokenization is typically used. (See "Tokenization.") The user is then enabled to check out in retail stores (via smartphone and specially equipped cash registers/POS) and online, without the need to enter payment account data. Biometric data such as a fingerprint is often used to ID the user on a smartphone. On a PC, account login is typically required. The end result is enhanced payment data security, plus reduced time checking out, as the consumer doesn't need to key-in account numbers, which often leads to errors on small screens. Top digital wallets include Apple Pay, Google Pay and LG Pay.

Direct Broadcast Satellite (DBS): A high-powered satellite authorized to broadcast television programming directly to homes. Home subscribers use a dish and a converter to receive and translate the TV signal. An example is the DirecTV service. DBS operates in the 11.70- to 12.40-GHz range.

Direct Marketing: A form of non-store retailing in which customers are exposed to merchandise and services through such media catalogs, direct mail, telemarketing, email, infomercials or television. Direct marketing may be used to generate purchases, store traffic, sales leads or a combination thereof.

Disaster Recovery: A set of rules and procedures that allow a computer site to be put back in operation after a disaster has occurred. Moving backups off-site constitutes the minimum basic precaution for disaster recovery. The remote copy is used to recover data if the local storage is inaccessible after a disaster.

Discount Broker: A broker or brokerage firm that executes buy and sell transactions at commission rates lower than a full-service broker or brokerage.

Disintermediate: A business or distribution model that bypasses the middleman in marketing or retailing. For example, a web site that enables end-consumers to purchase apparel direct from a designer or manufacturer, bypassing retail stores and traditional catalogs, is attempting to disintermediate the supply chain.

Disk Mirroring: A data redundancy technique in which data is recorded identically on multiple separate disk drives at the same time. When the primary disk is off-line, the alternate takes over, providing continuous access to data. Disk mirroring is sometimes referred to as RAID.

Disruptive: A new technology or business model that unexpectedly threatens to displace existing products or services. For example, the manner in which email has disrupted standard postal service. By some estimates, in order to be disruptive, a new service or product must provide most of the value of existing methods, and ideally even enhanced value, while reducing costs and/or speeding delivery.

Distributed Internet applications Architecture (DNA): A current Microsoft project, also known as Windows DNA, that is dependent on Active Directory and is designed to provide secure delivery of software components over the Internet and intranets.

Diverted Delivery: A type of ecommerce fraud. Because a website's shopping cart does not always utilize remote data services in order to verify that a consumer actually lives at the address stated in the order, fraudsters, using stolen cards or credentials, can have a delivery sent to an address not connected to the card/credential.

Domain: A name that has server records associated with it. See "Domain Name."

Domain (Top-Level): Either an ISO country code or a common domain name such as .com, .org or .net.

Domain Name: A unique web site name registered to a company, organization or individual (e.g., plunkettresearch.com).

Domain Name System Security Extensions (DNSSEC): A suite of specifications for securing data provided by the Domain Name System (DNS) as used on Internet Protocol (IP) networks. Based on specifications by the Internet Engineering Task Force (IETF), it provides origin authentication of DNS data and data integrity.

DS-1: A digital transmission format that transmits and receives information at a rate of 1,544,000 bits per second.

DSL: See "Digital Subscriber Line (DSL)."

Duplicate Host: A single host name that maps to duplicate IP addresses.

DX: See "Digital Transformation (DX)."

Dynamic HTML: Web content that changes with each individual viewing. For example, the same site could appear differently depending on geographic location of the reader, time of day, previous pages viewed or the user's profile.

Echo Boomers: See "Generation Y."

E-Commerce: The use of online, internet-based sales methods. The phrase is used to describe both business-to-consumer and business-to-business sales.

Ecosystem: In online platforms, an ecosystem is a business strategy wherein numerous complimentary services and tools are offered that create high levels of convenience for the user, who only has to login once to conduct multiple tasks. The ultimate ecosystem may be WeChat, based in China, which offers instant messaging, social media, streaming entertainment, payment services, access to government services, shopping and a very wide variety of additional services. In FinTech, Square (owned by Block), is an excellent example, where features include credit card processing, business marketing, and, within the related Venmo app, P2P payments, investments, debit cards and much more.

EFT: See "Electronic Funds Transfer (EFT)."

Electronic Data Interchange (EDI): An accepted standard format for the exchange of data between various companies' networks. EDI allows for the transfer of e-mail as well as orders, invoices and other files from one company to another.

Electronic Funds Transfer (EFT): Moving money from one account to another via electronic means.

E-Mail (eMail): The use of software that allows the posting of messages (text, audio or video) over a network. E-mail can be used on a LAN, a WAN or the Internet, as well as via online services or wireless devices that are Internet enabled. It can be used to send a message to a single recipient or may be broadcast to a large group of people at once.

EMEA: The region comprised of Europe, the Middle East and Africa.

Enterprise Application: A major software tool intended to manage data over an extremely large corporate or government user base (e.g., SAP, Oracle).

Enterprise Resource Planning (ERP): An integrated information system that helps manage all aspects of a business, including accounting, ordering and human resources, typically across all locations of a major corporation or organization. ERP is considered to be a critical tool for management of large organizations. Suppliers of ERP tools include SAP and Oracle.

ERP: See "Enterprise Resource Planning (ERP)."

E-Score: See "Buying Power Score."

Ethernet: The standard format on which local area network equipment works. Abiding by Ethernet standards allows equipment from various manufacturers to work together.

EU: See "European Union (EU)."

EU Competence: The jurisdiction in which the European Union (EU) can take legal action.

European Community (EC): See "European Union (EU)."

European Union (EU): A consolidation of European countries (member states) functioning as one body to facilitate trade. Previously known as the European

Community (EC). The EU has a unified currency, the Euro. See europa.eu.int.

EV-DO (CDMA 2000 1xEV-DO): A 3G (third generation) cellular telephone service standard that is an improved version of 1xRTT. The EV-DO (Evolution-Data Optimized) standard introduced in 2004 allows data download speeds of as much as 2.4 Mbps. A version introduced in 2006 allows up to 14.7 Mbps data download speeds. EV-DO is also known as CDMA 2000 1xEV-DO. EV-DO's capabilities are used by the entertainment industry to enable video via cell phone.

Exabyte: A measure of data equal to 1,024 petabytes, or 10 bytes to the 18th power (one billion billion, or one quintillion). Generally used to describe total volume of Internet traffic worldwide. Analysts estimate that all the world's printed material would fill five exabytes.

Expert Systems: A practical development of AI that requires creation of a knowledge base of facts and rules furnished by human experts and uses a defined set of rules to access this information in order to suggest solutions to problems. See "Artificial Intelligence (AI)."

Extended Reality (XR): Refers to the wide range of experiences from real to virtual (VR) to environments that are created through a combination of real experiences plus virtual or augmented reality (AR). For example, data or images from wearable devices might be combined in real-time with virtual reality to create a unique experience. Also, see "Mixed Reality".

Extensible Markup Language (XML): A programming language that enables designers to add extra functionality to documents that could not otherwise be utilized with standard HTML coding. XML was developed by the World Wide Web Consortium. It can communicate to various software programs the actual meanings contained in HTML documents. For example, it can enable the gathering and use of information from a large number of databases at once and place that information into one web site window. XML is an important protocol to web services. See "Web Services."

Extranet: A computer network that is accessible in part to authorized outside persons, as opposed to an intranet, which uses a firewall to limit accessibility.

FAQ: See "Frequently Asked Questions (FAQ)."

FASB: See "Financial Accounting Standards Board (FASB)."

FCC: See "Federal Communications Commission (FCC)."

FDDI: See "Fiber Distributed Data Interface (FDDI)."

Federal Communications Commission (FCC): The U.S. Government agency that regulates broadcast television and radio, as well as satellite transmission, telephony and all uses of radio spectrum.

Fiber Distributed Data Interface (FDDI): A token ring passing scheme that operates at 100 Mbps over fiber-optic lines with a built-in geographic limitation of 100 kilometers. This type of connection is faster than both Ethernet and T-3 connections. See "Token Ring."

Fiber to the Home (FTTH): Refers to the extension of a fiber-optic system through the last mile so that it touches the home or office where it will be used. This can provide high speed Internet access at speeds of 15 to 100 Mbps, much faster than typical T1 or DSL line. FTTH is now commonly installed in new communities where telecom infrastructure is being built for the first time. Another phrase used to describe such installations is FTTP, or Fiber to the Premises.

Fiber to the Node (FTTN): Refers to the extension of a fiber-optic system through the last mile so that it touches a central neighborhood junction close to the home or office where it will be used. The remaining distance is covered by existing copper phone line that uses DSL (digital subscriber line) technology to speed data transfer.

File Server: A computer that is modified to store and transfer large amounts of data to other computers. File servers often receive data from mainframes and store it for transfer to other, smaller computers, or from small computers to mainframes.

File Transfer Protocol (FTP): A widely used method of transferring data and files between two Internet sites.

Financial Accounting Standards Board (FASB): An independent organization that establishes the Generally Accepted Accounting Principles (GAAP).

Financial Technology (FinTech): A term used to broadly describe the utilization of advanced computer and communication technologies to enable more streamlined financial transactions for both consumers and businesses. FinTech service may include banking, insurance, investing, mortgages, credit cards, debit cards and related services. Typically, FinTech services are disruptive to established, traditional means (such as physical, store-front banks and offices), and are delivered to users via convenient smartphone apps.

FinTech: See "Financial Technology (FinTech)."

Firewall: Hardware or software that keeps unauthorized users from accessing a server or network. Firewalls are designed to prevent data theft and unauthorized web site manipulation by hackers.

Fixed Wireless: Refers to the use of Wi-Fi, WiMAX or other wireless receivers that remain fixed in a stationary place, to provide Internet service.

Flash Sale: Online sales events, generally advertised to by email to people who have asked to be notified. Flash sales are very limited in time. They tend to offer apparel, accessories and travel.

Folksonomy: A user-created taxonomy of Internet site content based on key words or concepts. This is a collaborative effort in a wiki-like environment that enables participants to organize data, such as photos, into categories. A widely known example is #hashtag system used on Twitter.

Form Abandonment: Occurs when an online customer or user begins filling out an information form on a website, but then abandons the effort without fully completing the form.

Fourth-Party Logistics (4PL): A service that integrates a company's third-party logistics providers into a single entity for ease of use. Often formed by a telecommunications company, a 4PL is also called a lead logistics provider. A 4PL service provider provides a top layer of business processes, generally technology-driven, to the client's supply chain. Also see "Third-Party Logistics (3PL)."

Frame Relay: An accepted standard for sending large amounts of data over phone lines and private datanets. The term refers to the way data is broken down into standard-size "frames" prior to transmission.

Freemium: A business model in which a product or service (usually a digital game, software or web service) is offered at no charge to the user, but advanced features and services are promoted for purchase.

Frequency: The number of times that an alternating current goes through its complete cycle in one second. One cycle per second is referred to as one hertz: 1,000 cycles per second, one kilohertz: 1 million cycles per second, one megahertz: and 1 billion cycles per second, one gigahertz.

Frequency Band: A term for designating a range of frequencies in the electromagnetic spectrum.

Frequently Asked Questions (FAQ): Answers inquiries about a given topic. Generally, FAQs come in the form of a help file or a hypertext document.

Front-Office Application: A computer program tailored to the needs of the customer relations portions of a business, such as sales and marketing.

FTP: See "File Transfer Protocol (FTP)."

FTTC: Fiber to the curb. See "Fiber to the Home (FTTH)."

FTTP: Fiber to the premises. See "Fiber to the Home (FTTH)."

Fuzzy Logic: Recognizes that some statements are not just "true" or "false," but also "more or less certain" or "very unlikely." Fuzzy logic is used in artificial intelligence. See "Artificial Intelligence (AI)."

GAAP: See "Generally Accepted Accounting Principles (GAAP)."

GAI: Generative Artificial Intelligence.

Gamification: The use of game design and practices to enhance non-game content in order to attract users and increase engagement. For example, the use of games in online advertising and marketing, or the use of games in online education.

Gateway: A device connecting two or more networks that may use different protocols and media. Gateways translate between the different networks and can connect locally or over wide area networks.

GDP: See "Gross Domestic Product (GDP)."

GDPR: See "General Data Protection Regulation (GDPR)."

General Data Protection Regulation (GDPR): Regulations that govern the collection and processing of personal information from individuals who live in the European Union (EU).

Generally Accepted Accounting Principles (GAAP): A set of accounting standards administered by the Financial Accounting Standards Board (FASB) and enforced by the U.S. Security and Exchange Commission (SEC). GAAP is primarily used in the U.S.

Generation C: Creative consumers who are active in unpaid, consumer-generated content, such as Wikipedia, blogging, YouTube and consumer-generated advertising.

Generation M: A very loosely defined term that is sometimes used to refer to young people who have grown up in the digital age. "M" may refer to any or all of media-saturated, mobile or multi-tasking. The term was most notably used in a Kaiser Family Foundation report published in 2005, "Generation M: Media in the Lives of 8-18 year olds." Also, see "Generation Y" and "Generation Z."

Generation X: A loosely-defined and variously-used term that describes people born between approximately 1965 and 1980, but other time frames are recited. Generation X is often referred to as a group influential in defining tastes in consumer goods, entertainment and/or political and social matters.

Generation Y: Refers to people born between approximately 1982 and 2002. In the U.S., they number more than 90 million, making them the largest generation segment in the nation's history. They are also known as Echo Boomers, Millennials or the Millennial Generation. These are children of the Baby Boom generation who will be filling the work force as Baby Boomers retire.

Generation Z: Some people refer to Generation Z as people born after 1991. Others use the beginning date of 2001, or refer to the era of 1994 to 2004. Members of Generation Z are considered to be natural and rapid adopters of the latest technologies.

Generative AI: Artificial intelligence (AI) and machine learning (ML)-driven tools that are capable of studying millions of digital groups of text, reference materials, photos/art and other items, and then generating new output, based on the user's statement about what the user is seeking. For example, a user could tell a system to "create a image of the Eiffel Tower in the style of Van Gogh" or "write a comparison of cancer therapies using radiation instead of surgery." The generative tools build the desired output in a matter of moments. Such platforms can be used to create music, write essays or magazine articles, complete homework assignments and generate computer software code. This also may create copyright, ownership and originality controversies. OpenAI is a pioneer in this technology.

Geofencing: The practice of setting virtual boundaries around a physical location and targeting mobile device users within those areas for a variety of purposes including search and rescue, advertising and social interaction.

Gigabyte: 1,024 megabytes.

Gigahertz (GHz): One billion cycles per second. See "Frequency."

Global System for Mobile Communications (GSM): The standard cellular format used throughout Europe, making one type of cellular phone usable in every nation on the continent and in the U.K. In the U.S., Cingular and T-Mobile also run GSM networks. The original GSM, introduced in 1991, has transfer speeds of only 9.6 kbps. GSM EDGE offers 2.75G data transfer speeds of up to 473.6 kbps. GSM GPRS offers slower 2.5G theoretical speeds of 144 kbps.

Graphic Interchange Format (GIF): A widely used format for image files.

Grid Computing: A computer network where each computer's resources are shared with every other computer in the system. Processing power, memory and data storage are all community resources that can be can tapped into and leveraged for specific tasks.

Gross Domestic Product (GDP): The total value of a nation's output, income and expenditures produced with a nation's physical borders.

Gross National Product (GNP): A country's total output of goods and services from all forms of economic activity measured at market prices for one calendar year. It differs from Gross Domestic Product (GDP) in that GNP includes income from investments made in foreign nations.

Groupware: A type of software that enables various people on a network to contribute to one document at the same time, sharing ideas, molding the final product and monitoring its progress along the way. Groupware is a new way of group "thinking" without physical meetings. Lotus Notes pioneered this market.

GSM: See "Global System for Mobile Communications (GSM)."

Handheld Devices Markup Language (HDML): A text-based markup language designed for display on a smaller screen (e.g., a cellular phone, PDA or pager). Enables the mobile user to send, receive and redirect e-mail as well as access the Internet (HDML-enabled web sites only).

HDML: See "Handheld Devices Markup Language (HDML)."

HDSL: See "High-Data-Rate Digital Subscriber Line (HDSL)."

Helper Applications: Applications that allow the user to view or play downloadable files.

HFC: Hybrid Fiber Coaxial. A type of cable system.

High-Data-Rate Digital Subscriber Line (HDSL): High-data-rate DSL, delivering up to T1 or E1 speeds.

Hosting: Maintaining a computer application for a third party. Hosting may include databases, web sites and proprietary applications.

Hot Spot: A location where access to the Internet is available via Wi-Fi.

HTML: See "Hypertext Markup Language (HTML)."

HTML5: A specification for Internet development that represents the fifth major revision of the Hypertext Markup Language, or HTML. HTML5 is designed to better handle the types of Internet content that are rapidly growing in popularity, such as online video, audio and interactive documents and pages. For example, HTML5 enables the designer to embed images, audio and video directly into a web-based document.

HTTP: See "Hypertext Transfer Protocol (HTTP)."

Hybrid Cloud: A data strategy where some applications and data are moved to cloud-based systems, while highly sensitive data or certain functions are kept on client-owned systems.

Hyperlink: On the Internet, an element in a web page that links to another page or to another place in the same document. Generally, the user clicks on the hyperlink in order to follow it.

Hypertext Markup Language (HTML): A language for coding text for viewing on the World Wide Web. HTML is unique because it enables the use of hyperlinks from one site to another, creating a web.

Hypertext Transfer Protocol (HTTP): The protocol used most frequently on the World Wide Web to move hypertext files between clients and servers on the Internet.

IAAS: Infrastructure as a Service. See "Cloud Computing."

IAM: Internet Access Management.

ICANN: The Internet Corporation for Assigned Names and Numbers. ICANN acts as the central coordinator for the Internet's technical operations.

ICT: See "Information and Communication Technologies (ICT)."

IDaaS: Identity-as-a-Service. Services, based in the cloud, that manage user authentication on a network or online service.

Idea Management: Software designed to enable employees, investors, management, customers and vendors to share ideas and opportunities for innovation in a secure environment. The goal is to foster faster development of new products and services. Idea management may be an adjunct to crowdsourcing. See "Crowdsourcing."

IDN: See "Integrated Digital Network (IDN)."

IEEE: See "Institute of Electrical and Electronic Engineers (IEEE)."

IFRS: See "International Financials Reporting Standards (IFRS)."

ILEC: See "Incumbent Local Exchange Carrier (ILEC)."

IM: See "Instant Messaging (IM)."

Impressions: In Internet advertising, the total number of times an ad is displayed on a web page. Impressions are not the same as "hits," which count the number of times each page or element in a page is retrieved. Since a single complicated page on a web site could consist of five or more individual elements, including graphics and text, one viewer calling up that page would register multiple hits but just a single impression.

Incumbent Local Exchange Carrier (ILEC): A traditional telephone company that was providing local service prior to the establishment of the Telecommunications Act of 1996, when upstart companies (CLECs, or competitive local exchange carriers) were enabled to compete against the ILECS and were granted access to their system wiring.

Industry Code: A descriptive code assigned to any company in order to group it with firms that operate in similar businesses. Common industry codes include the NAICS (North American Industrial Classification System) and the SIC (Standard Industrial Classification), both of which are standards widely used in America, as well as the International Standard Industrial Classification of all Economic Activities (ISIC), the Standard International Trade Classification established by the United Nations (SITC) and the General Industrial Classification of Economic Activities within the European Communities (NACE).

Information and Communication Technologies (ICT): A term used to describe the relationship between the myriad types of goods, services and networks that make up the global information and communications system. Sectors involved in ICT include landlines, data networks, the Internet, wireless communications, (including cellular and remote wireless sensors) and satellites.

Information Technology (IT): The systems, including hardware and software, that move and store voice, video and data via computers and telecommunications.

Infrastructure (Telecommunications): The entity made up of all the cable and equipment installed in the worldwide telecommunications market. Most of today's telecommunications infrastructure is connected by copper and fiber-optic cable, which represents a huge capital investment that telephone companies would like to continue to utilize in as many ways as possible.

Initial Public Offering (IPO): A company's first effort to sell its stock to investors (the public). Investors in an up-trending market eagerly seek stocks offered in many IPOs because the stocks of newly public companies that seem to have great promise may appreciate very rapidly in price, reaping great profits for those who were able to get the stock at the first offering. In the United States, IPOs are regulated by the SEC (U.S. Securities Exchange Commission) and by the state-level regulatory agencies of the states in which the IPO shares are offered.

Insourcing: A unique and increasingly popular business method. It is similar to "outsourcing," in that it is a continuing business service or process provided to a company by an outside organization. The intent is to enable the client company to focus on its core strengths, while hiring outside firms to provide other needs such as warehouse, call center or human resources management. However, with insourcing, the services provider moves into or near the client company's facility and sets up shop. For example, ARAMARK has a business unit that will set up and manage an employee cafeteria within a client company's facility. (Occasionally, the term "insourcing" has also been used to describe the creation of jobs in America by foreign firms.) Also see "Third-Party Logistics (3PL)."

Instant Messaging (IM): A type of e-mail that is viewed and then deleted. IM is used between opt-in networks of people for leisure or business purposes.

Institute of Electrical and Electronic Engineers (IEEE): An organization that sets global technical standards and acts as an authority in technical areas including computer engineering, biomedical technology, telecommunications, electric power, aerospace and consumer electronics, among others. www.ieee.org.

Integrated Digital Network (IDN): A network that uses both digital transmission and digital switching.

Integrated Services Digital Networks (ISDN): Internet connection services offered at higher speeds than standard "dial-up" service. While ISDN was considered to be an advanced service at one time, it has been eclipsed by much faster DSL, cable modem and T1 line service.

Intellectual Property (IP): The exclusive ownership of original concepts, ideas, designs, engineering plans or other assets that are protected by law. Examples include items covered by trademarks, copyrights and patents. Items such as software, engineering plans, fashion designs and architectural designs, as well as games, books, songs and other entertainment items are among the many things that may be considered to be intellectual property. (Also, see "Patent.")

Interactive: In entertainment, advertising and communications, interactive refers to systems that enable the viewer or user to interact via a response or two-way communication. For example, interactive television advertising may enable the viewer to respond via a set-top box, immediately purchasing the item being advertised.

Interactive TV (ITV): Allows two-way data flow between a viewer and the cable TV system. A user can exchange information with the cable system—for example, by ordering a product related to a show he/she is watching or by voting in an interactive survey.

Interexchange Carrier (IXC or IEC): Any company providing long-distance phone service between LECs and LATAs. See "Local Exchange Carrier (LEC)" and "Local Access and Transport Area (LATA)."

Interface: Refers to (1) a common boundary between two or more items of equipment or between a terminal and a communication channel, (2) the electronic device that interconnects two or more devices or items of equipment having similar or dissimilar characteristics or (3) the electronic device placed between a terminal and a communication channel to protect the network from the hazard of excess voltage levels.

International Financials Reporting Standards (IFRS): A set of accounting standards established by the International Accounting Standards Board (IASB) for the preparation of public financial statements. IFRS has been adopted by much of the world, including the European Union, Russia and Singapore.

International Telecommunications Union (ITU): The international body responsible for telephone and computer communications standards describing interface techniques and practices. These standards include those that define how a nation's telephone and data systems connect to the worldwide communications network.

Internet: A global computer network that provides an easily accessible way for hundreds of millions of users to send and receive data electronically when appropriately connected via computers or wireless devices. Access is generally through HTML-enabled sites on the World Wide Web. Also known as the Net.

Internet Appliance: A non-PC device that connects users to the Internet for specific or general purposes. A good example is an electronic game machine with a screen and Internet capabilities.

Internet of Things (IoT): A concept whereby individual objects, such as kitchen appliances, automobiles, manufacturing equipment, environmental sensors or air conditioners, are connected to the Internet. The objects must be able to identify themselves to other devices or to databases. The ultimate goals may include the collection and processing of data, the control of instruments and machinery, and eventually, a new level of synergies, artificial intelligence and operating efficiencies among the objects. The Internet of Things is often referred to as IoT. Related technologies and topics include RFID, remote wireless sensors, telecommunications and nanotechnology.

Internet Protocol (IP): A set of tools and/or systems used to communicate across the World Wide Web.

Internet Protocol Version 6 (IPv6): The next-generation of IP standard. IPv6 is intended to first work with, and eventually replace, IPv4. Version 6 will enable a vastly larger number of devices to each utilize one internet address (an IP address) at one time. Specifically, it will allow for 340 trillion, trillion, trillion addresses.

Internet Service Provider (ISP): A company that sells access to the Internet to individual subscribers. Leading examples are MSN and AOL.

Internet Telephony: See "Voice Over Internet Protocol (VOIP)."

Internet2: An advanced networking consortium led by the U.S. research and education community that develops and deploys cutting edge network applications.

Intranet: A network protected by a firewall for sharing data and e-mail within an organization or company. Usually, intranets are used by organizations for internal communication.

IoT: See "Internet of Things (IoT)."

IP: See "Intellectual Property (IP)."

IP Number/IP Address: A number or address with four parts that are separated by dots. Each machine on the Internet has its own IP (Internet protocol) number, which serves as an identifier.

IPL: International Private Line.

IPv6: See "Internet Protocol Version 6 (IPv6)."

ISDN: See "Integrated Services Digital Networks (ISDN)."

ISO 9000, 9001, 9002, 9003: Standards set by the International Organization for Standardization. ISO 9000, 9001, 9002 and 9003 are the highest quality certifications awarded to organizations that meet exacting standards in their operating practices and procedures.

IT: See "Information Technology (IT)."

IT-Enabled Services (ITES): The portion of the Information Technology industry focused on providing business services, such as call centers, insurance claims processing and medical records transcription, by utilizing the power of IT, especially the Internet. Most ITES functions are considered to be back-office procedures. Also, see "Business Process Outsourcing (BPO)."

ITES: See "IT-Enabled Services (ITES)."

ITU: See "International Telecommunications Union (ITU)."

ITV: See "Interactive TV (ITV)."

Java: A programming language developed by Sun Microsystems that allows web pages to display interactive graphics. Any type of computer or operating systems can read Java.

Joint Photographic Experts Group (JPEG): A widely used format for digital image files.

Just-in-Time (JIT) Delivery: Refers to a supply chain practice whereby manufacturers receive components on or just before the time that they are needed on the assembly line, rather than bearing the cost of maintaining several days' or weeks' supply in a warehouse. This adds greatly to the cost-effectiveness of a manufacturing plant and puts the burden of warehousing and timely delivery on the supplier of the components.

Kilobyte: One thousand (or 1,024) bytes.

Kilohertz (kHz): A measure of frequency equal to 1,000 Hertz.

Knowledge Management (KM): Includes techniques and technologies that help users find their way through existing information. Also defined as capturing and growing knowledge as employees in an organization interact with customers, partners and products.

Knowledge Process Outsourcing (KPO): The use of outsourced and/or offshore workers to perform business tasks that require judgment and analysis. Examples include such professional tasks as patent research, legal research, architecture, design, engineering, market research, scientific research, accounting and tax return preparation. Also, see "Business Process Outsourcing (BPO)."

LAC: An acronym for Latin America and the Caribbean.

Large-Scale Integration (LSI): The placement of thousands of electronic gates on a single chip. This makes the manufacture of powerful computers possible.

LATA: See "Local Access and Transport Area (LATA)."

LDAP: Lightweight Directory Access Protocol. An advanced technology for storing managing authentication information.

LDCs: See "Least Developed Countries (LDCs)."

Leased Line: A phone line that is rented for use in continuous, long-term data connections.

Least Developed Countries (LDCs): Nations determined by the U.N. Economic and Social Council to be the poorest and weakest members of the international community. There are currently 50 LDCs, of which 34 are in Africa, 15 are in Asia Pacific and the remaining one (Haiti) is in Latin America. The top 10 on the LDC list, in descending order from top to 10th, are Afghanistan, Angola, Bangladesh, Benin, Bhutan, Burkina Faso, Burundi, Cambodia, Cape Verde and the Central African Republic. Sixteen of the LDCs are also Landlocked Least Developed Countries (LLDCs) which present them with additional difficulties often due to the high cost of transporting trade goods. Eleven of the LDCs are Small Island Developing States (SIDS), which are often at risk of extreme weather phenomenon (hurricanes, typhoons, Tsunami): have fragile ecosystems: are often dependent on foreign energy sources: can have high disease rates for HIV/AIDS and malaria: and can have poor market access and trade terms.

LEC: See "Local Exchange Carrier (LEC)."

Li-Fi: Optical wireless systems that operate somewhat like Wi-Fi, but they utilize light to transfer data.

LINUX: An open, free operating system that is shared readily with millions of users worldwide. These users continuously improve and add to the software's code. It can be used to operate computer networks and Internet appliances as well as servers and PCs.

Livestream Shopping: Interactive online content on which viewers may chat and click to buy retail merchandise. Also called interactive shopping, it combines entertainment, social interaction and shopping.

LMDS: Local Multipoint Distribution Service. A fixed, wireless, point-to-multipoint technology designed to distribute television signals.

Local Access and Transport Area (LATA): An operational service area established after the breakup of AT&T to distinguish local telephone service from long-distance service. The U.S. is divided into over 160 LATAs.

Local Area Network (LAN): A computer network that is generally within one office or one building. A LAN can be very inexpensive and efficient to set up when small numbers of computers are involved. It may require a network administrator and a serious investment if hundreds of computers are hooked up to the LAN. A LAN enables all computers within the office to share files and printers, to access common databases and to send e-mail to others on the network.

Local Exchange Carrier (LEC): Any local telephone company, i.e., a carrier, that provides ordinary phone service under regulation within a service area. Also see "Incumbent Local Exchange Carrier (ILEC)" and "Competitive Local Exchange Carrier (CLEC)."

Location Based Advertising (LBA): The ability for advertisers and information providers to push information to mobile consumers based on their locations. For example, GPS equipped cell phones have the potential to alert consumers on the go to nearby restaurants, entertainment attractions, and special sale events at retailers.

Log-in Friction: A cumulation of steps, fields to be filled-in or security checks that slow an online account user's ability to log-in or establish the account.

LOHAS: Lifestyles of Health and Sustainability. A marketing term that refers to consumers who choose to purchase and/or live with items that are natural, organic, less polluting, etc. Such consumers may also prefer products powered by alternative energy, such as hybrid cars.

LoRa: A long range, low power, wide-area wireless platform (such as NB-IoT and LTE Cat M1) utilized to build Internet of Things (IoT) networks in smart cities.

LSI: See "Large-Scale Integration (LSI)."

M2M: See "Machine-to-Machine (M2M)."

M2M2P: Machine-to-machine-to-people. Also, see "Machine-to-Machine (M2M)."

Machine-to-Machine (M2M): Refers to communications from one device to another (or to a collection of devices). It is typically through wireless means such as Wi-Fi or cellular. Wireless sensor networks (WSNs) will be a major growth factor in M2M communications, in everything from factory automation to agriculture and transportation. In

logistics and retailing, M2M can refer to the advanced use of RFID tags. See "Radio Frequency Identification (RFID)." The Internet of Things is based on the principle of M2M communications. Also, see "Internet of Things (IoT)."

Mainframe Computer: One of the largest types of computer, usually capable of serving many users simultaneously, with exceptional processing speed.

MAN: See "Metropolitan Area Network (MAN)."

Managed Service Provider (MSP): An outsourcer that deploys, manages and maintains the back-end software and hardware infrastructure for Internet businesses.

Market Segmentation: The division of a consumer market into specific groups of buyers based on demographic factors.

Marketing: Marketing includes all planning and management activities and expenses associated with the promotion of a product or service. Marketing can encompass advertising, customer surveys, public relations, special events and many other methods. Marketing is distinct from selling, which is the process of generating a final to the customer. While advertising is a form of marketing, it is a distinct form in which messaging is inserted into some sort of media for a fee. Marketing in general can be much more subtle, such as a public relations campaign.

Mashup: A web page that takes data from two or more web sites and joins them together to create a new point of view. For example, weather forecasts from weather.com, a beach camera from Miami, Miami restaurant reviews from Zagat.com and sports news from ESPN.com might be overlaid on a mashup to create a new site that would provide data for people who were traveling to a Super Bowl in Miami.

Massively Multiplayer Online Role Playing Games (MMORPG): A genre of games in which users from anywhere in the world can connect to a central server, which hosts a virtual game environment. Players can then interact with one another in cooperative or adversarial game settings. Users often pay monthly subscription fees to access the content.

MAU: Monthly Average Users.

Mbps (Megabits per second): One million bits transmitted per second.

M-Commerce: Mobile e-commerce over wireless devices.

Megabytes: One million bytes, or 1,024 kilobytes.

Megahertz (MHz): A measure of frequency equal to 1 million Hertz.

Meme: Content that spreads rapidly through Internet communities such as social networking web sites to achieve a high level of popularity.

Merchant Services: Credit card transaction processing services, typically provided by a retail bank. Merchant services include the processing and clearing of credit card transactions and the forwarding of the funds received to the client's bank account.

Mesh Network: A network that uses multiple Wi-Fi repeaters or "nodes" to deploy a wireless Internet access network. Typically, a mesh network is operated by the users themselves. Each user installs a node at his or her locale, and plugs the node into his/her local Internet access, whether DSL, cable or satellite. Other users within the mesh can access all other nodes as needed, or as they travel about. A mesh network can provide access to an apartment complex, an office building, a campus or an entire city. Meraki is a leading node brand in this sector.

Metasearch: Online search platforms that search several third-party travel sites at once. They then display the combined search results in a consolidated page. Metasearch sites may also sell advertising. This type of search platform is particularly common in the travel industry.

Metaverse: The world as seen through virtual reality. See "Virtual Reality."

Metropolitan Area Network (MAN): A data and communications network that operates over metropolitan areas and recently has been expanded to nationwide and even worldwide connectivity of high-speed data networks. A MAN can carry video and data.

MFA: See "Multifiber Agreement (MFA)".

Microprocessor: A computer on a digital semiconductor chip. It performs math and logic operations and executes instructions from memory. (Also known as a central processing unit or CPU.)

Middleware: Software that interprets requests between applications. Also used to describe software that helps an application communicate with an underlying operating system. Generally, middleware integrates various types of systems by acting as a conversion or translation layer.

Millenials: See "Generation Y."

Millions of Instructions per Second (MIPS): A unit used to compare relative computing power, measured in millions. For example, 25 MIPS is 25 million machine instructions per second.

MIME: See "Multipurpose Internet Mail Extensions (MIME)."

MIMO: See "802.11n (MIMO)."

Mixed Reality (MR): A concept that converges several technologies at once, perhaps into one very advanced headset or pair of glasses. For example, Artificial Reality (AR) and Virtual Reality (VR) features might be melded. The result would be very immersive and responsive experiences for education, manufacturing, design, entertainment and games. The phrase Mixed Reality is somewhat interchangeable with the phrase Extended Reality.

MMS: See "Multimedia Messaging System (MMS)."

Mobile Apps: See "Apps."

Moblog: Mobile blog. This is a blog created by cell phone or other mobile device. It often consists largely of photos taken by a cell phone's built-in camera. Also, see "Blog (Web Log)."

Modem: A device that allows a computer to be connected to a phone line, which in turn enables the computer to receive and exchange data with other machines via the Internet.

Modulator: A device that modulates a carrier. Modulators are found in broadcasting transmitters and satellite transponders. The devices are also used by cable TV companies to place a baseband video television signal onto a desired VHF or UHF channel.

Home video tape recorders also have built-in modulators that enable the recorded video information to be played back using a television receiver tuned to VHF channel 3 or 4.

MOOC: Massive open online course. An online educational course designed to be open to the public with the potential to attract an extremely large, global audience.

Moppers: Mobile shoppers.

MP3: A subsystem of MPEG used to compress sound into digital files. It is the most commonly used format for downloading music and audio books. MP3 compresses music significantly while retaining CD-like quality. MP3 players are personal, portable devices used for listening to music and audio book files. See "MPEG."

MPEG, MPEG-1, MPEG-2, MPEG-3, MPEG-4: Moving Picture Experts Group. It is a digital standard for the compression of motion or still video for transmission or storage. MPEGs are used in digital cameras and for Internet-based viewing.

MSP: See "Managed Service Provider (MSP)."

Multicasting: Sending data, audio or video simultaneously to a number of clients. Also known as broadcasting.

Multi-Factor Authentication: A strategy wherein additional levels of ID are required after a username and password have been provided. For example, the requirement that the user enter a code that has been pushed to him/her via a text message.

Multimedia: Refers to a presentation using several different media at once. For example, an encyclopedia in CD-ROM format is generally multimedia because it features written text, video and sound in one package.

Multimedia Messaging System (MMS): See "Text Messaging."

Multi-Protocol Label Switching (MPLS): A technology that enables network operators to route Internet traffic around network failures and bottlenecks.

Multipurpose Internet Mail Extensions (MIME): A widely used method for attaching non-text files to e-mails.

MU-MIMO: Mulit-User, Mutiple-Inut, Multiple-Output. See "802.11n (MIMO)."

NAICS: North American Industrial Classification System. See "Industry Code."

Nanosecond (NS): A billionth of a second. A common unit of measure of computer operating speed.

National Telecommunications and Information Administration (NTIA): A unit of the Department of Commerce that addresses U.S. government telecommunications policy, standards setting and radio spectrum allocation. www.ntia.doc.gov.

Network: In computing, a network is created when two or more computers are connected. Computers may be connected by wireless methods, using such technologies as 802.11b, or by a system of cables, switches and routers.

Network Effect: A phenomenon whereby each additional user added to a system brings disproportionately greater utility to the existing user base. Excellent examples include the telephone, fax machine and social media. This is a business effect that can rapidly and exponentially grow a user base.

Network Effect: A phenomenon whereby each additional user added to a system brings disproportionately greater utility to the existing user base. Excellent examples include the telephone, fax machine and social media. This is a business effect that can rapidly and exponentially grow a user base.

Network Information Center (NIC): Any organization responsible for supplying information about a network.

Network Numbers: The first portion of an IP address, which identifies the network to which hosts in the rest of the address are connected.

Neural Networks: Computer architecture that enables redundancy and self-repair of communications paths and supports high traffic loads through routing decisions.

New Media: A wide array of digital communication technologies, including Internet development tools and services, desktop and portable personal computers, workstations, servers, audio/video compression and editing equipment, graphics hardware and software, high-density storage services and video conferencing systems.

Node: Any single computer connected to a network or a junction of communications paths in a network.

Non-Store Retailing: A form of retailing that is not store-based. Non-store retailing can be conducted through vending machines, direct-selling, direct-marketing, party-based selling, catalogs, television programming, telemarketing and Internet-based selling.

NS: See "Nanosecond (NS)."

NTIA: See "National Telecommunications and Information Administration (NTIA)."

Object Technology: By merging data and software into "objects," a programming system becomes object-oriented. For example, an object called "weekly inventory sold" would have the data and programming needed to construct a flow chart. Some new programming systems–including Java–contain this feature. Object technology is also featured in many Microsoft products. See "Java."

OC3, up to OC768: Very high-speed data lines that run at speeds from 155 to 39,813.12 Mbps.

ODM: See "Original Design Manufacturer (ODM)."

OECD: See "Organisation for Economic Co-operation and Development (OECD)."

OEM: See "Original Equipment Manufacturer (OEM)."

OFDMA: Orthogonal Frequency-Division Multiple Access. See "802.11n (MIMO)."

Offshoring: The rapidly growing tendency among U.S., Japanese and Western European firms to send knowledge-based and manufacturing work overseas. The intent is to take advantage of lower wages and operating costs in such nations as China, India, Hungary and Russia. The choice of a nation for offshore work may be influenced by such factors as language and education of the local workforce, transportation systems or natural resources. For example, China and India are graduating high numbers of skilled engineers and scientists from their universities. Also, some nations are noted for large numbers of workers skilled in the English language, such as the Philippines and India. Also see "Captive Offshoring" and "Outsourcing."

Onshoring: The opposite of "offshoring." Providing or maintaining manufacturing or services within or nearby a company's domestic location. Sometimes referred to as reshoring.

Open Source (Open Standards): A software program for which the source code is openly available for modification and enhancement as various users and developers see fit. Open software is typically developed as a public collaboration and grows in usefulness over time. See "LINUX."

Operating System (OS): The software that allows applications like word processors or web browsers to run on a computer. For example, Microsoft Windows and Apple iOS are operating systems.

Organisation for Economic Co-operation and Development (OECD): A group of more than 30 nations that are strongly committed to the market economy and democracy. Some of the OECD members include Japan, the U.S., Spain, Germany, Australia, Korea, the U.K., Canada and Mexico. Although not members, Estonia, Israel and Russia are invited to member talks: and Brazil, China, India, Indonesia and South Africa have enhanced engagement policies with the OECD. The Organisation provides statistics, as well as social and economic data: and researches social changes, including patterns in evolving fiscal policy, agriculture, technology, trade, the environment and other areas. It publishes over 250 titles annually, including a corporate magazine, the OECD Observer. It also has radio and TV studios, and has centers in Tokyo, Washington, D.C., Berlin and Mexico City that distribute the Organisation's work and organizes events.

Original Design Manufacturer (ODM): A contract manufacturer that offers complete, end-to-end design, engineering and manufacturing services. ODMs design and build products, such as consumer electronics, that client companies can then brand and sell as their own. For example, a large percentage of laptop computers, cell phones and PDAs are made by ODMs. Also see "Original Equipment Manufacturer (OEM)" and "Contract Manufacturing."

Original Equipment Manufacturer (OEM): 1) A company that manufactures a component (or a completed product) for sale to a customer that will integrate the component into a final product. The OEM's customer will put its own brand name on the end product and distribute or resell it to end users. 2) A firm that buys a component and then incorporates it into a final product, or buys a completed product and then resells it under the firm's own brand name. This usage is most often found in the computer industry, where OEM is sometimes used as a verb. Also see "Original Design Manufacturer (ODM)" and "Contract Manufacturing."

OS: See "Operating System (OS)."

Outsourcing: The hiring of an outside company to perform a task otherwise performed internally by the company, generally with the goal of lowering costs and/or streamlining work flow. Outsourcing contracts are generally several years in length. Companies that hire outsourced services providers often prefer to focus on their core strengths while sending more routine tasks outside for others to perform. Typical outsourced services include the running of human resources departments, telephone call centers and computer departments. When outsourcing is performed overseas, it may be referred to as offshoring. Also see "Offshoring."

OWL: See "Web Ontology Language (OWL)."

P2P Network: See "Peer-to-Peer (P2P) Network."

Packet Switching: A higher-speed way to move data through a network, in which files are broken down into smaller "packets" that are reassembled electronically after transmission.

PAM: Privileged Access Management.

Participatory Sensing: The use of cell phones to gather information from a wide variety of users who transmit photos or comments about local conditions to a central repository. The information is then processed and analyzed by a database. For example, whatsinvasive.com is an effort to gather user generated data that documents invasive plants in America's national parks.

Passive Optical Network (PON): A telecommunications network that brings high speed fiber optic cable all the way (or most of the way) to the end user. Also, see "Fiber to the Home (FTTH)."

Passive Wi-Fi: An 802.11 wireless technology that requires dramatically less electric power than traditional Wi-Fi requires. This makes passive Wi-Fi ideal for widespread use in remote wireless sensor networks and other high-volume applications. This technology has wide applications in the Internet of Things where multitudes of remote data sensors needs the ability to gather and transmit information, independent of outside power supplies. Various methods are being developed for this technology, including the use of central power sources that can transmit electricity wirelessly to nearby sensors, as well as devices that can generate tiny amounts of power through changes in local temperature. Also see "Ambient Backscatter".

Patent: An intellectual property right granted by a national government to an inventor to exclude others from making, using, offering for sale, or selling the invention throughout that nation or importing the invention into the nation for a limited time in exchange for public disclosure of the invention when the patent is granted. In addition to national patenting agencies, such as the United States Patent and Trademark Office, and regional organizations such as the European Patent Office, there is a cooperative international patent organization, the World Intellectual Property Organization, or WIPO, established by the United Nations.

Payment Service Directive Two (PSD2): Regulations that force European payments processors and gateways to utilized advanced customer and account authentication at the time of payment in order to reduce fraud.

Paywall: A system that restricts access to a web site to only those with paid subscriptions to the sites.

PC: See "Personal Computer (PC)."

PCMCIA: Personal Computer Memory Card International Association.

Peer-to-Peer (P2P) Network: Refers to a connection between computers that creates equal status between the computers. P2P can be used in an office or home to create a simple computer network. However, P2P more commonly refers to networks of computers that share information online. For example, peer-to-peer music sharing networks enable one member to search the hard drives of other members to locate music files and then download those files.

Performance Marketing: Performance marketing is focused on actual results. The intent is to get a message's reader, listener or viewer to take a specific action, such as a click on a link or an actual purchase of a product or service. Some advertising methods are based on pay-for-performance, such as pay-per-click online ads.

Personal Communication Service (PCS): A type of cellular mobile telephone service.

Personal Computer (PC): An affordable, efficient computer meant to be used by one person. The device may be a desktop computer or a laptop. Frequently, the PC is connected to a local area network (LAN), or uses wireless methods such as Wi-Fi to access the Internet. PCs are used both in the home and in the office. There is no firm agreement on whether tablets should be regarded as PCs.

Personal Television (PTV): Television programming that has been manipulated to a viewer's personal taste. For example, the TiVo service allows viewers to eliminate commercials, watch programming stored in memory or watch selected real-time moments in slow motion.

Petabyte: 1,024 terabytes, or about 1 million gigabytes.

PLM: See "Product Lifecyle Management (PLM)."

Plug-In: Any small piece of software that adds extra functions to a larger piece of software.

Podcasting: The creation of audio files as webcasts. Podcasts can be anything from unique radio-like programming to sales pitches to audio press releases. Audio RSS (Real Simple Syndication) enables the broadcast of these audio files to appropriate parties. Also see "Real Simple Syndication (RSS)," "Video Blog (VLOG)" and "Blog (Web Log)."

Point-of-Sale (POS): A cash register with the capability to scan a UPC code, electronically record a sale and accept payment via multiple means, including the scanning of a credit card or digital wallet. It may

utilize NFC, near field communications, to read cards and digital wallets.

Point-to-Point Protocol (PPP): A protocol that enables a computer to use the combination of a standard telephone line and a modem to make TCP/IP connections.

PON: See "Passive Optical Networking (PON)."

POP: An acronym for both "Point of Presence" and "Post Office Protocol." Point of presence refers to a location that a network can be connected to (generally used to count the potential subscriber base of a cellular phone system). Post office protocol refers to the way in which e-mail software obtains mail from a mail server.

Port: An interface (or connector) between the computer and the outside world. The number of ports on a communications controller or front-end processor determines the number of communications channels that can be connected to it. The number of ports on a computer determines the number of peripheral devices that can be attached to it.

Portal: A comprehensive web site for general or specific purposes.

POS: See "Point of Sale (POS)."

Positioning: The design and implementation of a merchandising mix, price structure and style of selling to create an image of the retailer, relative to its competitors, in the customer's mind.

Predictive Analytics: See "Analytics."

Pre-N: A wireless technology introduced in 2004 before the higher-speed 802.11n standard was completed. See "802.11n (MIMO)."

Product Lifecycle (Product Life Cycle): The prediction of the life of a product or brand. Stages are described as Introduction, Growth, Maturity and finally Sales Decline. These stages track a product from its initial introduction to the market through to the end of its usefulness as a commercially viable product. The goal of Product Lifecycle Management is to maximize production efficiency, consumer acceptance and profits. Consequently, critical processes around the product need to be adjusted during its lifecycle, including pricing, advertising, promotion, distribution and packaging.

Product Lifecycle Management (PLM): See "Product Lifecycle (Product Life Cycle)."

Programmatic Buying: An automated method of placing advertising that enables advertisers to closely define the amount of money they want to spend along with the type of audience and behavior of the audience in which they are willing to invest. While programmatic buying was initially used in online advertising, it has since migrated to TV and other types of ads.

Protocol: A set of rules for communicating between computers. The use of standard protocols allows products from different vendors to communicate on a common network.

PTV: See "Personal Television (PTV)."

Public Switched Telephone Network (PSTN): A term that refers to the traditional telephone system.

Quantified Self: An evolving concept that refers to the use of electronic devices and electronic communications to gather, record and transmit personal information. An extreme practice of quantified self would be a person who uses a wearable, digital camera to record his surroundings 24/7, and who blogs, tweets or posts to social media his daily activities on a continuous basis. The most practical application of quantified self will most likely be in mobile health, (the personal health Internet). Examples include the wearing of wireless heart monitors, sleep monitors or pedometers that record daily health and exercise data in order to manage health problems or improve fitness.

R&D: Research and development. Also see "Applied Research" and "Basic Research."

Radio Frequency Identification (RFID): A technology that applies a special microchip-enabled tag to an individual item or piece of merchandise or inventory. RFID technology enables wireless, computerized tracking of that inventory item as it moves through the supply chain from factory to transport to warehouse to retail store or end user. Also known as radio tags.

RAM: See "Random Access Memory (RAM)."

Random Access Memory (RAM): Computer memory used to hold programs and data temporarily.

RDF: See "Resource Description Framework (RDF)."

Real Audio: A helper software application that enables the user to hear real-time audio via the Internet.

Real Simple Syndication (RSS): Uses XML programming language to let web logs and other data be broadcast to appropriate web sites and users. Formerly referred to as RDF Site Summary or Rich Site Summary, RSS also enables the publisher to create a description of the content and its location in the form of an RSS document. Also useful for distributing audio files. See "Podcasting."

Real Time: A system or software product specially designed to acquire, process, store and display large amounts of rapidly changing information almost instantaneously, with microsecond responses as changes occur.

Real-Time Bidding (RTB): RTB is a function on advanced exchanges that buy and sell online ads. This RTB technology enables an advertiser to automatically place a bid, in real time, based on various attributes of a web page and its visitors. (Also see "Programmatic Buying.")

Reshoring: See "Onshoring."

Resource Description Framework (RDF): A software concept that integrates many different software applications using XML as a syntax for the exchange of data. It is a core concept for development of the Semantic Web, an enhanced World Wide Web envisioned by W3C, the global organization that oversees development of the web. RDF may be useful for the syndication of news or the aggregation of all types of data for specific uses.

Responsive Web Design: Also known as RWD, responsive web design eliminates the need for separate web sites for viewing by desktop computers and the smaller screens found on various types of wireless devices. RWD automatically presents the correct web page based on the type of device that is accessing the site. RWD utilizes CSS3 media queries. Older browsers may not be able to view responsive web pages correctly. Consequently, the best design practice is to include a specific file that is able to handle and convert the CSS3 queries into pages that are viewable in older browsers.

Router: An electronic device that enables networks to communicate with each other. For example, the local area network (LAN) in an office connects to a router to give the LAN access to an Internet connection such as a T1 or DSL. Routers can be bundled with several added features, such as firewalls.

RSS: See "Real Simple Syndication (RSS)."

Ruby: An open source programming language first released in Japan in 1995. It is an object-oriented scripting language. "Ruby on Rails" is a framework that enables very rapid web site development. See www.rubyonrails.org.

SaaS: See "Software as a Service (SaaS)."

Satellite Broadcasting: The use of Earth-orbiting satellites to transmit, over a wide area, TV, radio, telephony, video and other data in digitized format.

Scalable: Refers to a network that can grow and adapt as the total customer count increases and as customer needs increase and change. Scalable websites (and the hardware and software behind them) are extremely vital to rapidly-growing online services. Scalable networks can easily manage increasing numbers of workstations, servers, user workloads and added functionality.

S-Commerce: The sale of goods and services through social media such as Facebook.

SCSI: See "Small Computer System Interface (SCSI)."

SDSL: See "Digital Subscriber Line (DSL)."

Search Engine Optimization (SEO): The process of improving a website's positioning in search engines such as Google, Yahoo, and Bing. SEO is used to drive more traffic to a website.

Semantic Web: An initiative started by the World Wide Web Consortium (W3C) that is focused on improving the way users access databases and online content by adding semantic metadata to content that will clearly define the relationships between data. Users see much better search results, and web site developers are able to create pages that update results and content based on related data on-the-fly. Data is automatically shared across applications and across organizations. While the Semantic Web is sometimes referred to as Web 3.0, it should not be confused with Web3.

Semiconductor: A generic term for a device that controls electrical signals. It specifically refers to a material (such as silicon, germanium or gallium arsenide) that can be altered either to conduct electrical current or to block its passage. Carbon nanotubes may eventually be used as semiconductors. Semiconductors are partly responsible for the miniaturization of modern electronic devices, as they are vital components in computer memory and processor chips. The manufacture of semiconductors is carried out by small firms, and by industry giants such as Intel and Advanced Micro Devices.

SEO: See "Search Engine Optimization (SEO)."

Serial Line Internet Protocol (SLIP): The connection of a traditional telephone line, or serial line, and modem to connect a computer to an Internet site.

Server: A computer that performs and manages specific duties for a central network such as a LAN. It may include storage devices and other peripherals. Competition within the server manufacturing industry is intense among leaders Dell, IBM, HP and others.

Service Level Agreement (SLA): A detail in a contract between a service provider and the client. The agreement specifies the level of service that is expected during the service contract term. For example, computer or Internet service contracts generally stipulate a maximum amount of time that a system may be unusable.

Servicemark (Service Mark): Similar to a trademark, except that it identifies and distinguishes the source of a service rather than a product. The servicemark may include a logo or other identifying word or mark meant to distinguish a service from others and indicate the provider of the service. An "SM" indicates that a servicemark has been applied for (or that the owner intends to protect the servicemark) but is still pending, while ® indicates it has been processed and is legally upheld. Servicemarks must be renewed on a regular basis with the appropriate regulatory authorities. In America, trademarks are registered with the U.S. Patent and

Trademark Office. There are also cooperative, international servicemark and trademark agreements and agencies. (Also, see "Trademark, (Trade Mark).")

Set-Top Box: Sits on top of a TV set and provides enhancement to cable TV or other television reception. Typically a cable modem, this box may enable interactive enhancements to television viewing. For example, a cable modem is a set-top box that enables Internet access via TV cable. See "Cable Modem."

Shareware: Software that is available for users to download for free from the Internet, usually with the expectation that they will register or pay for the software if they continue to use it. Many shareware programs are set to expire after a period of time.

Shockwave: An authoring tool that allows multimedia presentations to appear on the Internet. Shockwave enables interactive graphics, sound and animation to be viewed on the web.

Shopping Cart Abandonment: Occurs when an online customer places items in a website's shopping cart, but then abandons the transaction without completing the purchase.

SIC: Standard Industrial Classification. See "Industry Code."

Simple Mail Transfer Protocol (SMTP): The primary form of protocol used in the transference of e-mail.

Simple Network Management Protocol (SNMP): A set of communication standards for use between computers connected to TCP/IP networks.

Simple Object Access Protocol (SOAP): A method for applications to communicate with each other using HTTP web protocols. SOAP is an important protocol in web services.

SLA: See "Service Level Agreement (SLA)."

SLIP: See "Serial Line Internet Protocol (SLIP)."

Slugs: Small graphical icons that are frequently used in order to establish a visual language. They often function as buttons, such as sound slugs, which inform the user of the size of a sound file and, when clicked, download the file.

Small Computer System Interface (SCSI): A dominant, international standard interface used by UNIX servers and many desktop computers to connect to storage devices: a physical connection between devices.

Small to Medium Enterprise (SME): A term used to refer to smaller businesses. For example, in the European Union, SME businesses are officially considered to have fewer than 250 employees and less that 50 million Euros in annual sales. SMEs make up the vast majority of all businesses and provide the vast majority of all employment.

Smart Dust: The use of vast quantities of self-powered, remote wireless sensors to gather local data and transmit it to a central database for predictive analytics purposes, and for monitoring of environmental, structural stress and other local conditions.

SMDS: See "Switched Multimegabit Data Service (SMDS)."

SME: See "Small to Medium Enterprise (SME)."

SNMP: See "Simple Network Management Protocol (SNMP)."

Social Graph: An analysis of relationships between individuals, generally within the realm of the Internet. Social graphs track different kids of relationships such as coworkers, users of specific web sites or enthusiasts of a particular hobby. Advertise hope to devise technologies that exploit social graphs in order to reach targeted customers.

Social Media: Sites on the Internet that feature user generated content (UGC). Such media include wikis, blogs and specialty web sites such as MySpace.com, Facebook, YouTube, Yelp and Friendster.com. Social media are seen as powerful online tools because all or most of the content is user-generated.

Social, Mobile, Analytics and Cloud (SMAC): Refers to four of the fastest growing trends in computing and data technologies.

Software as a Service (SaaS): Refers to the practice of providing users with software applications that are hosted on remote servers and accessed via the Internet. Excellent examples include the CRM (Customer Relationship Management) software provided in SaaS format by Salesforce. An earlier technology that operated in a similar, but less sophisticated, manner was called ASP or Application Service Provider.

SONET: See "Synchronous Optical Network Technology (SONET)."

Spam: A term used to refer to generally unwanted, solicitous, bulk-sent e-mail. In recent years, significant amounts of government legislation have been passed in an attempt to limit the use of spam. Also, many types of software filters have been introduced in an effort to block spam on the receiving end. In addition to use for general advertising purposes, spam may be used in an effort to spread computer viruses or to commit financial or commercial fraud.

SRDF: See "Symmetrix Remote Data Facility (SRDF)."

SSO: See "Single Sign-On (SSO)."

Storage Area Network (SAN): Links host computers to advanced data storage systems.

Streaming Media: One-way audio and/or video that is compressed and transmitted over a broadband internet connction or wireless service. The media is viewed or heard almost as soon as data is fed to the receiver: there is usually a buffer period of a few seconds. Leading streaming media platforms provide movies, sports and other entertainment, typically at much lower monthly subscription cost that traditional cable or satellite TV. Also, see vMVPD.

Strong Customer Authentication (SCA): A technology that ensures that online payment transactions are secure and that fraud is significantly reduced. SCA took effect beginning in 2022.

Structured Query Language (SQL): A language set that defines a way of organizing and calling data in a computer database. SQL is becoming the standard for use in client/server databases.

Subsidiary, Wholly-Owned: A company that is wholly controlled by another company through stock ownership.

Supply Chain: The complete set of suppliers of goods and services required for a company to operate its business. For example, a manufacturer's supply chain may include providers of raw materials, components, custom-made parts and packaging materials.

Switch: A network device that directs packets of data between multiple ports, often filtering the data so that it travels more quickly.

Switched Multimegabit Data Service (SMDS): A method of extremely high-speed transference of data.

Symmetrix Remote Data Facility (SRDF): A high-performance, host-independent business solution that enables users to maintain a duplicate copy of all or some of their data at a remote site.

Synchronous Optical Network Technology (SONET): A mode of high-speed transmission meant to take full advantage of the wide bandwidth in fiber-optic cables.

T1: A standard for broadband digital transmission over phone lines. Generally, it can transmit at least 24 voice channels at once over copper wires, at a high speed of 1.5 Mbps. Higher speed versions include T3 and OC3 lines.

T3: Transmission over phone lines that supports data rates of 45 Mbps. T3 lines consist of 672 channels, and such lines are generally used by Internet service providers. They are also referred to as DS3 lines.

Tagging: A method of describing web sites with simple words so that links can be grouped by categories and easily found again in the future for access. Also, groups of tagged links can be shared for viewing by others. See http://del.icio.us.

TCP/IP: Transmission Control Protocol/Internet Protocol. The combination of a network and transport protocol developed by ARPANet for internetworking IP-based networks.

Telecommunications: Systems and networks of hardware and software used to carry voice, video and/or data within buildings and between locations around the world. This includes telephone wires, satellite signals, wireless networks, fiber networks, Internet networks and related devices.

Telepresence: The use of highly sophisticated digital video cameras, microphones and high speed Internet connections to create a video conference for remote participants that is nearly life-like. Conference participants may consult with each other from specially-equipped rooms that can be almost anywhere in the world. With the most advanced equipment, such as that produced by Cisco, the images on screens can be near life-size and the results can be of almost face-to-face quality.

Telnet: A terminal emulation program for TCP/IP networks like the Internet, which runs on a computer and connects to a particular network. Directions entered on a computer that is connected using Telnet will be read and followed just as if they had been entered on the server itself. Through Telnet, users are able to control a server and communicate with other servers on the same network at the same time. Telnet is commonly used to control web servers remotely.

Terabyte: A measure of data equal to 1,024 gigabytes, or about 1 trillion bytes of data.

Text Messaging: The transmission of very short, text messages in a format similar to e-mail. Generally, text messaging is used as an additional service on cell phones. The format has typically been SMS (Short Messaging System), but a newer standard is evolving: MMS (Multimedia Messaging System). MMS can transmit pictures, sound and video as well as text.

Third-Party Fulfillment (3PF): A 3PL company that focuses on warehousing, order processing and shipping, especially for retail and online sellers. See "Third-Party Logistics (3PL)" and "Insourcing."

Third-Party Logistics (3PL): A specialist firm in logistics, which may provide a variety of transportation, warehousing and logistics-related services to buyers or sellers. These tasks were previously performed in-house by the customer. When 3PL services are provided within the client's own facilities, it can also be referred to as insourcing. Also see "Fourth-Party Logistics (4PL)."

TIME: Telecommunications, Information Technology, Media and Electronics.

Token Ring: A local area network architecture in which a token, or continuously repeating frame, is passed sequentially from station to station. Only the station possessing the token can communicate on the network.

Trademark (Trade Mark): A name or phrase that has been registered by a company or organization for its exclusive use. A "TM" indicates that a trademark has been applied for (or that the owner intends to protect the trademark) but is still pending, while ® indicates it has been processed and is legally upheld. A trademark may or may not include an accompanying, distinctive design or font for the word or phrase. Trademarks must be renewed on a regular basis with the appropriate regulatory authorities. In America, trademarks are registered with the U.S. Patent and Trademark Office. There are also cooperative, international trademark agreements and agencies.

Transaction Authority Markup Language (XAML): A computer programming code (developer language) created by Microsoft as part of its effort to launch the operating system code named Longhorn to facilitate the processing of online transactions.

Two-Factor Authentication (2FA): A strategy wherein two levels of ID are required after a username and password have been provided. For example, the requirement that the user enter a code that has been pushed to him/her via a text message.

U-Commerce (U Commerce): Ubiquitous Commerce, Universal Commerce or Ultimate Commerce (ubiquitous meaning ever-present), depending on whom you ask. It describes the concept that buyers and sellers have the potential to interact anywhere, anytime thanks to the use of wireless devices, such as cell phones, by buyers to connect with sellers via the Internet where orders can be placed online and payments can be made via credit card or PayPal. The Association for Information Systems states that the qualities of U-Commerce include ubiquity, uniqueness, universality and unison.

UDDI: See "Universal Description, Discovery and Integration (UDDI)."

UGC: See "User Generated Content (UGC)."

UI: See "User Interface (UI)."

Unified Communications: The use of advanced technology to replace traditional telecommunications infrastructure such as PBX, fax and even the desktop telephone. Special software operating on a local or remote server enables each office worker to have access, via the desktop PC, to communications tools that include VOIP phone service, email, voice mail, fax, instant messaging (IM), collaborative calendars and schedules, contact information such as address books, audio conferencing and video conferencing.

Uniform Resource Locator (URL): The address that allows an Internet browser to locate a homepage or web site.

Universal Description, Discovery and Integration (UDDI): A vital protocol used in web services. UDDI enables businesses to create a standard description of their activities so that they can be searched for appropriately by automatic software tools.

UNIX: A multi-user, multitasking operating system that runs on a wide variety of computer systems, from PCs to mainframes.

URL: See "Uniform Resource Locator (URL)."

User Experience (UX): An overall interaction that a user has with a product or service: the human-device interaction is a key point of differentiation for most tech companies.

User Generated Content (UGC): Data contributed by users of interactive web sites. Such sites can include wikis, blogs, entertainment sites, shopping sites or social networks such as Facebook. UGC data can also include such things as product reviews, photos, videos, comments on forums, and how-to advice. Also see "Social Media."

User Interface (UI): The software and hardware that enable humans to interact with machines: typically a great user interface is a key differentiator for companies. For example, Windows is a user interface that enables users to access computers.

UX: See "User Experience (UX)."

VDSL: Very high-data-rate digital subscriber line, operating at data rates from 55 to 100 Mbps.

Vendor Relationship Management (VRM): A process whereby consumers can use online tools and other means to manage their relationships with the firms ("vendors") that they buy from. An example is the ability of a consumer to set personal preferences in an online account. Some observers expect VRM to rapidly evolve into sophisticated technology that enables the consumer to be in control of the buyer-

seller cycle while enjoying maximum-possible choices and lowest-possible prices.

Vertical Integration: A business model in which one company owns many (or all) of the means of production of the many goods that comprise its product line. For example, founder Henry Ford designed Ford Motor Company's early River Rogue plant so that coal, iron ore and other needed raw materials arrived at one end of the plant and were processed into steel, which was then converted on-site into finished components. At the final stage of the plant, completed automobiles were assembled.

Video Blog (VLOG): The creation of video files as webcasts. VLOGs can be viewed on personal computers and wireless devices that are Internet-enabled. They can include anything from unique TV-like programming to sales pitches to music videos, news coverage or audio press releases. Online video is one of the fastest-growing segments in Internet usage. Leading e-commerce companies such as Microsoft, through its MSN service, Google and Yahoo!, as well as mainstream media firms such as Reuters, are making significant investments in online video services. Real Simple Syndication (RSS) enables the broadcasting of these files to appropriate parties. Also see "Real Simple Syndication (RSS)," "Podcasting" and "Blog (Web Log)."

Viral Marketing: A marketing strategy in which the consumer is the vehicle for sales and marketing efforts, thus, spreading word of a company's message. This is otherwise known as word-of-mouth marketing. Viral marketing is an excellent way to capitalize on social media. Memes are an example of digital viral marketing, in which an image, video, text or icon (often humorous) is spread by consumers.

Virtual Private Network (VPN): Cordons off part of a public network to create a private LAN. It is a common way of increasing login security.

Virtual Reality (VR): A life-like scene, representation or virtual world that has been generated by specialized software. Viewing and participating in virtual reality through special equipment (such as a helmet/googles with 3-D viewing screens and earphones, sometimes used with gloves that contain sensors) creates an experience that is immersive to the user. Many observers consider the emerging "metaverse" to be a segment of virtual reality.

Virtual Storage Access Method (VSAM): A data storage and retrieval mechanism designed to maintain large quantities of data on external disks or drums on computers designed for virtual storage systems.

VLOG: See "Video Blog (VLOG)."

vMVPD: Virtual Multichannel Video Programming Distributors. Firms like Hulu and Netflix that distribute movies, sports and other video entertainment as a streaming service over a broadband internet connection. These services are an alternative to tradiitional satellite and cable TV, and they are typically sold at much lower cost per monthly subscription, with no long-term contracts or credit applications required.

Voice Over Internet Protocol (VOIP): The ability to make telephone calls and send faxes over IP-based data networks, i.e., real-time voice between computers via the Internet. Leading providers of VOIP service include independent firms Skype and Vonage. However, all major telecom companies, such as SBC are planning or offering VOIP service. VOIP can offer greatly reduced telephone bills to users, since toll charges, certain taxes and other fees can be bypassed. Long-distance calls can pass to anywhere in the world using VOIP. Over the mid-term, many telephone handsets, including cellular phones, will have the ability to detect wireless networks offering VOIP connections and will switch seamlessly between landline and VOIP or cellular and VOIP as needed.

VOIP: See "Voice Over Internet Protocol (VOIP)."

VPN: See "Virtual Private Network (VPN)."

VRM: See "Vendor Relationship Management (VRM)."

WAN: See "Wide Area Network (WAN)."

WAP: See "Wireless Access Protocol (WAP)."

Web 2.0: The second stage of development of the World Wide Web. Services include collaborative sites that emphasize dynamic user-generated content such as those for social media.

Web 3.0: See "Semantic Web" and "Web3."

Web of Things: See "Internet of Things (IoT)."

Web Ontology Language (OWL): A markup language that is related to RDF. See "Resource Description Framework (RDF)" and "Semantic Web."

Web Services: Self-contained modular applications that can be described, published, located and invoked over the World Wide Web or another network. Web services architecture evolved from object-oriented design and is geared toward e-business solutions. Microsoft Corporation is focusing on web services with its .NET initiative. Also see "Extensible Markup Language (XML)."

Web Services Description Language (WSDL): An important protocol to web services that describes the web service being offered.

Web3: Not to be confused with the Semantic Web (which has, from time-to-time in the past, been called Web 3.0), a version of the world wide web based on blockchain technology. Also known as Web 3.0.

Weblog: See "Blog (Web Log)."

Webmaster: Any individual who runs a web site. Webmasters generally perform maintenance and upkeep.

Website Meta-Language (WML): A free HTML generation toolkit for the Unix operating system.

WFH: Work from home.

Wide Area Network (WAN): A regional or global network that provides links between all local area networks within a company. For example, Ford Motor Company might use a WAN to enable its factory in Detroit to talk to its sales offices in New York and Chicago, its plants in England and its buying offices in Taiwan. Also see "Local Area Network (LAN)."

Widget: A small software application that can be embedded into a web page. These applications can be designed to contain games, cartoons, entertainment, helpful data or just about anything that might engage the user's attention.

WiFi: See "Wi-Fi."

Wi-Fi: Wireless Fidelity. Refers to 802.11 wireless network specifications. The 802.XX standards are set by the IEEE (Institute of Electrical and Electronics Engineers). Wi-Fi enables very high-speed local networks in homes, businesses, factories, industrial and transportation infrastructure, public spaces and vehicles. Wi-Fi networks enable computing devices of all types to connect to each other and to the internet, including smartphones, laptops, desktops and tablet computers. In addition, Wi-Fi enables machine-to-machine (M2M) communication between devices, providing a backbone for the Internet of Things. These networks can be made reasonably secure when strong passwords are required, and additional cybersecurity measures are in place. (Also, see "Internet of Things.")

Wiki: A web site that enables large or small groups of users to create and co-edit data. The best known example is Wikipedia, a high traffic web site that presents a public encyclopedia that is continuously written and edited by a vast number of volunteer contributors and editors who include both experts and enthusiasts in various subjects. Also, see "User Generated Content (UGC)."

WiMAX: An advanced wireless standard with significant speed and distance capabilities, WiMAX is officially known as the 802.16 standard. Using microwave technologies, it has the theoretical potential to broadcast at distances up to 30 miles and speeds of up to 70 Mbps. The 802.XX standards are set by the IEEE (Institute of Electrical and Electronics Engineers).

Wireless: Transmission of voice, video or data by a cellular telephone or other wireless device, as opposed to landline, fiber or cable. It includes Bluetooth, Cellular, Wi-Fi, WiMAX and other local or long-distance wireless methods.

Wireless Access Protocol (WAP): A technology that enables the delivery of internet pages in a smaller format readable by screens on smartphones.

Wireless Cable: A pay television service that delivers multiple programming services to subscribers equipped with special antennae and tuners. It is an alternative to traditional, wired cable TV systems.

Wireless LAN (WLAN): A wireless local area network. WLANs frequently operate on 802.11-enabled equipment (Wi-Fi).

Wireless Sensor Network (WSN): Consists of a grouping of remote sensors that transmit data wirelessly to a receiver that is collecting data into a database. Special controls may alert the network's manager to changes in the environment, traffic or hazardous conditions. Long-term collection of data from remote sensors can be used to establish patterns and make predictions. The use of WSNs is growing rapidly, in such applications as environmental monitoring, agriculture, military intelligence, surveillance, factory automation, home automation and traffic control. (Also, see "Internet of Things".)

WLAN: See "Wireless LAN (WLAN)."

WML: See "Website Meta-Language (WML)."

Workstation: A high-powered desktop computer, usually used by engineers.

World Trade Organization (WTO): One of the only globally active international organizations dealing with the trade rules between nations. Its goal is to assist the free flow of trade goods, ensuring a smooth, predictable supply of goods to help raise the quality of life of member citizens. Members form consensus decisions that are then ratified by their respective parliaments. The WTO's conflict resolution process generally emphasizes interpreting existing commitments and agreements, and discovers how to ensure trade policies to conform to those agreements, with the ultimate aim of avoiding military or political conflict.

World Wide Web: A system (the internet) that provides enhanced access to various sites on the Internet through the use of hyperlinks. Clicking on a link displayed in one document takes you to a related document. The World Wide Web is governed by the World Wide Web Consortium, located at www.w3.org. Also known as the web.

WoT: Web of Things. See "Internet of Things."

WPA: Wireless Protected Access. A basic security standard for wireless networking, including Wi-Fi.

WSDL: See "Web Services Description Language (WSDL)."

WTO: See "World Trade Organization (WTO)."

XML: See "Extensible Markup Language (XML)."

YouTube: A web site that allows any user to post video content to be shared with others. Other users can then rate or comment on the video to share their views. Most YouTube videos can be embedded in outside web sites for others to view without having to visit YouTube. The site offers videos ranging from news to entertainment to training and education. The YouTube firm is owned by Google.

Zero Trust: A strategy wherein networks should never automatically assume that anything either within or outside the network is valid or trustworthy. This requires continual user authentication at a higher level. That is, access to an account or a network should not be provided until authorization and identity are well verified. This verification can be against a database of multiple ID factors. For example, a user with a verified user name/password should be attempting access from a device that is typically utilized by that person, in a geolocation that is typical and from an IP address that is not blacklisted. Any access attempt that doesn't pass such real-time tests should be forced to pass through additional verification steps.

Printed in the USA
CPSIA information can be obtained
at www.ICGtesting.com
CBHW080726180324
5457CB00004B/17